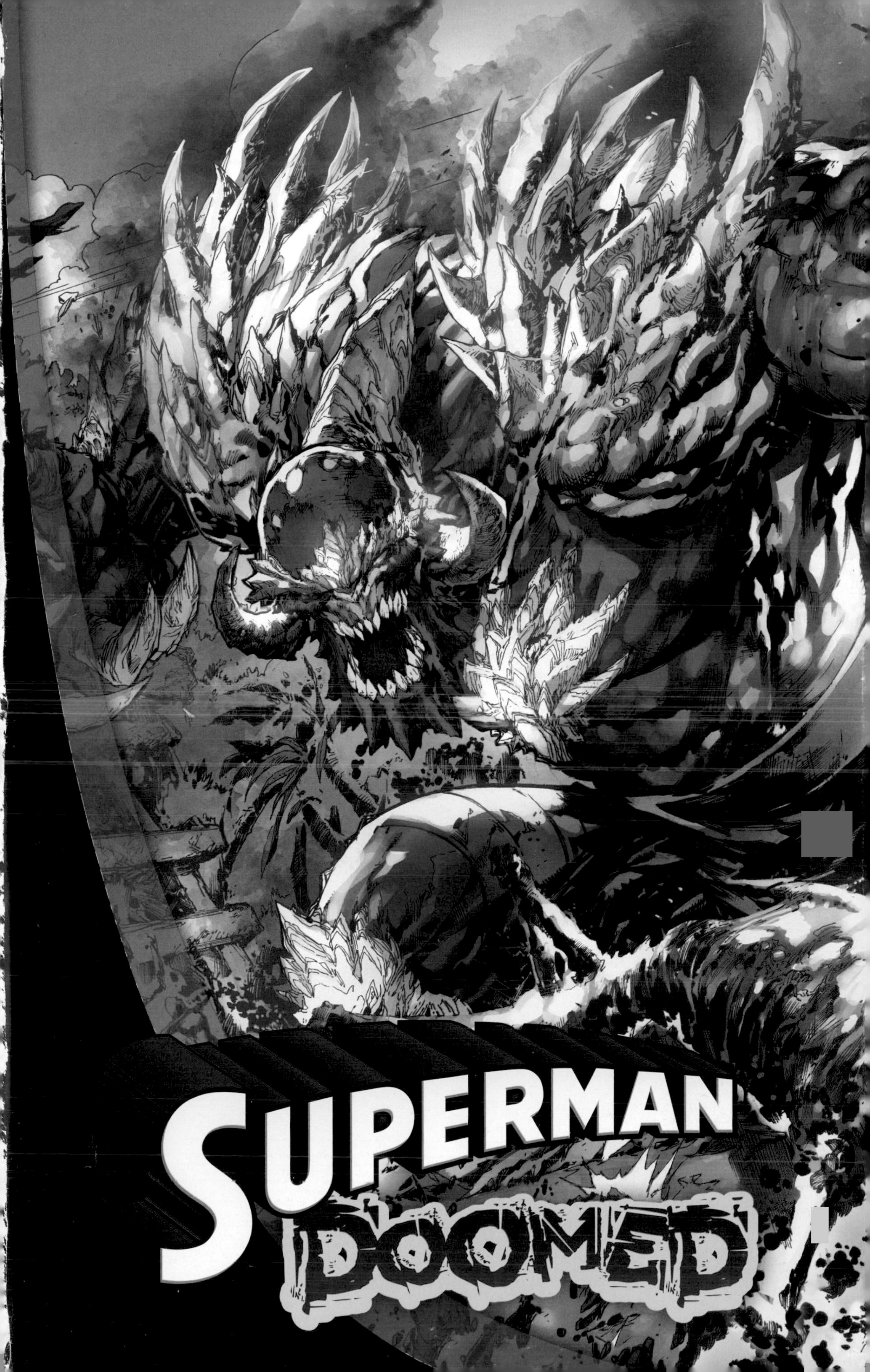
SUPERMAN
DOOMED

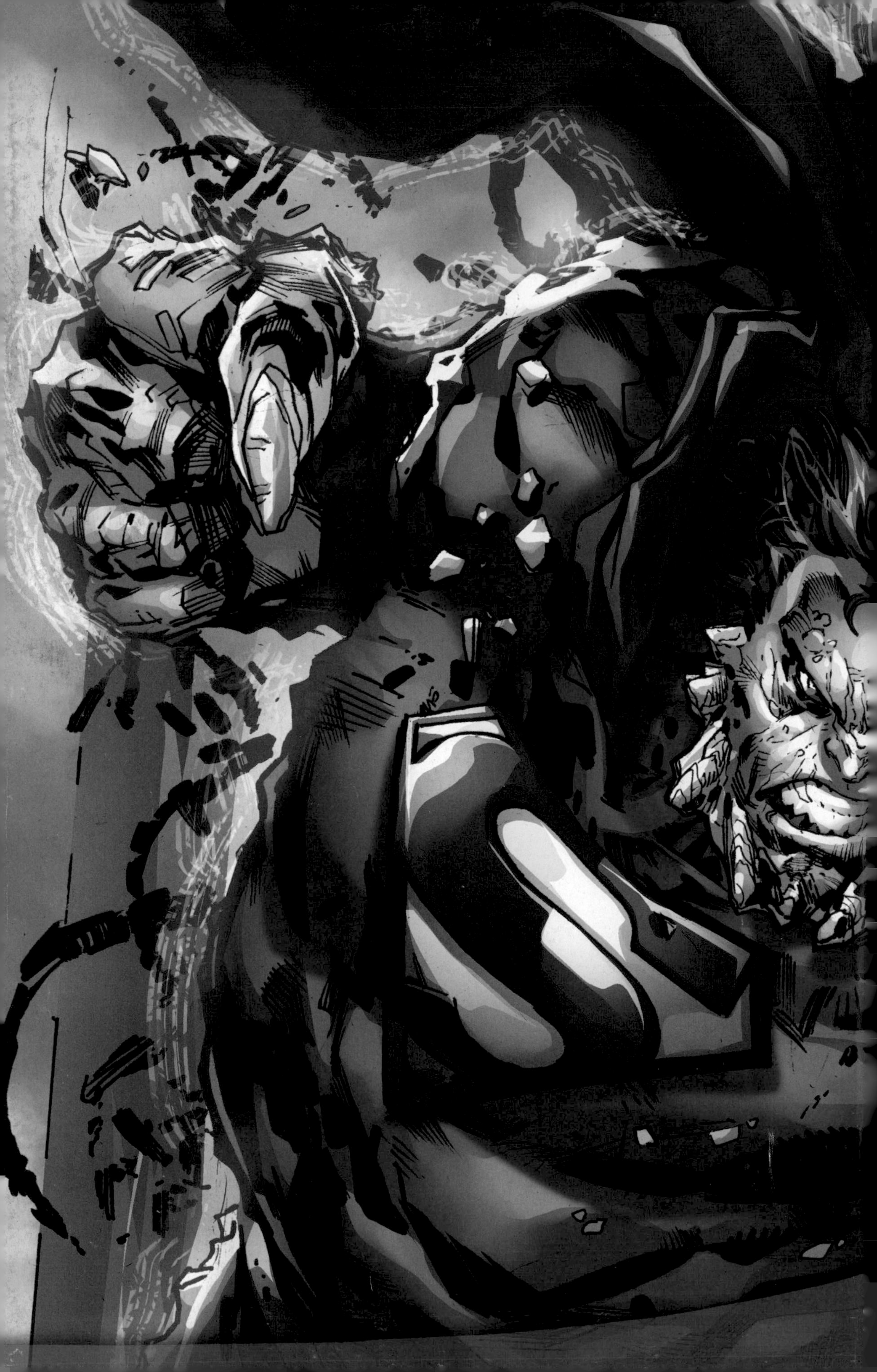

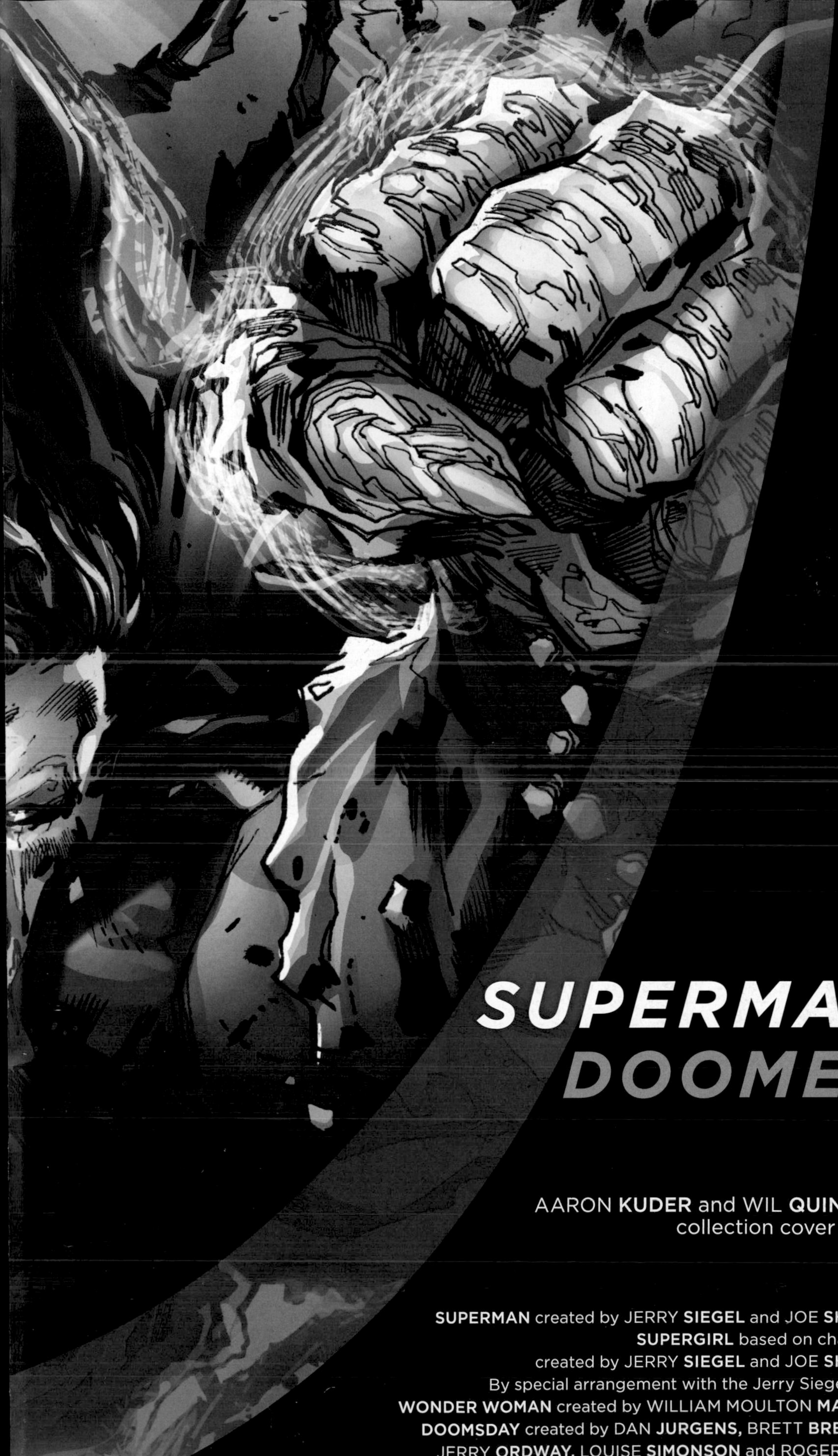

SUPERMAN
DOOMED

AARON **KUDER** and WIL **QUINTANA**
collection cover artists

SUPERMAN created by JERRY **SIEGEL** and JOE **SHUSTER**
SUPERGIRL based on characters
created by JERRY **SIEGEL** and JOE **SHUSTER**
By special arrangement with the Jerry Siegel family
WONDER WOMAN created by WILLIAM MOULTON **MARSTON**
DOOMSDAY created by DAN **JURGENS,** BRETT **BREEDING,**
JERRY **ORDWAY,** LOUISE **SIMONSON** and ROGER **STERN**

EDDIE BERGANZA Editor – Original Series RICKEY PURDIN Associate Editor – Original Series
ANTHONY MARQUES Assistant Editor – Original Series   ROBIN WILDMAN Editor
ROBBIN BROSTERMAN Design Director – Books ROBBIE BIEDERMAN Publication Design

BOB HARRAS Senior VP – Editor-in-Chief, DC Comics

DIANE NELSON President DAN DIDIO and JIM LEE Co-Publishers GEOFF JOHNS Chief Creative Officer
AMIT DESAI Senior VP – Marketing and Franchise Management
AMY GENKINS Senior VP – Business and Legal Affairs NAIRI GARDINER Senior VP – Finance
JEFF BOISON VP – Publishing Planning MARK CHIARELLO VP – Art Direction and Design
JOHN CUNNINGHAM VP – Marketing TERRI CUNNINGHAM VP – Editorial Administration
LARRY GANEM VP – Talent Relations and Services ALISON GILL Senior VP – Manufacturing and Operations
HANK KANALZ Senior VP – Vertigo and Integrated Publishing JAY KOGAN VP – Business and Legal Affairs, Publishing
JACK MAHAN VP – Business Affairs, Talent NICK NAPOLITANO VP – Manufacturing Administration SUE POHJA VP – Book Sales
FRED RUIZ VP – Manufacturing Operations COURTNEY SIMMONS Senior VP – Publicity BOB WAYNE Senior VP – Sales

SUPERMAN: DOOMED

DC Comics, 1700 Broadway, New York, NY 10019
A Warner Bros. Entertainment Company.
Printed by RR Donnelley, Salem, VA, USA. 3/25/15. First Printing.

ISBN: 978-1-4012-5240-3

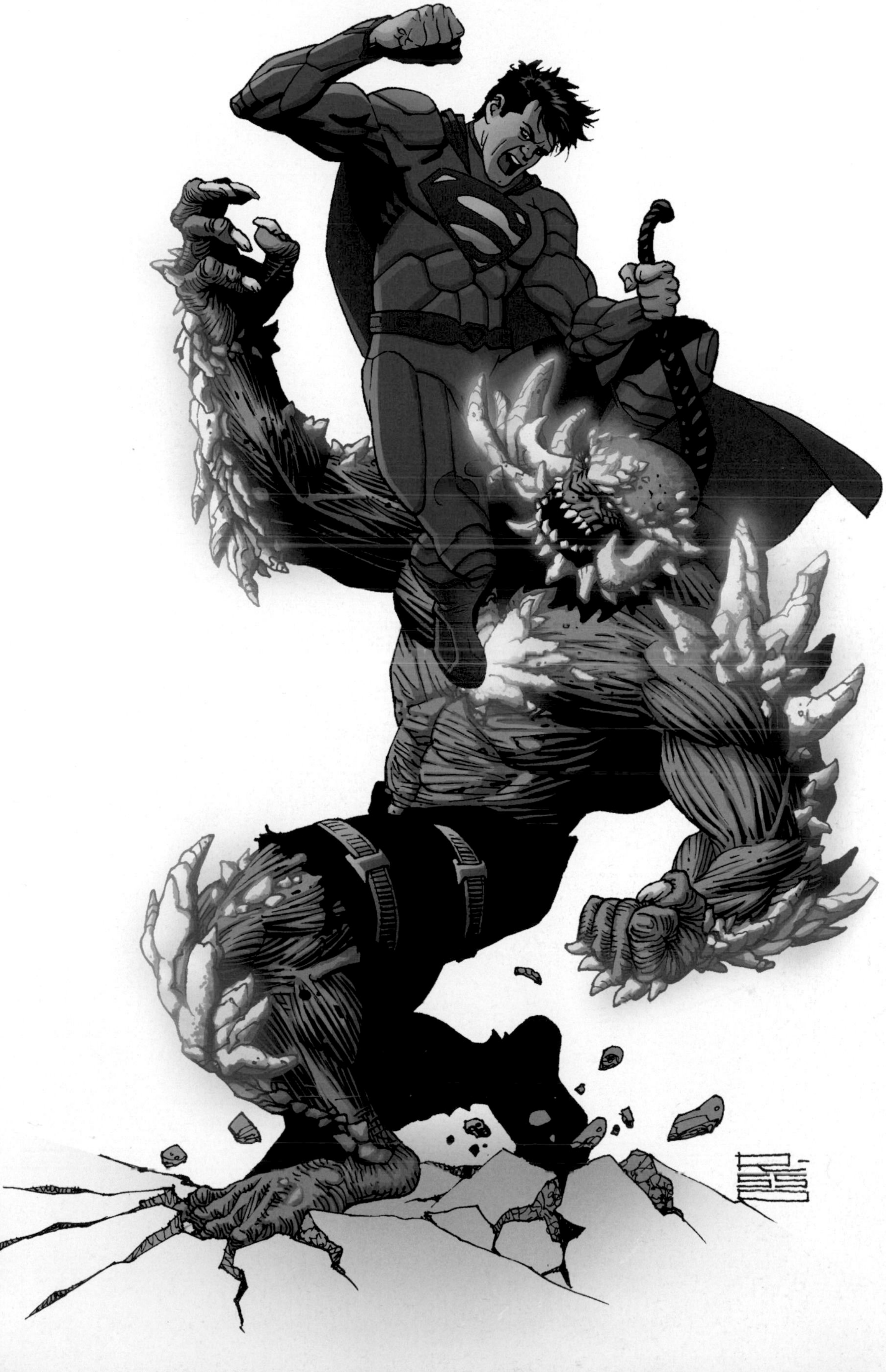

SUPERMAN

DOOMED

[PRELUDE] part 1

PAGES 1-5

STORY
GREG PAK

ART
AARON KUDER

COLORS
WIL QUINTANA

LETTERS
TRAVIS LANHAM

PAGES 6-12

STORY
CHARLES SOULE

PENCILS
EDDY BARROWS

INKS
EBER FERREIRA

COLORS
HI-FI

LETTERS
CARLOS M. MANGUAL

COVER
EDUARDO RISSO AND **TRISH MULVIHILL**

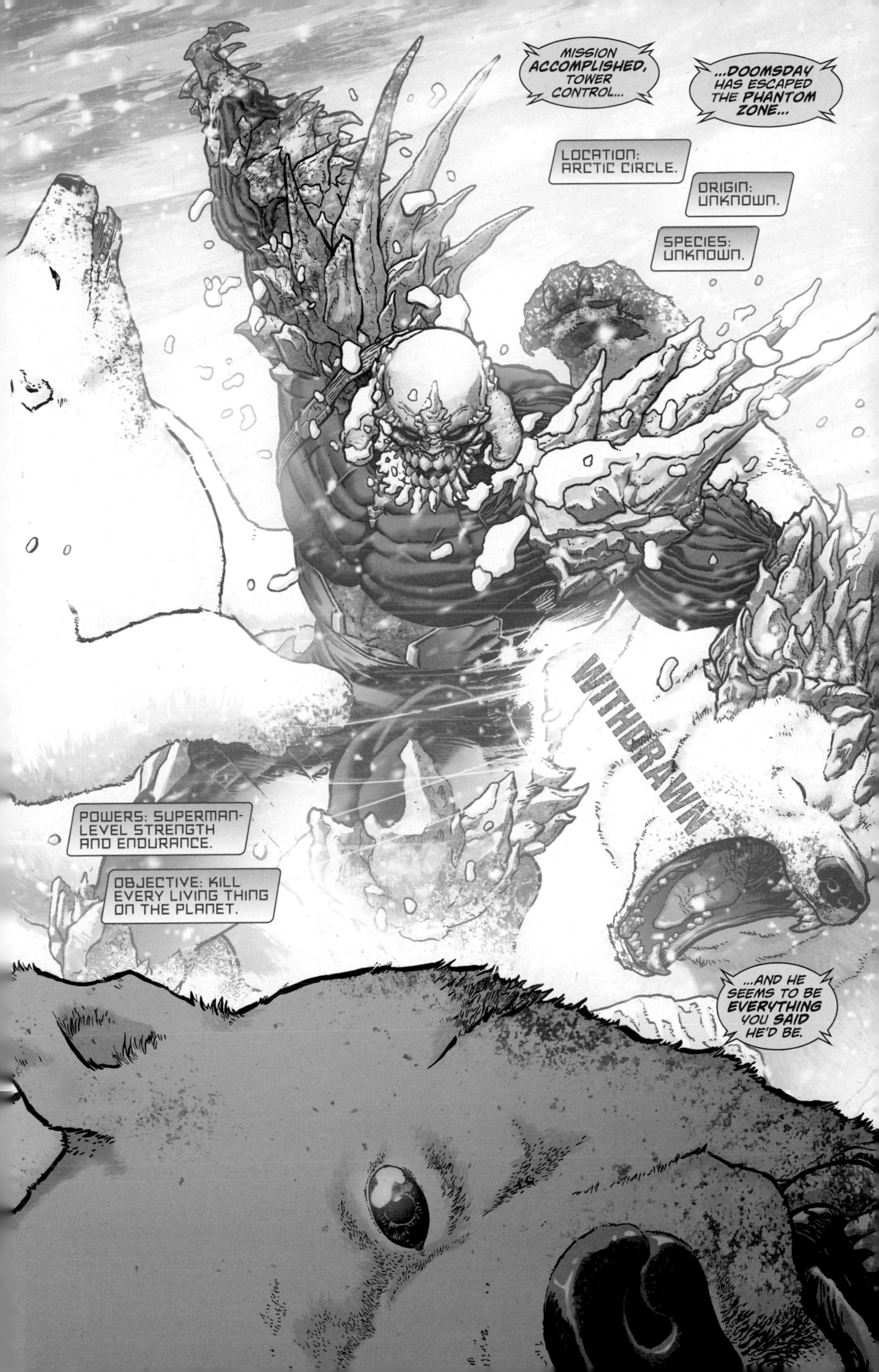
MISSION ACCOMPLISHED, TOWER CONTROL...
...DOOMSDAY HAS ESCAPED THE PHANTOM ZONE...
LOCATION: ARCTIC CIRCLE.
ORIGIN: UNKNOWN.
SPECIES: UNKNOWN.
POWERS: SUPERMAN-LEVEL STRENGTH AND ENDURANCE.
OBJECTIVE: KILL EVERY LIVING THING ON THE PLANET.
...AND HE SEEMS TO BE EVERYTHING YOU SAID HE'D BE.
WITHDRAWN

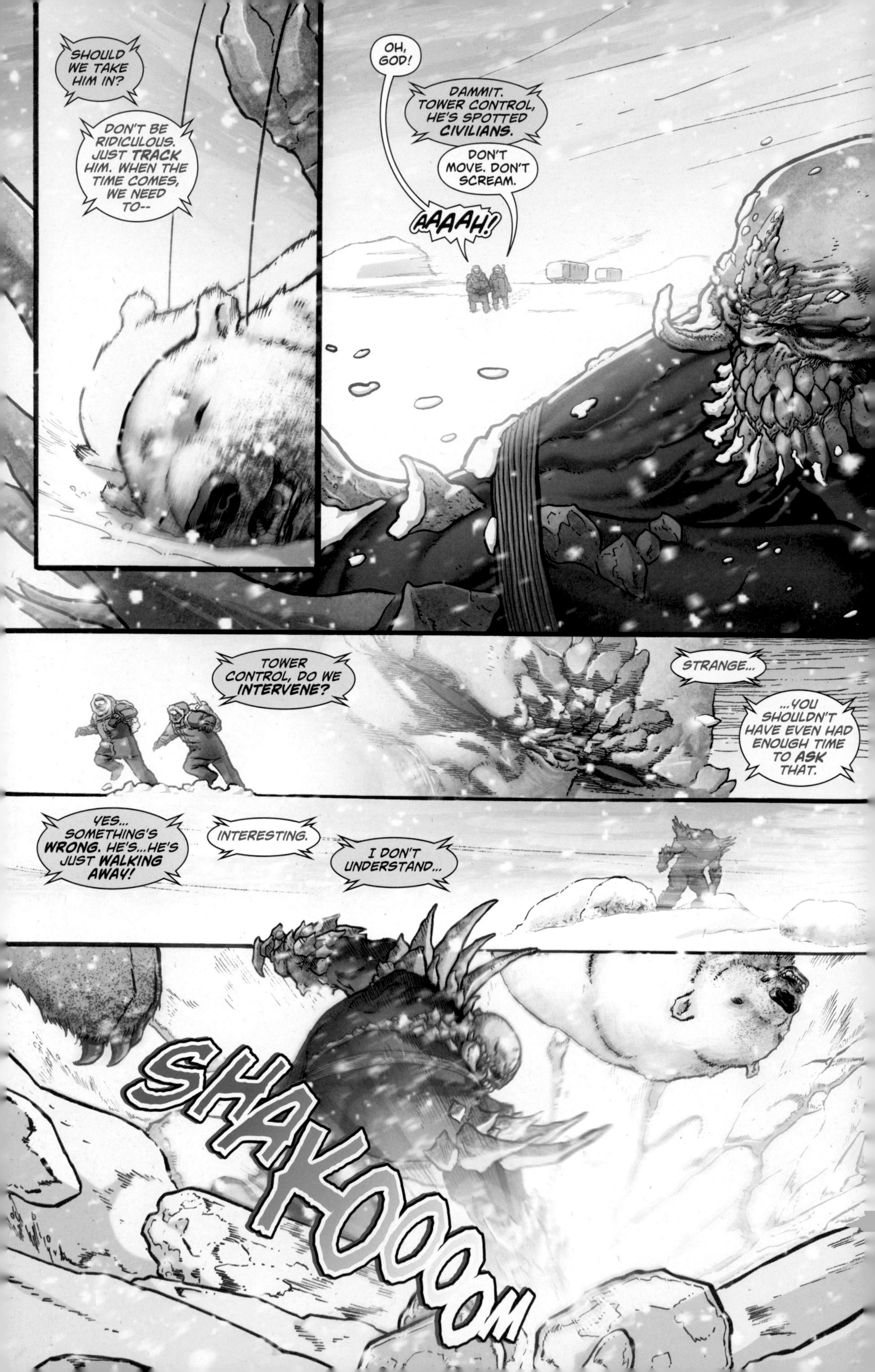
SHOULD WE TAKE HIM IN?
DON'T BE RIDICULOUS. JUST TRACK HIM. WHEN THE TIME COMES, WE NEED TO--
OH, GOD!
DAMMIT. TOWER CONTROL, HE'S SPOTTED CIVILIANS.
DON'T MOVE. DON'T SCREAM.
AAAAH!
TOWER CONTROL, DO WE INTERVENE?
STRANGE...
...YOU SHOULDN'T HAVE EVEN HAD ENOUGH TIME TO ASK THAT.
YES... SOMETHING'S WRONG. HE'S...HE'S JUST WALKING AWAY!
INTERESTING.
I DON'T UNDERSTAND...
SHAKOOOOM

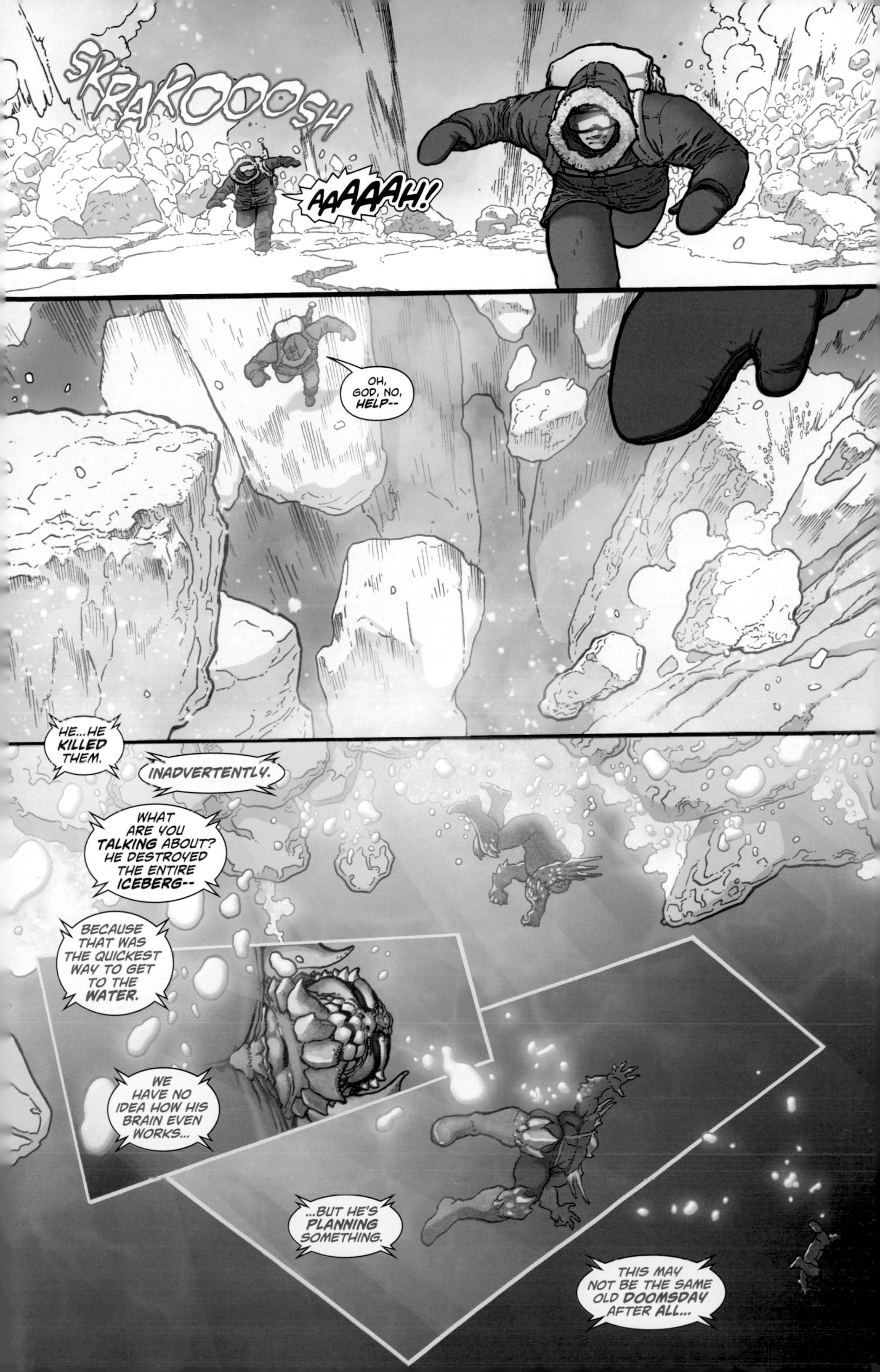
SKRAKOOOOSH
AAAAAH!
OH, GOD, NO, HELP--
HE...HE KILLED THEM.
INADVERTENTLY.
WHAT ARE YOU TALKING ABOUT? HE DESTROYED THE ENTIRE ICEBERG--
BECAUSE THAT WAS THE QUICKEST WAY TO GET TO THE WATER.
WE HAVE NO IDEA HOW HIS BRAIN EVEN WORKS...
...BUT HE'S PLANNING SOMETHING.
THIS MAY NOT BE THE SAME OLD DOOMSDAY AFTER ALL...

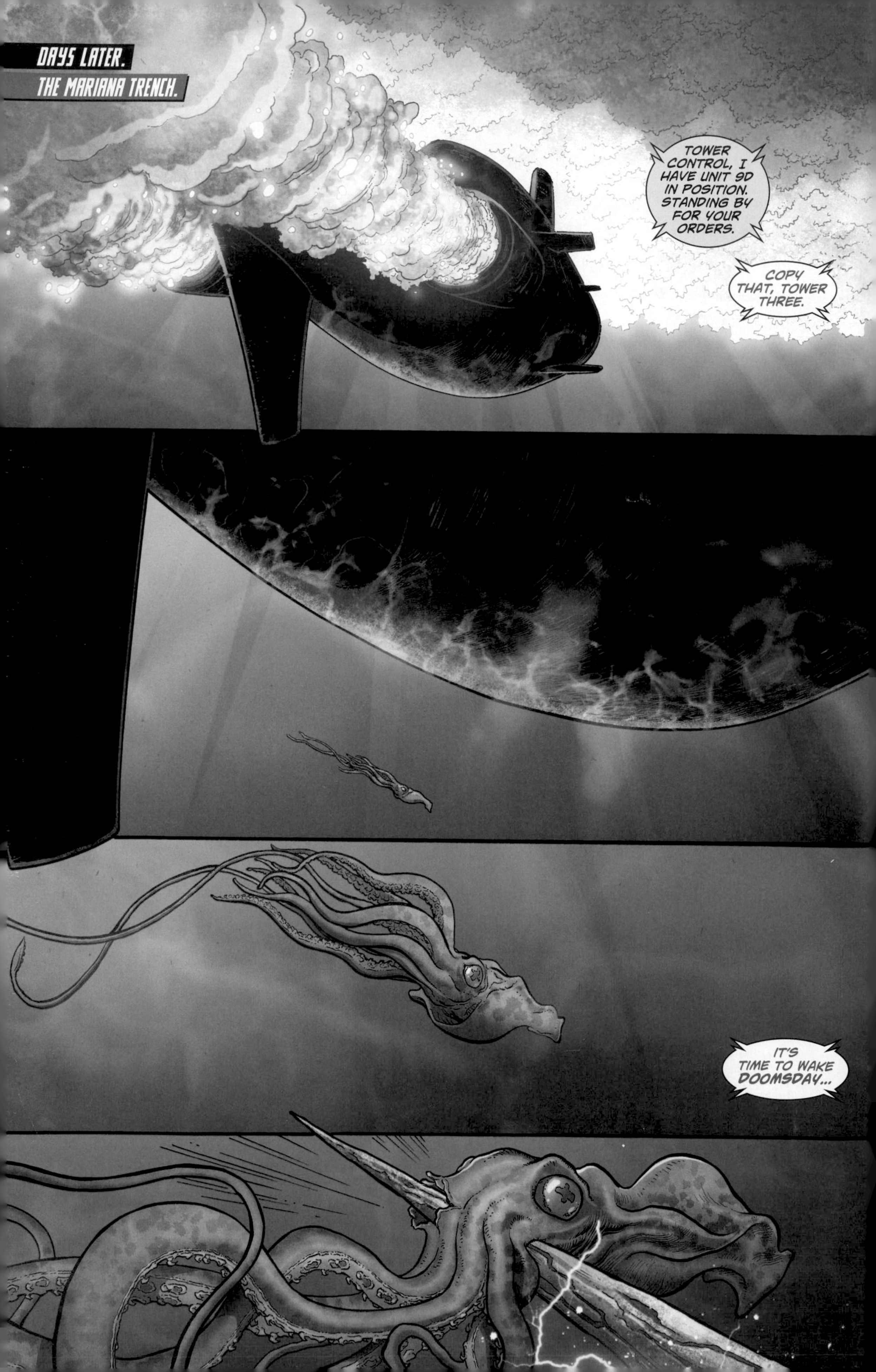
DAYS LATER.
THE MARIANA TRENCH.
TOWER CONTROL, I HAVE UNIT 9D IN POSITION. STANDING BY FOR YOUR ORDERS.
COPY THAT, TOWER THREE.
IT'S TIME TO WAKE DOOMSDAY...

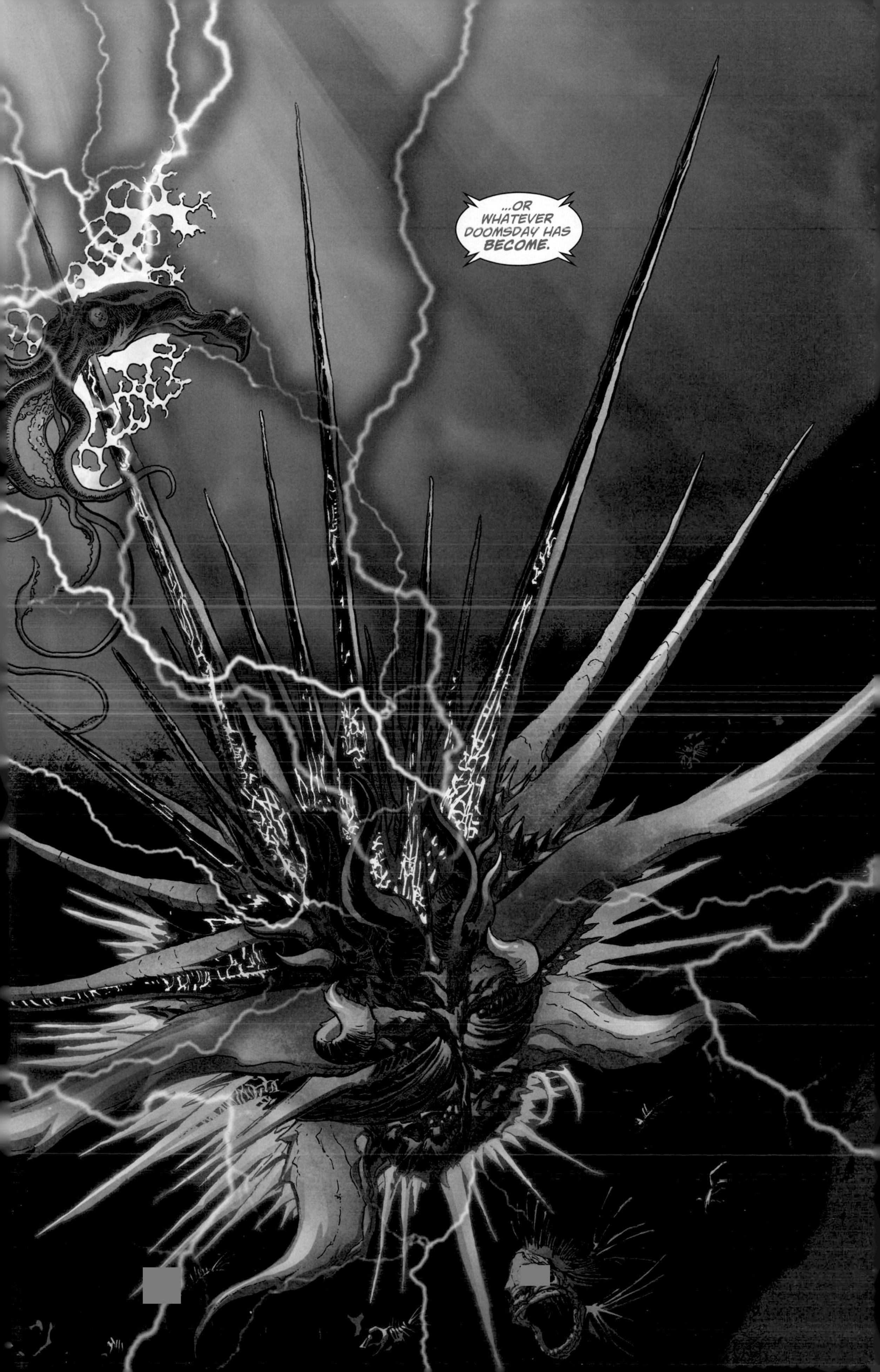
...OR WHATEVER DOOMSDAY HAS BECOME.

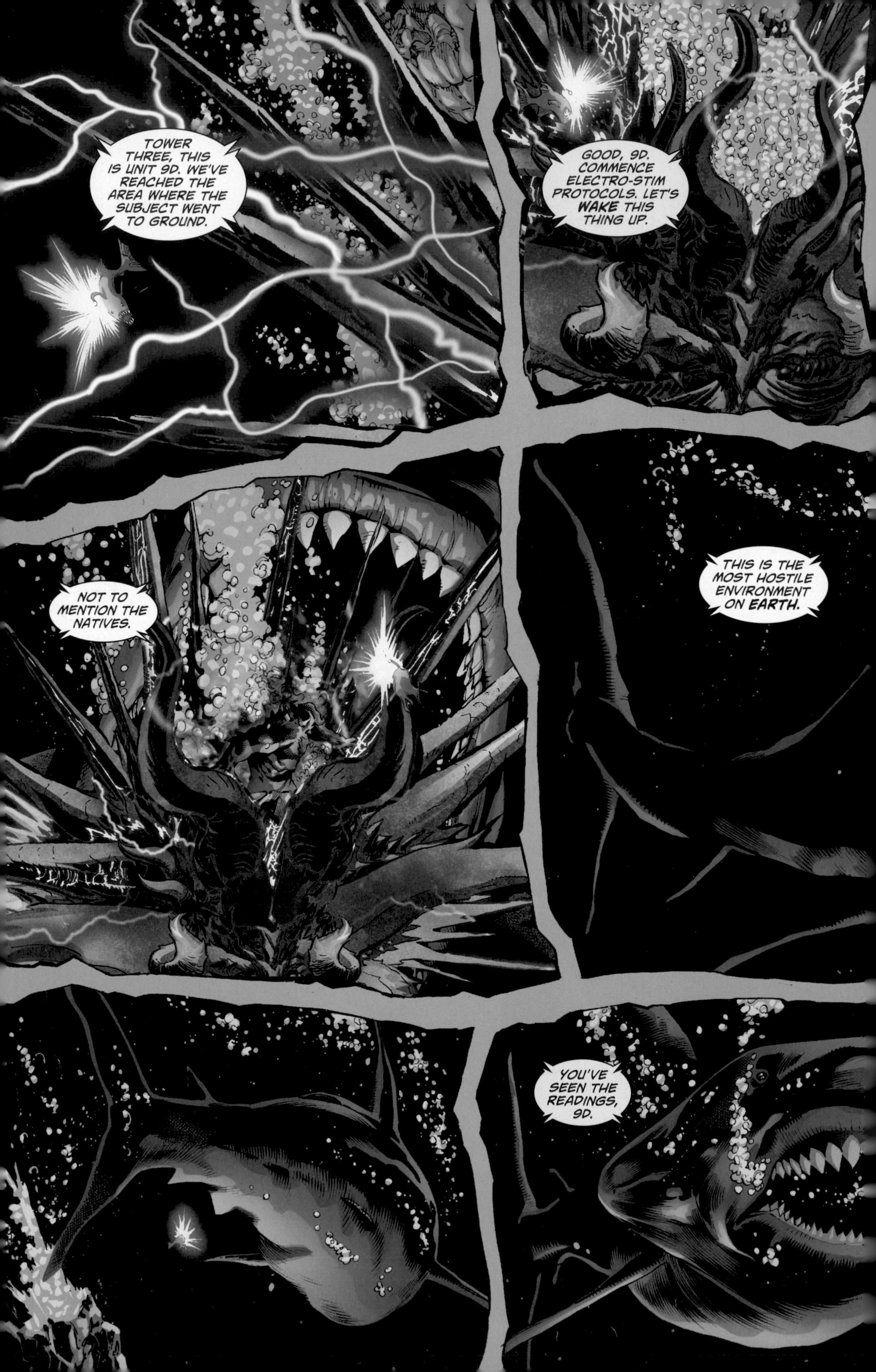
TOWER THREE, THIS IS UNIT 9D. WE'VE REACHED THE AREA WHERE THE SUBJECT WENT TO GROUND.
GOOD, 9D. COMMENCE ELECTRO-STIM PROTOCOLS. LET'S WAKE THIS THING UP.
NOT TO MENTION THE NATIVES.
THIS IS THE MOST HOSTILE ENVIRONMENT ON EARTH.
YOU'VE SEEN THE READINGS, 9D.

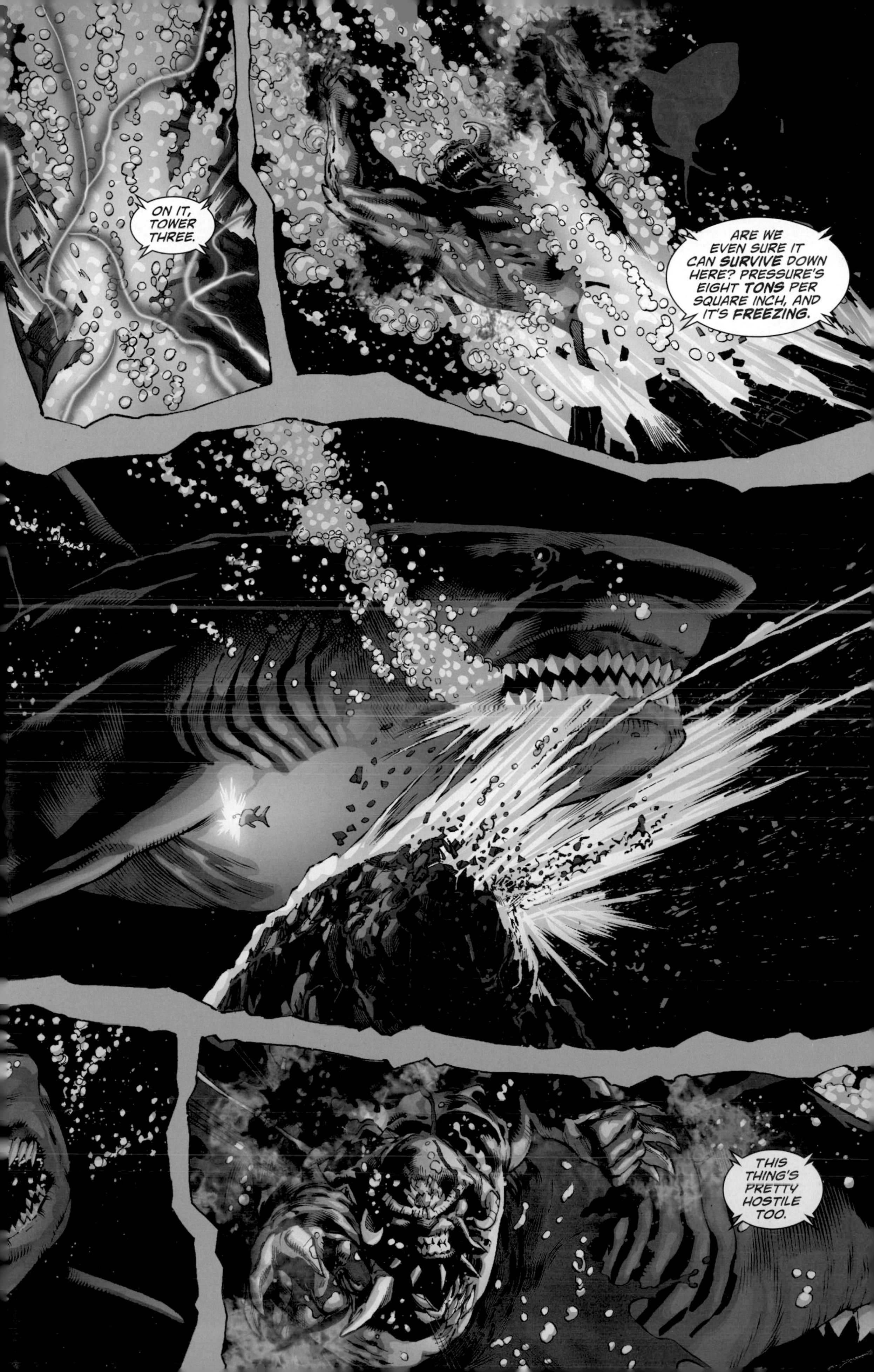
ON IT, TOWER THREE.
ARE WE EVEN SURE IT CAN SURVIVE DOWN HERE? PRESSURE'S EIGHT TONS PER SQUARE INCH, AND IT'S FREEZING.
THIS THING'S PRETTY HOSTILE TOO.

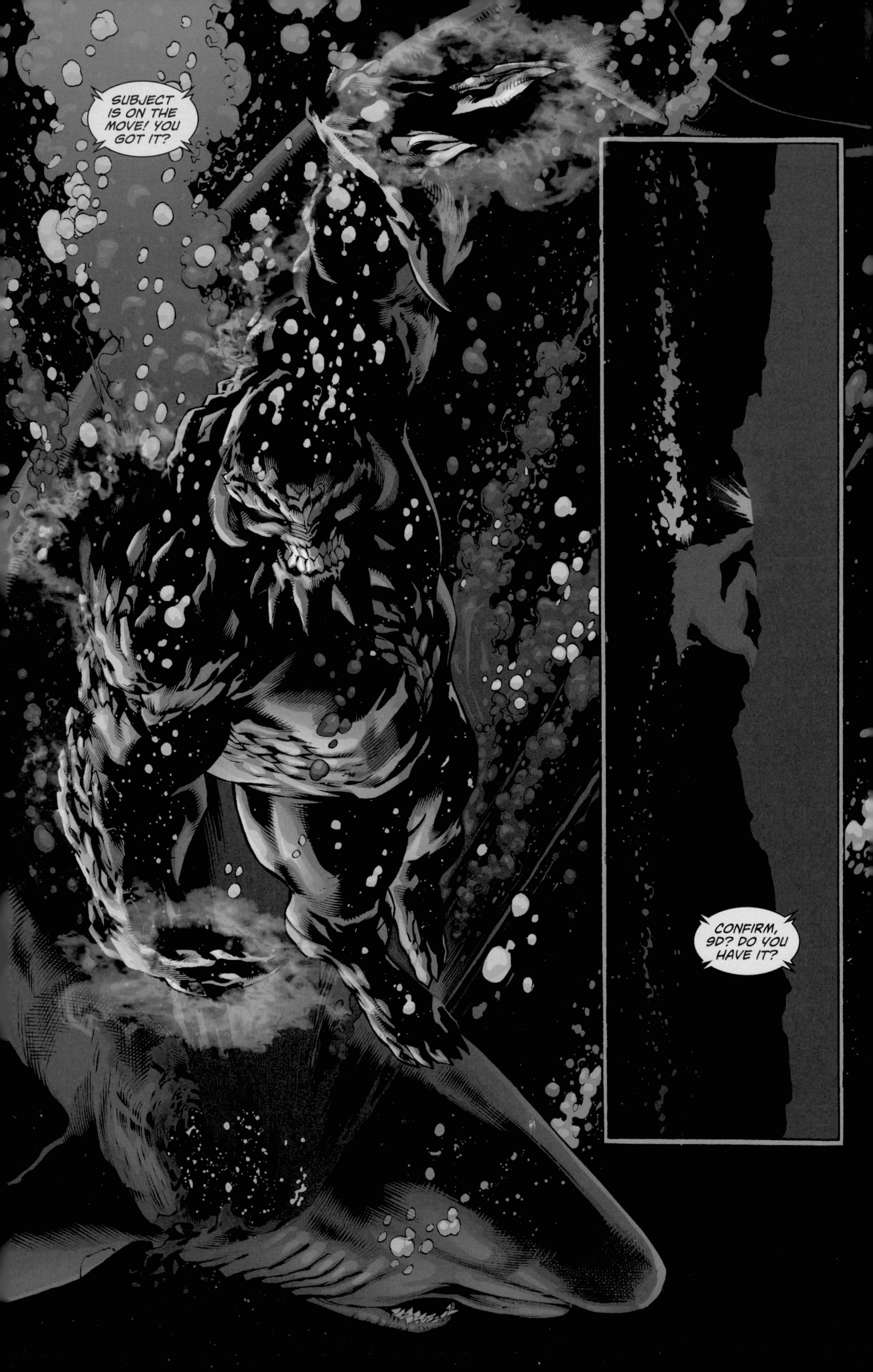
SUBJECT IS ON THE MOVE! YOU GOT IT?
CONFIRM, 9D? DO YOU HAVE IT?

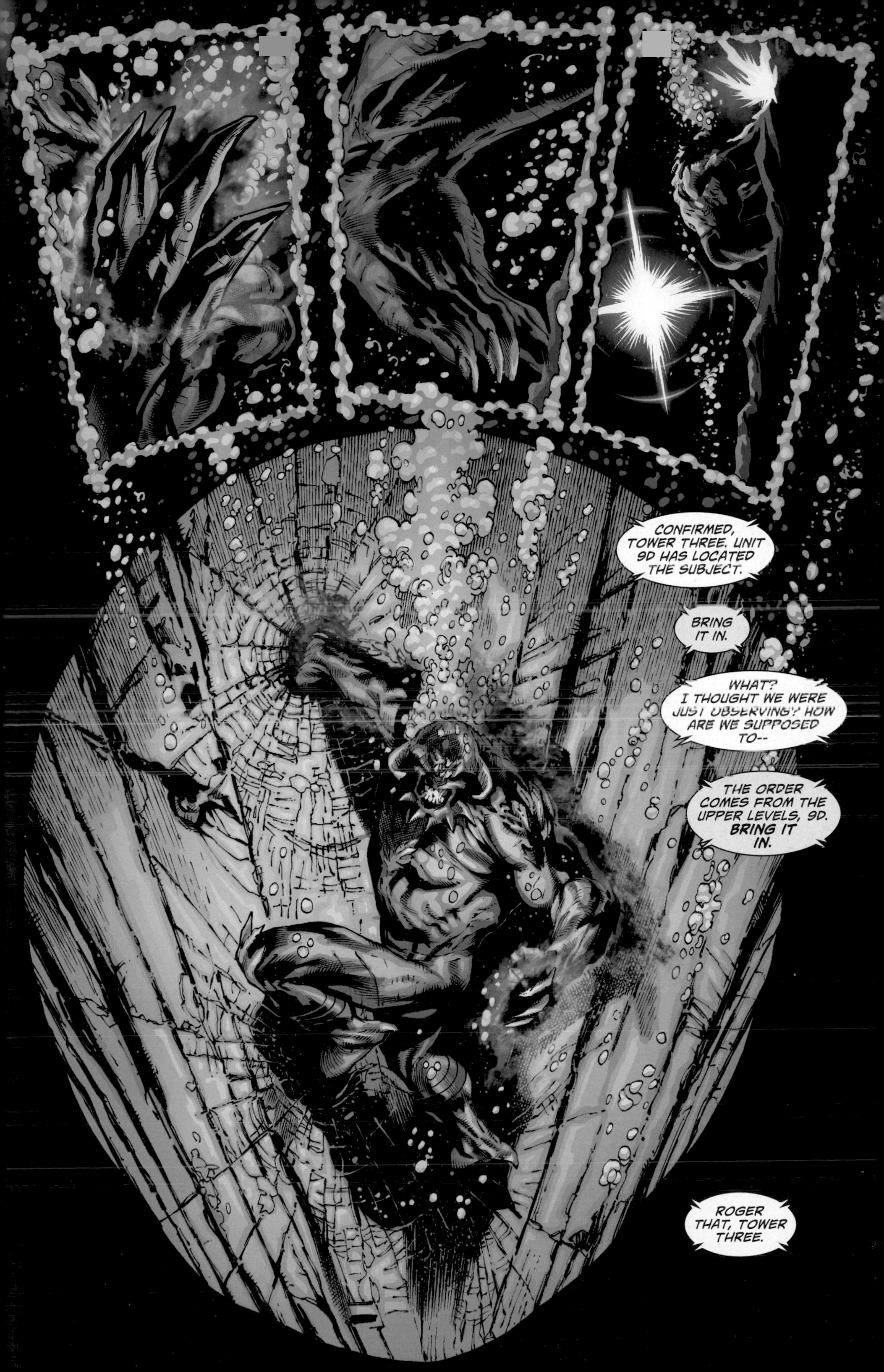
CONFIRMED, TOWER THREE. UNIT 9D HAS LOCATED THE SUBJECT.
BRING IT IN.
WHAT? I THOUGHT WE WERE JUST OBSERVING? HOW ARE WE SUPPOSED TO--
THE ORDER COMES FROM THE UPPER LEVELS, 9D. BRING IT IN.
ROGER THAT, TOWER THREE.

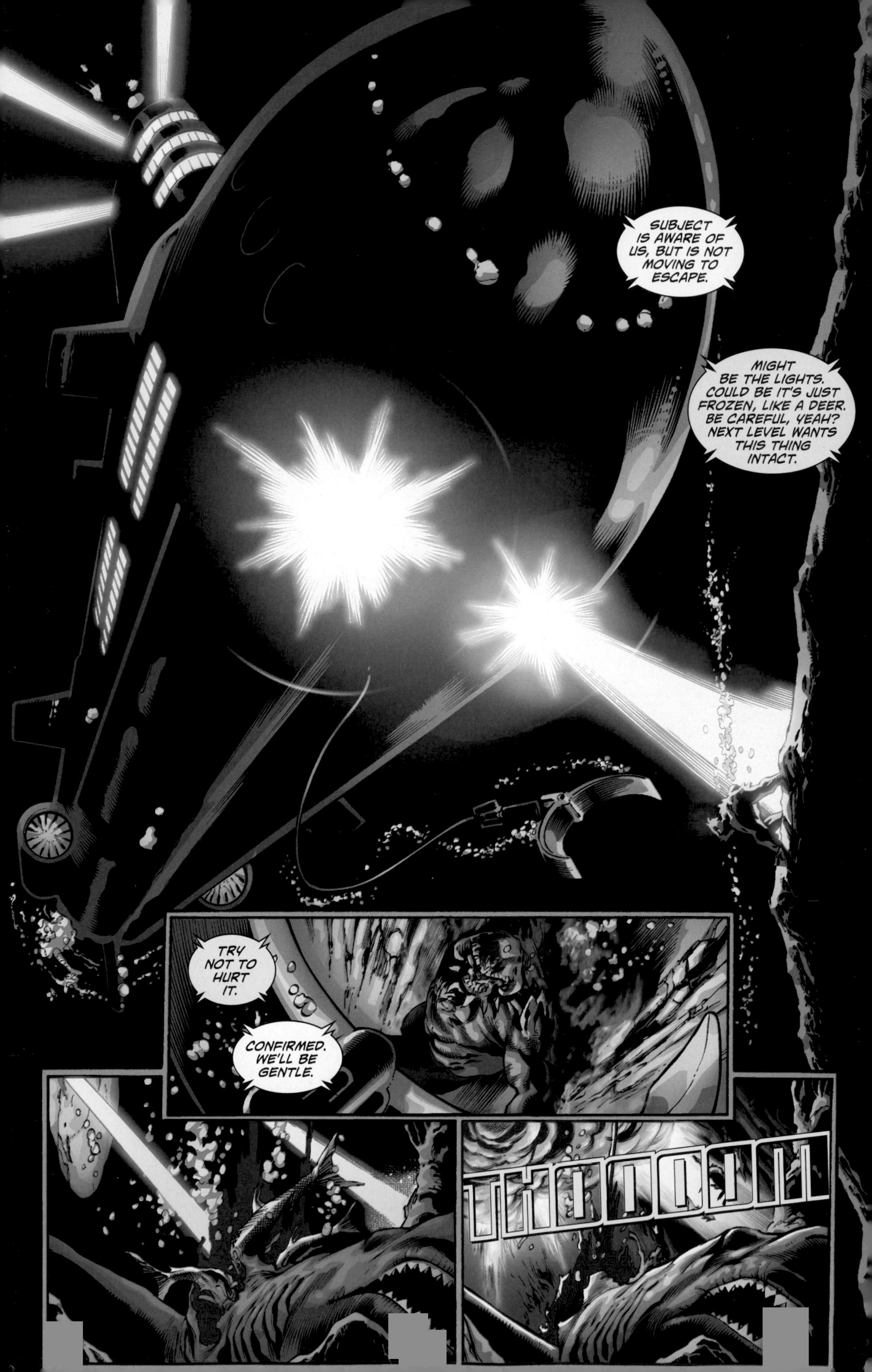
SUBJECT IS AWARE OF US, BUT IS NOT MOVING TO ESCAPE.
MIGHT BE THE LIGHTS. COULD BE IT'S JUST FROZEN, LIKE A DEER. BE CAREFUL, YEAH? NEXT LEVEL WANTS THIS THING INTACT.
TRY NOT TO HURT IT.
CONFIRMED. WE'LL BE GENTLE.
THOOOOM

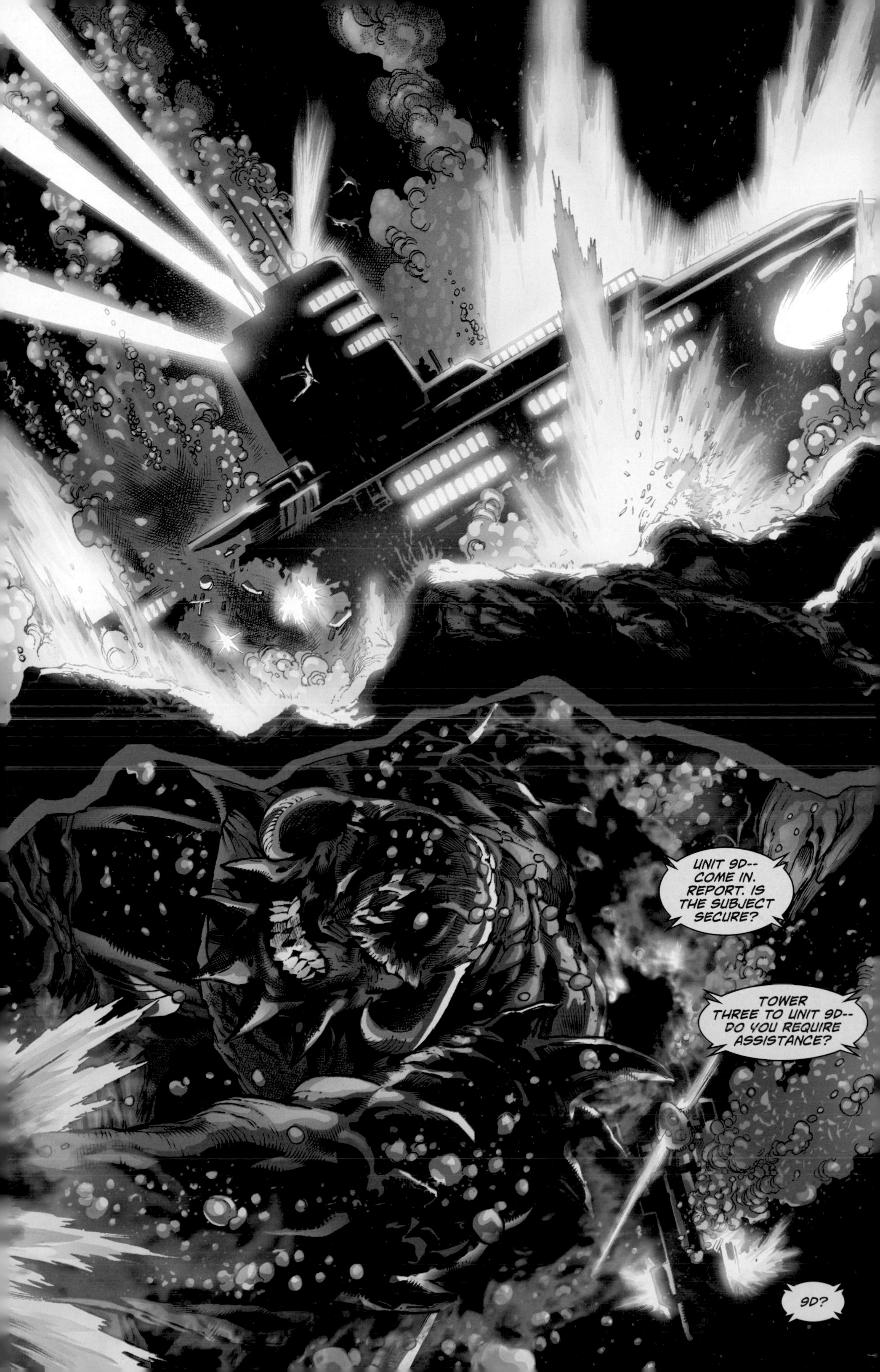
UNIT 9D-- COME IN. REPORT. IS THE SUBJECT SECURE?
TOWER THREE TO UNIT 9D-- DO YOU REQUIRE ASSISTANCE?
9D?

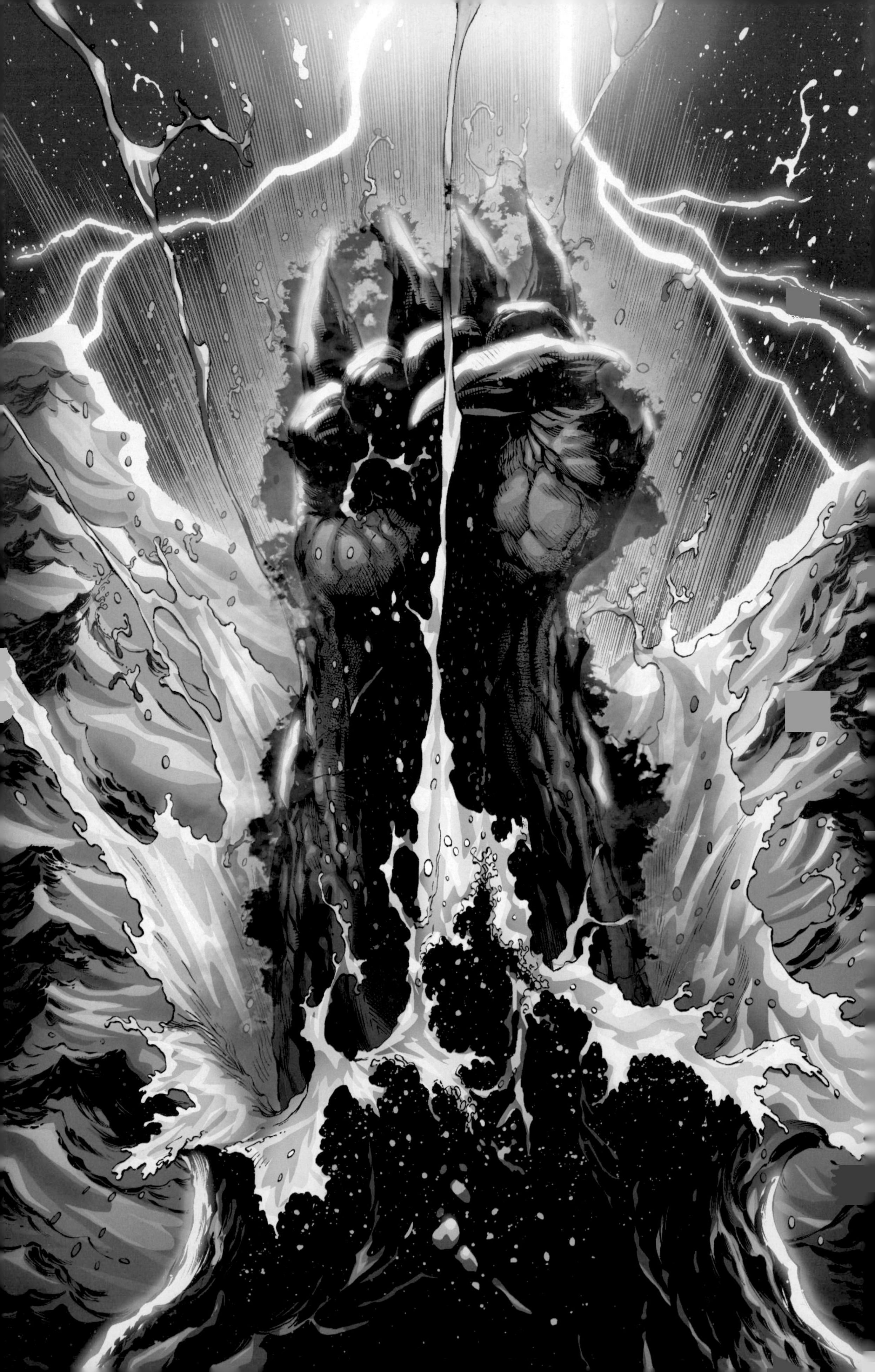

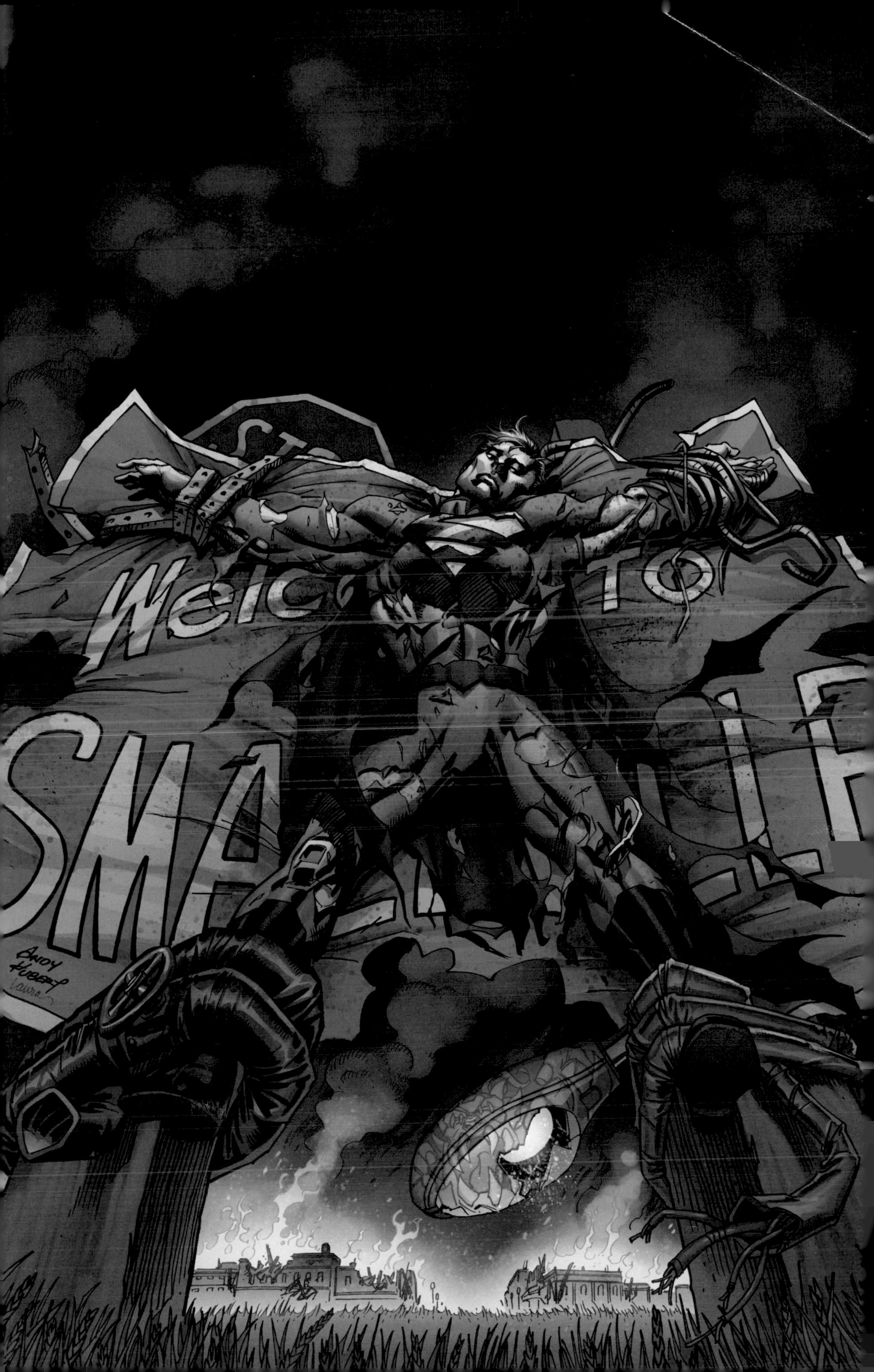
Welc
TO
SMA
ANDY KUBERT

SUPERMAN DOOMED

[PRELUDE] part 2

STORY
SCOTT LOBDELL

PENCILS
ED BENES

INKS
NORM RAPMUND

COLORS
PETE PANTAZIS

LETTERS
ROB LEIGH

COVER
ANDY KUBERT AND **BRAD ANDERSON**

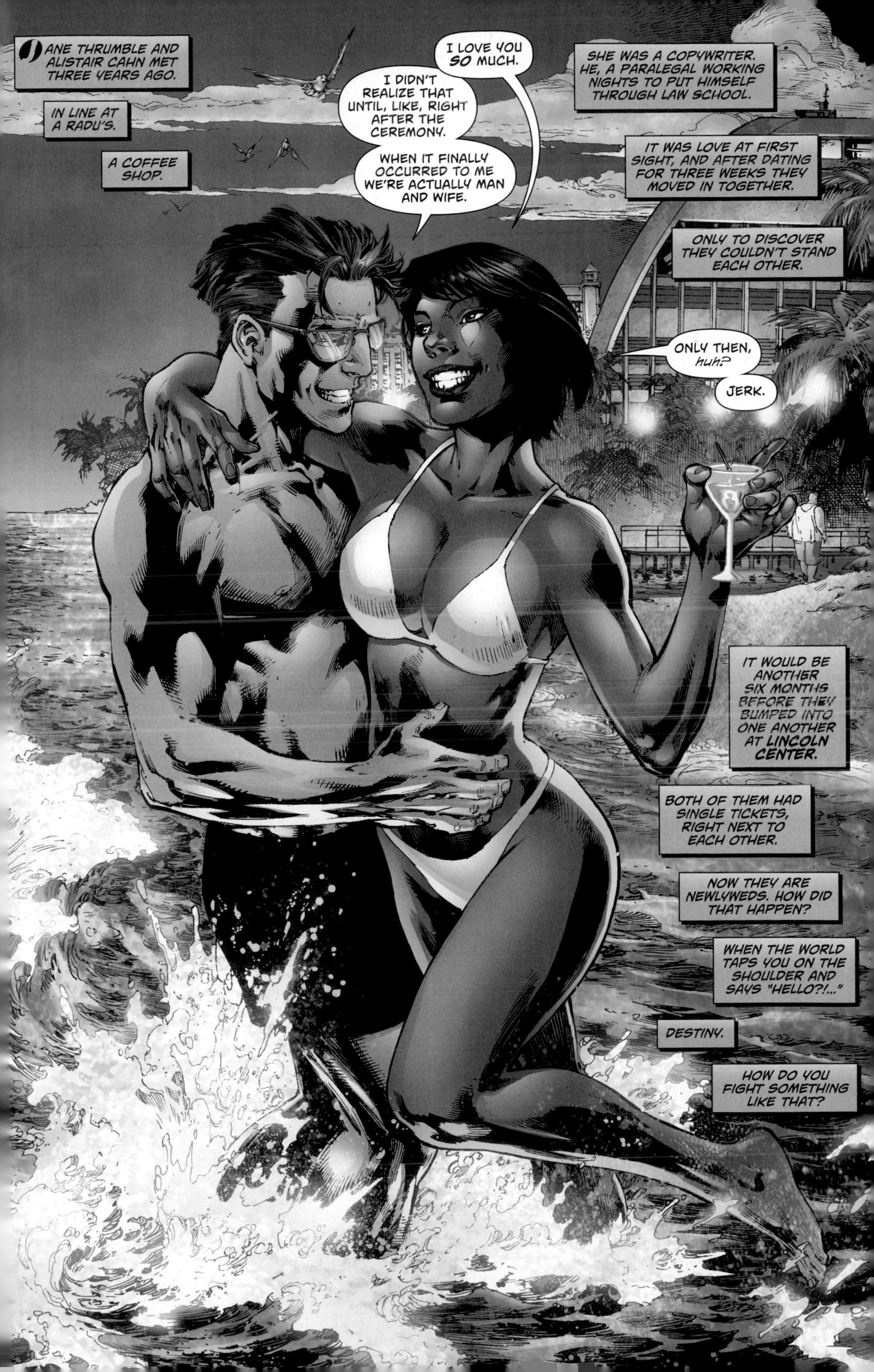
JANE THRUMBLE AND ALISTAIR CAHN MET THREE YEARS AGO.
IN LINE AT A RADU'S.
A COFFEE SHOP.
I LOVE YOU SO MUCH.
I DIDN'T REALIZE THAT UNTIL, LIKE, RIGHT AFTER THE CEREMONY.
WHEN IT FINALLY OCCURRED TO ME WE'RE ACTUALLY MAN AND WIFE.
SHE WAS A COPYWRITER. HE, A PARALEGAL WORKING NIGHTS TO PUT HIMSELF THROUGH LAW SCHOOL.
IT WAS LOVE AT FIRST SIGHT, AND AFTER DATING FOR THREE WEEKS THEY MOVED IN TOGETHER.
ONLY TO DISCOVER THEY COULDN'T STAND EACH OTHER.
ONLY THEN, *huh?*
JERK.
IT WOULD BE ANOTHER SIX MONTHS BEFORE THEY BUMPED INTO ONE ANOTHER AT **LINCOLN CENTER.**
BOTH OF THEM HAD SINGLE TICKETS, RIGHT NEXT TO EACH OTHER.
NOW THEY ARE NEWLYWEDS. HOW DID THAT HAPPEN?
WHEN THE WORLD TAPS YOU ON THE SHOULDER AND SAYS "HELLO?!..."
DESTINY.
HOW DO YOU FIGHT SOMETHING LIKE THAT?

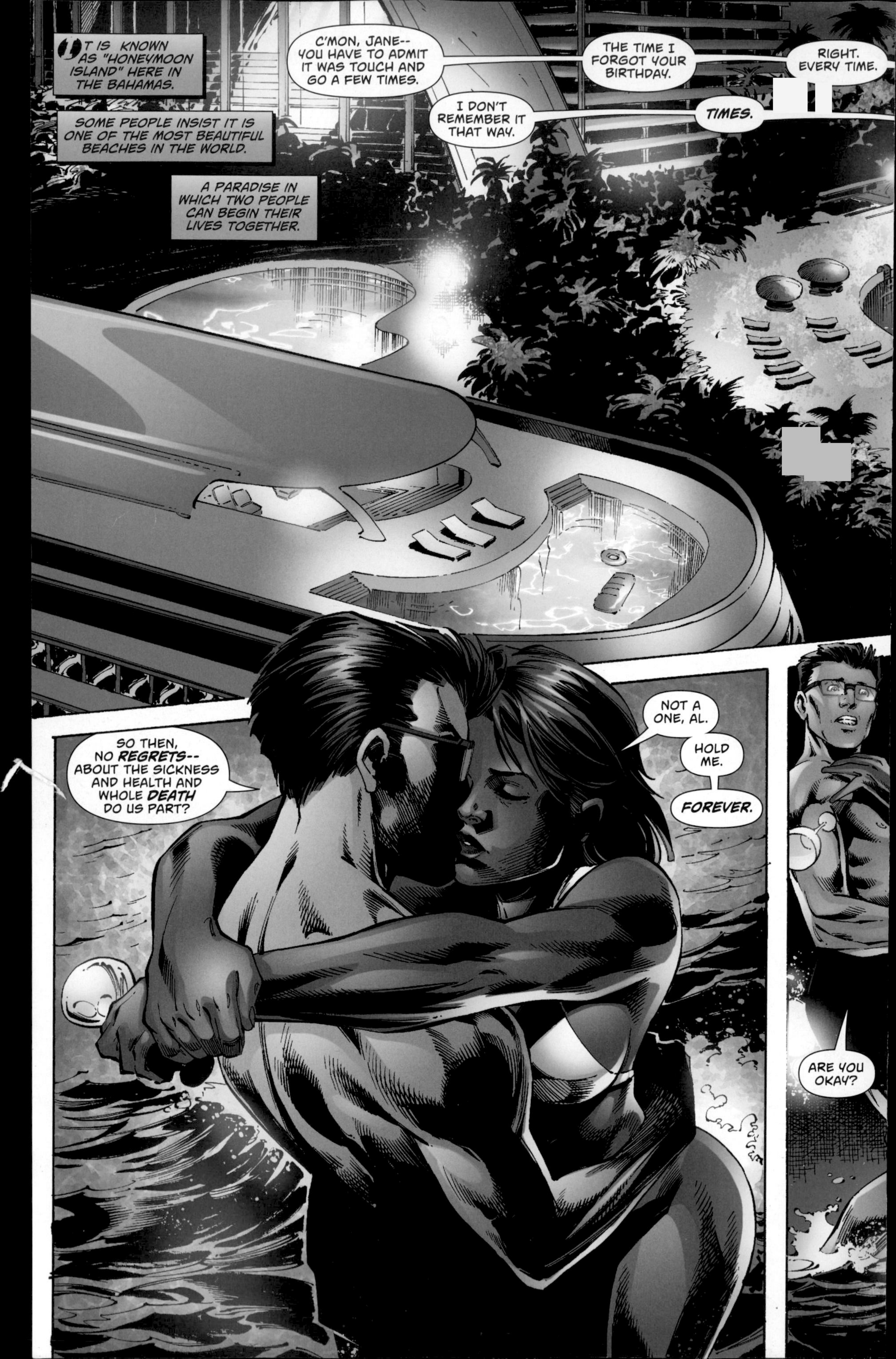

IT IS KNOWN AS "HONEYMOON ISLAND" HERE IN THE BAHAMAS.
SOME PEOPLE INSIST IT IS ONE OF THE MOST BEAUTIFUL BEACHES IN THE WORLD.
A PARADISE IN WHICH TWO PEOPLE CAN BEGIN THEIR LIVES TOGETHER.
C'MON, JANE-- YOU HAVE TO ADMIT IT WAS TOUCH AND GO A FEW TIMES.
I DON'T REMEMBER IT THAT WAY.
THE TIME I FORGOT YOUR BIRTHDAY.
TIMES.
RIGHT. EVERY TIME.
SO THEN, NO REGRETS-- ABOUT THE SICKNESS AND HEALTH AND WHOLE DEATH DO US PART?
NOT A ONE, AL.
HOLD ME.
FOREVER.
ARE YOU OKAY?

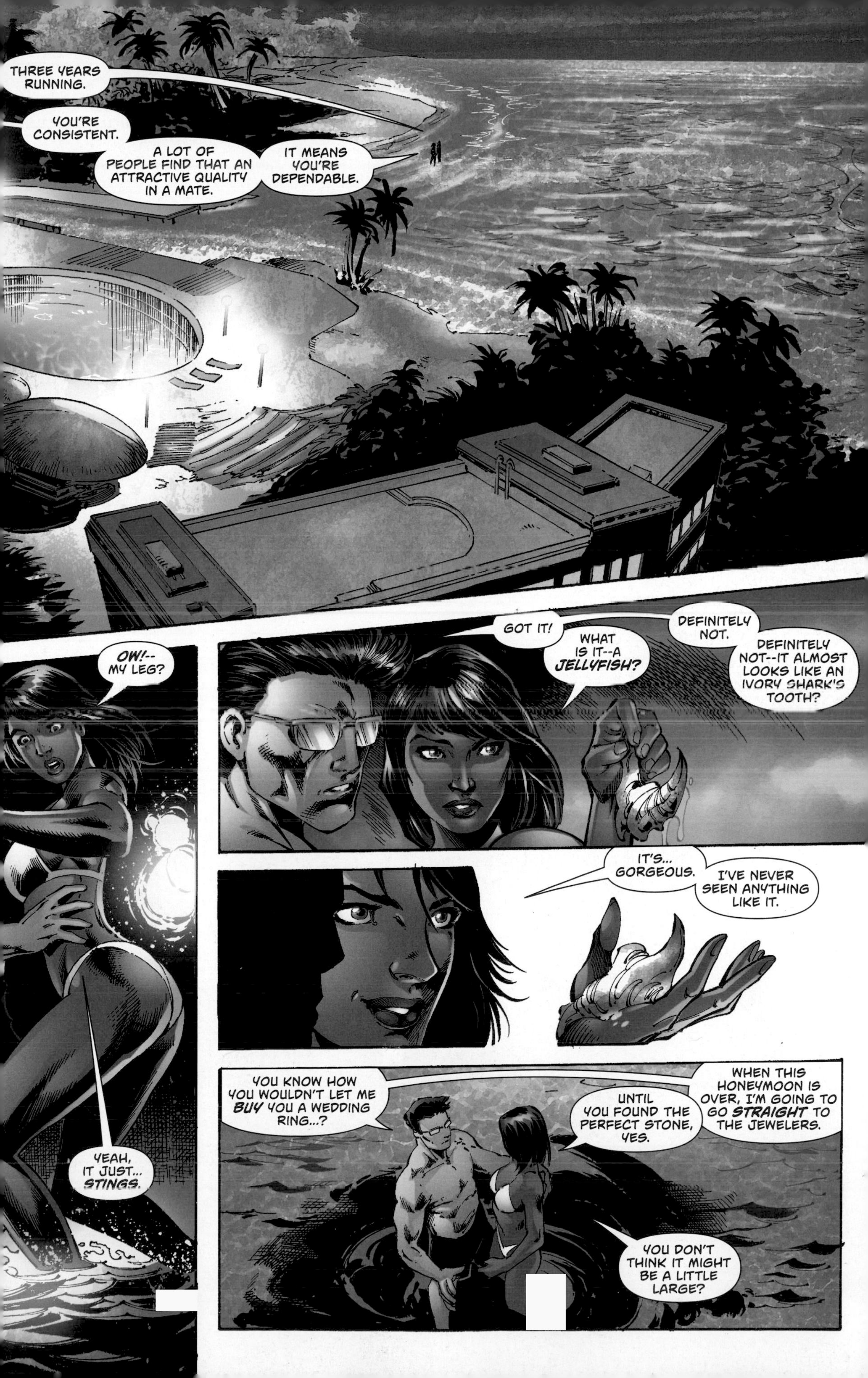
THREE YEARS RUNNING.
YOU'RE CONSISTENT.
A LOT OF PEOPLE FIND THAT AN ATTRACTIVE QUALITY IN A MATE.
IT MEANS YOU'RE DEPENDABLE.
OW!-- MY LEG?
YEAH, IT JUST... STINGS.
GOT IT!
WHAT IS IT--A JELLYFISH?
DEFINITELY NOT.
DEFINITELY NOT--IT ALMOST LOOKS LIKE AN IVORY SHARK'S TOOTH?
IT'S... GORGEOUS.
I'VE NEVER SEEN ANYTHING LIKE IT.
YOU KNOW HOW YOU WOULDN'T LET ME BUY YOU A WEDDING RING...?
UNTIL YOU FOUND THE PERFECT STONE, YES.
WHEN THIS HONEYMOON IS OVER, I'M GOING TO GO STRAIGHT TO THE JEWELERS.
YOU DON'T THINK IT MIGHT BE A LITTLE LARGE?

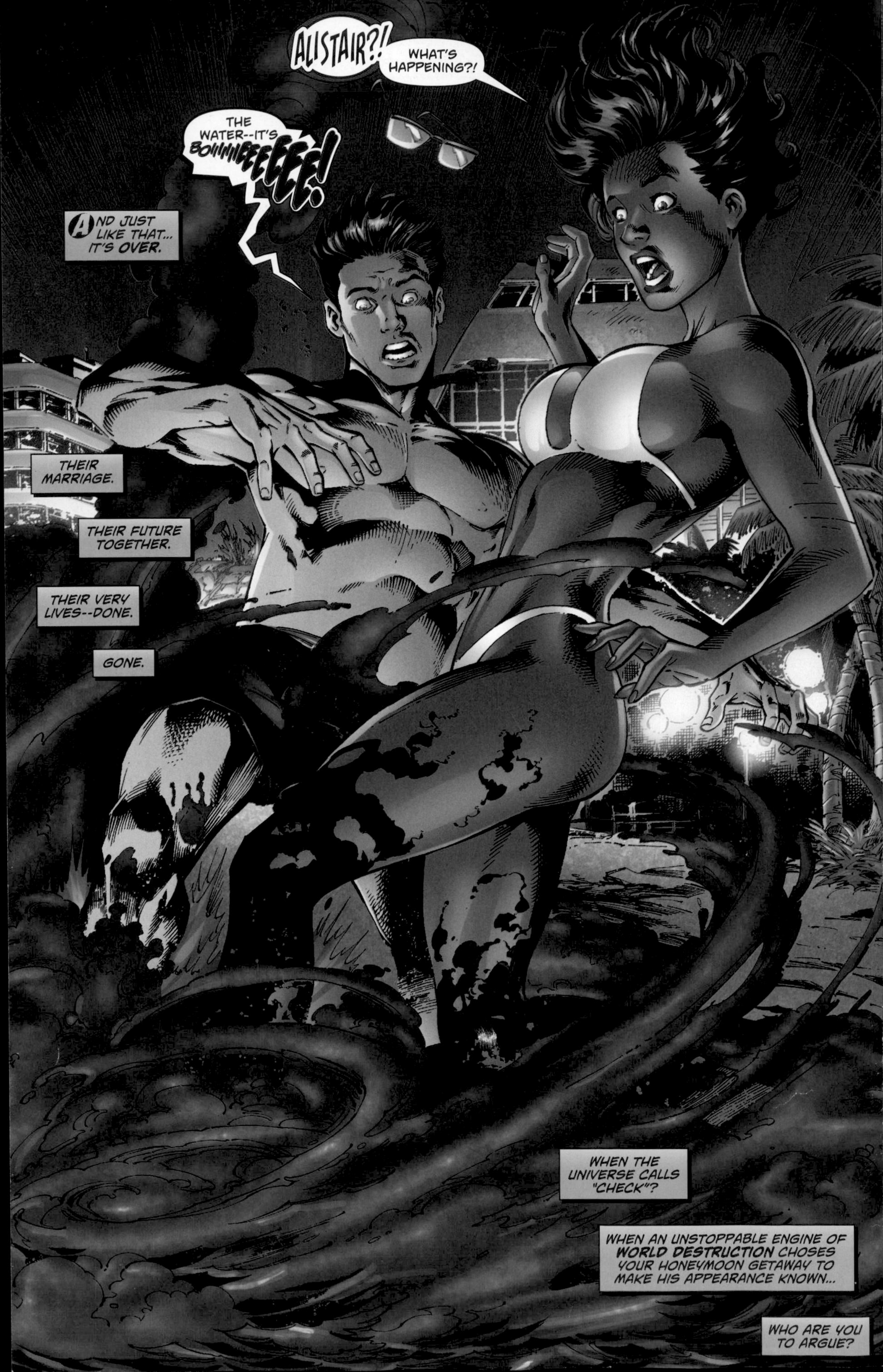
ALISTAIR?!
WHAT'S HAPPENING?!
THE WATER--IT'S BOIIIIIEEEEEEE!
AND JUST LIKE THAT... IT'S OVER.
THEIR MARRIAGE.
THEIR FUTURE TOGETHER.
THEIR VERY LIVES--DONE.
GONE.
WHEN THE UNIVERSE CALLS "CHECK"?
WHEN AN UNSTOPPABLE ENGINE OF WORLD DESTRUCTION CHOSES YOUR HONEYMOON GETAWAY TO MAKE HIS APPEARANCE KNOWN...
WHO ARE YOU TO ARGUE?

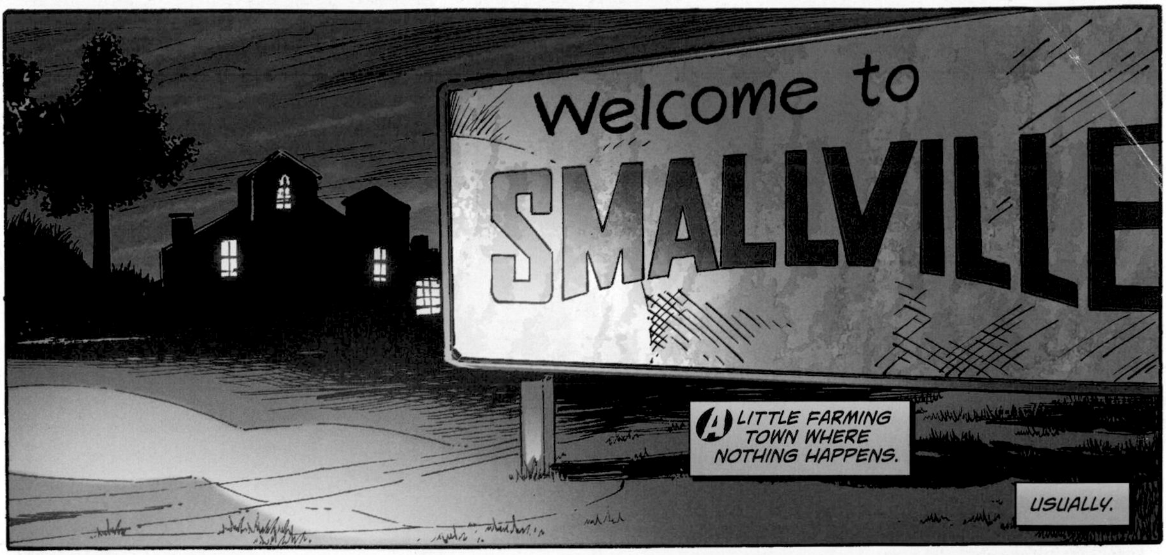
Welcome to
SMALLVILLE
A LITTLE FARMING TOWN WHERE NOTHING HAPPENS.
USUALLY.

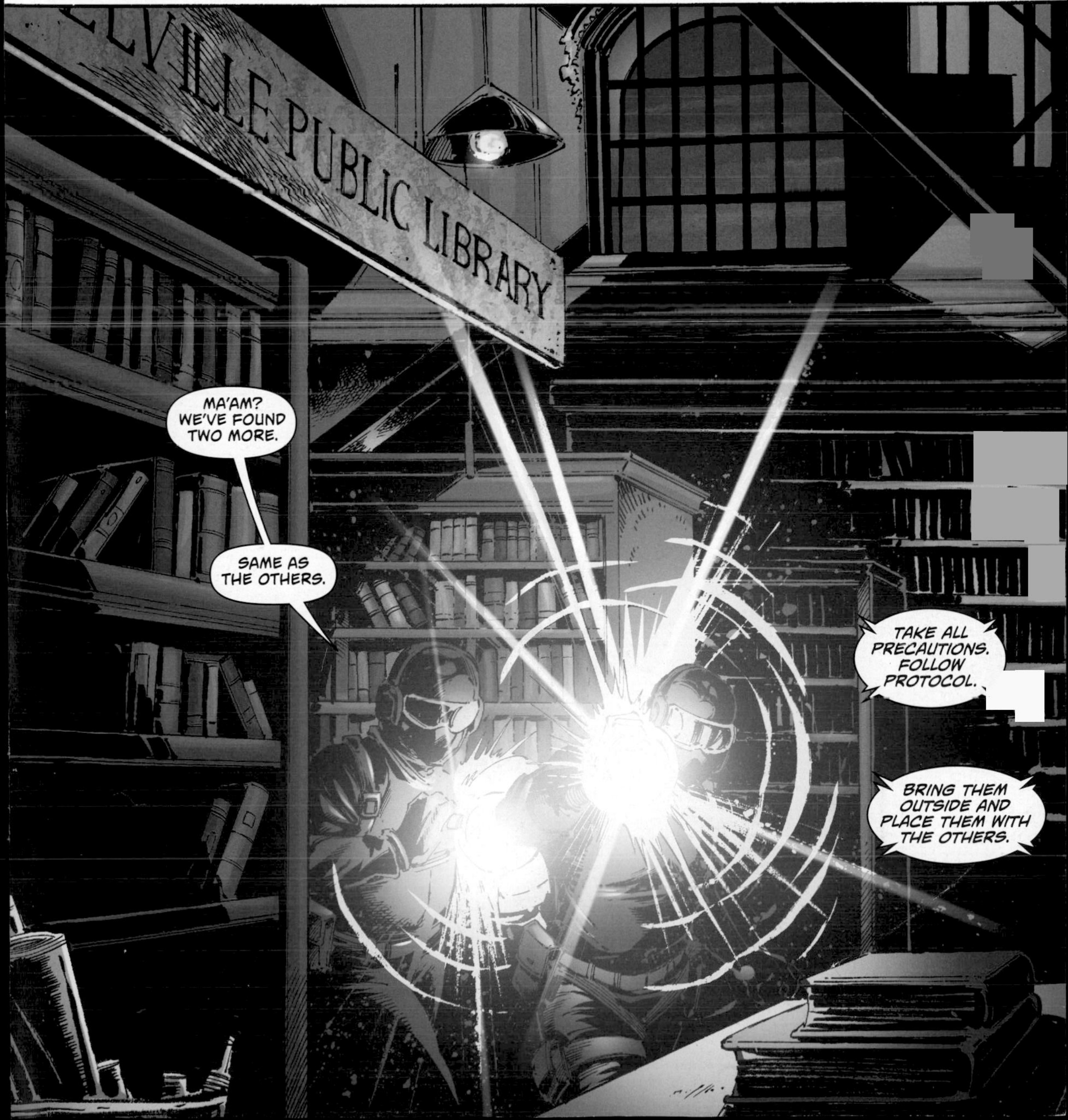
LLVILLE PUBLIC LIBRARY
MA'AM? WE'VE FOUND TWO MORE.
SAME AS THE OTHERS.
TAKE ALL PRECAUTIONS. FOLLOW PROTOCOL.
BRING THEM OUTSIDE AND PLACE THEM WITH THE OTHERS.

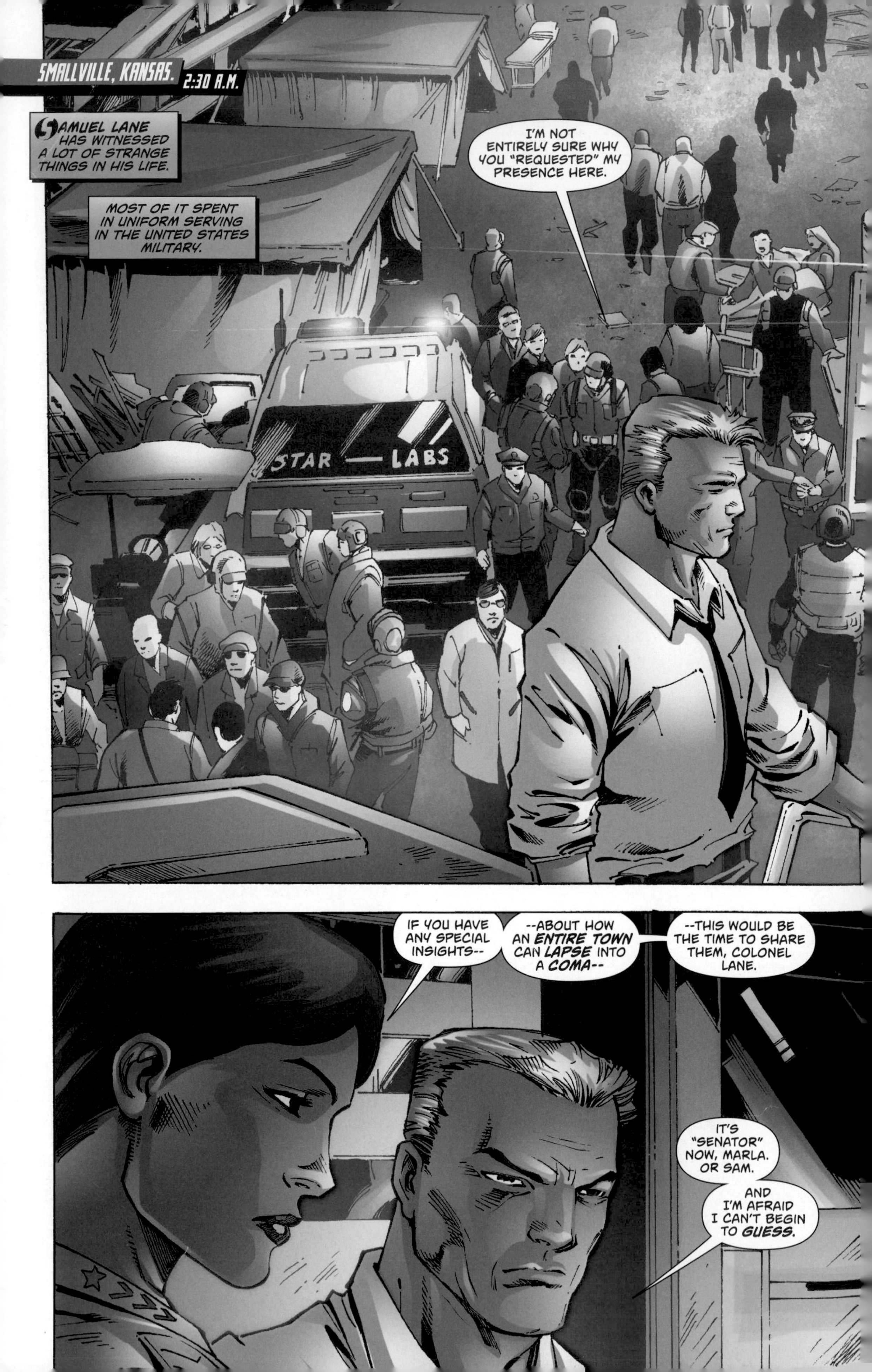
SMALLVILLE, KANSAS.
2:30 A.M.
SAMUEL LANE HAS WITNESSED A LOT OF STRANGE THINGS IN HIS LIFE.
MOST OF IT SPENT IN UNIFORM SERVING IN THE UNITED STATES MILITARY.
I'M NOT ENTIRELY SURE WHY YOU "REQUESTED" MY PRESENCE HERE.
STAR LABS
IF YOU HAVE ANY SPECIAL INSIGHTS--
--ABOUT HOW AN ENTIRE TOWN CAN LAPSE INTO A COMA--
--THIS WOULD BE THE TIME TO SHARE THEM, COLONEL LANE.
IT'S "SENATOR" NOW, MARLA. OR SAM.
AND I'M AFRAID I CAN'T BEGIN TO GUESS.

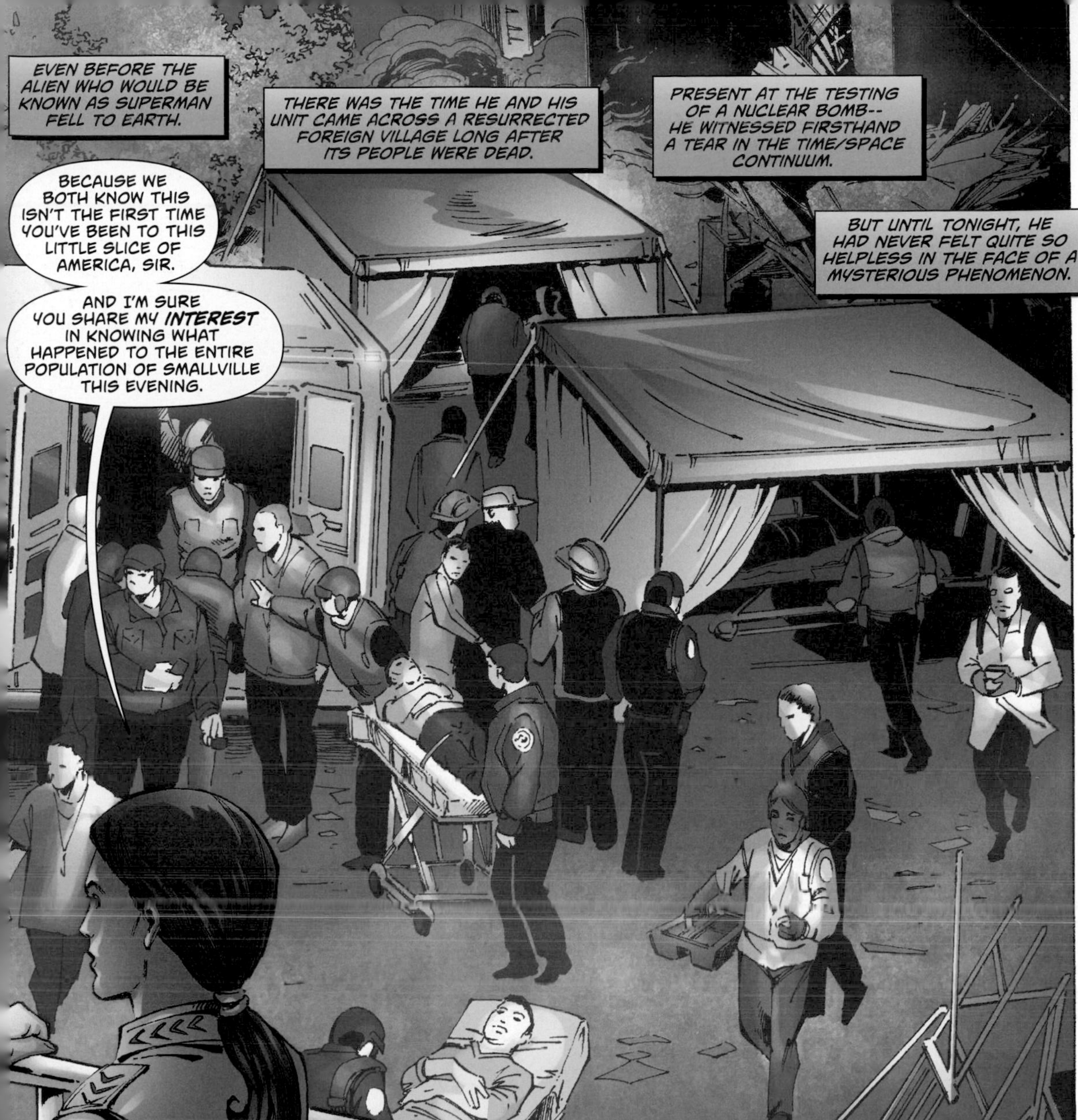
EVEN BEFORE THE ALIEN WHO WOULD BE KNOWN AS SUPERMAN FELL TO EARTH.
THERE WAS THE TIME HE AND HIS UNIT CAME ACROSS A RESURRECTED FOREIGN VILLAGE LONG AFTER ITS PEOPLE WERE DEAD.
PRESENT AT THE TESTING OF A NUCLEAR BOMB-- HE WITNESSED FIRSTHAND A TEAR IN THE TIME/SPACE CONTINUUM.
BUT UNTIL TONIGHT, HE HAD NEVER FELT QUITE SO HELPLESS IN THE FACE OF A MYSTERIOUS PHENOMENON.
BECAUSE WE BOTH KNOW THIS ISN'T THE FIRST TIME YOU'VE BEEN TO THIS LITTLE SLICE OF AMERICA, SIR.
AND I'M SURE YOU SHARE MY INTEREST IN KNOWING WHAT HAPPENED TO THE ENTIRE POPULATION OF SMALLVILLE THIS EVENING.

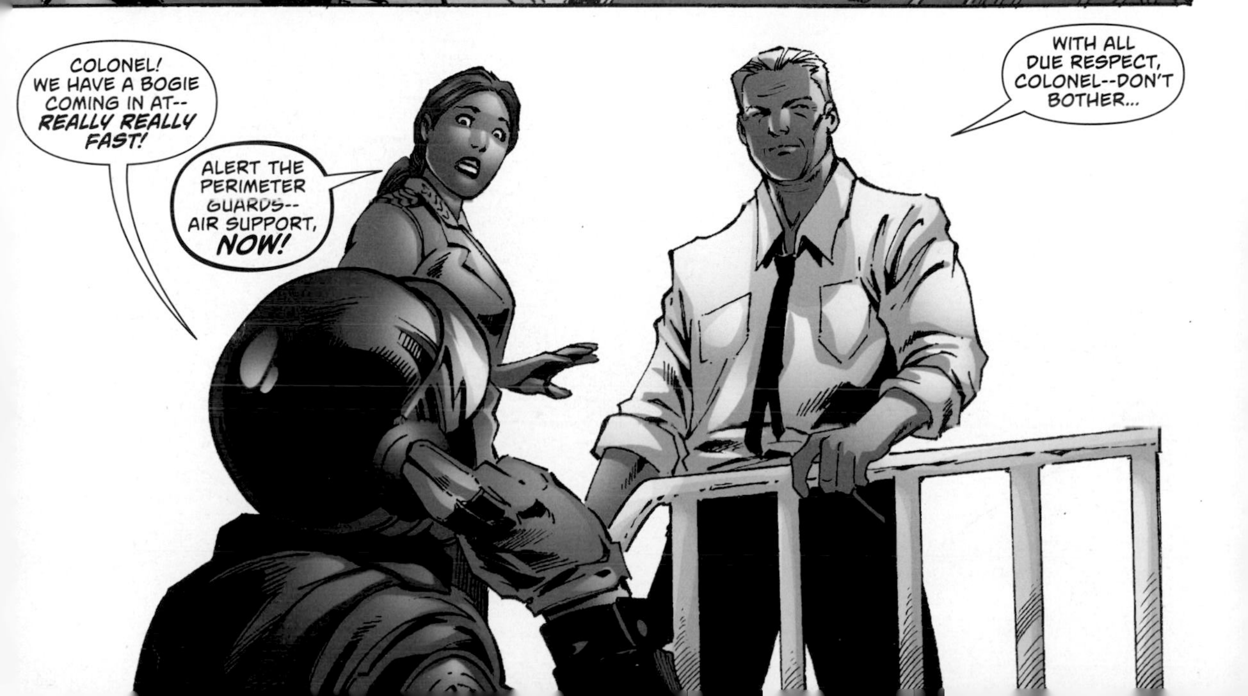
COLONEL! WE HAVE A BOGIE COMING IN AT-- REALLY REALLY FAST!
ALERT THE PERIMETER GUARDS-- AIR SUPPORT, NOW!
WITH ALL DUE RESPECT, COLONEL--DON'T BOTHER...

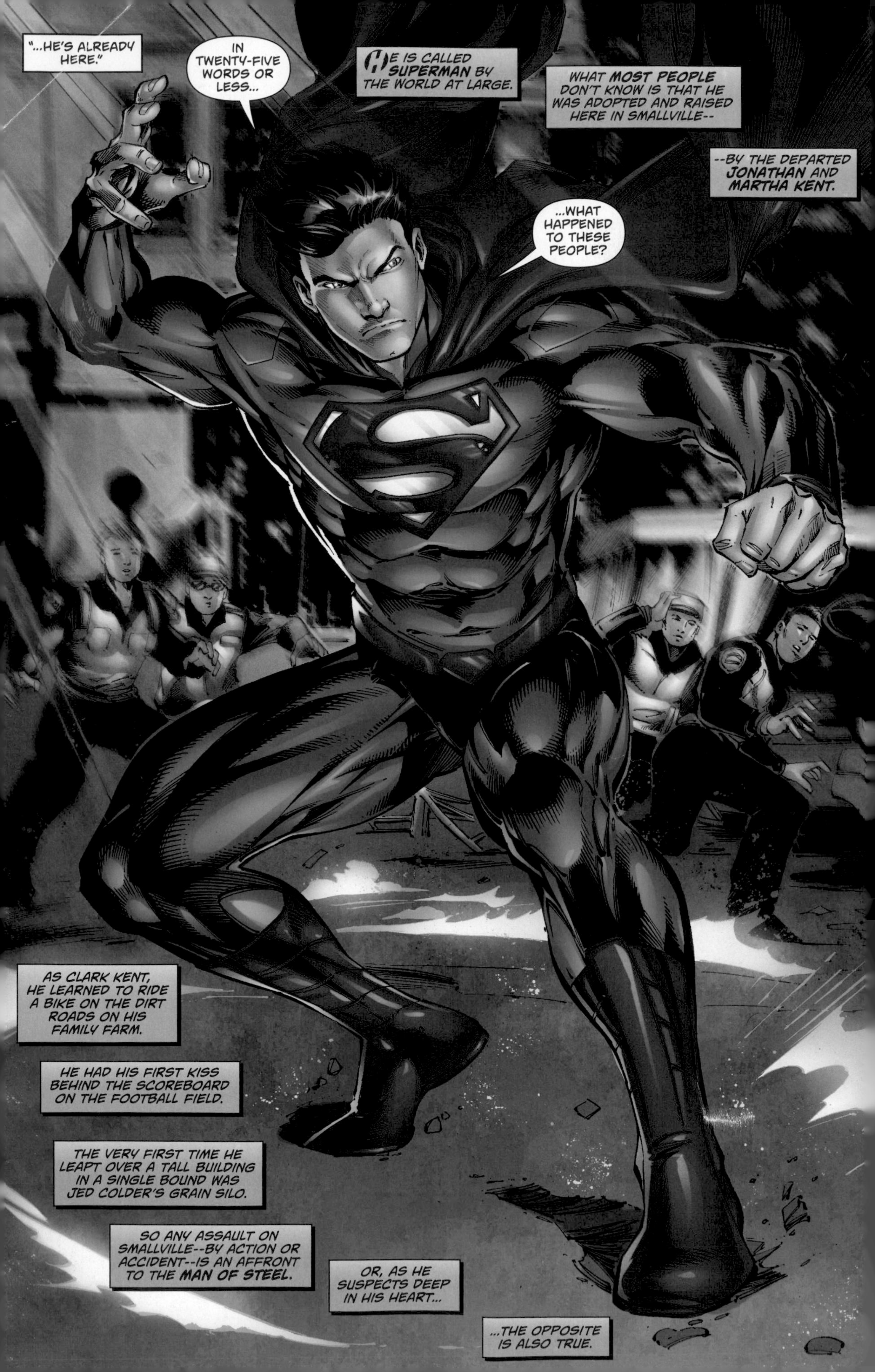
"...HE'S ALREADY HERE."
IN TWENTY-FIVE WORDS OR LESS...
HE IS CALLED SUPERMAN BY THE WORLD AT LARGE.
WHAT MOST PEOPLE DON'T KNOW IS THAT HE WAS ADOPTED AND RAISED HERE IN SMALLVILLE--
--BY THE DEPARTED JONATHAN AND MARTHA KENT.
...WHAT HAPPENED TO THESE PEOPLE?
AS CLARK KENT, HE LEARNED TO RIDE A BIKE ON THE DIRT ROADS ON HIS FAMILY FARM.
HE HAD HIS FIRST KISS BEHIND THE SCOREBOARD ON THE FOOTBALL FIELD.
THE VERY FIRST TIME HE LEAPT OVER A TALL BUILDING IN A SINGLE BOUND WAS JED COLDER'S GRAIN SILO.
SO ANY ASSAULT ON SMALLVILLE--BY ACTION OR ACCIDENT--IS AN AFFRONT TO THE MAN OF STEEL.
OR, AS HE SUSPECTS DEEP IN HIS HEART...
...THE OPPOSITE IS ALSO TRUE.

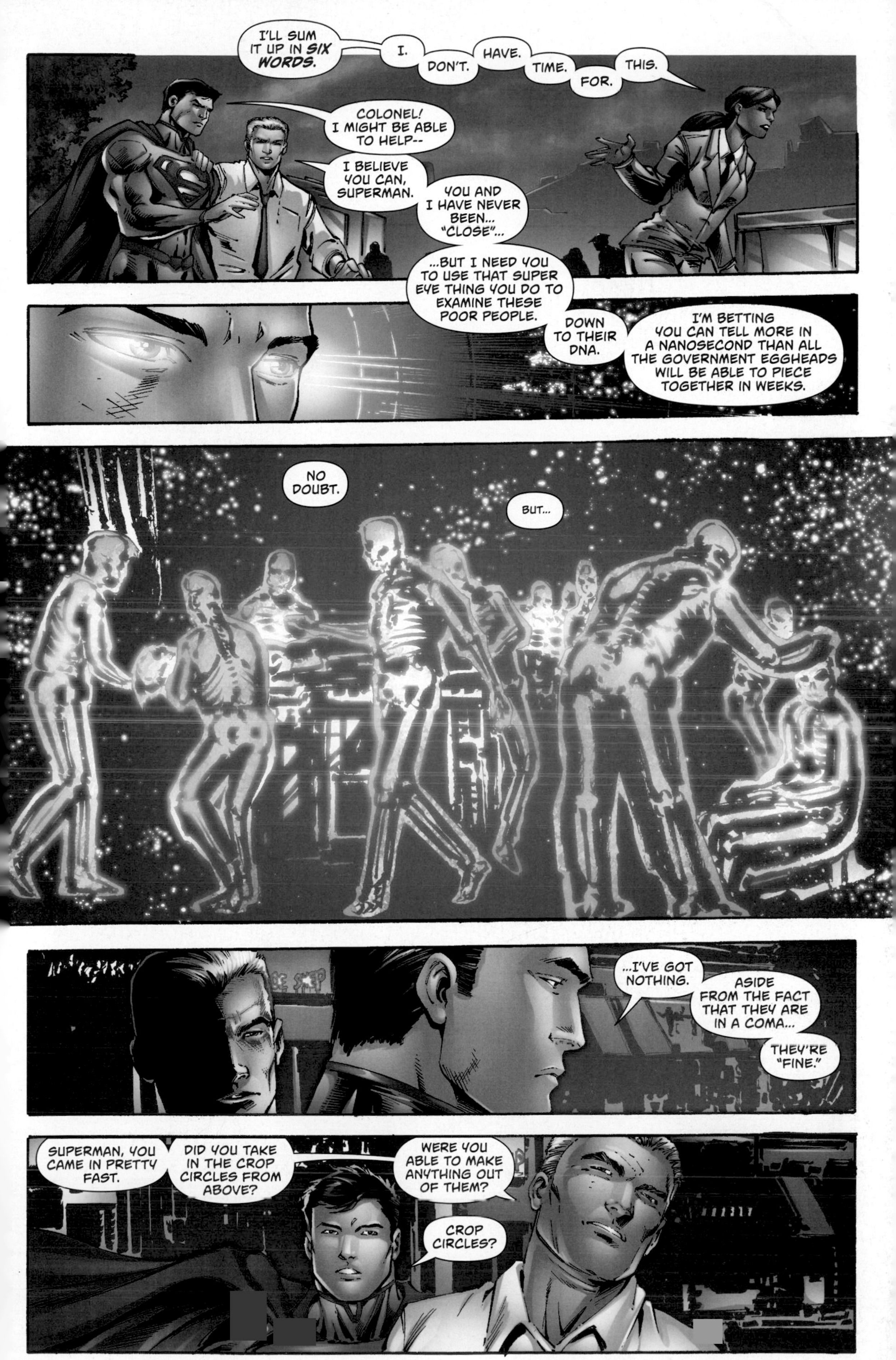
I'LL SUM IT UP IN SIX WORDS.
I.
DON'T.
HAVE.
TIME.
FOR.
THIS.
COLONEL! I MIGHT BE ABLE TO HELP--
I BELIEVE YOU CAN, SUPERMAN.
YOU AND I HAVE NEVER BEEN... "CLOSE"...
...BUT I NEED YOU TO USE THAT SUPER EYE THING YOU DO TO EXAMINE THESE POOR PEOPLE.
DOWN TO THEIR DNA.
I'M BETTING YOU CAN TELL MORE IN A NANOSECOND THAN ALL THE GOVERNMENT EGGHEADS WILL BE ABLE TO PIECE TOGETHER IN WEEKS.
NO DOUBT.
BUT...
...I'VE GOT NOTHING.
ASIDE FROM THE FACT THAT THEY ARE IN A COMA...
THEY'RE "FINE."
SUPERMAN, YOU CAME IN PRETTY FAST.
DID YOU TAKE IN THE CROP CIRCLES FROM ABOVE?
WERE YOU ABLE TO MAKE ANYTHING OUT OF THEM?
CROP CIRCLES?

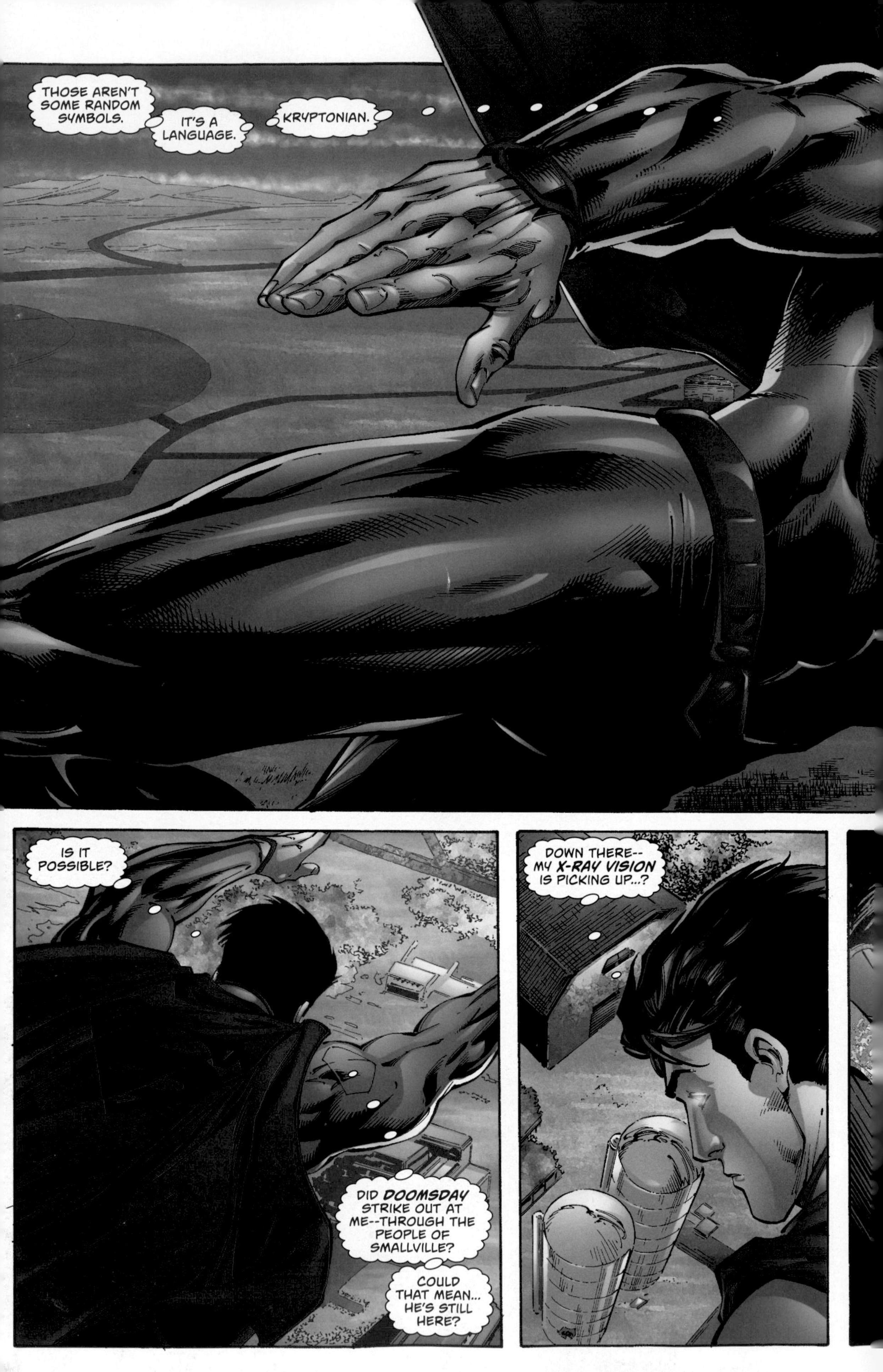
THOSE AREN'T SOME RANDOM SYMBOLS.
IT'S A LANGUAGE.
KRYPTONIAN.
IS IT POSSIBLE?
DID DOOMSDAY STRIKE OUT AT ME--THROUGH THE PEOPLE OF SMALLVILLE?
COULD THAT MEAN... HE'S STILL HERE?
DOWN THERE-- MY X-RAY VISION IS PICKING UP...?

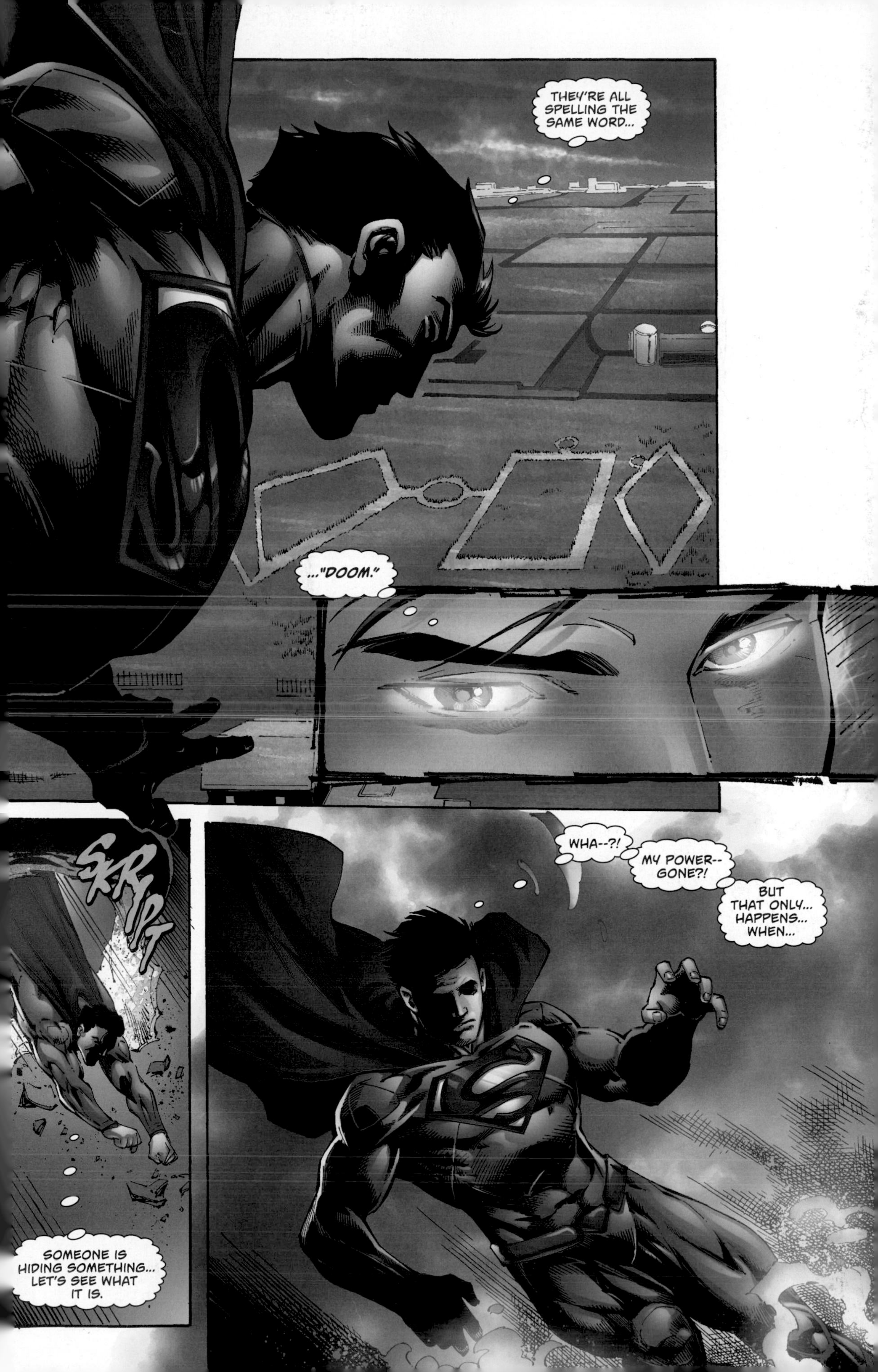
THEY'RE ALL SPELLING THE SAME WORD...
..."DOOM."
SKRIPT
SOMEONE IS HIDING SOMETHING... LET'S SEE WHAT IT IS.
WHA--?!
MY POWER-- GONE?!
BUT THAT ONLY... HAPPENS... WHEN...

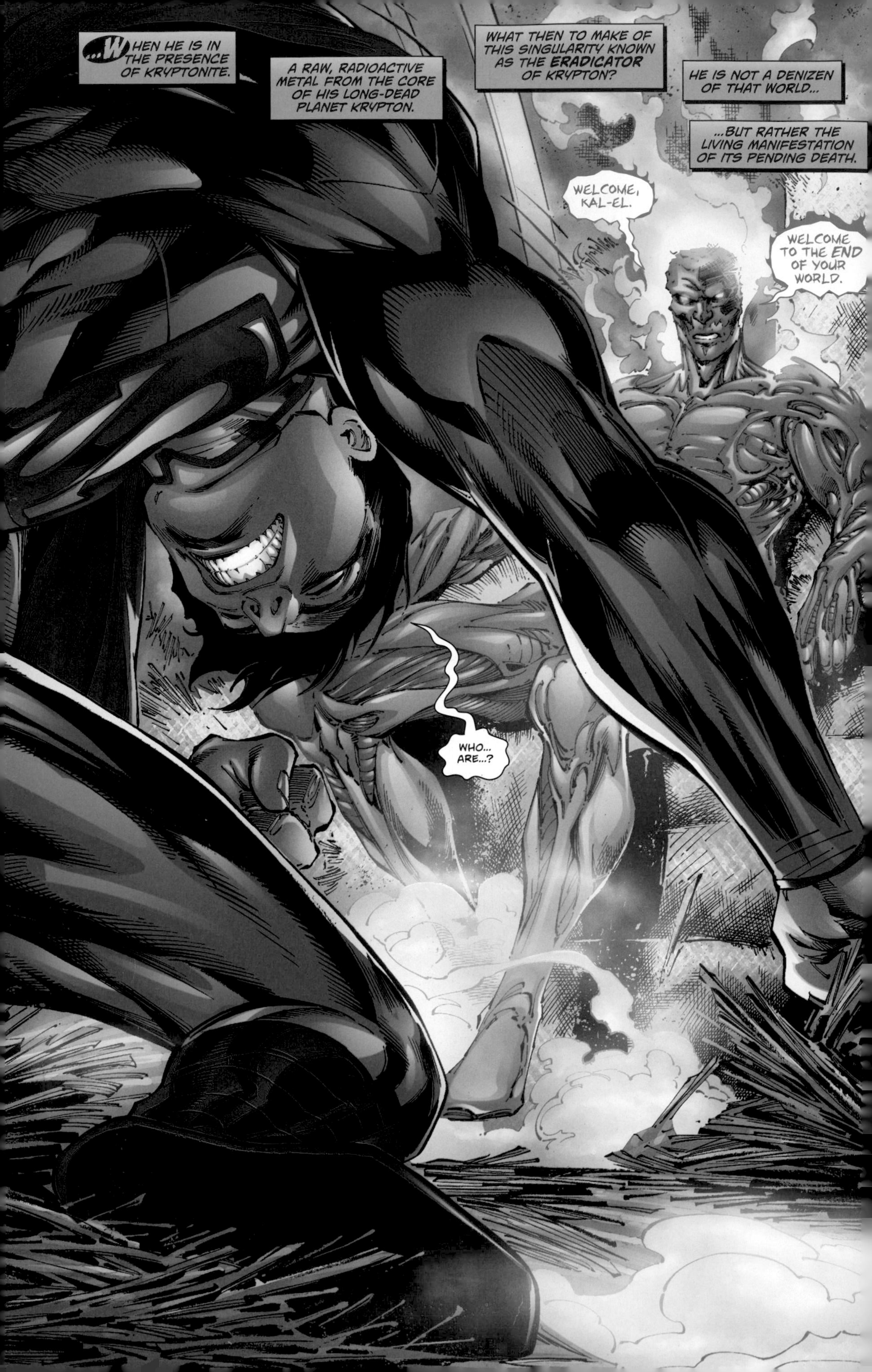
...WHEN HE IS IN THE PRESENCE OF KRYPTONITE.
A RAW, RADIOACTIVE METAL FROM THE CORE OF HIS LONG-DEAD PLANET KRYPTON.
WHAT THEN TO MAKE OF THIS SINGULARITY KNOWN AS THE ERADICATOR OF KRYPTON?
HE IS NOT A DENIZEN OF THAT WORLD...
...BUT RATHER THE LIVING MANIFESTATION OF ITS PENDING DEATH.
WELCOME, KAL-EL.
WELCOME TO THE END OF YOUR WORLD.
WHO... ARE...?

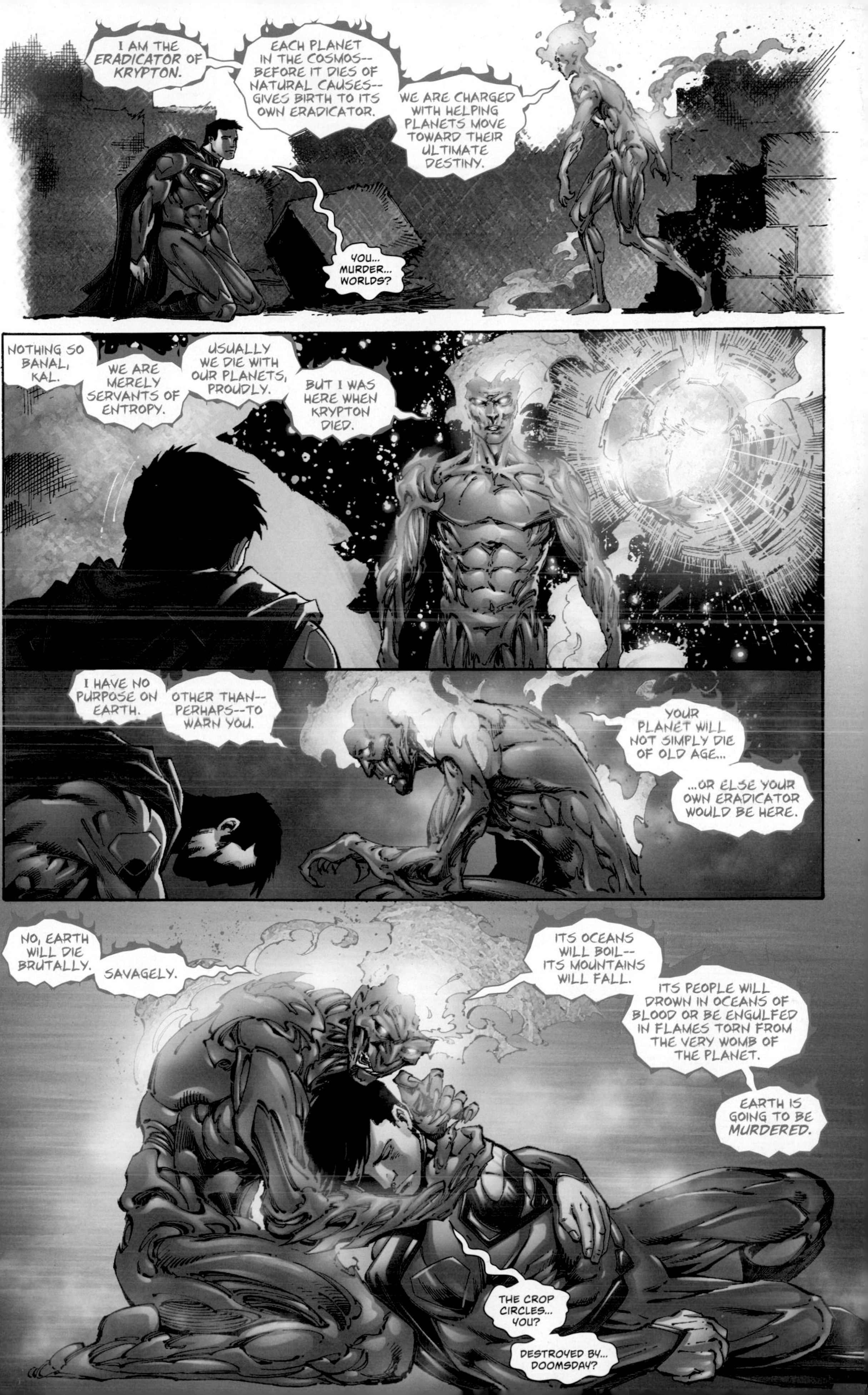
I AM THE ERADICATOR OF KRYPTON.
EACH PLANET IN THE COSMOS-- BEFORE IT DIES OF NATURAL CAUSES-- GIVES BIRTH TO ITS OWN ERADICATOR.
WE ARE CHARGED WITH HELPING PLANETS MOVE TOWARD THEIR ULTIMATE DESTINY.
YOU... MURDER... WORLDS?
NOTHING SO BANAL, KAL.
WE ARE MERELY SERVANTS OF ENTROPY.
USUALLY WE DIE WITH OUR PLANETS, PROUDLY.
BUT I WAS HERE WHEN KRYPTON DIED.
I HAVE NO PURPOSE ON EARTH.
OTHER THAN-- PERHAPS--TO WARN YOU.
YOUR PLANET WILL NOT SIMPLY DIE OF OLD AGE...
...OR ELSE YOUR OWN ERADICATOR WOULD BE HERE.
NO, EARTH WILL DIE BRUTALLY.
SAVAGELY.
ITS OCEANS WILL BOIL-- ITS MOUNTAINS WILL FALL.
ITS PEOPLE WILL DROWN IN OCEANS OF BLOOD OR BE ENGULFED IN FLAMES TORN FROM THE VERY WOMB OF THE PLANET.
EARTH IS GOING TO BE MURDERED.
THE CROP CIRCLES... YOU?
DESTROYED BY... DOOMSDAY?

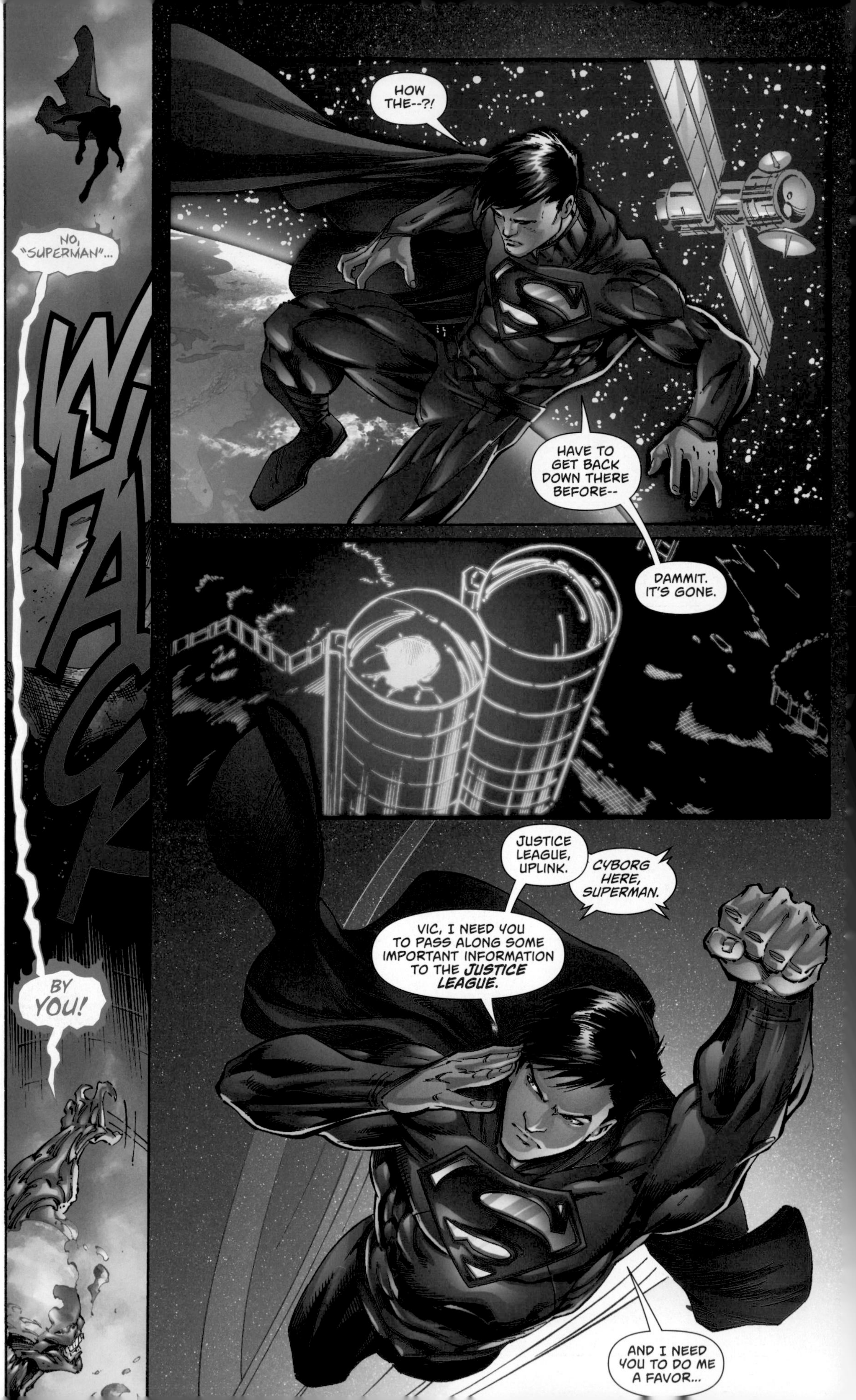
HOW THE--?!
HAVE TO GET BACK DOWN THERE BEFORE--
DAMMIT. IT'S GONE.
NO, "SUPERMAN"...
BY YOU!
JUSTICE LEAGUE, UPLINK.
CYBORG HERE, SUPERMAN.
VIC, I NEED YOU TO PASS ALONG SOME IMPORTANT INFORMATION TO THE JUSTICE LEAGUE.
AND I NEED YOU TO DO ME A FAVOR...

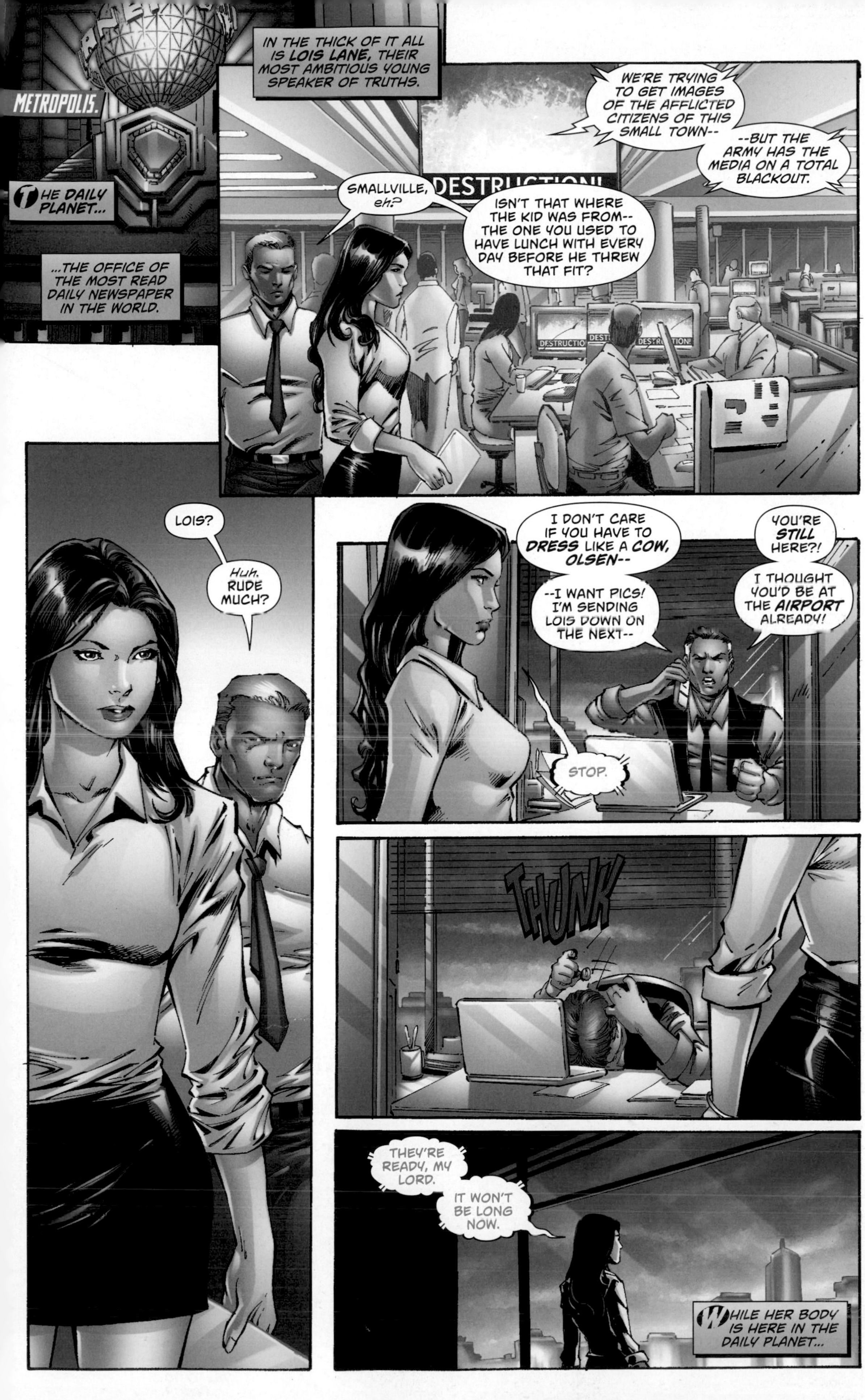
METROPOLIS.
THE DAILY PLANET...
...THE OFFICE OF THE MOST READ DAILY NEWSPAPER IN THE WORLD.
IN THE THICK OF IT ALL IS LOIS LANE, THEIR MOST AMBITIOUS YOUNG SPEAKER OF TRUTHS.
WE'RE TRYING TO GET IMAGES OF THE AFFLICTED CITIZENS OF THIS SMALL TOWN--
--BUT THE ARMY HAS THE MEDIA ON A TOTAL BLACKOUT.
DESTRUCTION!
SMALLVILLE, eh?
ISN'T THAT WHERE THE KID WAS FROM-- THE ONE YOU USED TO HAVE LUNCH WITH EVERY DAY BEFORE HE THREW THAT FIT?
LOIS?
Huh. RUDE MUCH?
I DON'T CARE IF YOU HAVE TO DRESS LIKE A COW, OLSEN--
--I WANT PICS! I'M SENDING LOIS DOWN ON THE NEXT--
YOU'RE STILL HERE?!
I THOUGHT YOU'D BE AT THE AIRPORT ALREADY!
STOP.
THUNK
THEY'RE READY, MY LORD.
IT WON'T BE LONG NOW.
WHILE HER BODY IS HERE IN THE DAILY PLANET...

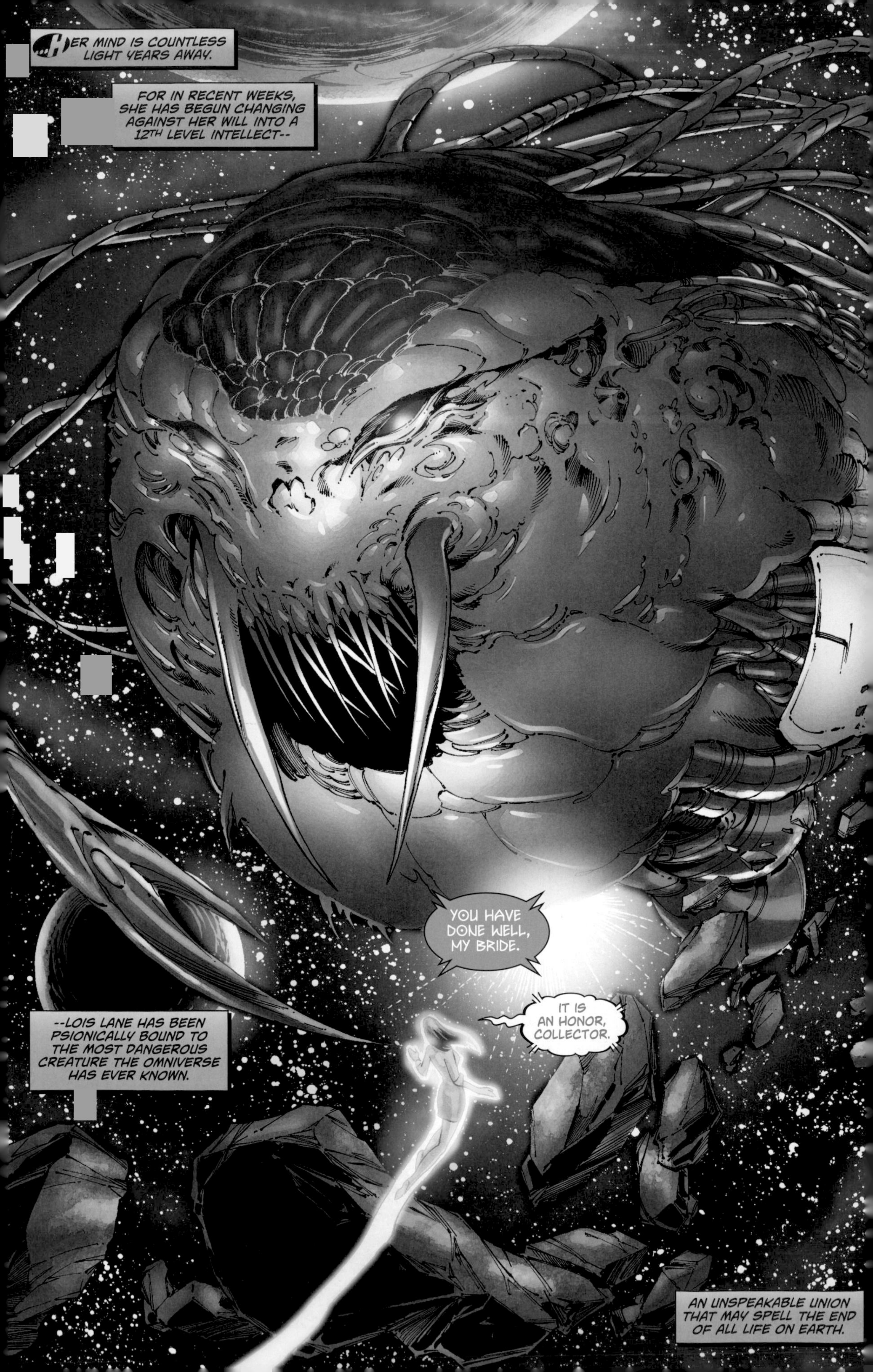
HER MIND IS COUNTLESS LIGHT YEARS AWAY.
FOR IN RECENT WEEKS, SHE HAS BEGUN CHANGING AGAINST HER WILL INTO A 12TH LEVEL INTELLECT--
YOU HAVE DONE WELL, MY BRIDE.
IT IS AN HONOR, COLLECTOR.
--LOIS LANE HAS BEEN PSIONICALLY BOUND TO THE MOST DANGEROUS CREATURE THE OMNIVERSE HAS EVER KNOWN.
AN UNSPEAKABLE UNION THAT MAY SPELL THE END OF ALL LIFE ON EARTH.

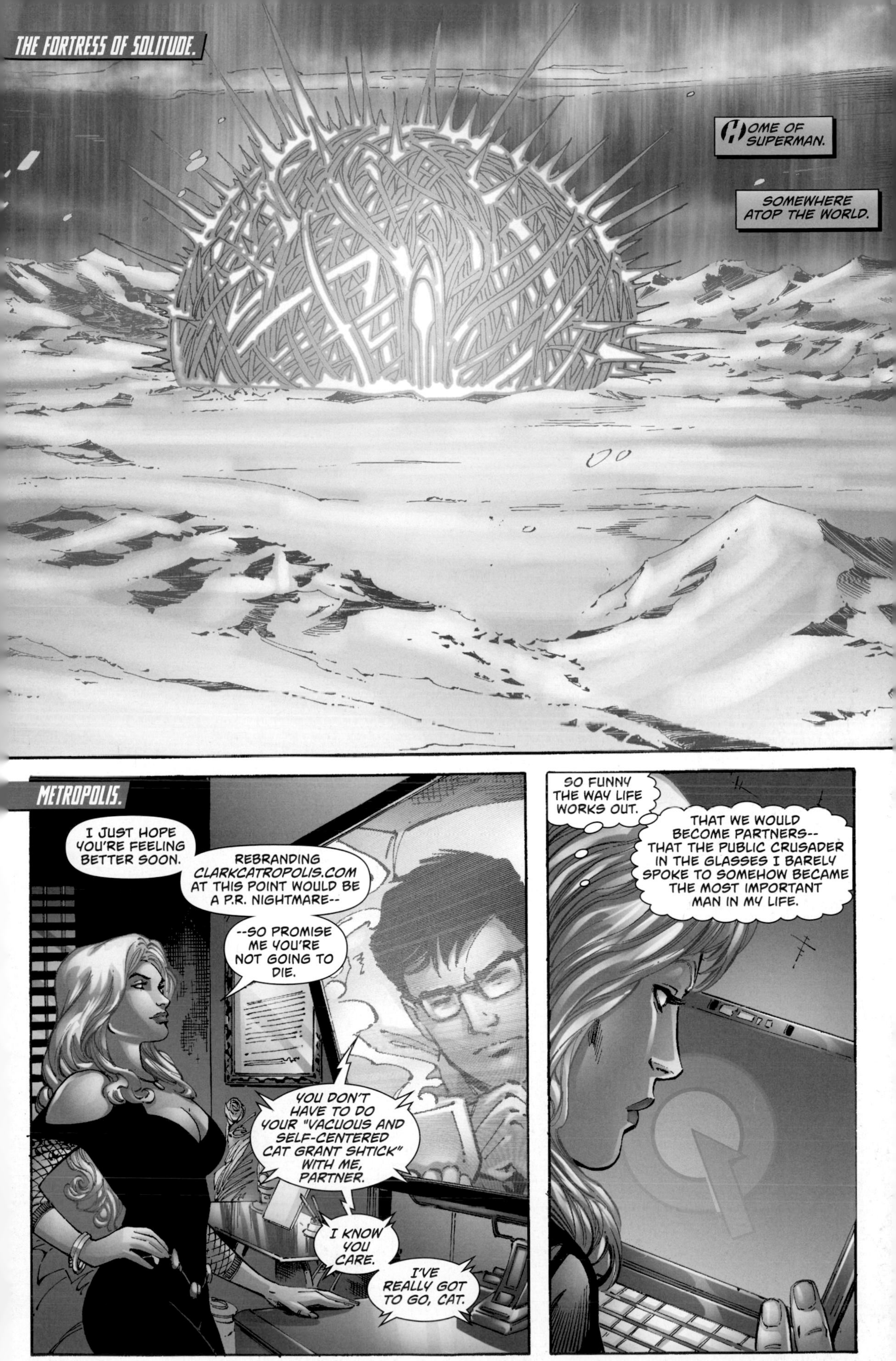
THE FORTRESS OF SOLITUDE.
HOME OF SUPERMAN.
SOMEWHERE ATOP THE WORLD.
METROPOLIS.
I JUST HOPE YOU'RE FEELING BETTER SOON.
REBRANDING CLARKCATROPOLIS.COM AT THIS POINT WOULD BE A P.R. NIGHTMARE--
--SO PROMISE ME YOU'RE NOT GOING TO DIE.
YOU DON'T HAVE TO DO YOUR "VACUOUS AND SELF-CENTERED CAT GRANT SHTICK" WITH ME, PARTNER.
I KNOW YOU CARE.
I'VE REALLY GOT TO GO, CAT.
SO FUNNY THE WAY LIFE WORKS OUT.
THAT WE WOULD BECOME PARTNERS-- THAT THE PUBLIC CRUSADER IN THE GLASSES I BARELY SPOKE TO SOMEHOW BECAME THE MOST IMPORTANT MAN IN MY LIFE.

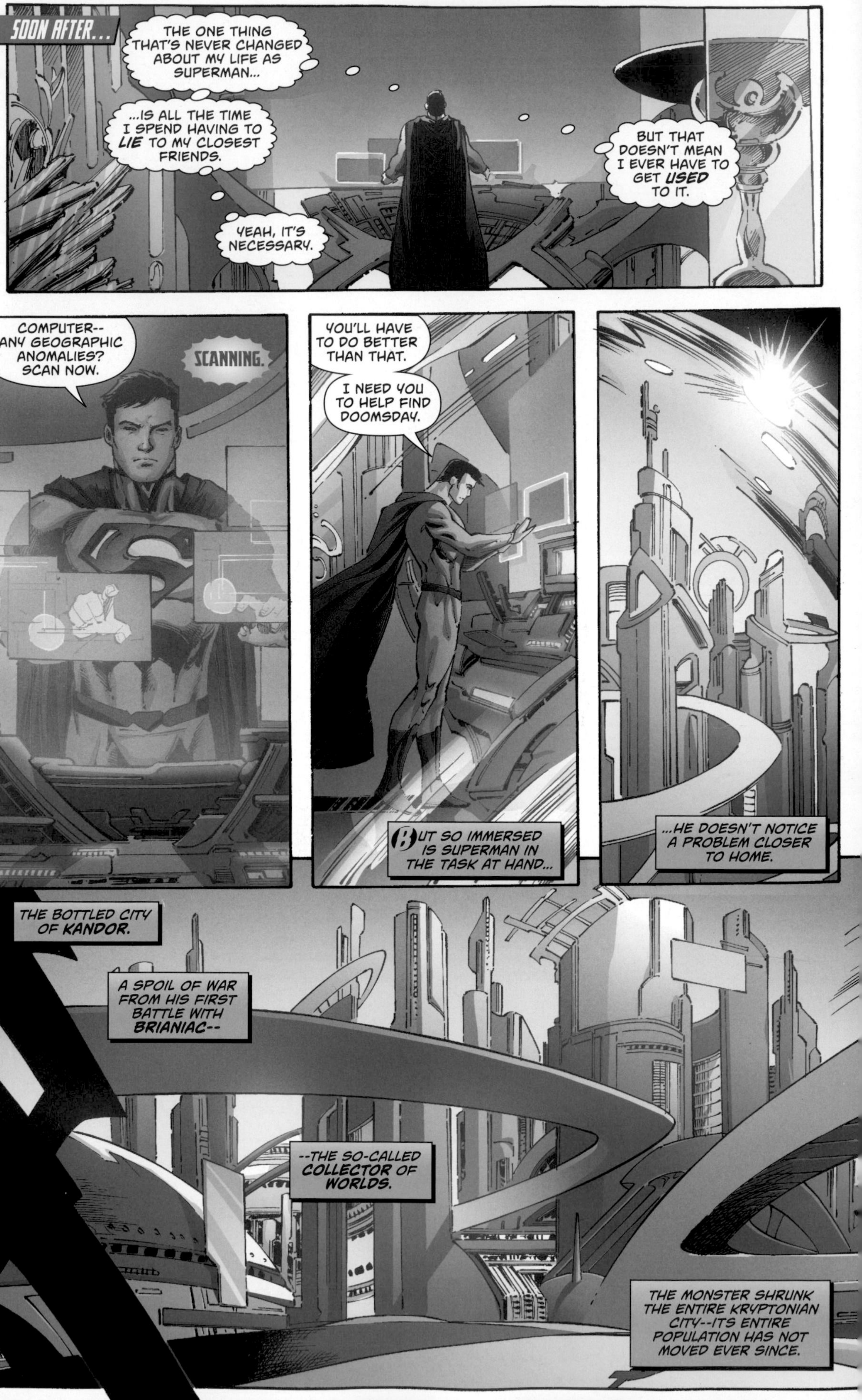
SOON AFTER...
THE ONE THING THAT'S NEVER CHANGED ABOUT MY LIFE AS SUPERMAN...
...IS ALL THE TIME I SPEND HAVING TO LIE TO MY CLOSEST FRIENDS.
YEAH, IT'S NECESSARY.
BUT THAT DOESN'T MEAN I EVER HAVE TO GET USED TO IT.
COMPUTER-- ANY GEOGRAPHIC ANOMALIES? SCAN NOW.
SCANNING.
YOU'LL HAVE TO DO BETTER THAN THAT.
I NEED YOU TO HELP FIND DOOMSDAY.
BUT SO IMMERSED IS SUPERMAN IN THE TASK AT HAND...
...HE DOESN'T NOTICE A PROBLEM CLOSER TO HOME.
THE BOTTLED CITY OF KANDOR.
A SPOIL OF WAR FROM HIS FIRST BATTLE WITH BRIANIAC--
--THE SO-CALLED COLLECTOR OF WORLDS.
THE MONSTER SHRUNK THE ENTIRE KRYPTONIAN CITY--ITS ENTIRE POPULATION HAS NOT MOVED EVER SINCE.

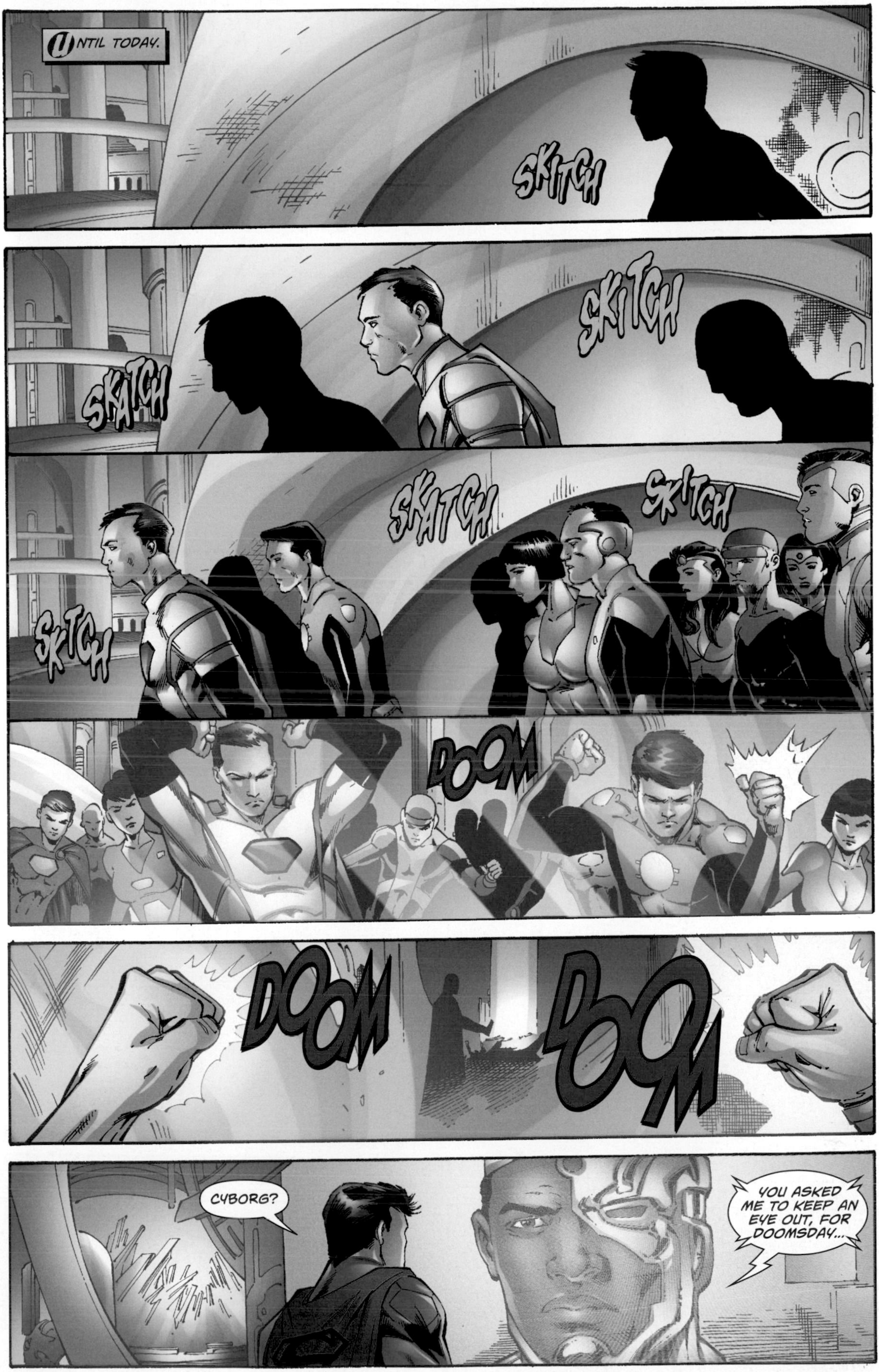
UNTIL TODAY.
SKITCH
SKATCH
SKITCH
SKTCH
SKATCH
SKITCH
DOOM
DOOM
DOOM
CYBORG?
YOU ASKED ME TO KEEP AN EYE OUT, FOR DOOMSDAY...

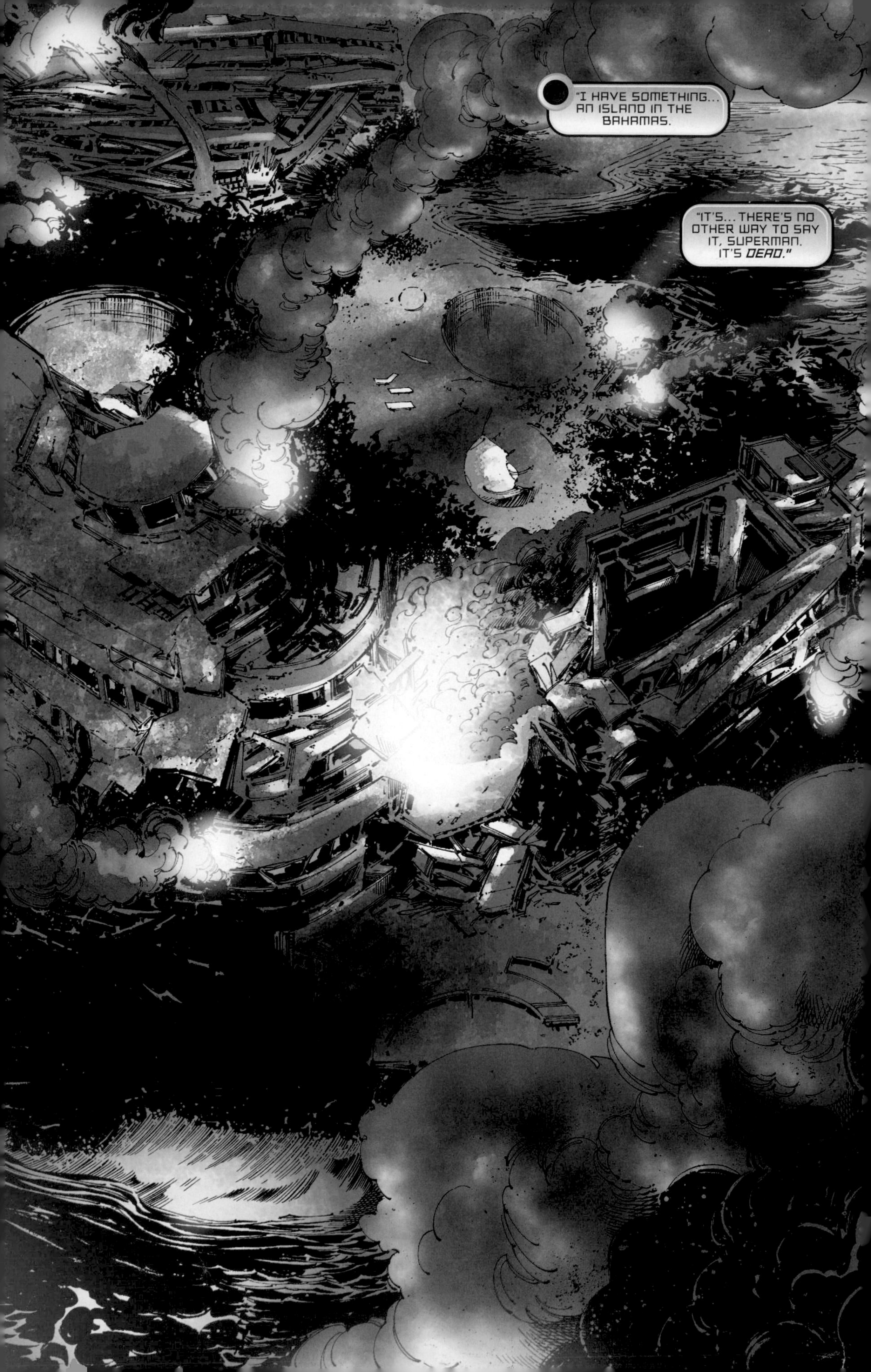
"I HAVE SOMETHING... AN ISLAND IN THE BAHAMAS.
"IT'S... THERE'S NO OTHER WAY TO SAY IT, SUPERMAN. IT'S DEAD."

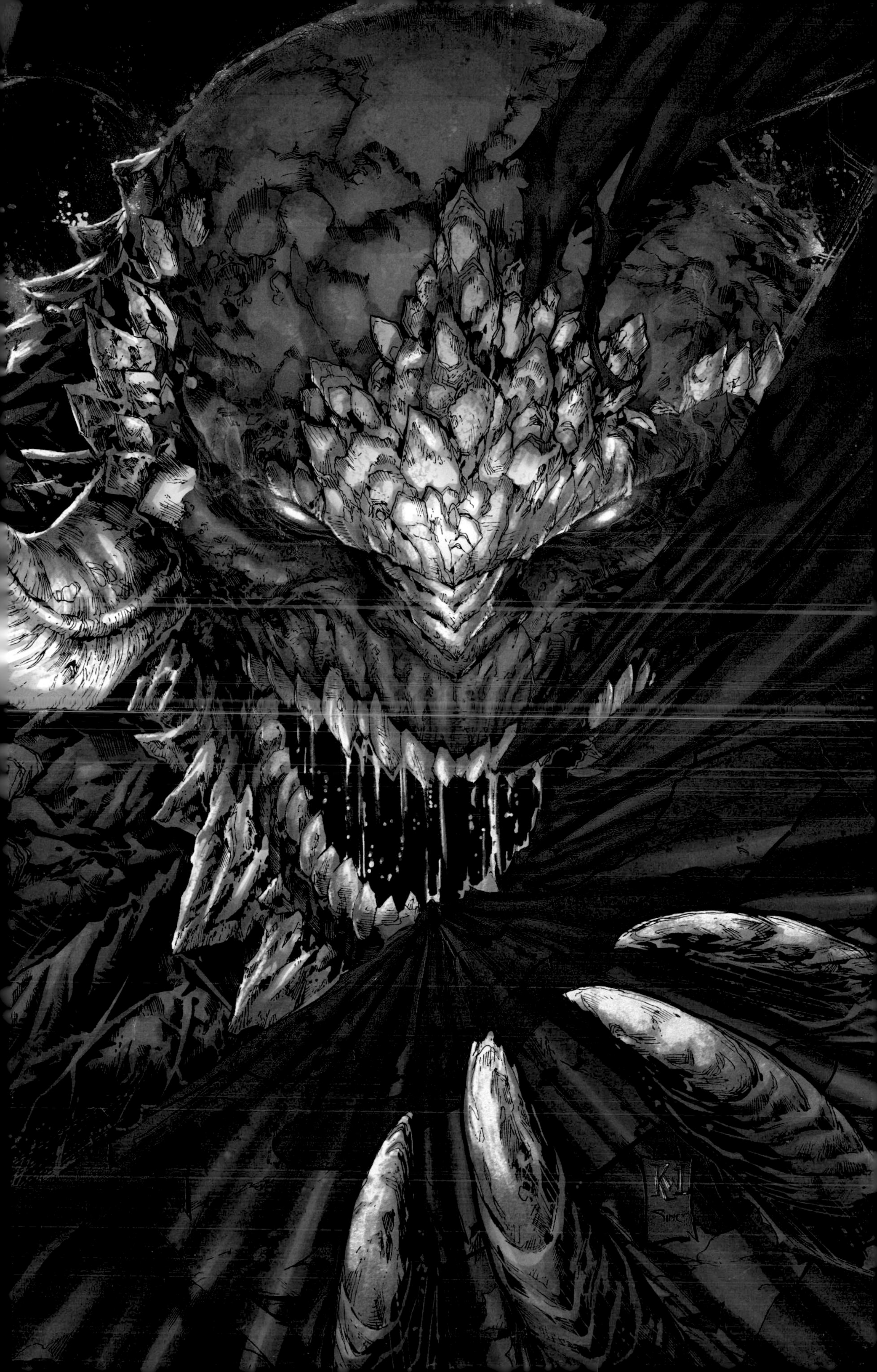

SUPERMAN DOOMED

STORY
SCOTT LOBDELL, GREG PAK AND **CHARLES SOULE**

ART
KEN LASHLEY

COLORS
SUNNY GHO

LETTERS
CARLOS M. MANGUAL

COVER
KEN LASHLEY AND **ALEX SINCLAIR,**
AFTER DAN JURGENS AND BRETT BREEDING

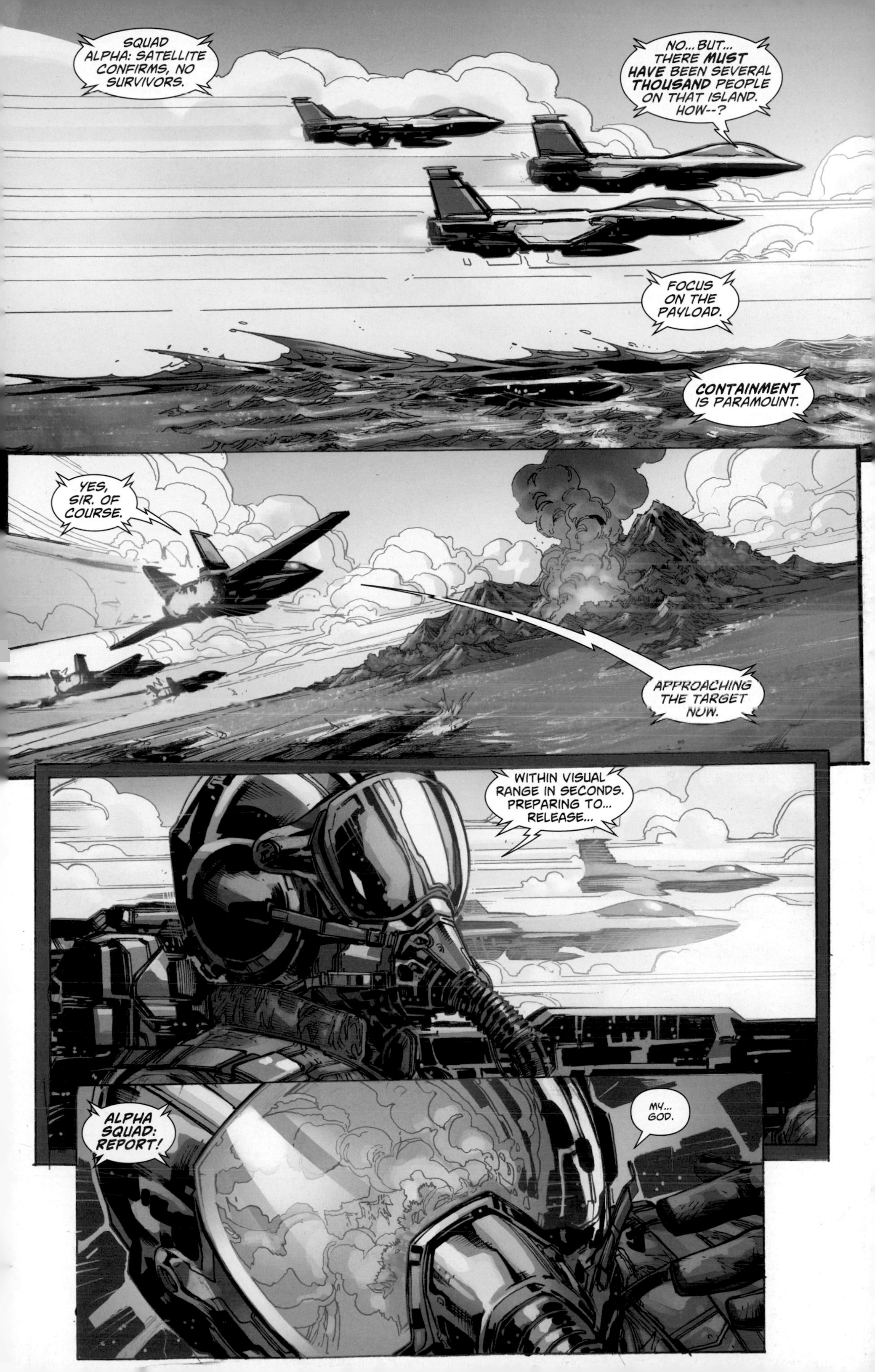
SQUAD ALPHA: SATELLITE CONFIRMS, NO SURVIVORS.
NO... BUT... THERE **MUST HAVE** BEEN SEVERAL **THOUSAND** PEOPLE ON THAT ISLAND. HOW--?
FOCUS ON THE PAYLOAD.
CONTAINMENT IS PARAMOUNT.
YES, SIR. OF COURSE.
APPROACHING THE TARGET NOW.
WITHIN VISUAL RANGE IN SECONDS. PREPARING TO... RELEASE...
ALPHA SQUAD: REPORT!
MY... GOD.

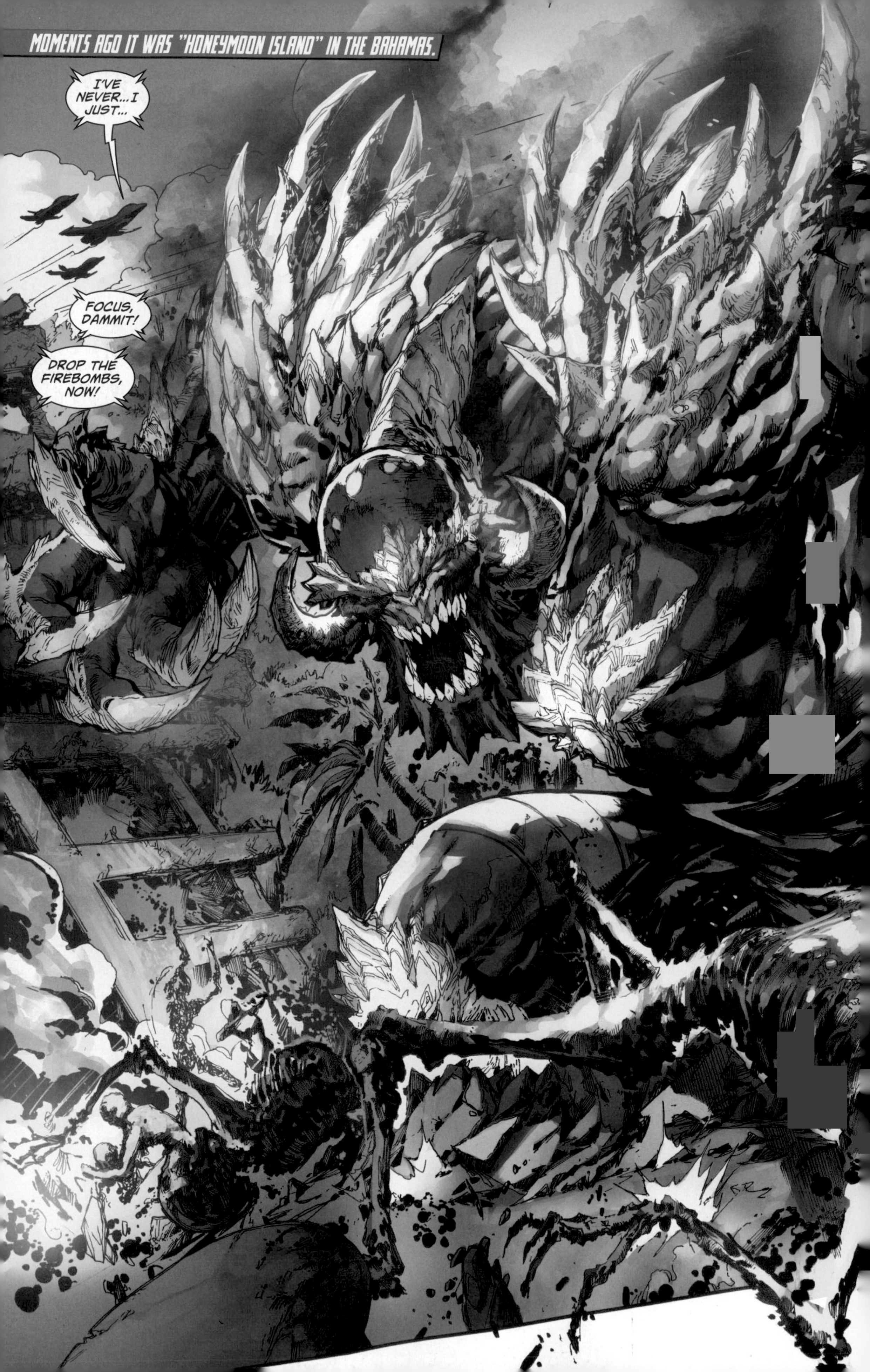
MOMENTS AGO IT WAS "HONEYMOON ISLAND" IN THE BAHAMAS.
I'VE NEVER... I JUST...
FOCUS, DAMMIT!
DROP THE FIREBOMBS, NOW!

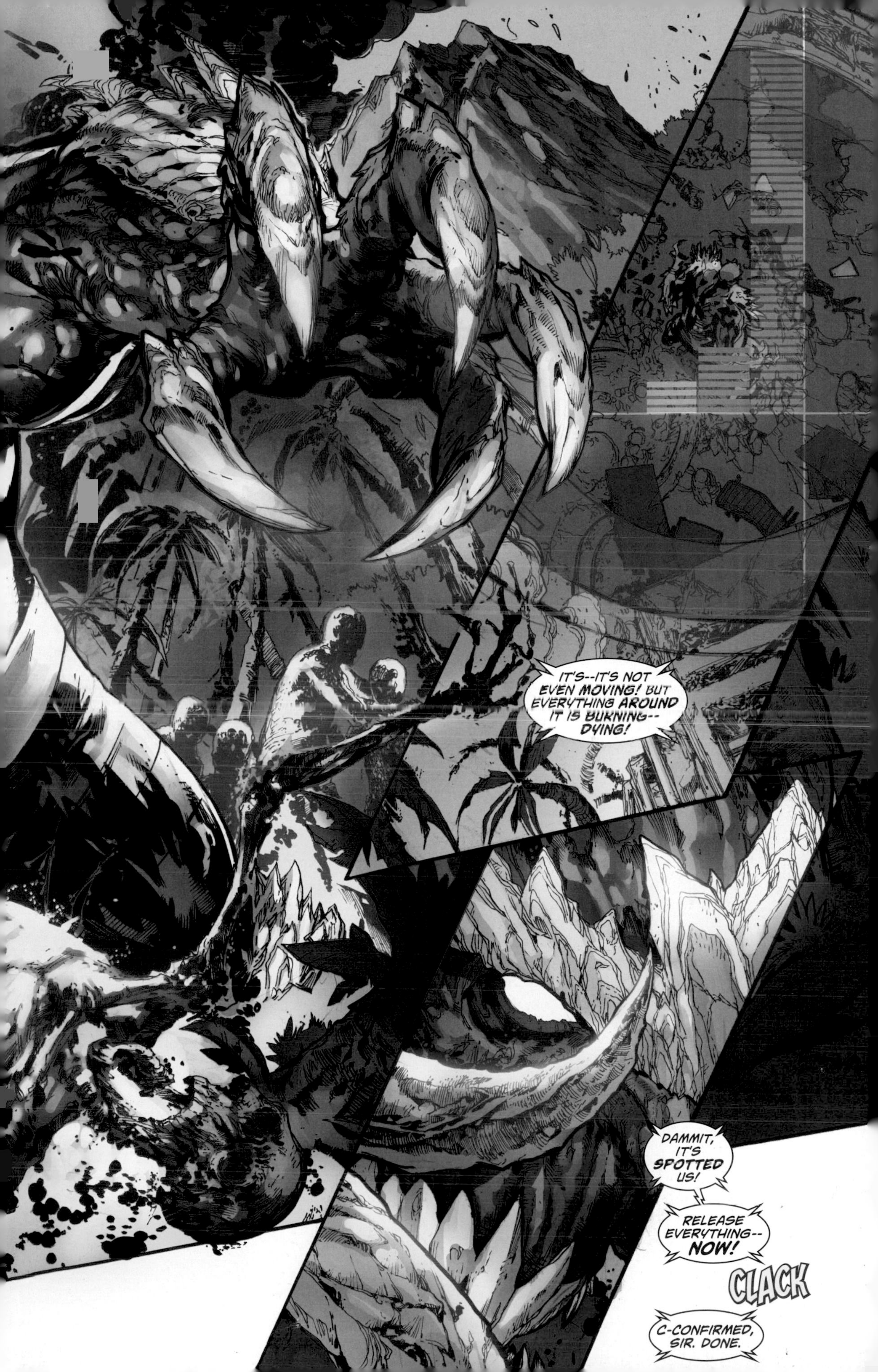
IT'S--IT'S NOT EVEN MOVING! BUT EVERYTHING AROUND IT IS BURNING--DYING!
DAMMIT, IT'S SPOTTED US!
RELEASE EVERYTHING--NOW!
CLACK
C-CONFIRMED, SIR. DONE.

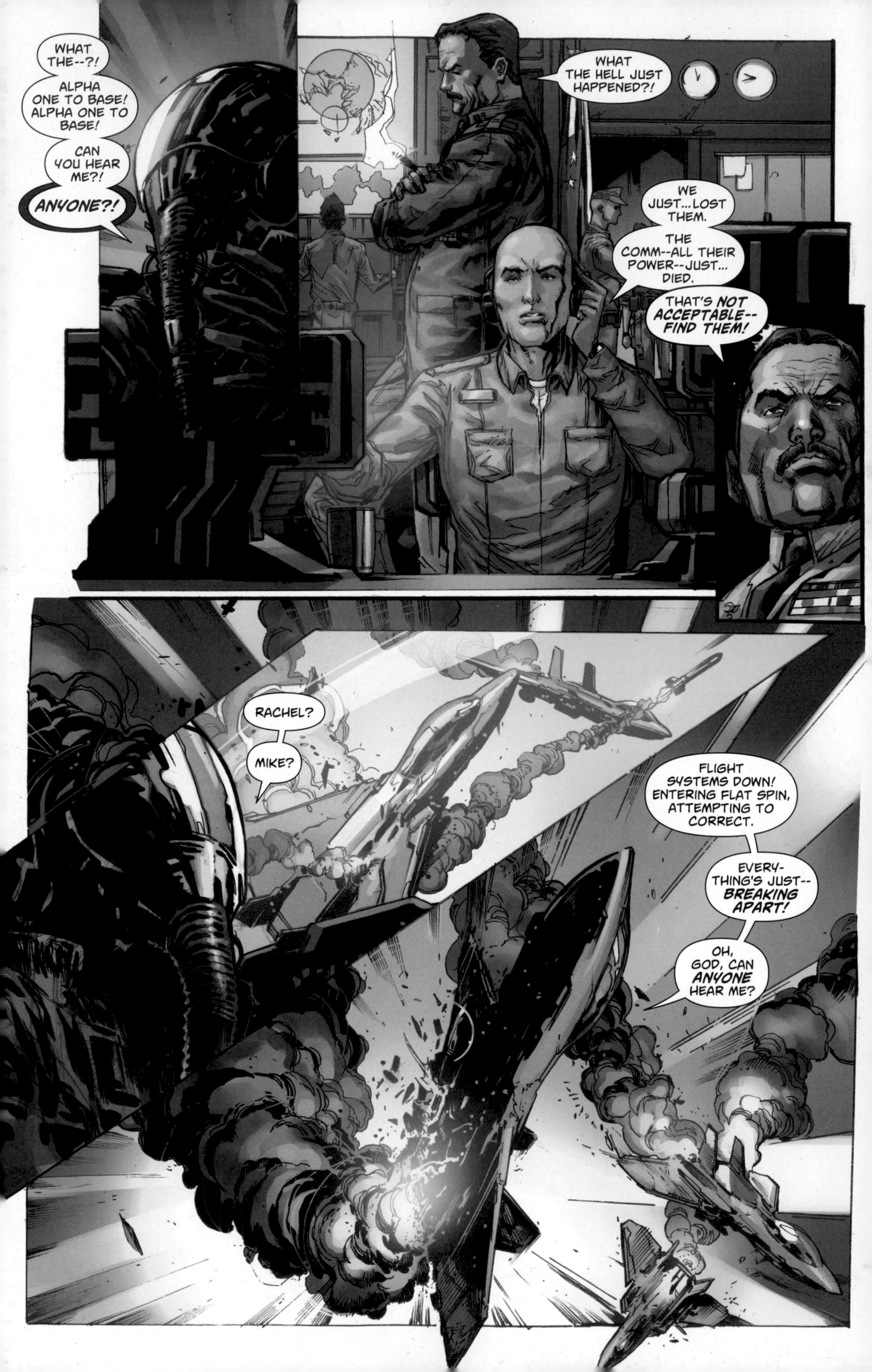
WHAT THE--?!
ALPHA ONE TO BASE! ALPHA ONE TO BASE!
CAN YOU HEAR ME?!
ANYONE?!
WHAT THE HELL JUST HAPPENED?!
WE JUST...LOST THEM.
THE COMM--ALL THEIR POWER--JUST... DIED.
THAT'S NOT ACCEPTABLE-- FIND THEM!
RACHEL?
MIKE?
FLIGHT SYSTEMS DOWN! ENTERING FLAT SPIN, ATTEMPTING TO CORRECT.
EVERY-THING'S JUST-- BREAKING APART!
OH, GOD, CAN ANYONE HEAR ME?

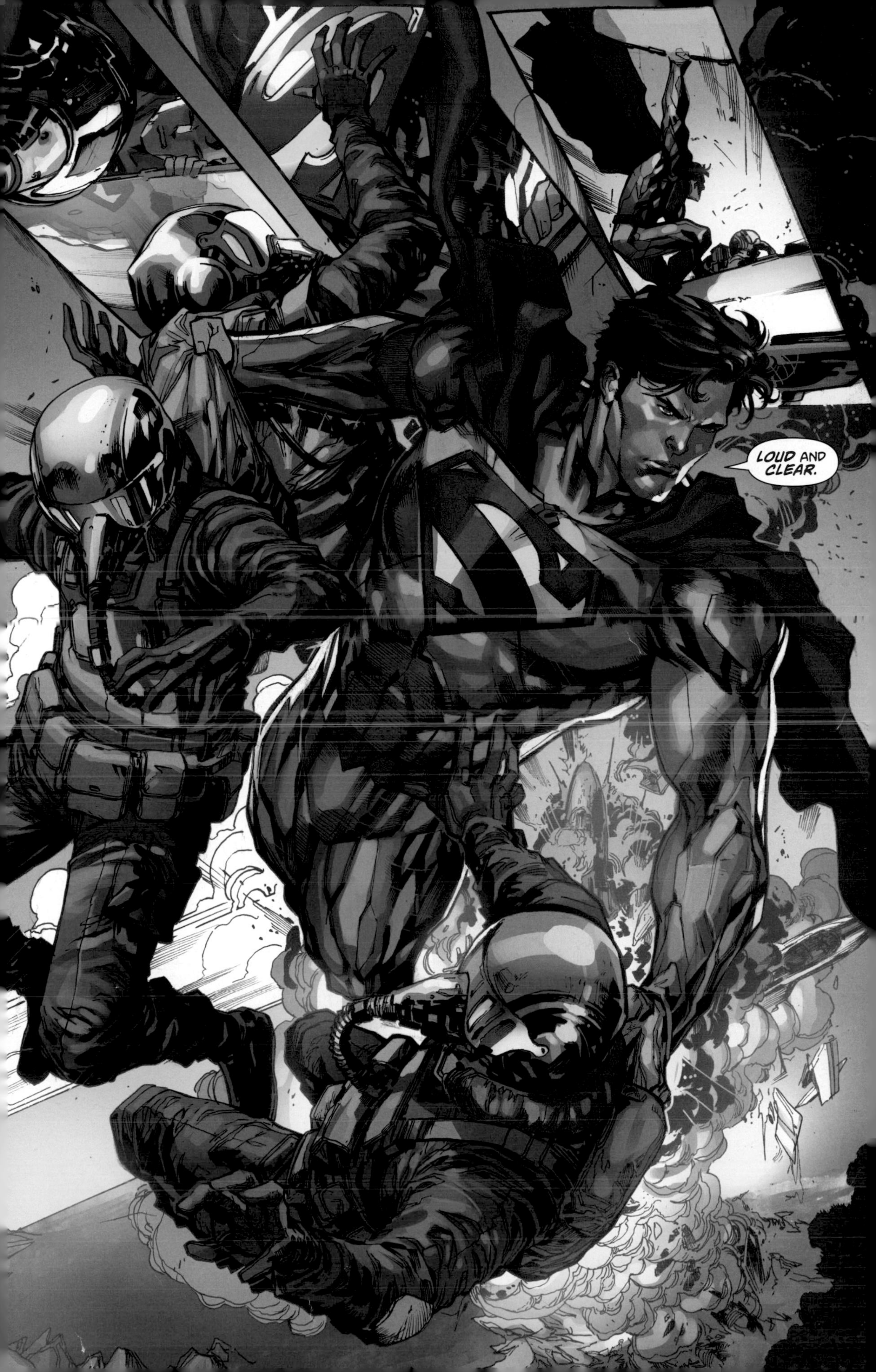
LOUD AND CLEAR.

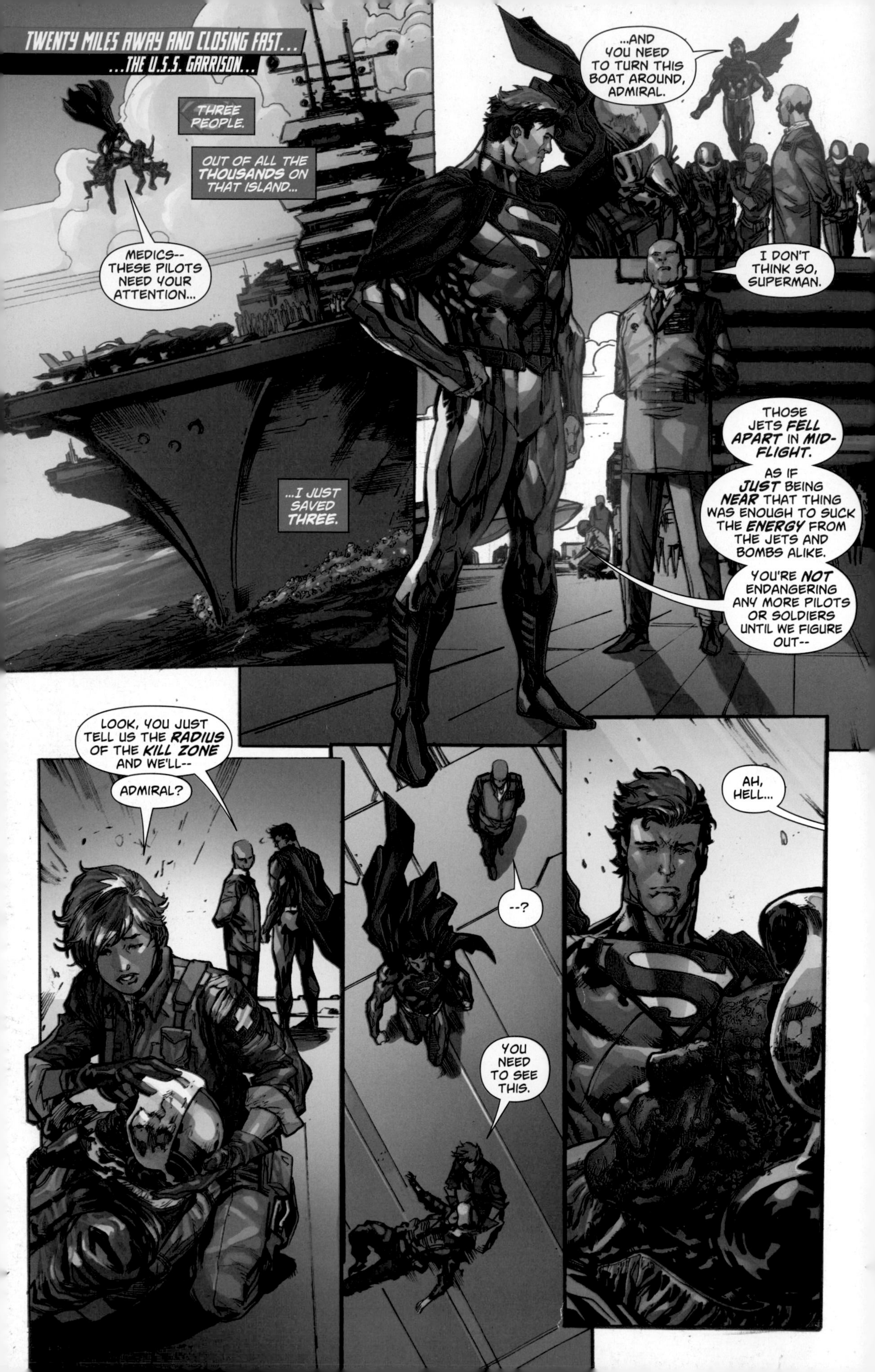
TWENTY MILES AWAY AND CLOSING FAST...
...THE U.S.S. GARRISON...
THREE PEOPLE.
OUT OF ALL THE THOUSANDS ON THAT ISLAND...
MEDICS-- THESE PILOTS NEED YOUR ATTENTION...
...I JUST SAVED THREE.
...AND YOU NEED TO TURN THIS BOAT AROUND, ADMIRAL.
I DON'T THINK SO, SUPERMAN.
THOSE JETS FELL APART IN MID-FLIGHT.
AS IF JUST BEING NEAR THAT THING WAS ENOUGH TO SUCK THE ENERGY FROM THE JETS AND BOMBS ALIKE.
YOU'RE NOT ENDANGERING ANY MORE PILOTS OR SOLDIERS UNTIL WE FIGURE OUT--
LOOK, YOU JUST TELL US THE RADIUS OF THE KILL ZONE AND WE'LL--
ADMIRAL?
--?
YOU NEED TO SEE THIS.
AH, HELL...

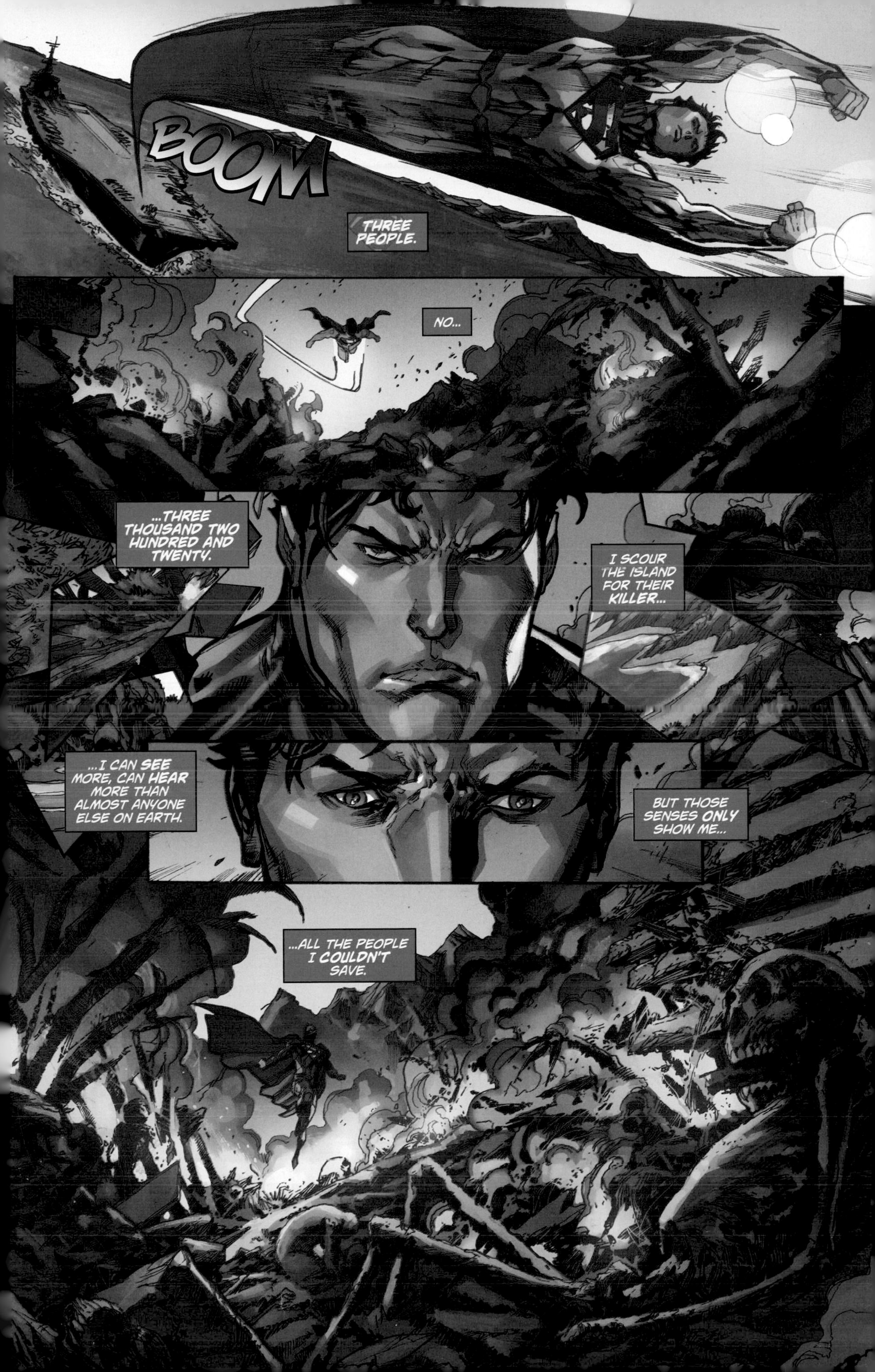
BOOM
THREE PEOPLE.
NO...
...THREE THOUSAND TWO HUNDRED AND TWENTY.
I SCOUR THE ISLAND FOR THEIR KILLER...
...I CAN SEE MORE, CAN HEAR MORE THAN ALMOST ANYONE ELSE ON EARTH.
BUT THOSE SENSES ONLY SHOW ME...
...ALL THE PEOPLE I COULDN'T SAVE.

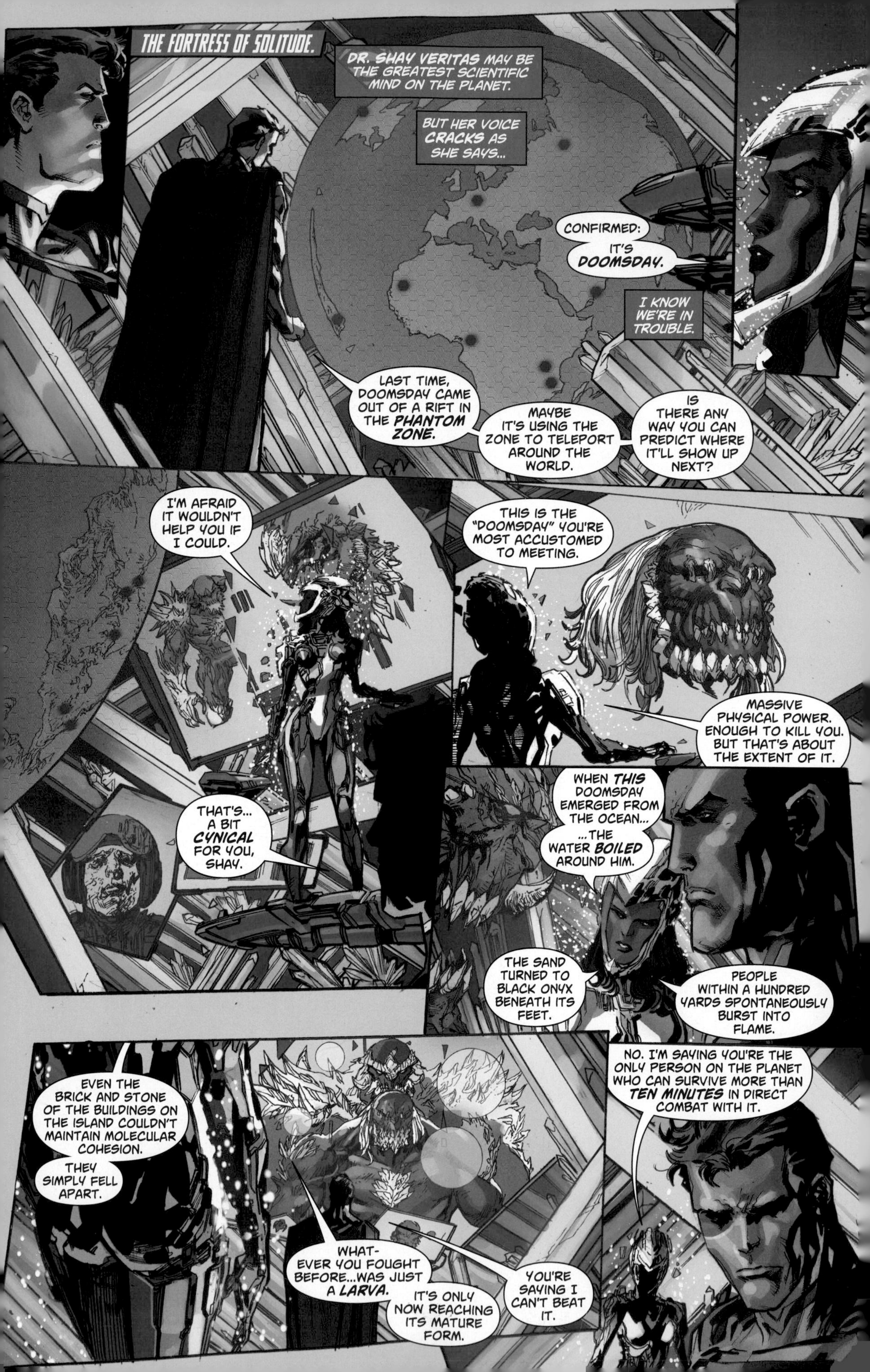
THE FORTRESS OF SOLITUDE.
DR. SHAY VERITAS MAY BE THE GREATEST SCIENTIFIC MIND ON THE PLANET.
BUT HER VOICE CRACKS AS SHE SAYS...
CONFIRMED: IT'S DOOMSDAY.
I KNOW WE'RE IN TROUBLE.
LAST TIME, DOOMSDAY CAME OUT OF A RIFT IN THE PHANTOM ZONE.
MAYBE IT'S USING THE ZONE TO TELEPORT AROUND THE WORLD.
IS THERE ANY WAY YOU CAN PREDICT WHERE IT'LL SHOW UP NEXT?
I'M AFRAID IT WOULDN'T HELP YOU IF I COULD.
THIS IS THE "DOOMSDAY" YOU'RE MOST ACCUSTOMED TO MEETING.
MASSIVE PHYSICAL POWER. ENOUGH TO KILL YOU. BUT THAT'S ABOUT THE EXTENT OF IT.
THAT'S... A BIT CYNICAL FOR YOU, SHAY.
WHEN THIS DOOMSDAY EMERGED FROM THE OCEAN...
...THE WATER BOILED AROUND HIM.
THE SAND TURNED TO BLACK ONYX BENEATH ITS FEET.
PEOPLE WITHIN A HUNDRED YARDS SPONTANEOUSLY BURST INTO FLAME.
EVEN THE BRICK AND STONE OF THE BUILDINGS ON THE ISLAND COULDN'T MAINTAIN MOLECULAR COHESION.
THEY SIMPLY FELL APART.
WHAT-EVER YOU FOUGHT BEFORE...WAS JUST A LARVA.
IT'S ONLY NOW REACHING ITS MATURE FORM.
YOU'RE SAYING I CAN'T BEAT IT.
NO. I'M SAYING YOU'RE THE ONLY PERSON ON THE PLANET WHO CAN SURVIVE MORE THAN TEN MINUTES IN DIRECT COMBAT WITH IT.

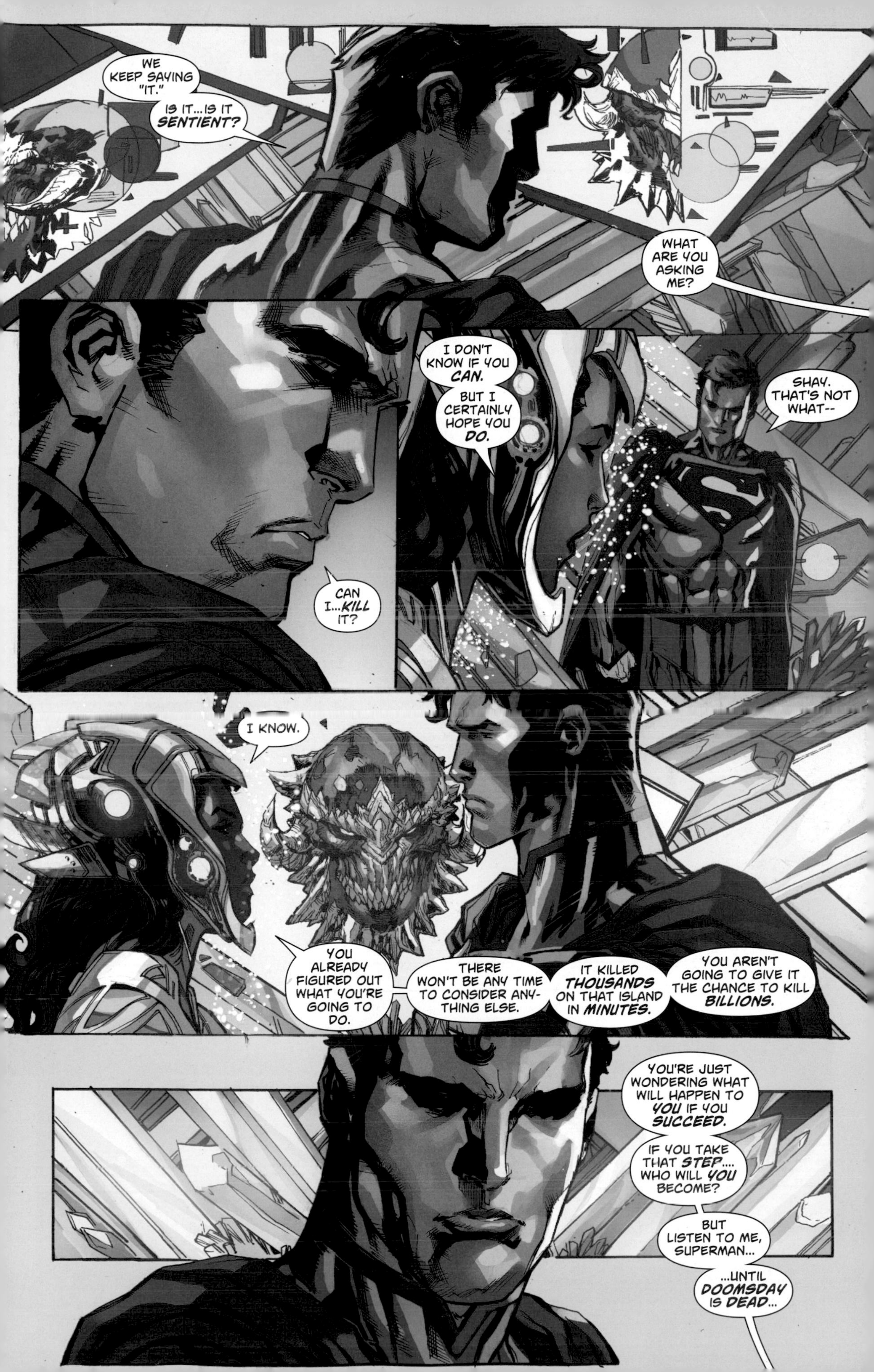
WE KEEP SAYING "IT."
IS IT...IS IT SENTIENT?
WHAT ARE YOU ASKING ME?
CAN I...KILL IT?
I DON'T KNOW IF YOU CAN.
BUT I CERTAINLY HOPE YOU DO.
SHAY. THAT'S NOT WHAT--
I KNOW.
YOU ALREADY FIGURED OUT WHAT YOU'RE GOING TO DO.
THERE WON'T BE ANY TIME TO CONSIDER ANY-THING ELSE.
IT KILLED THOUSANDS ON THAT ISLAND IN MINUTES.
YOU AREN'T GOING TO GIVE IT THE CHANCE TO KILL BILLIONS.
YOU'RE JUST WONDERING WHAT WILL HAPPEN TO YOU IF YOU SUCCEED.
IF YOU TAKE THAT STEP.... WHO WILL YOU BECOME?
BUT LISTEN TO ME, SUPERMAN...
...UNTIL DOOMSDAY IS DEAD...

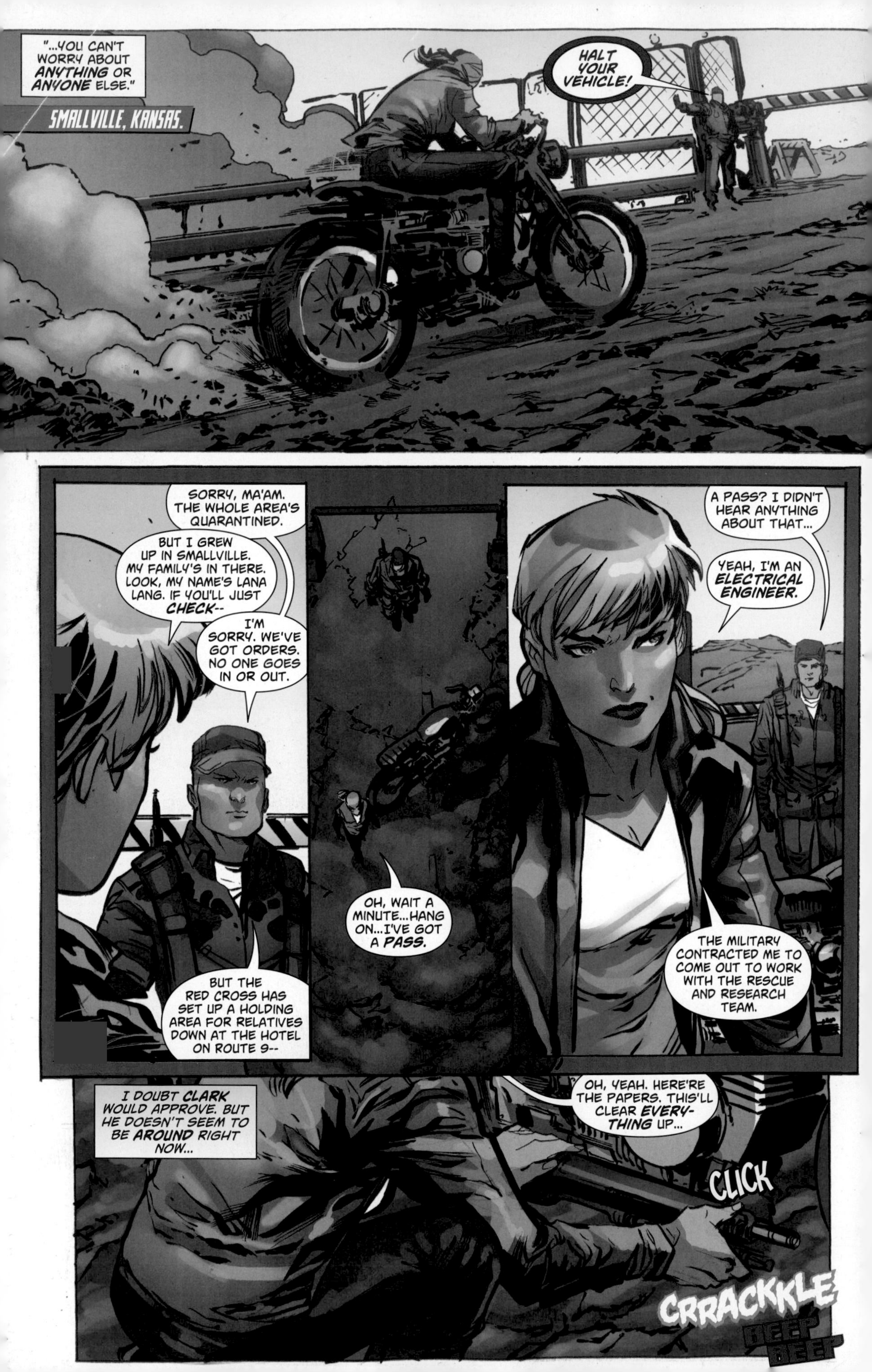

"...YOU! CAN'T WORRY ABOUT ANYTHING OR ANYONE ELSE."
SMALLVILLE, KANSAS.
HALT YOUR VEHICLE!
SORRY, MA'AM. THE WHOLE AREA'S QUARANTINED.
BUT I GREW UP IN SMALLVILLE. MY FAMILY'S IN THERE. LOOK, MY NAME'S LANA LANG. IF YOU'LL JUST CHECK--
I'M SORRY. WE'VE GOT ORDERS. NO ONE GOES IN OR OUT.
BUT THE RED CROSS HAS SET UP A HOLDING AREA FOR RELATIVES DOWN AT THE HOTEL ON ROUTE 9--
OH, WAIT A MINUTE...HANG ON...I'VE GOT A PASS.
A PASS? I DIDN'T HEAR ANYTHING ABOUT THAT...
YEAH, I'M AN ELECTRICAL ENGINEER.
THE MILITARY CONTRACTED ME TO COME OUT TO WORK WITH THE RESCUE AND RESEARCH TEAM.
I DOUBT CLARK WOULD APPROVE. BUT HE DOESN'T SEEM TO BE AROUND RIGHT NOW...
OH, YEAH. HERE'RE THE PAPERS. THIS'LL CLEAR EVERY-THING UP...
CLICK
CRRACKKLE

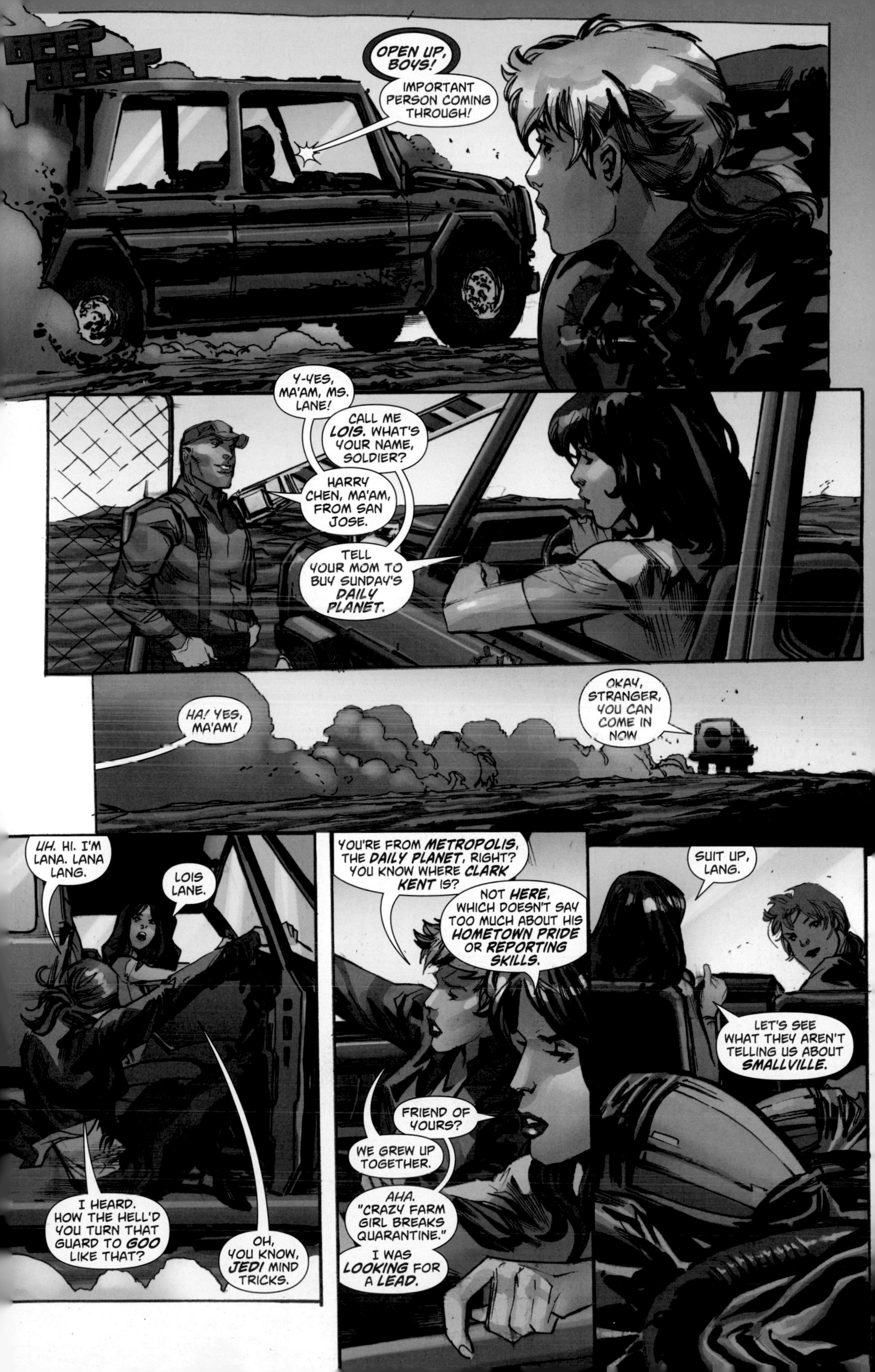
BEEP BEEEP
OPEN UP, BOYS!
IMPORTANT PERSON COMING THROUGH!
Y-YES, MA'AM, MS. LANE!
CALL ME LOIS. WHAT'S YOUR NAME, SOLDIER?
HARRY CHEN, MA'AM, FROM SAN JOSE.
TELL YOUR MOM TO BUY SUNDAY'S DAILY PLANET.
HA! YES, MA'AM!
OKAY, STRANGER, YOU CAN COME IN NOW
UH. HI. I'M LANA. LANA LANG.
LOIS LANE.
I HEARD. HOW THE HELL'D YOU TURN THAT GUARD TO GOO LIKE THAT?
OH, YOU KNOW, JEDI MIND TRICKS.
YOU'RE FROM METROPOLIS, THE DAILY PLANET, RIGHT? YOU KNOW WHERE CLARK KENT IS?
NOT HERE, WHICH DOESN'T SAY TOO MUCH ABOUT HIS HOMETOWN PRIDE OR REPORTING SKILLS.
FRIEND OF YOURS?
WE GREW UP TOGETHER.
AHA. "CRAZY FARM GIRL BREAKS QUARANTINE."
I WAS LOOKING FOR A LEAD.
SUIT UP, LANG.
LET'S SEE WHAT THEY AREN'T TELLING US ABOUT SMALLVILLE.

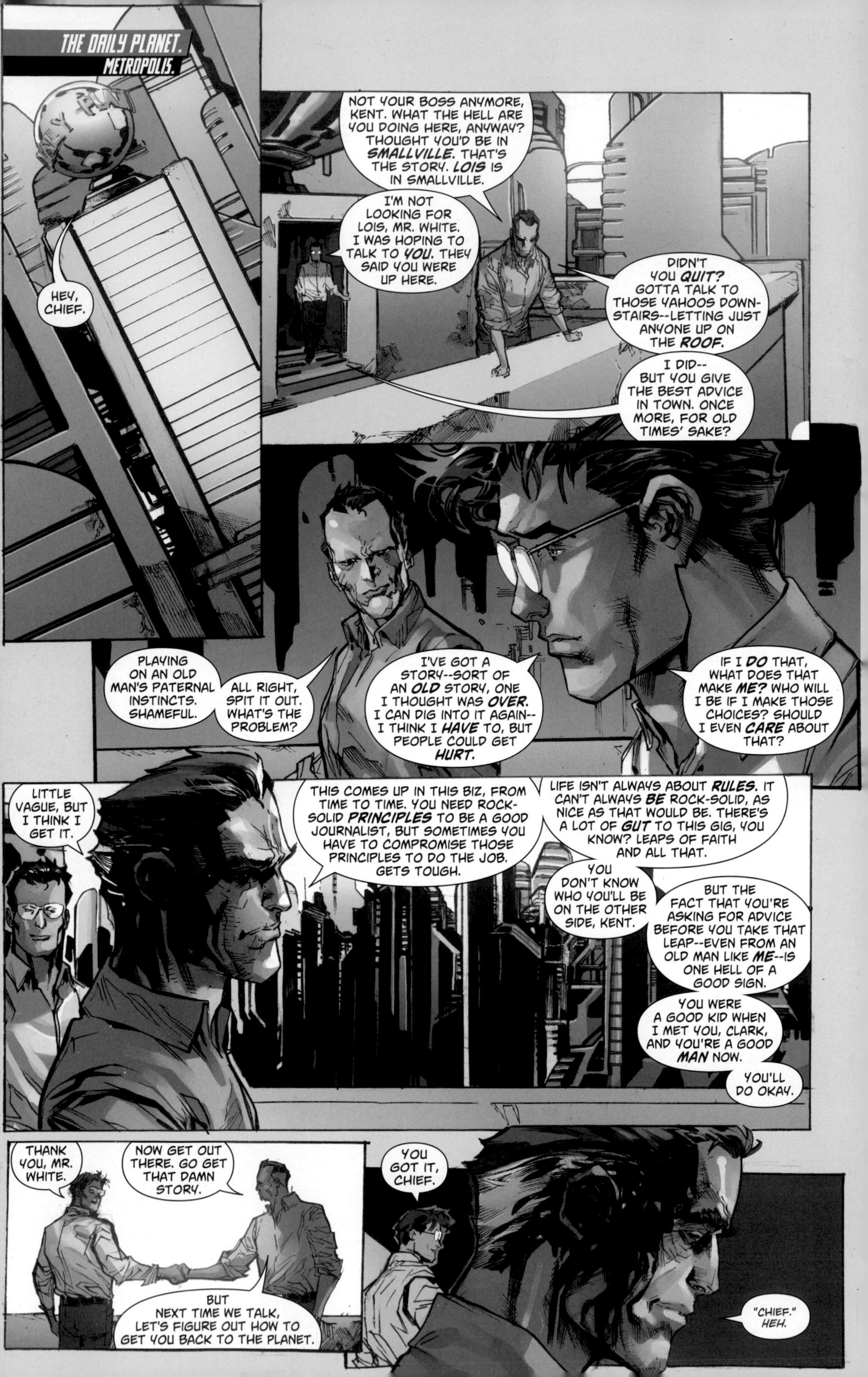
THE DAILY PLANET.
METROPOLIS.
HEY, CHIEF.
NOT YOUR BOSS ANYMORE, KENT. WHAT THE HELL ARE YOU DOING HERE, ANYWAY? THOUGHT YOU'D BE IN SMALLVILLE. THAT'S THE STORY. LOIS IS IN SMALLVILLE.
I'M NOT LOOKING FOR LOIS, MR. WHITE. I WAS HOPING TO TALK TO YOU. THEY SAID YOU WERE UP HERE.
DIDN'T YOU QUIT? GOTTA TALK TO THOSE YAHOOS DOWN-STAIRS--LETTING JUST ANYONE UP ON THE ROOF.
I DID-- BUT YOU GIVE THE BEST ADVICE IN TOWN. ONCE MORE, FOR OLD TIMES' SAKE?
PLAYING ON AN OLD MAN'S PATERNAL INSTINCTS. SHAMEFUL.
ALL RIGHT, SPIT IT OUT. WHAT'S THE PROBLEM?
I'VE GOT A STORY--SORT OF AN OLD STORY, ONE I THOUGHT WAS OVER. I CAN DIG INTO IT AGAIN-- I THINK I HAVE TO, BUT PEOPLE COULD GET HURT.
IF I DO THAT, WHAT DOES THAT MAKE ME? WHO WILL I BE IF I MAKE THOSE CHOICES? SHOULD I EVEN CARE ABOUT THAT?
LITTLE VAGUE, BUT I THINK I GET IT.
THIS COMES UP IN THIS BIZ, FROM TIME TO TIME. YOU NEED ROCK-SOLID PRINCIPLES TO BE A GOOD JOURNALIST, BUT SOMETIMES YOU HAVE TO COMPROMISE THOSE PRINCIPLES TO DO THE JOB. GETS TOUGH.
LIFE ISN'T ALWAYS ABOUT RULES. IT CAN'T ALWAYS BE ROCK-SOLID, AS NICE AS THAT WOULD BE. THERE'S A LOT OF GUT TO THIS GIG, YOU KNOW? LEAPS OF FAITH AND ALL THAT.
YOU DON'T KNOW WHO YOU'LL BE ON THE OTHER SIDE, KENT.
BUT THE FACT THAT YOU'RE ASKING FOR ADVICE BEFORE YOU TAKE THAT LEAP--EVEN FROM AN OLD MAN LIKE ME--IS ONE HELL OF A GOOD SIGN.
YOU WERE A GOOD KID WHEN I MET YOU, CLARK, AND YOU'RE A GOOD MAN NOW.
YOU'LL DO OKAY.
THANK YOU, MR. WHITE.
NOW GET OUT THERE. GO GET THAT DAMN STORY.
BUT NEXT TIME WE TALK, LET'S FIGURE OUT HOW TO GET YOU BACK TO THE PLANET.
YOU GOT IT, CHIEF.
"CHIEF." HEH.

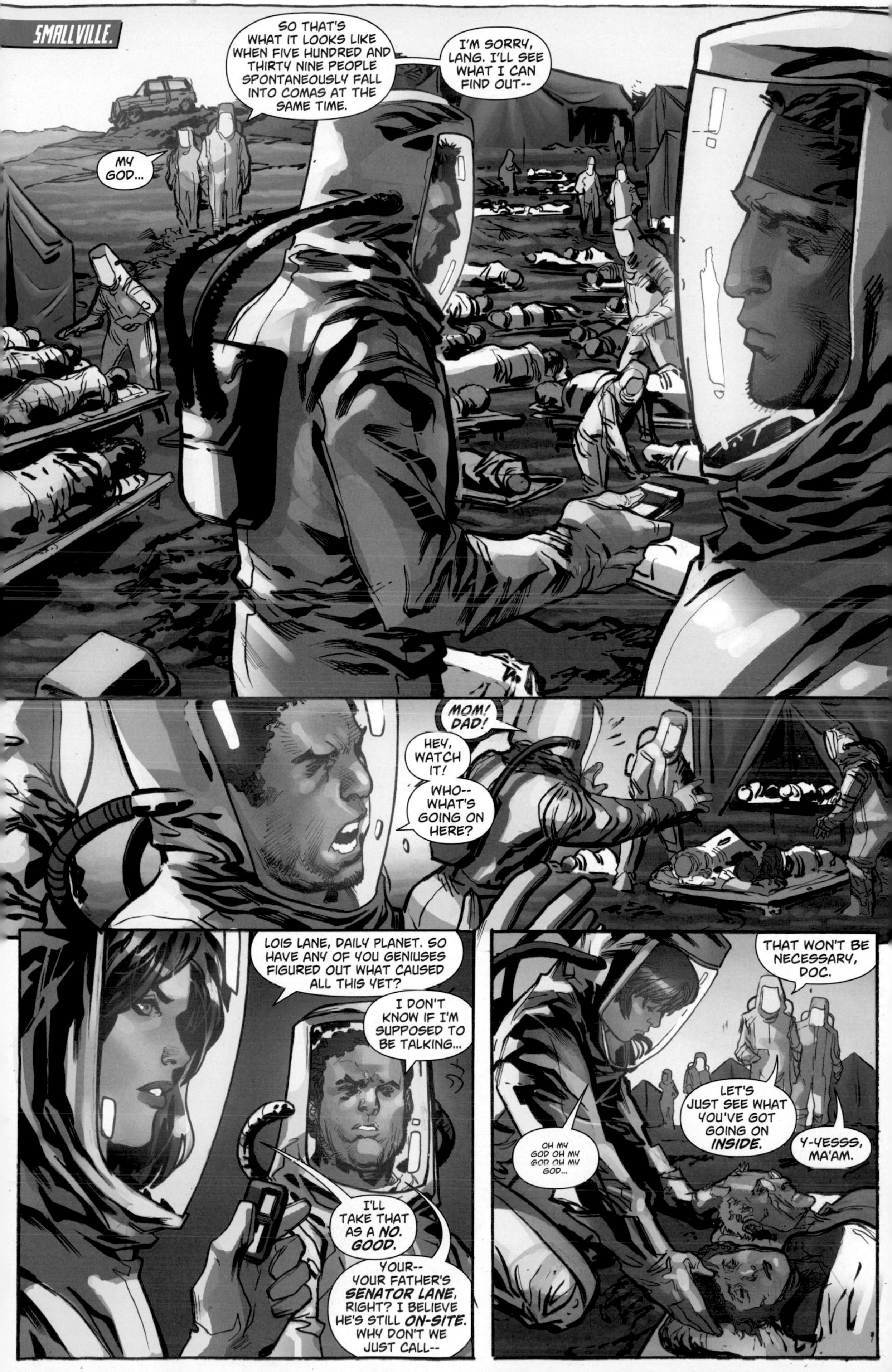
SMALLVILLE.
SO THAT'S WHAT IT LOOKS LIKE WHEN FIVE HUNDRED AND THIRTY NINE PEOPLE SPONTANEOUSLY FALL INTO COMAS AT THE SAME TIME.
I'M SORRY, LANG. I'LL SEE WHAT I CAN FIND OUT--
MY GOD...
MOM! DAD!
HEY, WATCH IT!
WHO-- WHAT'S GOING ON HERE?
LOIS LANE, DAILY PLANET. SO HAVE ANY OF YOU GENIUSES FIGURED OUT WHAT CAUSED ALL THIS YET?
I DON'T KNOW IF I'M SUPPOSED TO BE TALKING...
I'LL TAKE THAT AS A NO. GOOD.
YOUR-- YOUR FATHER'S SENATOR LANE, RIGHT? I BELIEVE HE'S STILL ON-SITE. WHY DON'T WE JUST CALL--
THAT WON'T BE NECESSARY, DOC.
OH MY GOD OH MY GOD OH MY GOD...
LET'S JUST SEE WHAT YOU'VE GOT GOING ON INSIDE.
Y-YESSS, MA'AM.

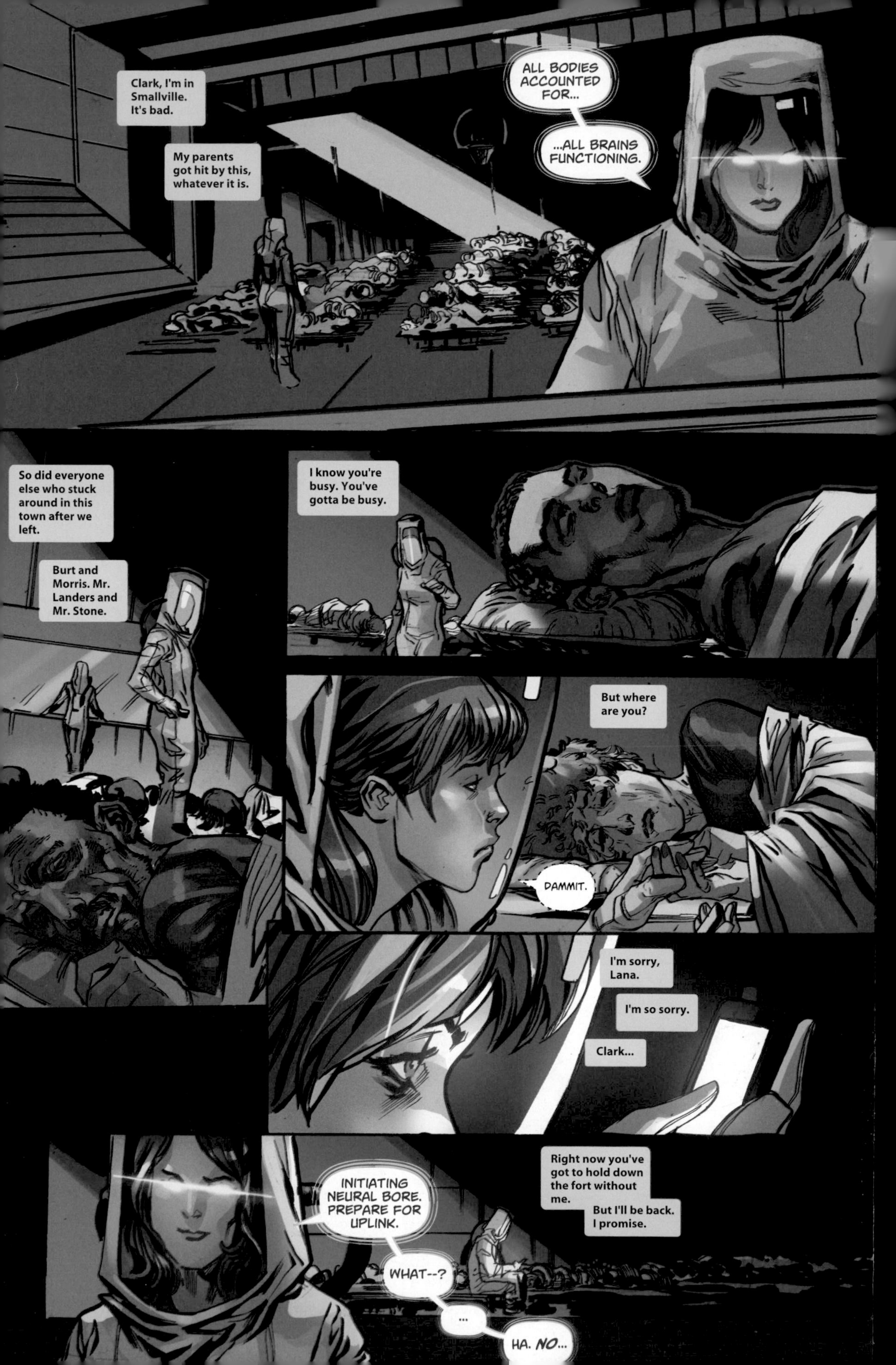
Clark, I'm in Smallville. It's bad.
My parents got hit by this, whatever it is.
ALL BODIES ACCOUNTED FOR...
...ALL BRAINS FUNCTIONING.
So did everyone else who stuck around in this town after we left.
Burt and Morris. Mr. Landers and Mr. Stone.
I know you're busy. You've gotta be busy.
But where are you?
DAMMIT.
I'm sorry, Lana.
I'm so sorry.
Clark...
INITIATING NEURAL BORE. PREPARE FOR UPLINK.
Right now you've got to hold down the fort without me.
But I'll be back. I promise.
WHAT--?
...
HA. NO...

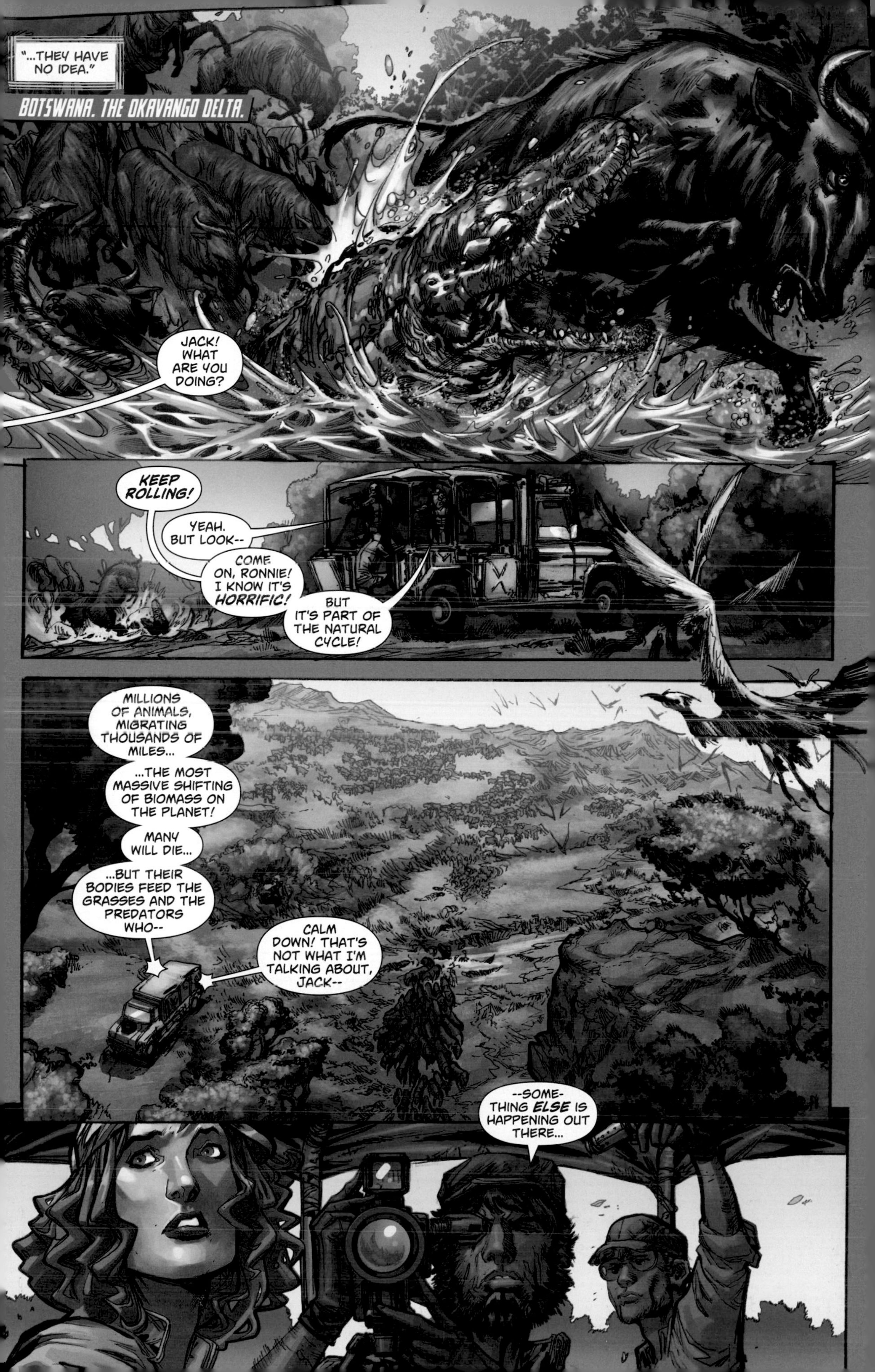
"...THEY HAVE NO IDEA."
BOTSWANA. THE OKAVANGO DELTA.
JACK! WHAT ARE YOU DOING?
KEEP ROLLING!
YEAH. BUT LOOK--
COME ON, RONNIE! I KNOW IT'S HORRIFIC!
BUT IT'S PART OF THE NATURAL CYCLE!
MILLIONS OF ANIMALS, MIGRATING THOUSANDS OF MILES...
...THE MOST MASSIVE SHIFTING OF BIOMASS ON THE PLANET!
MANY WILL DIE...
...BUT THEIR BODIES FEED THE GRASSES AND THE PREDATORS WHO--
CALM DOWN! THAT'S NOT WHAT I'M TALKING ABOUT, JACK--
--SOME-THING ELSE IS HAPPENING OUT THERE...

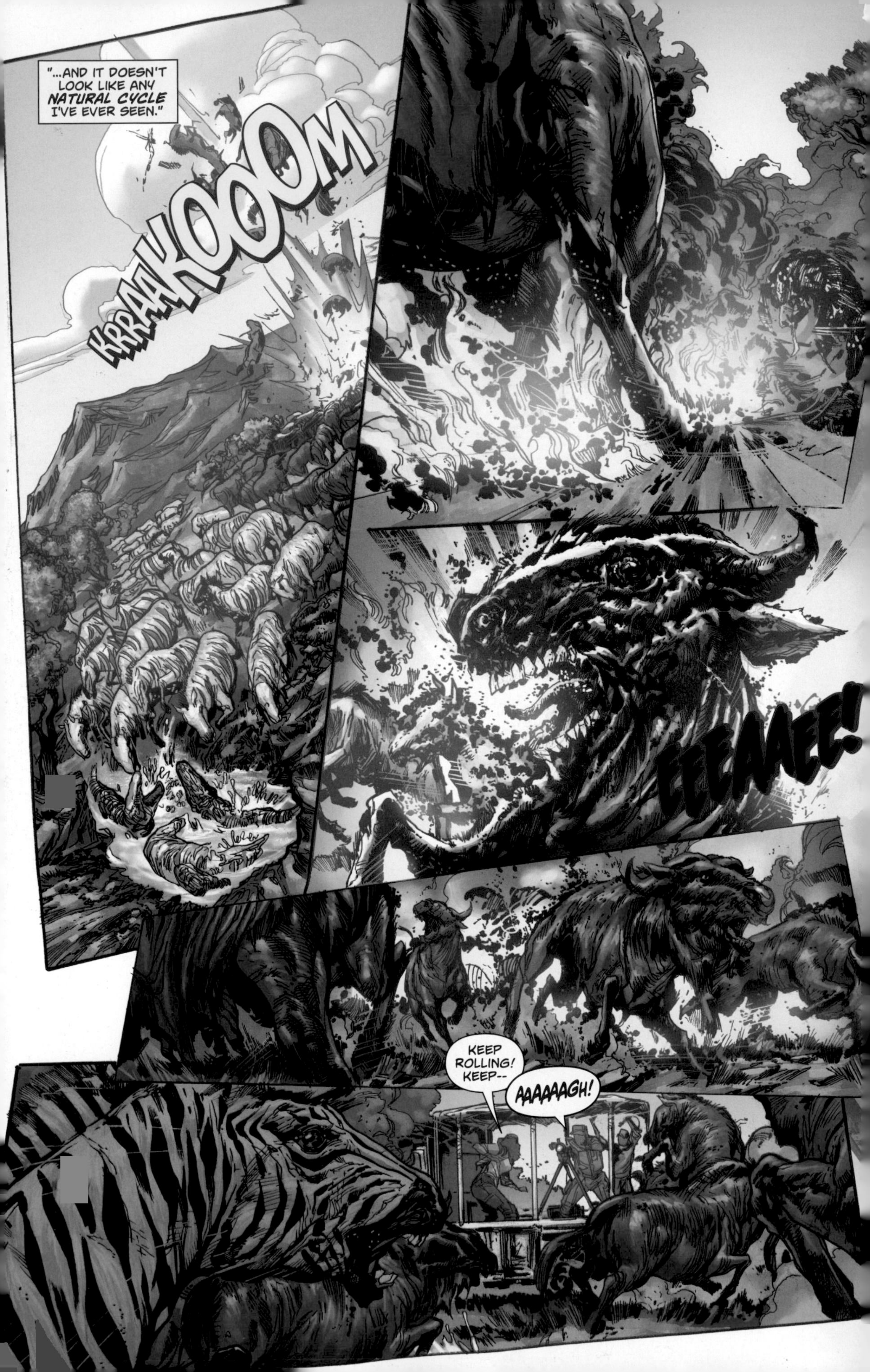
"...AND IT DOESN'T LOOK LIKE ANY *NATURAL CYCLE* I'VE EVER SEEN."
KRAAKOOOM
EEEAAEE!
KEEP ROLLING! KEEP--
AAAAAAGH!

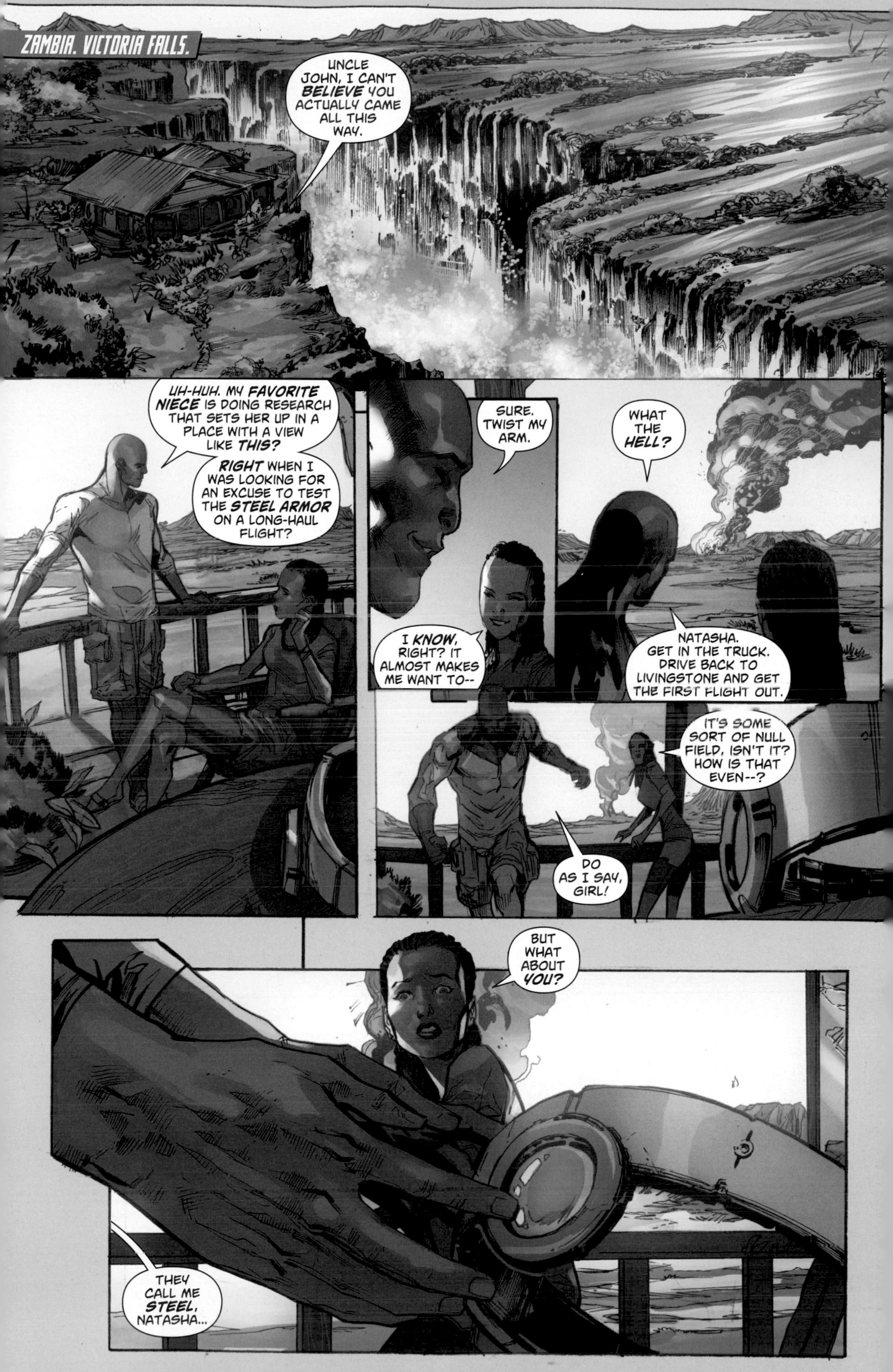
ZAMBIA. VICTORIA FALLS.
UNCLE JOHN, I CAN'T BELIEVE YOU ACTUALLY CAME ALL THIS WAY.
UH-HUH. MY FAVORITE NIECE IS DOING RESEARCH THAT SETS HER UP IN A PLACE WITH A VIEW LIKE THIS?
RIGHT WHEN I WAS LOOKING FOR AN EXCUSE TO TEST THE STEEL ARMOR ON A LONG-HAUL FLIGHT?
SURE. TWIST MY ARM.
I KNOW, RIGHT? IT ALMOST MAKES ME WANT TO--
WHAT THE HELL?
NATASHA. GET IN THE TRUCK. DRIVE BACK TO LIVINGSTONE AND GET THE FIRST FLIGHT OUT.
IT'S SOME SORT OF NULL FIELD, ISN'T IT? HOW IS THAT EVEN--?
DO AS I SAY, GIRL!
BUT WHAT ABOUT YOU?
THEY CALL ME STEEL, NATASHA...

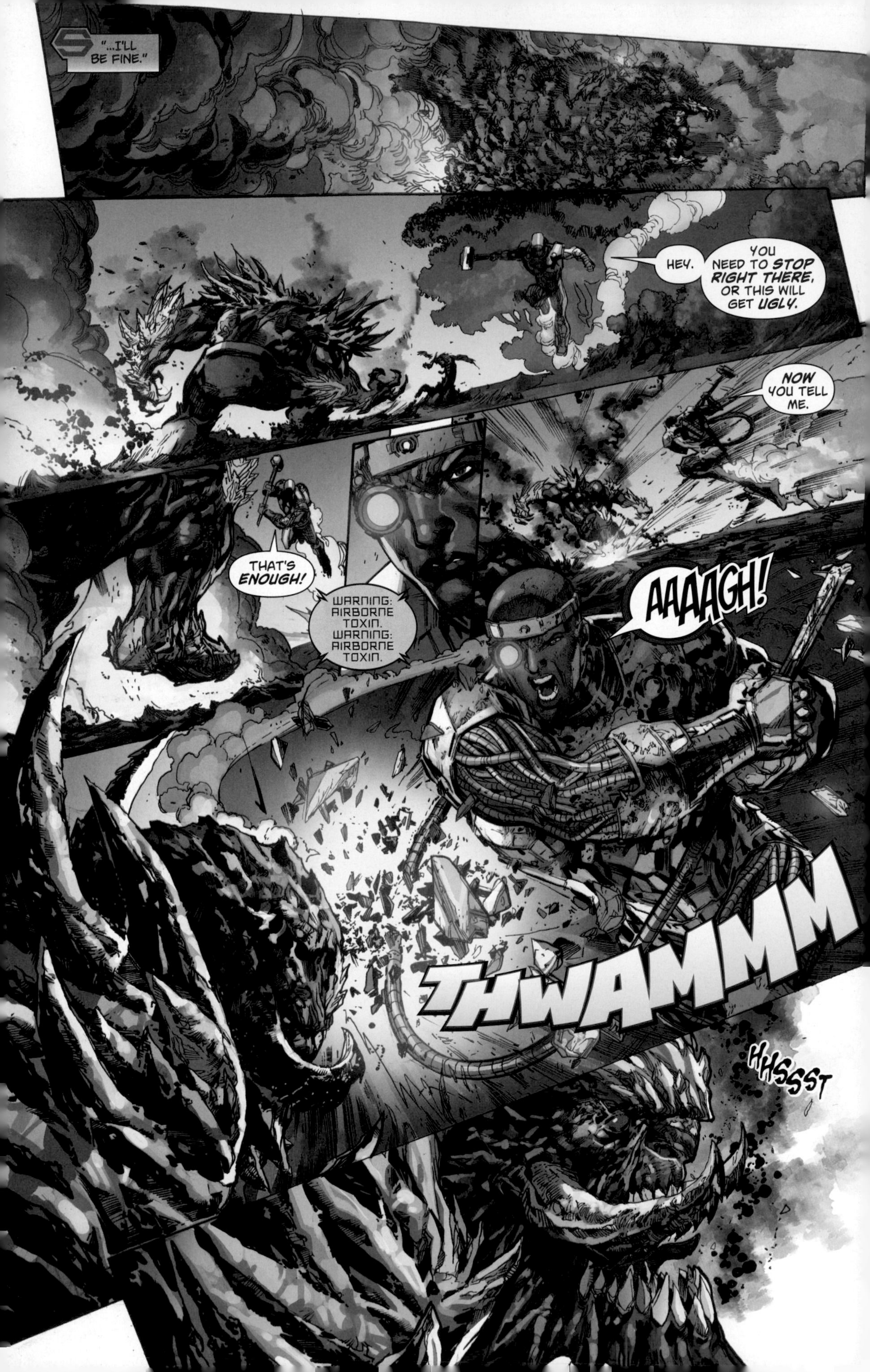
"...I'LL BE FINE."
HEY.
YOU NEED TO STOP RIGHT THERE, OR THIS WILL GET UGLY.
NOW YOU TELL ME.
THAT'S ENOUGH!
WARNING: AIRBORNE TOXIN. WARNING: AIRBORNE TOXIN.
AAAAGH!
THWAMMM
HHSSST

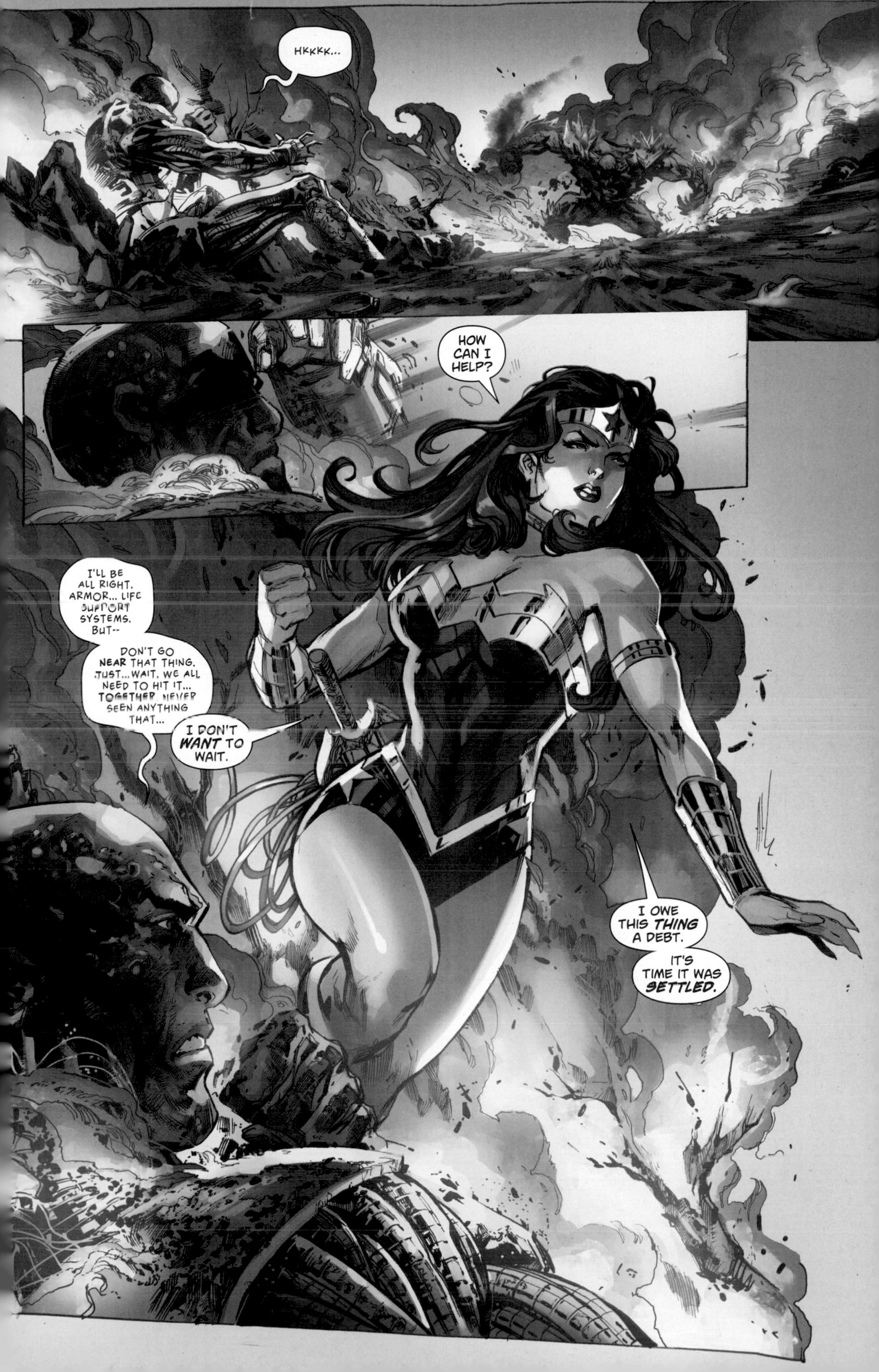
HKKKK...
HOW CAN I HELP?
I'LL BE ALL RIGHT. ARMOR... LIFE SUPPORT SYSTEMS. BUT--
DON'T GO NEAR THAT THING. JUST...WAIT. WE ALL NEED TO HIT IT... TOGETHER. NEVER SEEN ANYTHING THAT...
I DON'T WANT TO WAIT.
I OWE THIS THING A DEBT.
IT'S TIME IT WAS SETTLED.

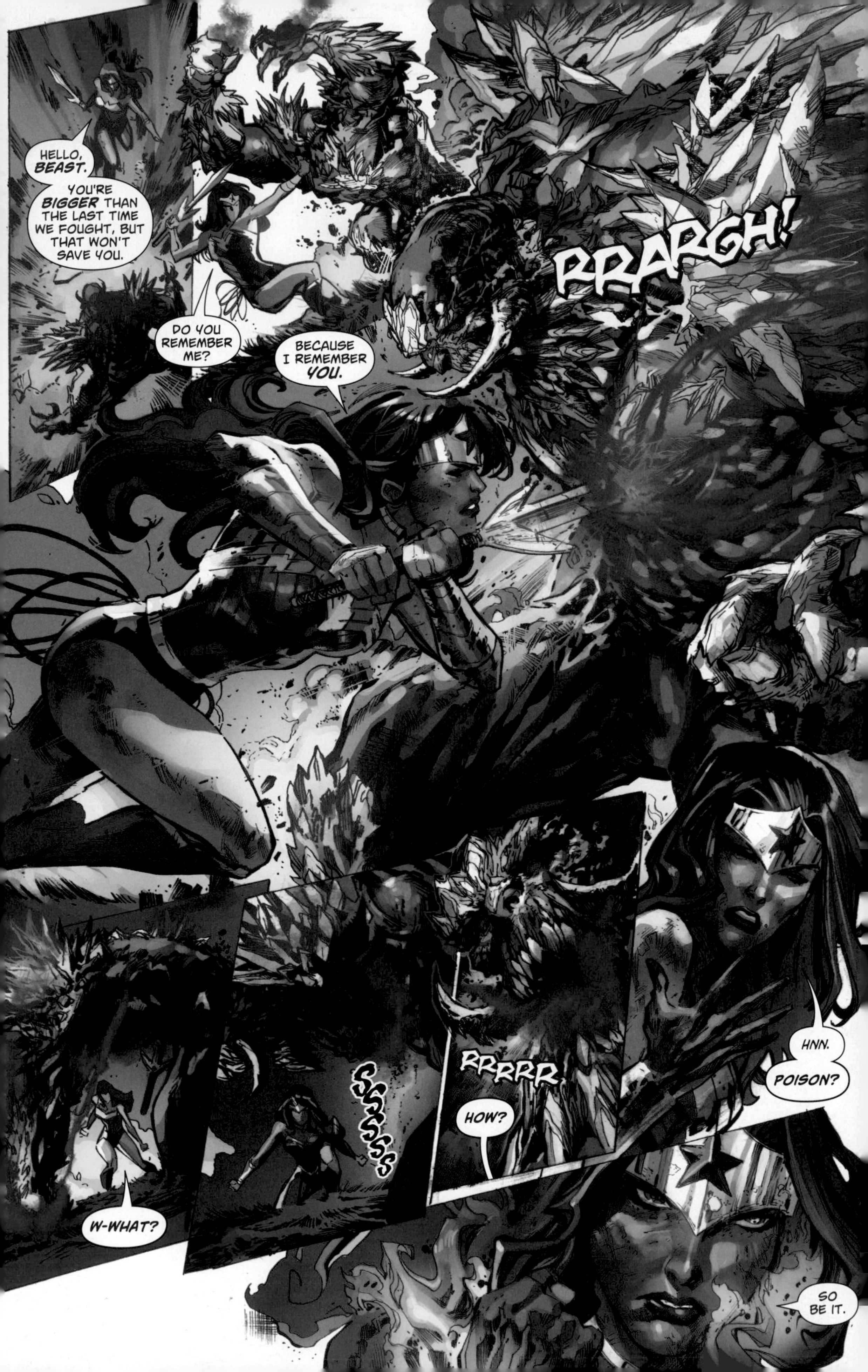
HELLO, BEAST.
YOU'RE BIGGER THAN THE LAST TIME WE FOUGHT, BUT THAT WON'T SAVE YOU.
RRARGH!
DO YOU REMEMBER ME?
BECAUSE I REMEMBER YOU.
W-WHAT?
SSSSSS
RRRRR!
HOW?
HNN.
POISON?
SO BE IT.

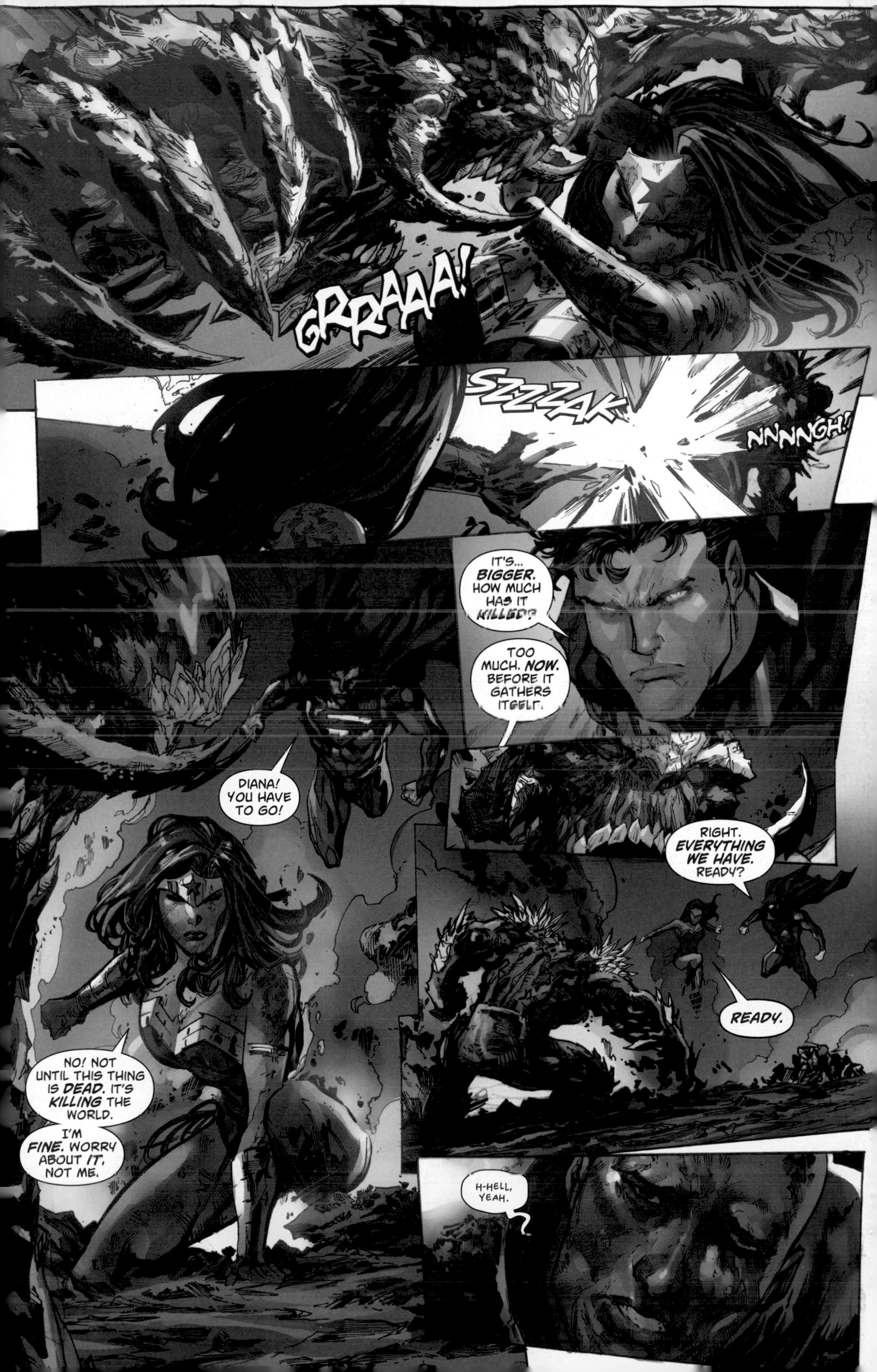
GRRAAA!
SZZZAK
NNNNGH!
IT'S... BIGGER. HOW MUCH HAS IT KILLED?
TOO MUCH. NOW. BEFORE IT GATHERS ITSELF.
DIANA! YOU HAVE TO GO!
NO! NOT UNTIL THIS THING IS DEAD. IT'S KILLING THE WORLD.
I'M FINE. WORRY ABOUT IT, NOT ME.
RIGHT. EVERYTHING WE HAVE. READY?
READY.
H-HELL, YEAH.

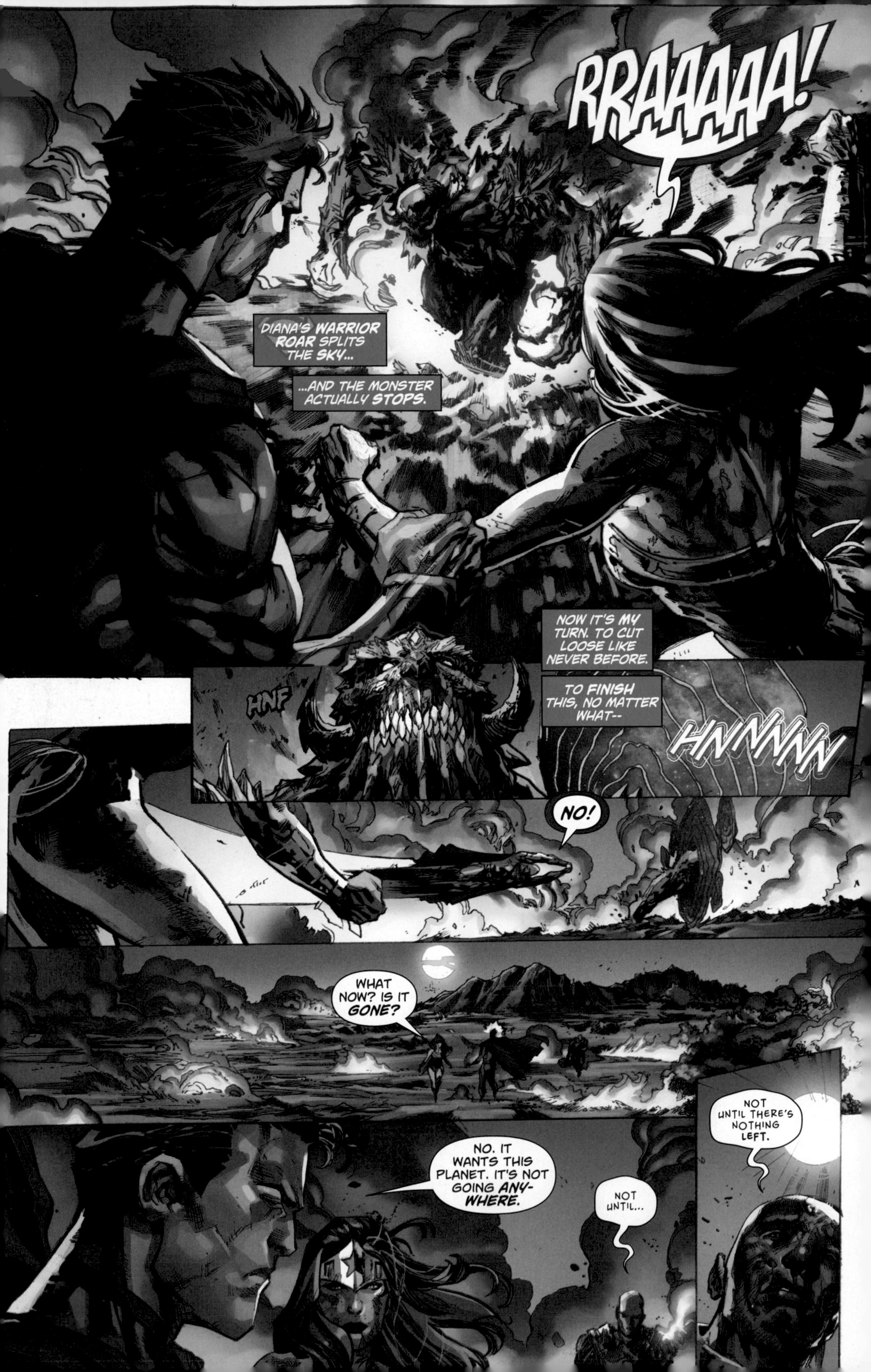
RRAAAAA!
DIANA'S WARRIOR ROAR SPLITS THE SKY...
...AND THE MONSTER ACTUALLY STOPS.
NOW IT'S MY TURN. TO CUT LOOSE LIKE NEVER BEFORE.
HNF
TO FINISH THIS, NO MATTER WHAT--
HNNNNN
NO!
WHAT NOW? IS IT GONE?
NO. IT WANTS THIS PLANET. IT'S NOT GOING ANY-WHERE.
NOT UNTIL...
NOT UNTIL THERE'S NOTHING LEFT.

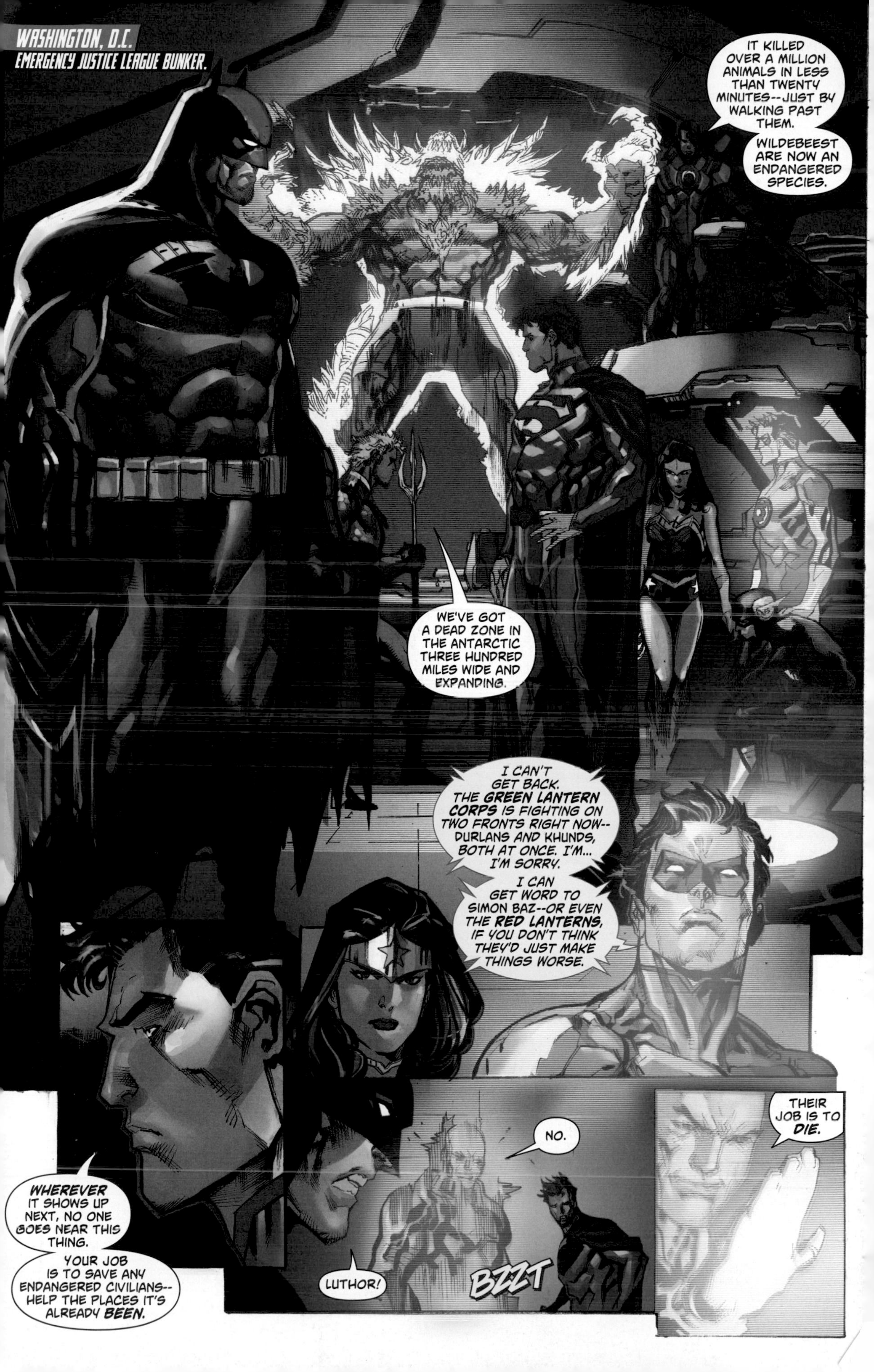
WASHINGTON, D.C.
EMERGENCY JUSTICE LEAGUE BUNKER.
IT KILLED OVER A MILLION ANIMALS IN LESS THAN TWENTY MINUTES--JUST BY WALKING PAST THEM.
WILDEBEEST ARE NOW AN ENDANGERED SPECIES.
WE'VE GOT A DEAD ZONE IN THE ANTARCTIC THREE HUNDRED MILES WIDE AND EXPANDING.
I CAN'T GET BACK. THE GREEN LANTERN CORPS IS FIGHTING ON TWO FRONTS RIGHT NOW--DURLANS AND KHUNDS, BOTH AT ONCE. I'M... I'M SORRY.
I CAN GET WORD TO SIMON BAZ--OR EVEN THE RED LANTERNS, IF YOU DON'T THINK THEY'D JUST MAKE THINGS WORSE.
WHEREVER IT SHOWS UP NEXT, NO ONE GOES NEAR THIS THING.
YOUR JOB IS TO SAVE ANY ENDANGERED CIVILIANS--HELP THE PLACES IT'S ALREADY BEEN.
LUTHOR!
NO.
BZZT
THEIR JOB IS TO DIE.

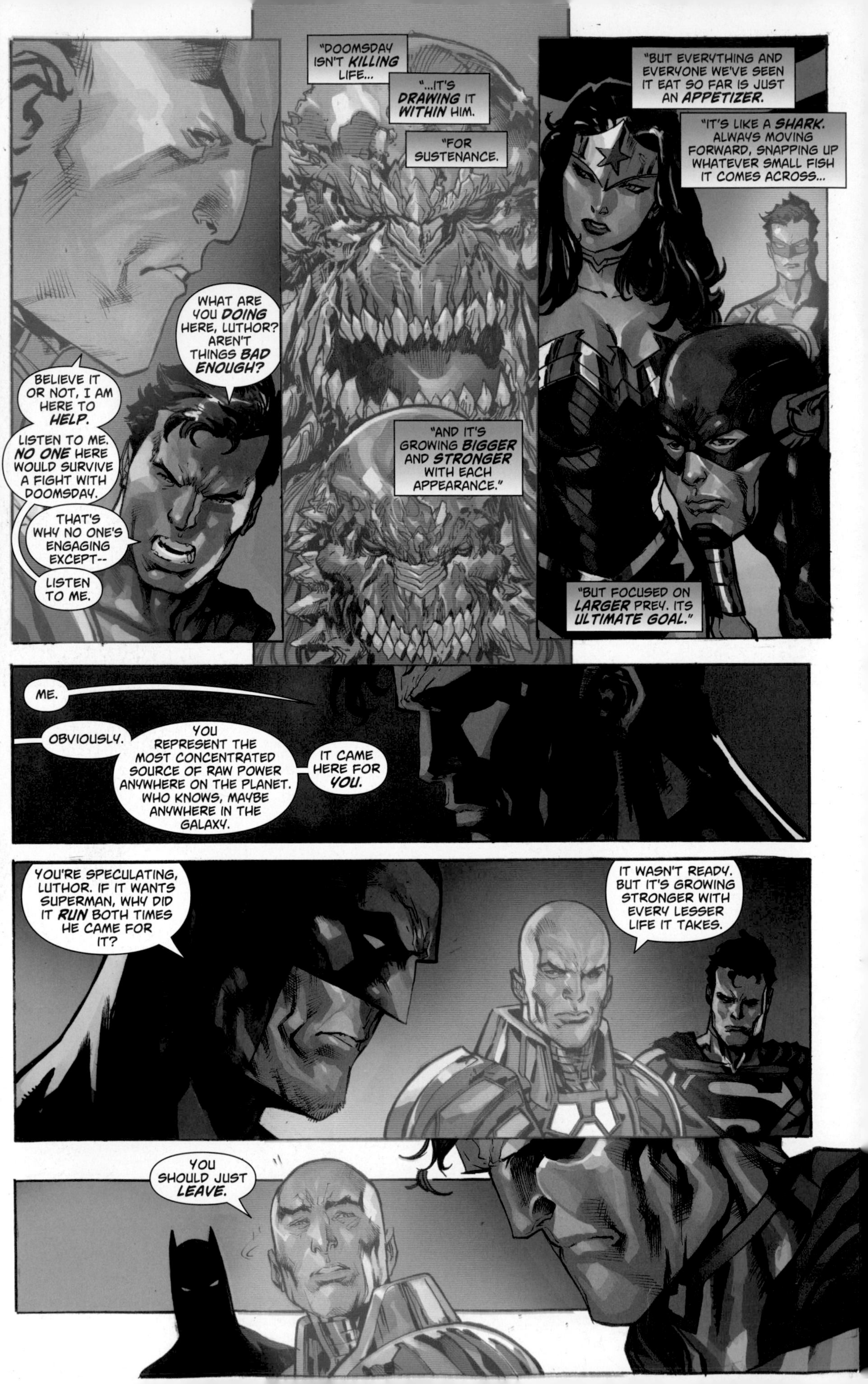

WHAT ARE YOU DOING HERE, LUTHOR? AREN'T THINGS BAD ENOUGH?
BELIEVE IT OR NOT, I AM HERE TO HELP.
LISTEN TO ME. NO ONE HERE WOULD SURVIVE A FIGHT WITH DOOMSDAY.
THAT'S WHY NO ONE'S ENGAGING EXCEPT--
LISTEN TO ME.
"DOOMSDAY ISN'T KILLING LIFE...
"...IT'S DRAWING IT WITHIN HIM.
"FOR SUSTENANCE.
"AND IT'S GROWING BIGGER AND STRONGER WITH EACH APPEARANCE."
"BUT EVERYTHING AND EVERYONE WE'VE SEEN IT EAT SO FAR IS JUST AN APPETIZER.
"IT'S LIKE A SHARK. ALWAYS MOVING FORWARD, SNAPPING UP WHATEVER SMALL FISH IT COMES ACROSS...
"BUT FOCUSED ON LARGER PREY. ITS ULTIMATE GOAL."
ME.
OBVIOUSLY.
YOU REPRESENT THE MOST CONCENTRATED SOURCE OF RAW POWER ANYWHERE ON THE PLANET. WHO KNOWS, MAYBE ANYWHERE IN THE GALAXY.
IT CAME HERE FOR YOU.
YOU'RE SPECULATING, LUTHOR. IF IT WANTS SUPERMAN, WHY DID IT RUN BOTH TIMES HE CAME FOR IT?
IT WASN'T READY. BUT IT'S GROWING STRONGER WITH EVERY LESSER LIFE IT TAKES.
YOU SHOULD JUST LEAVE.

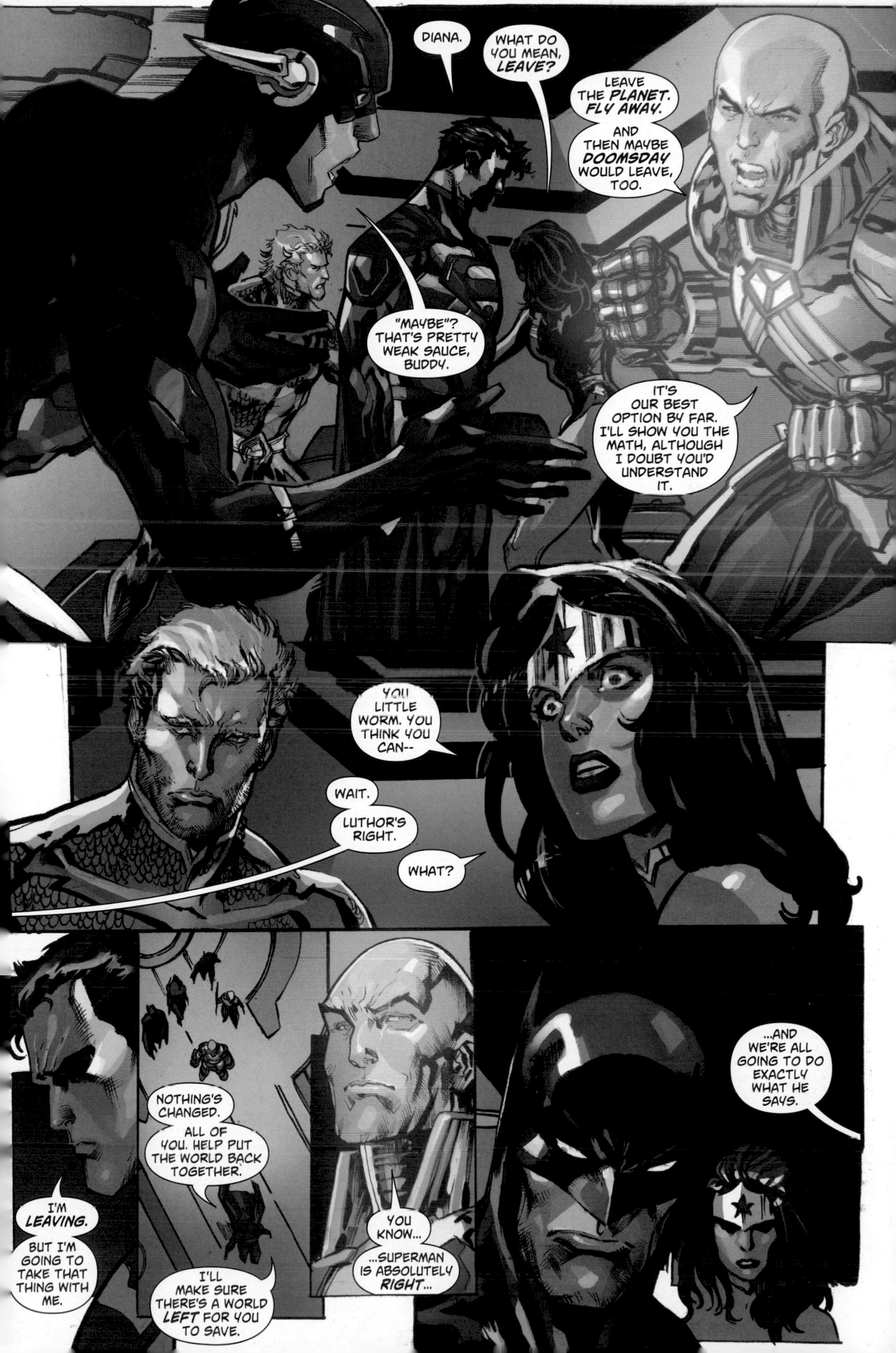
DIANA.
WHAT DO YOU MEAN, LEAVE?
LEAVE THE PLANET. FLY AWAY.
AND THEN MAYBE DOOMSDAY WOULD LEAVE, TOO.
"MAYBE"? THAT'S PRETTY WEAK SAUCE, BUDDY.
IT'S OUR BEST OPTION BY FAR. I'LL SHOW YOU THE MATH, ALTHOUGH I DOUBT YOU'D UNDERSTAND IT.
YOU LITTLE WORM. YOU THINK YOU CAN--
WAIT.
LUTHOR'S RIGHT.
WHAT?
I'M LEAVING.
BUT I'M GOING TO TAKE THAT THING WITH ME.
NOTHING'S CHANGED.
ALL OF YOU. HELP PUT THE WORLD BACK TOGETHER.
I'LL MAKE SURE THERE'S A WORLD LEFT FOR YOU TO SAVE.
YOU KNOW...
...SUPERMAN IS ABSOLUTELY RIGHT...
...AND WE'RE ALL GOING TO DO EXACTLY WHAT HE SAYS.

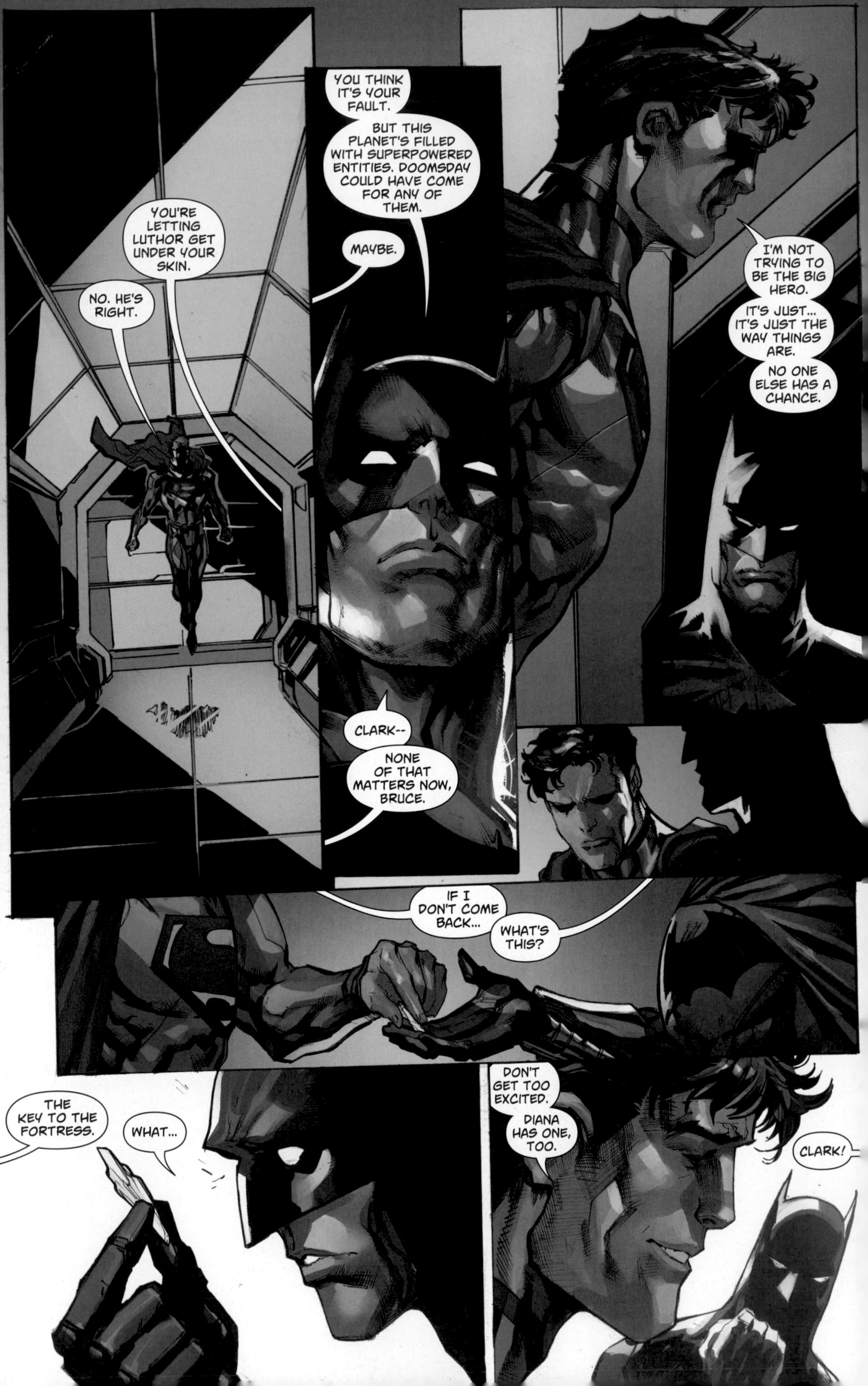
YOU'RE LETTING LUTHOR GET UNDER YOUR SKIN.
NO. HE'S RIGHT.
YOU THINK IT'S YOUR FAULT.
BUT THIS PLANET'S FILLED WITH SUPERPOWERED ENTITIES. DOOMSDAY COULD HAVE COME FOR ANY OF THEM.
MAYBE.
I'M NOT TRYING TO BE THE BIG HERO.
IT'S JUST... IT'S JUST THE WAY THINGS ARE.
NO ONE ELSE HAS A CHANCE.
CLARK--
NONE OF THAT MATTERS NOW, BRUCE.
IF I DON'T COME BACK...
WHAT'S THIS?
THE KEY TO THE FORTRESS.
WHAT...
DON'T GET TOO EXCITED.
DIANA HAS ONE, TOO.
CLARK!

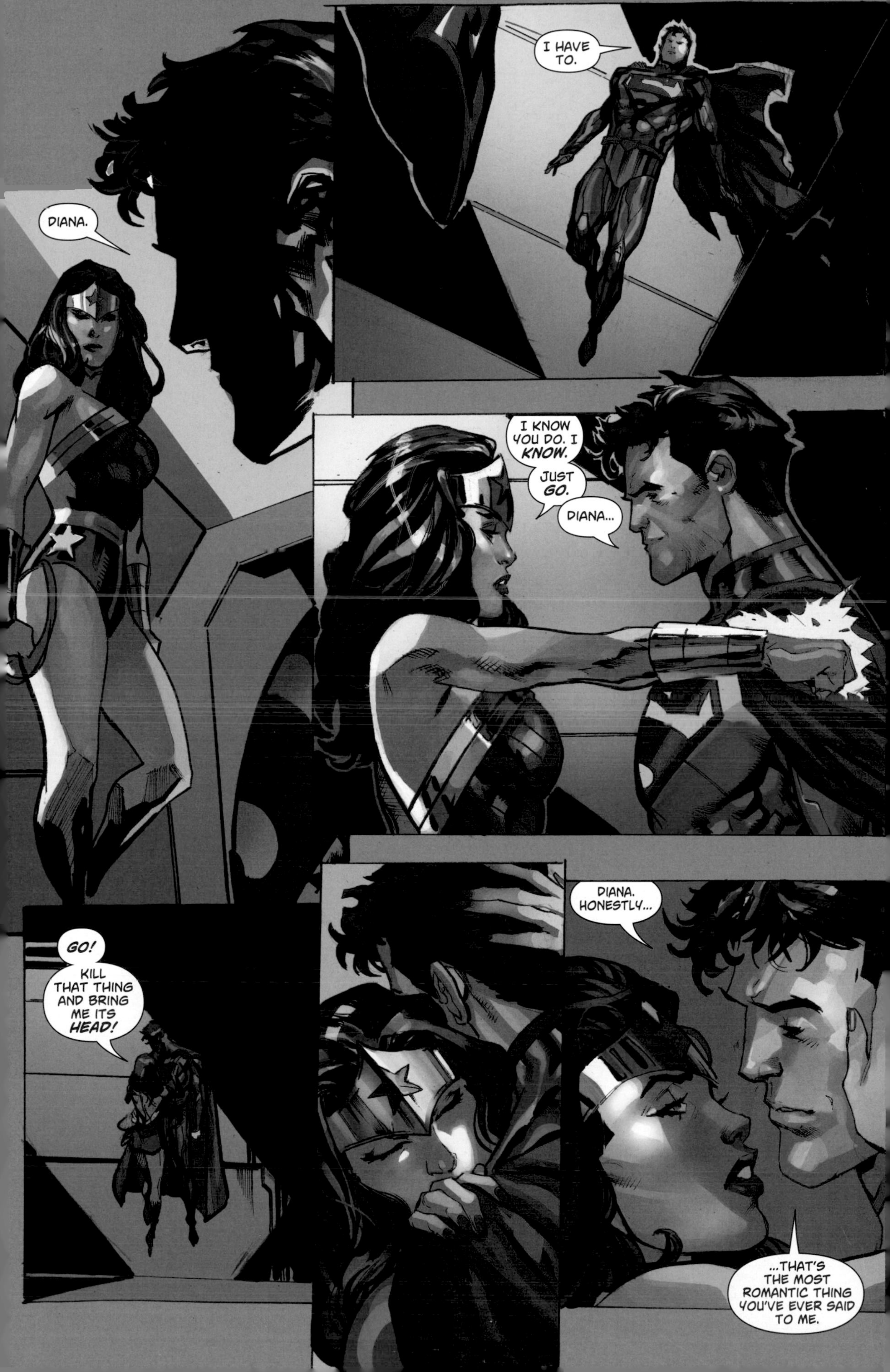
DIANA.
I HAVE TO.
I KNOW YOU DO. I KNOW.
JUST GO.
DIANA...
GO! KILL THAT THING AND BRING ME ITS HEAD!
DIANA. HONESTLY...
...THAT'S THE MOST ROMANTIC THING YOU'VE EVER SAID TO ME.

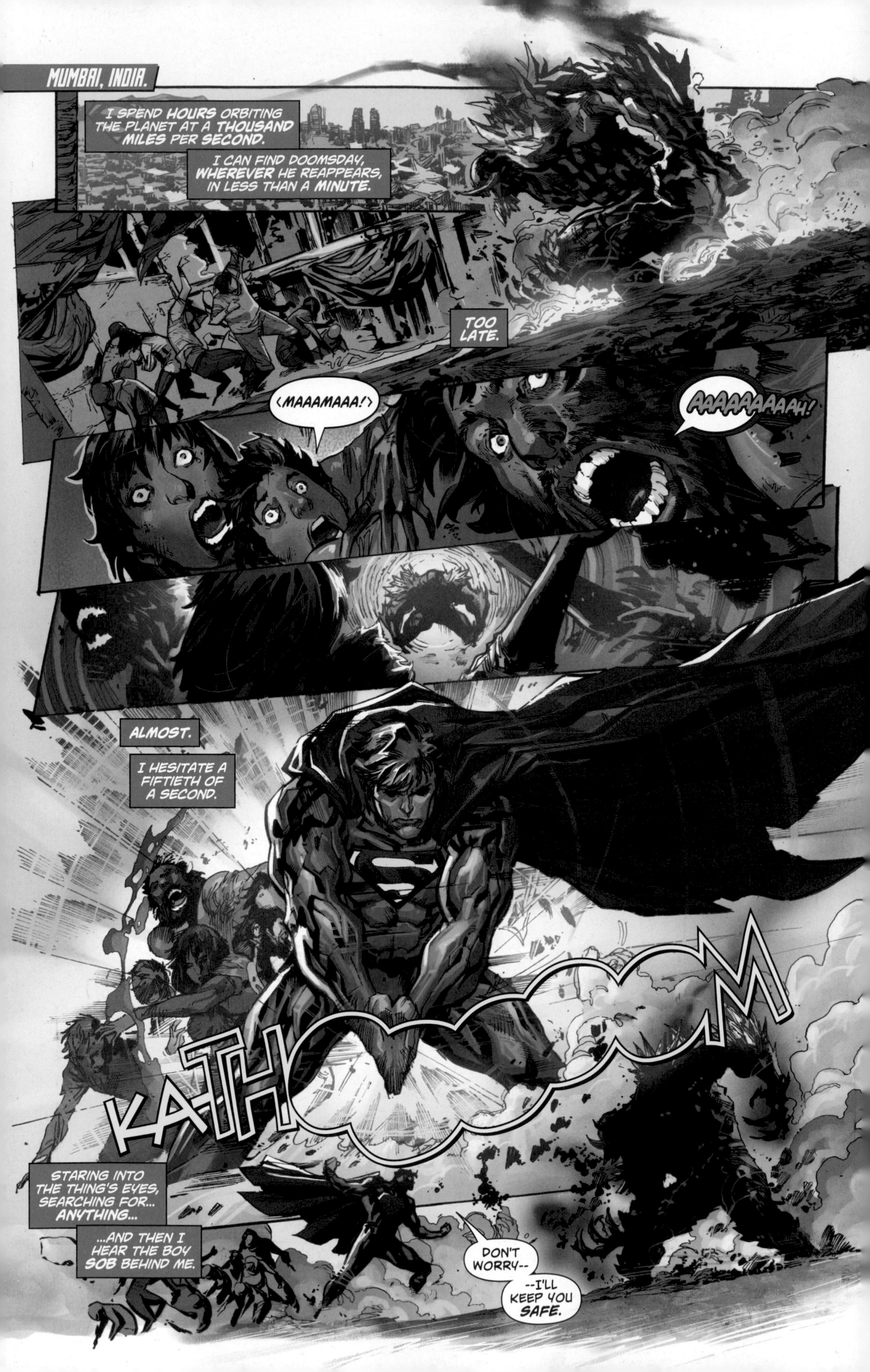
MUMBAI, INDIA.
I SPEND HOURS ORBITING THE PLANET AT A THOUSAND MILES PER SECOND.
I CAN FIND DOOMSDAY, WHEREVER HE REAPPEARS, IN LESS THAN A MINUTE.
TOO LATE.
<MAAAMAAA!>
AAAAAAAAAH!
ALMOST.
I HESITATE A FIFTIETH OF A SECOND.
KA-THOOOOOM
STARING INTO THE THING'S EYES, SEARCHING FOR... ANYTHING...
...AND THEN I HEAR THE BOY SOB BEHIND ME.
DON'T WORRY--
--I'LL KEEP YOU SAFE.

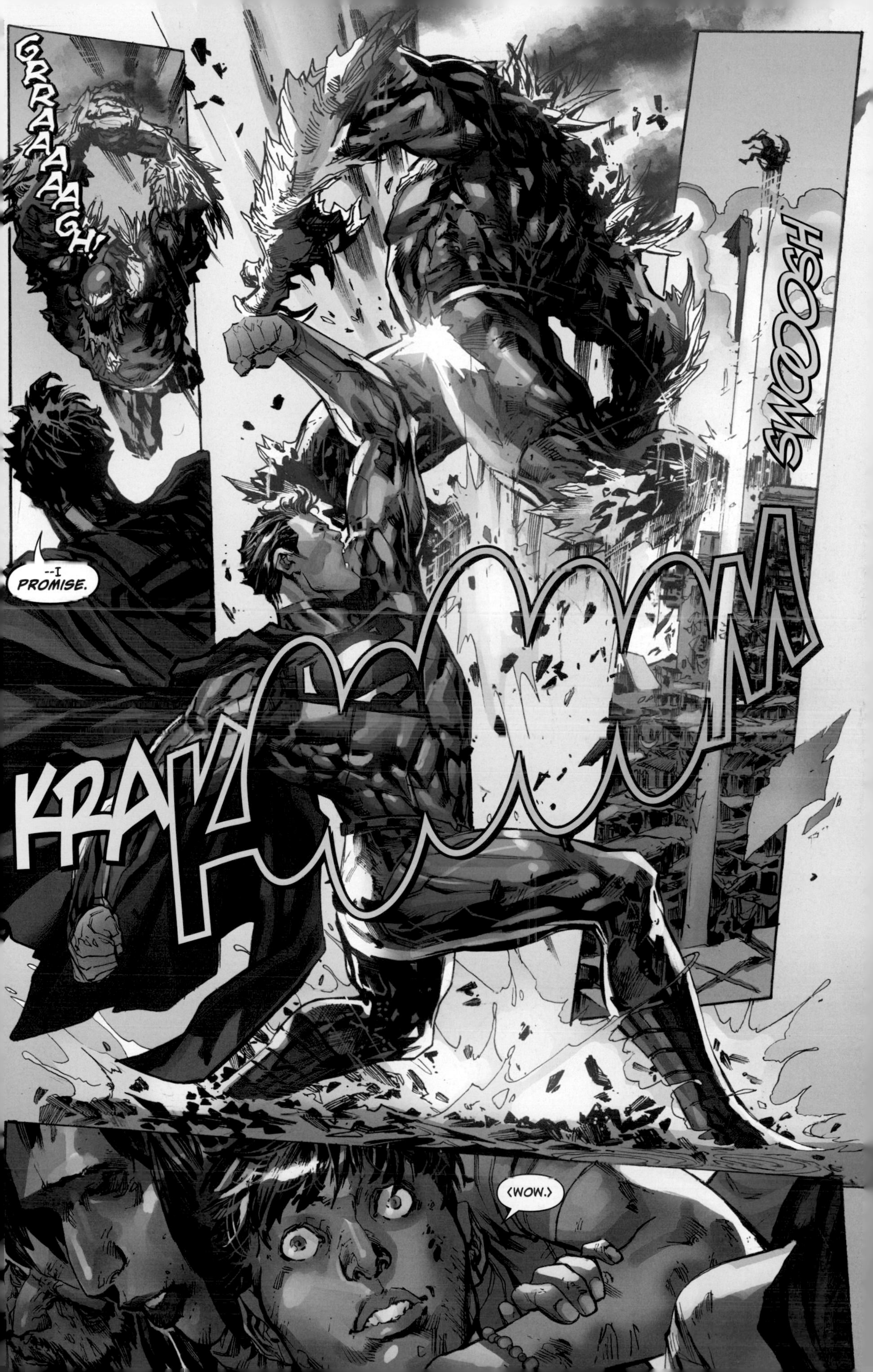
GRRAAAAAGH!
SWOOSH
--I PROMISE.
KRAKOOOOM
‹WOW.›

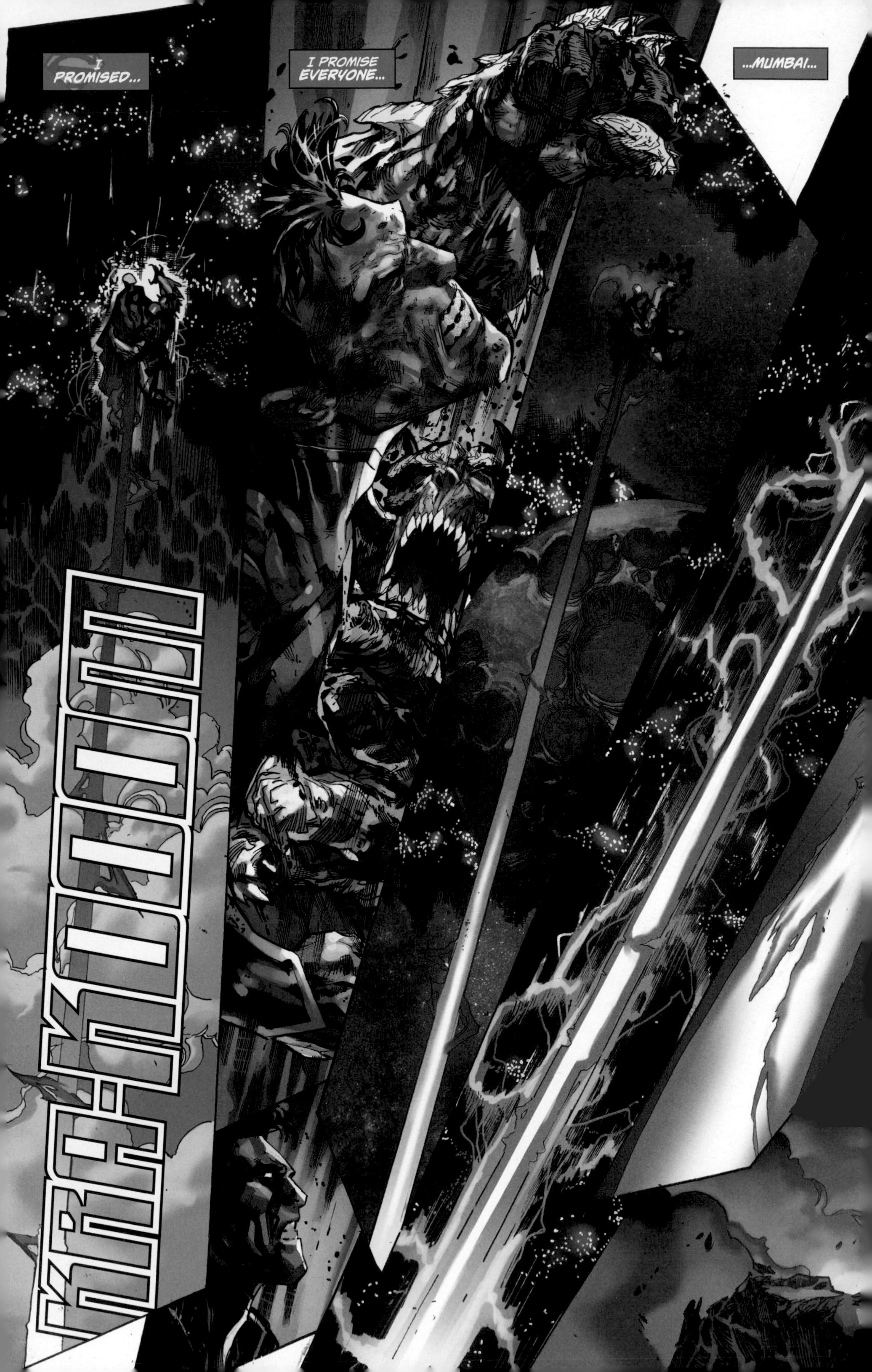
I PROMISED...
I PROMISE EVERYONE...
...MUMBAI...

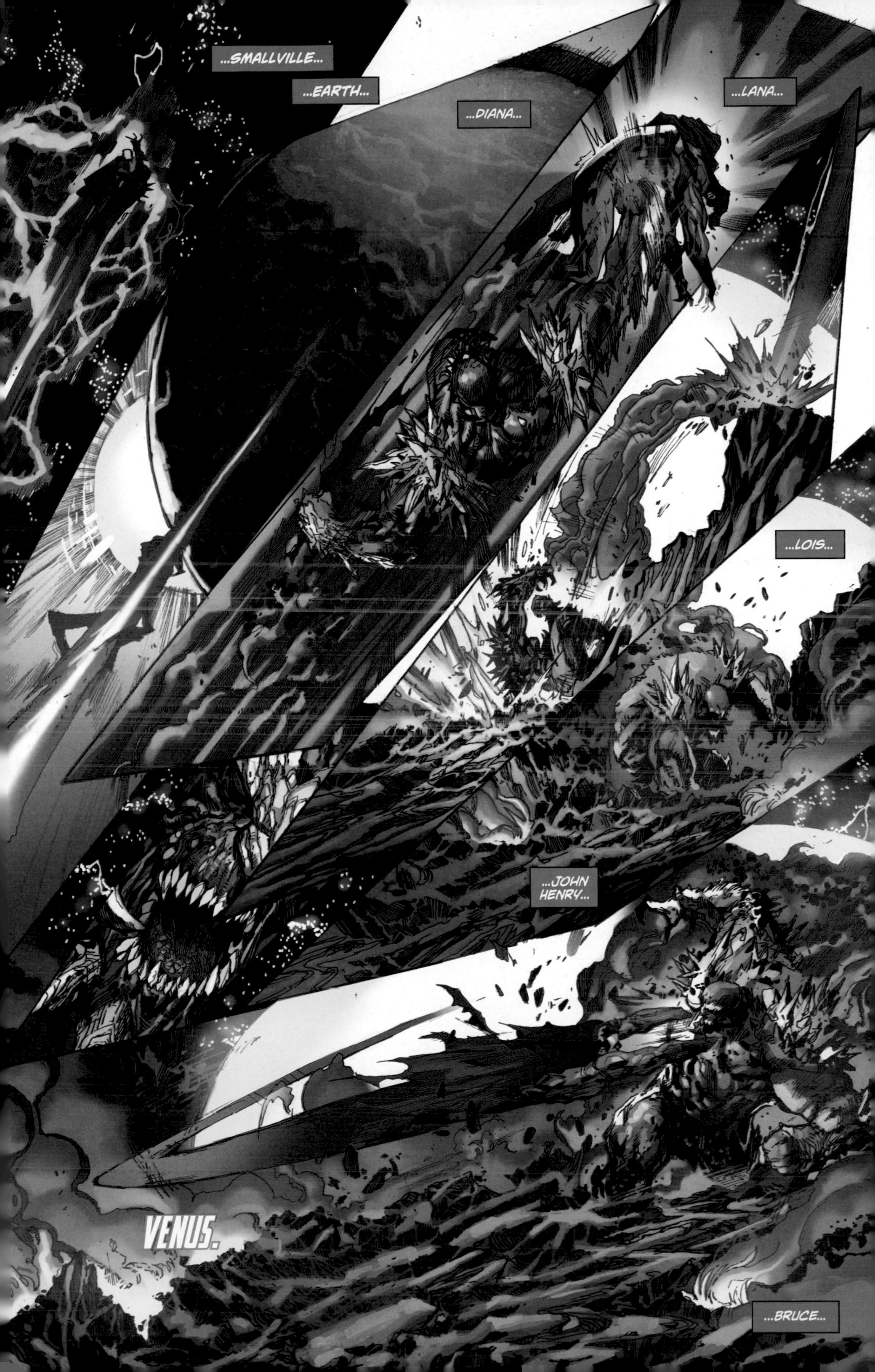

...SMALLVILLE...
...EARTH...
...DIANA...
...LANA...
...LOIS...
...JOHN HENRY...
VENUS.
...BRUCE...

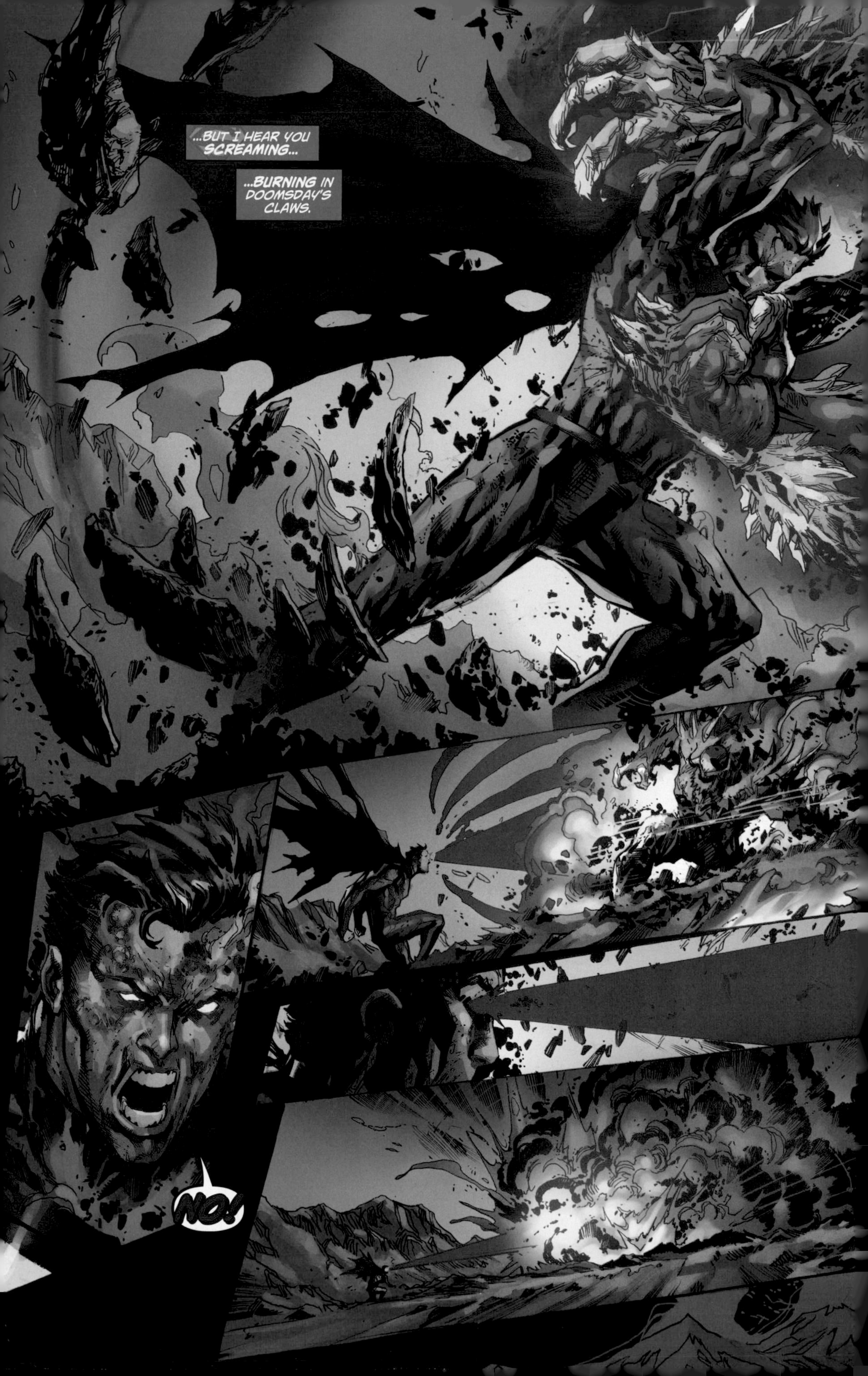
...BUT I HEAR YOU SCREAMING...
...BURNING IN DOOMSDAY'S CLAWS.
NO!

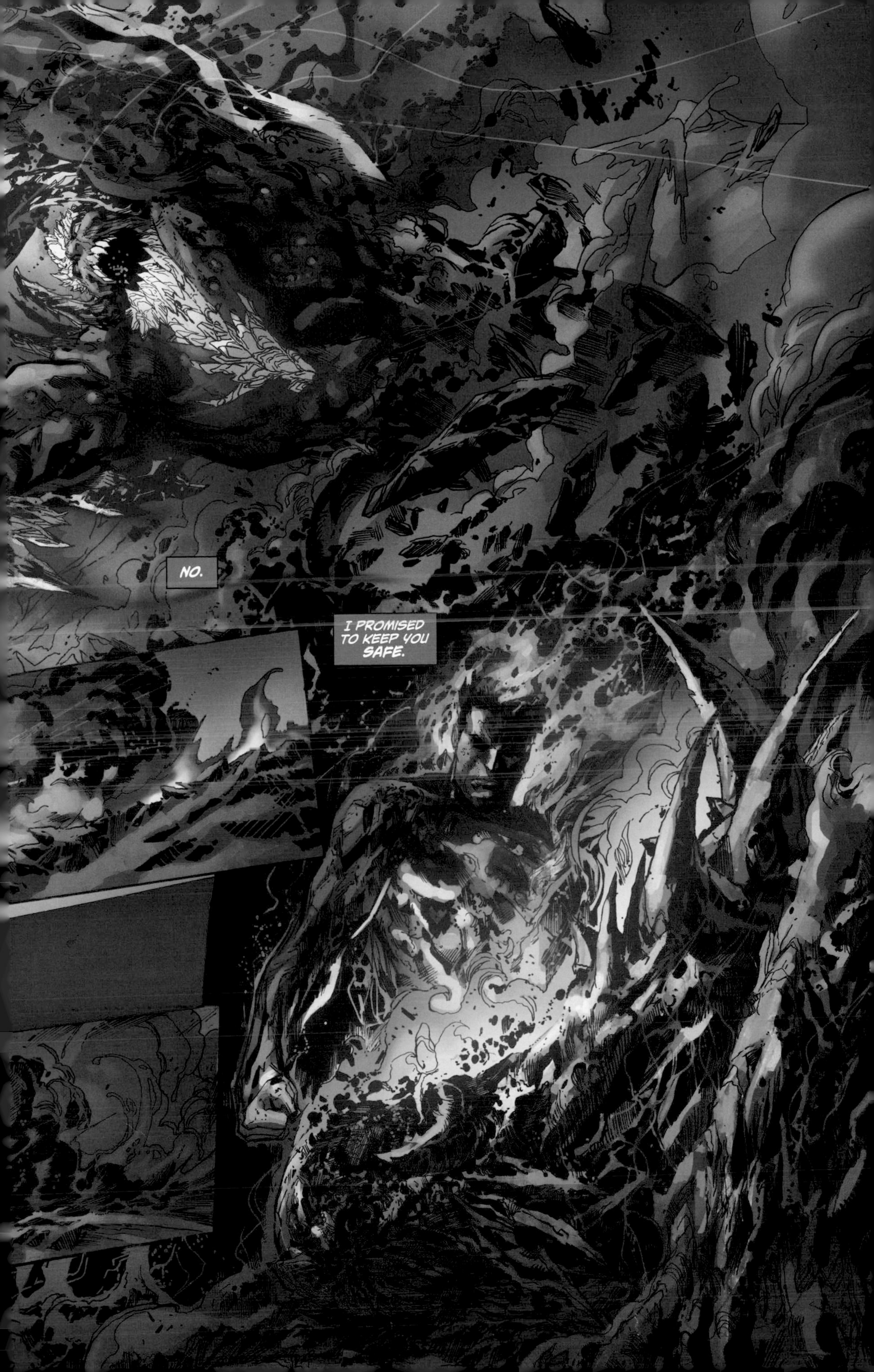
NO.
I PROMISED TO KEEP YOU SAFE.

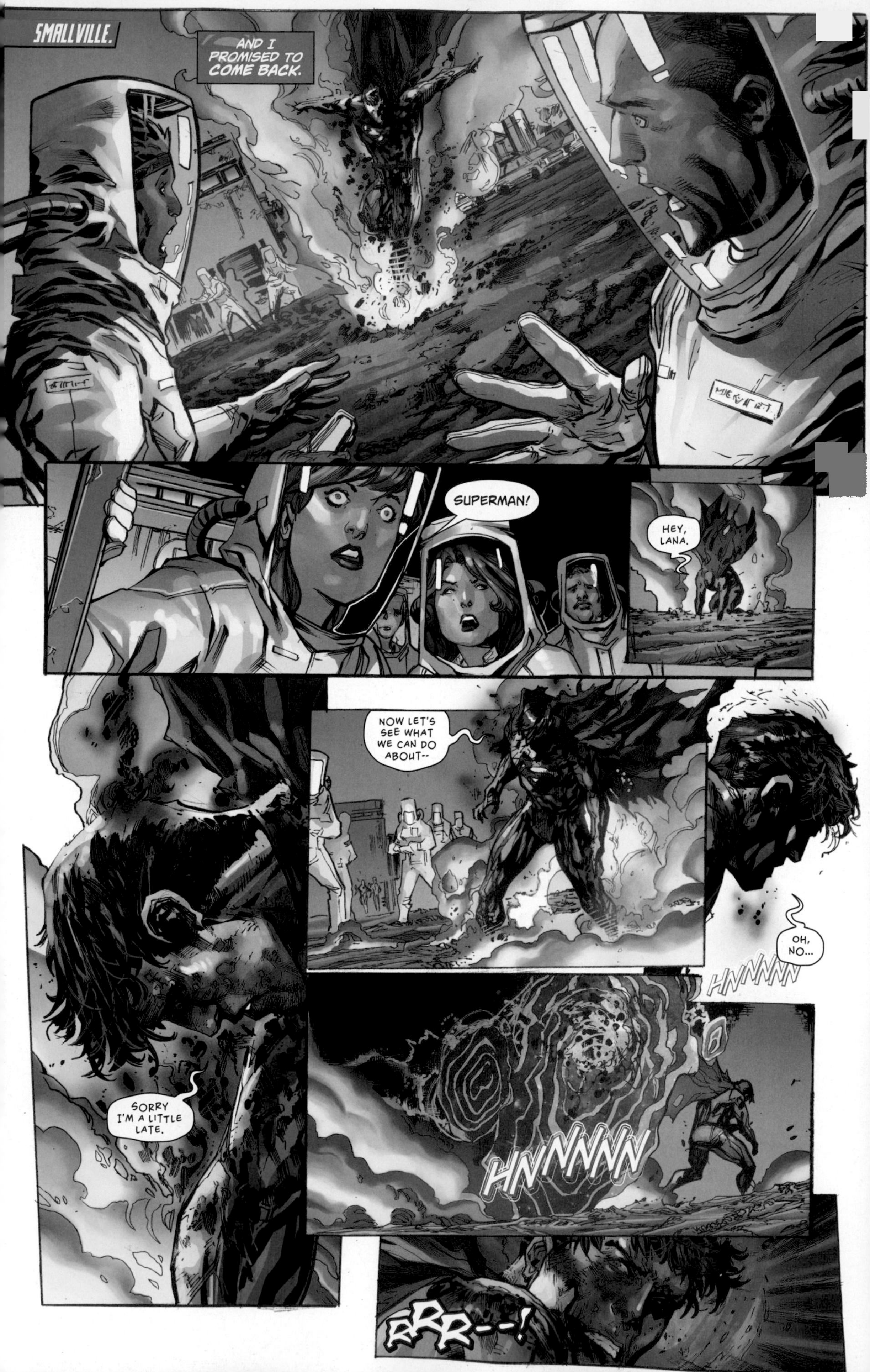
SMALLVILLE.
AND I PROMISED TO COME BACK.
SUPERMAN!
HEY, LANA.
SORRY I'M A LITTLE LATE.
NOW LET'S SEE WHAT WE CAN DO ABOUT--
OH, NO...
HNNNNN
HNNNNN
RRR--!

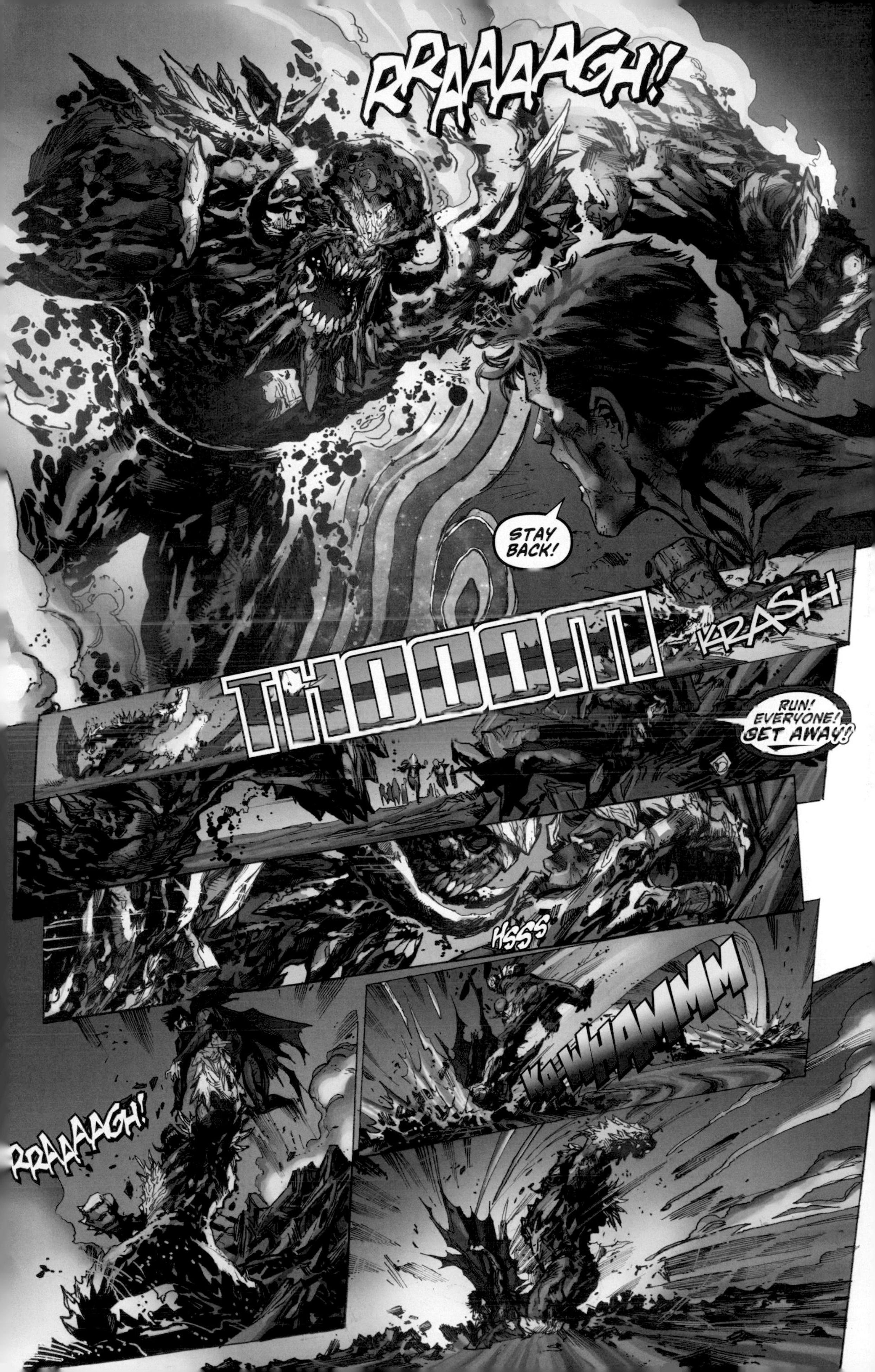
RRAAAAGH!
STAY BACK!
THOOOM
KRASH
RUN! EVERYONE! GET AWAY!
HSSS
KA-WHAMMM
RRAAAAGH!

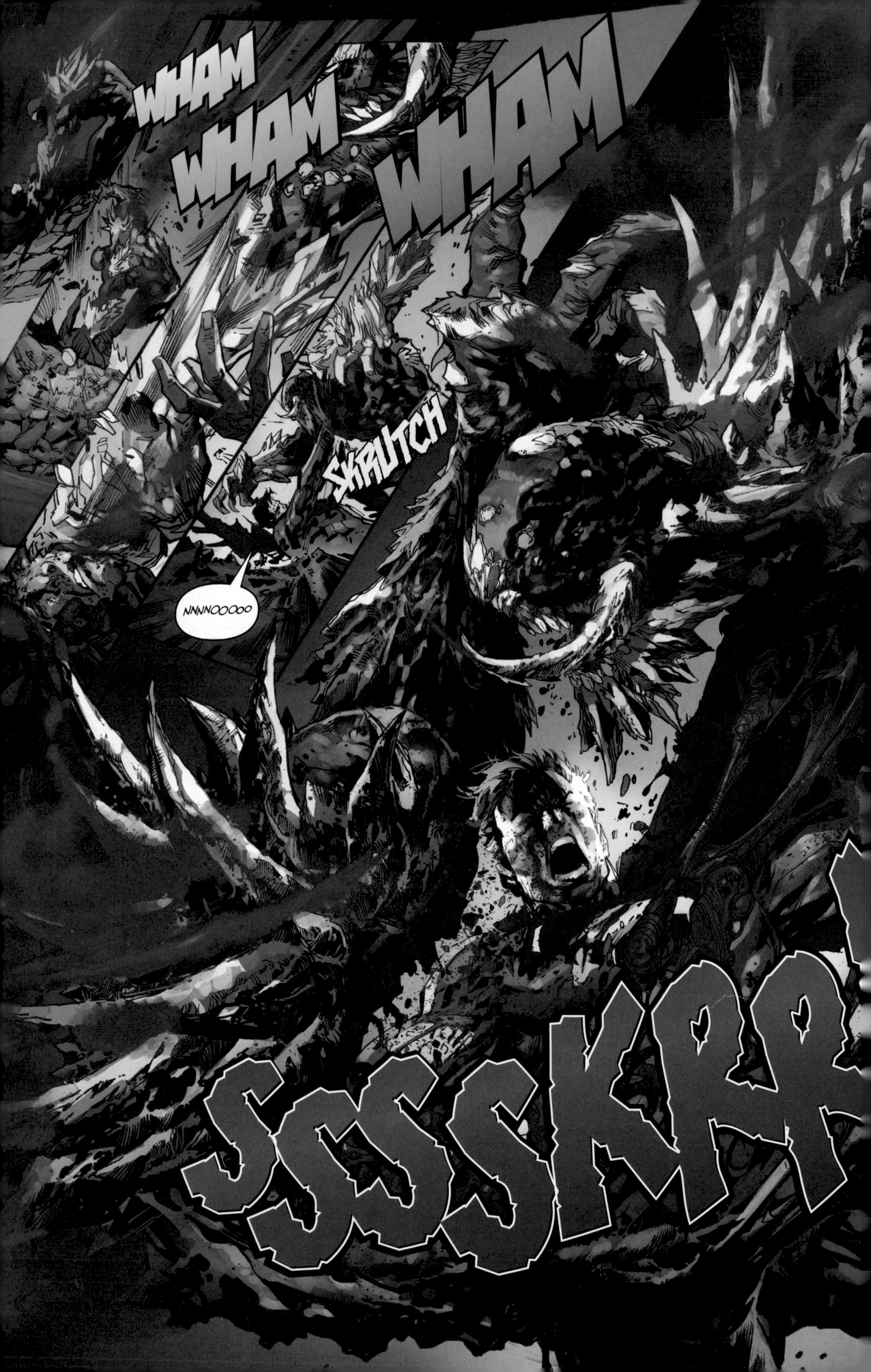
WHAM
WHAM
WHAM
SKRUTCH
NNNNOOOOO
SSSSKRR

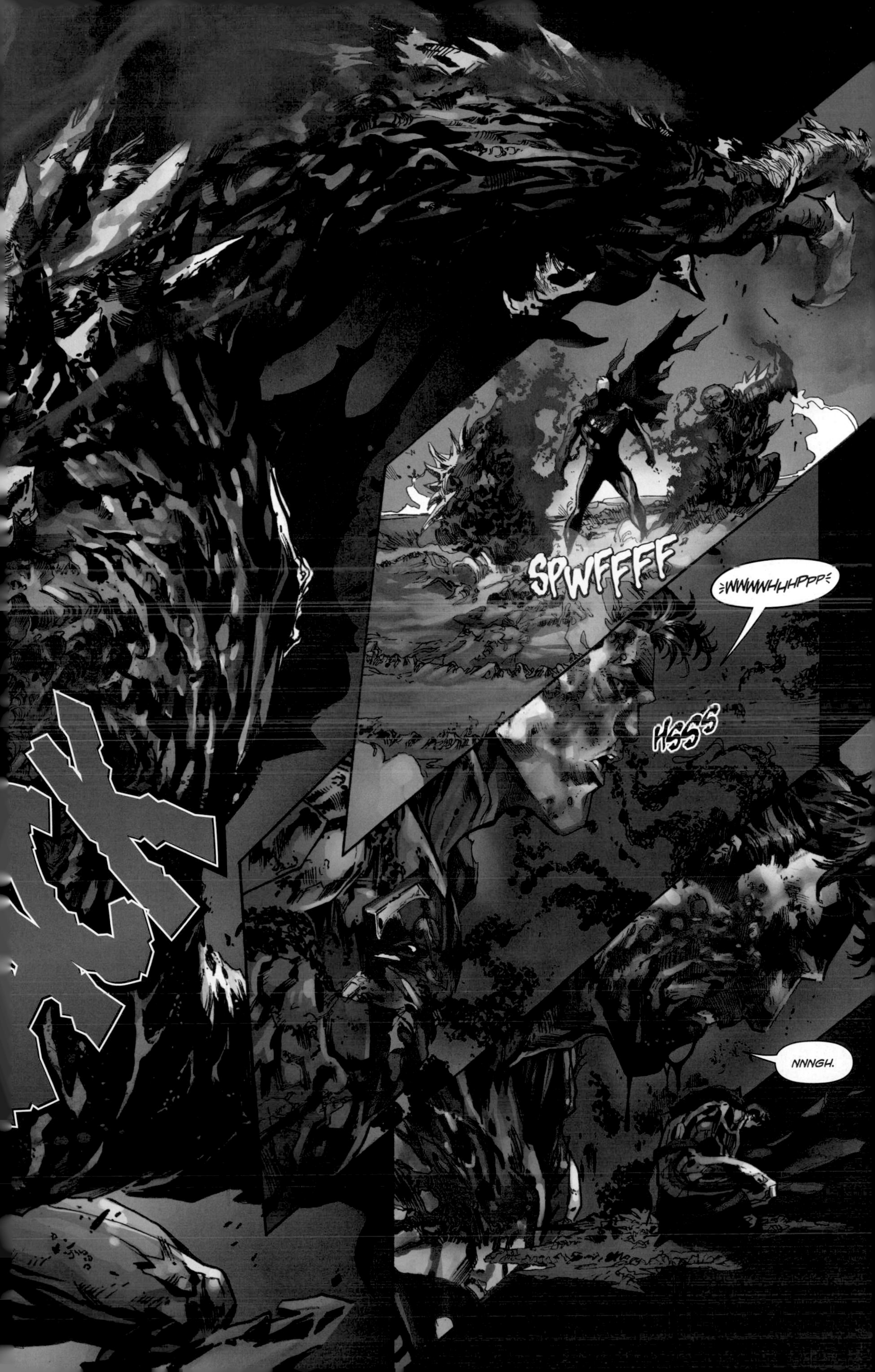
SPWFFFF
WWWWHHPPP
HSSS
NNNGH.

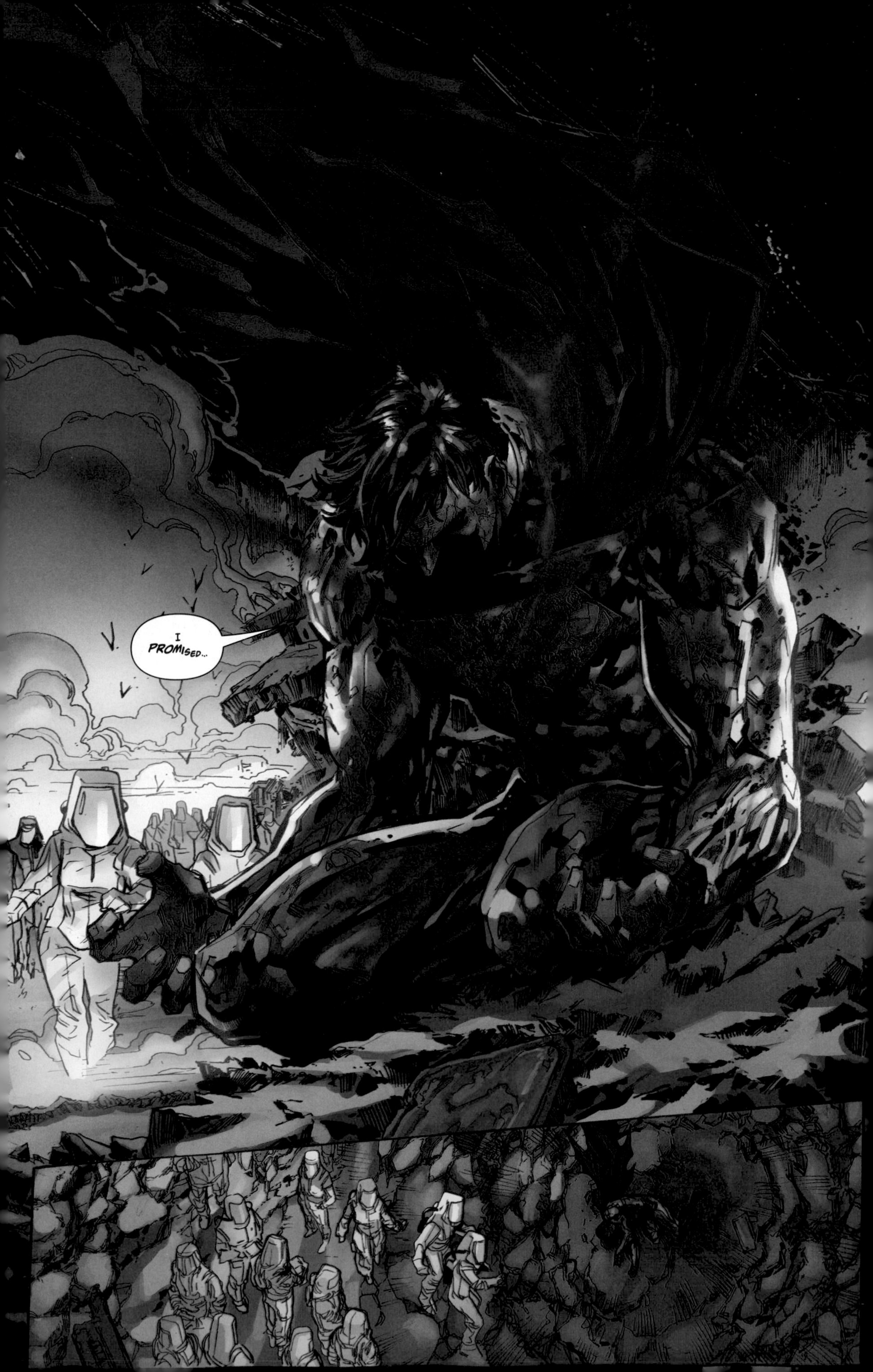
I PROMISED...

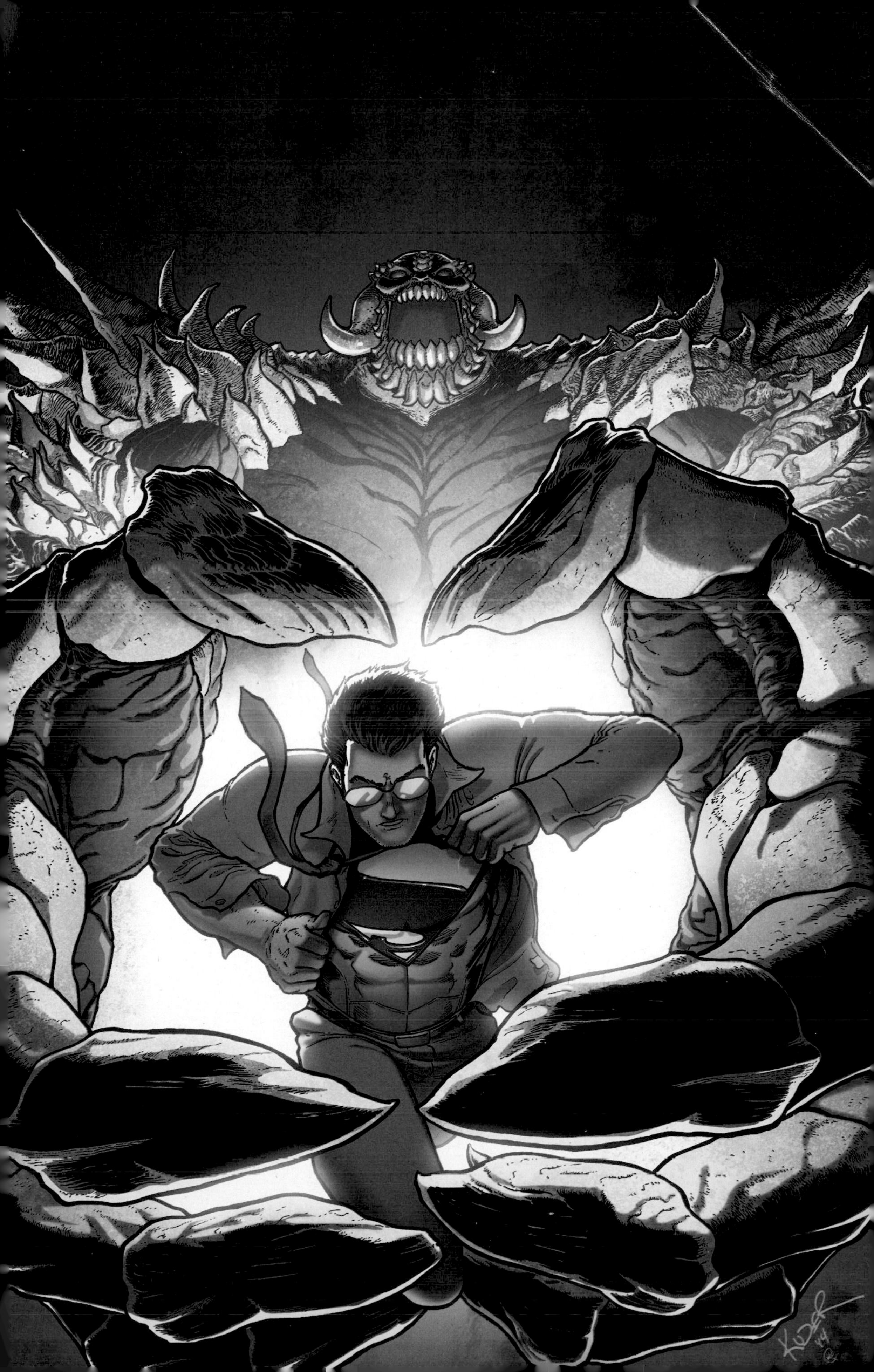

SUPERMAN

DOOMED

[INFECTED] chapter 1

"TRUE BELIEVERS"

STORY
GREG PAK

PENCILS
AARON KUDER, RAFA SANDOVAL & CAMERON STEWART

INKS
KUDER, VICENTE CIFUENTES, & CAMERON STEWART

COLORS
WIL QUINTANA

LETTERS
DEZI SIENTY & TAYLOR ESPOSITO

COVER
AARON KUDER AND WIL QUINTANA

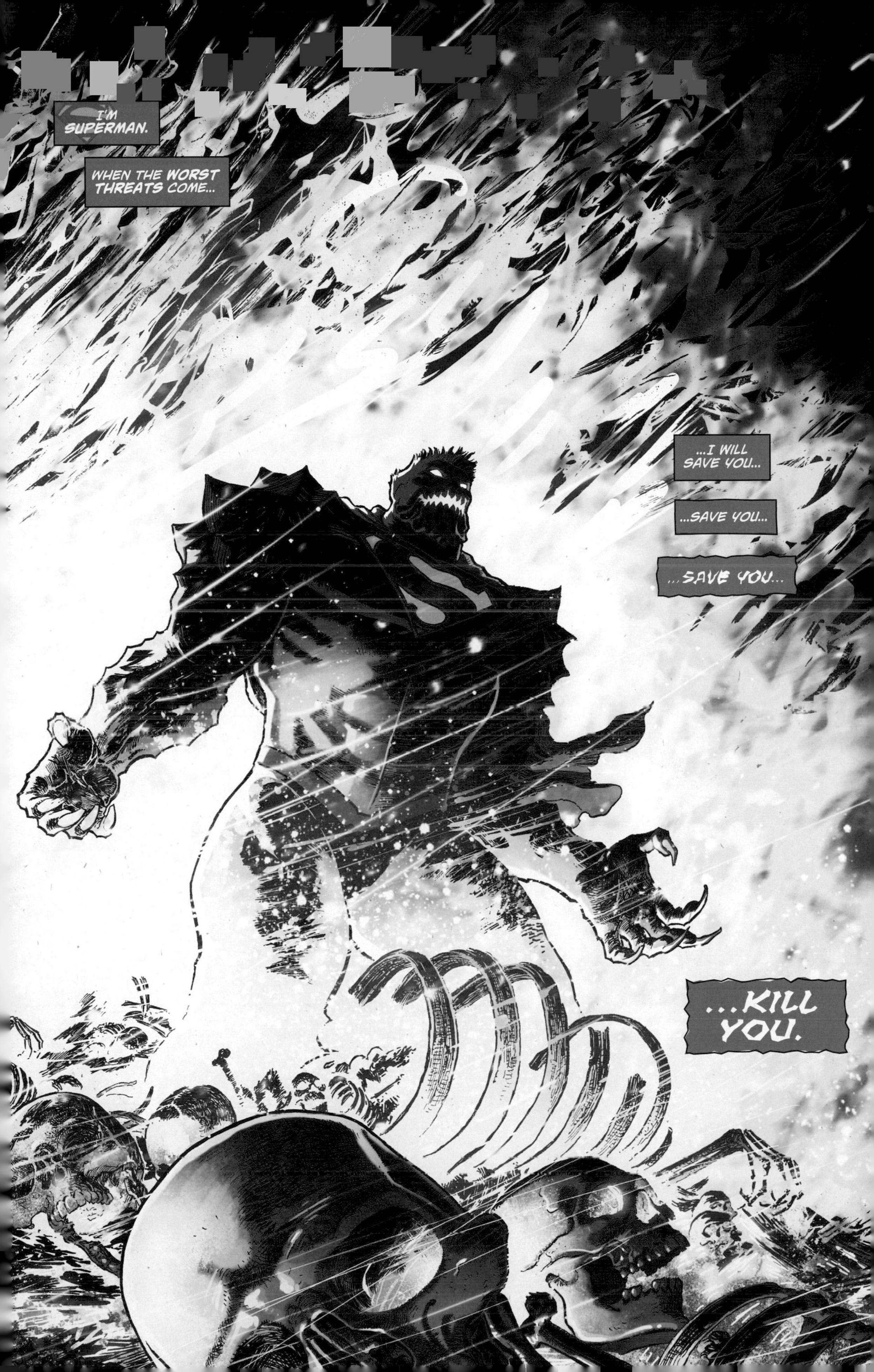
I'M SUPERMAN.
WHEN THE WORST THREATS COME...
...I WILL SAVE YOU...
...SAVE YOU...
...SAVE YOU...
...KILL YOU.

WAIT...

...NO.

I DIDN'T KILL ANYONE.

DOOMSDAY DID.

AND I STOPPED HIM.

SMALLVILLE, KANSAS.

I'M NOT A MONSTER.

I'M NOT THE KILLER.

I'M...I'M...

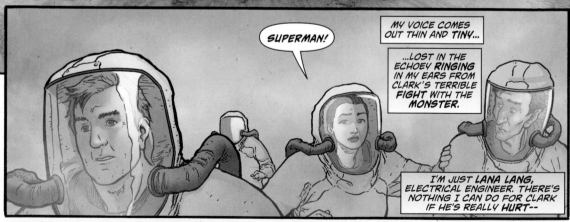

SUPERMAN!

MY VOICE COMES OUT THIN AND TINY...

...LOST IN THE ECHOEY RINGING IN MY EARS FROM CLARK'S TERRIBLE FIGHT WITH THE MONSTER.

I'M JUST LANA LANG, ELECTRICAL ENGINEER. THERE'S NOTHING I CAN DO FOR CLARK IF HE'S REALLY HURT--

--BUT I'M NOT GONNA HANG BACK AND LEAVE HIM ALL ALONE TO BLEED TO--

SHAAKOOM

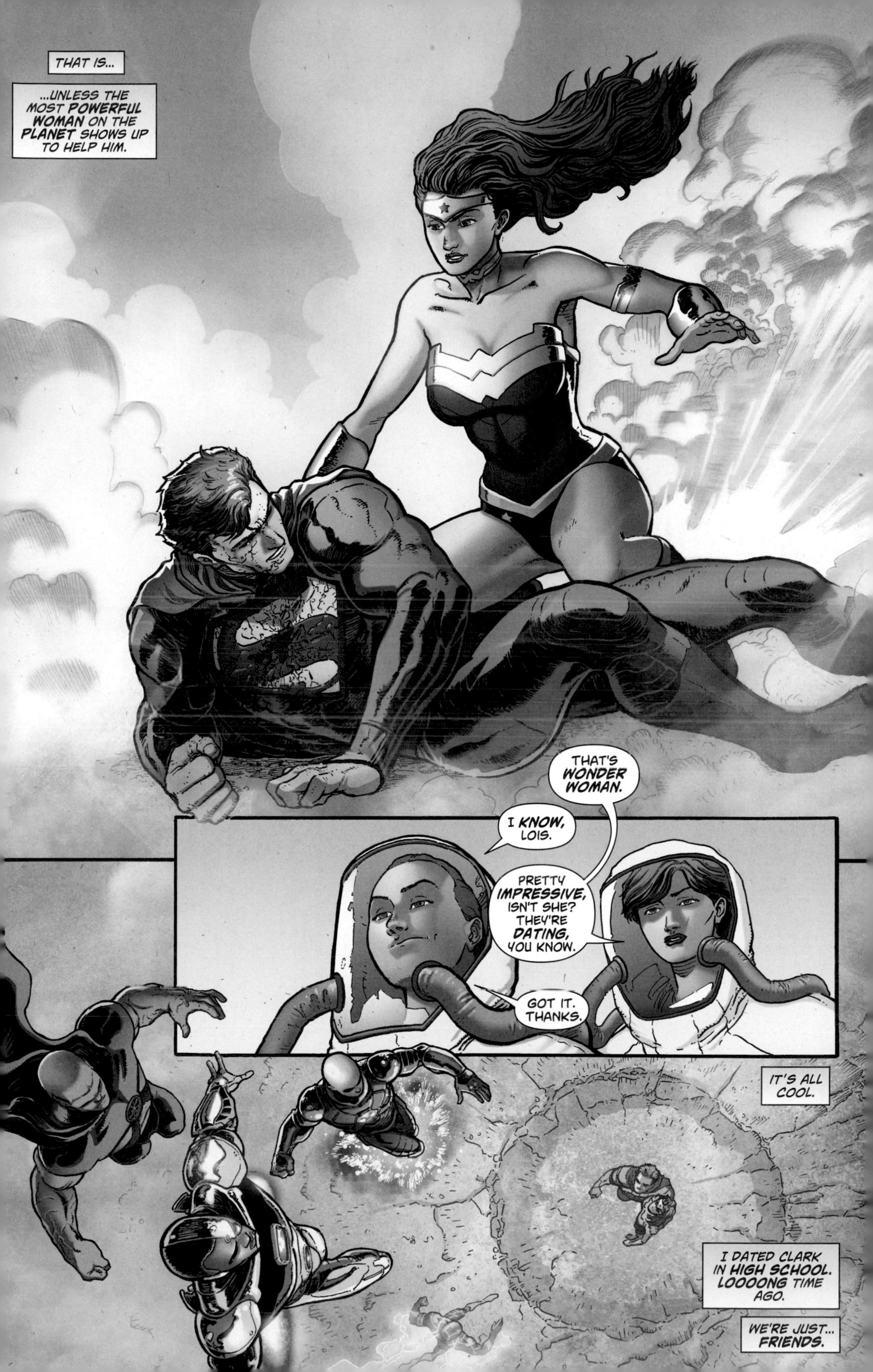
THAT IS...
...UNLESS THE MOST POWERFUL WOMAN ON THE PLANET SHOWS UP TO HELP HIM.
THAT'S WONDER WOMAN.
I KNOW, LOIS.
PRETTY IMPRESSIVE, ISN'T SHE? THEY'RE DATING, YOU KNOW.
GOT IT. THANKS.
IT'S ALL COOL.
I DATED CLARK IN HIGH SCHOOL. LOOOONG TIME AGO.
WE'RE JUST... FRIENDS.

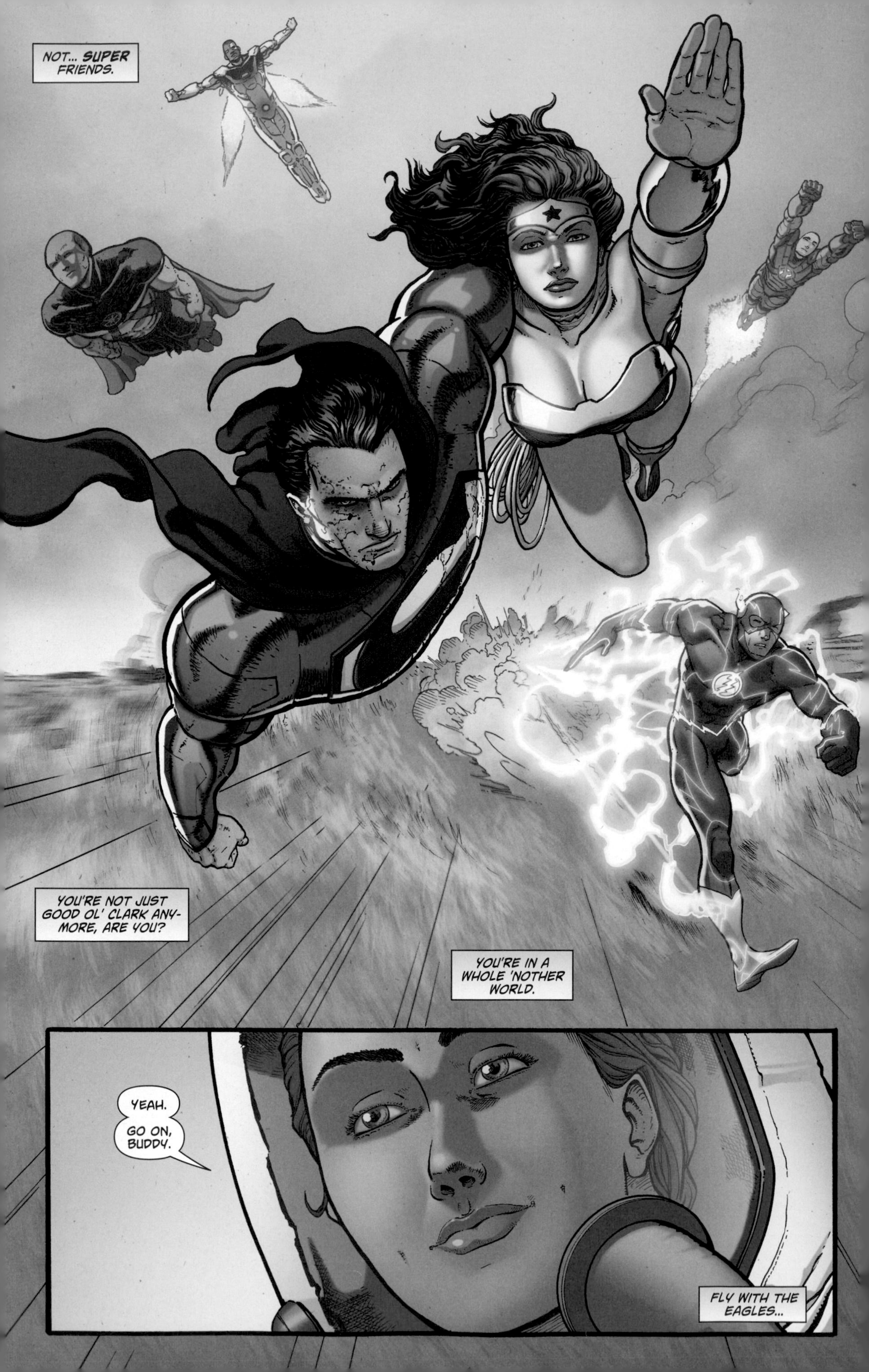
NOT... SUPER FRIENDS.
YOU'RE NOT JUST GOOD OL' CLARK ANY-MORE, ARE YOU?
YOU'RE IN A WHOLE 'NOTHER WORLD.
YEAH.
GO ON, BUDDY.
FLY WITH THE EAGLES...

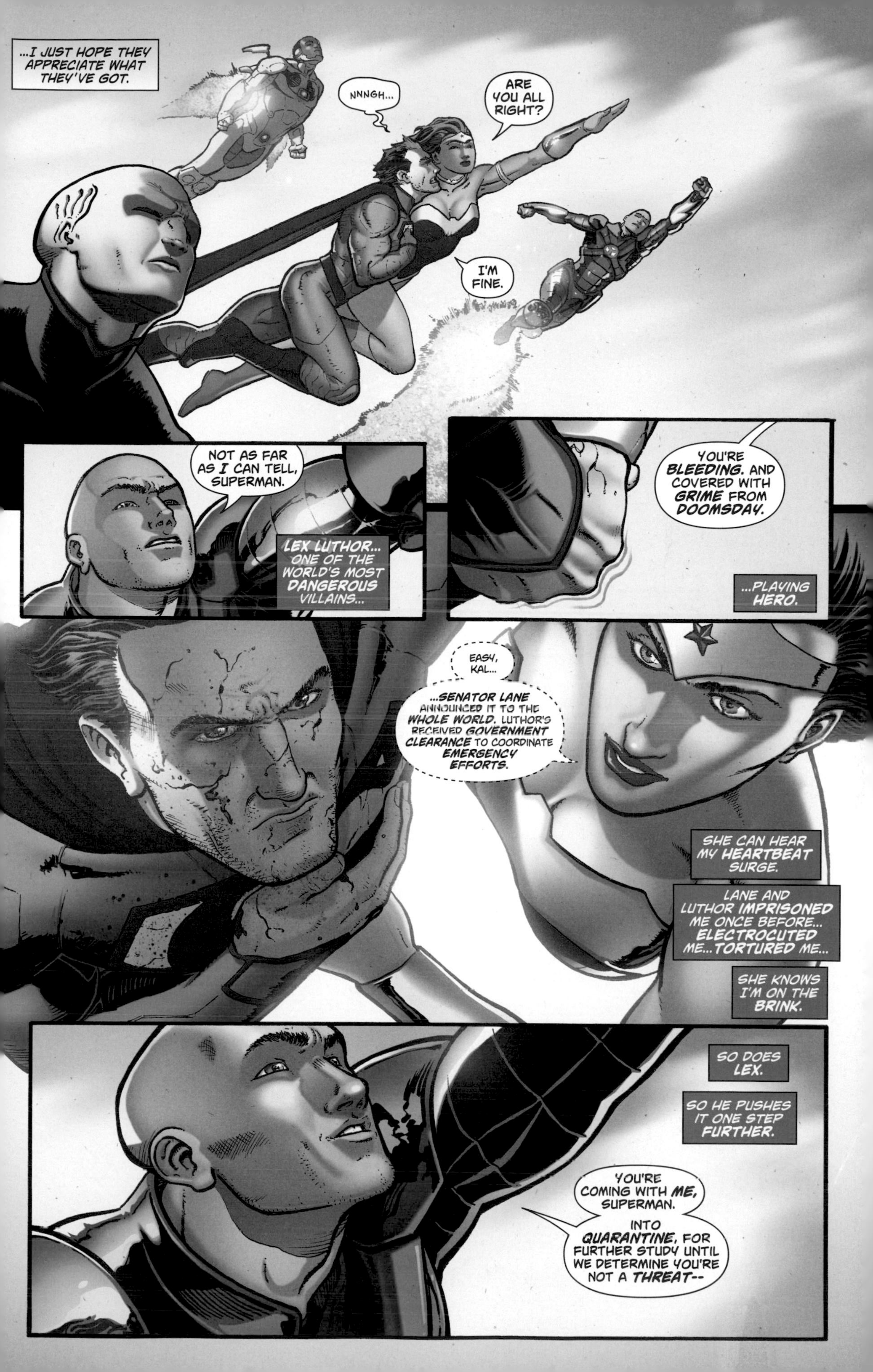
...I JUST HOPE THEY APPRECIATE WHAT THEY'VE GOT.
NNNGH...
ARE YOU ALL RIGHT?
I'M FINE.
NOT AS FAR AS I CAN TELL, SUPERMAN.
LEX LUTHOR... ONE OF THE WORLD'S MOST DANGEROUS VILLAINS...
YOU'RE BLEEDING. AND COVERED WITH GRIME FROM DOOMSDAY.
...PLAYING HERO.
EASY, KAL...
...SENATOR LANE ANNOUNCED IT TO THE WHOLE WORLD. LUTHOR'S RECEIVED GOVERNMENT CLEARANCE TO COORDINATE EMERGENCY EFFORTS.
SHE CAN HEAR MY HEARTBEAT SURGE.
LANE AND LUTHOR IMPRISONED ME ONCE BEFORE... ELECTROCUTED ME...TORTURED ME...
SHE KNOWS I'M ON THE BRINK.
SO DOES LEX.
SO HE PUSHES IT ONE STEP FURTHER.
YOU'RE COMING WITH ME, SUPERMAN.
INTO QUARANTINE, FOR FURTHER STUDY UNTIL WE DETERMINE YOU'RE NOT A THREAT--

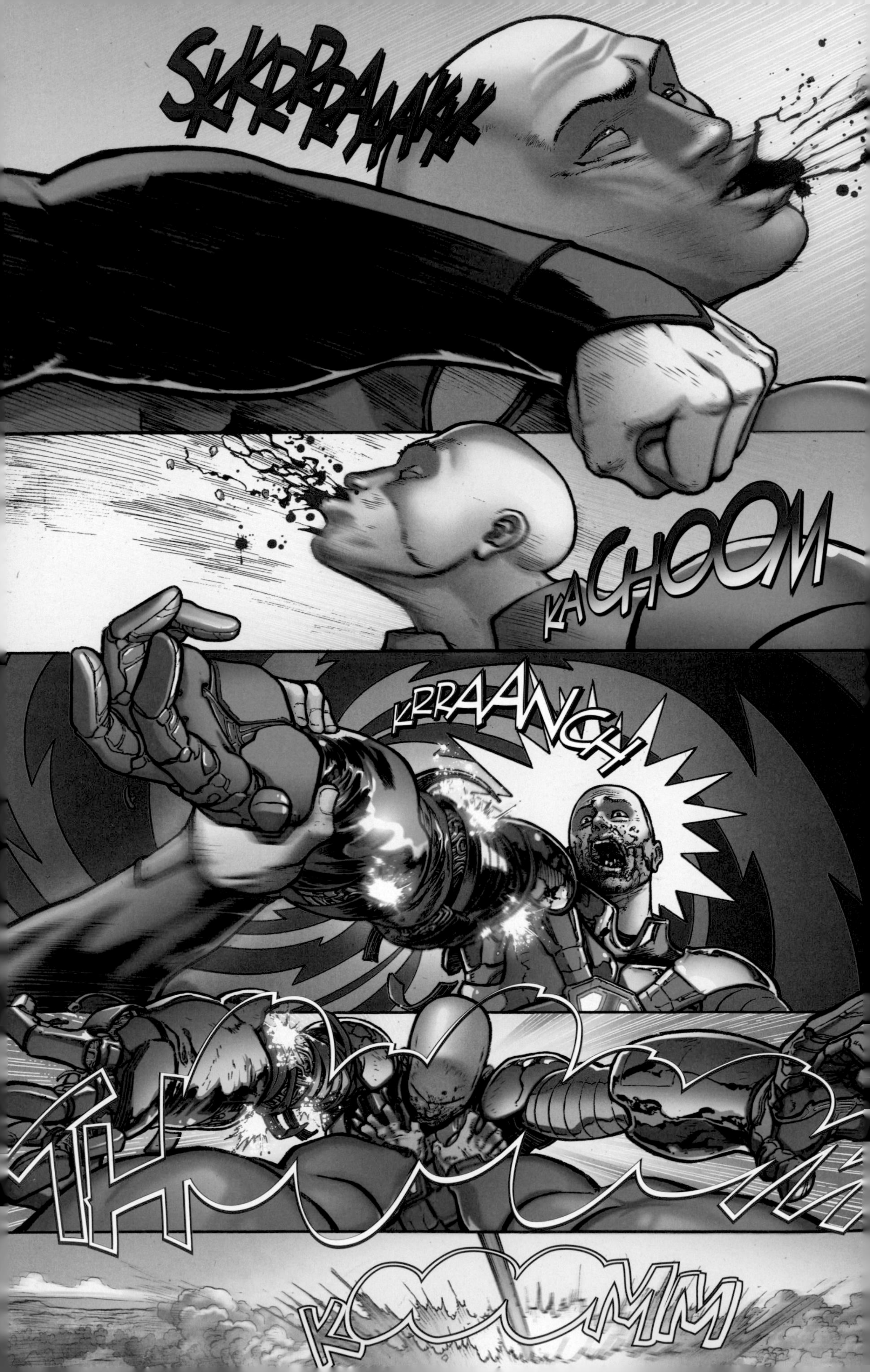
SKKRRAAAKK
KACHOOM
KRRAANCH
THHUMM
KOOOMM

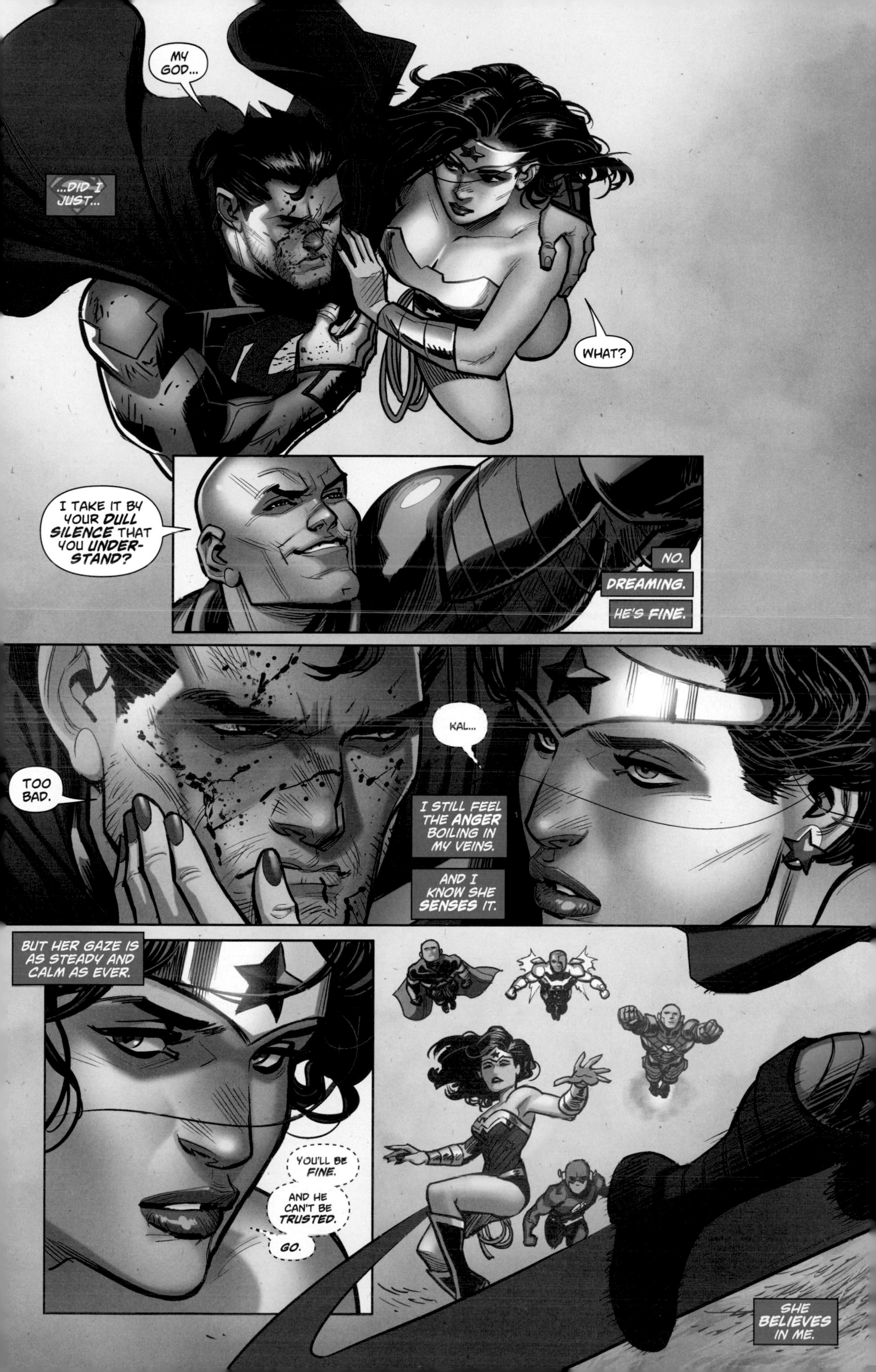
MY GOD...
...DID I JUST...
WHAT?
I TAKE IT BY YOUR DULL SILENCE THAT YOU UNDER-STAND?
NO.
DREAMING.
HE'S FINE.
TOO BAD.
KAL...
I STILL FEEL THE ANGER BOILING IN MY VEINS.
AND I KNOW SHE SENSES IT.
BUT HER GAZE IS AS STEADY AND CALM AS EVER.
YOU'LL BE FINE.
AND HE CAN'T BE TRUSTED.
GO.
SHE BELIEVES IN ME.

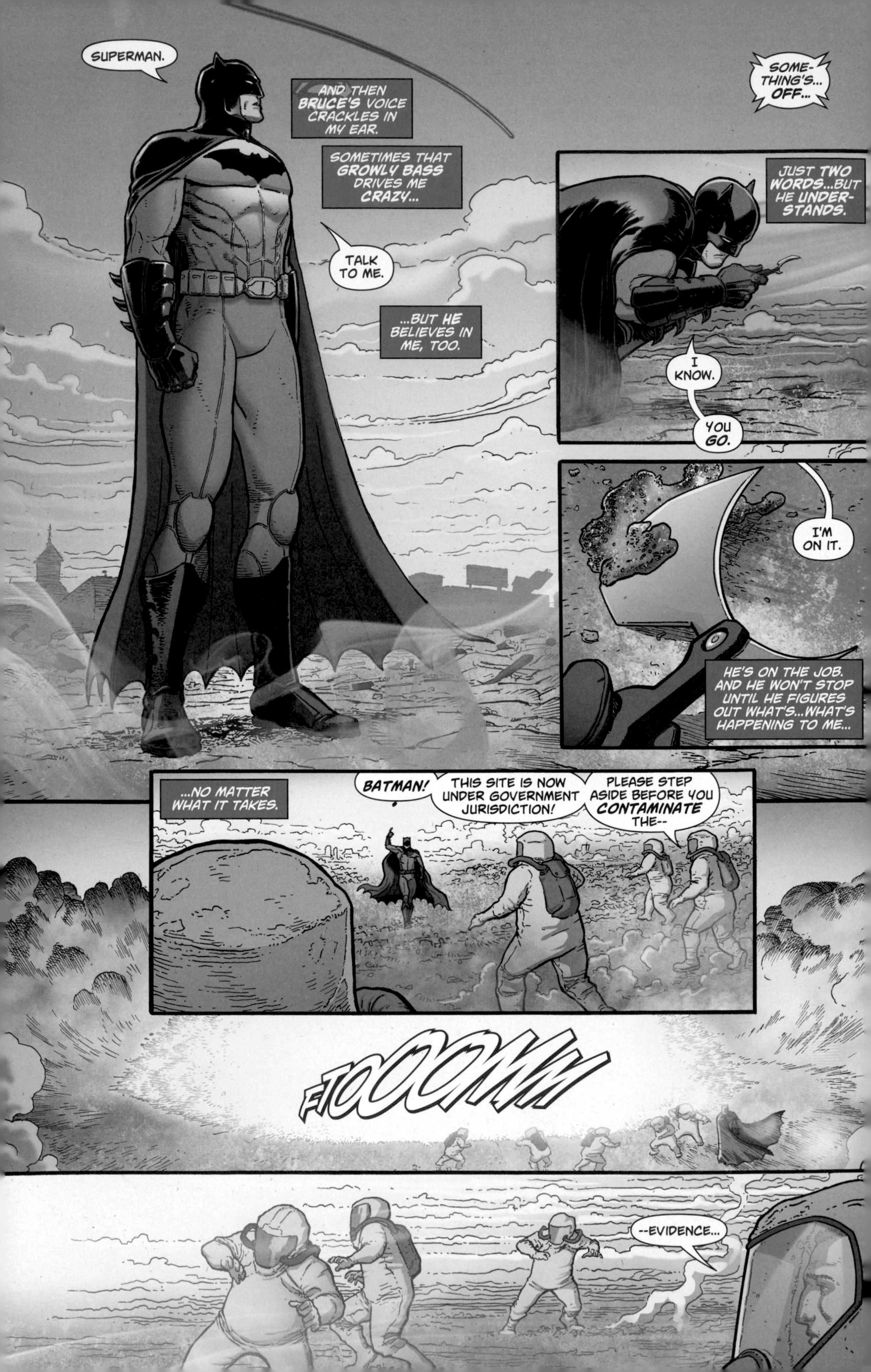
SUPERMAN.
AND THEN BRUCE'S VOICE CRACKLES IN MY EAR.
SOMETIMES THAT GROWLY BASS DRIVES ME CRAZY...
TALK TO ME.
...BUT HE BELIEVES IN ME, TOO.
SOME-THING'S... OFF...
JUST TWO WORDS...BUT HE UNDER-STANDS.
I KNOW.
YOU GO.
I'M ON IT.
HE'S ON THE JOB. AND HE WON'T STOP UNTIL HE FIGURES OUT WHAT'S...WHAT'S HAPPENING TO ME...
...NO MATTER WHAT IT TAKES.
BATMAN!
THIS SITE IS NOW UNDER GOVERNMENT JURISDICTION!
PLEASE STEP ASIDE BEFORE YOU CONTAMINATE THE--
FTOOOOMM
--EVIDENCE...

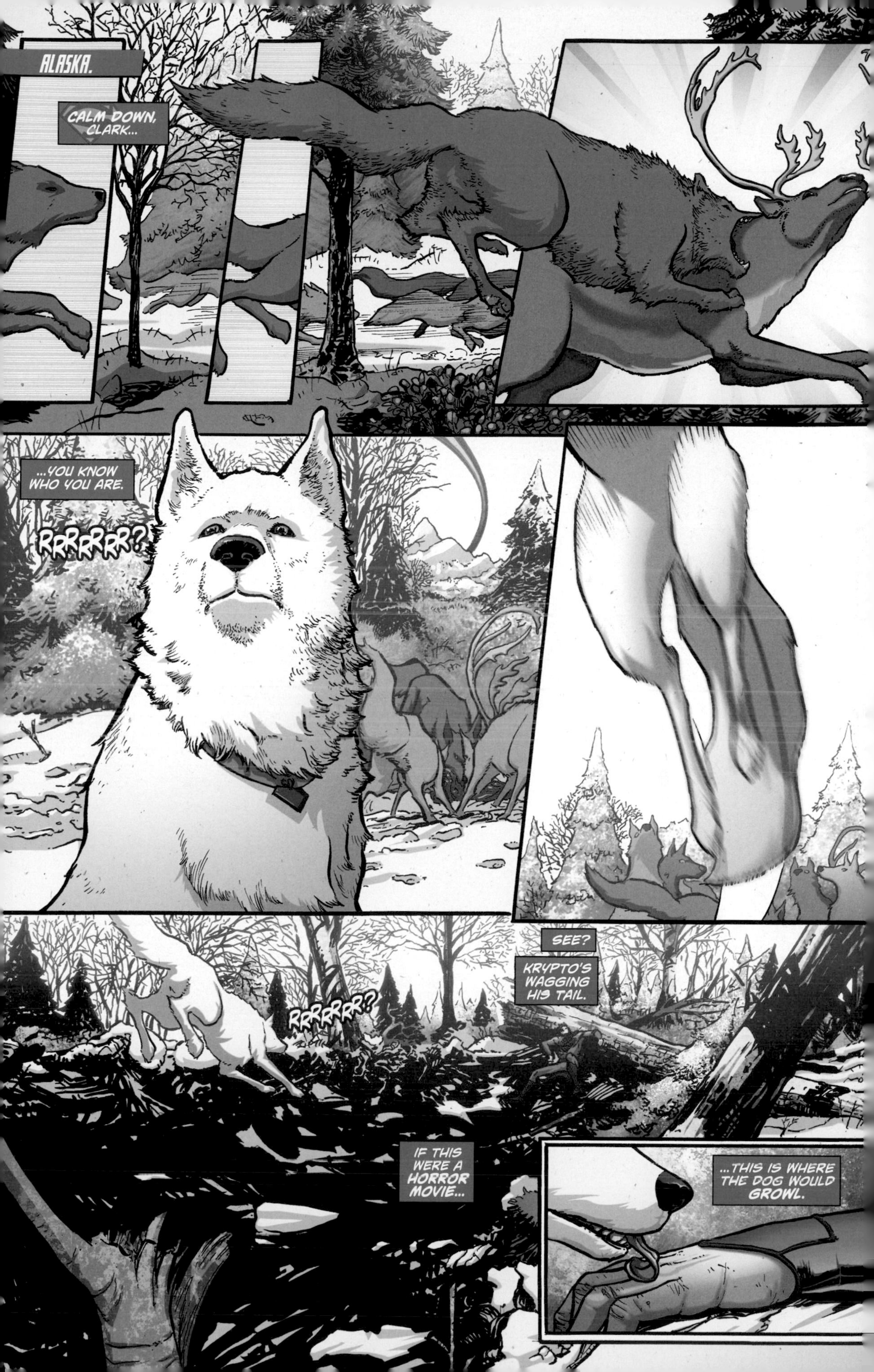

ALASKA.
CALM DOWN, CLARK...
...YOU KNOW WHO YOU ARE.
RRRRRRR?
SEE?
KRYPTO'S WAGGING HIS TAIL.
RRRRRRR?
IF THIS WERE A HORROR MOVIE...
...THIS IS WHERE THE DOG WOULD GROWL.

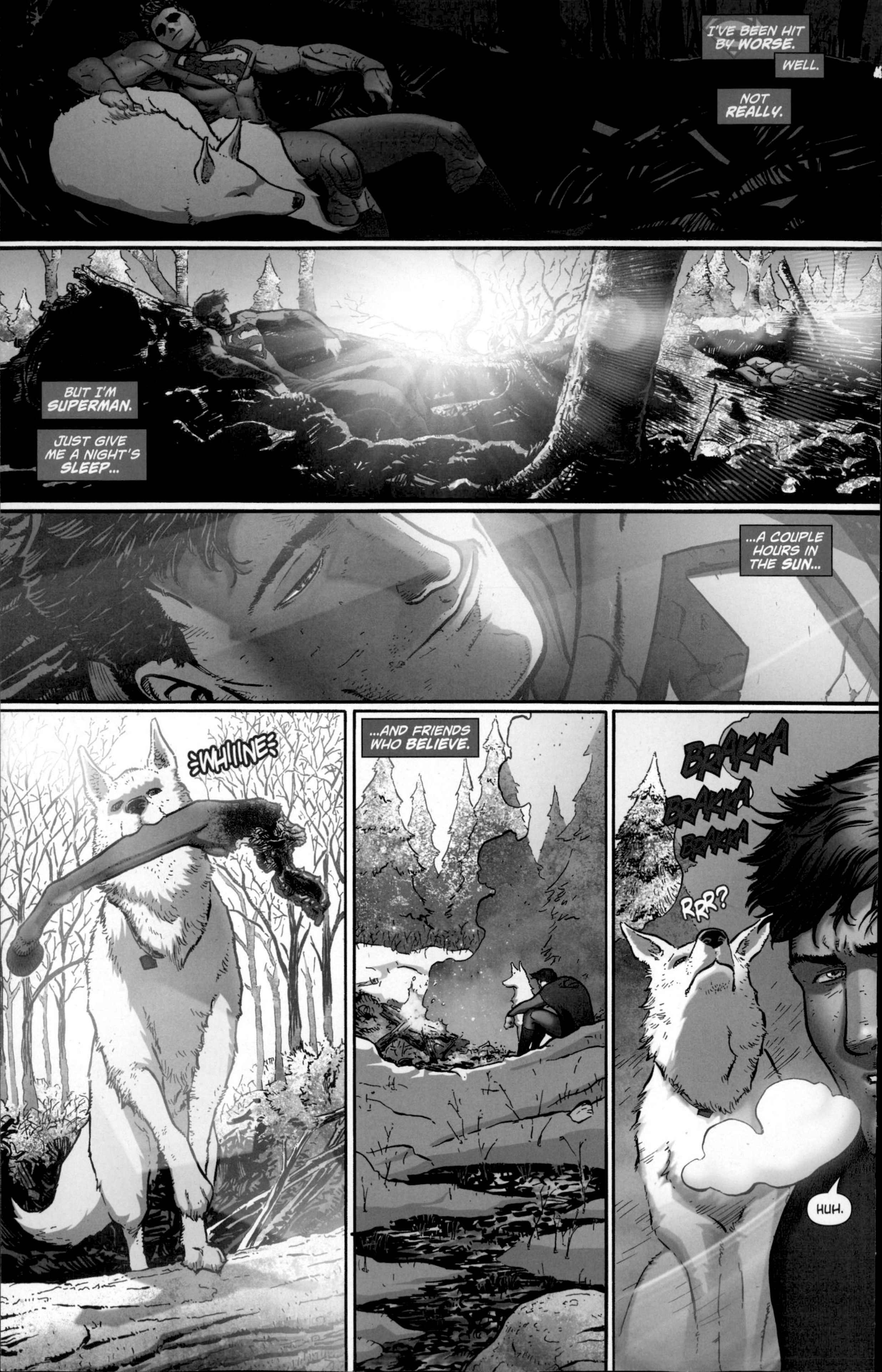
I'VE BEEN HIT BY WORSE.
WELL.
NOT REALLY.
BUT I'M SUPERMAN.
JUST GIVE ME A NIGHT'S SLEEP...
...A COUPLE HOURS IN THE SUN...
WHIIINE
...AND FRIENDS WHO BELIEVE.
BRAKKA BRAKKA BRAKKA
RRR?
HUH.

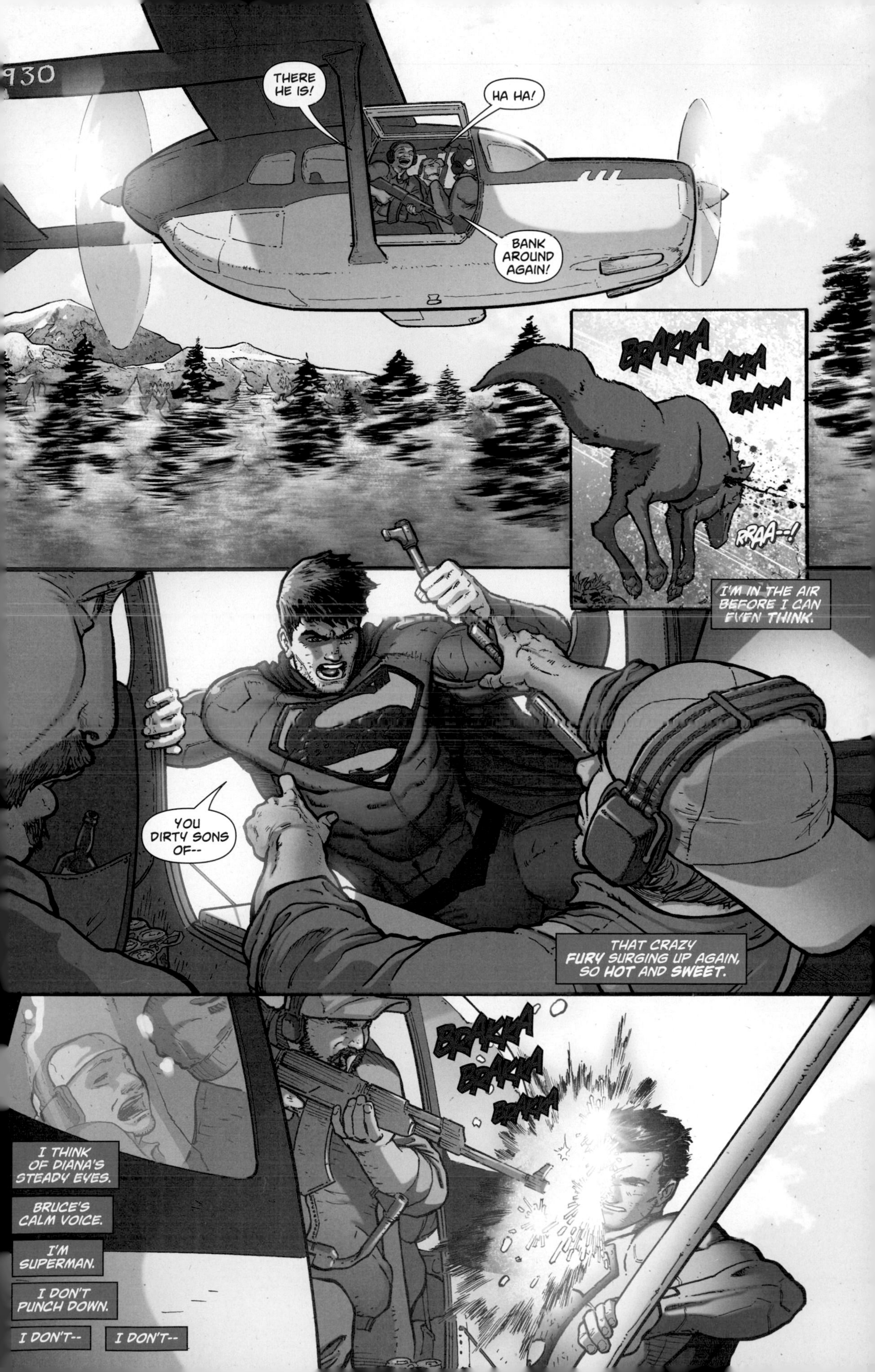

930
THERE HE IS!
HA HA!
BANK AROUND AGAIN!
BRAKKA BRAKKA BRAKKA
RRAA--!
I'M IN THE AIR BEFORE I CAN EVEN THINK.
YOU DIRTY SONS OF--
THAT CRAZY FURY SURGING UP AGAIN, SO HOT AND SWEET.
BRAKKA BRAKKA BRAKKA
I THINK OF DIANA'S STEADY EYES.
BRUCE'S CALM VOICE.
I'M SUPERMAN.
I DON'T PUNCH DOWN.
I DON'T--
I DON'T--

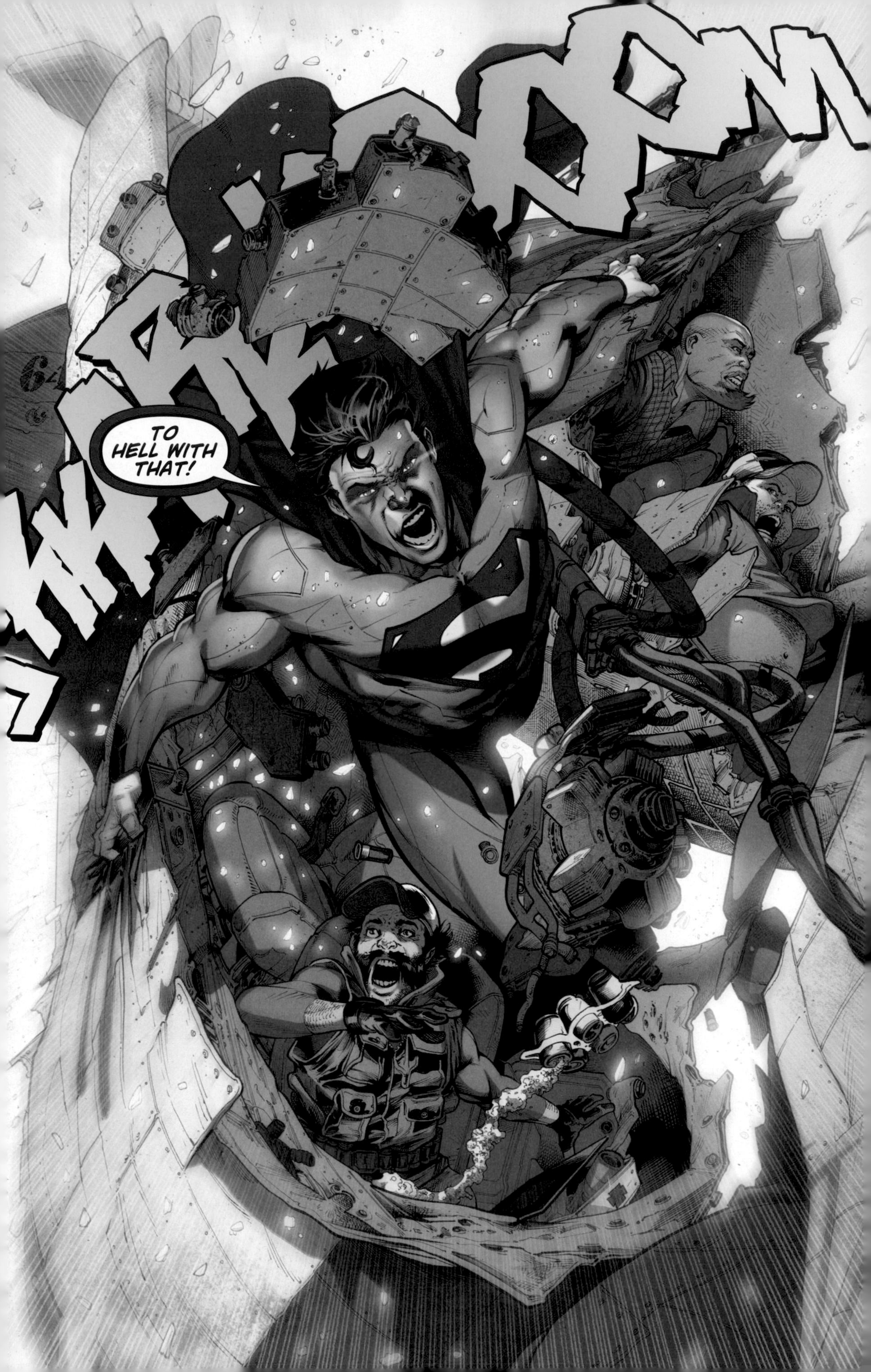
TO HELL WITH THAT!

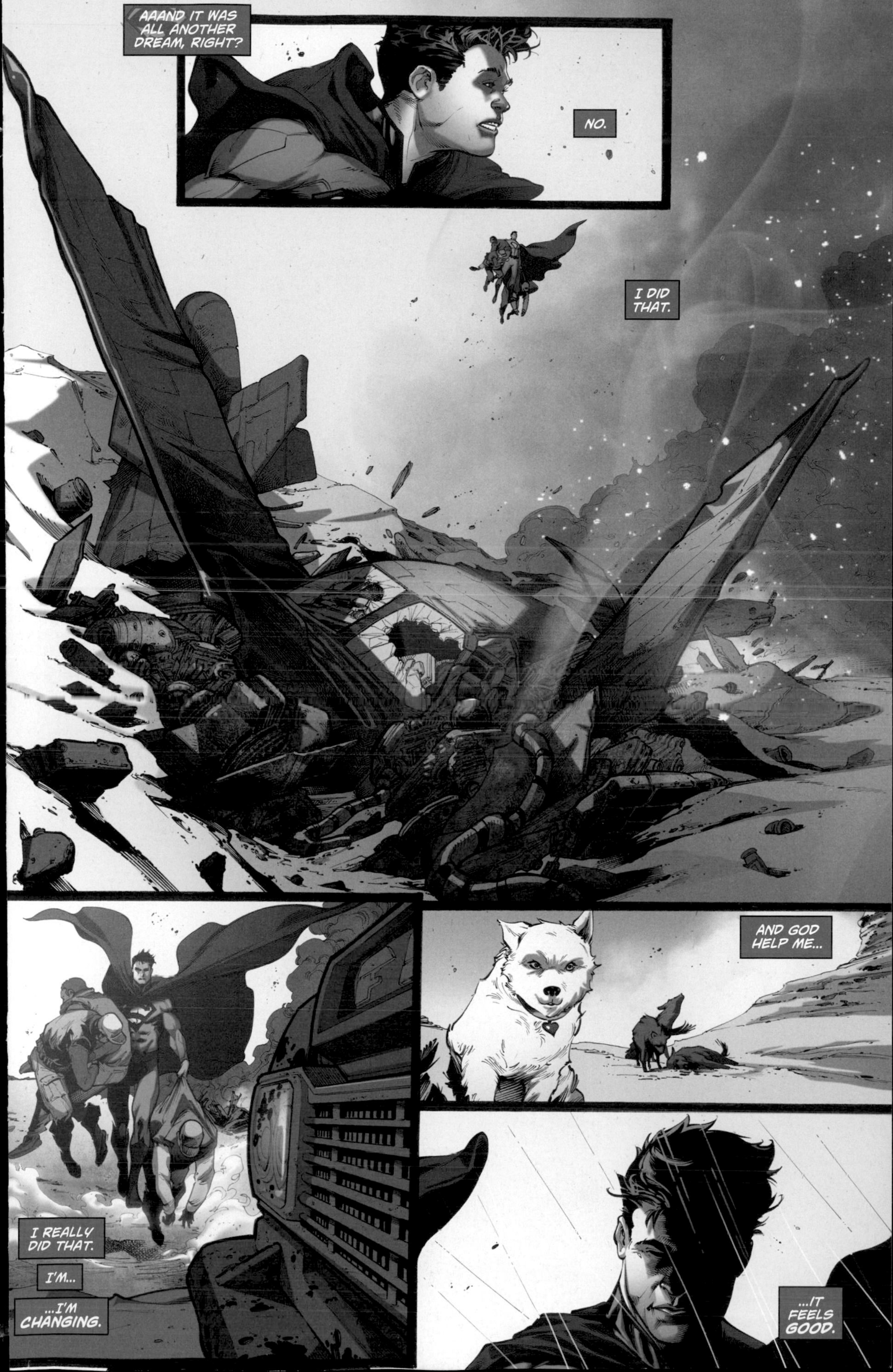
AAAND IT WAS ALL ANOTHER DREAM, RIGHT?
NO.
I DID THAT.
I REALLY DID THAT.
I'M...
...I'M CHANGING.
AND GOD HELP ME...
...IT FEELS GOOD.

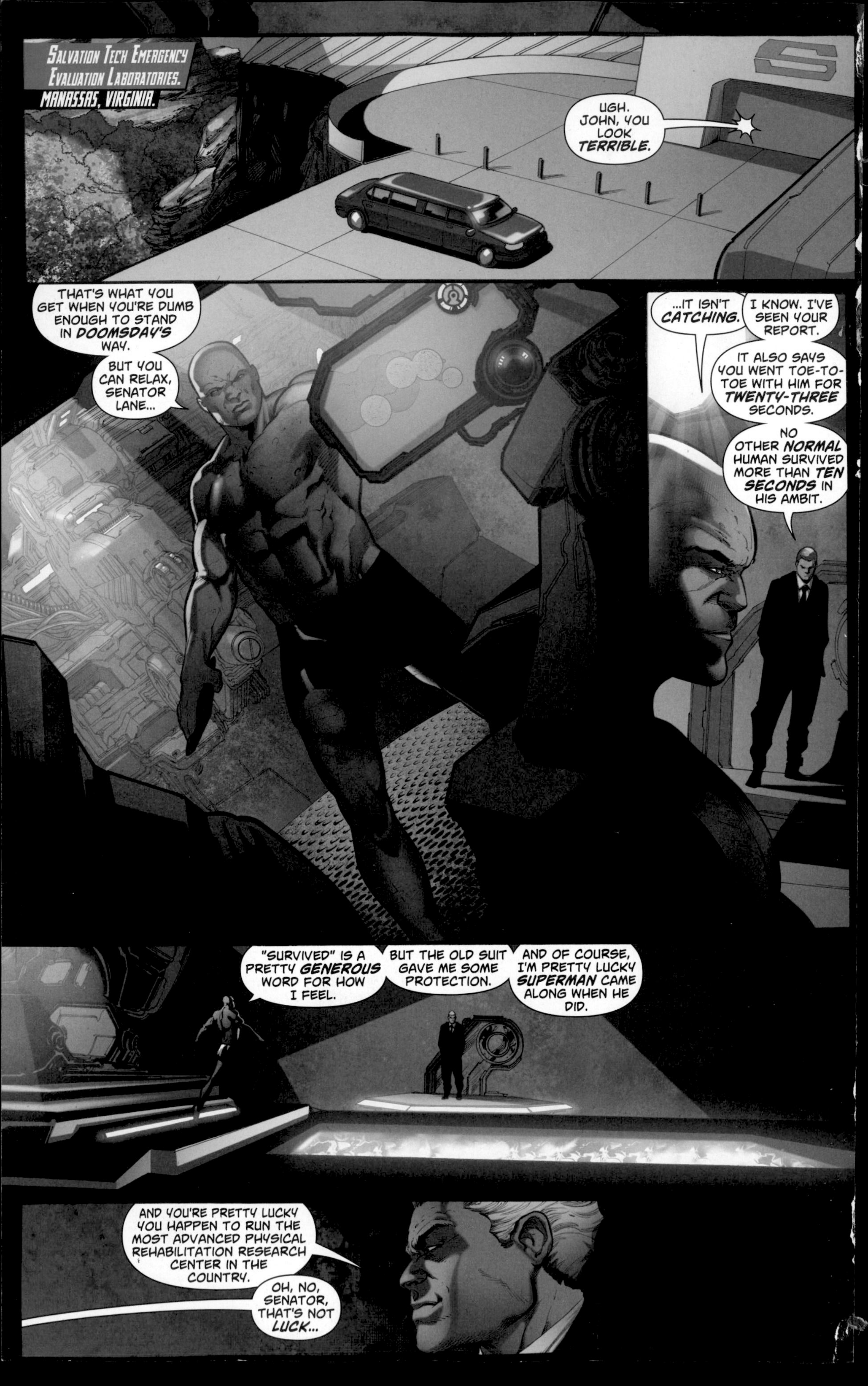
SALVATION TECH EMERGENCY EVALUATION LABORATORIES.
MANASSAS, VIRGINIA.
UGH. JOHN, YOU LOOK TERRIBLE.
THAT'S WHAT YOU GET WHEN YOU'RE DUMB ENOUGH TO STAND IN DOOMSDAY'S WAY.
BUT YOU CAN RELAX, SENATOR LANE...
...IT ISN'T CATCHING.
I KNOW. I'VE SEEN YOUR REPORT.
IT ALSO SAYS YOU WENT TOE-TO-TOE WITH HIM FOR TWENTY-THREE SECONDS.
NO OTHER NORMAL HUMAN SURVIVED MORE THAN TEN SECONDS IN HIS AMBIT.
"SURVIVED" IS A PRETTY GENEROUS WORD FOR HOW I FEEL.
BUT THE OLD SUIT GAVE ME SOME PROTECTION.
AND OF COURSE, I'M PRETTY LUCKY SUPERMAN CAME ALONG WHEN HE DID.
AND YOU'RE PRETTY LUCKY YOU HAPPEN TO RUN THE MOST ADVANCED PHYSICAL REHABILITATION RESEARCH CENTER IN THE COUNTRY.
OH, NO, SENATOR, THAT'S NOT LUCK...

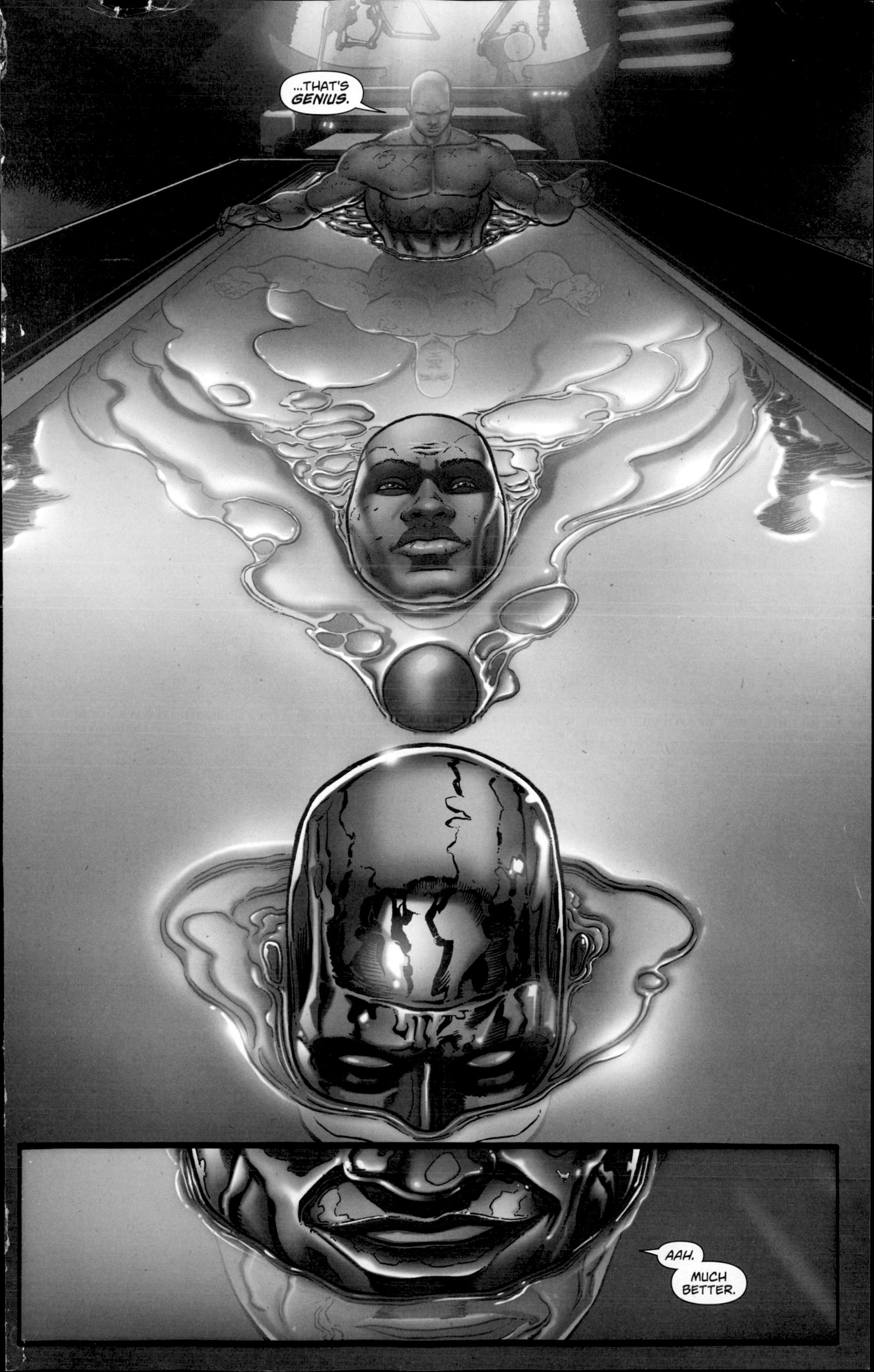
...THAT'S GENIUS.
AAH.
MUCH BETTER.

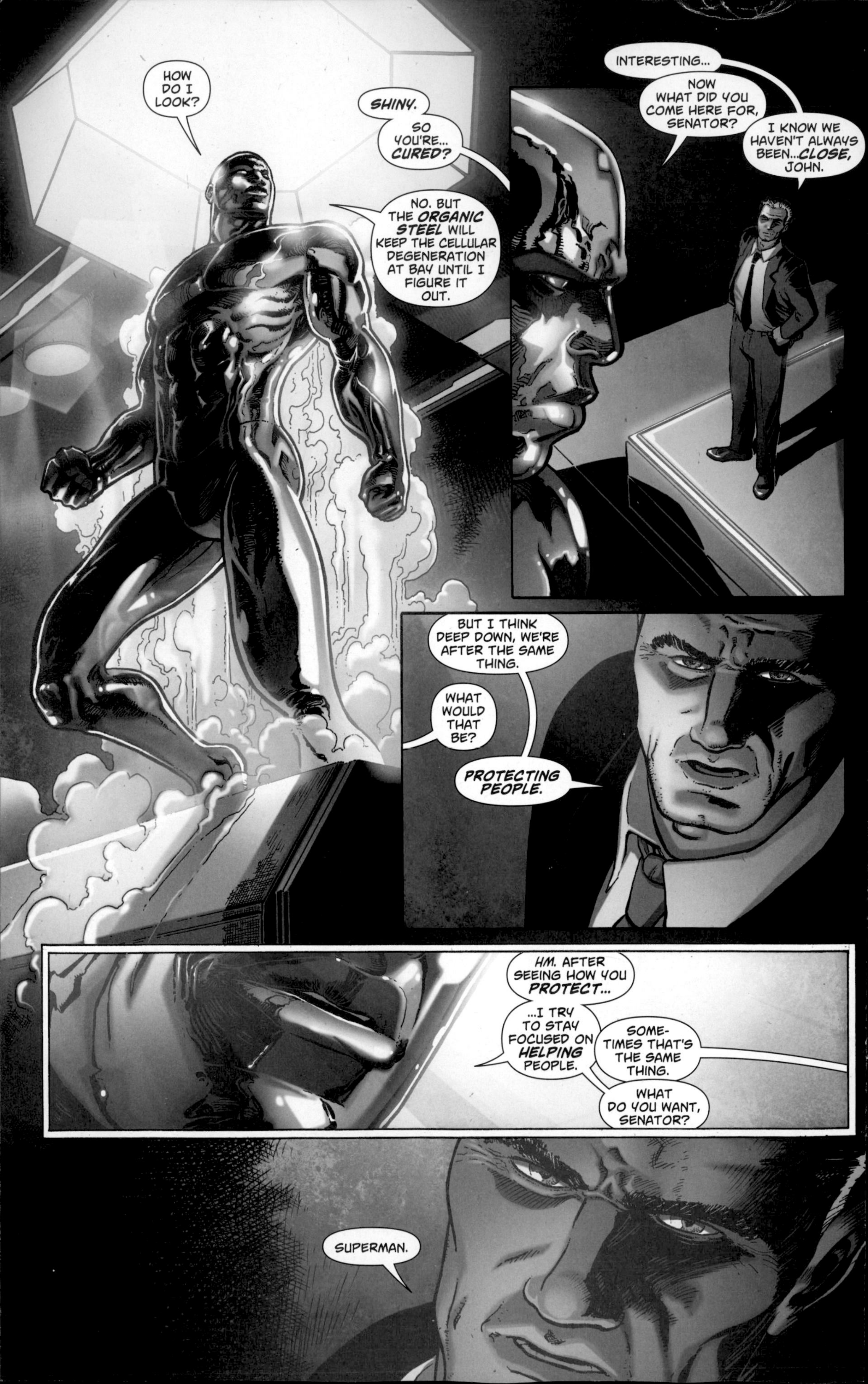
HOW DO I LOOK?
SHINY.
SO YOU'RE... CURED?
NO. BUT THE ORGANIC STEEL WILL KEEP THE CELLULAR DEGENERATION AT BAY UNTIL I FIGURE IT OUT.
INTERESTING...
NOW WHAT DID YOU COME HERE FOR, SENATOR?
I KNOW WE HAVEN'T ALWAYS BEEN...CLOSE, JOHN.
BUT I THINK DEEP DOWN, WE'RE AFTER THE SAME THING.
WHAT WOULD THAT BE?
PROTECTING PEOPLE.
HM. AFTER SEEING HOW YOU PROTECT...
...I TRY TO STAY FOCUSED ON HELPING PEOPLE.
SOME-TIMES THAT'S THE SAME THING.
WHAT DO YOU WANT, SENATOR?
SUPERMAN.

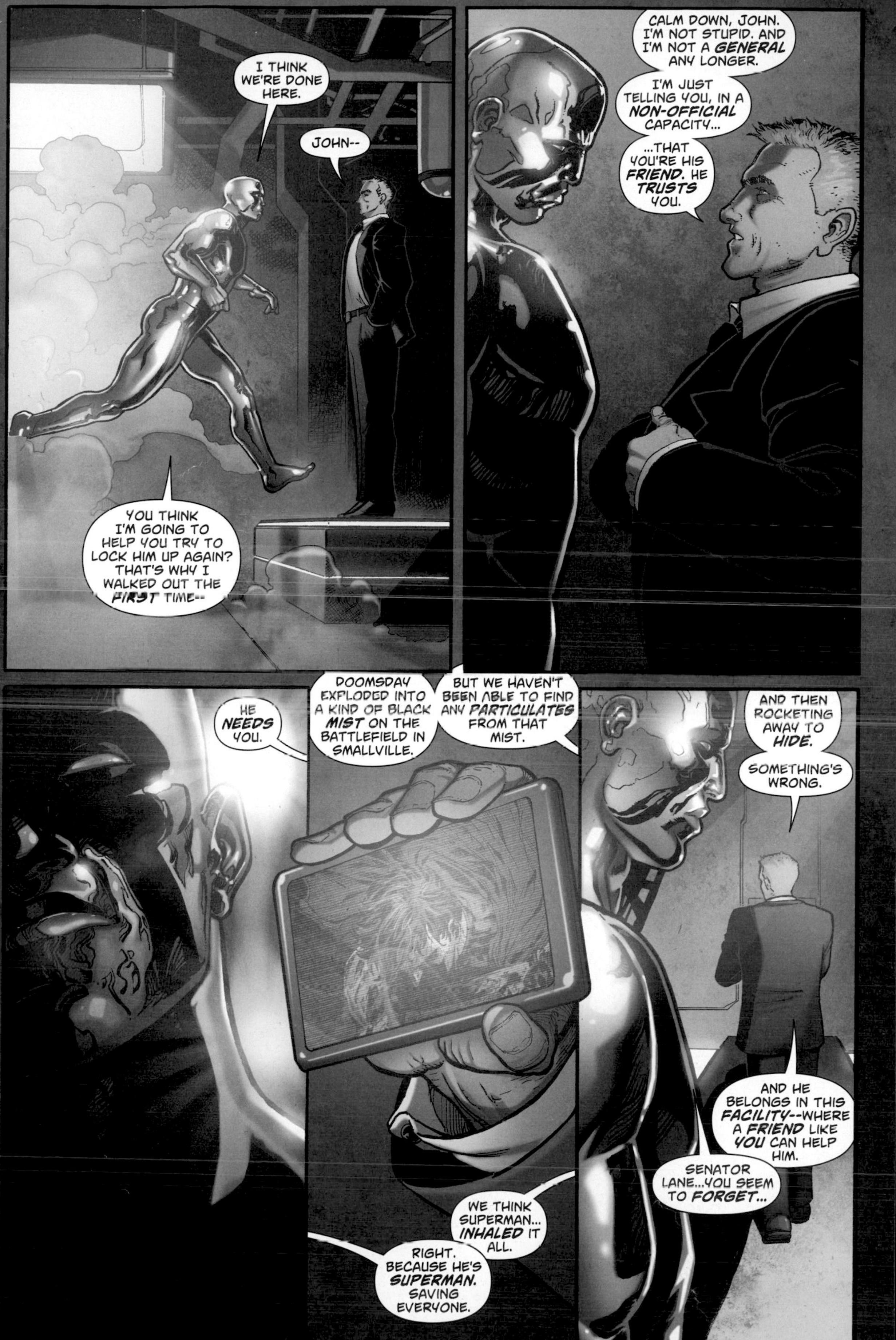

I THINK WE'RE DONE HERE.
JOHN--
YOU THINK I'M GOING TO HELP YOU TRY TO LOCK HIM UP AGAIN? THAT'S WHY I WALKED OUT THE FIRST TIME--
CALM DOWN, JOHN. I'M NOT STUPID. AND I'M NOT A GENERAL ANY LONGER.
I'M JUST TELLING YOU, IN A NON-OFFICIAL CAPACITY...
...THAT YOU'RE HIS FRIEND. HE TRUSTS YOU.
HE NEEDS YOU.
DOOMSDAY EXPLODED INTO A KIND OF BLACK MIST ON THE BATTLEFIELD IN SMALLVILLE.
BUT WE HAVEN'T BEEN ABLE TO FIND ANY PARTICULATES FROM THAT MIST.
WE THINK SUPERMAN... INHALED IT ALL.
RIGHT. BECAUSE HE'S SUPERMAN. SAVING EVERYONE.
AND THEN ROCKETING AWAY TO HIDE.
SOMETHING'S WRONG.
AND HE BELONGS IN THIS FACILITY--WHERE A FRIEND LIKE YOU CAN HELP HIM.
SENATOR LANE...YOU SEEM TO FORGET...

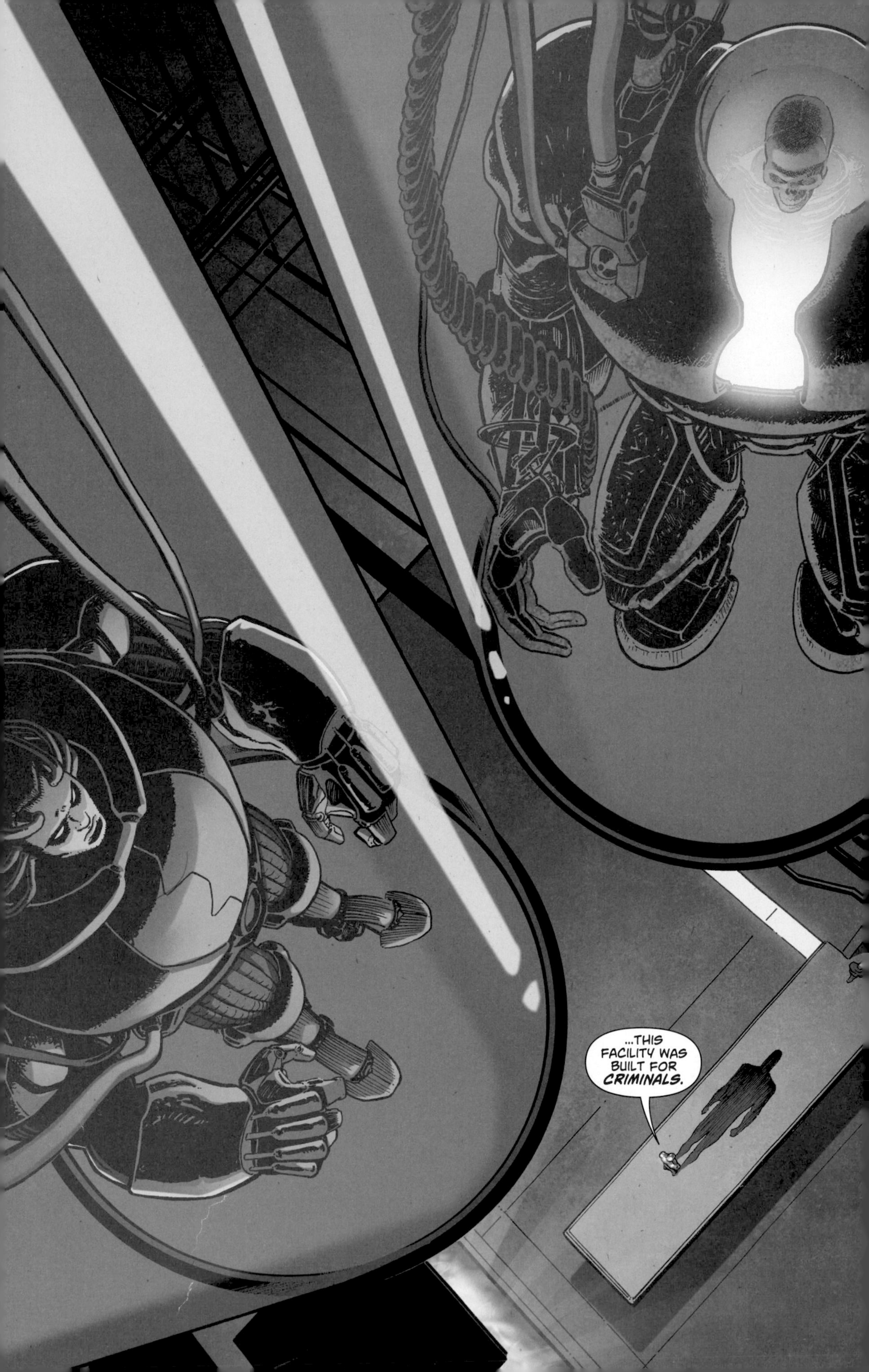
...THIS FACILITY WAS BUILT FOR CRIMINALS.

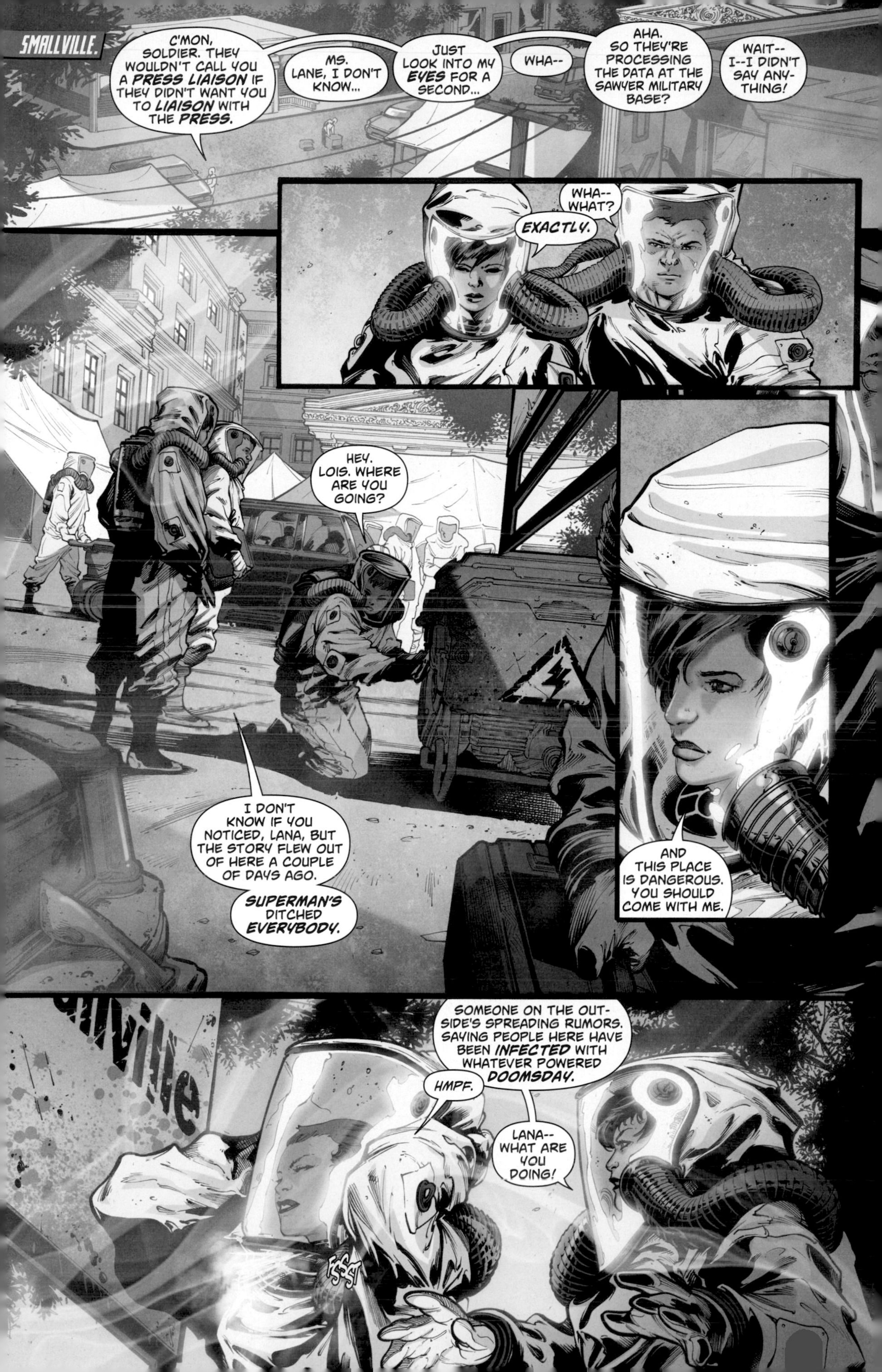
SMALLVILLE.
C'MON, SOLDIER. THEY WOULDN'T CALL YOU A PRESS LIAISON IF THEY DIDN'T WANT YOU TO LIAISON WITH THE PRESS.
MS. LANE, I DON'T KNOW...
JUST LOOK INTO MY EYES FOR A SECOND...
WHA--
AHA. SO THEY'RE PROCESSING THE DATA AT THE SAWYER MILITARY BASE?
WAIT-- I--I DIDN'T SAY ANY-THING!
WHA-- WHAT?
EXACTLY.
HEY. LOIS. WHERE ARE YOU GOING?
I DON'T KNOW IF YOU NOTICED, LANA, BUT THE STORY FLEW OUT OF HERE A COUPLE OF DAYS AGO.
SUPERMAN'S DITCHED EVERYBODY.
AND THIS PLACE IS DANGEROUS. YOU SHOULD COME WITH ME.
SOMEONE ON THE OUT-SIDE'S SPREADING RUMORS. SAYING PEOPLE HERE HAVE BEEN INFECTED WITH WHATEVER POWERED DOOMSDAY.
HMPF.
LANA-- WHAT ARE YOU DOING!

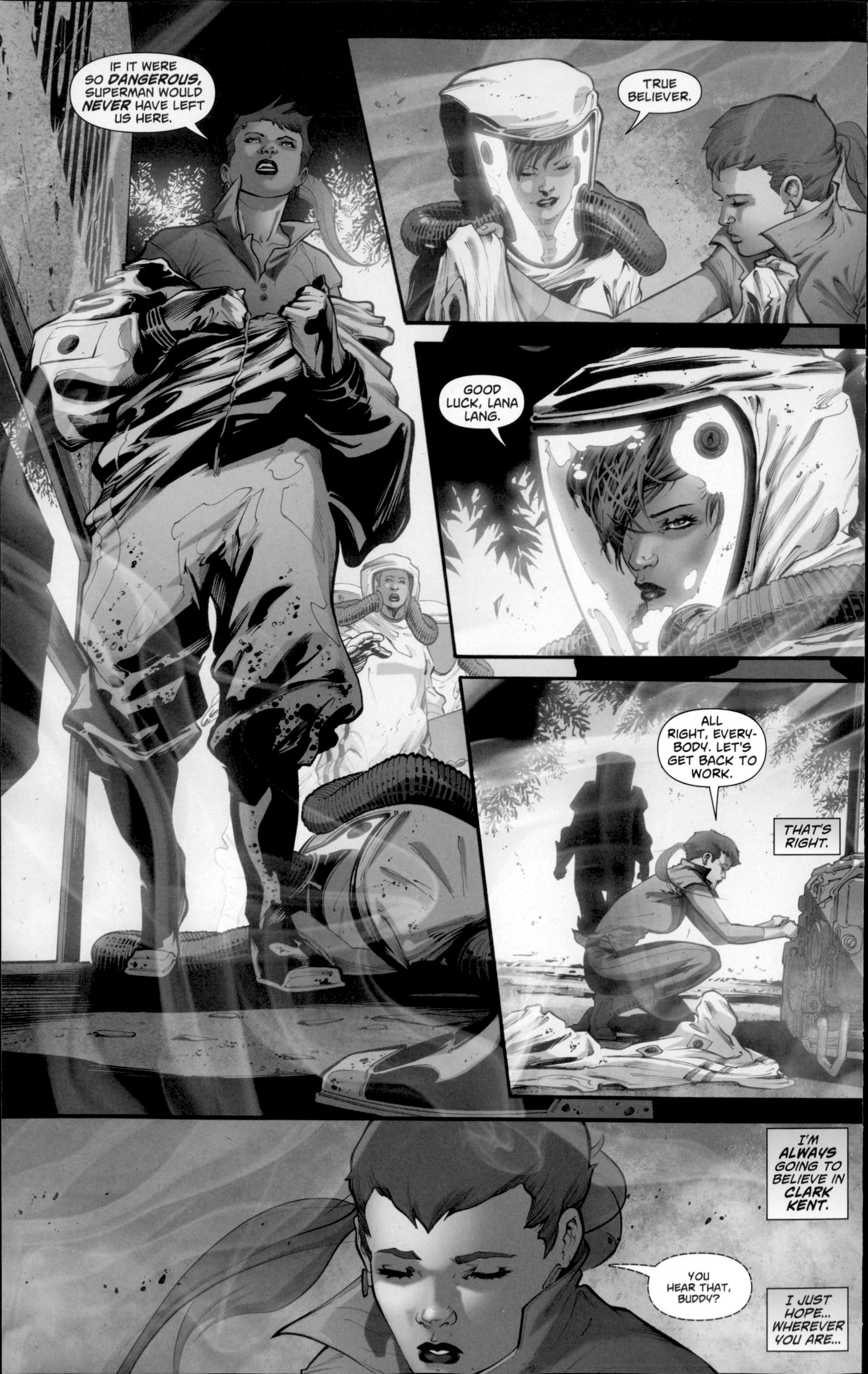
IF IT WERE SO DANGEROUS, SUPERMAN WOULD NEVER HAVE LEFT US HERE.
TRUE BELIEVER.
GOOD LUCK, LANA LANG.
ALL RIGHT, EVERY-BODY. LET'S GET BACK TO WORK.
THAT'S RIGHT.
I'M ALWAYS GOING TO BELIEVE IN CLARK KENT.
YOU HEAR THAT, BUDDY?
I JUST HOPE... WHEREVER YOU ARE...

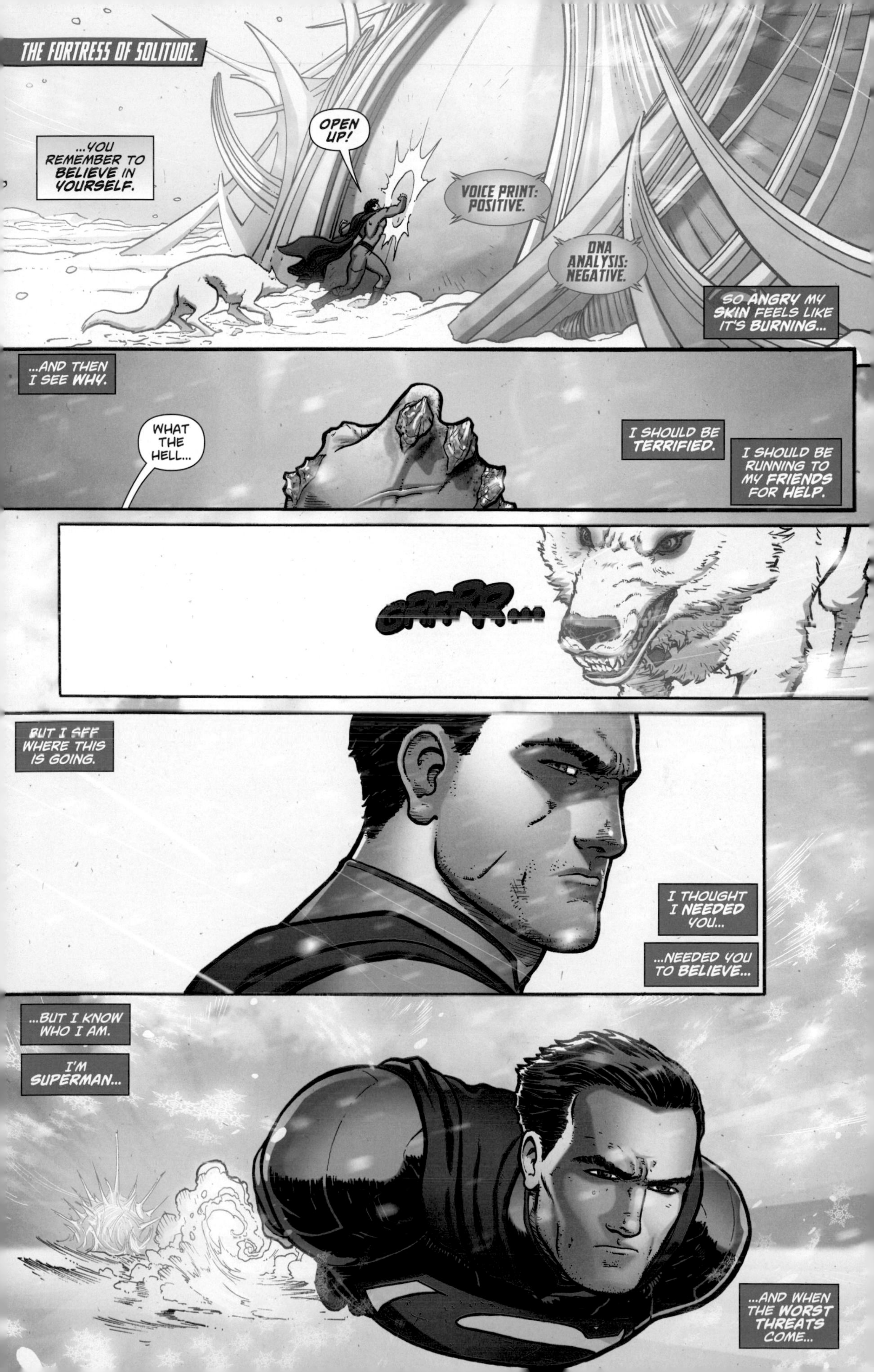

THE FORTRESS OF SOLITUDE.
...YOU REMEMBER TO BELIEVE IN YOURSELF.
OPEN UP!
VOICE PRINT: POSITIVE.
DNA ANALYSIS: NEGATIVE.
SO ANGRY MY SKIN FEELS LIKE IT'S BURNING...
...AND THEN I SEE WHY.
WHAT THE HELL...
I SHOULD BE TERRIFIED.
I SHOULD BE RUNNING TO MY FRIENDS FOR HELP.
GRRRR...
BUT I SEE WHERE THIS IS GOING.
I THOUGHT I NEEDED YOU...
...NEEDED YOU TO BELIEVE...
...BUT I KNOW WHO I AM.
I'M SUPERMAN...
...AND WHEN THE WORST THREATS COME...

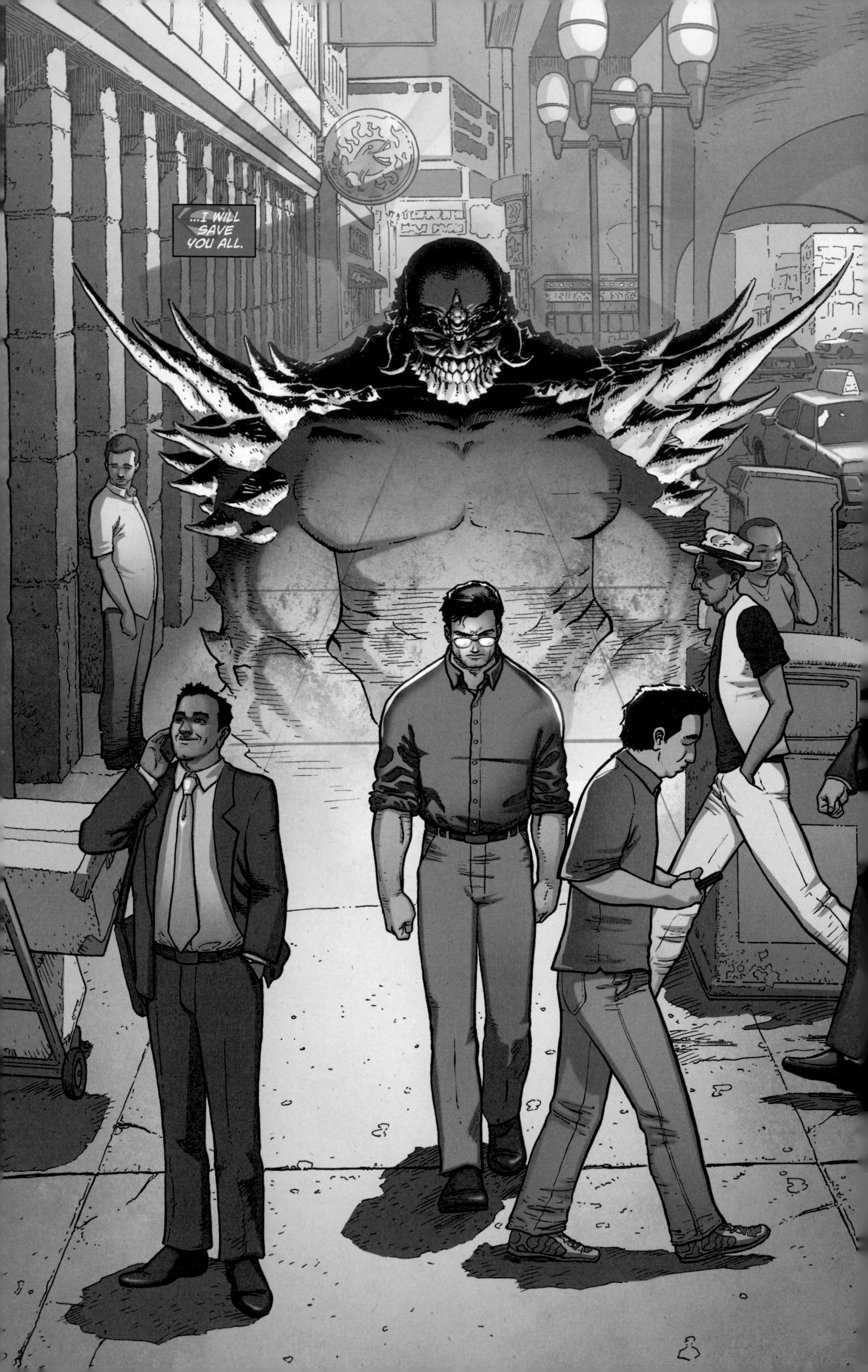
...I WILL SAVE YOU ALL.

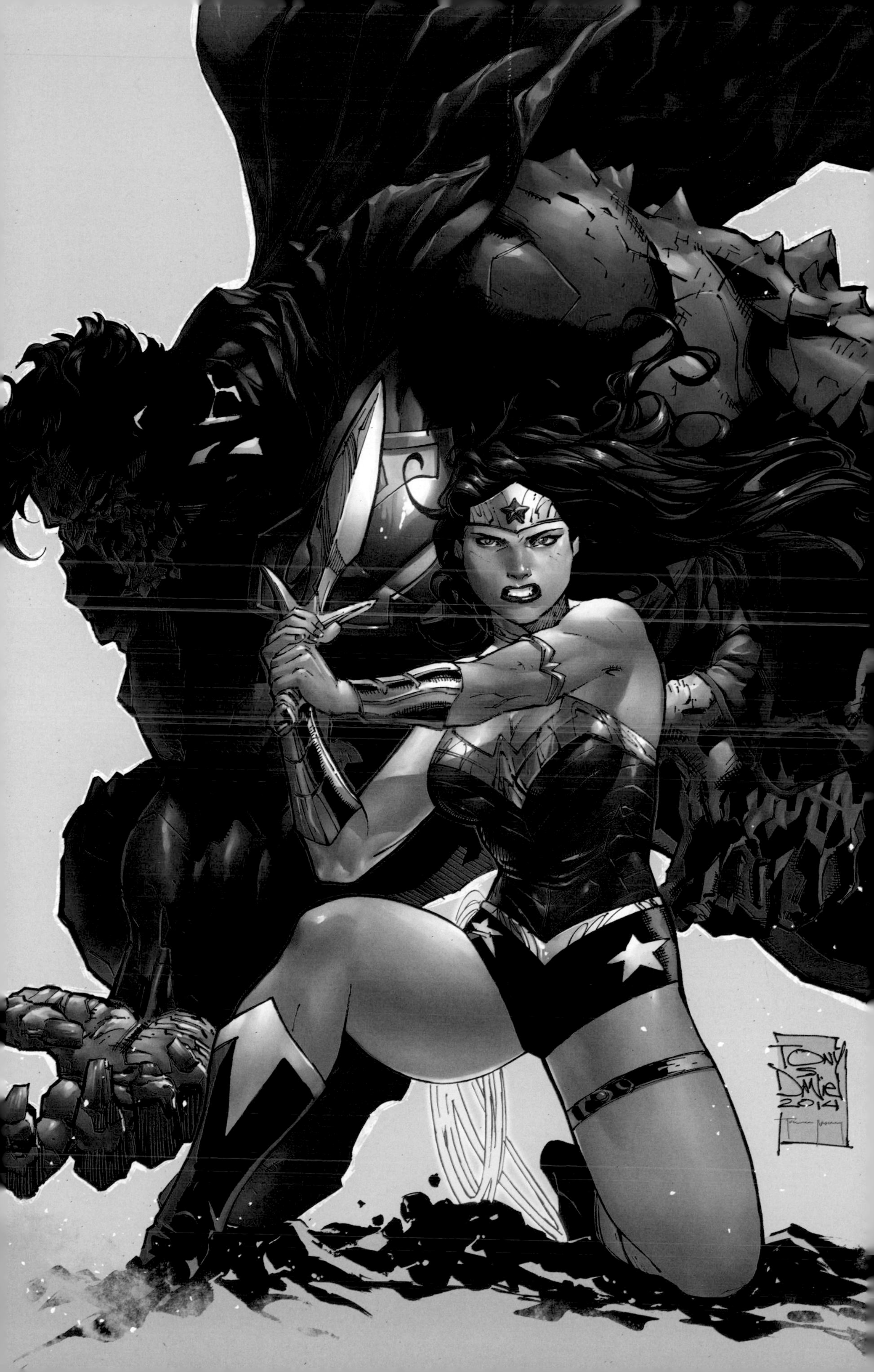
TONY S. DANIEL 2014

SUPERMAN DOOMED

[INFECTED] chapter 2

"EVOLUTIONS"

STORY
CHARLES SOULE

PENCILS
TONY DANIEL

INKS
MATT BANNING AND **SANDU FLOREA**

COLORS
TOMEU MOREY

LETTERS
CARLOS M. MANGUAL

COVER
TONY DANIEL AND **TOMEU MOREY**

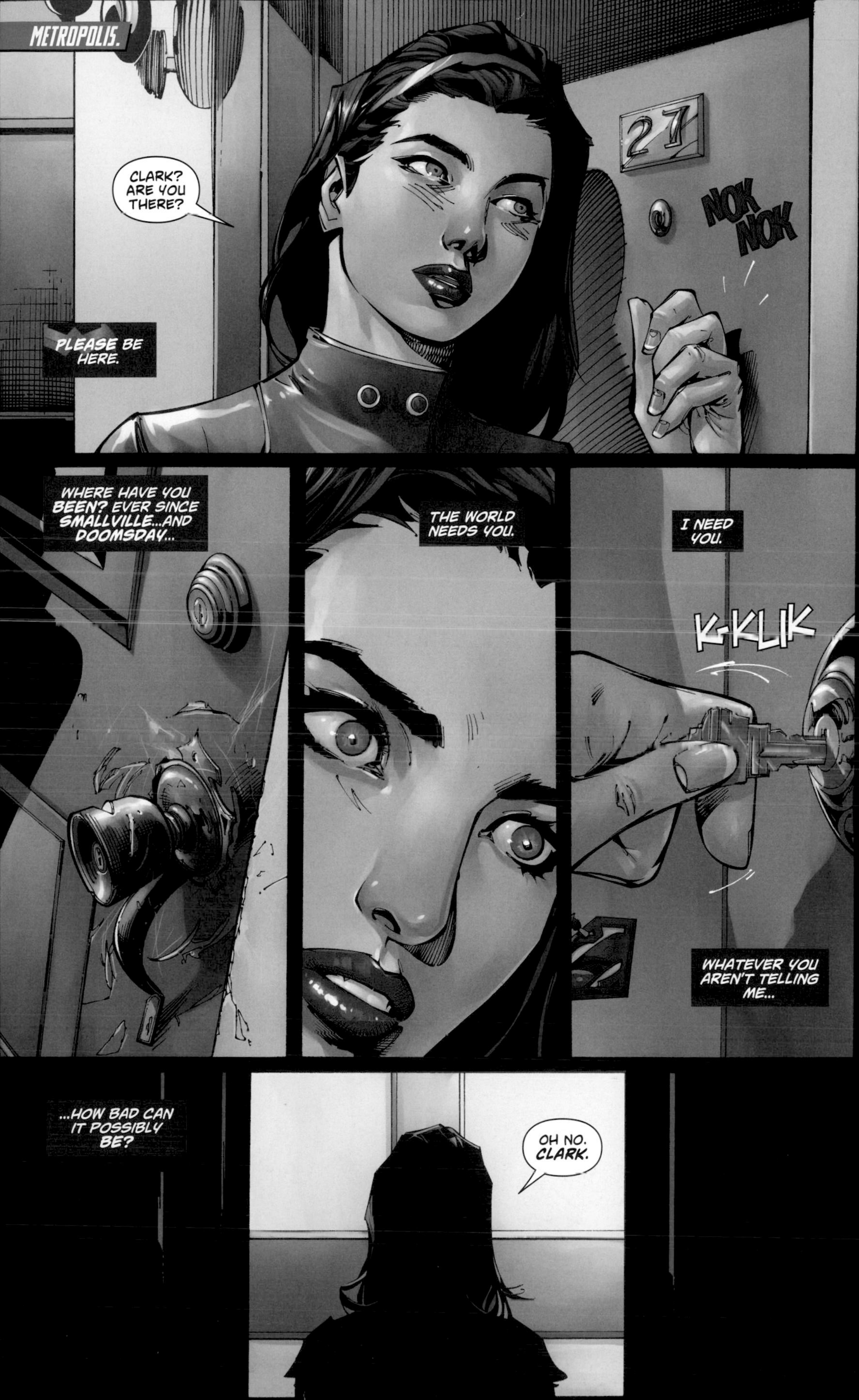
METROPOLIS.
CLARK? ARE YOU THERE?
NOK NOK
PLEASE BE HERE.
WHERE HAVE YOU BEEN? EVER SINCE SMALLVILLE...AND DOOMSDAY...
THE WORLD NEEDS YOU.
I NEED YOU.
K-KLIK
WHATEVER YOU AREN'T TELLING ME...
...HOW BAD CAN IT POSSIBLY BE?
OH NO. CLARK.

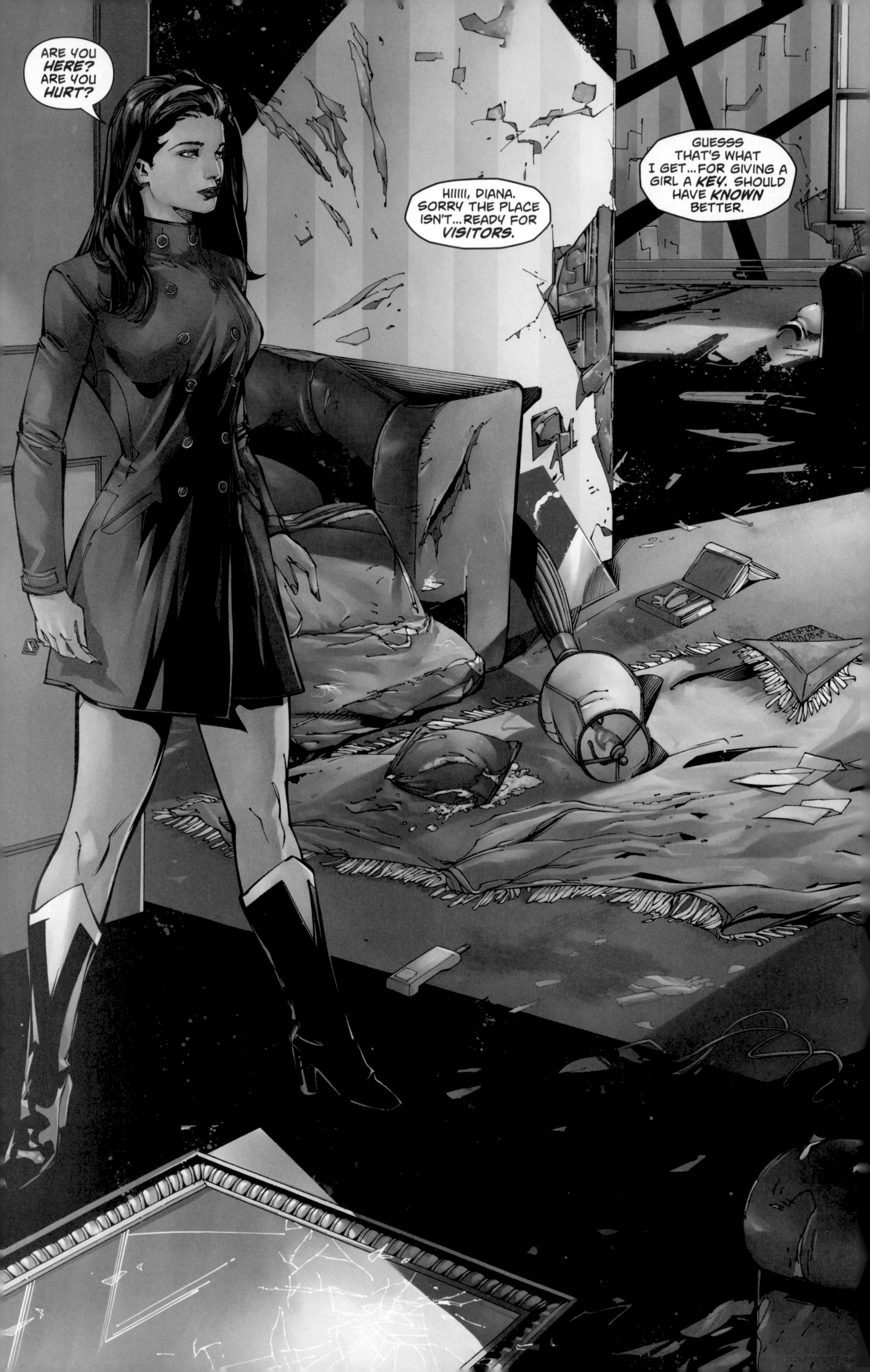
ARE YOU HERE? ARE YOU HURT?
HIIIII, DIANA. SORRY THE PLACE ISN'T...READY FOR VISITORS.
GUESSS THAT'S WHAT I GET...FOR GIVING A GIRL A KEY. SHOULD HAVE KNOWN BETTER.

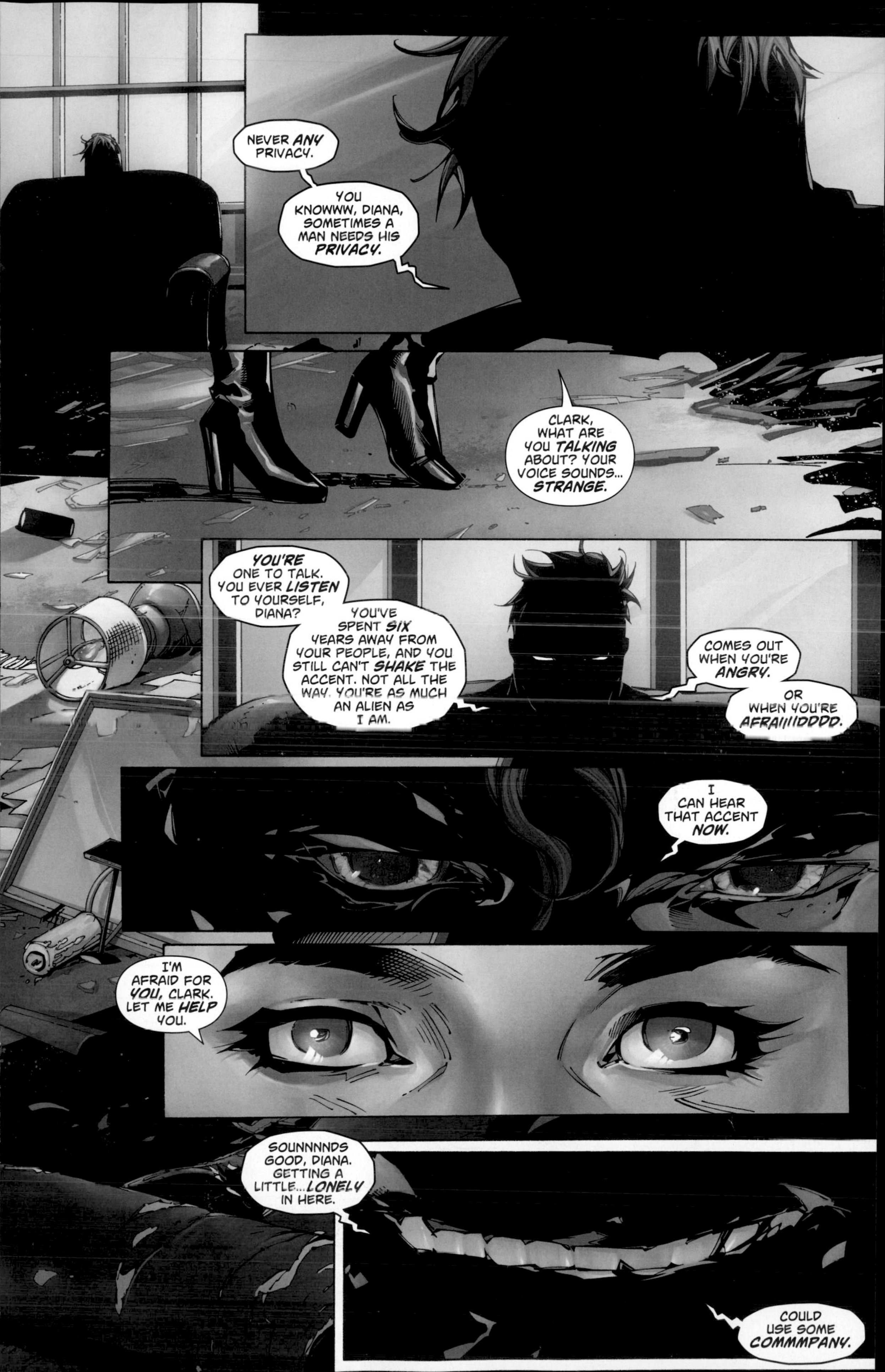
NEVER ANY PRIVACY.
YOU KNOWWW, DIANA, SOMETIMES A MAN NEEDS HIS PRIVACY.
CLARK, WHAT ARE YOU TALKING ABOUT? YOUR VOICE SOUNDS... STRANGE.
YOU'RE ONE TO TALK. YOU EVER LISTEN TO YOURSELF, DIANA?
YOU'VE SPENT SIX YEARS AWAY FROM YOUR PEOPLE, AND YOU STILL CAN'T SHAKE THE ACCENT. NOT ALL THE WAY. YOU'RE AS MUCH AN ALIEN AS I AM.
COMES OUT WHEN YOU'RE ANGRY.
OR WHEN YOU'RE AFRAIIIIDDDD.
I CAN HEAR THAT ACCENT NOW.
I'M AFRAID FOR YOU, CLARK. LET ME HELP YOU.
SOUNNNNDS GOOD, DIANA. GETTING A LITTLE...LONELY IN HERE.
COULD USE SOME COMMMPANY.

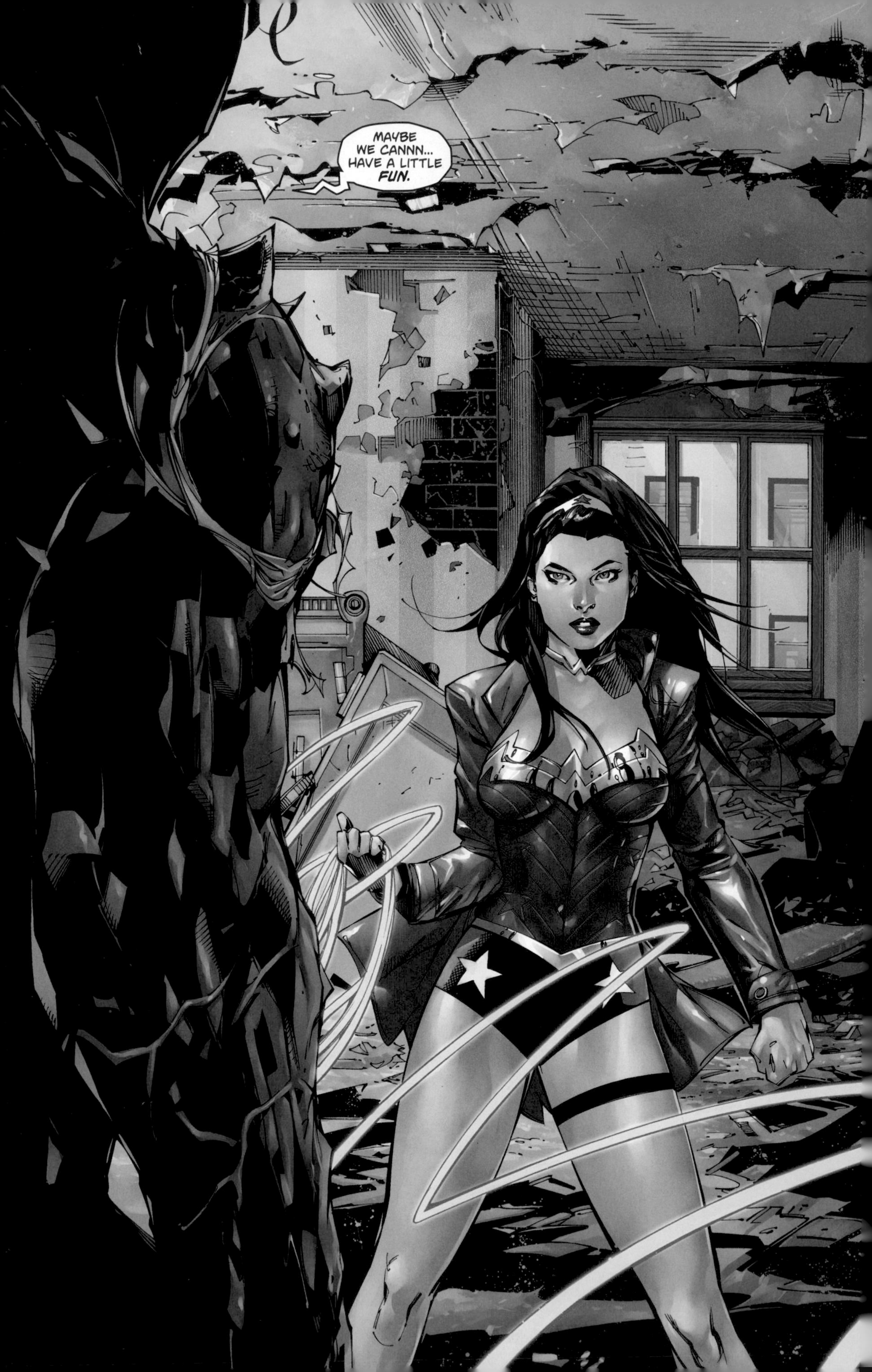
MAYBE WE CANNN... HAVE A LITTLE FUN.

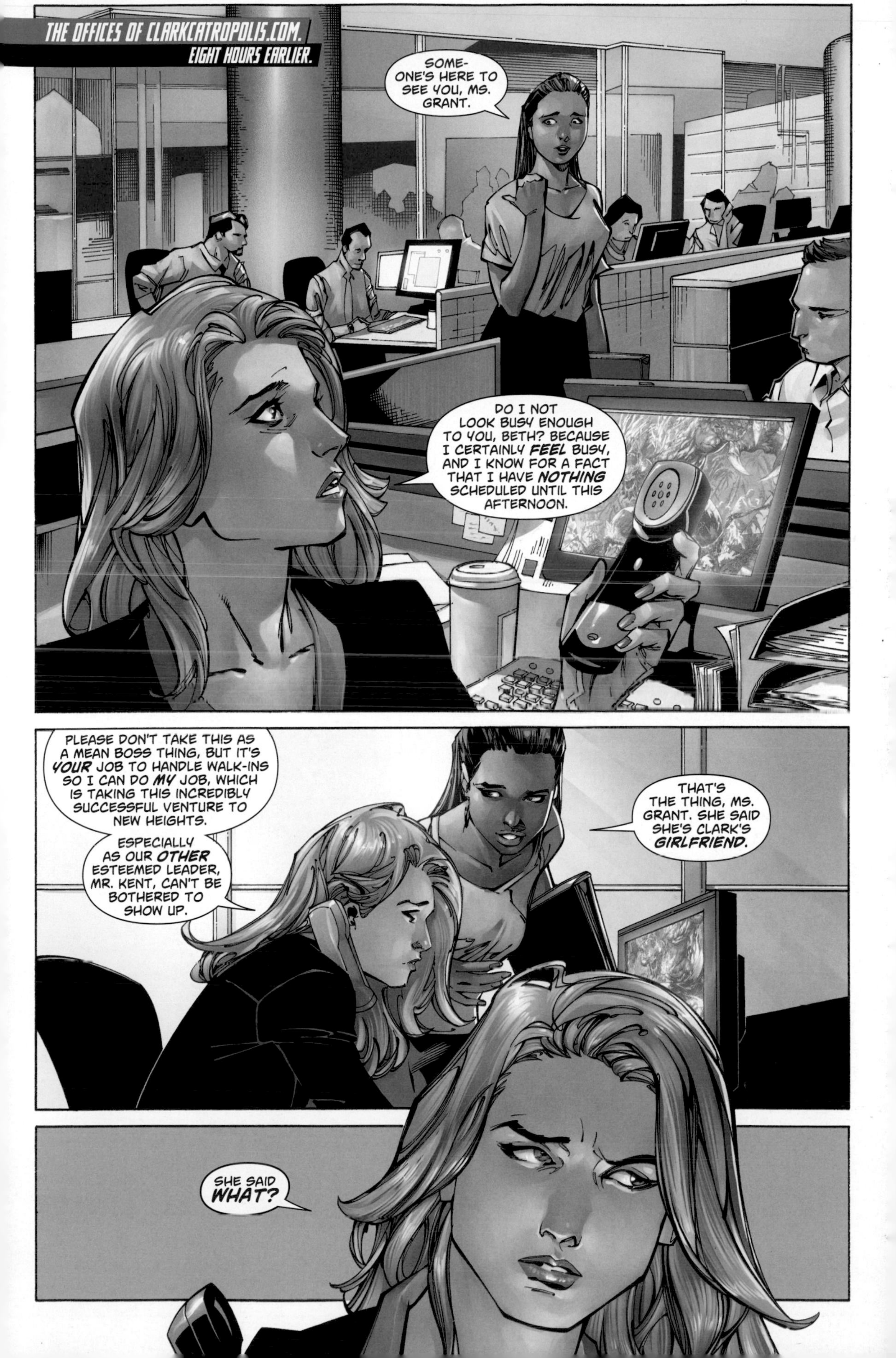
THE OFFICES OF CLARKCATROPOLIS.COM.
EIGHT HOURS EARLIER.
SOME-ONE'S HERE TO SEE YOU, MS. GRANT.
DO I NOT LOOK BUSY ENOUGH TO YOU, BETH? BECAUSE I CERTAINLY FEEL BUSY, AND I KNOW FOR A FACT THAT I HAVE NOTHING SCHEDULED UNTIL THIS AFTERNOON.
PLEASE DON'T TAKE THIS AS A MEAN BOSS THING, BUT IT'S YOUR JOB TO HANDLE WALK-INS SO I CAN DO MY JOB, WHICH IS TAKING THIS INCREDIBLY SUCCESSFUL VENTURE TO NEW HEIGHTS.
ESPECIALLY AS OUR OTHER ESTEEMED LEADER, MR. KENT, CAN'T BE BOTHERED TO SHOW UP.
THAT'S THE THING, MS. GRANT. SHE SAID SHE'S CLARK'S GIRLFRIEND.
SHE SAID WHAT?

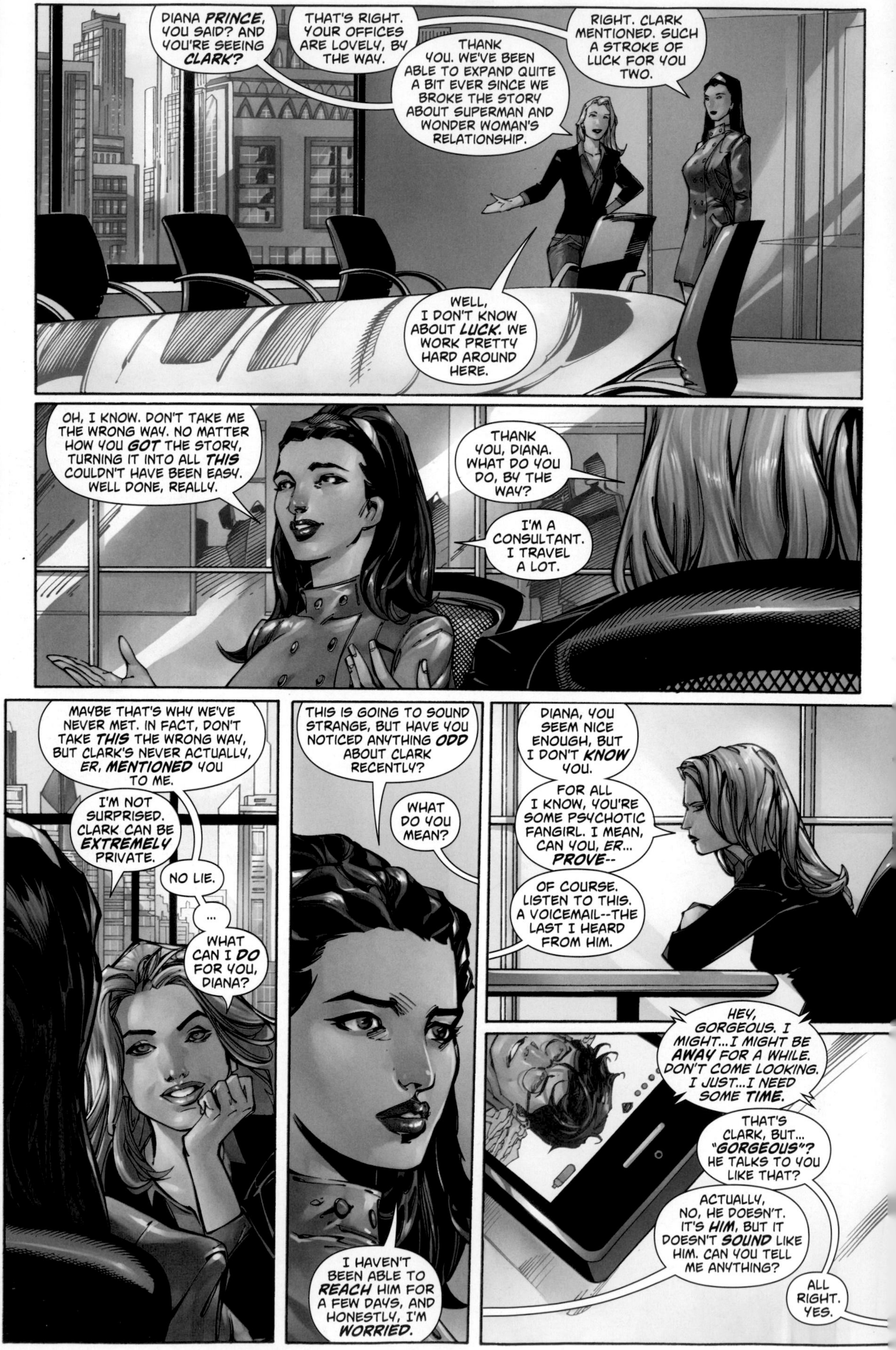
DIANA PRINCE, YOU SAID? AND YOU'RE SEEING CLARK?
THAT'S RIGHT. YOUR OFFICES ARE LOVELY, BY THE WAY.
THANK YOU. WE'VE BEEN ABLE TO EXPAND QUITE A BIT EVER SINCE WE BROKE THE STORY ABOUT SUPERMAN AND WONDER WOMAN'S RELATIONSHIP.
RIGHT. CLARK MENTIONED. SUCH A STROKE OF LUCK FOR YOU TWO.
WELL, I DON'T KNOW ABOUT LUCK. WE WORK PRETTY HARD AROUND HERE.
OH, I KNOW. DON'T TAKE ME THE WRONG WAY. NO MATTER HOW YOU GOT THE STORY, TURNING IT INTO ALL THIS COULDN'T HAVE BEEN EASY. WELL DONE, REALLY.
THANK YOU, DIANA. WHAT DO YOU DO, BY THE WAY?
I'M A CONSULTANT. I TRAVEL A LOT.
MAYBE THAT'S WHY WE'VE NEVER MET. IN FACT, DON'T TAKE THIS THE WRONG WAY, BUT CLARK'S NEVER ACTUALLY, ER, MENTIONED YOU TO ME.
I'M NOT SURPRISED. CLARK CAN BE EXTREMELY PRIVATE.
NO LIE.
...
WHAT CAN I DO FOR YOU, DIANA?
THIS IS GOING TO SOUND STRANGE, BUT HAVE YOU NOTICED ANYTHING ODD ABOUT CLARK RECENTLY?
WHAT DO YOU MEAN?
I HAVEN'T BEEN ABLE TO REACH HIM FOR A FEW DAYS, AND HONESTLY, I'M WORRIED.
DIANA, YOU SEEM NICE ENOUGH, BUT I DON'T KNOW YOU.
FOR ALL I KNOW, YOU'RE SOME PSYCHOTIC FANGIRL. I MEAN, CAN YOU, ER... PROVE--
OF COURSE. LISTEN TO THIS. A VOICEMAIL--THE LAST I HEARD FROM HIM.
HEY, GORGEOUS. I MIGHT...I MIGHT BE AWAY FOR A WHILE. DON'T COME LOOKING. I JUST...I NEED SOME TIME.
THAT'S CLARK, BUT... "GORGEOUS"? HE TALKS TO YOU LIKE THAT?
ACTUALLY, NO, HE DOESN'T. IT'S HIM, BUT IT DOESN'T SOUND LIKE HIM. CAN YOU TELL ME ANYTHING?
ALL RIGHT. YES.

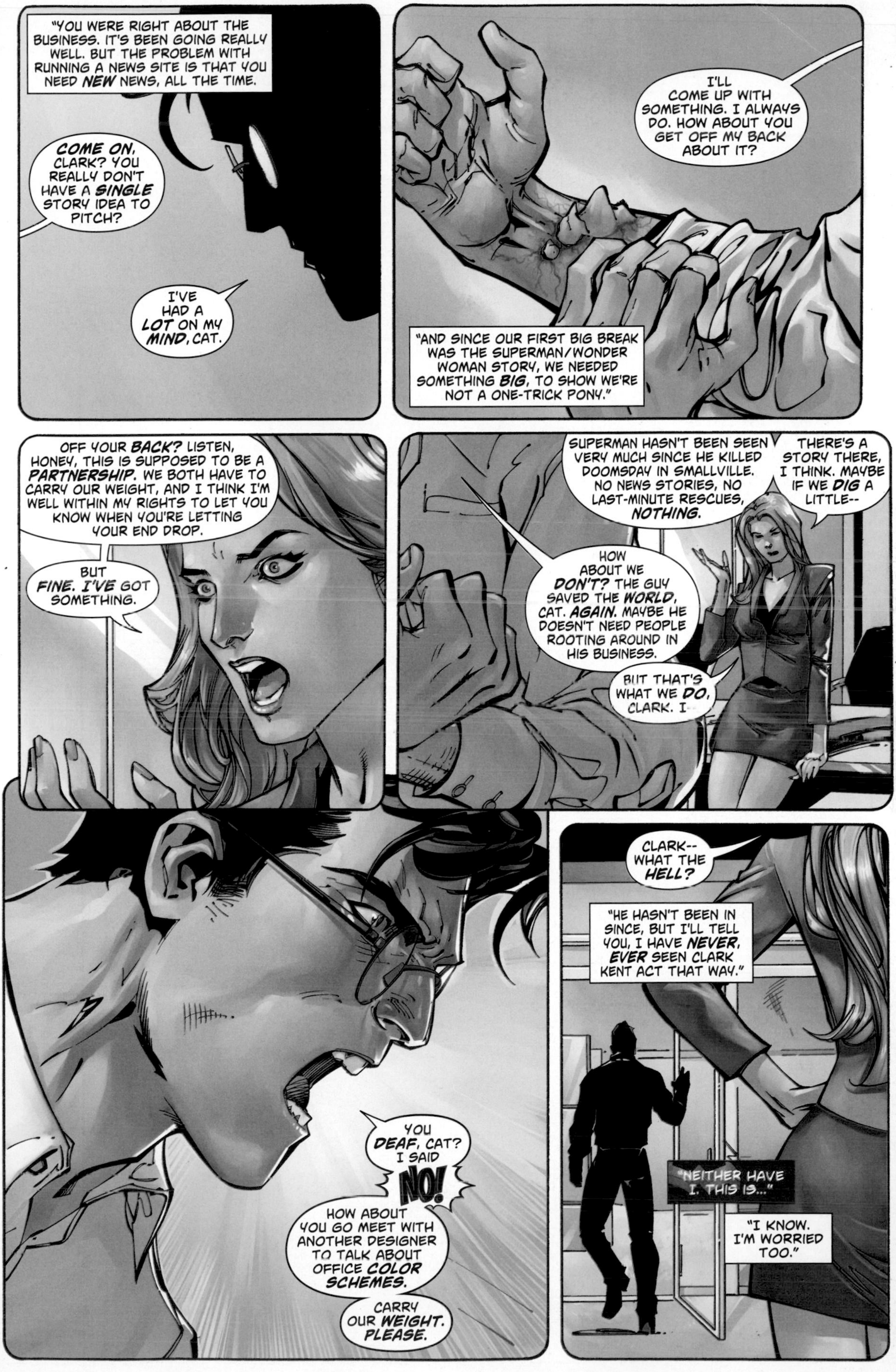
"YOU WERE RIGHT ABOUT THE BUSINESS. IT'S BEEN GOING REALLY WELL. BUT THE PROBLEM WITH RUNNING A NEWS SITE IS THAT YOU NEED NEW NEWS, ALL THE TIME.
COME ON, CLARK? YOU REALLY DON'T HAVE A SINGLE STORY IDEA TO PITCH?
I'VE HAD A LOT ON MY MIND, CAT.
I'LL COME UP WITH SOMETHING. I ALWAYS DO. HOW ABOUT YOU GET OFF MY BACK ABOUT IT?
"AND SINCE OUR FIRST BIG BREAK WAS THE SUPERMAN/WONDER WOMAN STORY, WE NEEDED SOMETHING BIG, TO SHOW WE'RE NOT A ONE-TRICK PONY."
OFF YOUR BACK? LISTEN, HONEY, THIS IS SUPPOSED TO BE A PARTNERSHIP. WE BOTH HAVE TO CARRY OUR WEIGHT, AND I THINK I'M WELL WITHIN MY RIGHTS TO LET YOU KNOW WHEN YOU'RE LETTING YOUR END DROP.
BUT FINE. I'VE GOT SOMETHING.
SUPERMAN HASN'T BEEN SEEN VERY MUCH SINCE HE KILLED DOOMSDAY IN SMALLVILLE. NO NEWS STORIES, NO LAST-MINUTE RESCUES, NOTHING.
THERE'S A STORY THERE, I THINK. MAYBE IF WE DIG A LITTLE--
HOW ABOUT WE DON'T? THE GUY SAVED THE WORLD, CAT. AGAIN. MAYBE HE DOESN'T NEED PEOPLE ROOTING AROUND IN HIS BUSINESS.
BUT THAT'S WHAT WE DO, CLARK. I--
YOU DEAF, CAT? I SAID NO!
HOW ABOUT YOU GO MEET WITH ANOTHER DESIGNER TO TALK ABOUT OFFICE COLOR SCHEMES.
CARRY OUR WEIGHT. PLEASE.
CLARK-- WHAT THE HELL?
"HE HASN'T BEEN IN SINCE, BUT I'LL TELL YOU, I HAVE NEVER, EVER SEEN CLARK KENT ACT THAT WAY."
"NEITHER HAVE I. THIS IS..."
"I KNOW. I'M WORRIED TOO."

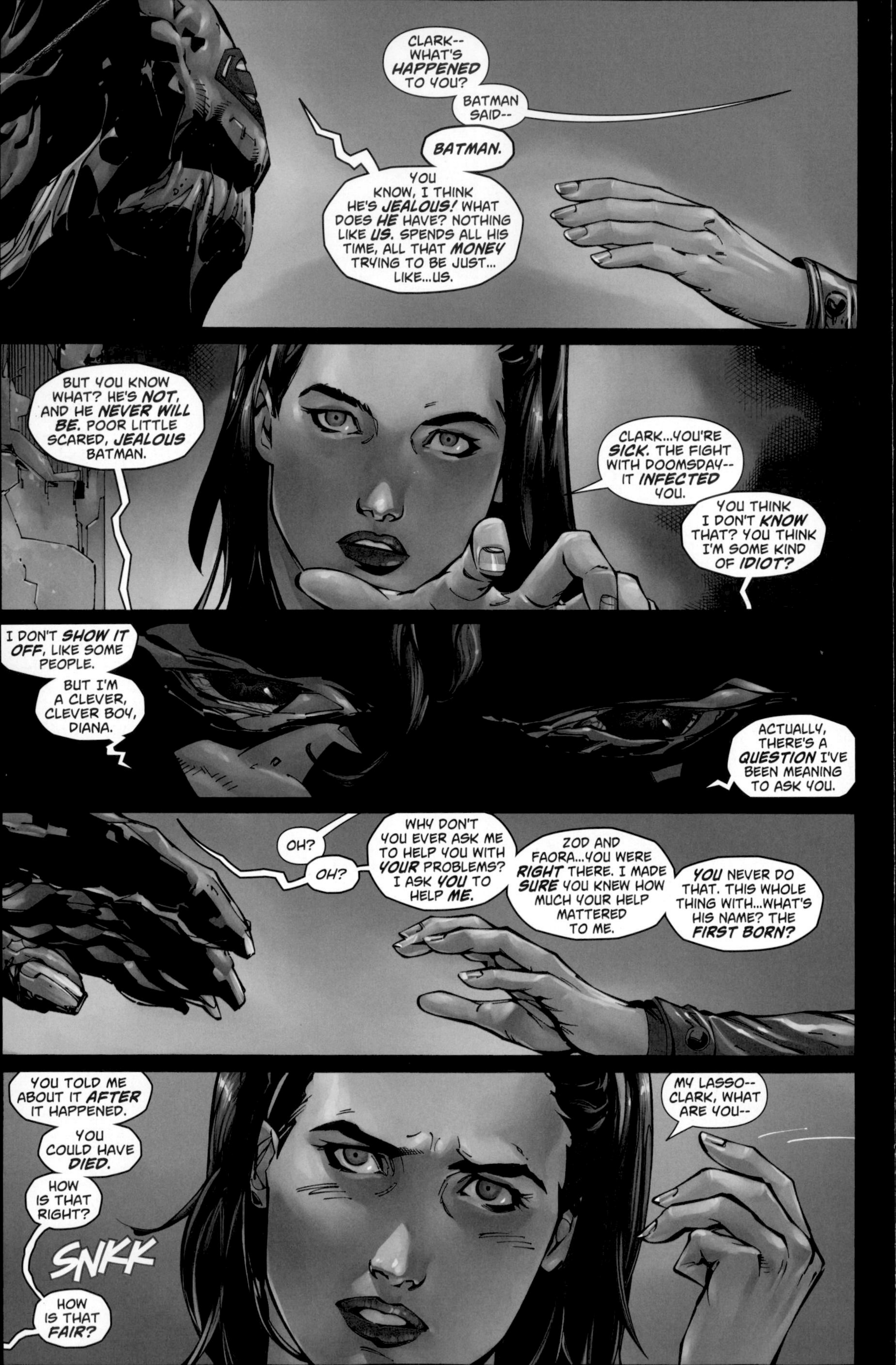
CLARK-- WHAT'S HAPPENED TO YOU?
BATMAN SAID--
BATMAN.
YOU KNOW, I THINK HE'S JEALOUS! WHAT DOES HE HAVE? NOTHING LIKE US. SPENDS ALL HIS TIME, ALL THAT MONEY TRYING TO BE JUST... LIKE...US.
BUT YOU KNOW WHAT? HE'S NOT, AND HE NEVER WILL BE. POOR LITTLE SCARED, JEALOUS BATMAN.
CLARK...YOU'RE SICK. THE FIGHT WITH DOOMSDAY-- IT INFECTED YOU.
YOU THINK I DON'T KNOW THAT? YOU THINK I'M SOME KIND OF IDIOT?
I DON'T SHOW IT OFF, LIKE SOME PEOPLE.
BUT I'M A CLEVER, CLEVER BOY, DIANA.
ACTUALLY, THERE'S A QUESTION I'VE BEEN MEANING TO ASK YOU.
OH?
OH?
WHY DON'T YOU EVER ASK ME TO HELP YOU WITH YOUR PROBLEMS? I ASK YOU TO HELP ME.
ZOD AND FAORA...YOU WERE RIGHT THERE. I MADE SURE YOU KNEW HOW MUCH YOUR HELP MATTERED TO ME.
YOU NEVER DO THAT. THIS WHOLE THING WITH...WHAT'S HIS NAME? THE FIRST BORN?
YOU TOLD ME ABOUT IT AFTER IT HAPPENED.
YOU COULD HAVE DIED.
HOW IS THAT RIGHT?
SNKK
HOW IS THAT FAIR?
MY LASSO-- CLARK, WHAT ARE YOU--

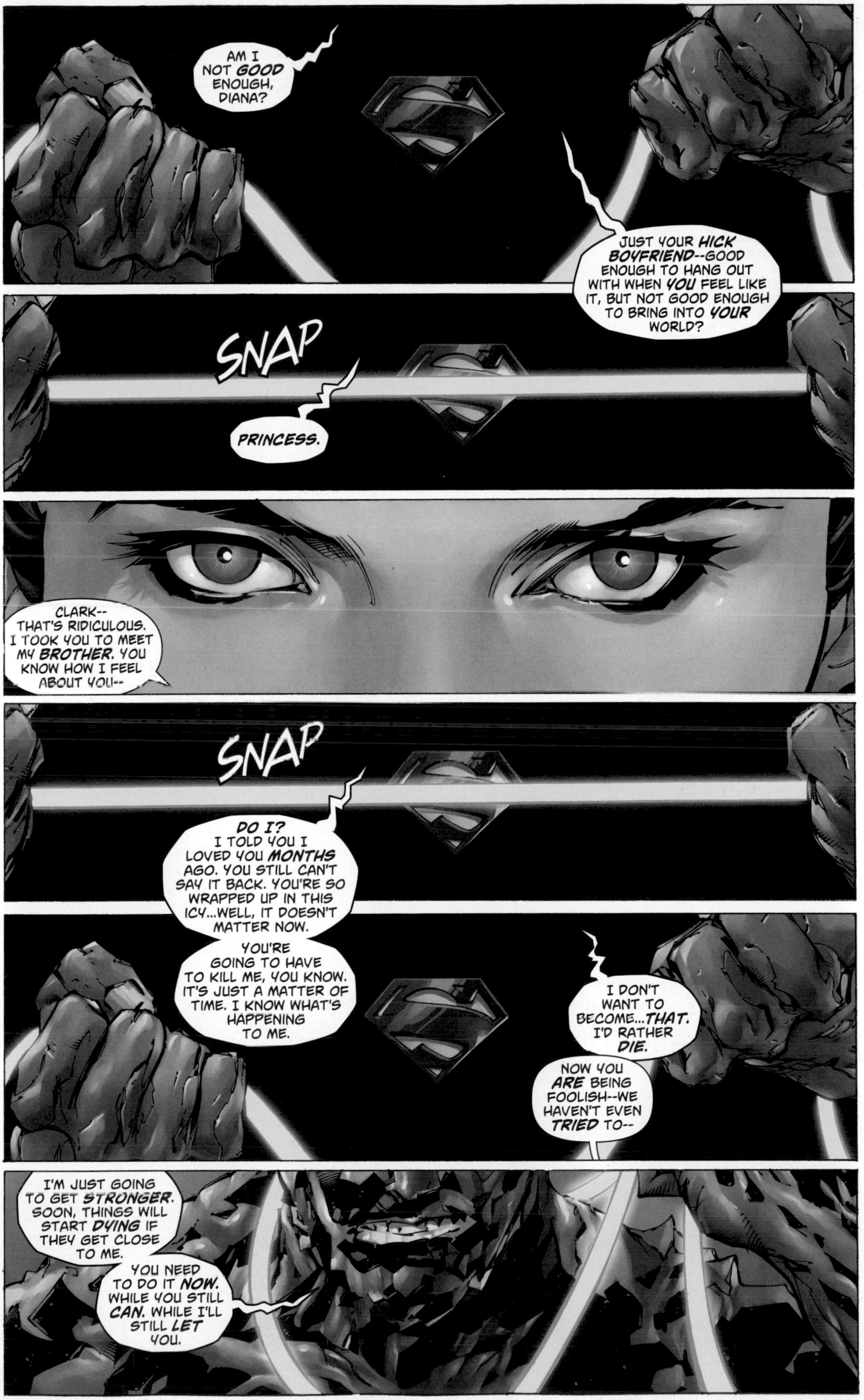
AM I NOT GOOD ENOUGH, DIANA?
JUST YOUR HICK BOYFRIEND--GOOD ENOUGH TO HANG OUT WITH WHEN YOU FEEL LIKE IT, BUT NOT GOOD ENOUGH TO BRING INTO YOUR WORLD?
SNAP
PRINCESS.
CLARK-- THAT'S RIDICULOUS. I TOOK YOU TO MEET MY BROTHER. YOU KNOW HOW I FEEL ABOUT YOU--
SNAP
DO I? I TOLD YOU I LOVED YOU MONTHS AGO. YOU STILL CAN'T SAY IT BACK. YOU'RE SO WRAPPED UP IN THIS ICY...WELL, IT DOESN'T MATTER NOW.
YOU'RE GOING TO HAVE TO KILL ME, YOU KNOW. IT'S JUST A MATTER OF TIME. I KNOW WHAT'S HAPPENING TO ME.
I DON'T WANT TO BECOME...THAT. I'D RATHER DIE.
NOW YOU ARE BEING FOOLISH--WE HAVEN'T EVEN TRIED TO--
I'M JUST GOING TO GET STRONGER. SOON, THINGS WILL START DYING IF THEY GET CLOSE TO ME.
YOU NEED TO DO IT NOW. WHILE YOU STILL CAN. WHILE I'LL STILL LET YOU.

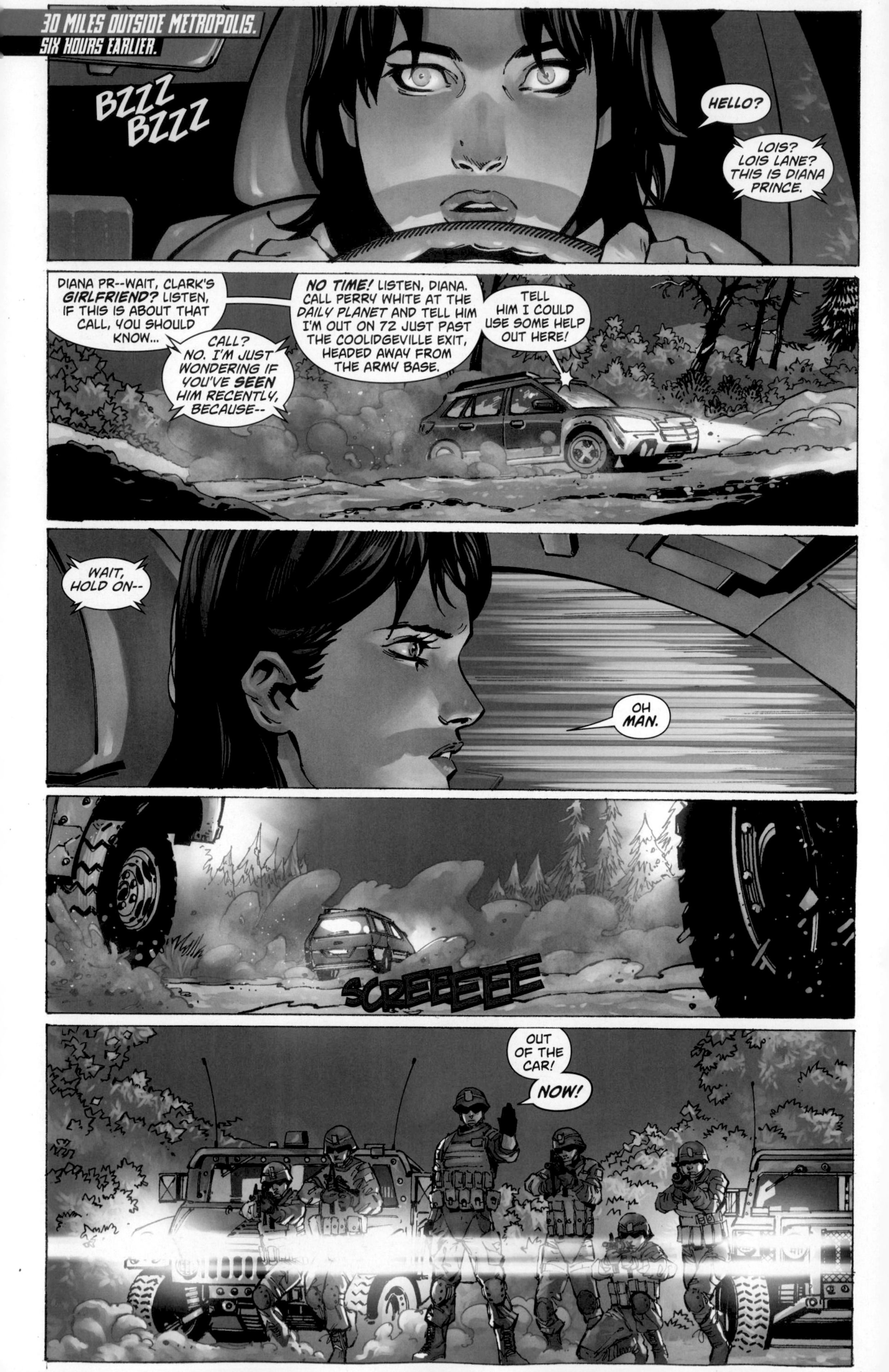

30 MILES OUTSIDE METROPOLIS.
SIX HOURS EARLIER.
BZZZ BZZZ
HELLO?
LOIS? LOIS LANE? THIS IS DIANA PRINCE.
DIANA PR--WAIT, CLARK'S GIRLFRIEND? LISTEN, IF THIS IS ABOUT THAT CALL, YOU SHOULD KNOW...
CALL? NO. I'M JUST WONDERING IF YOU'VE SEEN HIM RECENTLY, BECAUSE--
NO TIME! LISTEN, DIANA. CALL PERRY WHITE AT THE DAILY PLANET AND TELL HIM I'M OUT ON 72 JUST PAST THE COOLIDGEVILLE EXIT, HEADED AWAY FROM THE ARMY BASE.
TELL HIM I COULD USE SOME HELP OUT HERE!
WAIT, HOLD ON--
OH MAN.
SCREEEEEE
OUT OF THE CAR!
NOW!

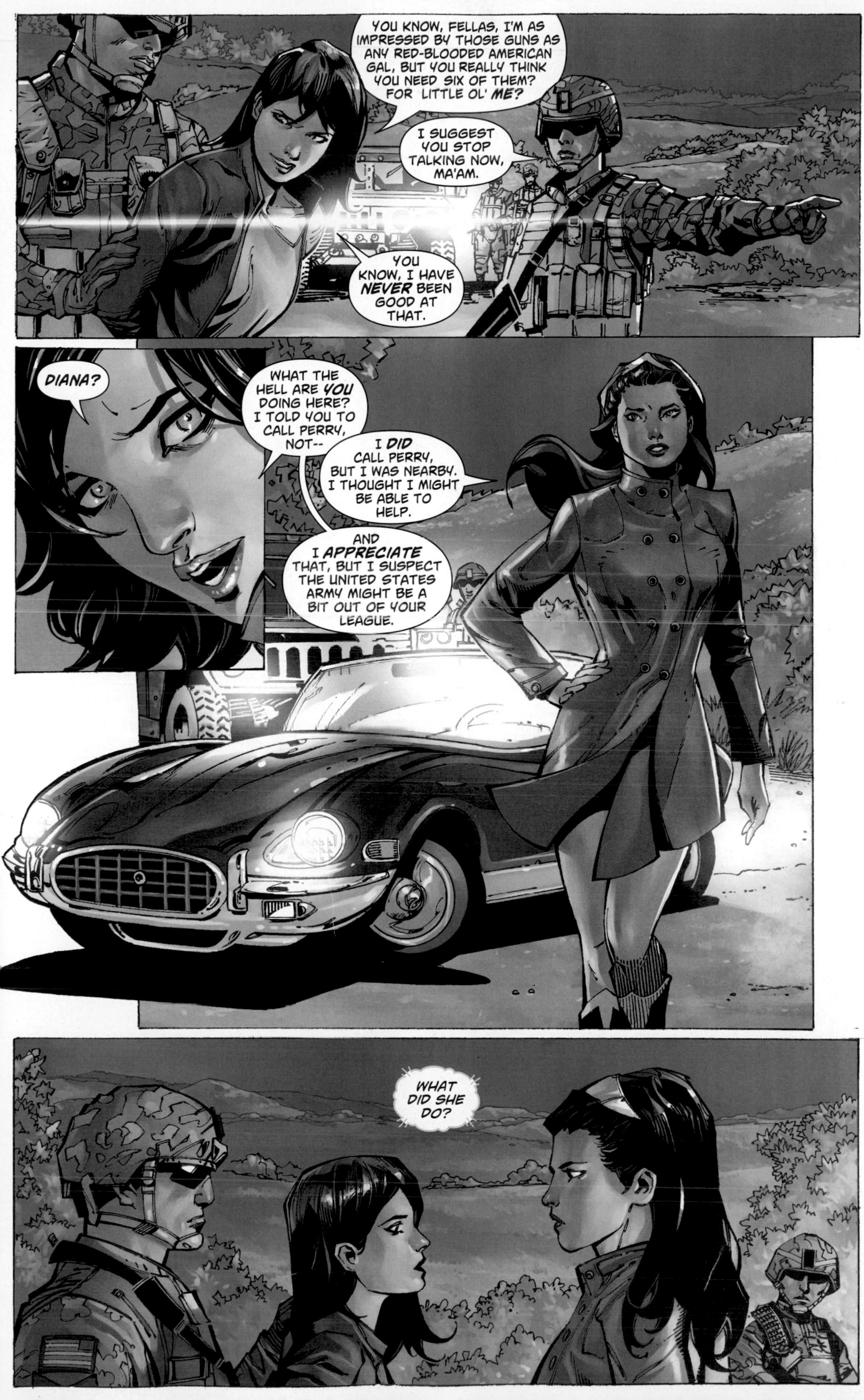

YOU KNOW, FELLAS, I'M AS IMPRESSED BY THOSE GUNS AS ANY RED-BLOODED AMERICAN GAL, BUT YOU REALLY THINK YOU NEED SIX OF THEM? FOR LITTLE OL' ME?
I SUGGEST YOU STOP TALKING NOW, MA'AM.
YOU KNOW, I HAVE NEVER BEEN GOOD AT THAT.
DIANA?
WHAT THE HELL ARE YOU DOING HERE? I TOLD YOU TO CALL PERRY, NOT--
I DID CALL PERRY, BUT I WAS NEARBY. I THOUGHT I MIGHT BE ABLE TO HELP.
AND I APPRECIATE THAT, BUT I SUSPECT THE UNITED STATES ARMY MIGHT BE A BIT OUT OF YOUR LEAGUE.
WHAT DID SHE DO?

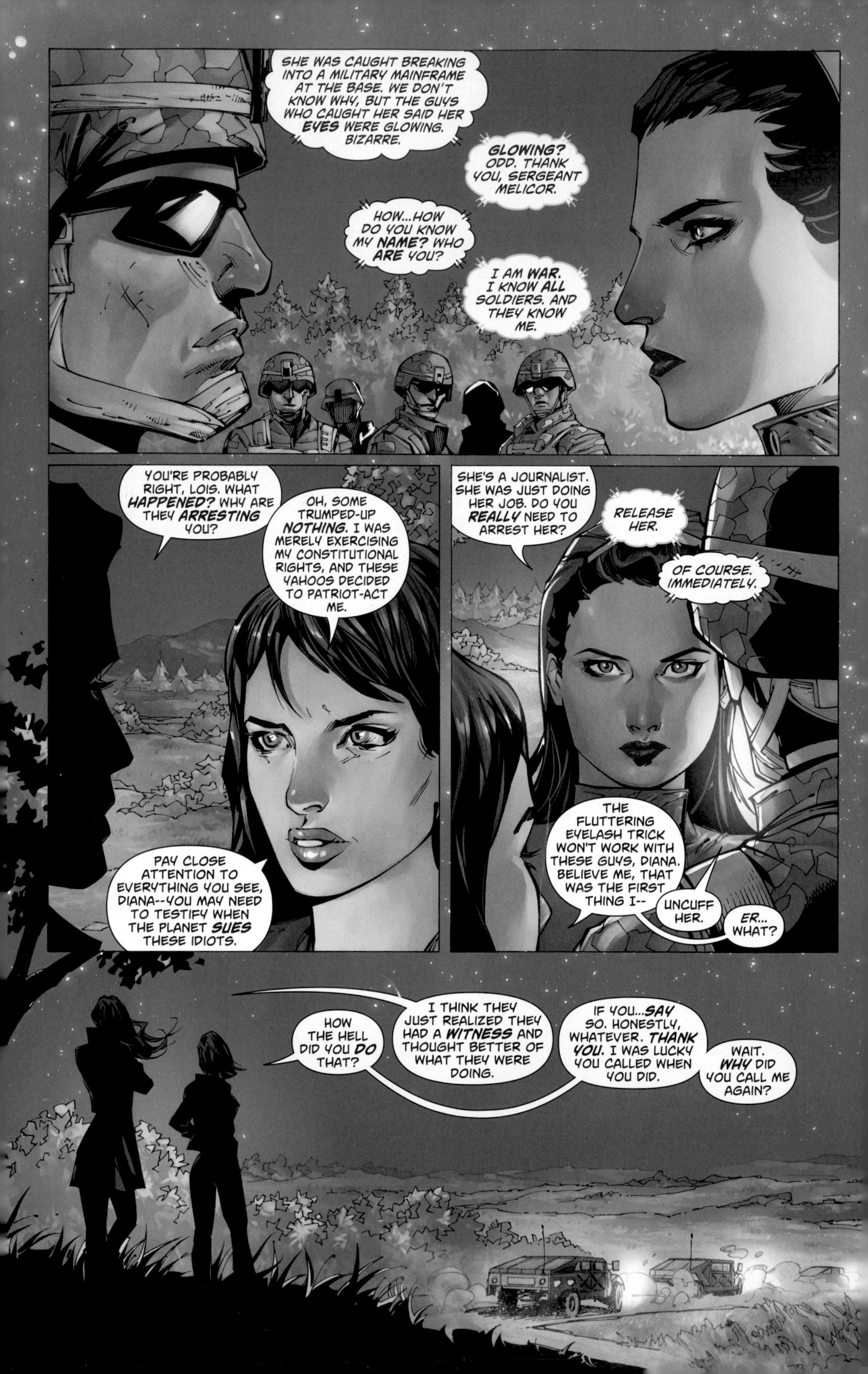
SHE WAS CAUGHT BREAKING INTO A MILITARY MAINFRAME AT THE BASE. WE DON'T KNOW WHY, BUT THE GUYS WHO CAUGHT HER SAID HER EYES WERE GLOWING. BIZARRE.
GLOWING? ODD. THANK YOU, SERGEANT MELICOR.
HOW...HOW DO YOU KNOW MY NAME? WHO ARE YOU?
I AM WAR. I KNOW ALL SOLDIERS. AND THEY KNOW ME.
YOU'RE PROBABLY RIGHT, LOIS. WHAT HAPPENED? WHY ARE THEY ARRESTING YOU?
OH, SOME TRUMPED-UP NOTHING. I WAS MERELY EXERCISING MY CONSTITUTIONAL RIGHTS, AND THESE YAHOOS DECIDED TO PATRIOT-ACT ME.
PAY CLOSE ATTENTION TO EVERYTHING YOU SEE, DIANA--YOU MAY NEED TO TESTIFY WHEN THE PLANET SUES THESE IDIOTS.
SHE'S A JOURNALIST. SHE WAS JUST DOING HER JOB. DO YOU REALLY NEED TO ARREST HER?
RELEASE HER.
OF COURSE. IMMEDIATELY.
THE FLUTTERING EYELASH TRICK WON'T WORK WITH THESE GUYS, DIANA. BELIEVE ME, THAT WAS THE FIRST THING I--
UNCUFF HER.
ER... WHAT?
HOW THE HELL DID YOU DO THAT?
I THINK THEY JUST REALIZED THEY HAD A WITNESS AND THOUGHT BETTER OF WHAT THEY WERE DOING.
IF YOU...SAY SO. HONESTLY, WHATEVER. THANK YOU. I WAS LUCKY YOU CALLED WHEN YOU DID.
WAIT. WHY DID YOU CALL ME AGAIN?

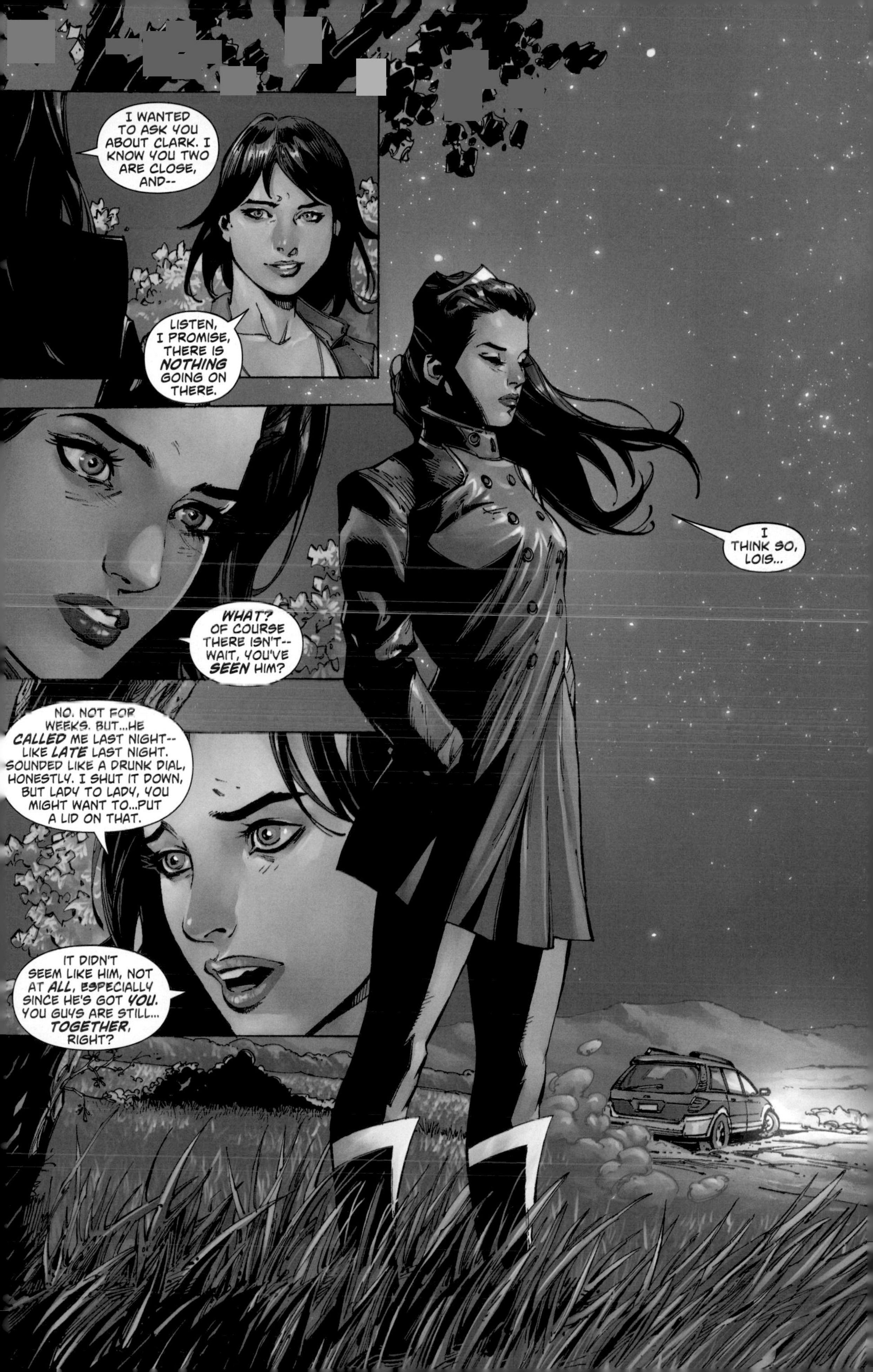
I WANTED TO ASK YOU ABOUT CLARK. I KNOW YOU TWO ARE CLOSE, AND--
LISTEN, I PROMISE, THERE IS NOTHING GOING ON THERE.
WHAT? OF COURSE THERE ISN'T-- WAIT, YOU'VE SEEN HIM?
NO. NOT FOR WEEKS. BUT...HE CALLED ME LAST NIGHT-- LIKE LATE LAST NIGHT. SOUNDED LIKE A DRUNK DIAL, HONESTLY. I SHUT IT DOWN, BUT LADY TO LADY, YOU MIGHT WANT TO...PUT A LID ON THAT.
IT DIDN'T SEEM LIKE HIM, NOT AT ALL, ESPECIALLY SINCE HE'S GOT YOU. YOU GUYS ARE STILL... TOGETHER, RIGHT?
I THINK SO, LOIS...

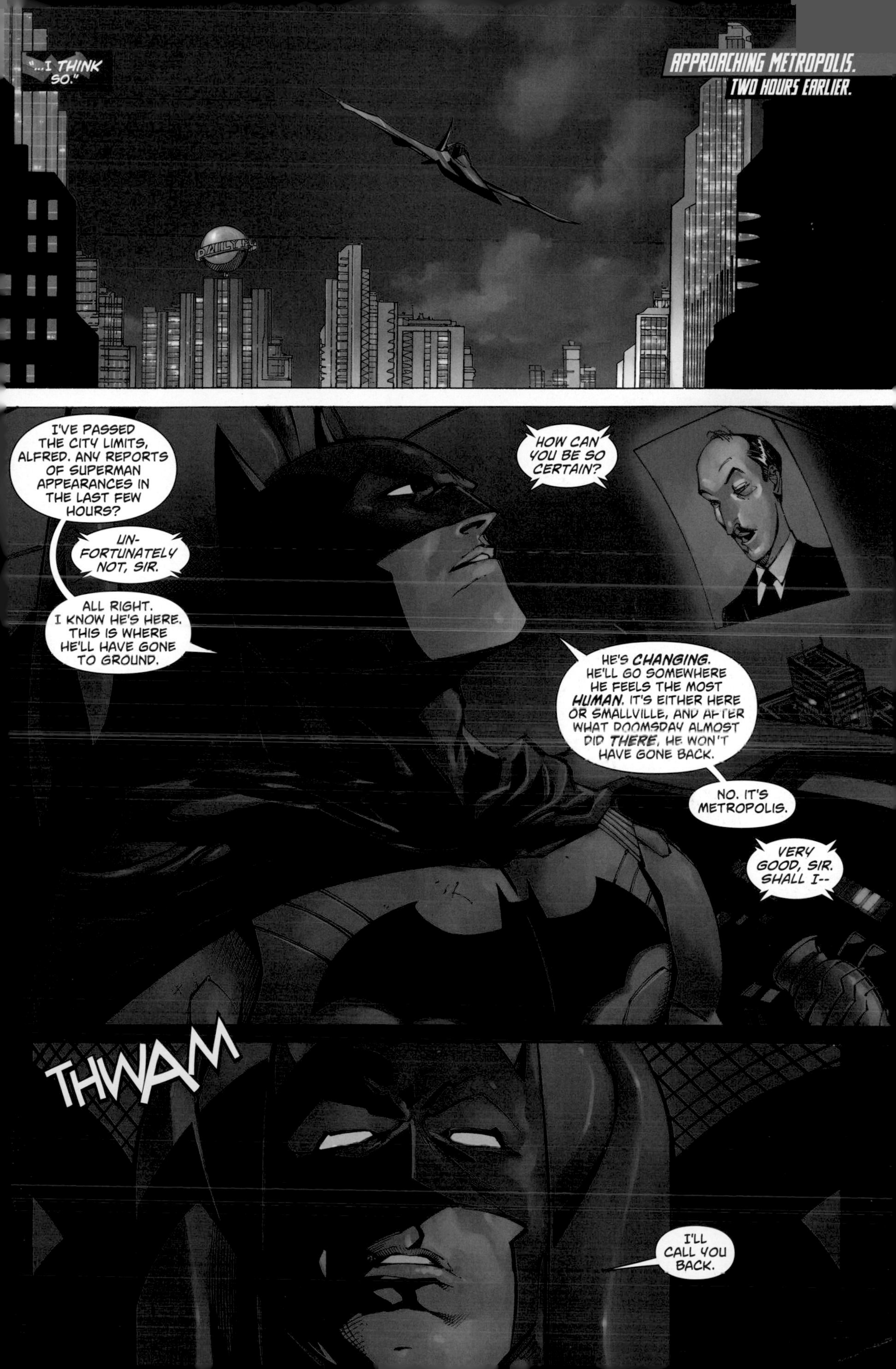
"...I THINK SO."
APPROACHING METROPOLIS.
TWO HOURS EARLIER.
I'VE PASSED THE CITY LIMITS, ALFRED. ANY REPORTS OF SUPERMAN APPEARANCES IN THE LAST FEW HOURS?
UN-FORTUNATELY NOT, SIR.
ALL RIGHT. I KNOW HE'S HERE. THIS IS WHERE HE'LL HAVE GONE TO GROUND.
HOW CAN YOU BE SO CERTAIN?
HE'S CHANGING. HE'LL GO SOMEWHERE HE FEELS THE MOST HUMAN. IT'S EITHER HERE OR SMALLVILLE, AND AFTER WHAT DOOMSDAY ALMOST DID THERE, HE WON'T HAVE GONE BACK.
NO. IT'S METROPOLIS.
VERY GOOD, SIR. SHALL I--
THWAM
I'LL CALL YOU BACK.

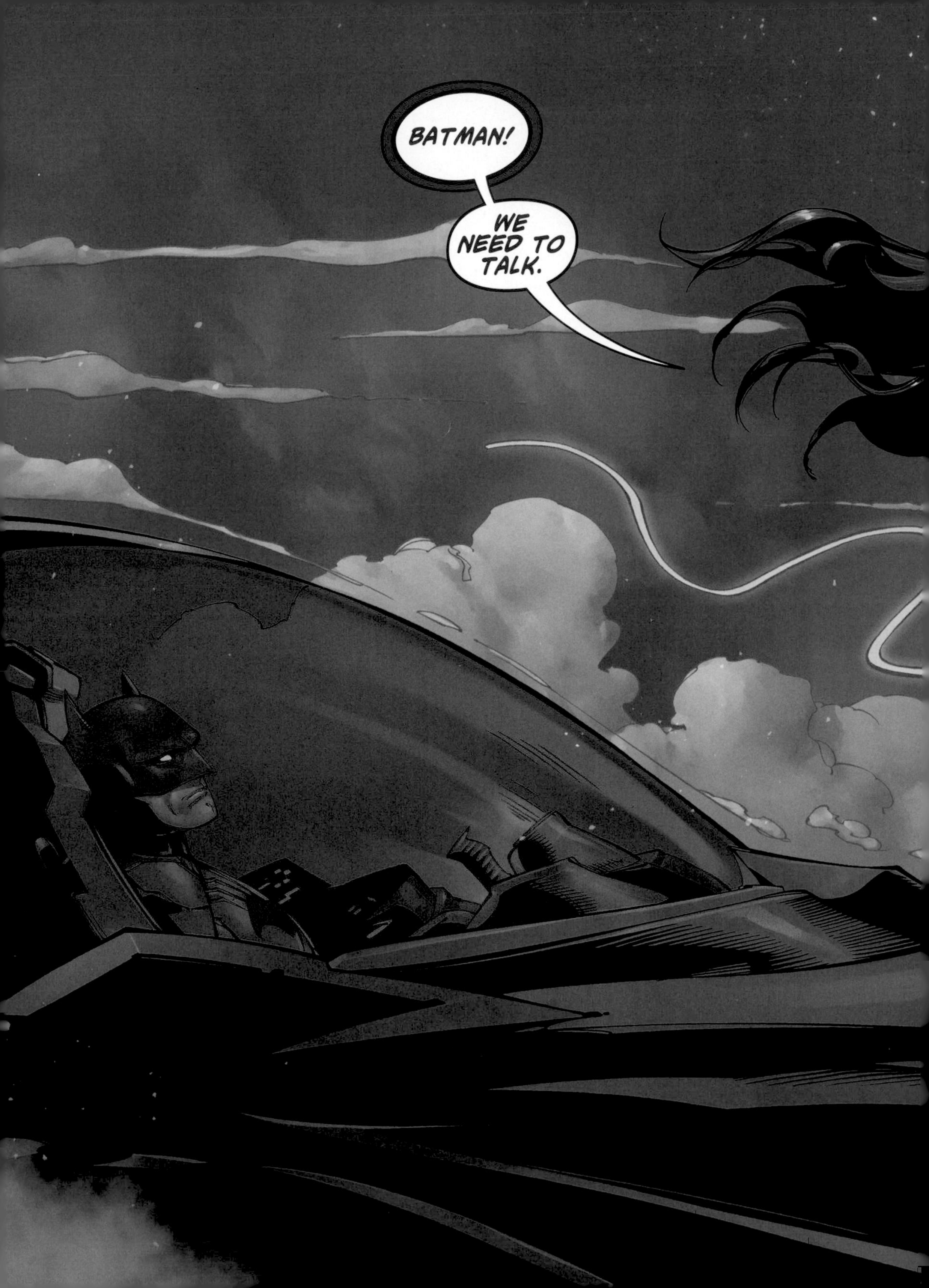
BATMAN!
WE NEED TO TALK.

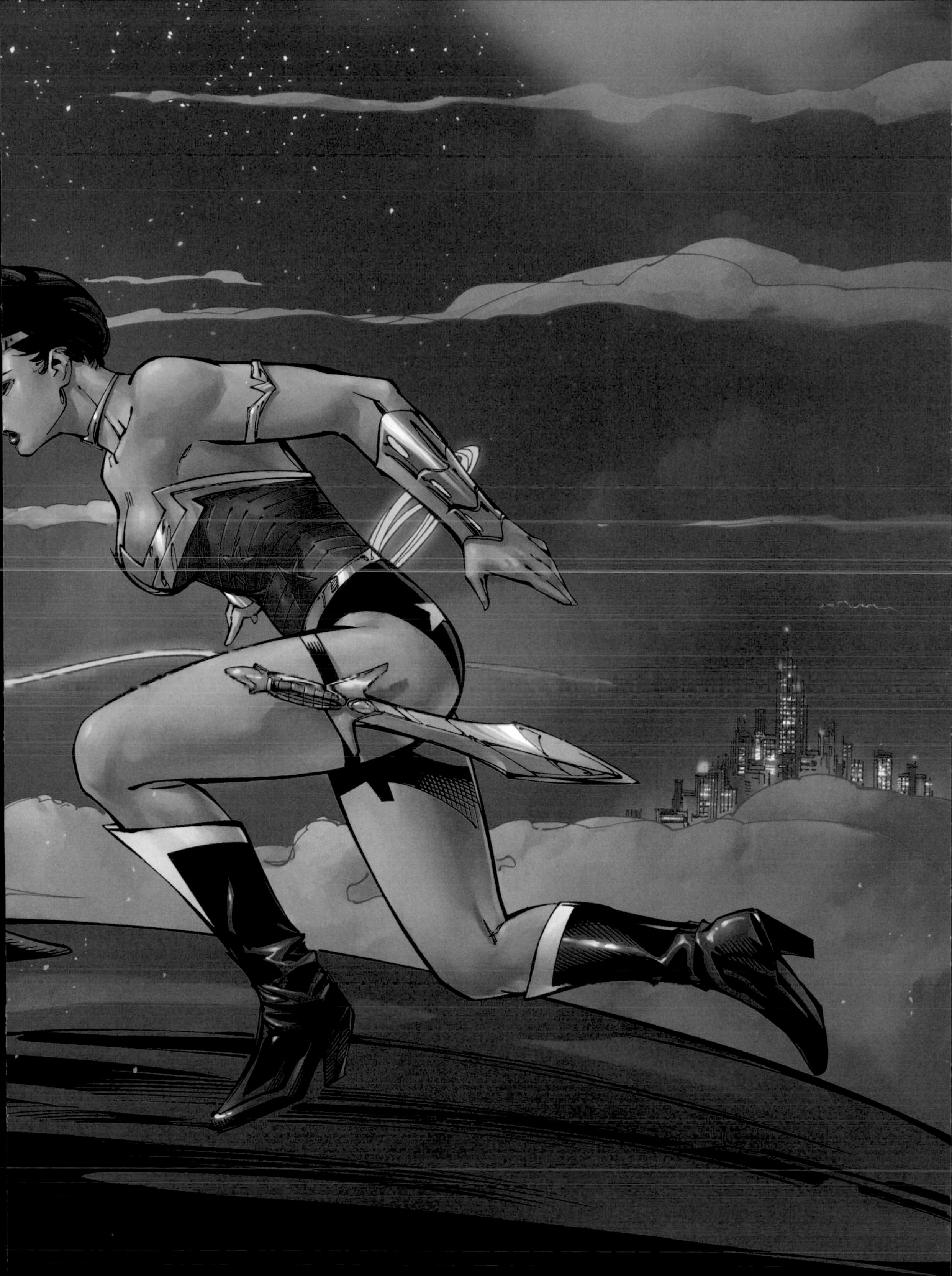

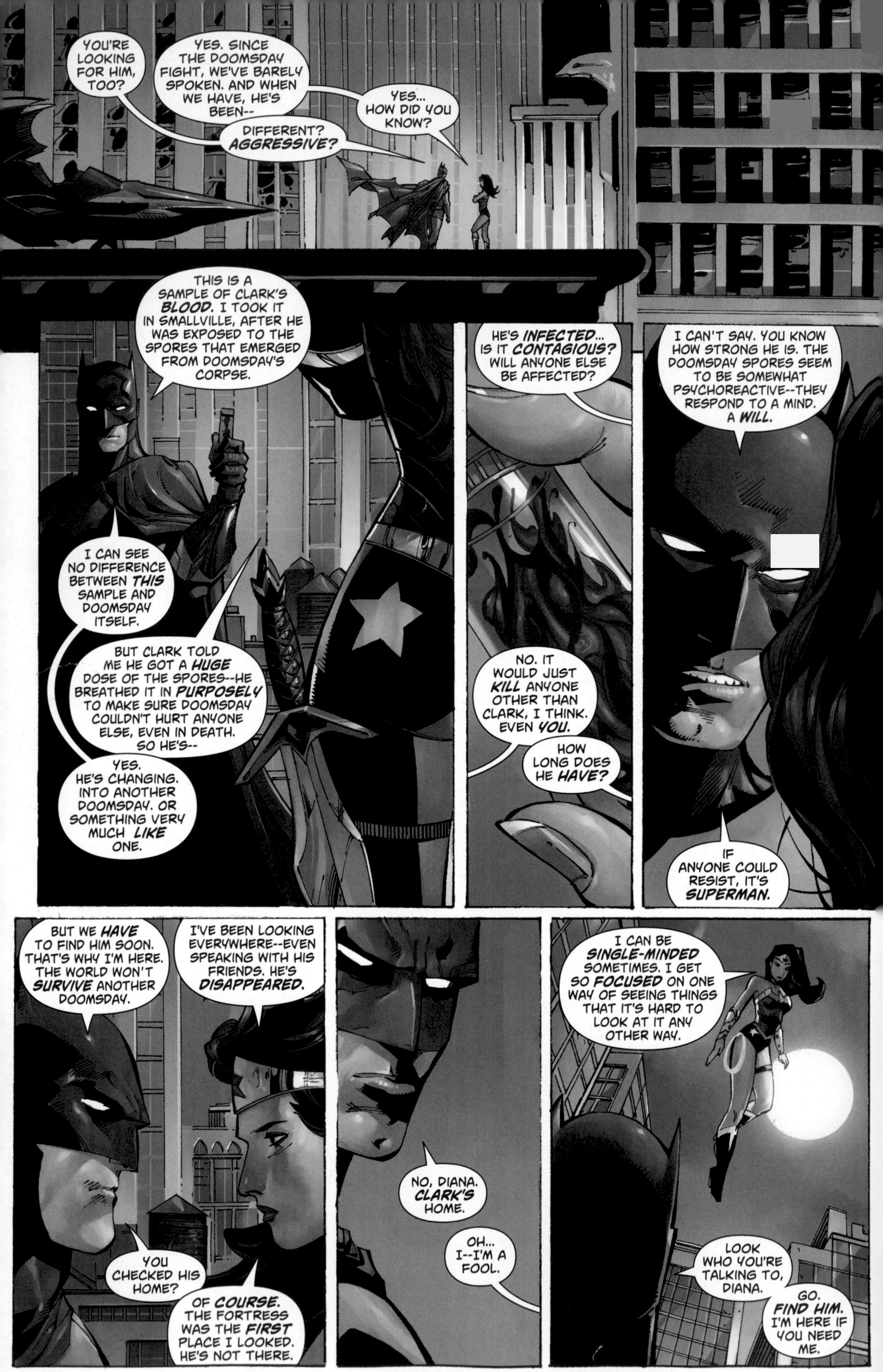

YOU'RE LOOKING FOR HIM, TOO?
YES. SINCE THE DOOMSDAY FIGHT, WE'VE BARELY SPOKEN. AND WHEN WE HAVE, HE'S BEEN--
DIFFERENT? AGGRESSIVE?
YES... HOW DID YOU KNOW?
THIS IS A SAMPLE OF CLARK'S BLOOD. I TOOK IT IN SMALLVILLE, AFTER HE WAS EXPOSED TO THE SPORES THAT EMERGED FROM DOOMSDAY'S CORPSE.
I CAN SEE NO DIFFERENCE BETWEEN THIS SAMPLE AND DOOMSDAY ITSELF.
BUT CLARK TOLD ME HE GOT A HUGE DOSE OF THE SPORES--HE BREATHED IT IN PURPOSELY TO MAKE SURE DOOMSDAY COULDN'T HURT ANYONE ELSE, EVEN IN DEATH. SO HE'S--
YES. HE'S CHANGING. INTO ANOTHER DOOMSDAY. OR SOMETHING VERY MUCH LIKE ONE.
HE'S INFECTED... IS IT CONTAGIOUS? WILL ANYONE ELSE BE AFFECTED?
NO. IT WOULD JUST KILL ANYONE OTHER THAN CLARK, I THINK. EVEN YOU.
HOW LONG DOES HE HAVE?
I CAN'T SAY. YOU KNOW HOW STRONG HE IS. THE DOOMSDAY SPORES SEEM TO BE SOMEWHAT PSYCHOREACTIVE--THEY RESPOND TO A MIND. A WILL.
IF ANYONE COULD RESIST, IT'S SUPERMAN.
BUT WE HAVE TO FIND HIM SOON. THAT'S WHY I'M HERE. THE WORLD WON'T SURVIVE ANOTHER DOOMSDAY.
I'VE BEEN LOOKING EVERYWHERE--EVEN SPEAKING WITH HIS FRIENDS. HE'S DISAPPEARED.
YOU CHECKED HIS HOME?
OF COURSE. THE FORTRESS WAS THE FIRST PLACE I LOOKED. HE'S NOT THERE.
NO, DIANA. CLARK'S HOME.
OH... I--I'M A FOOL.
I CAN BE SINGLE-MINDED SOMETIMES. I GET SO FOCUSED ON ONE WAY OF SEEING THINGS THAT IT'S HARD TO LOOK AT IT ANY OTHER WAY.
LOOK WHO YOU'RE TALKING TO, DIANA.
GO. FIND HIM. I'M HERE IF YOU NEED ME.

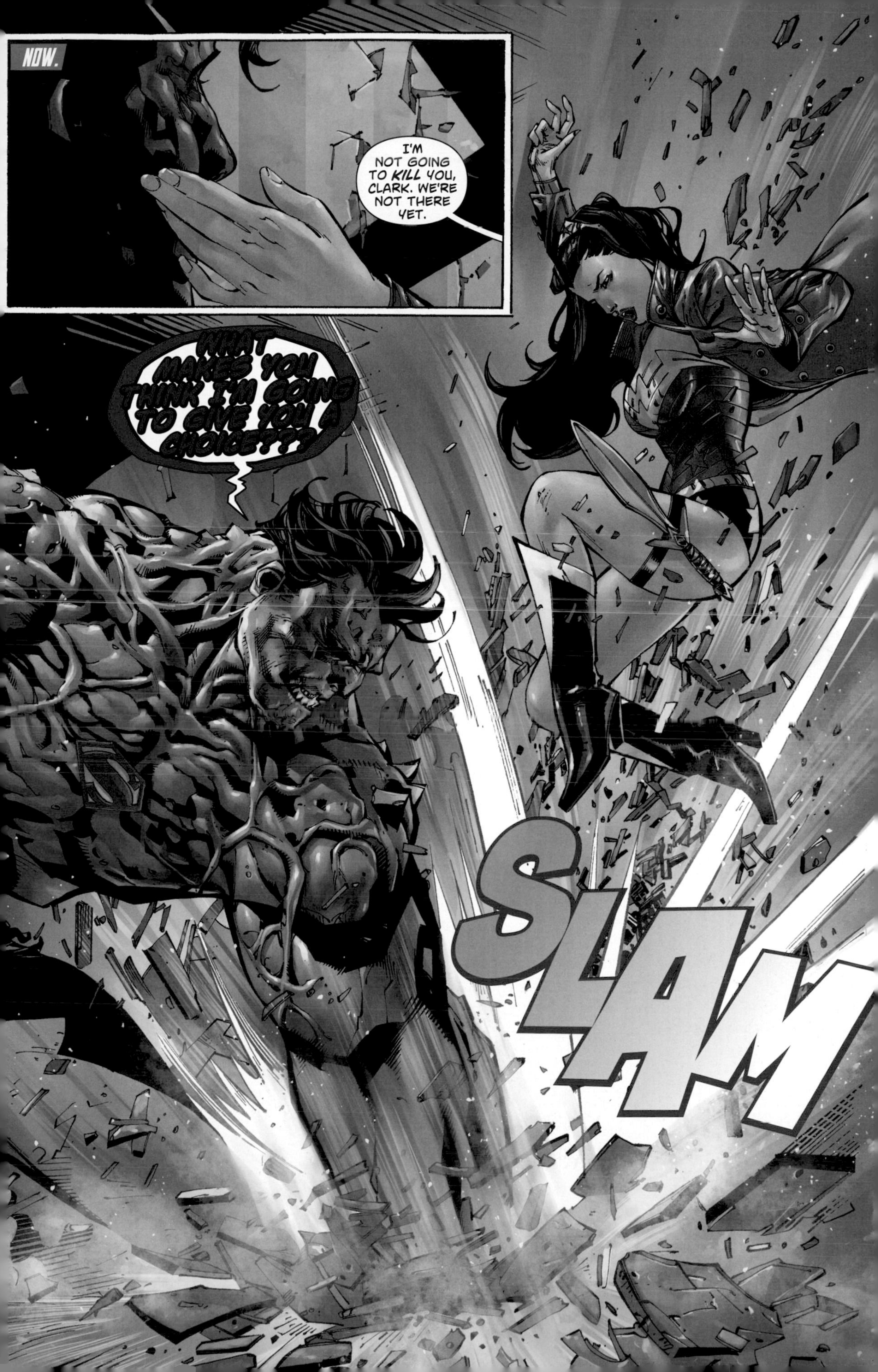
NOW.
I'M NOT GOING TO KILL YOU, CLARK. WE'RE NOT THERE YET.
WHAT MAKES YOU THINK I'M GOING TO GIVE YOU A CHOICE???
SLAM

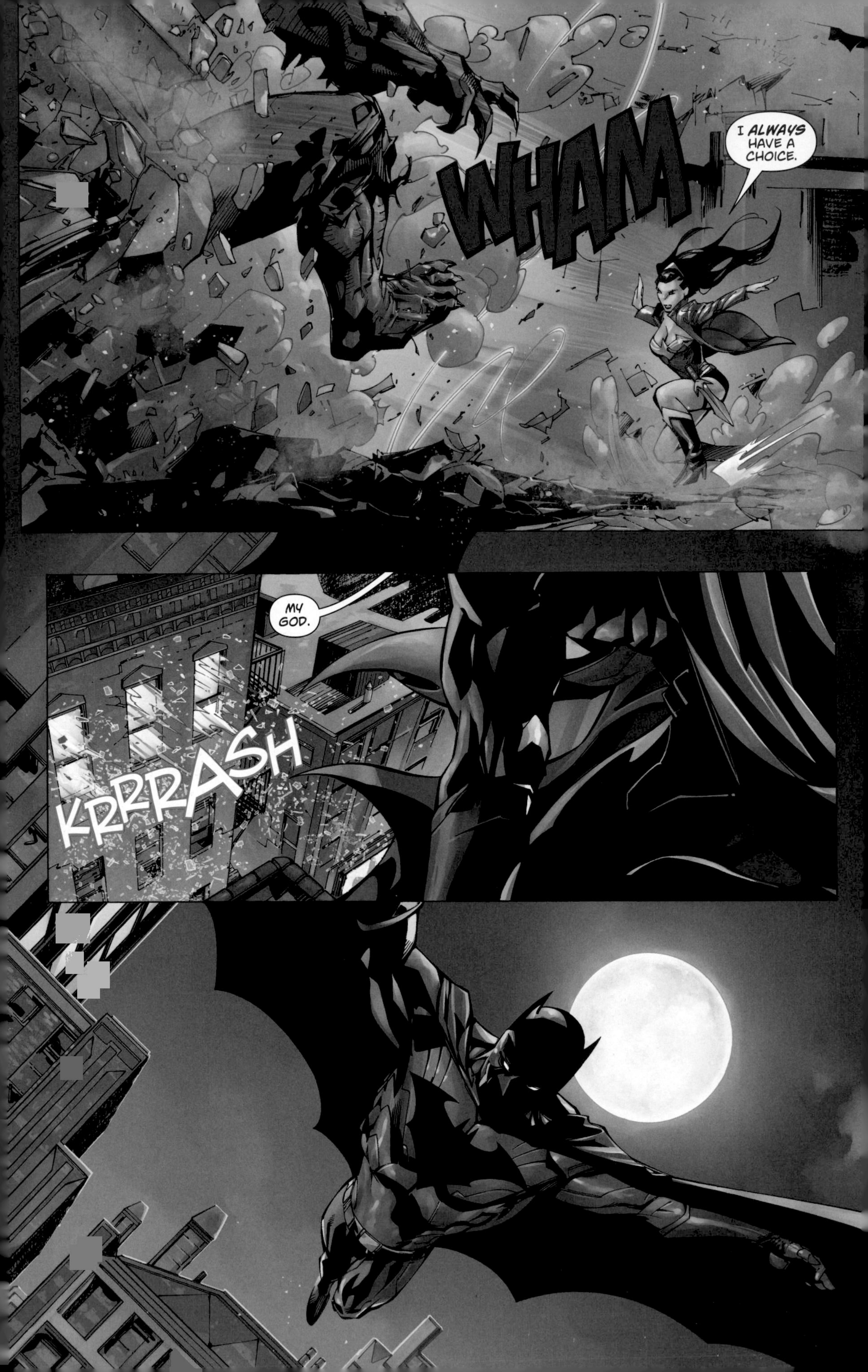
WHAM
I ALWAYS HAVE A CHOICE.
MY GOD.
KRRRASH

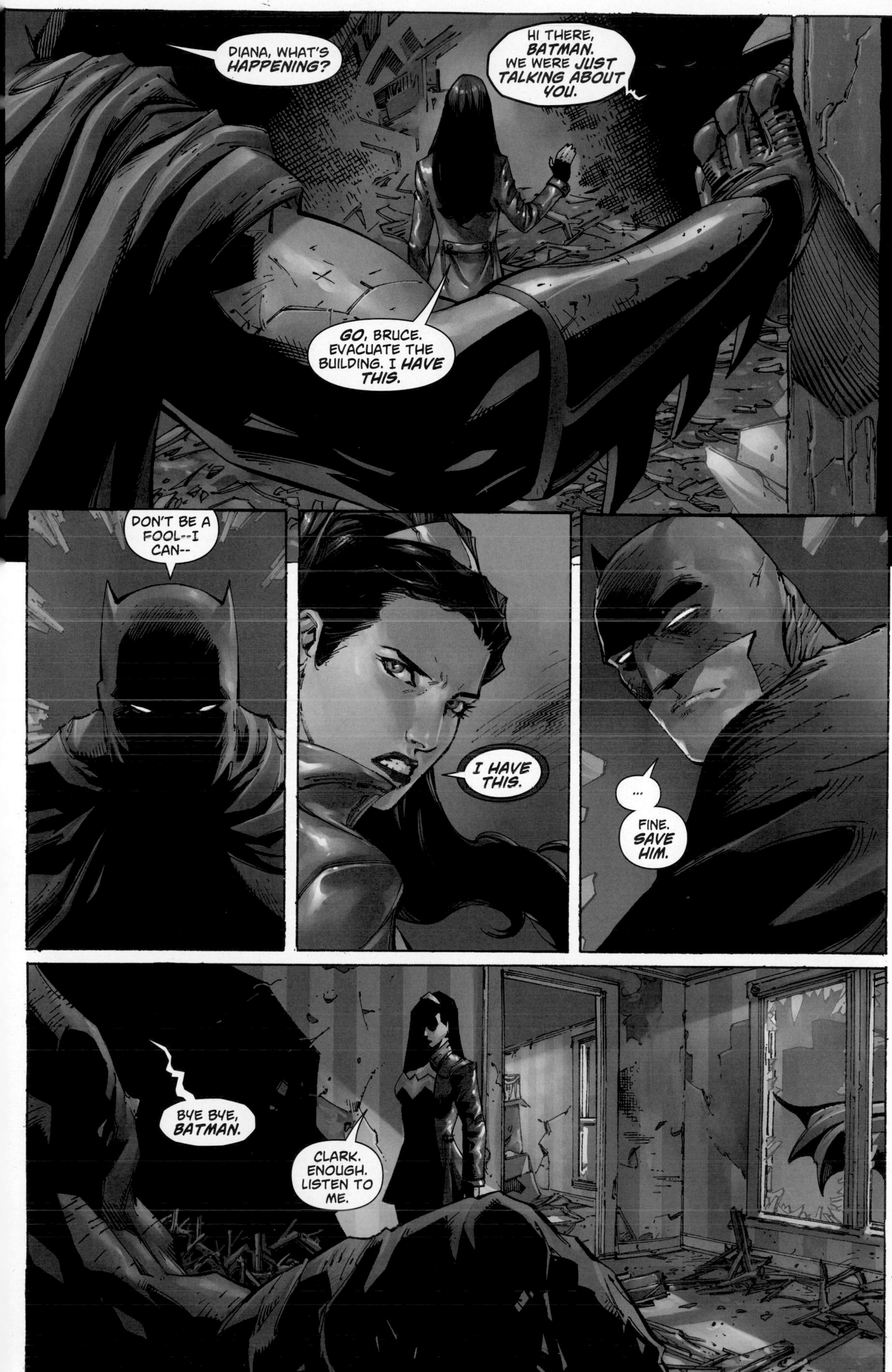
DIANA, WHAT'S HAPPENING?
HI THERE, BATMAN. WE WERE JUST TALKING ABOUT YOU.
GO, BRUCE. EVACUATE THE BUILDING. I HAVE THIS.
DON'T BE A FOOL--I CAN--
I HAVE THIS.
...
FINE. SAVE HIM.
BYE BYE, BATMAN.
CLARK. ENOUGH. LISTEN TO ME.

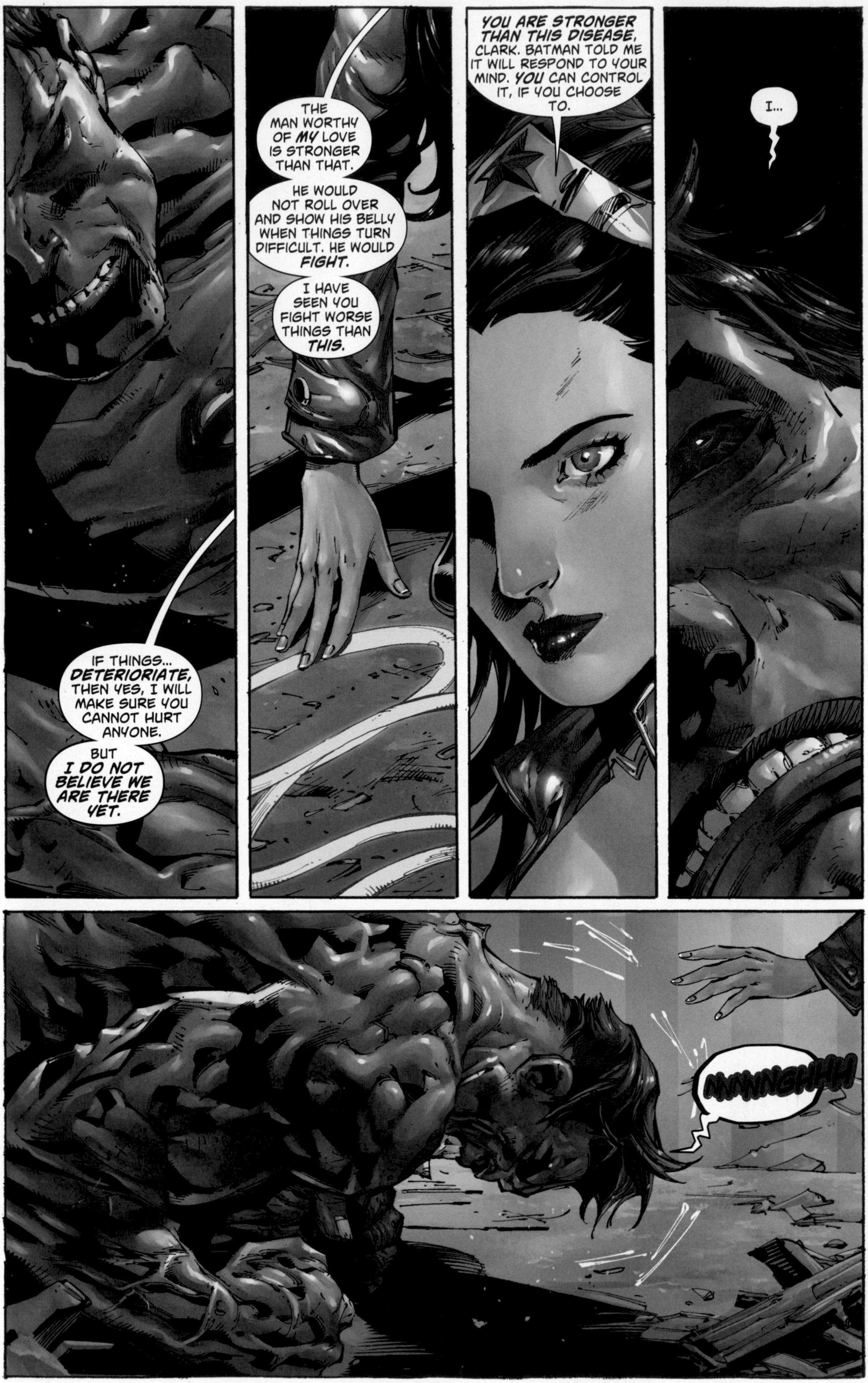
THE MAN WORTHY OF MY LOVE IS STRONGER THAN THAT.
HE WOULD NOT ROLL OVER AND SHOW HIS BELLY WHEN THINGS TURN DIFFICULT. HE WOULD FIGHT.
I HAVE SEEN YOU FIGHT WORSE THINGS THAN THIS.
IF THINGS... DETERIORIATE, THEN YES, I WILL MAKE SURE YOU CANNOT HURT ANYONE.
BUT I DO NOT BELIEVE WE ARE THERE YET.
YOU ARE STRONGER THAN THIS DISEASE, CLARK. BATMAN TOLD ME IT WILL RESPOND TO YOUR MIND. YOU CAN CONTROL IT, IF YOU CHOOSE TO.
I...
NNNNGHHH

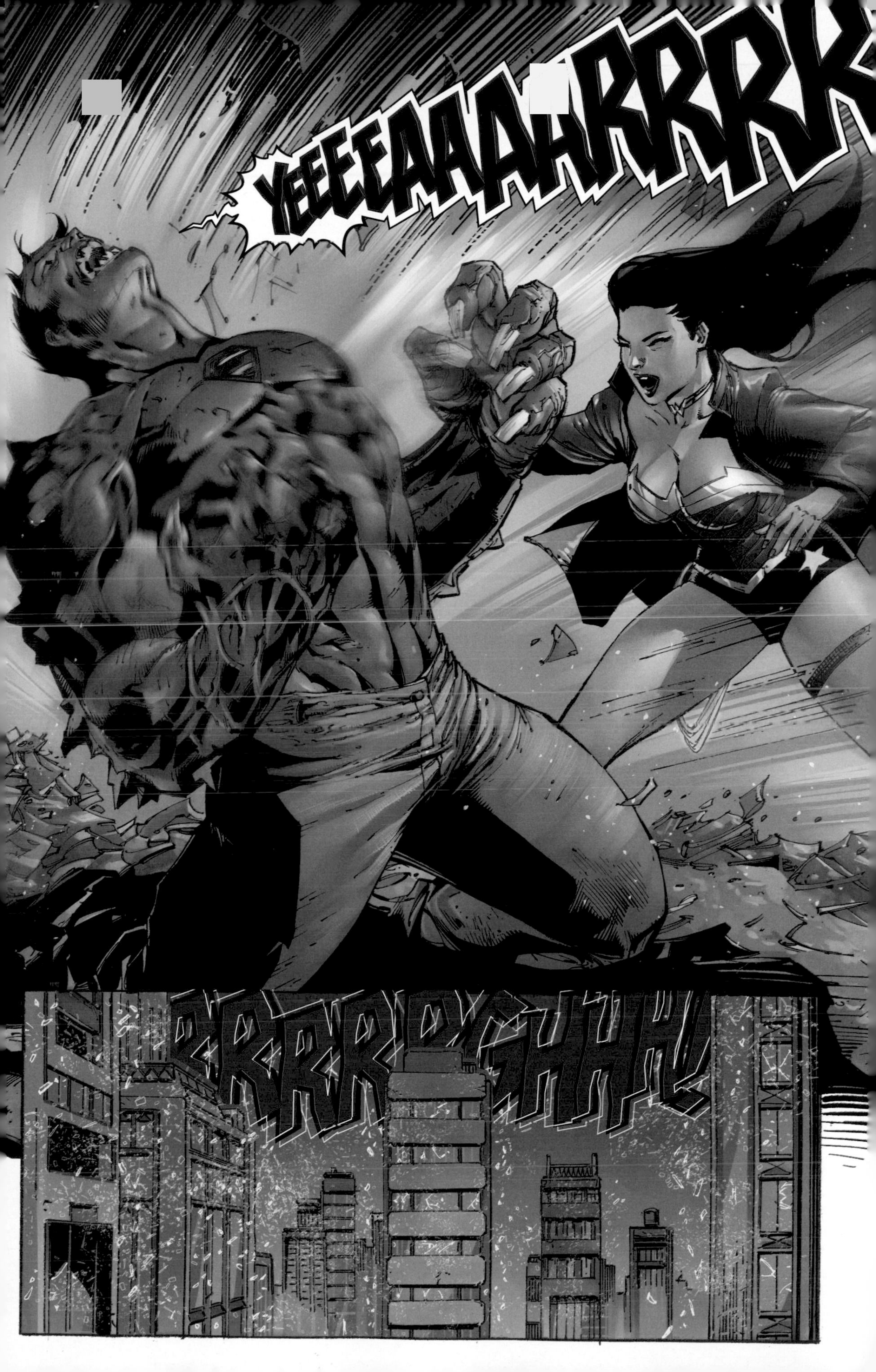
YEEEEAAAARRRK

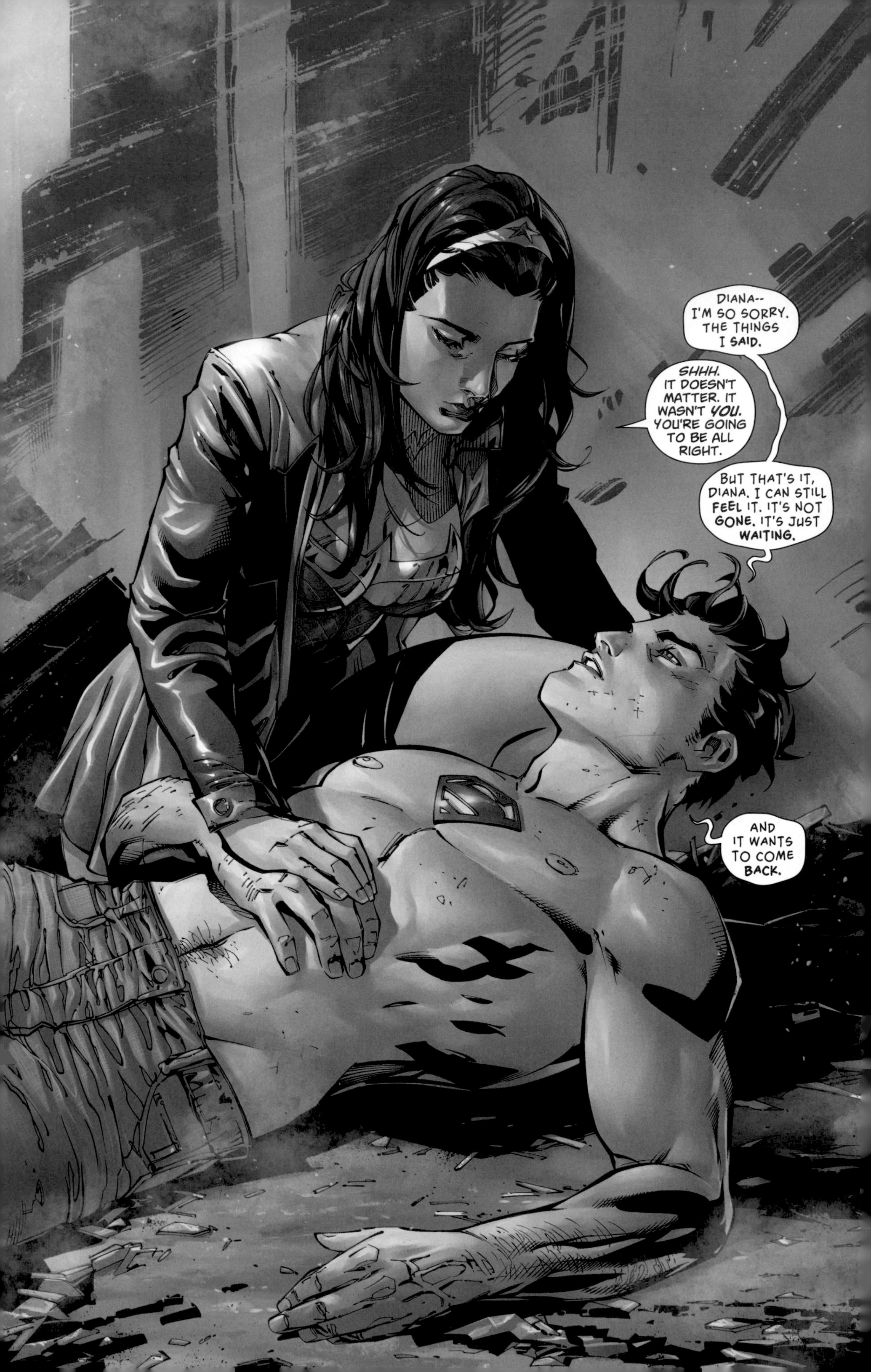
DIANA-- I'M SO SORRY. THE THINGS I SAID.
SHHH. IT DOESN'T MATTER. IT WASN'T YOU. YOU'RE GOING TO BE ALL RIGHT.
BUT THAT'S IT, DIANA. I CAN STILL FEEL IT. IT'S NOT GONE. IT'S JUST WAITING.
AND IT WANTS TO COME BACK.

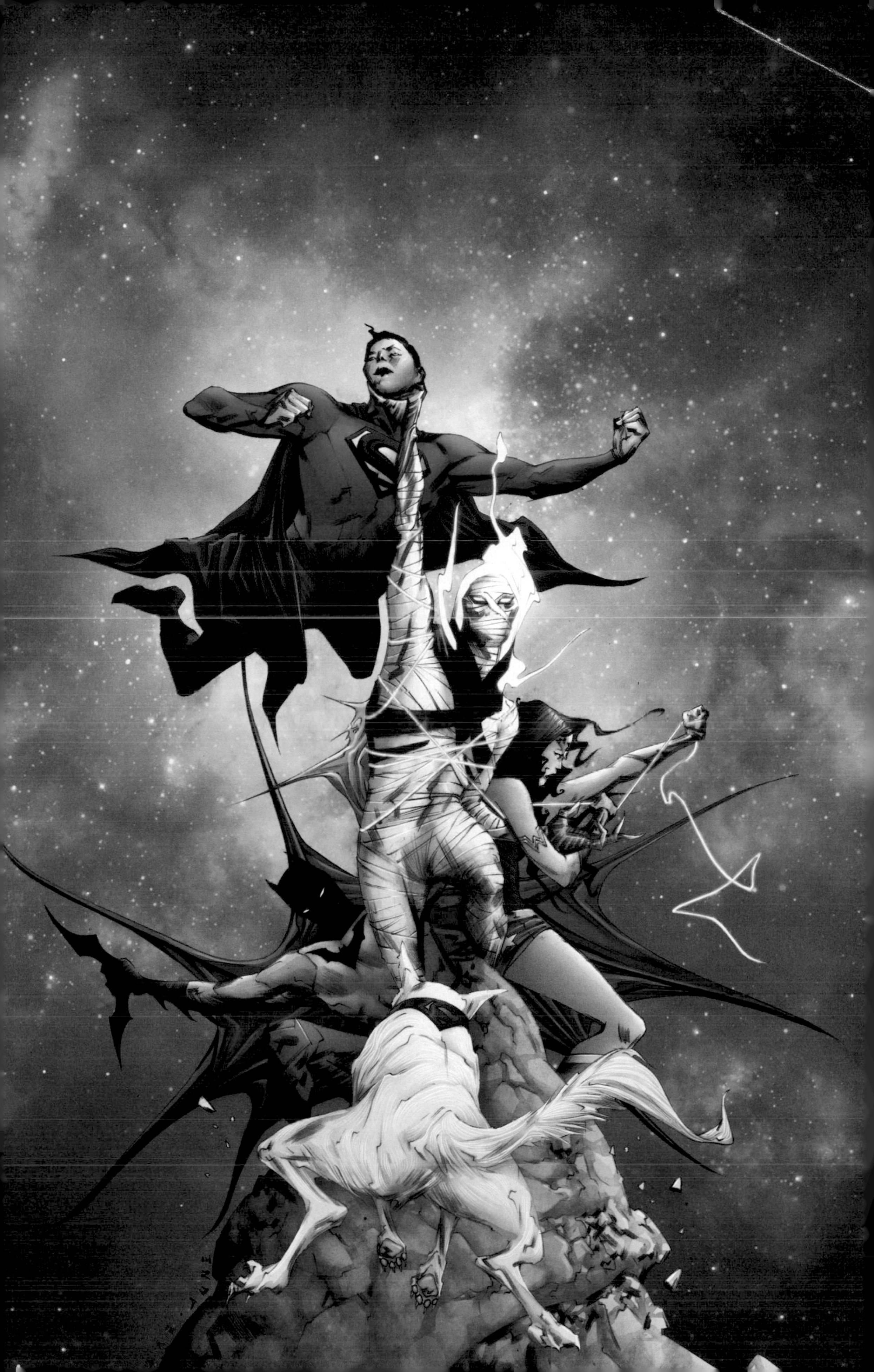

SUPERMAN

DOOMED

[INFECTED] chapter 3

"DANGER ZONE"

STORY
GREG PAK

PENCILS
KARL KERSCHL, TOM DERENICK & DANIEL SAMPERE

INKS
**KARL KERSCHL, VICENTE CIFUENTES, MARC DEERING,
WAYNE FAUCHER & DANIEL SAMPERE**

COLORS
HI-FI

LETTERS
ROB LEIGH

COVER
JAE LEE AND JUNE CHUNG

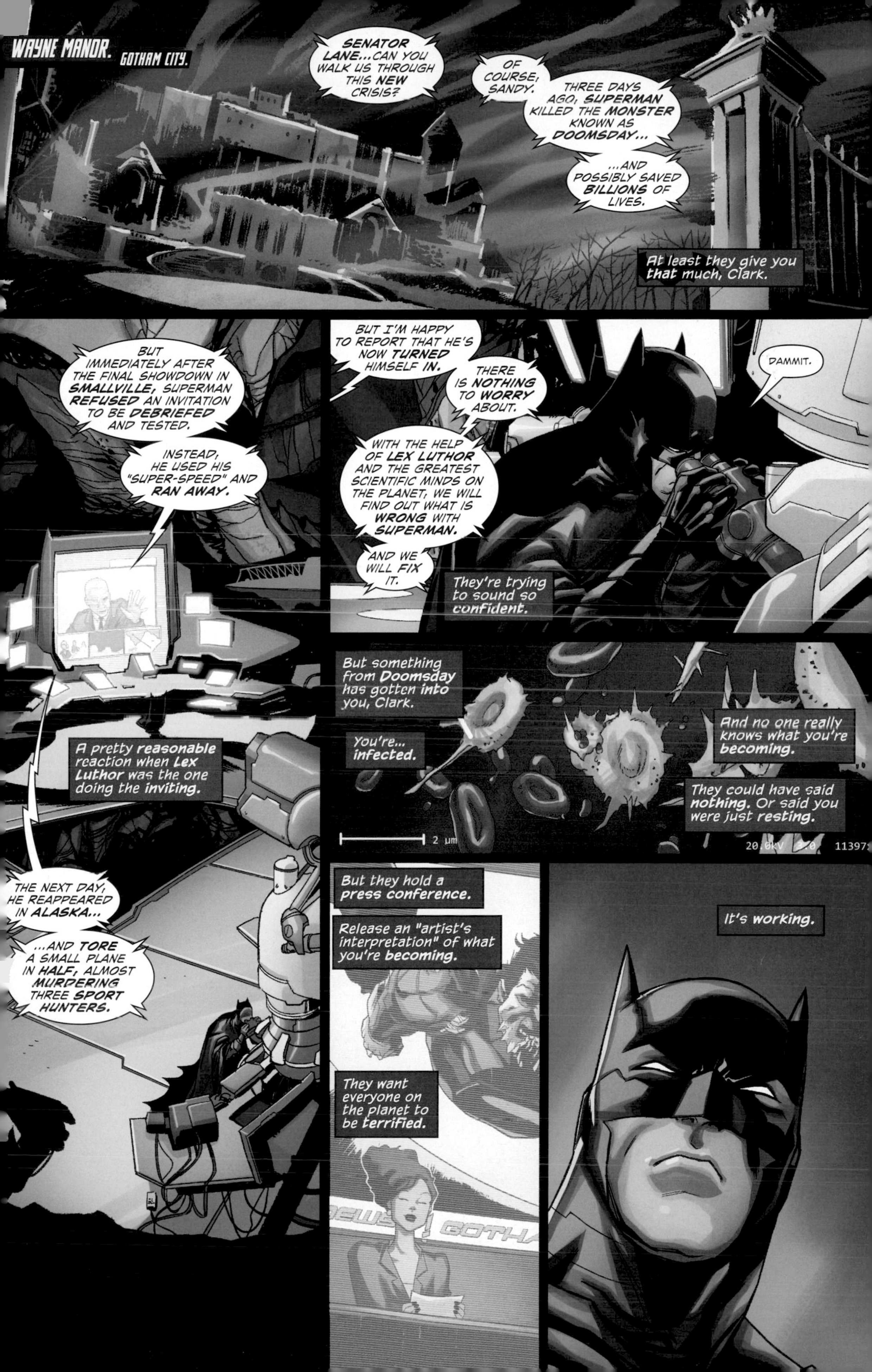
WAYNE MANOR. GOTHAM CITY.
SENATOR LANE...CAN YOU WALK US THROUGH THIS NEW CRISIS?
OF COURSE, SANDY.
THREE DAYS AGO, SUPERMAN KILLED THE MONSTER KNOWN AS DOOMSDAY...
...AND POSSIBLY SAVED BILLIONS OF LIVES.
At least they give you that much, Clark.
BUT IMMEDIATELY AFTER THE FINAL SHOWDOWN IN SMALLVILLE, SUPERMAN REFUSED AN INVITATION TO BE DEBRIEFED AND TESTED.
INSTEAD, HE USED HIS "SUPER-SPEED" AND RAN AWAY.
A pretty reasonable reaction when Lex Luthor was the one doing the inviting.
THE NEXT DAY, HE REAPPEARED IN ALASKA...
...AND TORE A SMALL PLANE IN HALF, ALMOST MURDERING THREE SPORT HUNTERS.
BUT I'M HAPPY TO REPORT THAT HE'S NOW TURNED HIMSELF IN.
THERE IS NOTHING TO WORRY ABOUT.
WITH THE HELP OF LEX LUTHOR AND THE GREATEST SCIENTIFIC MINDS ON THE PLANET, WE WILL FIND OUT WHAT IS WRONG WITH SUPERMAN.
AND WE WILL FIX IT.
They're trying to sound so confident.
DAMMIT.
But something from Doomsday has gotten into you, Clark.
You're... infected.
And no one really knows what you're becoming.
They could have said nothing. Or said you were just resting.
2 µm
But they hold a press conference.
Release an "artist's interpretation" of what you're becoming.
They want everyone on the planet to be terrified.
It's working.

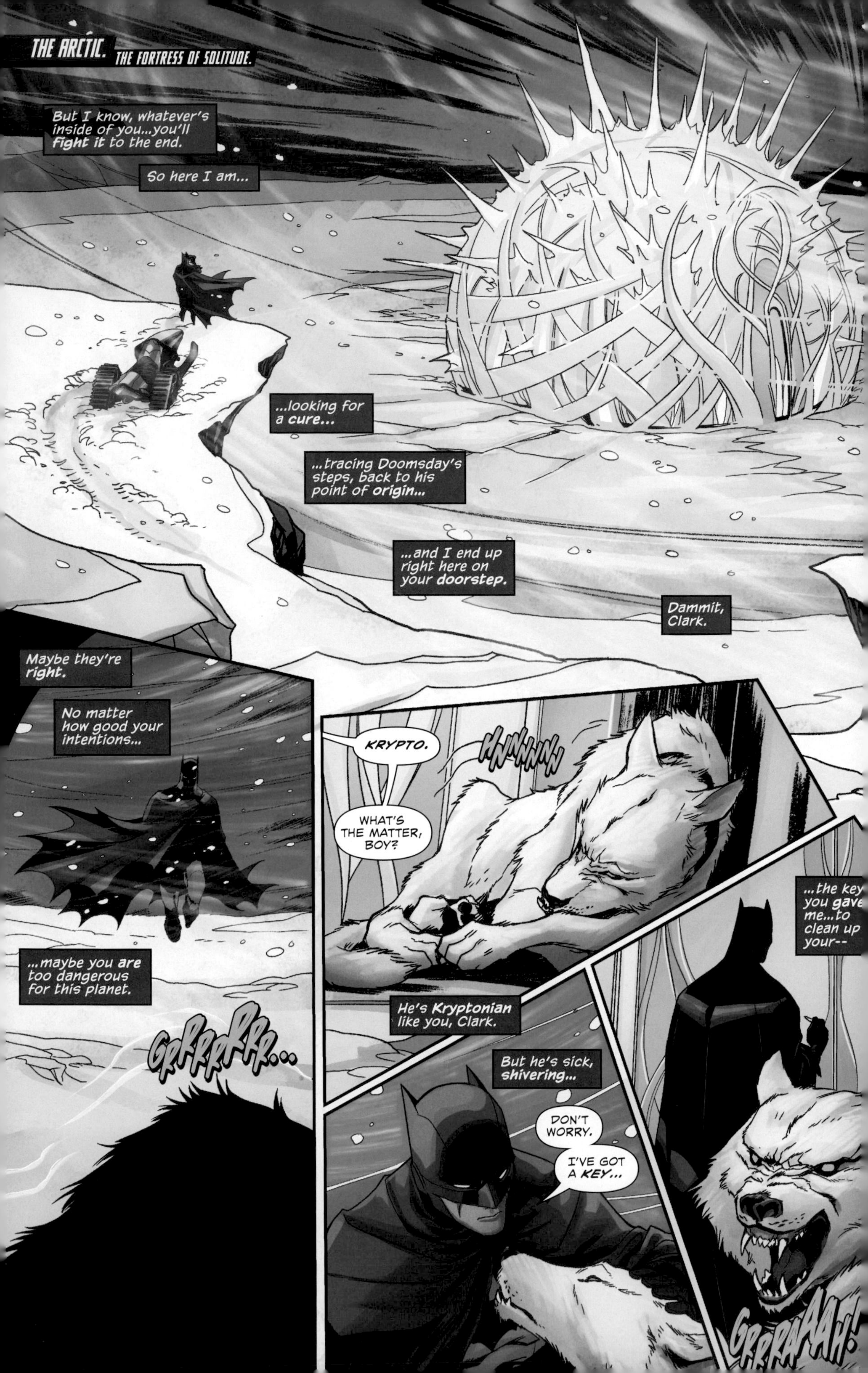
THE ARCTIC. THE FORTRESS OF SOLITUDE.
But I know, whatever's inside of you...you'll fight it to the end.
So here I am...
...looking for a cure...
...tracing Doomsday's steps, back to his point of origin...
...and I end up right here on your doorstep.
Dammit, Clark.
Maybe they're right.
No matter how good your intentions...
...maybe you are too dangerous for this planet.
GRRRRRR...
KRYPTO.
HNNNNNN
WHAT'S THE MATTER, BOY?
He's Kryptonian like you, Clark.
But he's sick, shivering...
DON'T WORRY.
I'VE GOT A KEY...
...the key you gave me...to clean up your--
GRRAAAH!

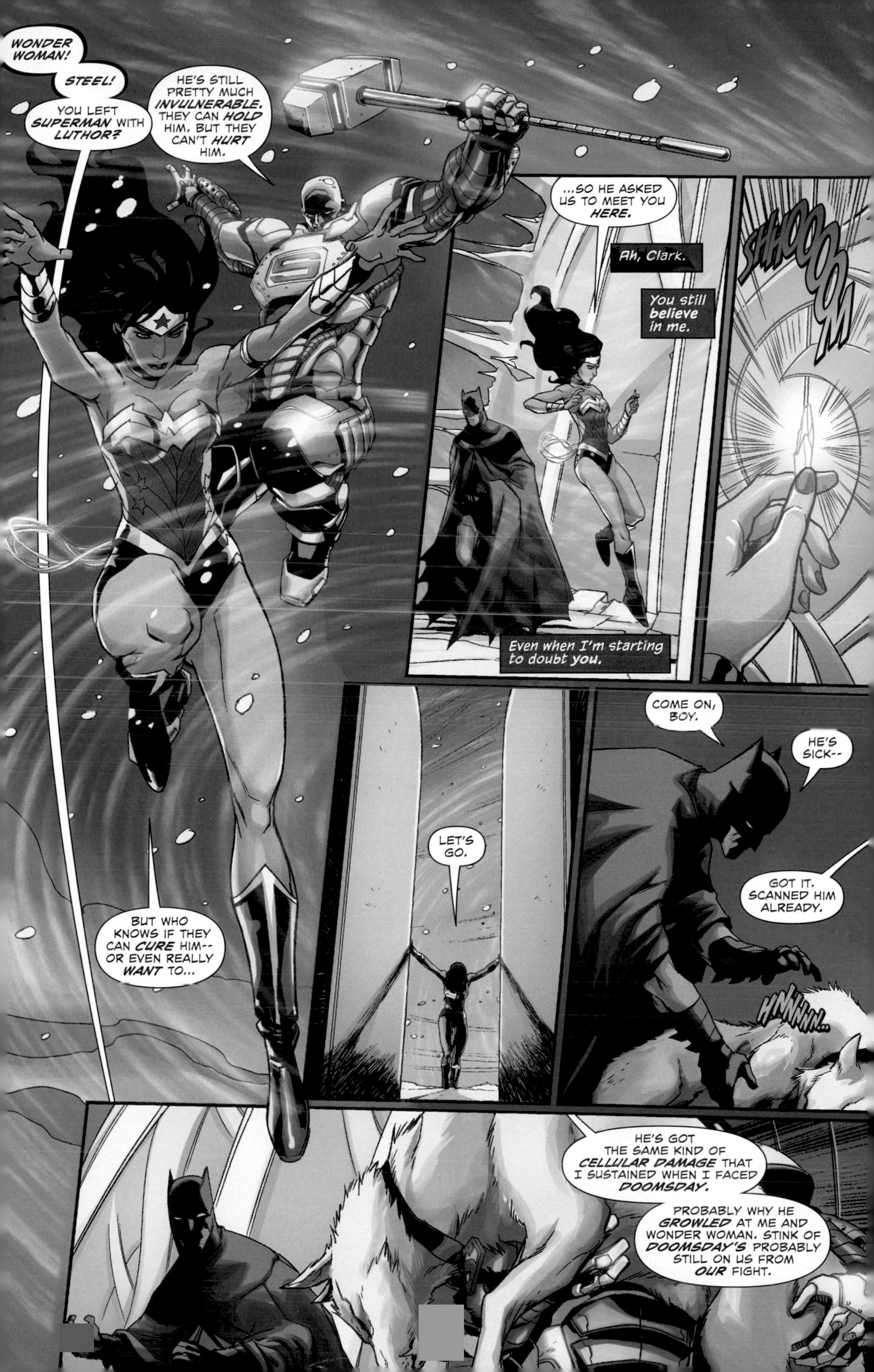
WONDER WOMAN!
STEEL!
YOU LEFT SUPERMAN WITH LUTHOR?
HE'S STILL PRETTY MUCH INVULNERABLE. THEY CAN HOLD HIM. BUT THEY CAN'T HURT HIM.
BUT WHO KNOWS IF THEY CAN CURE HIM-- OR EVEN REALLY WANT TO...
...SO HE ASKED US TO MEET YOU HERE.
Ah, Clark.
You still believe in me.
Even when I'm starting to doubt you.
SHHOOOOM
LET'S GO.
COME ON, BOY.
HE'S SICK--
GOT IT. SCANNED HIM ALREADY.
HNNNN...
HE'S GOT THE SAME KIND OF CELLULAR DAMAGE THAT I SUSTAINED WHEN I FACED DOOMSDAY.
PROBABLY WHY HE GROWLED AT ME AND WONDER WOMAN. STINK OF DOOMSDAY'S PROBABLY STILL ON US FROM OUR FIGHT.

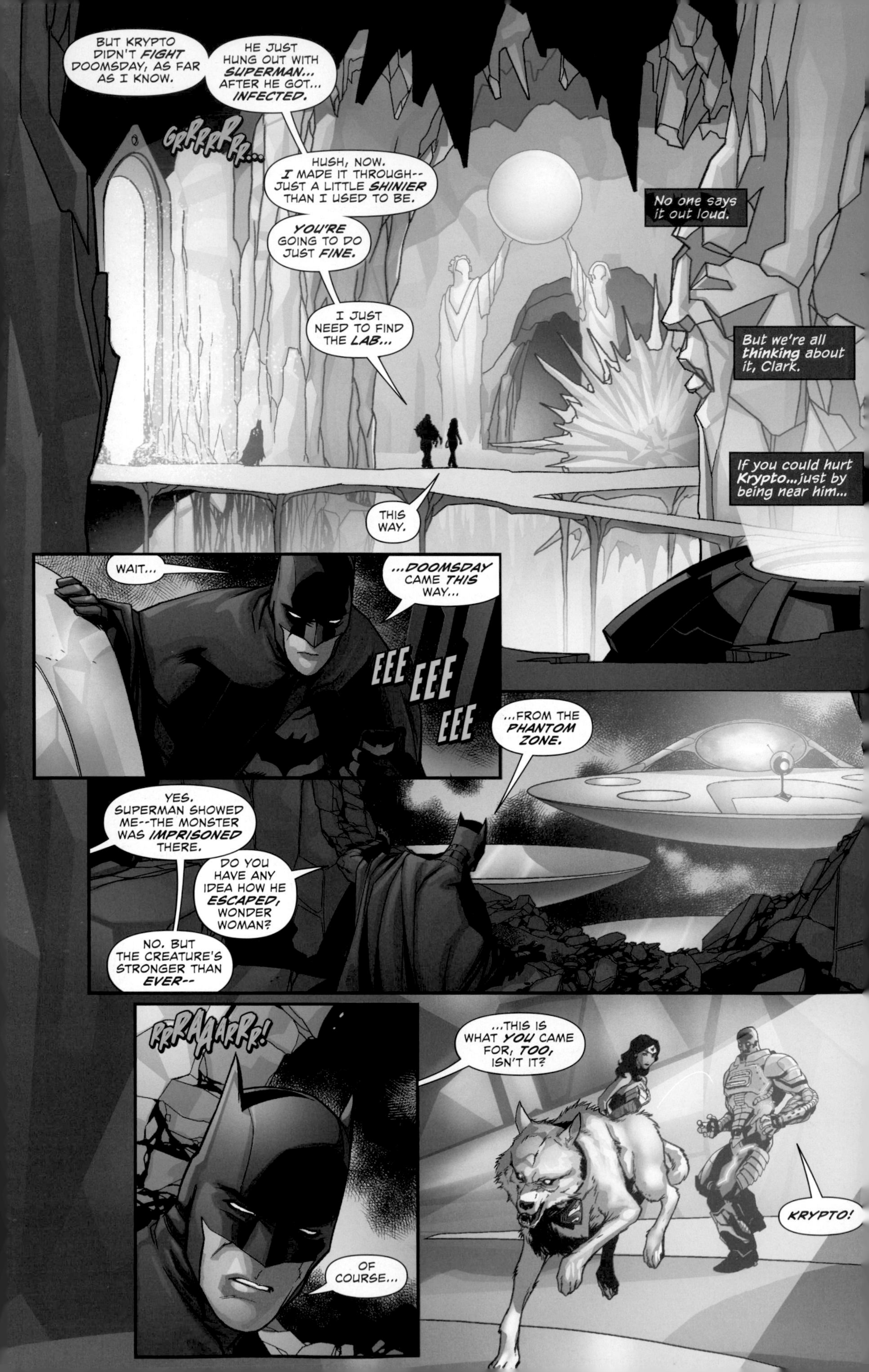
BUT KRYPTO DIDN'T FIGHT DOOMSDAY, AS FAR AS I KNOW.
HE JUST HUNG OUT WITH SUPERMAN... AFTER HE GOT... INFECTED.
GRRRRRRR...
HUSH, NOW. I MADE IT THROUGH-- JUST A LITTLE SHINIER THAN I USED TO BE.
YOU'RE GOING TO DO JUST FINE.
I JUST NEED TO FIND THE LAB...
No one says it out loud.
But we're all thinking about it, Clark.
If you could hurt Krypto...just by being near him...
THIS WAY.
WAIT...
...DOOMSDAY CAME THIS WAY...
EEE EEE EEE
...FROM THE PHANTOM ZONE.
YES. SUPERMAN SHOWED ME--THE MONSTER WAS IMPRISONED THERE.
DO YOU HAVE ANY IDEA HOW HE ESCAPED, WONDER WOMAN?
NO. BUT THE CREATURE'S STRONGER THAN EVER--
RRRAAARRR!
...THIS IS WHAT YOU CAME FOR, TOO, ISN'T IT?
OF COURSE...
KRYPTO!

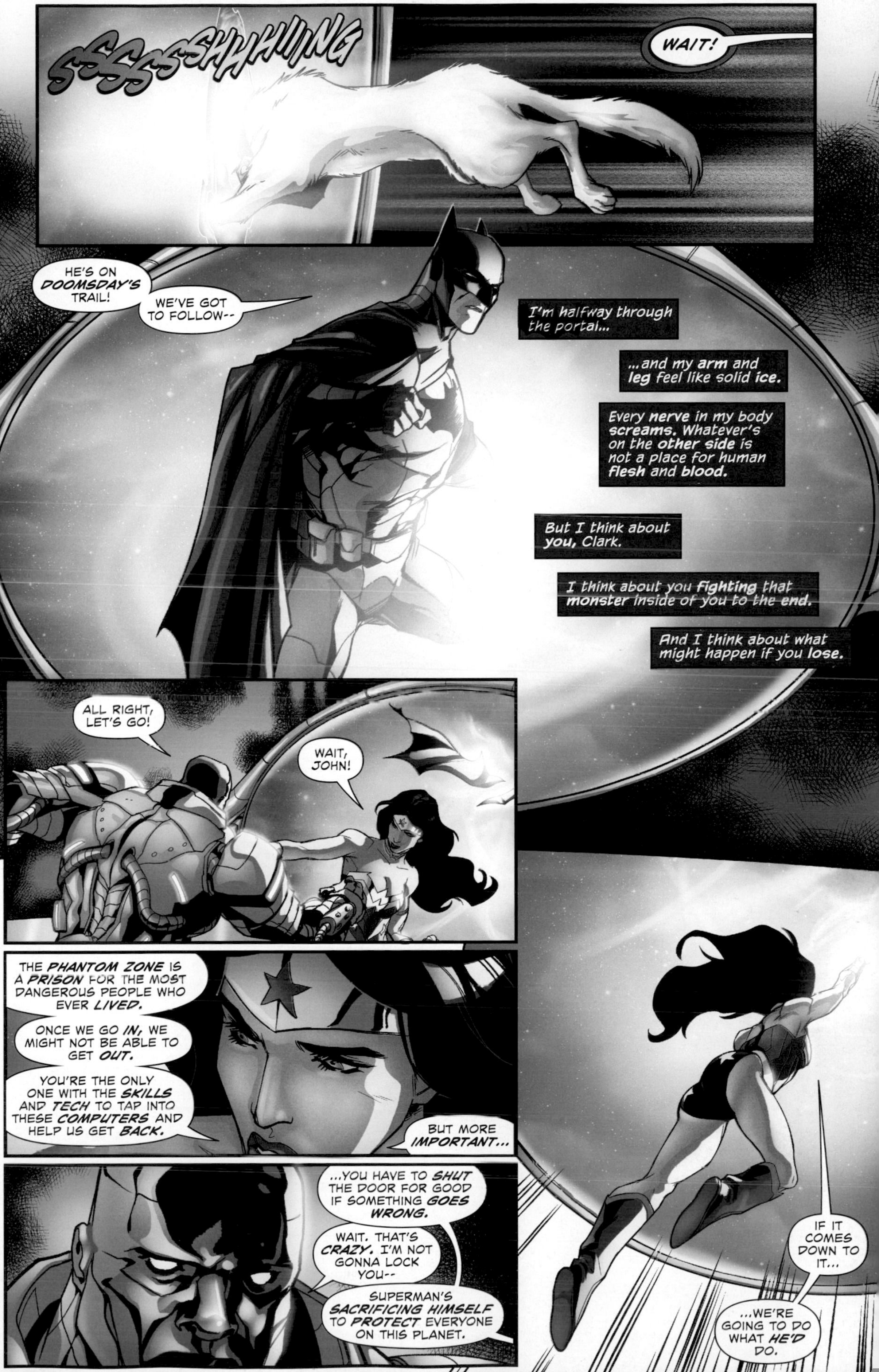
SSSSSSHUHUING
WAIT!
HE'S ON DOOMSDAY'S TRAIL!
WE'VE GOT TO FOLLOW--
I'm halfway through the portal...
...and my arm and leg feel like solid ice.
Every nerve in my body screams. Whatever's on the other side is not a place for human flesh and blood.
But I think about you, Clark.
I think about you fighting that monster inside of you to the end.
And I think about what might happen if you lose.
ALL RIGHT, LET'S GO!
WAIT, JOHN!
THE PHANTOM ZONE IS A PRISON FOR THE MOST DANGEROUS PEOPLE WHO EVER LIVED.
ONCE WE GO IN, WE MIGHT NOT BE ABLE TO GET OUT.
YOU'RE THE ONLY ONE WITH THE SKILLS AND TECH TO TAP INTO THESE COMPUTERS AND HELP US GET BACK.
BUT MORE IMPORTANT...
...YOU HAVE TO SHUT THE DOOR FOR GOOD IF SOMETHING GOES WRONG.
WAIT. THAT'S CRAZY. I'M NOT GONNA LOCK YOU--
SUPERMAN'S SACRIFICING HIMSELF TO PROTECT EVERYONE ON THIS PLANET.
IF IT COMES DOWN TO IT...
...WE'RE GOING TO DO WHAT HE'D DO.

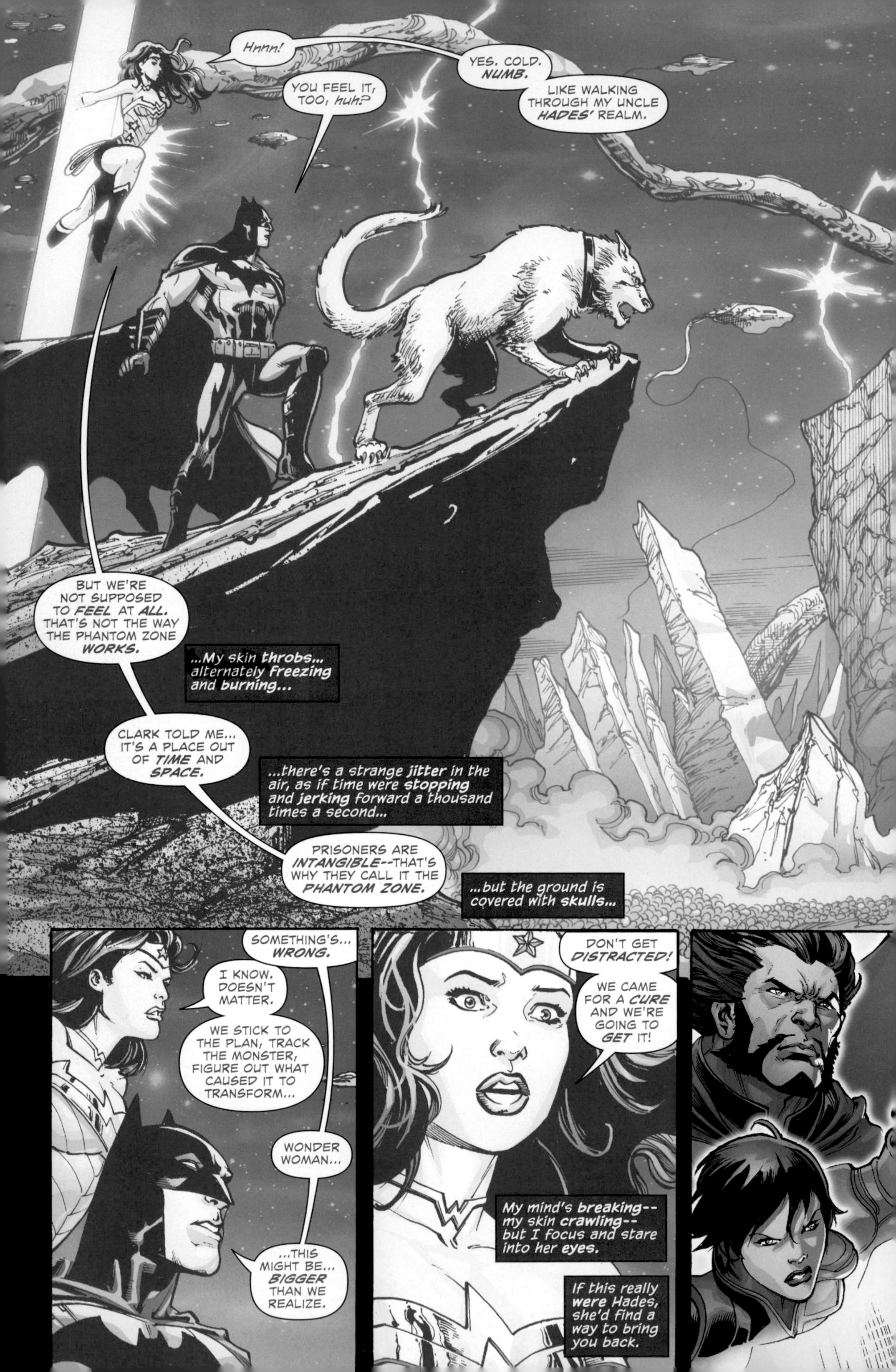

Hnnn!
YOU FEEL IT, TOO, huh?
YES. COLD. NUMB.
LIKE WALKING THROUGH MY UNCLE HADES' REALM.
BUT WE'RE NOT SUPPOSED TO FEEL AT ALL. THAT'S NOT THE WAY THE PHANTOM ZONE WORKS.
...My skin throbs... alternately freezing and burning...
CLARK TOLD ME... IT'S A PLACE OUT OF TIME AND SPACE.
...there's a strange jitter in the air, as if time were stopping and jerking forward a thousand times a second...
PRISONERS ARE INTANGIBLE--THAT'S WHY THEY CALL IT THE PHANTOM ZONE.
...but the ground is covered with skulls...
SOMETHING'S... WRONG.
I KNOW. DOESN'T MATTER.
WE STICK TO THE PLAN, TRACK THE MONSTER, FIGURE OUT WHAT CAUSED IT TO TRANSFORM...
WONDER WOMAN...
...THIS MIGHT BE... BIGGER THAN WE REALIZE.
DON'T GET DISTRACTED!
WE CAME FOR A CURE AND WE'RE GOING TO GET IT!
My mind's breaking-- my skin crawling-- but I focus and stare into her eyes.
If this really were Hades, she'd find a way to bring you back.

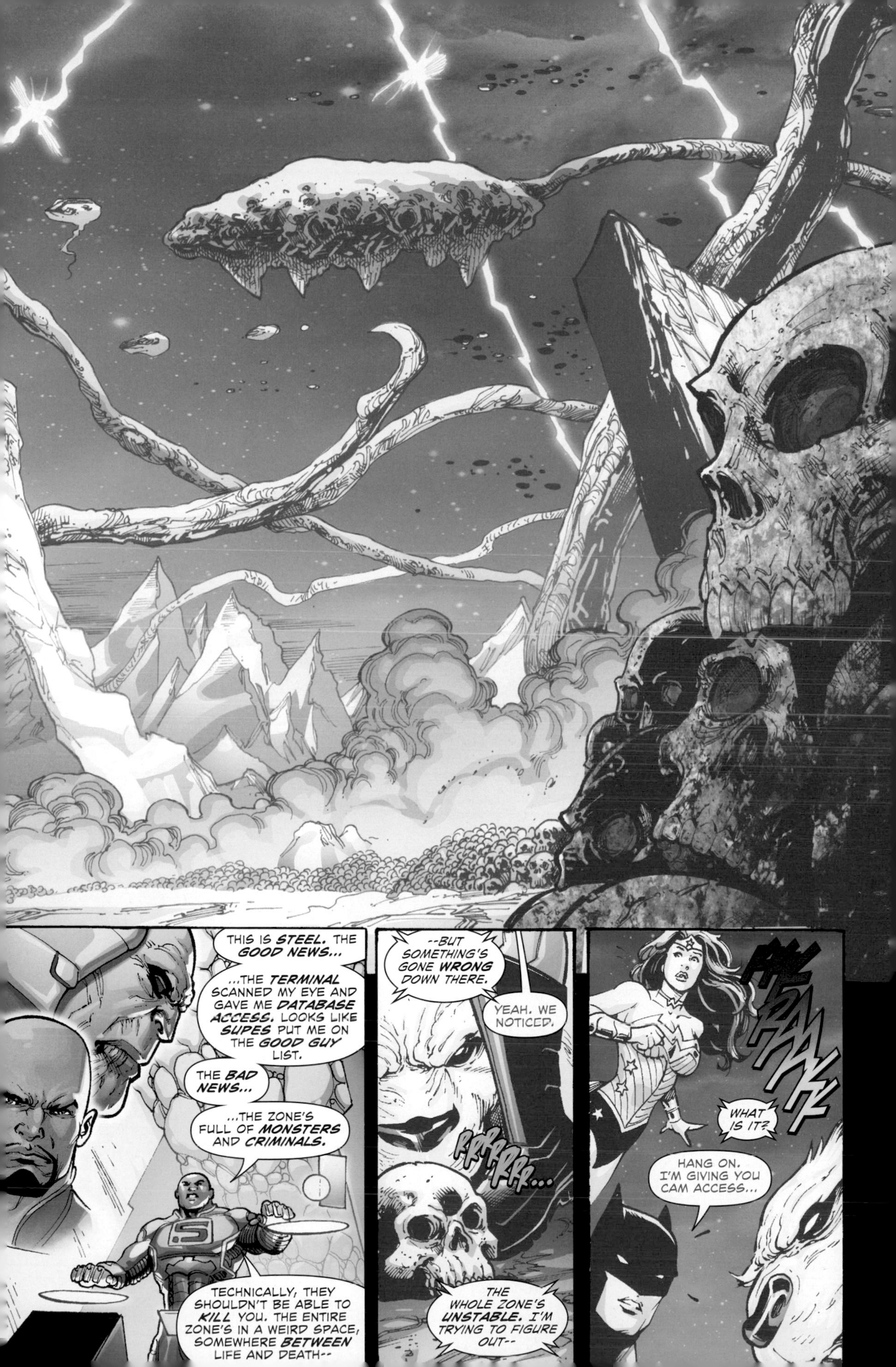

THIS IS STEEL. THE GOOD NEWS...
...THE TERMINAL SCANNED MY EYE AND GAVE ME DATABASE ACCESS. LOOKS LIKE SUPES PUT ME ON THE GOOD GUY LIST.
THE BAD NEWS...
...THE ZONE'S FULL OF MONSTERS AND CRIMINALS.
TECHNICALLY, THEY SHOULDN'T BE ABLE TO KILL YOU. THE ENTIRE ZONE'S IN A WEIRD SPACE, SOMEWHERE BETWEEN LIFE AND DEATH--
--BUT SOMETHING'S GONE WRONG DOWN THERE.
YEAH. WE NOTICED.
THE WHOLE ZONE'S UNSTABLE. I'M TRYING TO FIGURE OUT--
WHAT IS IT?
HANG ON. I'M GIVING YOU CAM ACCESS...

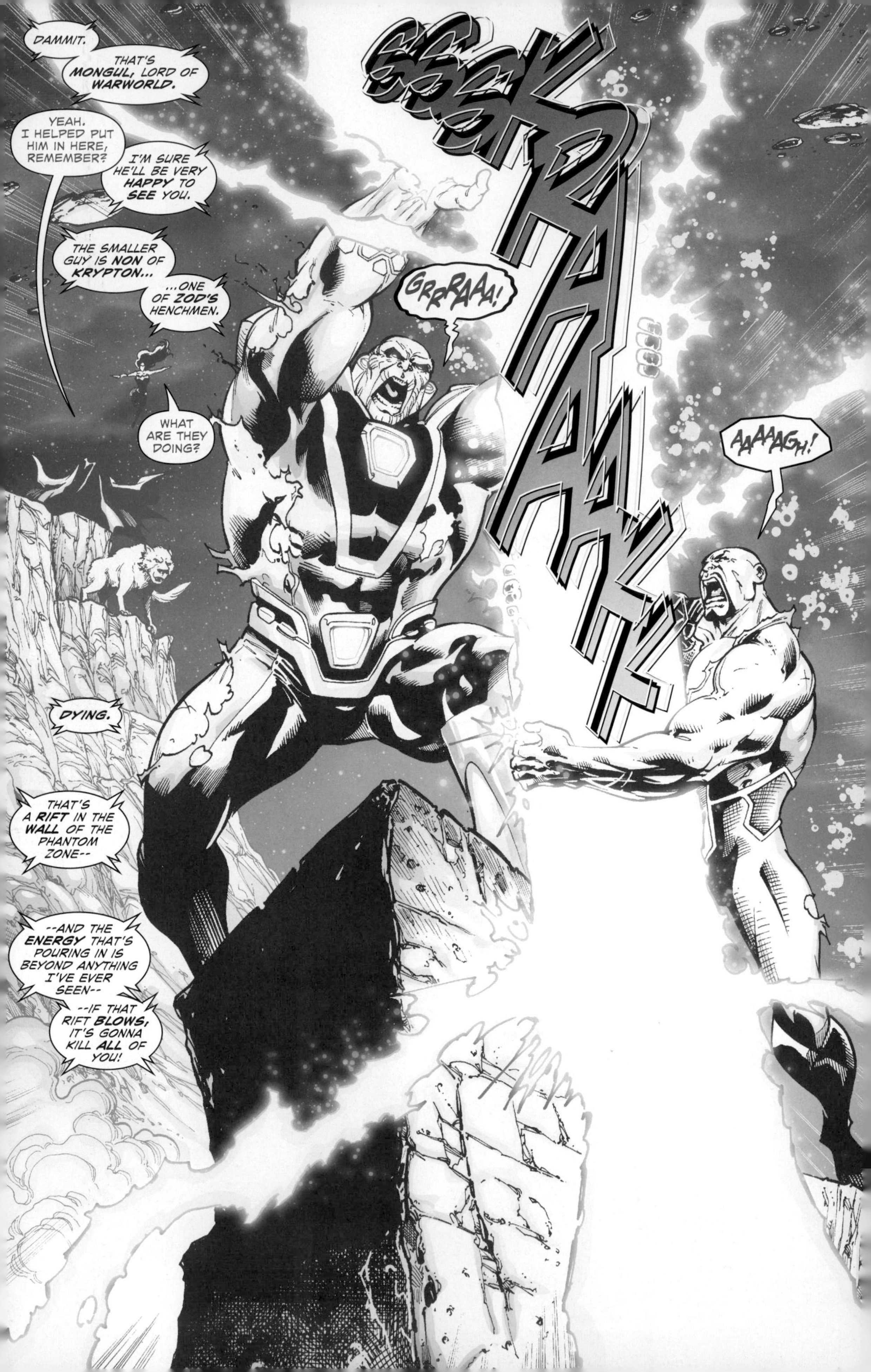
DAMMIT.
THAT'S MONGUL, LORD OF WARWORLD.
YEAH. I HELPED PUT HIM IN HERE, REMEMBER?
I'M SURE HE'LL BE VERY HAPPY TO SEE YOU.
THE SMALLER GUY IS NON OF KRYPTON...
...ONE OF ZOD'S HENCHMEN.
WHAT ARE THEY DOING?
GRRRAAA!
AAAAAGH!
DYING.
THAT'S A RIFT IN THE WALL OF THE PHANTOM ZONE--
--AND THE ENERGY THAT'S POURING IN IS BEYOND ANYTHING I'VE EVER SEEN--
--IF THAT RIFT BLOWS, IT'S GONNA KILL ALL OF YOU!

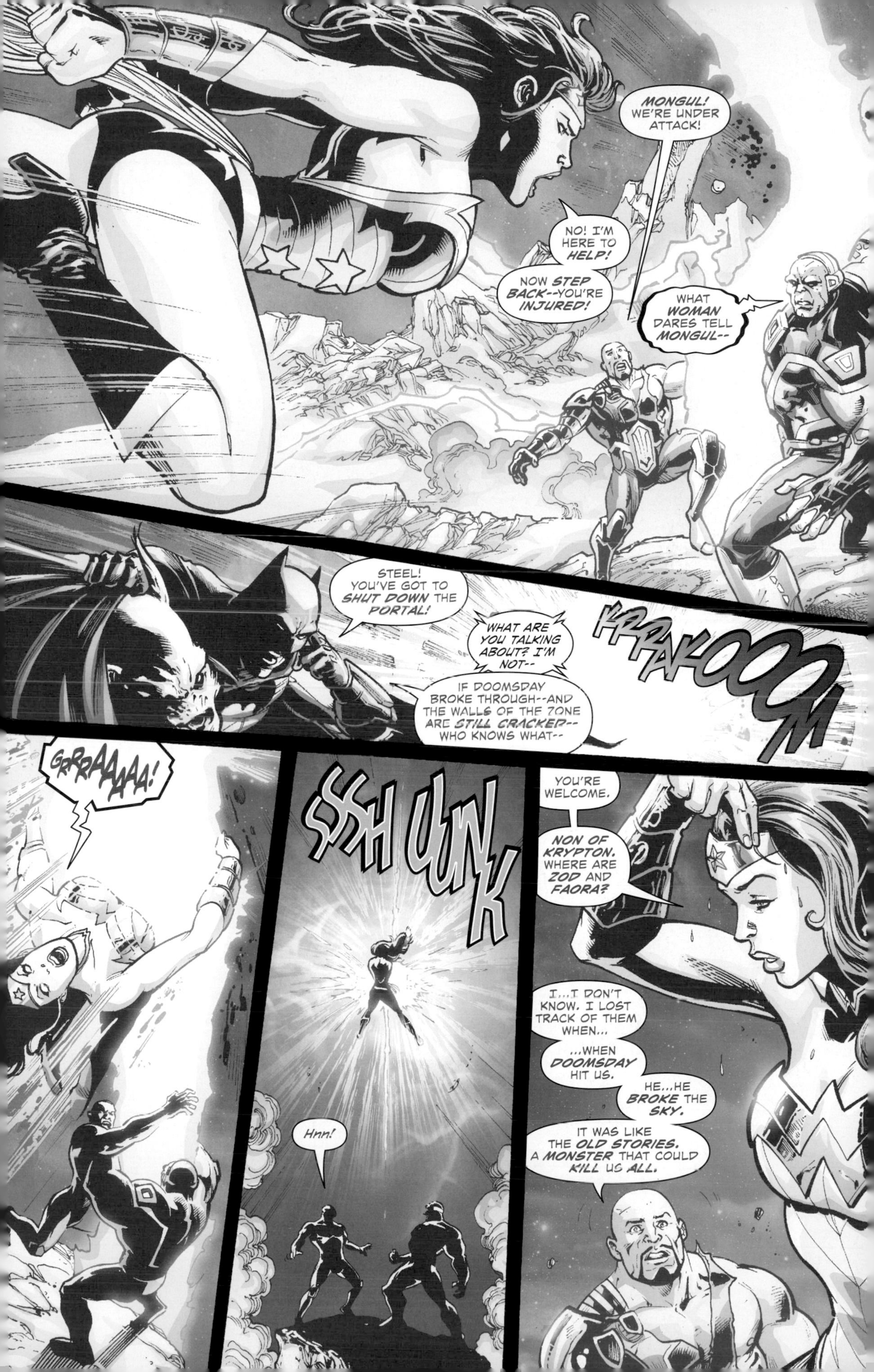
MONGUL! WE'RE UNDER ATTACK!
NO! I'M HERE TO HELP!
NOW STEP BACK--YOU'RE INJURED!
WHAT WOMAN DARES TELL MONGUL--
STEEL! YOU'VE GOT TO SHUT DOWN THE PORTAL!
WHAT ARE YOU TALKING ABOUT? I'M NOT--
IF DOOMSDAY BROKE THROUGH--AND THE WALLS OF THE ZONE ARE STILL CRACKED--WHO KNOWS WHAT--
KRRAKOOOM
GRRRAAAAAA!
SSHUUNK
Hnn!
YOU'RE WELCOME.
NON OF KRYPTON. WHERE ARE ZOD AND FAORA?
I...I DON'T KNOW. I LOST TRACK OF THEM WHEN...
...WHEN DOOMSDAY HIT US.
HE...HE BROKE THE SKY.
IT WAS LIKE THE OLD STORIES. A MONSTER THAT COULD KILL US ALL.

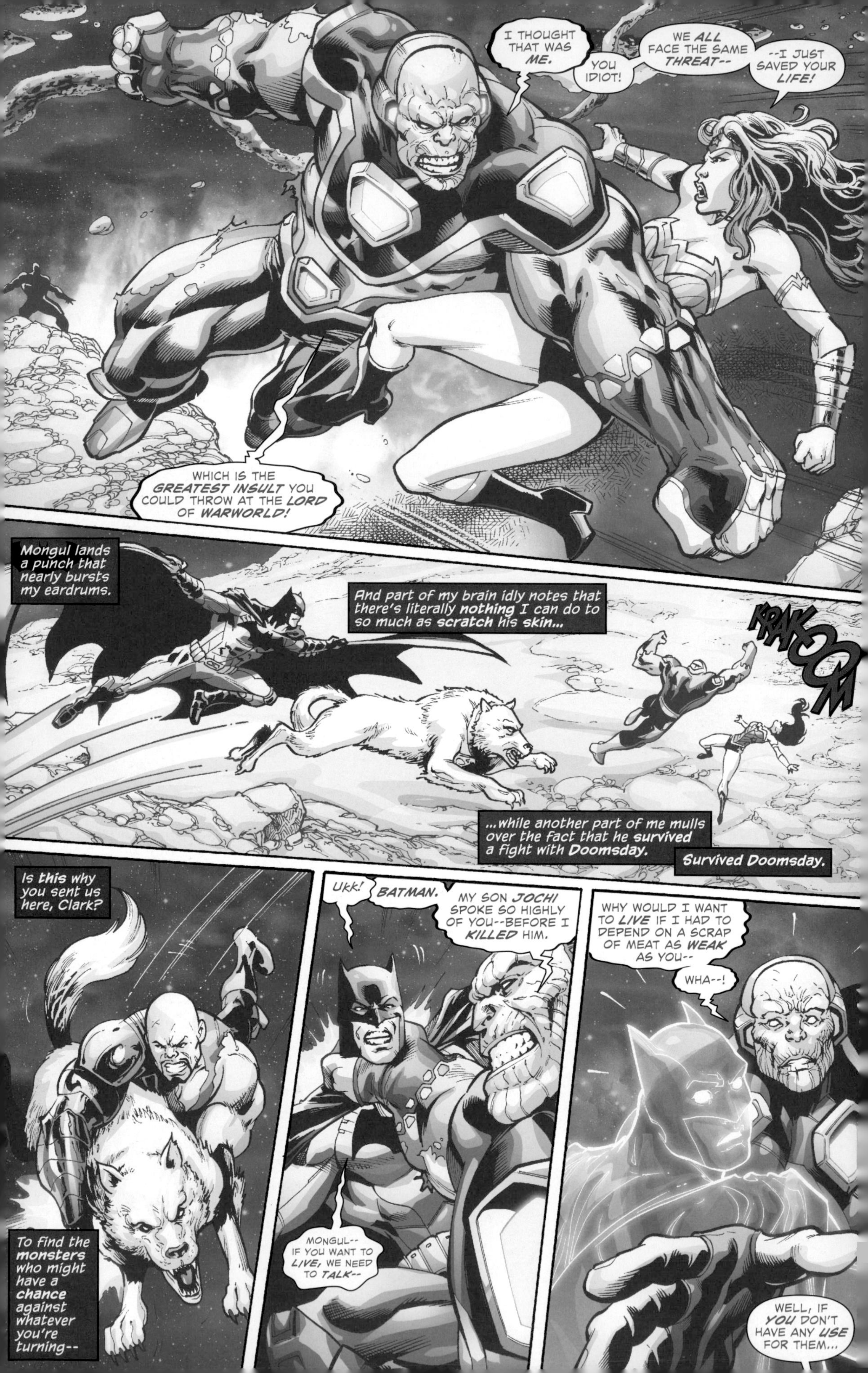

I THOUGHT THAT WAS ME.
YOU IDIOT!
WE ALL FACE THE SAME THREAT--
--I JUST SAVED YOUR LIFE!
WHICH IS THE GREATEST INSULT YOU COULD THROW AT THE LORD OF WARWORLD!
Mongul lands a punch that nearly bursts my eardrums.
And part of my brain idly notes that there's literally nothing I can do to so much as scratch his skin...
KRAKOOM
...while another part of me mulls over the fact that he survived a fight with Doomsday.
Survived Doomsday.
Is this why you sent us here, Clark?
To find the monsters who might have a chance against whatever you're turning--
Ukk!
BATMAN.
MY SON JOCHI SPOKE SO HIGHLY OF YOU--BEFORE I KILLED HIM.
MONGUL-- IF YOU WANT TO LIVE, WE NEED TO TALK--
WHY WOULD I WANT TO LIVE IF I HAD TO DEPEND ON A SCRAP OF MEAT AS WEAK AS YOU--
WHA--!
WELL, IF YOU DON'T HAVE ANY USE FOR THEM...

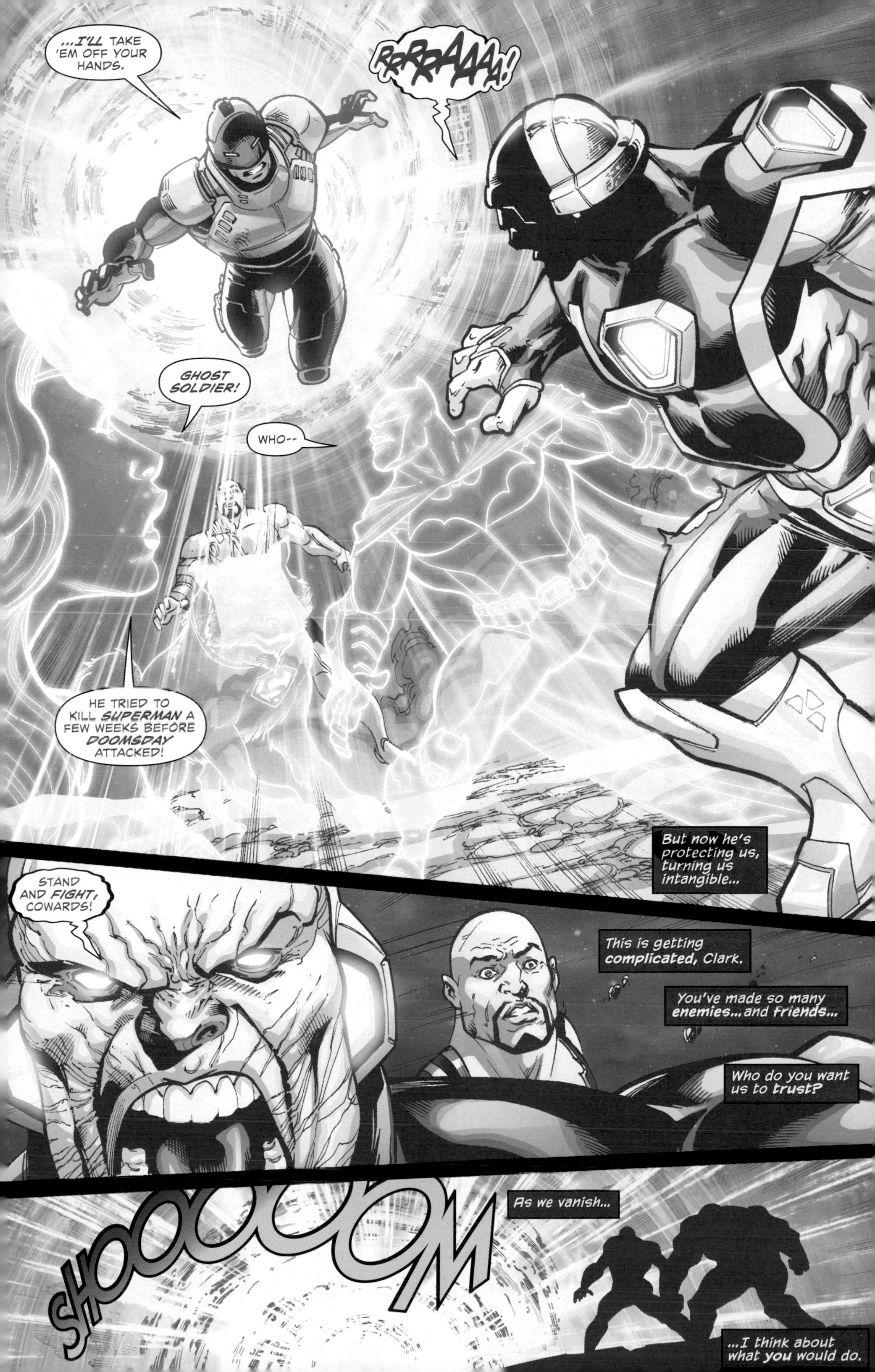
...I'LL TAKE 'EM OFF YOUR HANDS.
RRRRAAAAA!
GHOST SOLDIER!
WHO--
HE TRIED TO KILL SUPERMAN A FEW WEEKS BEFORE DOOMSDAY ATTACKED!
But now he's protecting us, turning us intangible...
STAND AND FIGHT, COWARDS!
This is getting complicated, Clark.
You've made so many enemies...and friends...
Who do you want us to trust?
SHOOOOOM
As we vanish...
...I think about what you would do.

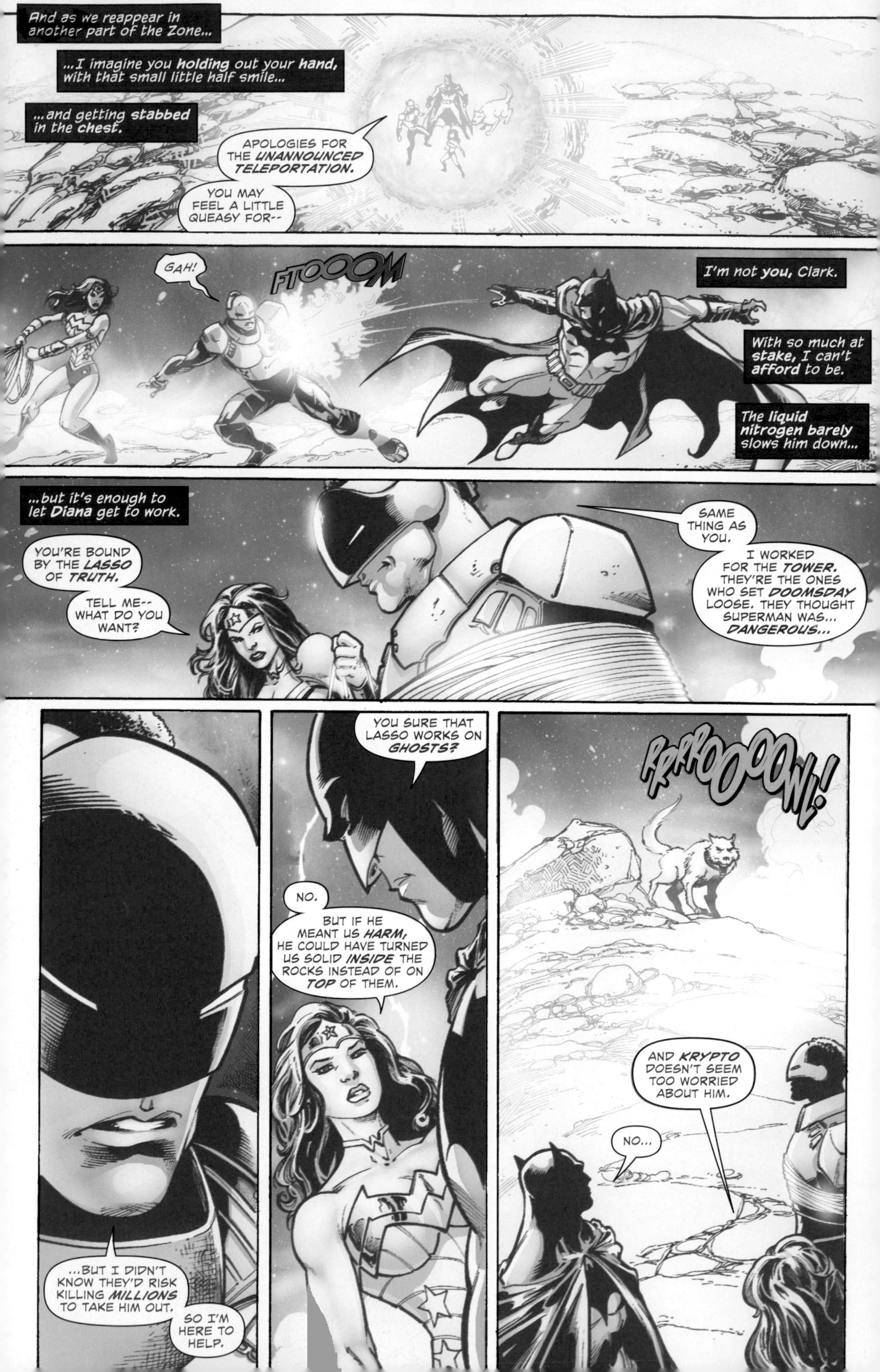

And as we reappear in another part of the Zone...
...I imagine you holding out your hand, with that small little half smile...
...and getting stabbed in the chest.
APOLOGIES FOR THE UNANNOUNCED TELEPORTATION.
YOU MAY FEEL A LITTLE QUEASY FOR--
GAH!
FTOOOOM
I'm not you, Clark.
With so much at stake, I can't afford to be.
The liquid nitrogen barely slows him down...
...but it's enough to let Diana get to work.
YOU'RE BOUND BY THE LASSO OF TRUTH.
TELL ME-- WHAT DO YOU WANT?
SAME THING AS YOU.
I WORKED FOR THE TOWER. THEY'RE THE ONES WHO SET DOOMSDAY LOOSE. THEY THOUGHT SUPERMAN WAS... DANGEROUS...
...BUT I DIDN'T KNOW THEY'D RISK KILLING MILLIONS TO TAKE HIM OUT.
SO I'M HERE TO HELP.
YOU SURE THAT LASSO WORKS ON GHOSTS?
NO.
BUT IF HE MEANT US HARM, HE COULD HAVE TURNED US SOLID INSIDE THE ROCKS INSTEAD OF ON TOP OF THEM.
RRRROOOOOWL!
AND KRYPTO DOESN'T SEEM TOO WORRIED ABOUT HIM.
NO...

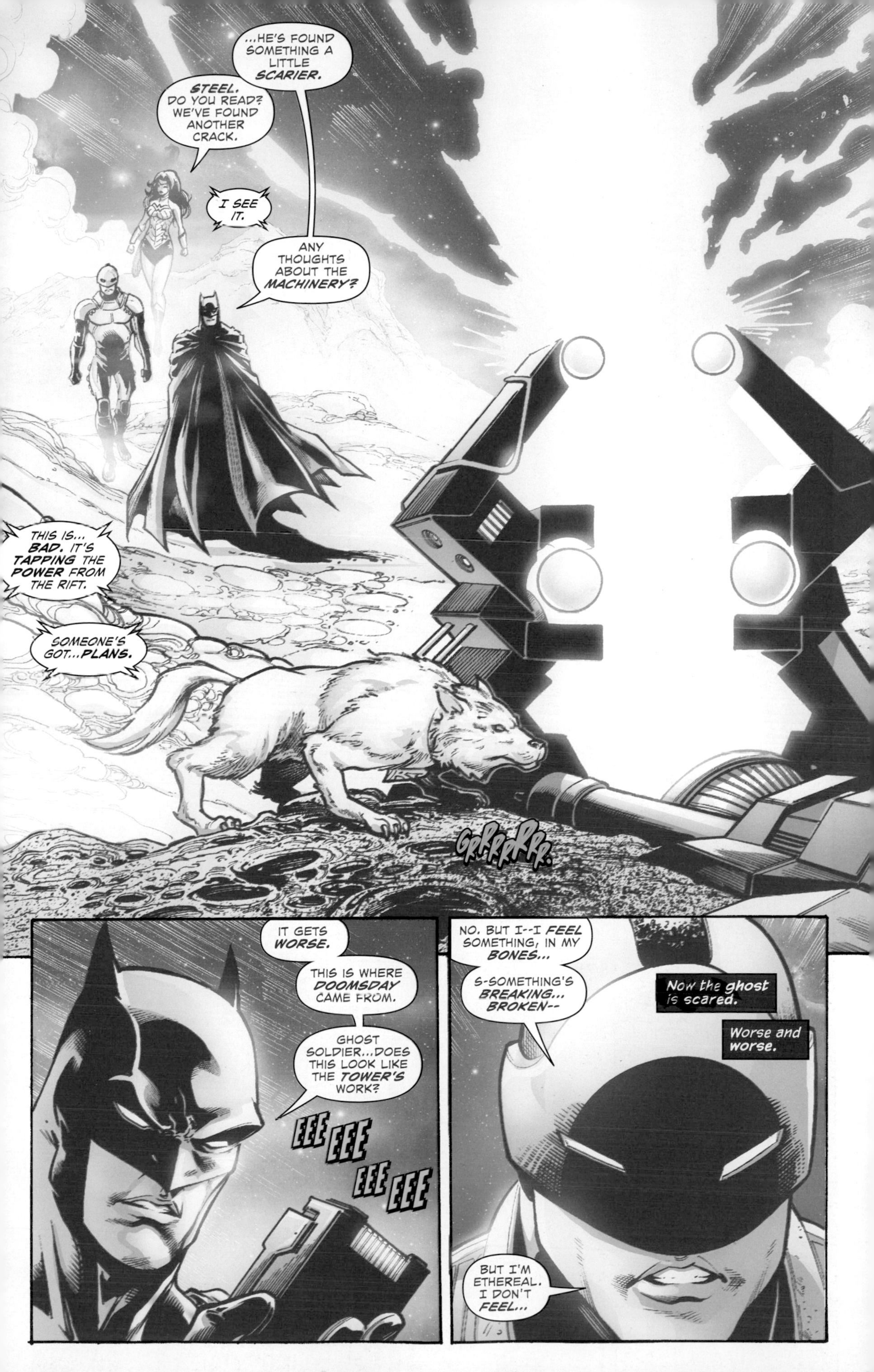
STEEL. DO YOU READ? WE'VE FOUND ANOTHER CRACK.
...HE'S FOUND SOMETHING A LITTLE SCARIER.
I SEE IT.
ANY THOUGHTS ABOUT THE MACHINERY?
THIS IS... BAD. IT'S TAPPING THE POWER FROM THE RIFT.
SOMEONE'S GOT...PLANS.
GRRRRRRR.
IT GETS WORSE.
THIS IS WHERE DOOMSDAY CAME FROM.
GHOST SOLDIER...DOES THIS LOOK LIKE THE TOWER'S WORK?
EEE EEE EEE EEE
NO. BUT I--I FEEL SOMETHING, IN MY BONES...
S-SOMETHING'S BREAKING... BROKEN--
Now the ghost is scared.
Worse and worse.
BUT I'M ETHEREAL. I DON'T FEEL...

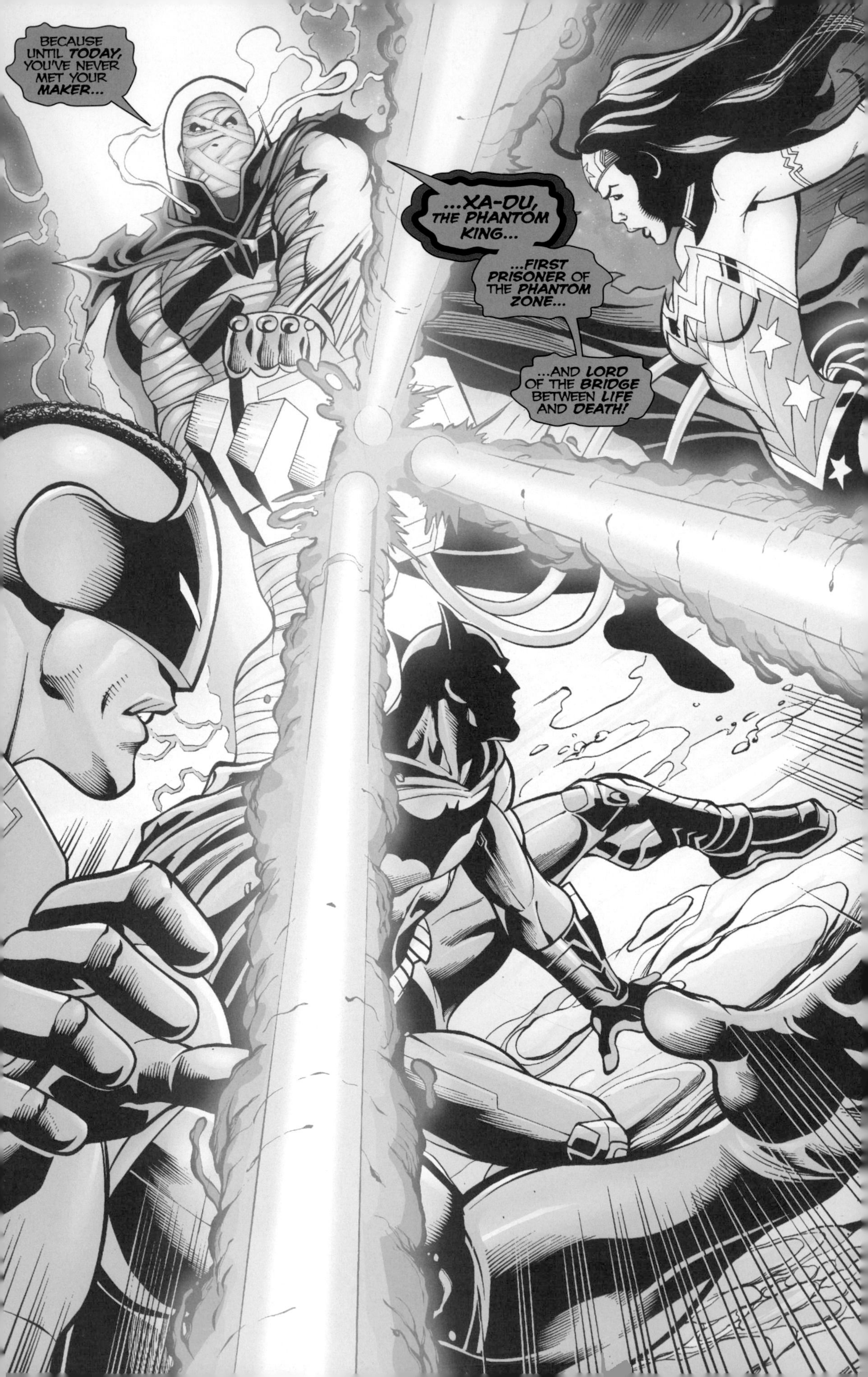

BECAUSE UNTIL TODAY, YOU'VE NEVER MET YOUR MAKER...
...XA-DU, THE PHANTOM KING...
...FIRST PRISONER OF THE PHANTOM ZONE...
...AND LORD OF THE BRIDGE BETWEEN LIFE AND DEATH!

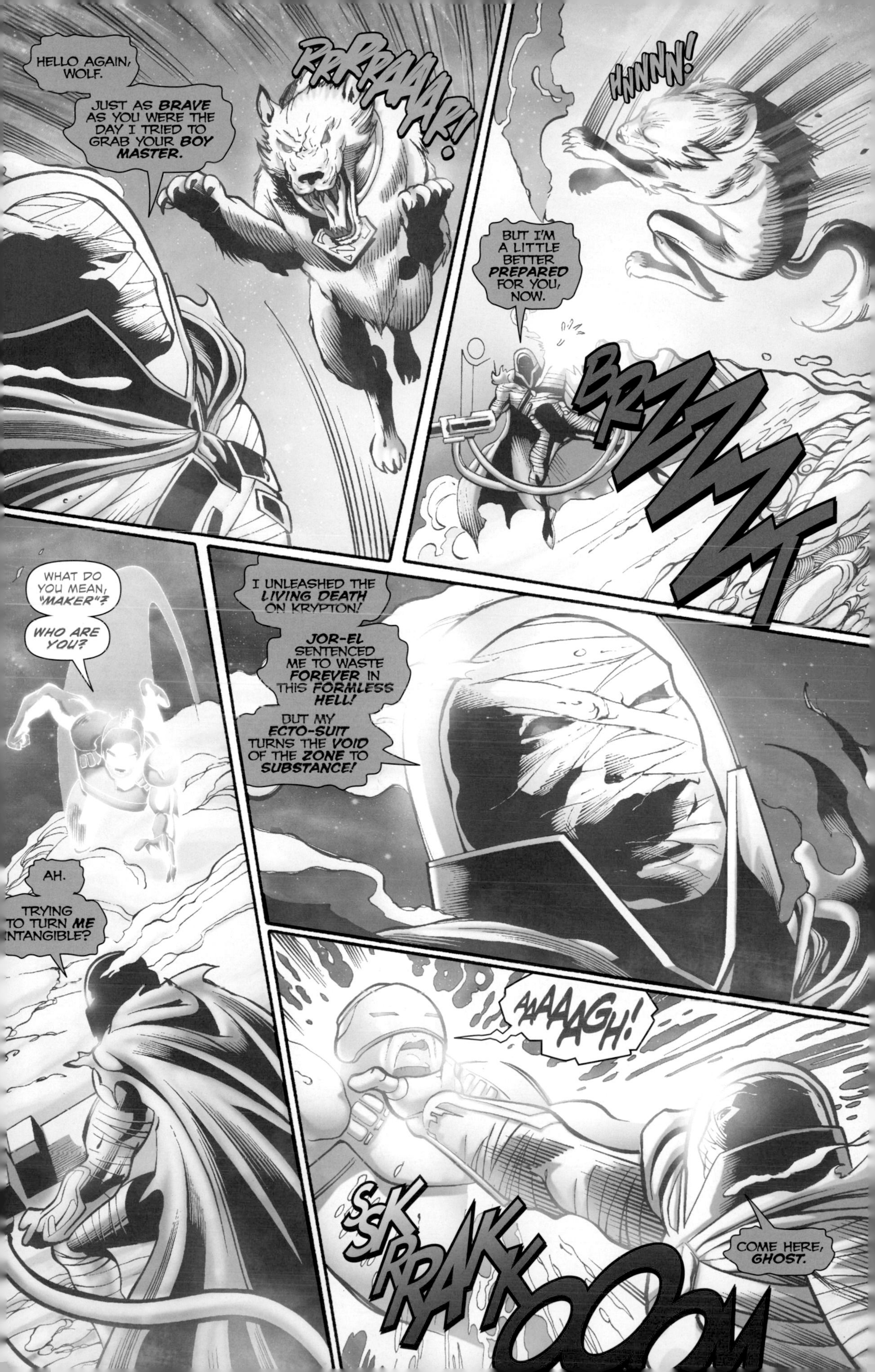
HELLO AGAIN, WOLF.
JUST AS BRAVE AS YOU WERE THE DAY I TRIED TO GRAB YOUR BOY MASTER.
RRRRAAAAR!
HNNNN!
BUT I'M A LITTLE BETTER PREPARED FOR YOU, NOW.
BRZZZZM
WHAT DO YOU MEAN, "MAKER"?
WHO ARE YOU?
I UNLEASHED THE LIVING DEATH ON KRYPTON!
JOR-EL SENTENCED ME TO WASTE FOREVER IN THIS FORMLESS HELL!
BUT MY ECTO-SUIT TURNS THE VOID OF THE ZONE TO SUBSTANCE!
AH.
TRYING TO TURN ME INTANGIBLE?
AAAAAGH!
COME HERE, GHOST.
SSKRRAKKOOOM

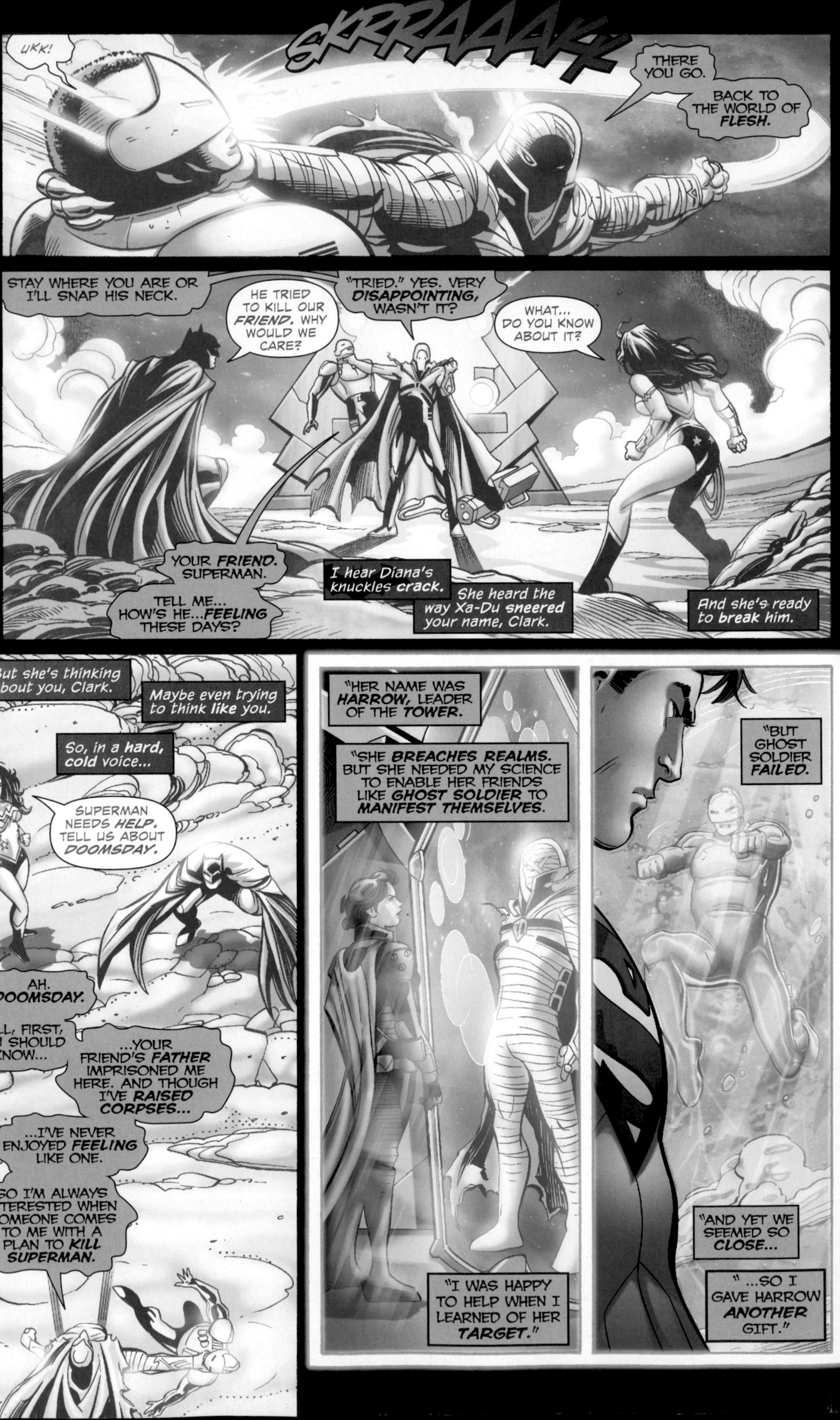
SKRRAAAKK
UKK!
THERE YOU GO.
BACK TO THE WORLD OF FLESH.
STAY WHERE YOU ARE OR I'LL SNAP HIS NECK.
HE TRIED TO KILL OUR FRIEND. WHY WOULD WE CARE?
"TRIED." YES. VERY DISAPPOINTING, WASN'T IT?
WHAT... DO YOU KNOW ABOUT IT?
YOUR FRIEND. SUPERMAN.
TELL ME... HOW'S HE...FEELING THESE DAYS?
I hear Diana's knuckles crack.
She heard the way Xa-Du sneered your name, Clark.
And she's ready to break him.
But she's thinking about you, Clark.
Maybe even trying to think like you.
So, in a hard, cold voice...
SUPERMAN NEEDS HELP. TELL US ABOUT DOOMSDAY.
AH. DOOMSDAY.
WELL, FIRST, YOU SHOULD KNOW...
...YOUR FRIEND'S FATHER IMPRISONED ME HERE. AND THOUGH I'VE RAISED CORPSES...
...I'VE NEVER ENJOYED FEELING LIKE ONE.
SO I'M ALWAYS INTERESTED WHEN SOMEONE COMES TO ME WITH A PLAN TO KILL SUPERMAN.
"HER NAME WAS HARROW, LEADER OF THE TOWER.
"SHE BREACHES REALMS. BUT SHE NEEDED MY SCIENCE TO ENABLE HER FRIENDS LIKE GHOST SOLDIER TO MANIFEST THEMSELVES.
"I WAS HAPPY TO HELP WHEN I LEARNED OF HER TARGET."
"BUT GHOST SOLDIER FAILED.
"AND YET WE SEEMED SO CLOSE...
"...SO I GAVE HARROW ANOTHER GIFT."

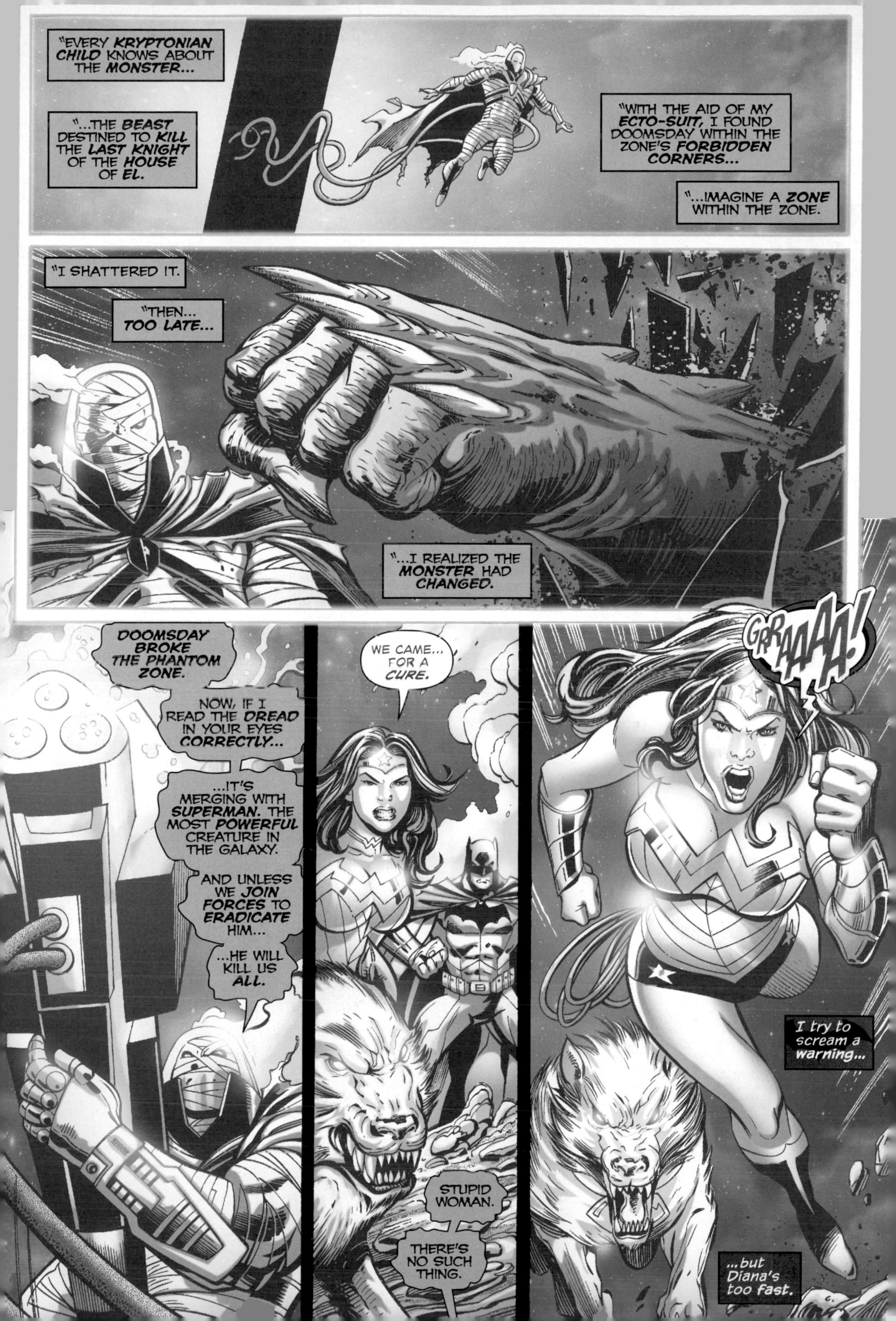
"EVERY KRYPTONIAN CHILD KNOWS ABOUT THE MONSTER...
"...THE BEAST DESTINED TO KILL THE LAST KNIGHT OF THE HOUSE OF EL.
"WITH THE AID OF MY ECTO-SUIT, I FOUND DOOMSDAY WITHIN THE ZONE'S FORBIDDEN CORNERS...
"...IMAGINE A ZONE WITHIN THE ZONE.
"I SHATTERED IT.
"THEN... TOO LATE...
"...I REALIZED THE MONSTER HAD CHANGED.
DOOMSDAY BROKE THE PHANTOM ZONE.
NOW, IF I READ THE DREAD IN YOUR EYES CORRECTLY...
...IT'S MERGING WITH SUPERMAN. THE MOST POWERFUL CREATURE IN THE GALAXY.
AND UNLESS WE JOIN FORCES TO ERADICATE HIM...
...HE WILL KILL US ALL.
WE CAME... FOR A CURE.
STUPID WOMAN.
THERE'S NO SUCH THING.
GRRAAAA!
I try to scream a warning...
...but Diana's too fast.

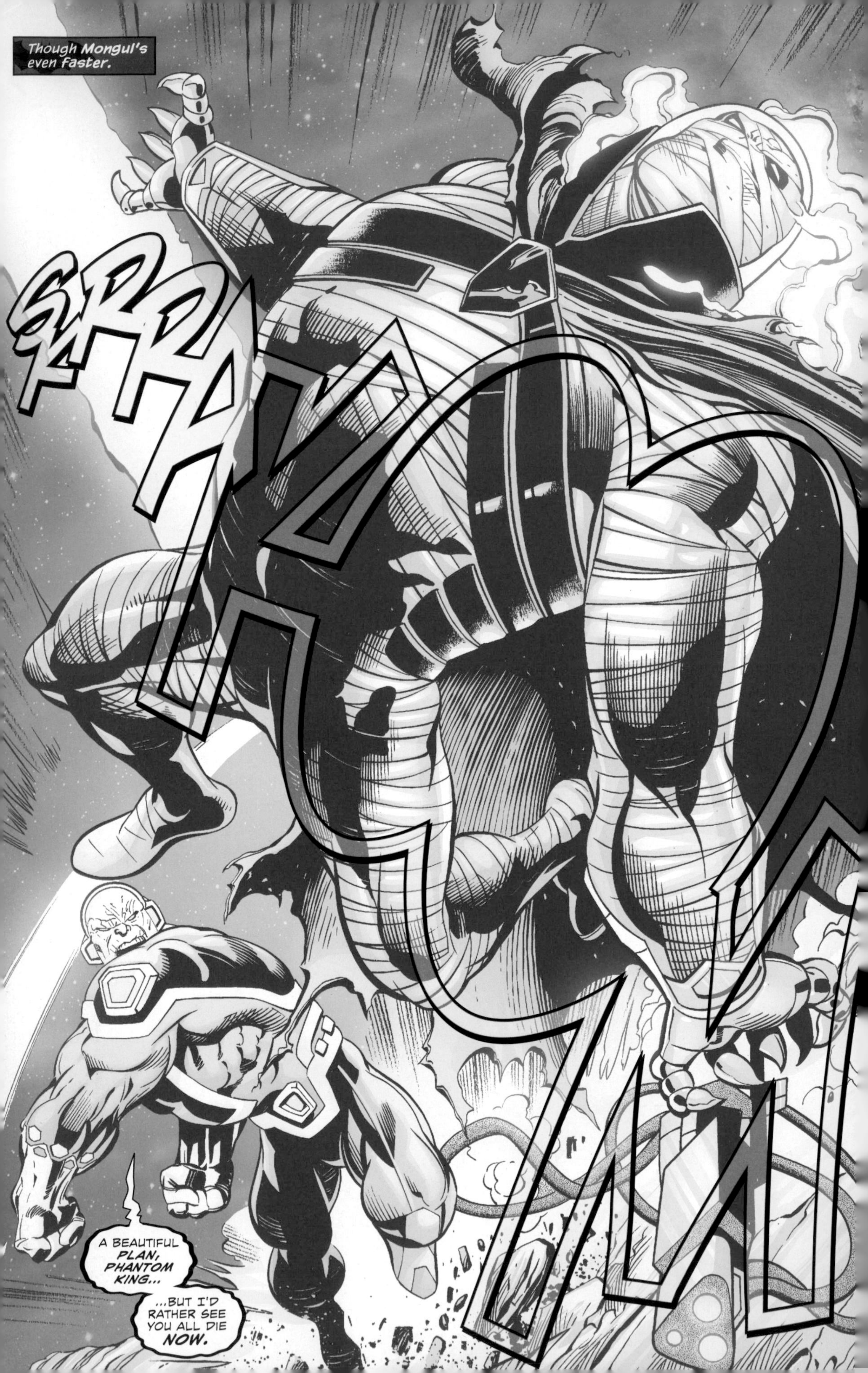

Though Mongul's even faster.
SPRAKOOM
A BEAUTIFUL PLAN, PHANTOM KING...
...BUT I'D RATHER SEE YOU ALL DIE NOW.

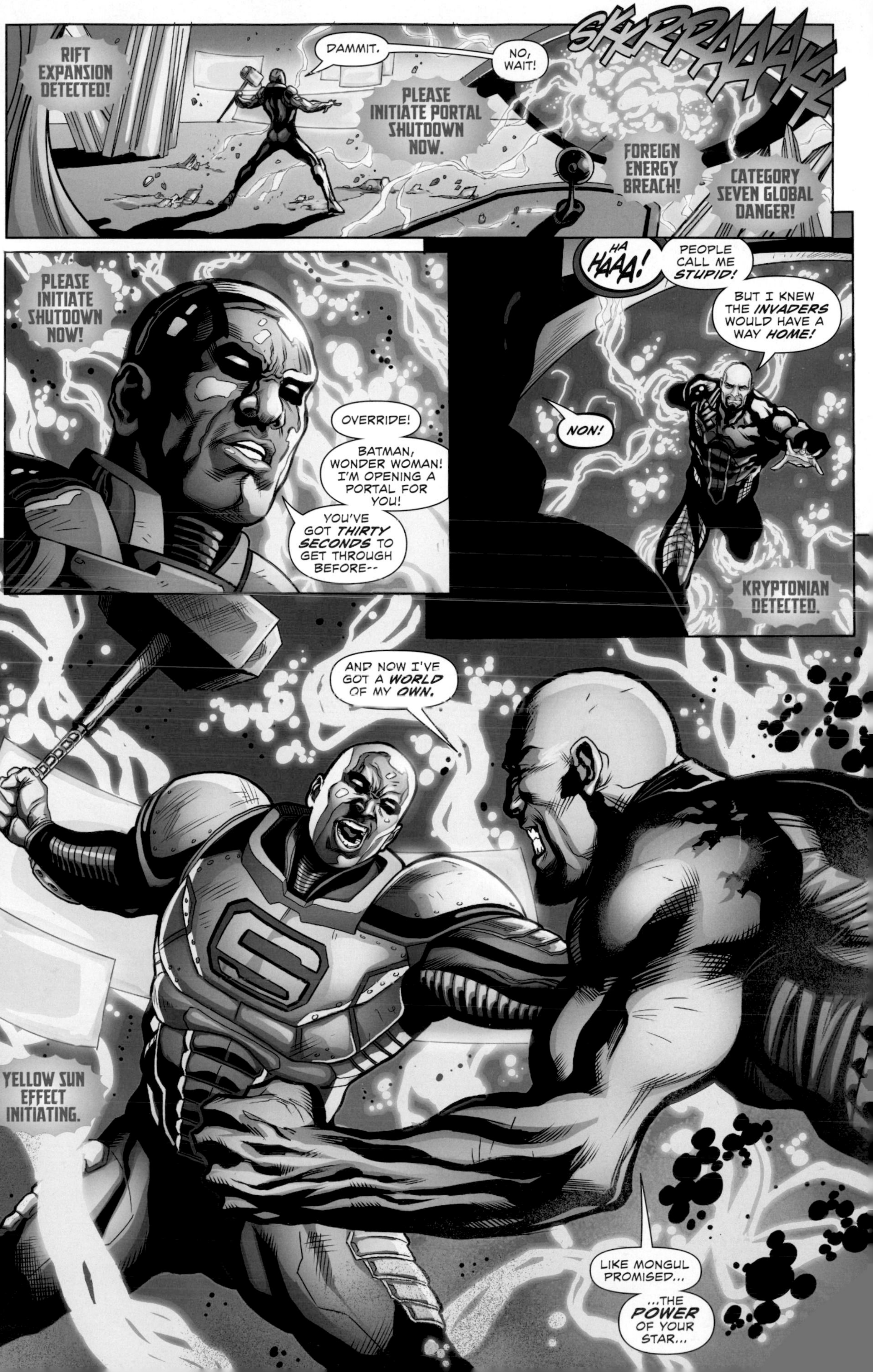
RIFT EXPANSION DETECTED!
DAMMIT.
NO, WAIT!
SKKRRAAAKK
PLEASE INITIATE PORTAL SHUTDOWN NOW.
FOREIGN ENERGY BREACH!
CATEGORY SEVEN GLOBAL DANGER!
PLEASE INITIATE SHUTDOWN NOW!
OVERRIDE!
BATMAN, WONDER WOMAN! I'M OPENING A PORTAL FOR YOU!
YOU'VE GOT THIRTY SECONDS TO GET THROUGH BEFORE--
HA HAAA!
PEOPLE CALL ME STUPID!
BUT I KNEW THE INVADERS WOULD HAVE A WAY HOME!
NON!
KRYPTONIAN DETECTED.
AND NOW I'VE GOT A WORLD OF MY OWN.
YELLOW SUN EFFECT INITIATING.
LIKE MONGUL PROMISED...
...THE POWER OF YOUR STAR...

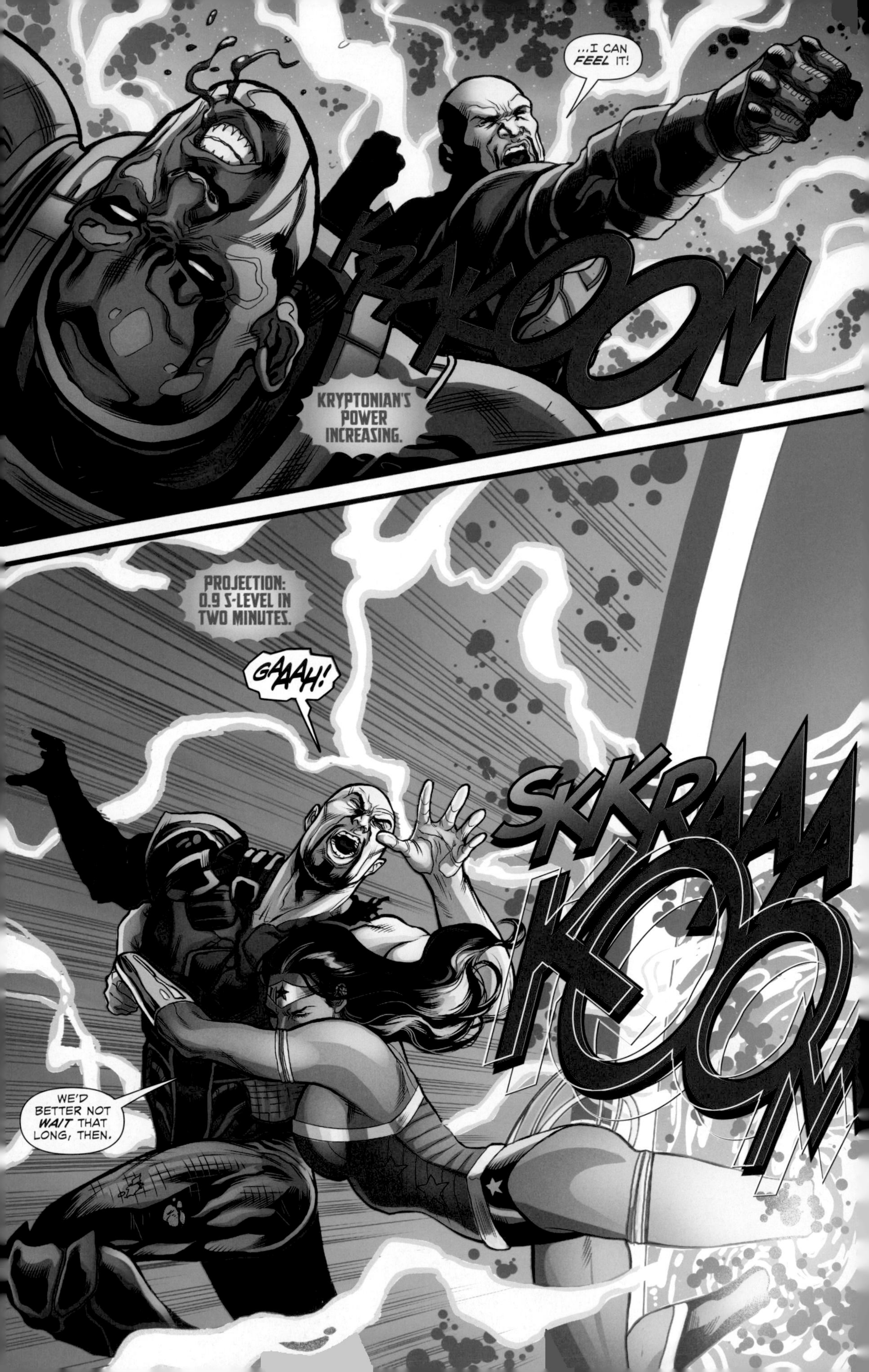
...I CAN *FEEL* IT!
KRAKOOM
KRYPTONIAN'S POWER INCREASING.
PROJECTION: 0.9 S-LEVEL IN TWO MINUTES.
GAAAH!
SKKRAAAA
KOOOM
WE'D BETTER NOT *WAIT* THAT LONG, THEN.

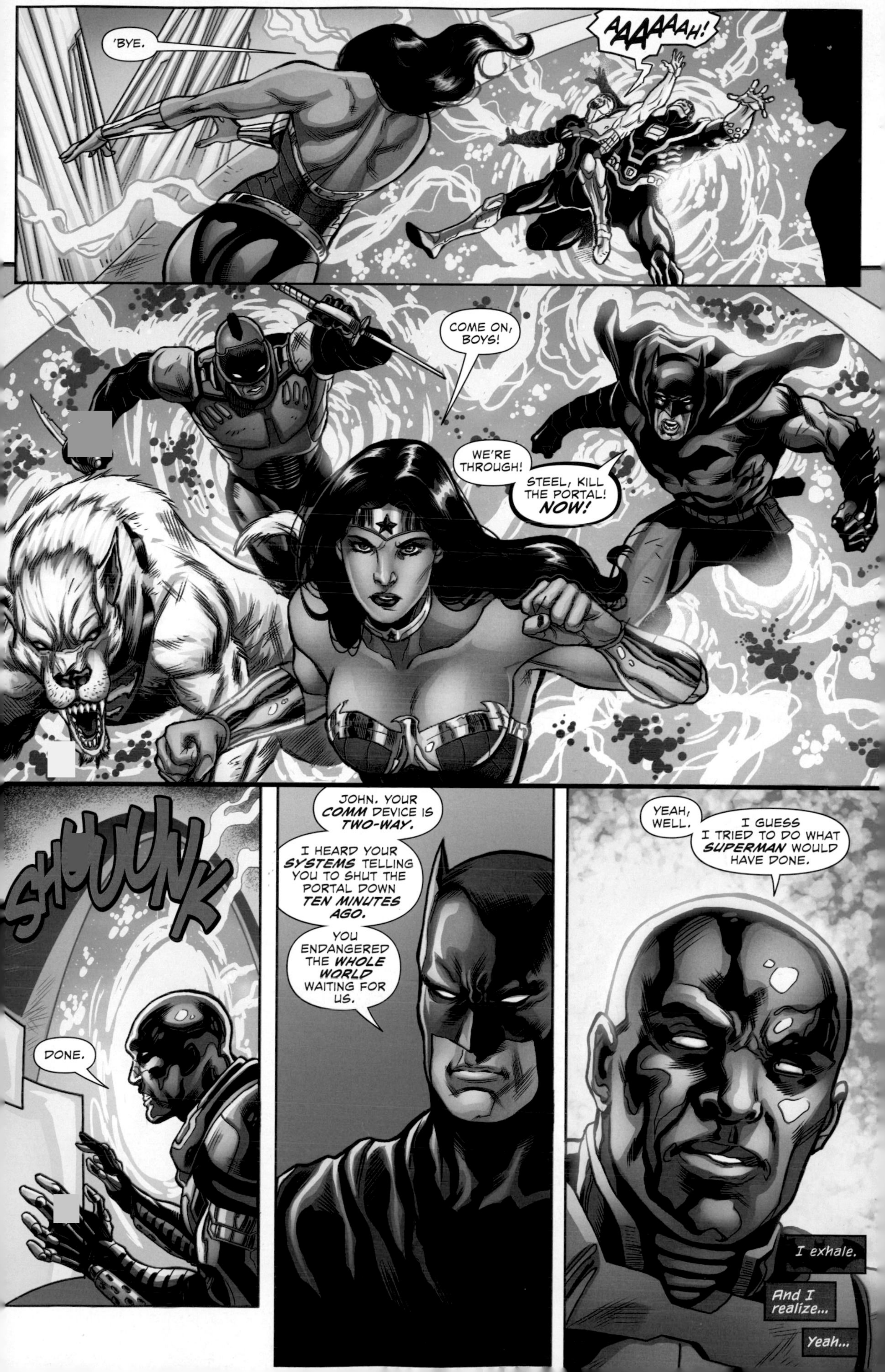

'BYE.
AAAAAAH!
COME ON, BOYS!
WE'RE THROUGH!
STEEL, KILL THE PORTAL! NOW!
SHUUNK
DONE.
JOHN. YOUR COMM DEVICE IS TWO-WAY.
I HEARD YOUR SYSTEMS TELLING YOU TO SHUT THE PORTAL DOWN TEN MINUTES AGO.
YOU ENDANGERED THE WHOLE WORLD WAITING FOR US.
YEAH, WELL.
I GUESS I TRIED TO DO WHAT SUPERMAN WOULD HAVE DONE.
I exhale.
And I realize...
Yeah...

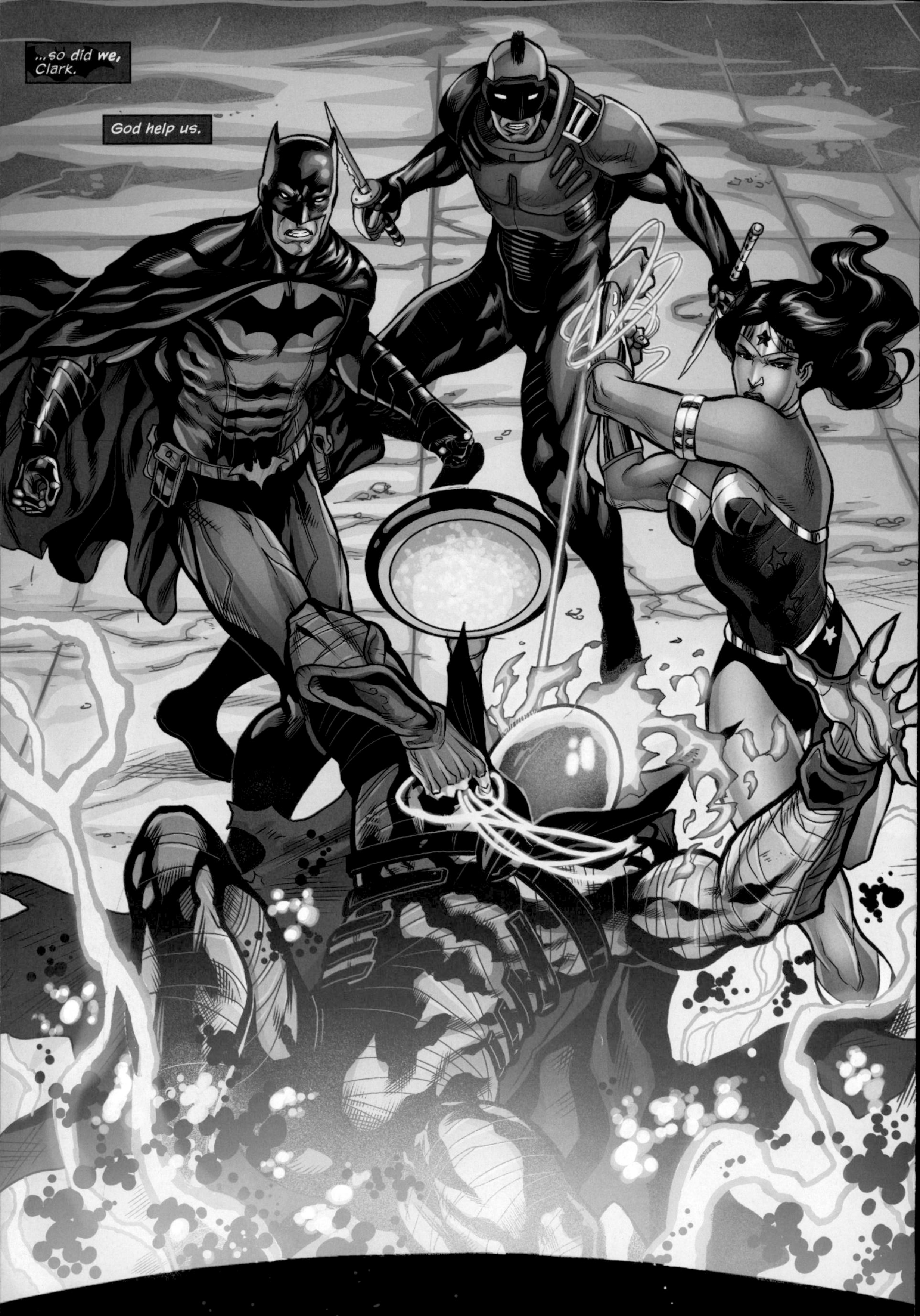

...so did we, Clark.
God help us.

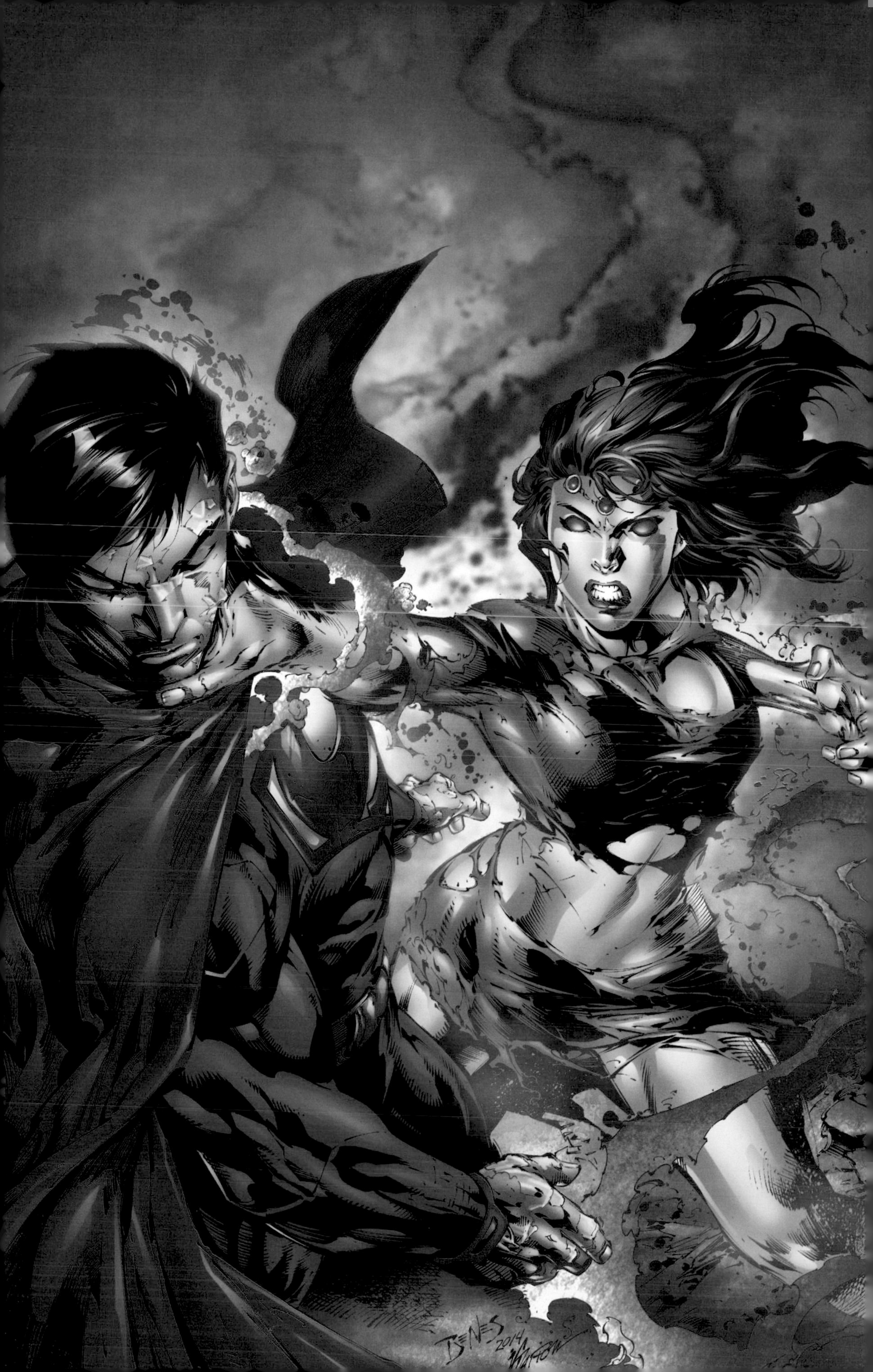

SUPERMAN DOOMED

[INFECTED] chapter 4

"LOCKDOWN"

STORY
SCOTT LOBDELL

PENCILS
ED BENES AND **JACK HERBERT**

INKS
JAIME MENDOZA & **VICENTE CIFUENTES**

COLORS
PETE PANTAZIS AND **JEROMY COX**

LETTERS
ROB LEIGH

COVER
ED BENES, JONATHAN GLAPION AND **PETE PANTAZIS**

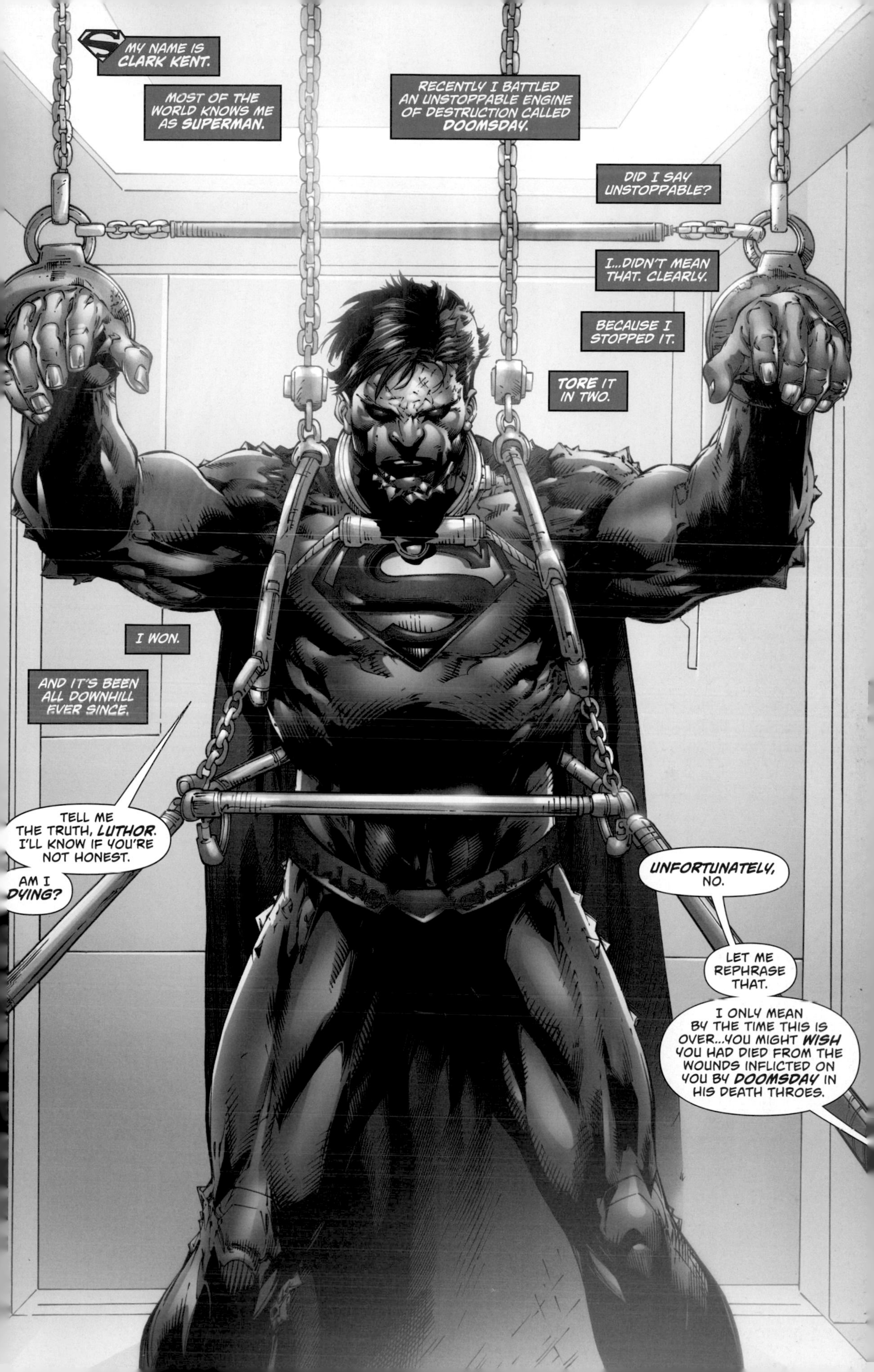
MY NAME IS CLARK KENT.
MOST OF THE WORLD KNOWS ME AS SUPERMAN.
RECENTLY I BATTLED AN UNSTOPPABLE ENGINE OF DESTRUCTION CALLED DOOMSDAY.
DID I SAY UNSTOPPABLE?
I...DIDN'T MEAN THAT. CLEARLY.
BECAUSE I STOPPED IT.
TORE IT IN TWO.
I WON.
AND IT'S BEEN ALL DOWNHILL EVER SINCE.
TELL ME THE TRUTH, LUTHOR. I'LL KNOW IF YOU'RE NOT HONEST.
AM I DYING?
UNFORTUNATELY, NO.
LET ME REPHRASE THAT.
I ONLY MEAN BY THE TIME THIS IS OVER...YOU MIGHT WISH YOU HAD DIED FROM THE WOUNDS INFLICTED ON YOU BY DOOMSDAY IN HIS DEATH THROES.

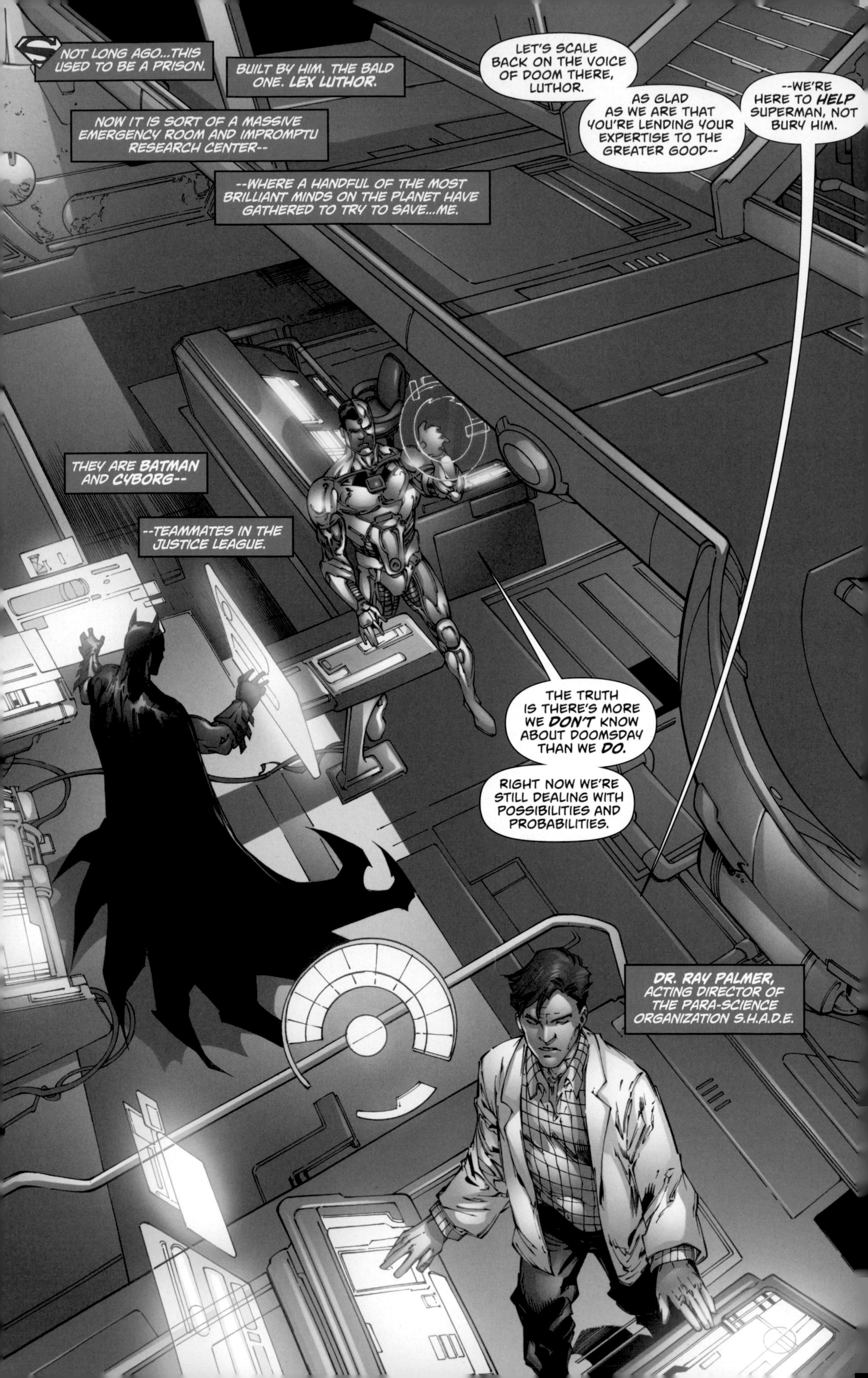
NOT LONG AGO...THIS USED TO BE A PRISON.
BUILT BY HIM. THE BALD ONE. LEX LUTHOR.
NOW IT IS SORT OF A MASSIVE EMERGENCY ROOM AND IMPROMPTU RESEARCH CENTER--
--WHERE A HANDFUL OF THE MOST BRILLIANT MINDS ON THE PLANET HAVE GATHERED TO TRY TO SAVE...ME.
LET'S SCALE BACK ON THE VOICE OF DOOM THERE, LUTHOR.
AS GLAD AS WE ARE THAT YOU'RE LENDING YOUR EXPERTISE TO THE GREATER GOOD--
--WE'RE HERE TO HELP SUPERMAN, NOT BURY HIM.
THEY ARE BATMAN AND CYBORG--
--TEAMMATES IN THE JUSTICE LEAGUE.
THE TRUTH IS THERE'S MORE WE DON'T KNOW ABOUT DOOMSDAY THAN WE DO.
RIGHT NOW WE'RE STILL DEALING WITH POSSIBILITIES AND PROBABILITIES.
DR. RAY PALMER, ACTING DIRECTOR OF THE PARA-SCIENCE ORGANIZATION S.H.A.D.E.

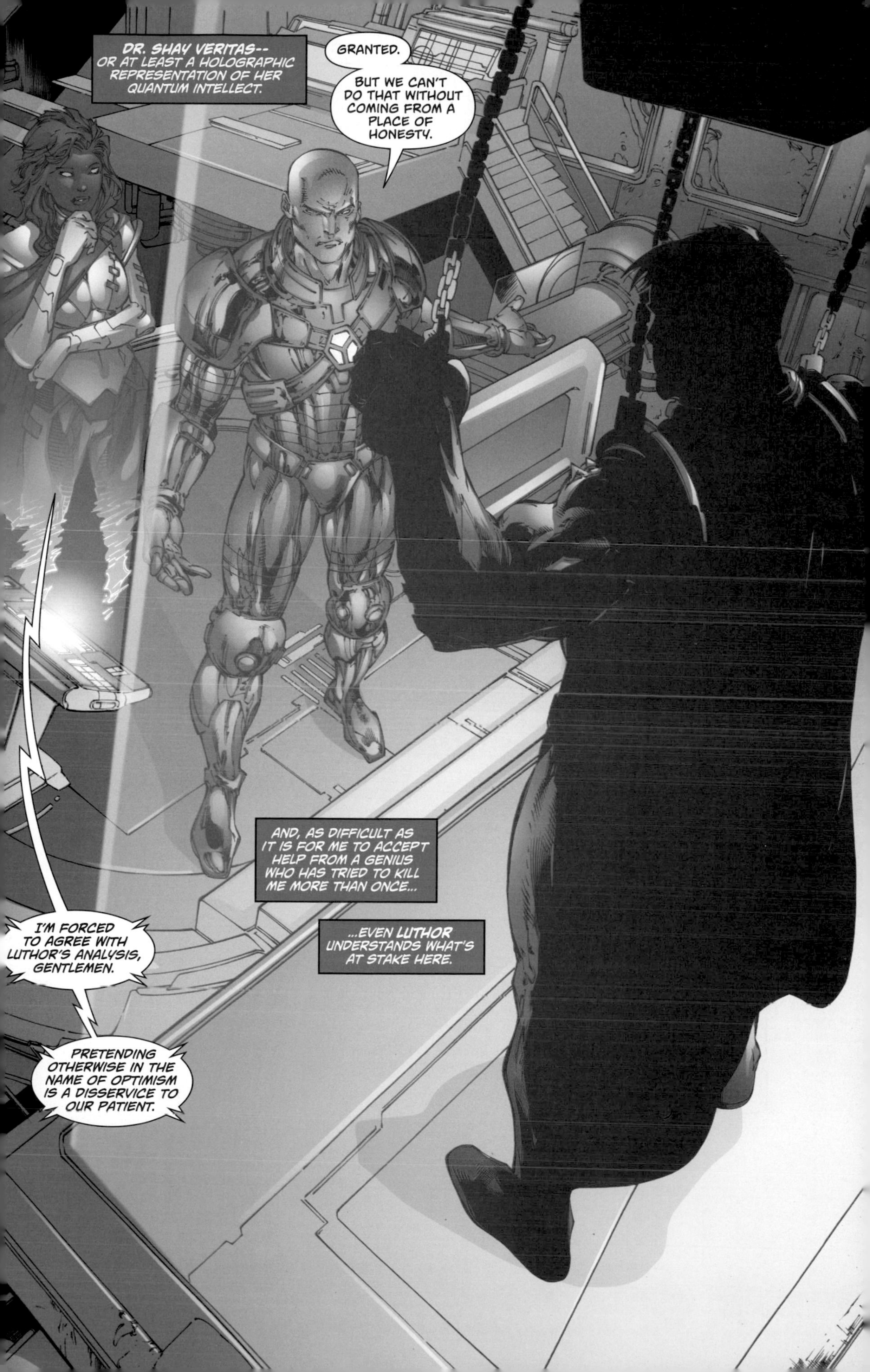
DR. SHAY VERITAS--
OR AT LEAST A HOLOGRAPHIC REPRESENTATION OF HER QUANTUM INTELLECT.
GRANTED.
BUT WE CAN'T DO THAT WITHOUT COMING FROM A PLACE OF HONESTY.
AND, AS DIFFICULT AS IT IS FOR ME TO ACCEPT HELP FROM A GENIUS WHO HAS TRIED TO KILL ME MORE THAN ONCE...
...EVEN LUTHOR UNDERSTANDS WHAT'S AT STAKE HERE.
I'M FORCED TO AGREE WITH LUTHOR'S ANALYSIS, GENTLEMEN.
PRETENDING OTHERWISE IN THE NAME OF OPTIMISM IS A DISSERVICE TO OUR PATIENT.

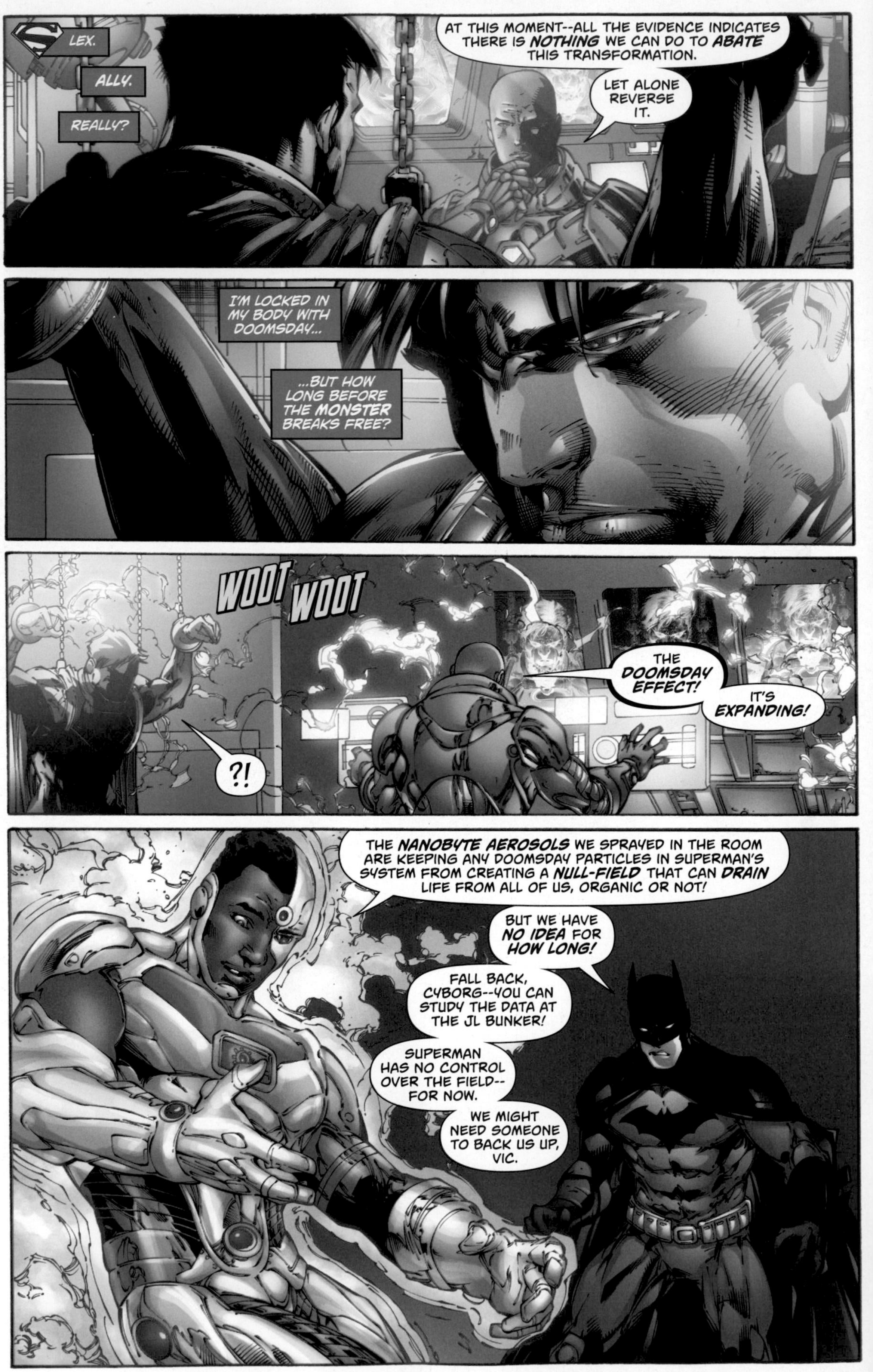
LEX.
ALLY.
REALLY?
AT THIS MOMENT--ALL THE EVIDENCE INDICATES THERE IS NOTHING WE CAN DO TO ABATE THIS TRANSFORMATION.
LET ALONE REVERSE IT.
I'M LOCKED IN MY BODY WITH DOOMSDAY...
...BUT HOW LONG BEFORE THE MONSTER BREAKS FREE?
WOOT WOOT
?!
THE DOOMSDAY EFFECT!
IT'S EXPANDING!
THE NANOBYTE AEROSOLS WE SPRAYED IN THE ROOM ARE KEEPING ANY DOOMSDAY PARTICLES IN SUPERMAN'S SYSTEM FROM CREATING A NULL-FIELD THAT CAN DRAIN LIFE FROM ALL OF US, ORGANIC OR NOT!
BUT WE HAVE NO IDEA FOR HOW LONG!
FALL BACK, CYBORG--YOU CAN STUDY THE DATA AT THE JL BUNKER!
SUPERMAN HAS NO CONTROL OVER THE FIELD-- FOR NOW.
WE MIGHT NEED SOMEONE TO BACK US UP, VIC.

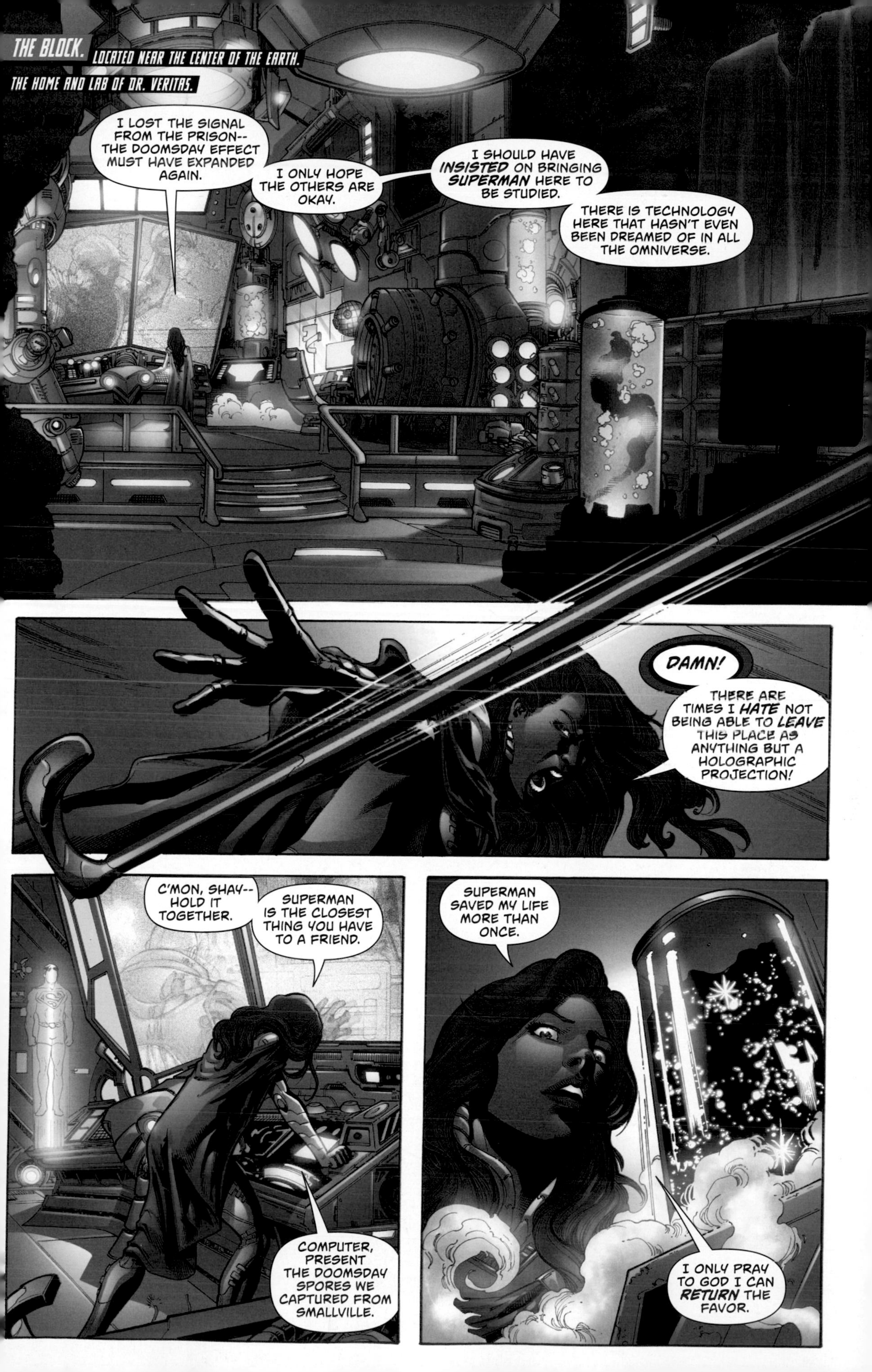
THE BLOCK. LOCATED NEAR THE CENTER OF THE EARTH.
THE HOME AND LAB OF DR. VERITAS.
I LOST THE SIGNAL FROM THE PRISON-- THE DOOMSDAY EFFECT MUST HAVE EXPANDED AGAIN.
I ONLY HOPE THE OTHERS ARE OKAY.
I SHOULD HAVE INSISTED ON BRINGING SUPERMAN HERE TO BE STUDIED.
THERE IS TECHNOLOGY HERE THAT HASN'T EVEN BEEN DREAMED OF IN ALL THE OMNIVERSE.
DAMN!
THERE ARE TIMES I HATE NOT BEING ABLE TO LEAVE THIS PLACE AS ANYTHING BUT A HOLOGRAPHIC PROJECTION!
C'MON, SHAY-- HOLD IT TOGETHER.
SUPERMAN IS THE CLOSEST THING YOU HAVE TO A FRIEND.
COMPUTER, PRESENT THE DOOMSDAY SPORES WE CAPTURED FROM SMALLVILLE.
SUPERMAN SAVED MY LIFE MORE THAN ONCE.
I ONLY PRAY TO GOD I CAN RETURN THE FAVOR.

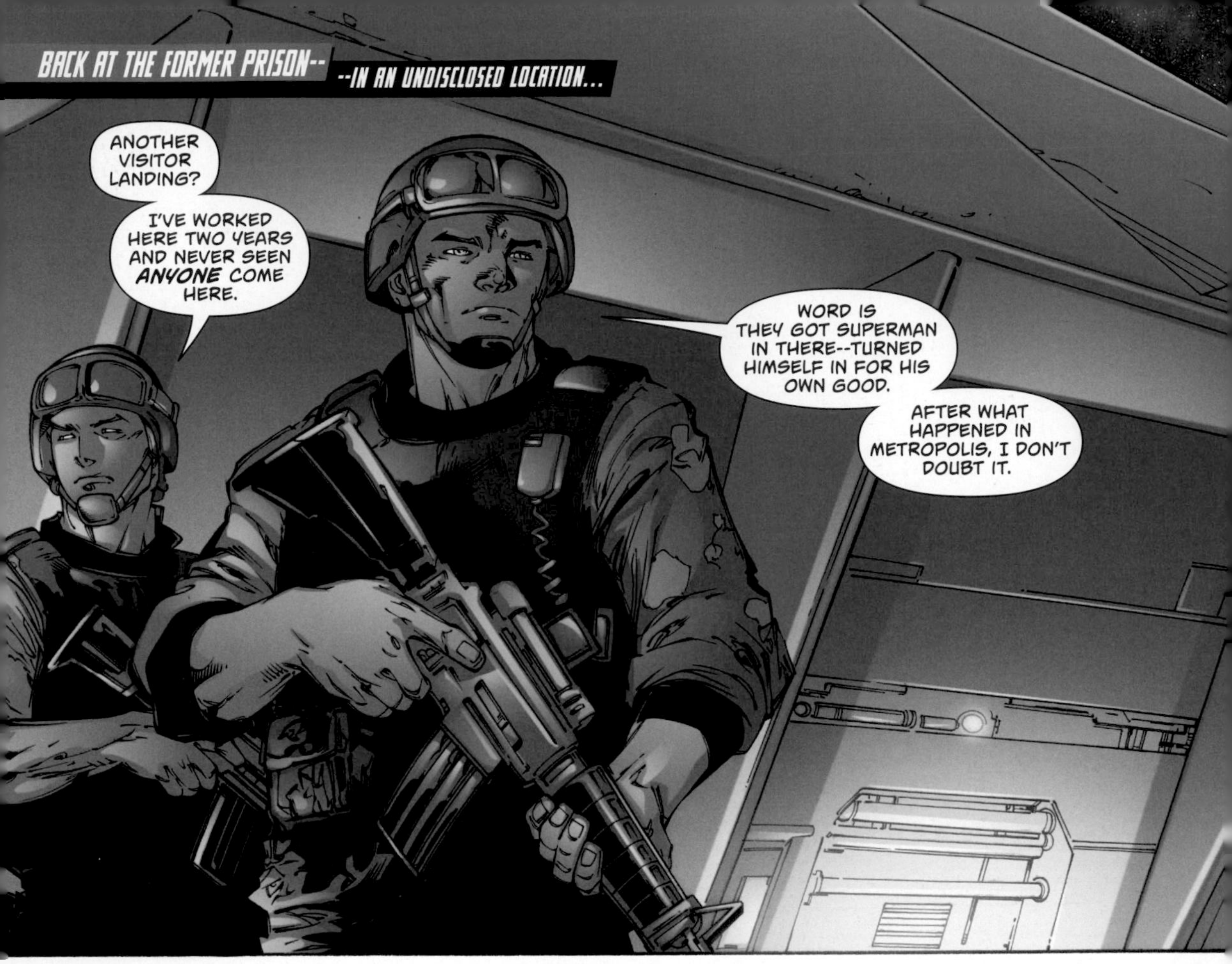
BACK AT THE FORMER PRISON--
--IN AN UNDISCLOSED LOCATION...
ANOTHER VISITOR LANDING?
I'VE WORKED HERE TWO YEARS AND NEVER SEEN ANYONE COME HERE.
WORD IS THEY GOT SUPERMAN IN THERE--TURNED HIMSELF IN FOR HIS OWN GOOD.
AFTER WHAT HAPPENED IN METROPOLIS, I DON'T DOUBT IT.

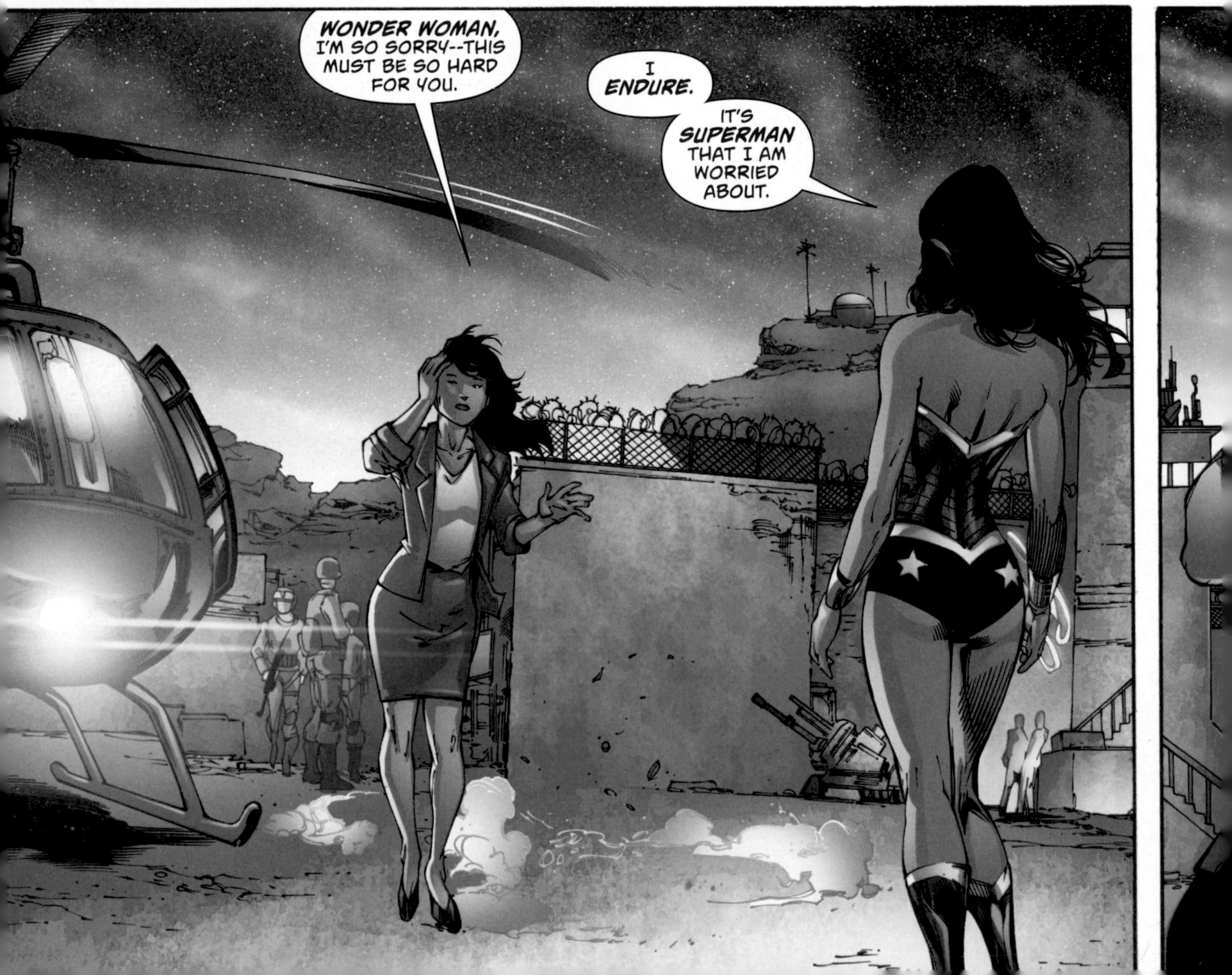
WONDER WOMAN, I'M SO SORRY--THIS MUST BE SO HARD FOR YOU.
I ENDURE.
IT'S SUPERMAN THAT I AM WORRIED ABOUT.

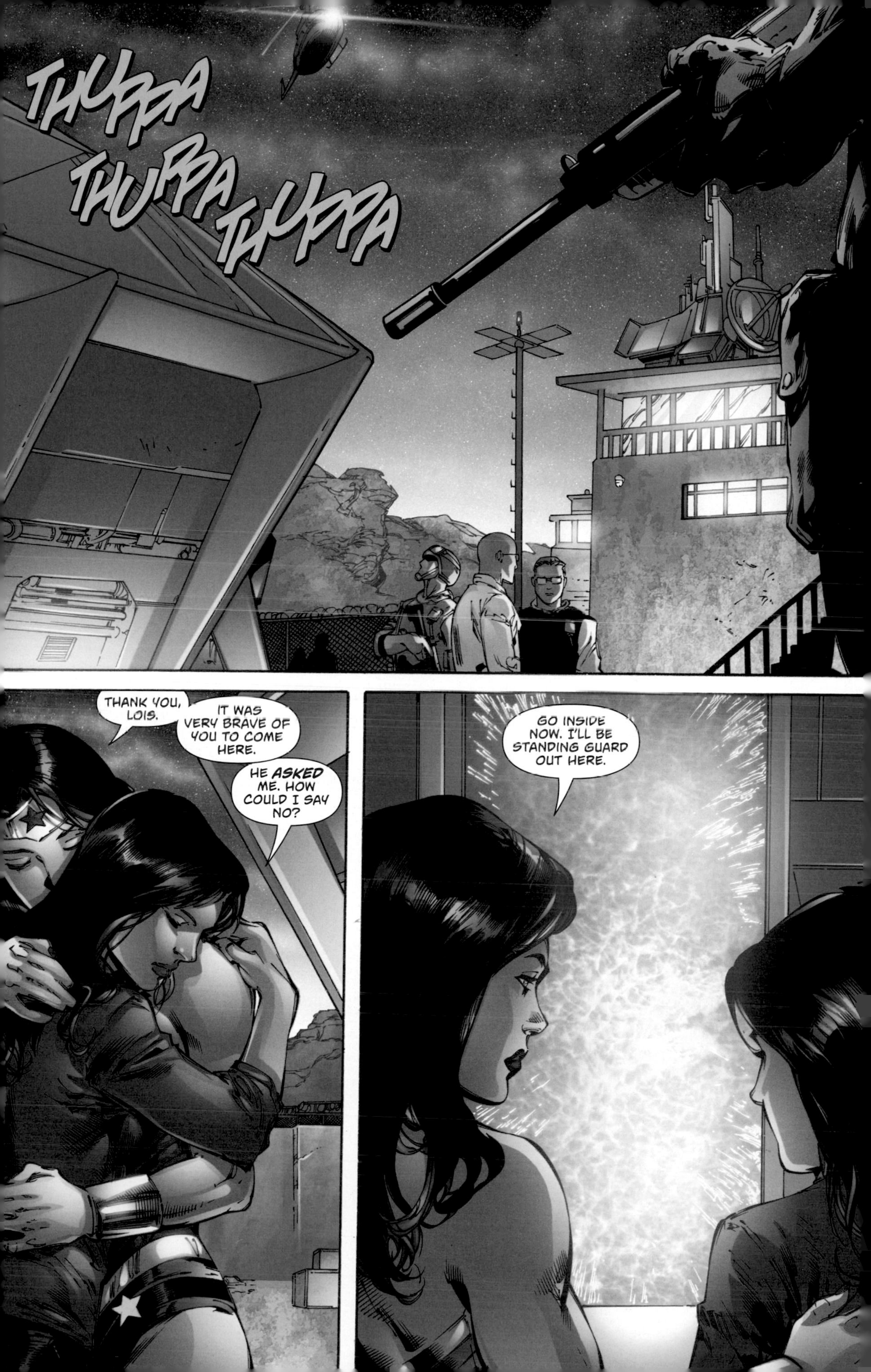
THUPPA THUPPA THUPPA
THANK YOU, LOIS.
IT WAS VERY BRAVE OF YOU TO COME HERE.
HE ASKED ME. HOW COULD I SAY NO?
GO INSIDE NOW. I'LL BE STANDING GUARD OUT HERE.

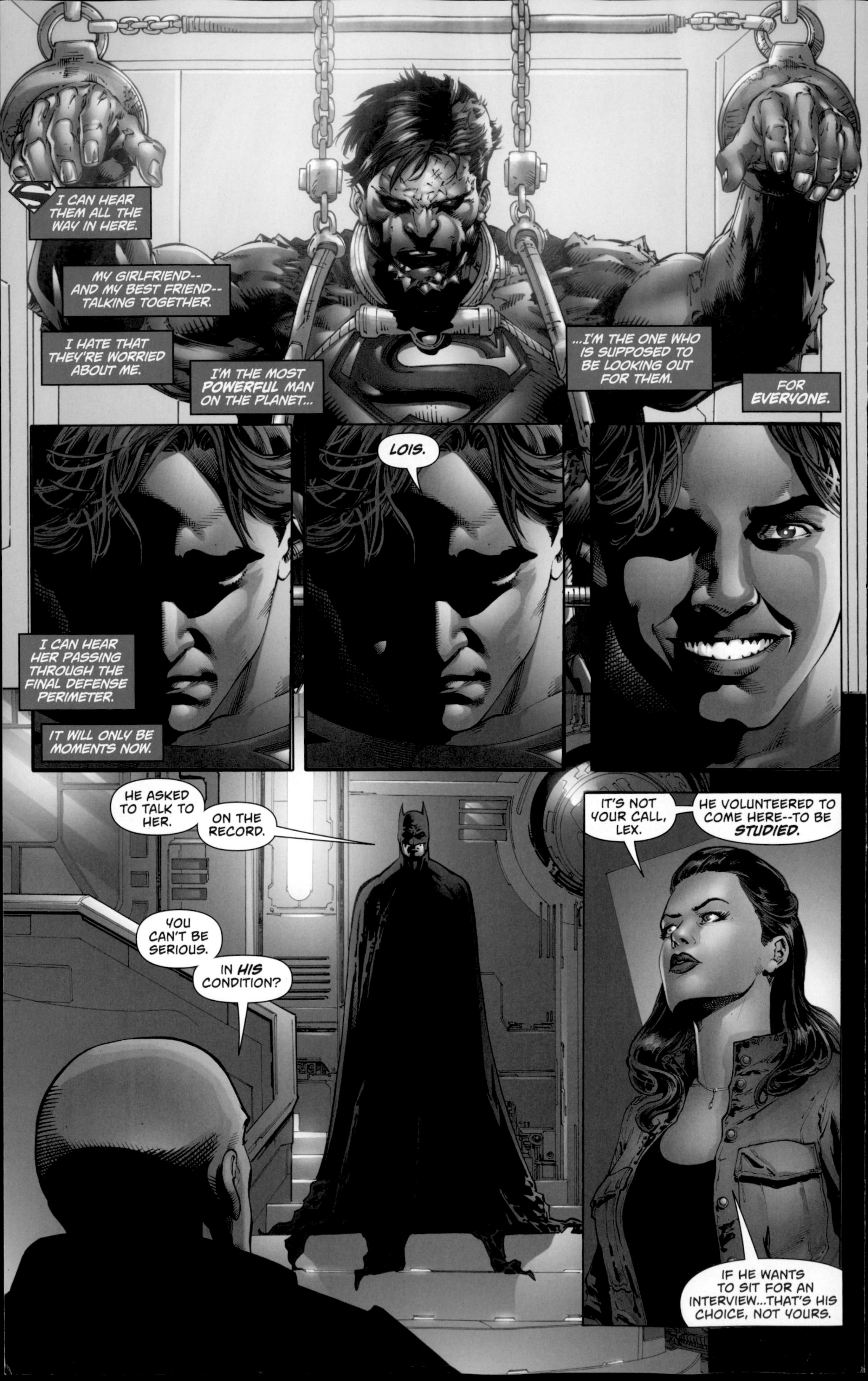
I CAN HEAR THEM ALL THE WAY IN HERE.
MY GIRLFRIEND-- AND MY BEST FRIEND-- TALKING TOGETHER.
I HATE THAT THEY'RE WORRIED ABOUT ME.
I'M THE MOST POWERFUL MAN ON THE PLANET...
...I'M THE ONE WHO IS SUPPOSED TO BE LOOKING OUT FOR THEM.
FOR EVERYONE.
I CAN HEAR HER PASSING THROUGH THE FINAL DEFENSE PERIMETER.
IT WILL ONLY BE MOMENTS NOW.
LOIS.
HE ASKED TO TALK TO HER.
ON THE RECORD.
YOU CAN'T BE SERIOUS.
IN HIS CONDITION?
IT'S NOT YOUR CALL, LEX.
HE VOLUNTEERED TO COME HERE--TO BE STUDIED.
IF HE WANTS TO SIT FOR AN INTERVIEW...THAT'S HIS CHOICE, NOT YOURS.

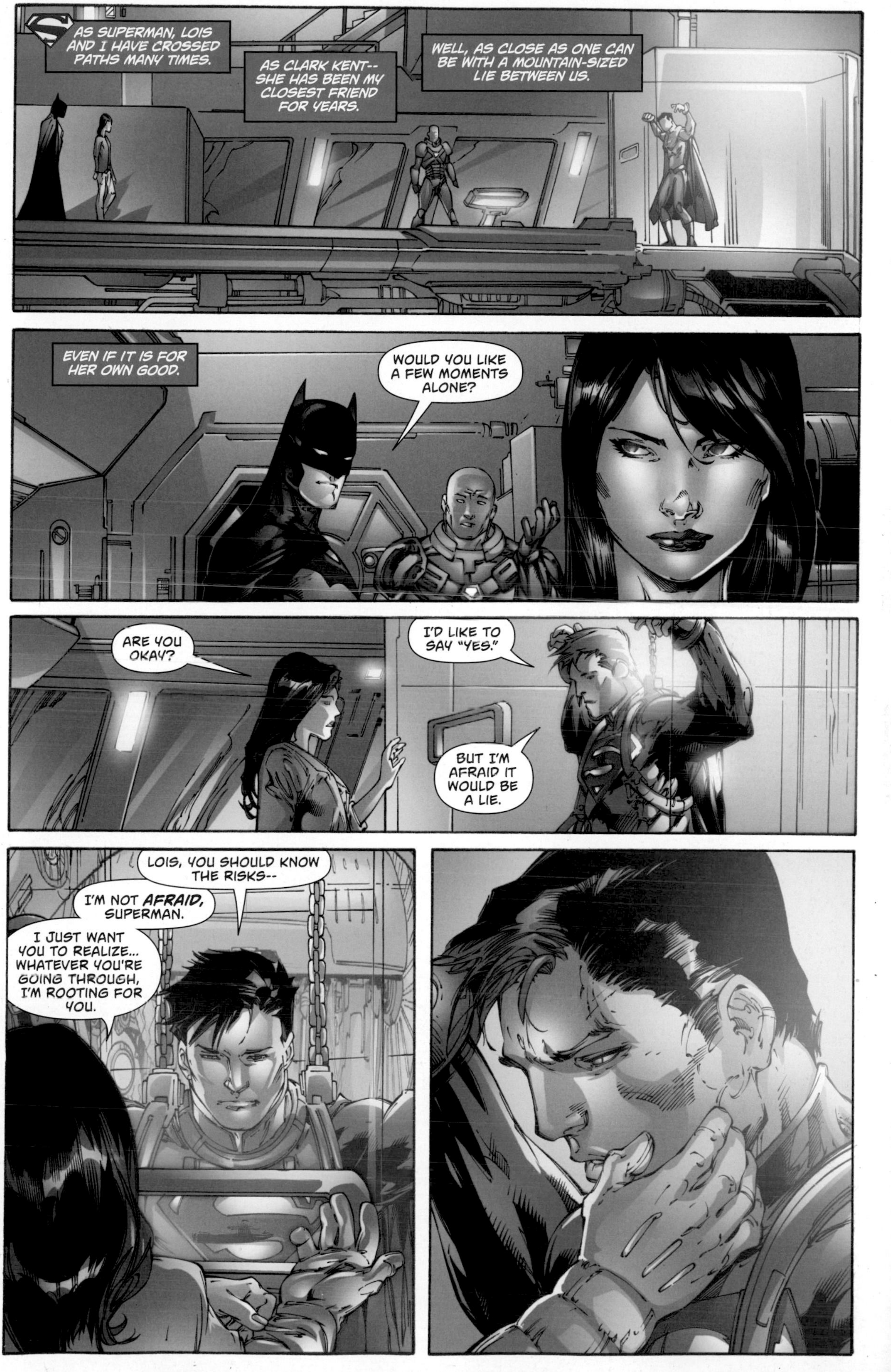
AS SUPERMAN, LOIS AND I HAVE CROSSED PATHS MANY TIMES.
AS CLARK KENT--SHE HAS BEEN MY CLOSEST FRIEND FOR YEARS.
WELL, AS CLOSE AS ONE CAN BE WITH A MOUNTAIN-SIZED LIE BETWEEN US.
EVEN IF IT IS FOR HER OWN GOOD.
WOULD YOU LIKE A FEW MOMENTS ALONE?
ARE YOU OKAY?
I'D LIKE TO SAY "YES."
BUT I'M AFRAID IT WOULD BE A LIE.
LOIS, YOU SHOULD KNOW THE RISKS--
I'M NOT AFRAID, SUPERMAN.
I JUST WANT YOU TO REALIZE... WHATEVER YOU'RE GOING THROUGH, I'M ROOTING FOR YOU.

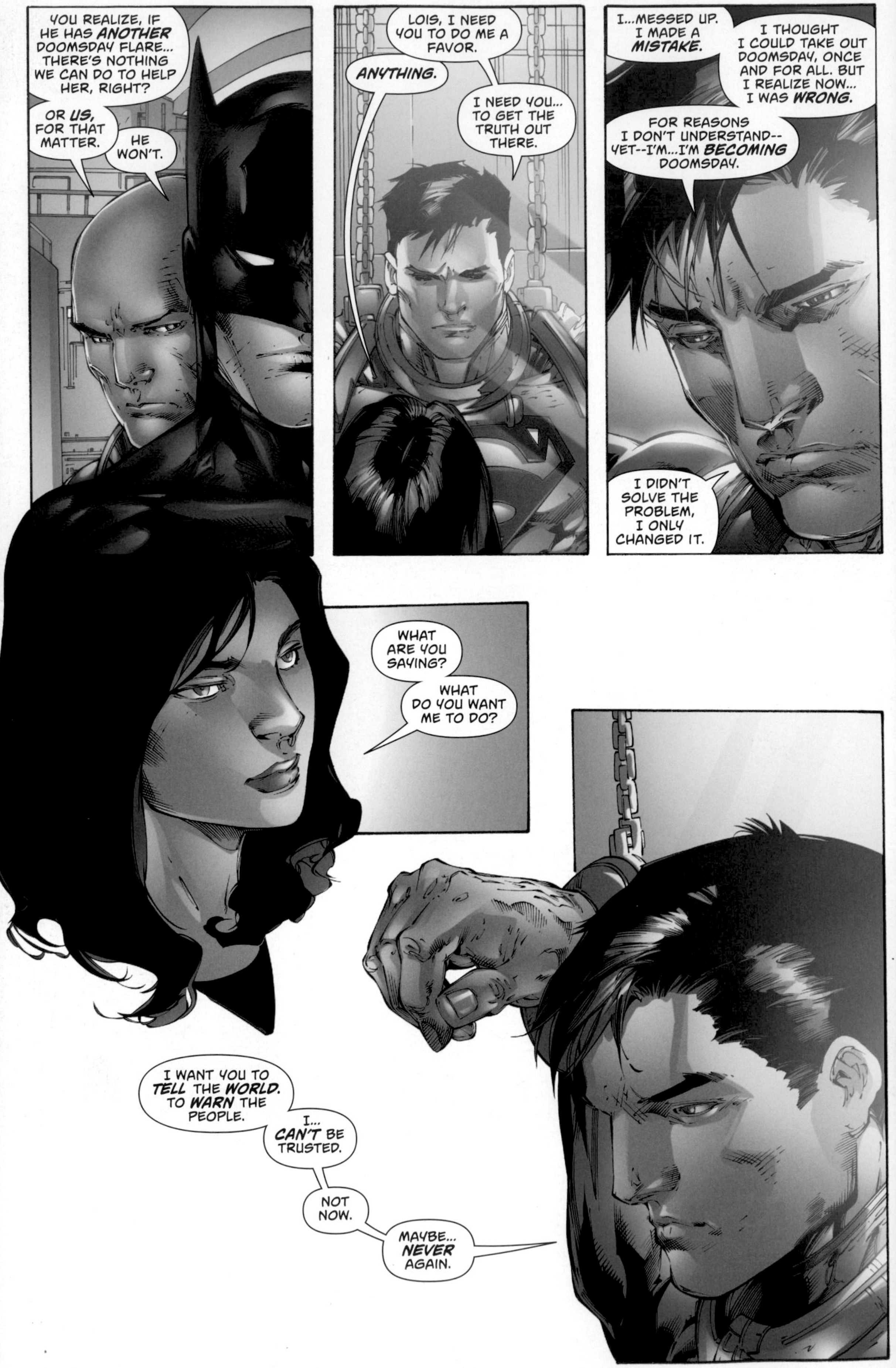
YOU REALIZE, IF HE HAS ANOTHER DOOMSDAY FLARE... THERE'S NOTHING WE CAN DO TO HELP HER, RIGHT?
OR US, FOR THAT MATTER.
HE WON'T.
LOIS, I NEED YOU TO DO ME A FAVOR.
ANYTHING.
I NEED YOU... TO GET THE TRUTH OUT THERE.
I...MESSED UP. I MADE A MISTAKE.
I THOUGHT I COULD TAKE OUT DOOMSDAY, ONCE AND FOR ALL. BUT I REALIZE NOW... I WAS WRONG.
FOR REASONS I DON'T UNDERSTAND-- YET--I'M...I'M BECOMING DOOMSDAY.
I DIDN'T SOLVE THE PROBLEM, I ONLY CHANGED IT.
WHAT ARE YOU SAYING?
WHAT DO YOU WANT ME TO DO?
I WANT YOU TO TELL THE WORLD. TO WARN THE PEOPLE.
I... CAN'T BE TRUSTED.
NOT NOW.
MAYBE... NEVER AGAIN.

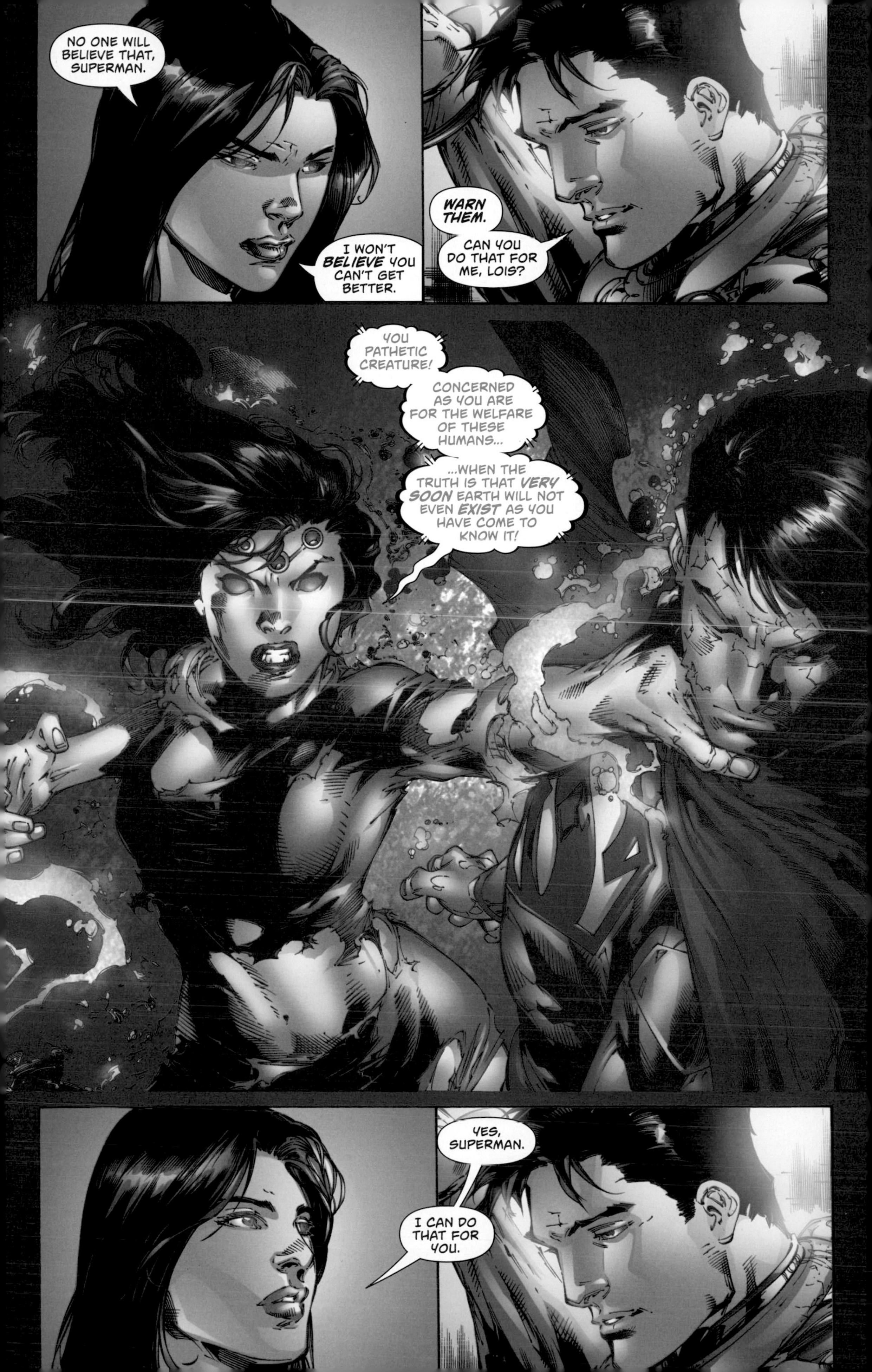

NO ONE WILL BELIEVE THAT, SUPERMAN.
I WON'T BELIEVE YOU CAN'T GET BETTER.
WARN THEM.
CAN YOU DO THAT FOR ME, LOIS?
YOU PATHETIC CREATURE!
CONCERNED AS YOU ARE FOR THE WELFARE OF THESE HUMANS...
...WHEN THE TRUTH IS THAT VERY SOON EARTH WILL NOT EVEN EXIST AS YOU HAVE COME TO KNOW IT!
YES, SUPERMAN.
I CAN DO THAT FOR YOU.

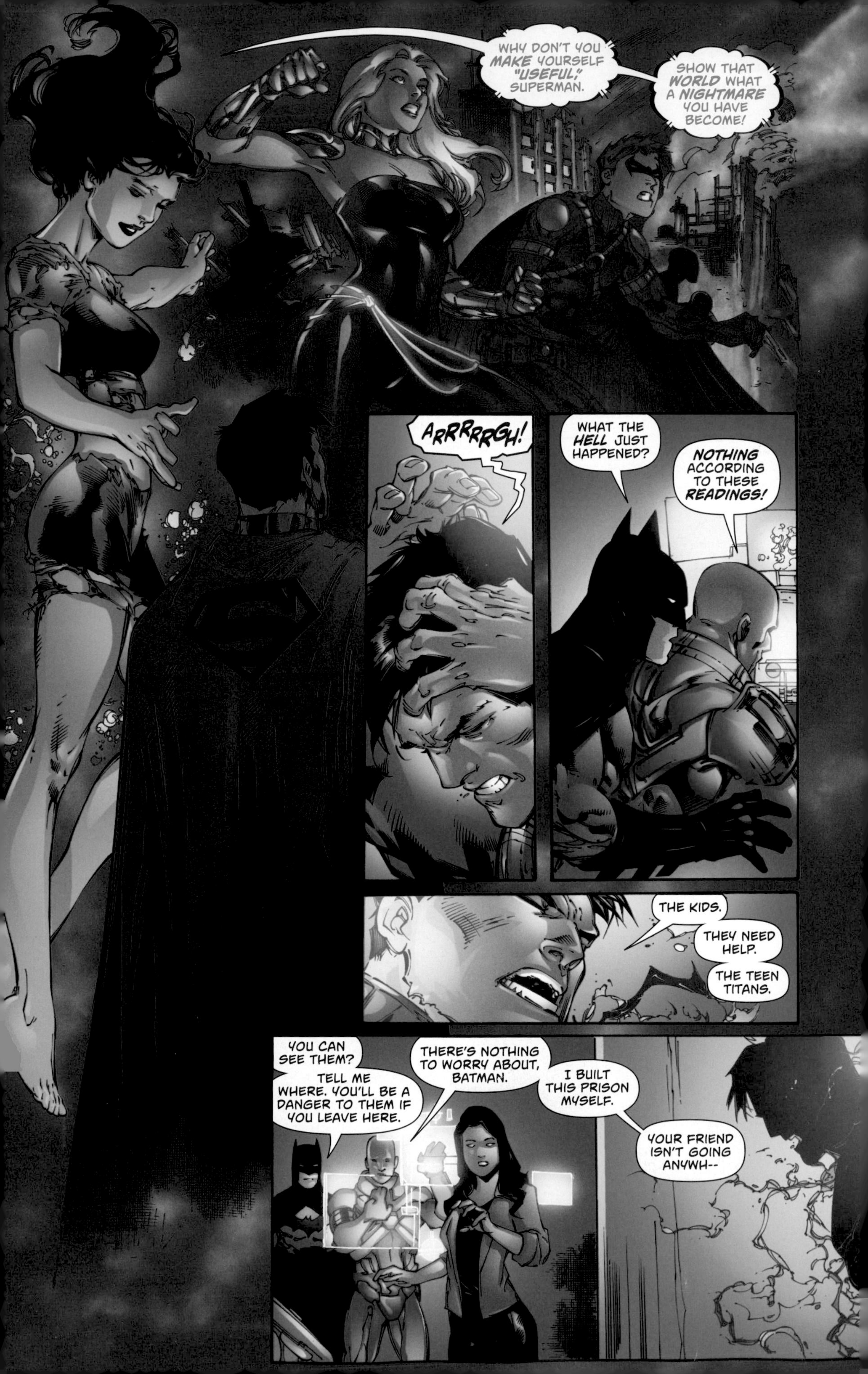

WHY DON'T YOU MAKE YOURSELF "USEFUL," SUPERMAN.
SHOW THAT WORLD WHAT A NIGHTMARE YOU HAVE BECOME!
ARRRRRGH!
WHAT THE HELL JUST HAPPENED?
NOTHING ACCORDING TO THESE READINGS!
THE KIDS.
THEY NEED HELP.
THE TEEN TITANS.
YOU CAN SEE THEM?
TELL ME WHERE. YOU'LL BE A DANGER TO THEM IF YOU LEAVE HERE.
THERE'S NOTHING TO WORRY ABOUT, BATMAN.
I BUILT THIS PRISON MYSELF.
YOUR FRIEND ISN'T GOING ANYWH--

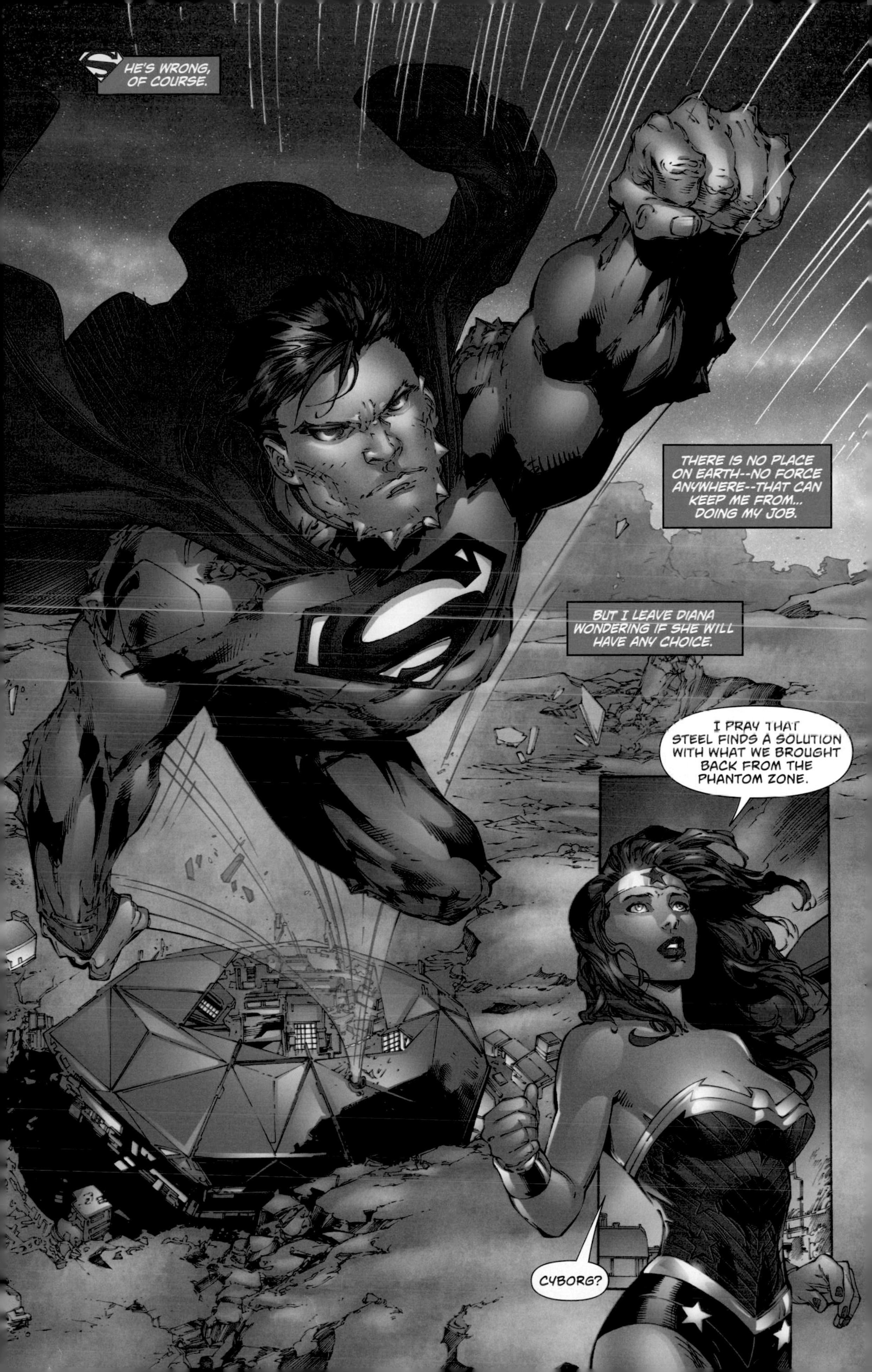
HE'S WRONG, OF COURSE.
THERE IS NO PLACE ON EARTH--NO FORCE ANYWHERE--THAT CAN KEEP ME FROM... DOING MY JOB.
BUT I LEAVE DIANA WONDERING IF SHE WILL HAVE ANY CHOICE.
I PRAY THAT STEEL FINDS A SOLUTION WITH WHAT WE BROUGHT BACK FROM THE PHANTOM ZONE.
CYBORG?

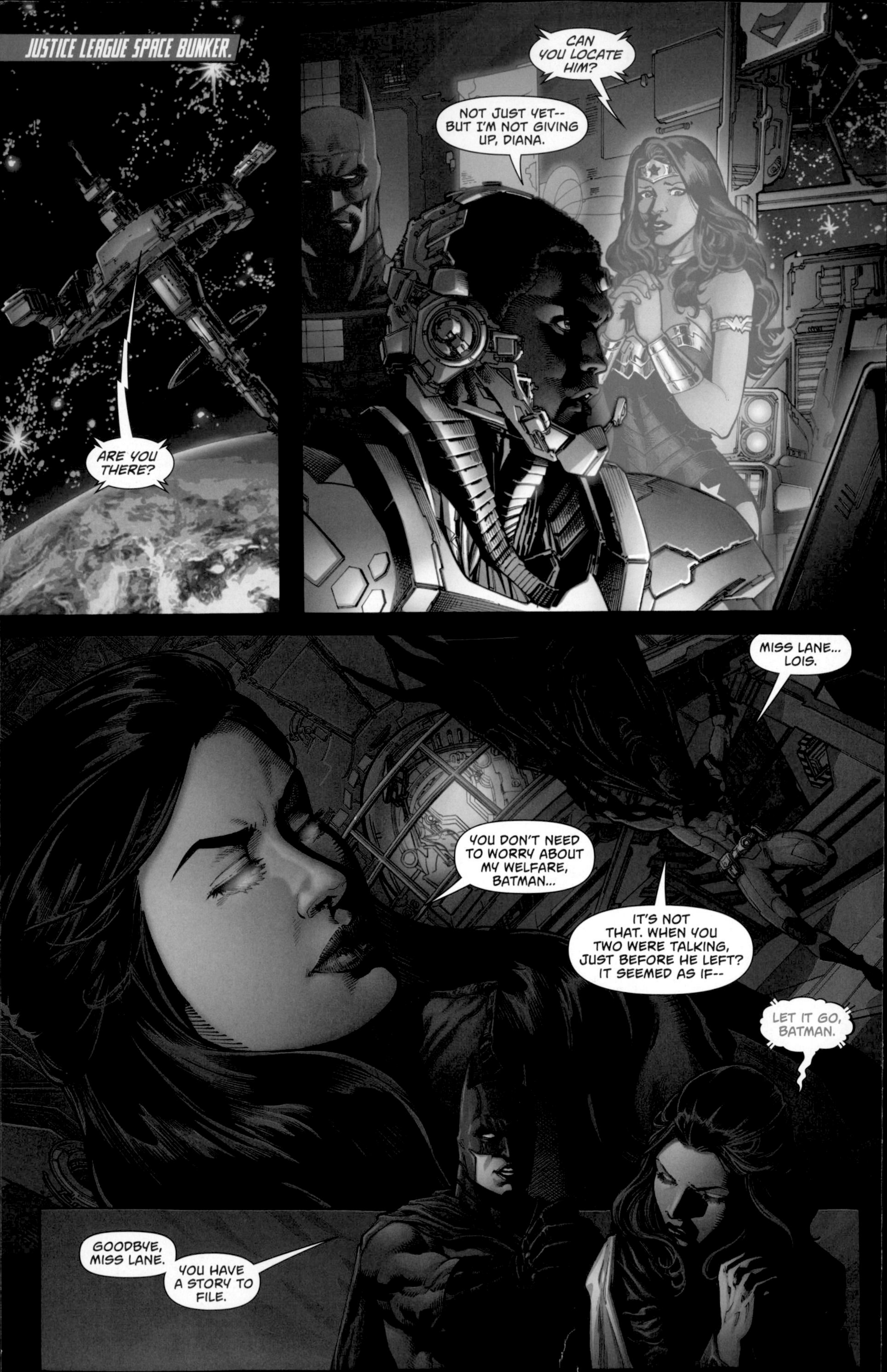
JUSTICE LEAGUE SPACE BUNKER.
ARE YOU THERE?
CAN YOU LOCATE HIM?
NOT JUST YET-- BUT I'M NOT GIVING UP, DIANA.
MISS LANE... LOIS.
YOU DON'T NEED TO WORRY ABOUT MY WELFARE, BATMAN...
IT'S NOT THAT. WHEN YOU TWO WERE TALKING, JUST BEFORE HE LEFT? IT SEEMED AS IF--
LET IT GO, BATMAN.
GOODBYE, MISS LANE.
YOU HAVE A STORY TO FILE.

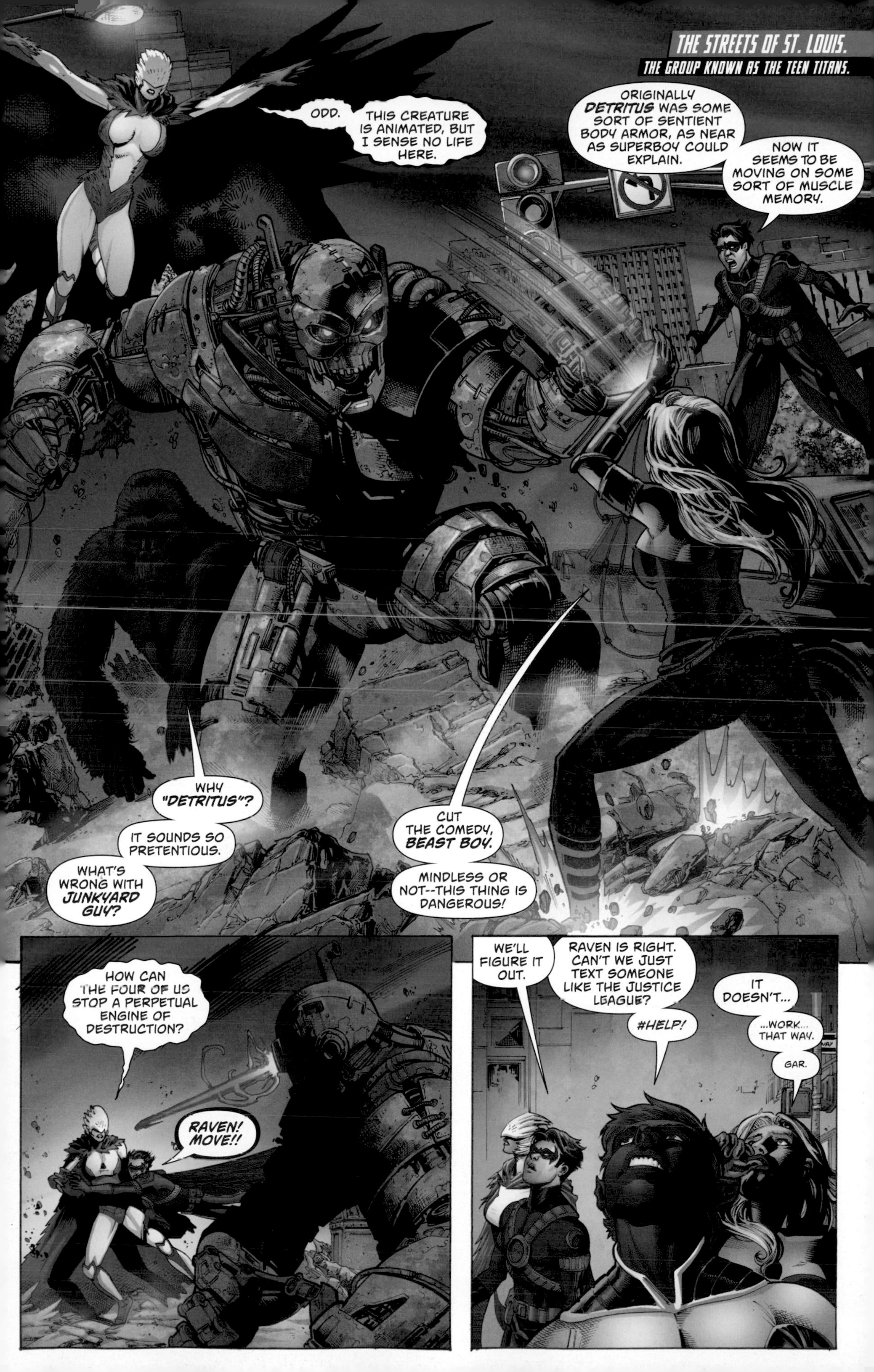
THE STREETS OF ST. LOUIS.
THE GROUP KNOWN AS THE TEEN TITANS.
ODD.
THIS CREATURE IS ANIMATED, BUT I SENSE NO LIFE HERE.
ORIGINALLY *DETRITUS* WAS SOME SORT OF SENTIENT BODY ARMOR, AS NEAR AS SUPERBOY COULD EXPLAIN.
NOW IT SEEMS TO BE MOVING ON SOME SORT OF MUSCLE MEMORY.
WHY *"DETRITUS"*?
IT SOUNDS SO PRETENTIOUS.
WHAT'S WRONG WITH *JUNKYARD GUY?*
CUT THE COMEDY, *BEAST BOY.*
MINDLESS OR NOT--THIS THING IS DANGEROUS!
HOW CAN THE FOUR OF US STOP A PERPETUAL ENGINE OF DESTRUCTION?
RAVEN! MOVE!!
WE'LL FIGURE IT OUT.
RAVEN IS RIGHT. CAN'T WE JUST TEXT SOMEONE LIKE THE JUSTICE LEAGUE?
#HELP!
IT DOESN'T...
...WORK... THAT WAY.
GAR.

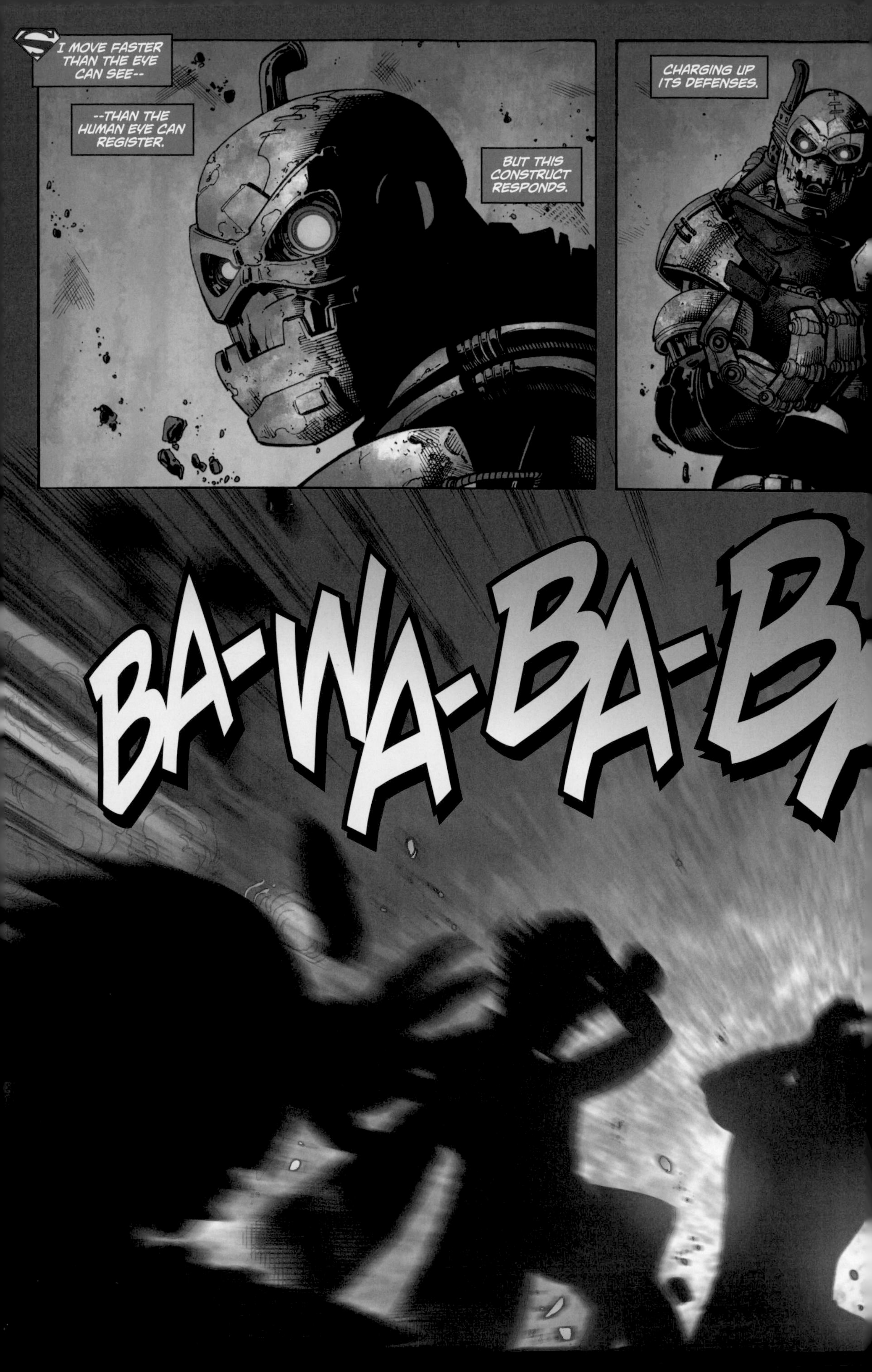
I MOVE FASTER THAN THE EYE CAN SEE--
--THAN THE HUMAN EYE CAN REGISTER.
BUT THIS CONSTRUCT RESPONDS.
CHARGING UP ITS DEFENSES.
BA-WA-BA-B

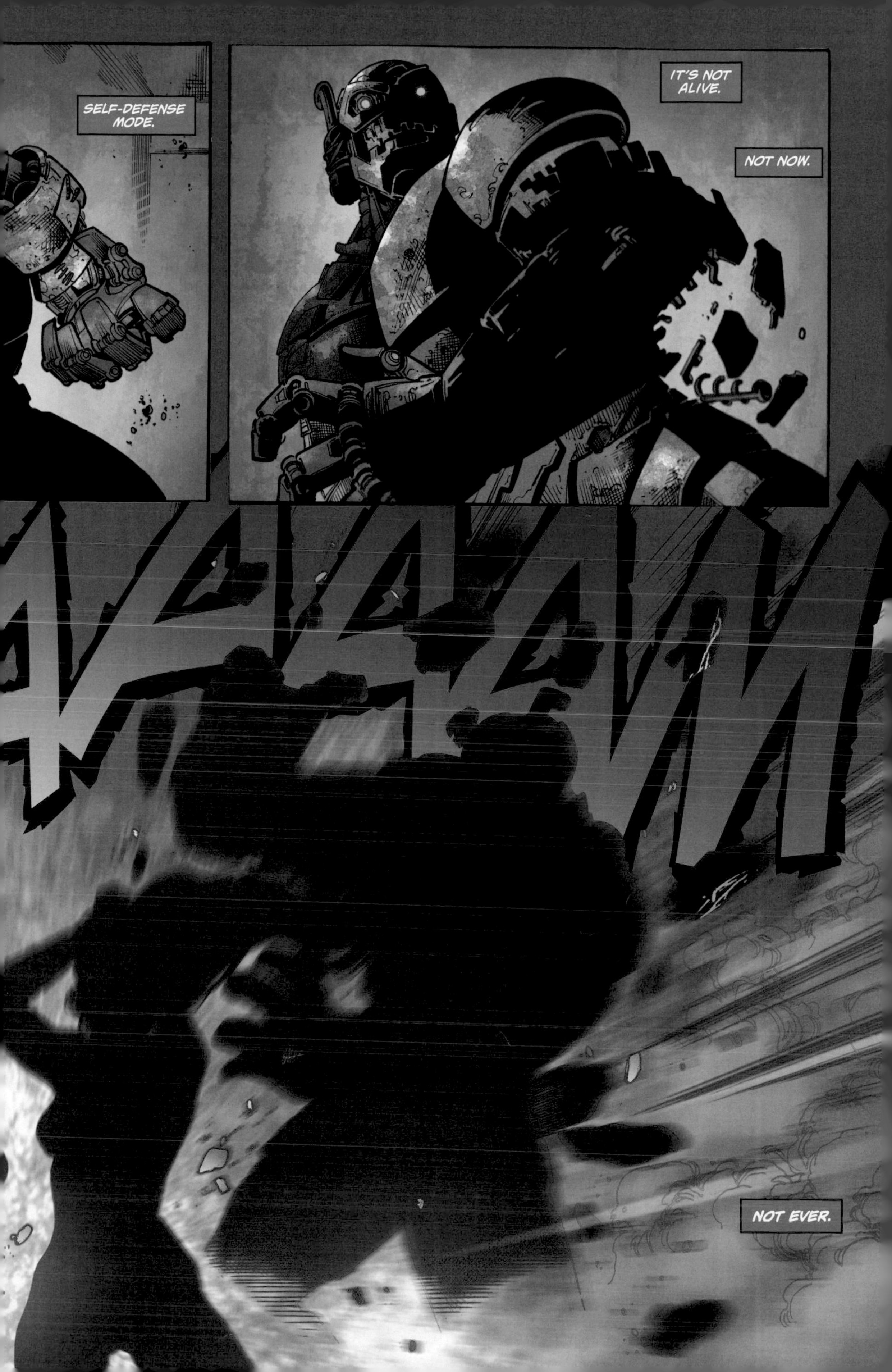
SELF-DEFENSE MODE.
IT'S NOT ALIVE.
NOT NOW.
NOT EVER.

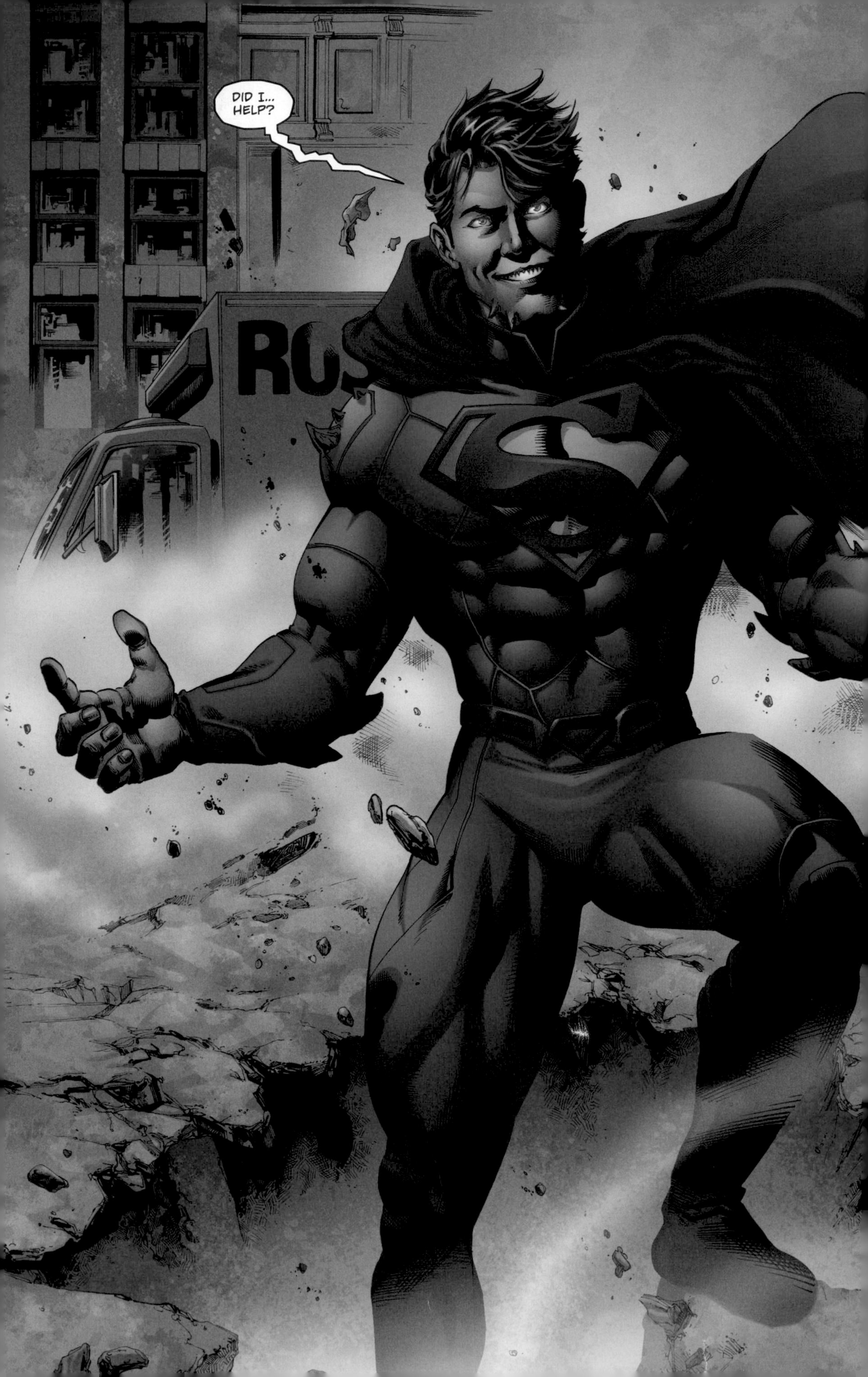
DID I... HELP?

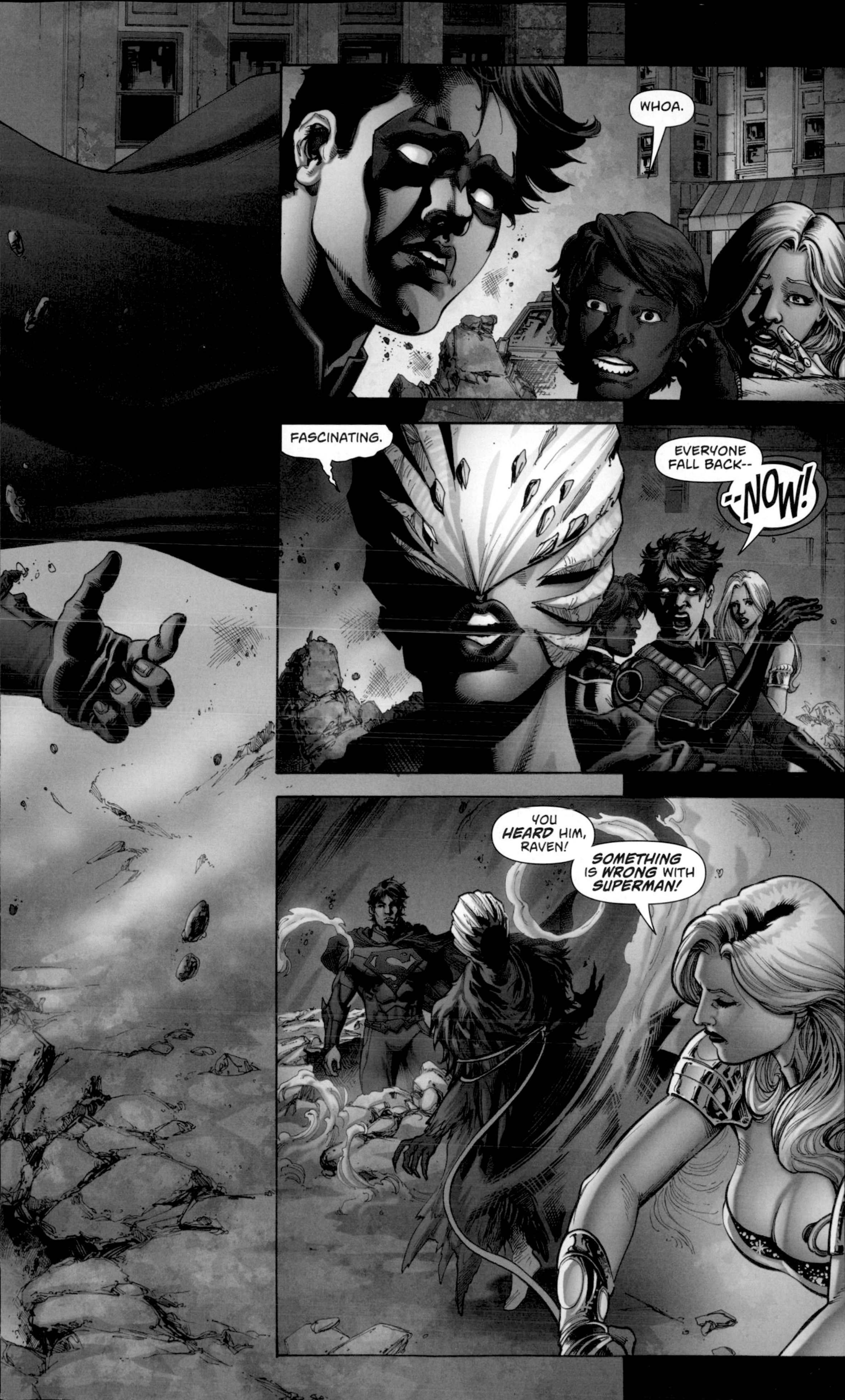

WHOA.
FASCINATING.
EVERYONE FALL BACK--
--NOW!
YOU HEARD HIM, RAVEN!
SOMETHING IS WRONG WITH SUPERMAN!

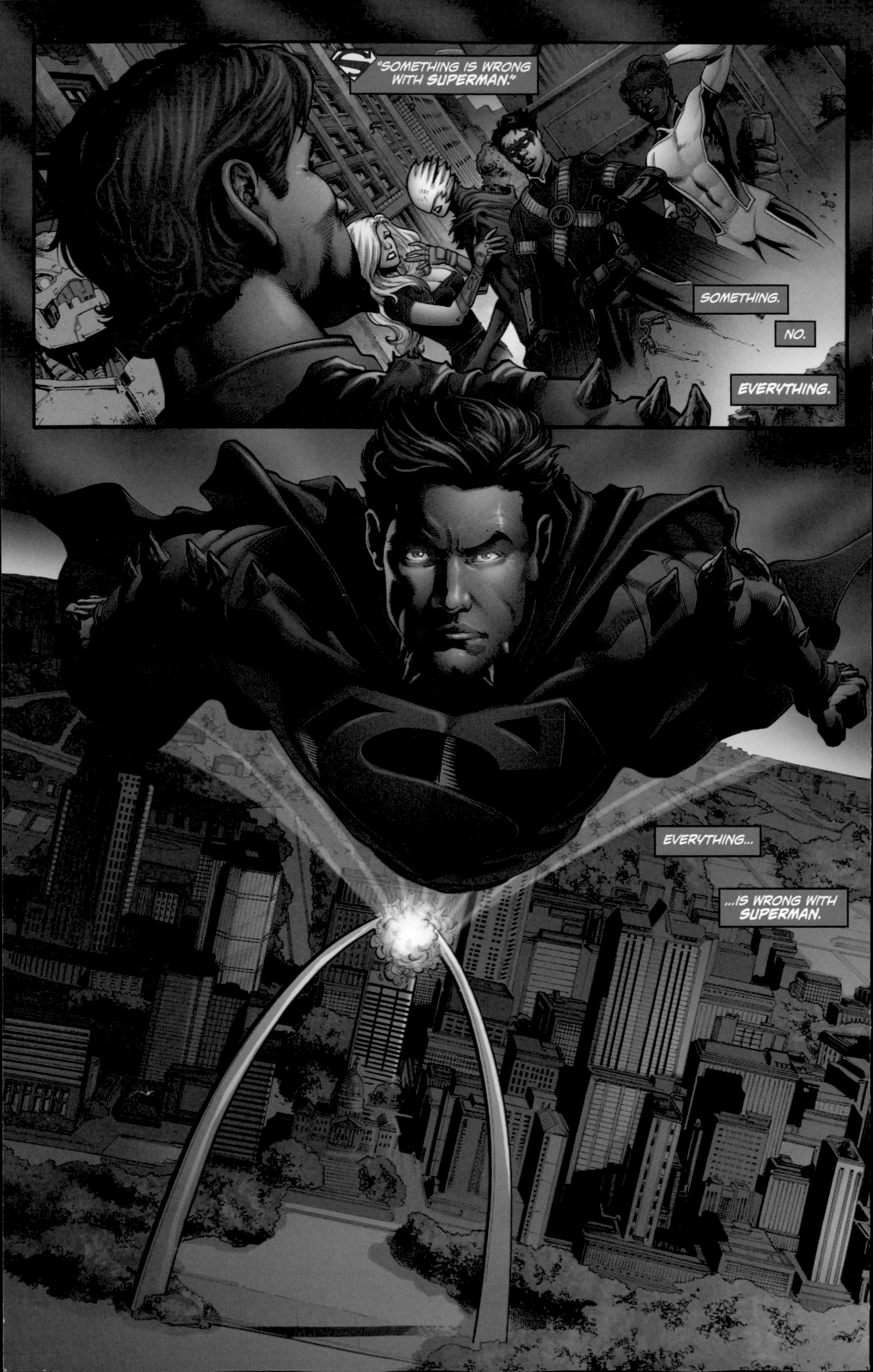
"SOMETHING IS WRONG WITH SUPERMAN."
SOMETHING.
NO.
EVERYTHING.
EVERYTHING...
...IS WRONG WITH SUPERMAN.

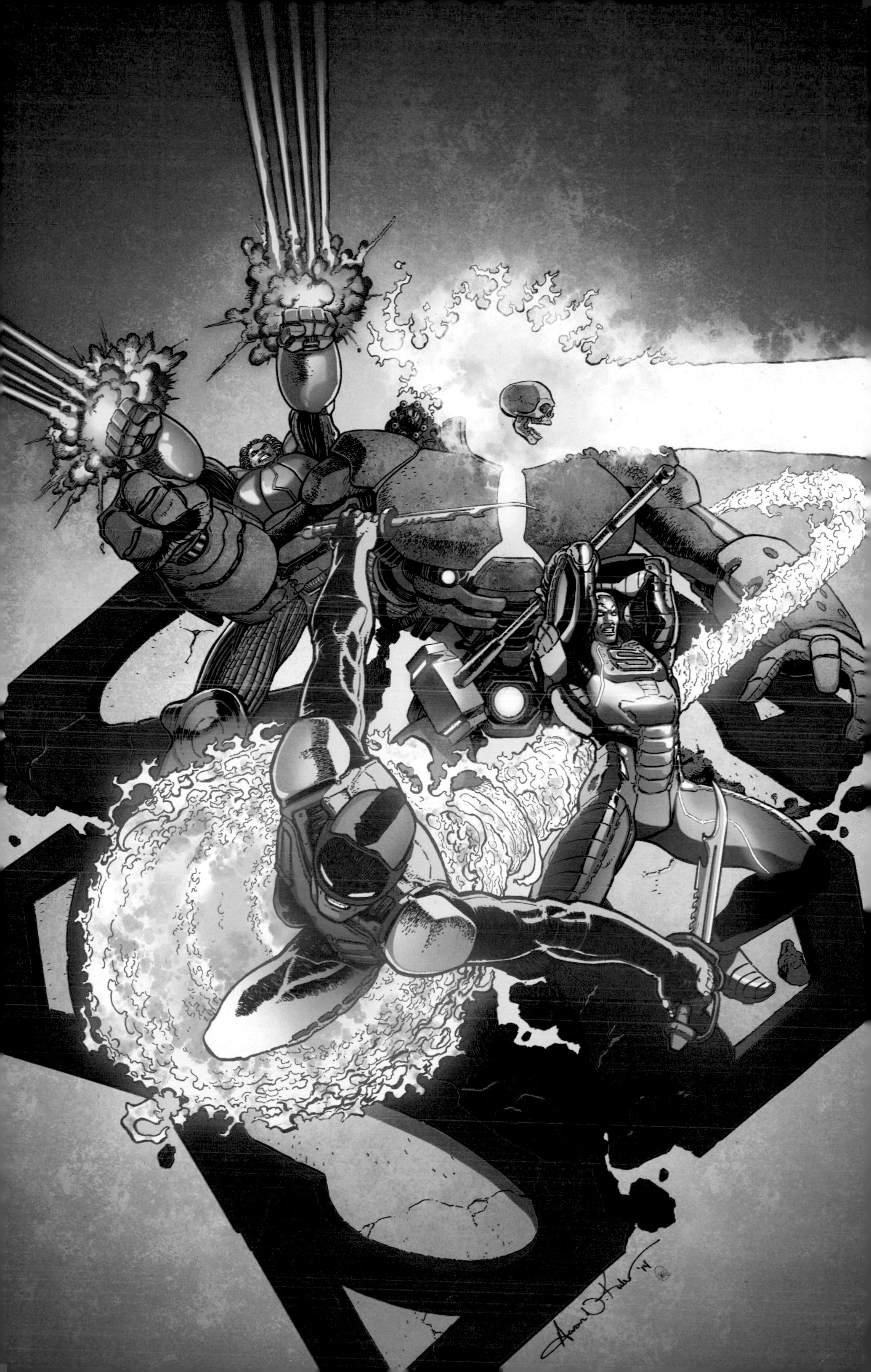

SUPERMAN

DOOMED

[ENEMY OF THE STATE] chapter 1

"NIGHTMARE"

STORY
GREG PAK

ART
SCOTT KOLINS

COLORS
WIL QUINTANA

LETTERS
CARLOS M. MANGUAL

COVER
AARON KUDER AND **WIL QUINTANA**

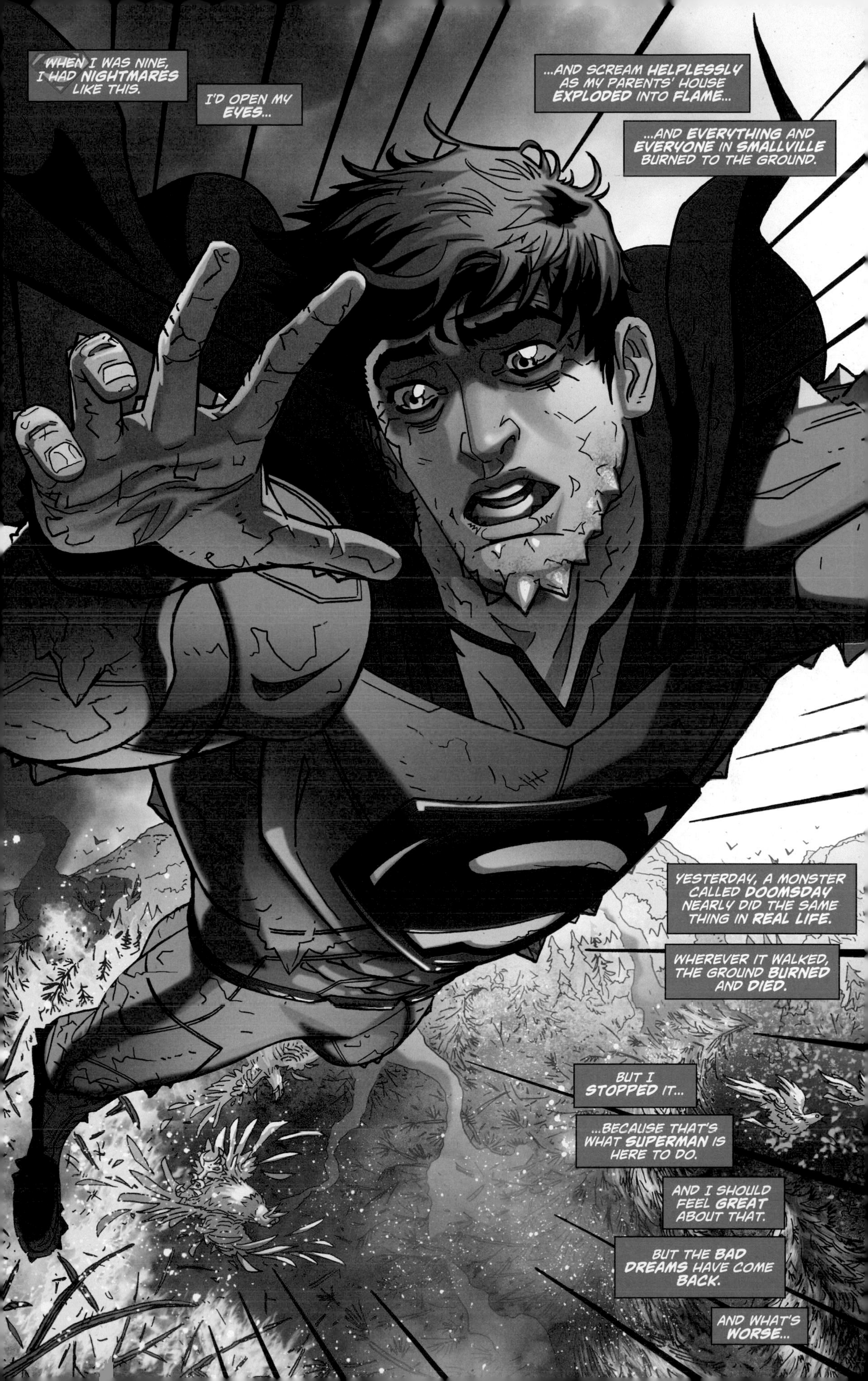
WHEN I WAS NINE, I HAD NIGHTMARES LIKE THIS.
I'D OPEN MY EYES...
...AND SCREAM HELPLESSLY AS MY PARENTS' HOUSE EXPLODED INTO FLAME...
...AND EVERYTHING AND EVERYONE IN SMALLVILLE BURNED TO THE GROUND.
YESTERDAY, A MONSTER CALLED DOOMSDAY NEARLY DID THE SAME THING IN REAL LIFE.
WHEREVER IT WALKED, THE GROUND BURNED AND DIED.
BUT I STOPPED IT...
...BECAUSE THAT'S WHAT SUPERMAN IS HERE TO DO.
AND I SHOULD FEEL GREAT ABOUT THAT.
BUT THE BAD DREAMS HAVE COME BACK.
AND WHAT'S WORSE...

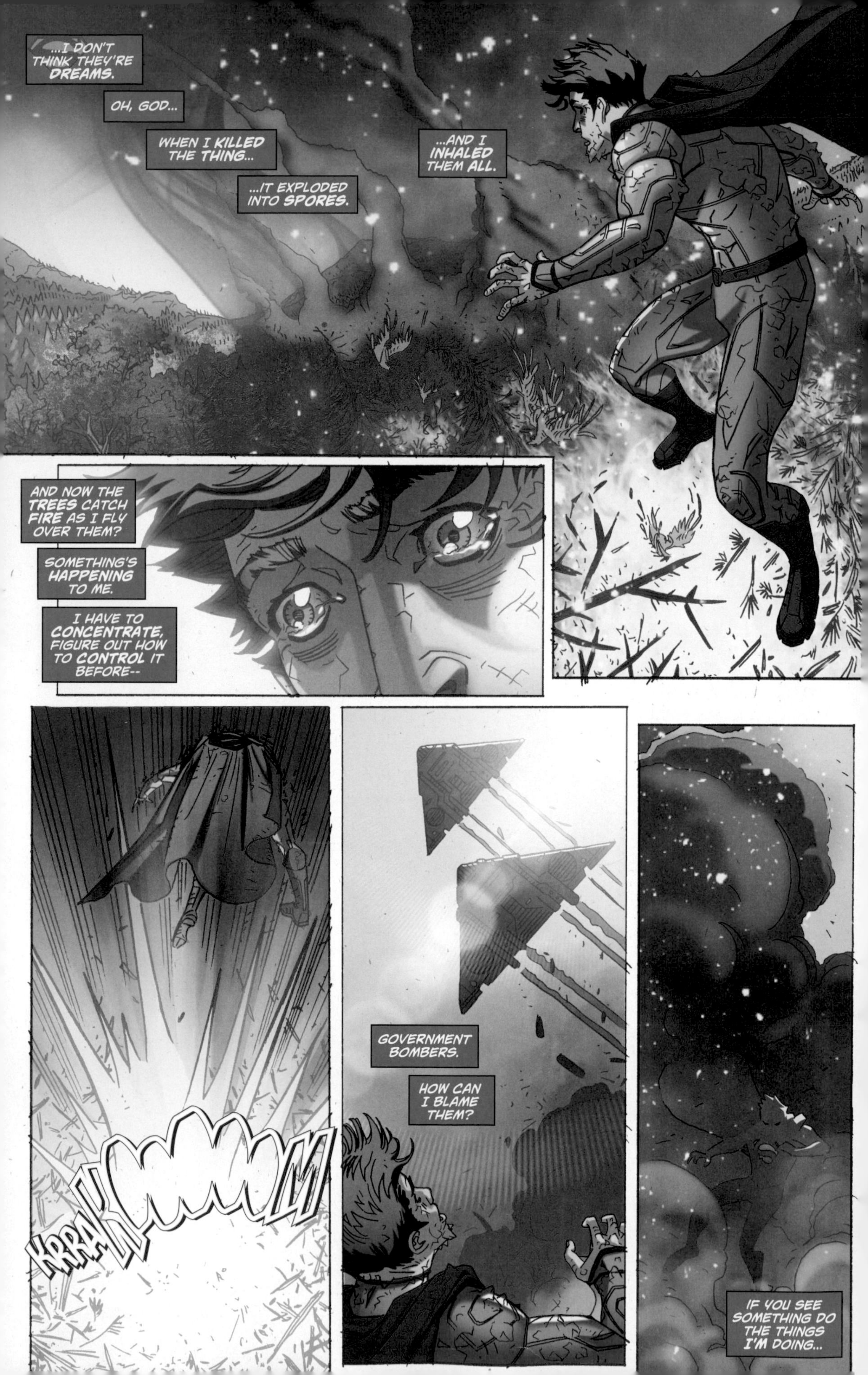
...I DON'T THINK THEY'RE DREAMS.
OH, GOD...
WHEN I KILLED THE THING...
...IT EXPLODED INTO SPORES.
...AND I INHALED THEM ALL.
AND NOW THE TREES CATCH FIRE AS I FLY OVER THEM?
SOMETHING'S HAPPENING TO ME.
I HAVE TO CONCENTRATE, FIGURE OUT HOW TO CONTROL IT BEFORE--
KRRABOOOOOM
GOVERNMENT BOMBERS.
HOW CAN I BLAME THEM?
IF YOU SEE SOMETHING DO THE THINGS I'M DOING...

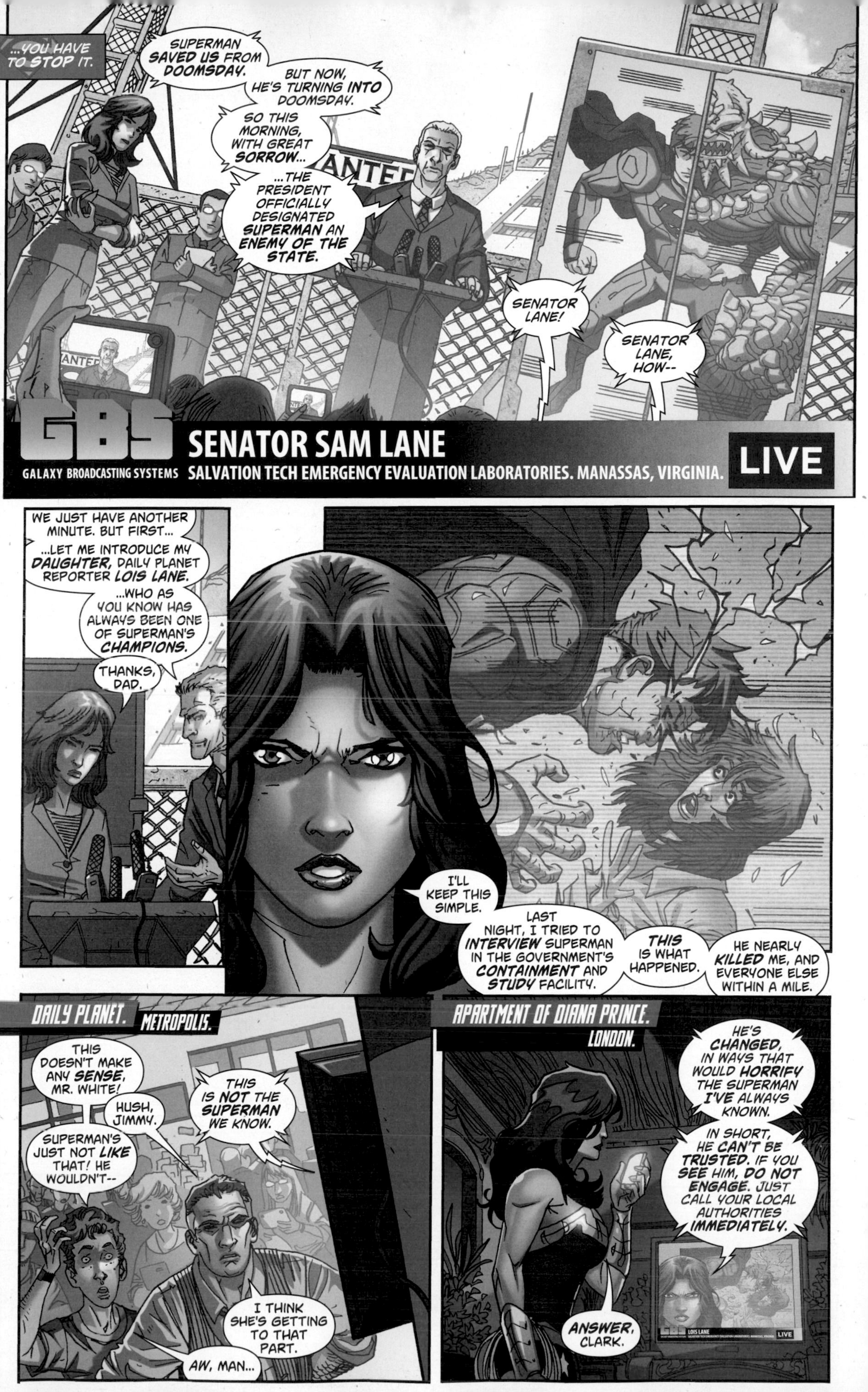

...YOU HAVE TO STOP IT.
SUPERMAN SAVED US FROM DOOMSDAY.
BUT NOW, HE'S TURNING INTO DOOMSDAY.
SO THIS MORNING, WITH GREAT SORROW...
...THE PRESIDENT OFFICIALLY DESIGNATED SUPERMAN AN ENEMY OF THE STATE.
SENATOR LANE!
SENATOR LANE, HOW--
GBS
GALAXY BROADCASTING SYSTEMS
SENATOR SAM LANE
SALVATION TECH EMERGENCY EVALUATION LABORATORIES. MANASSAS, VIRGINIA.
LIVE
WE JUST HAVE ANOTHER MINUTE. BUT FIRST...
...LET ME INTRODUCE MY DAUGHTER, DAILY PLANET REPORTER LOIS LANE.
...WHO AS YOU KNOW HAS ALWAYS BEEN ONE OF SUPERMAN'S CHAMPIONS.
THANKS, DAD.
I'LL KEEP THIS SIMPLE.
LAST NIGHT, I TRIED TO INTERVIEW SUPERMAN IN THE GOVERNMENT'S CONTAINMENT AND STUDY FACILITY.
THIS IS WHAT HAPPENED.
HE NEARLY KILLED ME, AND EVERYONE ELSE WITHIN A MILE.
DAILY PLANET. METROPOLIS.
THIS DOESN'T MAKE ANY SENSE, MR. WHITE!
HUSH, JIMMY.
THIS IS NOT THE SUPERMAN WE KNOW.
SUPERMAN'S JUST NOT LIKE THAT! HE WOULDN'T--
I THINK SHE'S GETTING TO THAT PART.
AW, MAN...
APARTMENT OF DIANA PRINCE. LONDON.
HE'S CHANGED, IN WAYS THAT WOULD HORRIFY THE SUPERMAN I'VE ALWAYS KNOWN.
IN SHORT, HE CAN'T BE TRUSTED. IF YOU SEE HIM, DO NOT ENGAGE. JUST CALL YOUR LOCAL AUTHORITIES IMMEDIATELY.
ANSWER, CLARK.

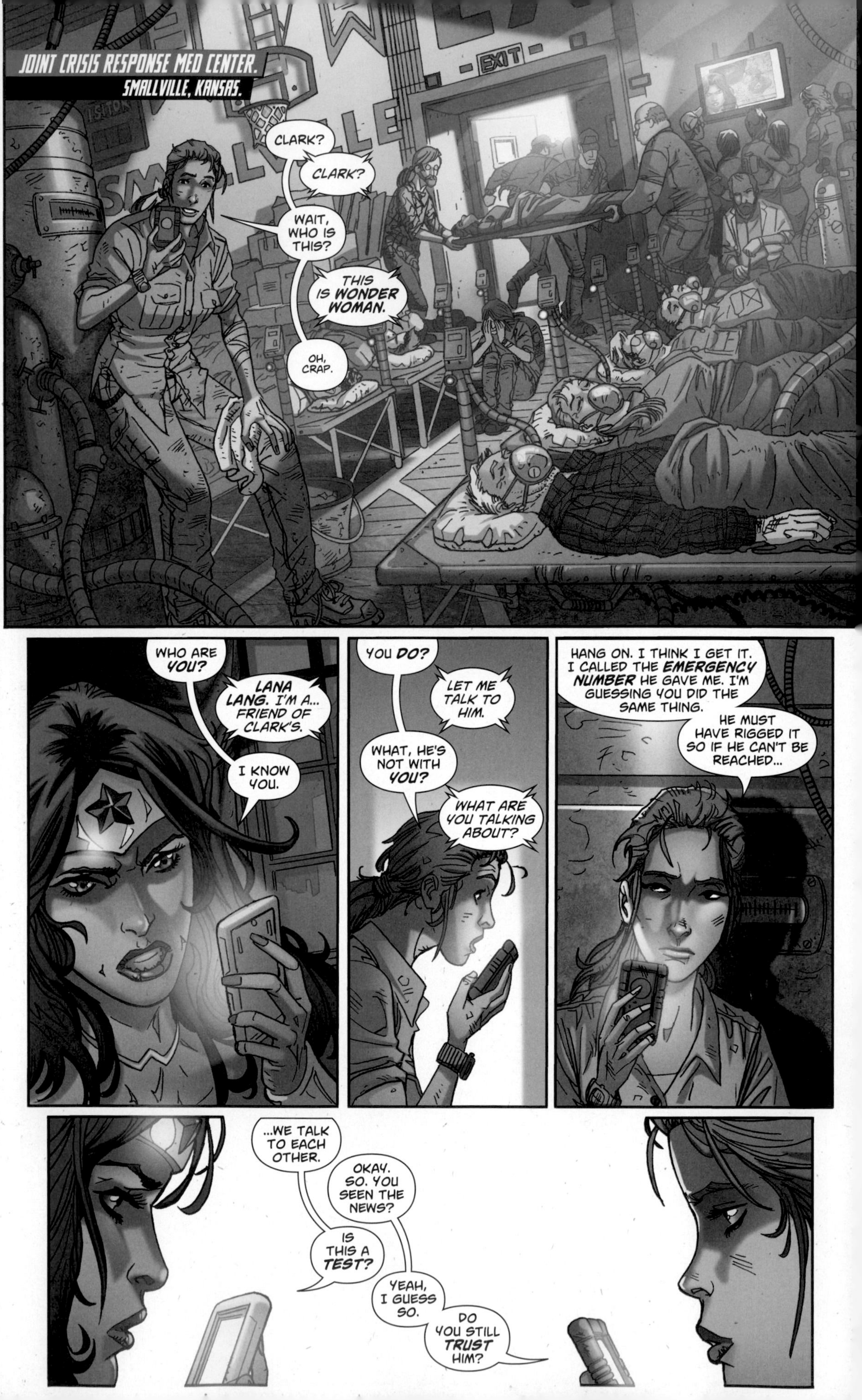
JOINT CRISIS RESPONSE MED CENTER.
SMALLVILLE, KANSAS.
EXIT
CLARK?
CLARK?
WAIT, WHO IS THIS?
THIS IS WONDER WOMAN.
OH, CRAP.
WHO ARE YOU?
LANA LANG. I'M A... FRIEND OF CLARK'S.
I KNOW YOU.
YOU DO?
LET ME TALK TO HIM.
WHAT, HE'S NOT WITH YOU?
WHAT ARE YOU TALKING ABOUT?
HANG ON. I THINK I GET IT. I CALLED THE EMERGENCY NUMBER HE GAVE ME. I'M GUESSING YOU DID THE SAME THING.
HE MUST HAVE RIGGED IT SO IF HE CAN'T BE REACHED...
...WE TALK TO EACH OTHER.
OKAY. SO. YOU SEEN THE NEWS?
IS THIS A TEST?
YEAH, I GUESS SO.
DO YOU STILL TRUST HIM?

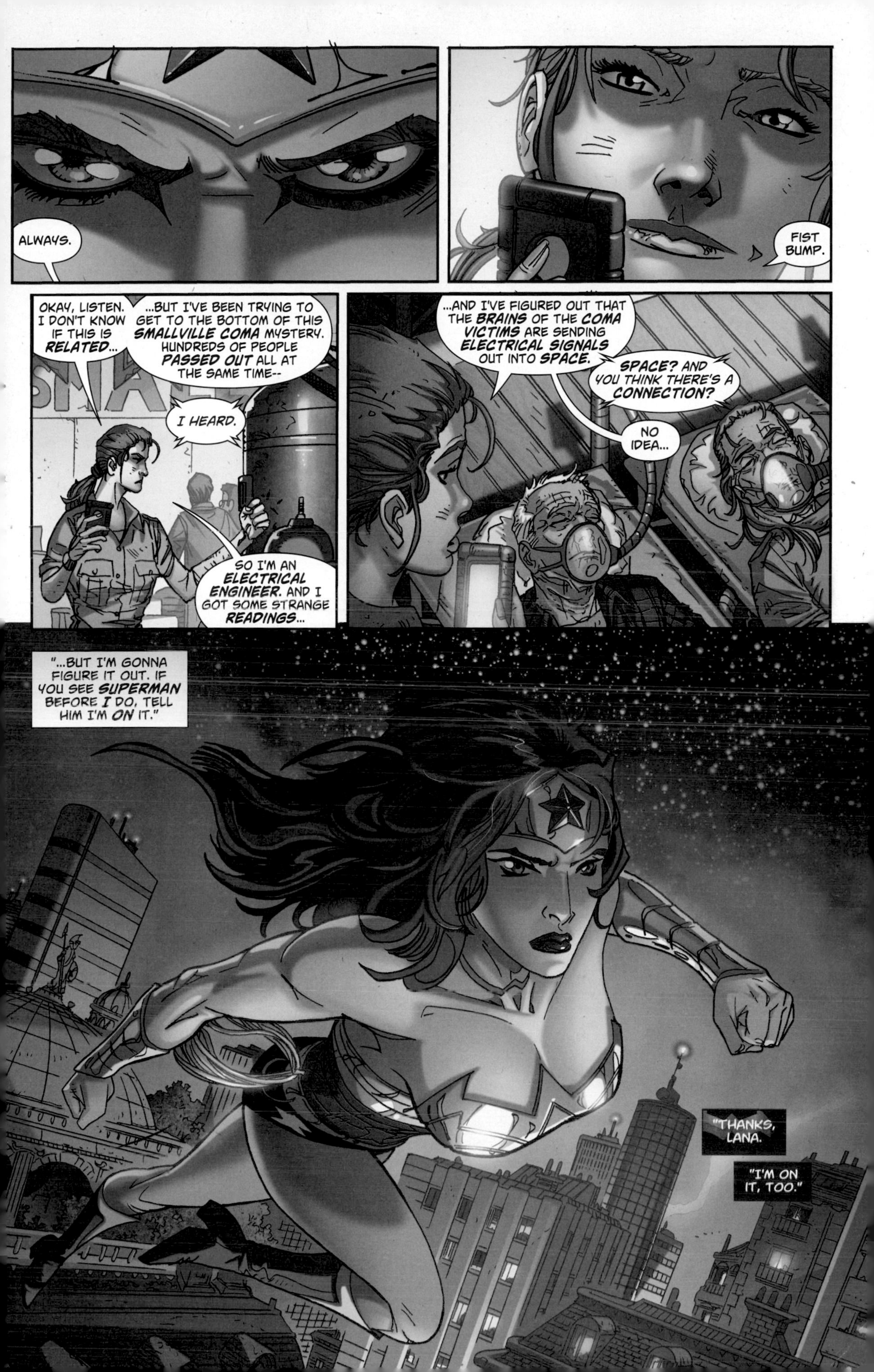
ALWAYS.
FIST BUMP.
OKAY, LISTEN. I DON'T KNOW IF THIS IS RELATED...
...BUT I'VE BEEN TRYING TO GET TO THE BOTTOM OF THIS SMALLVILLE COMA MYSTERY. HUNDREDS OF PEOPLE PASSED OUT ALL AT THE SAME TIME--
I HEARD.
SO I'M AN ELECTRICAL ENGINEER. AND I GOT SOME STRANGE READINGS...
...AND I'VE FIGURED OUT THAT THE BRAINS OF THE COMA VICTIMS ARE SENDING ELECTRICAL SIGNALS OUT INTO SPACE.
SPACE? AND YOU THINK THERE'S A CONNECTION?
NO IDEA...
"...BUT I'M GONNA FIGURE IT OUT. IF YOU SEE SUPERMAN BEFORE I DO, TELL HIM I'M ON IT."
"THANKS, LANA.
"I'M ON IT, TOO."

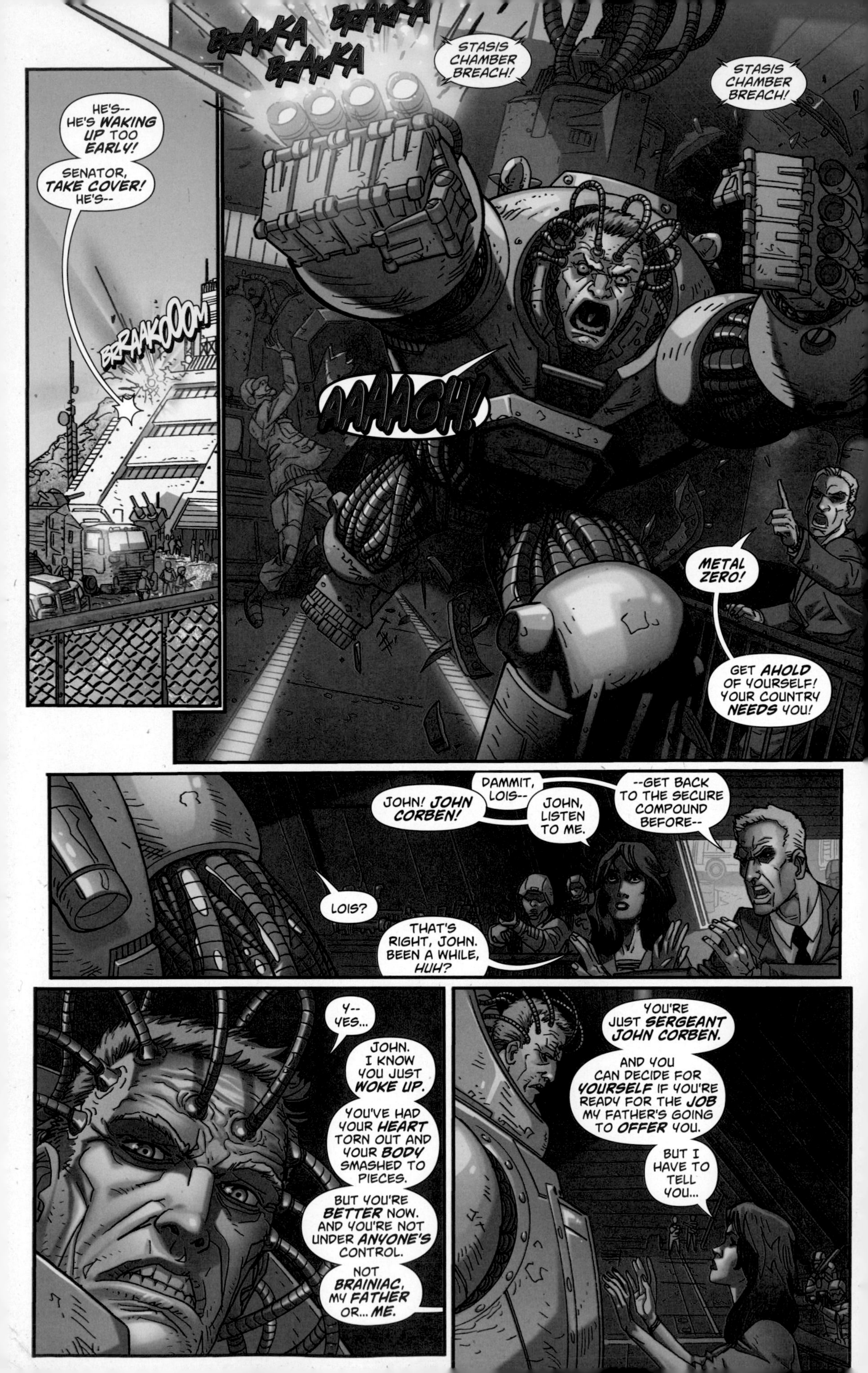

HE'S-- HE'S WAKING UP TOO EARLY!
SENATOR, TAKE COVER! HE'S--
BRRAAKOOOM
BRAKKA BRAKKA BRAKKA
STASIS CHAMBER BREACH!
STASIS CHAMBER BREACH!
AAAAAGH!
METAL ZERO!
GET AHOLD OF YOURSELF! YOUR COUNTRY NEEDS YOU!
JOHN! JOHN CORBEN!
DAMMIT, LOIS--
JOHN, LISTEN TO ME.
--GET BACK TO THE SECURE COMPOUND BEFORE--
LOIS?
THAT'S RIGHT, JOHN. BEEN A WHILE, HUH?
Y-- YES...
JOHN. I KNOW YOU JUST WOKE UP.
YOU'VE HAD YOUR HEART TORN OUT AND YOUR BODY SMASHED TO PIECES.
BUT YOU'RE BETTER NOW. AND YOU'RE NOT UNDER ANYONE'S CONTROL.
NOT BRAINIAC, MY FATHER OR... ME.
YOU'RE JUST SERGEANT JOHN CORBEN.
AND YOU CAN DECIDE FOR YOURSELF IF YOU'RE READY FOR THE JOB MY FATHER'S GOING TO OFFER YOU.
BUT I HAVE TO TELL YOU...

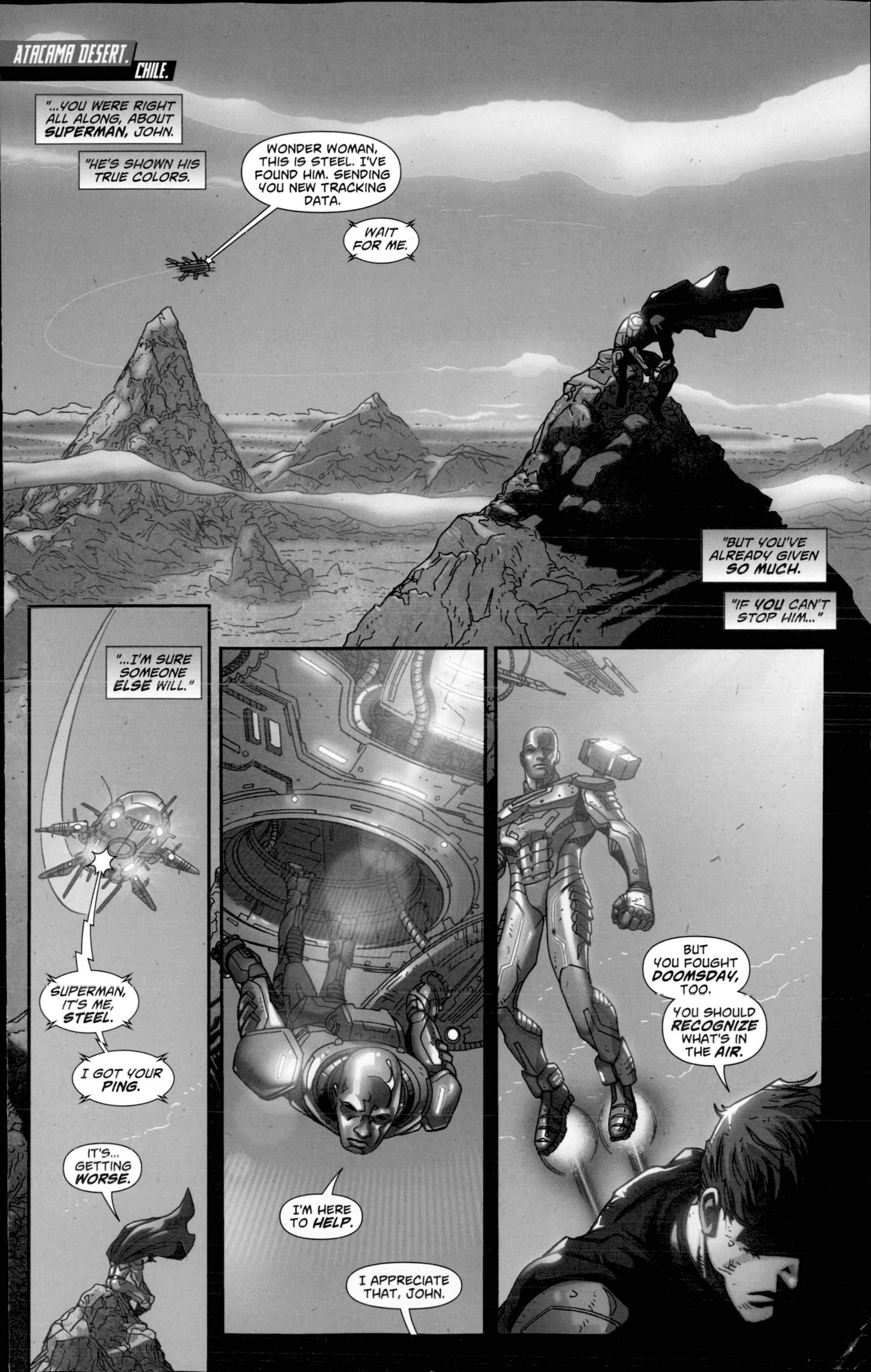
ATACAMA DESERT.
CHILE.
"...YOU WERE RIGHT ALL ALONG, ABOUT SUPERMAN, JOHN.
"HE'S SHOWN HIS TRUE COLORS.
WONDER WOMAN, THIS IS STEEL. I'VE FOUND HIM. SENDING YOU NEW TRACKING DATA.
WAIT FOR ME.
"BUT YOU'VE ALREADY GIVEN SO MUCH.
"IF YOU CAN'T STOP HIM...
"...I'M SURE SOMEONE ELSE WILL."
SUPERMAN, IT'S ME, STEEL.
I GOT YOUR PING.
IT'S... GETTING WORSE.
I'M HERE TO HELP.
I APPRECIATE THAT, JOHN.
BUT YOU FOUGHT DOOMSDAY, TOO.
YOU SHOULD RECOGNIZE WHAT'S IN THE AIR.

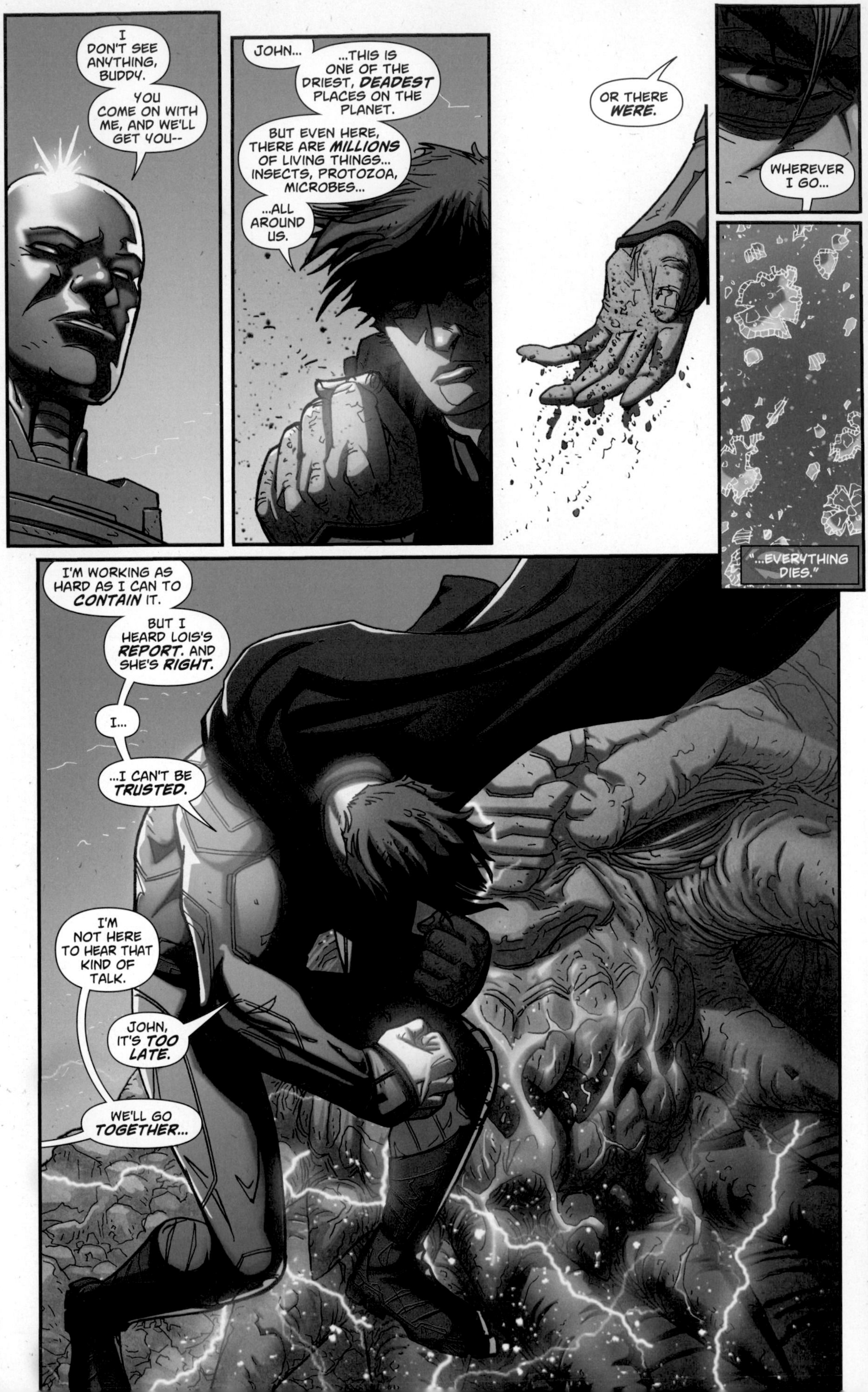
I DON'T SEE ANYTHING, BUDDY.
YOU COME ON WITH ME, AND WE'LL GET YOU--
JOHN...
...THIS IS ONE OF THE DRIEST, DEADEST PLACES ON THE PLANET.
BUT EVEN HERE, THERE ARE MILLIONS OF LIVING THINGS... INSECTS, PROTOZOA, MICROBES...
...ALL AROUND US.
OR THERE WERE.
WHEREVER I GO...
"...EVERYTHING DIES."
I'M WORKING AS HARD AS I CAN TO CONTAIN IT.
BUT I HEARD LOIS'S REPORT. AND SHE'S RIGHT.
I...
...I CAN'T BE TRUSTED.
I'M NOT HERE TO HEAR THAT KIND OF TALK.
JOHN, IT'S TOO LATE.
WE'LL GO TOGETHER...

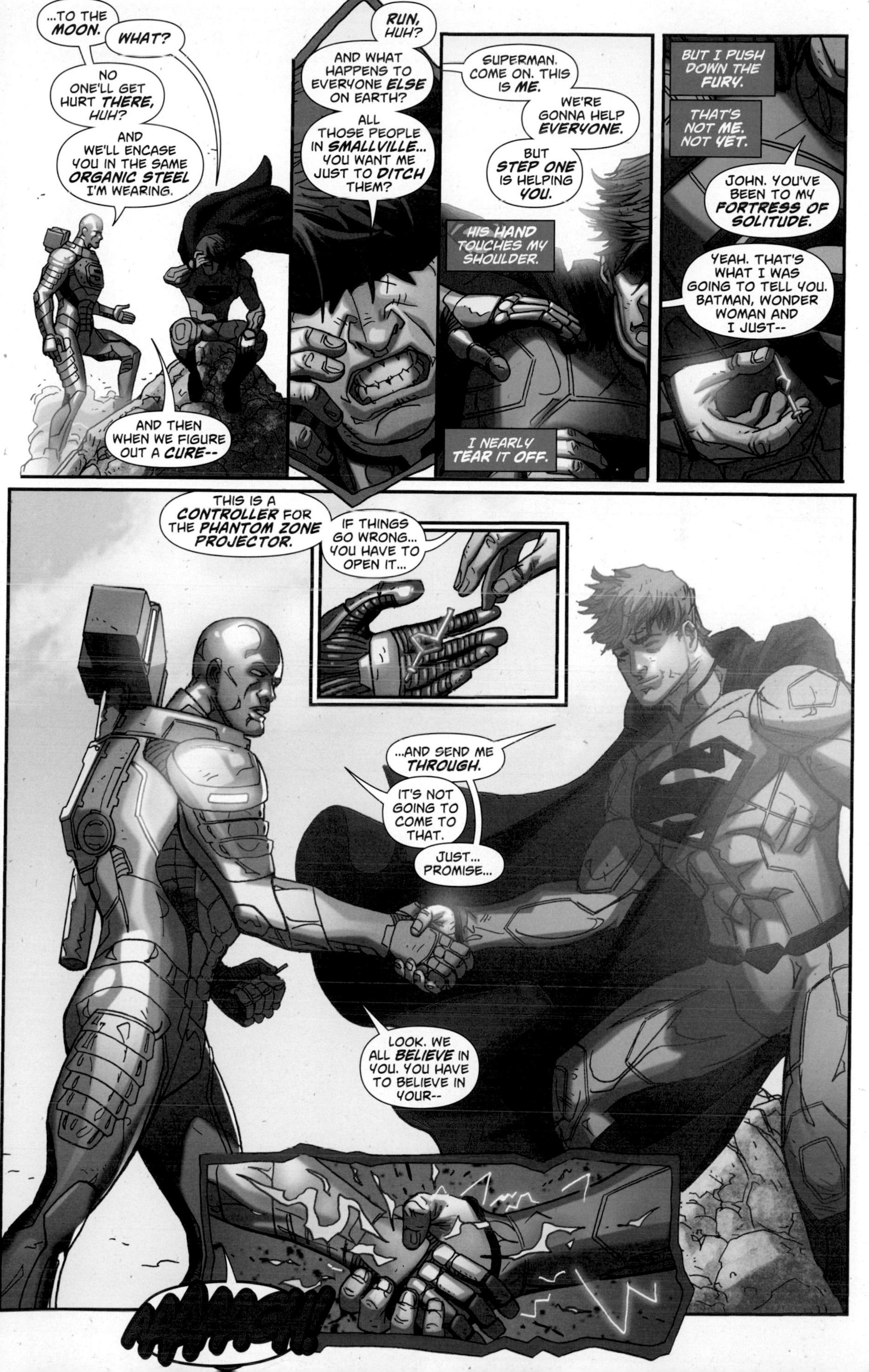
...TO THE MOON.
WHAT?
NO ONE'LL GET HURT THERE, HUH?
AND WE'LL ENCASE YOU IN THE SAME ORGANIC STEEL I'M WEARING.
AND THEN WHEN WE FIGURE OUT A CURE--
RUN, HUH?
AND WHAT HAPPENS TO EVERYONE ELSE ON EARTH?
ALL THOSE PEOPLE IN SMALLVILLE... YOU WANT ME JUST TO DITCH THEM?
SUPERMAN. COME ON. THIS IS ME.
WE'RE GONNA HELP EVERYONE.
BUT STEP ONE IS HELPING YOU.
HIS HAND TOUCHES MY SHOULDER.
I NEARLY TEAR IT OFF.
BUT I PUSH DOWN THE FURY.
THAT'S NOT ME. NOT YET.
JOHN. YOU'VE BEEN TO MY FORTRESS OF SOLITUDE.
YEAH. THAT'S WHAT I WAS GOING TO TELL YOU. BATMAN, WONDER WOMAN AND I JUST--
THIS IS A CONTROLLER FOR THE PHANTOM ZONE PROJECTOR.
IF THINGS GO WRONG... YOU HAVE TO OPEN IT...
...AND SEND ME THROUGH.
IT'S NOT GOING TO COME TO THAT.
JUST... PROMISE...
LOOK. WE ALL BELIEVE IN YOU. YOU HAVE TO BELIEVE IN YOUR--

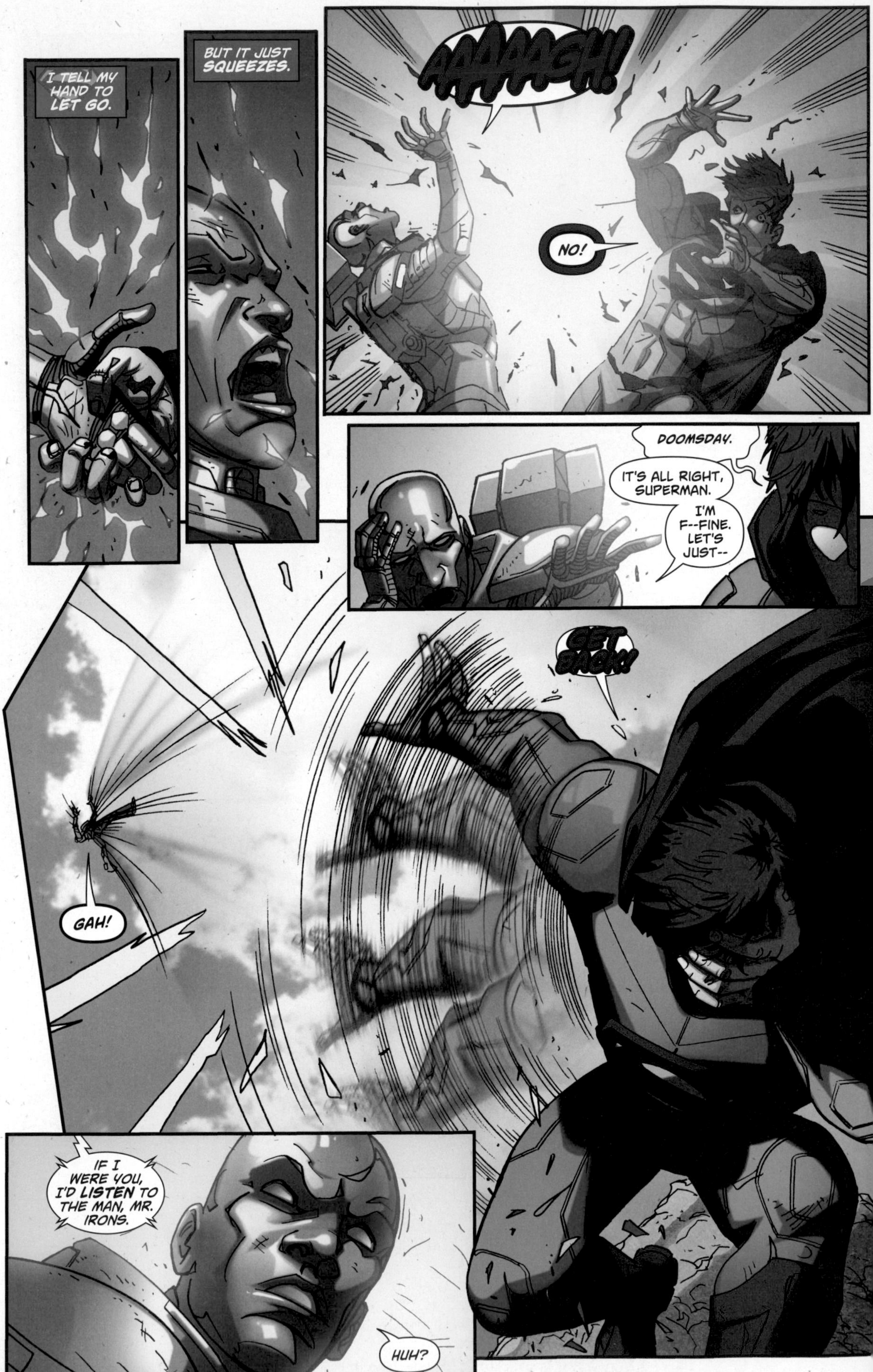

I TELL MY HAND TO LET GO.
BUT IT JUST SQUEEZES.
AAAAAGH!
NO!
DOOMSDAY.
IT'S ALL RIGHT, SUPERMAN.
I'M F--FINE. LET'S JUST--
GET BACK!
GAH!
IF I WERE YOU, I'D LISTEN TO THE MAN, MR. IRONS.
HUH?

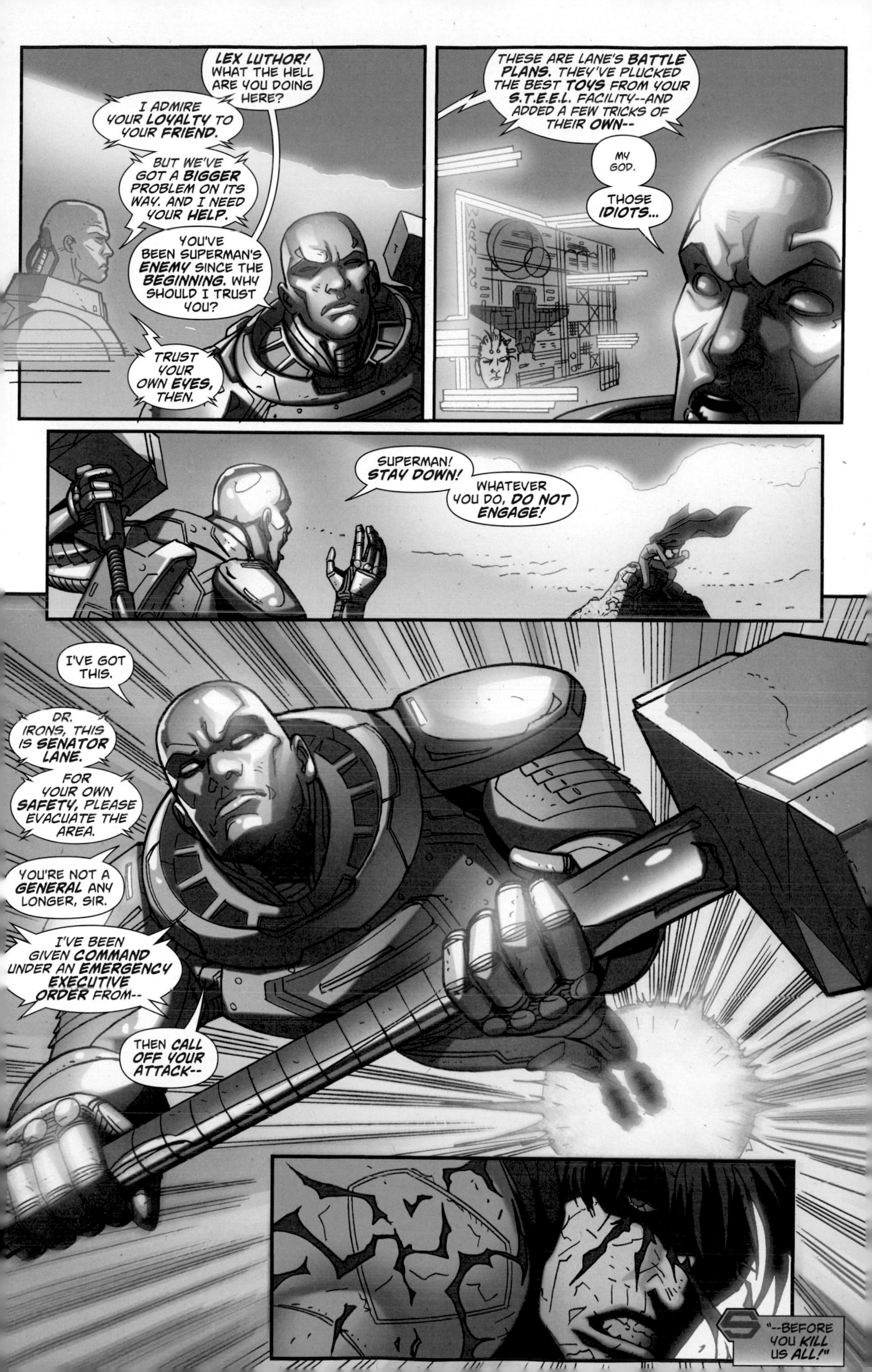
LEX LUTHOR! WHAT THE HELL ARE YOU DOING HERE?
I ADMIRE YOUR LOYALTY TO YOUR FRIEND.
BUT WE'VE GOT A BIGGER PROBLEM ON ITS WAY. AND I NEED YOUR HELP.
YOU'VE BEEN SUPERMAN'S ENEMY SINCE THE BEGINNING. WHY SHOULD I TRUST YOU?
TRUST YOUR OWN EYES, THEN.
THESE ARE LANE'S BATTLE PLANS. THEY'VE PLUCKED THE BEST TOYS FROM YOUR S.T.E.E.L. FACILITY--AND ADDED A FEW TRICKS OF THEIR OWN--
MY GOD.
THOSE IDIOTS...
WARNING
SUPERMAN! STAY DOWN!
WHATEVER YOU DO, DO NOT ENGAGE!
I'VE GOT THIS.
DR. IRONS, THIS IS SENATOR LANE.
FOR YOUR OWN SAFETY, PLEASE EVACUATE THE AREA.
YOU'RE NOT A GENERAL ANY LONGER, SIR.
I'VE BEEN GIVEN COMMAND UNDER AN EMERGENCY EXECUTIVE ORDER FROM--
THEN CALL OFF YOUR ATTACK--
"--BEFORE YOU KILL US ALL!"

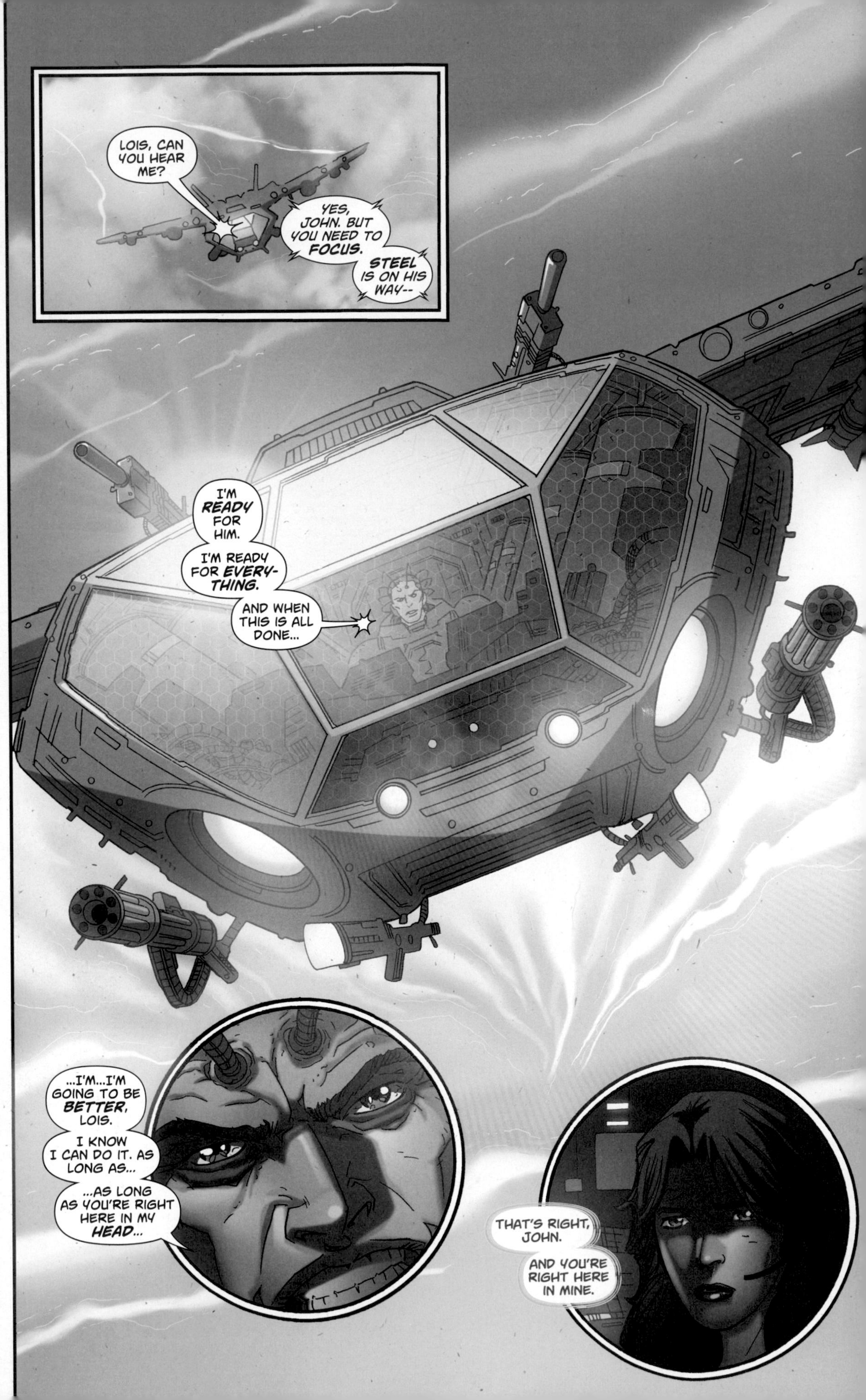

LOIS, CAN YOU HEAR ME?
YES, JOHN. BUT YOU NEED TO FOCUS.
STEEL IS ON HIS WAY--
I'M READY FOR HIM.
I'M READY FOR EVERY-THING.
AND WHEN THIS IS ALL DONE...
...I'M...I'M GOING TO BE BETTER, LOIS.
I KNOW I CAN DO IT. AS LONG AS...
...AS LONG AS YOU'RE RIGHT HERE IN MY HEAD...
THAT'S RIGHT, JOHN.
AND YOU'RE RIGHT HERE IN MINE.

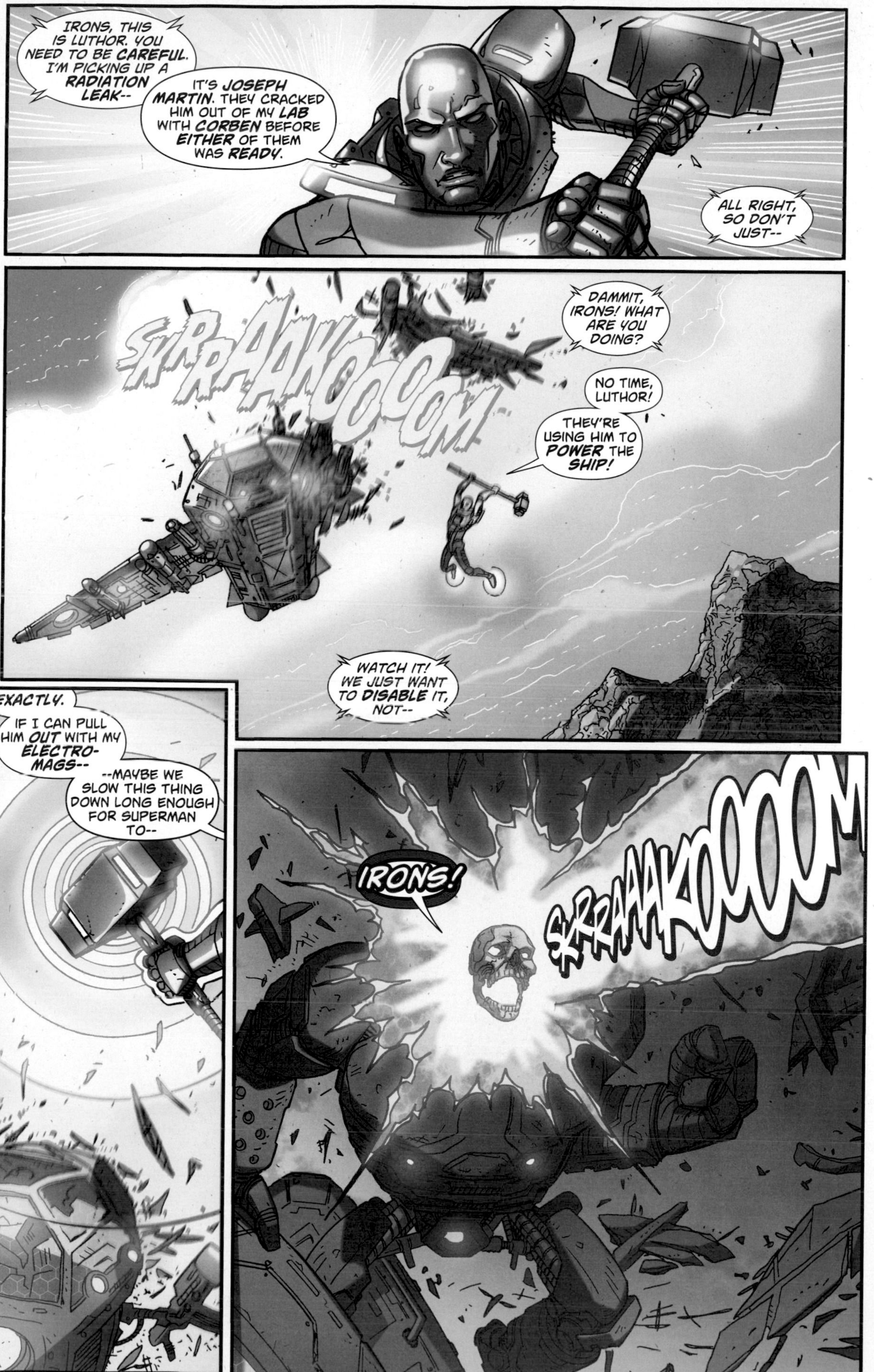
IRONS, THIS IS LUTHOR. YOU NEED TO BE CAREFUL. I'M PICKING UP A RADIATION LEAK--
IT'S JOSEPH MARTIN. THEY CRACKED HIM OUT OF MY LAB WITH CORBEN BEFORE EITHER OF THEM WAS READY.
ALL RIGHT, SO DON'T JUST--
SKRRAAKOOOOM
DAMMIT, IRONS! WHAT ARE YOU DOING?
NO TIME, LUTHOR!
THEY'RE USING HIM TO POWER THE SHIP!
WATCH IT! WE JUST WANT TO DISABLE IT, NOT--
EXACTLY.
IF I CAN PULL HIM OUT WITH MY ELECTRO-MAGS--
--MAYBE WE SLOW THIS THING DOWN LONG ENOUGH FOR SUPERMAN TO--
IRONS!
SKRRAAAKOOOOM

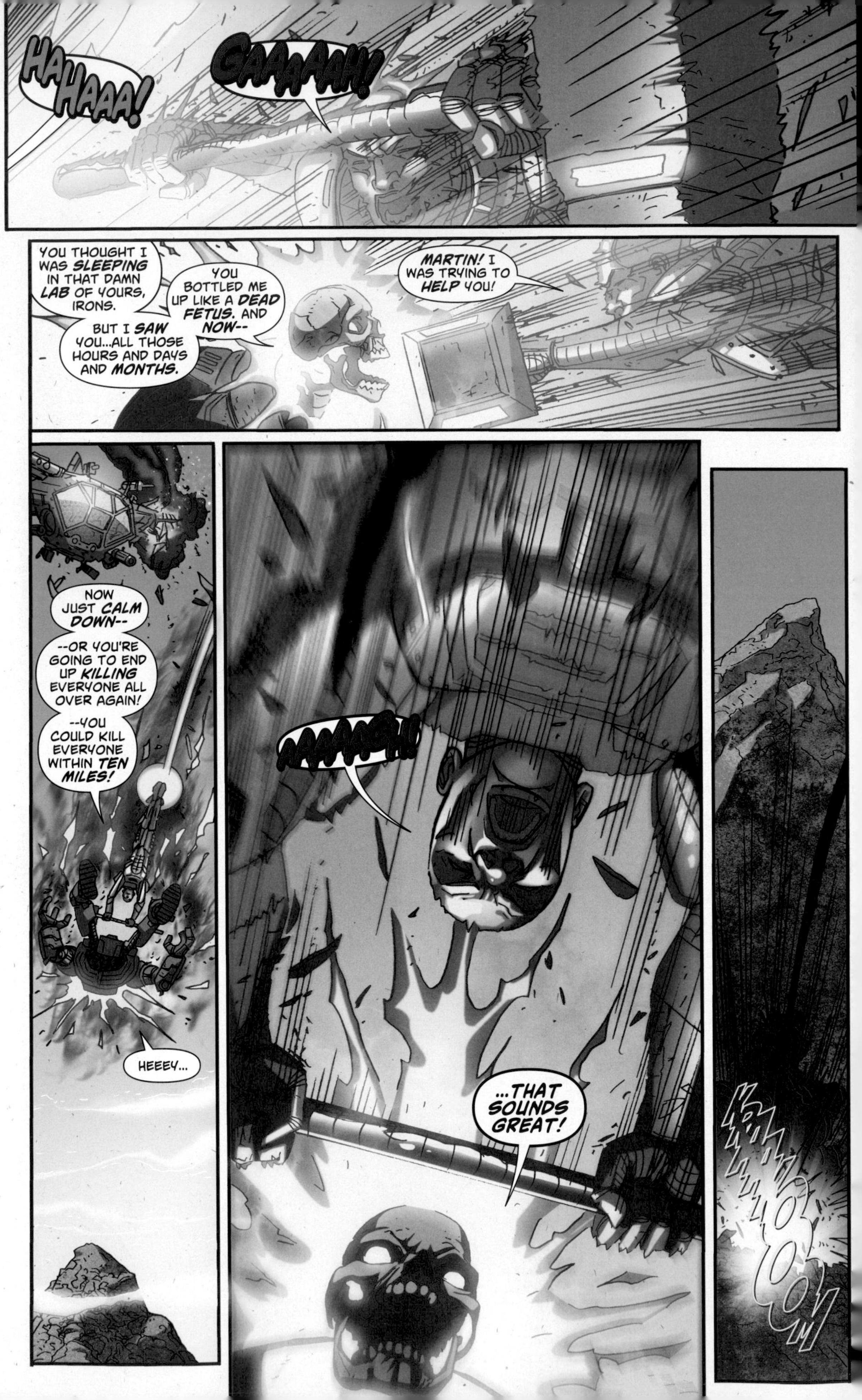
HA HAAA!
GAAAAAH!
YOU THOUGHT I WAS SLEEPING IN THAT DAMN LAB OF YOURS, IRONS.
BUT I SAW YOU...ALL THOSE HOURS AND DAYS AND MONTHS.
YOU BOTTLED ME UP LIKE A DEAD FETUS. AND NOW--
MARTIN! I WAS TRYING TO HELP YOU!
NOW JUST CALM DOWN--
--OR YOU'RE GOING TO END UP KILLING EVERYONE ALL OVER AGAIN!
--YOU COULD KILL EVERYONE WITHIN TEN MILES!
HEEEY...
...THAT SOUNDS GREAT!

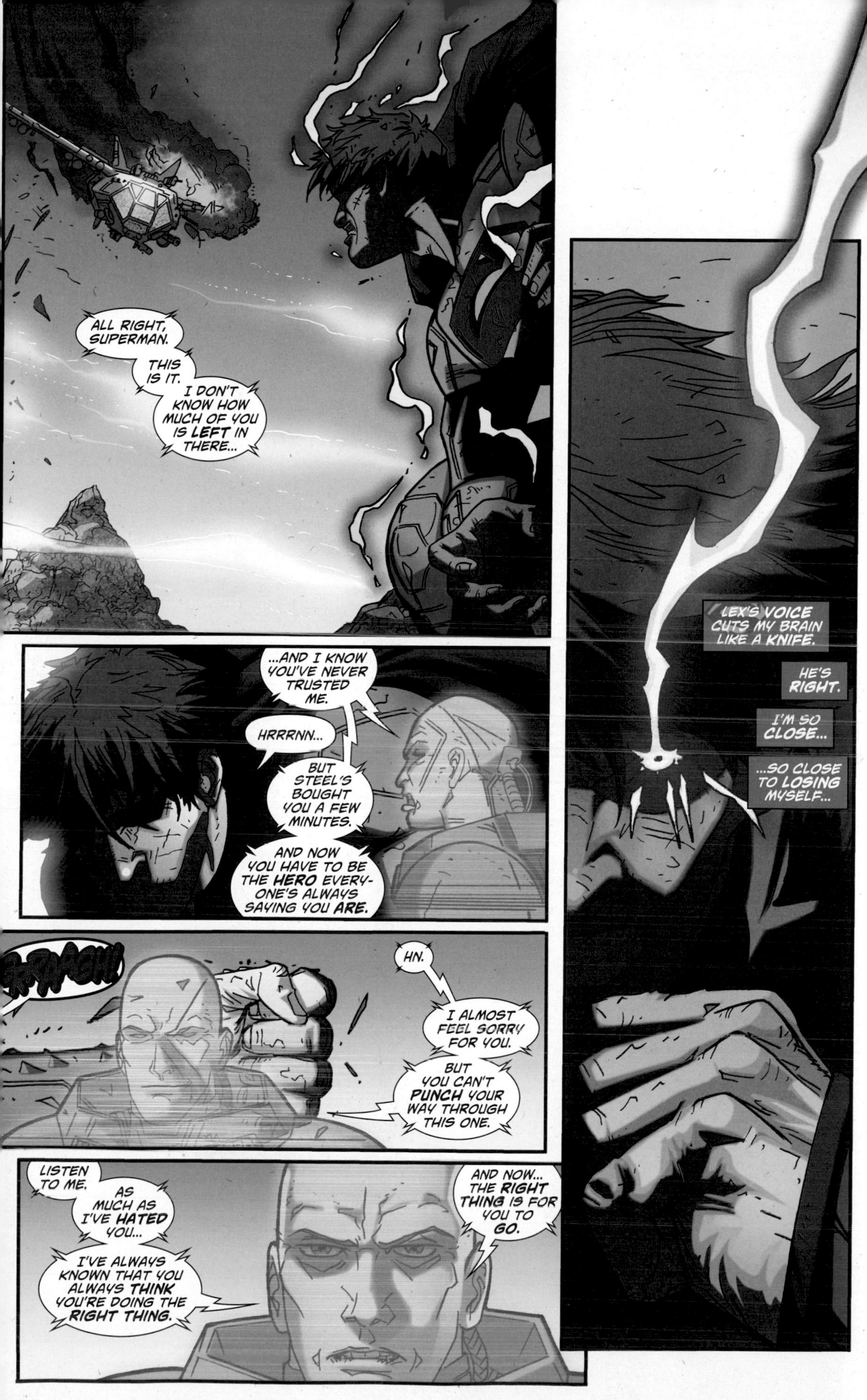

ALL RIGHT, SUPERMAN.
THIS IS IT.
I DON'T KNOW HOW MUCH OF YOU IS LEFT IN THERE...
...AND I KNOW YOU'VE NEVER TRUSTED ME.
HRRRNN...
BUT STEEL'S BOUGHT YOU A FEW MINUTES.
AND NOW YOU HAVE TO BE THE HERO EVERY-ONE'S ALWAYS SAYING YOU ARE.
HN.
I ALMOST FEEL SORRY FOR YOU.
BUT YOU CAN'T PUNCH YOUR WAY THROUGH THIS ONE.
LISTEN TO ME.
AS MUCH AS I'VE HATED YOU...
I'VE ALWAYS KNOWN THAT YOU ALWAYS THINK YOU'RE DOING THE RIGHT THING.
AND NOW... THE RIGHT THING IS FOR YOU TO GO.
LEX'S VOICE CUTS MY BRAIN LIKE A KNIFE.
HE'S RIGHT.
I'M SO CLOSE...
...SO CLOSE TO LOSING MYSELF...

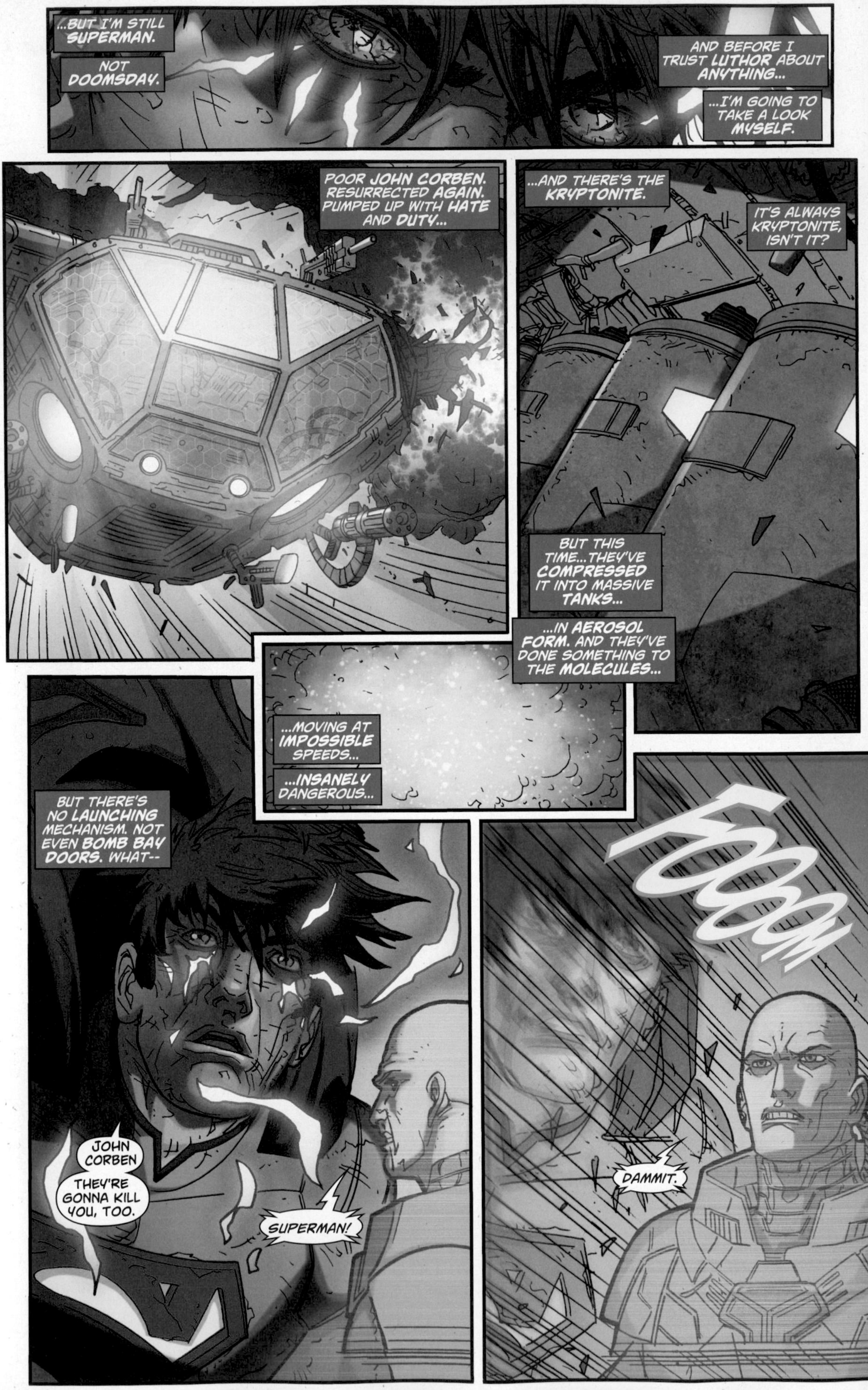
...BUT I'M STILL SUPERMAN.
NOT DOOMSDAY.
AND BEFORE I TRUST LUTHOR ABOUT ANYTHING...
...I'M GOING TO TAKE A LOOK MYSELF.
POOR JOHN CORBEN. RESURRECTED AGAIN. PUMPED UP WITH HATE AND DUTY...
...AND THERE'S THE KRYPTONITE.
IT'S ALWAYS KRYPTONITE, ISN'T IT?
BUT THIS TIME...THEY'VE COMPRESSED IT INTO MASSIVE TANKS...
...IN AEROSOL FORM. AND THEY'VE DONE SOMETHING TO THE MOLECULES...
...MOVING AT IMPOSSIBLE SPEEDS...
...INSANELY DANGEROUS...
BUT THERE'S NO LAUNCHING MECHANISM. NOT EVEN BOMB BAY DOORS. WHAT--
JOHN CORBEN
THEY'RE GONNA KILL YOU, TOO.
SUPERMAN!
FOOOOM
DAMMIT.

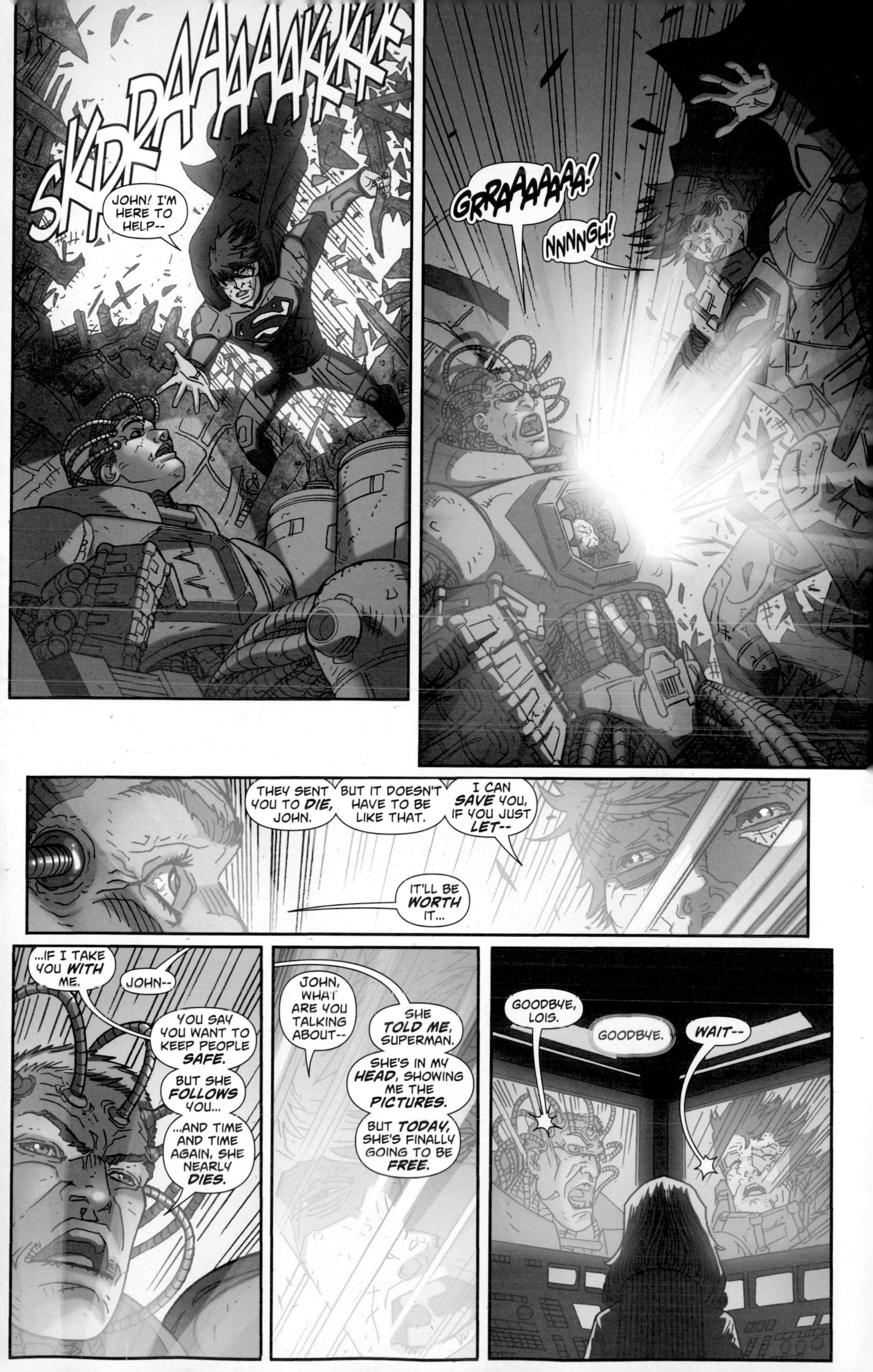
SKDRAAAAKKKK
JOHN! I'M HERE TO HELP--
GRRAAAAAAA!
NNNNGH!
THEY SENT YOU TO DIE, JOHN.
BUT IT DOESN'T HAVE TO BE LIKE THAT.
I CAN SAVE YOU, IF YOU JUST LET--
IT'LL BE WORTH IT...
...IF I TAKE YOU WITH ME.
JOHN--
YOU SAY YOU WANT TO KEEP PEOPLE SAFE.
BUT SHE FOLLOWS YOU...
...AND TIME AND TIME AGAIN, SHE NEARLY DIES.
JOHN, WHAT ARE YOU TALKING ABOUT--
SHE TOLD ME, SUPERMAN.
SHE'S IN MY HEAD, SHOWING ME THE PICTURES.
BUT TODAY, SHE'S FINALLY GOING TO BE FREE.
GOODBYE, LOIS.
GOODBYE.
WAIT--

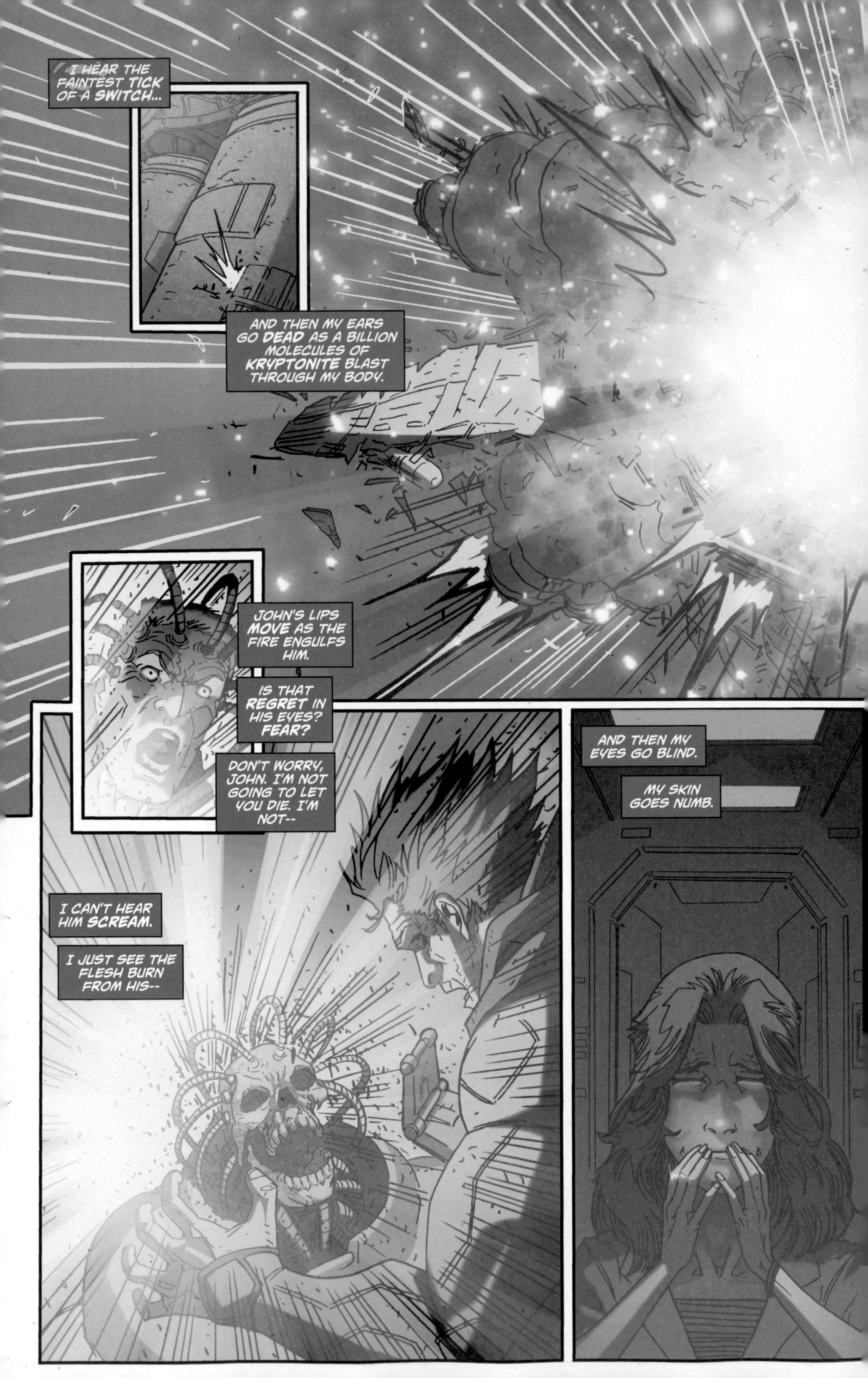
I HEAR THE FAINTEST TICK OF A SWITCH...
AND THEN MY EARS GO DEAD AS A BILLION MOLECULES OF KRYPTONITE BLAST THROUGH MY BODY.
JOHN'S LIPS MOVE AS THE FIRE ENGULFS HIM.
IS THAT REGRET IN HIS EYES? FEAR?
DON'T WORRY, JOHN. I'M NOT GOING TO LET YOU DIE. I'M NOT--
I CAN'T HEAR HIM SCREAM.
I JUST SEE THE FLESH BURN FROM HIS--
AND THEN MY EYES GO BLIND.
MY SKIN GOES NUMB.

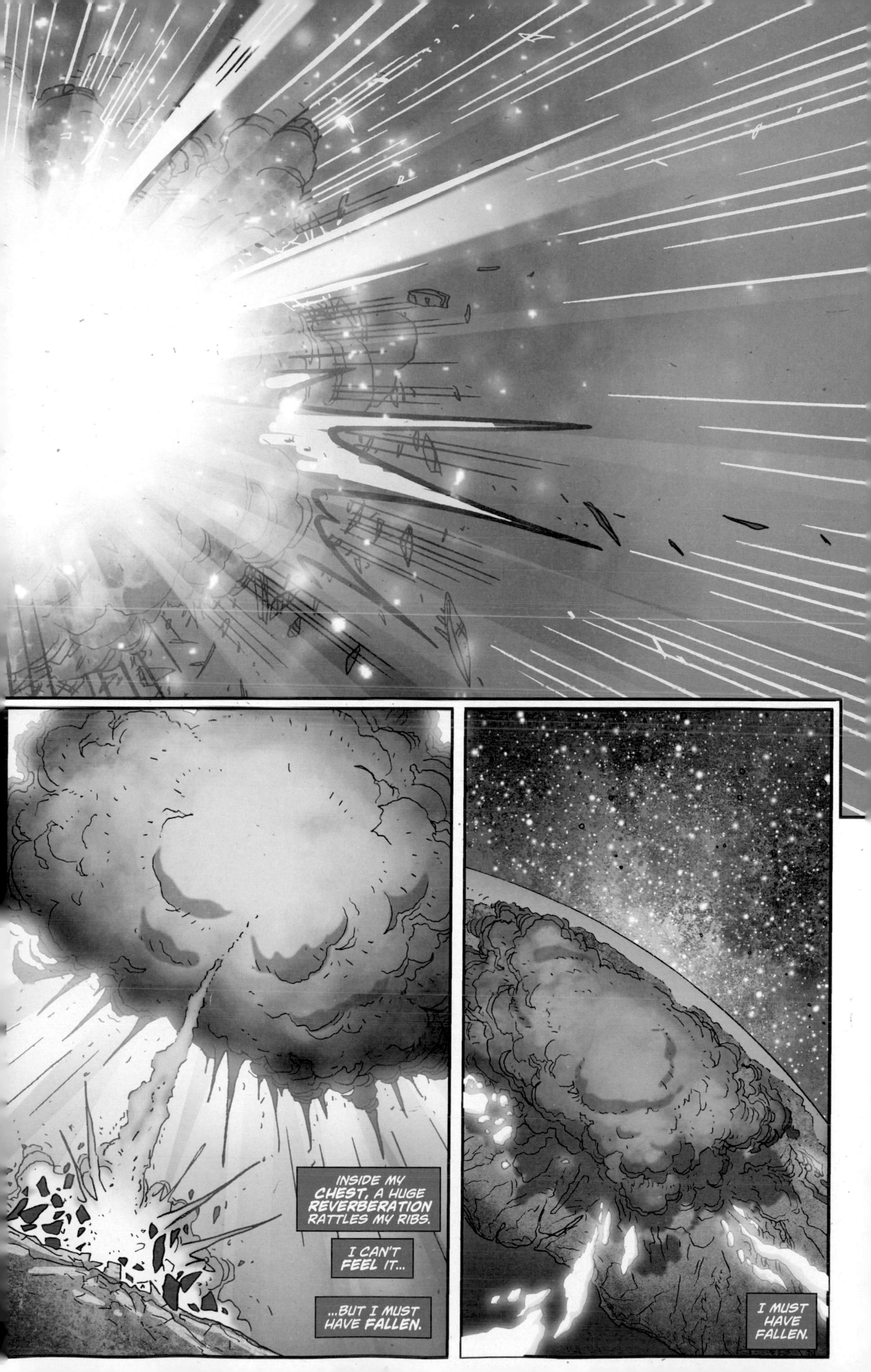
INSIDE MY CHEST, A HUGE REVERBERATION RATTLES MY RIBS.
I CAN'T FEEL IT...
...BUT I MUST HAVE FALLEN.
I MUST HAVE FALLEN.

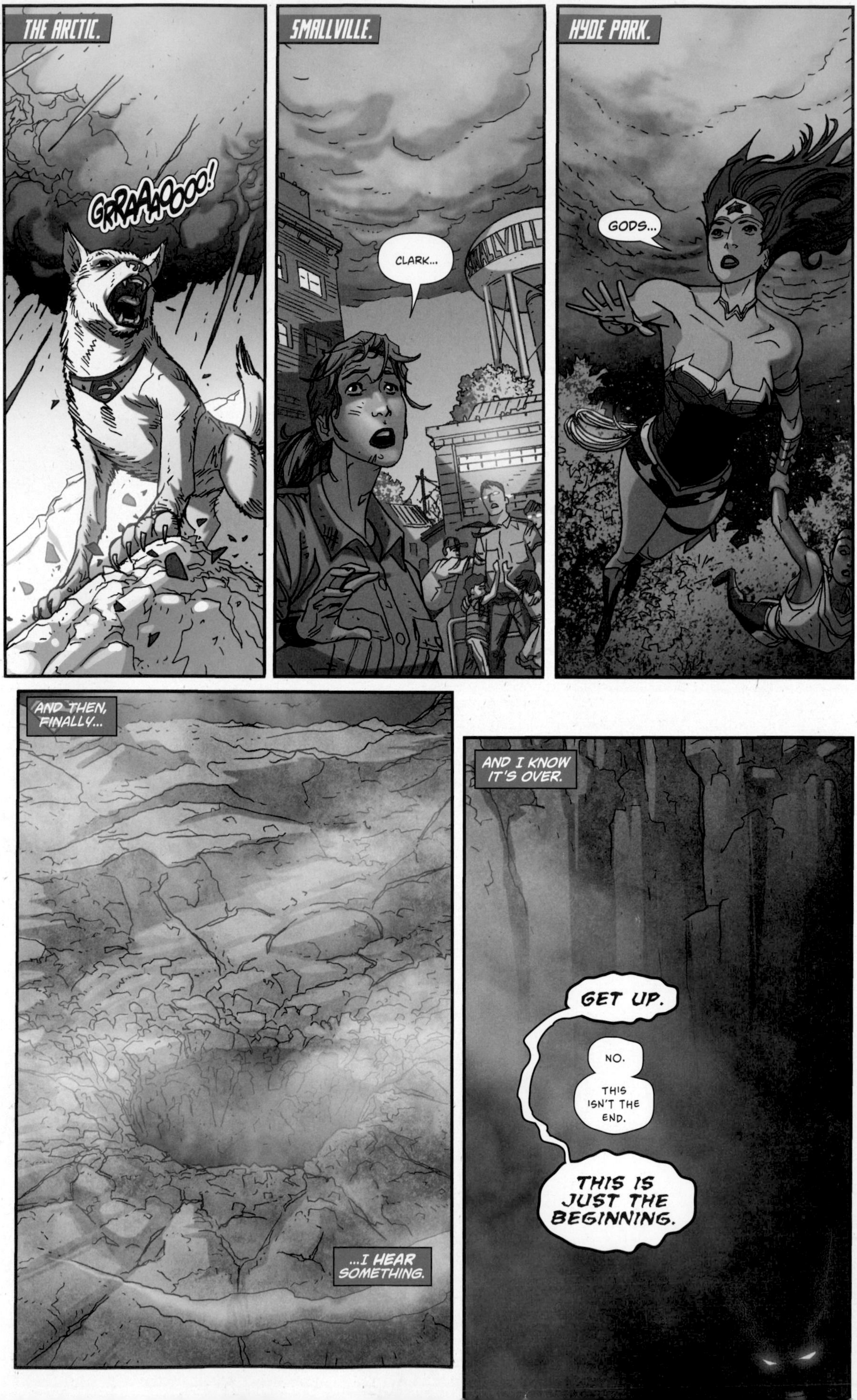
THE ARCTIC.
GRRAAAOOOO!
SMALLVILLE.
CLARK...
HYDE PARK.
GODS...
AND THEN, FINALLY...
...I HEAR SOMETHING.
AND I KNOW IT'S OVER.
GET UP.
NO.
THIS ISN'T THE END.
THIS IS JUST THE BEGINNING.

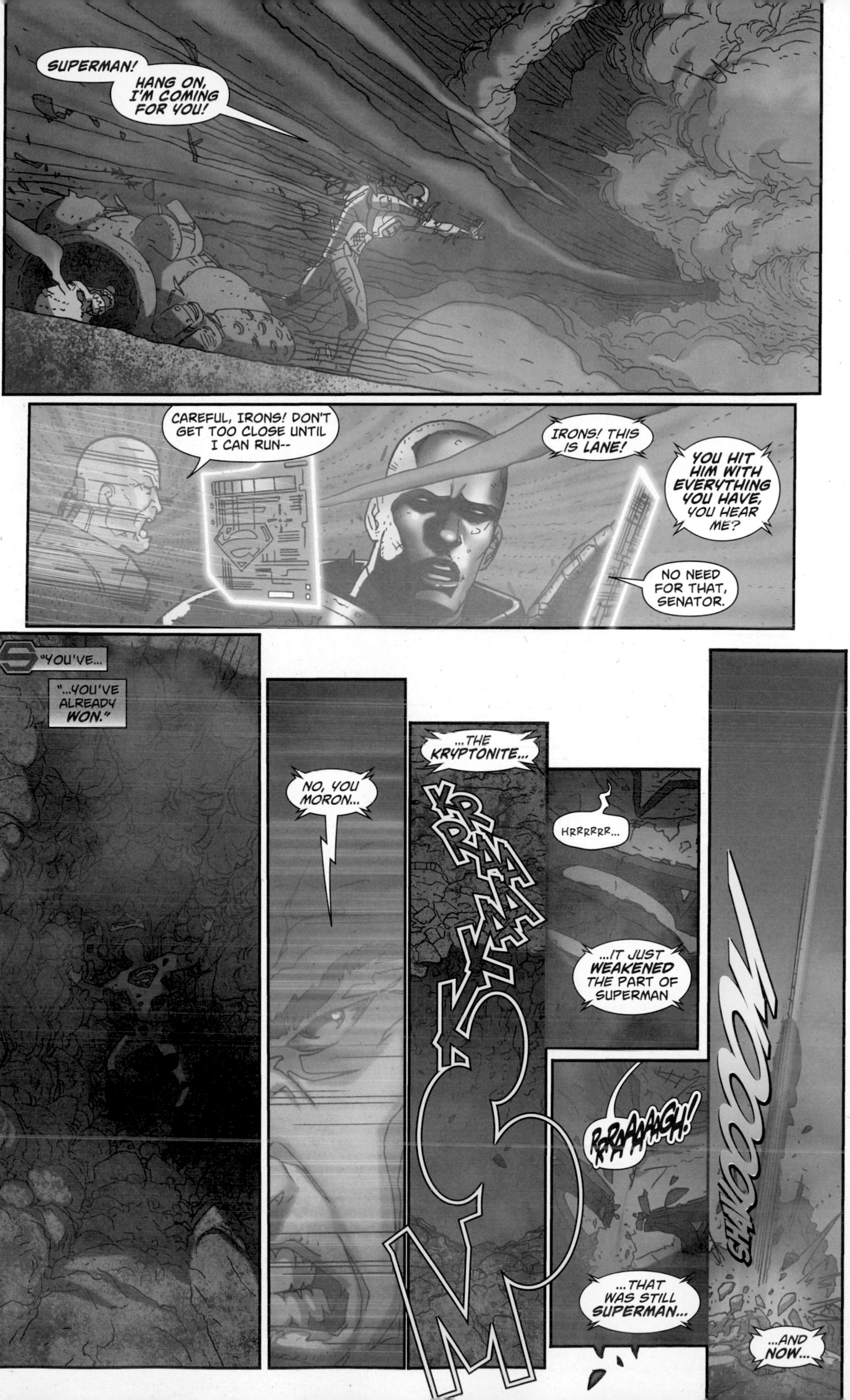
SUPERMAN!
HANG ON, I'M COMING FOR YOU!
CAREFUL, IRONS! DON'T GET TOO CLOSE UNTIL I CAN RUN--
IRONS! THIS IS LANE!
YOU HIT HIM WITH EVERYTHING YOU HAVE, YOU HEAR ME?
NO NEED FOR THAT, SENATOR.
"YOU'VE...
"...YOU'VE ALREADY WON."
NO, YOU MORON...
...THE KRYPTONITE...
KRRAAKKASSSHHHHH
HRRRRRR...
...IT JUST WEAKENED THE PART OF SUPERMAN
RRRAAAAAGH!
...THAT WAS STILL SUPERMAN...
SHHHOOOOM
...AND NOW...

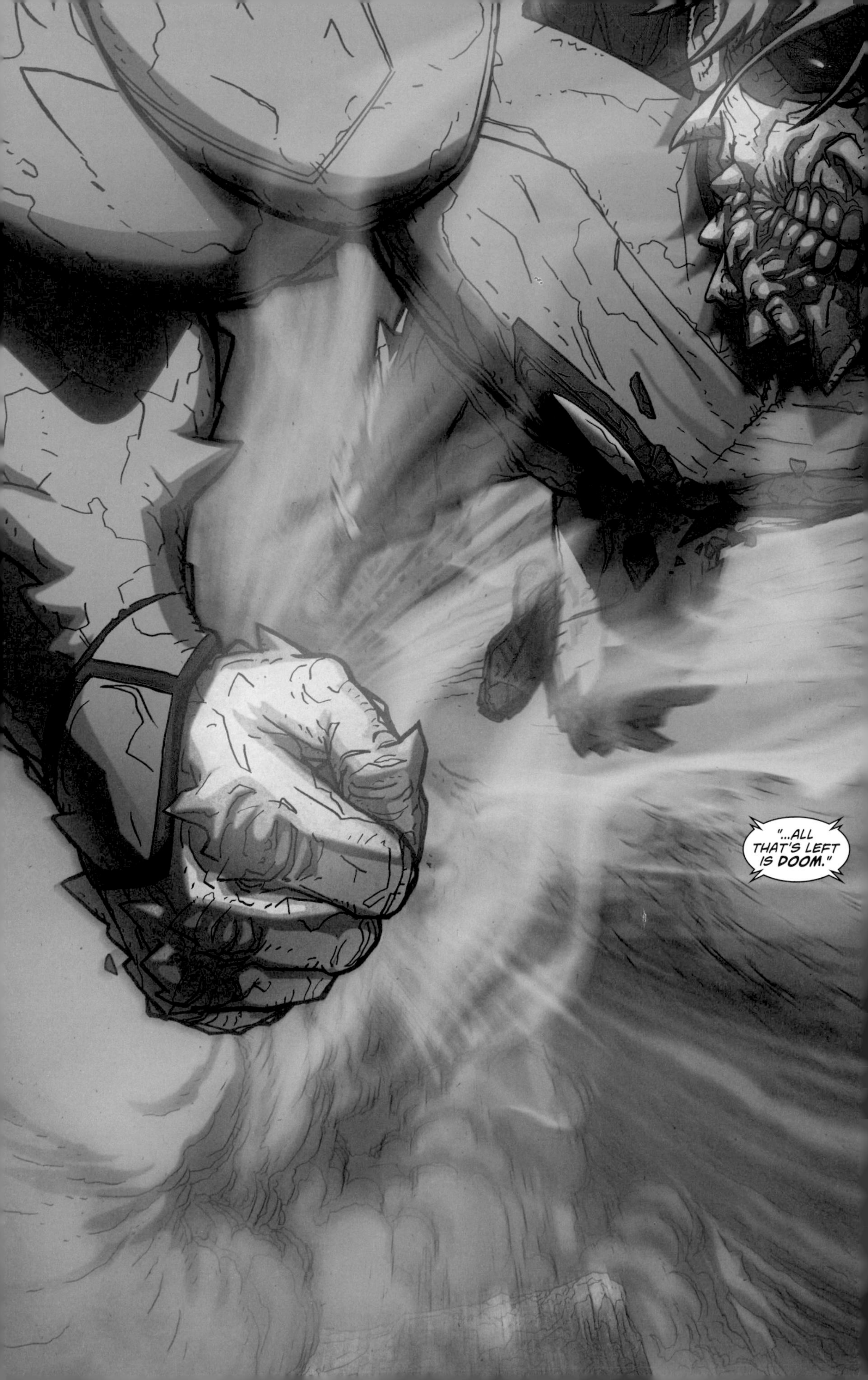
"...ALL THAT'S LEFT IS DOOM."

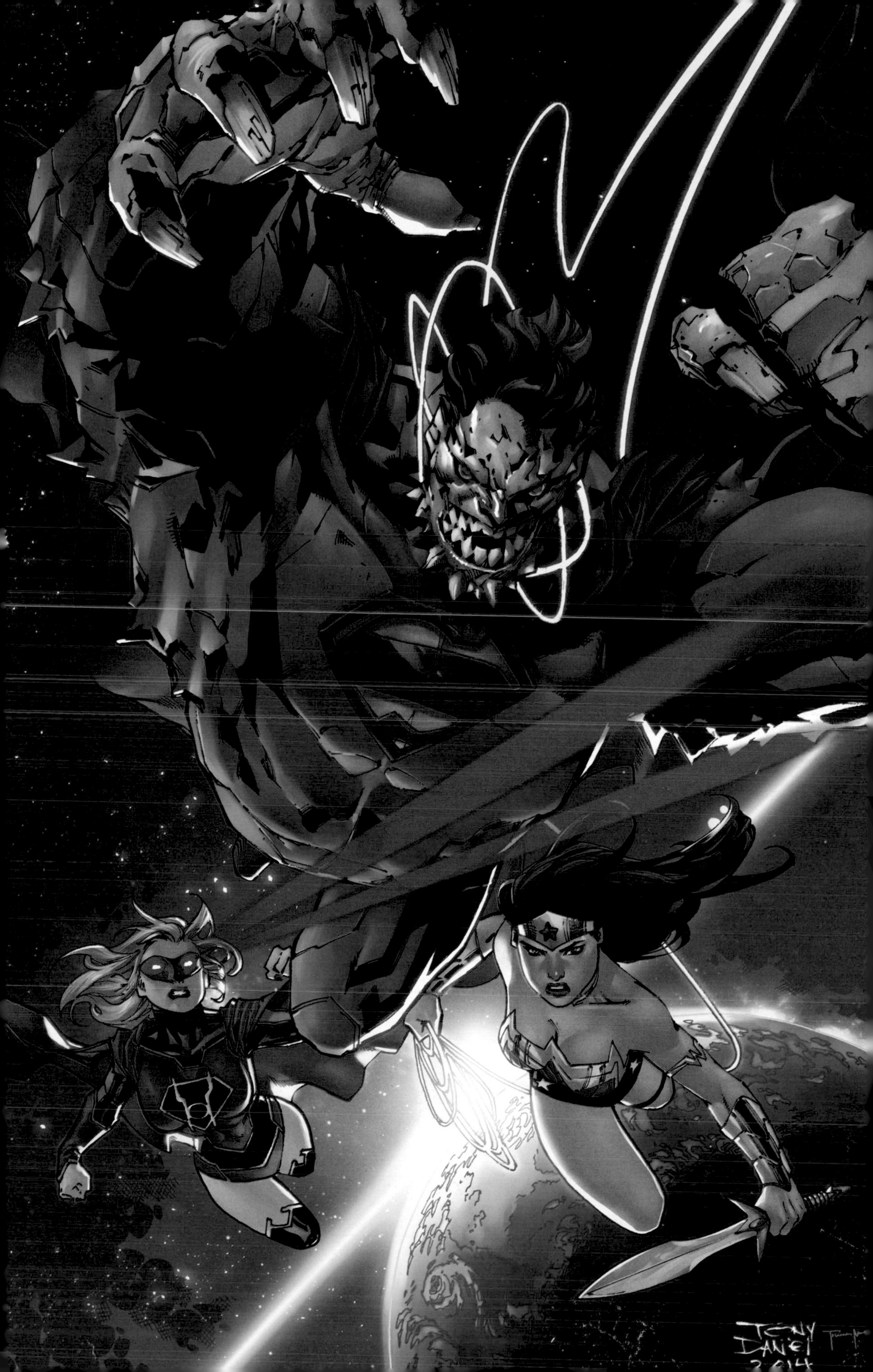
TONY DANIEL

SUPERMAN DOOMED

[ENEMY OF THE STATE] chapter 2

"ESCAPE"

STORY
CHARLES SOULE

PENCILS
TONY DANIEL

INKS
MATT BANNING AND **SANDU FLOREA**

COLORS
TOMEU MOREY

LETTERS
DEZI SIENTY

COVER
TONY DANIEL AND **TOMEU MOREY**

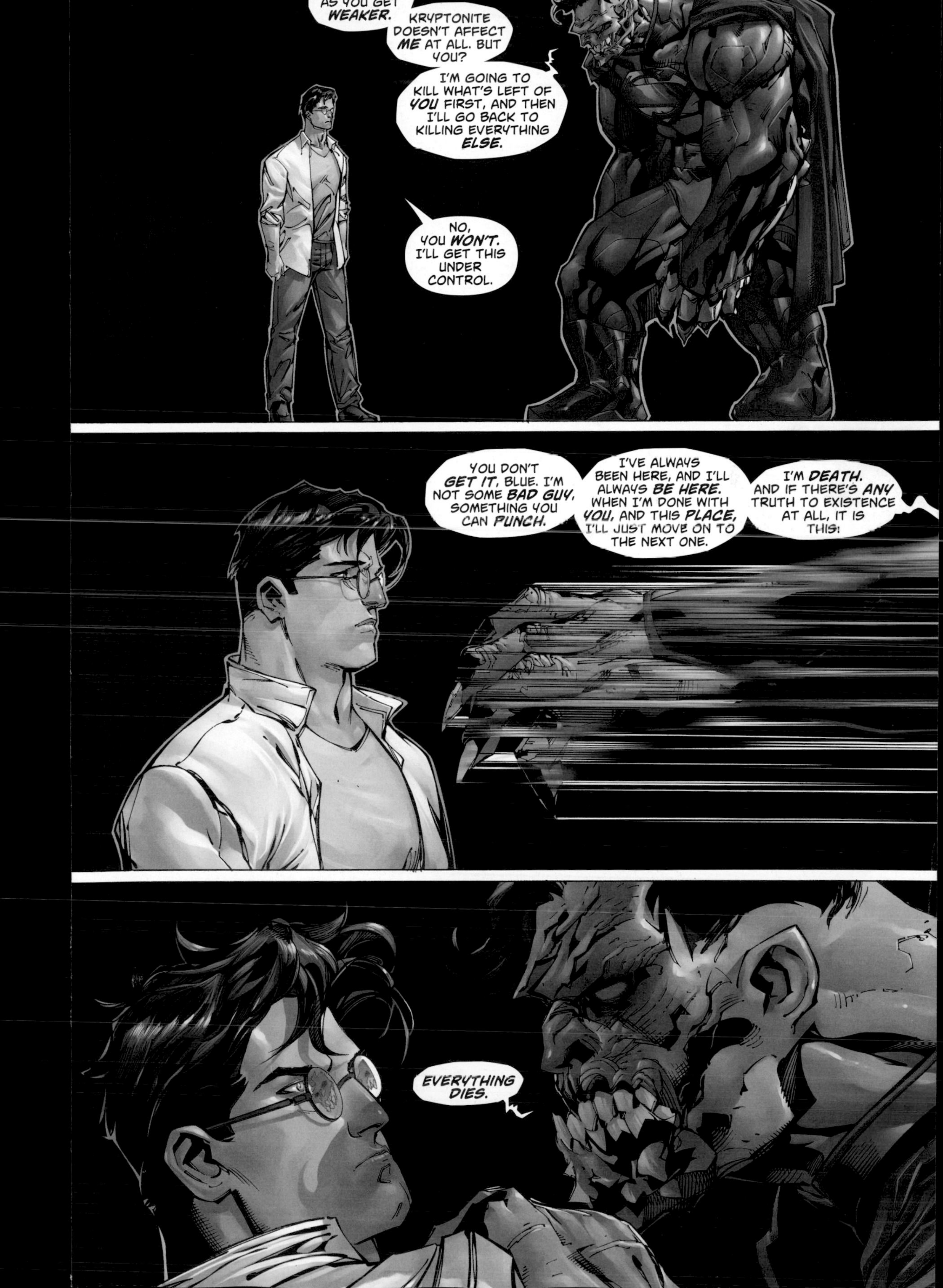
AS YOU GET WEAKER.
KRYPTONITE DOESN'T AFFECT ME AT ALL. BUT YOU?
I'M GOING TO KILL WHAT'S LEFT OF YOU FIRST, AND THEN I'LL GO BACK TO KILLING EVERYTHING ELSE.
NO, YOU WON'T. I'LL GET THIS UNDER CONTROL.
YOU DON'T GET IT, BLUE. I'M NOT SOME BAD GUY, SOMETHING YOU CAN PUNCH.
I'VE ALWAYS BEEN HERE, AND I'LL ALWAYS BE HERE. WHEN I'M DONE WITH YOU, AND THIS PLACE, I'LL JUST MOVE ON TO THE NEXT ONE.
I'M DEATH. AND IF THERE'S ANY TRUTH TO EXISTENCE AT ALL, IT IS THIS:
EVERYTHING DIES.

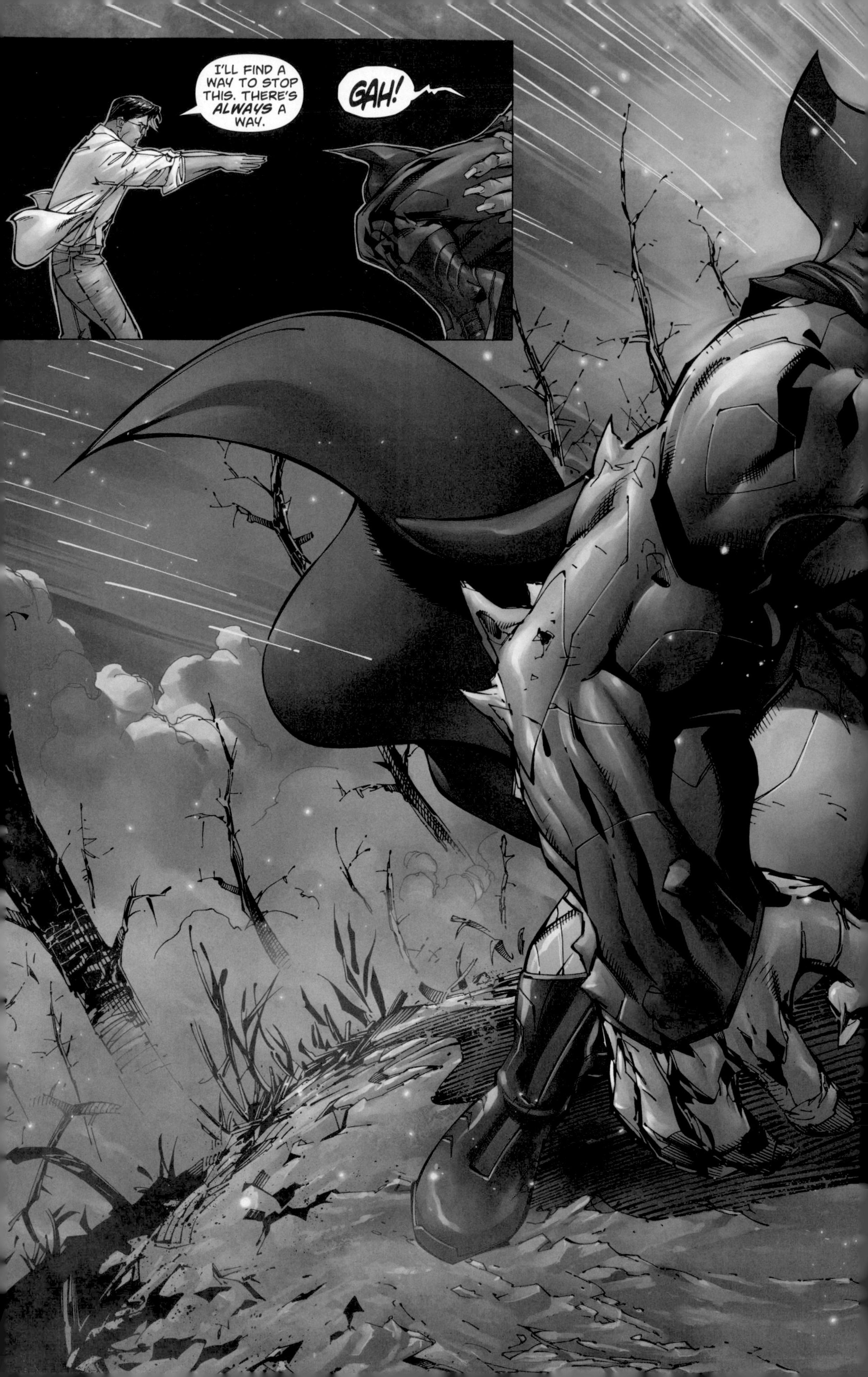
I'LL FIND A WAY TO STOP THIS. THERE'S ALWAYS A WAY.
GAH!

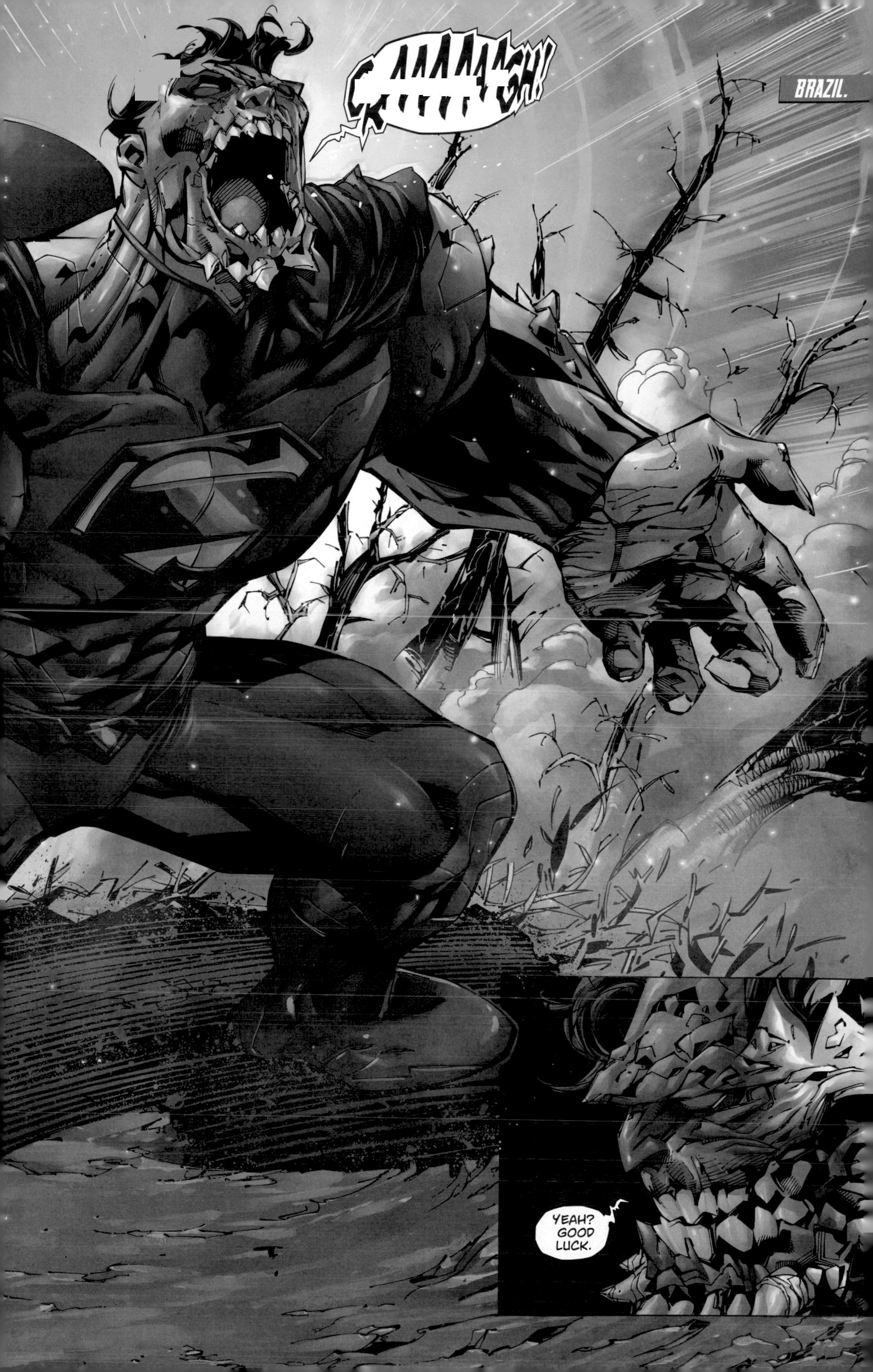
BRAZIL.
YEAH? GOOD LUCK.

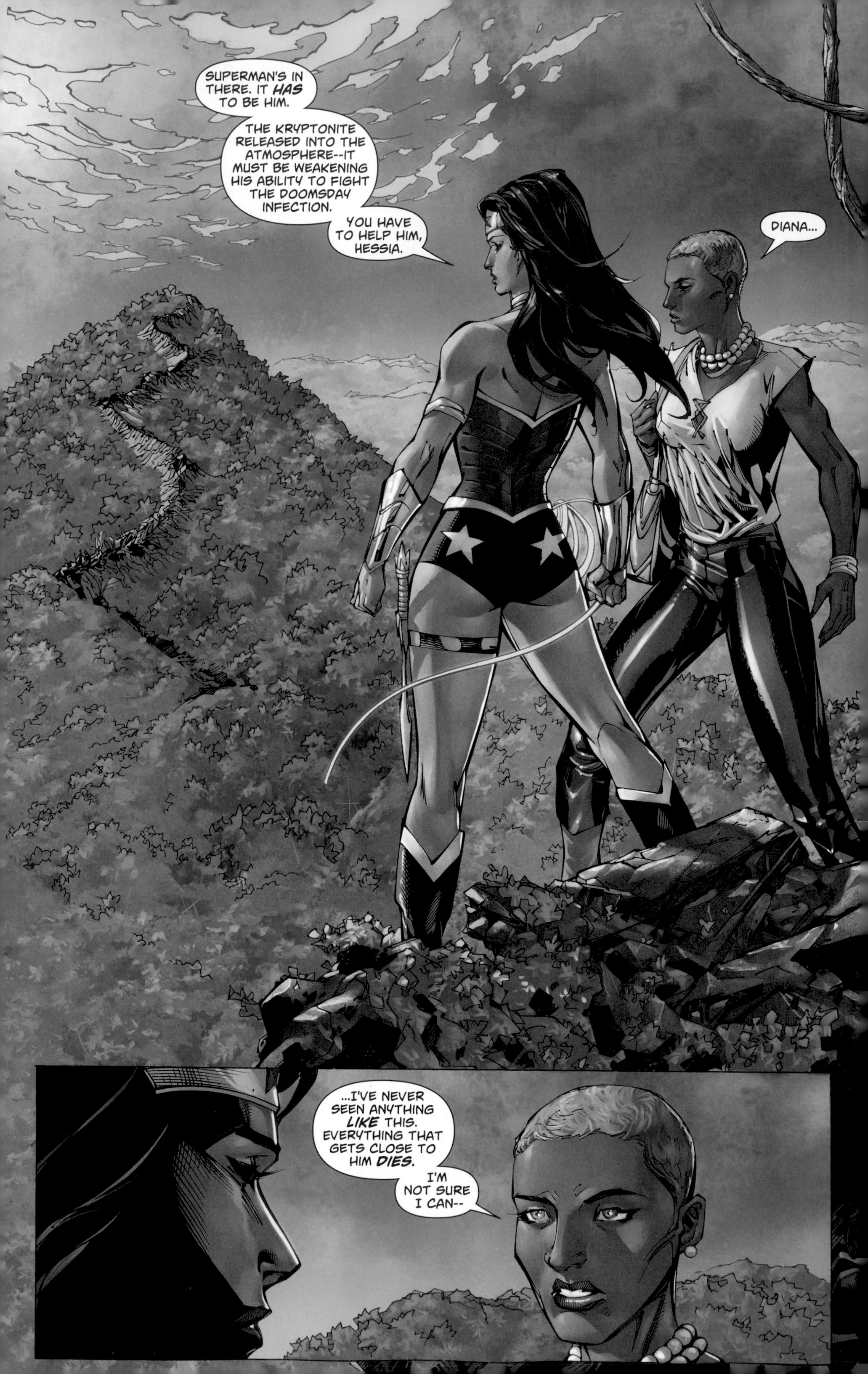
SUPERMAN'S IN THERE. IT HAS TO BE HIM.
THE KRYPTONITE RELEASED INTO THE ATMOSPHERE--IT MUST BE WEAKENING HIS ABILITY TO FIGHT THE DOOMSDAY INFECTION.
YOU HAVE TO HELP HIM, HESSIA.
DIANA...
...I'VE NEVER SEEN ANYTHING LIKE THIS. EVERYTHING THAT GETS CLOSE TO HIM DIES.
I'M NOT SURE I CAN--

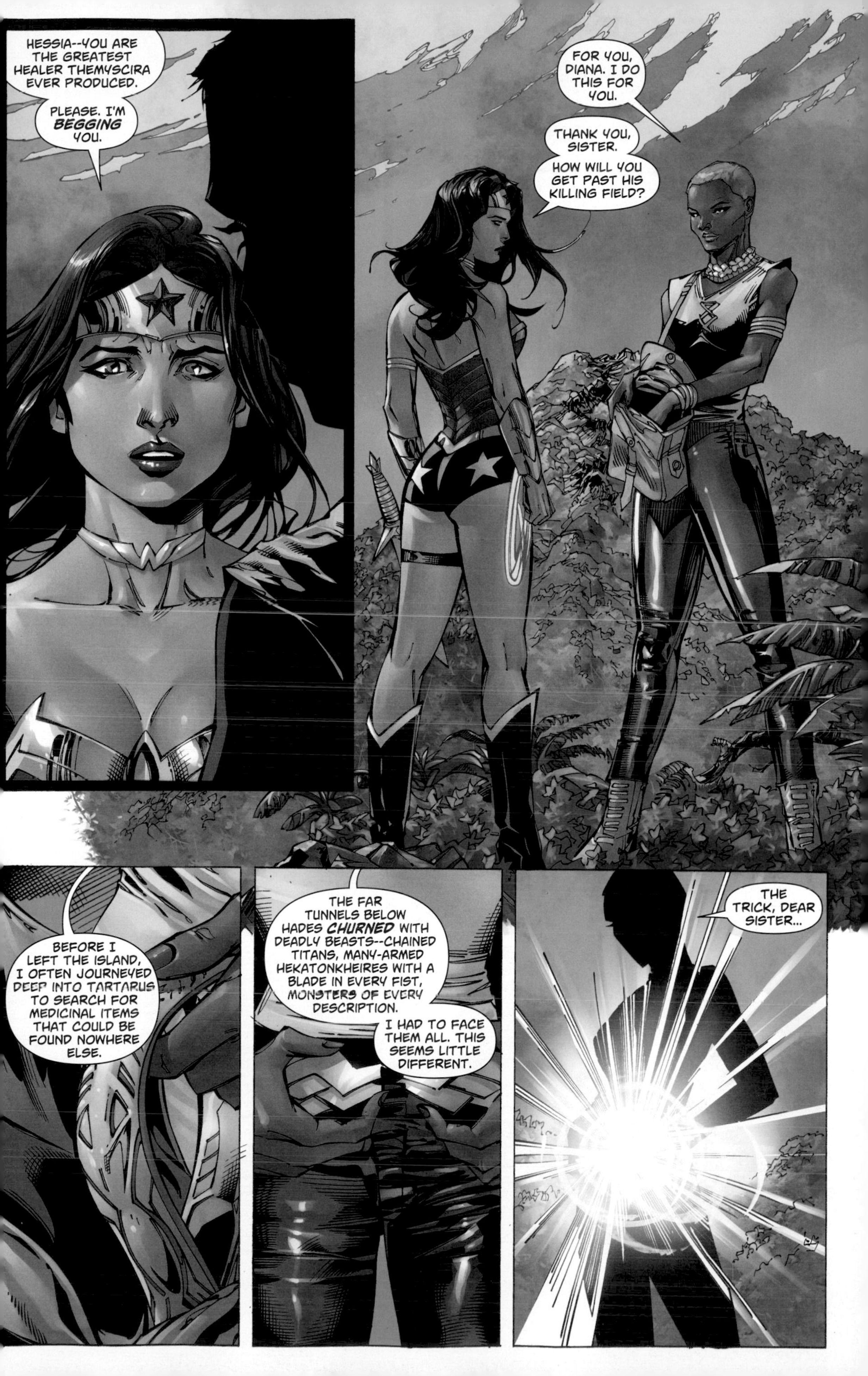
HESSIA--YOU ARE THE GREATEST HEALER THEMYSCIRA EVER PRODUCED.
PLEASE. I'M *BEGGING* YOU.
FOR YOU, DIANA. I DO THIS FOR YOU.
THANK YOU, SISTER.
HOW WILL YOU GET PAST HIS KILLING FIELD?
BEFORE I LEFT THE ISLAND, I OFTEN JOURNEYED DEEP INTO TARTARUS TO SEARCH FOR MEDICINAL ITEMS THAT COULD BE FOUND NOWHERE ELSE.
THE FAR TUNNELS BELOW HADES *CHURNED* WITH DEADLY BEASTS--CHAINED TITANS, MANY-ARMED HEKATONKHEIRES WITH A BLADE IN EVERY FIST, MONSTERS OF EVERY DESCRIPTION.
I HAD TO FACE THEM ALL. THIS SEEMS LITTLE DIFFERENT.
THE TRICK, DEAR SISTER...

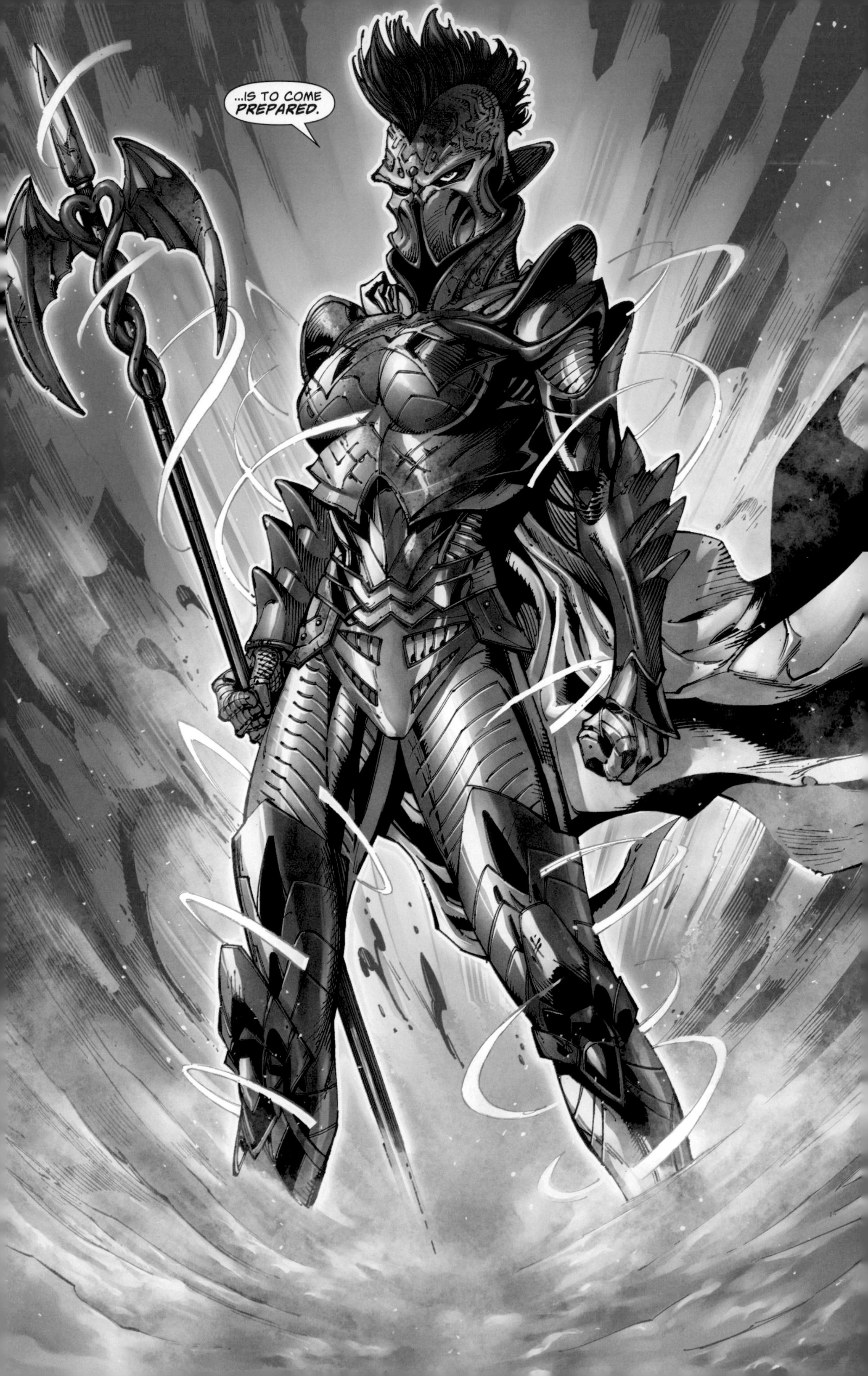
...IS TO COME PREPARED.

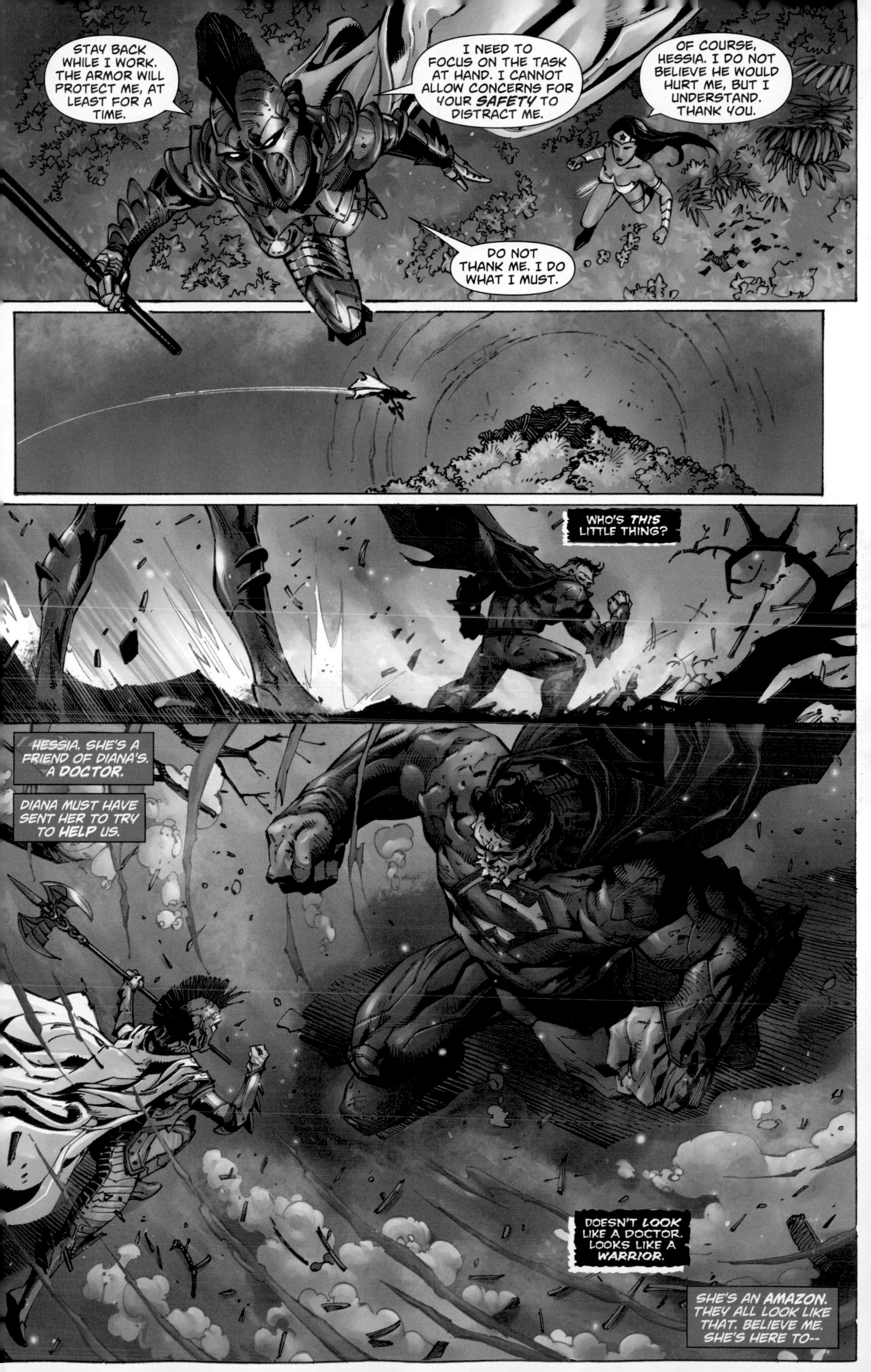
STAY BACK WHILE I WORK. THE ARMOR WILL PROTECT ME, AT LEAST FOR A TIME.
I NEED TO FOCUS ON THE TASK AT HAND. I CANNOT ALLOW CONCERNS FOR YOUR SAFETY TO DISTRACT ME.
OF COURSE, HESSIA. I DO NOT BELIEVE HE WOULD HURT ME, BUT I UNDERSTAND. THANK YOU.
DO NOT THANK ME. I DO WHAT I MUST.
WHO'S THIS LITTLE THING?
HESSIA. SHE'S A FRIEND OF DIANA'S. A DOCTOR.
DIANA MUST HAVE SENT HER TO TRY TO HELP US.
DOESN'T LOOK LIKE A DOCTOR. LOOKS LIKE A WARRIOR.
SHE'S AN AMAZON. THEY ALL LOOK LIKE THAT. BELIEVE ME. SHE'S HERE TO--

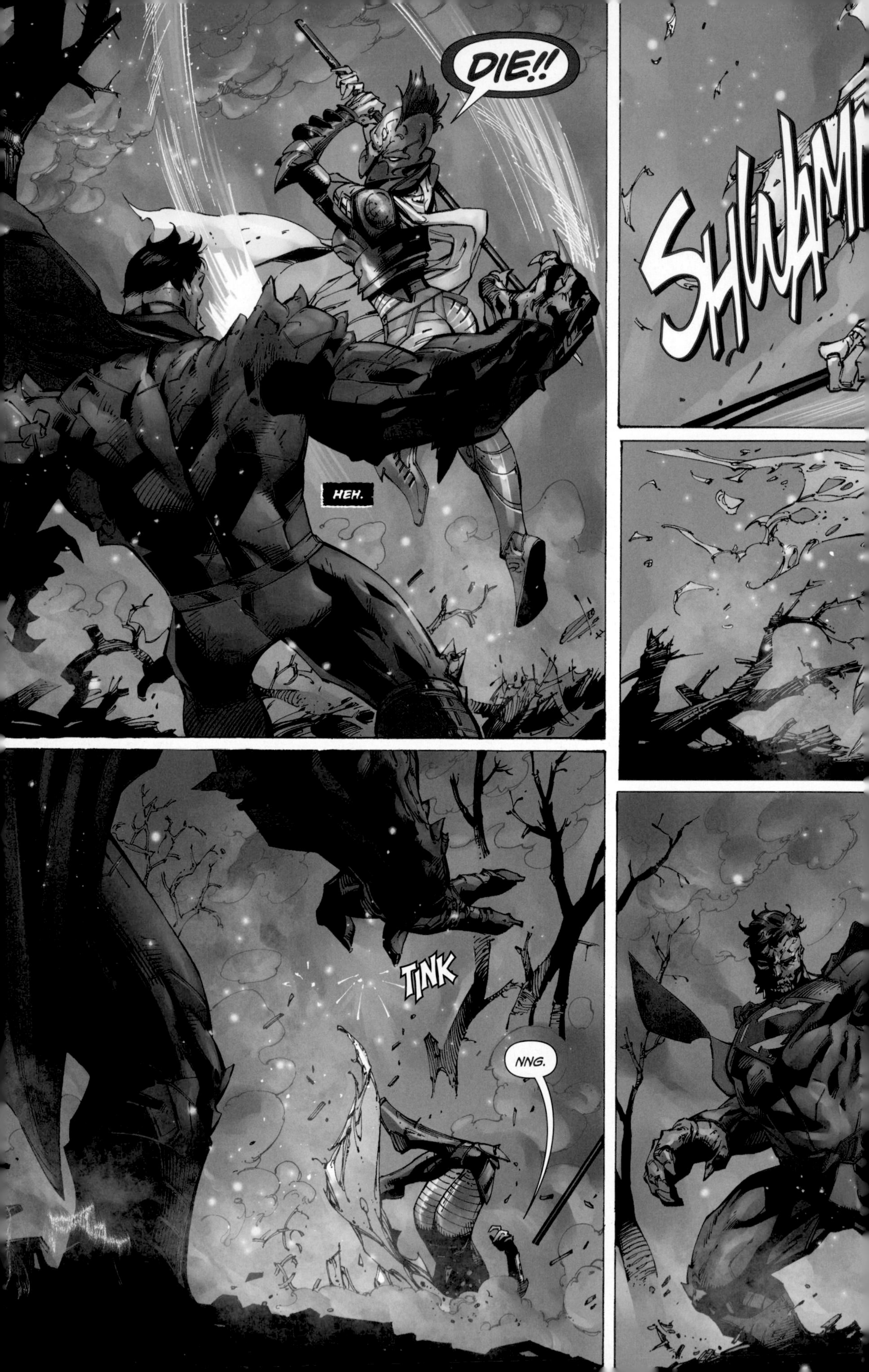
DIE!!
HEH.
SHWAM
TINK
NNG.

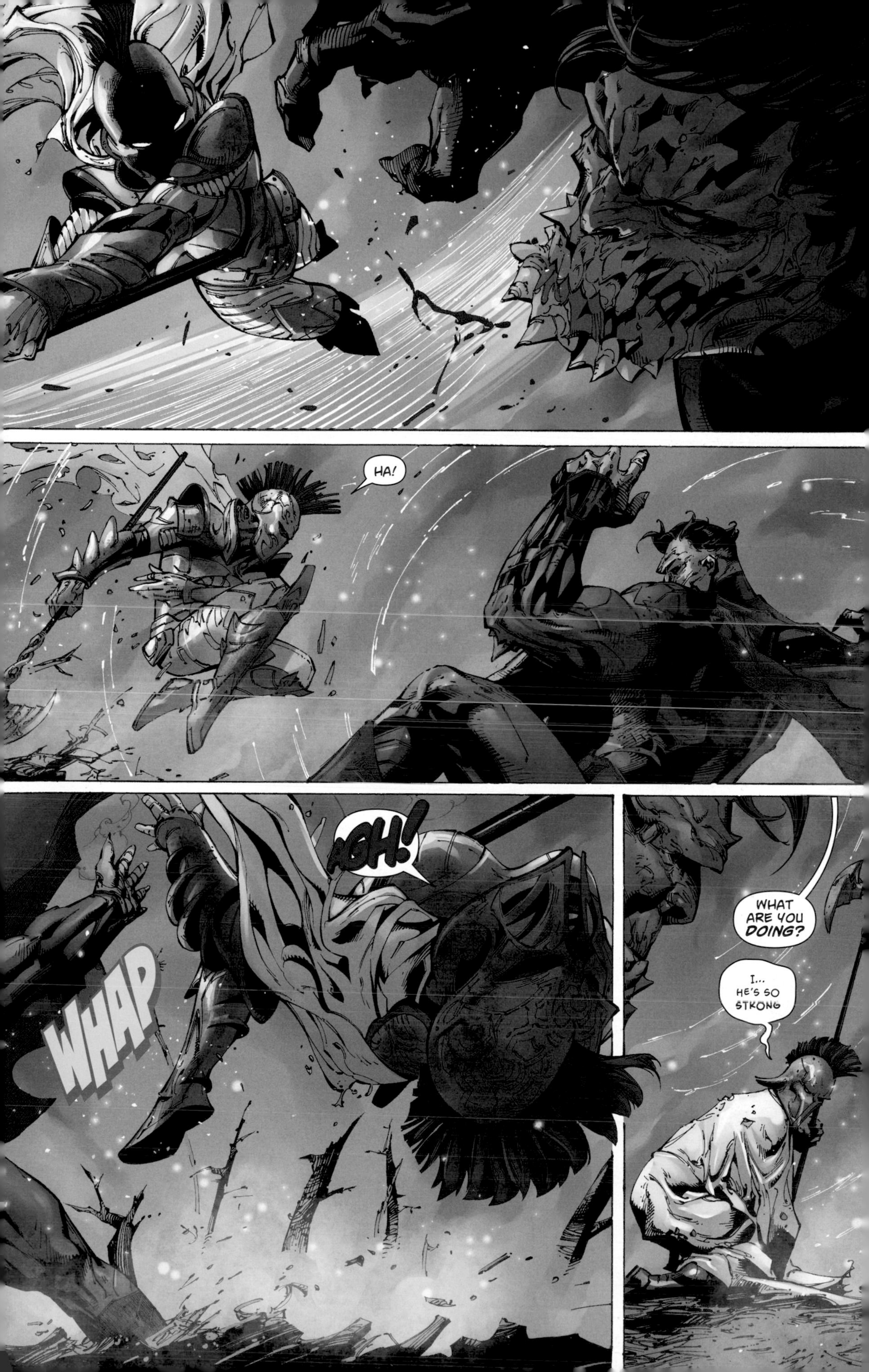
HA!
AGH!
WHAP
WHAT ARE YOU *DOING?*
I... HE'S SO STKONG

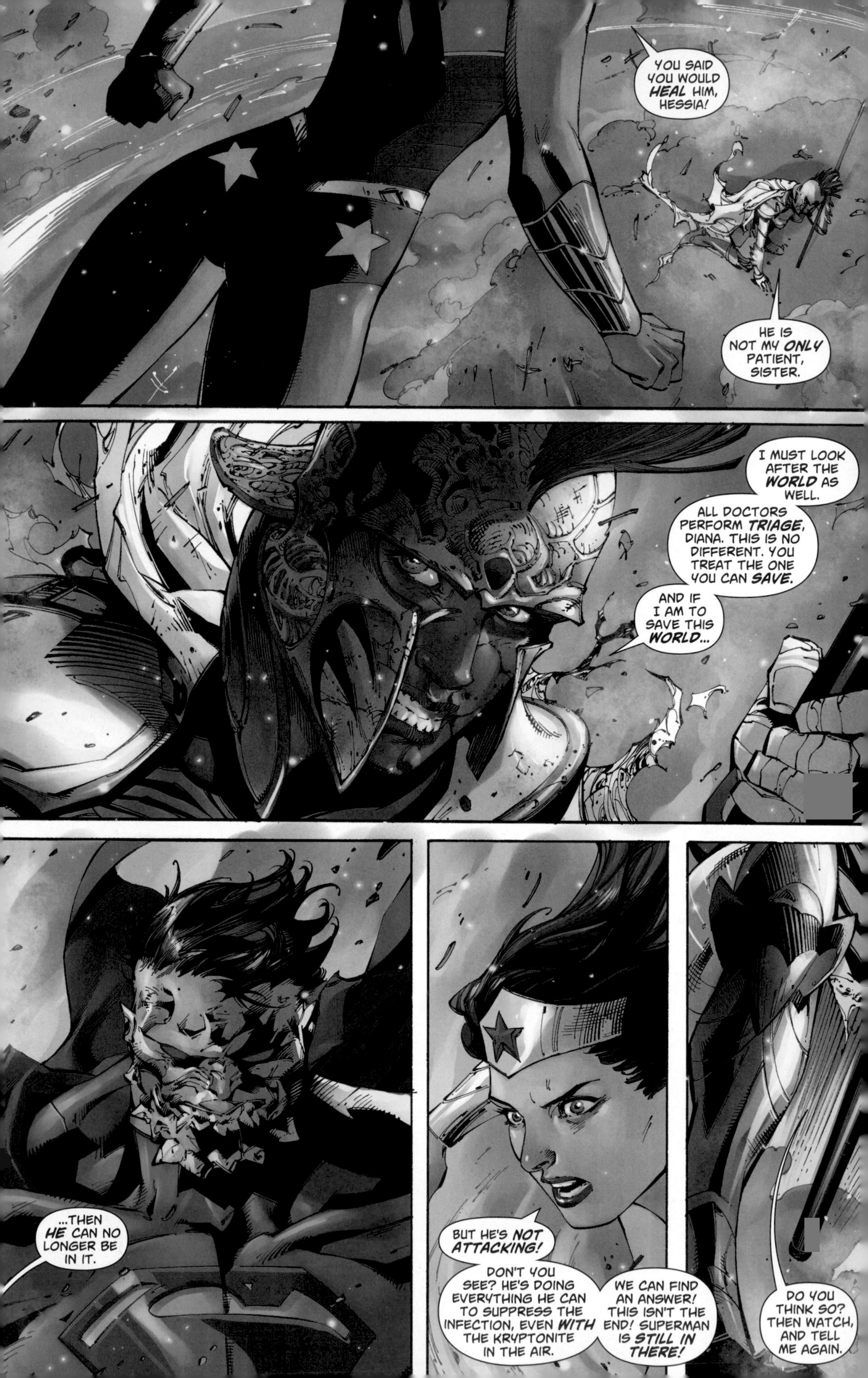
YOU SAID YOU WOULD HEAL HIM, HESSIA!
HE IS NOT MY ONLY PATIENT, SISTER.
I MUST LOOK AFTER THE WORLD AS WELL.
ALL DOCTORS PERFORM TRIAGE, DIANA. THIS IS NO DIFFERENT. YOU TREAT THE ONE YOU CAN SAVE.
AND IF I AM TO SAVE THIS WORLD...
...THEN HE CAN NO LONGER BE IN IT.
BUT HE'S NOT ATTACKING!
DON'T YOU SEE? HE'S DOING EVERYTHING HE CAN TO SUPPRESS THE INFECTION, EVEN WITH THE KRYPTONITE IN THE AIR.
WE CAN FIND AN ANSWER! THIS ISN'T THE END! SUPERMAN IS STILL IN THERE!
DO YOU THINK SO? THEN WATCH, AND TELL ME AGAIN.

HEAR ME!

I REVEALED YOUR RELATIONSHIP WITH WONDER WOMAN TO THE WORLD, SUPERMAN.

I DID IT FOR DIANA --AND FOR *YOU.* IT WAS WHAT YOU *NEEDED.*

I *HATE* THIS. I THOUGHT YOU WERE *GOOD* FOR EACH OTHER.

I WAS *WRONG.*

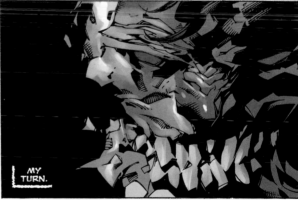

MY TURN.

KRACK

RRRAGGG!!

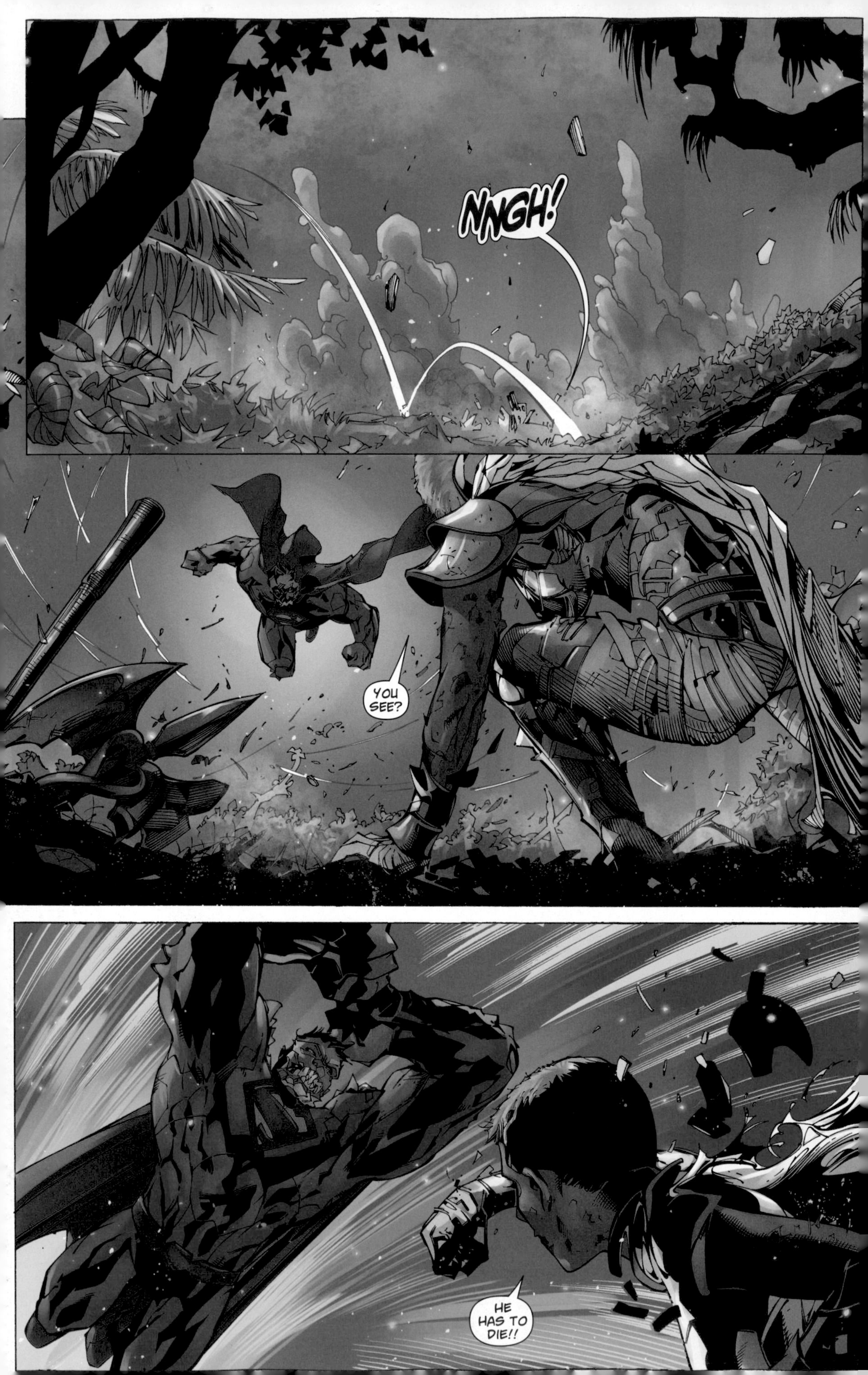
NNGH!
YOU SEE?
HE HAS TO DIE!!

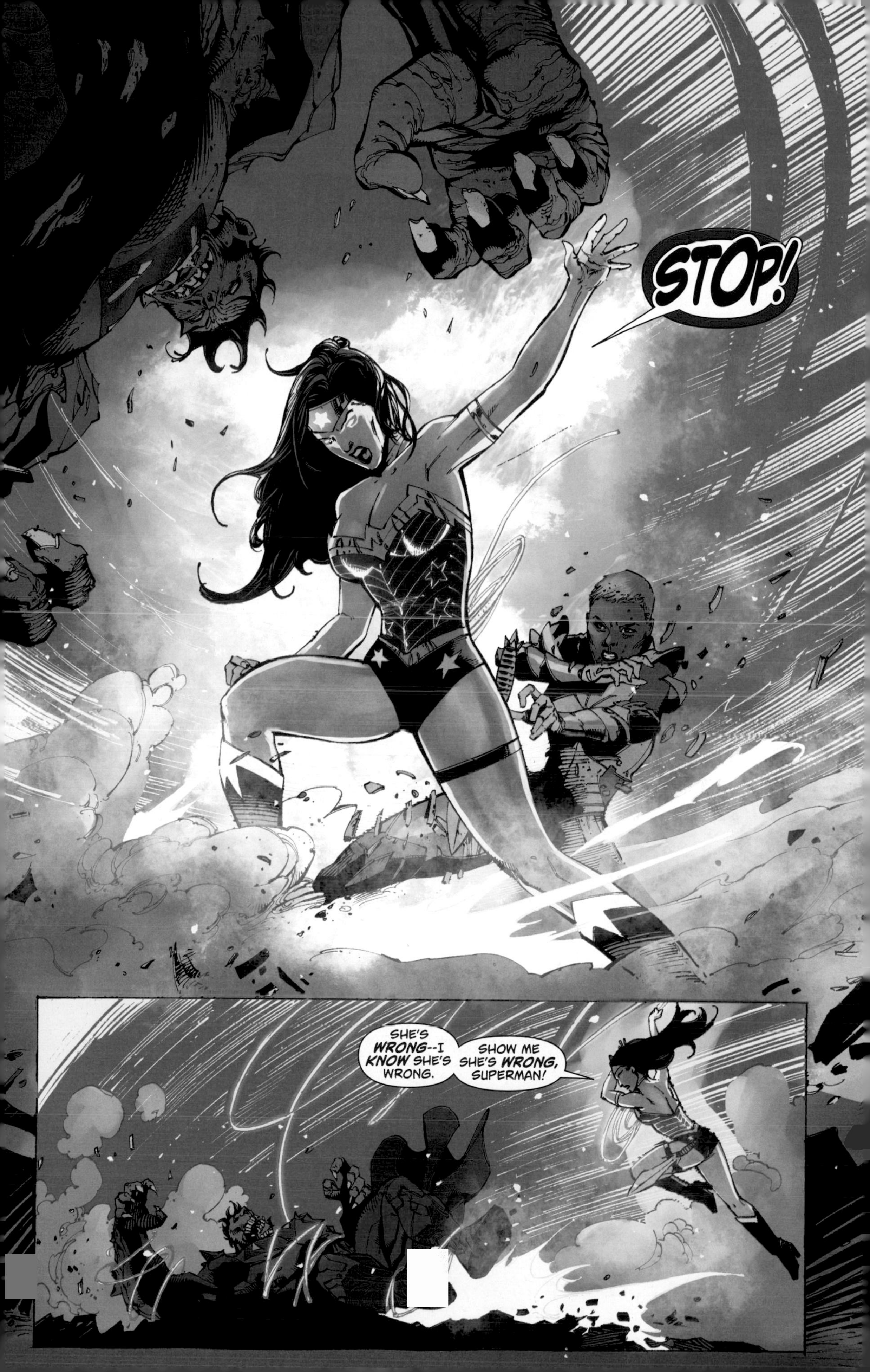
STOP!
SHE'S WRONG--I KNOW SHE'S WRONG.
SHOW ME SHE'S WRONG, SUPERMAN!

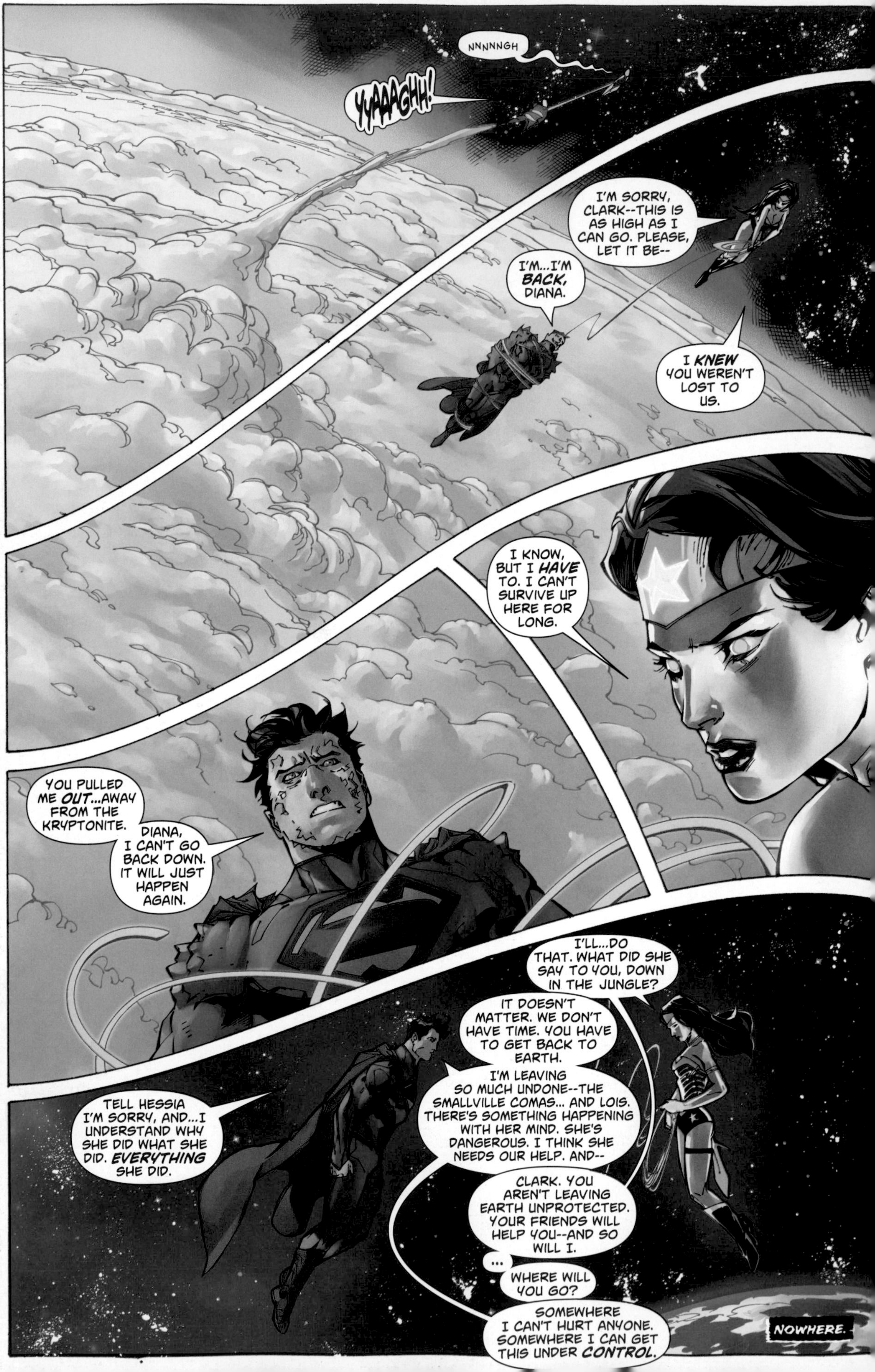
NNNNNGH
YYAAAGHH!
I'M SORRY, CLARK--THIS IS AS HIGH AS I CAN GO. PLEASE, LET IT BE--
I'M...I'M BACK, DIANA.
I KNEW YOU WEREN'T LOST TO US.
I KNOW, BUT I HAVE TO. I CAN'T SURVIVE UP HERE FOR LONG.
YOU PULLED ME OUT...AWAY FROM THE KRYPTONITE.
DIANA, I CAN'T GO BACK DOWN. IT WILL JUST HAPPEN AGAIN.
I'LL...DO THAT. WHAT DID SHE SAY TO YOU, DOWN IN THE JUNGLE?
IT DOESN'T MATTER. WE DON'T HAVE TIME. YOU HAVE TO GET BACK TO EARTH.
TELL HESSIA I'M SORRY, AND...I UNDERSTAND WHY SHE DID WHAT SHE DID. EVERYTHING SHE DID.
I'M LEAVING SO MUCH UNDONE--THE SMALLVILLE COMAS... AND LOIS. THERE'S SOMETHING HAPPENING WITH HER MIND. SHE'S DANGEROUS. I THINK SHE NEEDS OUR HELP. AND--
CLARK. YOU AREN'T LEAVING EARTH UNPROTECTED. YOUR FRIENDS WILL HELP YOU--AND SO WILL I.
...
WHERE WILL YOU GO?
SOMEWHERE I CAN'T HURT ANYONE. SOMEWHERE I CAN GET THIS UNDER CONTROL.
NOWHERE.

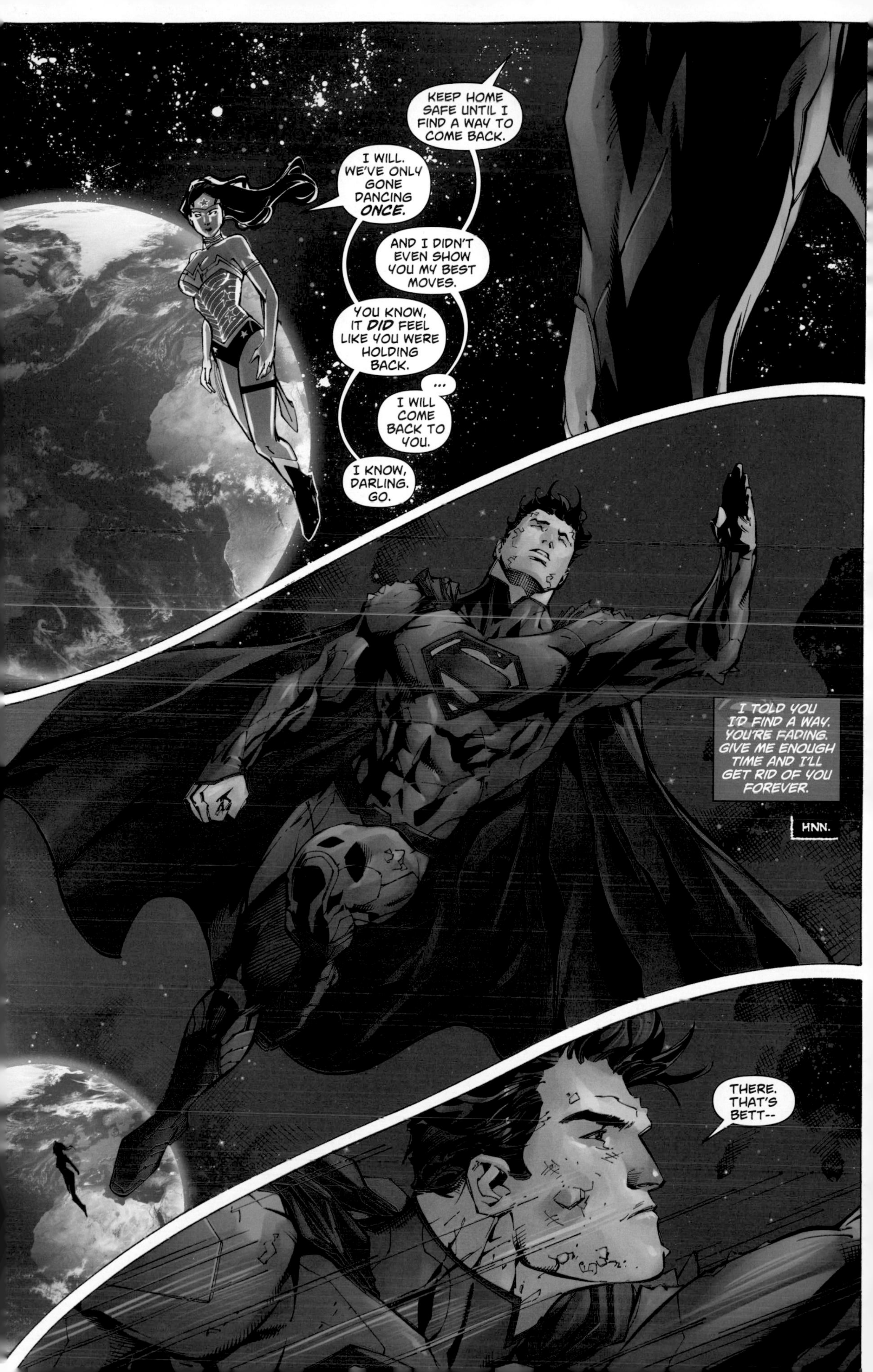
KEEP HOME SAFE UNTIL I FIND A WAY TO COME BACK.
I WILL. WE'VE ONLY GONE DANCING ONCE.
AND I DIDN'T EVEN SHOW YOU MY BEST MOVES.
YOU KNOW, IT DID FEEL LIKE YOU WERE HOLDING BACK.
...
I WILL COME BACK TO YOU.
I KNOW, DARLING. GO.
I TOLD YOU I'D FIND A WAY. YOU'RE FADING. GIVE ME ENOUGH TIME AND I'LL GET RID OF YOU FOREVER.
HNN.
THERE. THAT'S BETT--

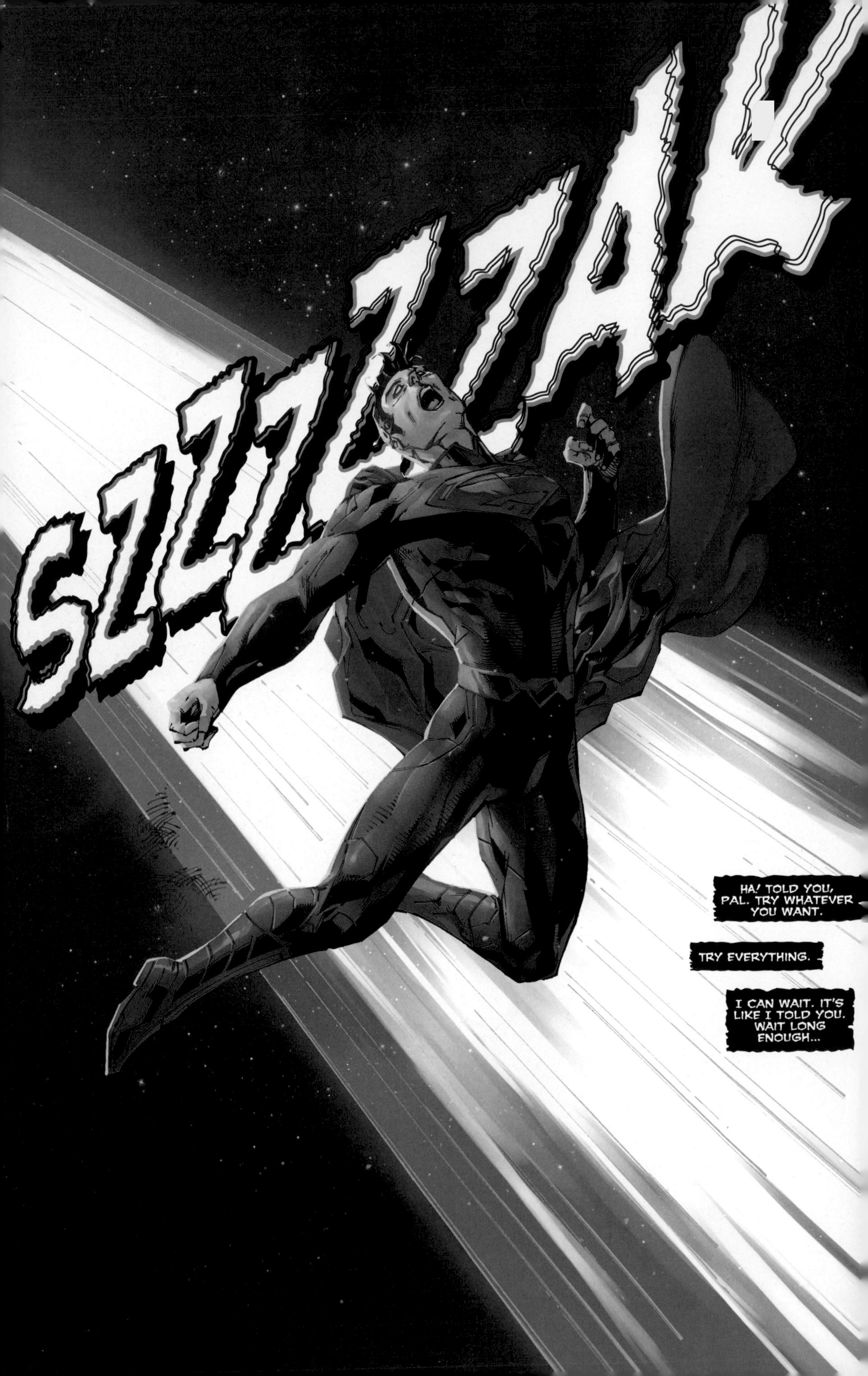
SZZZZZAK
HA! TOLD YOU, PAL. TRY WHATEVER YOU WANT.
TRY EVERYTHING.
I CAN WAIT. IT'S LIKE I TOLD YOU. WAIT LONG ENOUGH...

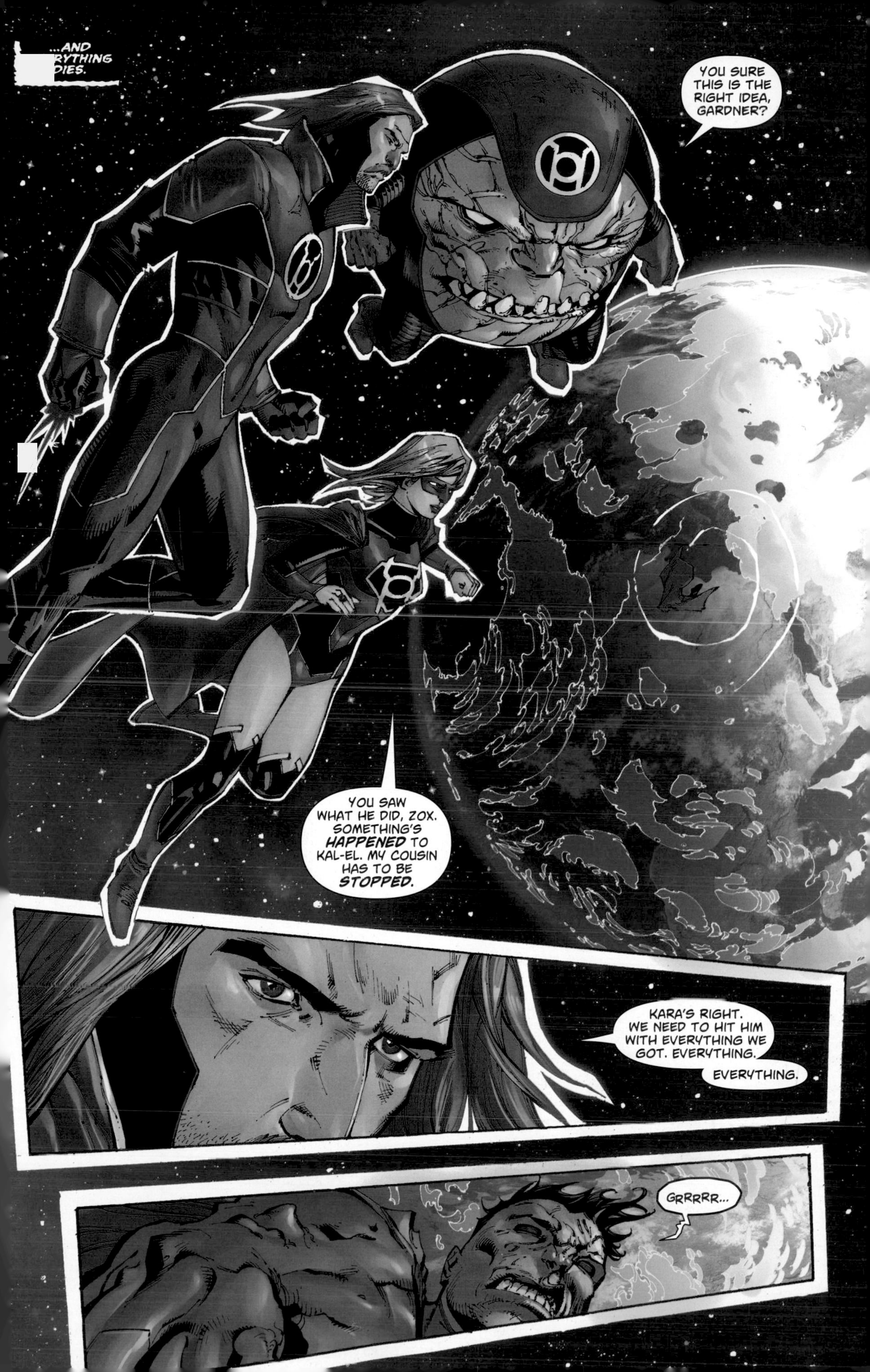
...AND
RYTHING
DIES.
YOU SURE THIS IS THE RIGHT IDEA, GARDNER?
YOU SAW WHAT HE DID, ZOX. SOMETHING'S **HAPPENED** TO KAL-EL. MY COUSIN HAS TO BE **STOPPED**.
KARA'S RIGHT. WE NEED TO HIT HIM WITH EVERYTHING WE GOT. EVERYTHING.
EVERYTHING.
GRRRRR...

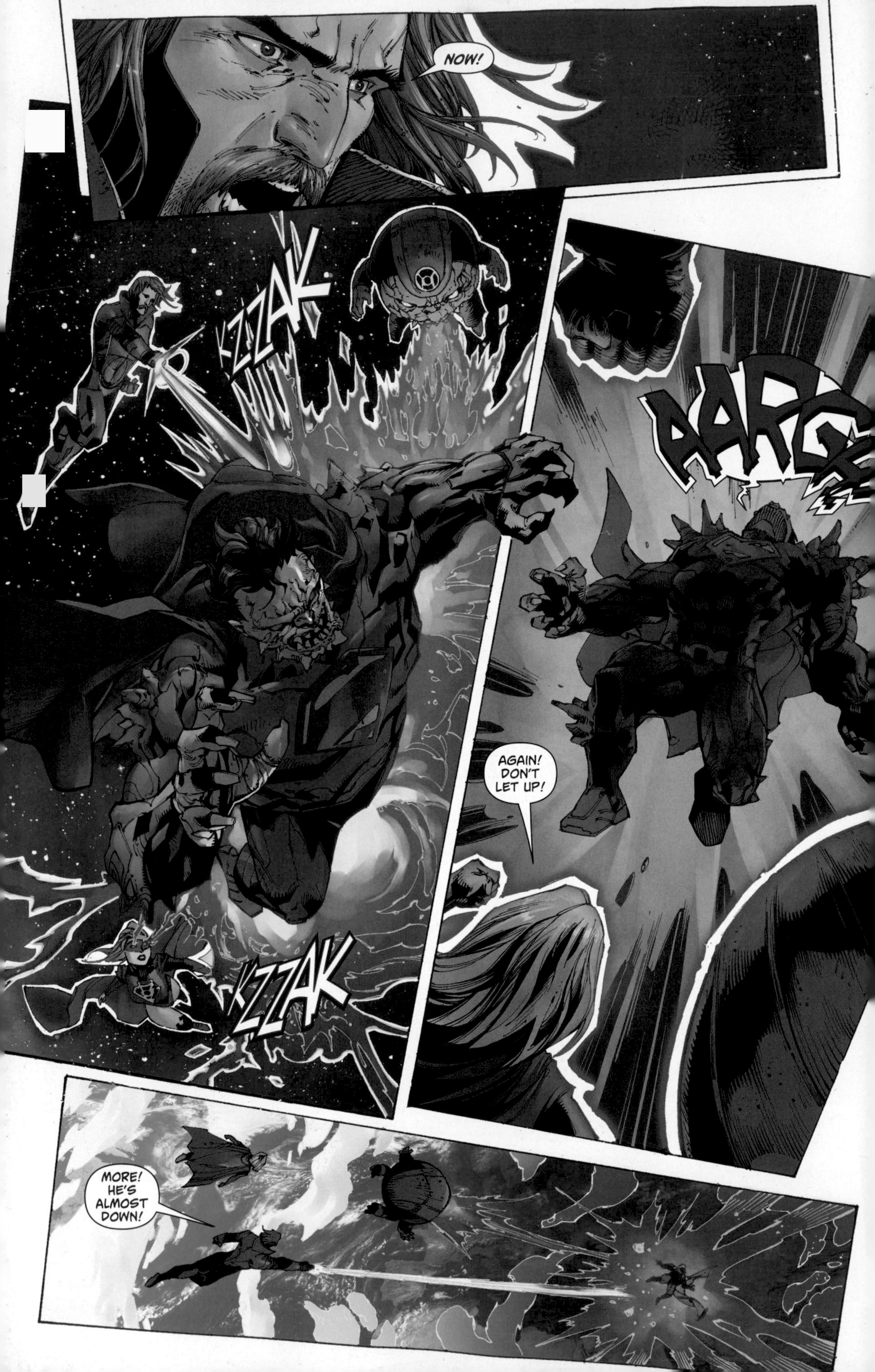

NOW!
K'ZZAK
K'ZZAK
AARGH
AGAIN! DON'T LET UP!
MORE! HE'S ALMOST DOWN!

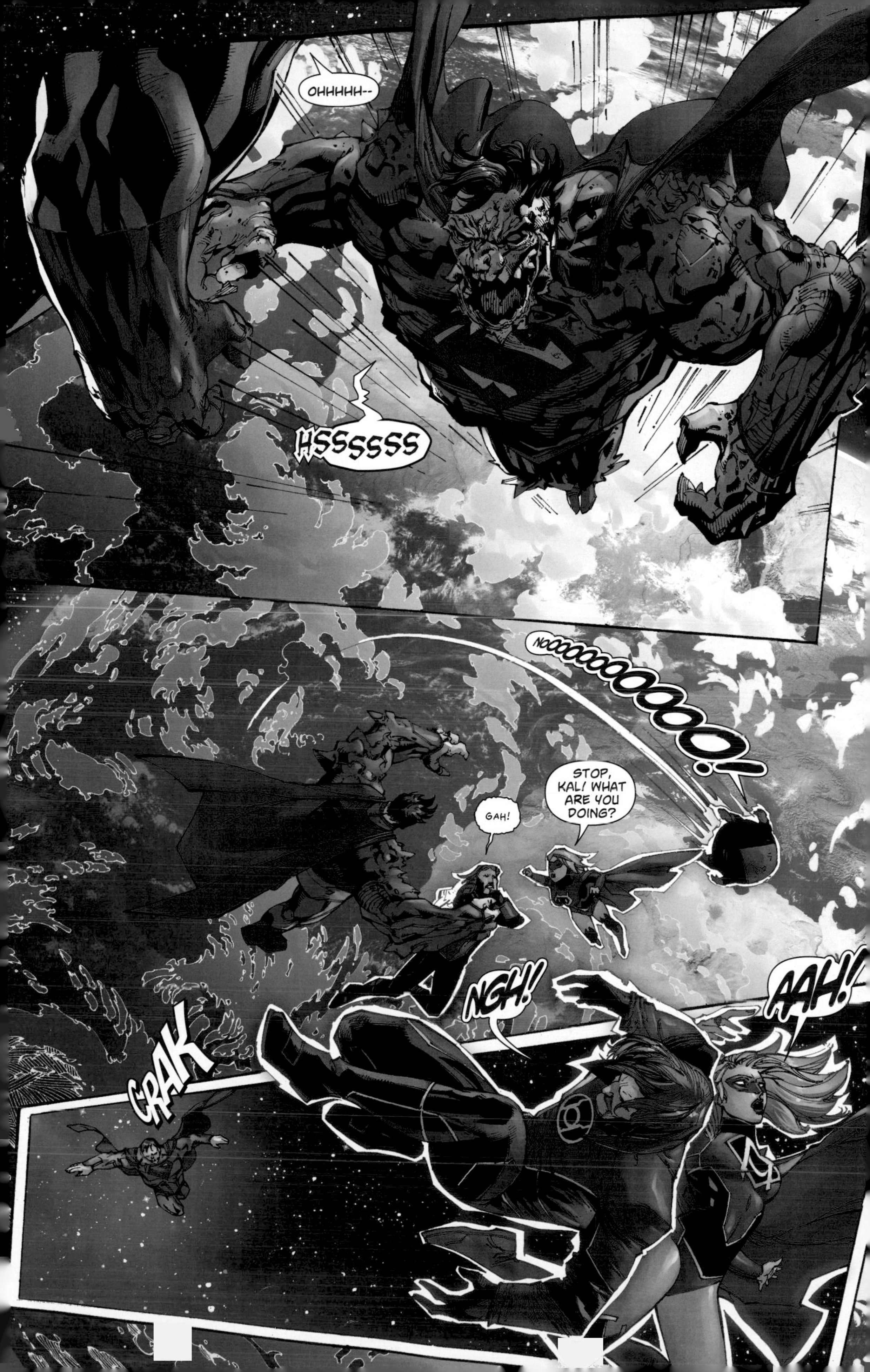
OHHHHH--
HSSSSSS
NOOOOOOOOOOOOOOO!
GAH!
STOP, KAL! WHAT ARE YOU DOING?
CRAK
NGH!
AAH!

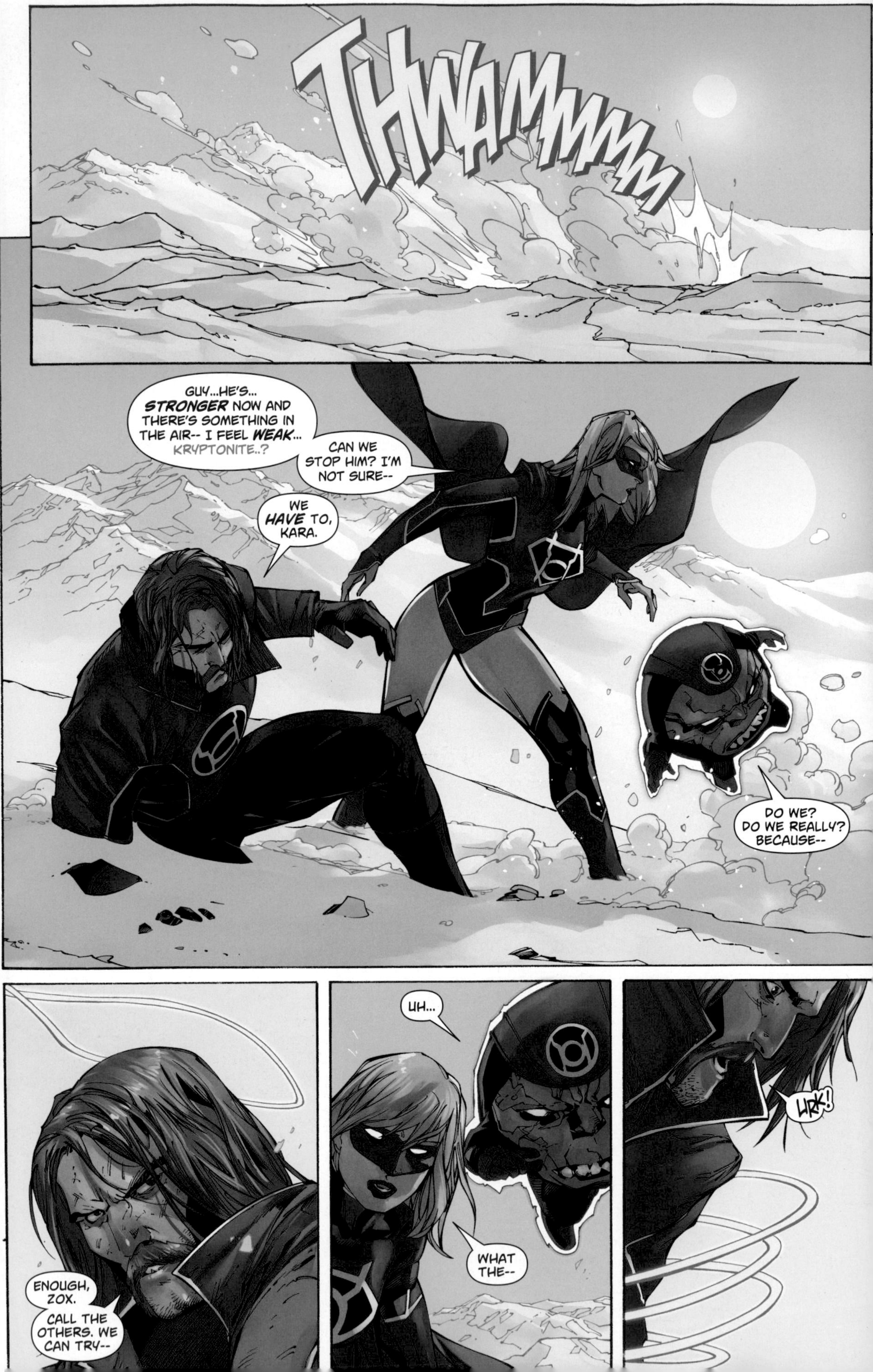
THWAMMMMM
GUY...HE'S... STRONGER NOW AND THERE'S SOMETHING IN THE AIR-- I FEEL WEAK... KRYPTONITE..?
CAN WE STOP HIM? I'M NOT SURE--
WE HAVE TO, KARA.
DO WE? DO WE REALLY? BECAUSE--
ENOUGH, ZOX.
CALL THE OTHERS. WE CAN TRY--
UH...
WHAT THE--
URK!

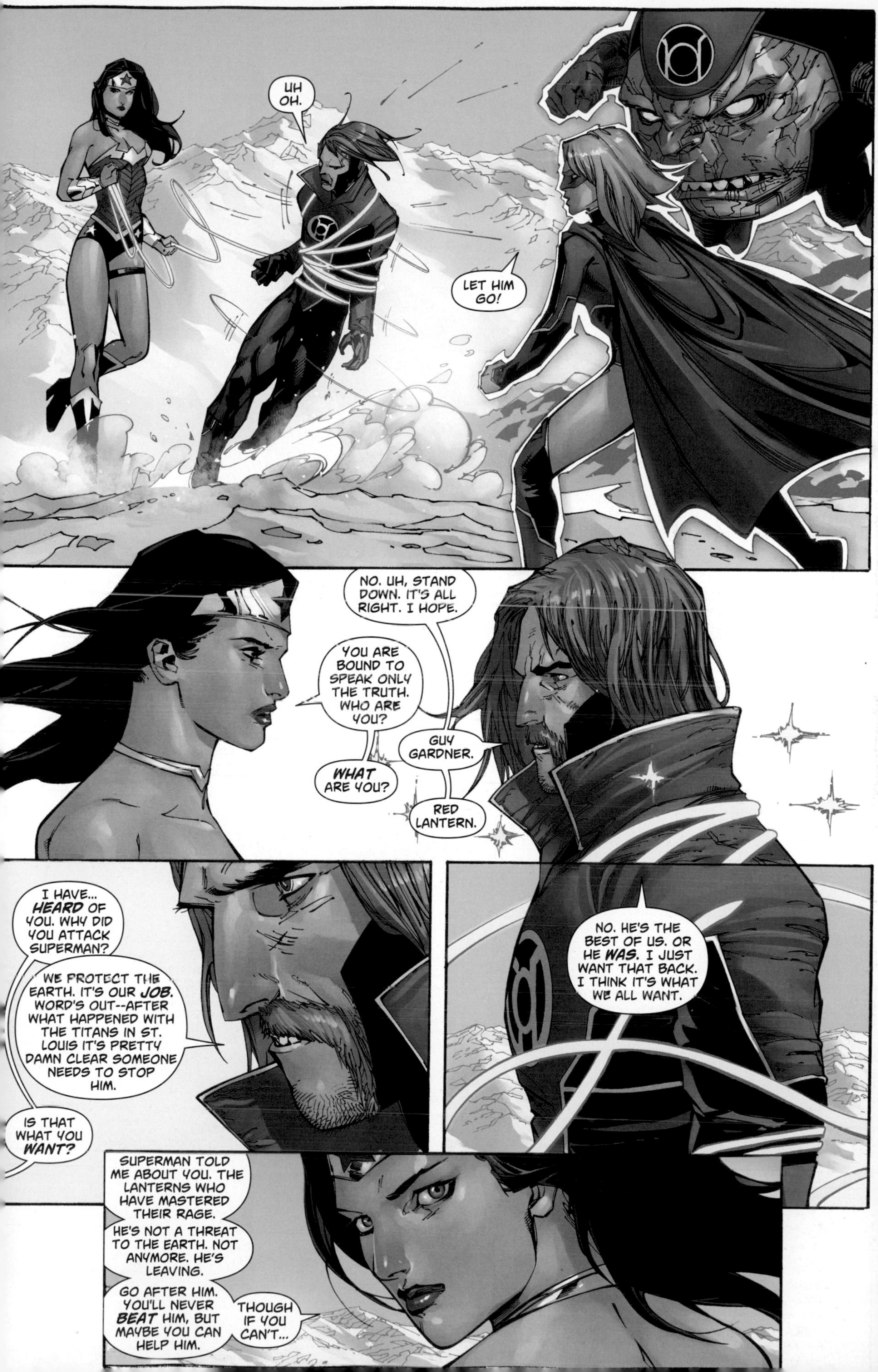
UH OH.
LET HIM GO!
NO. UH, STAND DOWN. IT'S ALL RIGHT. I HOPE.
YOU ARE BOUND TO SPEAK ONLY THE TRUTH. WHO ARE YOU?
GUY GARDNER.
WHAT ARE YOU?
RED LANTERN.
I HAVE... HEARD OF YOU. WHY DID YOU ATTACK SUPERMAN?
WE PROTECT THE EARTH. IT'S OUR JOB. WORD'S OUT--AFTER WHAT HAPPENED WITH THE TITANS IN ST. LOUIS IT'S PRETTY DAMN CLEAR SOMEONE NEEDS TO STOP HIM.
IS THAT WHAT YOU WANT?
NO. HE'S THE BEST OF US. OR HE WAS. I JUST WANT THAT BACK. I THINK IT'S WHAT WE ALL WANT.
SUPERMAN TOLD ME ABOUT YOU. THE LANTERNS WHO HAVE MASTERED THEIR RAGE.
HE'S NOT A THREAT TO THE EARTH. NOT ANYMORE. HE'S LEAVING.
GO AFTER HIM. YOU'LL NEVER BEAT HIM, BUT MAYBE YOU CAN HELP HIM.
THOUGH IF YOU CAN'T...

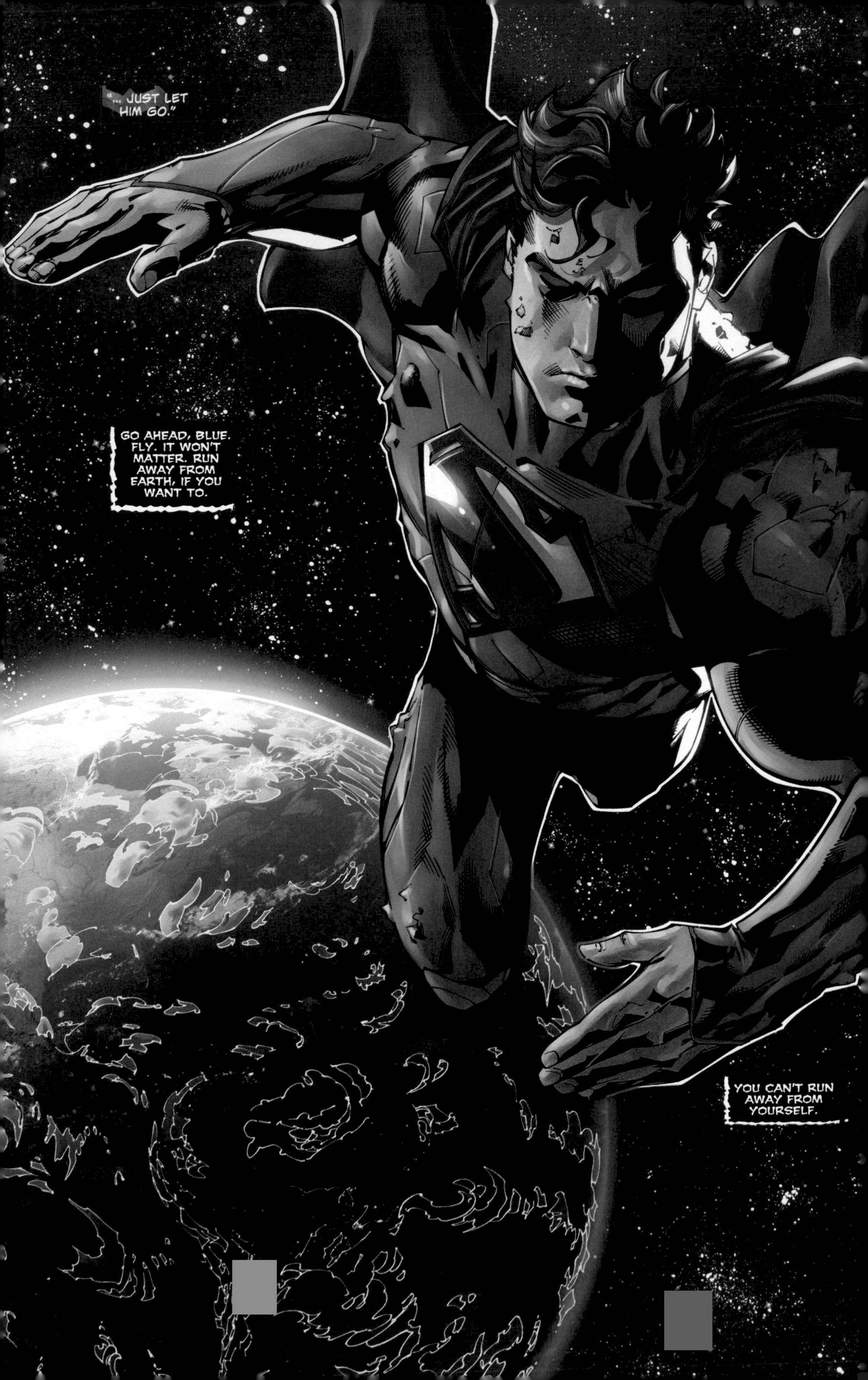
"... JUST LET HIM GO."
GO AHEAD, BLUE. FLY. IT WON'T MATTER. RUN AWAY FROM EARTH, IF YOU WANT TO.
YOU CAN'T RUN AWAY FROM YOURSELF.

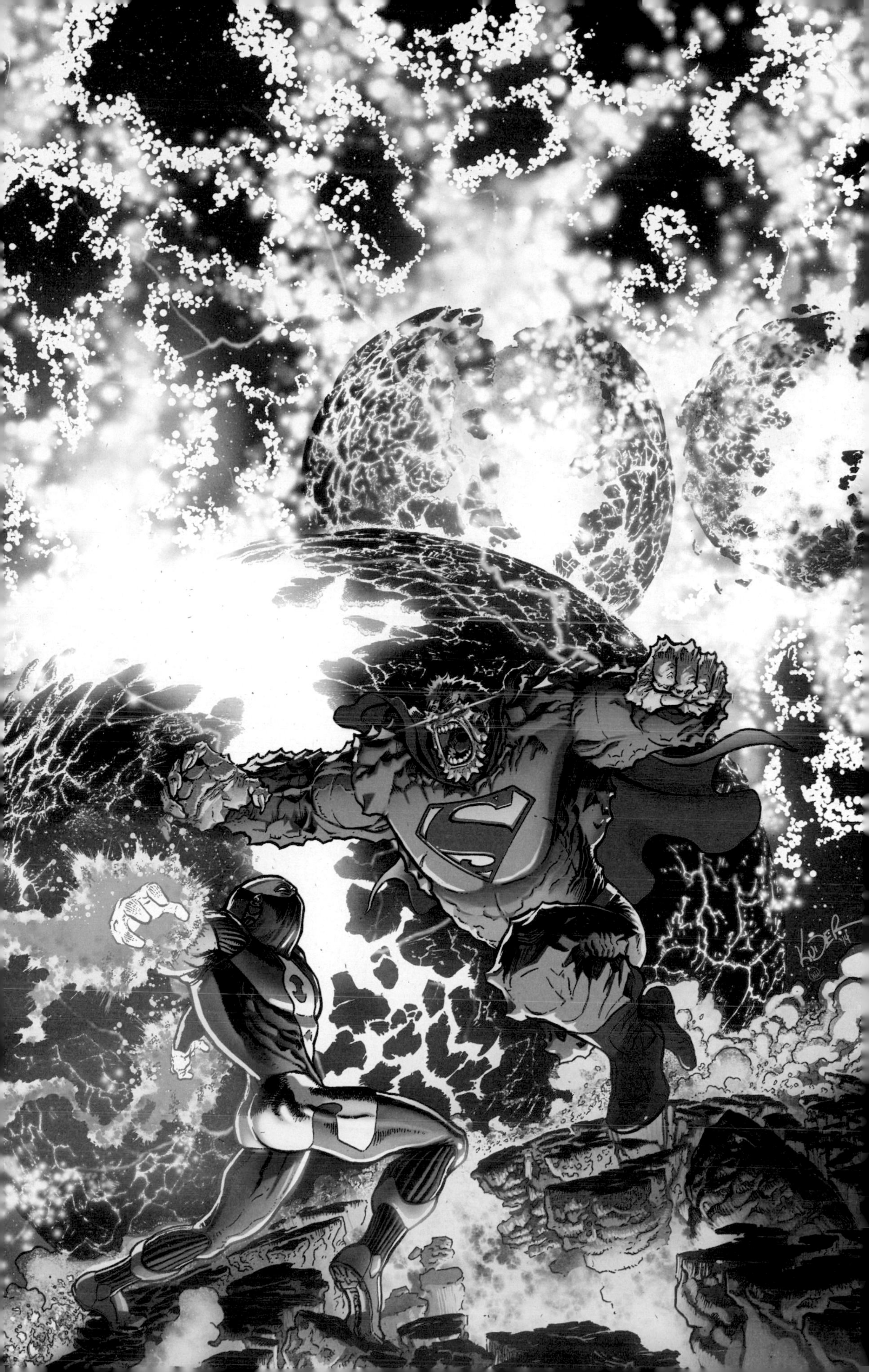

SUPERMAN DOOMED

[SUPERDOOM] chapter 1
"UNBOUND"

STORY
GREG PAK

ART
AARON KUDER

COLORS
WIL QUINTANA

LETTERS
DC LETTERING

COVER
AARON KUDER AND **WIL QUINTANA**

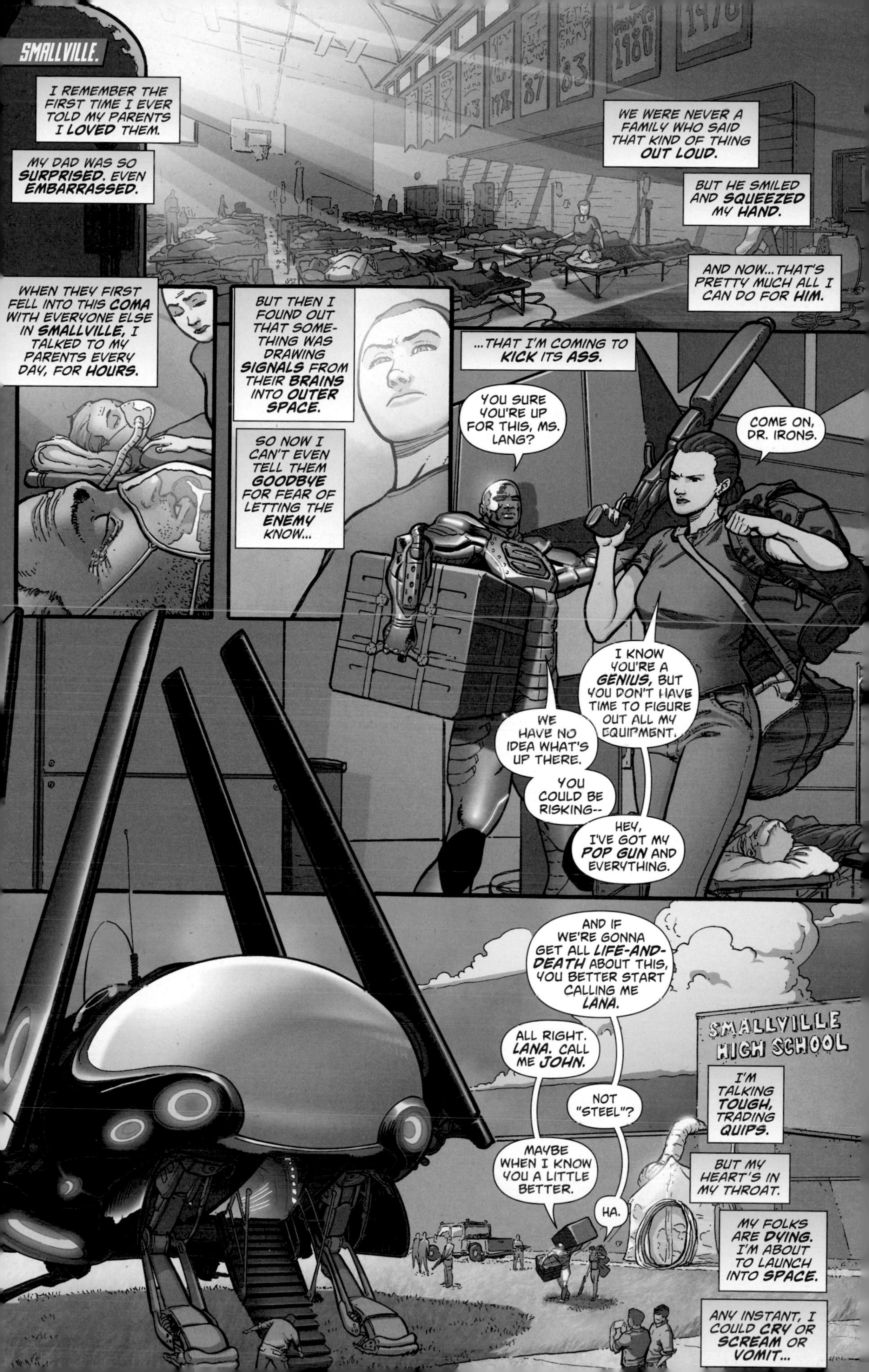
SMALLVILLE.
I REMEMBER THE FIRST TIME I EVER TOLD MY PARENTS I LOVED THEM.
MY DAD WAS SO SURPRISED. EVEN EMBARRASSED.
WE WERE NEVER A FAMILY WHO SAID THAT KIND OF THING OUT LOUD.
BUT HE SMILED AND SQUEEZED MY HAND.
AND NOW...THAT'S PRETTY MUCH ALL I CAN DO FOR HIM.
WHEN THEY FIRST FELL INTO THIS COMA WITH EVERYONE ELSE IN SMALLVILLE, I TALKED TO MY PARENTS EVERY DAY, FOR HOURS.
BUT THEN I FOUND OUT THAT SOMETHING WAS DRAWING SIGNALS FROM THEIR BRAINS INTO OUTER SPACE.
SO NOW I CAN'T EVEN TELL THEM GOODBYE FOR FEAR OF LETTING THE ENEMY KNOW...
...THAT I'M COMING TO KICK ITS ASS.
YOU SURE YOU'RE UP FOR THIS, MS. LANG?
COME ON, DR. IRONS.
I KNOW YOU'RE A GENIUS, BUT YOU DON'T HAVE TIME TO FIGURE OUT ALL MY EQUIPMENT.
WE HAVE NO IDEA WHAT'S UP THERE.
YOU COULD BE RISKING--
HEY, I'VE GOT MY POP GUN AND EVERYTHING.
AND IF WE'RE GONNA GET ALL LIFE-AND-DEATH ABOUT THIS, YOU BETTER START CALLING ME LANA.
ALL RIGHT. LANA. CALL ME JOHN.
NOT "STEEL"?
MAYBE WHEN I KNOW YOU A LITTLE BETTER.
HA.
SMALLVILLE HIGH SCHOOL
I'M TALKING TOUGH, TRADING QUIPS.
BUT MY HEART'S IN MY THROAT.
MY FOLKS ARE DYING. I'M ABOUT TO LAUNCH INTO SPACE.
ANY INSTANT, I COULD CRY OR SCREAM OR VOMIT...

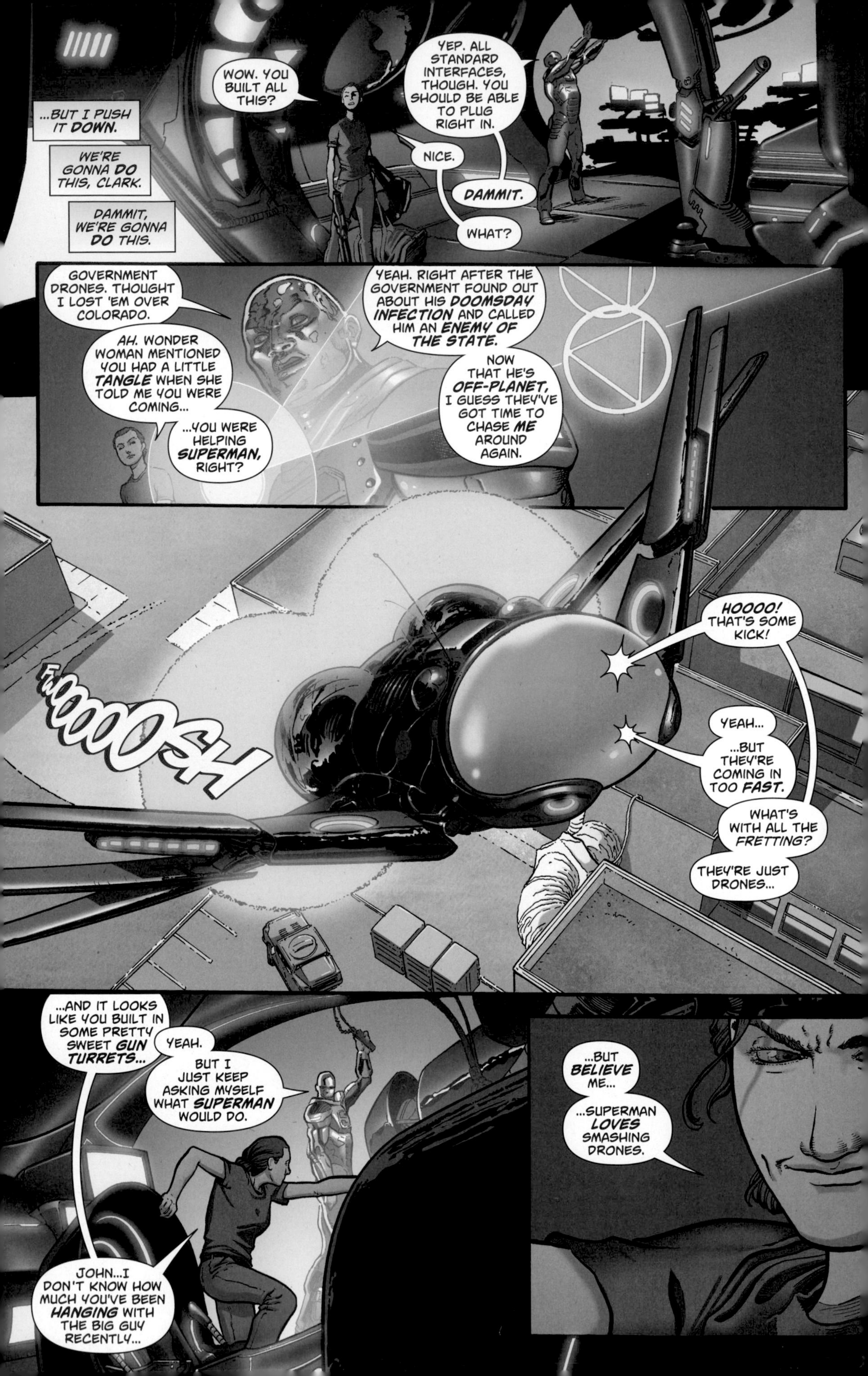
...BUT I PUSH IT DOWN.
WE'RE GONNA DO THIS, CLARK.
DAMMIT, WE'RE GONNA DO THIS.
WOW. YOU BUILT ALL THIS?
YEP. ALL STANDARD INTERFACES, THOUGH. YOU SHOULD BE ABLE TO PLUG RIGHT IN.
NICE.
DAMMIT.
WHAT?
GOVERNMENT DRONES. THOUGHT I LOST 'EM OVER COLORADO.
AH. WONDER WOMAN MENTIONED YOU HAD A LITTLE TANGLE WHEN SHE TOLD ME YOU WERE COMING...
...YOU WERE HELPING SUPERMAN, RIGHT?
YEAH. RIGHT AFTER THE GOVERNMENT FOUND OUT ABOUT HIS DOOMSDAY INFECTION AND CALLED HIM AN ENEMY OF THE STATE.
NOW THAT HE'S OFF-PLANET, I GUESS THEY'VE GOT TIME TO CHASE ME AROUND AGAIN.
FWOOOOOSH
HOOOO! THAT'S SOME KICK!
YEAH...
...BUT THEY'RE COMING IN TOO FAST.
WHAT'S WITH ALL THE FRETTING?
THEY'RE JUST DRONES...
...AND IT LOOKS LIKE YOU BUILT IN SOME PRETTY SWEET GUN TURRETS...
YEAH.
BUT I JUST KEEP ASKING MYSELF WHAT SUPERMAN WOULD DO.
JOHN...I DON'T KNOW HOW MUCH YOU'VE BEEN HANGING WITH THE BIG GUY RECENTLY...
...BUT BELIEVE ME...
...SUPERMAN LOVES SMASHING DRONES.

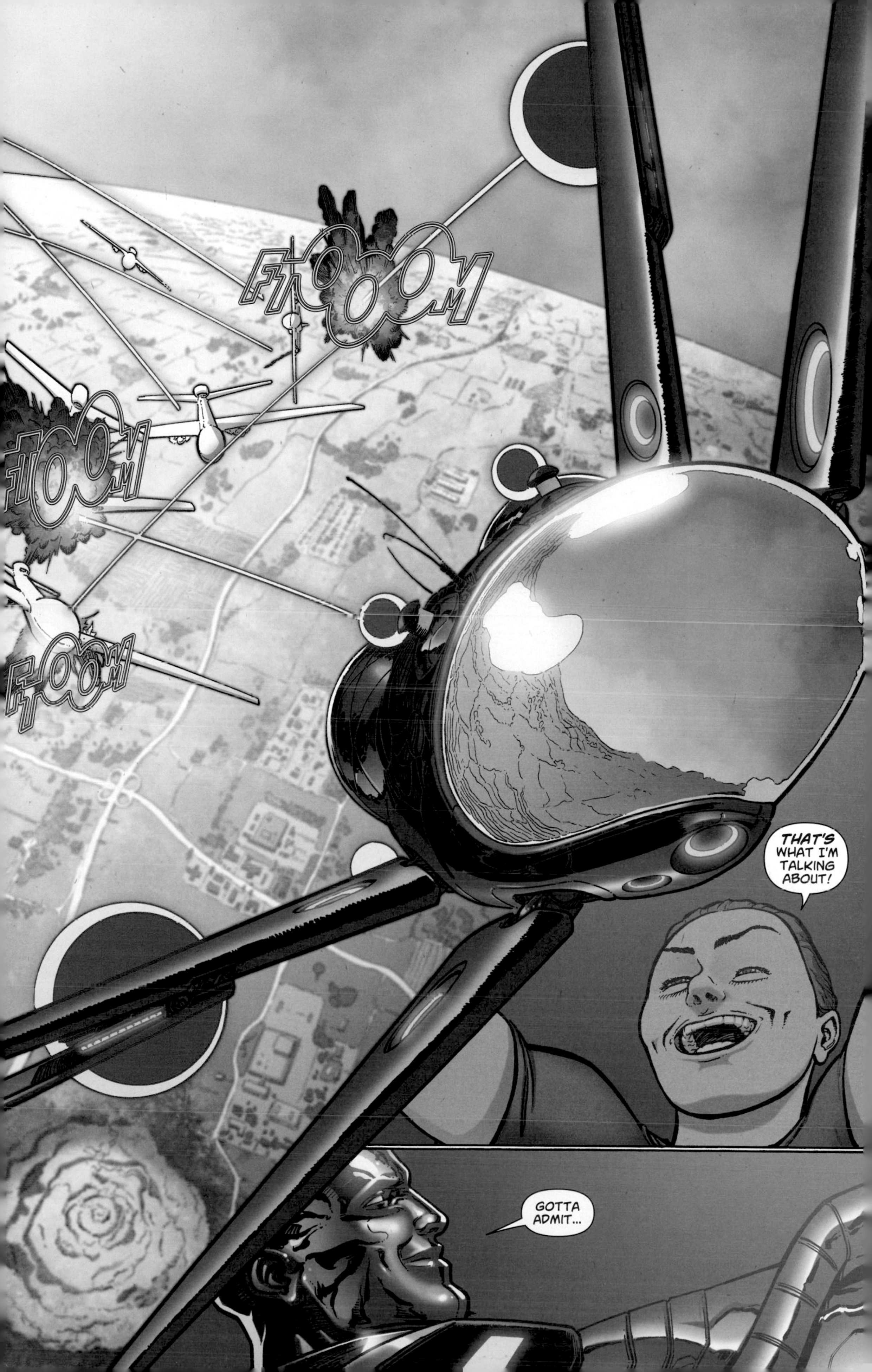
FTOOOOM
FTOOOM
FTOOOM
THAT'S WHAT I'M TALKING ABOUT!
GOTTA ADMIT...

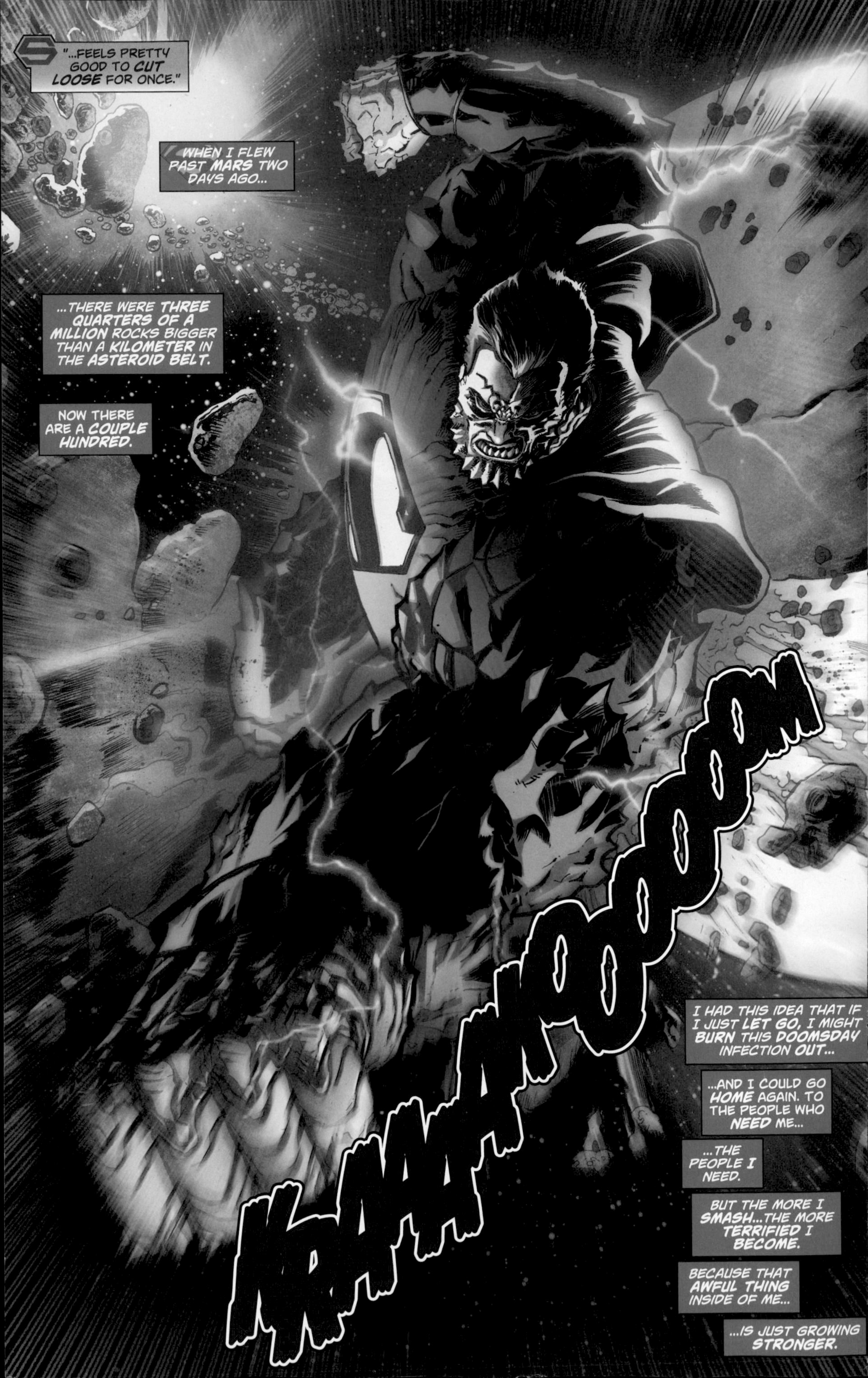
"...FEELS PRETTY GOOD TO CUT LOOSE FOR ONCE."
WHEN I FLEW PAST MARS TWO DAYS AGO...
...THERE WERE THREE QUARTERS OF A MILLION ROCKS BIGGER THAN A KILOMETER IN THE ASTEROID BELT.
NOW THERE ARE A COUPLE HUNDRED.
KRAAAKOOOOOOM
I HAD THIS IDEA THAT IF I JUST LET GO, I MIGHT BURN THIS DOOMSDAY INFECTION OUT...
...AND I COULD GO HOME AGAIN. TO THE PEOPLE WHO NEED ME...
...THE PEOPLE I NEED.
BUT THE MORE I SMASH...THE MORE TERRIFIED I BECOME.
BECAUSE THAT AWFUL THING INSIDE OF ME...
...IS JUST GROWING STRONGER.

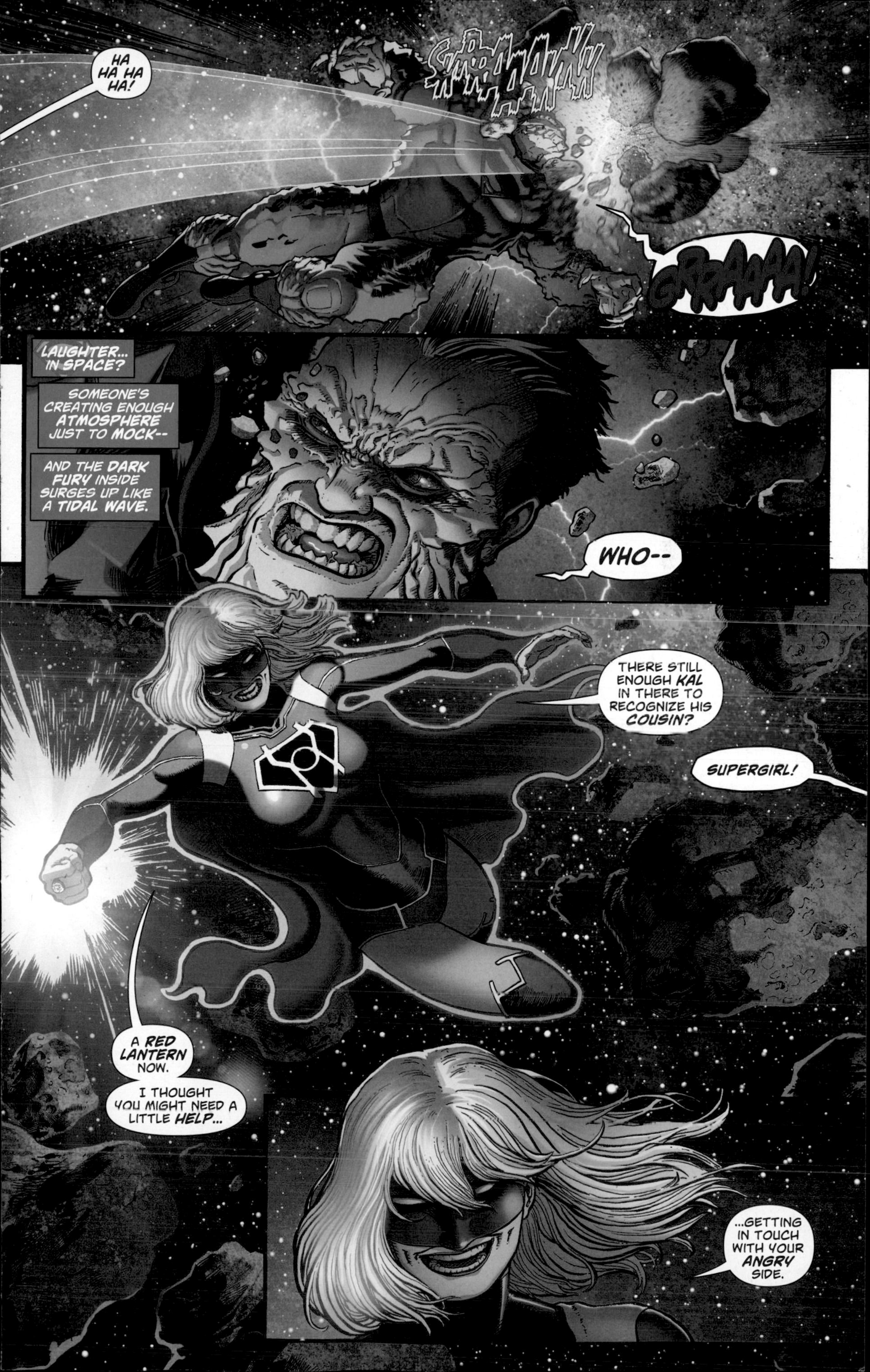
HA HA HA HA!
SHRAAAKK
GRRAAAA!
LAUGHTER... IN SPACE?
SOMEONE'S CREATING ENOUGH ATMOSPHERE JUST TO MOCK--
AND THE DARK FURY INSIDE SURGES UP LIKE A TIDAL WAVE.
WHO--
THERE STILL ENOUGH KAL IN THERE TO RECOGNIZE HIS COUSIN?
SUPERGIRL!
A RED LANTERN NOW.
I THOUGHT YOU MIGHT NEED A LITTLE HELP...
...GETTING IN TOUCH WITH YOUR ANGRY SIDE.

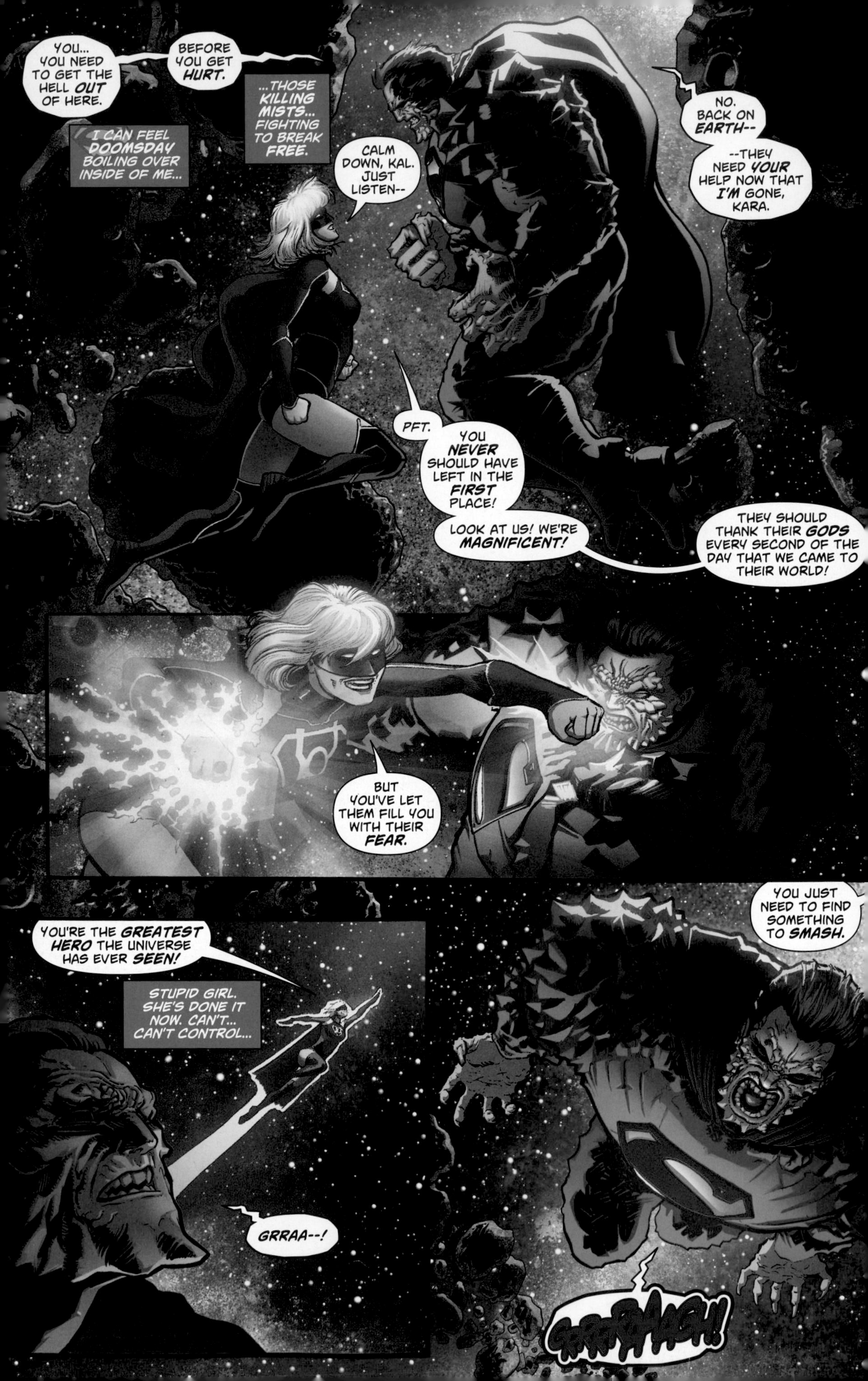
YOU... YOU NEED TO GET THE HELL OUT OF HERE.
BEFORE YOU GET HURT.
I CAN FEEL DOOMSDAY BOILING OVER INSIDE OF ME...
...THOSE KILLING MISTS... FIGHTING TO BREAK FREE.
CALM DOWN, KAL. JUST LISTEN--
NO. BACK ON EARTH--
--THEY NEED YOUR HELP NOW THAT I'M GONE, KARA.
PFT.
YOU NEVER SHOULD HAVE LEFT IN THE FIRST PLACE!
LOOK AT US! WE'RE MAGNIFICENT!
THEY SHOULD THANK THEIR GODS EVERY SECOND OF THE DAY THAT WE CAME TO THEIR WORLD!
BUT YOU'VE LET THEM FILL YOU WITH THEIR FEAR.
YOU'RE THE GREATEST HERO THE UNIVERSE HAS EVER SEEN!
STUPID GIRL. SHE'S DONE IT NOW. CAN'T... CAN'T CONTROL...
YOU JUST NEED TO FIND SOMETHING TO SMASH.
GRRAA--!

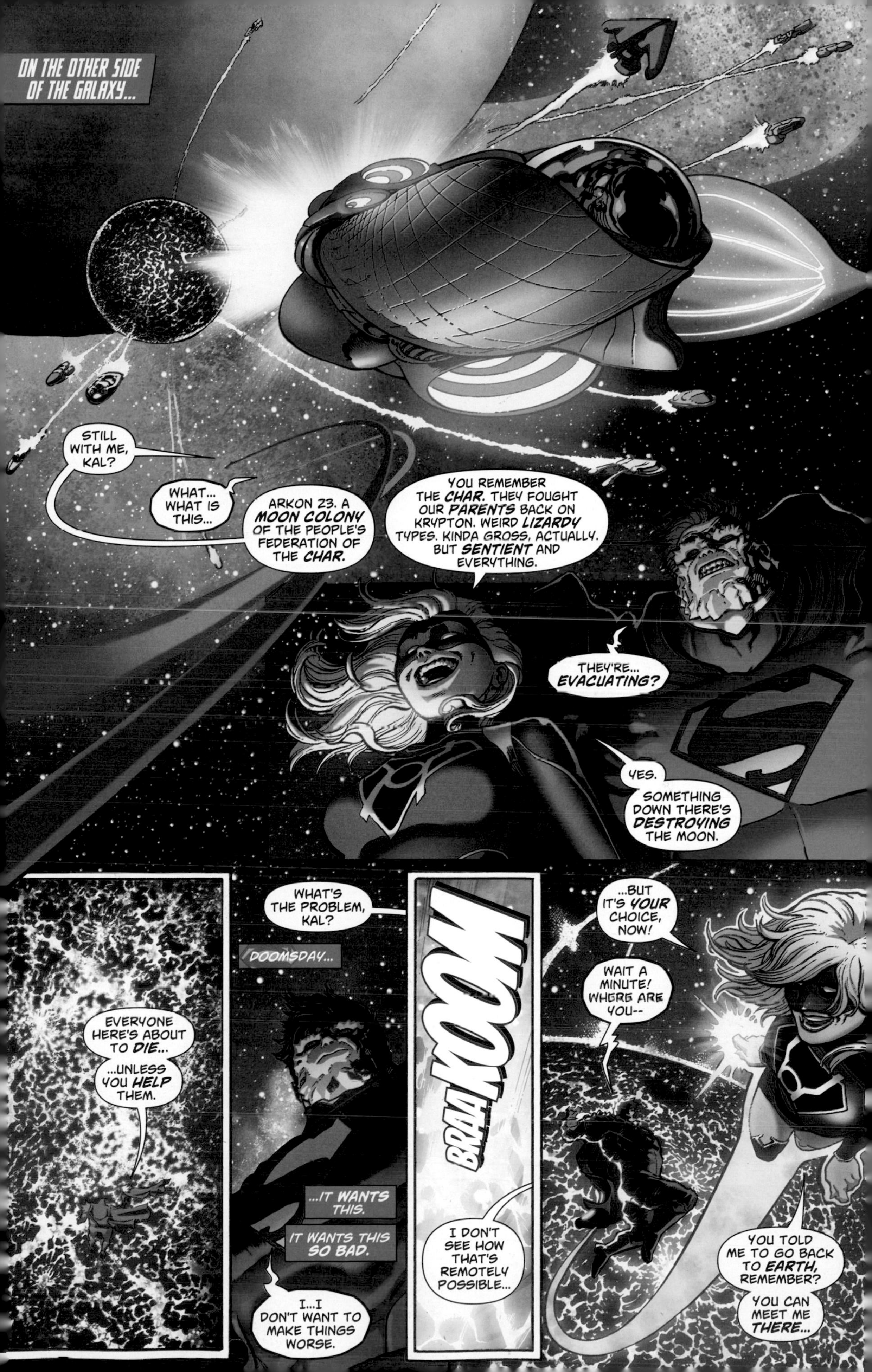
ON THE OTHER SIDE OF THE GALAXY...
STILL WITH ME, KAL?
WHAT... WHAT IS THIS...
ARKON 23. A MOON COLONY OF THE PEOPLE'S FEDERATION OF THE CHAR.
YOU REMEMBER THE CHAR. THEY FOUGHT OUR PARENTS BACK ON KRYPTON. WEIRD LIZARDY TYPES. KINDA GROSS, ACTUALLY. BUT SENTIENT AND EVERYTHING.
THEY'RE... EVACUATING?
YES.
SOMETHING DOWN THERE'S DESTROYING THE MOON.
EVERYONE HERE'S ABOUT TO DIE...
...UNLESS YOU HELP THEM.
WHAT'S THE PROBLEM, KAL?
DOOMSDAY...
...IT WANTS THIS.
IT WANTS THIS SO BAD.
I...I DON'T WANT TO MAKE THINGS WORSE.
BRAAKOOM
I DON'T SEE HOW THAT'S REMOTELY POSSIBLE...
...BUT IT'S YOUR CHOICE, NOW!
WAIT A MINUTE! WHERE ARE YOU--
YOU TOLD ME TO GO BACK TO EARTH, REMEMBER?
YOU CAN MEET ME THERE...

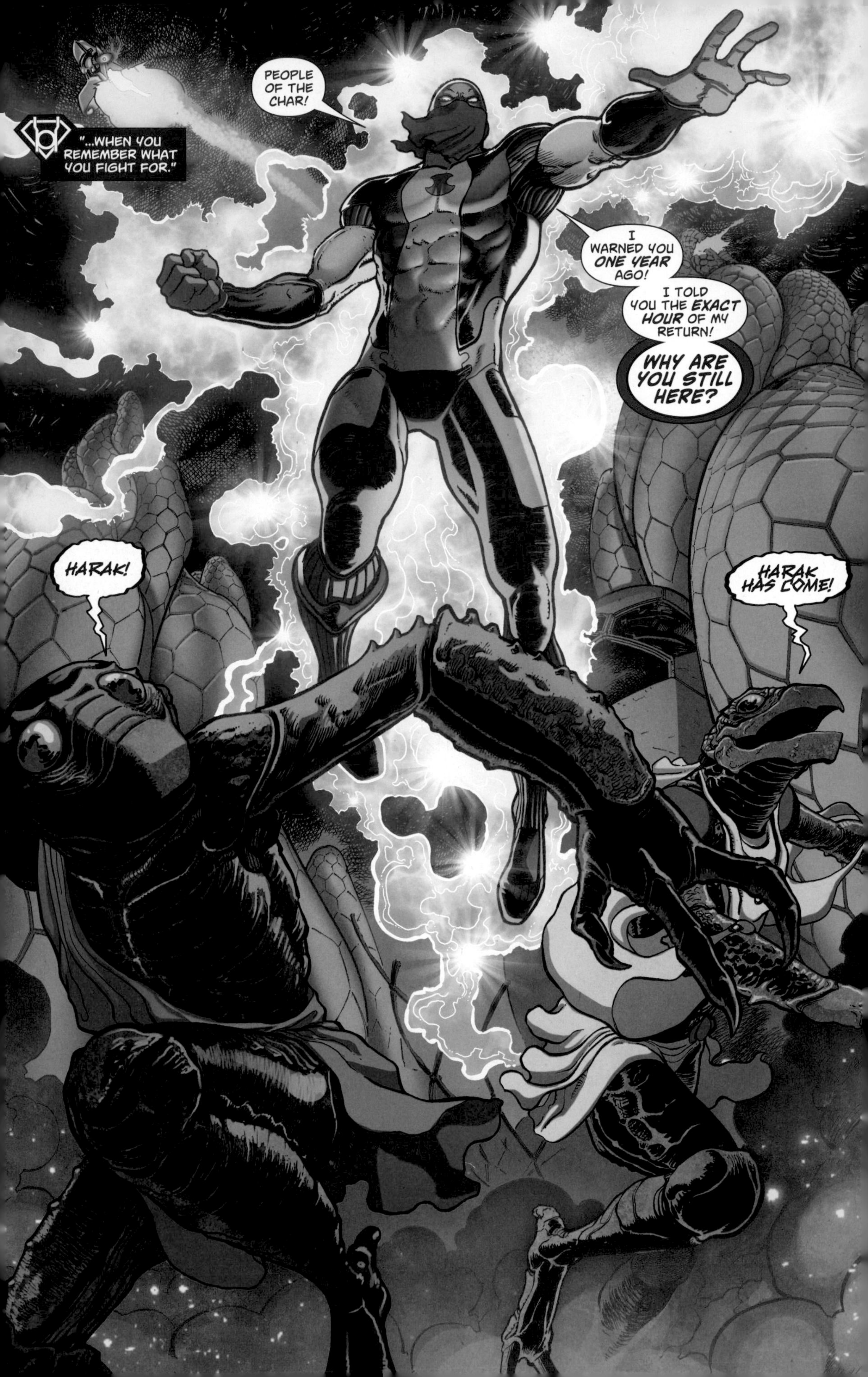
"...WHEN YOU REMEMBER WHAT YOU FIGHT FOR."
PEOPLE OF THE CHAR!
I WARNED YOU ONE YEAR AGO!
I TOLD YOU THE EXACT HOUR OF MY RETURN!
WHY ARE YOU STILL HERE?
HARAK!
HARAK HAS COME!

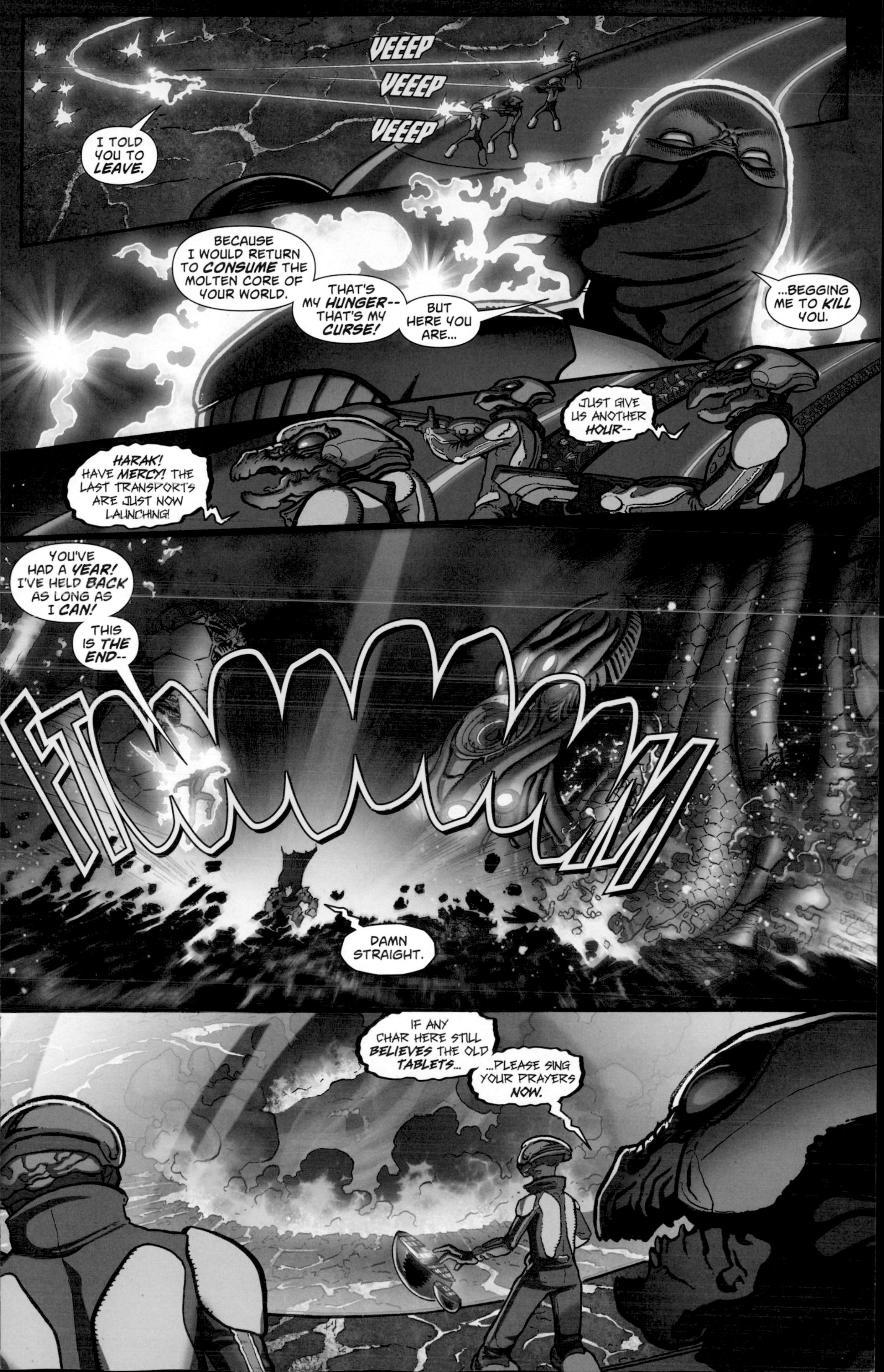
VEEEP
VEEEP
VEEEP
I TOLD YOU TO LEAVE.
BECAUSE I WOULD RETURN TO CONSUME THE MOLTEN CORE OF YOUR WORLD.
THAT'S MY HUNGER-- THAT'S MY CURSE!
BUT HERE YOU ARE...
...BEGGING ME TO KILL YOU.
JUST GIVE US ANOTHER HOUR--
HARAK! HAVE MERCY! THE LAST TRANSPORTS ARE JUST NOW LAUNCHING!
YOU'VE HAD A YEAR! I'VE HELD BACK AS LONG AS I CAN!
THIS IS THE END--
DAMN STRAIGHT.
IF ANY CHAR HERE STILL BELIEVES THE OLD TABLETS...
...PLEASE SING YOUR PRAYERS NOW.

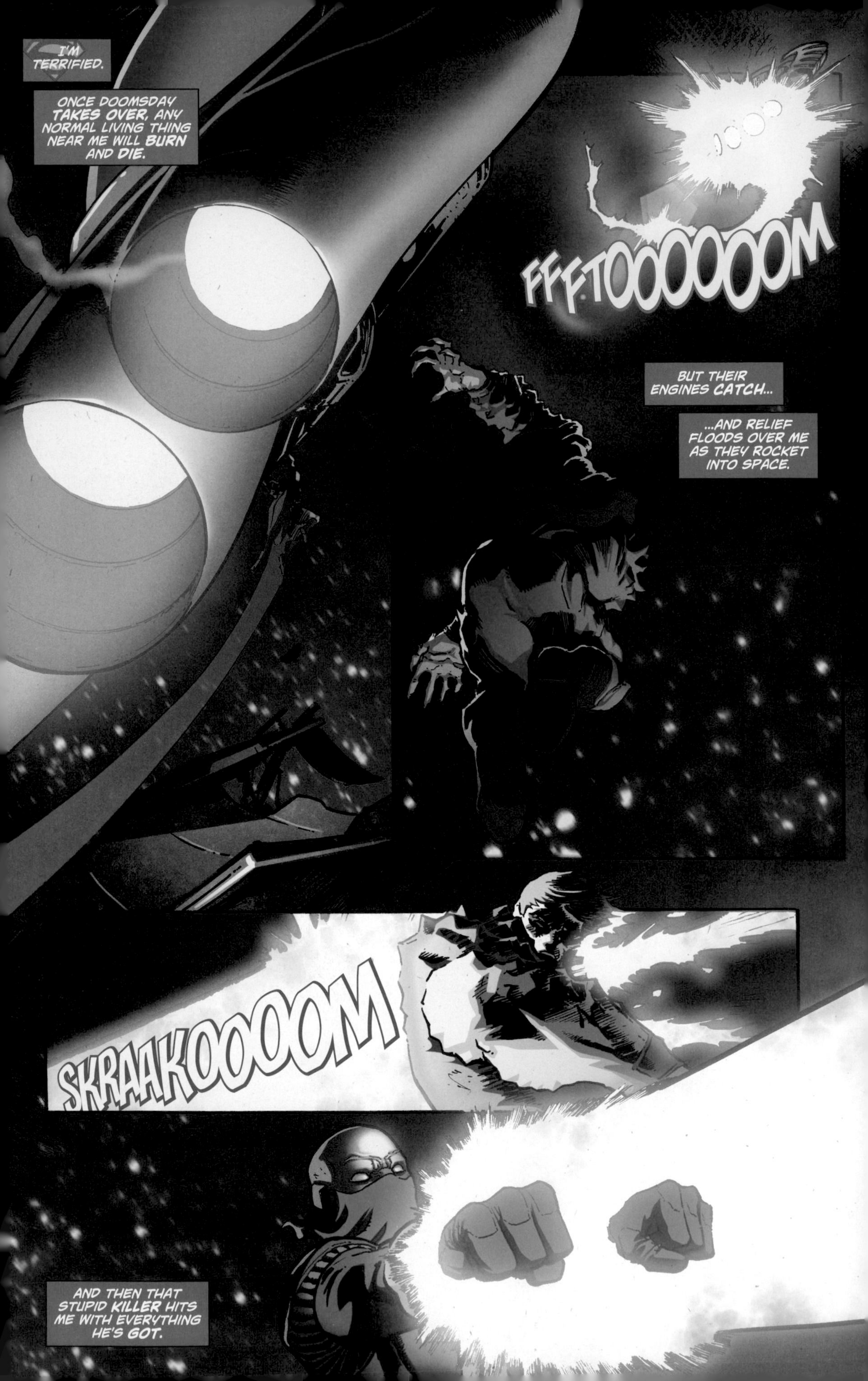
I'M TERRIFIED.
ONCE DOOMSDAY TAKES OVER, ANY NORMAL LIVING THING NEAR ME WILL BURN AND DIE.
FFFTOOOOOOOM
BUT THEIR ENGINES CATCH...
...AND RELIEF FLOODS OVER ME AS THEY ROCKET INTO SPACE.
SKRAAKOOOOM
AND THEN THAT STUPID KILLER HITS ME WITH EVERYTHING HE'S GOT.

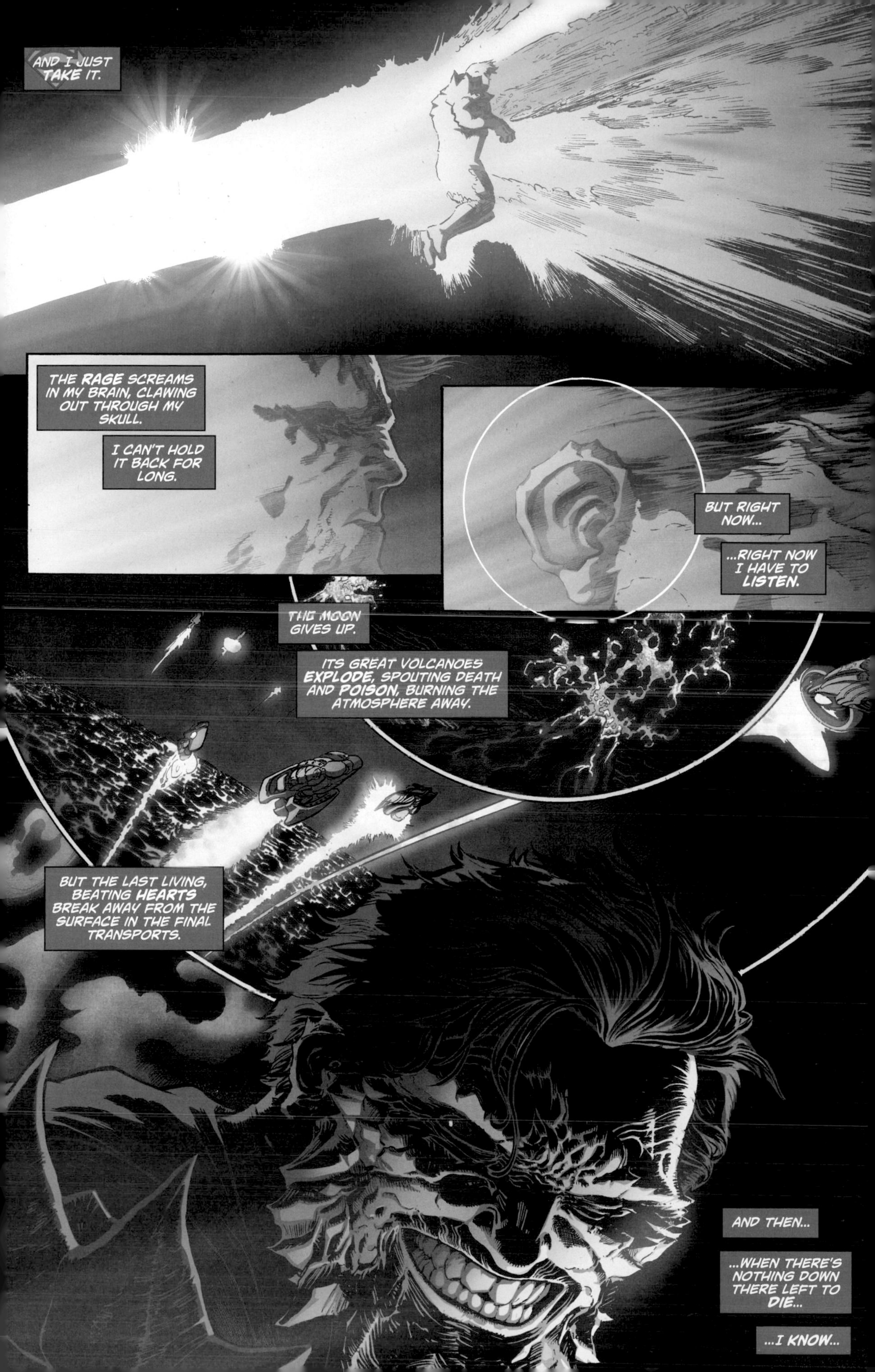
AND I JUST TAKE IT.
THE RAGE SCREAMS IN MY BRAIN, CLAWING OUT THROUGH MY SKULL.
I CAN'T HOLD IT BACK FOR LONG.
BUT RIGHT NOW...
...RIGHT NOW I HAVE TO LISTEN.
THE MOON GIVES UP.
ITS GREAT VOLCANOES EXPLODE, SPOUTING DEATH AND POISON, BURNING THE ATMOSPHERE AWAY.
BUT THE LAST LIVING, BEATING HEARTS BREAK AWAY FROM THE SURFACE IN THE FINAL TRANSPORTS.
AND THEN...
...WHEN THERE'S NOTHING DOWN THERE LEFT TO DIE...
...I KNOW...

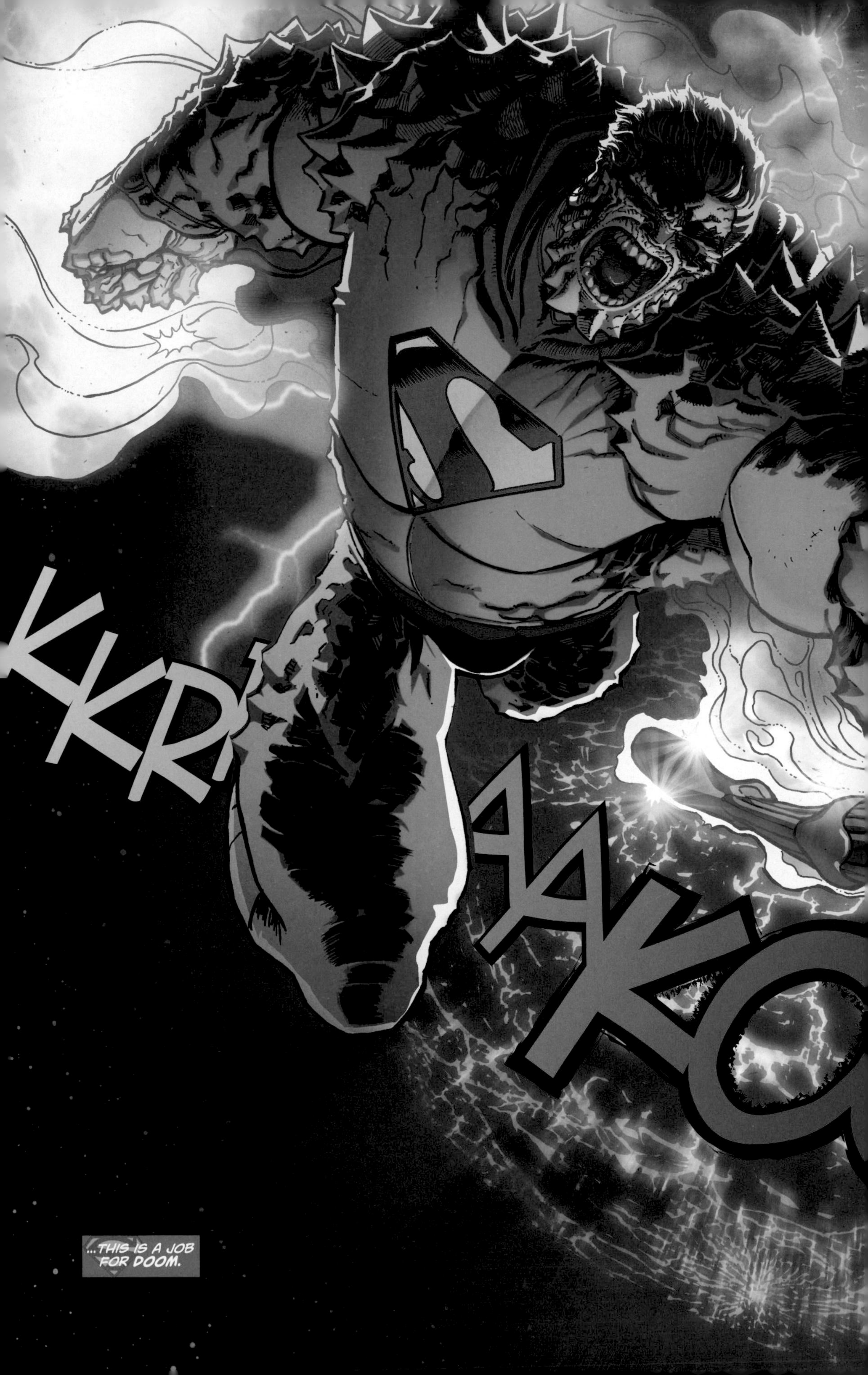

KKRAAKOO
...THIS IS A JOB FOR DOOM.

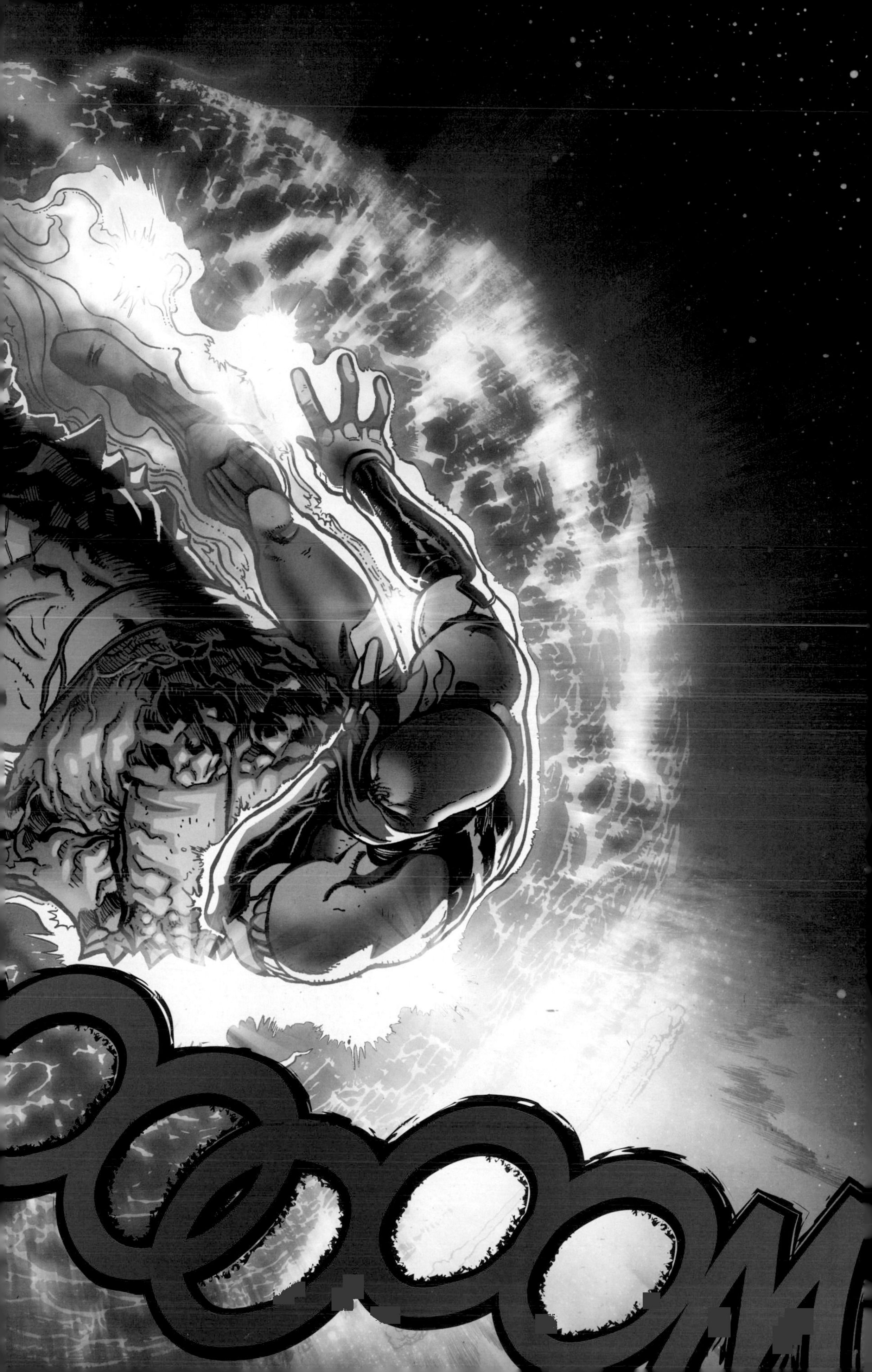
OOOOM

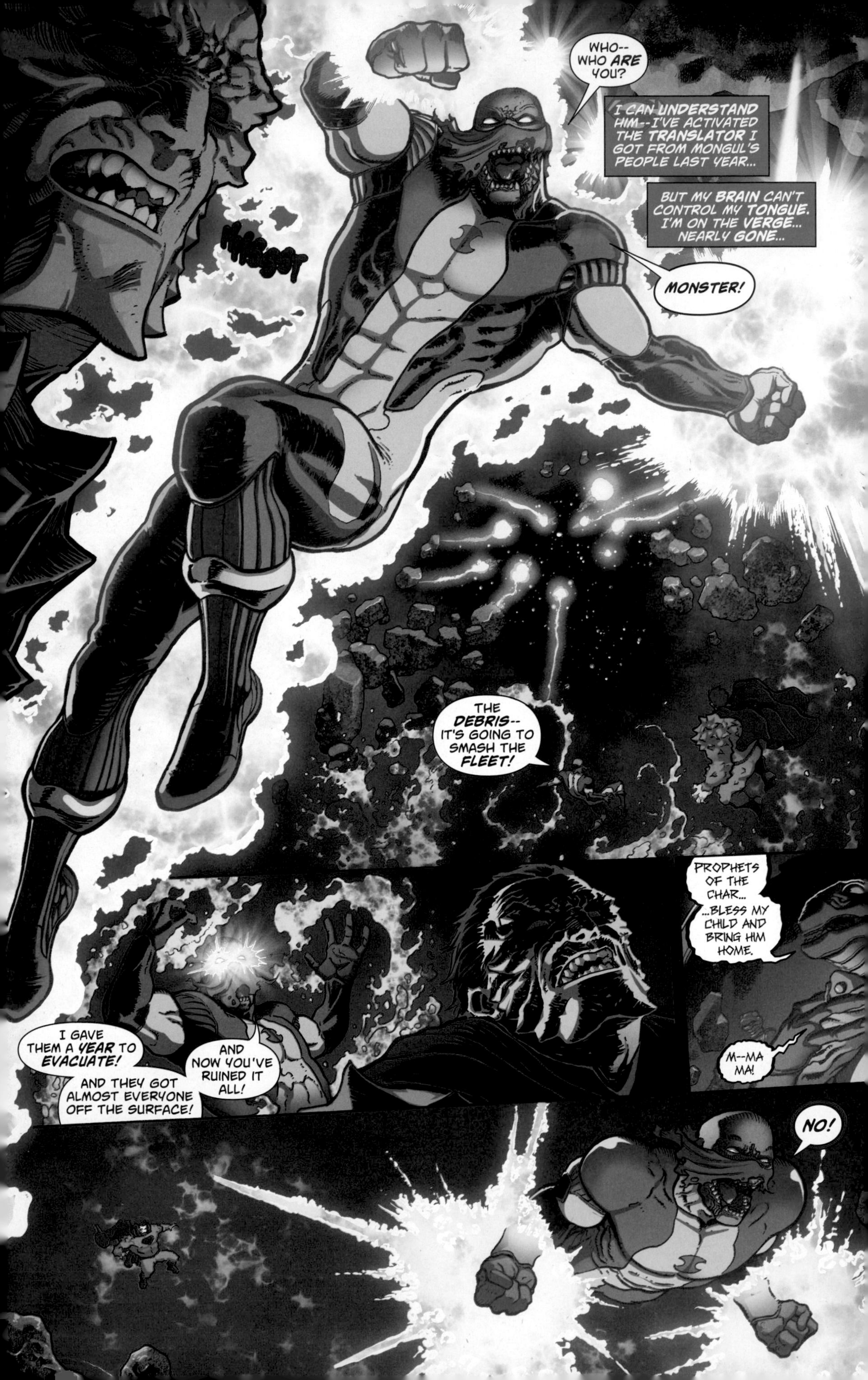
WHO-- WHO ARE YOU?
I CAN UNDERSTAND HIM--I'VE ACTIVATED THE TRANSLATOR I GOT FROM MONGUL'S PEOPLE LAST YEAR...
BUT MY BRAIN CAN'T CONTROL MY TONGUE. I'M ON THE VERGE... NEARLY GONE...
HISSST
MONSTER!
THE DEBRIS-- IT'S GOING TO SMASH THE FLEET!
I GAVE THEM A YEAR TO EVACUATE!
AND THEY GOT ALMOST EVERYONE OFF THE SURFACE!
AND NOW YOU'VE RUINED IT ALL!
PROPHETS OF THE CHAR...
...BLESS MY CHILD AND BRING HIM HOME.
M--MA MA!
NO!

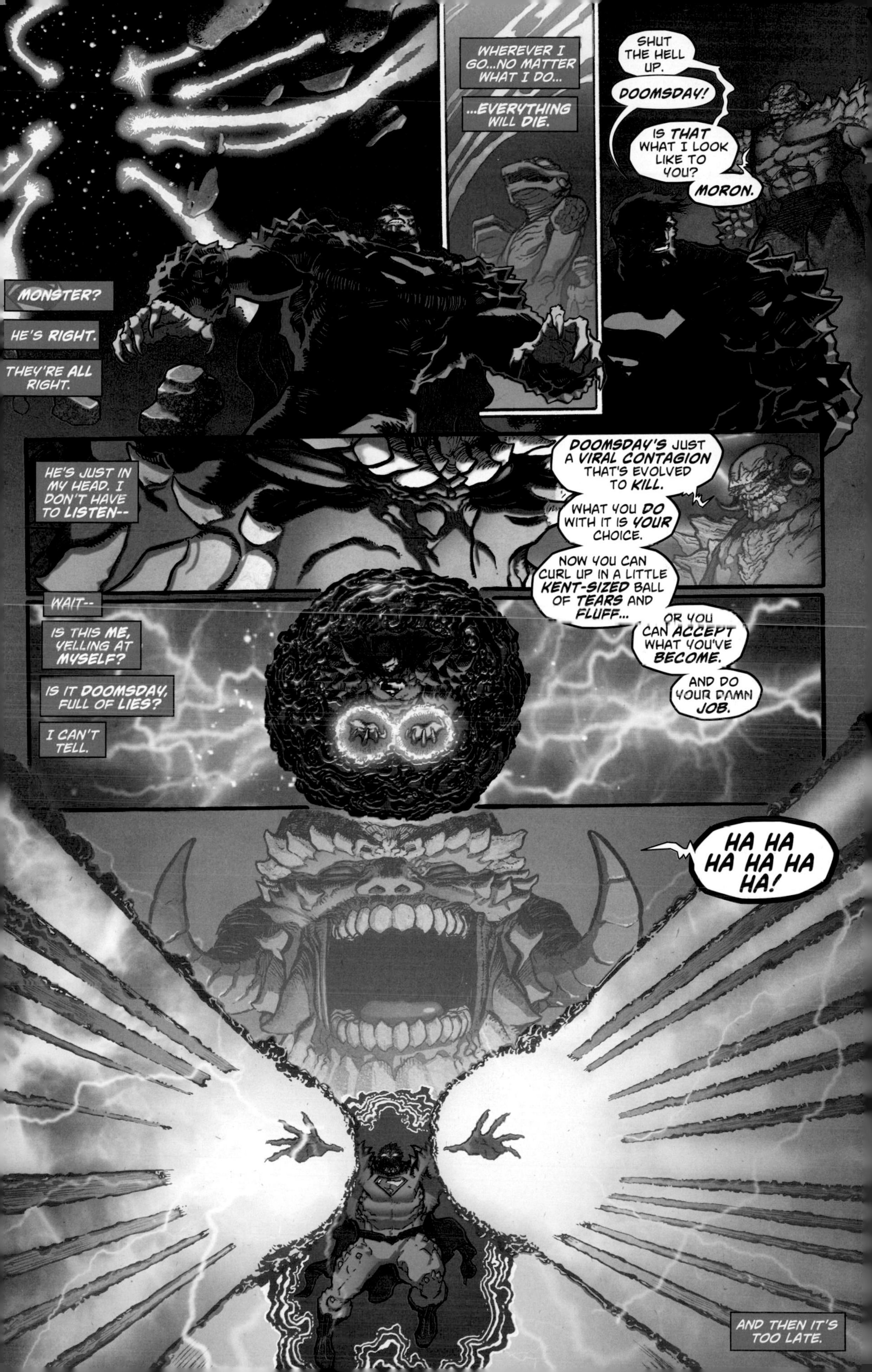
WHEREVER I GO...NO MATTER WHAT I DO...
...EVERYTHING WILL DIE.
SHUT THE HELL UP.
DOOMSDAY!
IS THAT WHAT I LOOK LIKE TO YOU?
MORON.
MONSTER?
HE'S RIGHT.
THEY'RE ALL RIGHT.
HE'S JUST IN MY HEAD. I DON'T HAVE TO LISTEN--
DOOMSDAY'S JUST A VIRAL CONTAGION THAT'S EVOLVED TO KILL.
WHAT YOU DO WITH IT IS YOUR CHOICE.
NOW YOU CAN CURL UP IN A LITTLE KENT-SIZED BALL OF TEARS AND FLUFF...
OR YOU CAN ACCEPT WHAT YOU'VE BECOME.
AND DO YOUR DAMN JOB.
WAIT--
IS THIS ME, YELLING AT MYSELF?
IS IT DOOMSDAY, FULL OF LIES?
I CAN'T TELL.
HA HA HA HA HA HA HA!
AND THEN IT'S TOO LATE.

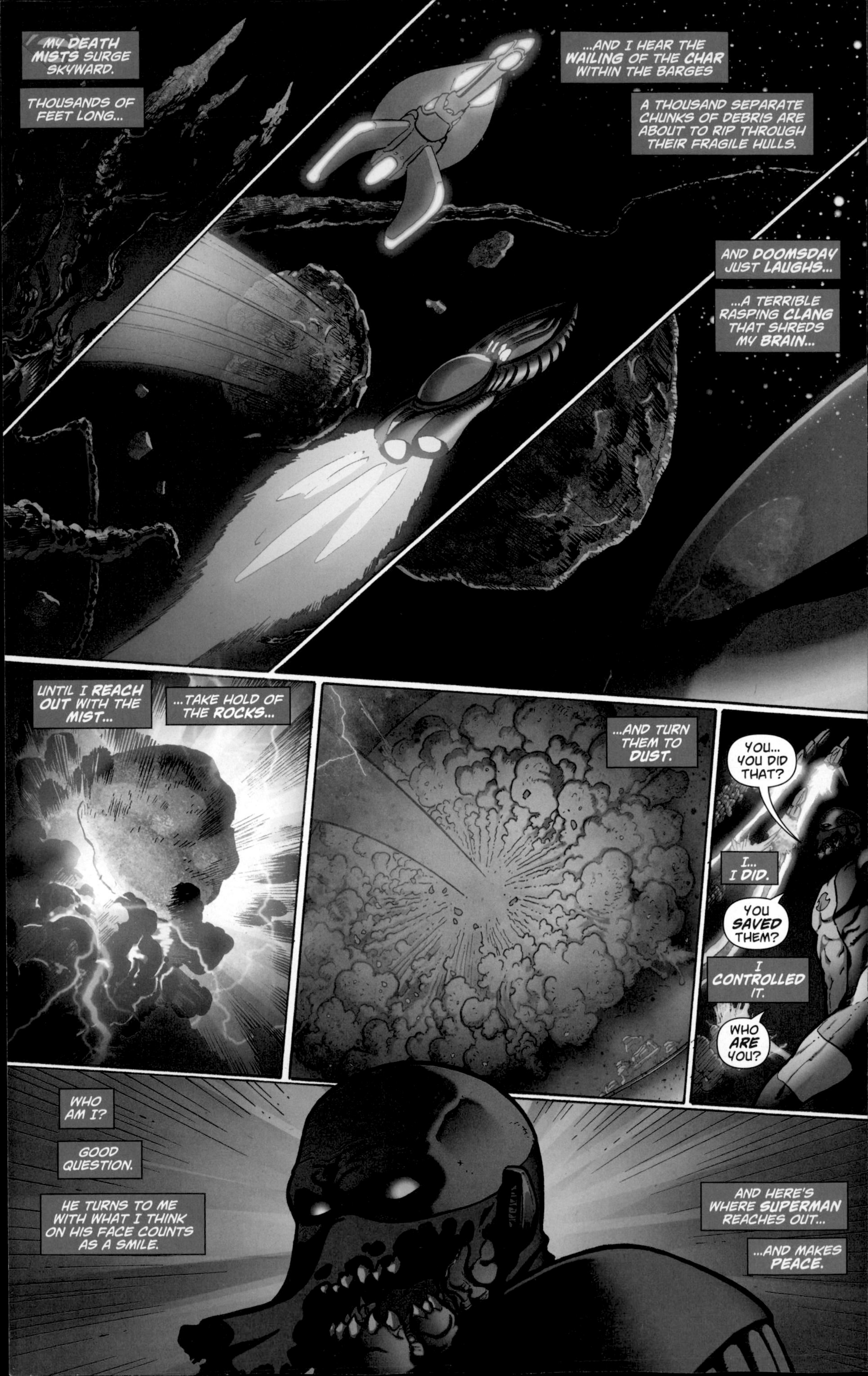
MY DEATH MISTS SURGE SKYWARD.
THOUSANDS OF FEET LONG...
...AND I HEAR THE WAILING OF THE CHAR WITHIN THE BARGES
A THOUSAND SEPARATE CHUNKS OF DEBRIS ARE ABOUT TO RIP THROUGH THEIR FRAGILE HULLS.
AND DOOMSDAY JUST LAUGHS...
...A TERRIBLE RASPING CLANG THAT SHREDS MY BRAIN...
UNTIL I REACH OUT WITH THE MIST...
...TAKE HOLD OF THE ROCKS...
...AND TURN THEM TO DUST.
YOU... YOU DID THAT?
I... I DID.
YOU SAVED THEM?
I CONTROLLED IT.
WHO ARE YOU?
WHO AM I?
GOOD QUESTION.
HE TURNS TO ME WITH WHAT I THINK ON HIS FACE COUNTS AS A SMILE.
AND HERE'S WHERE SUPERMAN REACHES OUT...
...AND MAKES PEACE.

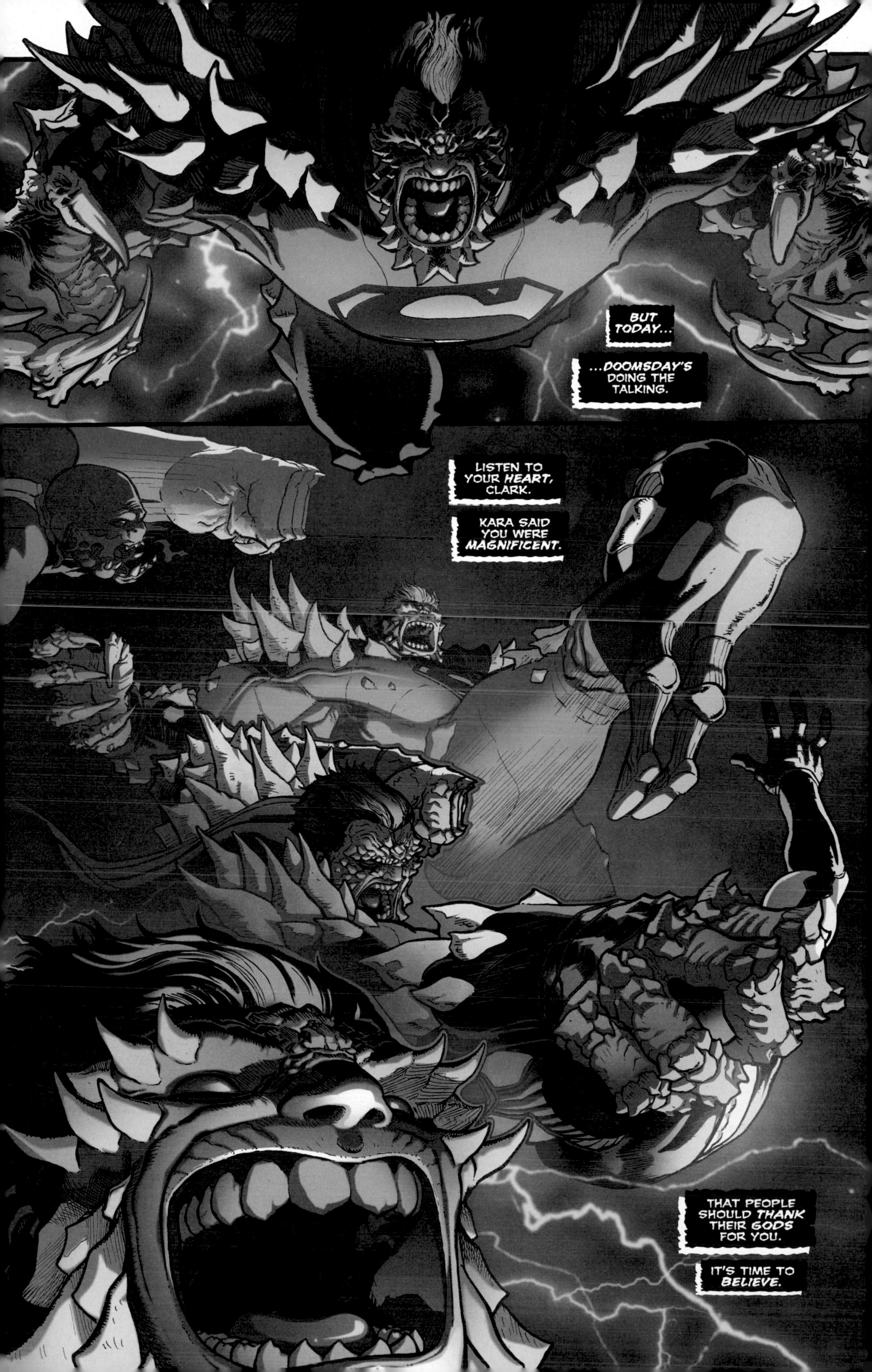
BUT TODAY...
...DOOMSDAY'S DOING THE TALKING.
LISTEN TO YOUR HEART, CLARK.
KARA SAID YOU WERE MAGNIFICENT.
THAT PEOPLE SHOULD THANK THEIR GODS FOR YOU.
IT'S TIME TO BELIEVE.

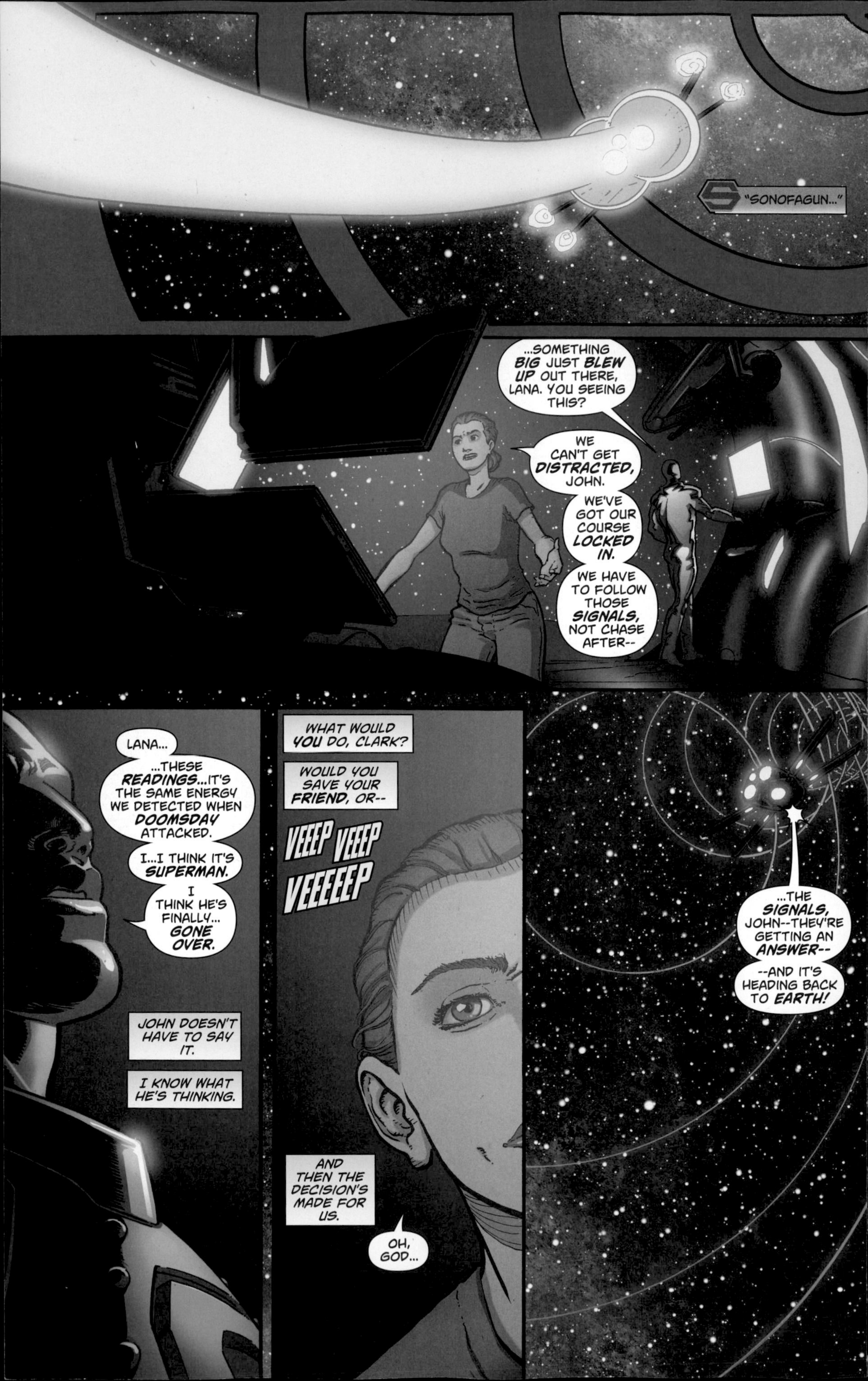
"SONOFAGUN..."
...SOMETHING BIG JUST BLEW UP OUT THERE, LANA. YOU SEEING THIS?
WE CAN'T GET DISTRACTED, JOHN.
WE'VE GOT OUR COURSE LOCKED IN.
WE HAVE TO FOLLOW THOSE SIGNALS, NOT CHASE AFTER--
LANA...
...THESE READINGS...IT'S THE SAME ENERGY WE DETECTED WHEN DOOMSDAY ATTACKED.
I...I THINK IT'S SUPERMAN.
I THINK HE'S FINALLY... GONE OVER.
JOHN DOESN'T HAVE TO SAY IT.
I KNOW WHAT HE'S THINKING.
WHAT WOULD YOU DO, CLARK?
WOULD YOU SAVE YOUR FRIEND, OR--
VEEEP VEEEP
VEEEEEP
AND THEN THE DECISION'S MADE FOR US.
OH, GOD...
...THE SIGNALS, JOHN--THEY'RE GETTING AN ANSWER--
--AND IT'S HEADING BACK TO EARTH!

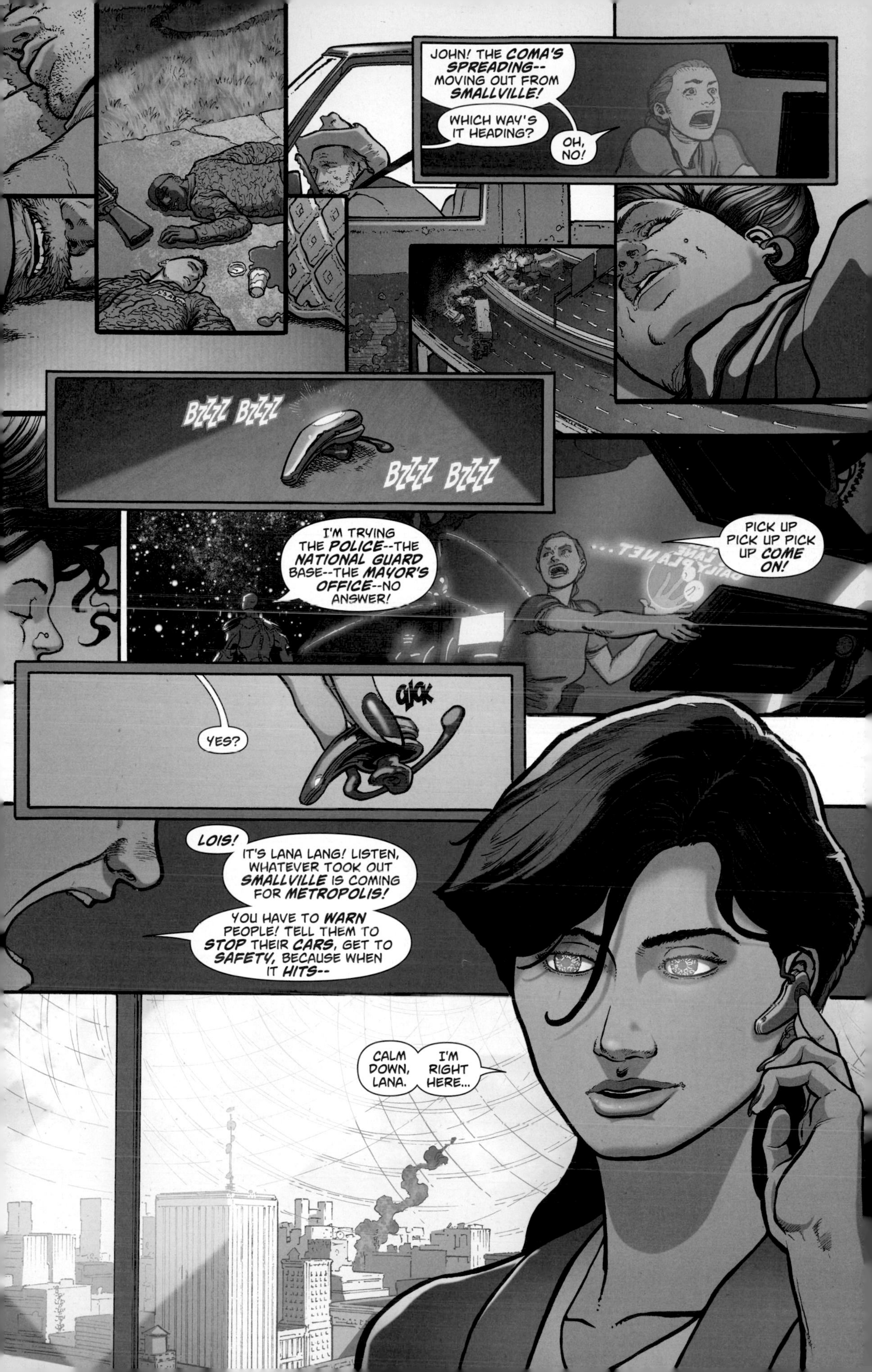
JOHN! THE COMA'S SPREADING-- MOVING OUT FROM SMALLVILLE!
WHICH WAY'S IT HEADING?
OH, NO!
BZZZZ BZZZZ
BZZZZ BZZZZ
I'M TRYING THE POLICE--THE NATIONAL GUARD BASE--THE MAYOR'S OFFICE--NO ANSWER!
PICK UP PICK UP PICK UP COME ON!
CLICK
YES?
LOIS!
IT'S LANA LANG! LISTEN, WHATEVER TOOK OUT SMALLVILLE IS COMING FOR METROPOLIS!
YOU HAVE TO WARN PEOPLE! TELL THEM TO STOP THEIR CARS, GET TO SAFETY, BECAUSE WHEN IT HITS--
CALM DOWN, LANA.
I'M RIGHT HERE...

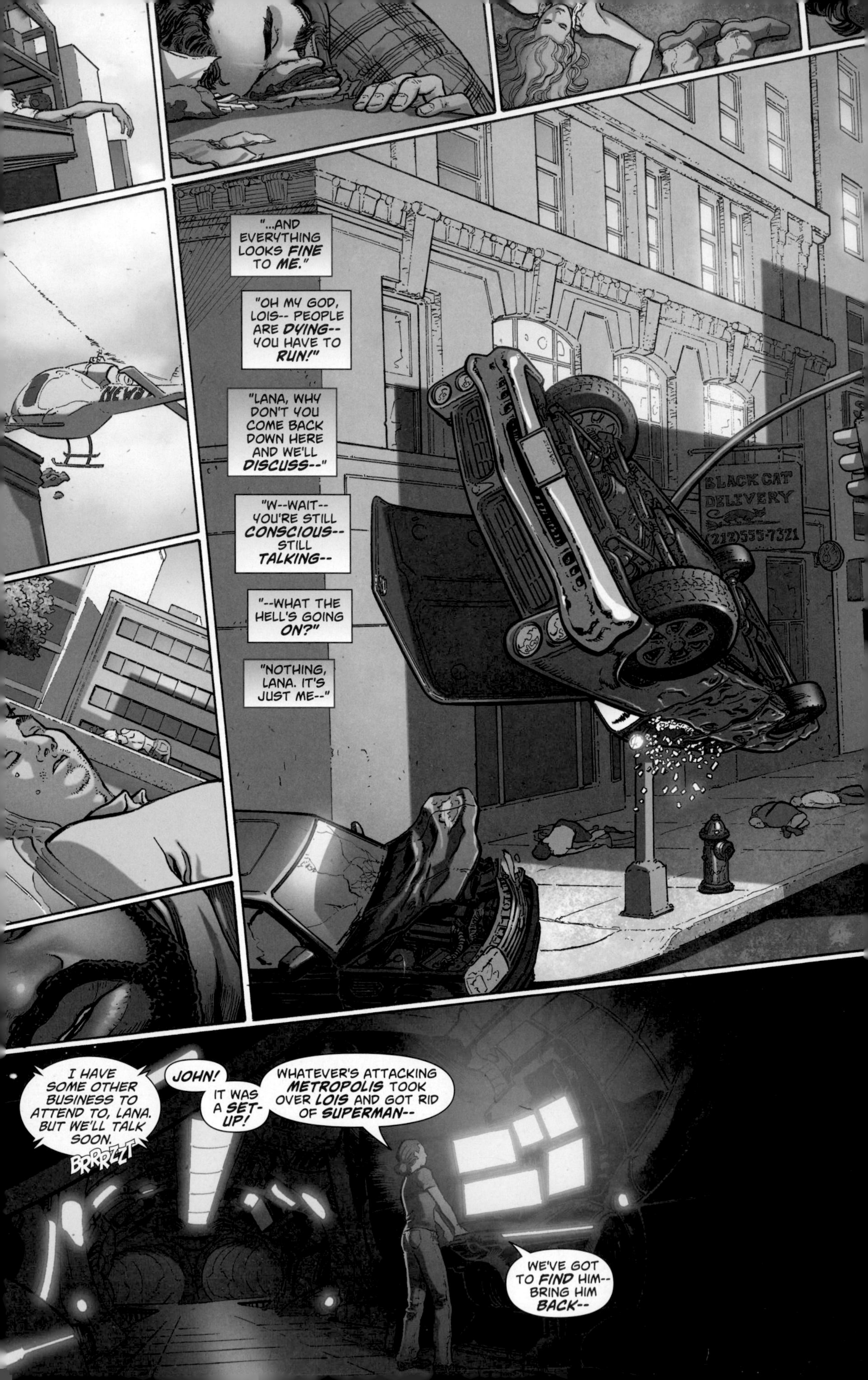
NEWS
"...AND EVERYTHING LOOKS FINE TO ME."
"OH MY GOD, LOIS-- PEOPLE ARE DYING-- YOU HAVE TO RUN!"
"LANA, WHY DON'T YOU COME BACK DOWN HERE AND WE'LL DISCUSS--"
"W--WAIT-- YOU'RE STILL CONSCIOUS-- STILL TALKING--
"--WHAT THE HELL'S GOING ON?"
"NOTHING, LANA. IT'S JUST ME--"
BLACK CAT DELIVERY
(212)555-7321
I HAVE SOME OTHER BUSINESS TO ATTEND TO, LANA. BUT WE'LL TALK SOON.
BRRRZZT
JOHN!
IT WAS A SET-UP!
WHATEVER'S ATTACKING METROPOLIS TOOK OVER LOIS AND GOT RID OF SUPERMAN--
WE'VE GOT TO FIND HIM-- BRING HIM BACK--

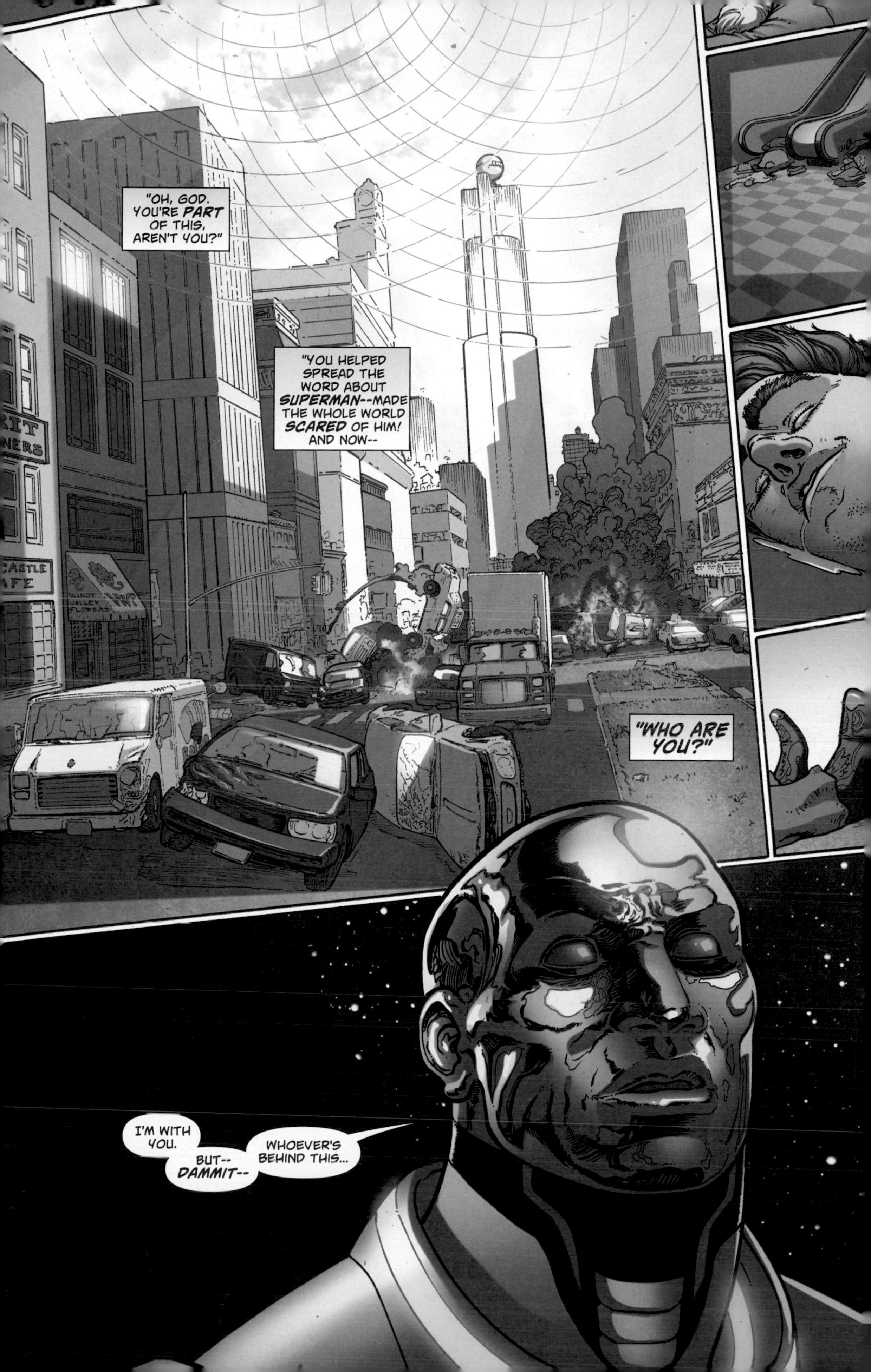
"OH, GOD. YOU'RE PART OF THIS, AREN'T YOU?"
"YOU HELPED SPREAD THE WORD ABOUT SUPERMAN--MADE THE WHOLE WORLD SCARED OF HIM! AND NOW--
"WHO ARE YOU?"
I'M WITH YOU.
BUT-- DAMMIT--
WHOEVER'S BEHIND THIS...

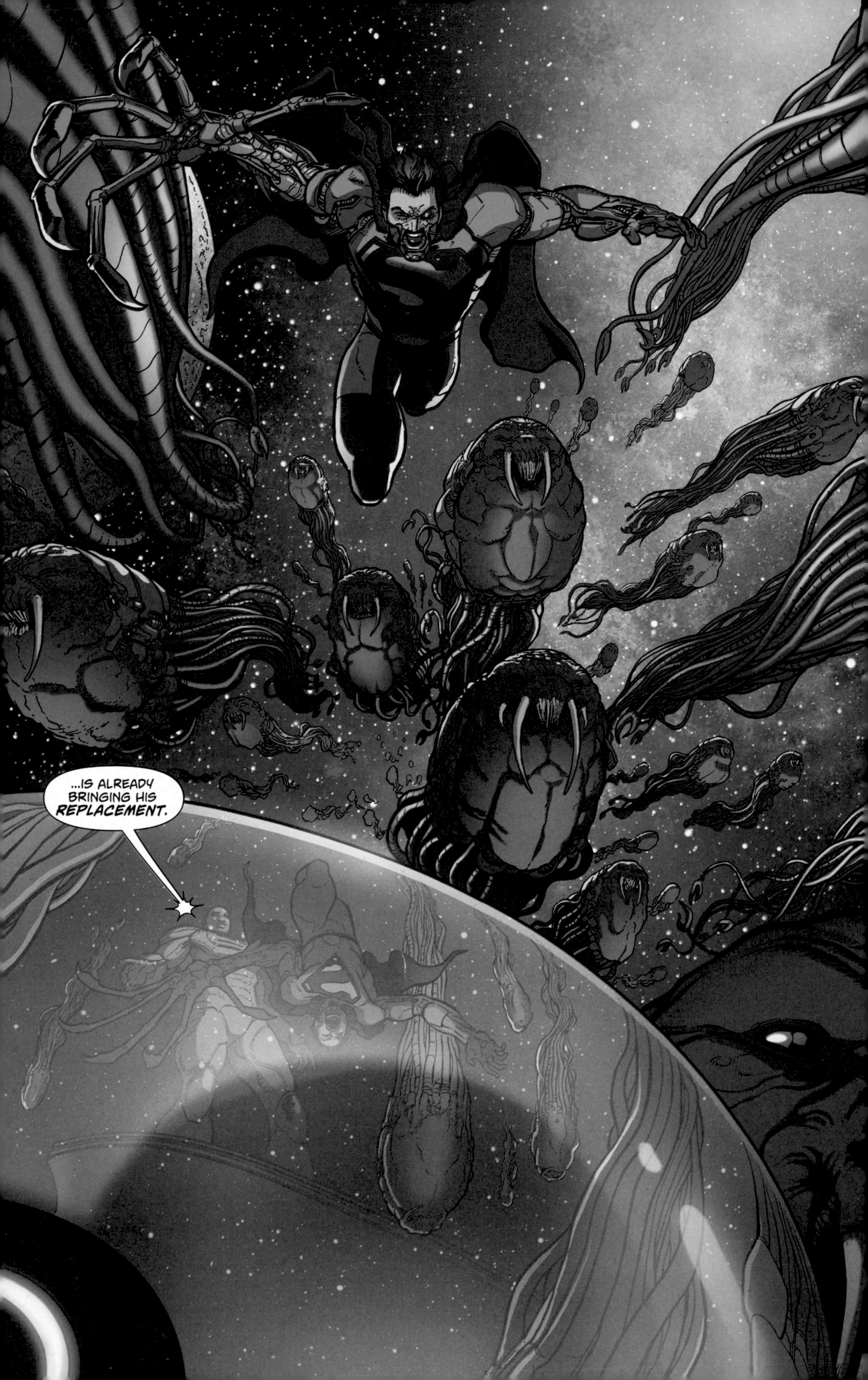
...IS ALREADY BRINGING HIS REPLACEMENT.

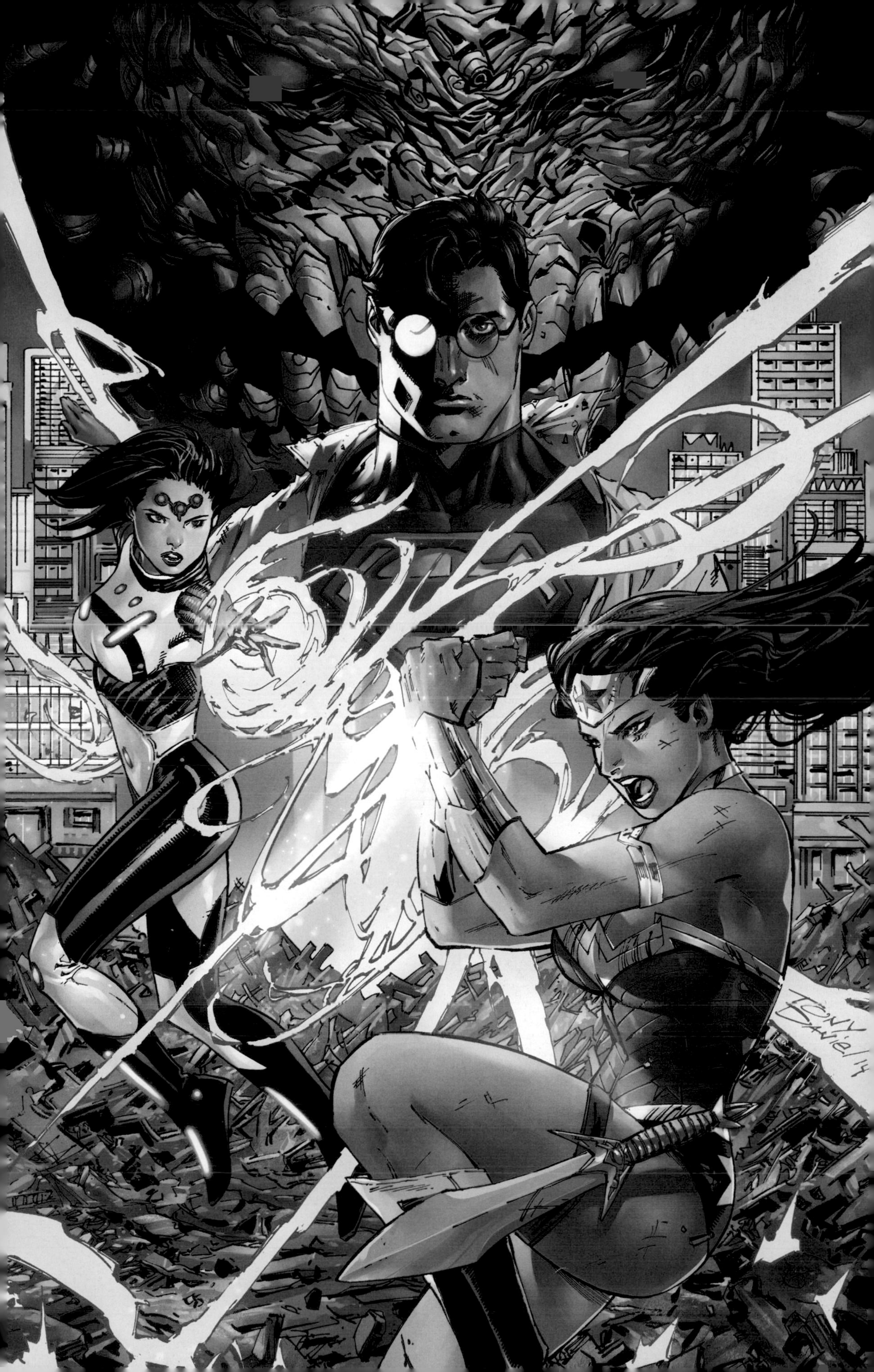

SUPERMAN DOOMED

[SUPERDOOM] chapter 2

"DISTANCE"

STORY
CHARLES SOULE

PENCILS
PAULO SIQUEIRA AND **PASCAL ALIXE**

INKS
PASCAL ALIXE

COLORS
HI-FI

LETTERS
CARLOS M. MANGUAL

COVER
TONY DANIEL AND **TOMEU MOREY**

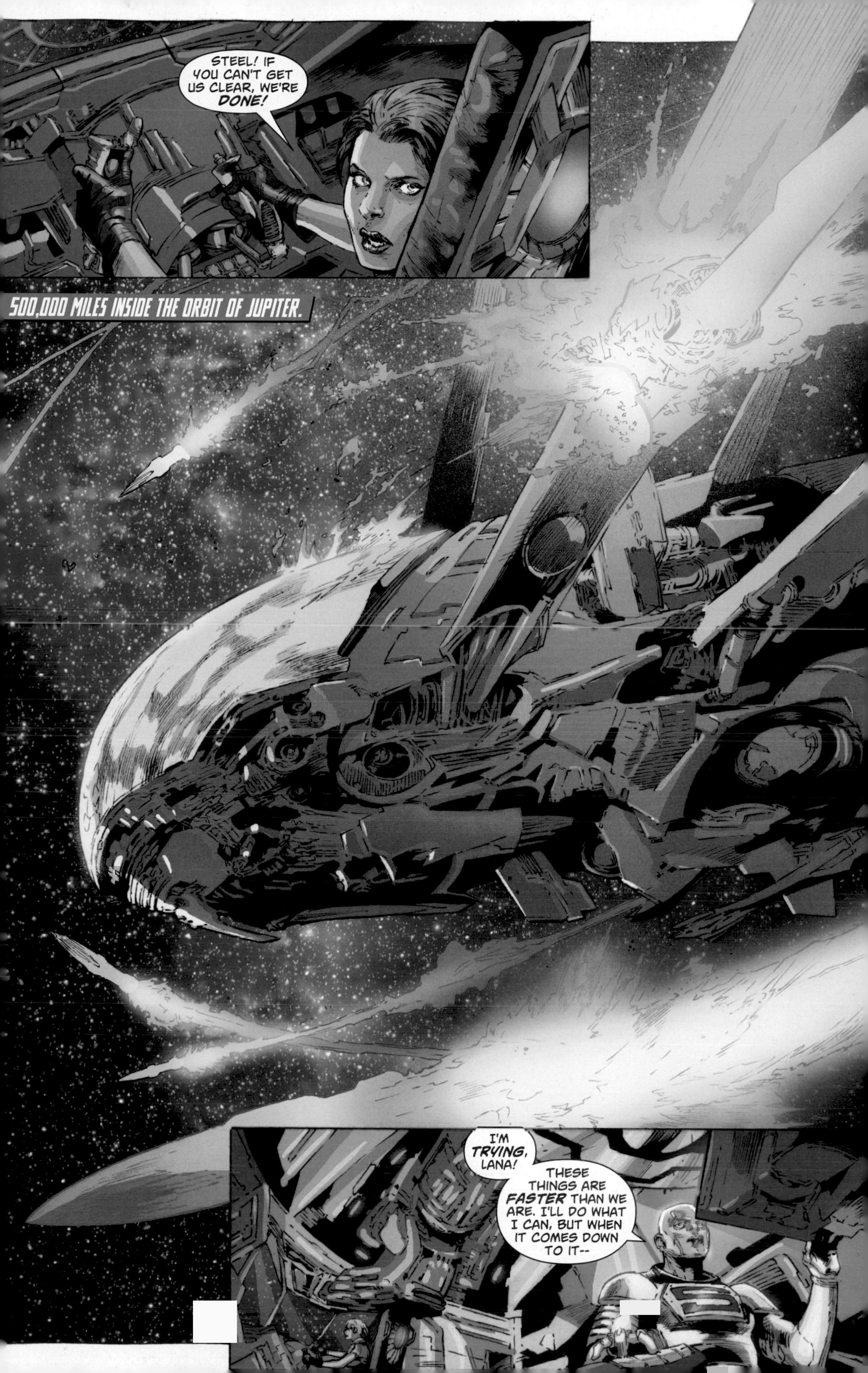
STEEL! IF YOU CAN'T GET US CLEAR, WE'RE DONE!
500,000 MILES INSIDE THE ORBIT OF JUPITER.
I'M TRYING, LANA!
THESE THINGS ARE FASTER THAN WE ARE. I'LL DO WHAT I CAN, BUT WHEN IT COMES DOWN TO IT--

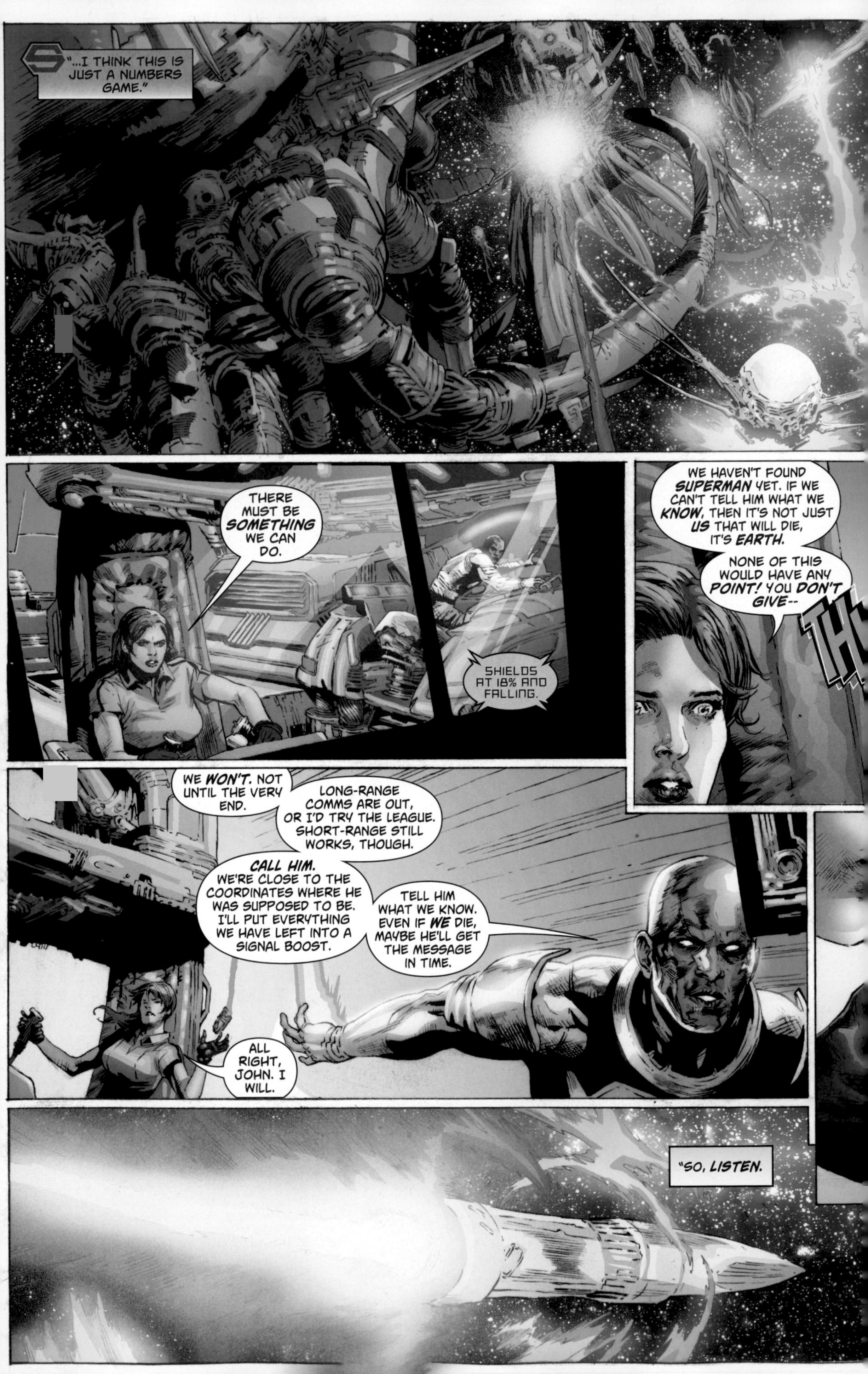
"...I THINK THIS IS JUST A NUMBERS GAME."
THERE MUST BE SOMETHING WE CAN DO.
SHIELDS AT 18% AND FALLING.
WE HAVEN'T FOUND SUPERMAN YET. IF WE CAN'T TELL HIM WHAT WE KNOW, THEN IT'S NOT JUST US THAT WILL DIE, IT'S EARTH.
NONE OF THIS WOULD HAVE ANY POINT! YOU DON'T GIVE--
WE WON'T. NOT UNTIL THE VERY END.
LONG-RANGE COMMS ARE OUT, OR I'D TRY THE LEAGUE. SHORT-RANGE STILL WORKS, THOUGH.
CALL HIM. WE'RE CLOSE TO THE COORDINATES WHERE HE WAS SUPPOSED TO BE. I'LL PUT EVERYTHING WE HAVE LEFT INTO A SIGNAL BOOST.
TELL HIM WHAT WE KNOW. EVEN IF WE DIE, MAYBE HE'LL GET THE MESSAGE IN TIME.
ALL RIGHT, JOHN. I WILL.
"SO, LISTEN.

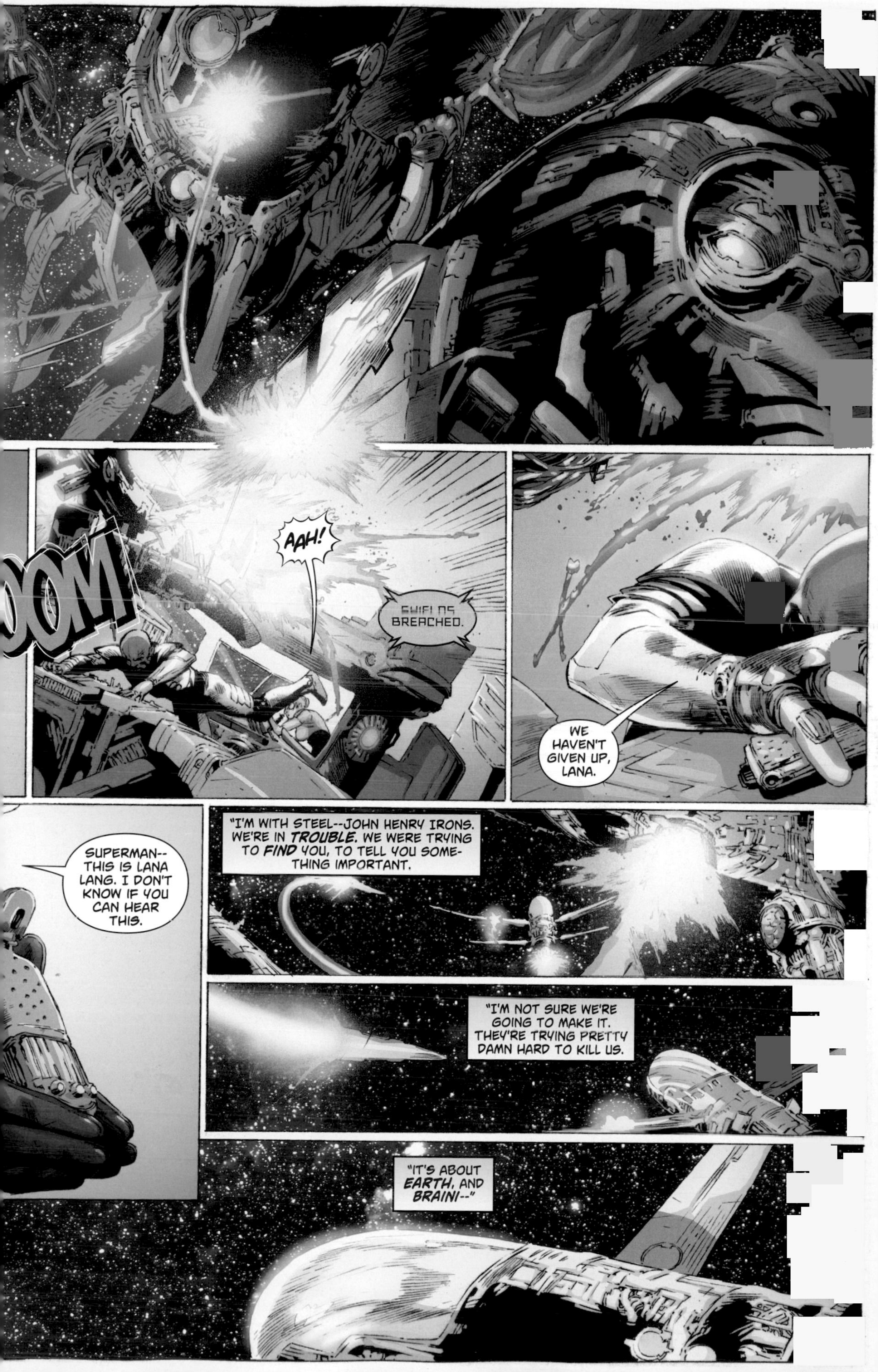
OOM
AAH!
SHIELDS BREACHED.
WE HAVEN'T GIVEN UP, LANA.
SUPERMAN-- THIS IS LANA LANG. I DON'T KNOW IF YOU CAN HEAR THIS.
"I'M WITH STEEL--JOHN HENRY IRONS. WE'RE IN TROUBLE. WE WERE TRYING TO FIND YOU, TO TELL YOU SOMETHING IMPORTANT.
"I'M NOT SURE WE'RE GOING TO MAKE IT. THEY'RE TRYING PRETTY DAMN HARD TO KILL US.
"IT'S ABOUT EARTH, AND BRAINI--"

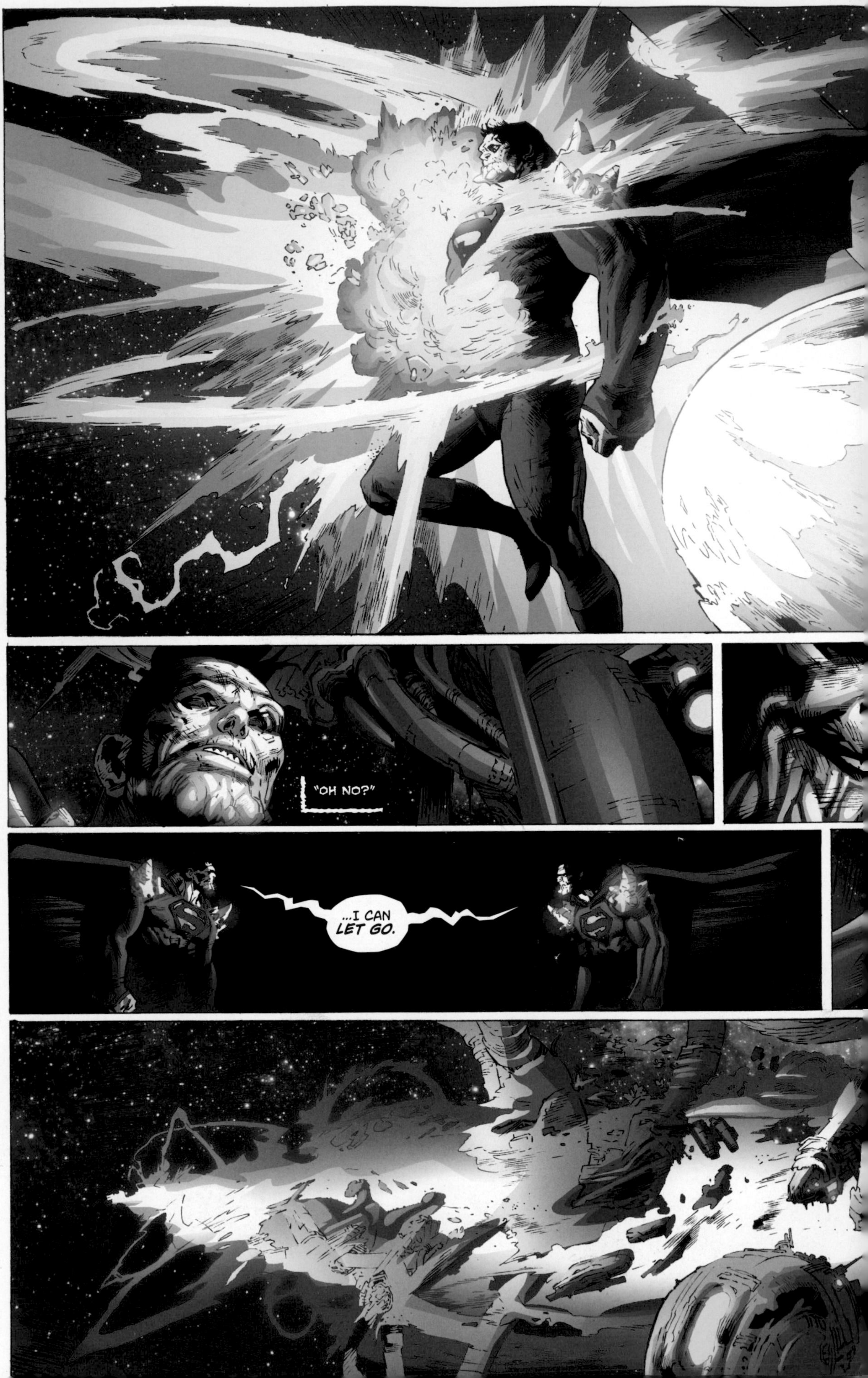
"OH NO?"
...I CAN LET GO.

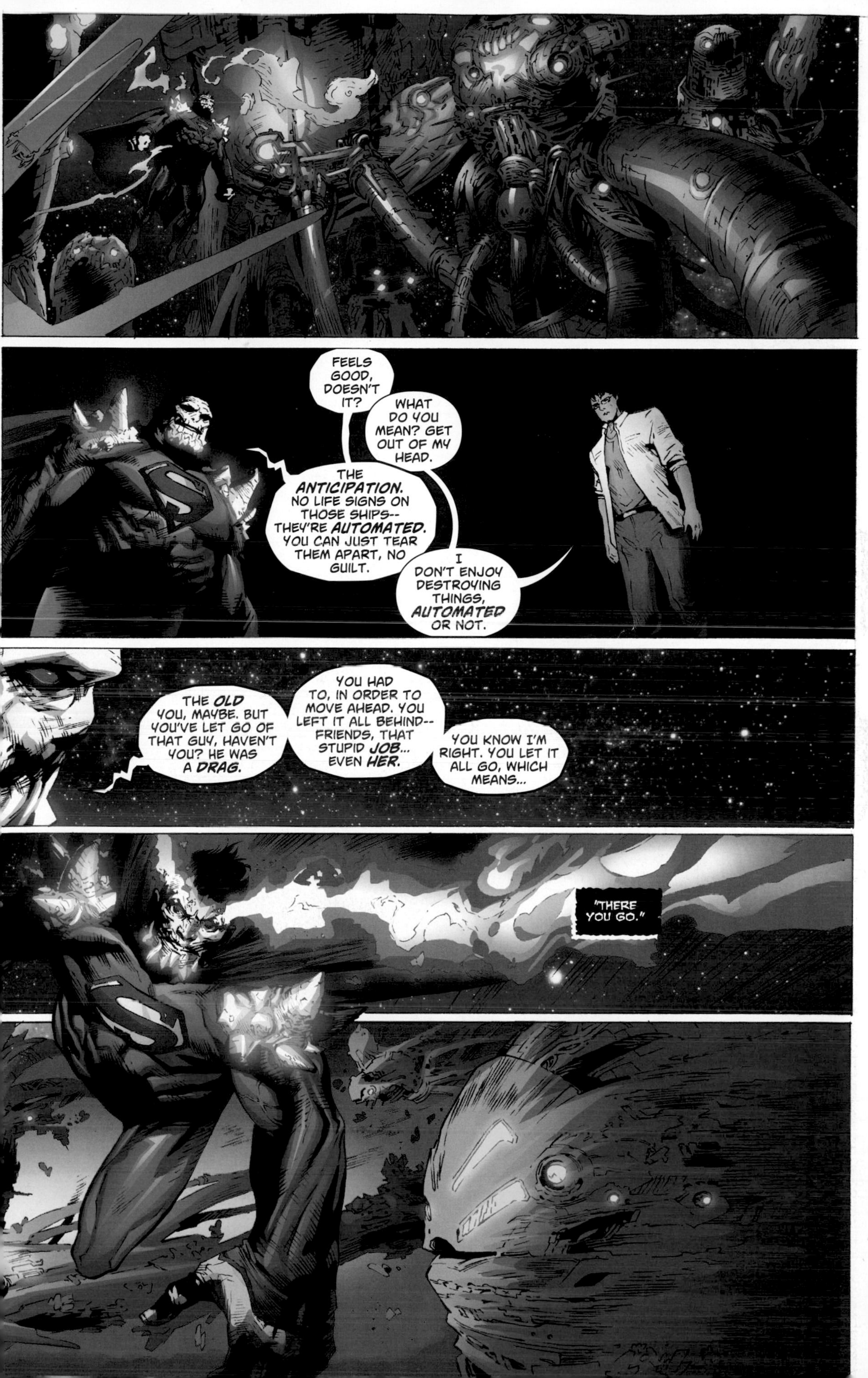
FEELS GOOD, DOESN'T IT?
WHAT DO YOU MEAN? GET OUT OF MY HEAD.
THE ANTICIPATION. NO LIFE SIGNS ON THOSE SHIPS-- THEY'RE AUTOMATED. YOU CAN JUST TEAR THEM APART, NO GUILT.
I DON'T ENJOY DESTROYING THINGS, AUTOMATED OR NOT.
THE OLD YOU, MAYBE. BUT YOU'VE LET GO OF THAT GUY, HAVEN'T YOU? HE WAS A DRAG.
YOU HAD TO, IN ORDER TO MOVE AHEAD. YOU LEFT IT ALL BEHIND-- FRIENDS, THAT STUPID JOB... EVEN HER.
YOU KNOW I'M RIGHT. YOU LET IT ALL GO, WHICH MEANS...
"THERE YOU GO."

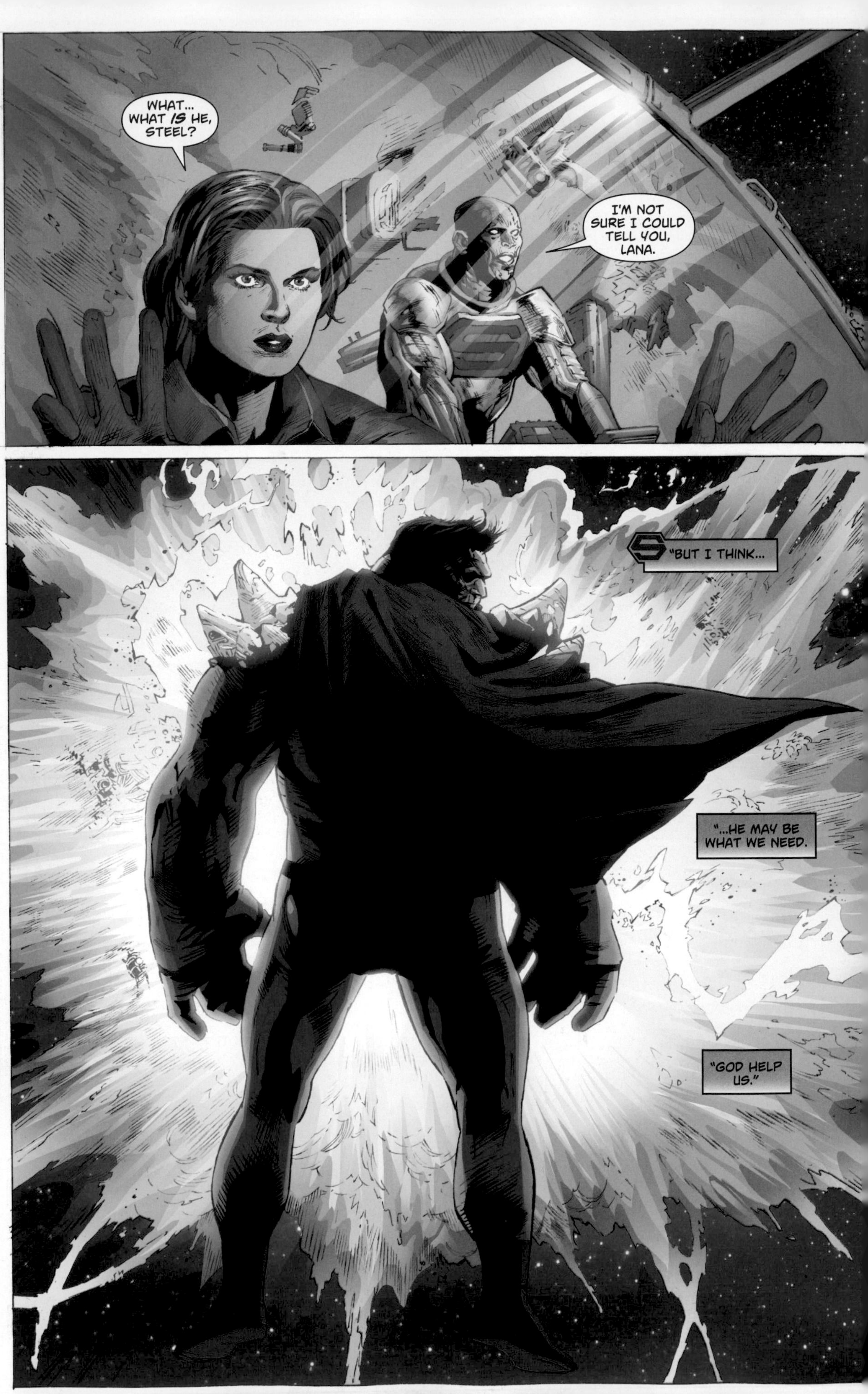
WHAT... WHAT IS HE, STEEL?
I'M NOT SURE I COULD TELL YOU, LANA.
"BUT I THINK...
"...HE MAY BE WHAT WE NEED.
"GOD HELP US."

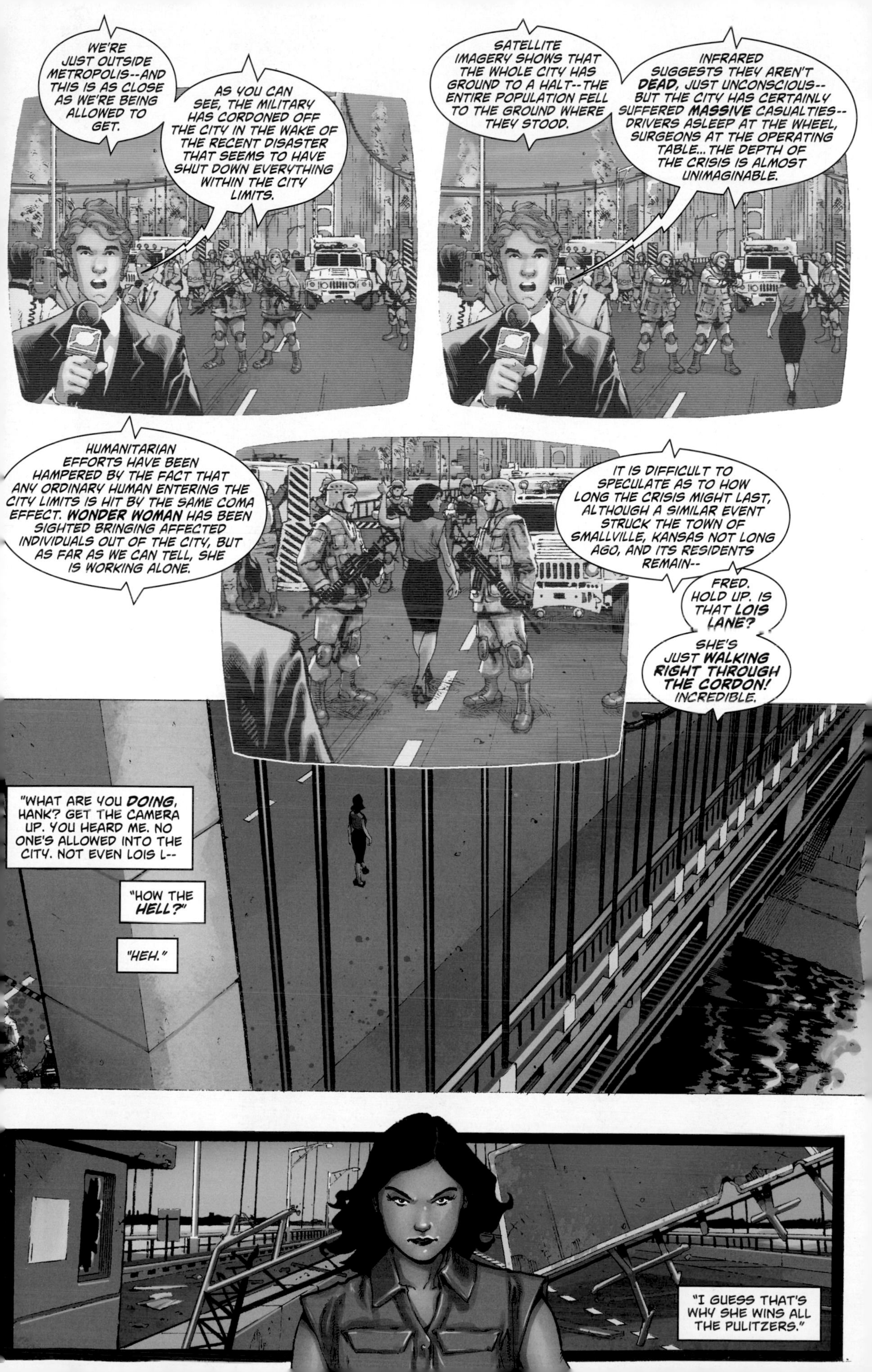
WE'RE JUST OUTSIDE METROPOLIS--AND THIS IS AS CLOSE AS WE'RE BEING ALLOWED TO GET.
AS YOU CAN SEE, THE MILITARY HAS CORDONED OFF THE CITY IN THE WAKE OF THE RECENT DISASTER THAT SEEMS TO HAVE SHUT DOWN EVERYTHING WITHIN THE CITY LIMITS.
SATELLITE IMAGERY SHOWS THAT THE WHOLE CITY HAS GROUND TO A HALT--THE ENTIRE POPULATION FELL TO THE GROUND WHERE THEY STOOD.
INFRARED SUGGESTS THEY AREN'T DEAD, JUST UNCONSCIOUS--BUT THE CITY HAS CERTAINLY SUFFERED MASSIVE CASUALTIES--DRIVERS ASLEEP AT THE WHEEL, SURGEONS AT THE OPERATING TABLE...THE DEPTH OF THE CRISIS IS ALMOST UNIMAGINABLE.
HUMANITARIAN EFFORTS HAVE BEEN HAMPERED BY THE FACT THAT ANY ORDINARY HUMAN ENTERING THE CITY LIMITS IS HIT BY THE SAME COMA EFFECT. WONDER WOMAN HAS BEEN SIGHTED BRINGING AFFECTED INDIVIDUALS OUT OF THE CITY, BUT AS FAR AS WE CAN TELL, SHE IS WORKING ALONE.
IT IS DIFFICULT TO SPECULATE AS TO HOW LONG THE CRISIS MIGHT LAST, ALTHOUGH A SIMILAR EVENT STRUCK THE TOWN OF SMALLVILLE, KANSAS NOT LONG AGO, AND ITS RESIDENTS REMAIN--
FRED. HOLD UP. IS THAT LOIS LANE?
SHE'S JUST WALKING RIGHT THROUGH THE CORDON! INCREDIBLE.
"WHAT ARE YOU DOING, HANK? GET THE CAMERA UP. YOU HEARD ME. NO ONE'S ALLOWED INTO THE CITY. NOT EVEN LOIS L--
"HOW THE HELL?"
"HEH."
"I GUESS THAT'S WHY SHE WINS ALL THE PULITZERS."

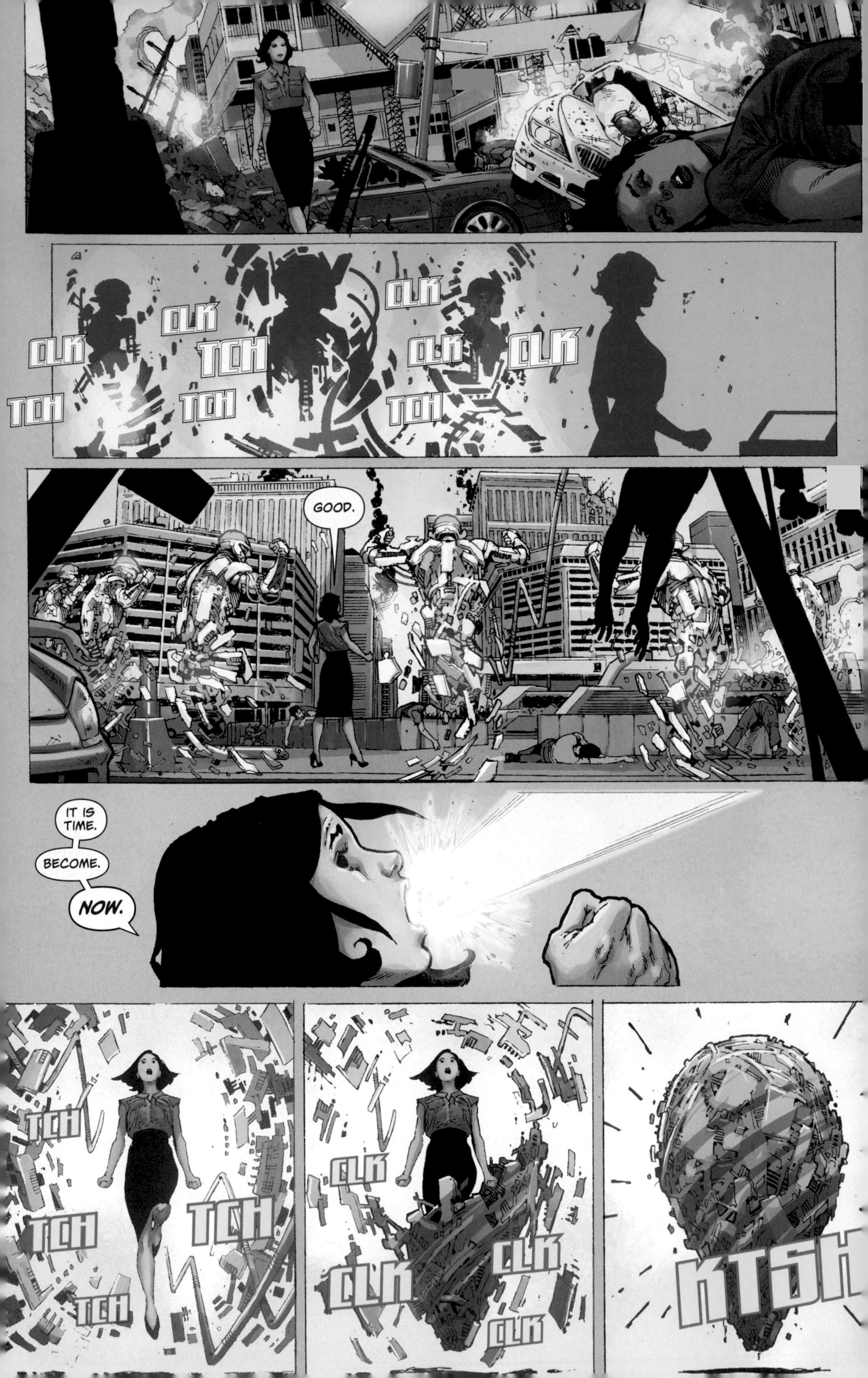

CLK
TCH
CLK
TCH
TCH
CLK
CLK
TCH
CLK
GOOD.
IT IS TIME.
BECOME.
NOW.
TCH
TCH
TCH
TCH
CLK
CLK
CLK
CLK
KTSH

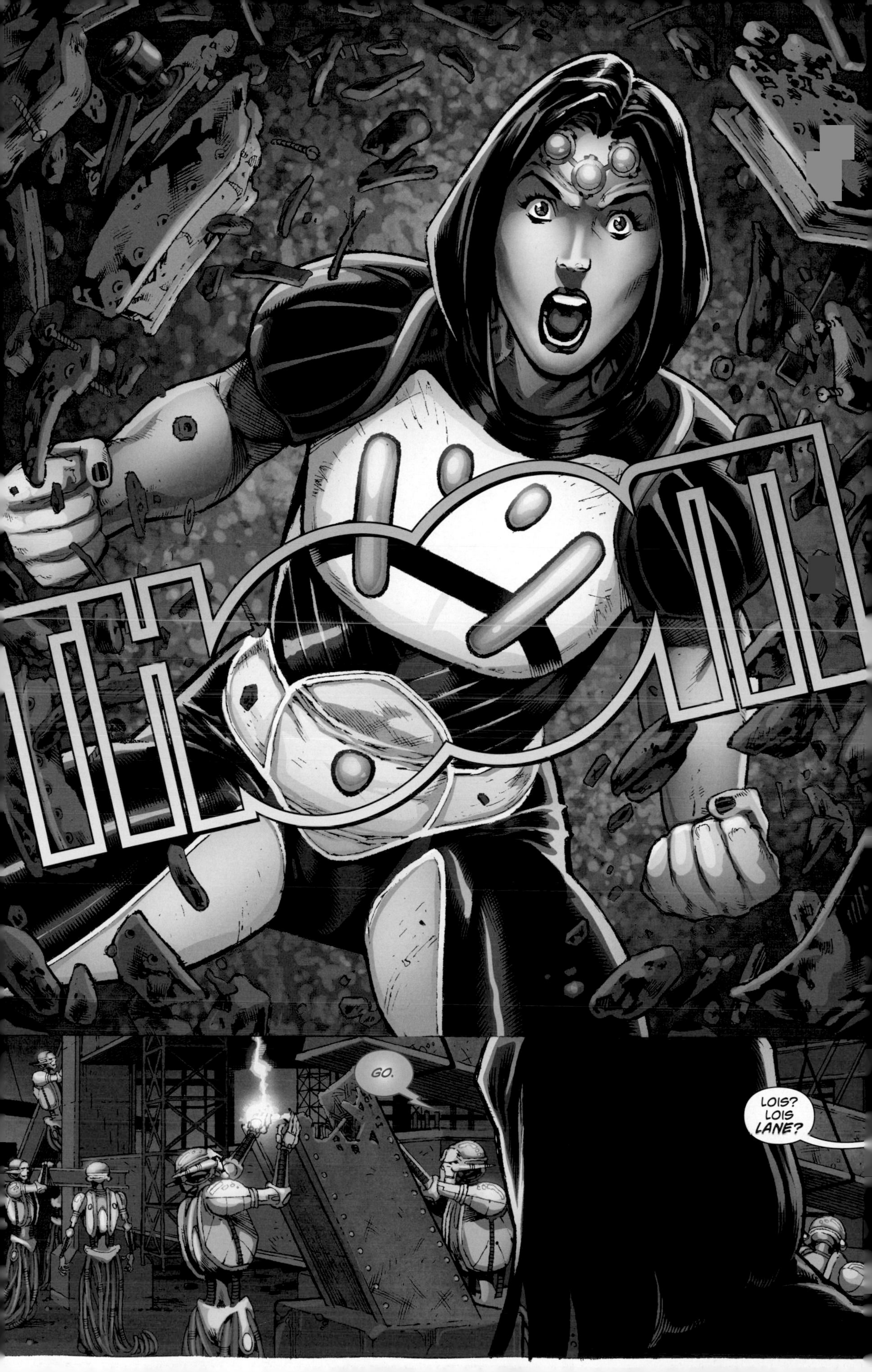
GO.
LOIS? LOIS LANE?

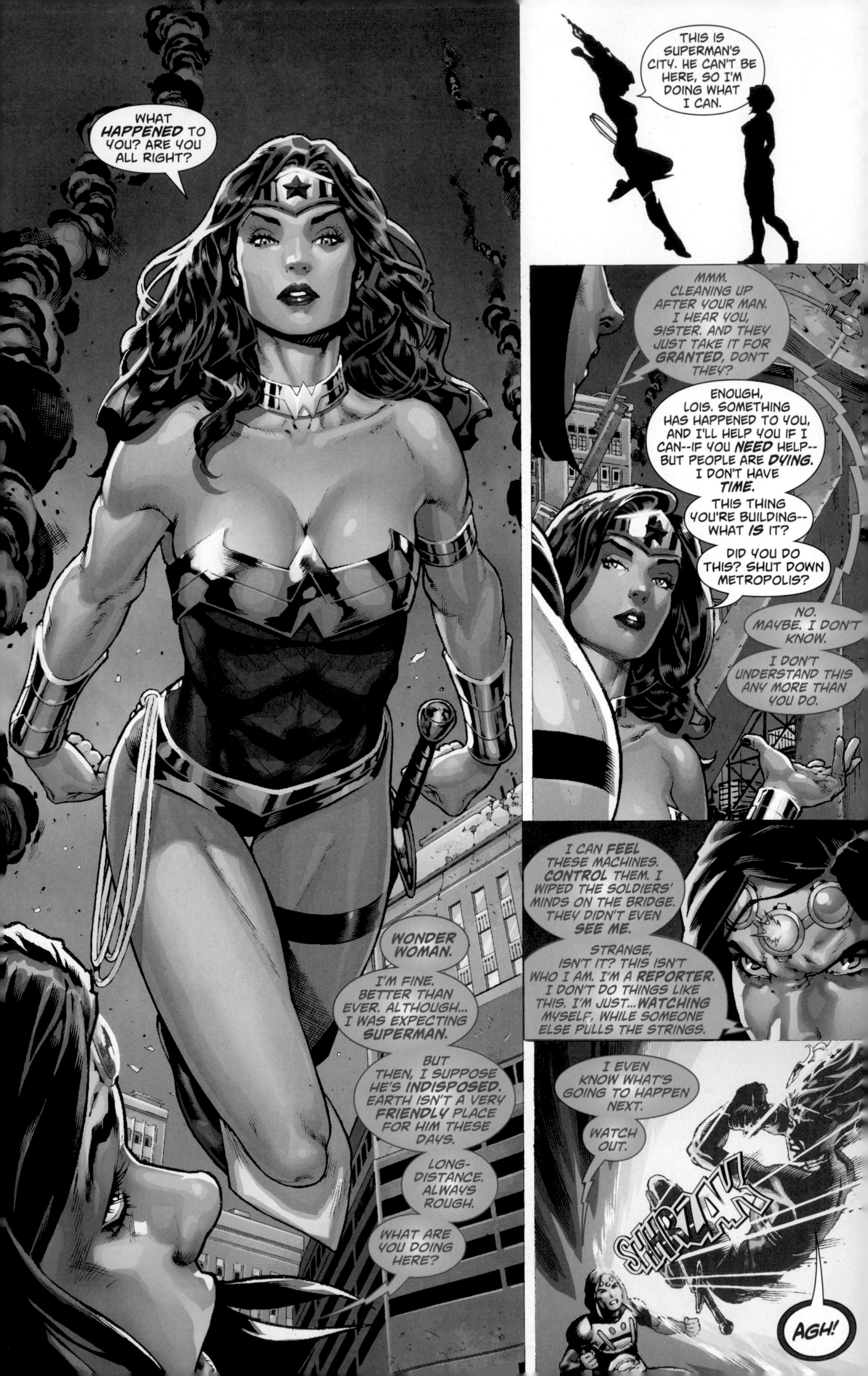
WHAT HAPPENED TO YOU? ARE YOU ALL RIGHT?
WONDER WOMAN.
I'M FINE. BETTER THAN EVER. ALTHOUGH... I WAS EXPECTING SUPERMAN.
BUT THEN, I SUPPOSE HE'S INDISPOSED. EARTH ISN'T A VERY FRIENDLY PLACE FOR HIM THESE DAYS.
LONG-DISTANCE. ALWAYS ROUGH.
WHAT ARE YOU DOING HERE?
THIS IS SUPERMAN'S CITY. HE CAN'T BE HERE, SO I'M DOING WHAT I CAN.
MMM. CLEANING UP AFTER YOUR MAN. I HEAR YOU, SISTER. AND THEY JUST TAKE IT FOR GRANTED, DON'T THEY?
ENOUGH, LOIS. SOMETHING HAS HAPPENED TO YOU, AND I'LL HELP YOU IF I CAN--IF YOU NEED HELP--BUT PEOPLE ARE DYING. I DON'T HAVE TIME.
THIS THING YOU'RE BUILDING--WHAT IS IT?
DID YOU DO THIS? SHUT DOWN METROPOLIS?
NO. MAYBE. I DON'T KNOW.
I DON'T UNDERSTAND THIS ANY MORE THAN YOU DO.
I CAN FEEL THESE MACHINES. CONTROL THEM. I WIPED THE SOLDIERS' MINDS ON THE BRIDGE. THEY DIDN'T EVEN SEE ME.
STRANGE, ISN'T IT? THIS ISN'T WHO I AM. I'M A REPORTER. I DON'T DO THINGS LIKE THIS. I'M JUST...WATCHING MYSELF, WHILE SOMEONE ELSE PULLS THE STRINGS.
I EVEN KNOW WHAT'S GOING TO HAPPEN NEXT.
WATCH OUT.
SHRZAK
AGH!

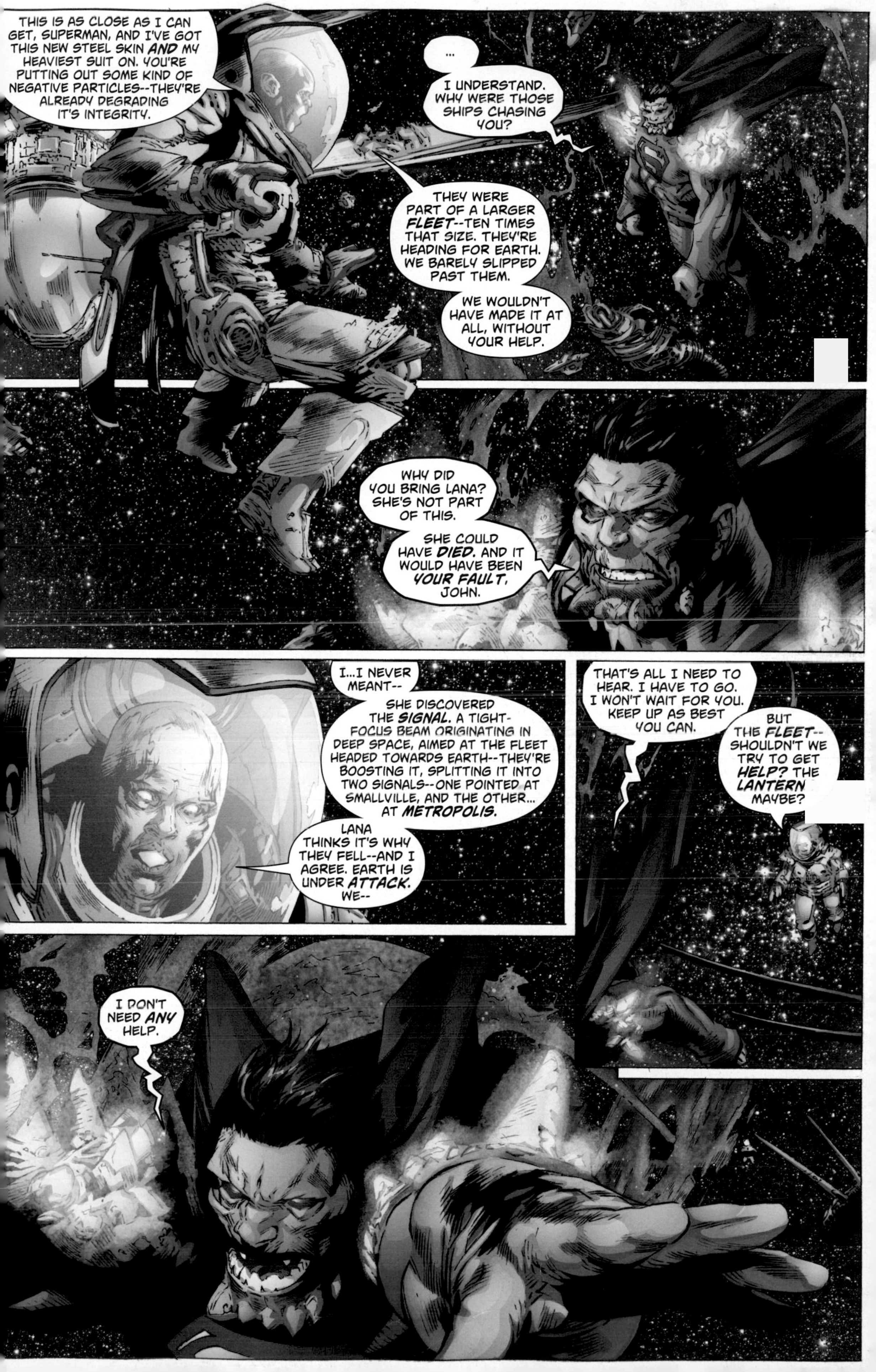
THIS IS AS CLOSE AS I CAN GET, SUPERMAN, AND I'VE GOT THIS NEW STEEL SKIN AND MY HEAVIEST SUIT ON. YOU'RE PUTTING OUT SOME KIND OF NEGATIVE PARTICLES--THEY'RE ALREADY DEGRADING IT'S INTEGRITY.
...
I UNDERSTAND. WHY WERE THOSE SHIPS CHASING YOU?
THEY WERE PART OF A LARGER FLEET--TEN TIMES THAT SIZE. THEY'RE HEADING FOR EARTH. WE BARELY SLIPPED PAST THEM.
WE WOULDN'T HAVE MADE IT AT ALL, WITHOUT YOUR HELP.
WHY DID YOU BRING LANA? SHE'S NOT PART OF THIS.
SHE COULD HAVE DIED. AND IT WOULD HAVE BEEN YOUR FAULT, JOHN.
I...I NEVER MEANT--
SHE DISCOVERED THE SIGNAL. A TIGHT-FOCUS BEAM ORIGINATING IN DEEP SPACE, AIMED AT THE FLEET HEADED TOWARDS EARTH--THEY'RE BOOSTING IT, SPLITTING IT INTO TWO SIGNALS--ONE POINTED AT SMALLVILLE, AND THE OTHER... AT METROPOLIS.
LANA THINKS IT'S WHY THEY FELL--AND I AGREE. EARTH IS UNDER ATTACK. WE--
THAT'S ALL I NEED TO HEAR. I HAVE TO GO. I WON'T WAIT FOR YOU. KEEP UP AS BEST YOU CAN.
BUT THE FLEET--SHOULDN'T WE TRY TO GET HELP? THE LANTERN MAYBE?
I DON'T NEED ANY HELP.

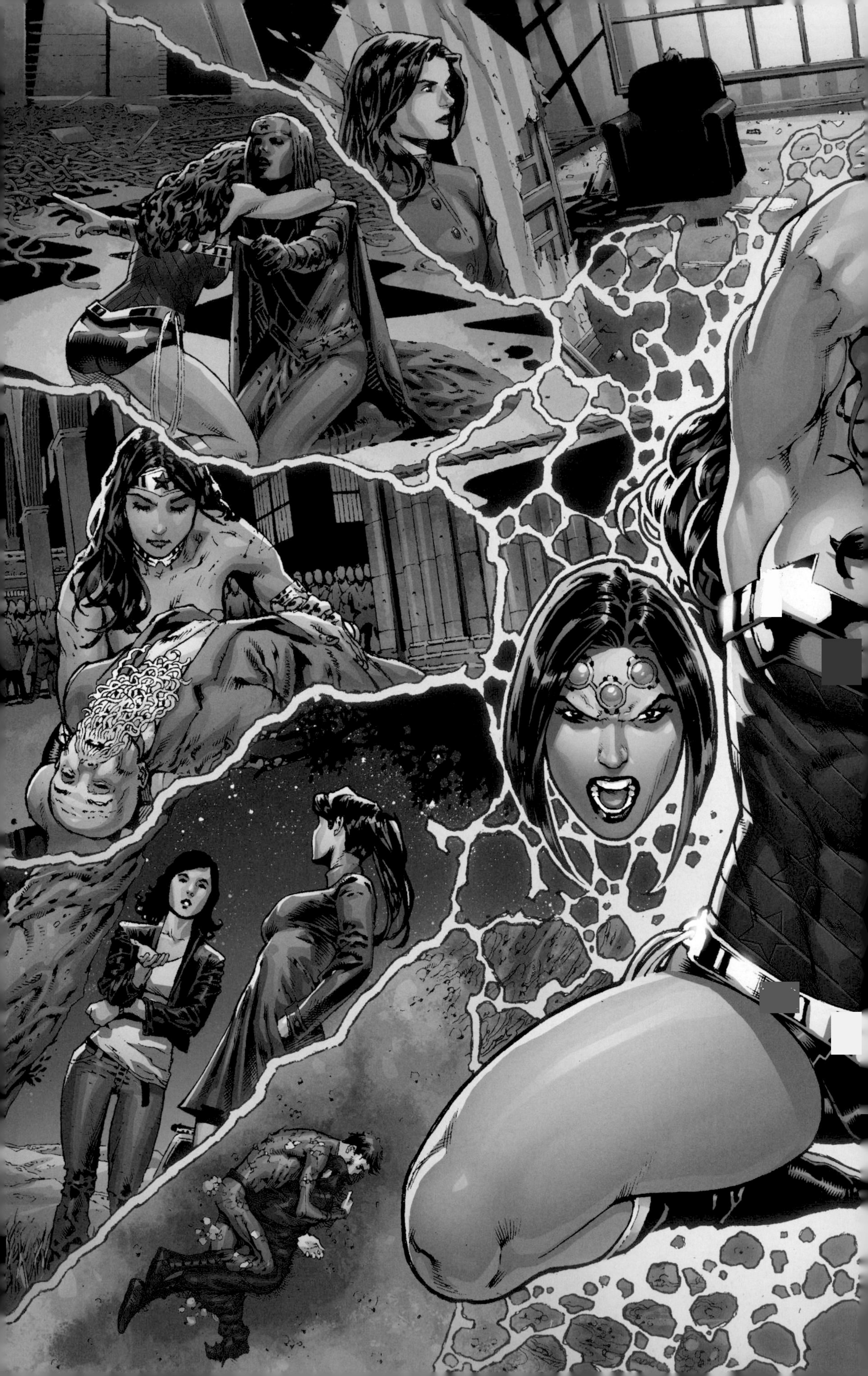

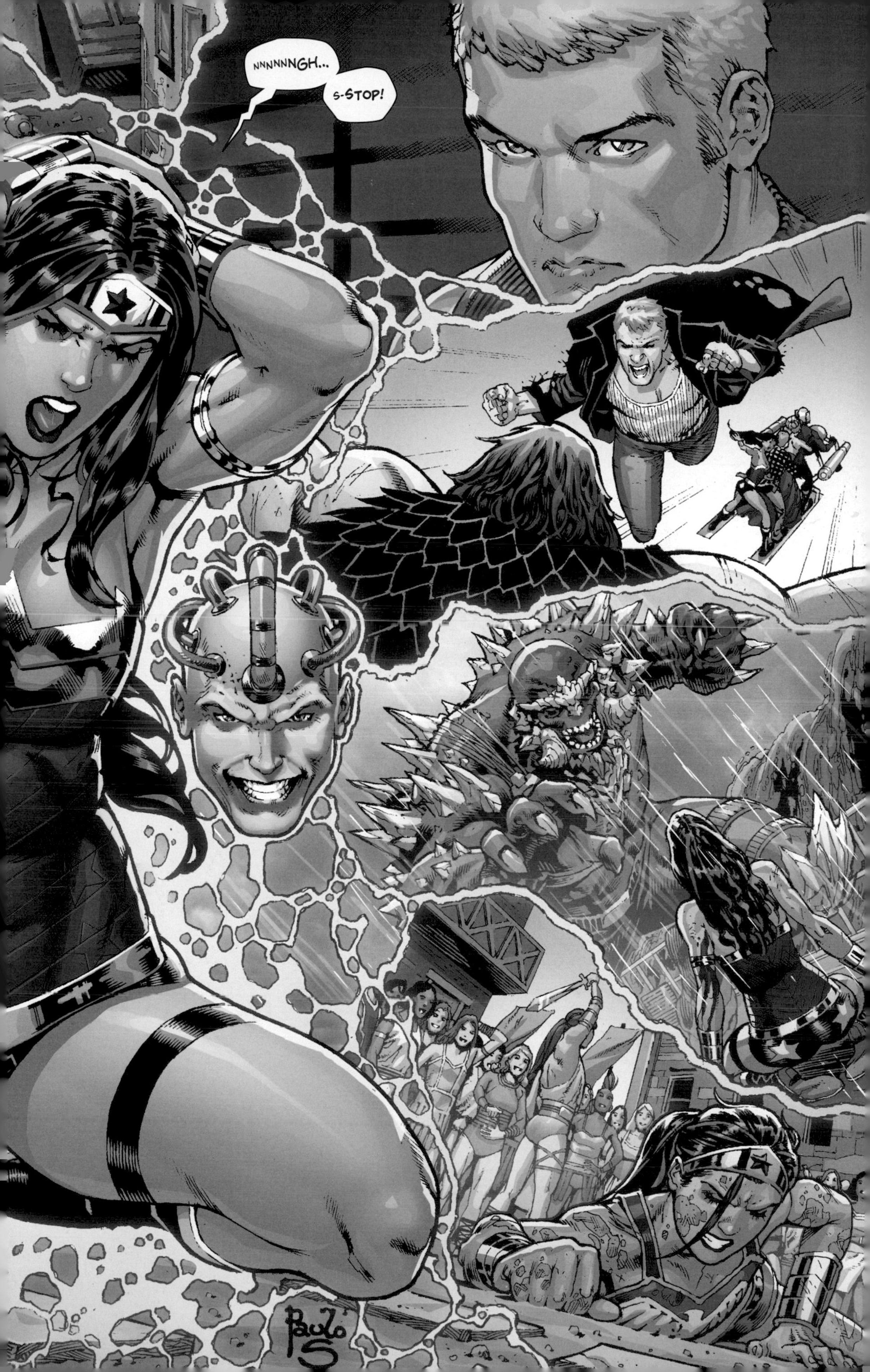
NNNNNNGH...
S-STOP!
Paulo S

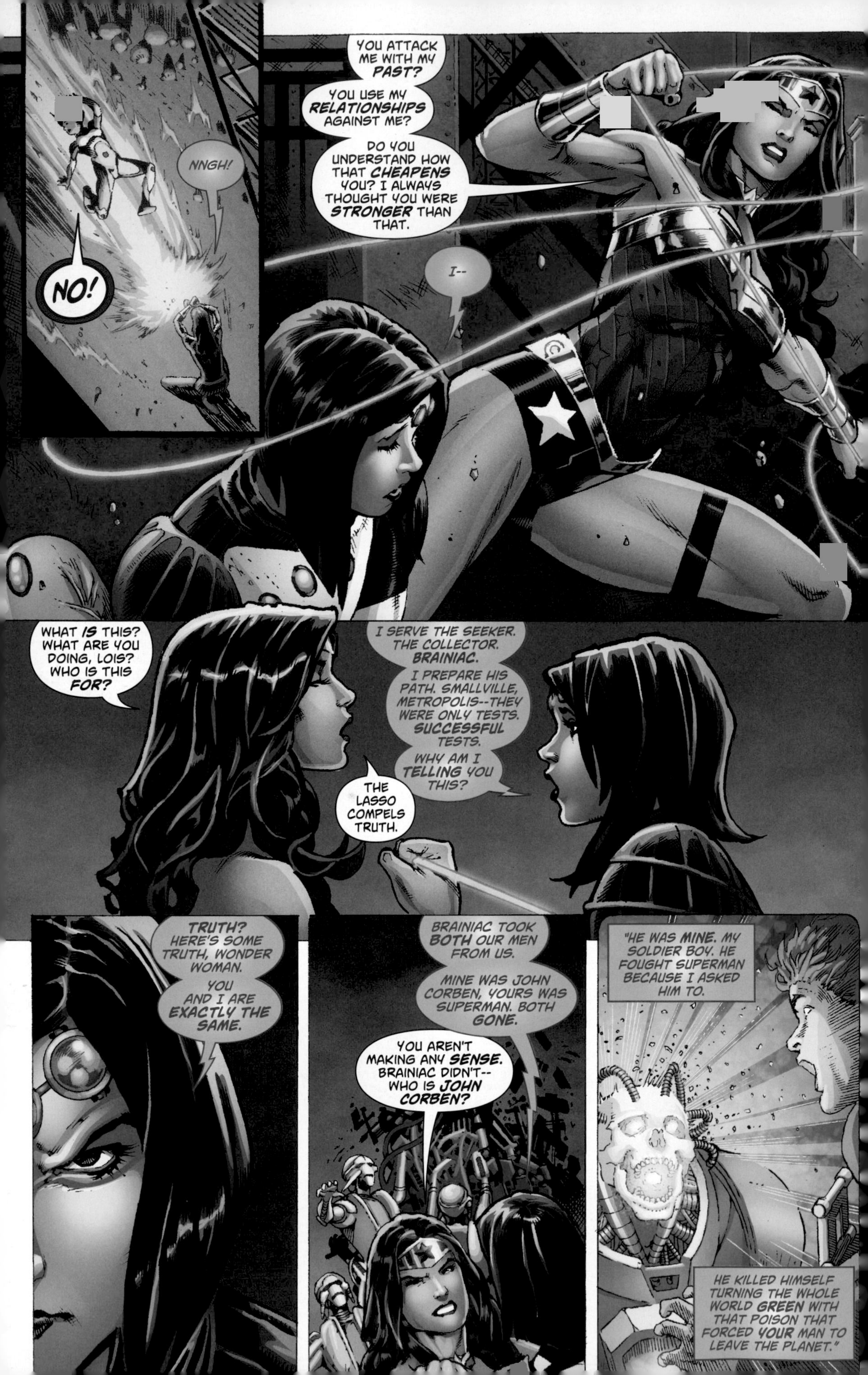
NNGH!
NO!
YOU ATTACK ME WITH MY PAST?
YOU USE MY RELATIONSHIPS AGAINST ME?
DO YOU UNDERSTAND HOW THAT CHEAPENS YOU? I ALWAYS THOUGHT YOU WERE STRONGER THAN THAT.
I--
WHAT IS THIS? WHAT ARE YOU DOING, LOIS? WHO IS THIS FOR?
I SERVE THE SEEKER. THE COLLECTOR. BRAINIAC.
I PREPARE HIS PATH. SMALLVILLE, METROPOLIS--THEY WERE ONLY TESTS. SUCCESSFUL TESTS.
WHY AM I TELLING YOU THIS?
THE LASSO COMPELS TRUTH.
TRUTH? HERE'S SOME TRUTH, WONDER WOMAN.
YOU AND I ARE EXACTLY THE SAME.
BRAINIAC TOOK BOTH OUR MEN FROM US.
MINE WAS JOHN CORBEN, YOURS WAS SUPERMAN. BOTH GONE.
YOU AREN'T MAKING ANY SENSE. BRAINIAC DIDN'T-- WHO IS JOHN CORBEN?
"HE WAS MINE. MY SOLDIER BOY. HE FOUGHT SUPERMAN BECAUSE I ASKED HIM TO.
HE KILLED HIMSELF TURNING THE WHOLE WORLD GREEN WITH THAT POISON THAT FORCED YOUR MAN TO LEAVE THE PLANET."

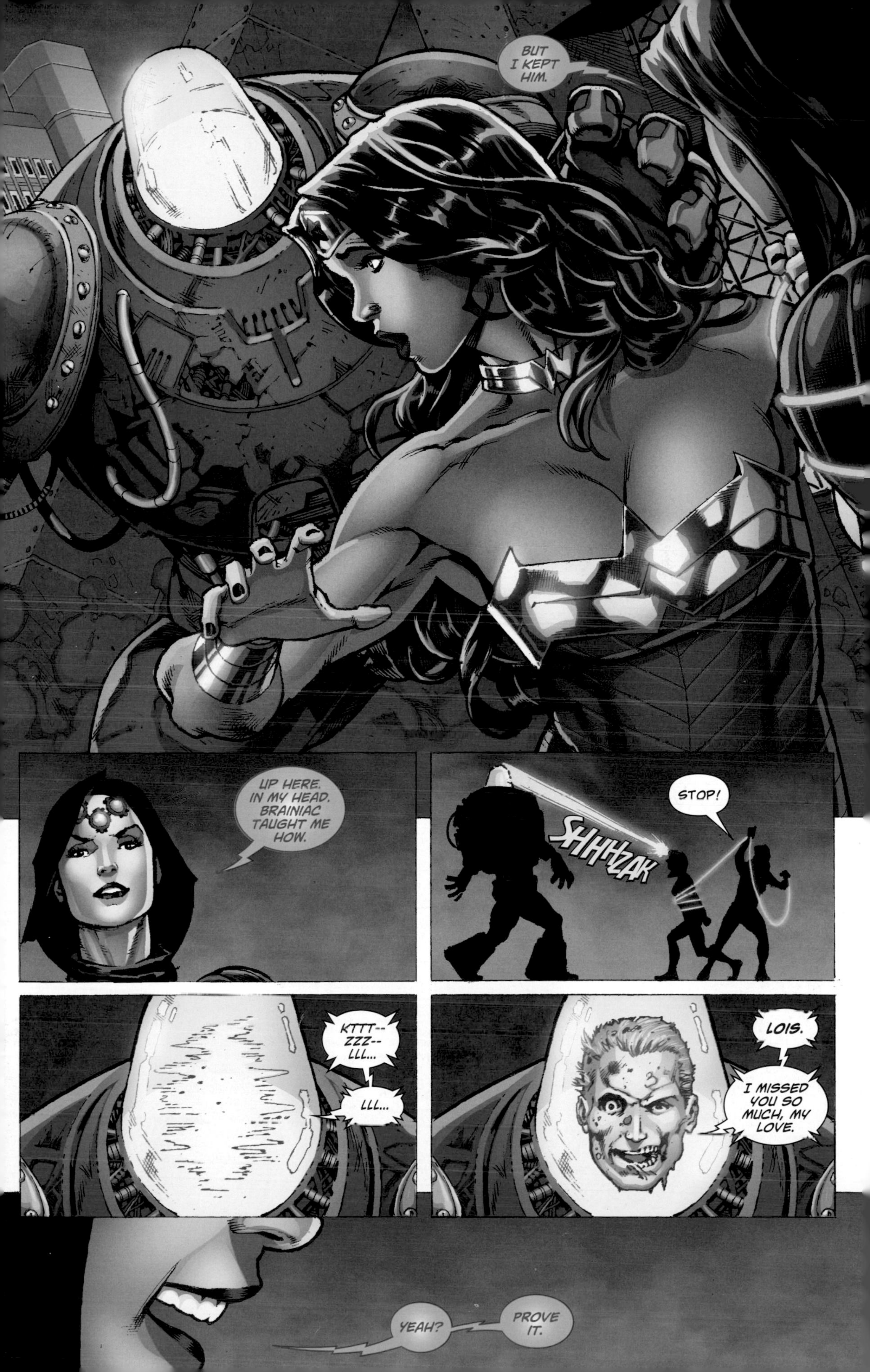
BUT I KEPT HIM.
UP HERE. IN MY HEAD. BRAINIAC TAUGHT ME HOW.
SHHHZAK
STOP!
KTTT-- ZZZ-- LLL...
LLL...
LOIS.
I MISSED YOU SO MUCH, MY LOVE.
YEAH?
PROVE IT.

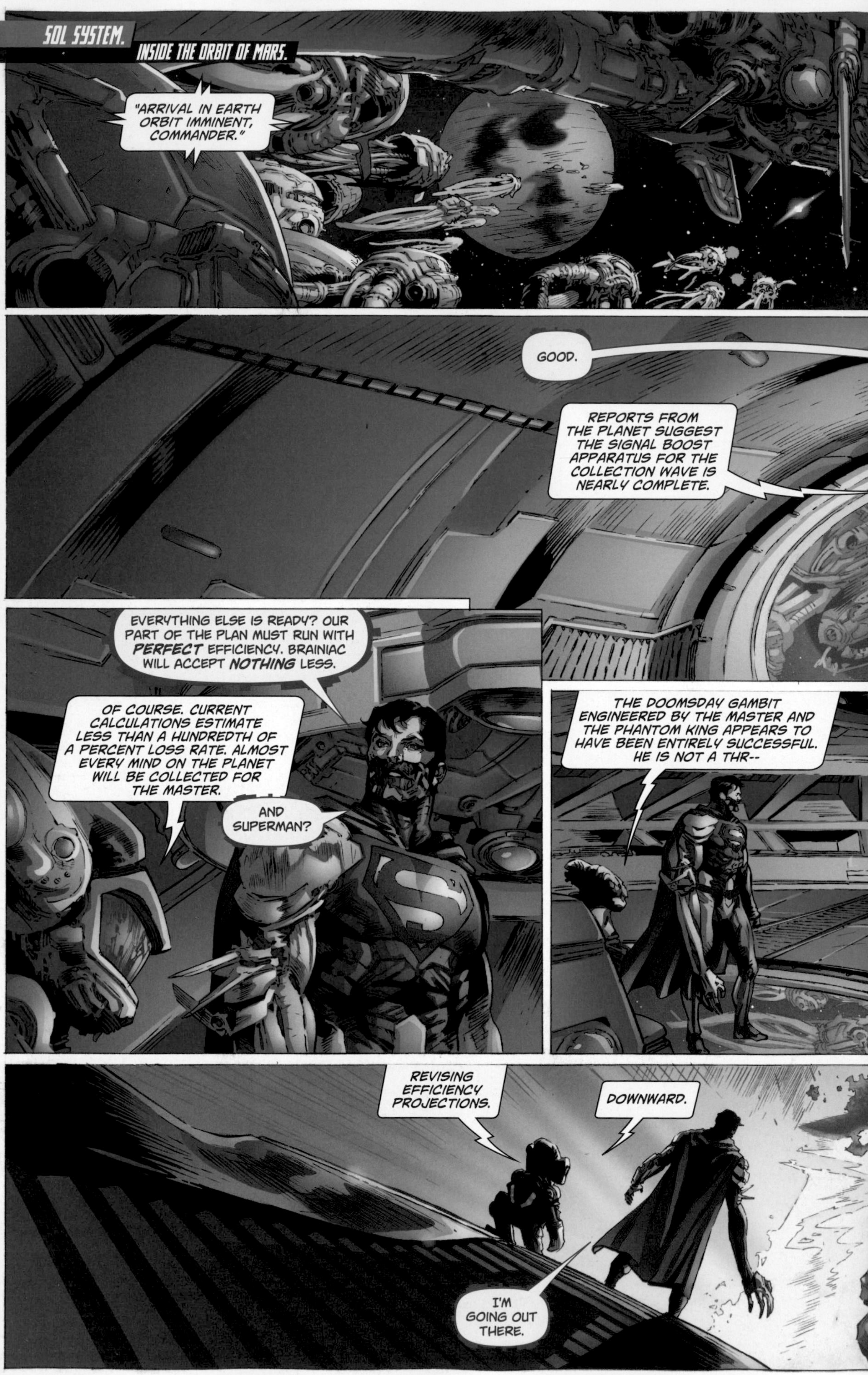
SOL SYSTEM.
INSIDE THE ORBIT OF MARS.
"ARRIVAL IN EARTH ORBIT IMMINENT, COMMANDER."
GOOD.
REPORTS FROM THE PLANET SUGGEST THE SIGNAL BOOST APPARATUS FOR THE COLLECTION WAVE IS NEARLY COMPLETE.
EVERYTHING ELSE IS READY? OUR PART OF THE PLAN MUST RUN WITH PERFECT EFFICIENCY. BRAINIAC WILL ACCEPT NOTHING LESS.
OF COURSE. CURRENT CALCULATIONS ESTIMATE LESS THAN A HUNDREDTH OF A PERCENT LOSS RATE. ALMOST EVERY MIND ON THE PLANET WILL BE COLLECTED FOR THE MASTER.
AND SUPERMAN?
THE DOOMSDAY GAMBIT ENGINEERED BY THE MASTER AND THE PHANTOM KING APPEARS TO HAVE BEEN ENTIRELY SUCCESSFUL. HE IS NOT A THR--
REVISING EFFICIENCY PROJECTIONS.
DOWNWARD.
I'M GOING OUT THERE.

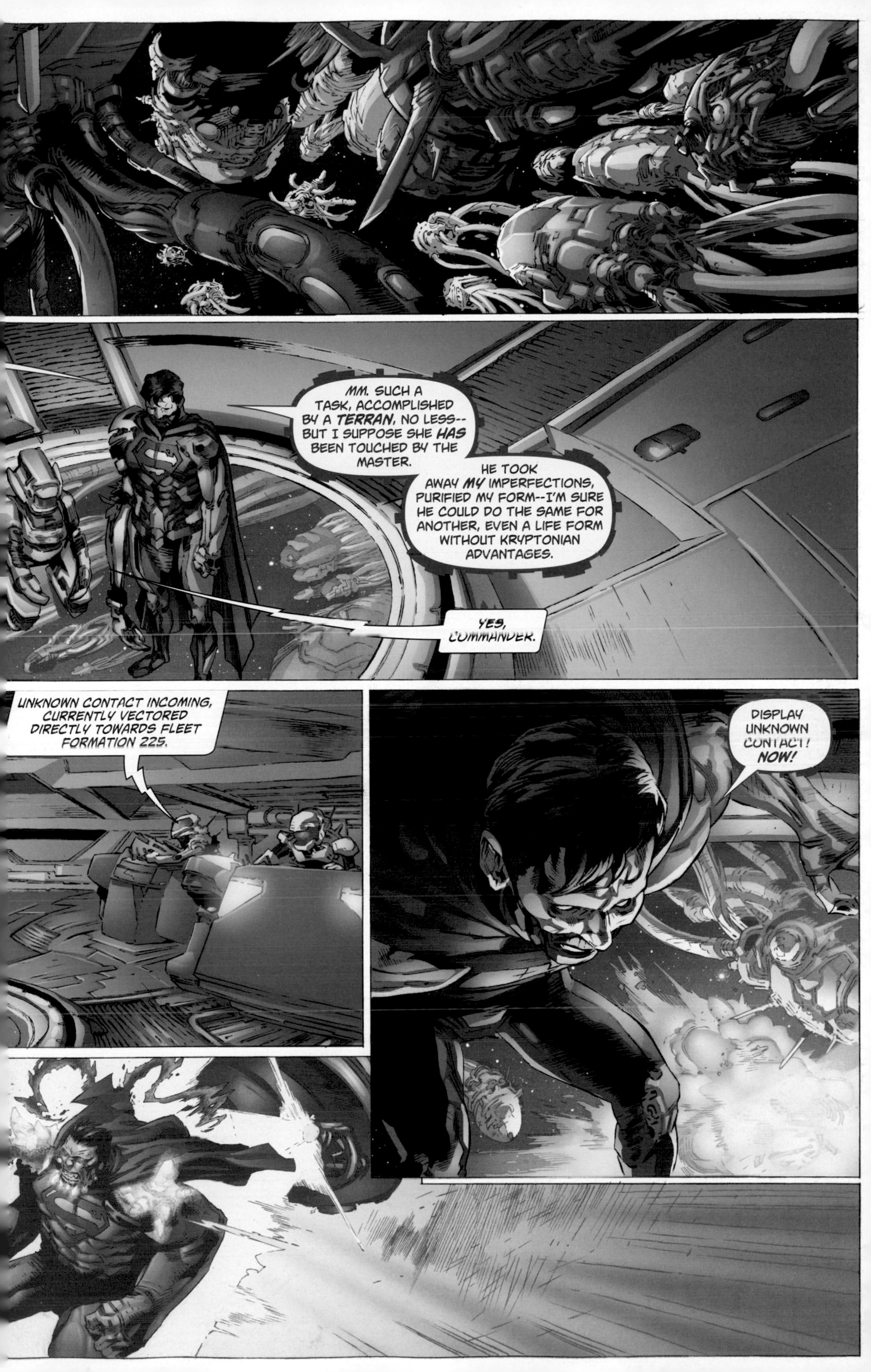
MM. SUCH A TASK, ACCOMPLISHED BY A TERRAN, NO LESS--BUT I SUPPOSE SHE HAS BEEN TOUCHED BY THE MASTER.
HE TOOK AWAY MY IMPERFECTIONS, PURIFIED MY FORM--I'M SURE HE COULD DO THE SAME FOR ANOTHER, EVEN A LIFE FORM WITHOUT KRYPTONIAN ADVANTAGES.
YES, COMMANDER.
UNKNOWN CONTACT INCOMING, CURRENTLY VECTORED DIRECTLY TOWARDS FLEET FORMATION 225.
DISPLAY UNKNOWN CONTACT! NOW!

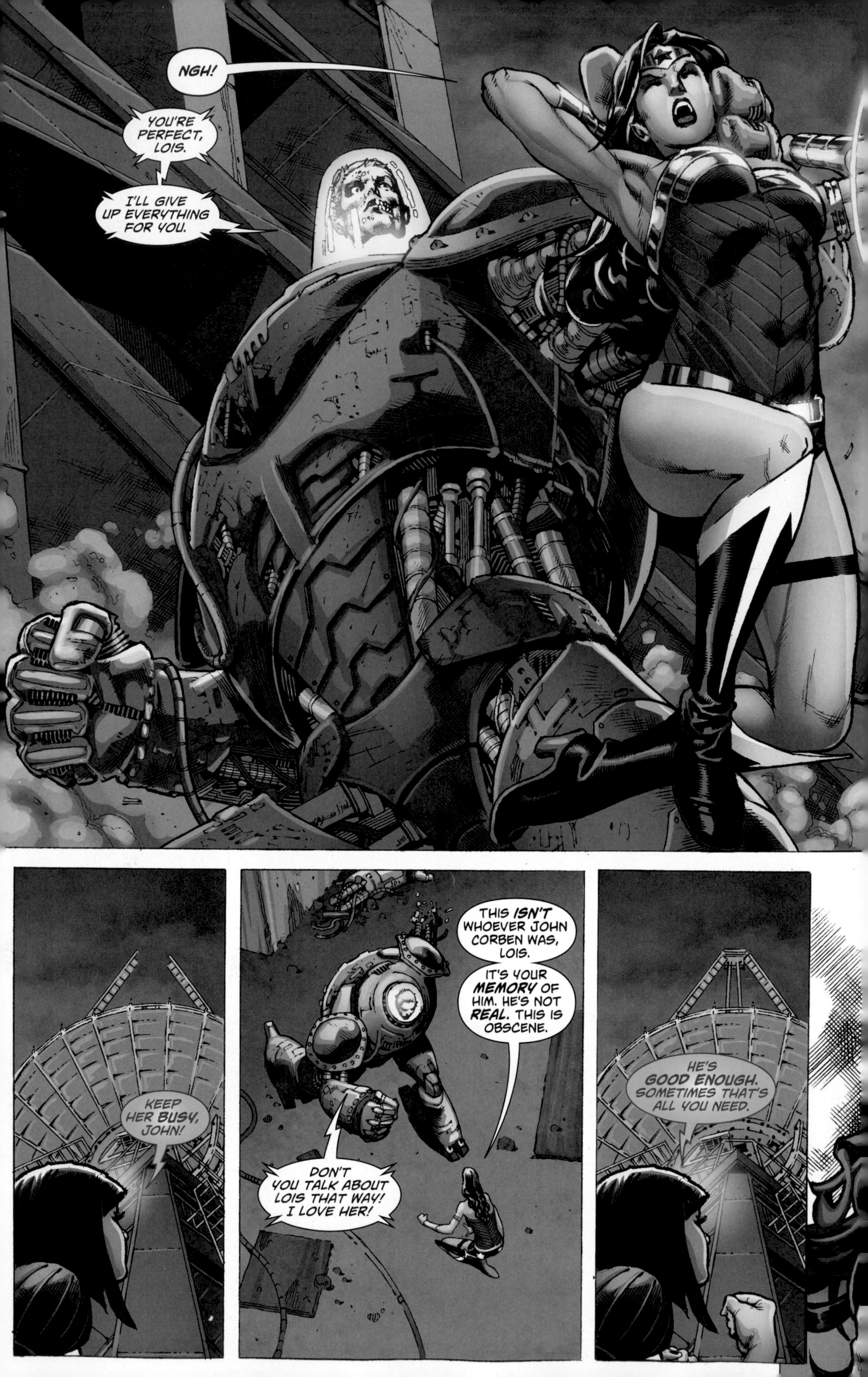
NGH!
YOU'RE PERFECT, LOIS.
I'LL GIVE UP EVERYTHING FOR YOU.
KEEP HER BUSY, JOHN!
THIS ISN'T WHOEVER JOHN CORBEN WAS, LOIS.
IT'S YOUR MEMORY OF HIM. HE'S NOT REAL. THIS IS OBSCENE.
DON'T YOU TALK ABOUT LOIS THAT WAY! I LOVE HER!
HE'S GOOD ENOUGH. SOMETIMES THAT'S ALL YOU NEED.

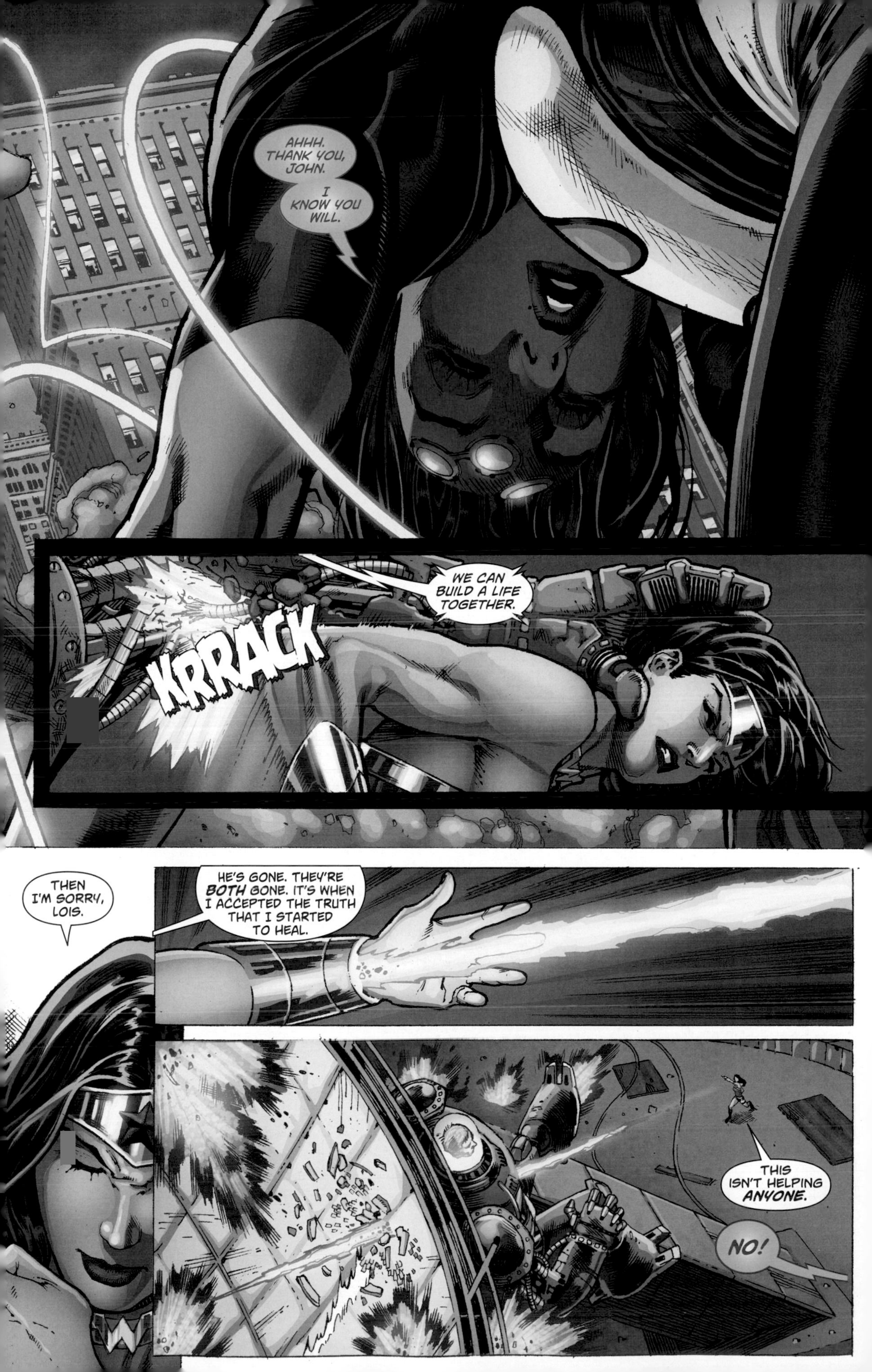
AHHH. THANK YOU, JOHN.
I KNOW YOU WILL.
WE CAN BUILD A LIFE TOGETHER.
KRRACK
THEN I'M SORRY, LOIS.
HE'S GONE. THEY'RE BOTH GONE. IT'S WHEN I ACCEPTED THE TRUTH THAT I STARTED TO HEAL.
THIS ISN'T HELPING ANYONE.
NO!

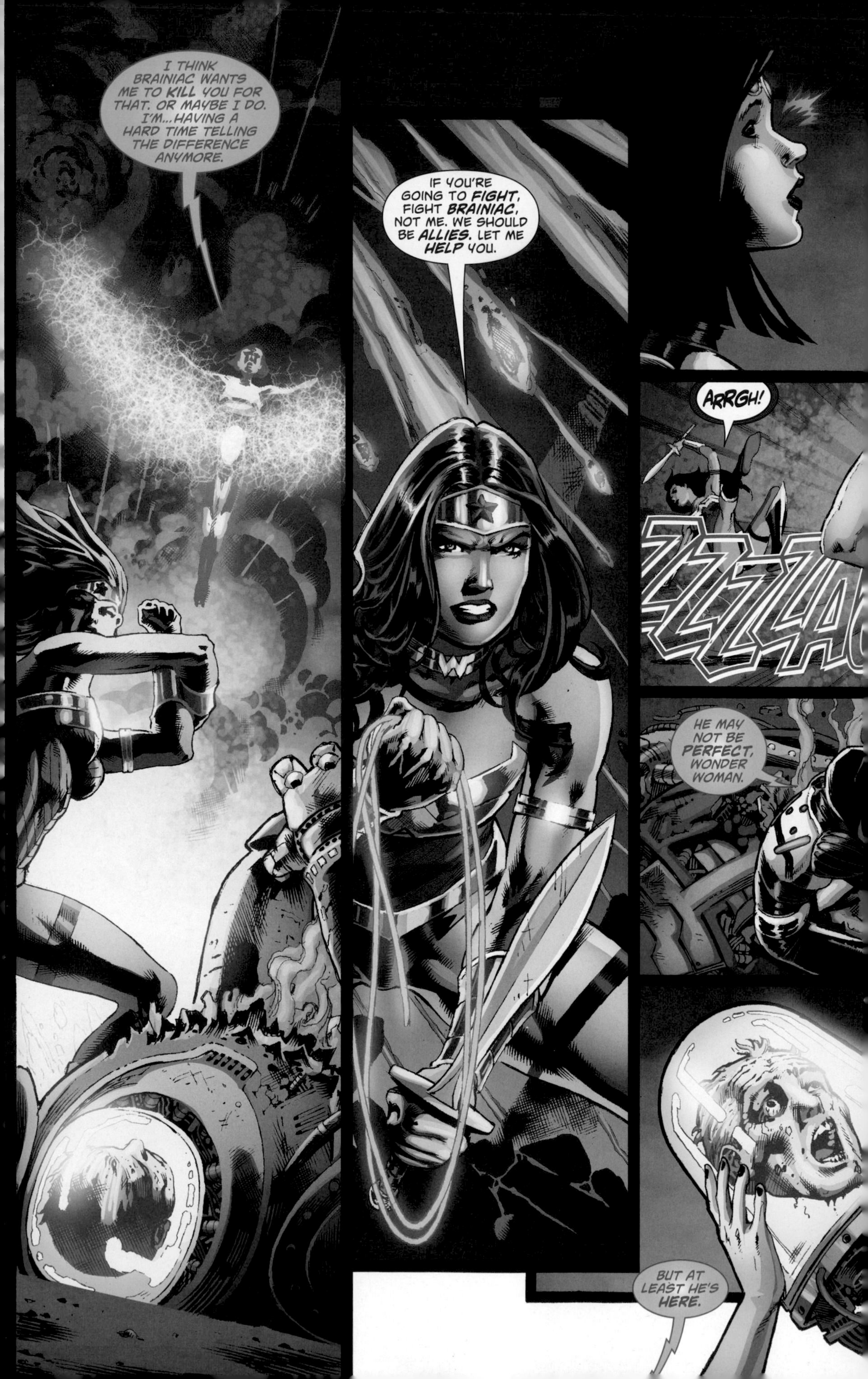
I THINK BRAINIAC WANTS ME TO KILL YOU FOR THAT. OR MAYBE I DO. I'M...HAVING A HARD TIME TELLING THE DIFFERENCE ANYMORE.
IF YOU'RE GOING TO FIGHT, FIGHT BRAINIAC, NOT ME. WE SHOULD BE ALLIES. LET ME HELP YOU.
ARRGH!
HE MAY NOT BE PERFECT, WONDER WOMAN.
BUT AT LEAST HE'S HERE.

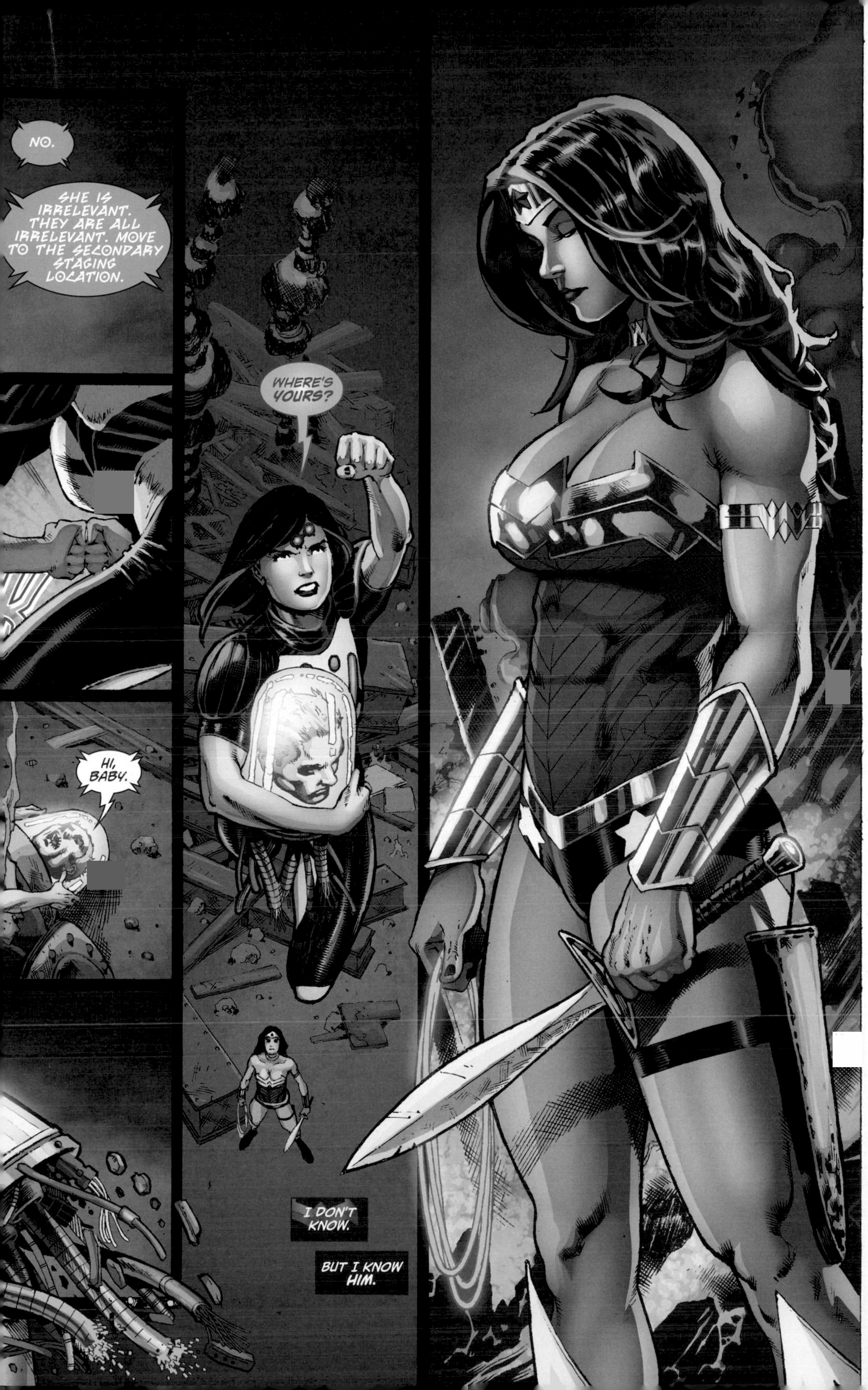
NO.
SHE IS IRRELEVANT. THEY ARE ALL IRRELEVANT. MOVE TO THE SECONDARY STAGING LOCATION.
HI, BABY.
WHERE'S YOURS?
I DON'T KNOW.
BUT I KNOW HIM.

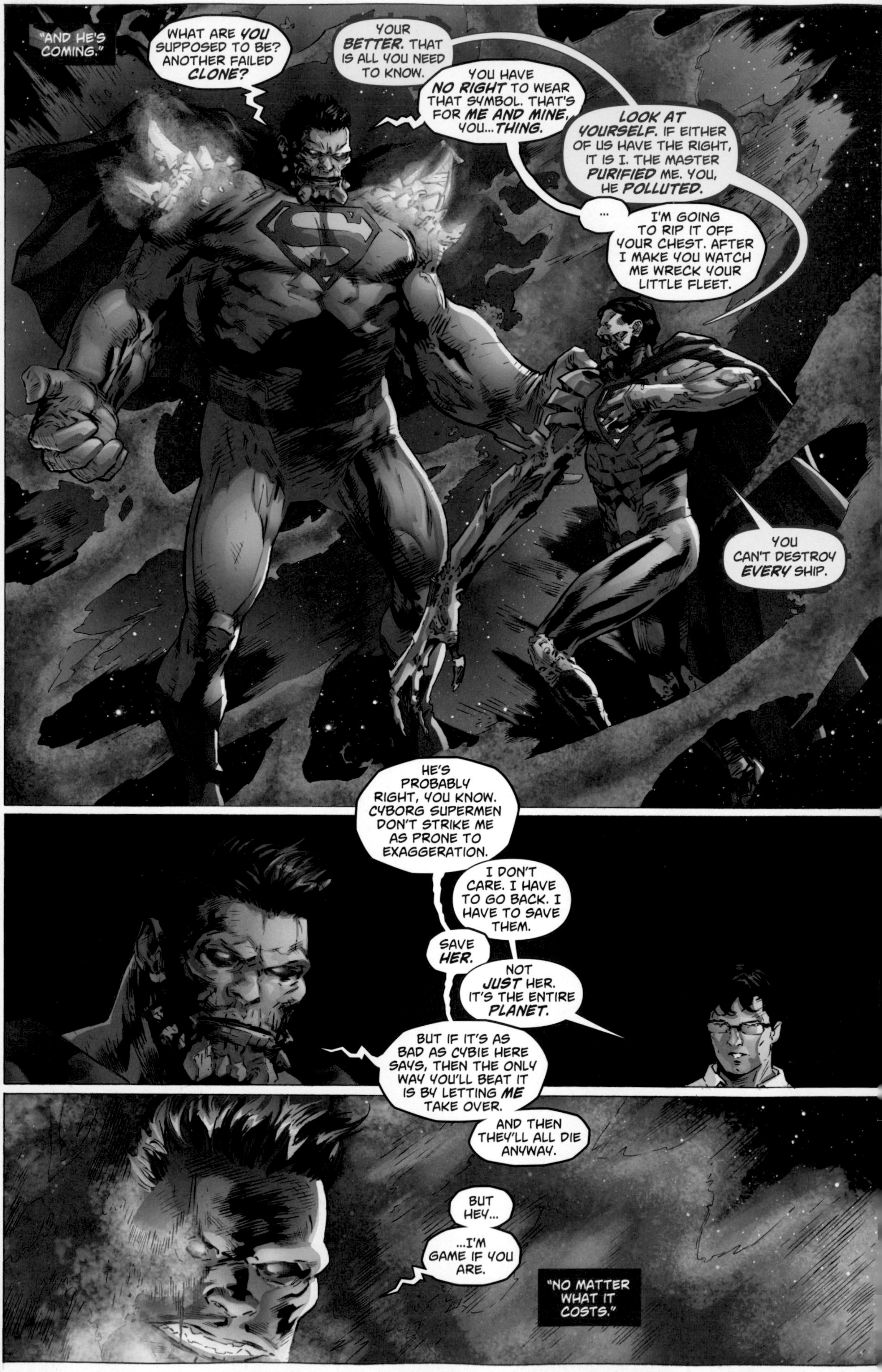
"AND HE'S COMING."
WHAT ARE YOU SUPPOSED TO BE? ANOTHER FAILED CLONE?
YOUR BETTER. THAT IS ALL YOU NEED TO KNOW.
YOU HAVE NO RIGHT TO WEAR THAT SYMBOL. THAT'S FOR ME AND MINE, YOU...THING.
LOOK AT YOURSELF. IF EITHER OF US HAVE THE RIGHT, IT IS I. THE MASTER PURIFIED ME. YOU, HE POLLUTED.
...
I'M GOING TO RIP IT OFF YOUR CHEST. AFTER I MAKE YOU WATCH ME WRECK YOUR LITTLE FLEET.
YOU CAN'T DESTROY EVERY SHIP.
HE'S PROBABLY RIGHT, YOU KNOW. CYBORG SUPERMEN DON'T STRIKE ME AS PRONE TO EXAGGERATION.
I DON'T CARE. I HAVE TO GO BACK. I HAVE TO SAVE THEM.
SAVE HER.
NOT JUST HER. IT'S THE ENTIRE PLANET.
BUT IF IT'S AS BAD AS CYBIE HERE SAYS, THEN THE ONLY WAY YOU'LL BEAT IT IS BY LETTING ME TAKE OVER.
AND THEN THEY'LL ALL DIE ANYWAY.
BUT HEY...
...I'M GAME IF YOU ARE.
"NO MATTER WHAT IT COSTS."

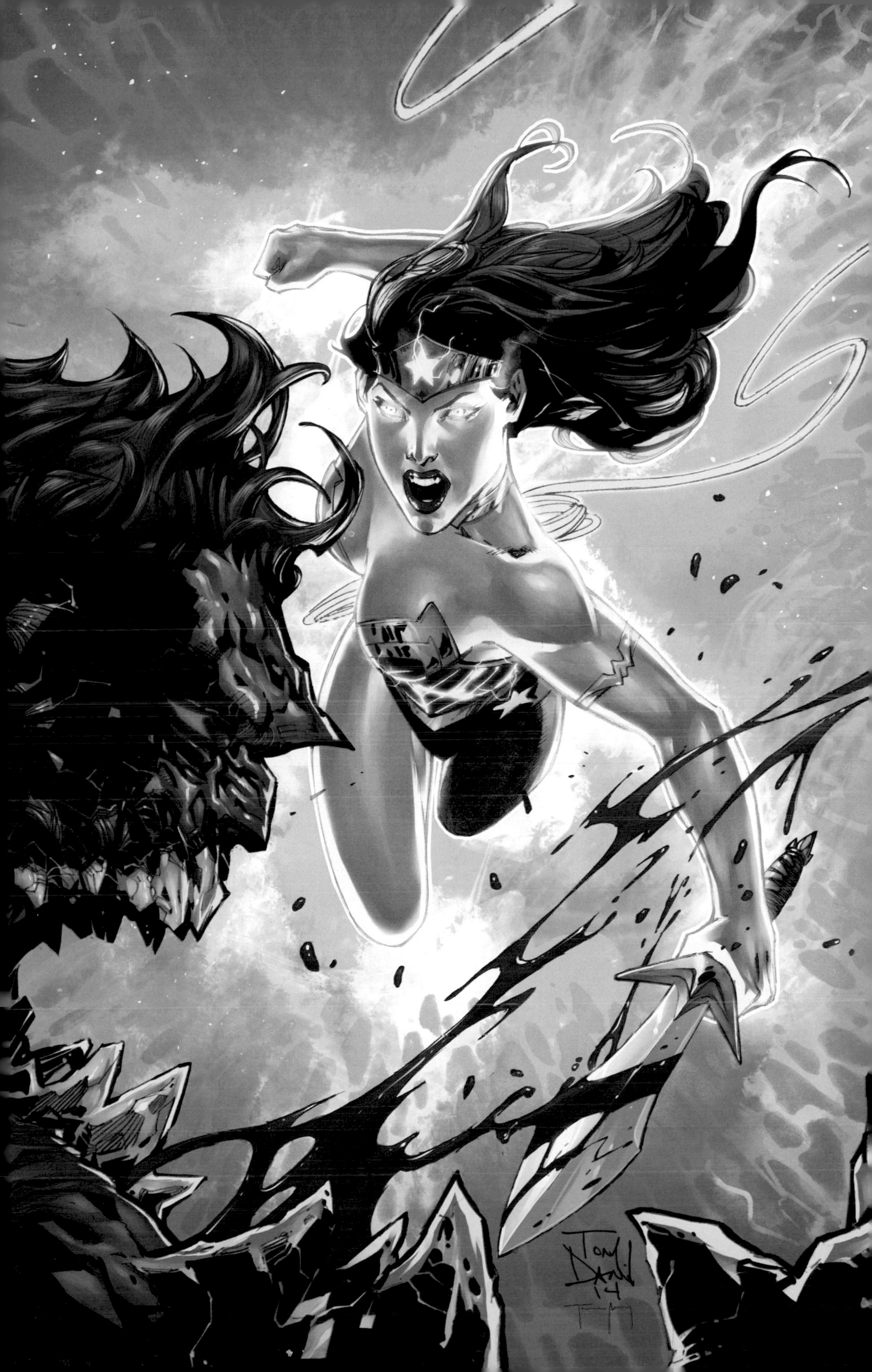

SUPERMAN

DOOMED

[SUPERDOOM] chapter 3

"THE PROMISE"

STORY
CHARLES SOULE

PENCILS
ED BENES, TONY DANIEL, PASCAL ALIXE, CLIFF RICHARDS, AND **JACK HERBERT**

INKS
JAIME MENDOZA, MATT BANNING, VICENTE CIFUENTES, PASCAL ALIXE, AND **CLIFF RICHARDS**

COLORS
JEROMY COX

LETTERS
CARLOS M. MANGUAL, DEZI SIENTY AND **TAYLOR ESPOSITO**

COVER
TONY DANIEL AND **TOMEU MOREY**

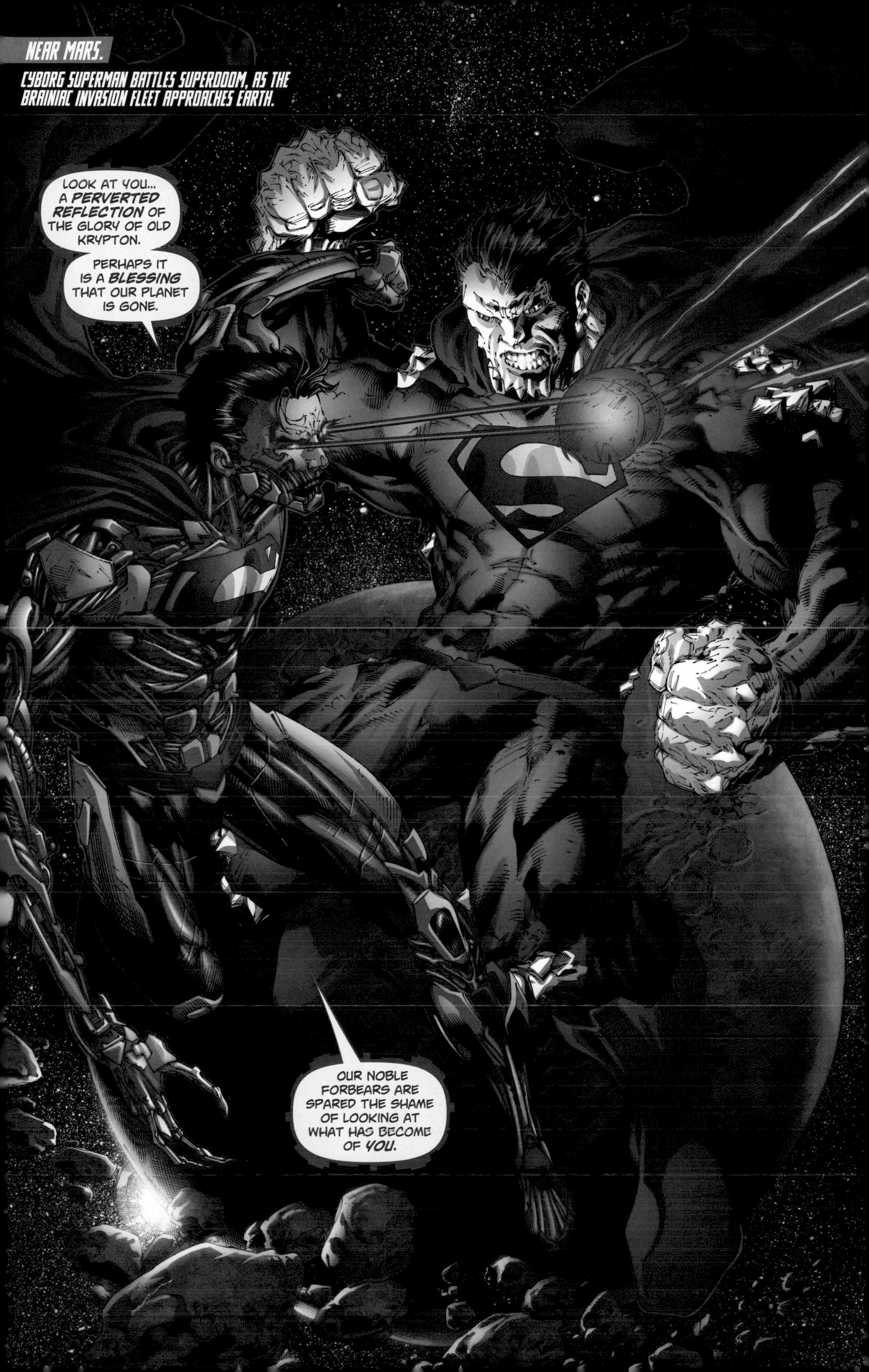
NEAR MARS.
CYBORG SUPERMAN BATTLES SUPERDOOM, AS THE BRAINIAC INVASION FLEET APPROACHES EARTH.
LOOK AT YOU... A PERVERTED REFLECTION OF THE GLORY OF OLD KRYPTON.
PERHAPS IT IS A BLESSING THAT OUR PLANET IS GONE.
OUR NOBLE FORBEARS ARE SPARED THE SHAME OF LOOKING AT WHAT HAS BECOME OF YOU.

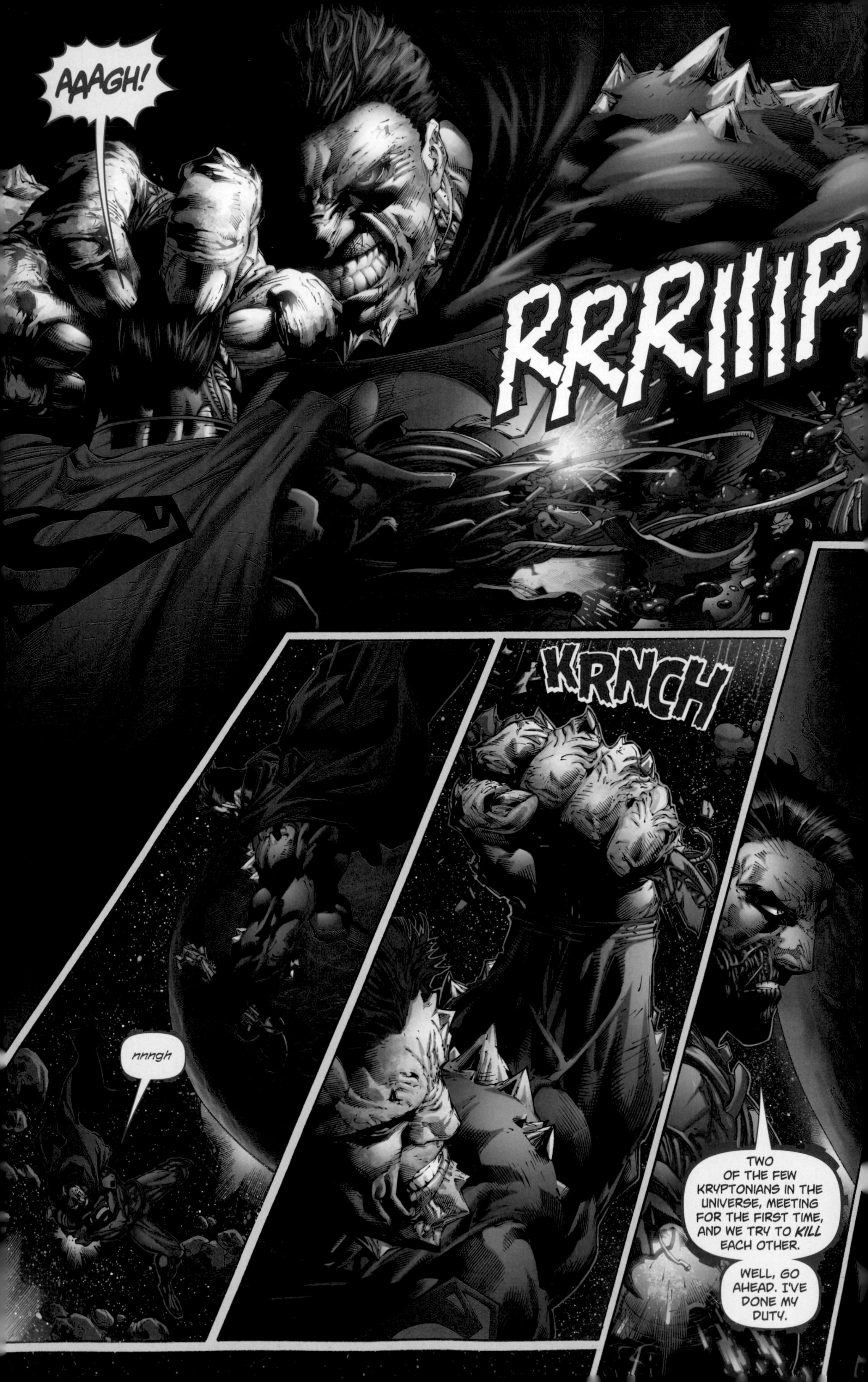
AAAGH!
RRRIIIP
nnngh
KRNCH
TWO OF THE FEW KRYPTONIANS IN THE UNIVERSE, MEETING FOR THE FIRST TIME, AND WE TRY TO KILL EACH OTHER.
WELL, GO AHEAD. I'VE DONE MY DUTY.

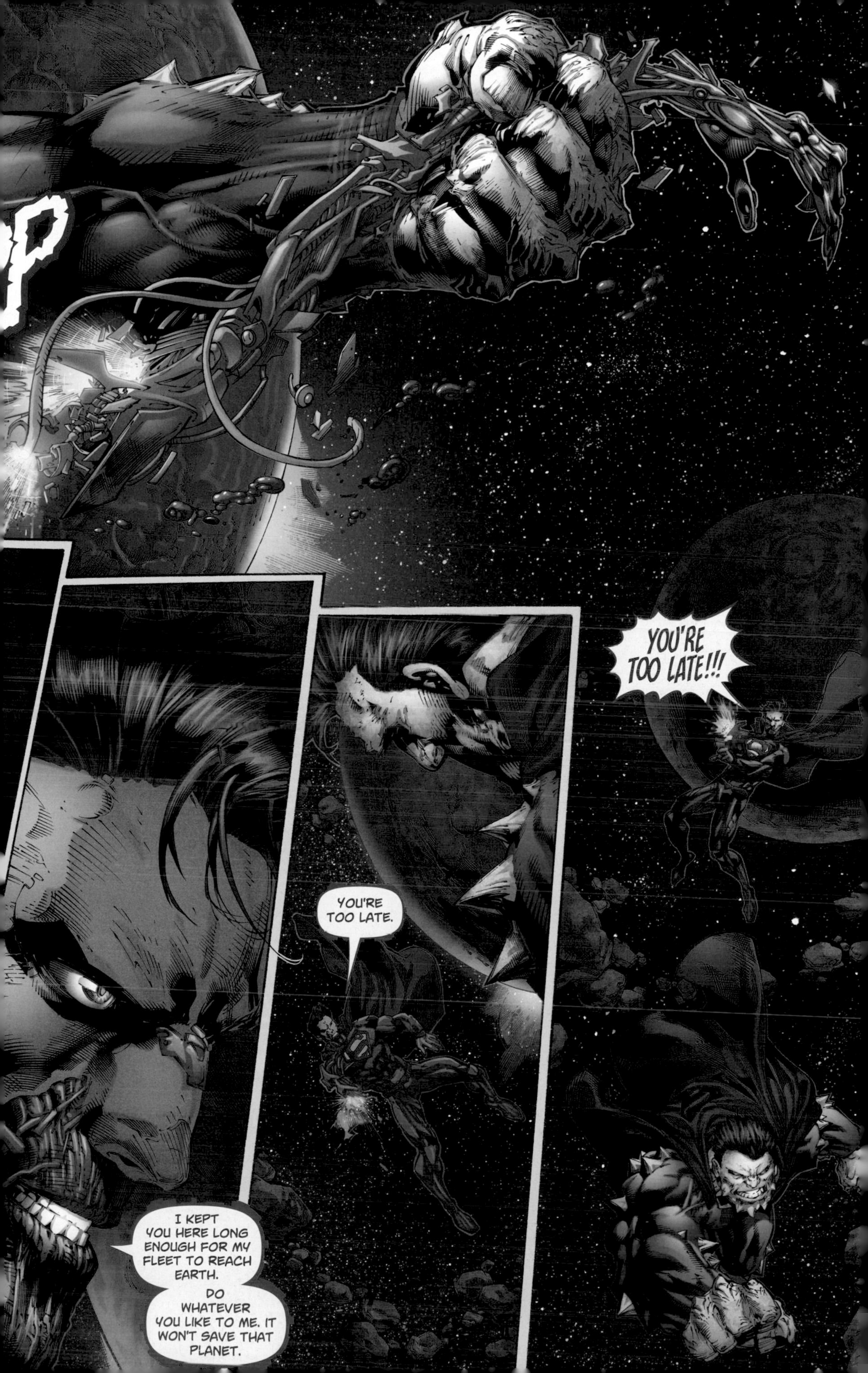

YOU'RE TOO LATE!!!
YOU'RE TOO LATE.
I KEPT YOU HERE LONG ENOUGH FOR MY FLEET TO REACH EARTH.
DO WHATEVER YOU LIKE TO ME. IT WON'T SAVE THAT PLANET.

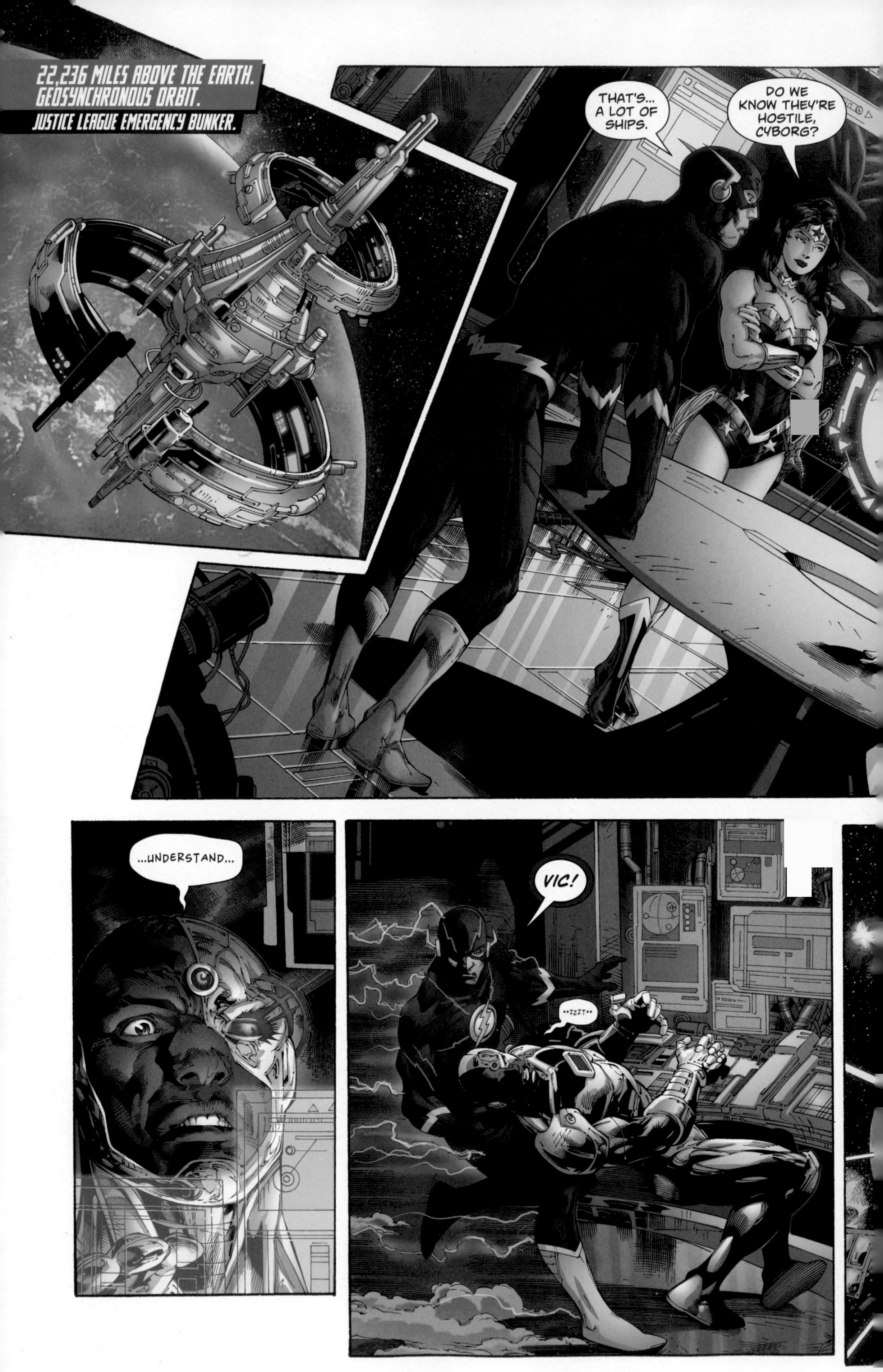
22,236 MILES ABOVE THE EARTH. GEOSYNCHRONOUS ORBIT.
JUSTICE LEAGUE EMERGENCY BUNKER.
THAT'S... A LOT OF SHIPS.
DO WE KNOW THEY'RE HOSTILE, CYBORG?
...UNDERSTAND...
VIC!
ZZZT

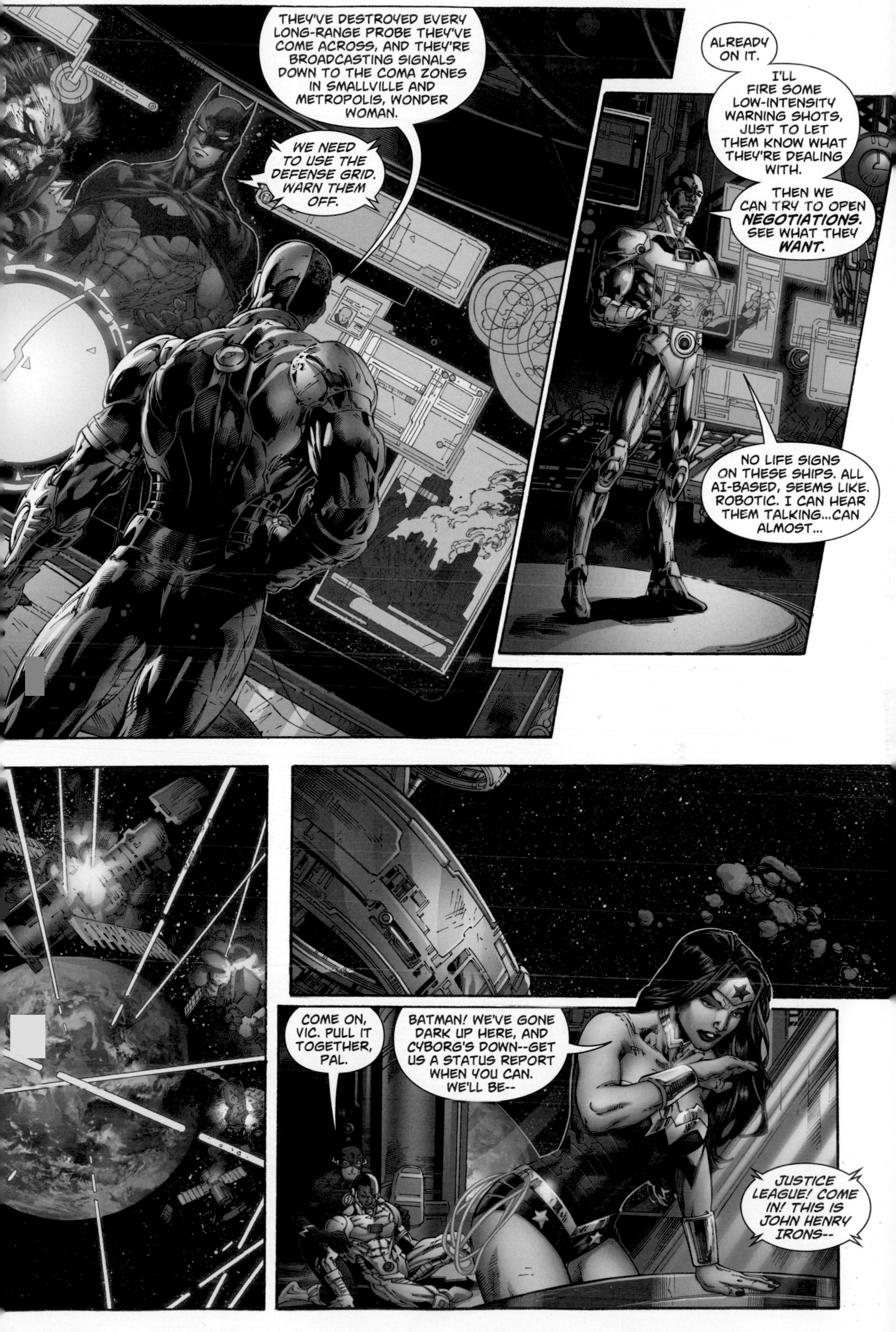

THEY'VE DESTROYED EVERY LONG-RANGE PROBE THEY'VE COME ACROSS, AND THEY'RE BROADCASTING SIGNALS DOWN TO THE COMA ZONES IN SMALLVILLE AND METROPOLIS, WONDER WOMAN.
WE NEED TO USE THE DEFENSE GRID. WARN THEM OFF.
ALREADY ON IT.
I'LL FIRE SOME LOW-INTENSITY WARNING SHOTS, JUST TO LET THEM KNOW WHAT THEY'RE DEALING WITH.
THEN WE CAN TRY TO OPEN NEGOTIATIONS. SEE WHAT THEY WANT.
NO LIFE SIGNS ON THESE SHIPS. ALL AI-BASED, SEEMS LIKE. ROBOTIC. I CAN HEAR THEM TALKING...CAN ALMOST...
COME ON, VIC. PULL IT TOGETHER, PAL.
BATMAN! WE'VE GONE DARK UP HERE, AND CYBORG'S DOWN--GET US A STATUS REPORT WHEN YOU CAN. WE'LL BE--
JUSTICE LEAGUE! COME IN! THIS IS JOHN HENRY IRONS--

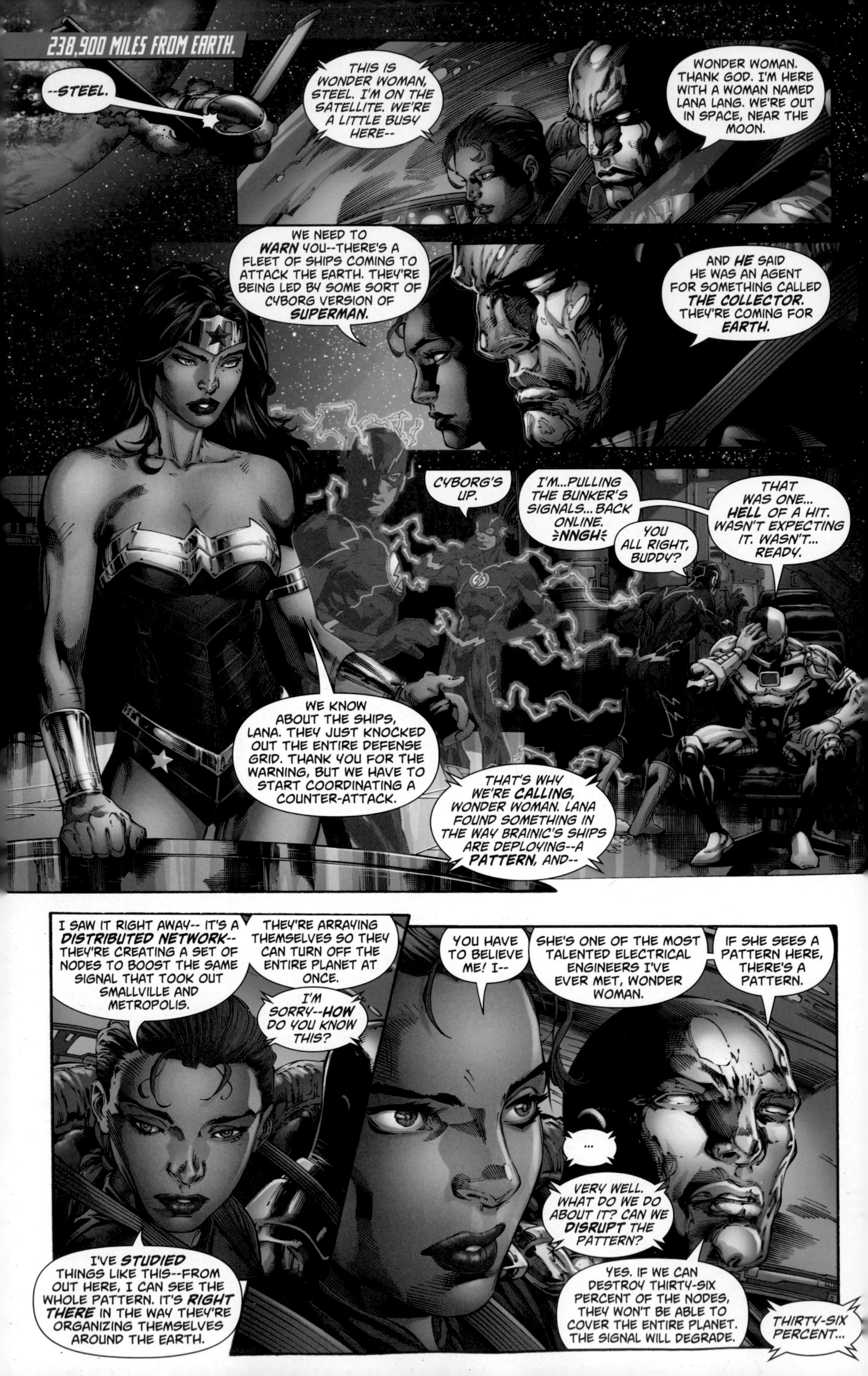
238,900 MILES FROM EARTH.
--STEEL.
THIS IS WONDER WOMAN, STEEL. I'M ON THE SATELLITE. WE'RE A LITTLE BUSY HERE--
WONDER WOMAN. THANK GOD. I'M HERE WITH A WOMAN NAMED LANA LANG. WE'RE OUT IN SPACE, NEAR THE MOON.
WE NEED TO WARN YOU--THERE'S A FLEET OF SHIPS COMING TO ATTACK THE EARTH. THEY'RE BEING LED BY SOME SORT OF CYBORG VERSION OF SUPERMAN.
AND HE SAID HE WAS AN AGENT FOR SOMETHING CALLED THE COLLECTOR. THEY'RE COMING FOR EARTH.
CYBORG'S UP.
I'M...PULLING THE BUNKER'S SIGNALS...BACK ONLINE. NNGH
YOU ALL RIGHT, BUDDY?
THAT WAS ONE... HELL OF A HIT. WASN'T EXPECTING IT. WASN'T... READY.
WE KNOW ABOUT THE SHIPS, LANA. THEY JUST KNOCKED OUT THE ENTIRE DEFENSE GRID. THANK YOU FOR THE WARNING, BUT WE HAVE TO START COORDINATING A COUNTER-ATTACK.
THAT'S WHY WE'RE CALLING, WONDER WOMAN. LANA FOUND SOMETHING IN THE WAY BRAINIC'S SHIPS ARE DEPLOYING--A PATTERN, AND--
I SAW IT RIGHT AWAY-- IT'S A DISTRIBUTED NETWORK-- THEY'RE CREATING A SET OF NODES TO BOOST THE SAME SIGNAL THAT TOOK OUT SMALLVILLE AND METROPOLIS.
THEY'RE ARRAYING THEMSELVES SO THEY CAN TURN OFF THE ENTIRE PLANET AT ONCE.
I'M SORRY--HOW DO YOU KNOW THIS?
YOU HAVE TO BELIEVE ME! I--
SHE'S ONE OF THE MOST TALENTED ELECTRICAL ENGINEERS I'VE EVER MET, WONDER WOMAN.
IF SHE SEES A PATTERN HERE, THERE'S A PATTERN.
I'VE STUDIED THINGS LIKE THIS--FROM OUT HERE, I CAN SEE THE WHOLE PATTERN. IT'S RIGHT THERE IN THE WAY THEY'RE ORGANIZING THEMSELVES AROUND THE EARTH.
...
VERY WELL. WHAT DO WE DO ABOUT IT? CAN WE DISRUPT THE PATTERN?
YES. IF WE CAN DESTROY THIRTY-SIX PERCENT OF THE NODES, THEY WON'T BE ABLE TO COVER THE ENTIRE PLANET. THE SIGNAL WILL DEGRADE.
THIRTY-SIX PERCENT...

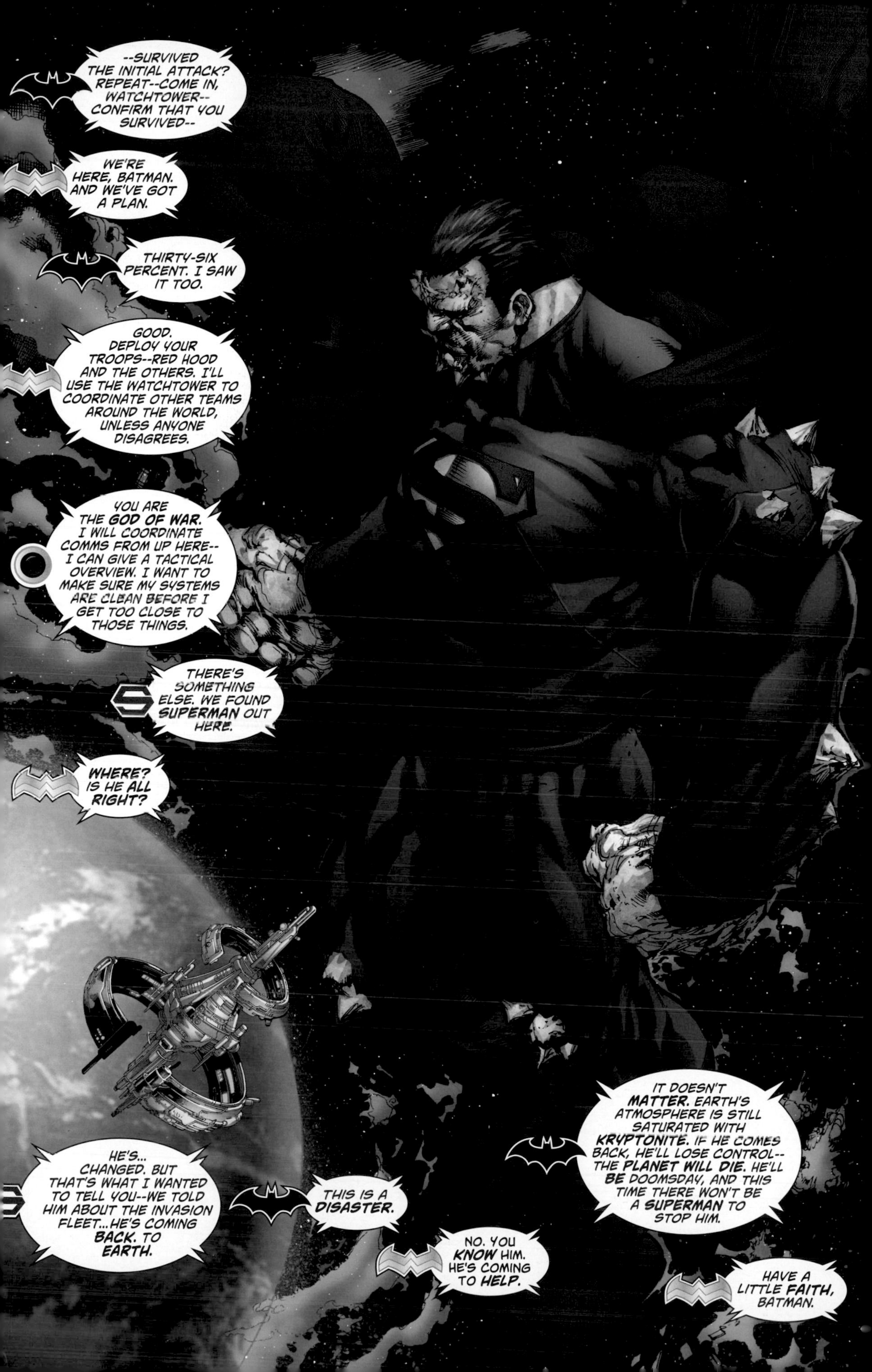

--SURVIVED THE INITIAL ATTACK? REPEAT--COME IN, WATCHTOWER-- CONFIRM THAT YOU SURVIVED--
WE'RE HERE, BATMAN. AND WE'VE GOT A PLAN.
THIRTY-SIX PERCENT. I SAW IT TOO.
GOOD. DEPLOY YOUR TROOPS--RED HOOD AND THE OTHERS. I'LL USE THE WATCHTOWER TO COORDINATE OTHER TEAMS AROUND THE WORLD, UNLESS ANYONE DISAGREES.
YOU ARE THE GOD OF WAR. I WILL COORDINATE COMMS FROM UP HERE-- I CAN GIVE A TACTICAL OVERVIEW. I WANT TO MAKE SURE MY SYSTEMS ARE CLEAN BEFORE I GET TOO CLOSE TO THOSE THINGS.
THERE'S SOMETHING ELSE. WE FOUND SUPERMAN OUT HERE.
WHERE? IS HE ALL RIGHT?
HE'S... CHANGED. BUT THAT'S WHAT I WANTED TO TELL YOU--WE TOLD HIM ABOUT THE INVASION FLEET...HE'S COMING BACK. TO EARTH.
THIS IS A DISASTER.
NO. YOU KNOW HIM. HE'S COMING TO HELP.
IT DOESN'T MATTER. EARTH'S ATMOSPHERE IS STILL SATURATED WITH KRYPTONITE. IF HE COMES BACK, HE'LL LOSE CONTROL-- THE PLANET WILL DIE. HE'LL BE DOOMSDAY, AND THIS TIME THERE WON'T BE A SUPERMAN TO STOP HIM.
HAVE A LITTLE FAITH, BATMAN.

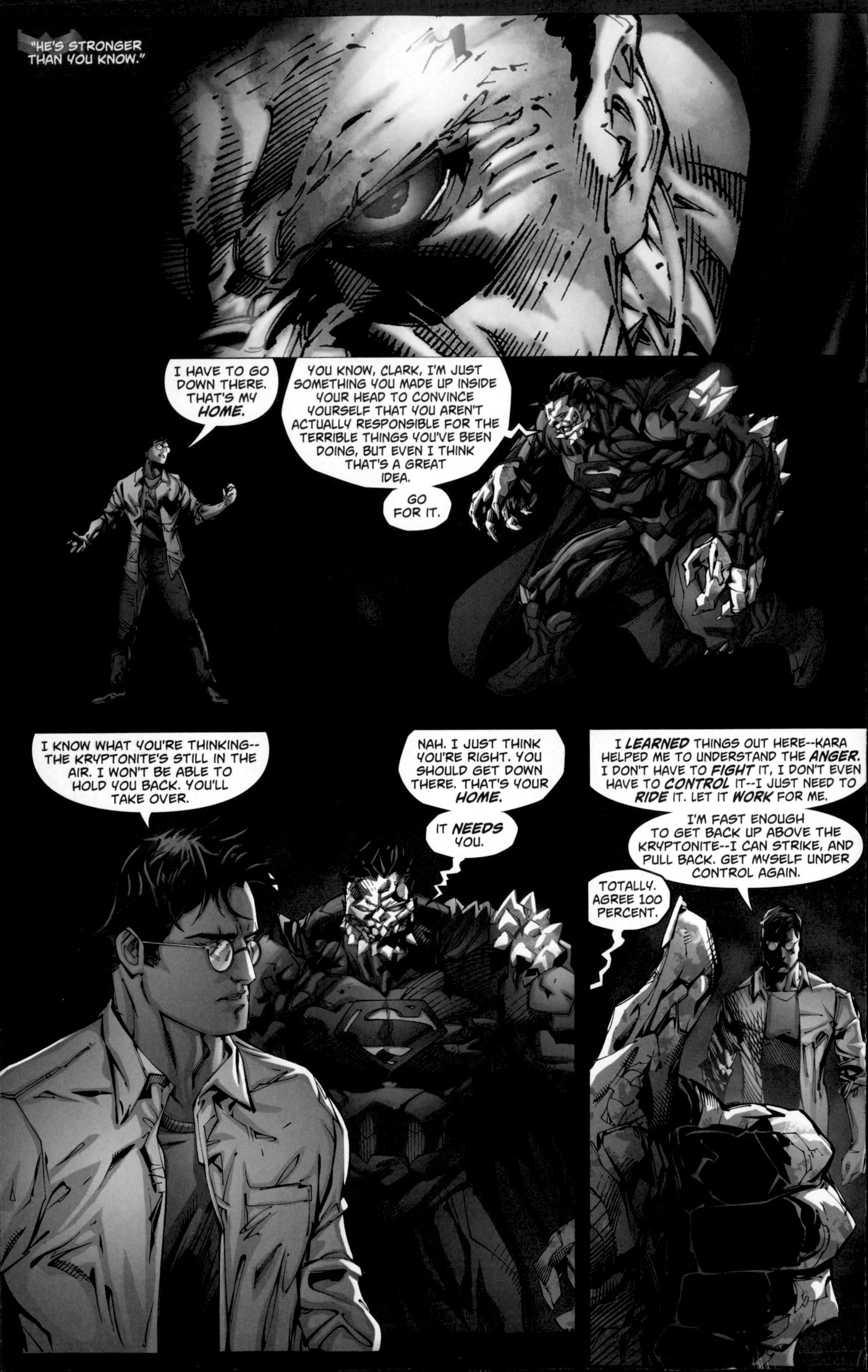
"HE'S STRONGER THAN YOU KNOW."
I HAVE TO GO DOWN THERE. THAT'S MY HOME.
YOU KNOW, CLARK, I'M JUST SOMETHING YOU MADE UP INSIDE YOUR HEAD TO CONVINCE YOURSELF THAT YOU AREN'T ACTUALLY RESPONSIBLE FOR THE TERRIBLE THINGS YOU'VE BEEN DOING, BUT EVEN I THINK THAT'S A GREAT IDEA.
GO FOR IT.
I KNOW WHAT YOU'RE THINKING-- THE KRYPTONITE'S STILL IN THE AIR. I WON'T BE ABLE TO HOLD YOU BACK. YOU'LL TAKE OVER.
NAH. I JUST THINK YOU'RE RIGHT. YOU SHOULD GET DOWN THERE. THAT'S YOUR HOME.
IT NEEDS YOU.
I LEARNED THINGS OUT HERE--KARA HELPED ME TO UNDERSTAND THE ANGER. I DON'T HAVE TO FIGHT IT, I DON'T EVEN HAVE TO CONTROL IT--I JUST NEED TO RIDE IT. LET IT WORK FOR ME.
I'M FAST ENOUGH TO GET BACK UP ABOVE THE KRYPTONITE--I CAN STRIKE, AND PULL BACK. GET MYSELF UNDER CONTROL AGAIN.
TOTALLY. AGREE 100 PERCENT.

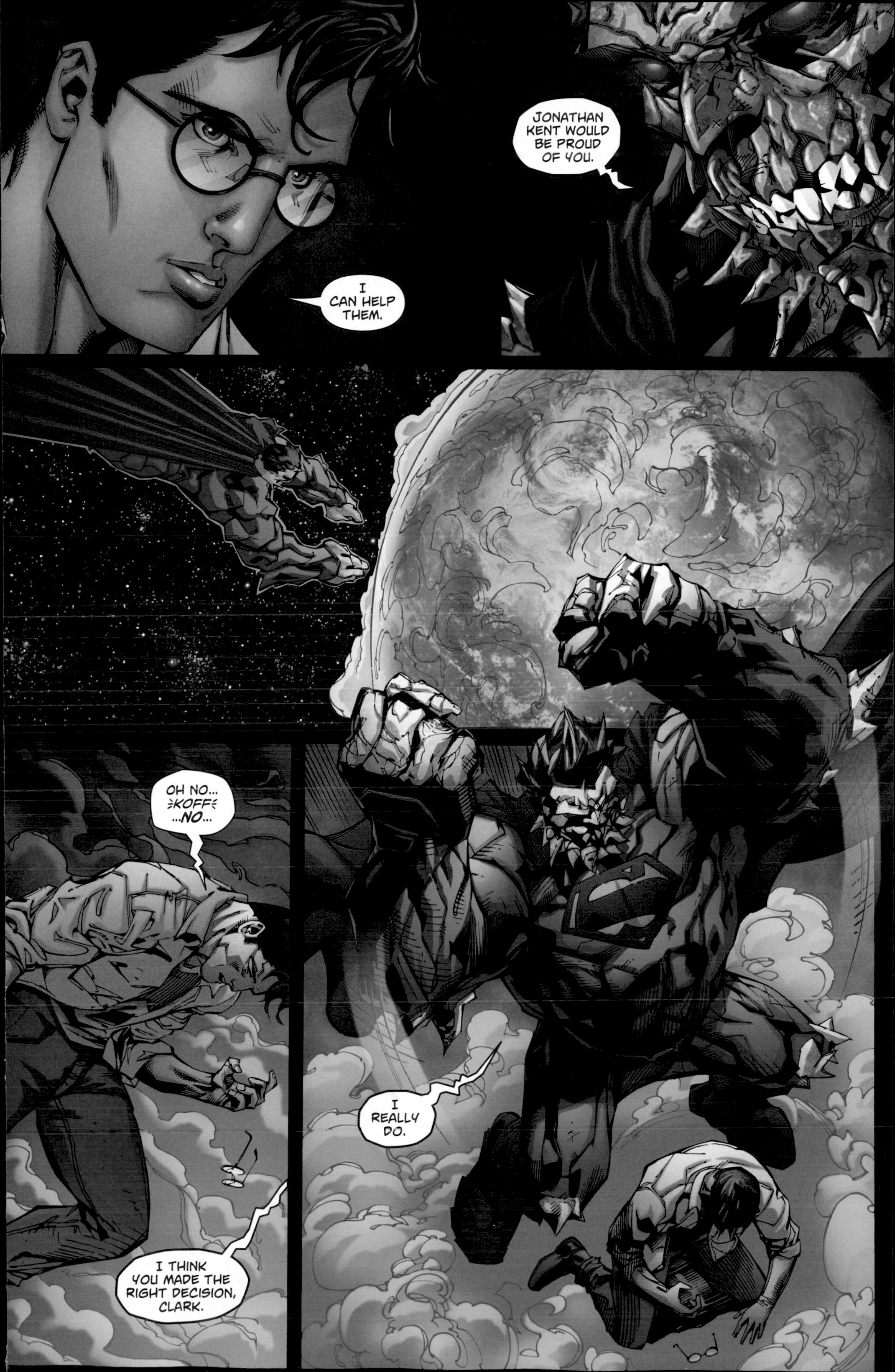
I CAN HELP THEM.
JONATHAN KENT WOULD BE PROUD OF YOU.
OH NO... ⁼KOFF⁼ ...NO...
I THINK YOU MADE THE RIGHT DECISION, CLARK.
I REALLY DO.

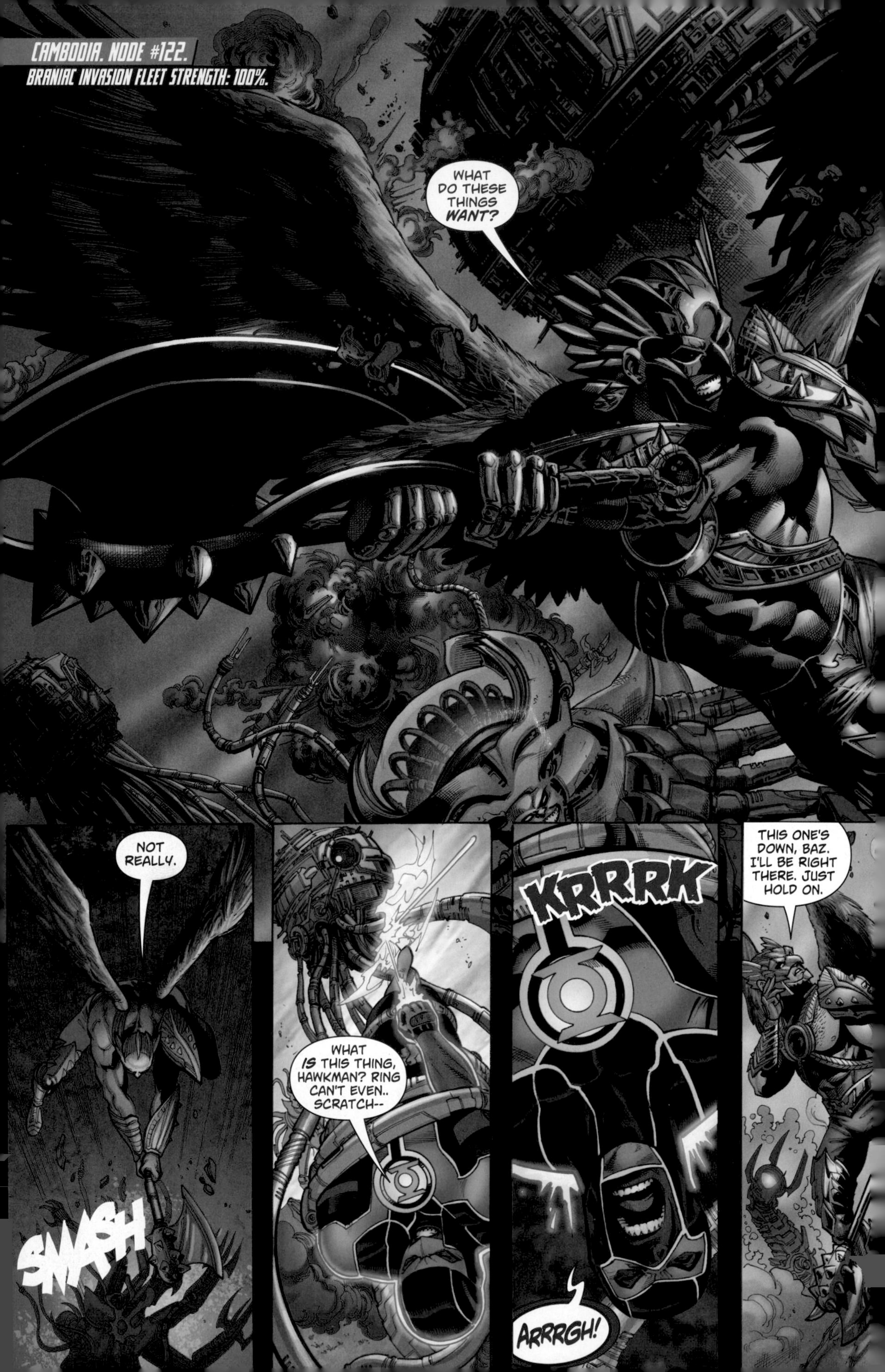
CAMBODIA. NODE #122.
BRANIAC INVASION FLEET STRENGTH: 100%.
WHAT DO THESE THINGS WANT?
NOT REALLY.
SMASH
WHAT IS THIS THING, HAWKMAN? RING CAN'T EVEN.. SCRATCH--
KRRRK
ARRRGH!
THIS ONE'S DOWN, BAZ. I'LL BE RIGHT THERE. JUST HOLD ON.

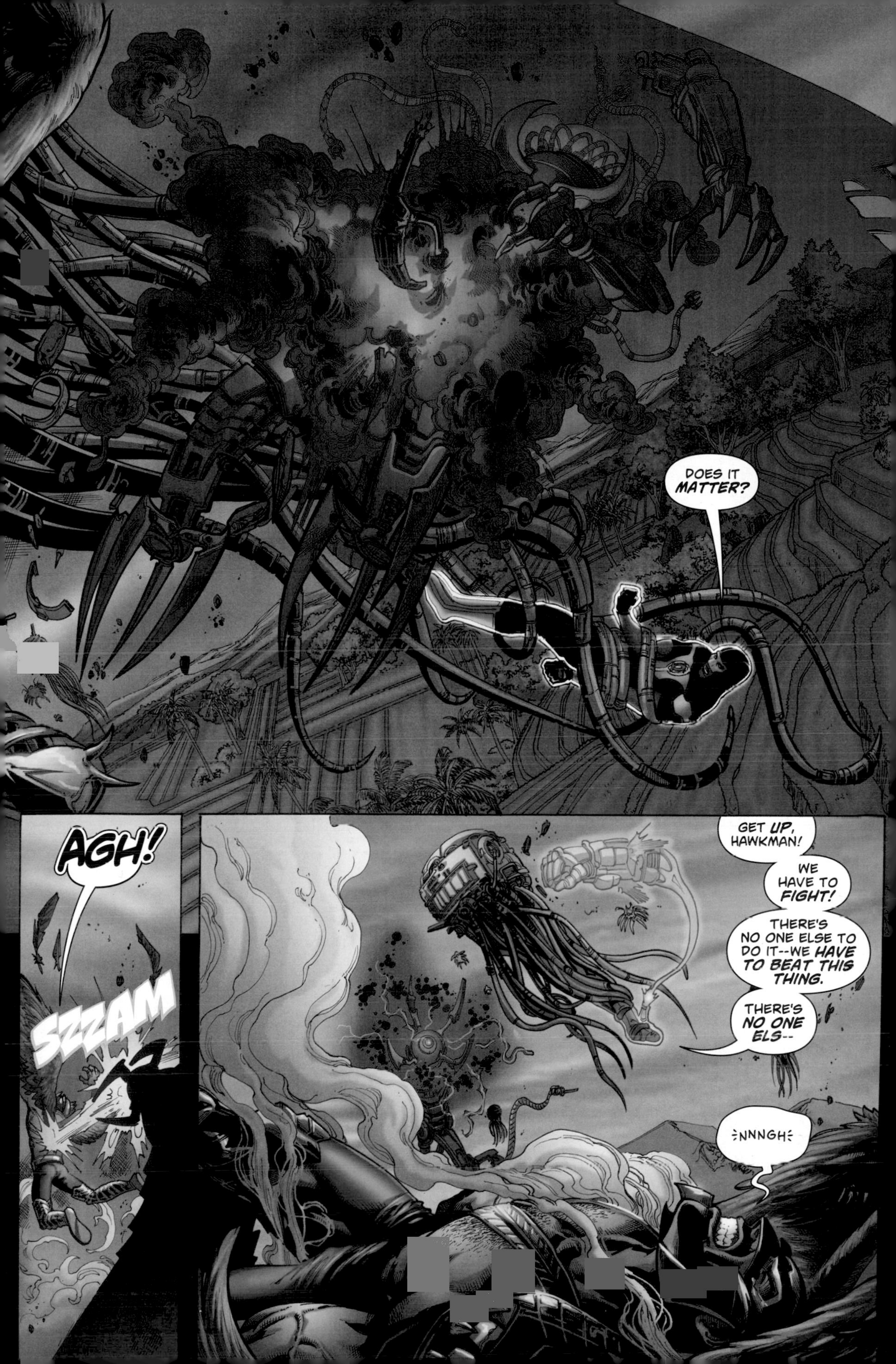
DOES IT MATTER?
AGH!
SZZAM
GET UP, HAWKMAN!
WE HAVE TO FIGHT!
THERE'S NO ONE ELSE TO DO IT--WE HAVE TO BEAT THIS THING.
THERE'S NO ONE ELS--
NNNGH

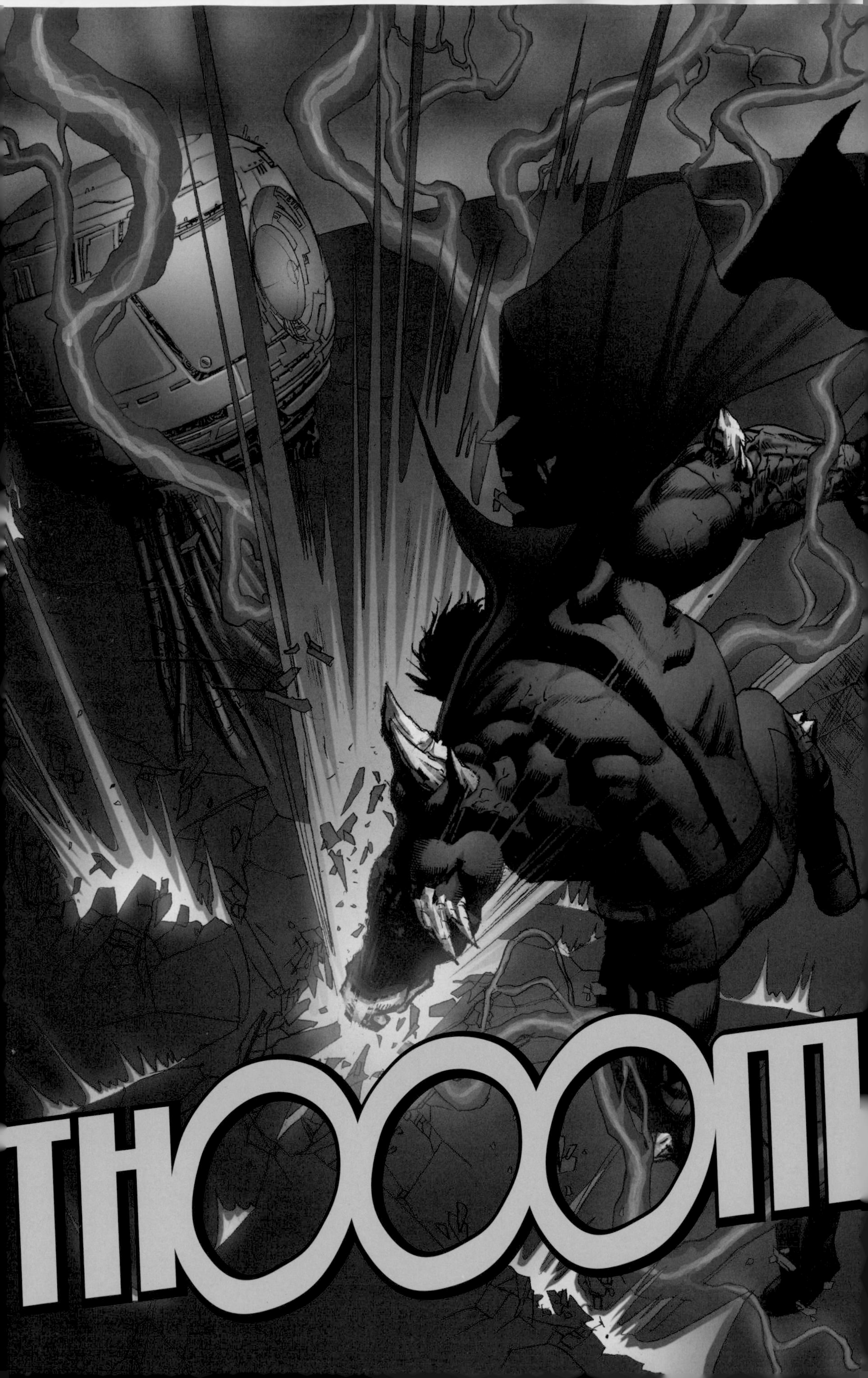
THOOOM

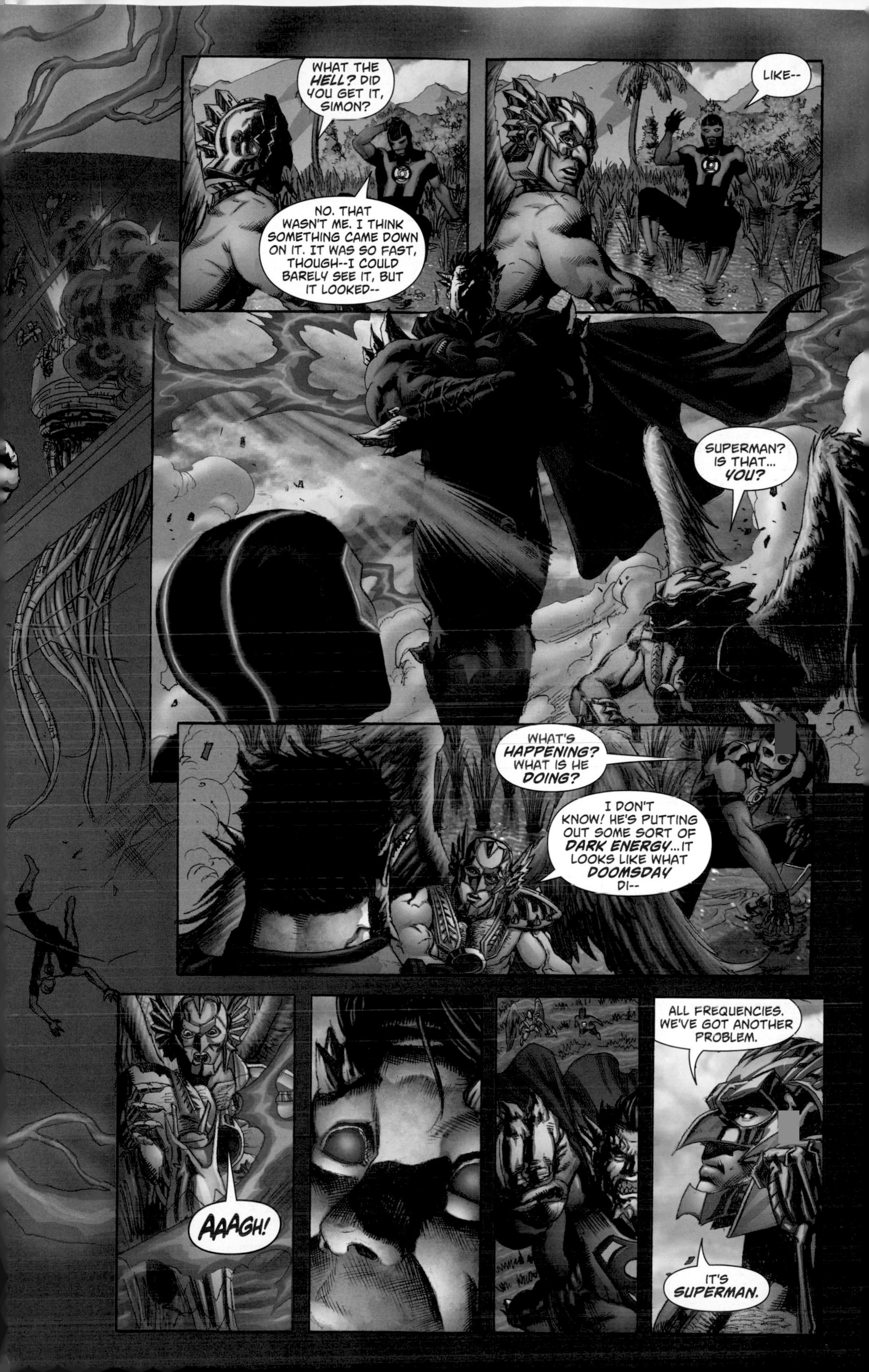
WHAT THE HELL? DID YOU GET IT, SIMON?
NO. THAT WASN'T ME. I THINK SOMETHING CAME DOWN ON IT. IT WAS SO FAST, THOUGH--I COULD BARELY SEE IT, BUT IT LOOKED--
LIKE--
SUPERMAN? IS THAT... YOU?
WHAT'S HAPPENING? WHAT IS HE DOING?
I DON'T KNOW! HE'S PUTTING OUT SOME SORT OF DARK ENERGY... IT LOOKS LIKE WHAT DOOMSDAY DI--
AAAGH!
ALL FREQUENCIES. WE'VE GOT ANOTHER PROBLEM.
IT'S SUPERMAN.

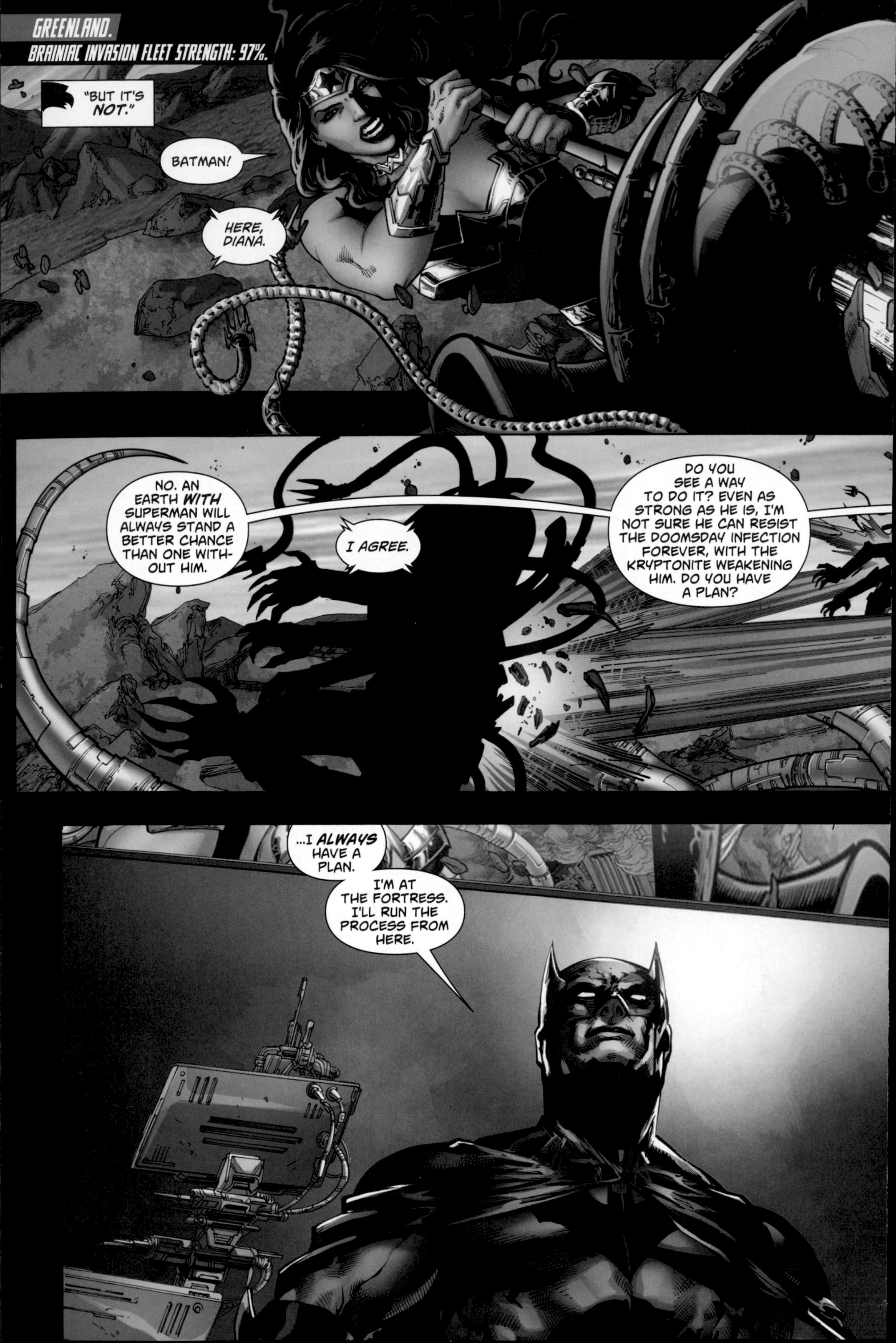
GREENLAND.
BRAINIAC INVASION FLEET STRENGTH: 97%.
"BUT IT'S NOT."
BATMAN!
HERE, DIANA.
NO. AN EARTH WITH SUPERMAN WILL ALWAYS STAND A BETTER CHANCE THAN ONE WITHOUT HIM.
I AGREE.
DO YOU SEE A WAY TO DO IT? EVEN AS STRONG AS HE IS, I'M NOT SURE HE CAN RESIST THE DOOMSDAY INFECTION FOREVER, WITH THE KRYPTONITE WEAKENING HIM. DO YOU HAVE A PLAN?
...I ALWAYS HAVE A PLAN.
I'M AT THE FORTRESS. I'LL RUN THE PROCESS FROM HERE.

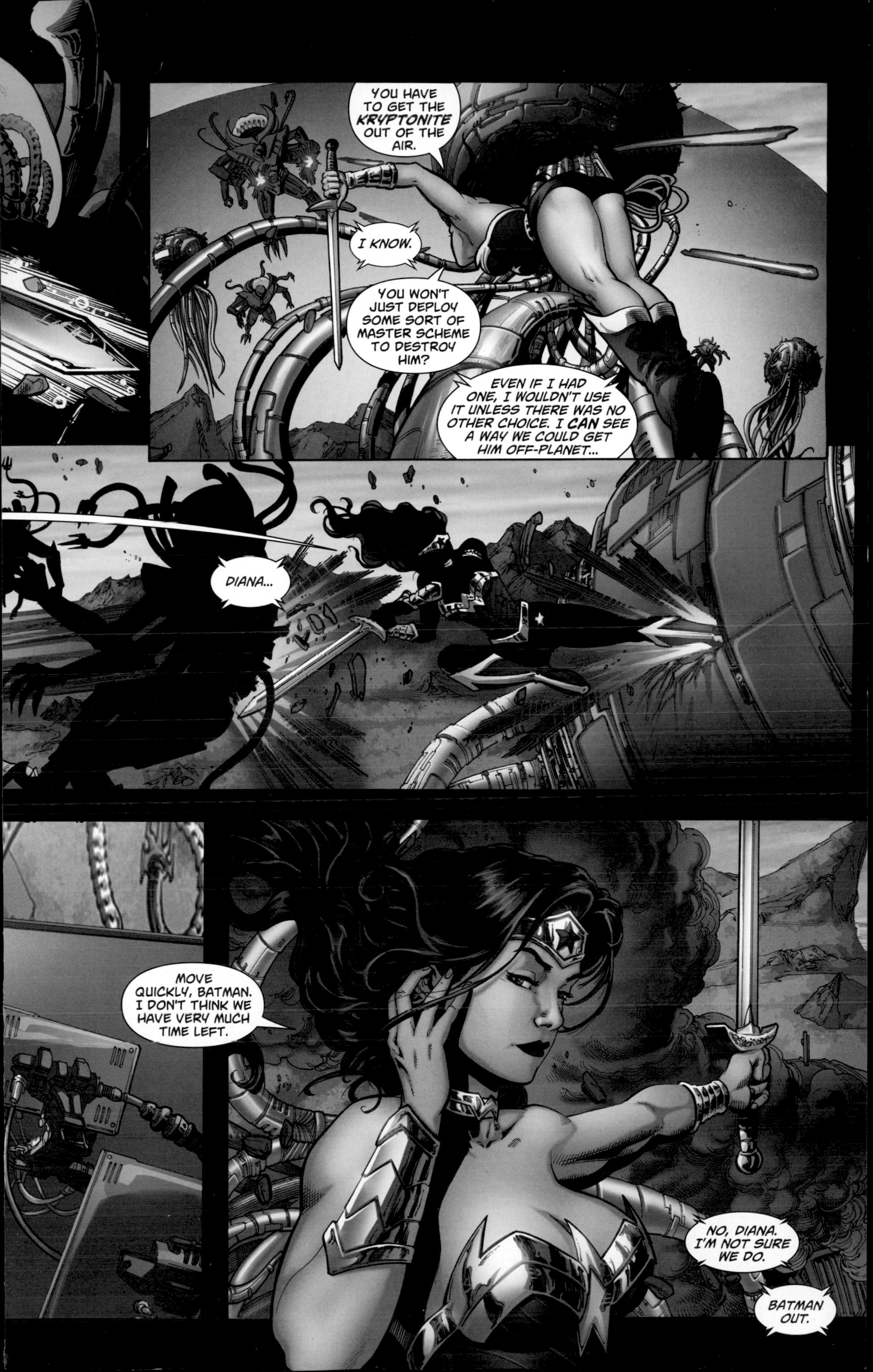
YOU HAVE TO GET THE KRYPTONITE OUT OF THE AIR.
I KNOW.
YOU WON'T JUST DEPLOY SOME SORT OF MASTER SCHEME TO DESTROY HIM?
EVEN IF I HAD ONE, I WOULDN'T USE IT UNLESS THERE WAS NO OTHER CHOICE. I CAN SEE A WAY WE COULD GET HIM OFF-PLANET...
DIANA...
MOVE QUICKLY, BATMAN. I DON'T THINK WE HAVE VERY MUCH TIME LEFT.
NO, DIANA. I'M NOT SURE WE DO.
BATMAN OUT.

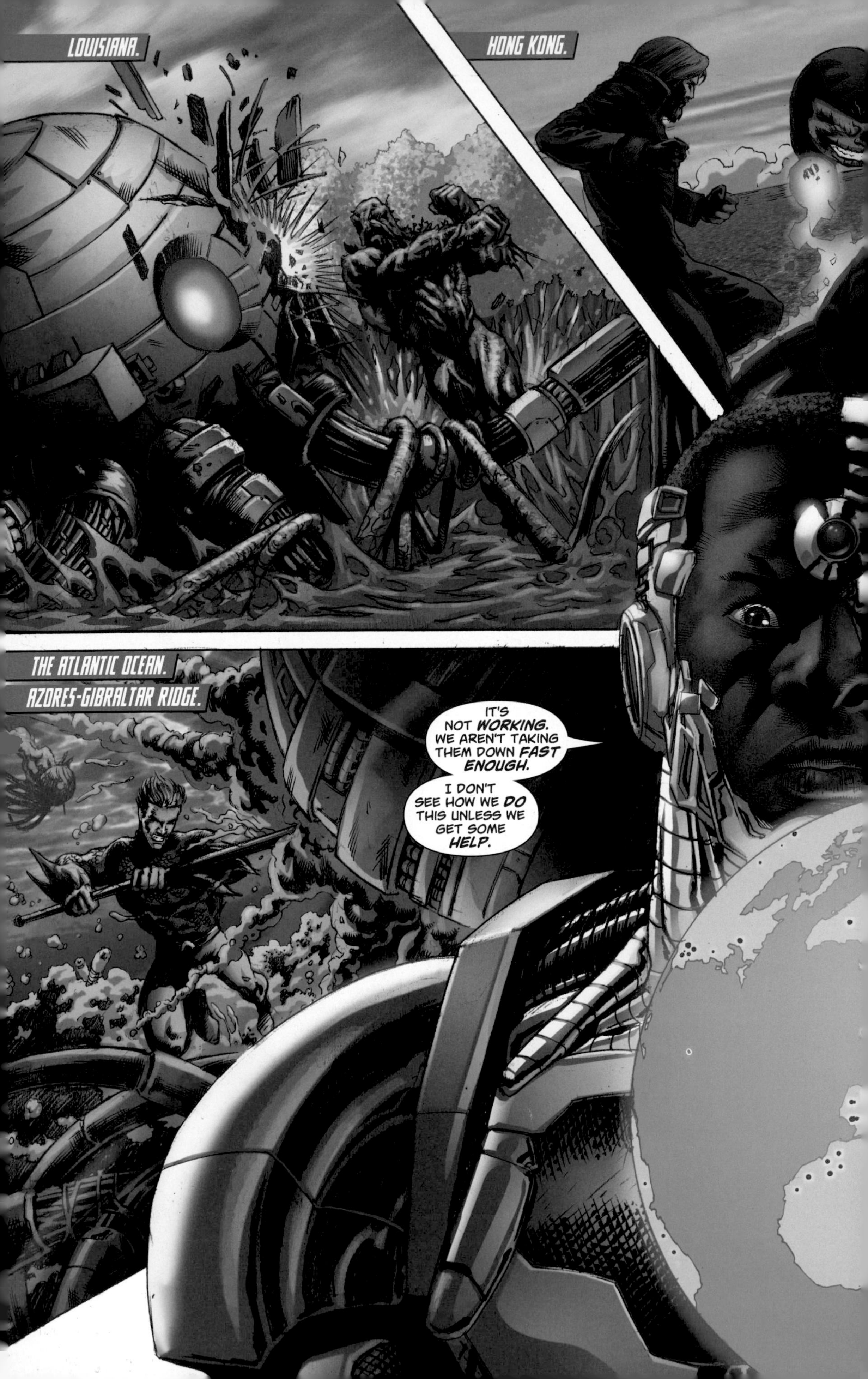
LOUISIANA.
HONG KONG.
THE ATLANTIC OCEAN.
AZORES-GIBRALTAR RIDGE.
IT'S NOT WORKING. WE AREN'T TAKING THEM DOWN FAST ENOUGH.
I DON'T SEE HOW WE DO THIS UNLESS WE GET SOME HELP.

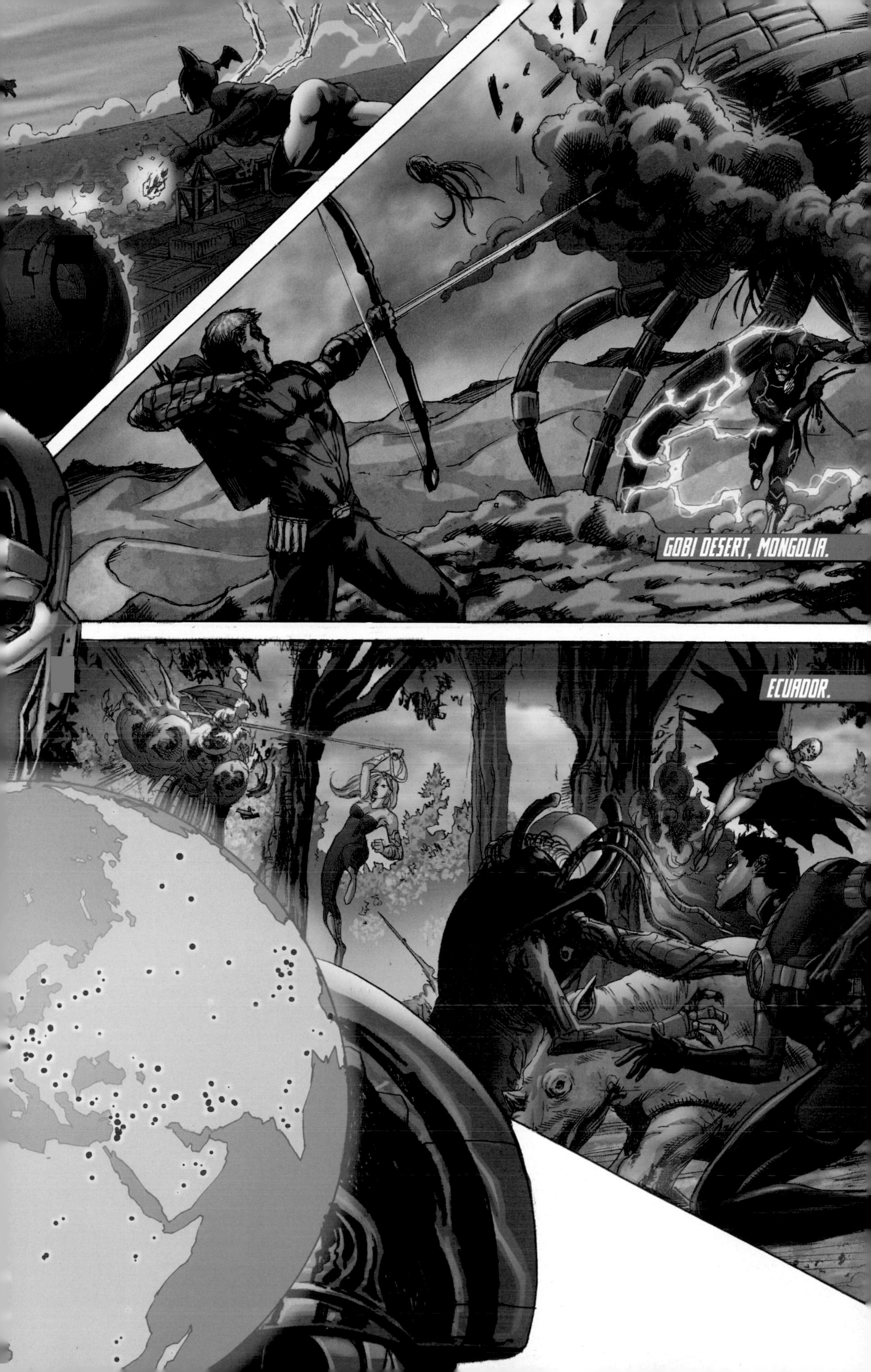
GOBI DESERT, MONGOLIA.
ECUADOR.

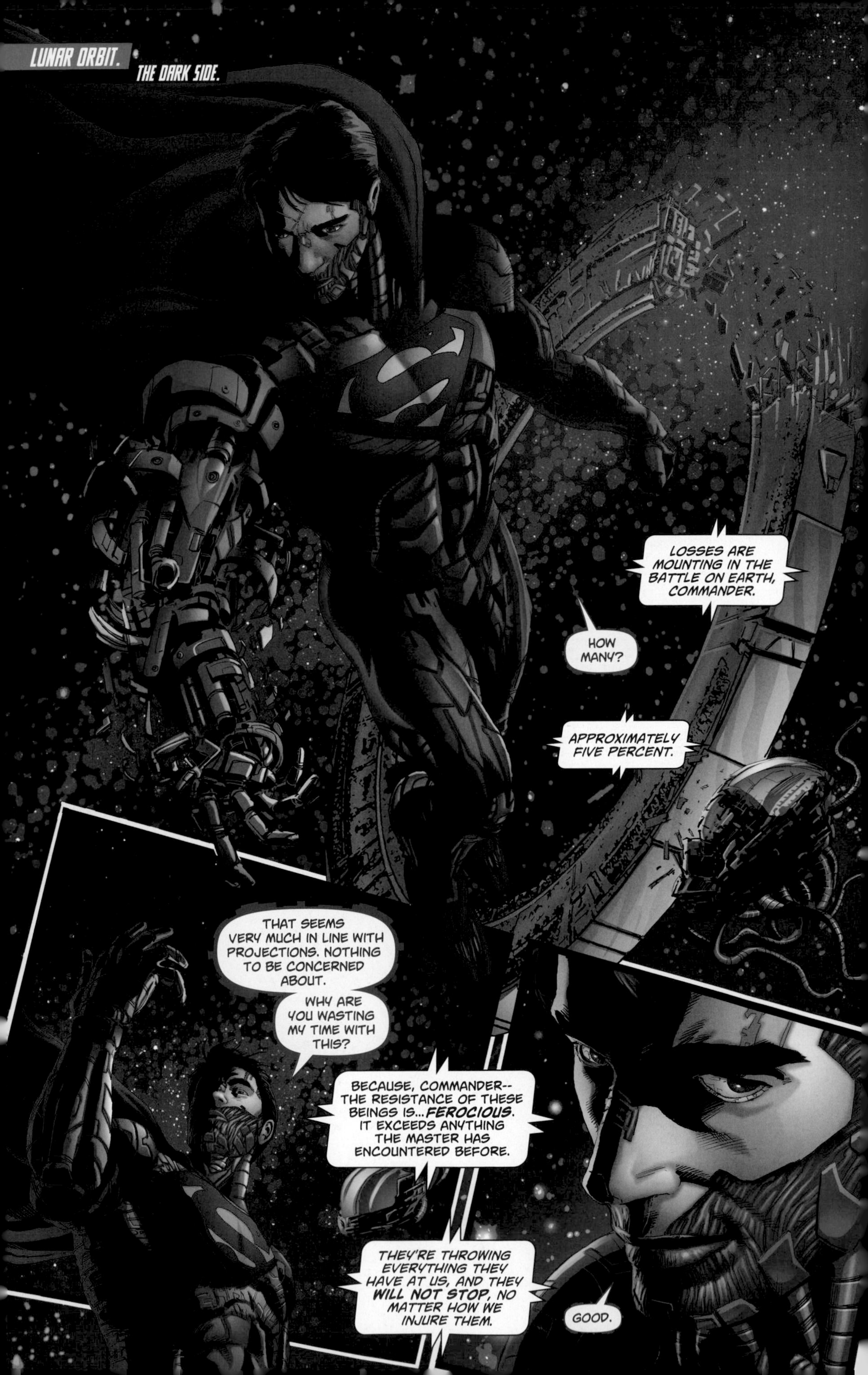
LUNAR ORBIT.
THE DARK SIDE.
LOSSES ARE MOUNTING IN THE BATTLE ON EARTH, COMMANDER.
HOW MANY?
APPROXIMATELY FIVE PERCENT.
THAT SEEMS VERY MUCH IN LINE WITH PROJECTIONS. NOTHING TO BE CONCERNED ABOUT.
WHY ARE YOU WASTING MY TIME WITH THIS?
BECAUSE, COMMANDER-- THE RESISTANCE OF THESE BEINGS IS...FEROCIOUS. IT EXCEEDS ANYTHING THE MASTER HAS ENCOUNTERED BEFORE.
THEY'RE THROWING EVERYTHING THEY HAVE AT US, AND THEY WILL NOT STOP, NO MATTER HOW WE INJURE THEM.
GOOD.

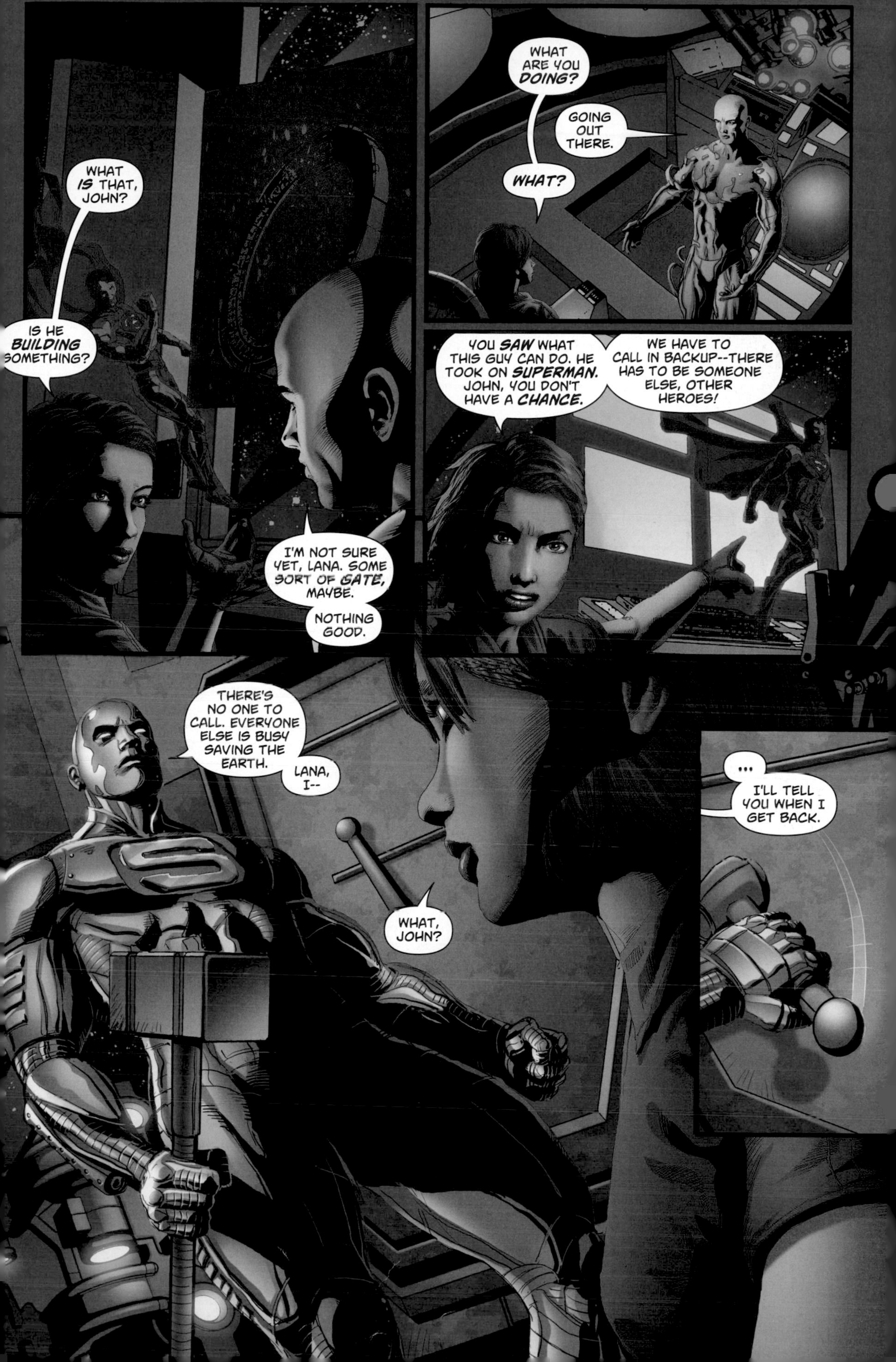

WHAT IS THAT, JOHN?
IS HE BUILDING SOMETHING?
I'M NOT SURE YET, LANA. SOME SORT OF GATE, MAYBE.
NOTHING GOOD.
WHAT ARE YOU DOING?
GOING OUT THERE.
WHAT?
YOU SAW WHAT THIS GUY CAN DO. HE TOOK ON SUPERMAN. JOHN, YOU DON'T HAVE A CHANCE.
WE HAVE TO CALL IN BACKUP--THERE HAS TO BE SOMEONE ELSE, OTHER HEROES!
THERE'S NO ONE TO CALL. EVERYONE ELSE IS BUSY SAVING THE EARTH.
LANA, I--
WHAT, JOHN?
...
I'LL TELL YOU WHEN I GET BACK.

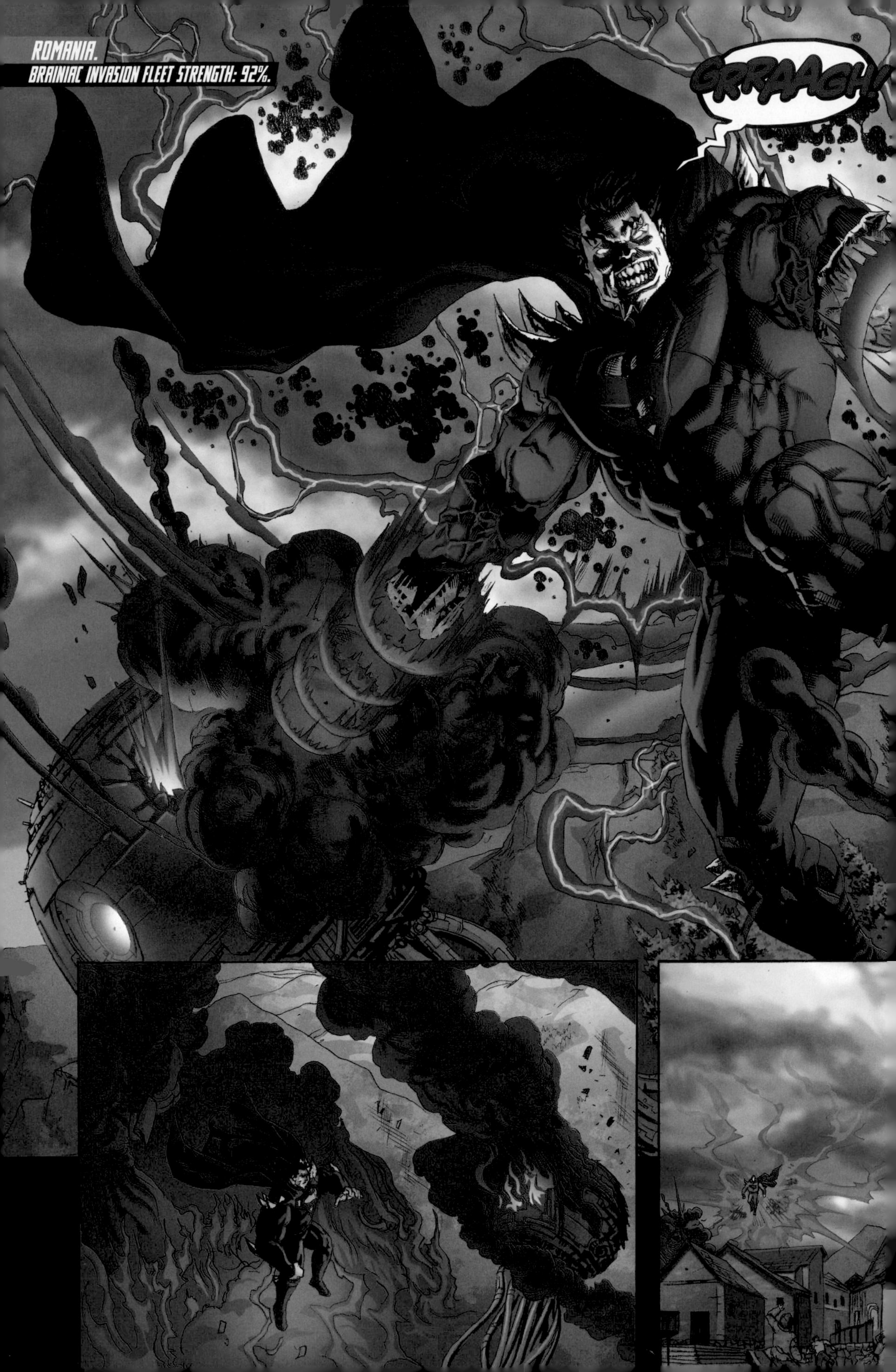
ROMANIA.
BRAINIAC INVASION FLEET STRENGTH: 92%.
GRRAAGH!

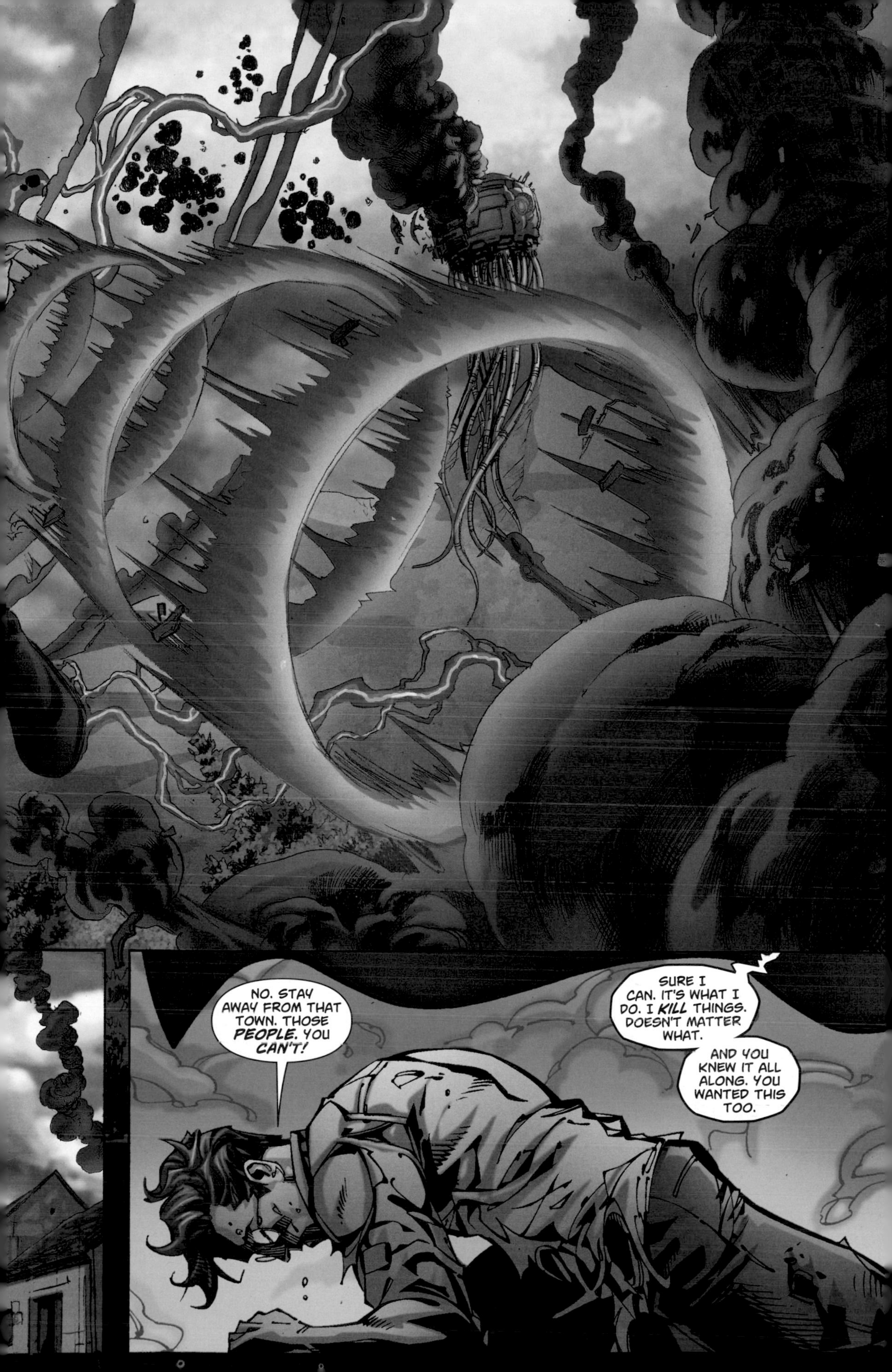
NO. STAY AWAY FROM THAT TOWN. THOSE PEOPLE. YOU CAN'T!
SURE I CAN. IT'S WHAT I DO. I KILL THINGS. DOESN'T MATTER WHAT.
AND YOU KNEW IT ALL ALONG. YOU WANTED THIS TOO.

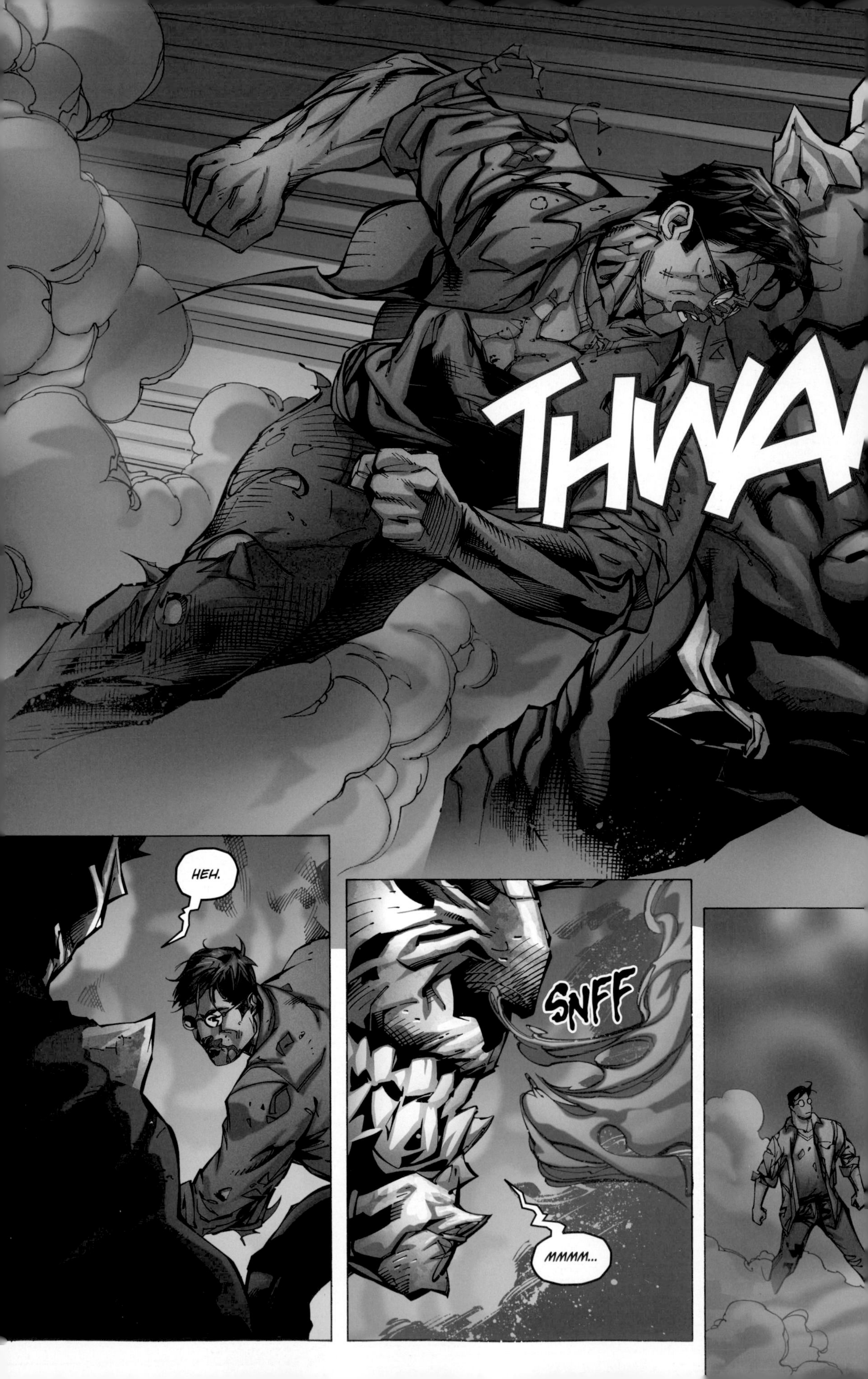
THWA
HEH.
SNFF
MMMM...

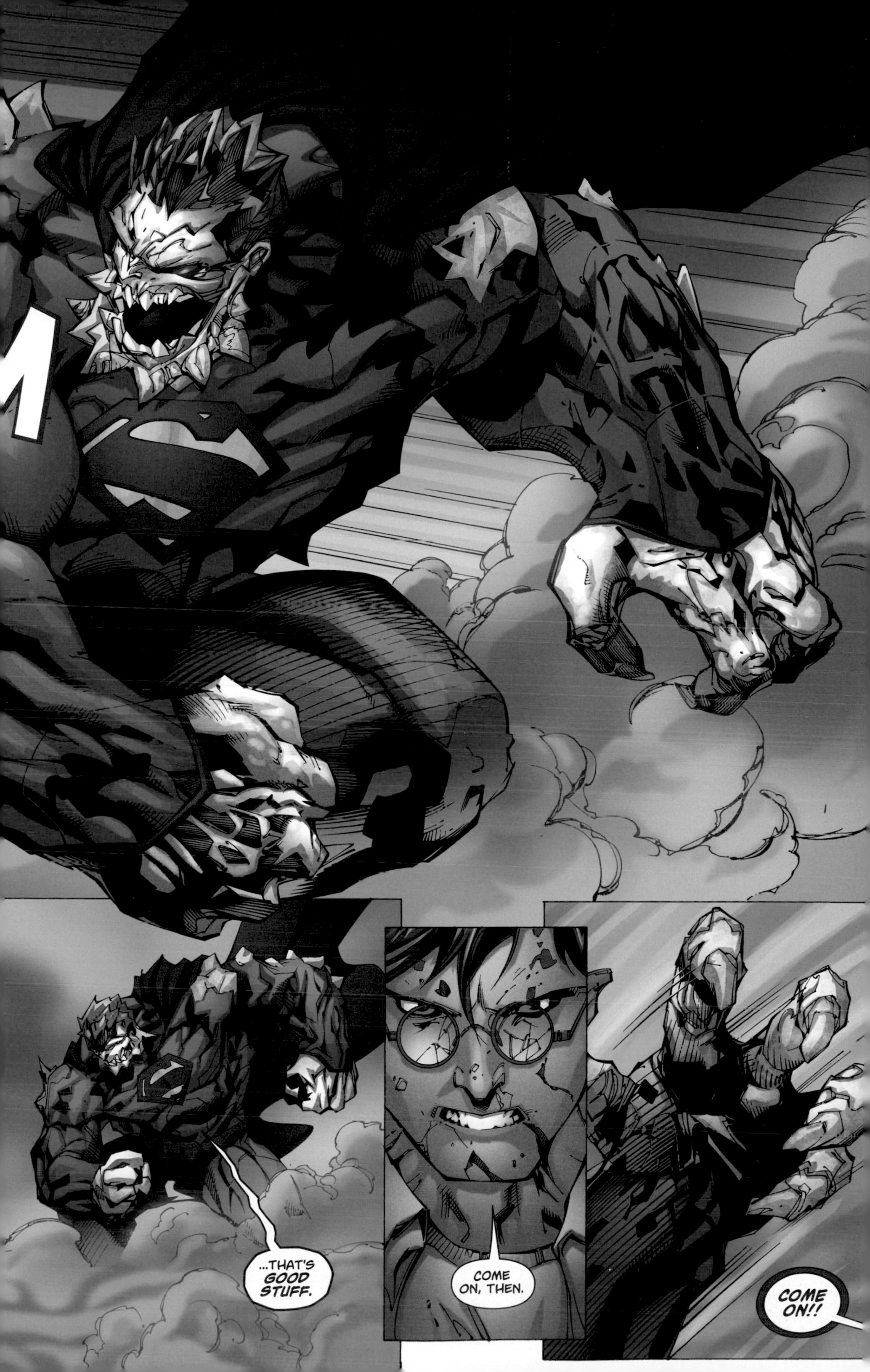
...THAT'S GOOD STUFF.
COME ON, THEN.
COME ON!!

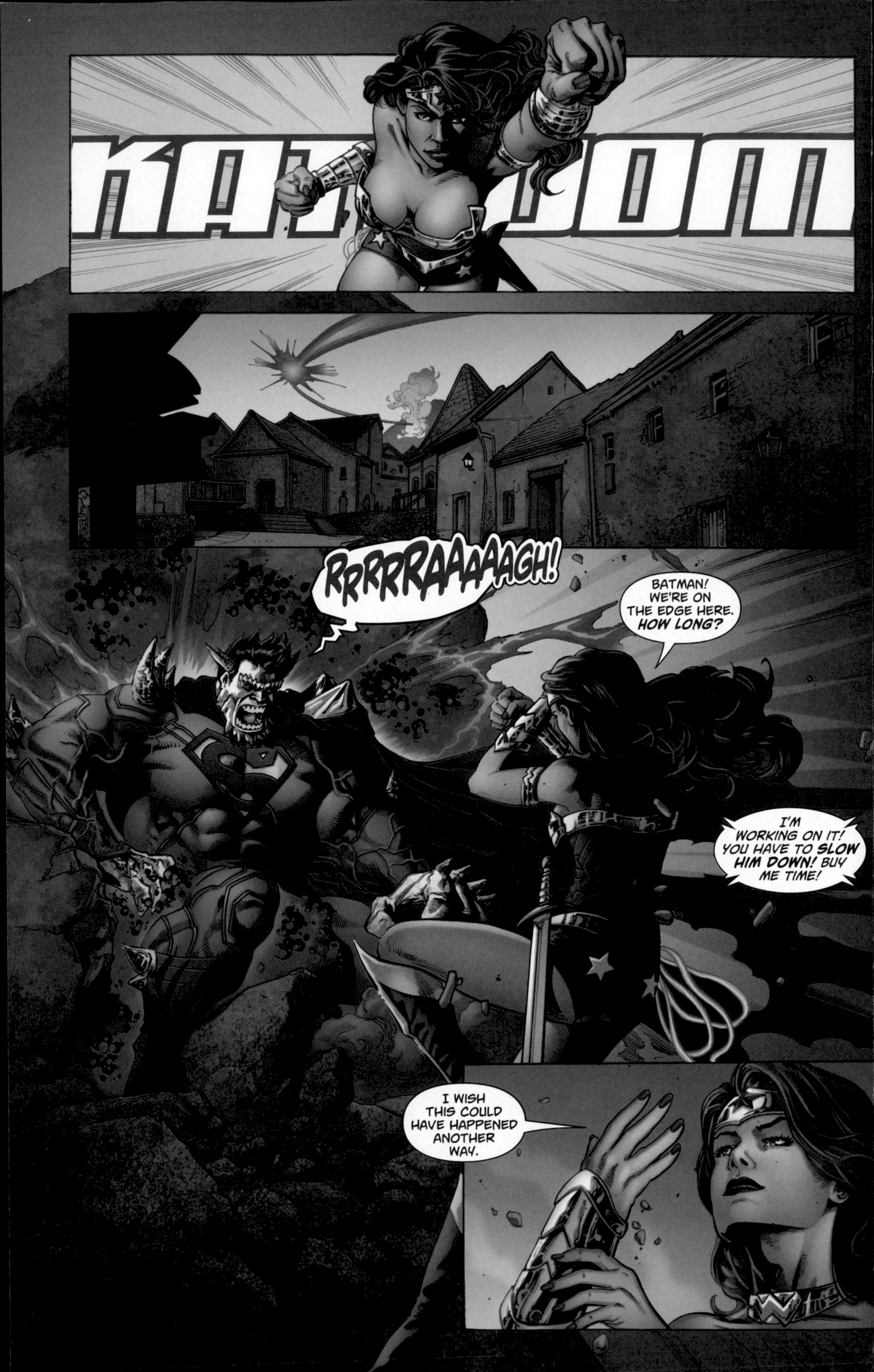
RRRRAAAAAGH!
BATMAN! WE'RE ON THE EDGE HERE. HOW LONG?
I'M WORKING ON IT! YOU HAVE TO SLOW HIM DOWN! BUY ME TIME!
I WISH THIS COULD HAVE HAPPENED ANOTHER WAY.

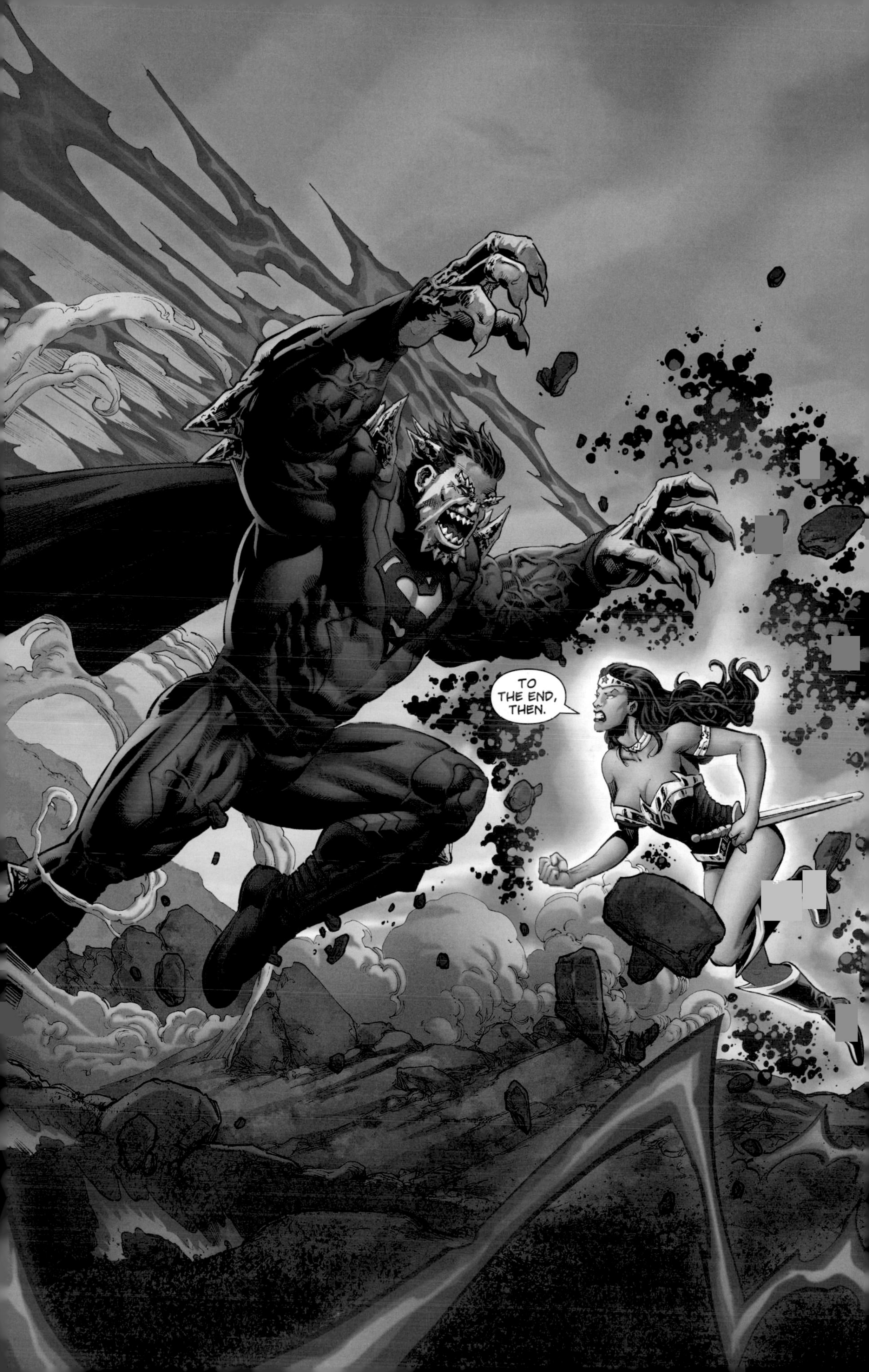
TO THE END, THEN.

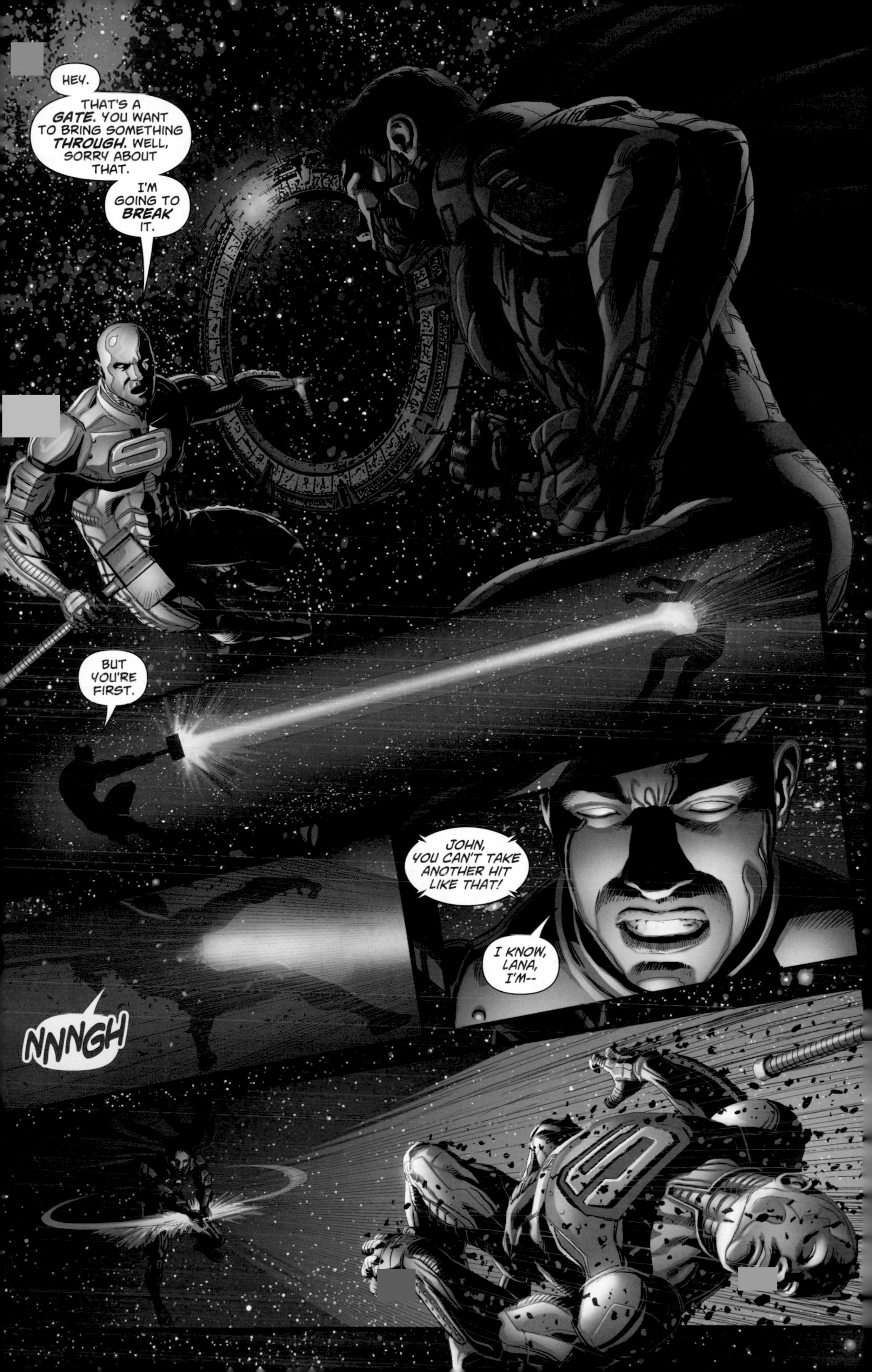

HEY.
THAT'S A GATE. YOU WANT TO BRING SOMETHING THROUGH. WELL, SORRY ABOUT THAT.
I'M GOING TO BREAK IT.
BUT YOU'RE FIRST.
JOHN, YOU CAN'T TAKE ANOTHER HIT LIKE THAT!
I KNOW, LANA, I'M--
NNNGH

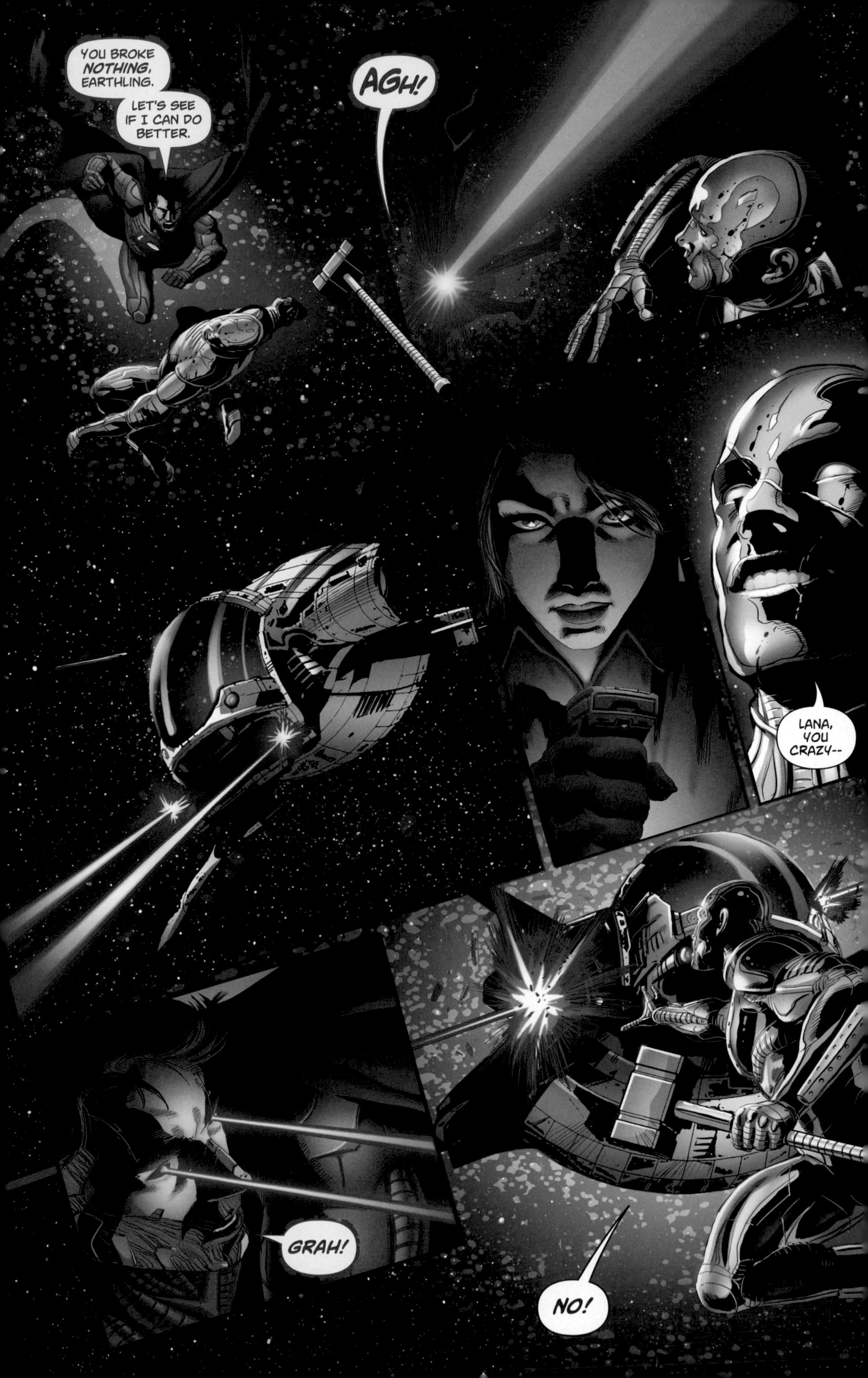
YOU BROKE *NOTHING*, EARTHLING.
LET'S SEE IF I CAN DO BETTER.
AGH!
LANA, YOU CRAZY--
GRAH!
NO!

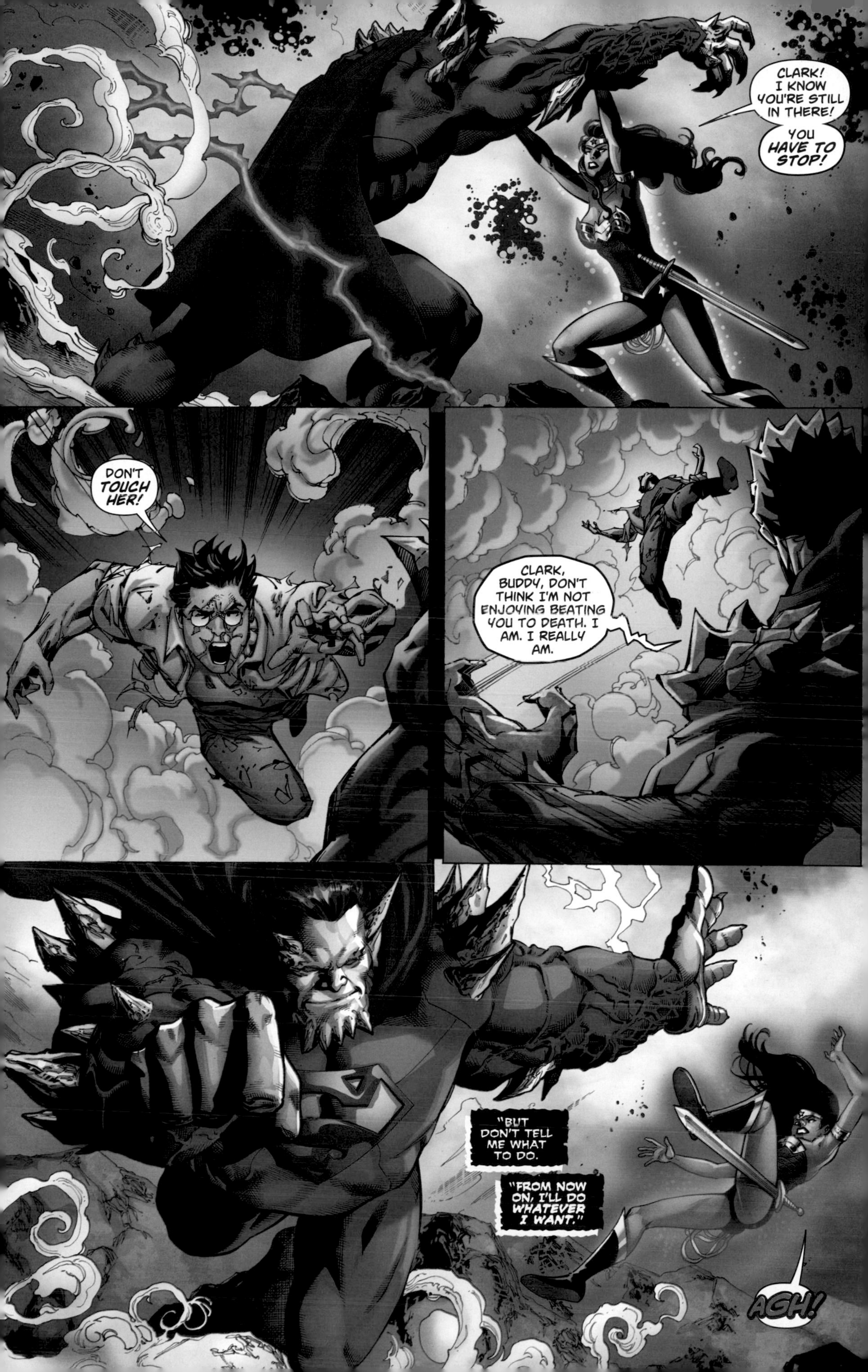
CLARK! I KNOW YOU'RE STILL IN THERE!
YOU HAVE TO STOP!
DON'T TOUCH HER!
CLARK, BUDDY, DON'T THINK I'M NOT ENJOYING BEATING YOU TO DEATH. I AM. I REALLY AM.
"BUT DON'T TELL ME WHAT TO DO.
"FROM NOW ON, I'LL DO WHATEVER I WANT."
AGH!

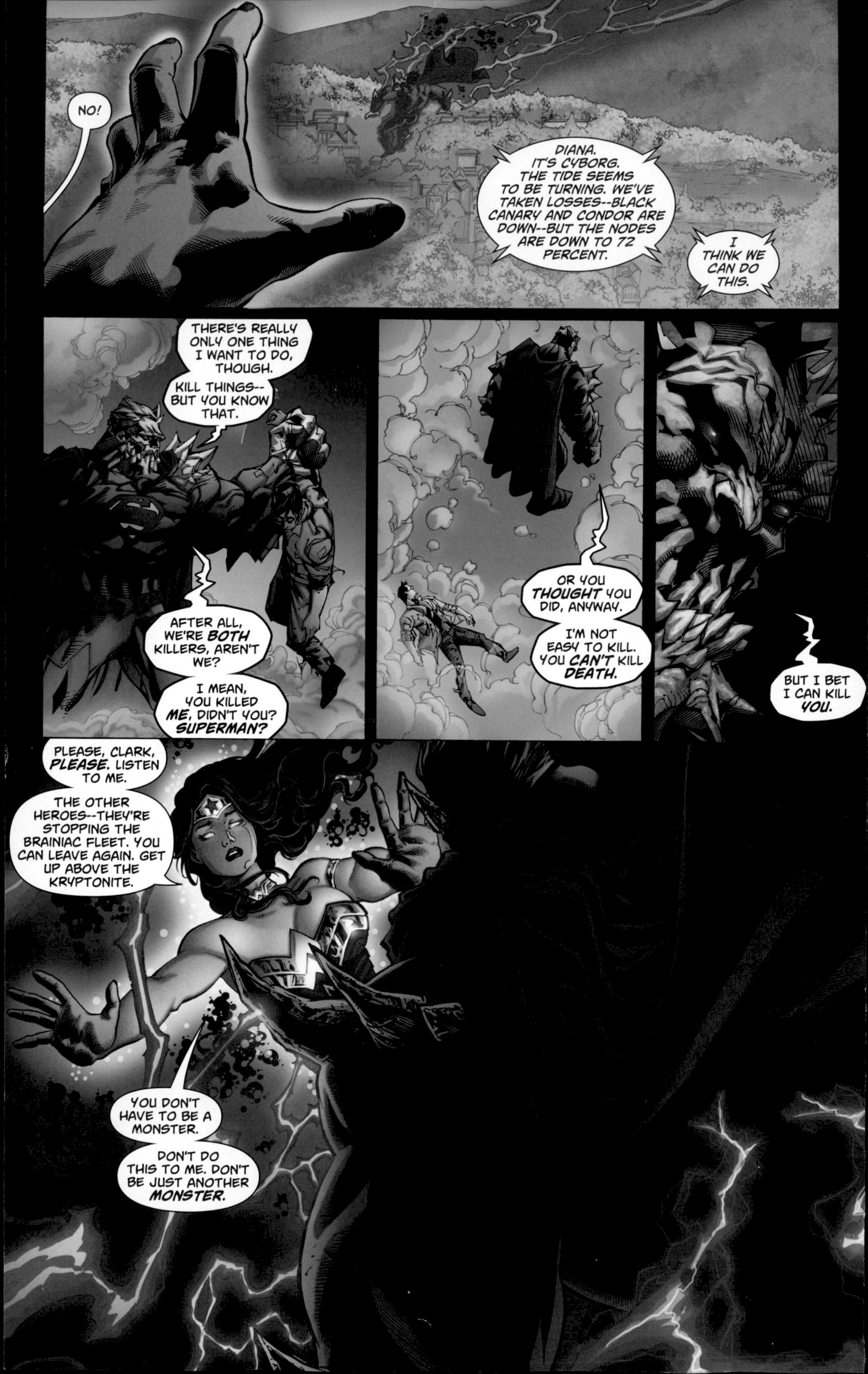
NO!
DIANA. IT'S CYBORG. THE TIDE SEEMS TO BE TURNING. WE'VE TAKEN LOSSES--BLACK CANARY AND CONDOR ARE DOWN--BUT THE NODES ARE DOWN TO 72 PERCENT.
I THINK WE CAN DO THIS.
THERE'S REALLY ONLY ONE THING I WANT TO DO, THOUGH.
KILL THINGS--BUT YOU KNOW THAT.
AFTER ALL, WE'RE **BOTH** KILLERS, AREN'T WE?
I MEAN, YOU KILLED **ME**, DIDN'T YOU? **SUPERMAN?**
OR YOU **THOUGHT** YOU DID, ANYWAY.
I'M NOT EASY TO KILL. YOU **CAN'T** KILL **DEATH**.
BUT I BET I CAN KILL **YOU**.
PLEASE, CLARK, **PLEASE**. LISTEN TO ME.
THE OTHER HEROES--THEY'RE STOPPING THE BRAINIAC FLEET. YOU CAN LEAVE AGAIN. GET UP ABOVE THE KRYPTONITE.
YOU DON'T HAVE TO BE A MONSTER.
DON'T DO THIS TO ME. DON'T BE JUST ANOTHER **MONSTER**.

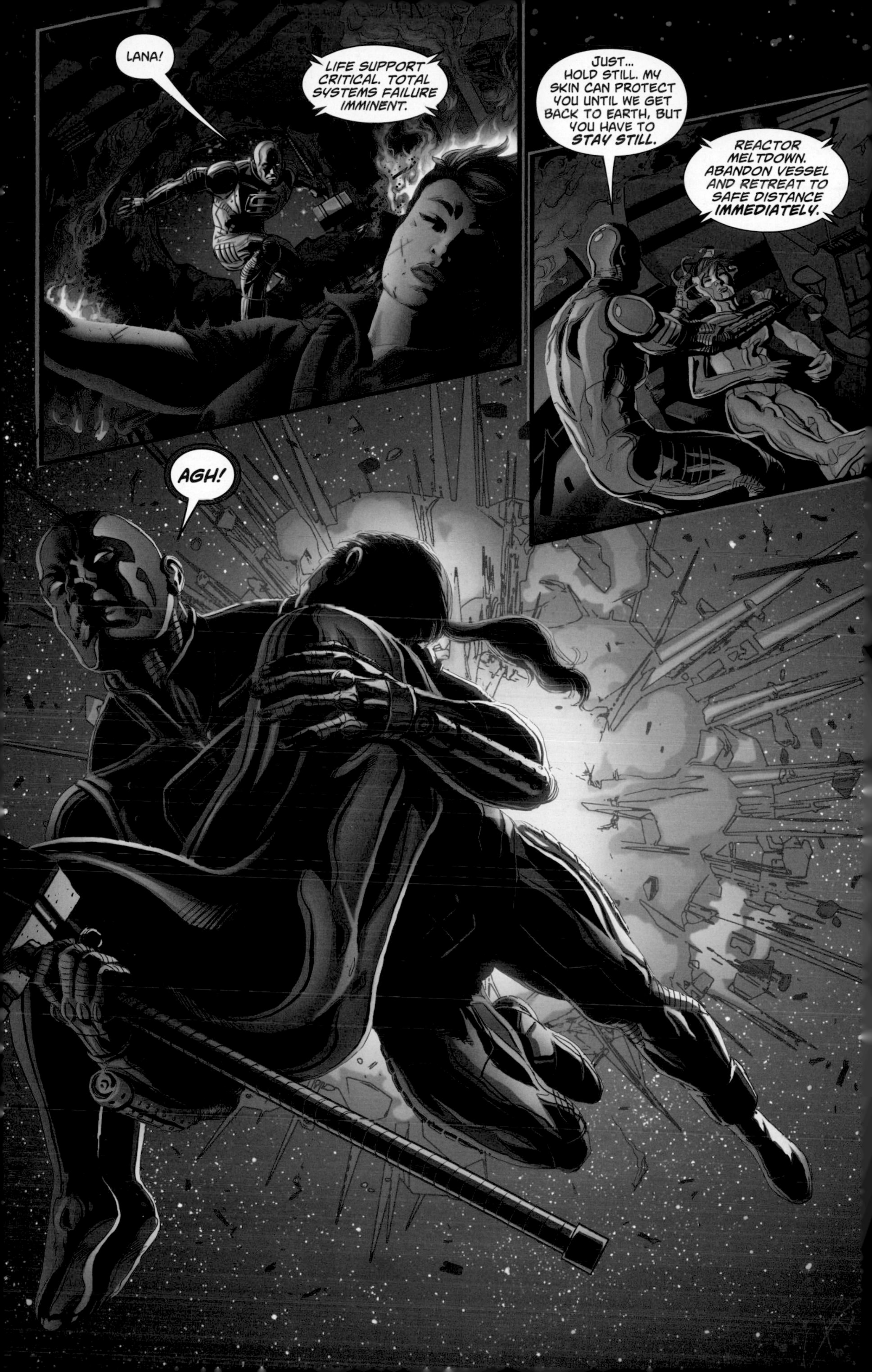
LANA!
LIFE SUPPORT CRITICAL. TOTAL SYSTEMS FAILURE IMMINENT.
JUST... HOLD STILL. MY SKIN CAN PROTECT YOU UNTIL WE GET BACK TO EARTH, BUT YOU HAVE TO STAY STILL.
REACTOR MELTDOWN. ABANDON VESSEL AND RETREAT TO SAFE DISTANCE IMMEDIATELY.
AGH!

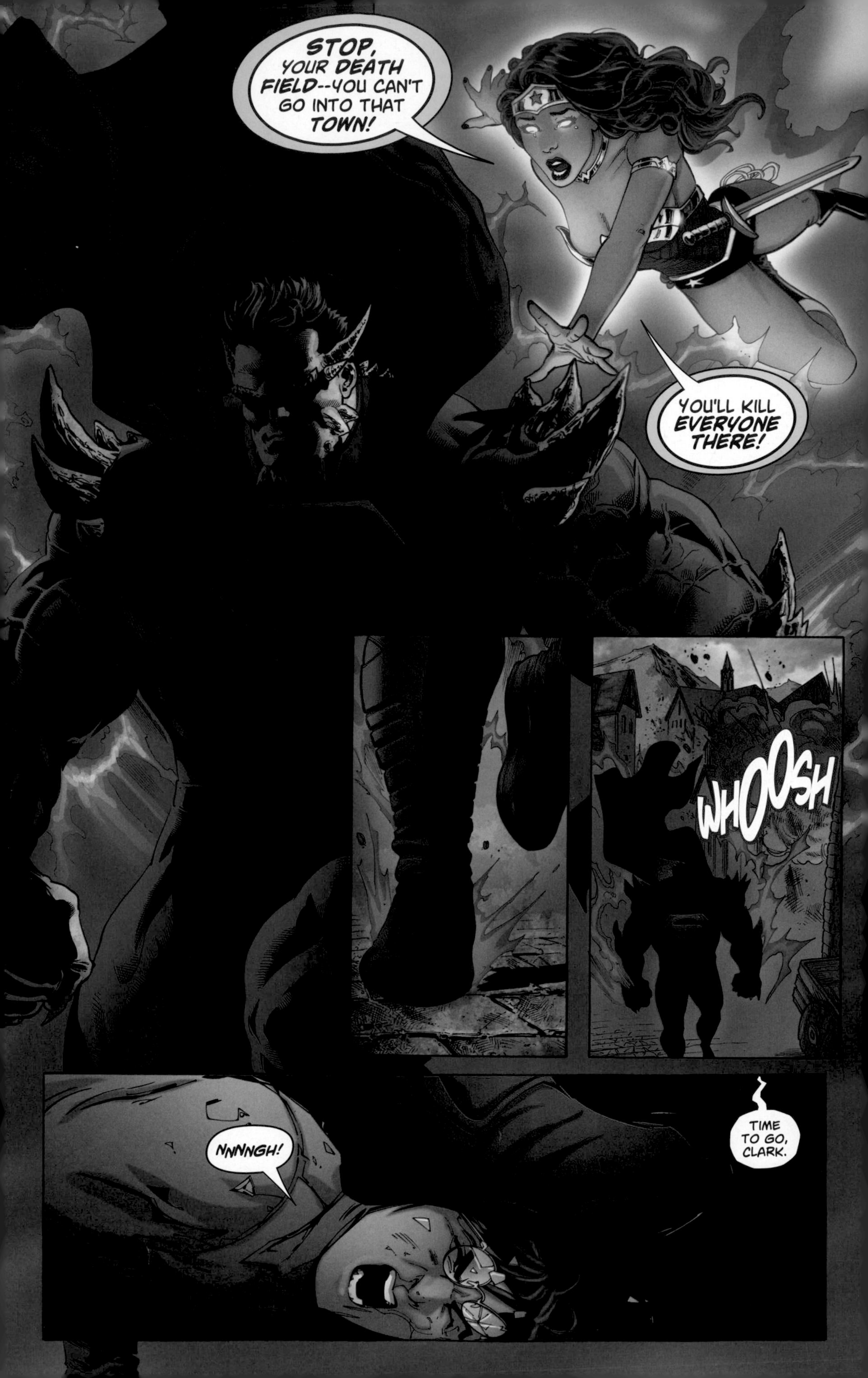
STOP, YOUR DEATH FIELD--YOU CAN'T GO INTO THAT TOWN!
YOU'LL KILL EVERYONE THERE!
WHOOSH
NNNNGH!
TIME TO GO, CLARK.

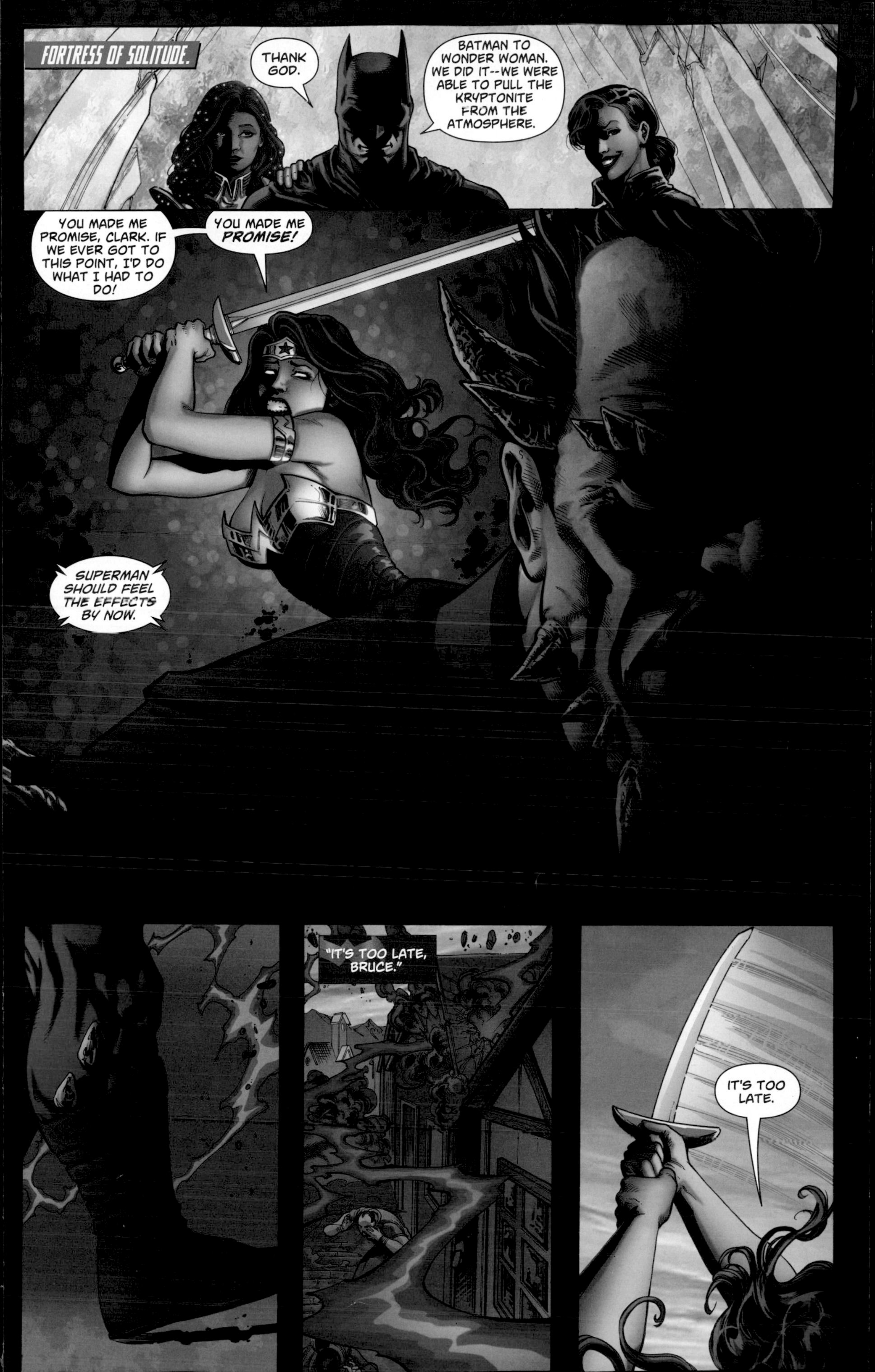
FORTRESS OF SOLITUDE.
THANK GOD.
BATMAN TO WONDER WOMAN. WE DID IT--WE WERE ABLE TO PULL THE KRYPTONITE FROM THE ATMOSPHERE.
YOU MADE ME PROMISE, CLARK. IF WE EVER GOT TO THIS POINT, I'D DO WHAT I HAD TO DO!
YOU MADE ME PROMISE!
SUPERMAN SHOULD FEEL THE EFFECTS BY NOW.
"IT'S TOO LATE, BRUCE."
IT'S TOO LATE.

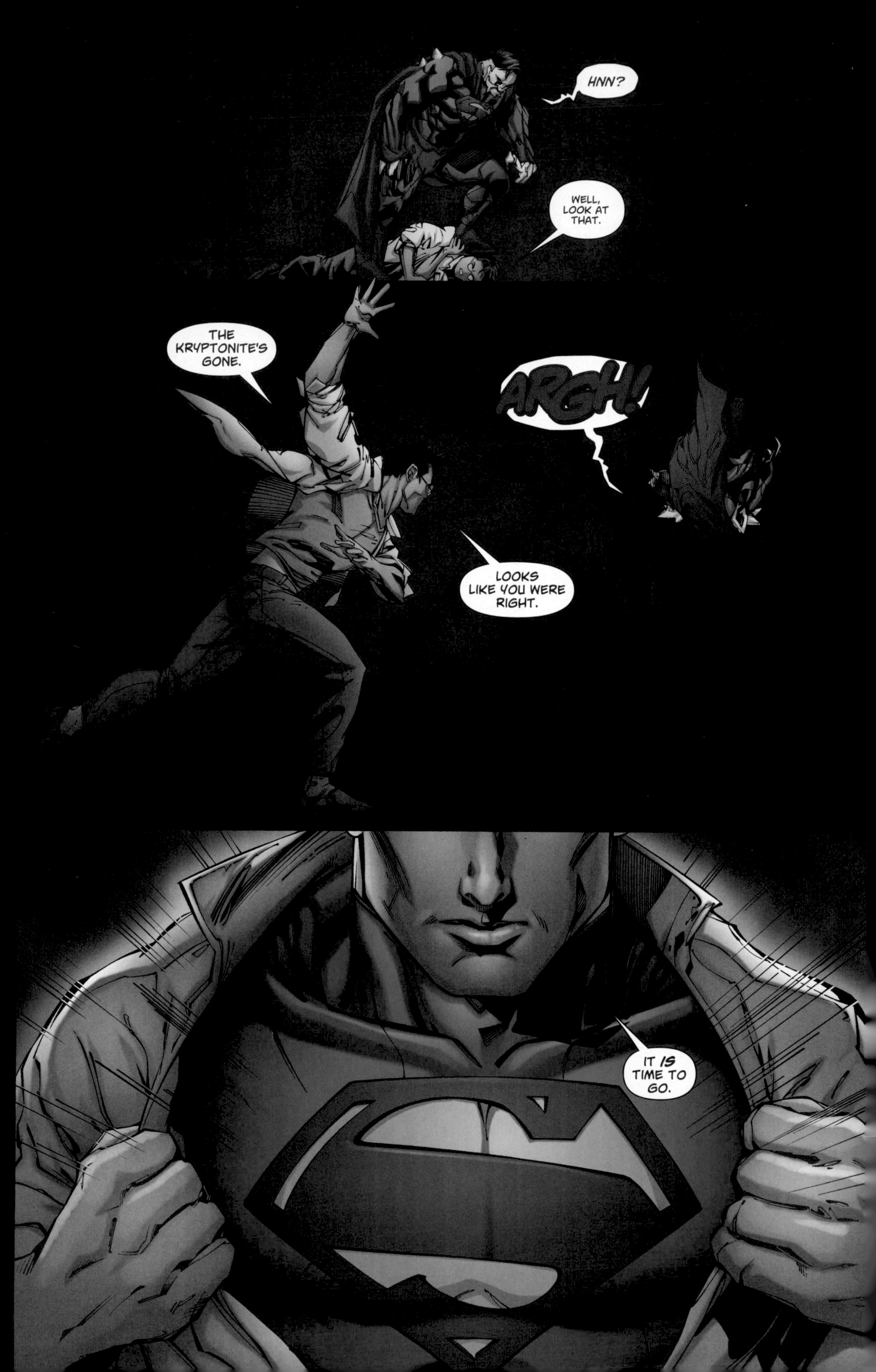
HNN?
WELL, LOOK AT THAT.
THE KRYPTONITE'S GONE.
ARGH!
LOOKS LIKE YOU WERE RIGHT.
IT IS TIME TO GO.

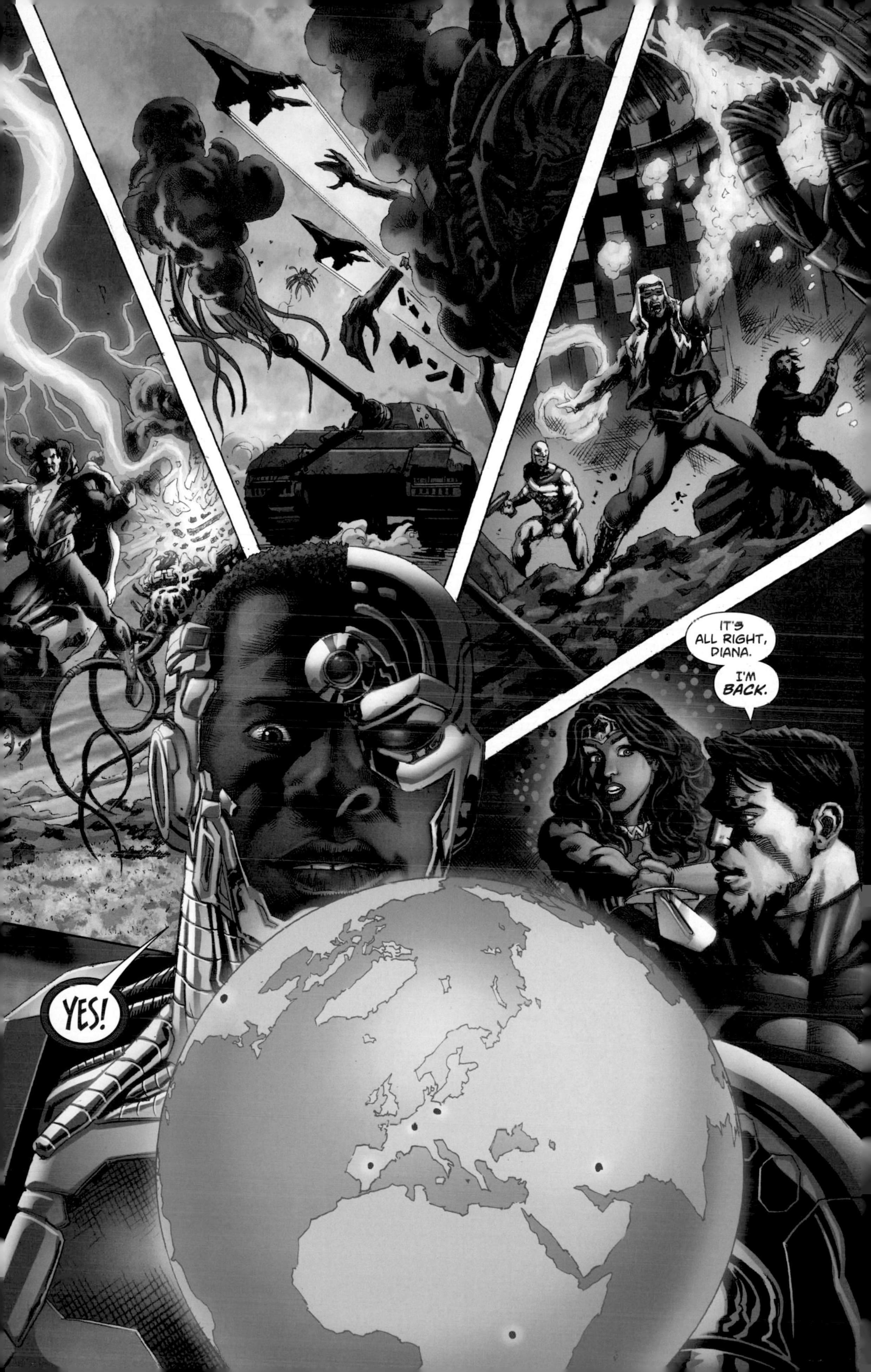

IT'S ALL RIGHT, DIANA.
I'M BACK.
YES!

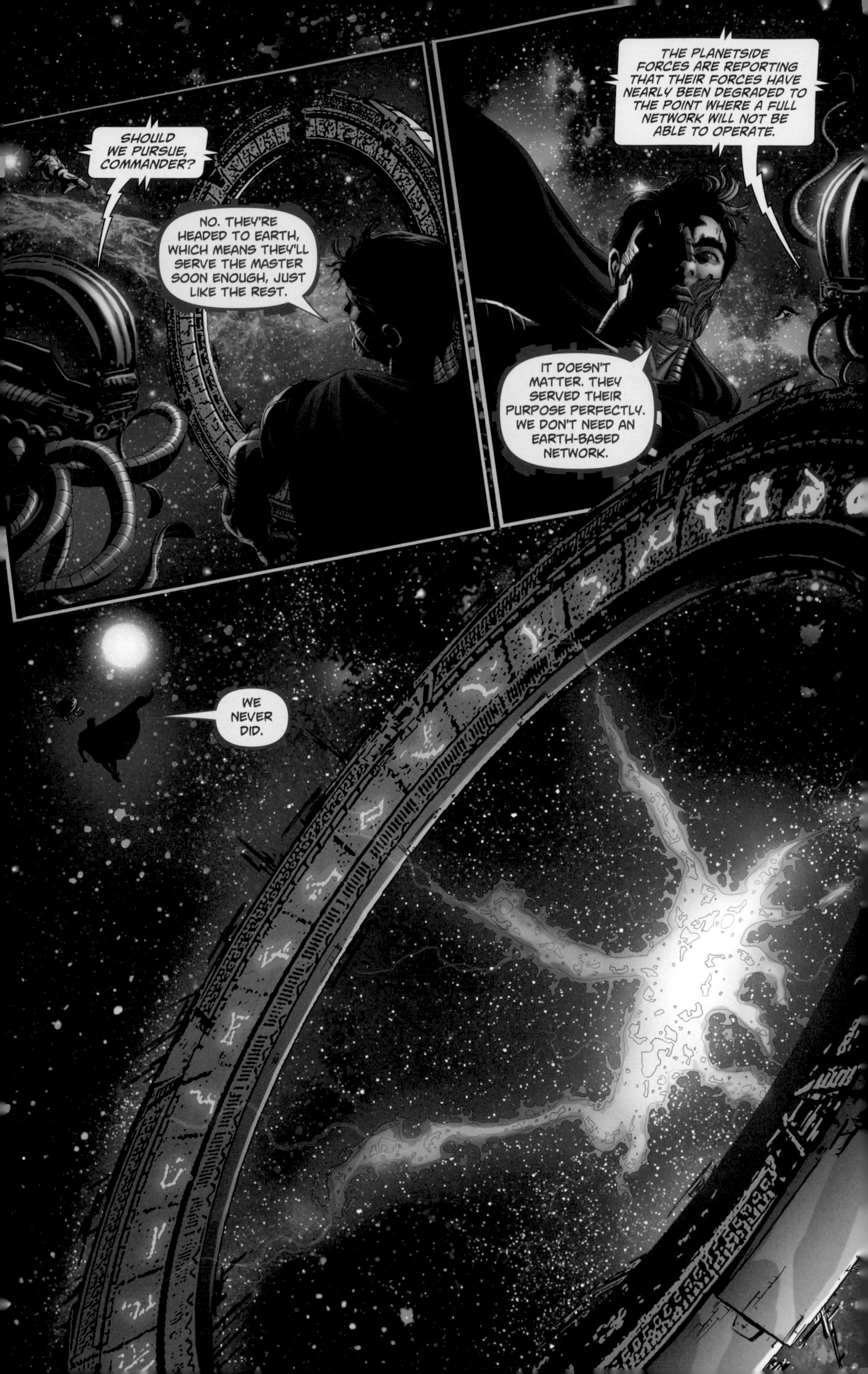
SHOULD WE PURSUE, COMMANDER?
NO. THEY'RE HEADED TO EARTH, WHICH MEANS THEY'LL SERVE THE MASTER SOON ENOUGH, JUST LIKE THE REST.
THE PLANETSIDE FORCES ARE REPORTING THAT THEIR FORCES HAVE NEARLY BEEN DEGRADED TO THE POINT WHERE A FULL NETWORK WILL NOT BE ABLE TO OPERATE.
IT DOESN'T MATTER. THEY SERVED THEIR PURPOSE PERFECTLY. WE DON'T NEED AN EARTH-BASED NETWORK.
WE NEVER DID.

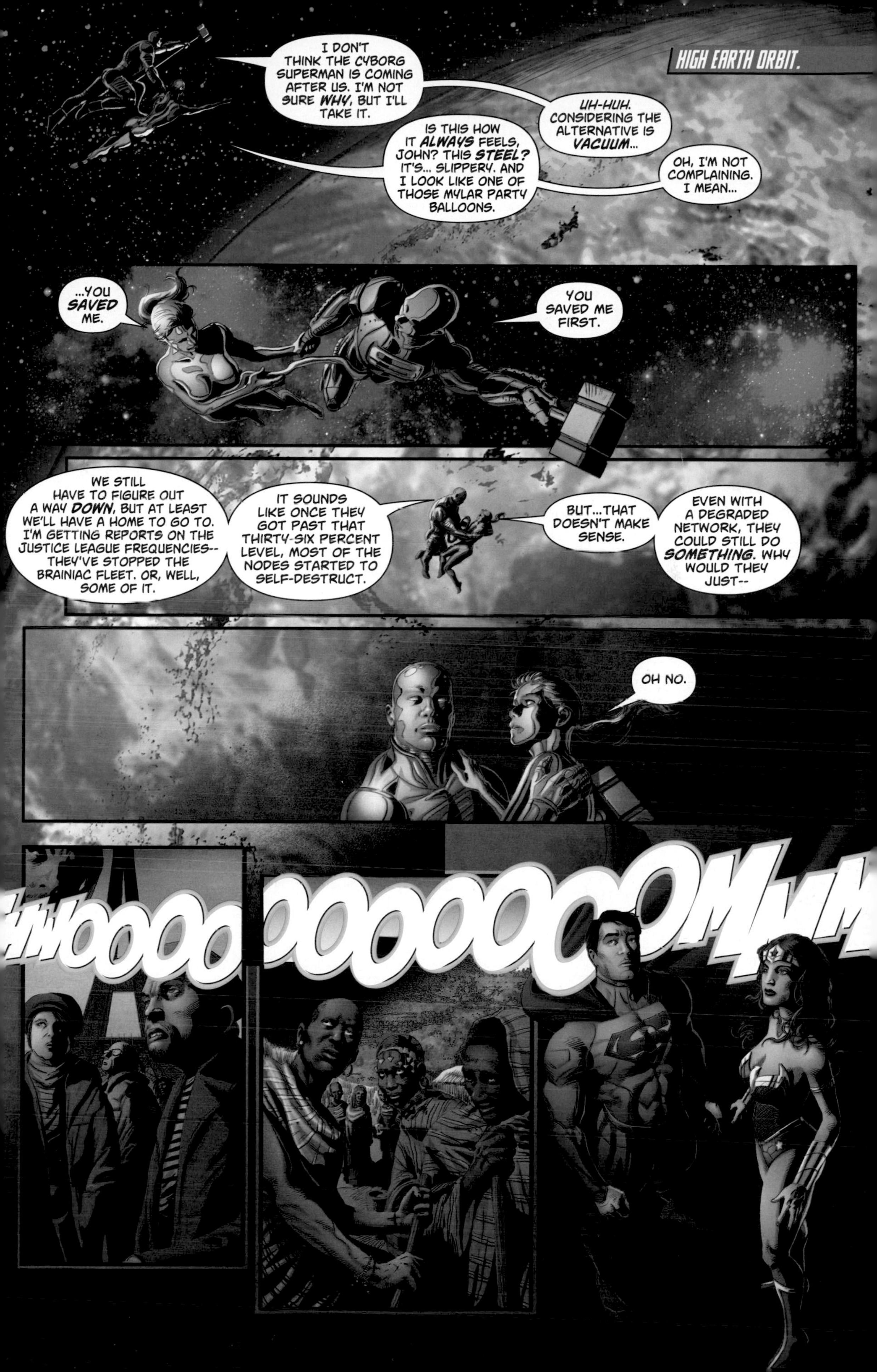
HIGH EARTH ORBIT.
I DON'T THINK THE CYBORG SUPERMAN IS COMING AFTER US. I'M NOT SURE WHY, BUT I'LL TAKE IT.
UH-HUH. CONSIDERING THE ALTERNATIVE IS VACUUM...
IS THIS HOW IT ALWAYS FEELS, JOHN? THIS STEEL? IT'S... SLIPPERY. AND I LOOK LIKE ONE OF THOSE MYLAR PARTY BALLOONS.
OH, I'M NOT COMPLAINING. I MEAN...
...YOU SAVED ME.
YOU SAVED ME FIRST.
WE STILL HAVE TO FIGURE OUT A WAY DOWN, BUT AT LEAST WE'LL HAVE A HOME TO GO TO. I'M GETTING REPORTS ON THE JUSTICE LEAGUE FREQUENCIES-- THEY'VE STOPPED THE BRAINIAC FLEET. OR, WELL, SOME OF IT.
IT SOUNDS LIKE ONCE THEY GOT PAST THAT THIRTY-SIX PERCENT LEVEL, MOST OF THE NODES STARTED TO SELF-DESTRUCT.
BUT...THAT DOESN'T MAKE SENSE.
EVEN WITH A DEGRADED NETWORK, THEY COULD STILL DO SOMETHING. WHY WOULD THEY JUST--
OH NO.
WHOOOOOOOOOOOOOMMM

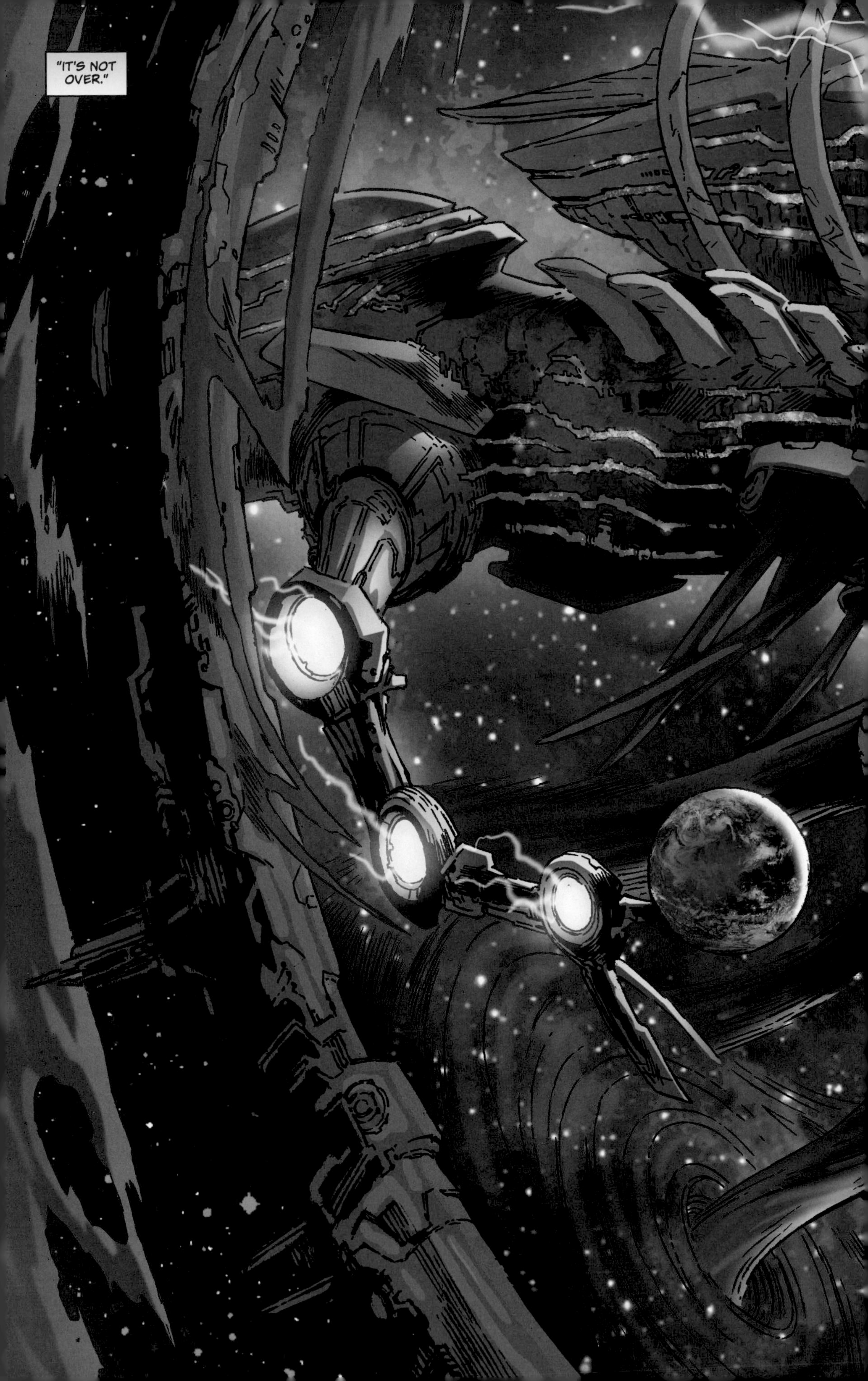
"IT'S NOT OVER."

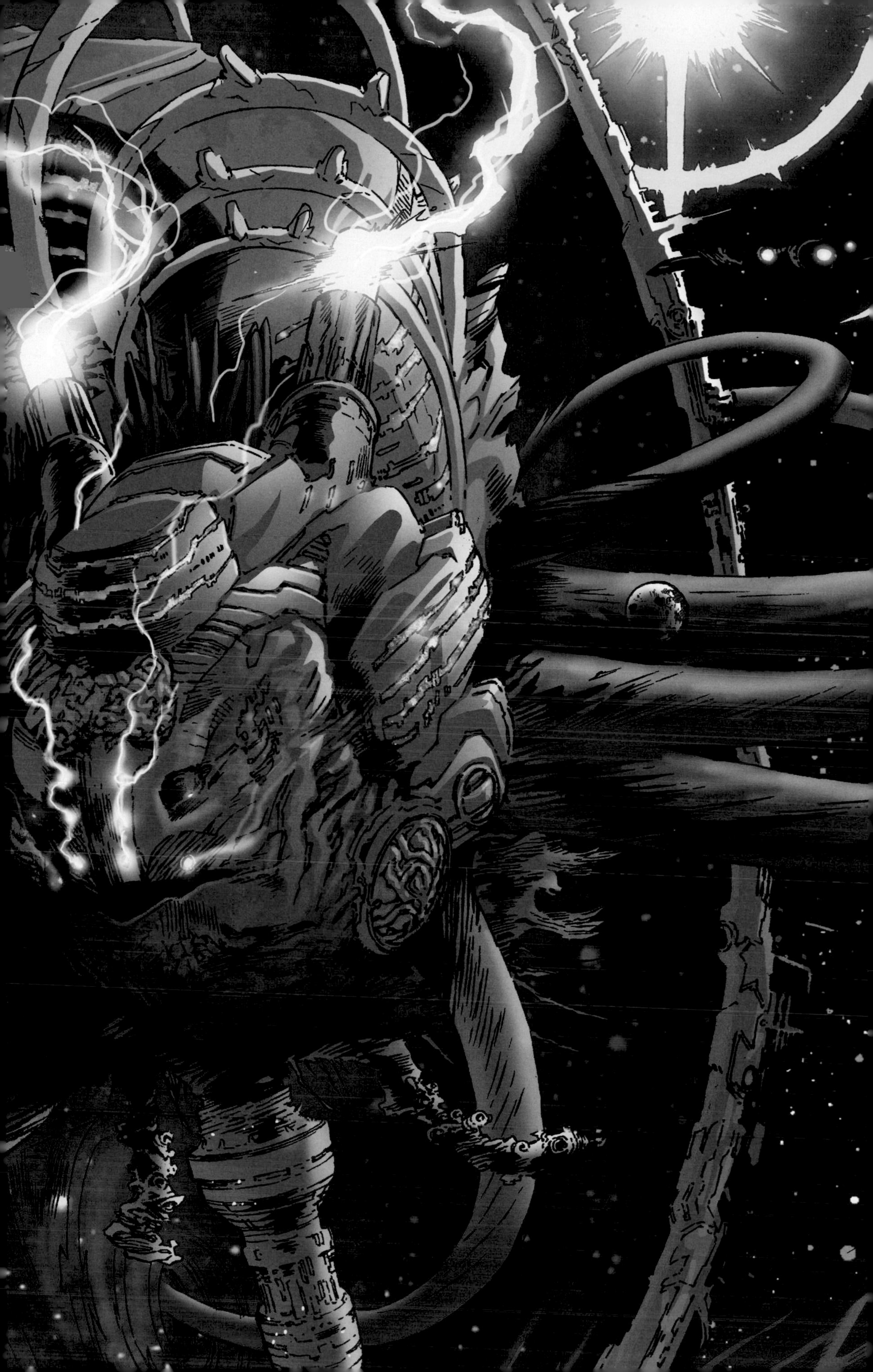

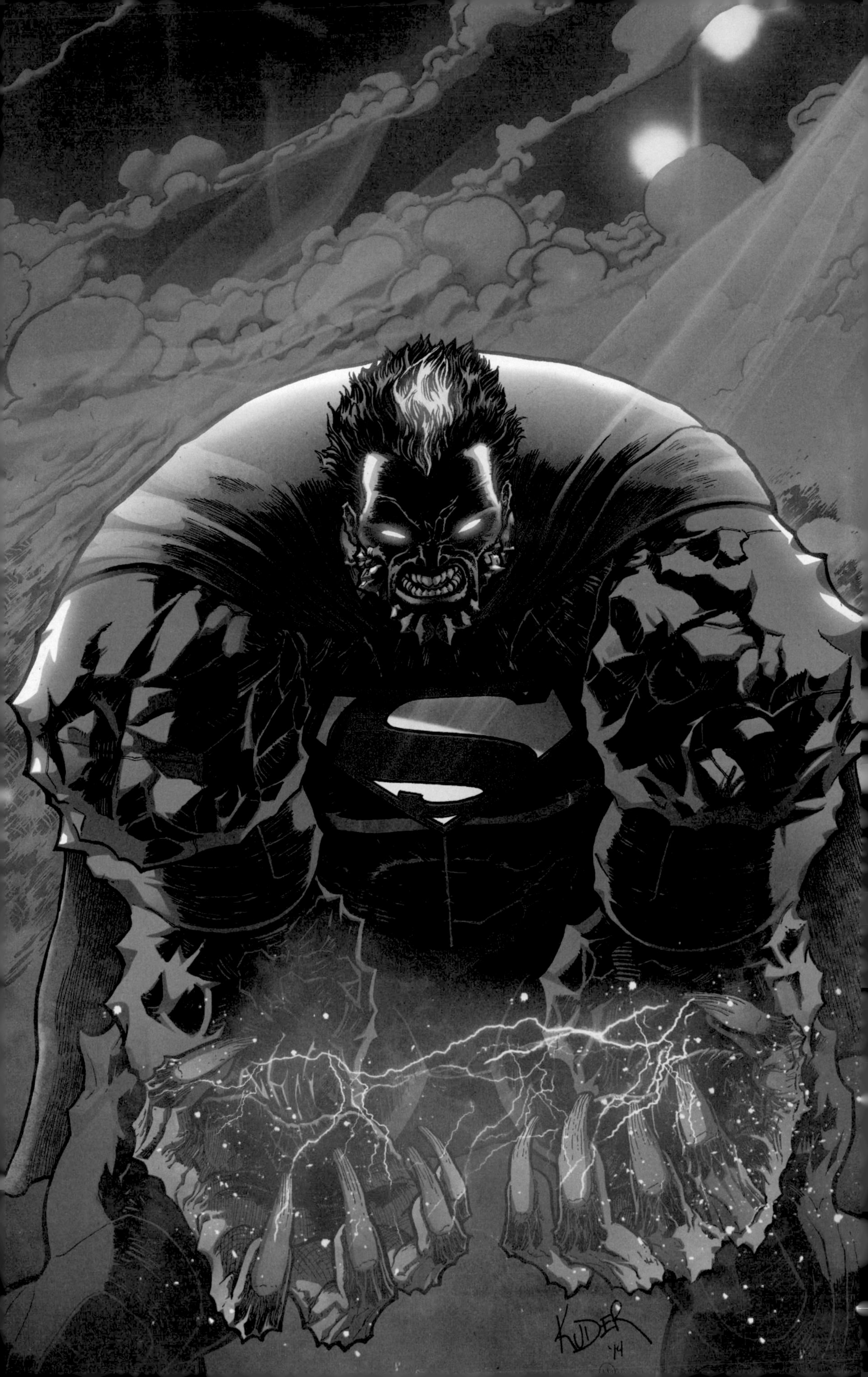
KUDER '14

SUPERMAN

[SUPERDOOM] chapter 4

"MY BODY IS A CAGE"

STORY
GREG PAK

PENCILS
KEN LASHLEY, AARON KUDER, JACK HERBERT, CLIFF RICHARDS, JULIUS GOPEZ, WILL CONRAD, AND PASCAL ALIXE

INKS
KEN LASHLEY, AARON KUDER, VICENTE CIFUENTE, CLIFF RICHARDS, WILL CONRAD, AND PASCAL ALIXE

COLORS
ULISES ARREOLA

LETTERS
STEVE WANDS

COVER
AARON KUDER AND WIL QUINTANA

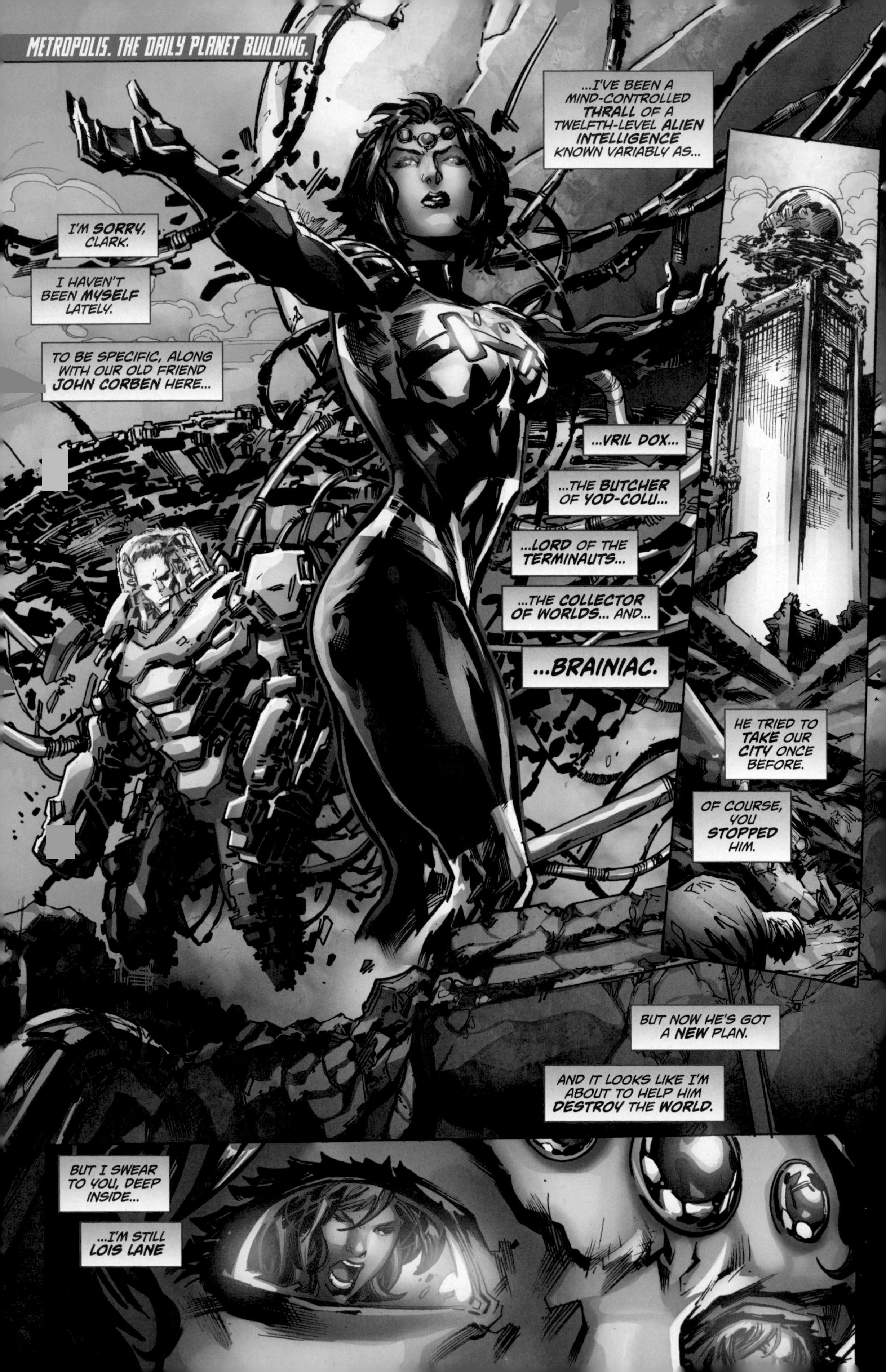
METROPOLIS. THE DAILY PLANET BUILDING.
I'M SORRY, CLARK.
I HAVEN'T BEEN MYSELF LATELY.
TO BE SPECIFIC, ALONG WITH OUR OLD FRIEND JOHN CORBEN HERE...
...I'VE BEEN A MIND-CONTROLLED THRALL OF A TWELFTH-LEVEL ALIEN INTELLIGENCE KNOWN VARIABLY AS...
...VRIL DOX...
...THE BUTCHER OF YOD-COLU...
...LORD OF THE TERMINAUTS...
...THE COLLECTOR OF WORLDS... AND...
...BRAINIAC.
HE TRIED TO TAKE OUR CITY ONCE BEFORE.
OF COURSE, YOU STOPPED HIM.
BUT NOW HE'S GOT A NEW PLAN.
AND IT LOOKS LIKE I'M ABOUT TO HELP HIM DESTROY THE WORLD.
BUT I SWEAR TO YOU, DEEP INSIDE...
...I'M STILL LOIS LANE

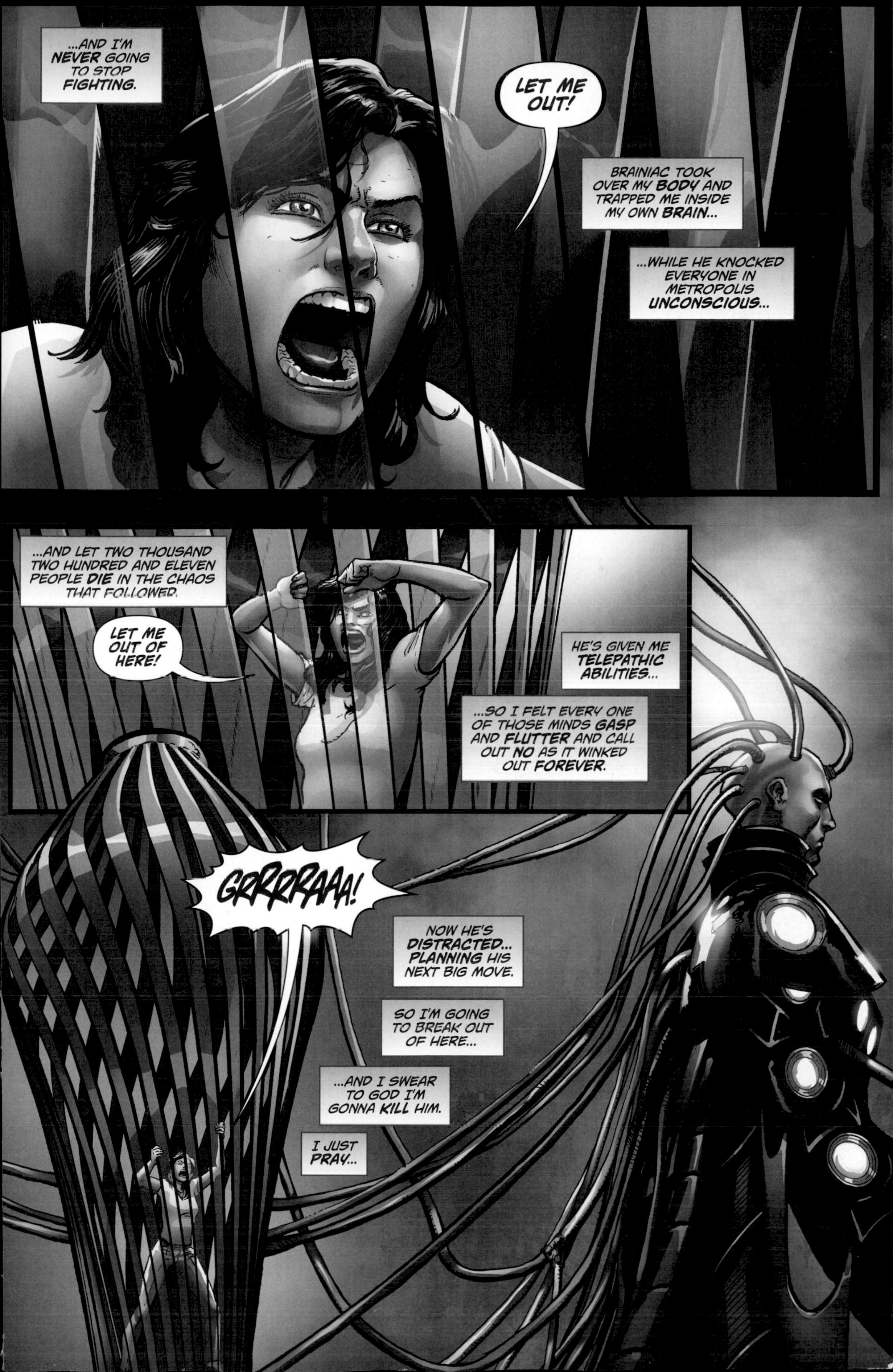
...AND I'M NEVER GOING TO STOP FIGHTING.
LET ME OUT!
BRAINIAC TOOK OVER MY BODY AND TRAPPED ME INSIDE MY OWN BRAIN...
...WHILE HE KNOCKED EVERYONE IN METROPOLIS UNCONSCIOUS...
...AND LET TWO THOUSAND TWO HUNDRED AND ELEVEN PEOPLE DIE IN THE CHAOS THAT FOLLOWED.
LET ME OUT OF HERE!
HE'S GIVEN ME TELEPATHIC ABILITIES...
...SO I FELT EVERY ONE OF THOSE MINDS GASP AND FLUTTER AND CALL OUT NO AS IT WINKED OUT FOREVER.
GRRRRAAA!
NOW HE'S DISTRACTED... PLANNING HIS NEXT BIG MOVE.
SO I'M GOING TO BREAK OUT OF HERE...
...AND I SWEAR TO GOD I'M GONNA KILL HIM.
I JUST PRAY...

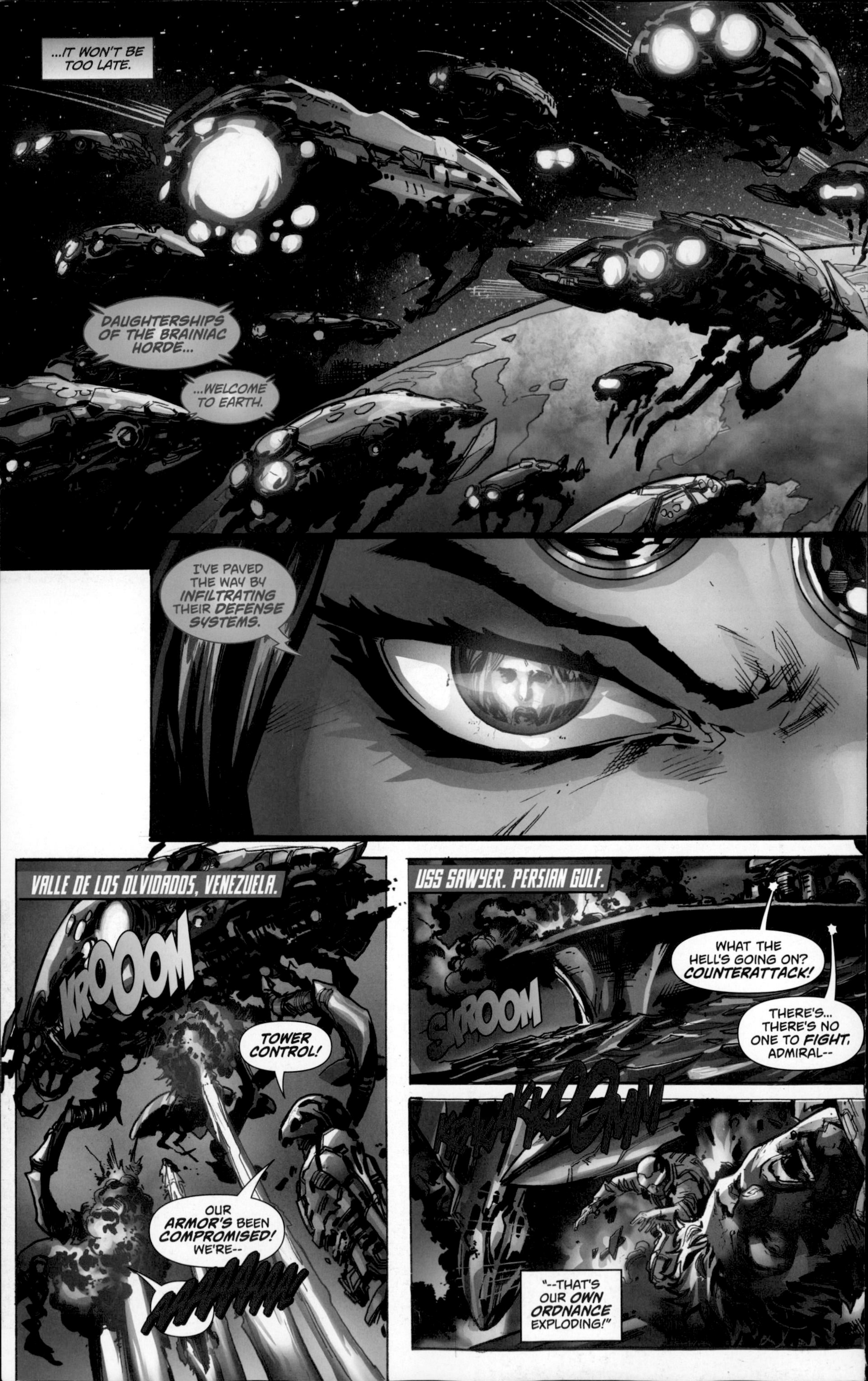

...IT WON'T BE TOO LATE.
DAUGHTERSHIPS OF THE BRAINIAC HORDE...
...WELCOME TO EARTH.
I'VE PAVED THE WAY BY INFILTRATING THEIR DEFENSE SYSTEMS.
VALLE DE LOS OLVIDADOS, VENEZUELA.
KROOOM
TOWER CONTROL!
OUR ARMOR'S BEEN COMPROMISED! WE'RE--
USS SAWYER. PERSIAN GULF.
WHAT THE HELL'S GOING ON? COUNTERATTACK!
SKROOM
THERE'S... THERE'S NO ONE TO FIGHT, ADMIRAL--
"--THAT'S OUR OWN ORDNANCE EXPLODING!"

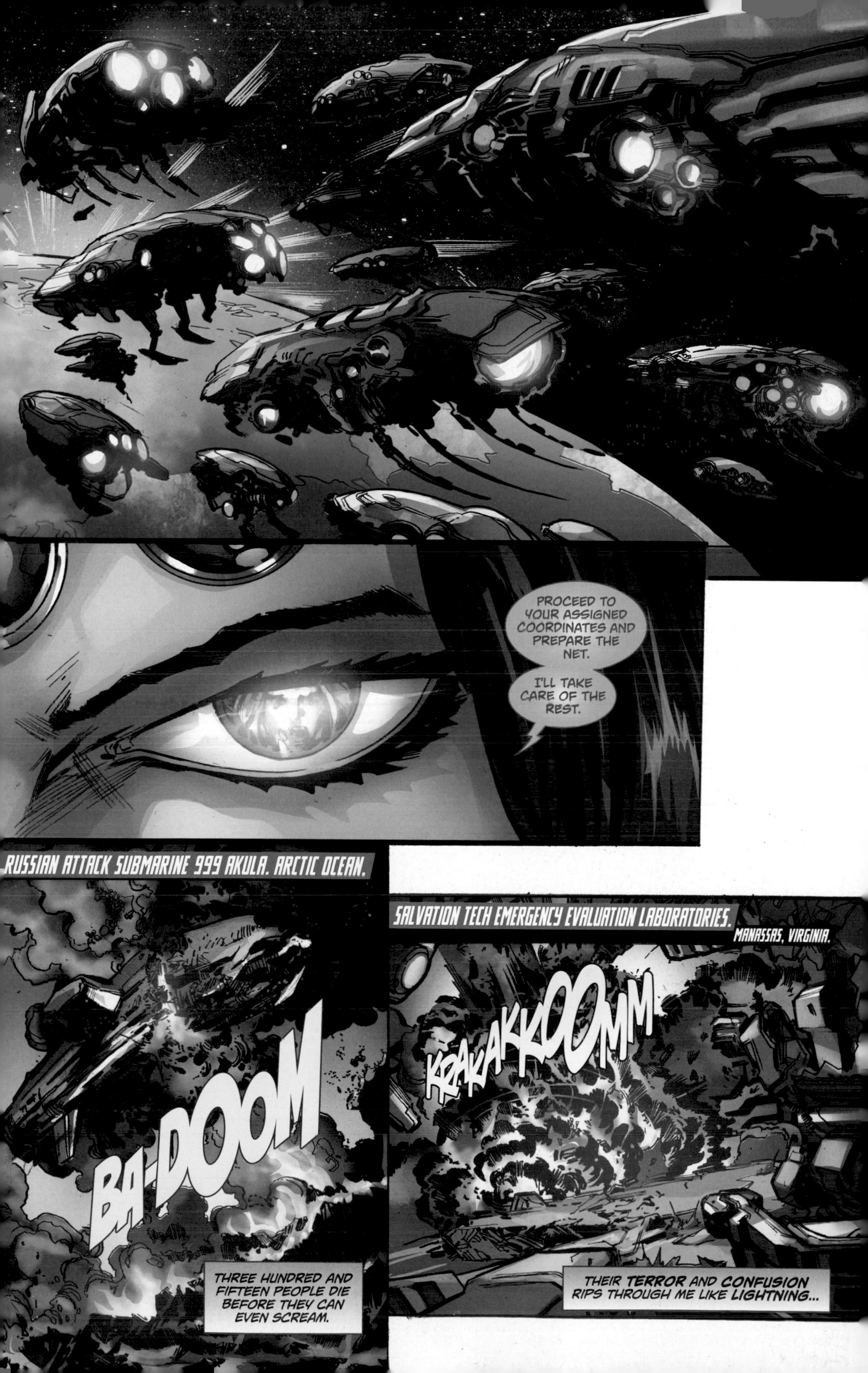
PROCEED TO YOUR ASSIGNED COORDINATES AND PREPARE THE NET.
I'LL TAKE CARE OF THE REST.
RUSSIAN ATTACK SUBMARINE 999 AKULA. ARCTIC OCEAN.
BA-DOOM
THREE HUNDRED AND FIFTEEN PEOPLE DIE BEFORE THEY CAN EVEN SCREAM.
SALVATION TECH EMERGENCY EVALUATION LABORATORIES.
MANASSAS, VIRGINIA.
KRAKAKKOOMM
THEIR TERROR AND CONFUSION RIPS THROUGH ME LIKE LIGHTNING...

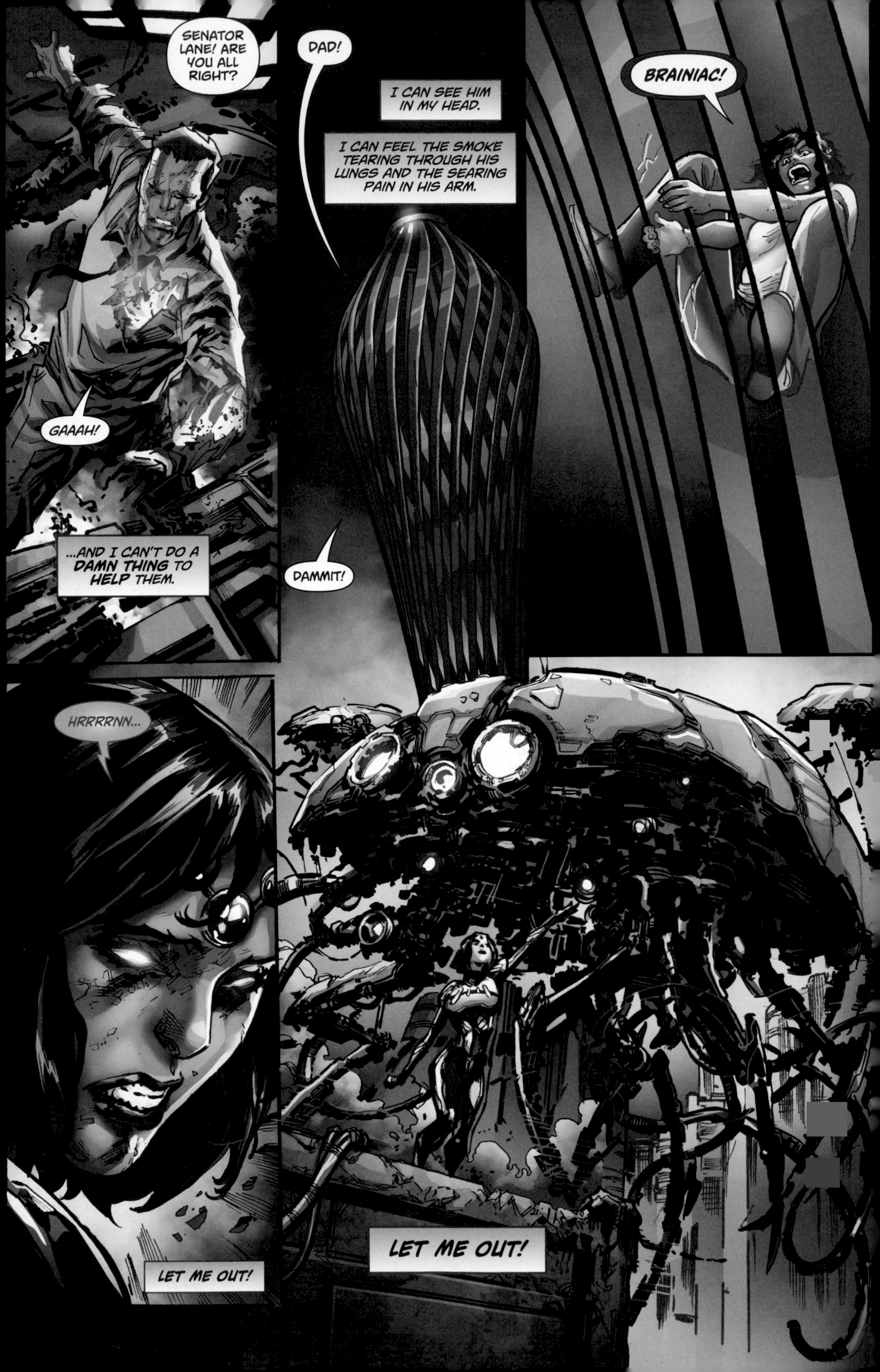

SENATOR LANE! ARE YOU ALL RIGHT?
GAAAH!
...AND I CAN'T DO A DAMN THING TO HELP THEM.
DAD!
I CAN SEE HIM IN MY HEAD.
I CAN FEEL THE SMOKE TEARING THROUGH HIS LUNGS AND THE SEARING PAIN IN HIS ARM.
DAMMIT!
BRAINIAC!
HRRRRNN...
LET ME OUT!
LET ME OUT!

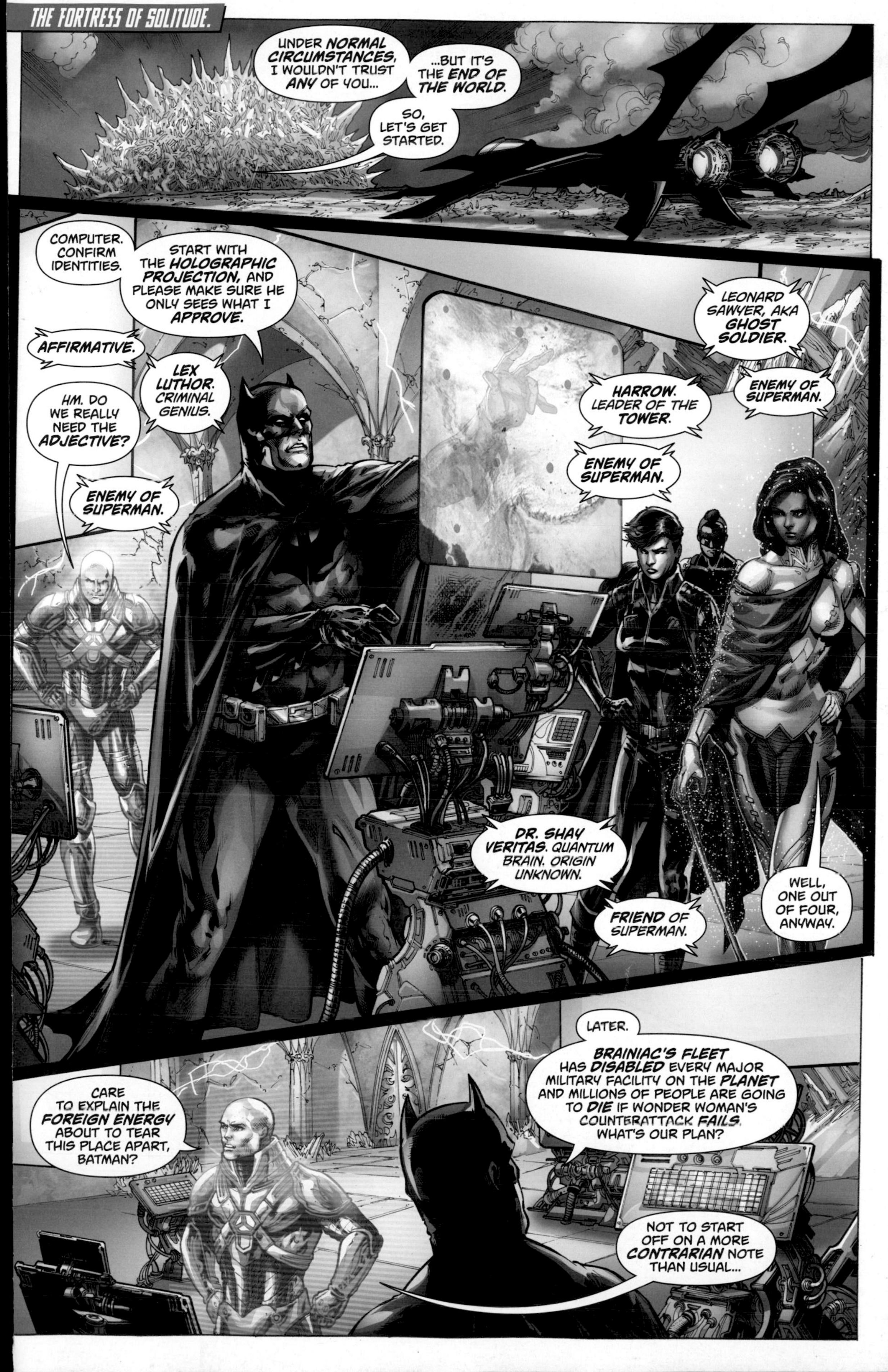
THE FORTRESS OF SOLITUDE.
UNDER NORMAL CIRCUMSTANCES, I WOULDN'T TRUST ANY OF YOU...
...BUT IT'S THE END OF THE WORLD.
SO, LET'S GET STARTED.
COMPUTER. CONFIRM IDENTITIES.
START WITH THE HOLOGRAPHIC PROJECTION, AND PLEASE MAKE SURE HE ONLY SEES WHAT I APPROVE.
AFFIRMATIVE.
LEX LUTHOR. CRIMINAL GENIUS.
HM. DO WE REALLY NEED THE ADJECTIVE?
ENEMY OF SUPERMAN.
LEONARD SAWYER, AKA GHOST SOLDIER.
ENEMY OF SUPERMAN.
HARROW. LEADER OF THE TOWER.
ENEMY OF SUPERMAN.
DR. SHAY VERITAS. QUANTUM BRAIN. ORIGIN UNKNOWN.
FRIEND OF SUPERMAN.
WELL, ONE OUT OF FOUR, ANYWAY.
LATER.
BRAINIAC'S FLEET HAS DISABLED EVERY MAJOR MILITARY FACILITY ON THE PLANET AND MILLIONS OF PEOPLE ARE GOING TO DIE IF WONDER WOMAN'S COUNTERATTACK FAILS. WHAT'S OUR PLAN?
CARE TO EXPLAIN THE FOREIGN ENERGY ABOUT TO TEAR THIS PLACE APART, BATMAN?
NOT TO START OFF ON A MORE CONTRARIAN NOTE THAN USUAL...

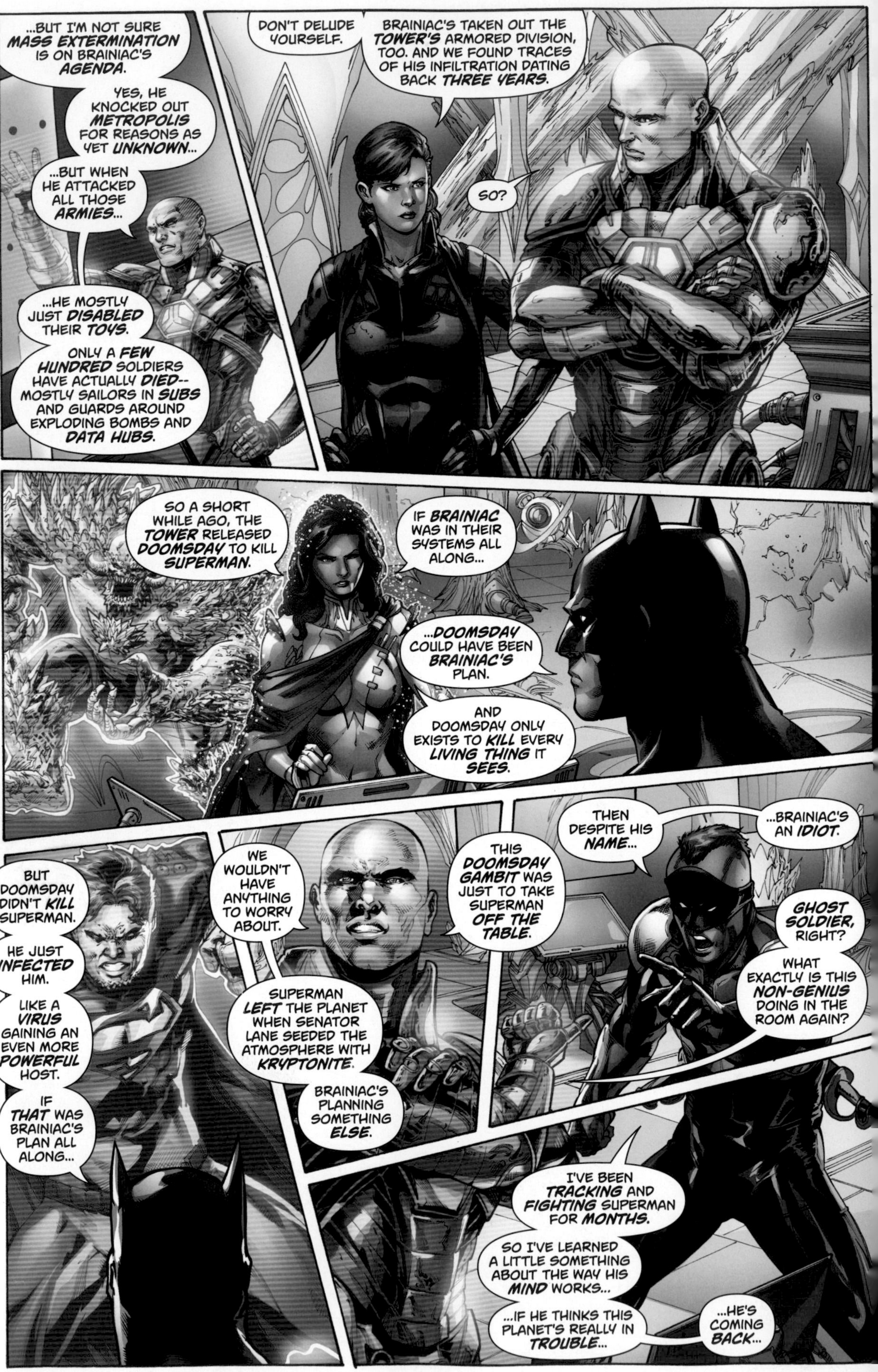
...BUT I'M NOT SURE MASS EXTERMINATION IS ON BRAINIAC'S AGENDA.
YES, HE KNOCKED OUT METROPOLIS FOR REASONS AS YET UNKNOWN...
...BUT WHEN HE ATTACKED ALL THOSE ARMIES...
...HE MOSTLY JUST DISABLED THEIR TOYS.
ONLY A FEW HUNDRED SOLDIERS HAVE ACTUALLY DIED--MOSTLY SAILORS IN SUBS AND GUARDS AROUND EXPLODING BOMBS AND DATA HUBS.
DON'T DELUDE YOURSELF.
BRAINIAC'S TAKEN OUT THE TOWER'S ARMORED DIVISION, TOO. AND WE FOUND TRACES OF HIS INFILTRATION DATING BACK THREE YEARS.
SO?
SO A SHORT WHILE AGO, THE TOWER RELEASED DOOMSDAY TO KILL SUPERMAN.
IF BRAINIAC WAS IN THEIR SYSTEMS ALL ALONG...
...DOOMSDAY COULD HAVE BEEN BRAINIAC'S PLAN.
AND DOOMSDAY ONLY EXISTS TO KILL EVERY LIVING THING IT SEES.
BUT DOOMSDAY DIDN'T KILL SUPERMAN.
HE JUST INFECTED HIM.
LIKE A VIRUS GAINING AN EVEN MORE POWERFUL HOST.
IF THAT WAS BRAINIAC'S PLAN ALL ALONG...
WE WOULDN'T HAVE ANYTHING TO WORRY ABOUT.
SUPERMAN LEFT THE PLANET WHEN SENATOR LANE SEEDED THE ATMOSPHERE WITH KRYPTONITE.
BRAINIAC'S PLANNING SOMETHING ELSE.
THIS DOOMSDAY GAMBIT WAS JUST TO TAKE SUPERMAN OFF THE TABLE.
THEN DESPITE HIS NAME...
...BRAINIAC'S AN IDIOT.
GHOST SOLDIER, RIGHT?
WHAT EXACTLY IS THIS NON-GENIUS DOING IN THE ROOM AGAIN?
I'VE BEEN TRACKING AND FIGHTING SUPERMAN FOR MONTHS.
SO I'VE LEARNED A LITTLE SOMETHING ABOUT THE WAY HIS MIND WORKS...
...IF HE THINKS THIS PLANET'S REALLY IN TROUBLE...
...HE'S COMING BACK...

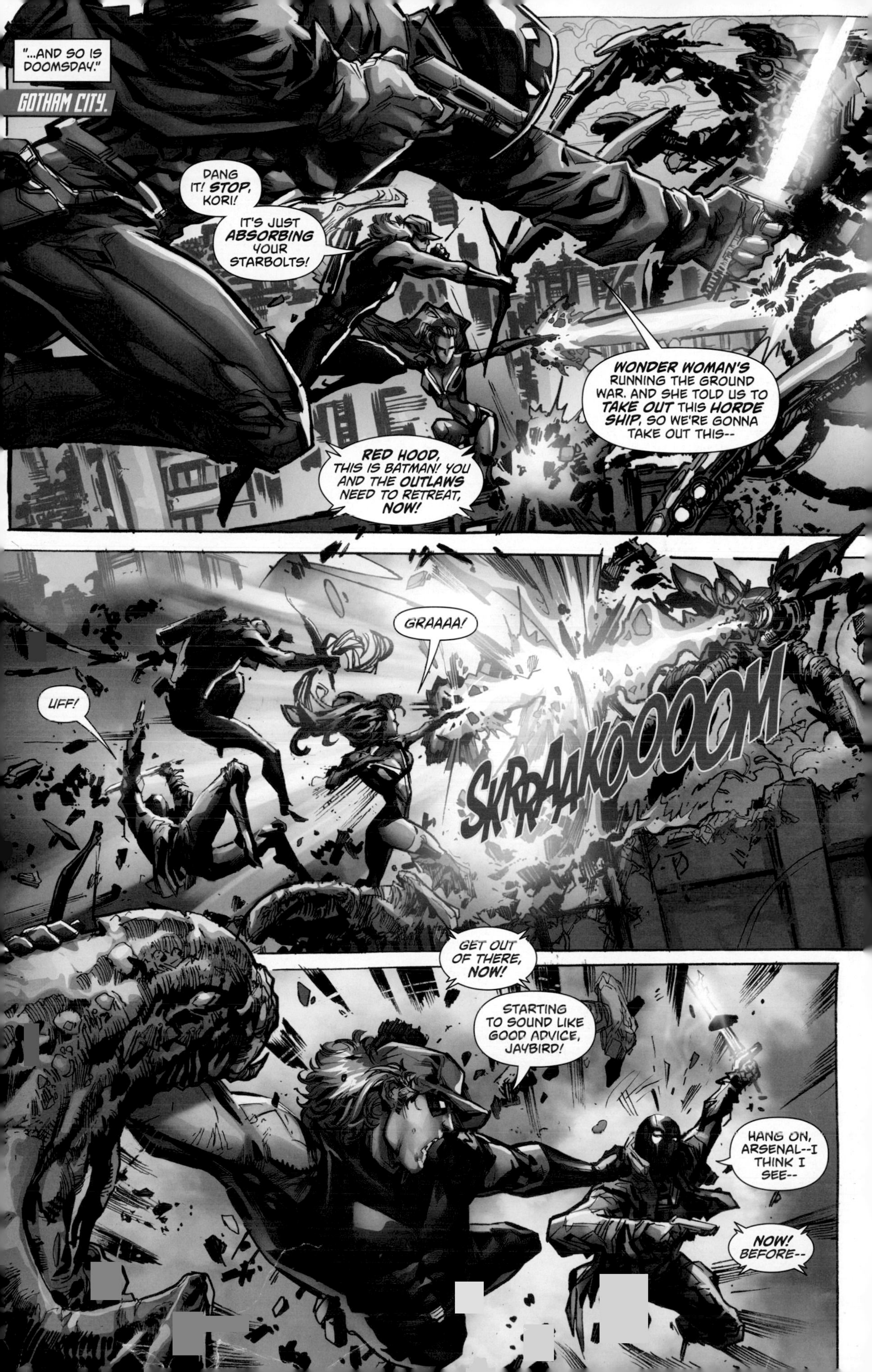
"...AND SO IS DOOMSDAY."
GOTHAM CITY.
DANG IT! STOP, KORI!
IT'S JUST ABSORBING YOUR STARBOLTS!
WONDER WOMAN'S RUNNING THE GROUND WAR. AND SHE TOLD US TO TAKE OUT THIS HORDE SHIP, SO WE'RE GONNA TAKE OUT THIS--
RED HOOD, THIS IS BATMAN! YOU AND THE OUTLAWS NEED TO RETREAT, NOW!
GRAAAA!
UFF!
SKRRAAKOOOOM
GET OUT OF THERE, NOW!
STARTING TO SOUND LIKE GOOD ADVICE, JAYBIRD!
HANG ON, ARSENAL--I THINK I SEE--
NOW! BEFORE--

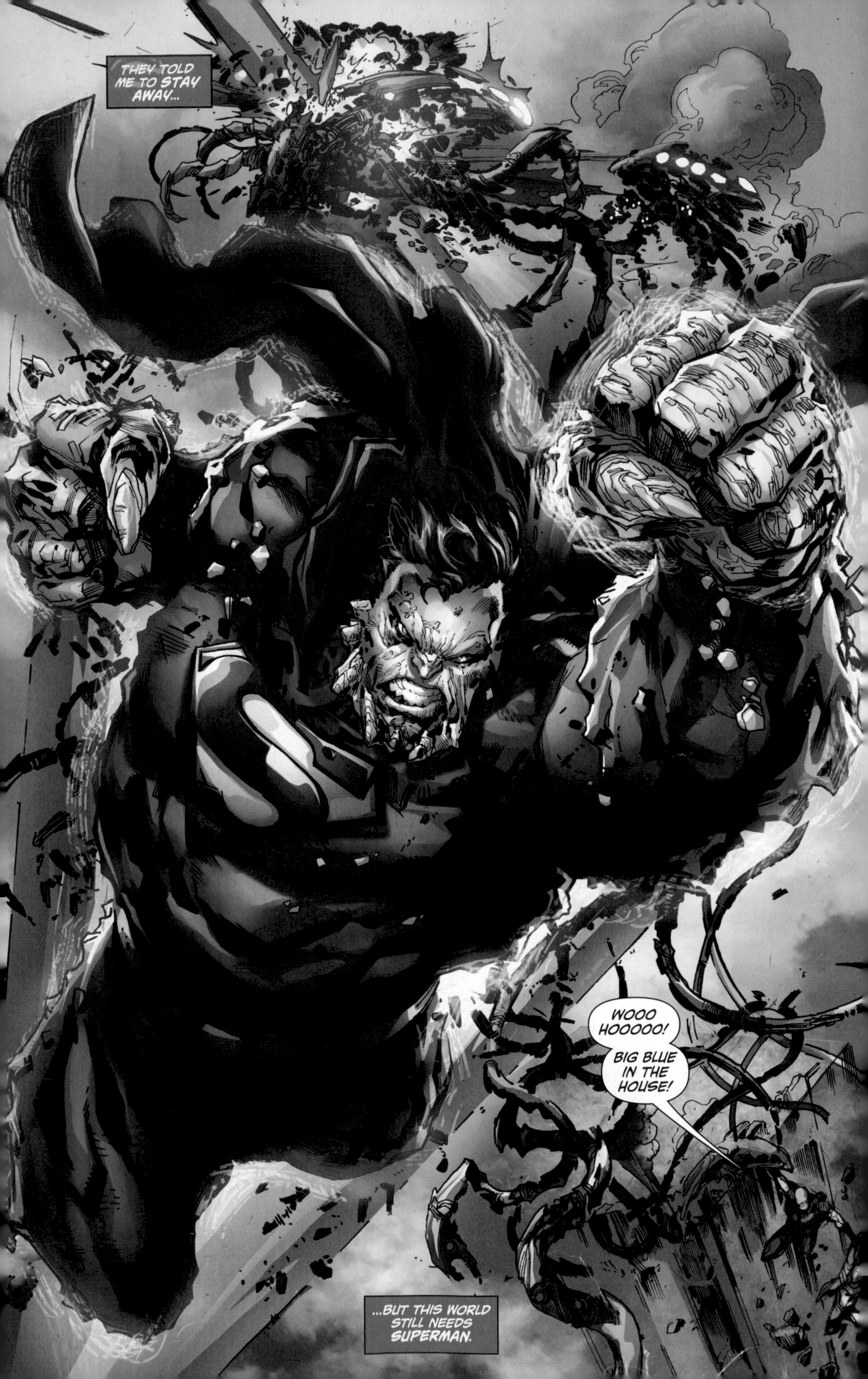
THEY TOLD ME TO STAY AWAY...
WOOO HOOOOO!
BIG BLUE IN THE HOUSE!
...BUT THIS WORLD STILL NEEDS SUPERMAN.

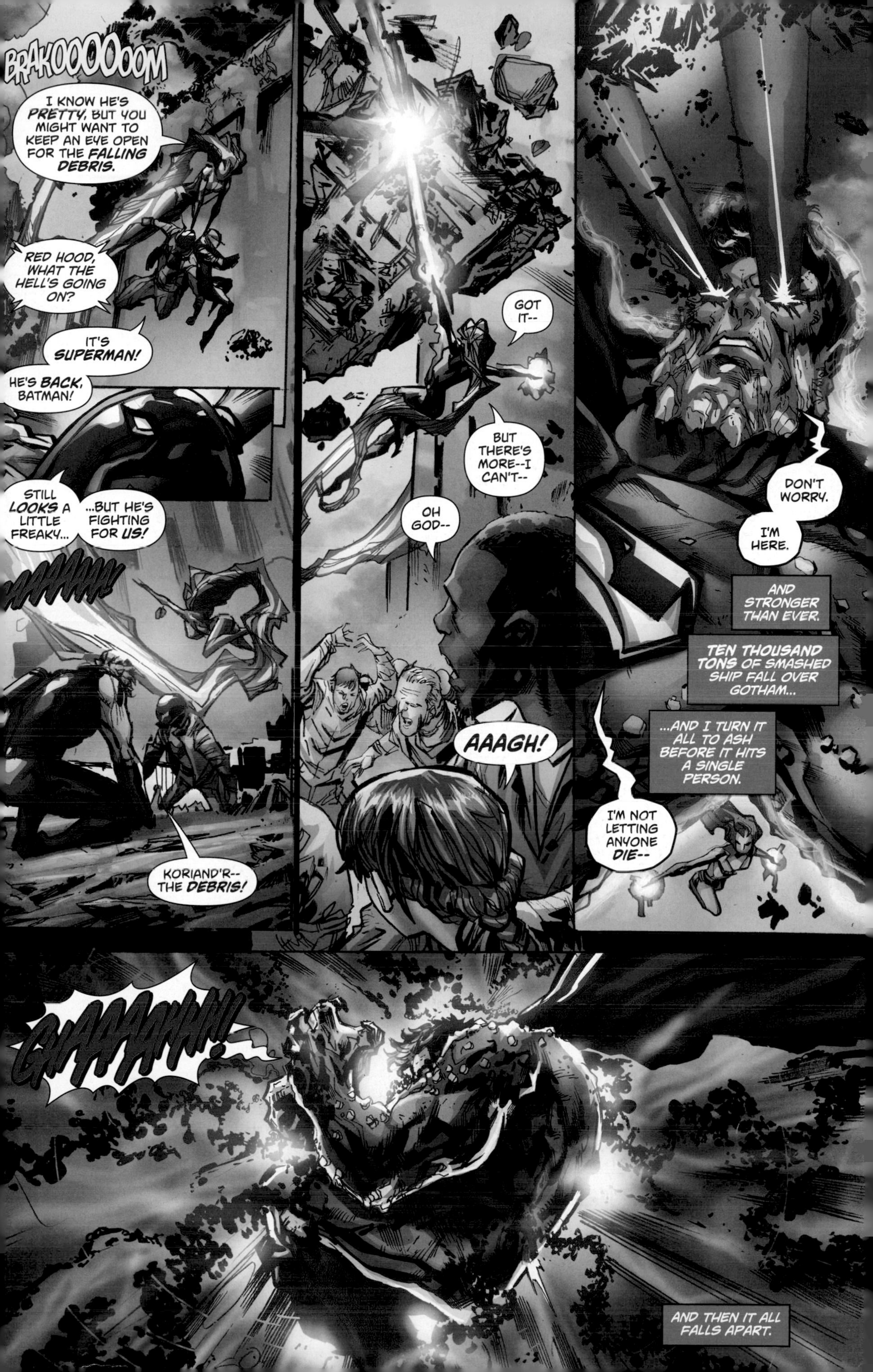
BRAKOOOOOoom
I KNOW HE'S PRETTY, BUT YOU MIGHT WANT TO KEEP AN EYE OPEN FOR THE FALLING DEBRIS.
RED HOOD, WHAT THE HELL'S GOING ON?
IT'S SUPERMAN!
HE'S BACK, BATMAN!
STILL LOOKS A LITTLE FREAKY...
...BUT HE'S FIGHTING FOR US!
KORIAND'R-- THE DEBRIS!
GOT IT--
BUT THERE'S MORE--I CAN'T--
OH GOD--
AAAGH!
DON'T WORRY.
I'M HERE.
AND STRONGER THAN EVER.
TEN THOUSAND TONS OF SMASHED SHIP FALL OVER GOTHAM...
...AND I TURN IT ALL TO ASH BEFORE IT HITS A SINGLE PERSON.
I'M NOT LETTING ANYONE DIE--
AND THEN IT ALL FALLS APART.

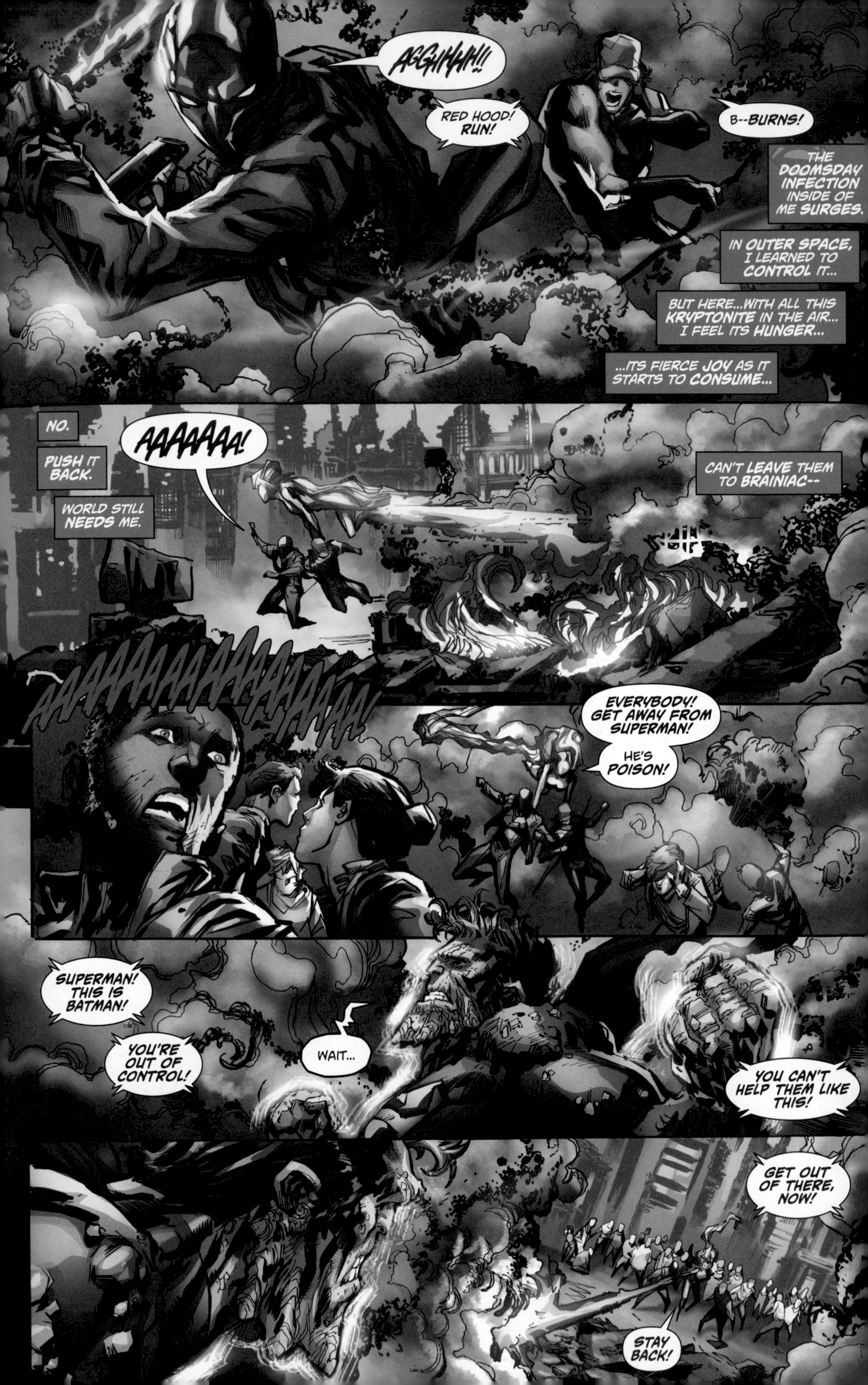
AGGHHH!!
RED HOOD! RUN!
B--BURNS!
THE DOOMSDAY INFECTION INSIDE OF ME SURGES.
IN OUTER SPACE, I LEARNED TO CONTROL IT...
BUT HERE...WITH ALL THIS KRYPTONITE IN THE AIR... I FEEL ITS HUNGER...
...ITS FIERCE JOY AS IT STARTS TO CONSUME...
NO.
PUSH IT BACK.
WORLD STILL NEEDS ME.
AAAAAAA!
CAN'T LEAVE THEM TO BRAINIAC--
AAAAAAAAAAAAAAAAAAAAA!
EVERYBODY! GET AWAY FROM SUPERMAN!
HE'S POISON!
SUPERMAN! THIS IS BATMAN!
YOU'RE OUT OF CONTROL!
WAIT...
YOU CAN'T HELP THEM LIKE THIS!
GET OUT OF THERE, NOW!
STAY BACK!

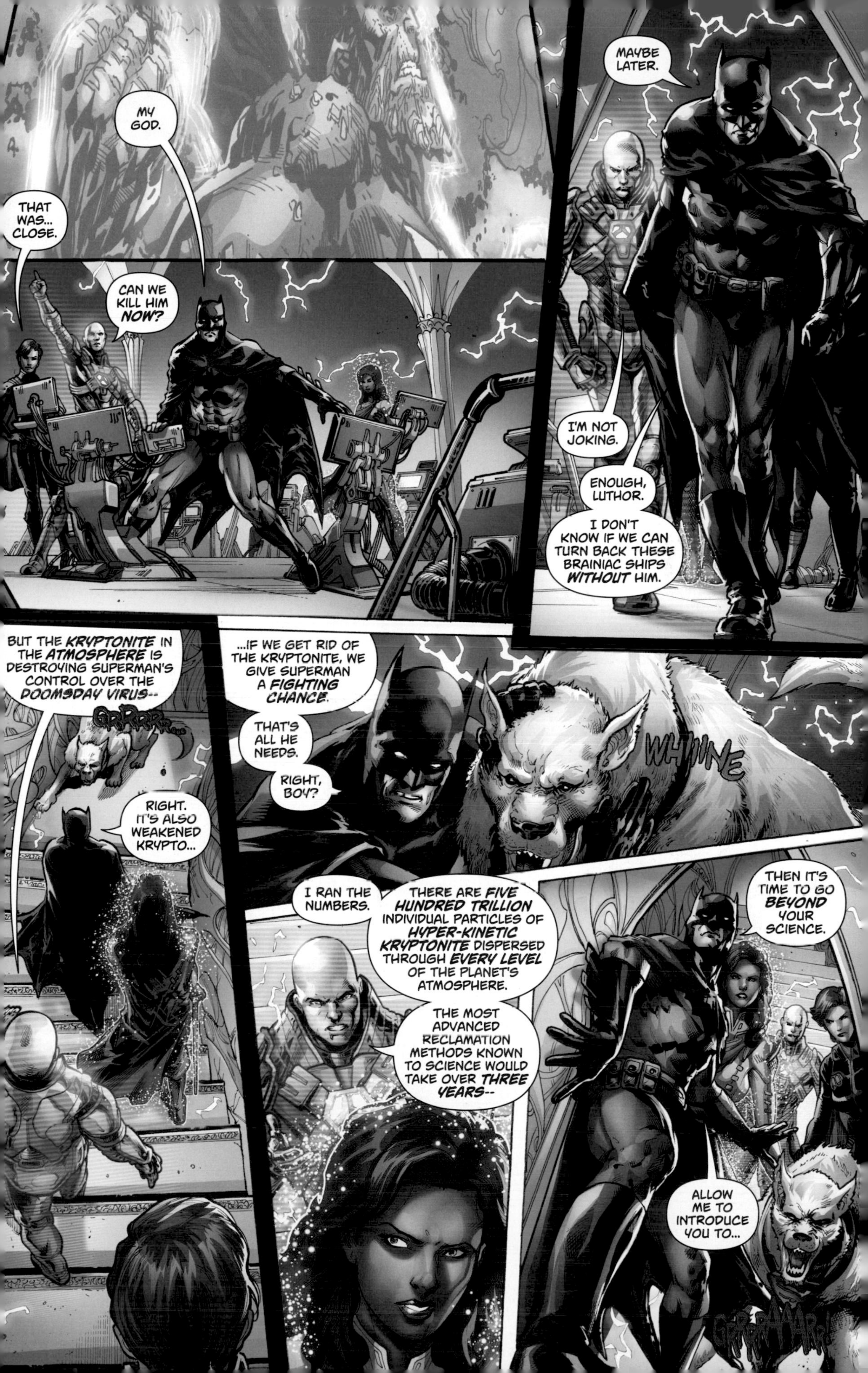
MY GOD.
THAT WAS... CLOSE.
CAN WE KILL HIM NOW?
MAYBE LATER.
I'M NOT JOKING.
ENOUGH, LUTHOR.
I DON'T KNOW IF WE CAN TURN BACK THESE BRAINIAC SHIPS WITHOUT HIM.
BUT THE KRYPTONITE IN THE ATMOSPHERE IS DESTROYING SUPERMAN'S CONTROL OVER THE DOOMSDAY VIRUS--
GRRRR...
RIGHT. IT'S ALSO WEAKENED KRYPTO...
...IF WE GET RID OF THE KRYPTONITE, WE GIVE SUPERMAN A FIGHTING CHANCE.
THAT'S ALL HE NEEDS.
RIGHT, BOY?
WHIINE
I RAN THE NUMBERS.
THERE ARE FIVE HUNDRED TRILLION INDIVIDUAL PARTICLES OF HYPER-KINETIC KRYPTONITE DISPERSED THROUGH EVERY LEVEL OF THE PLANET'S ATMOSPHERE.
THE MOST ADVANCED RECLAMATION METHODS KNOWN TO SCIENCE WOULD TAKE OVER THREE YEARS--
THEN IT'S TIME TO GO BEYOND YOUR SCIENCE.
ALLOW ME TO INTRODUCE YOU TO...
GRRRAAARR!

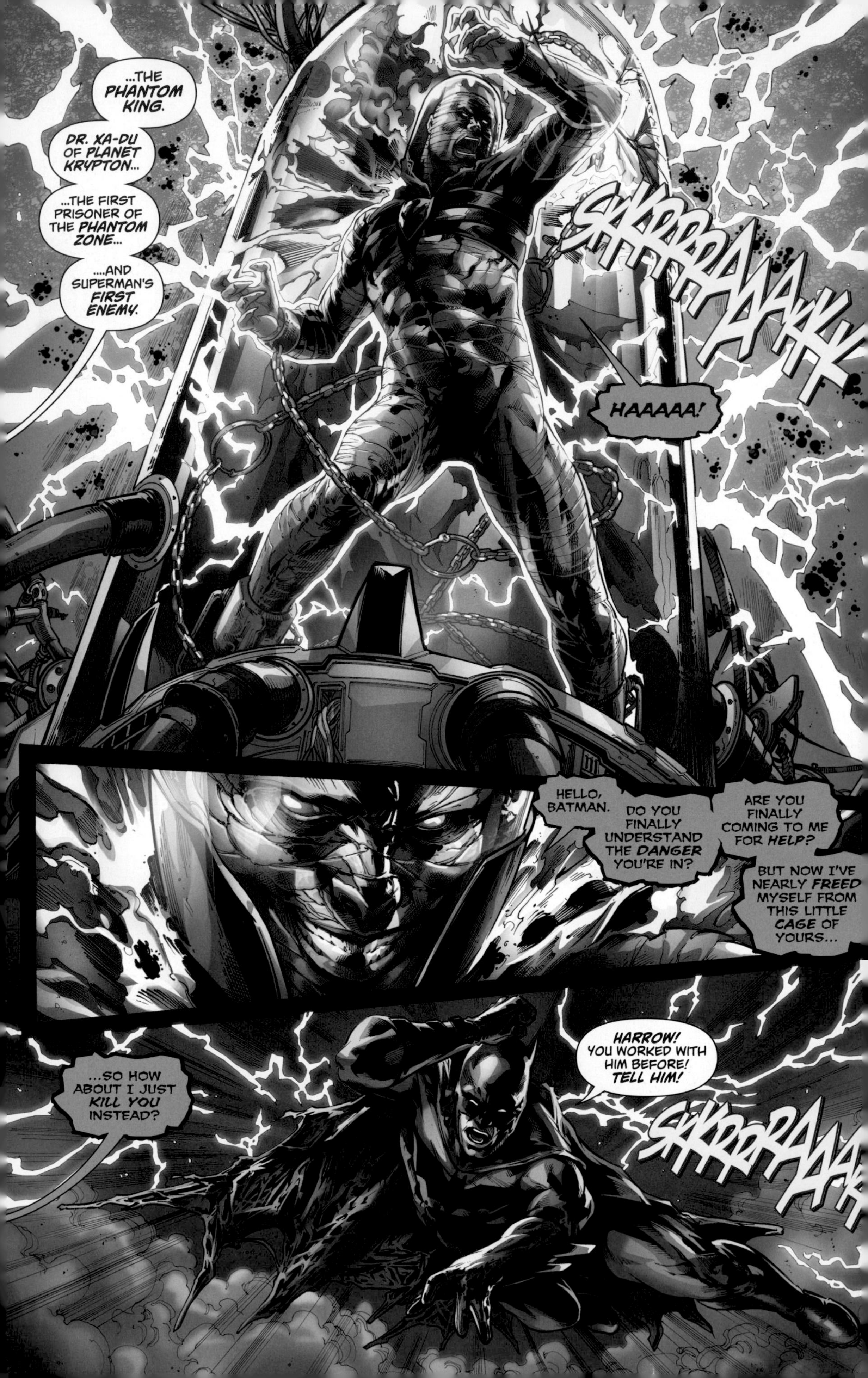
...THE PHANTOM KING.
DR. XA-DU OF PLANET KRYPTON...
...THE FIRST PRISONER OF THE PHANTOM ZONE...
....AND SUPERMAN'S FIRST ENEMY.
SKKRRRAAAKKK
HAAAAA!
HELLO, BATMAN.
DO YOU FINALLY UNDERSTAND THE DANGER YOU'RE IN?
ARE YOU FINALLY COMING TO ME FOR HELP?
BUT NOW I'VE NEARLY FREED MYSELF FROM THIS LITTLE CAGE OF YOURS...
...SO HOW ABOUT I JUST KILL YOU INSTEAD?
HARROW! YOU WORKED WITH HIM BEFORE! TELL HIM!
SKKRRRAAAK

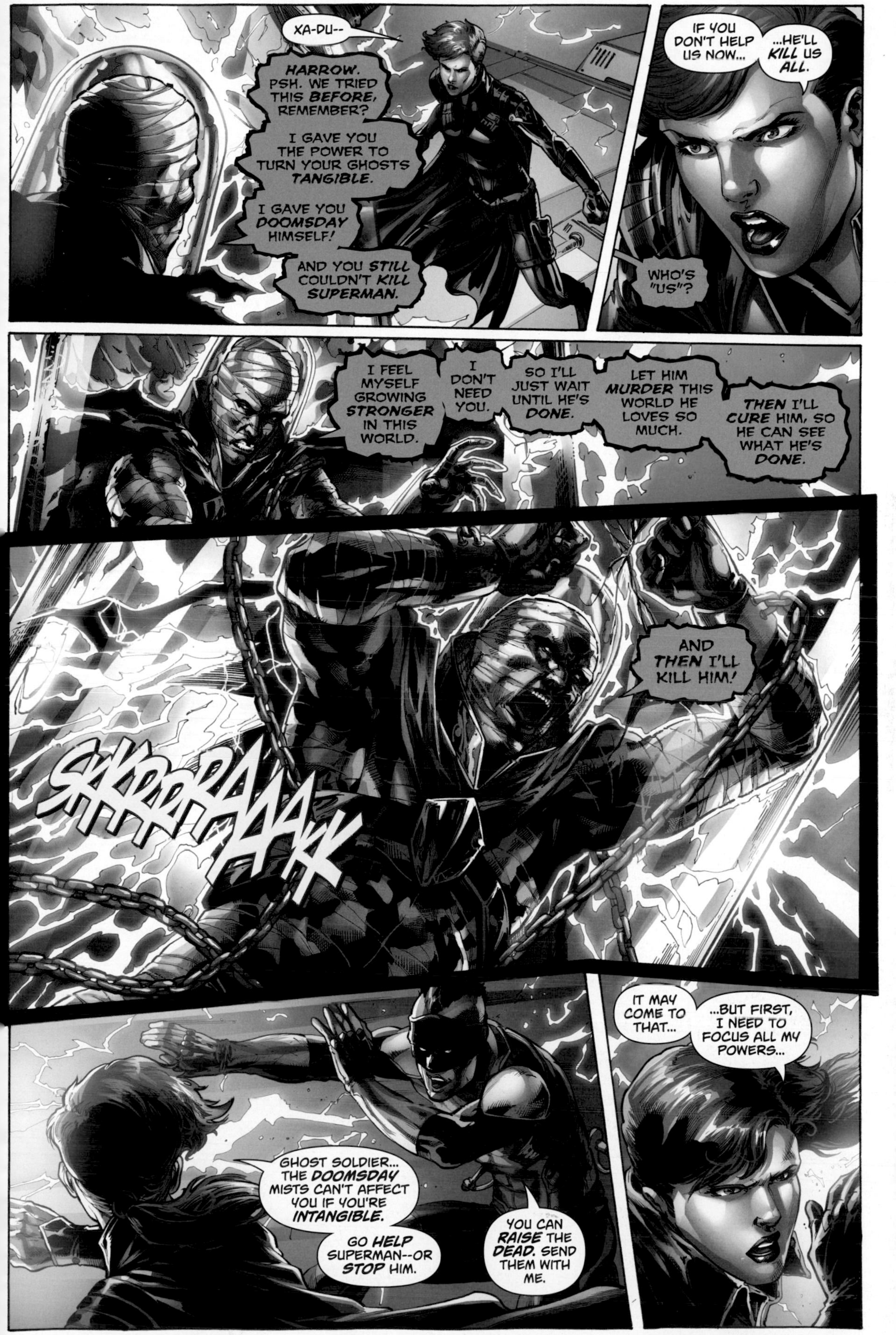
XA-DU--
HARROW. PSH. WE TRIED THIS BEFORE, REMEMBER?
I GAVE YOU THE POWER TO TURN YOUR GHOSTS TANGIBLE.
I GAVE YOU DOOMSDAY HIMSELF!
AND YOU STILL COULDN'T KILL SUPERMAN.
IF YOU DON'T HELP US NOW...
...HE'LL KILL US ALL.
WHO'S "US"?
I FEEL MYSELF GROWING STRONGER IN THIS WORLD.
I DON'T NEED YOU.
SO I'LL JUST WAIT UNTIL HE'S DONE.
LET HIM MURDER THIS WORLD HE LOVES SO MUCH.
THEN I'LL CURE HIM, SO HE CAN SEE WHAT HE'S DONE.
AND THEN I'LL KILL HIM!
SKKRRRAAAKK
GHOST SOLDIER... THE DOOMSDAY MISTS CAN'T AFFECT YOU IF YOU'RE INTANGIBLE.
GO HELP SUPERMAN--OR STOP HIM.
YOU CAN RAISE THE DEAD. SEND THEM WITH ME.
IT MAY COME TO THAT...
...BUT FIRST, I NEED TO FOCUS ALL MY POWERS...

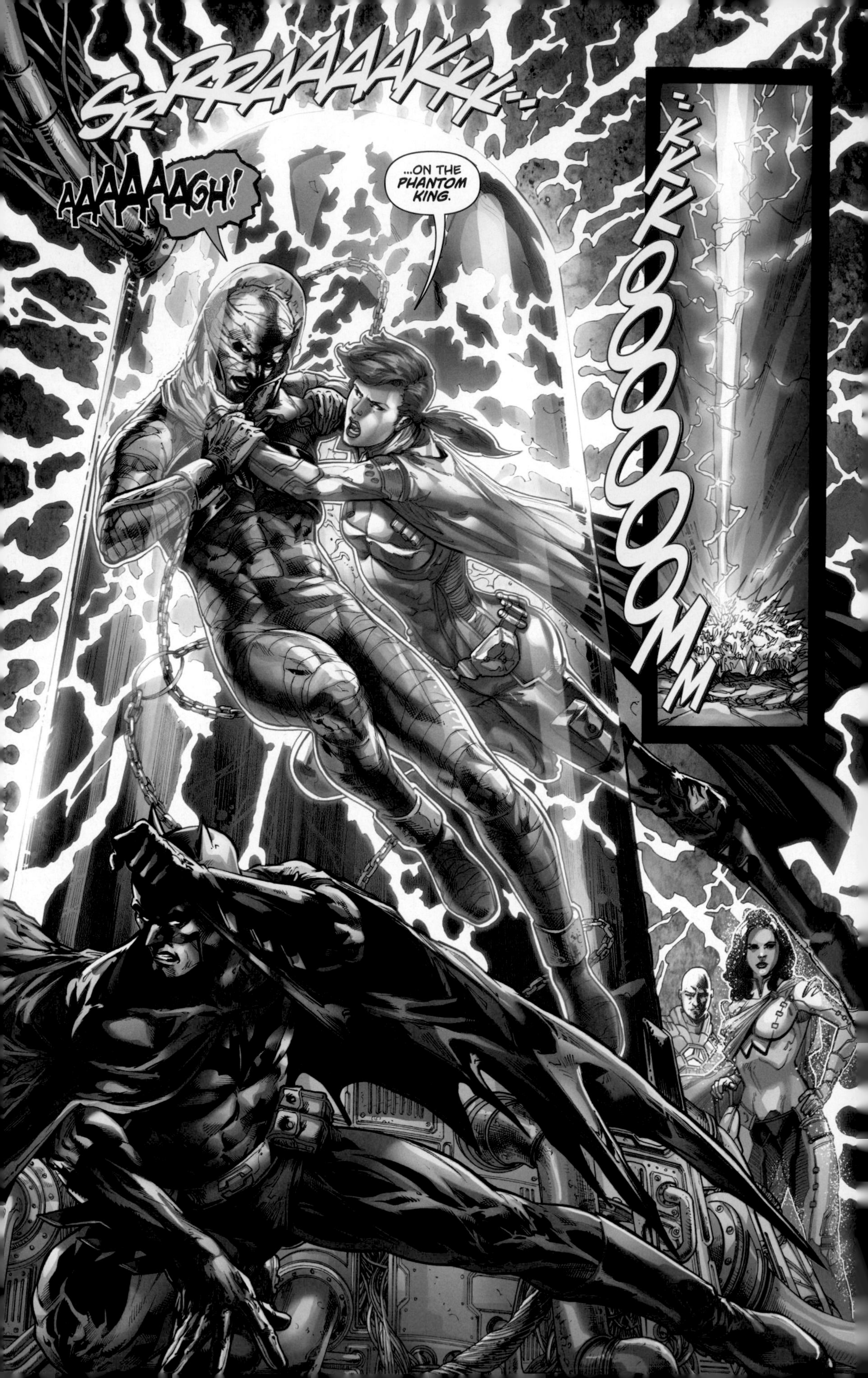
SRRRAAAAAKKK--
AAAAAAGH!
...ON THE PHANTOM KING.
--KKKOOOOOOOOMM

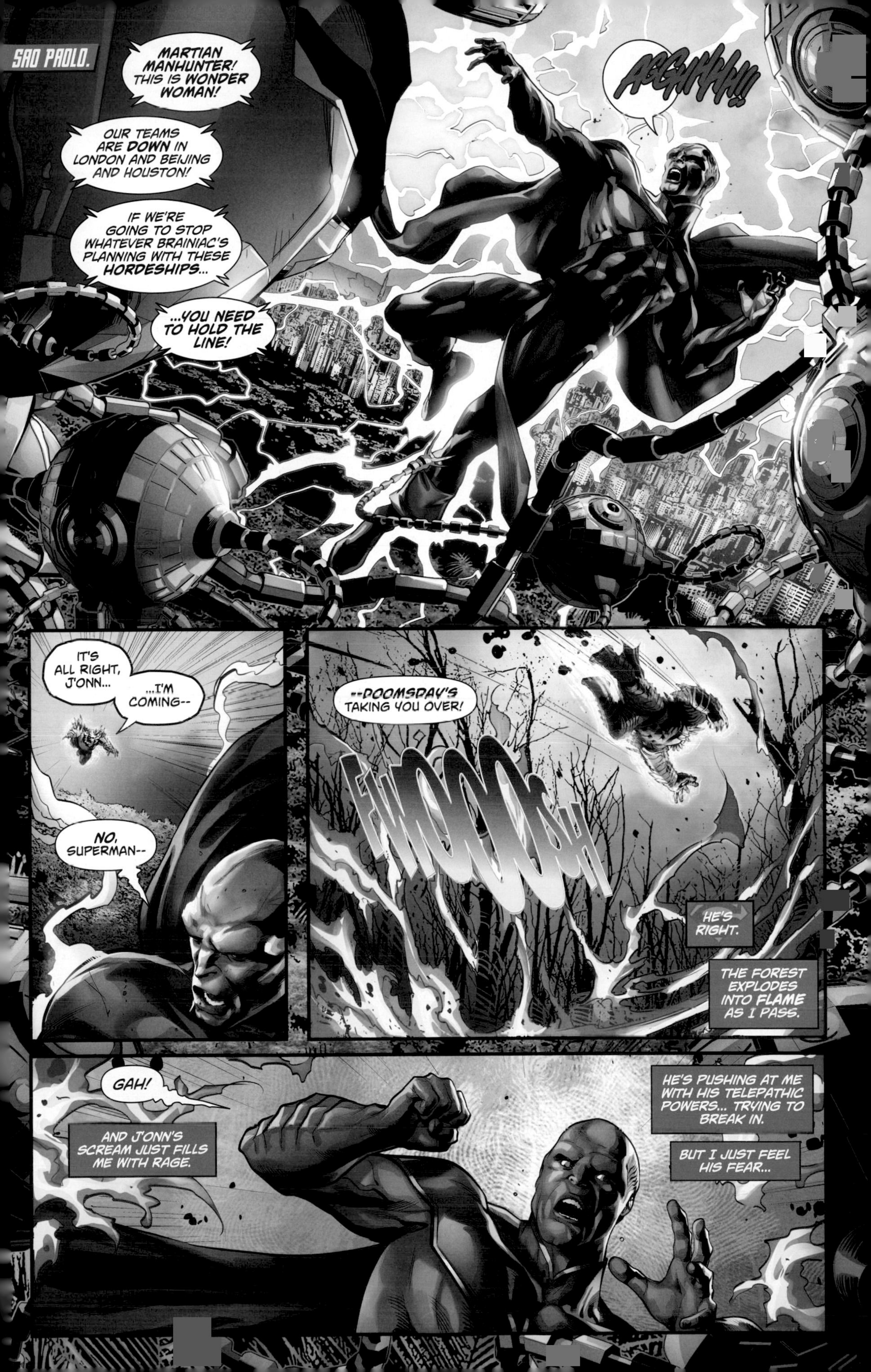
SAO PAOLO.
MARTIAN MANHUNTER! THIS IS WONDER WOMAN!
OUR TEAMS ARE DOWN IN LONDON AND BEIJING AND HOUSTON!
IF WE'RE GOING TO STOP WHATEVER BRAINIAC'S PLANNING WITH THESE HORDESHIPS...
...YOU NEED TO HOLD THE LINE!
IT'S ALL RIGHT, J'ONN...
...I'M COMING--
NO, SUPERMAN--
--DOOMSDAY'S TAKING YOU OVER!
HE'S RIGHT.
THE FOREST EXPLODES INTO FLAME AS I PASS.
GAH!
AND J'ONN'S SCREAM JUST FILLS ME WITH RAGE.
HE'S PUSHING AT ME WITH HIS TELEPATHIC POWERS... TRYING TO BREAK IN.
BUT I JUST FEEL HIS FEAR...

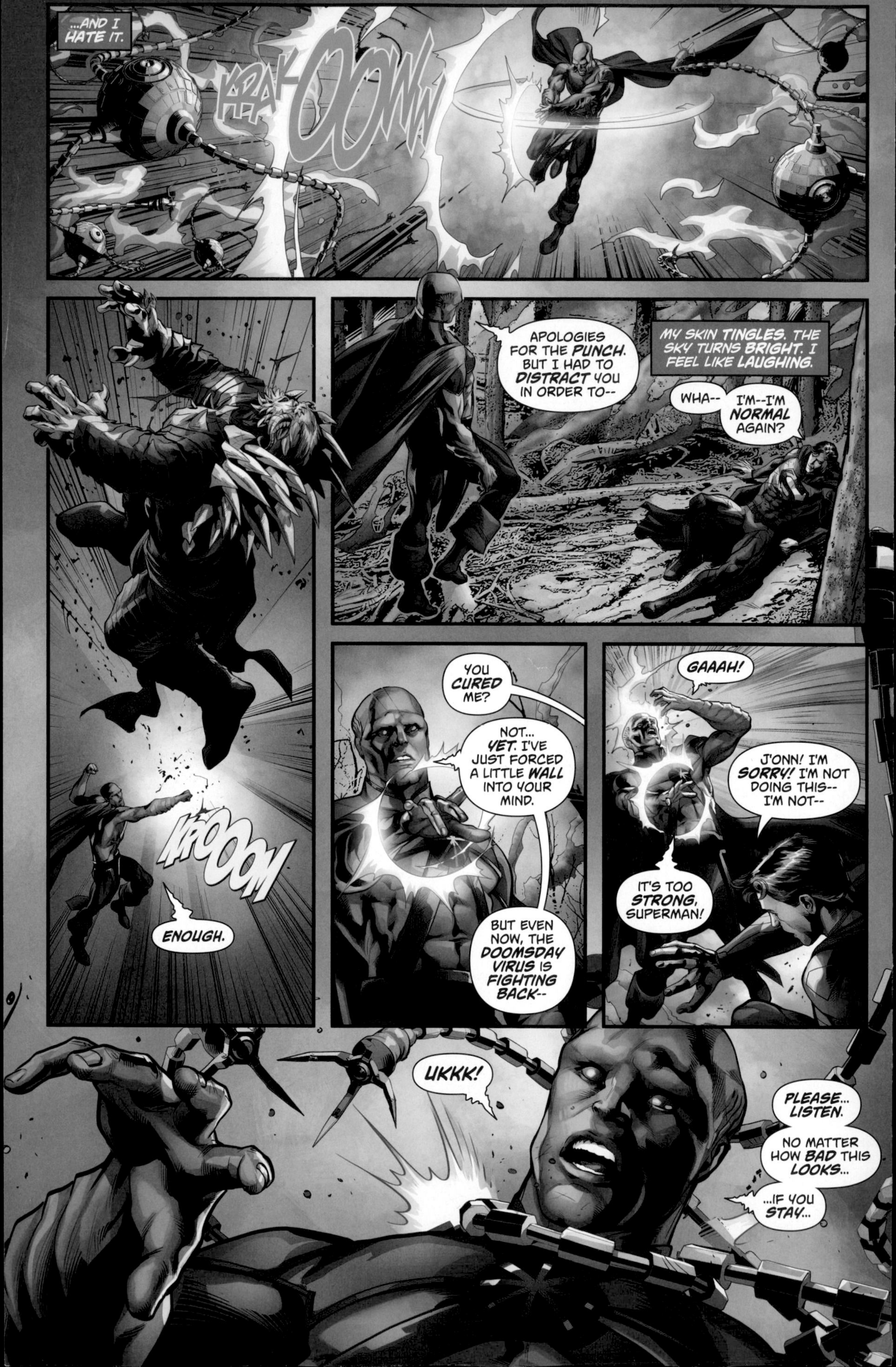
...AND I HATE IT.
KRAKOOOWW
KROOOOM
ENOUGH.
APOLOGIES FOR THE PUNCH. BUT I HAD TO DISTRACT YOU IN ORDER TO--
MY SKIN TINGLES. THE SKY TURNS BRIGHT. I FEEL LIKE LAUGHING.
WHA--
I'M--I'M NORMAL AGAIN?
YOU CURED ME?
NOT... YET. I'VE JUST FORCED A LITTLE WALL INTO YOUR MIND.
BUT EVEN NOW, THE DOOMSDAY VIRUS IS FIGHTING BACK--
GAAAH!
J'ONN! I'M SORRY! I'M NOT DOING THIS-- I'M NOT--
IT'S TOO STRONG, SUPERMAN!
UKKK!
PLEASE... LISTEN.
NO MATTER HOW BAD THIS LOOKS...
...IF YOU STAY...

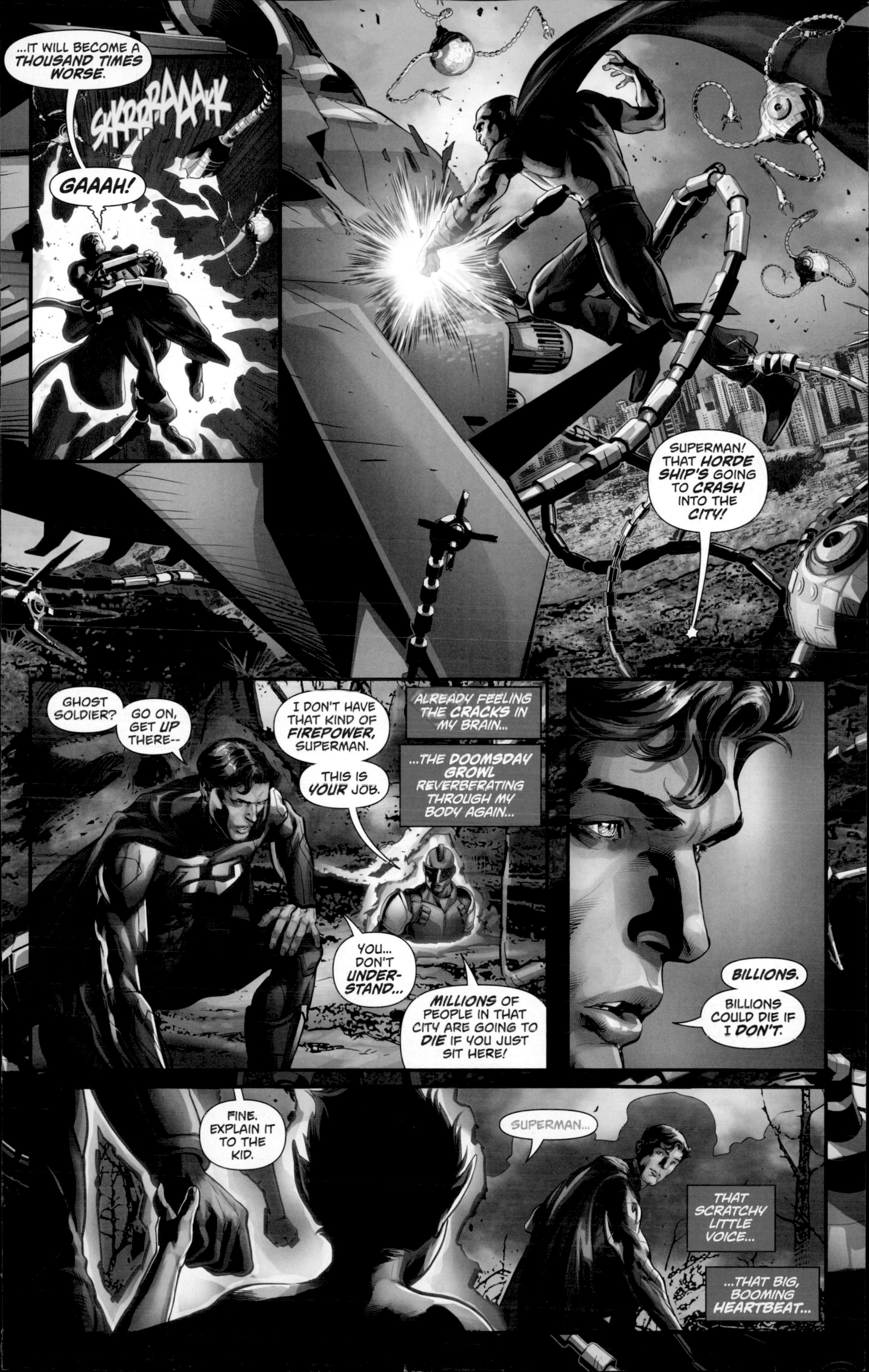

...IT WILL BECOME A THOUSAND TIMES WORSE.
SKRRRRAAAKK
GAAAH!
SUPERMAN! THAT HORDE SHIP'S GOING TO CRASH INTO THE CITY!
GHOST SOLDIER?
GO ON, GET UP THERE--
I DON'T HAVE THAT KIND OF FIREPOWER, SUPERMAN.
THIS IS YOUR JOB.
ALREADY FEELING THE CRACKS IN MY BRAIN...
...THE DOOMSDAY GROWL REVERBERATING THROUGH MY BODY AGAIN...
YOU... DON'T UNDER-STAND...
MILLIONS OF PEOPLE IN THAT CITY ARE GOING TO DIE IF YOU JUST SIT HERE!
BILLIONS.
BILLIONS COULD DIE IF I DON'T.
FINE. EXPLAIN IT TO THE KID.
SUPERMAN...
THAT SCRATCHY LITTLE VOICE...
...THAT BIG, BOOMING HEARTBEAT...

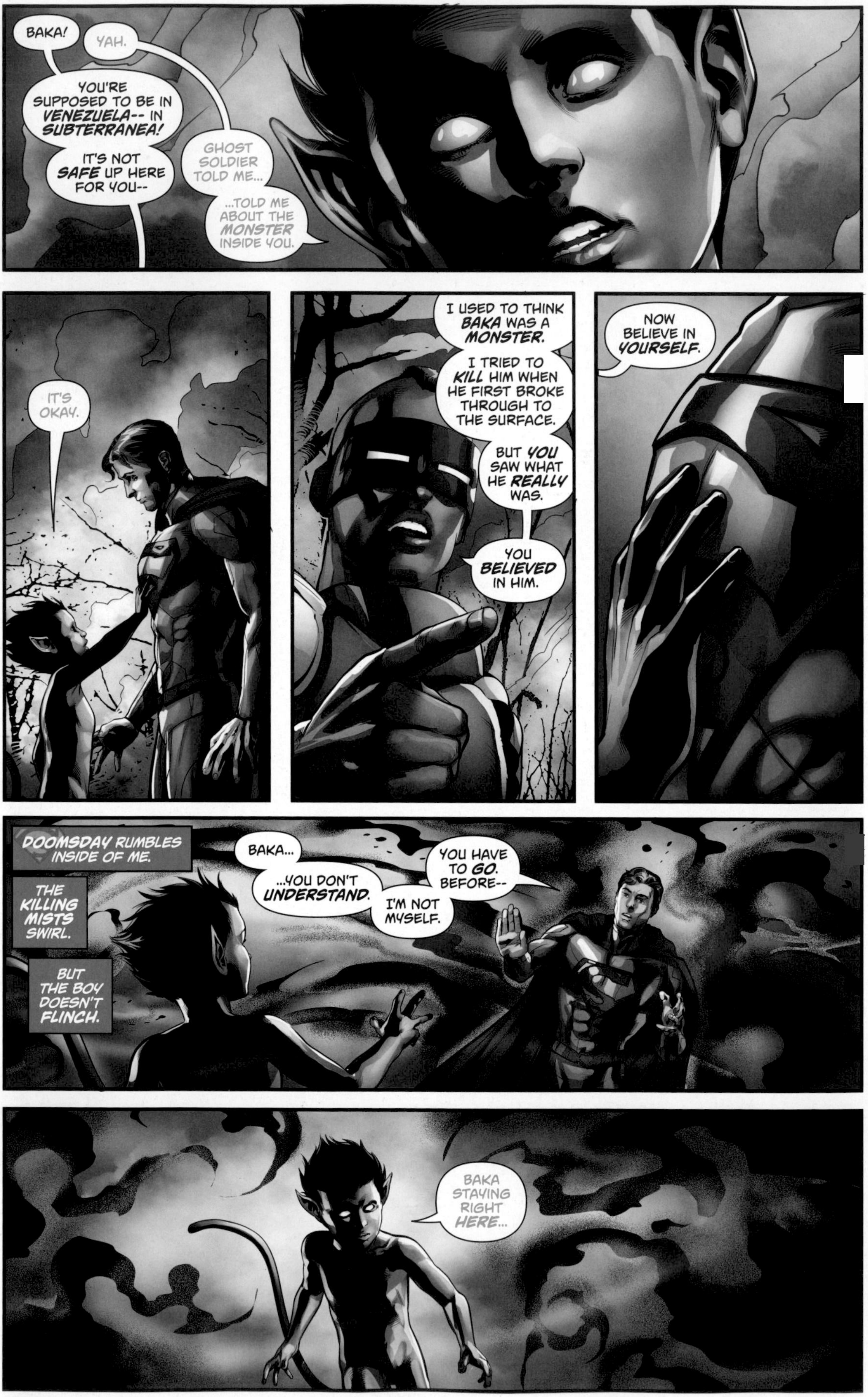
BAKA!
YAH.
YOU'RE SUPPOSED TO BE IN VENEZUELA-- IN SUBTERRANEA!
IT'S NOT SAFE UP HERE FOR YOU--
GHOST SOLDIER TOLD ME...
...TOLD ME ABOUT THE MONSTER INSIDE YOU.
IT'S OKAY.
I USED TO THINK BAKA WAS A MONSTER.
I TRIED TO KILL HIM WHEN HE FIRST BROKE THROUGH TO THE SURFACE.
BUT YOU SAW WHAT HE REALLY WAS.
YOU BELIEVED IN HIM.
NOW BELIEVE IN YOURSELF.
DOOMSDAY RUMBLES INSIDE OF ME.
THE KILLING MISTS SWIRL.
BUT THE BOY DOESN'T FLINCH.
BAKA...
...YOU DON'T UNDERSTAND.
I'M NOT MYSELF.
YOU HAVE TO GO. BEFORE--
BAKA STAYING RIGHT HERE...

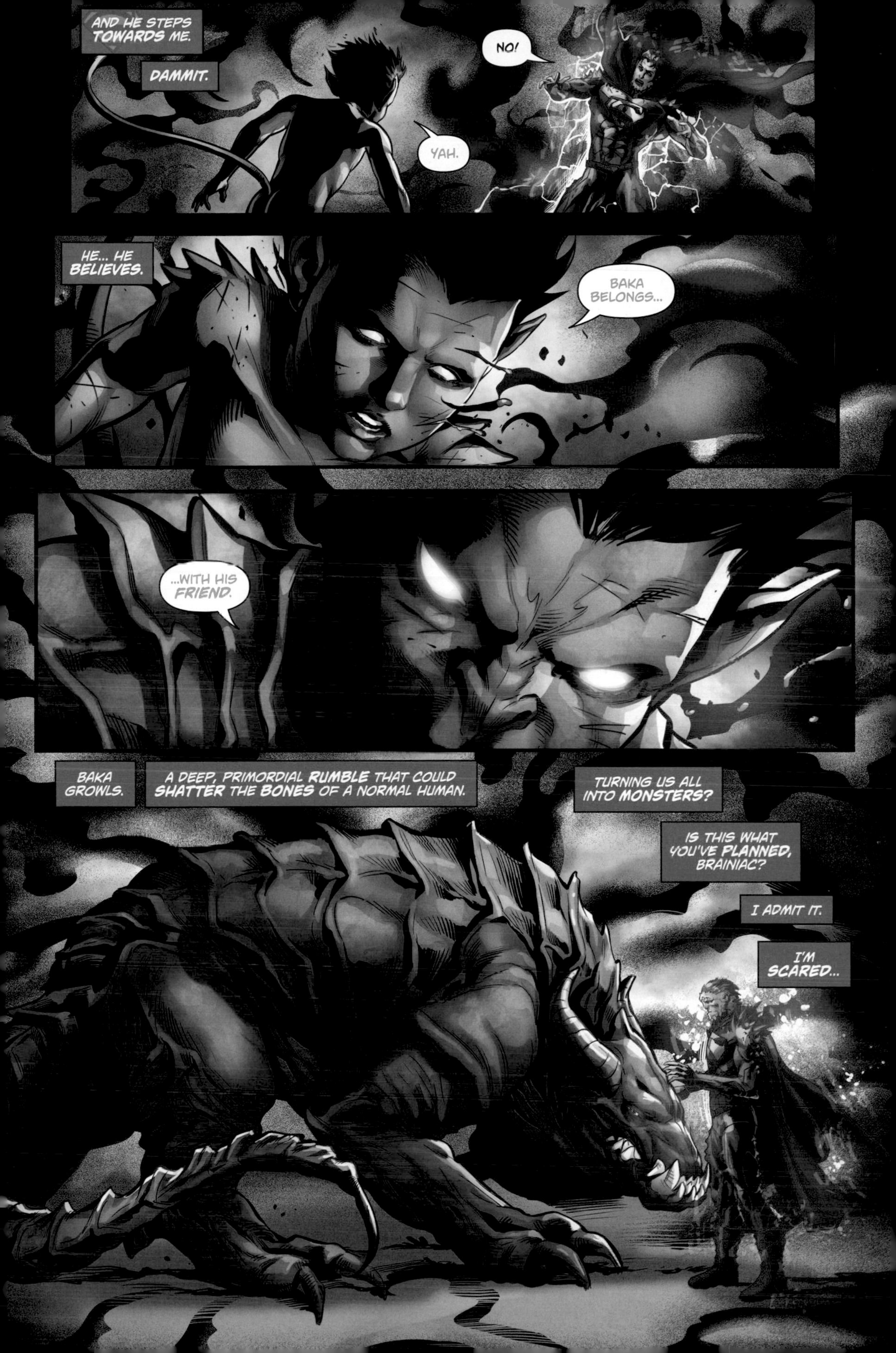
AND HE STEPS TOWARDS ME.
DAMMIT.
NO!
YAH.
HE... HE BELIEVES.
BAKA BELONGS...
...WITH HIS FRIEND.
BAKA GROWLS.
A DEEP, PRIMORDIAL RUMBLE THAT COULD SHATTER THE BONES OF A NORMAL HUMAN.
TURNING US ALL INTO MONSTERS?
IS THIS WHAT YOU'VE PLANNED, BRAINIAC?
I ADMIT IT.
I'M SCARED...

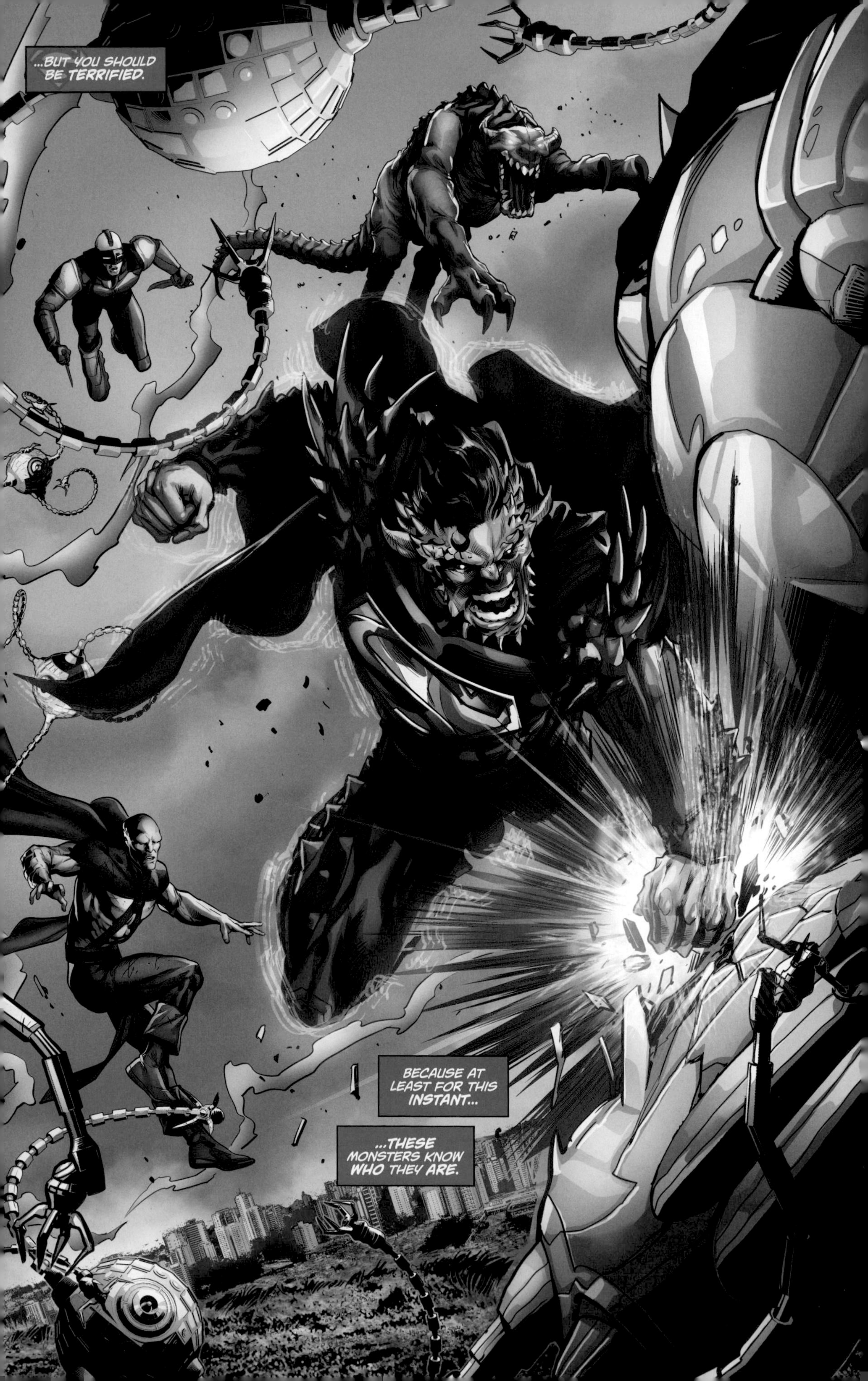
...BUT YOU SHOULD BE TERRIFIED.
BECAUSE AT LEAST FOR THIS INSTANT...
...THESE MONSTERS KNOW WHO THEY ARE.

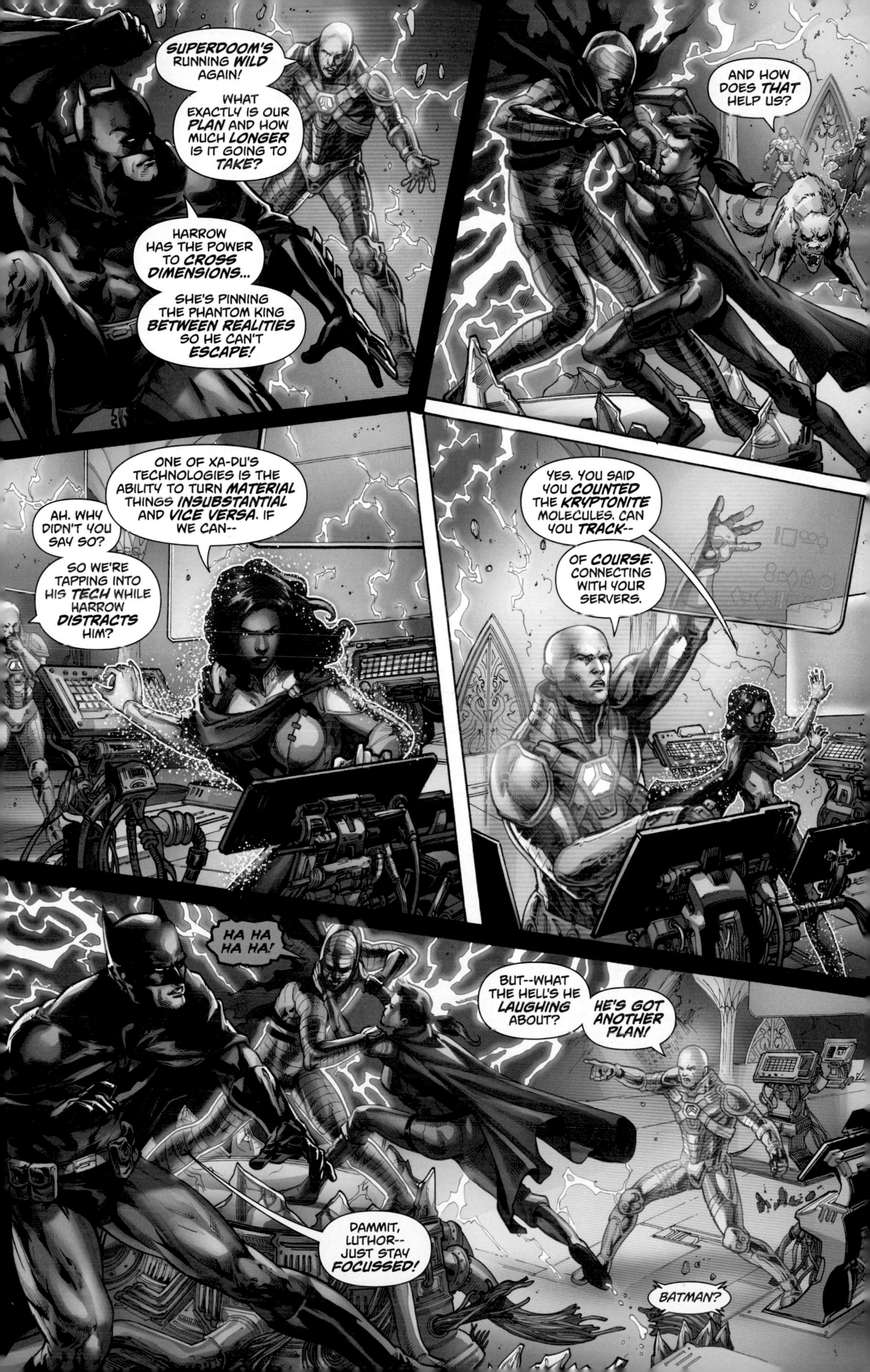
SUPERDOOM'S RUNNING WILD AGAIN!
WHAT EXACTLY IS OUR PLAN AND HOW MUCH LONGER IS IT GOING TO TAKE?
HARROW HAS THE POWER TO CROSS DIMENSIONS...
SHE'S PINNING THE PHANTOM KING BETWEEN REALITIES SO HE CAN'T ESCAPE!
AND HOW DOES THAT HELP US?
ONE OF XA-DU'S TECHNOLOGIES IS THE ABILITY TO TURN MATERIAL THINGS INSUBSTANTIAL AND VICE VERSA. IF WE CAN--
AH. WHY DIDN'T YOU SAY SO?
SO WE'RE TAPPING INTO HIS TECH WHILE HARROW DISTRACTS HIM?
YES. YOU SAID YOU COUNTED THE KRYPTONITE MOLECULES. CAN YOU TRACK--
OF COURSE. CONNECTING WITH YOUR SERVERS.
HA HA HA HA!
BUT--WHAT THE HELL'S HE LAUGHING ABOUT?
HE'S GOT ANOTHER PLAN!
DAMMIT, LUTHOR-- JUST STAY FOCUSSED!
BATMAN?

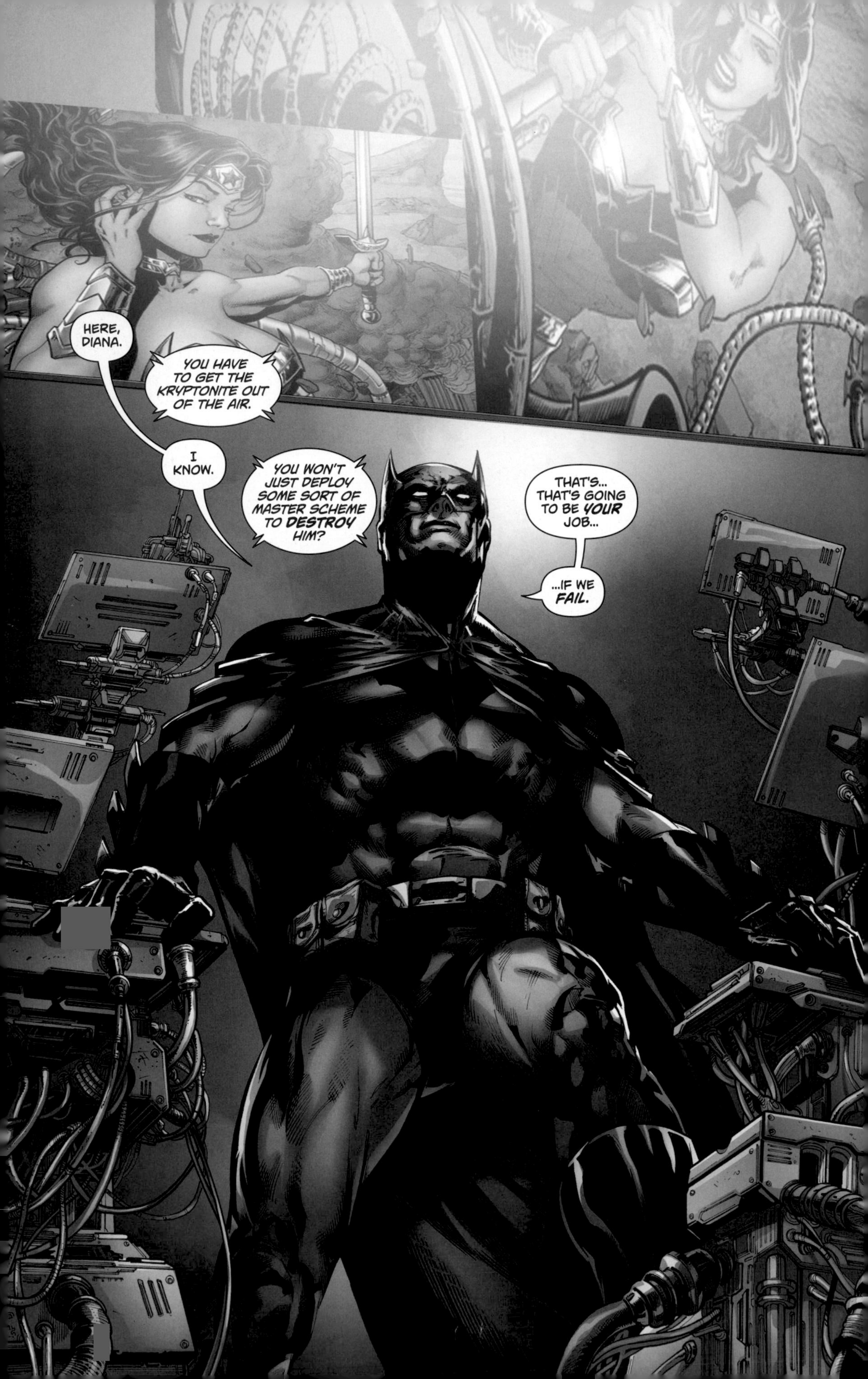
HERE, DIANA.
YOU HAVE TO GET THE KRYPTONITE OUT OF THE AIR.
I KNOW.
YOU WON'T JUST DEPLOY SOME SORT OF MASTER SCHEME TO DESTROY HIM?
THAT'S... THAT'S GOING TO BE YOUR JOB...
...IF WE FAIL.

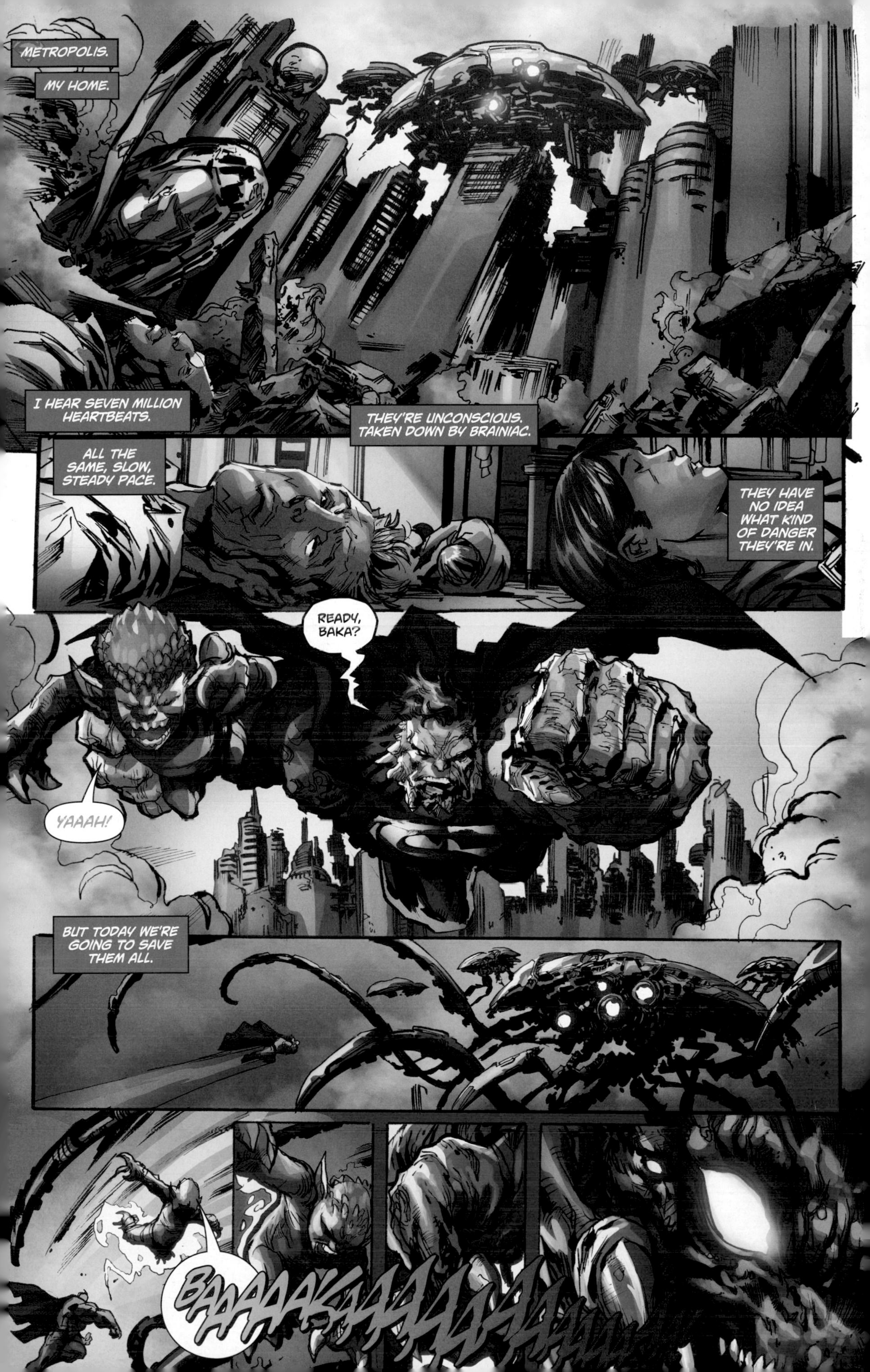
METROPOLIS.
MY HOME.
I HEAR SEVEN MILLION HEARTBEATS.
THEY'RE UNCONSCIOUS. TAKEN DOWN BY BRAINIAC.
ALL THE SAME, SLOW, STEADY PACE.
THEY HAVE NO IDEA WHAT KIND OF DANGER THEY'RE IN.
READY, BAKA?
YAAAH!
BUT TODAY WE'RE GOING TO SAVE THEM ALL.
BAAAAKAAAAAAAAAA

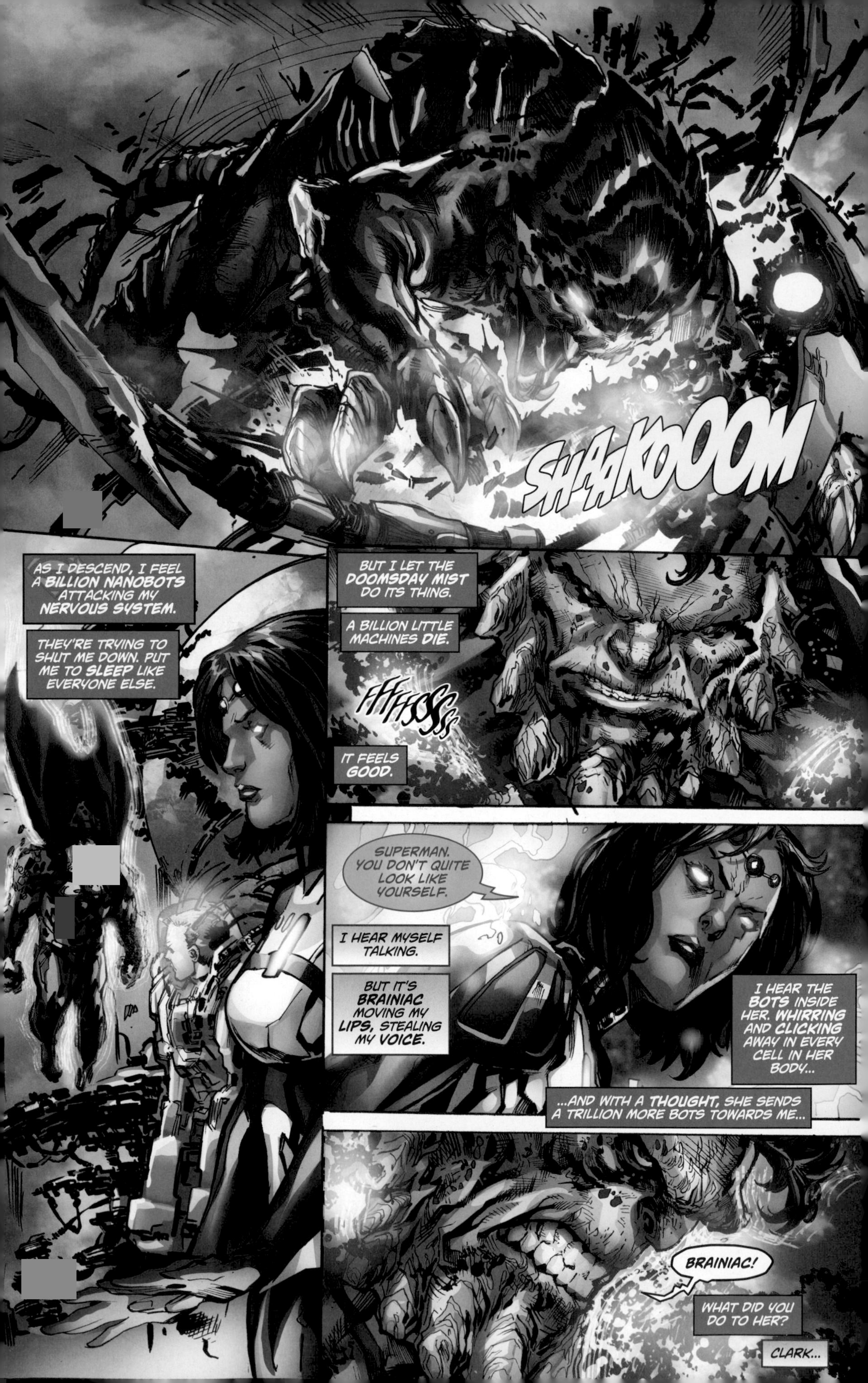
SHAAKOOOM
AS I DESCEND, I FEEL A BILLION NANOBOTS ATTACKING MY NERVOUS SYSTEM.
THEY'RE TRYING TO SHUT ME DOWN. PUT ME TO SLEEP LIKE EVERYONE ELSE.
BUT I LET THE DOOMSDAY MIST DO ITS THING.
A BILLION LITTLE MACHINES DIE.
FFFFSSSsss
IT FEELS GOOD.
SUPERMAN. YOU DON'T QUITE LOOK LIKE YOURSELF.
I HEAR MYSELF TALKING.
BUT IT'S BRAINIAC MOVING MY LIPS, STEALING MY VOICE.
I HEAR THE BOTS INSIDE HER. WHIRRING AND CLICKING AWAY IN EVERY CELL IN HER BODY...
...AND WITH A THOUGHT, SHE SENDS A TRILLION MORE BOTS TOWARDS ME...
BRAINIAC!
WHAT DID YOU DO TO HER?
CLARK...

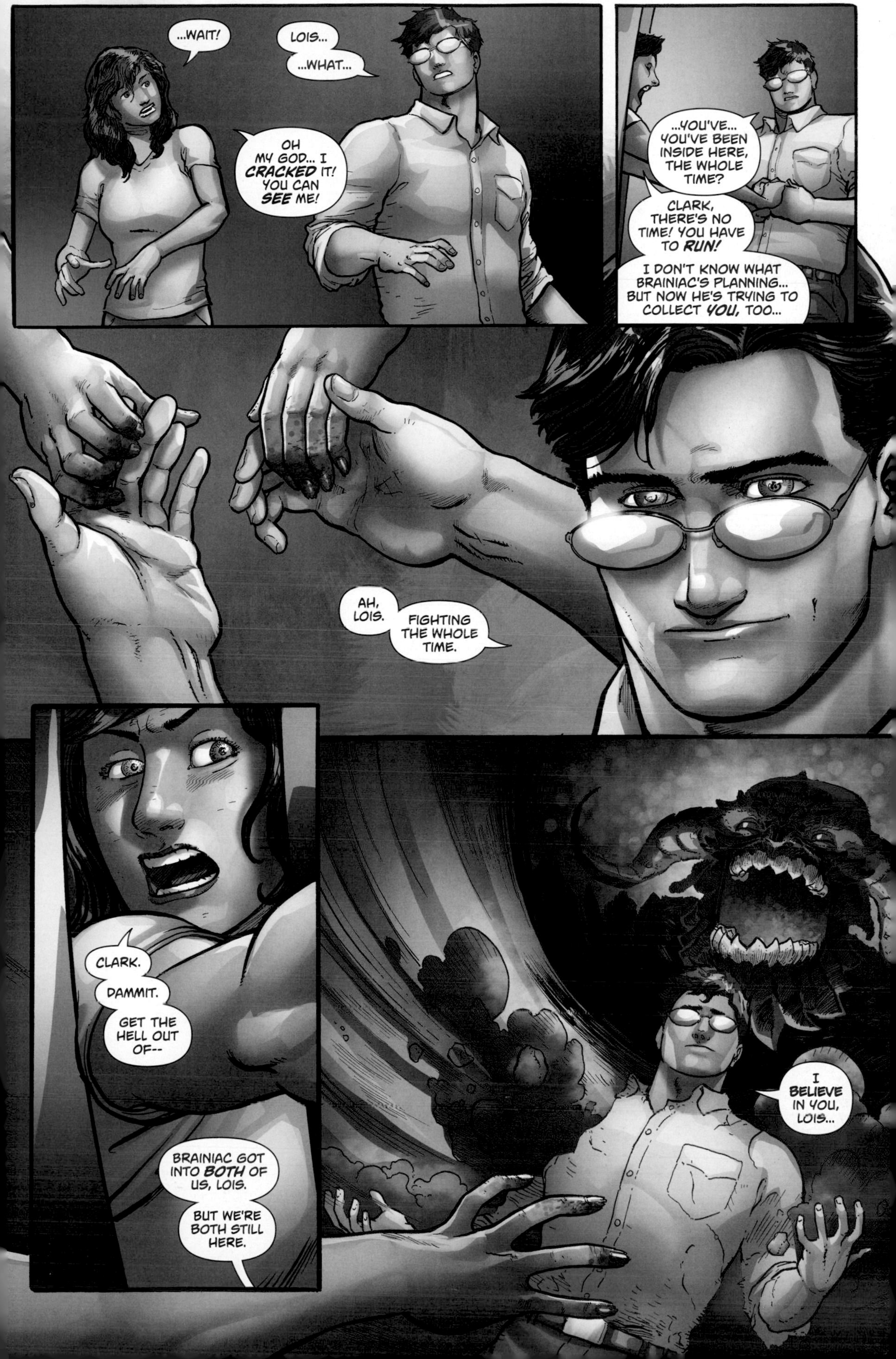
...WAIT!
LOIS...
...WHAT...
OH MY GOD... I CRACKED IT! YOU CAN SEE ME!
...YOU'VE... YOU'VE BEEN INSIDE HERE, THE WHOLE TIME?
CLARK, THERE'S NO TIME! YOU HAVE TO RUN!
I DON'T KNOW WHAT BRAINIAC'S PLANNING... BUT NOW HE'S TRYING TO COLLECT YOU, TOO...
AH, LOIS.
FIGHTING THE WHOLE TIME.
CLARK.
DAMMIT.
GET THE HELL OUT OF--
BRAINIAC GOT INTO BOTH OF US, LOIS.
BUT WE'RE BOTH STILL HERE.
I BELIEVE IN YOU, LOIS...

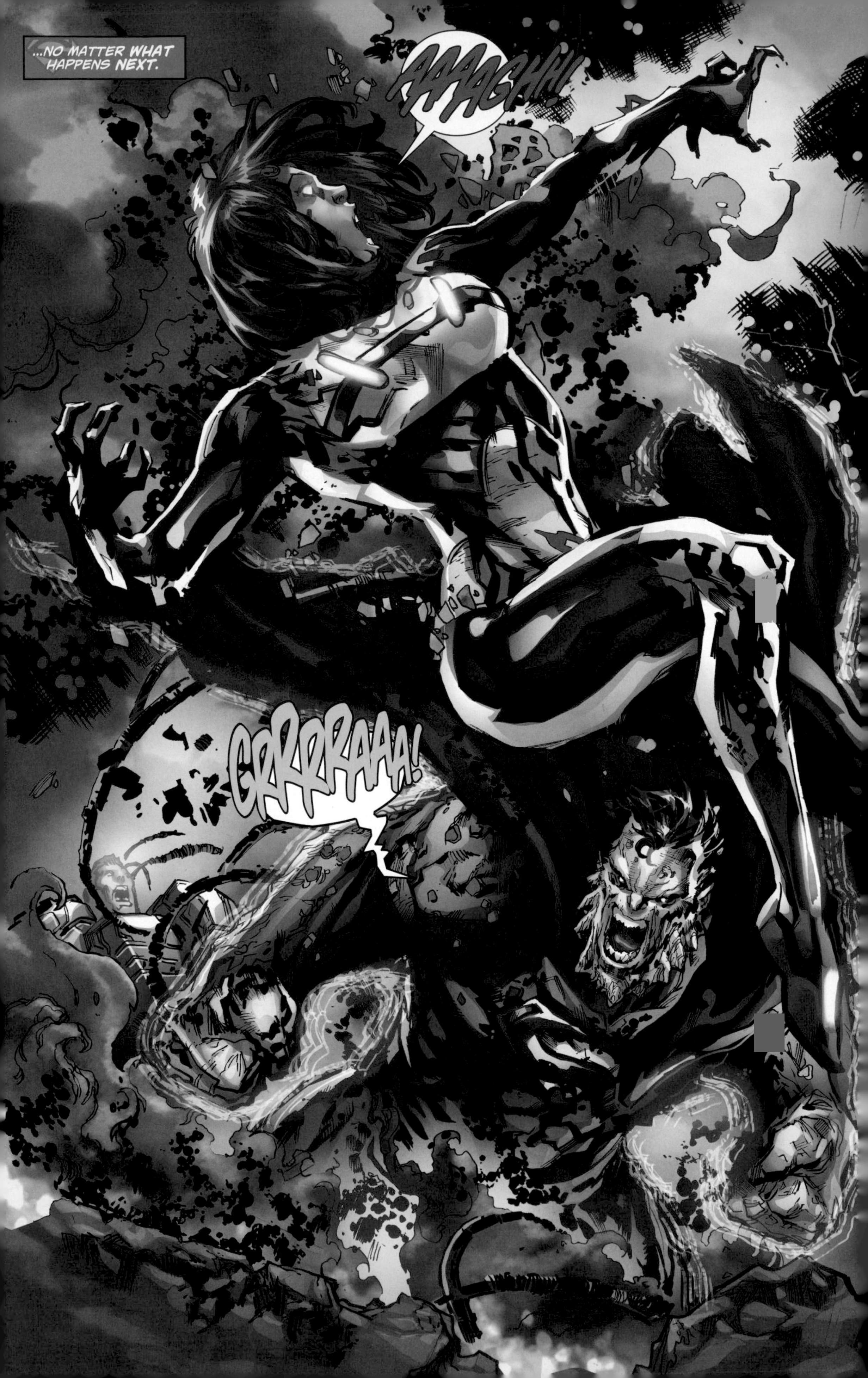
...NO MATTER WHAT HAPPENS NEXT.
AAAAGHH!
GRRRRAAA!

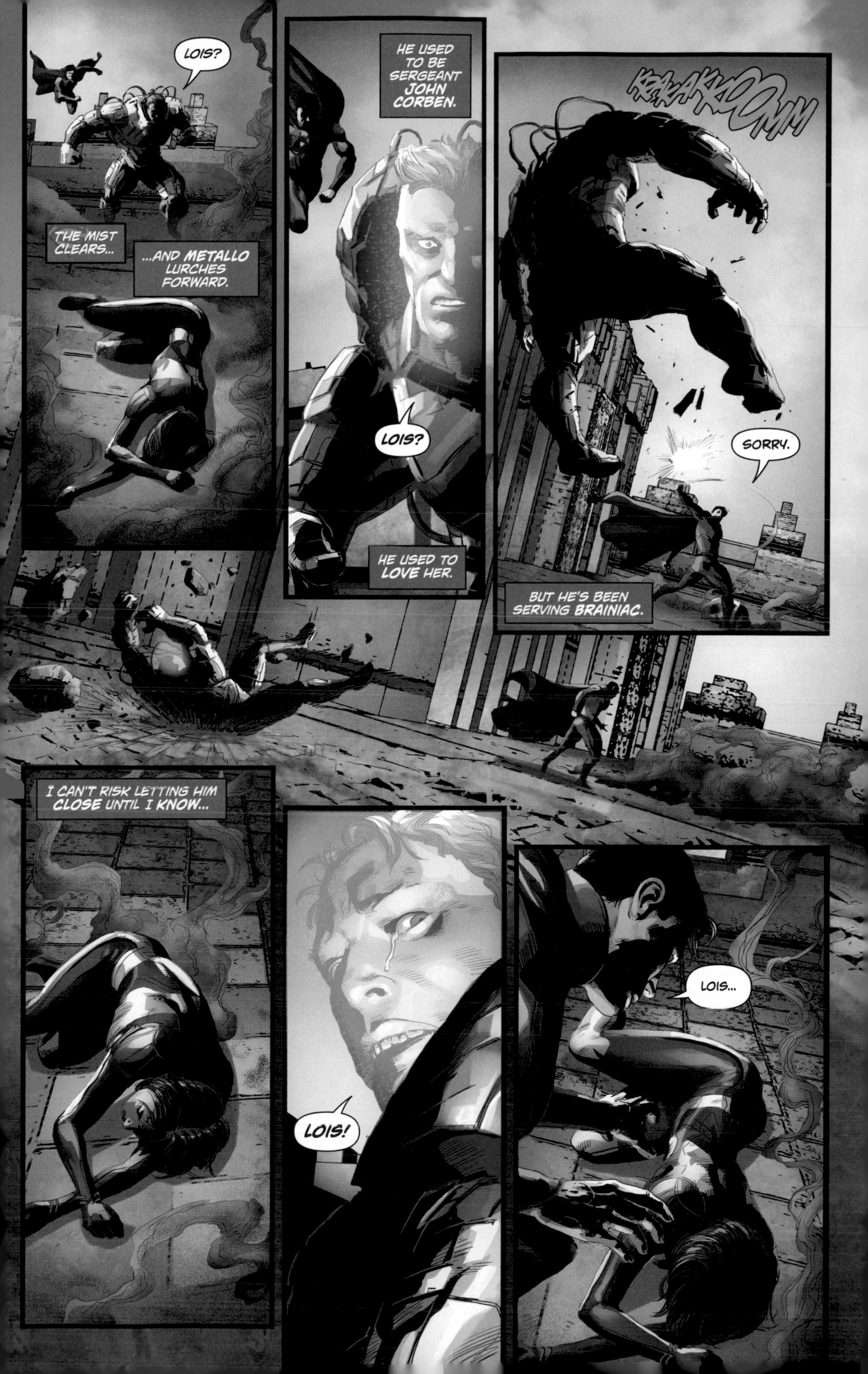
LOIS?
THE MIST CLEARS...
...AND METALLO LURCHES FORWARD.
HE USED TO BE SERGEANT JOHN CORBEN.
LOIS?
HE USED TO LOVE HER.
KRAKAKKOOMM
SORRY.
BUT HE'S BEEN SERVING BRAINIAC.
I CAN'T RISK LETTING HIM CLOSE UNTIL I KNOW...
LOIS!
LOIS...

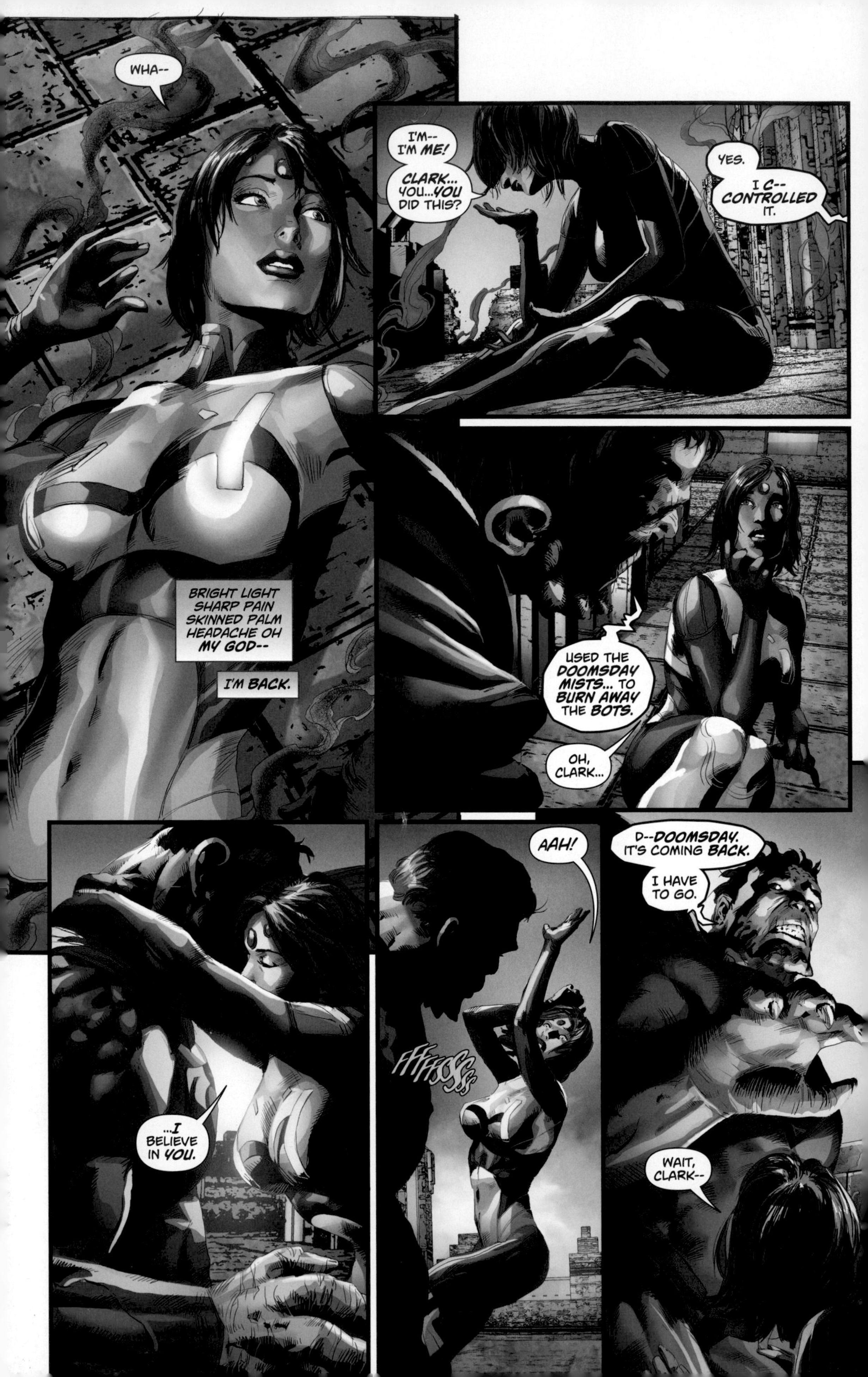
WHA--
I'M-- I'M ME!
CLARK... YOU...YOU DID THIS?
YES.
I C-- CONTROLLED IT.
BRIGHT LIGHT SHARP PAIN SKINNED PALM HEADACHE OH MY GOD--
I'M BACK.
USED THE DOOMSDAY MISTS... TO BURN AWAY THE BOTS.
OH, CLARK...
...I BELIEVE IN YOU.
AAH!
FFFFSSSSS
D--DOOMSDAY. IT'S COMING BACK.
I HAVE TO GO.
WAIT, CLARK--

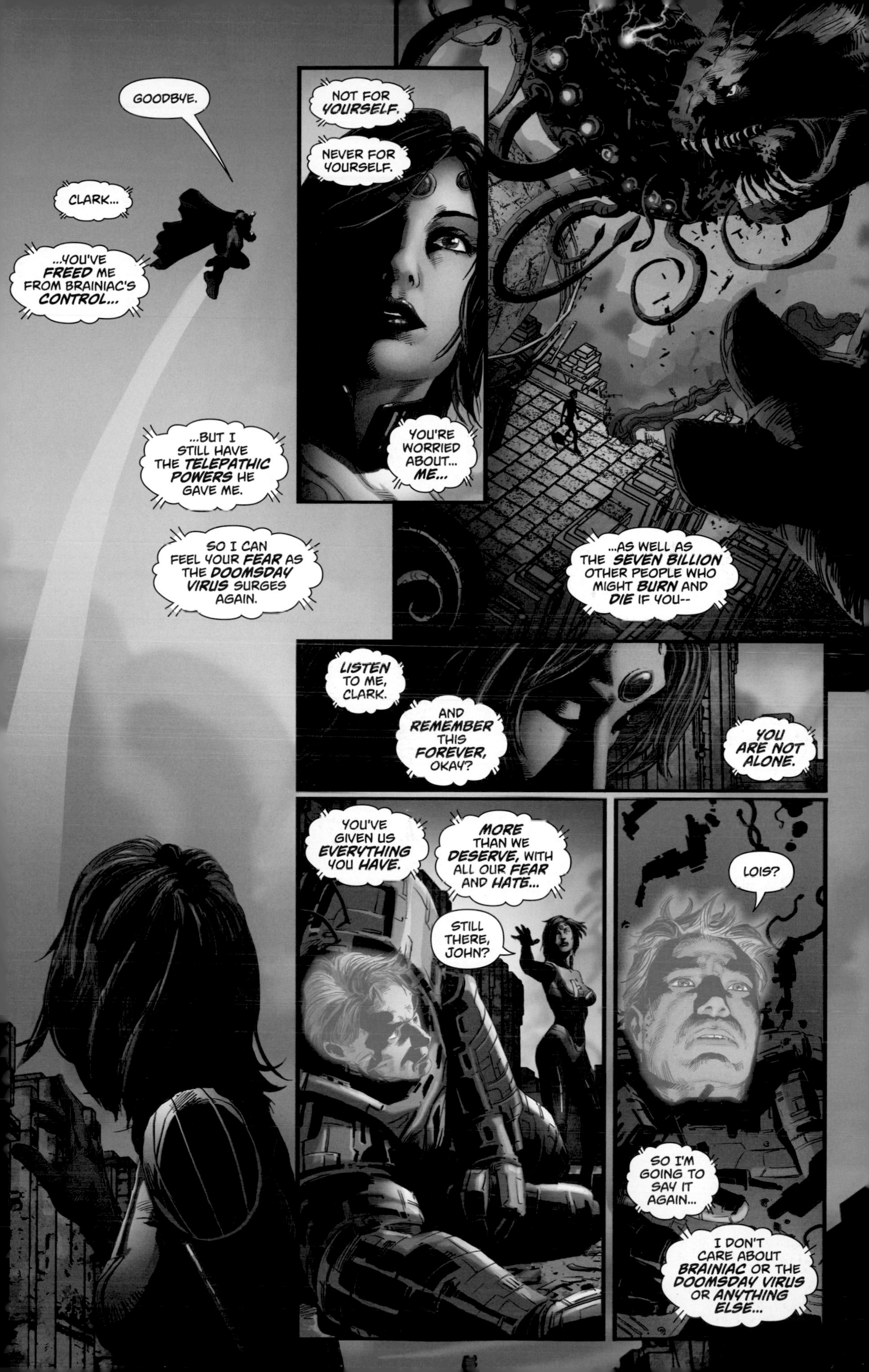
GOODBYE.
CLARK...
...YOU'VE FREED ME FROM BRAINIAC'S CONTROL...
...BUT I STILL HAVE THE TELEPATHIC POWERS HE GAVE ME.
SO I CAN FEEL YOUR FEAR AS THE DOOMSDAY VIRUS SURGES AGAIN.
NOT FOR YOURSELF.
NEVER FOR YOURSELF.
YOU'RE WORRIED ABOUT... ME...
...AS WELL AS THE SEVEN BILLION OTHER PEOPLE WHO MIGHT BURN AND DIE IF YOU--
LISTEN TO ME, CLARK.
AND REMEMBER THIS FOREVER, OKAY?
YOU ARE NOT ALONE.
YOU'VE GIVEN US EVERYTHING YOU HAVE.
MORE THAN WE DESERVE, WITH ALL OUR FEAR AND HATE...
STILL THERE, JOHN?
LOIS?
SO I'M GOING TO SAY IT AGAIN...
I DON'T CARE ABOUT BRAINIAC OR THE DOOMSDAY VIRUS OR ANYTHING ELSE...

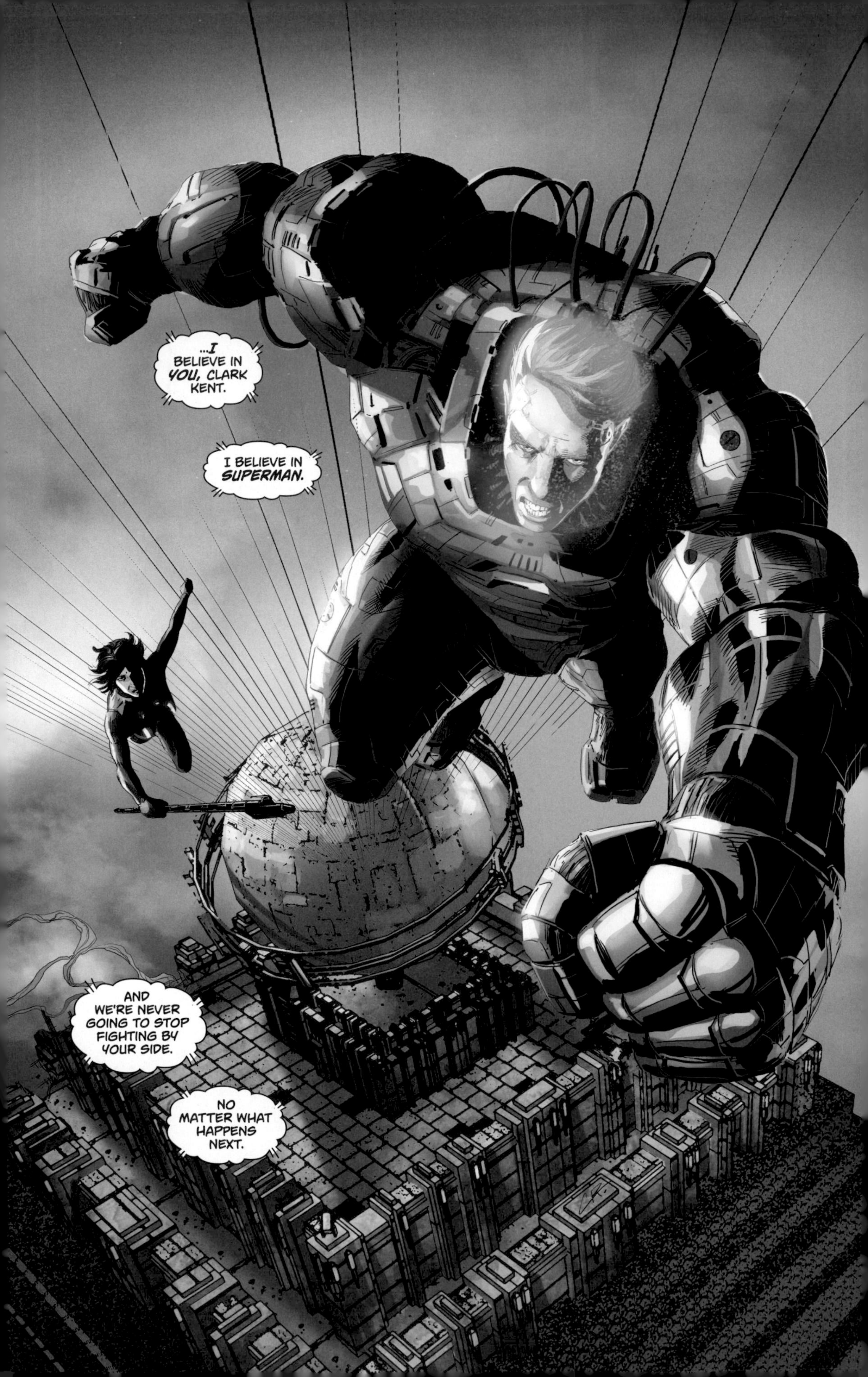
...I BELIEVE IN YOU, CLARK KENT.
I BELIEVE IN SUPERMAN.
AND WE'RE NEVER GOING TO STOP FIGHTING BY YOUR SIDE.
NO MATTER WHAT HAPPENS NEXT.

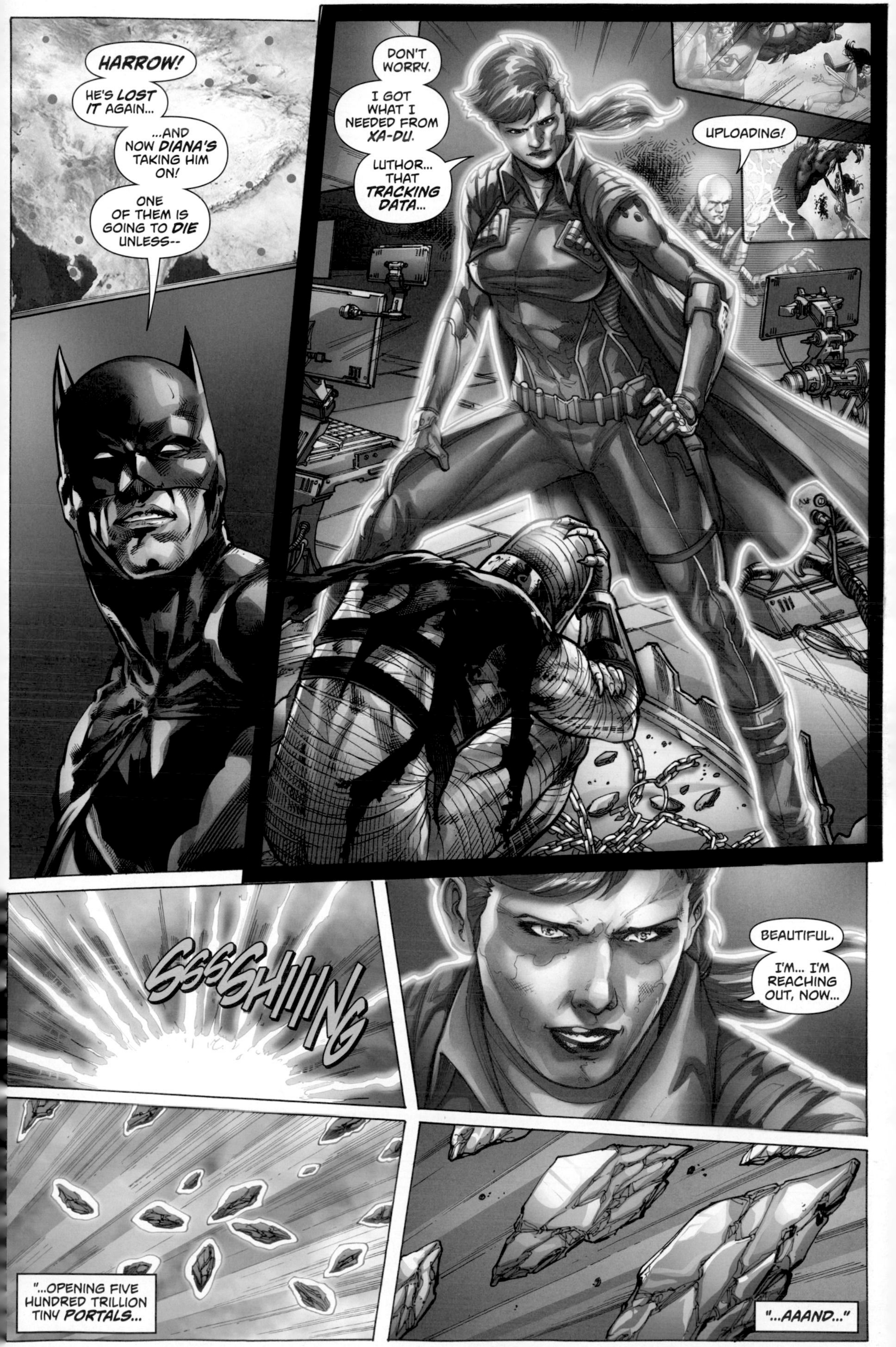
HARROW!
HE'S LOST IT AGAIN...
...AND NOW DIANA'S TAKING HIM ON!
ONE OF THEM IS GOING TO DIE UNLESS--
DON'T WORRY.
I GOT WHAT I NEEDED FROM XA-DU.
LUTHOR... THAT TRACKING DATA...
UPLOADING!
SSSSHIIIING
BEAUTIFUL.
I'M... I'M REACHING OUT, NOW...
"...OPENING FIVE HUNDRED TRILLION TINY PORTALS...
"...AAAND..."

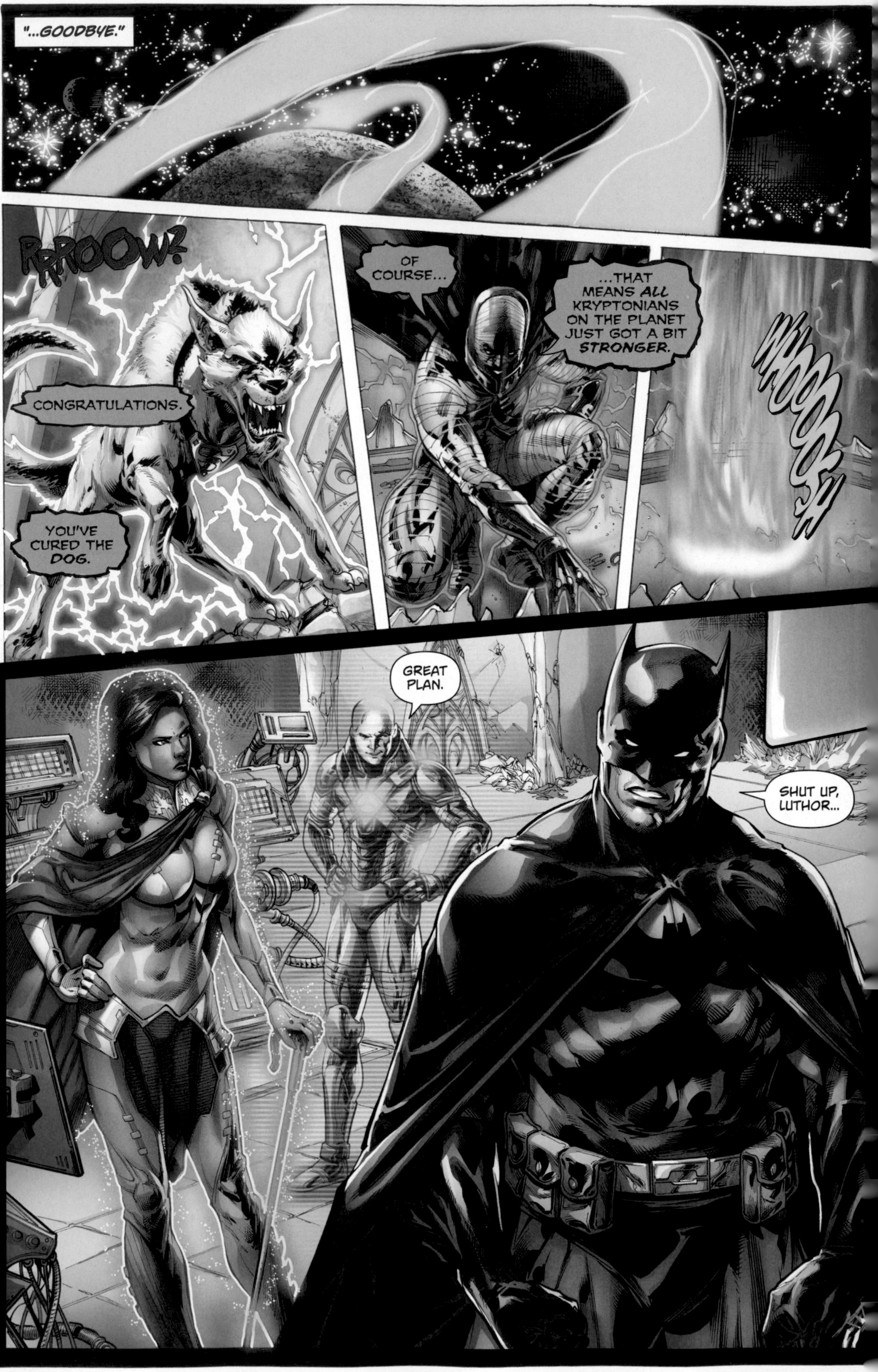
"...GOODBYE."
RRROOW?
CONGRATULATIONS.
YOU'VE CURED THE DOG.
OF COURSE...
...THAT MEANS ALL KRYPTONIANS ON THE PLANET JUST GOT A BIT STRONGER.
WHOOOOOSH
GREAT PLAN.
SHUT UP, LUTHOR...

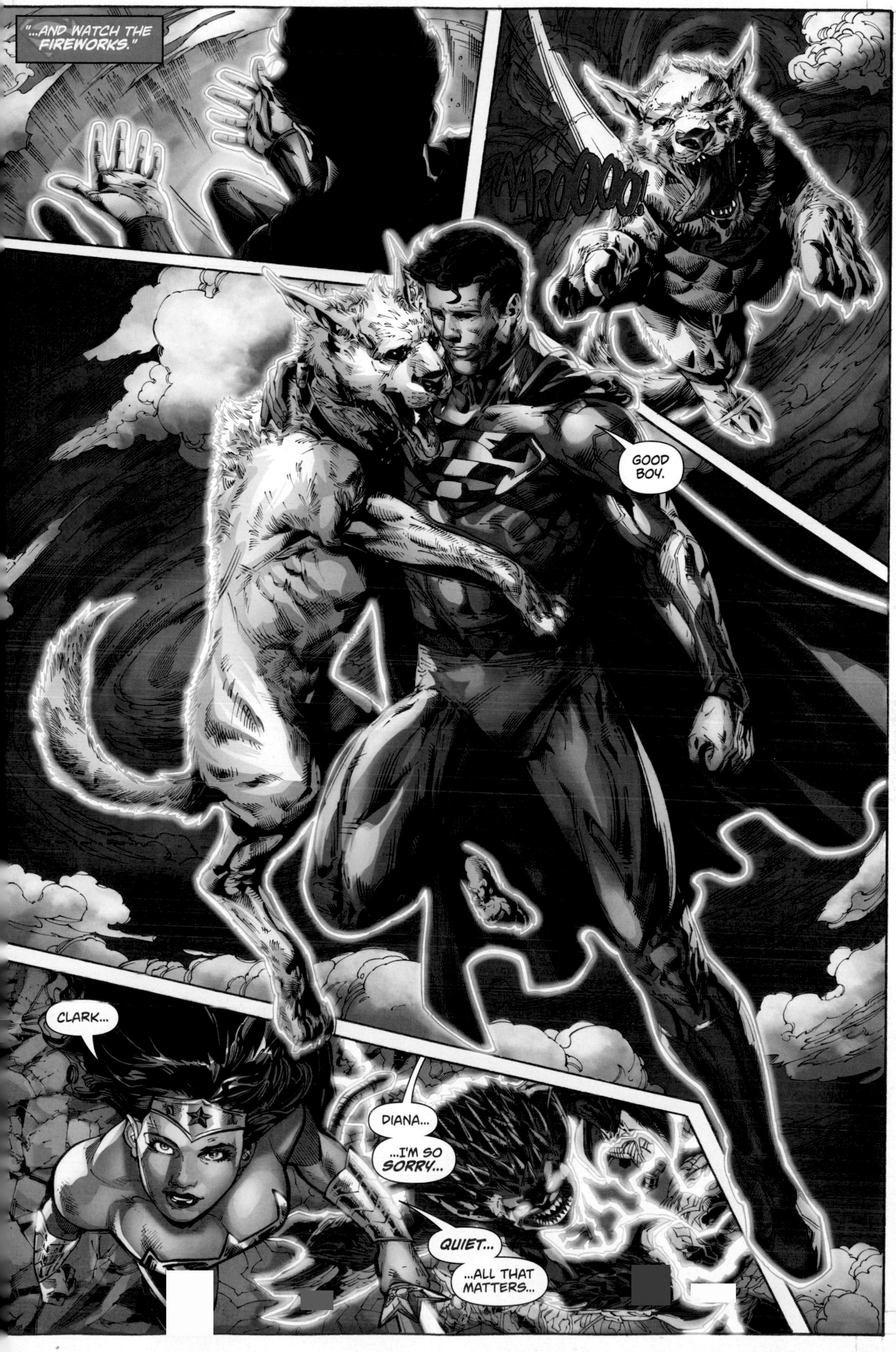
"...AND WATCH THE FIREWORKS."
AAROOOOO!
GOOD BOY.
CLARK...
DIANA...
...I'M SO SORRY...
QUIET...
...ALL THAT MATTERS...

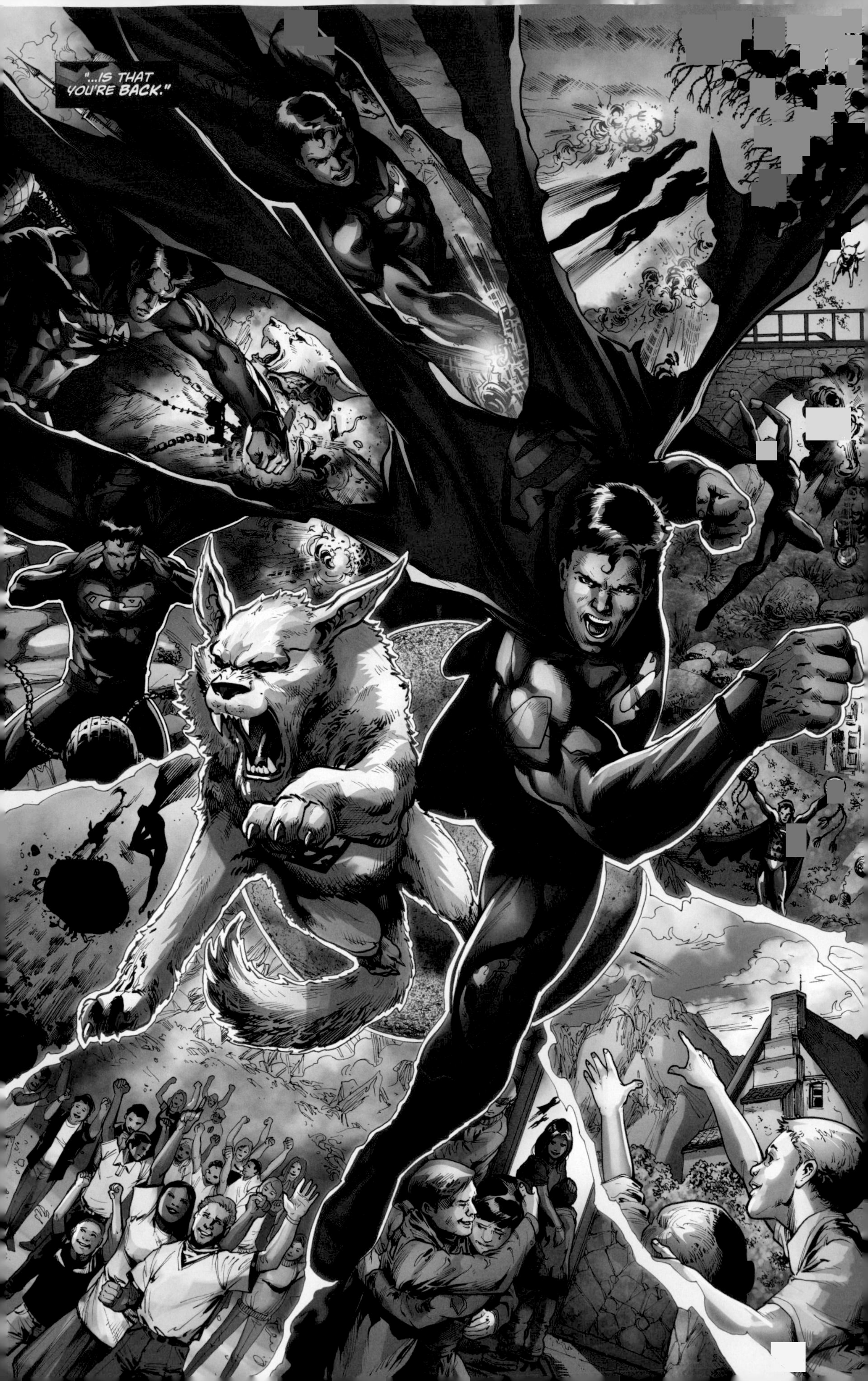
"...IS THAT YOU'RE BACK."

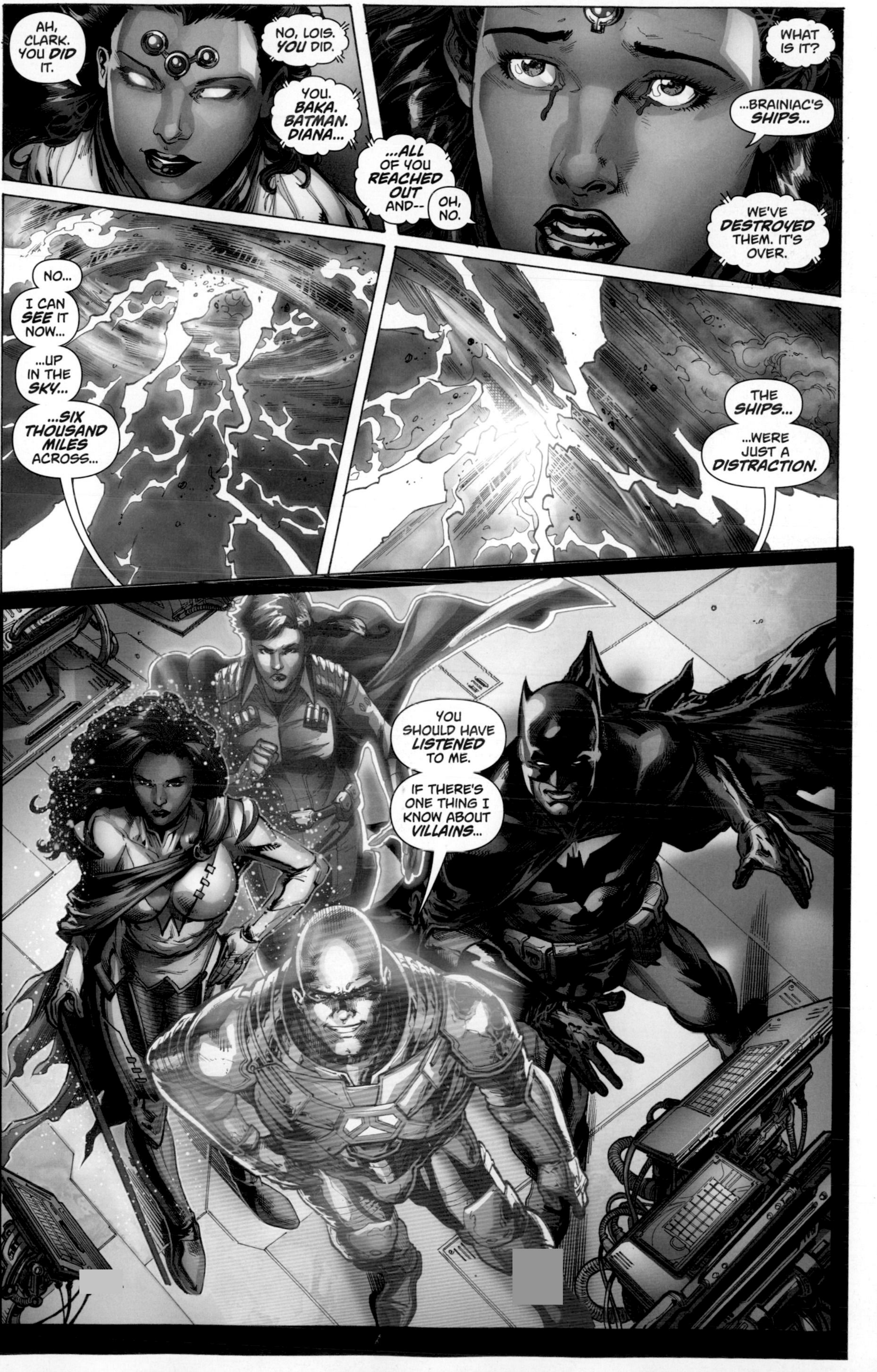
AH, CLARK. YOU DID IT.
NO, LOIS. YOU DID.
YOU. BAKA. BATMAN. DIANA...
...ALL OF YOU REACHED OUT AND--
OH, NO.
WHAT IS IT?
...BRAINIAC'S SHIPS...
WE'VE DESTROYED THEM. IT'S OVER.
NO...
I CAN SEE IT NOW...
...UP IN THE SKY...
...SIX THOUSAND MILES ACROSS...
THE SHIPS...
...WERE JUST A DISTRACTION.
YOU SHOULD HAVE LISTENED TO ME.
IF THERE'S ONE THING I KNOW ABOUT VILLAINS...

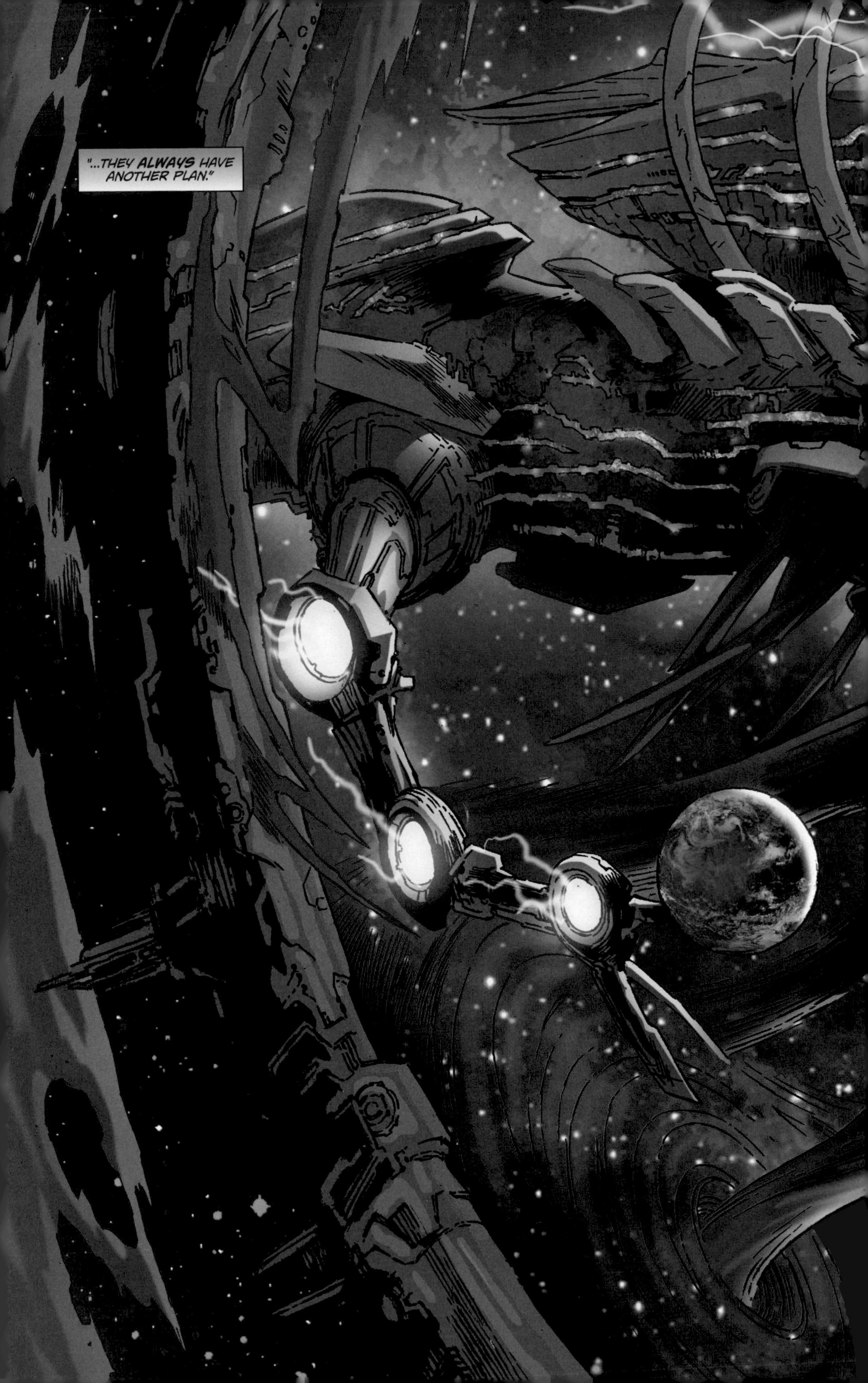
"...THEY ALWAYS HAVE ANOTHER PLAN."

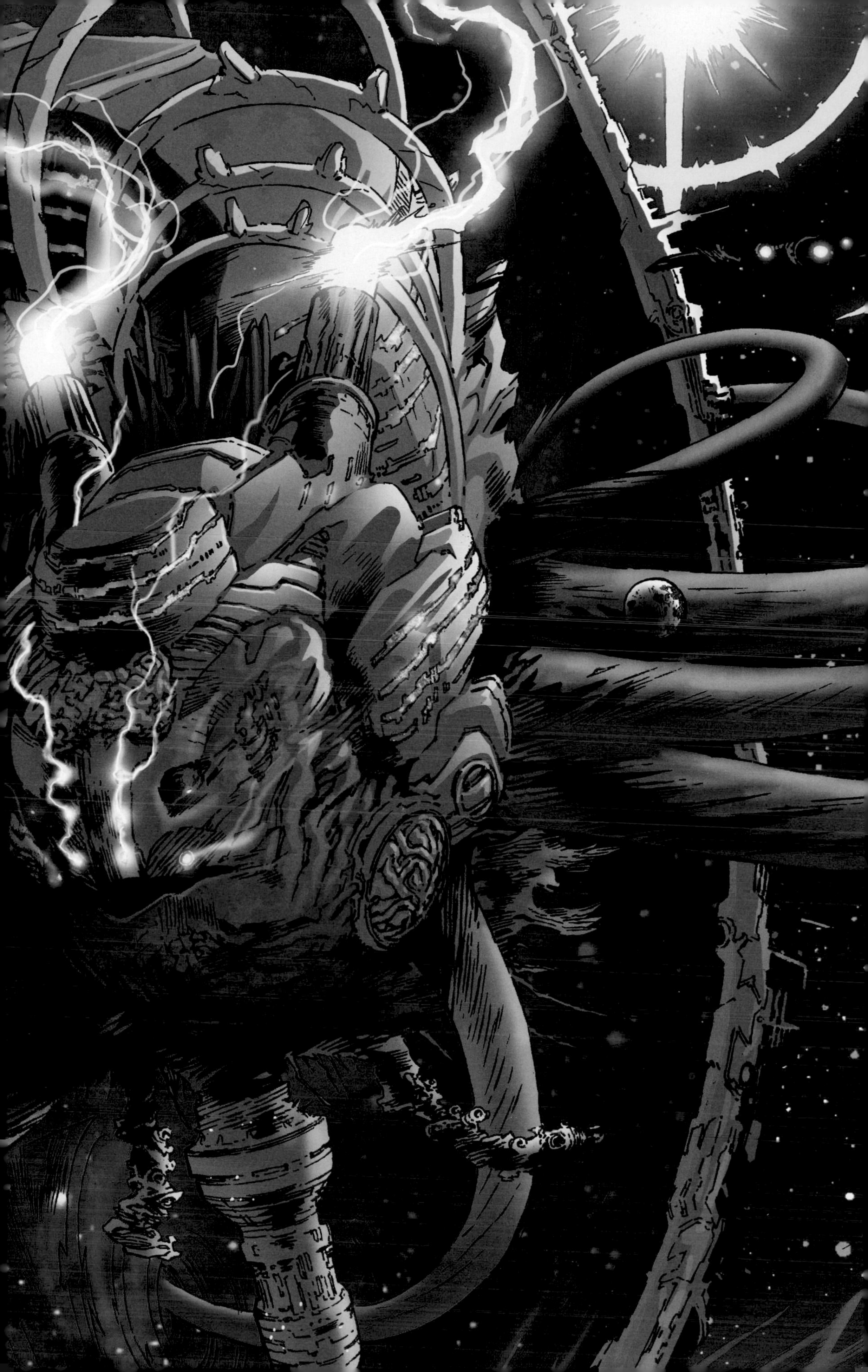

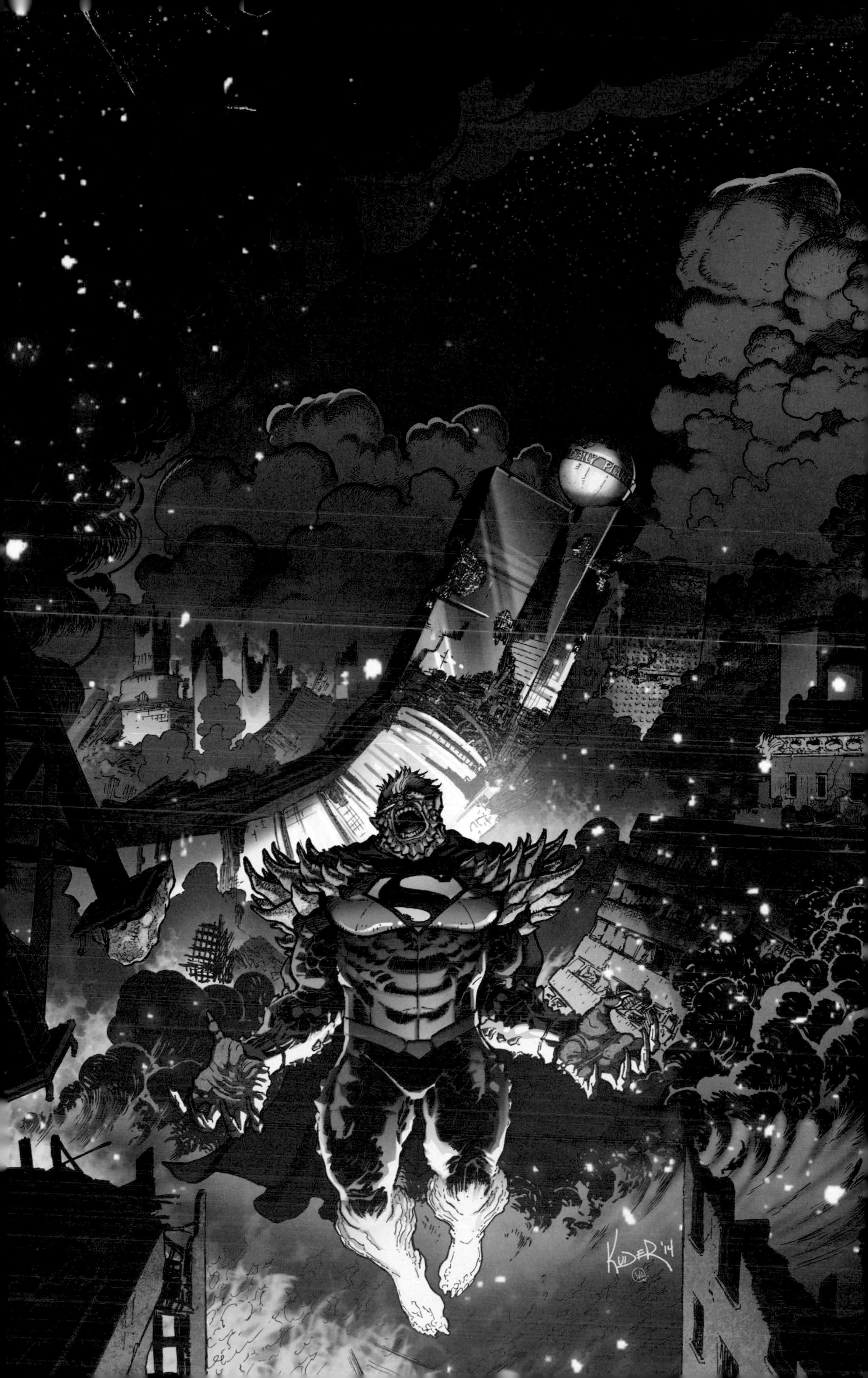
KUDER '14

SUPERMAN DOOMED

[LAST SUN] chapter 1

"ASSIMILATION"

STORY
GREG PAK

ART
AARON KUDER

& SCOTT KOLINS

COLORS
WIL QUINTANA

LETTERS
DEZI SIENTY & TAYLOR ESPOSITO

COVER
AARON KUDER & WIL QUINTANA

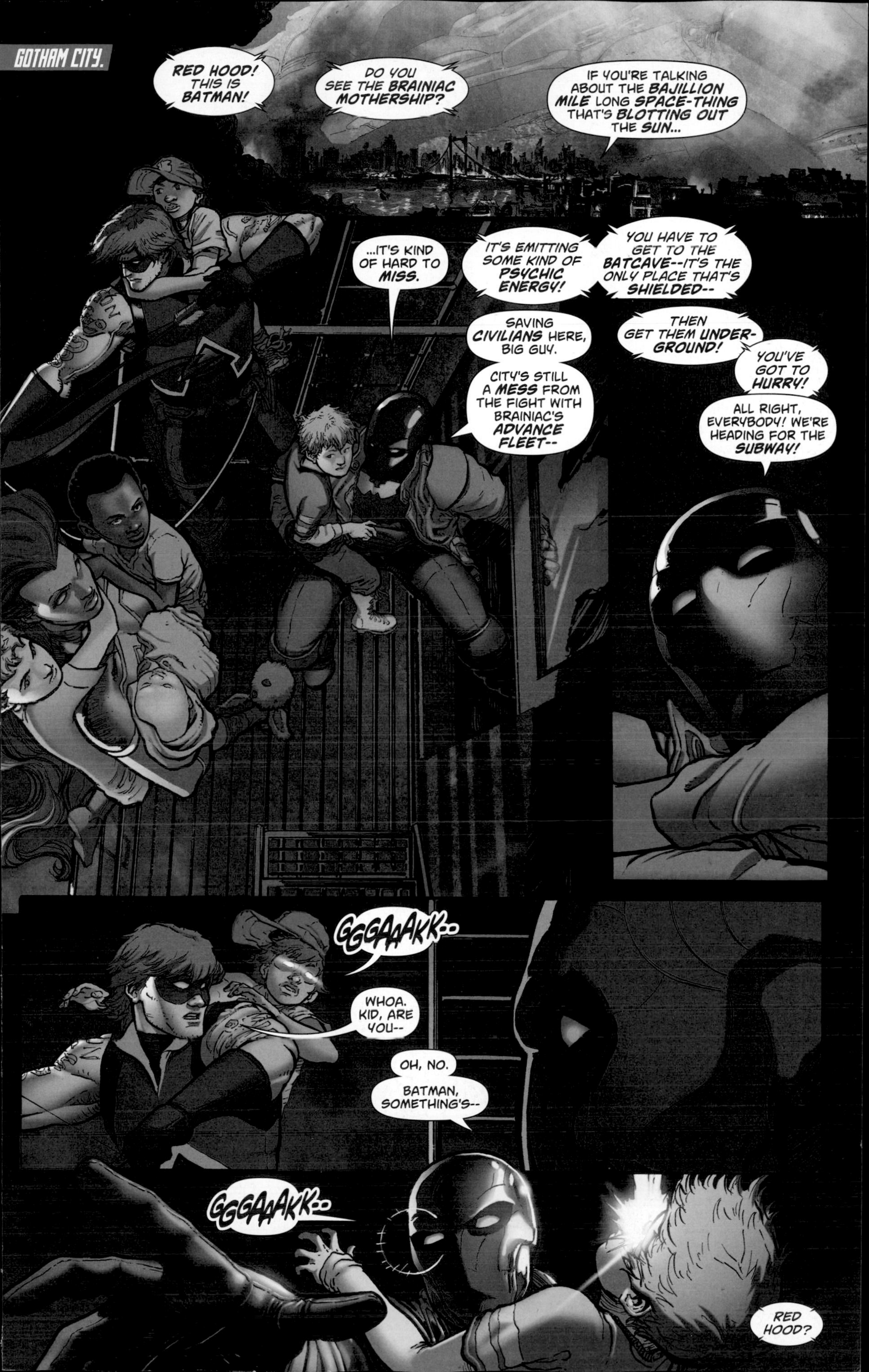
GOTHAM CITY.
RED HOOD! THIS IS BATMAN!
DO YOU SEE THE BRAINIAC MOTHERSHIP?
IF YOU'RE TALKING ABOUT THE BAJILLION MILE LONG SPACE-THING THAT'S BLOTTING OUT THE SUN...
...IT'S KIND OF HARD TO MISS.
IT'S EMITTING SOME KIND OF PSYCHIC ENERGY!
YOU HAVE TO GET TO THE BATCAVE--IT'S THE ONLY PLACE THAT'S SHIELDED--
SAVING CIVILIANS HERE, BIG GUY.
CITY'S STILL A MESS FROM THE FIGHT WITH BRAINIAC'S ADVANCE FLEET--
THEN GET THEM UNDER-GROUND!
YOU'VE GOT TO HURRY!
ALL RIGHT, EVERYBODY! WE'RE HEADING FOR THE SUBWAY!
GGGAAAKK--
WHOA. KID, ARE YOU--
OH, NO.
BATMAN, SOMETHING'S--
GGGAAAKK--
RED HOOD?

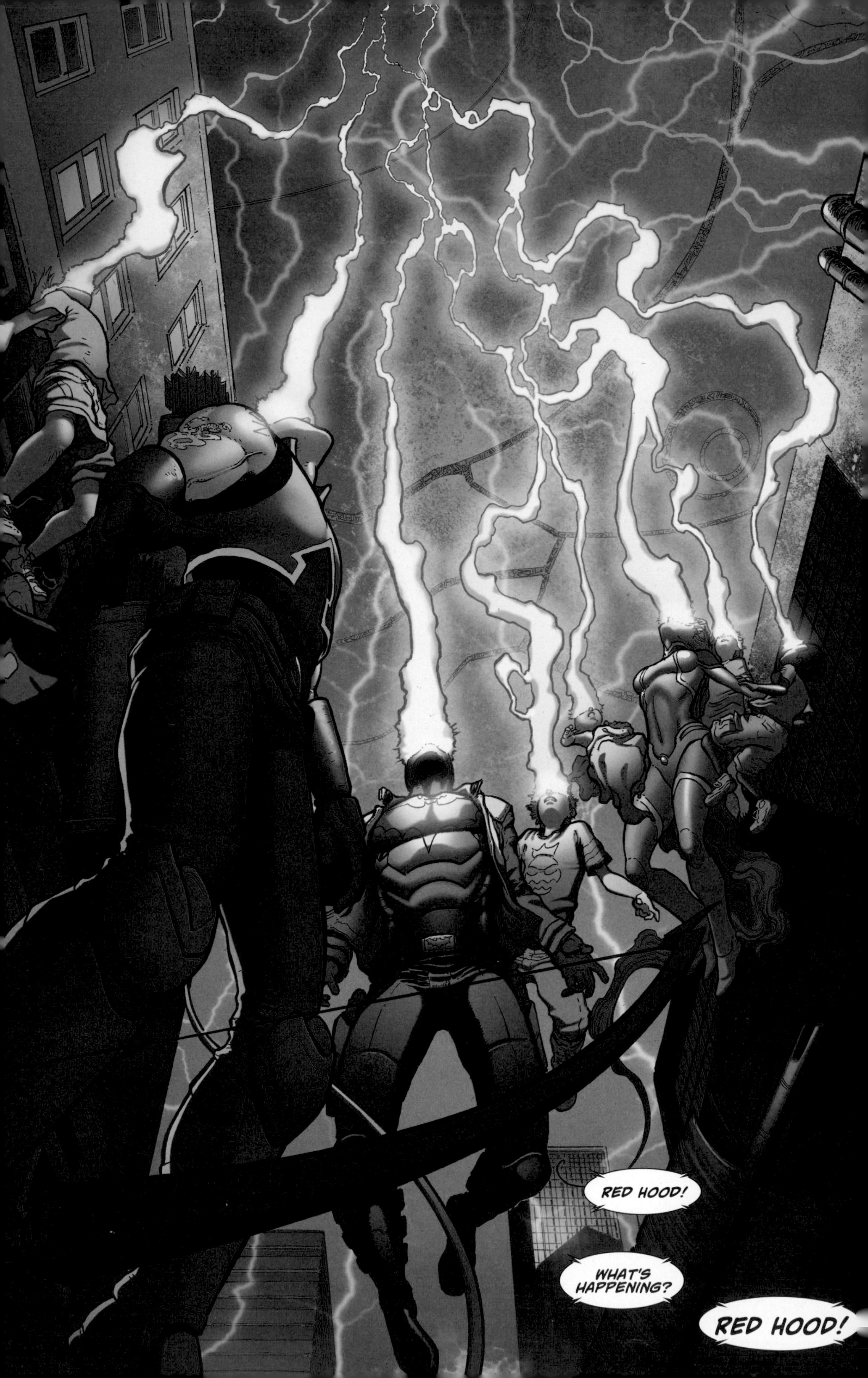
RED HOOD!
WHAT'S HAPPENING?
RED HOOD!

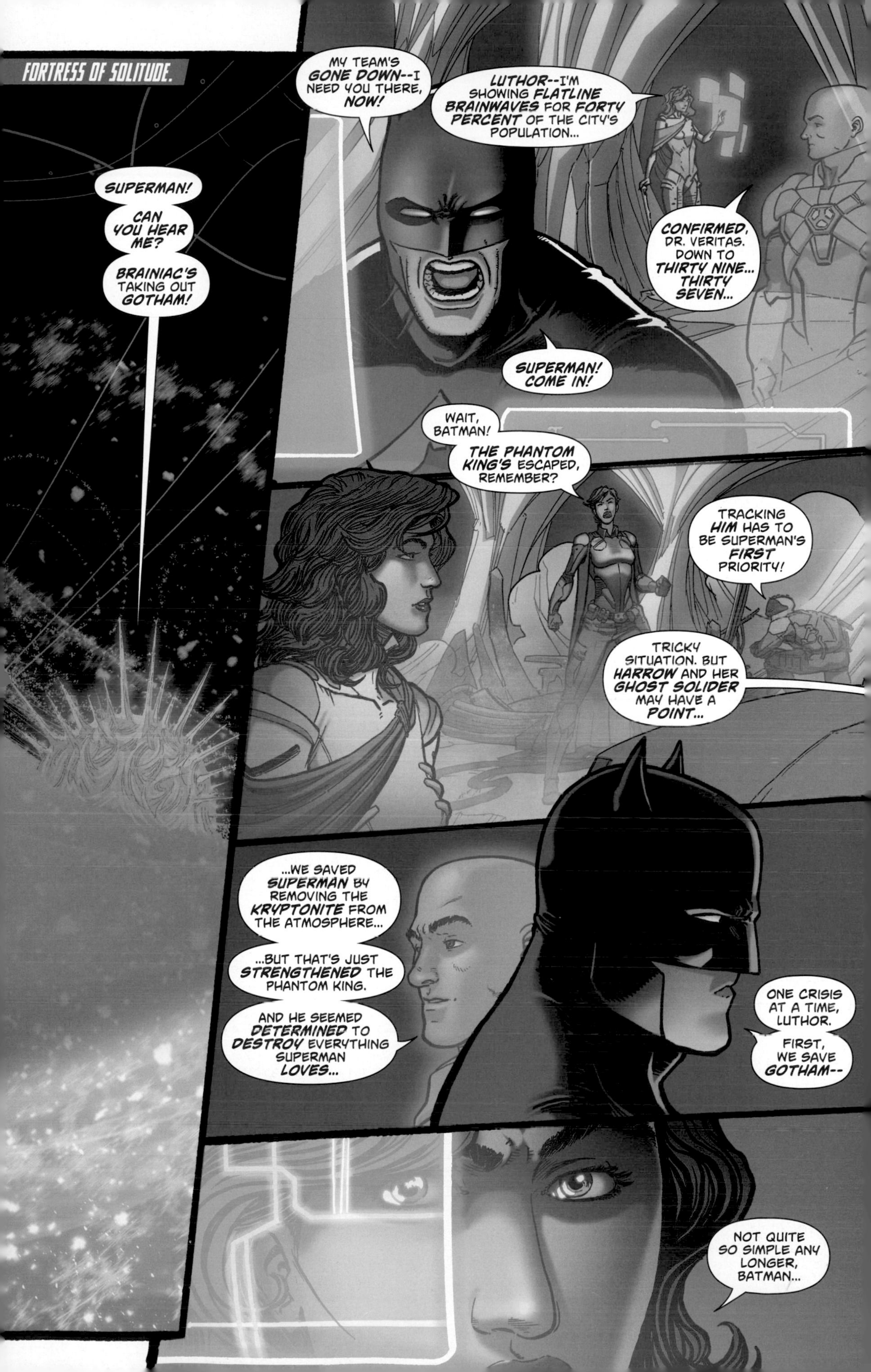

FORTRESS OF SOLITUDE.
SUPERMAN!
CAN YOU HEAR ME?
BRAINIAC'S TAKING OUT GOTHAM!
MY TEAM'S GONE DOWN--I NEED YOU THERE, NOW!
LUTHOR--I'M SHOWING FLATLINE BRAINWAVES FOR FORTY PERCENT OF THE CITY'S POPULATION...
CONFIRMED, DR. VERITAS. DOWN TO THIRTY NINE... THIRTY SEVEN...
SUPERMAN! COME IN!
WAIT, BATMAN!
THE PHANTOM KING'S ESCAPED, REMEMBER?
TRACKING HIM HAS TO BE SUPERMAN'S FIRST PRIORITY!
TRICKY SITUATION. BUT HARROW AND HER GHOST SOLIDER MAY HAVE A POINT...
...WE SAVED SUPERMAN BY REMOVING THE KRYPTONITE FROM THE ATMOSPHERE...
...BUT THAT'S JUST STRENGTHENED THE PHANTOM KING.
AND HE SEEMED DETERMINED TO DESTROY EVERYTHING SUPERMAN LOVES...
ONE CRISIS AT A TIME, LUTHOR.
FIRST, WE SAVE GOTHAM--
NOT QUITE SO SIMPLE ANY LONGER, BATMAN...

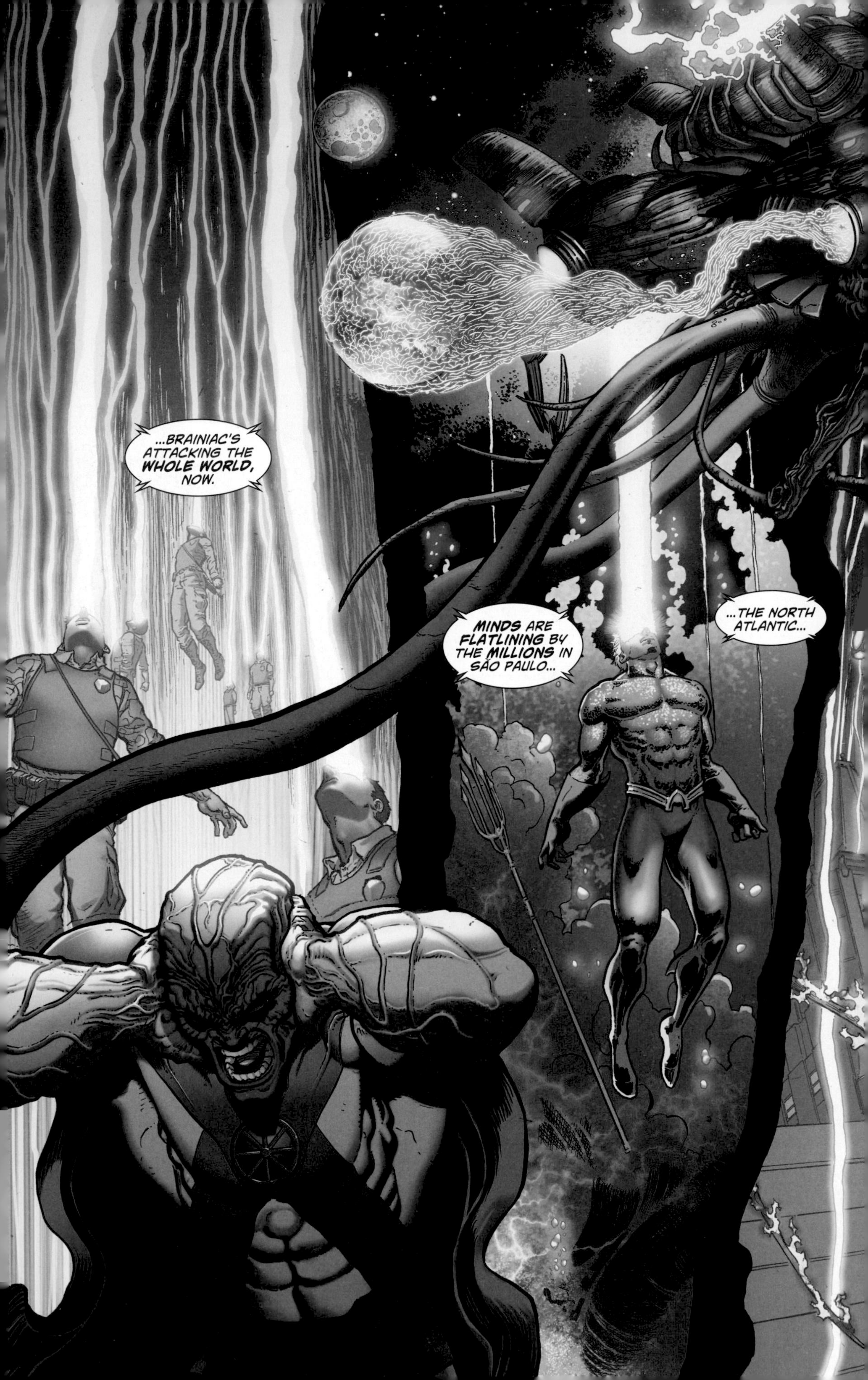
...BRAINIAC'S ATTACKING THE WHOLE WORLD, NOW.
MINDS ARE FLATLINING BY THE MILLIONS IN SÃO PAULO...
...THE NORTH ATLANTIC...

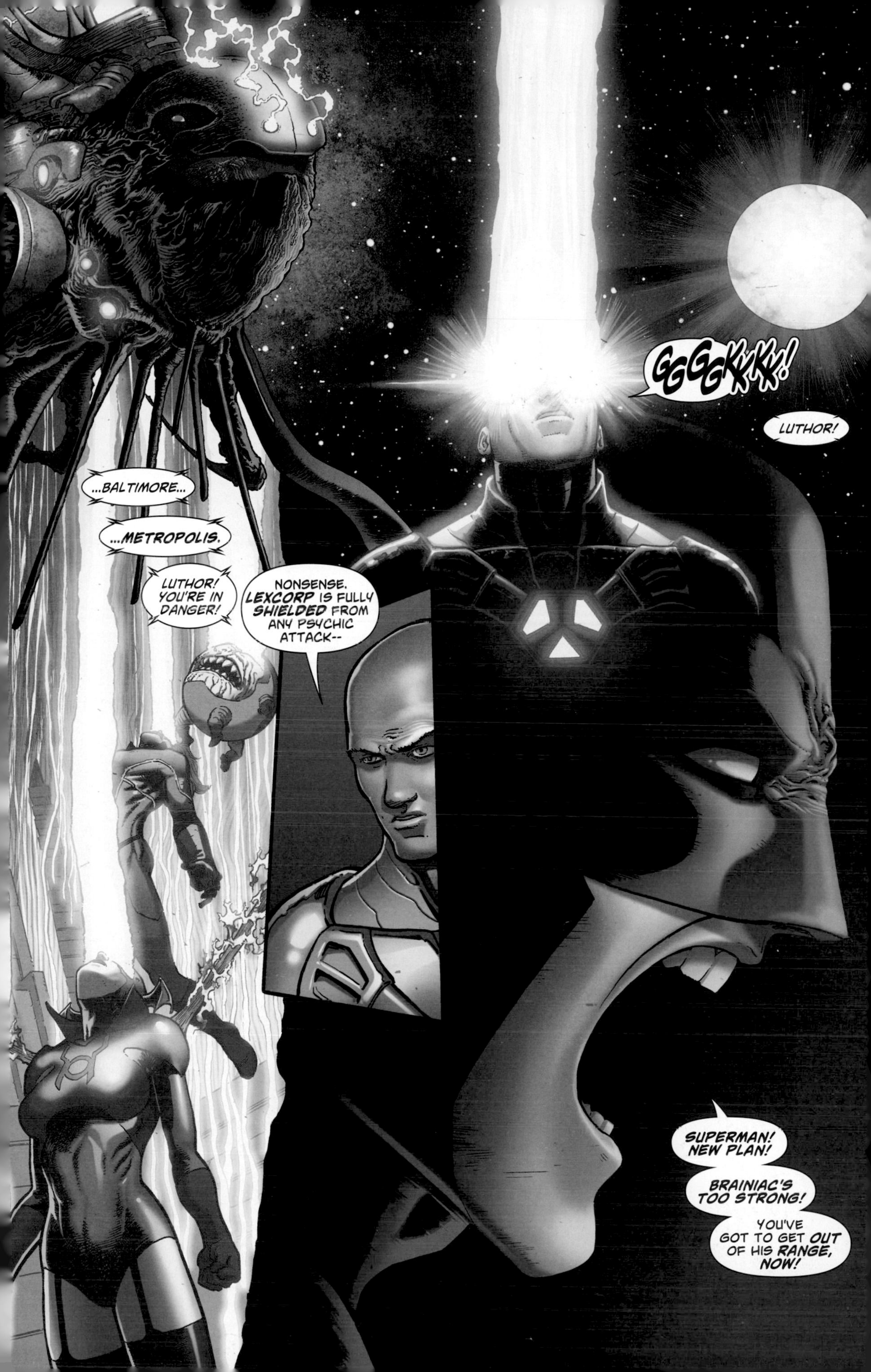
GGGGKKKKK!
LUTHOR!
...BALTIMORE...
...METROPOLIS.
LUTHOR! YOU'RE IN DANGER!
NONSENSE. LEXCORP IS FULLY SHIELDED FROM ANY PSYCHIC ATTACK--
SUPERMAN! NEW PLAN!
BRAINIAC'S TOO STRONG!
YOU'VE GOT TO GET OUT OF HIS RANGE, NOW!

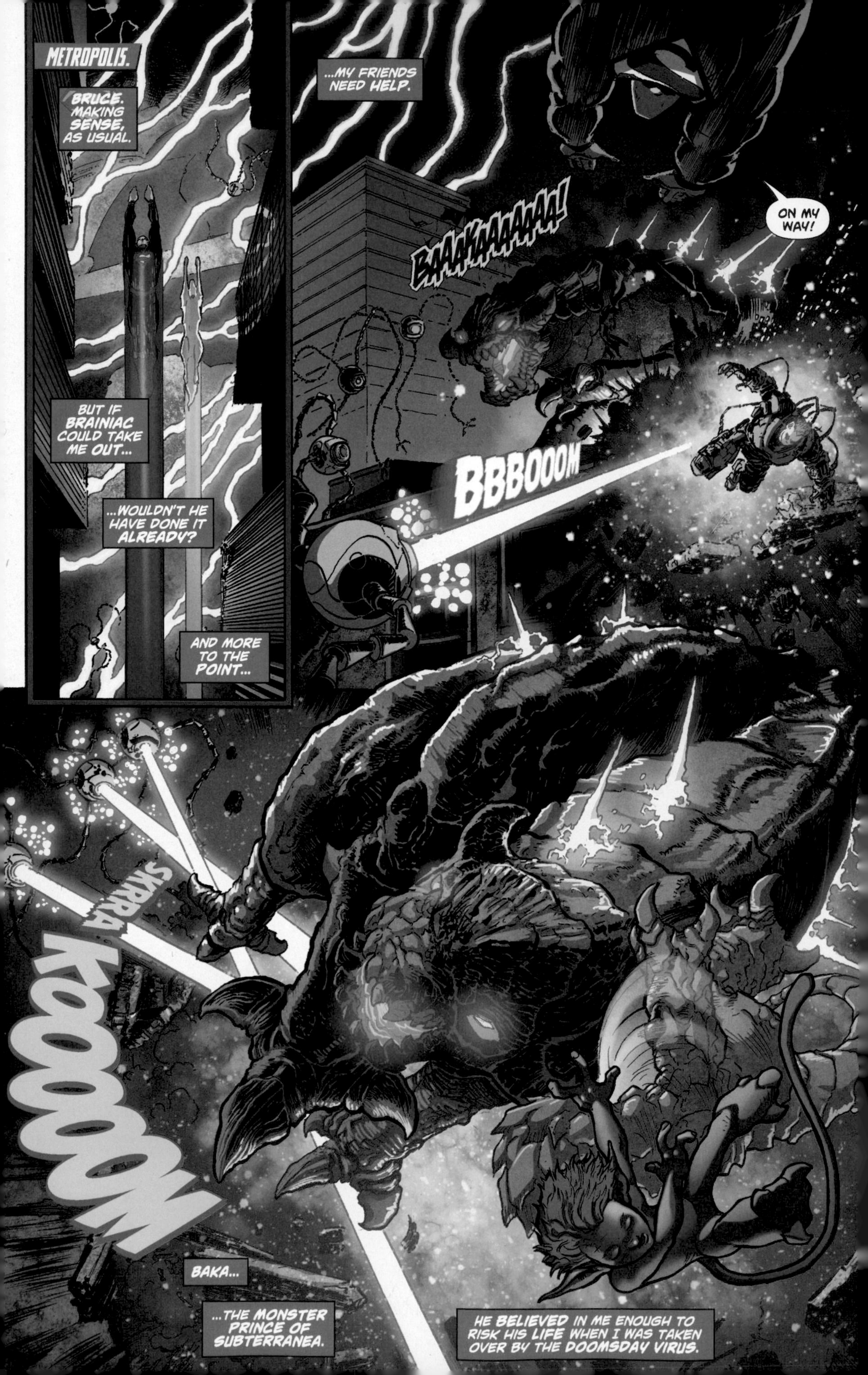
METROPOLIS.
BRUCE. MAKING SENSE, AS USUAL.
BUT IF BRAINIAC COULD TAKE ME OUT...
...WOULDN'T HE HAVE DONE IT ALREADY?
AND MORE TO THE POINT...
...MY FRIENDS NEED HELP.
ON MY WAY!
BAAAKAAAAAAA!
BBBOOOM
SKRRA
KOOOOOM
BAKA...
...THE MONSTER PRINCE OF SUBTERRANEA.
HE BELIEVED IN ME ENOUGH TO RISK HIS LIFE WHEN I WAS TAKEN OVER BY THE DOOMSDAY VIRUS.

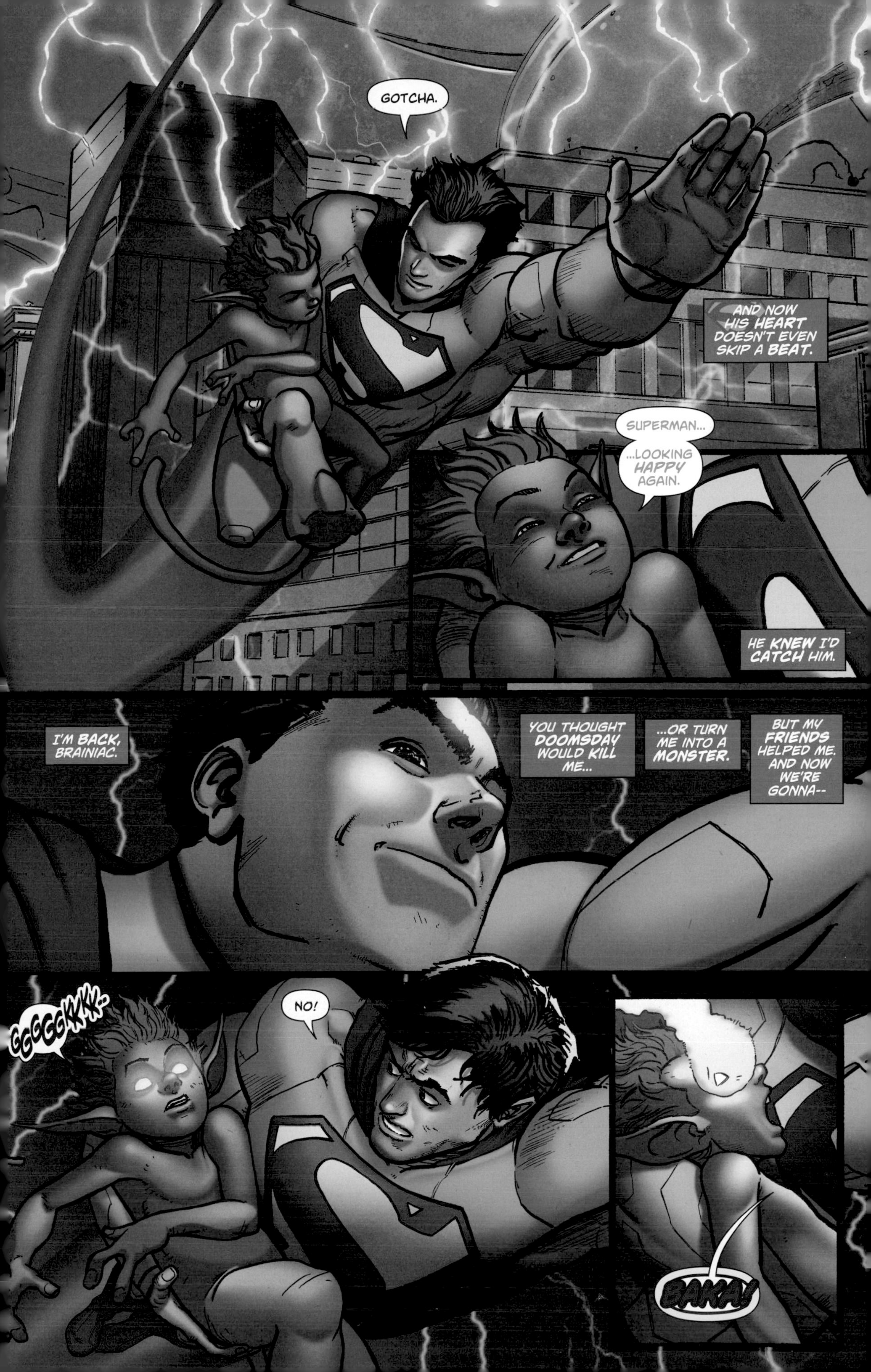
GOTCHA.
AND NOW HIS HEART DOESN'T EVEN SKIP A BEAT.
SUPERMAN...
...LOOKING HAPPY AGAIN.
HE KNEW I'D CATCH HIM.
I'M BACK, BRAINIAC.
YOU THOUGHT DOOMSDAY WOULD KILL ME...
...OR TURN ME INTO A MONSTER.
BUT MY FRIENDS HELPED ME. AND NOW WE'RE GONNA--
GGGGGKKK-
NO!
BAKA!

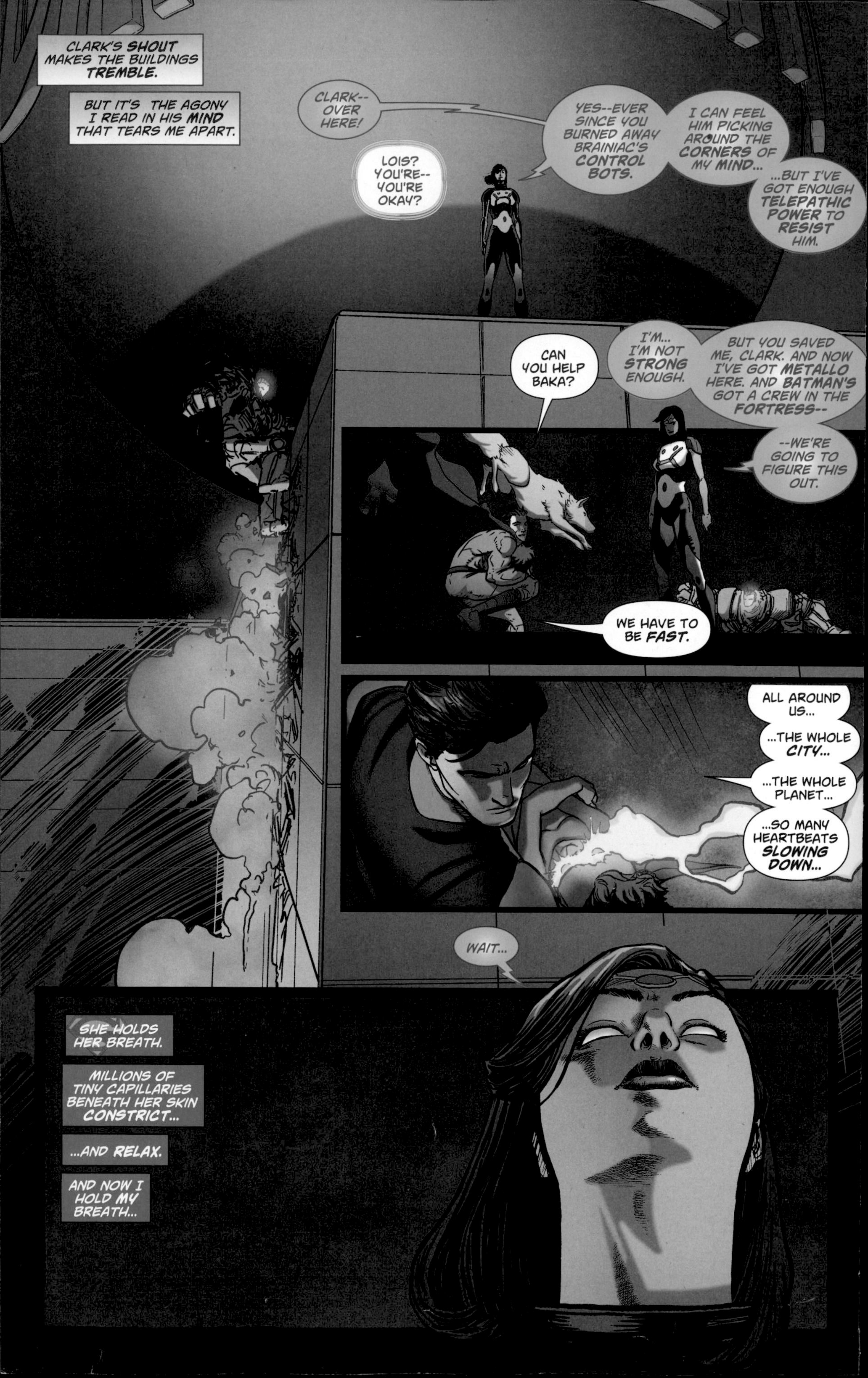
CLARK'S SHOUT MAKES THE BUILDINGS TREMBLE.
BUT IT'S THE AGONY I READ IN HIS MIND THAT TEARS ME APART.
CLARK-- OVER HERE!
LOIS? YOU'RE-- YOU'RE OKAY?
YES--EVER SINCE YOU BURNED AWAY BRAINIAC'S CONTROL BOTS.
I CAN FEEL HIM PICKING AROUND THE CORNERS OF MY MIND...
...BUT I'VE GOT ENOUGH TELEPATHIC POWER TO RESIST HIM.
CAN YOU HELP BAKA?
I'M... I'M NOT STRONG ENOUGH.
BUT YOU SAVED ME, CLARK. AND NOW I'VE GOT METALLO HERE. AND BATMAN'S GOT A CREW IN THE FORTRESS--
--WE'RE GOING TO FIGURE THIS OUT.
WE HAVE TO BE FAST.
ALL AROUND US...
...THE WHOLE CITY...
...THE WHOLE PLANET...
...SO MANY HEARTBEATS SLOWING DOWN...
WAIT...
SHE HOLDS HER BREATH.
MILLIONS OF TINY CAPILLARIES BENEATH HER SKIN CONSTRICT...
...AND RELAX.
AND NOW I HOLD MY BREATH...

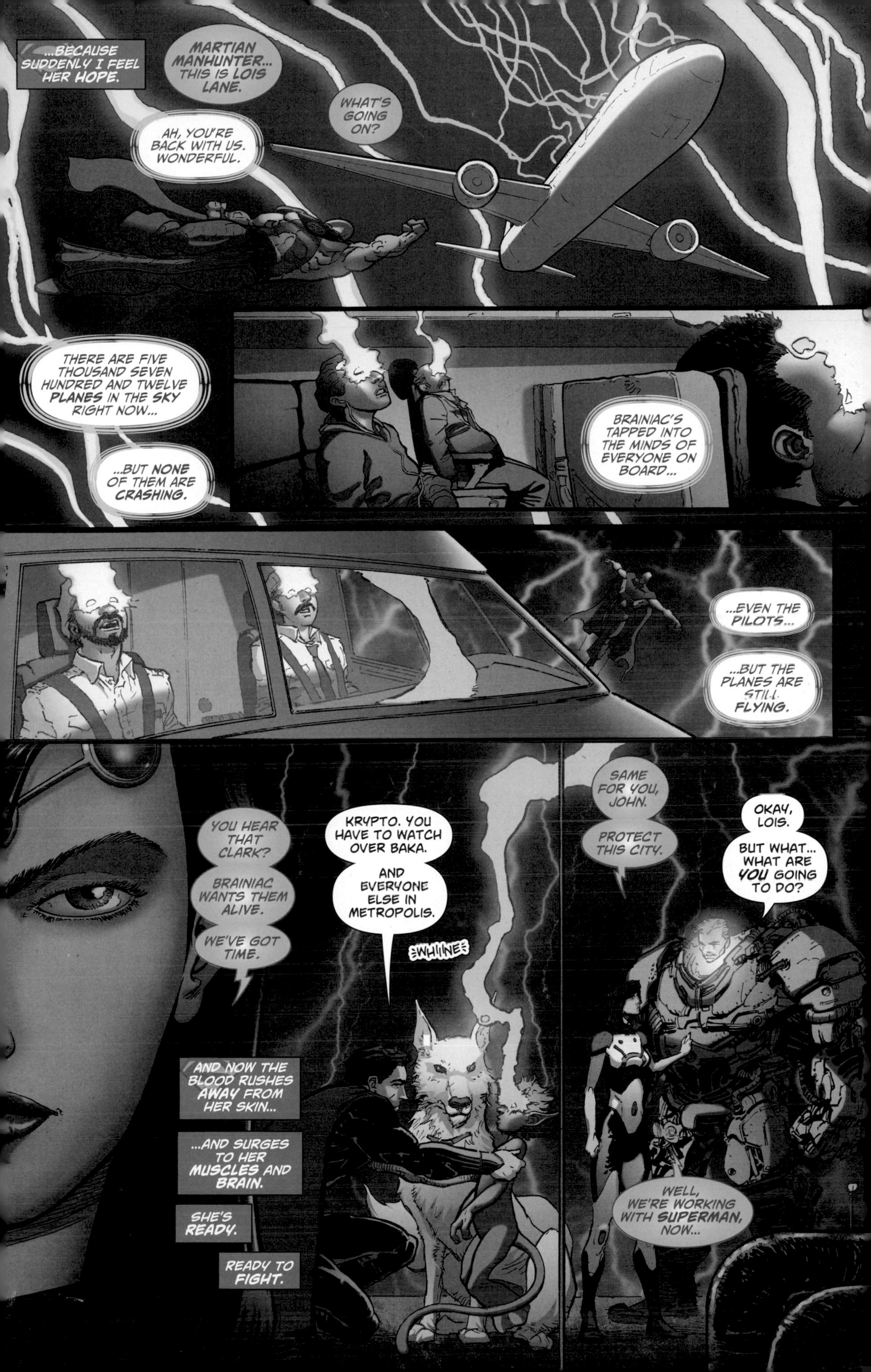
...BECAUSE SUDDENLY I FEEL HER HOPE.
MARTIAN MANHUNTER... THIS IS LOIS LANE.
WHAT'S GOING ON?
AH, YOU'RE BACK WITH US. WONDERFUL.
THERE ARE FIVE THOUSAND SEVEN HUNDRED AND TWELVE PLANES IN THE SKY RIGHT NOW...
...BUT NONE OF THEM ARE CRASHING.
BRAINIAC'S TAPPED INTO THE MINDS OF EVERYONE ON BOARD...
...EVEN THE PILOTS...
...BUT THE PLANES ARE STILL FLYING.
YOU HEAR THAT CLARK?
BRAINIAC WANTS THEM ALIVE.
WE'VE GOT TIME.
KRYPTO. YOU HAVE TO WATCH OVER BAKA.
AND EVERYONE ELSE IN METROPOLIS.
WHIINE
AND NOW THE BLOOD RUSHES AWAY FROM HER SKIN...
...AND SURGES TO HER MUSCLES AND BRAIN.
SHE'S READY.
READY TO FIGHT.
SAME FOR YOU, JOHN.
PROTECT THIS CITY.
OKAY, LOIS.
BUT WHAT... WHAT ARE YOU GOING TO DO?
WELL, WE'RE WORKING WITH SUPERMAN, NOW...

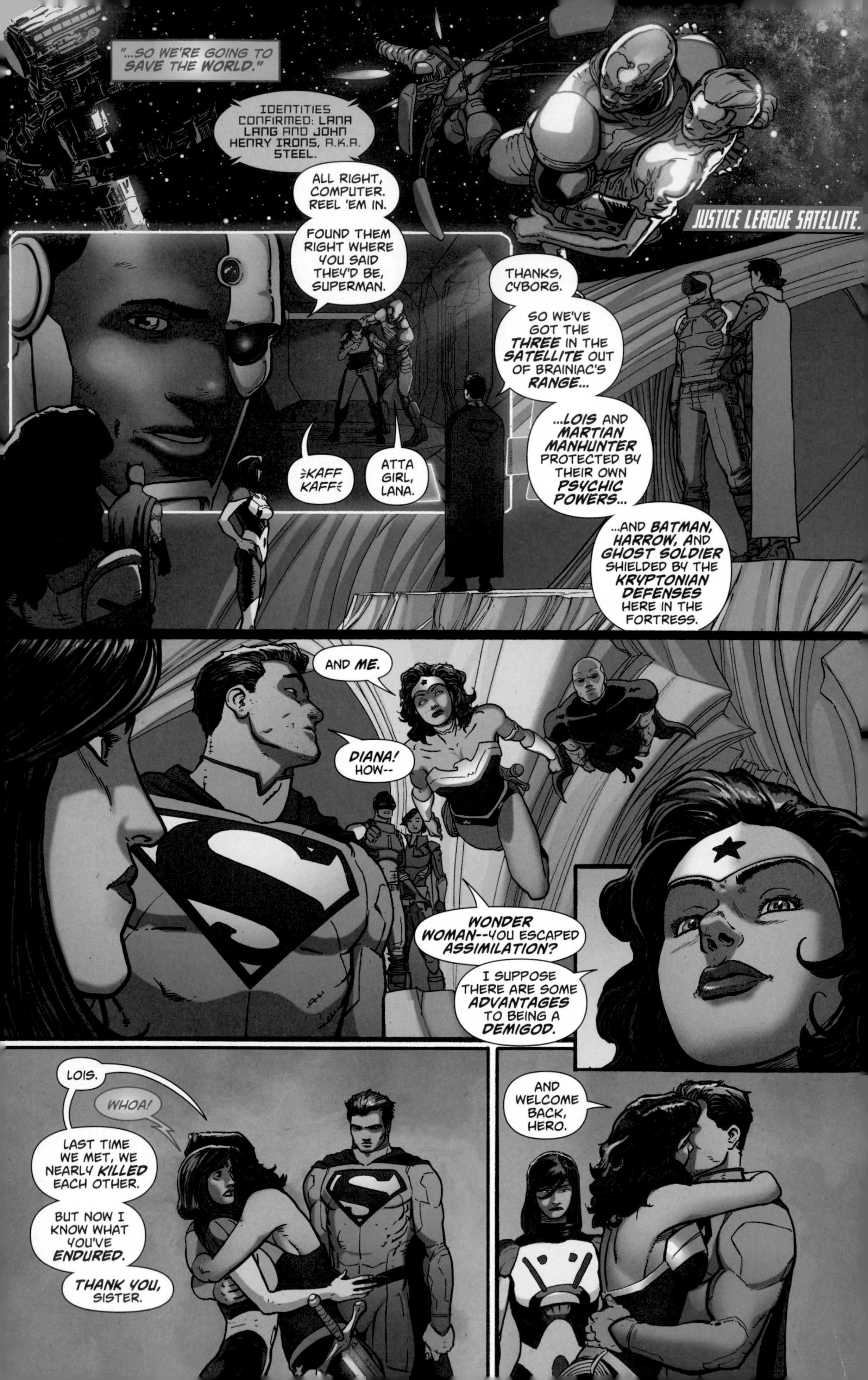
"...SO WE'RE GOING TO SAVE THE WORLD."
IDENTITIES CONFIRMED: LANA LANG AND JOHN HENRY IRONS, A.K.A. STEEL.
ALL RIGHT, COMPUTER. REEL 'EM IN.
JUSTICE LEAGUE SATELLITE.
FOUND THEM RIGHT WHERE YOU SAID THEY'D BE, SUPERMAN.
THANKS, CYBORG.
SO WE'VE GOT THE THREE IN THE SATELLITE OUT OF BRAINIAC'S RANGE...
KAFF KAFF
ATTA GIRL, LANA.
...LOIS AND MARTIAN MANHUNTER PROTECTED BY THEIR OWN PSYCHIC POWERS...
...AND BATMAN, HARROW, AND GHOST SOLDIER SHIELDED BY THE KRYPTONIAN DEFENSES HERE IN THE FORTRESS.
AND ME.
DIANA! HOW--
WONDER WOMAN--YOU ESCAPED ASSIMILATION?
I SUPPOSE THERE ARE SOME ADVANTAGES TO BEING A DEMIGOD.
LOIS.
WHOA!
LAST TIME WE MET, WE NEARLY KILLED EACH OTHER.
BUT NOW I KNOW WHAT YOU'VE ENDURED.
THANK YOU, SISTER.
AND WELCOME BACK, HERO.

Lana: HEY, GUYS! LANA LANG, HERE!

Lana: I'M GETTING A LOOK AT THIS NEW DATA...

Lana: ...AND I THINK BRAINIAC'S *NETWORKING* ALL THESE BRAINS!

Wonder Woman: *NETWORKING?* BUT I'M NOT PICKING UP ANY *INFORMATION EXCHANGE*...

Woman: NO, FOR *PROCESSING POWER!*

Wonder Woman: YES...THAT MAKES SENSE. I DON'T SENSE HIM *SEARCHING* THEIR MINDS...

Wonder Woman: ...HE'S JUST BUILDING THEM INTO HIS *SYSTEM*...BUT *WHY*...

Superman: *MONGUL* TRIED SOMETHING LIKE THIS A WHILE BACK.

Superman: TAPPED INTO MILLIONS OF BRAINS, TRIED TO TURN THE EARTH INTO A MASSIVE PSYCHIC *WEAPON*.

Superman: WE HAD TO THROW HIM INTO THE *PHANTOM ZONE* TO STOP HIM.

Batman: GUESSING THE *MOTHERSHIP'S* A LITTLE TO *BIG* FOR *THAT* SOLUTION.

Batman: BUT WE'VE GOT TO TAKE IT *DOWN*.

Batman: *HARROW* CAN *SUMMON* THE *DEAD*. WE CAN STAY *INTANGIBLE* UNTIL THE LAST MINUTE, WHICH SHOULD HELP US FROM GETTING *ASSIMILATED*.

Batman: JUST POINT US TO THE SHIP'S *SOFT SPOT* AND--

Superman: BELIEVE ME, I'D LOVE TO BREAK ALL OF BRAINIAC'S TOYS.

Superman: BUT RIGHT NOW, *SEVEN BILLION MINDS* ARE LINKED TO THAT MOTHERSHIP.

Superman: I...I DON'T KNOW WHAT'LL HAPPEN TO THEM IF WE JUST *SMASH* IT.

Batman: HRNN...

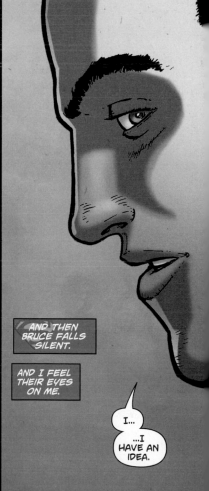

AND THEN BRUCE FALLS SILENT.

AND I FEEL THEIR EYES ON ME.

I...

...I HAVE AN IDEA.

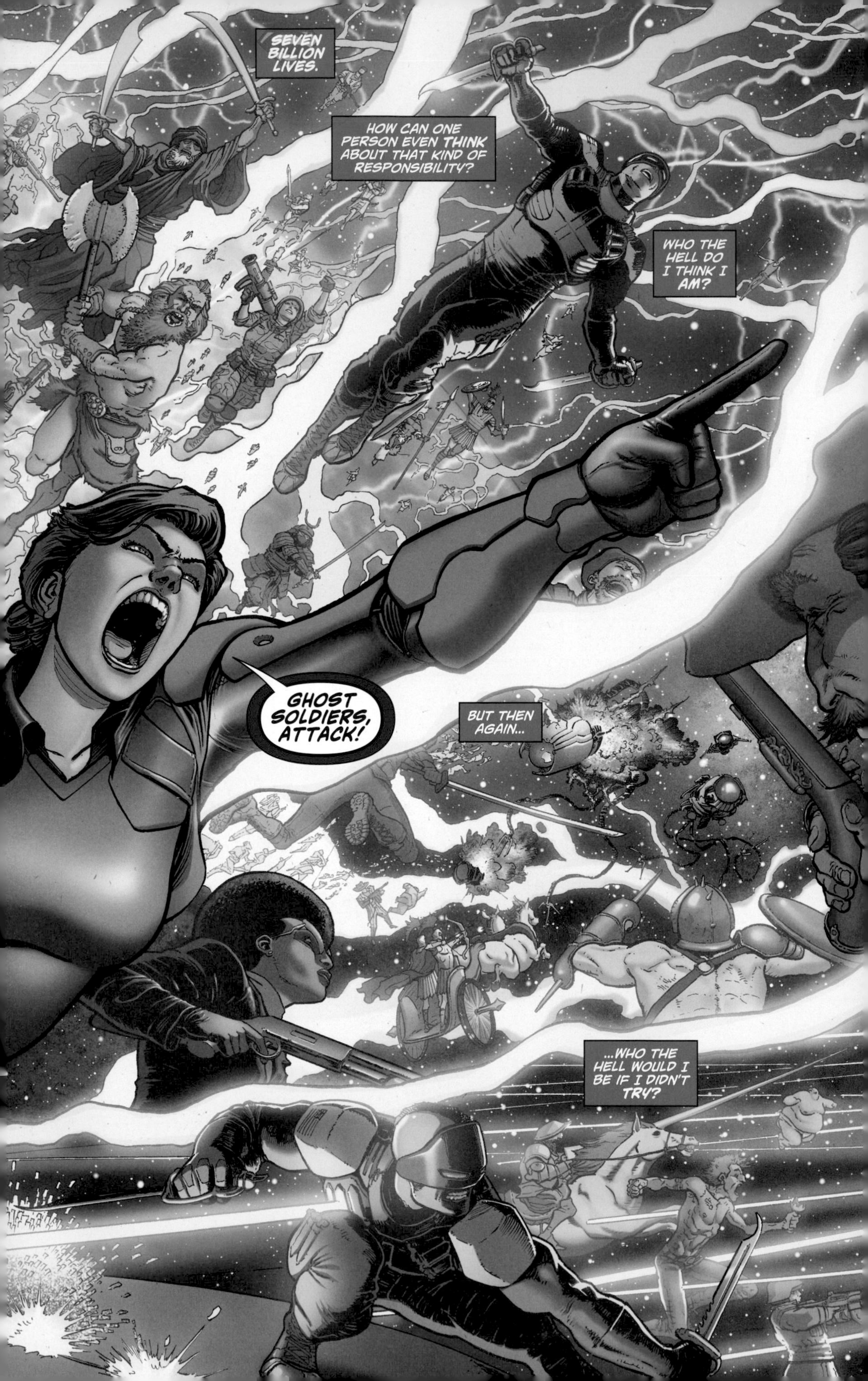
SEVEN BILLION LIVES.
HOW CAN ONE PERSON EVEN THINK ABOUT THAT KIND OF RESPONSIBILITY?
WHO THE HELL DO I THINK I AM?
GHOST SOLDIERS, ATTACK!
BUT THEN AGAIN...
...WHO THE HELL WOULD I BE IF I DIDN'T TRY?

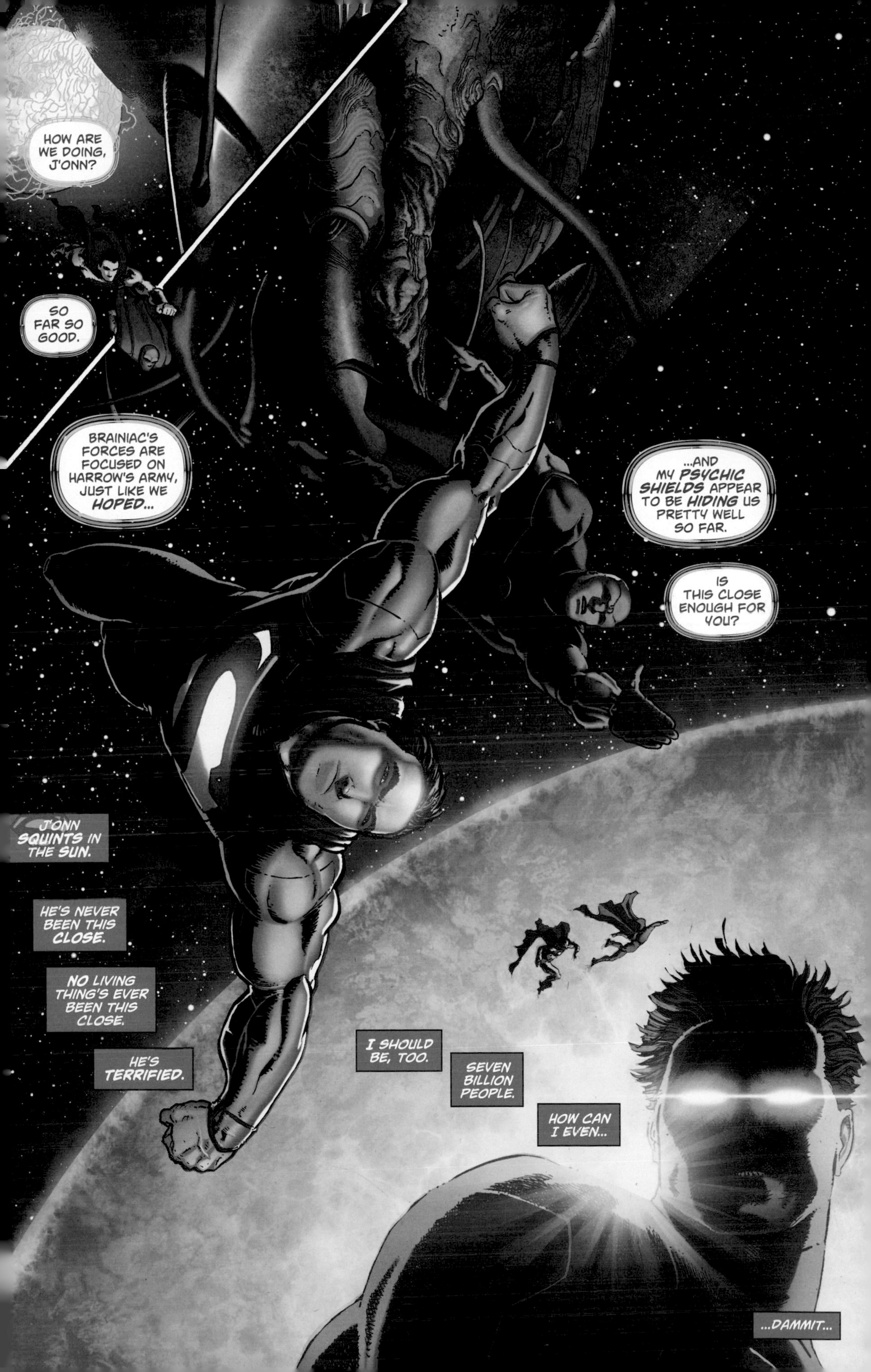
HOW ARE WE DOING, J'ONN?
SO FAR SO GOOD.
BRAINIAC'S FORCES ARE FOCUSED ON HARROW'S ARMY, JUST LIKE WE HOPED...
...AND MY PSYCHIC SHIELDS APPEAR TO BE HIDING US PRETTY WELL SO FAR.
IS THIS CLOSE ENOUGH FOR YOU?
J'ONN SQUINTS IN THE SUN.
HE'S NEVER BEEN THIS CLOSE.
NO LIVING THING'S EVER BEEN THIS CLOSE.
HE'S TERRIFIED.
I SHOULD BE, TOO.
SEVEN BILLION PEOPLE.
HOW CAN I EVEN...
...DAMMIT...

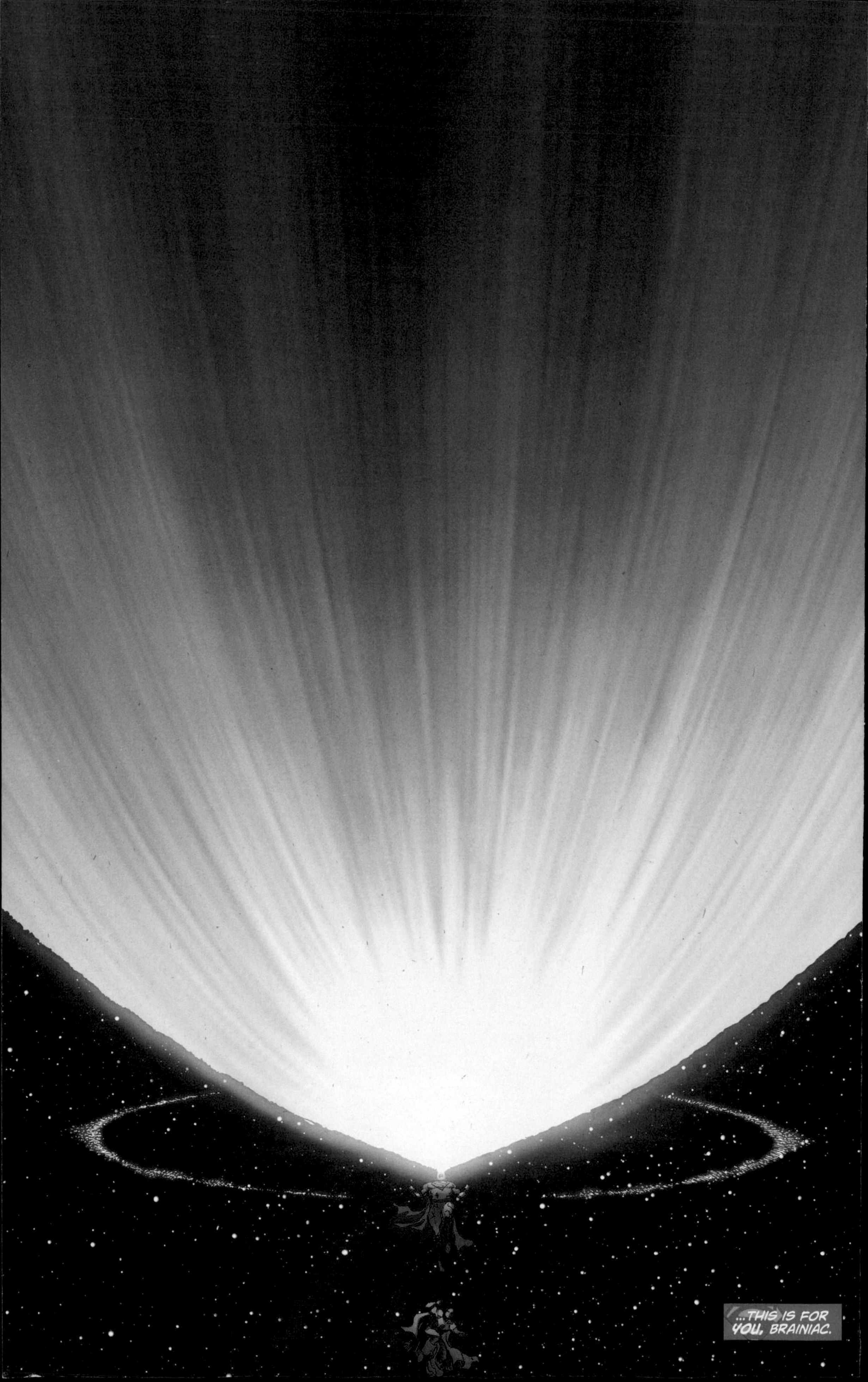
...THIS IS FOR YOU, BRAINIAC.

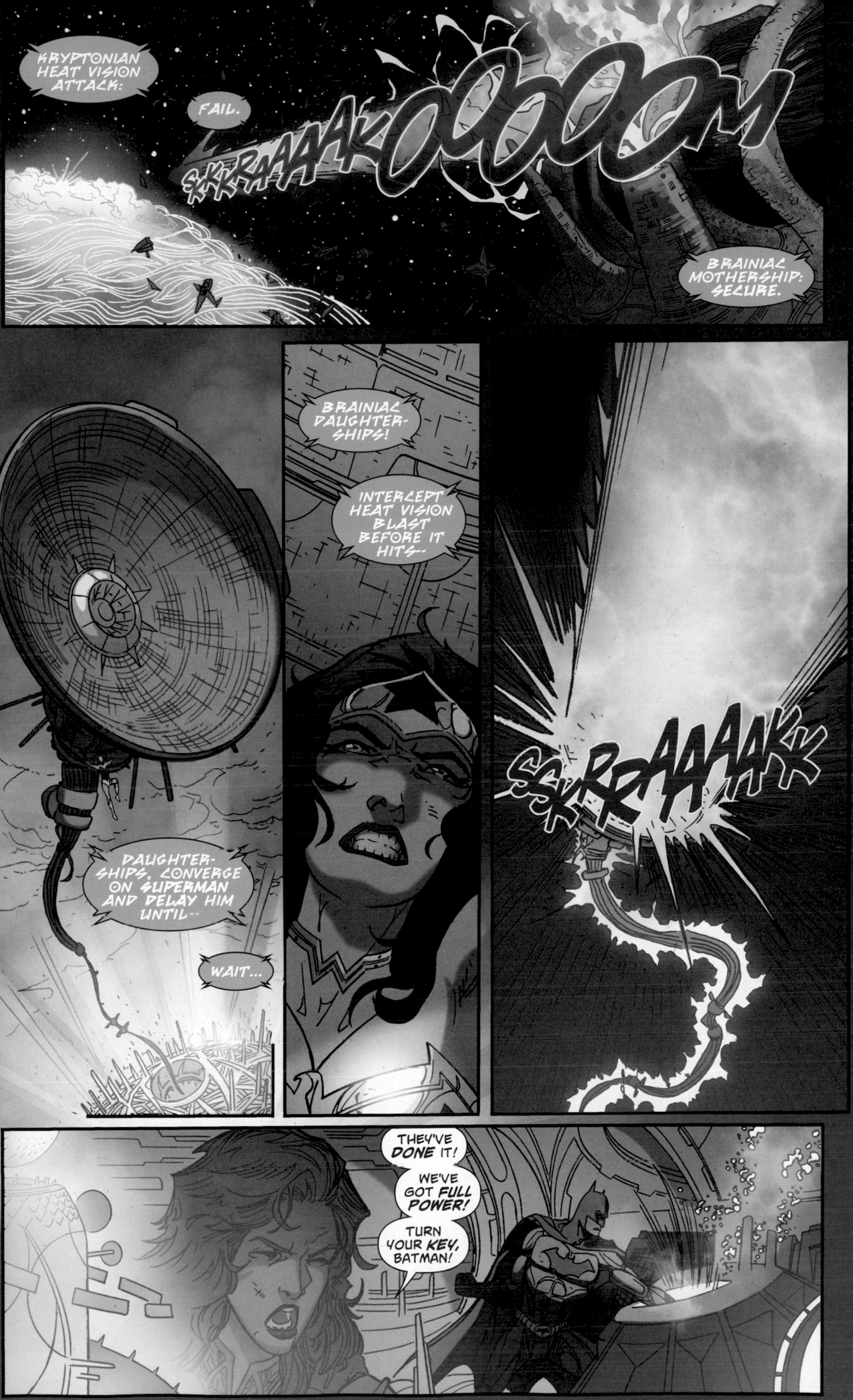
KRYPTONIAN HEAT VISION ATTACK:
FAIL.
SKKRAAAAKOOOOOM
BRAINIAC MOTHERSHIP: SECURE.
BRAINIAC DAUGHTER-SHIPS!
INTERCEPT HEAT VISION BLAST BEFORE IT HITS--
DAUGHTER-SHIPS, CONVERGE ON SUPERMAN AND DELAY HIM UNTIL--
WAIT...
SSKRRAAAAKK
THEY'VE DONE IT!
WE'VE GOT FULL POWER!
TURN YOUR KEY, BATMAN!

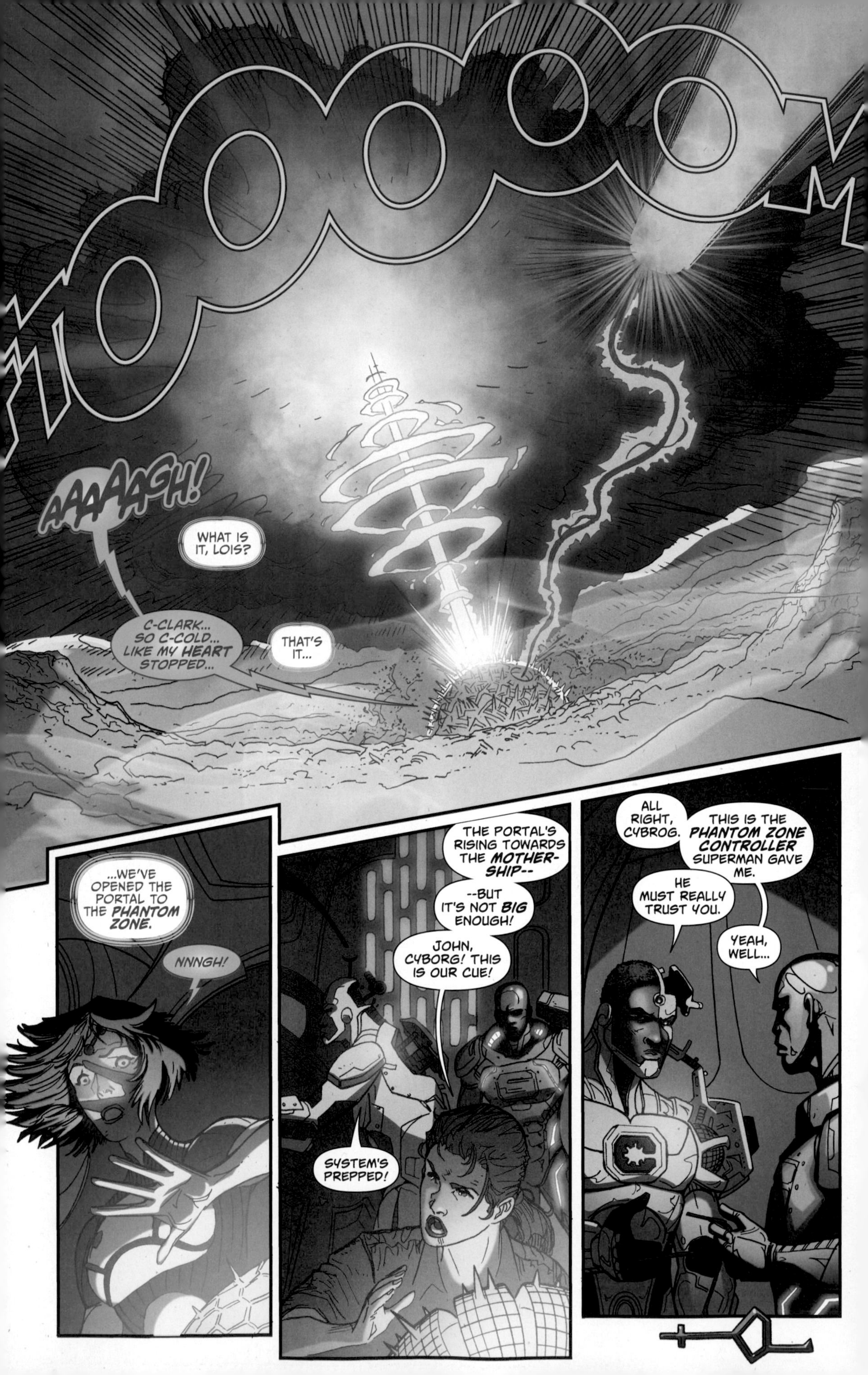

HOOOOOOOM
AAAAAGH!
WHAT IS IT, LOIS?
C-CLARK... SO C-COLD... LIKE MY HEART STOPPED...
THAT'S IT...
...WE'VE OPENED THE PORTAL TO THE PHANTOM ZONE.
NNNGH!
THE PORTAL'S RISING TOWARDS THE MOTHER-SHIP--
--BUT IT'S NOT BIG ENOUGH!
JOHN, CYBORG! THIS IS OUR CUE!
SYSTEM'S PREPPED!
ALL RIGHT, CYBROG.
THIS IS THE PHANTOM ZONE CONTROLLER SUPERMAN GAVE ME.
HE MUST REALLY TRUST YOU.
YEAH, WELL...

"...NOW I GUESS IT'S TIME FOR US TO TRUST *HIM*."

SECONDARY PHANTOM ENERGY SOURCE DETECTED!

CONVERGING WITH PRIMARY PORTAL!

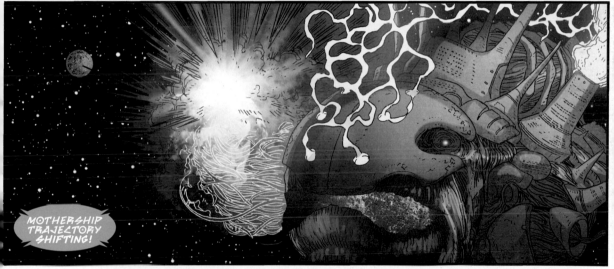

MOTHERSHIP TRAJECTORY SHIFTING!

SHAY.

PLEASE TELL ME SOMETHING *GOOD*.

HAPPY TO OBLIGE, SUPERMAN.

IT'S *WORKING*.

WE'RE GOING TO PULL BOTH THE *MOTHER-SHIP*...

...AND THE *ENTIRE PLANET*...

...INTO THE *PHANTOM ZONE*...

...A PLACE WITHOUT *TIME*...

...IN ORDER TO *BUY* THE *TIME* WE NEED TO SAVE *EVERYONE*.

INTRIGUING...

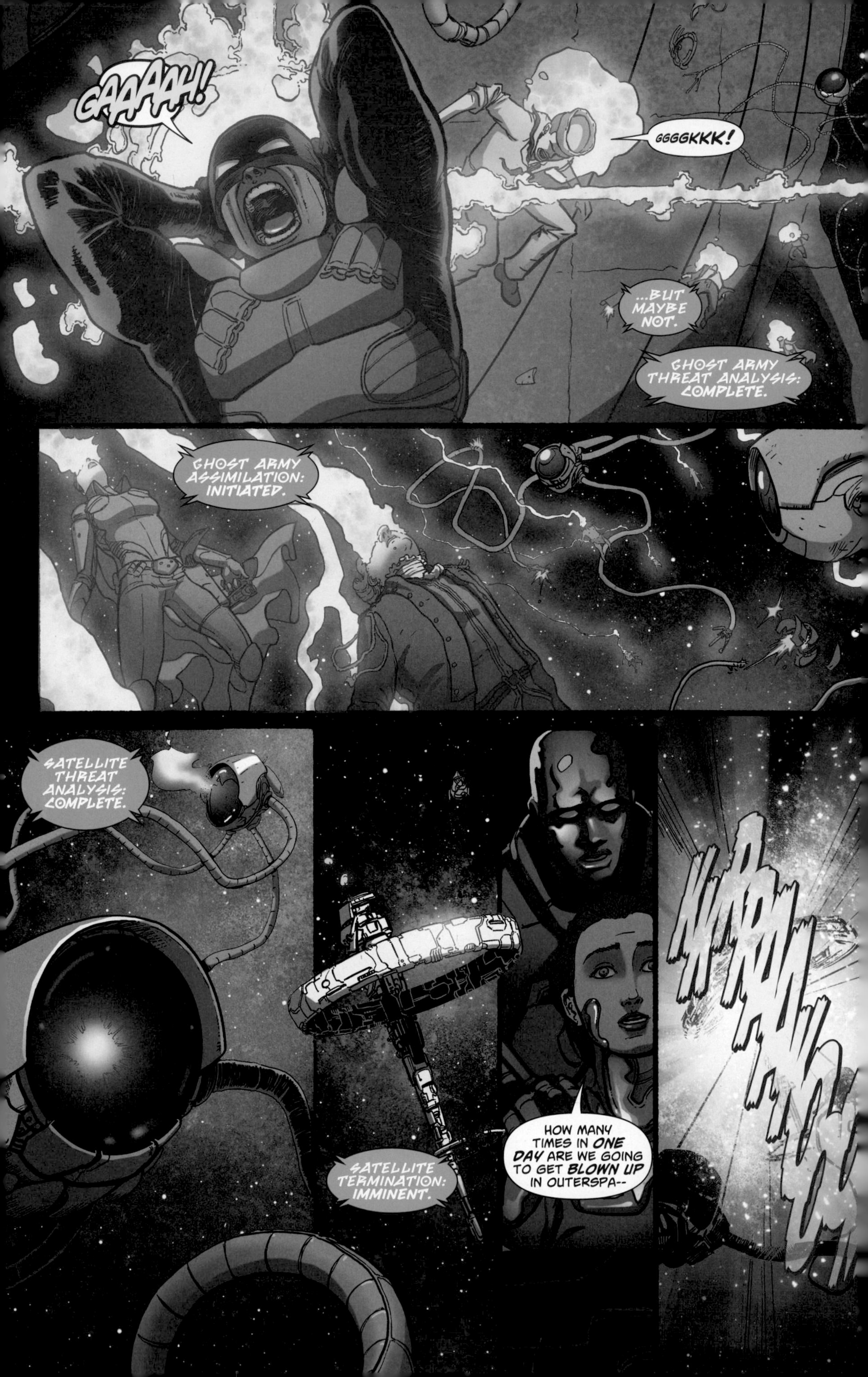
GAAAAH!
GGGGKKK!
...BUT MAYBE NOT.
GHOST ARMY THREAT ANALYSIS: COMPLETE.
GHOST ARMY ASSIMILATION: INITIATED.
SATELLITE THREAT ANALYSIS: COMPLETE.
SATELLITE TERMINATION: IMMINENT.
HOW MANY TIMES IN ONE DAY ARE WE GOING TO GET BLOWN UP IN OUTERSPA--

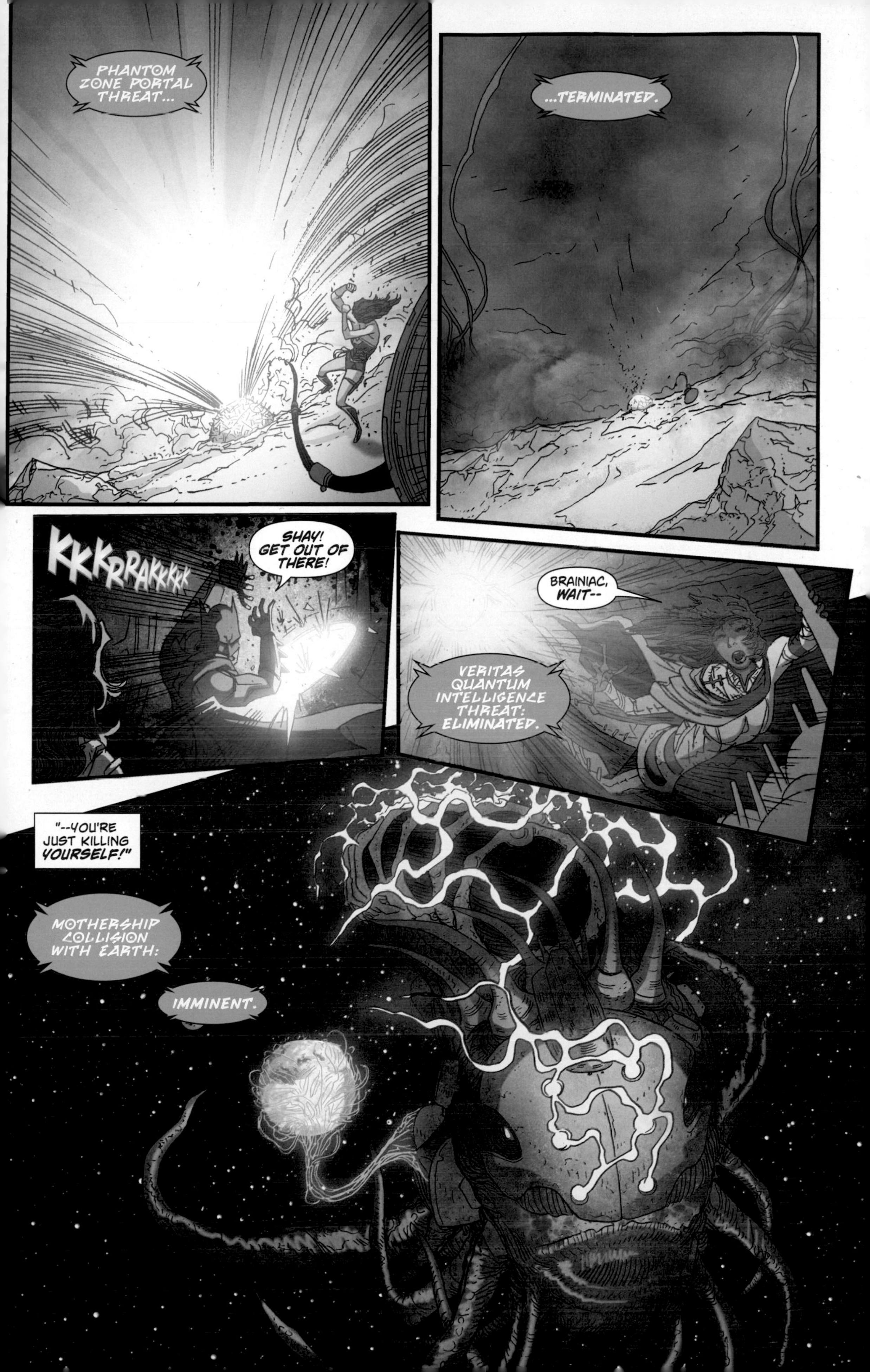
PHANTOM ZONE PORTAL THREAT...
...TERMINATED.
KKKRRAKKKKK
SHAY! GET OUT OF THERE!
BRAINIAC, WAIT--
VERITAS QUANTUM INTELLIGENCE THREAT: ELIMINATED.
"--YOU'RE JUST KILLING YOURSELF!"
MOTHERSHIP COLLISION WITH EARTH:
IMMINENT.

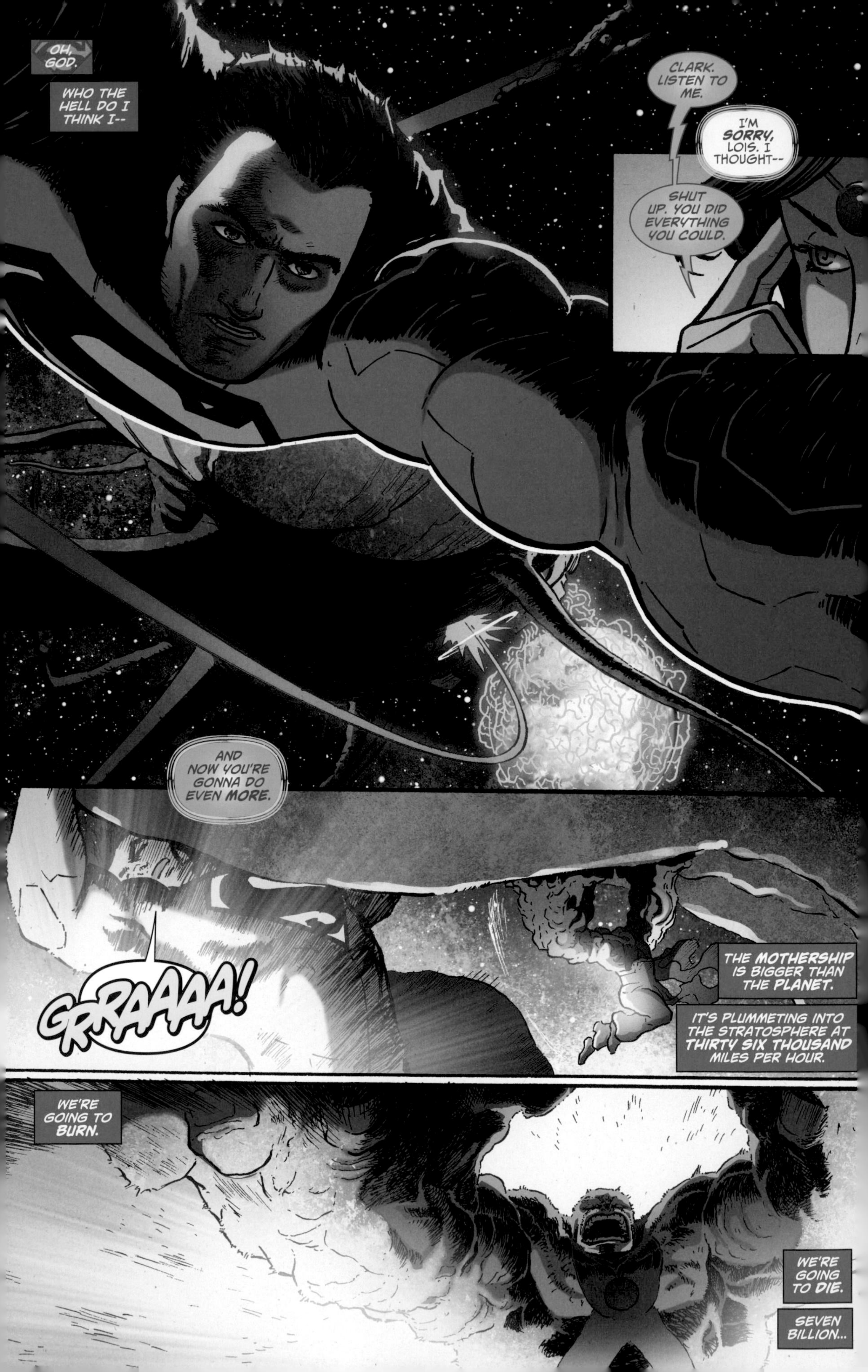
OH, GOD.
WHO THE HELL DO I THINK I--
CLARK. LISTEN TO ME.
I'M SORRY, LOIS. I THOUGHT--
SHUT UP. YOU DID EVERYTHING YOU COULD.
AND NOW YOU'RE GONNA DO EVEN MORE.
GRRAAAA!
THE MOTHERSHIP IS BIGGER THAN THE PLANET.
IT'S PLUMMETING INTO THE STRATOSPHERE AT THIRTY SIX THOUSAND MILES PER HOUR.
WE'RE GOING TO BURN.
WE'RE GOING TO DIE.
SEVEN BILLION...

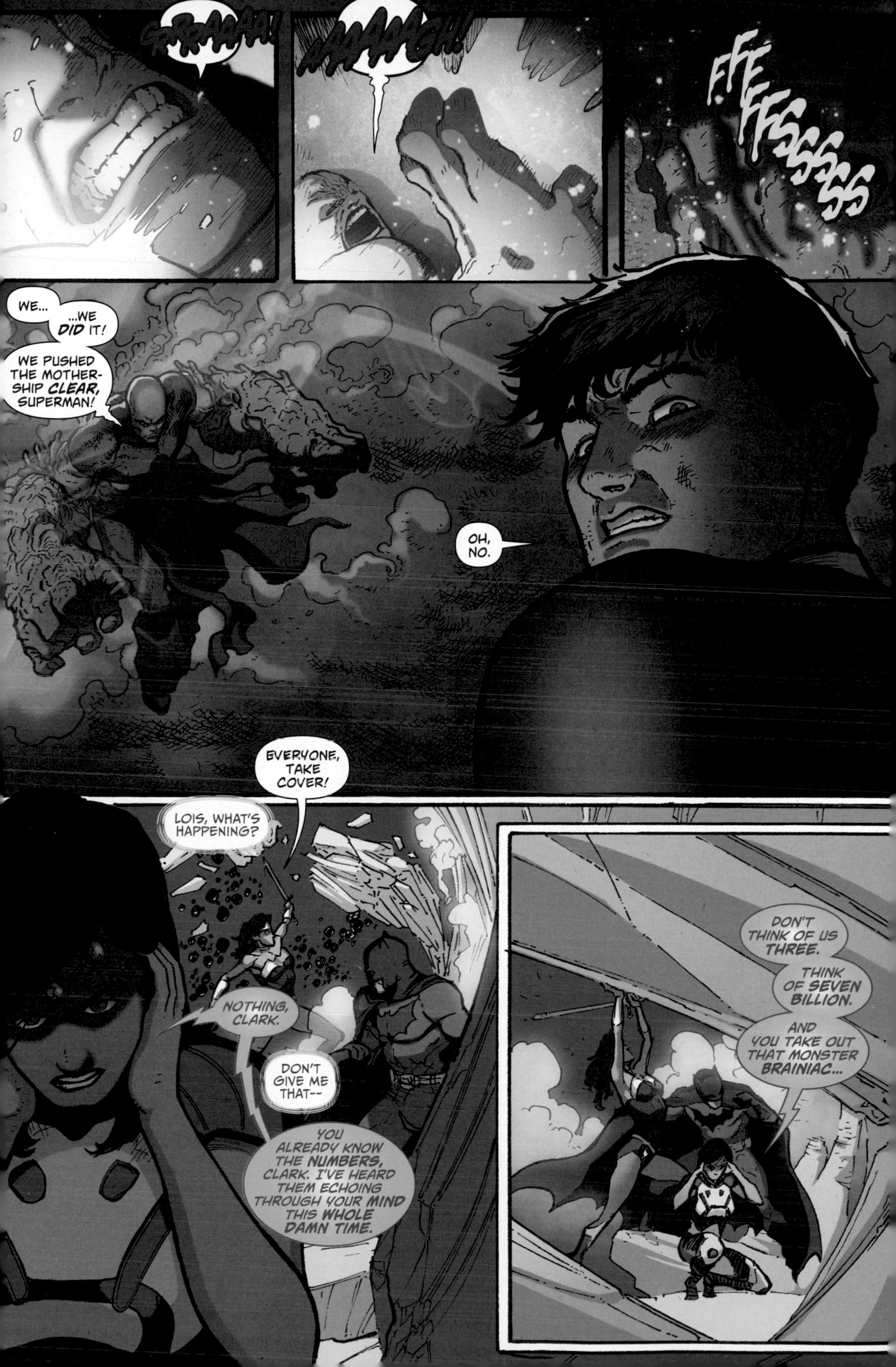
GRRAAAA!
AAAAAAGH!
FFFFFSSSSSS
WE...
...WE DID IT!
WE PUSHED THE MOTHER-SHIP CLEAR, SUPERMAN!
OH, NO.
EVERYONE, TAKE COVER!
LOIS, WHAT'S HAPPENING?
NOTHING, CLARK.
DON'T GIVE ME THAT--
YOU ALREADY KNOW THE NUMBERS, CLARK. I'VE HEARD THEM ECHOING THROUGH YOUR MIND THIS WHOLE DAMN TIME.
DON'T THINK OF US THREE.
THINK OF SEVEN BILLION.
AND YOU TAKE OUT THAT MONSTER BRAINIAC...

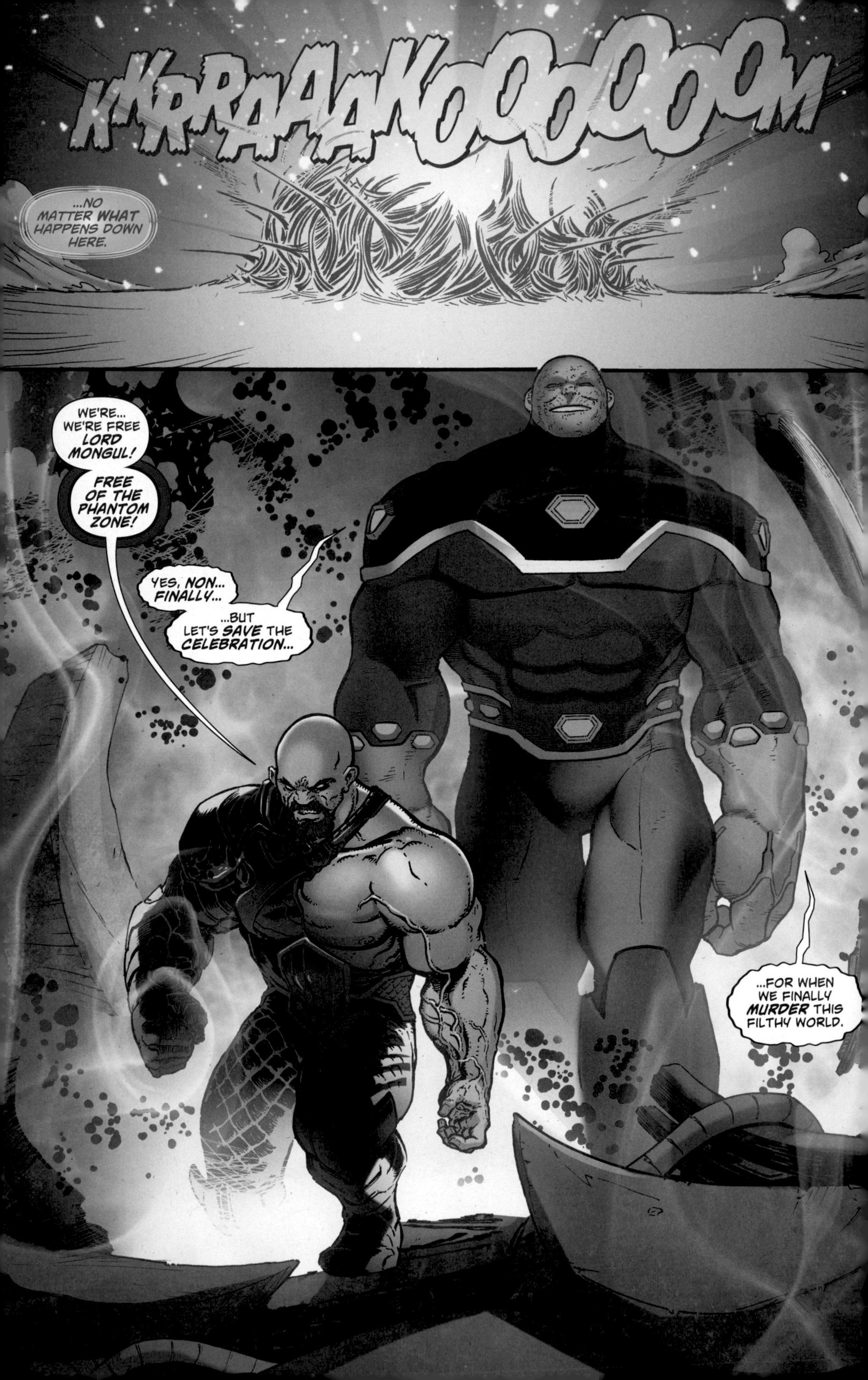

KKRRAAAKOOOOOOM
...NO MATTER WHAT HAPPENS DOWN HERE.
WE'RE... WE'RE FREE LORD MONGUL!
FREE OF THE PHANTOM ZONE!
YES, NON... FINALLY...
...BUT LET'S SAVE THE CELEBRATION...
...FOR WHEN WE FINALLY MURDER THIS FILTHY WORLD.

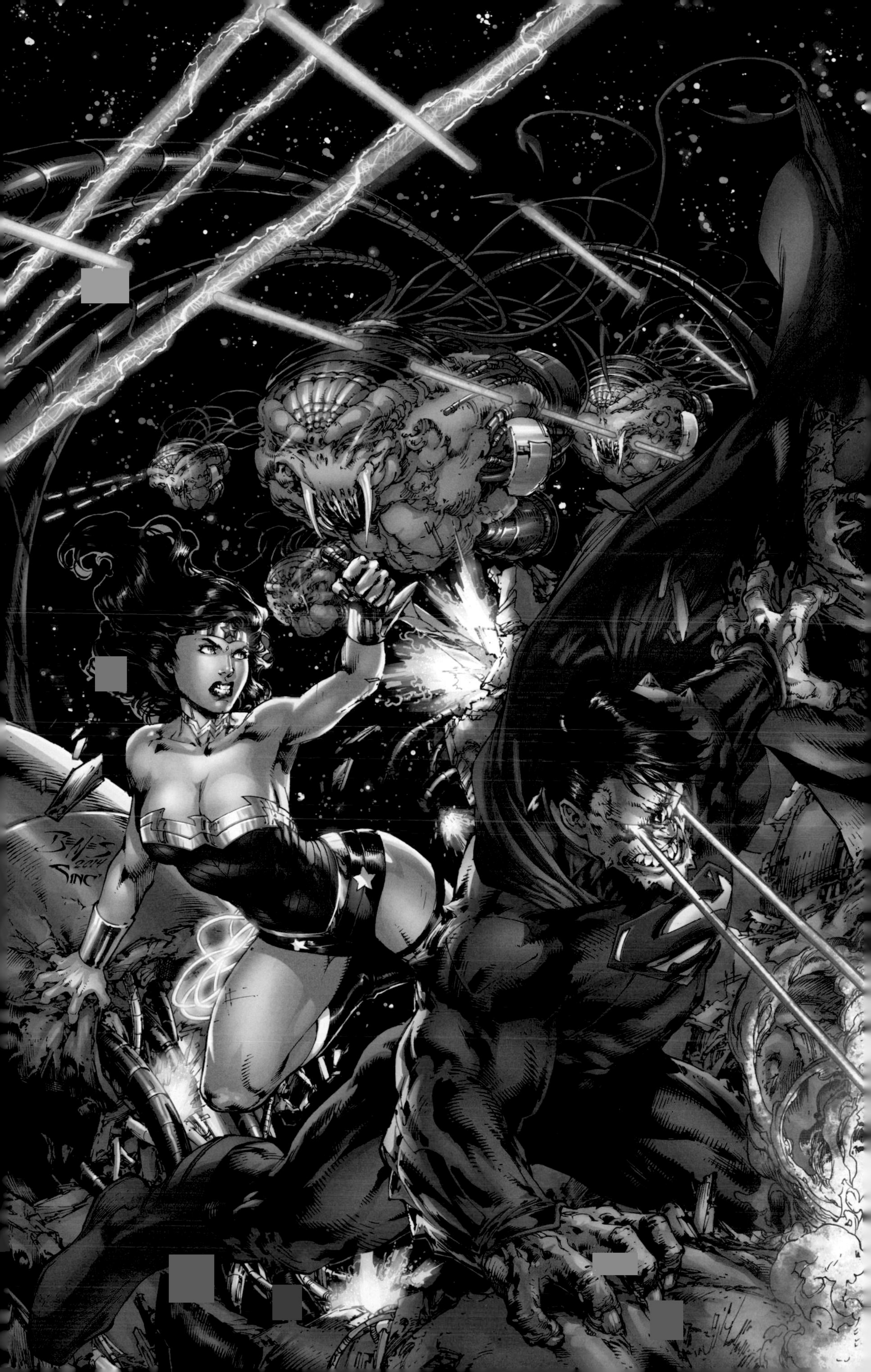

SUPERMAN DOOMED

[LAST SUN] chapter 2

"ASSIMILATION"

STORY
CHARLES SOULE

ART
THONY SILAS

COLORS
TOMEU MOREY AND **ULISES ARREOLA**

LETTERS
SAL CIPRIANO

COVER
ED BENES AND **ALEX SINCLAIR**

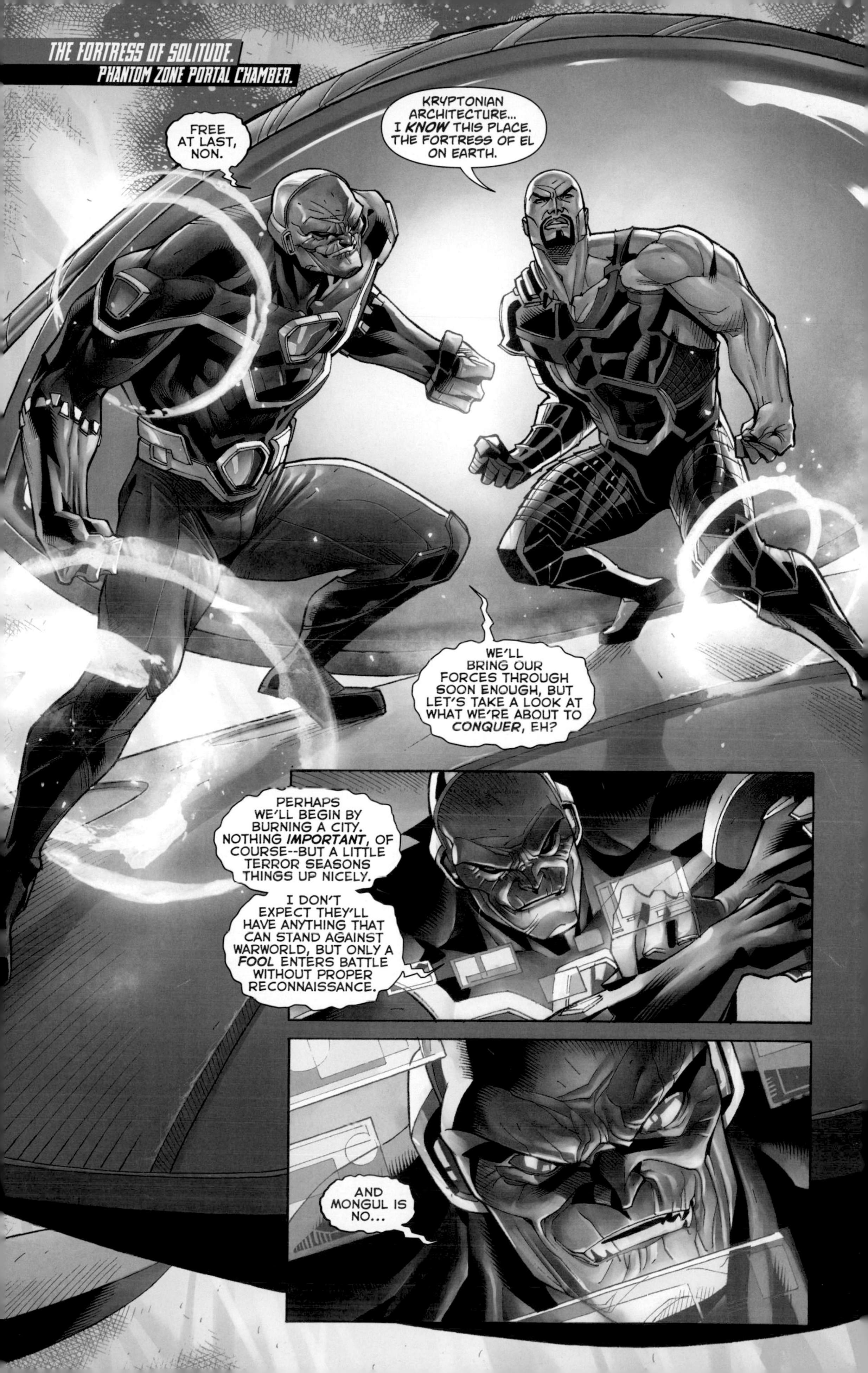
THE FORTRESS OF SOLITUDE.
PHANTOM ZONE PORTAL CHAMBER.
FREE AT LAST, NON.
KRYPTONIAN ARCHITECTURE... I KNOW THIS PLACE. THE FORTRESS OF EL ON EARTH.
WE'LL BRING OUR FORCES THROUGH SOON ENOUGH, BUT LET'S TAKE A LOOK AT WHAT WE'RE ABOUT TO CONQUER, EH?
PERHAPS WE'LL BEGIN BY BURNING A CITY. NOTHING IMPORTANT, OF COURSE--BUT A LITTLE TERROR SEASONS THINGS UP NICELY.
I DON'T EXPECT THEY'LL HAVE ANYTHING THAT CAN STAND AGAINST WARWORLD, BUT ONLY A FOOL ENTERS BATTLE WITHOUT PROPER RECONNAISSANCE.
AND MONGUL IS NO...

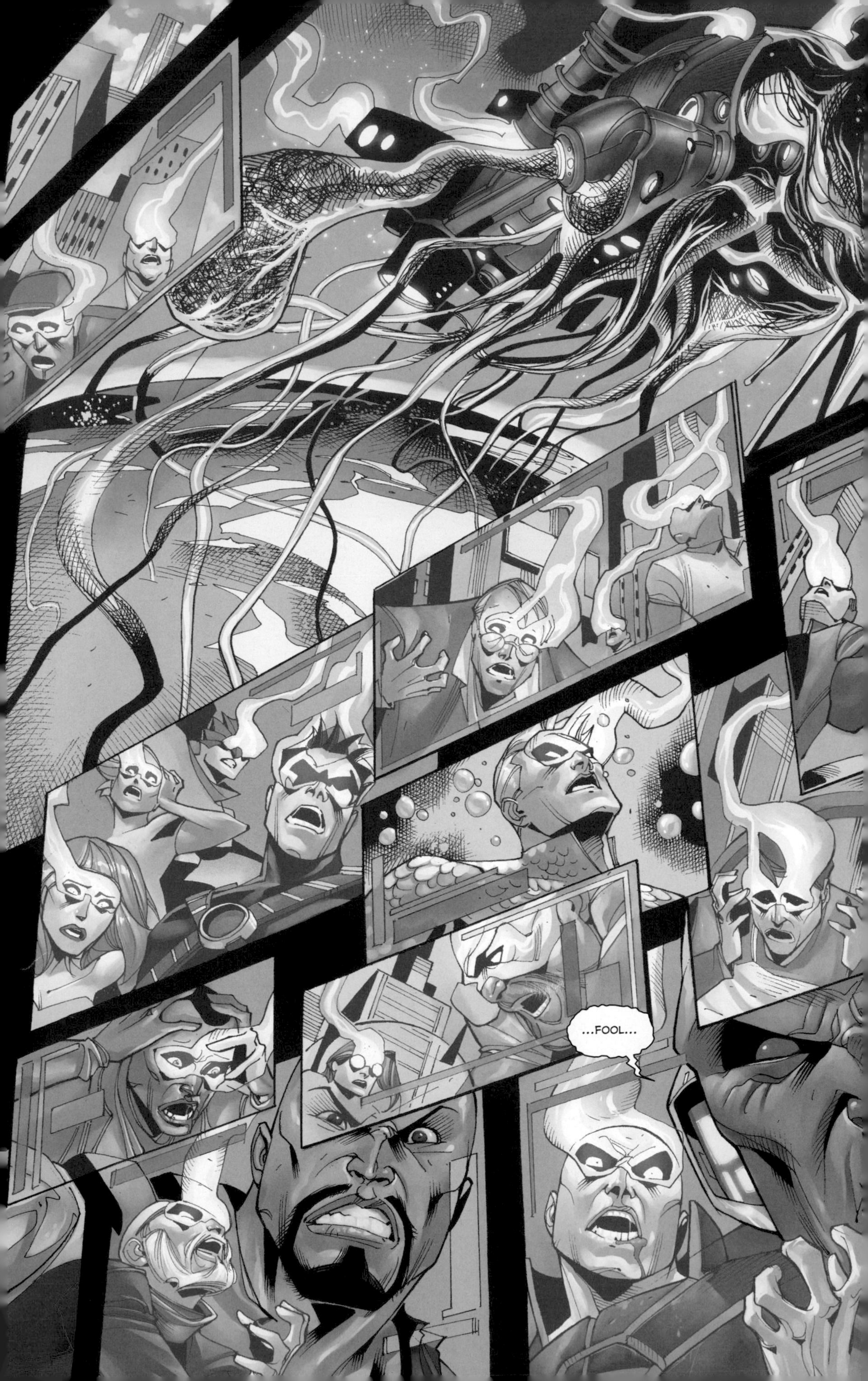
...FOOL...

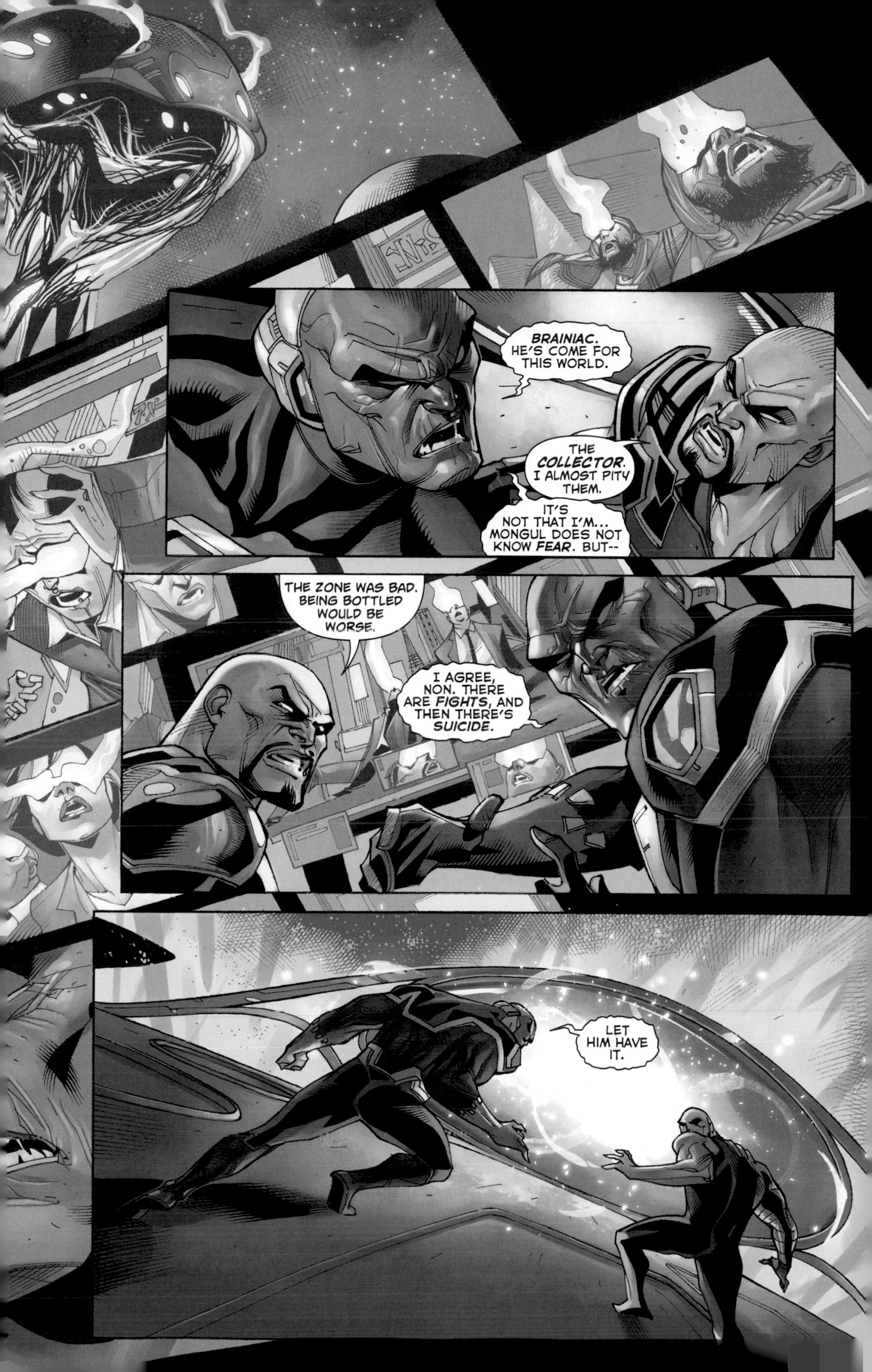

BRAINIAC. HE'S COME FOR THIS WORLD.
THE COLLECTOR. I ALMOST PITY THEM.
IT'S NOT THAT I'M... MONGUL DOES NOT KNOW FEAR. BUT--
THE ZONE WAS BAD. BEING BOTTLED WOULD BE WORSE.
I AGREE, NON. THERE ARE FIGHTS, AND THEN THERE'S SUICIDE.
LET HIM HAVE IT.

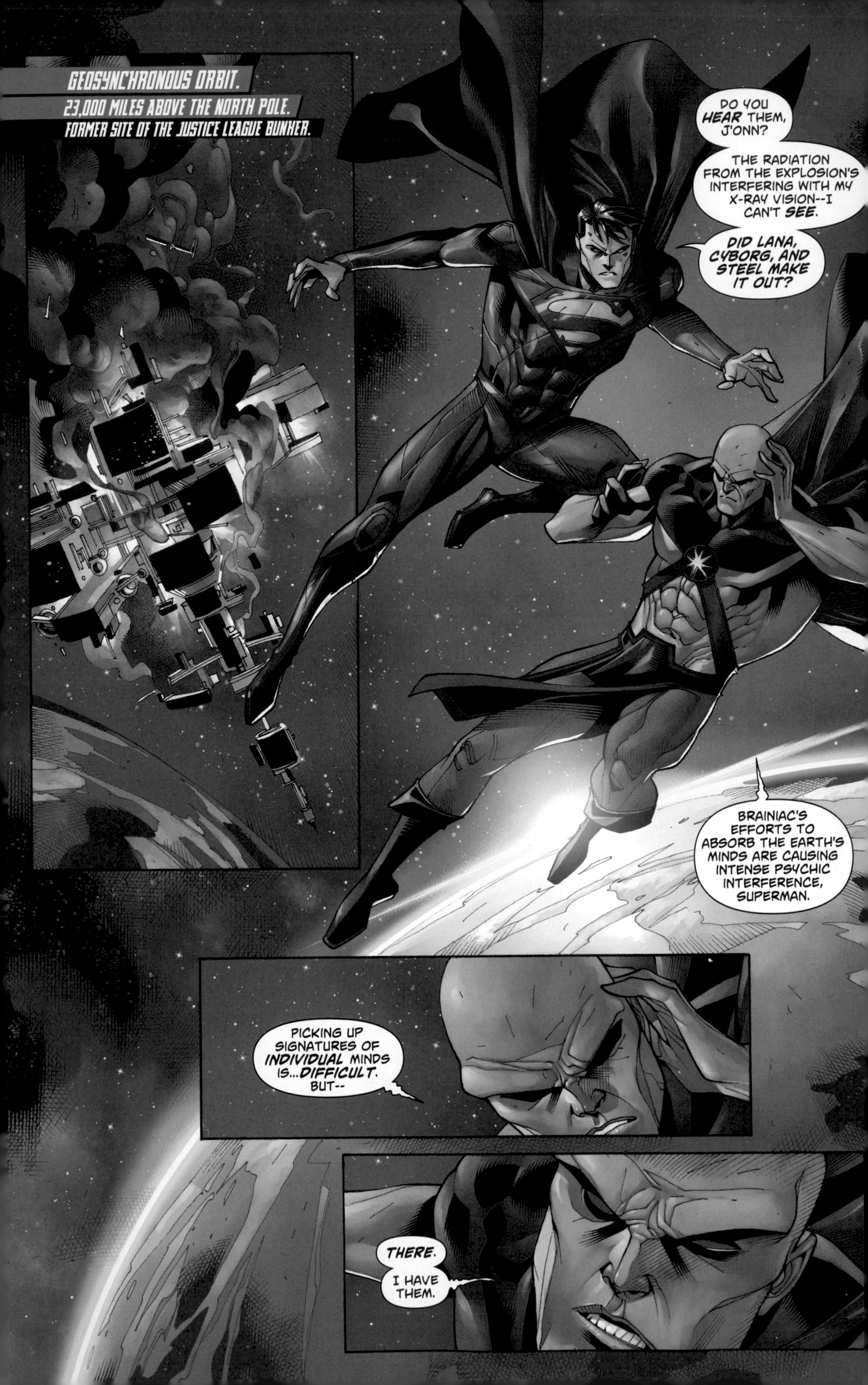
GEOSYNCHRONOUS ORBIT.
23,000 MILES ABOVE THE NORTH POLE.
FORMER SITE OF THE JUSTICE LEAGUE BUNKER.
DO YOU HEAR THEM, J'ONN?
THE RADIATION FROM THE EXPLOSION'S INTERFERING WITH MY X-RAY VISION--I CAN'T SEE.
DID LANA, CYBORG, AND STEEL MAKE IT OUT?
BRAINIAC'S EFFORTS TO ABSORB THE EARTH'S MINDS ARE CAUSING INTENSE PSYCHIC INTERFERENCE, SUPERMAN.
PICKING UP SIGNATURES OF INDIVIDUAL MINDS IS...DIFFICULT. BUT--
THERE.
I HAVE THEM.

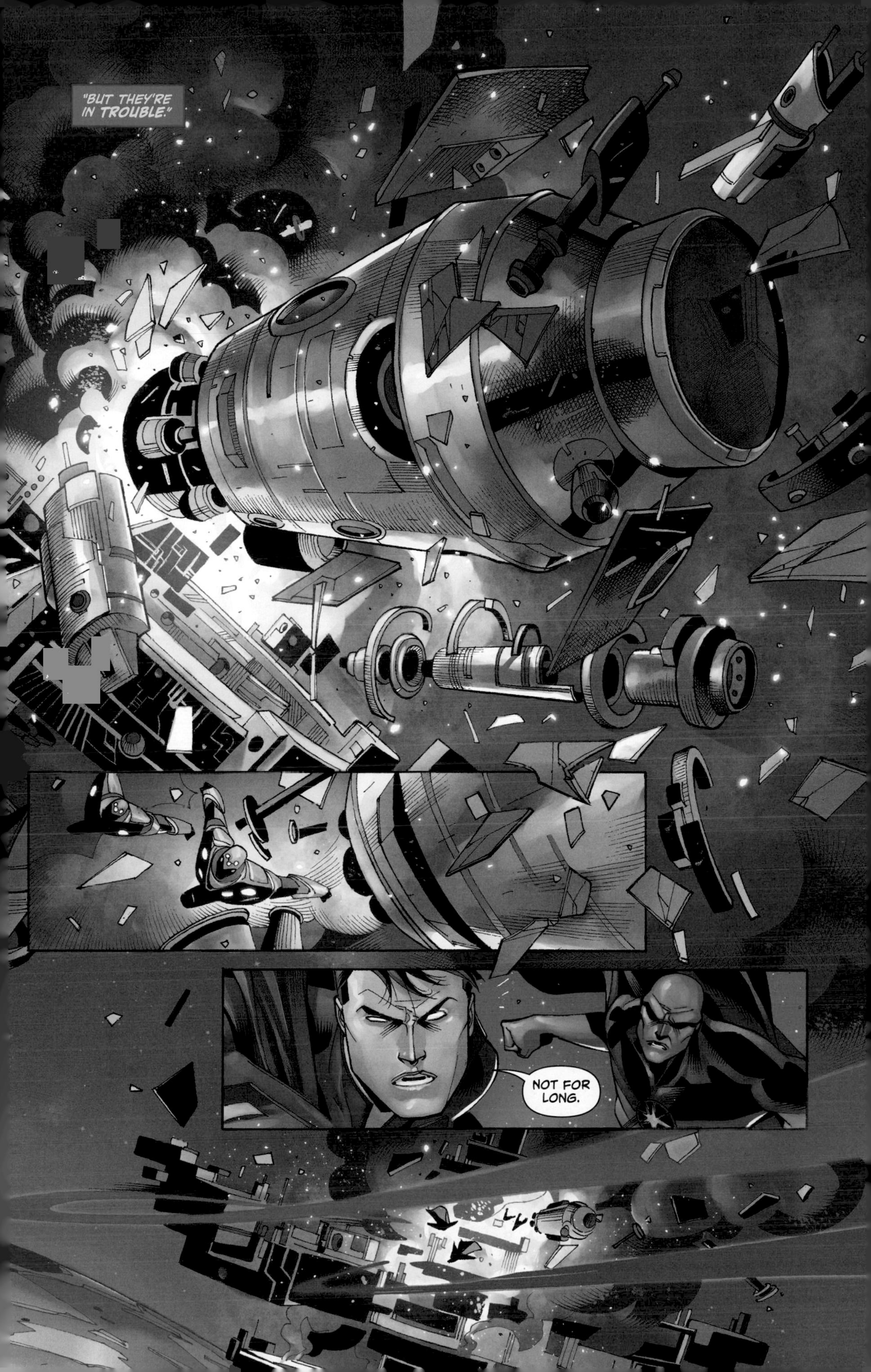
"BUT THEY'RE IN TROUBLE."
NOT FOR LONG.

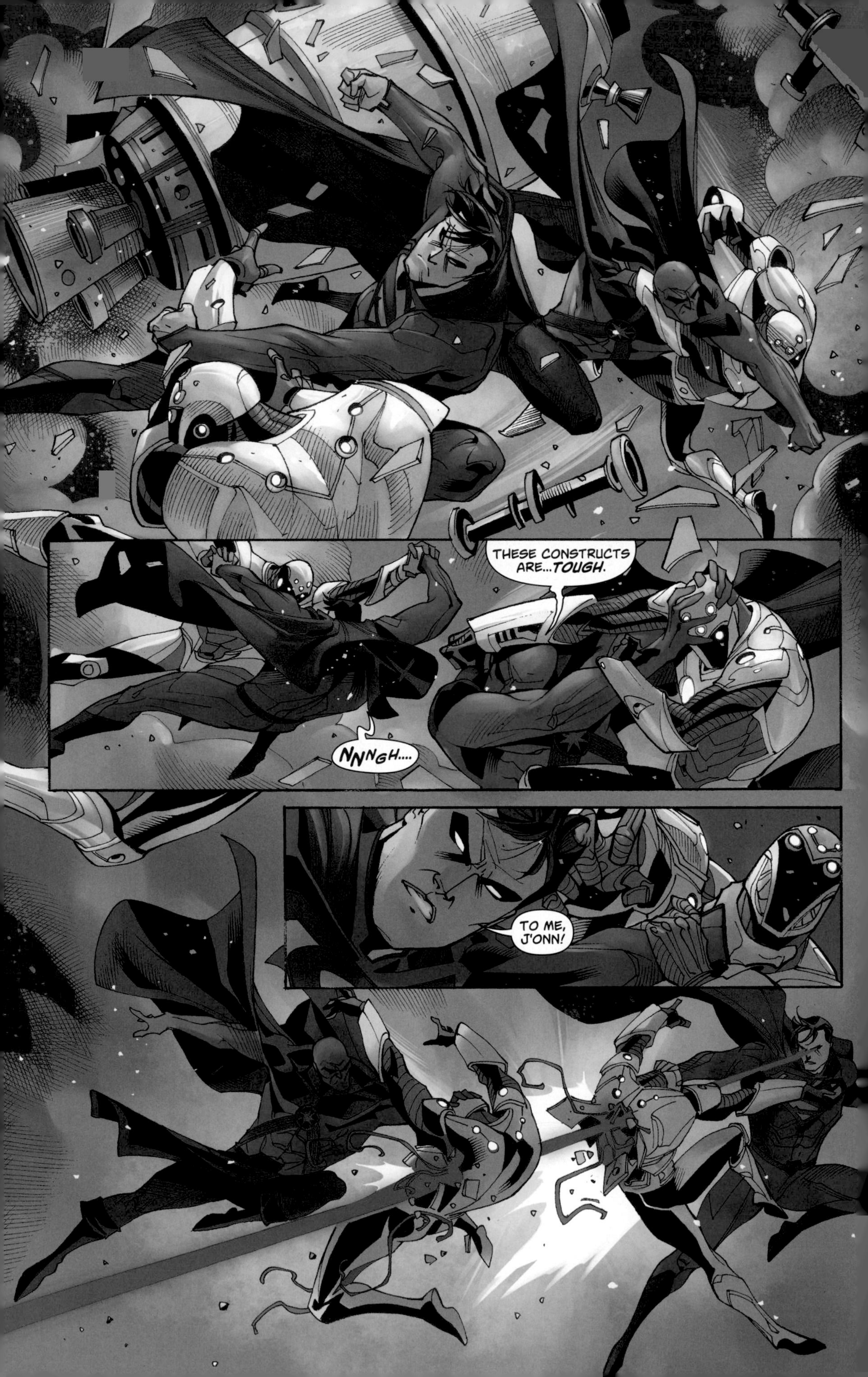
THESE CONSTRUCTS ARE...TOUGH.
NNNGH....
TO ME, J'ONN!

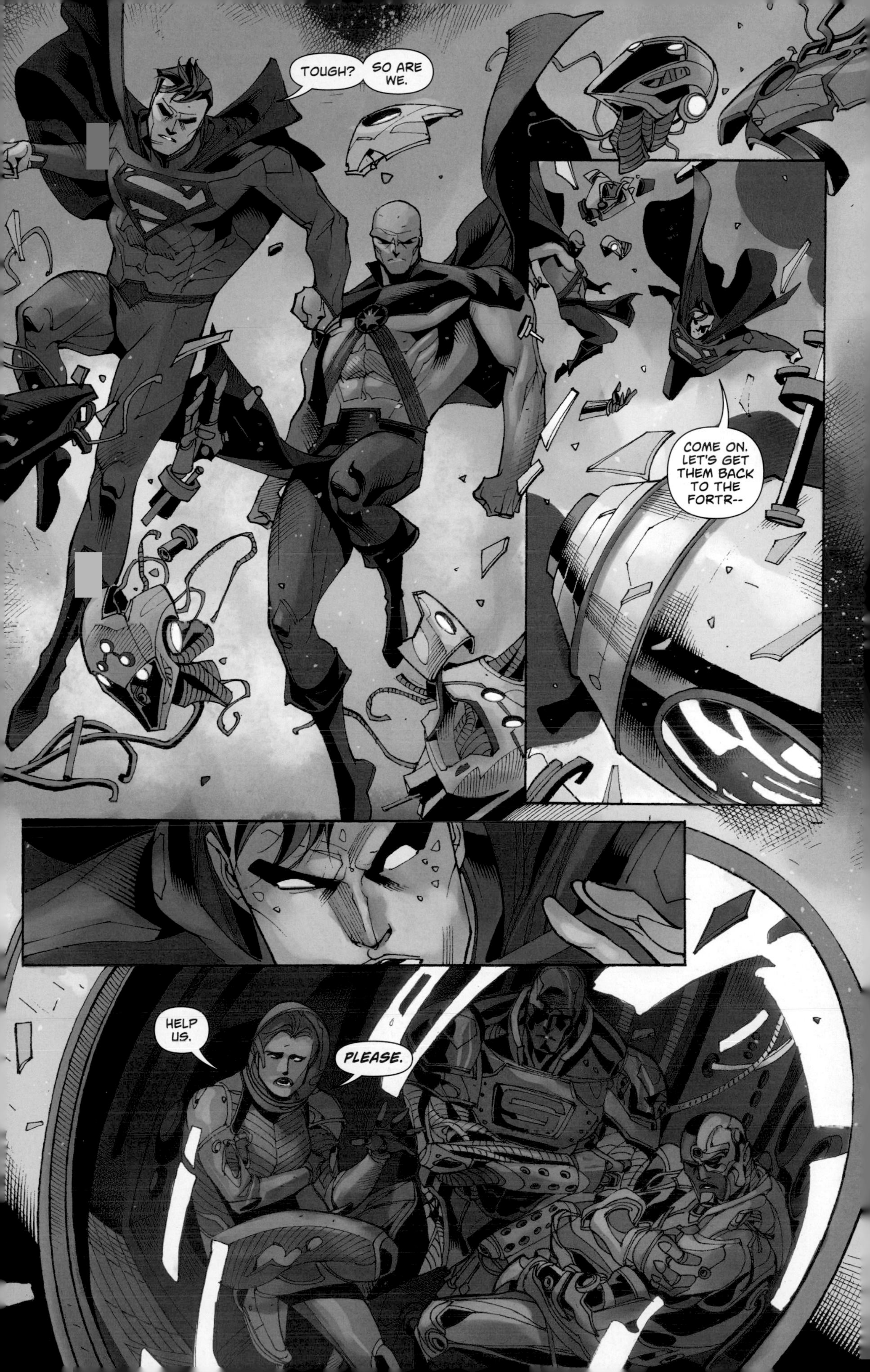
TOUGH?
SO ARE WE.
COME ON. LET'S GET THEM BACK TO THE FORTR--
HELP US.
PLEASE.

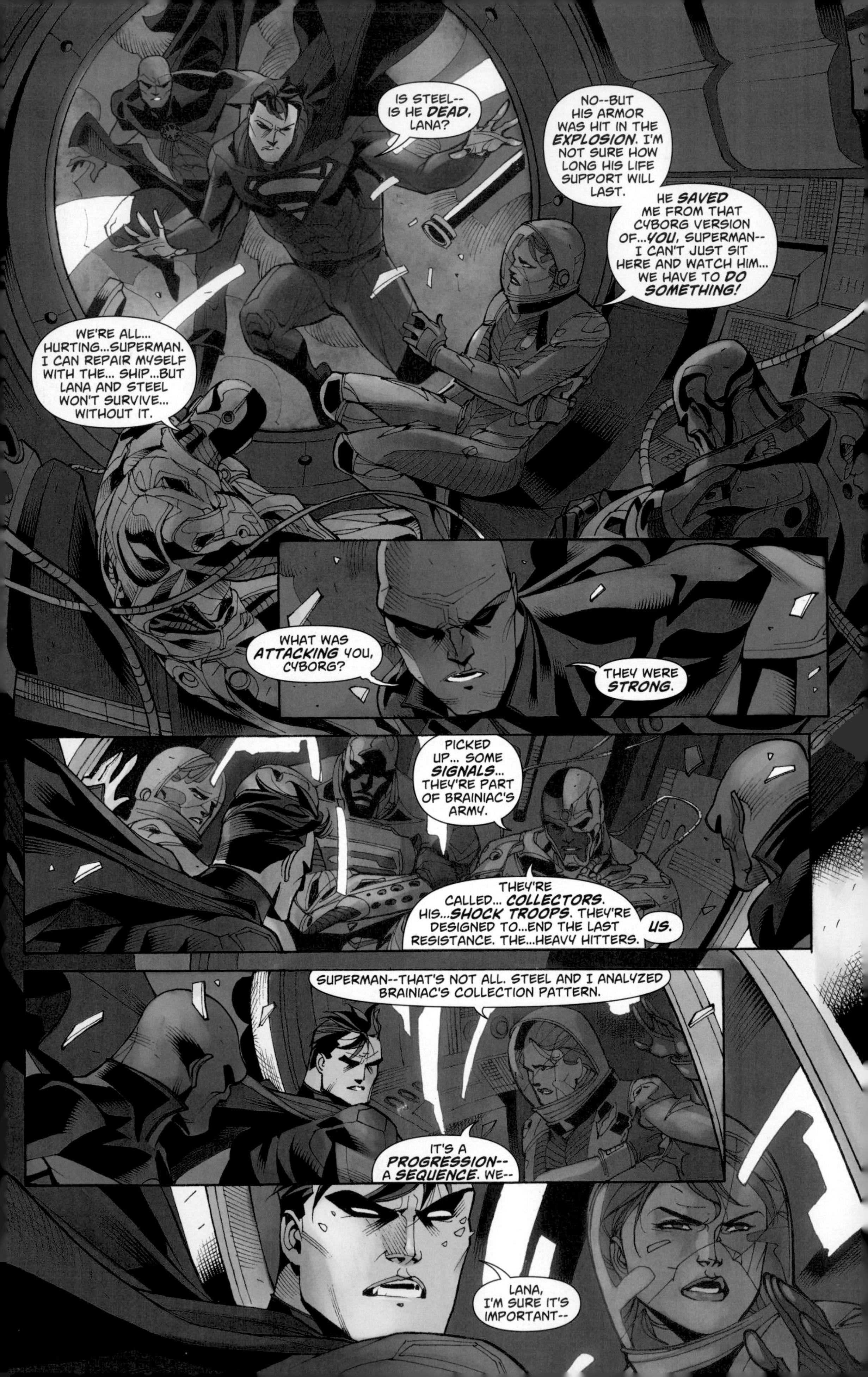
IS STEEL-- IS HE DEAD, LANA?
NO--BUT HIS ARMOR WAS HIT IN THE EXPLOSION. I'M NOT SURE HOW LONG HIS LIFE SUPPORT WILL LAST.
HE SAVED ME FROM THAT CYBORG VERSION OF...YOU, SUPERMAN-- I CAN'T JUST SIT HERE AND WATCH HIM... WE HAVE TO DO SOMETHING!
WE'RE ALL... HURTING...SUPERMAN. I CAN REPAIR MYSELF WITH THE... SHIP...BUT LANA AND STEEL WON'T SURVIVE... WITHOUT IT.
WHAT WAS ATTACKING YOU, CYBORG?
THEY WERE STRONG.
PICKED UP... SOME SIGNALS... THEY'RE PART OF BRAINIAC'S ARMY.
THEY'RE CALLED... COLLECTORS. HIS...SHOCK TROOPS. THEY'RE DESIGNED TO...END THE LAST RESISTANCE. THE...HEAVY HITTERS.
US.
SUPERMAN--THAT'S NOT ALL. STEEL AND I ANALYZED BRAINIAC'S COLLECTION PATTERN.
IT'S A PROGRESSION-- A SEQUENCE. WE--
LANA, I'M SURE IT'S IMPORTANT--

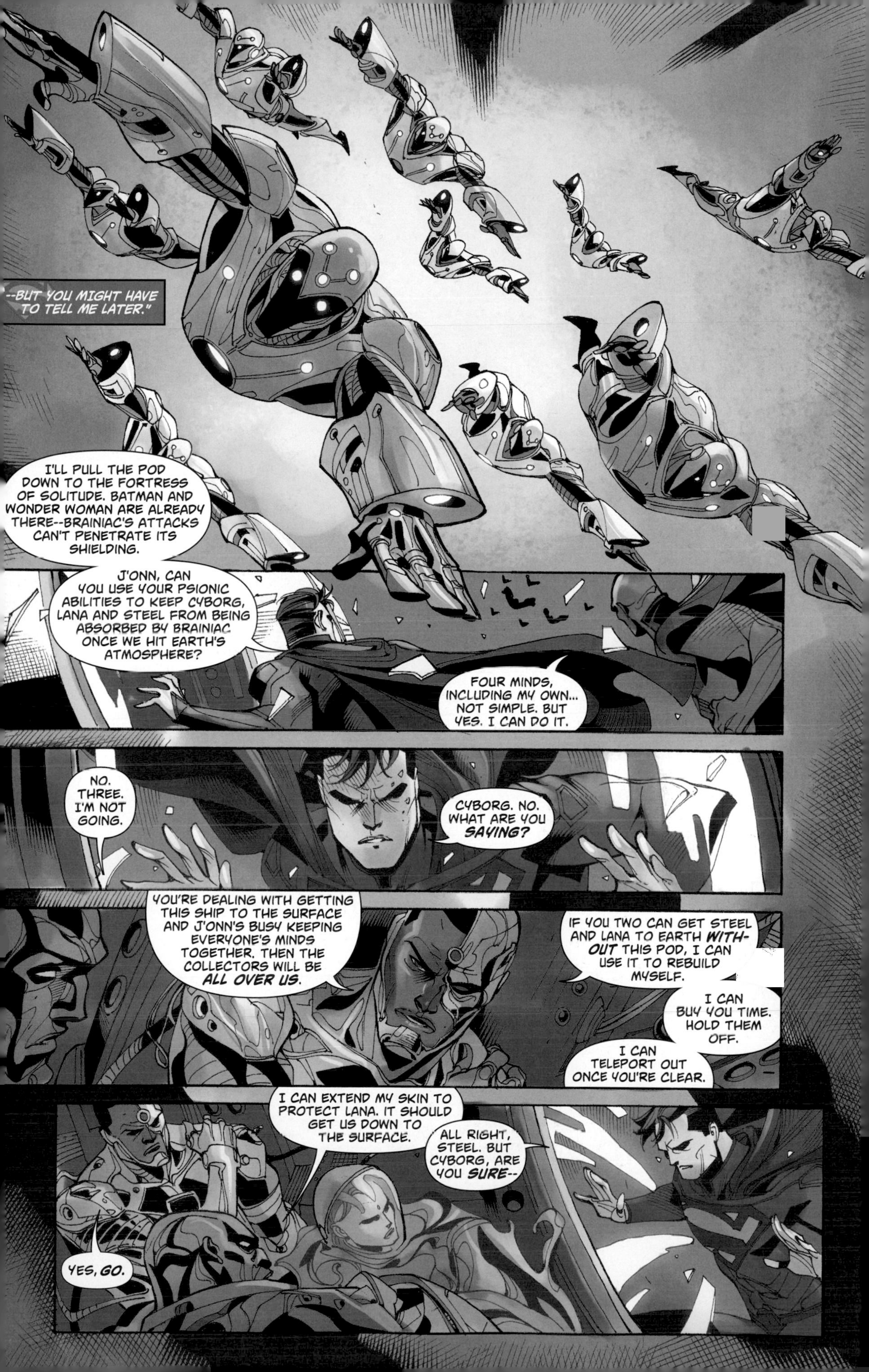
--BUT YOU MIGHT HAVE TO TELL ME LATER."
I'LL PULL THE POD DOWN TO THE FORTRESS OF SOLITUDE. BATMAN AND WONDER WOMAN ARE ALREADY THERE--BRAINIAC'S ATTACKS CAN'T PENETRATE ITS SHIELDING.
J'ONN, CAN YOU USE YOUR PSIONIC ABILITIES TO KEEP CYBORG, LANA AND STEEL FROM BEING ABSORBED BY BRAINIAC ONCE WE HIT EARTH'S ATMOSPHERE?
FOUR MINDS, INCLUDING MY OWN... NOT SIMPLE. BUT YES. I CAN DO IT.
NO. THREE. I'M NOT GOING.
CYBORG. NO. WHAT ARE YOU SAYING?
YOU'RE DEALING WITH GETTING THIS SHIP TO THE SURFACE AND J'ONN'S BUSY KEEPING EVERYONE'S MINDS TOGETHER. THEN THE COLLECTORS WILL BE ALL OVER US.
IF YOU TWO CAN GET STEEL AND LANA TO EARTH WITH-OUT THIS POD, I CAN USE IT TO REBUILD MYSELF.
I CAN BUY YOU TIME. HOLD THEM OFF.
I CAN TELEPORT OUT ONCE YOU'RE CLEAR.
I CAN EXTEND MY SKIN TO PROTECT LANA. IT SHOULD GET US DOWN TO THE SURFACE.
ALL RIGHT, STEEL. BUT CYBORG, ARE YOU SURE--
YES, GO.

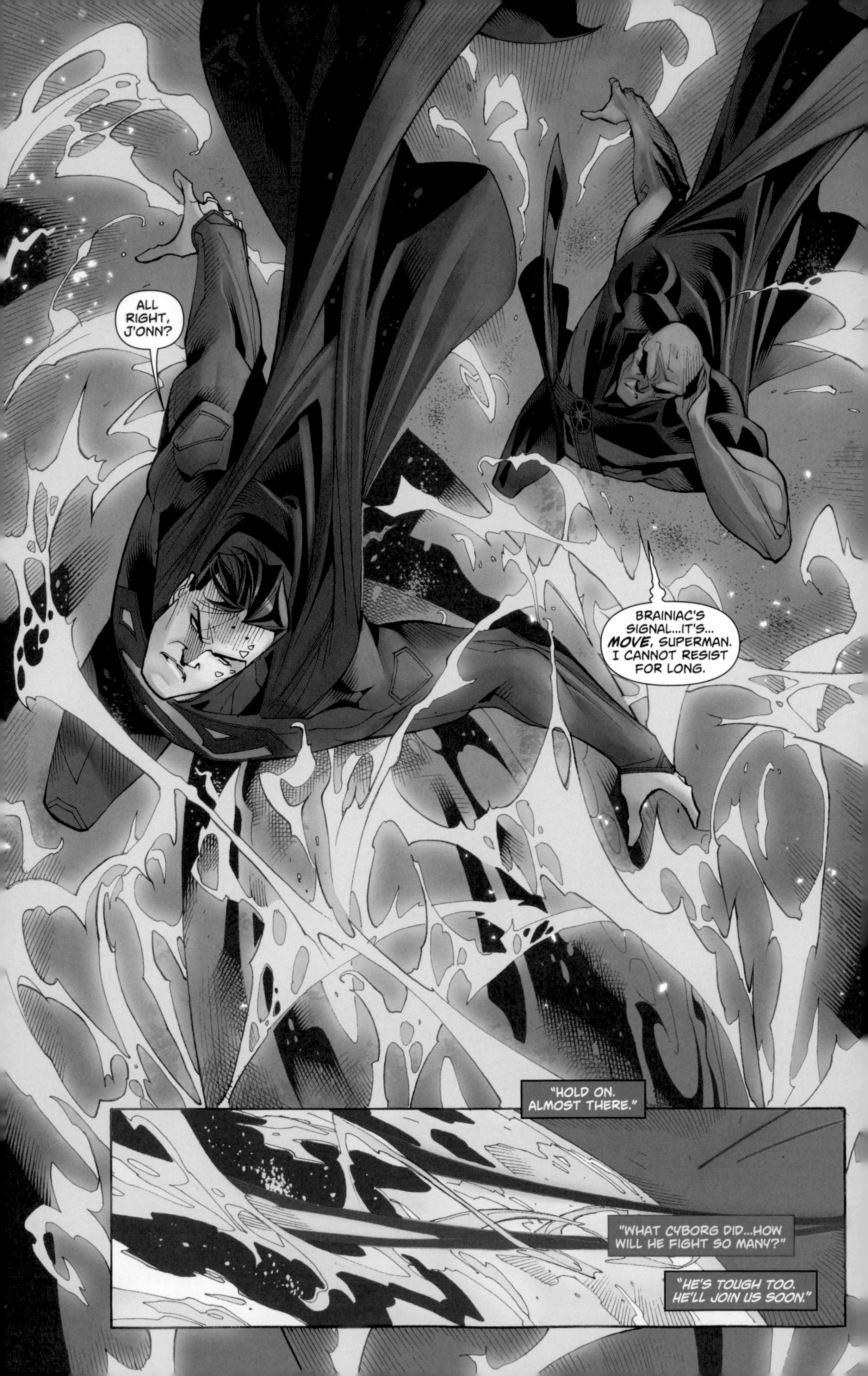
ALL RIGHT, J'ONN?
BRAINIAC'S SIGNAL...IT'S... MOVE, SUPERMAN. I CANNOT RESIST FOR LONG.
"HOLD ON. ALMOST THERE."
"WHAT CYBORG DID...HOW WILL HE FIGHT SO MANY?"
"HE'S TOUGH TOO. HE'LL JOIN US SOON."

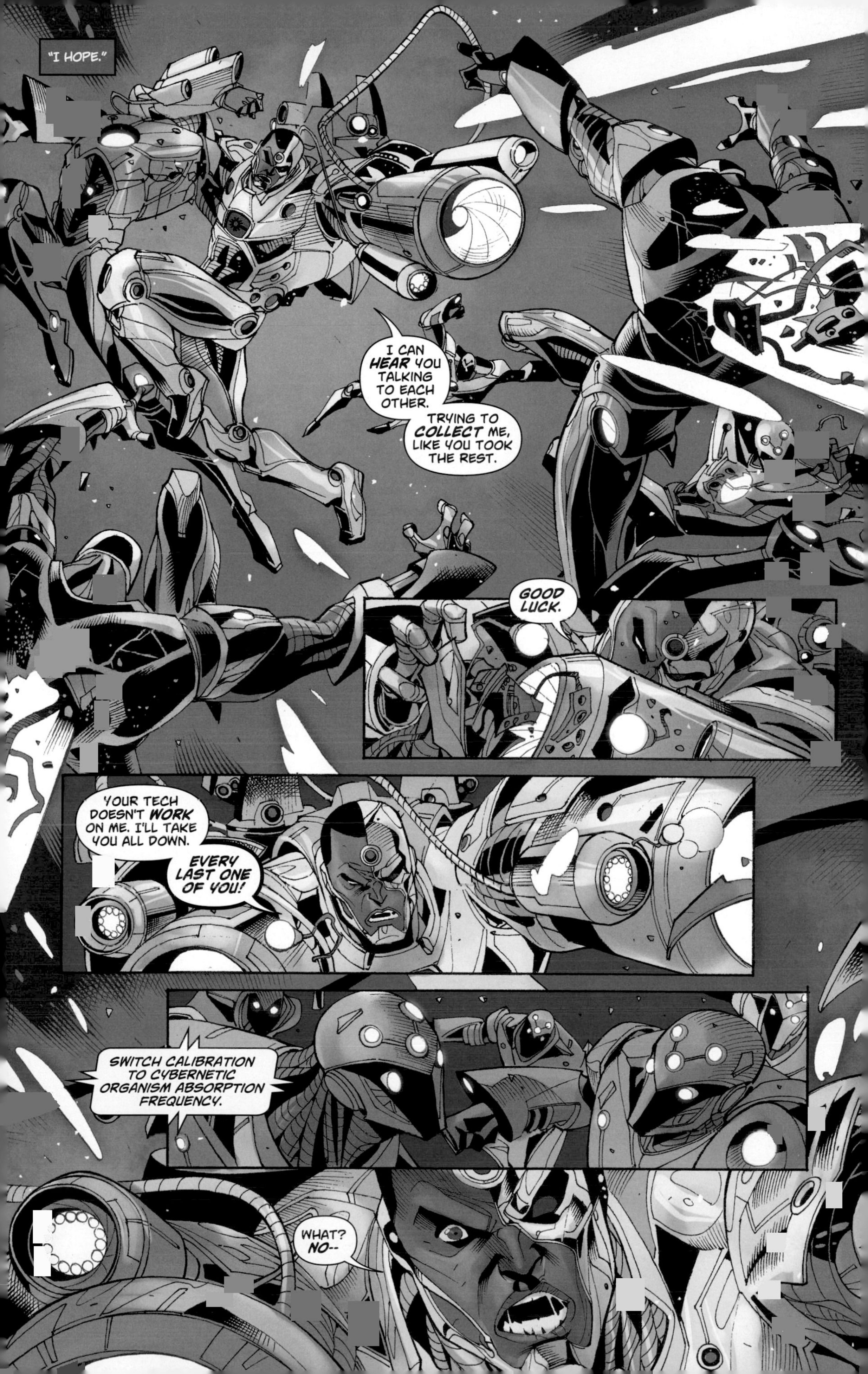
"I HOPE."
I CAN HEAR YOU TALKING TO EACH OTHER.
TRYING TO COLLECT ME, LIKE YOU TOOK THE REST.
GOOD LUCK.
YOUR TECH DOESN'T WORK ON ME. I'LL TAKE YOU ALL DOWN.
EVERY LAST ONE OF YOU!
SWITCH CALIBRATION TO CYBERNETIC ORGANISM ABSORPTION FREQUENCY.
WHAT? NO--

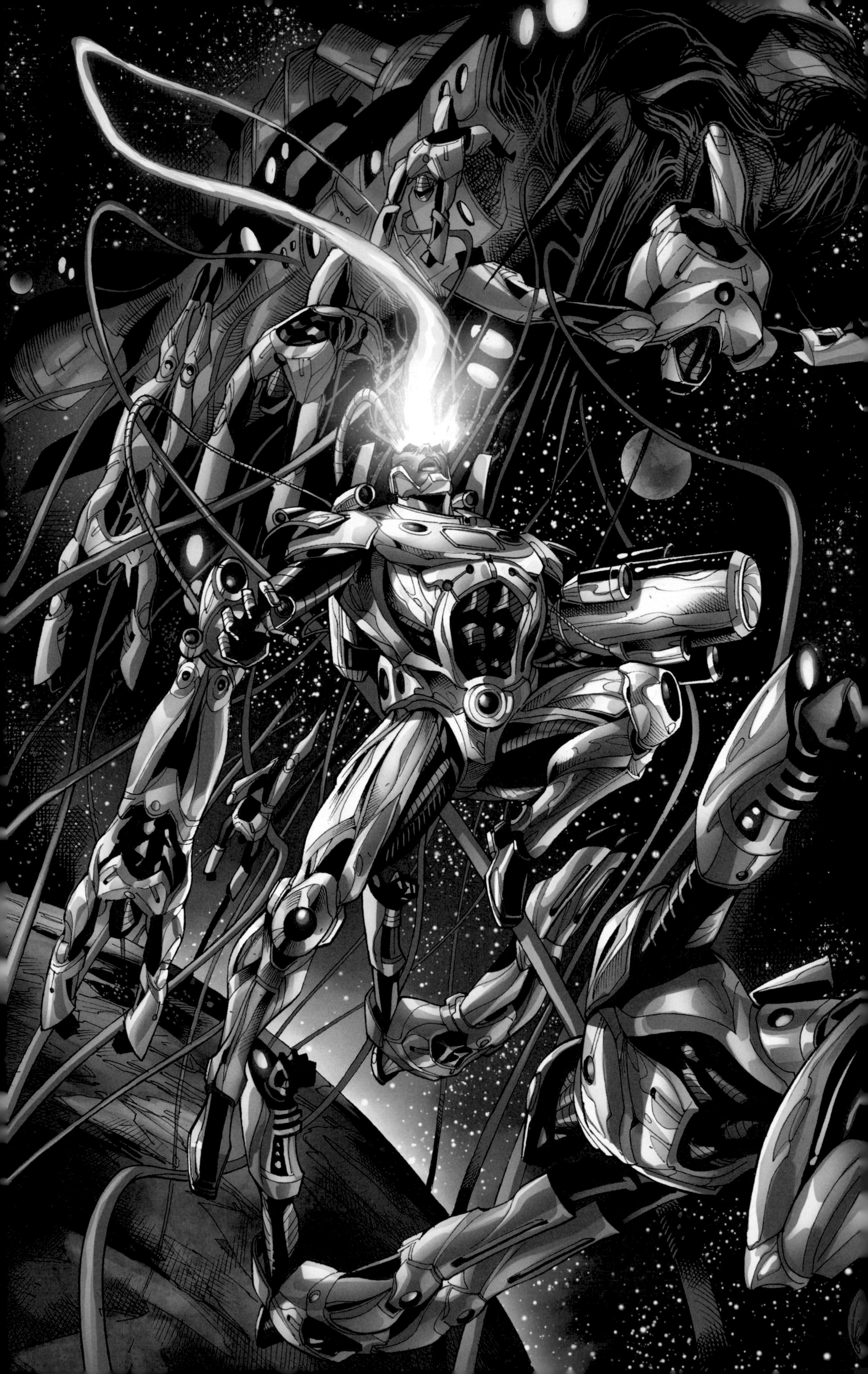

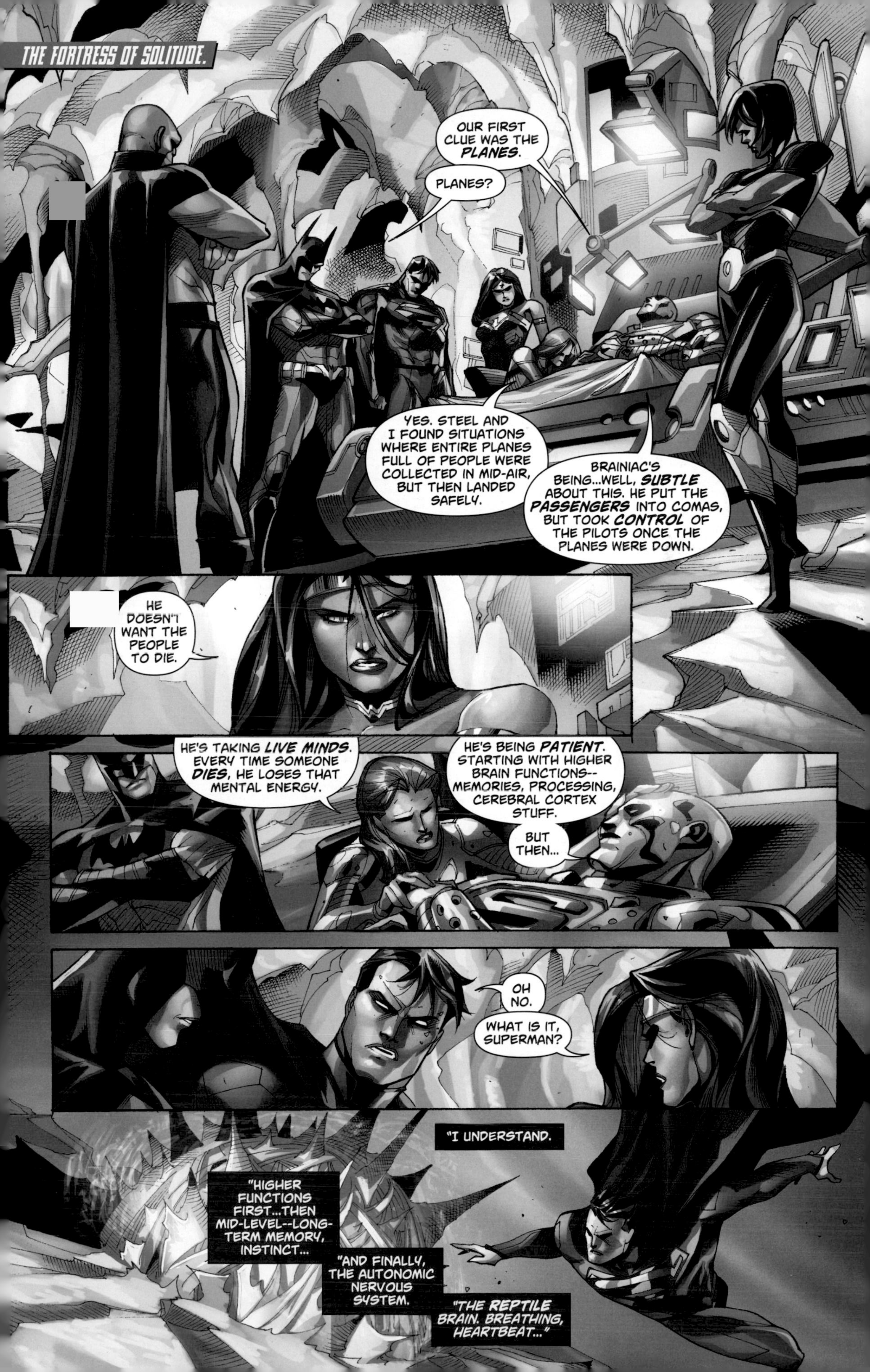
THE FORTRESS OF SOLITUDE.
OUR FIRST CLUE WAS THE PLANES.
PLANES?
YES. STEEL AND I FOUND SITUATIONS WHERE ENTIRE PLANES FULL OF PEOPLE WERE COLLECTED IN MID-AIR, BUT THEN LANDED SAFELY.
BRAINIAC'S BEING...WELL, SUBTLE ABOUT THIS. HE PUT THE PASSENGERS INTO COMAS, BUT TOOK CONTROL OF THE PILOTS ONCE THE PLANES WERE DOWN.
HE DOESN'T WANT THE PEOPLE TO DIE.
HE'S TAKING LIVE MINDS. EVERY TIME SOMEONE DIES, HE LOSES THAT MENTAL ENERGY.
HE'S BEING PATIENT. STARTING WITH HIGHER BRAIN FUNCTIONS-- MEMORIES, PROCESSING, CEREBRAL CORTEX STUFF.
BUT THEN...
OH NO.
WHAT IS IT, SUPERMAN?
"I UNDERSTAND.
"HIGHER FUNCTIONS FIRST...THEN MID-LEVEL--LONG-TERM MEMORY, INSTINCT...
"AND FINALLY, THE AUTONOMIC NERVOUS SYSTEM.
"THE REPTILE BRAIN. BREATHING, HEARTBEAT..."

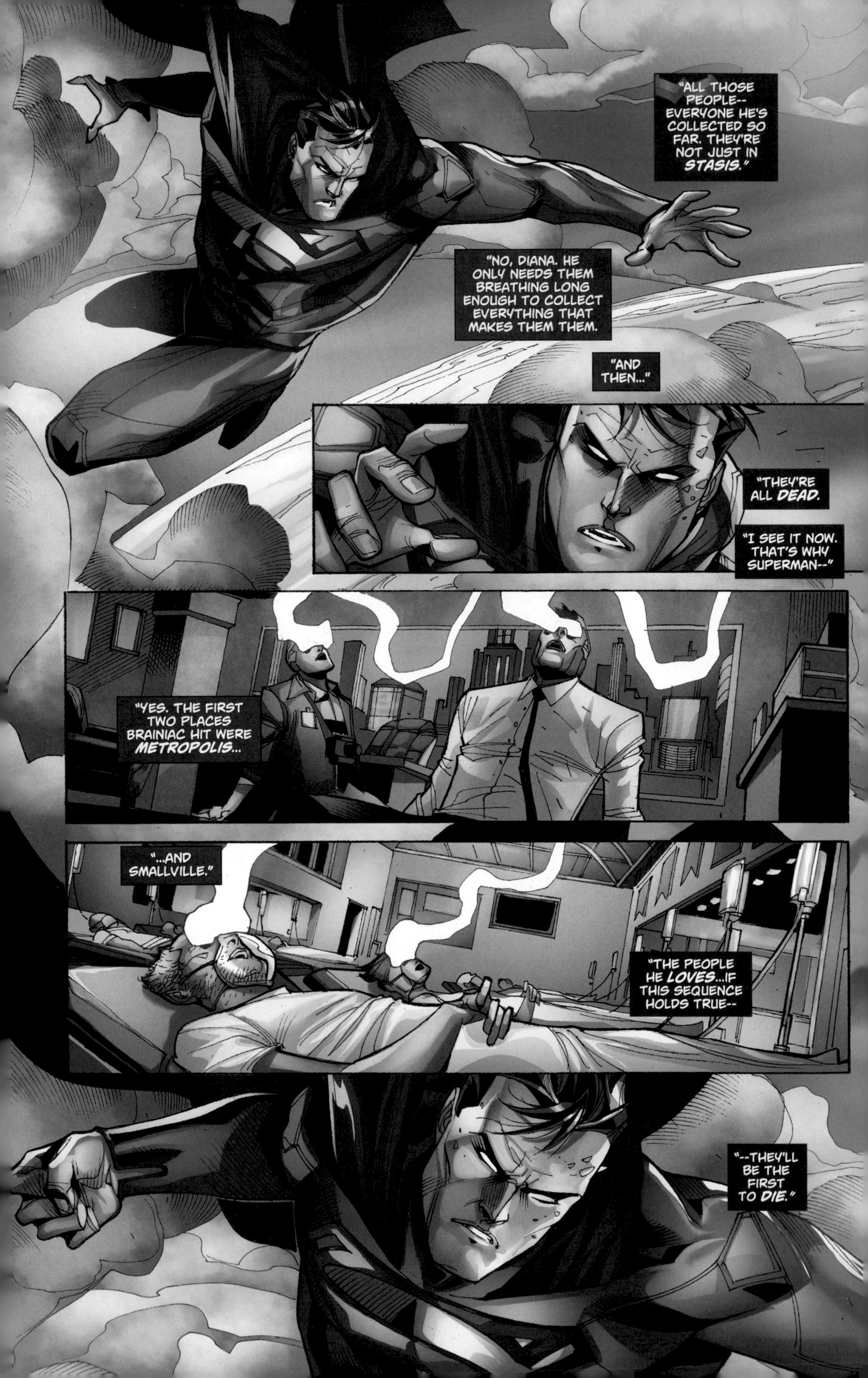
"ALL THOSE PEOPLE--EVERYONE HE'S COLLECTED SO FAR. THEY'RE NOT JUST IN STASIS."
"NO, DIANA. HE ONLY NEEDS THEM BREATHING LONG ENOUGH TO COLLECT EVERYTHING THAT MAKES THEM THEM.
"AND THEN..."
"THEY'RE ALL DEAD.
"I SEE IT NOW. THAT'S WHY SUPERMAN--"
"YES. THE FIRST TWO PLACES BRAINIAC HIT WERE METROPOLIS...
"...AND SMALLVILLE."
"THE PEOPLE HE LOVES...IF THIS SEQUENCE HOLDS TRUE--
"--THEY'LL BE THE FIRST TO DIE."

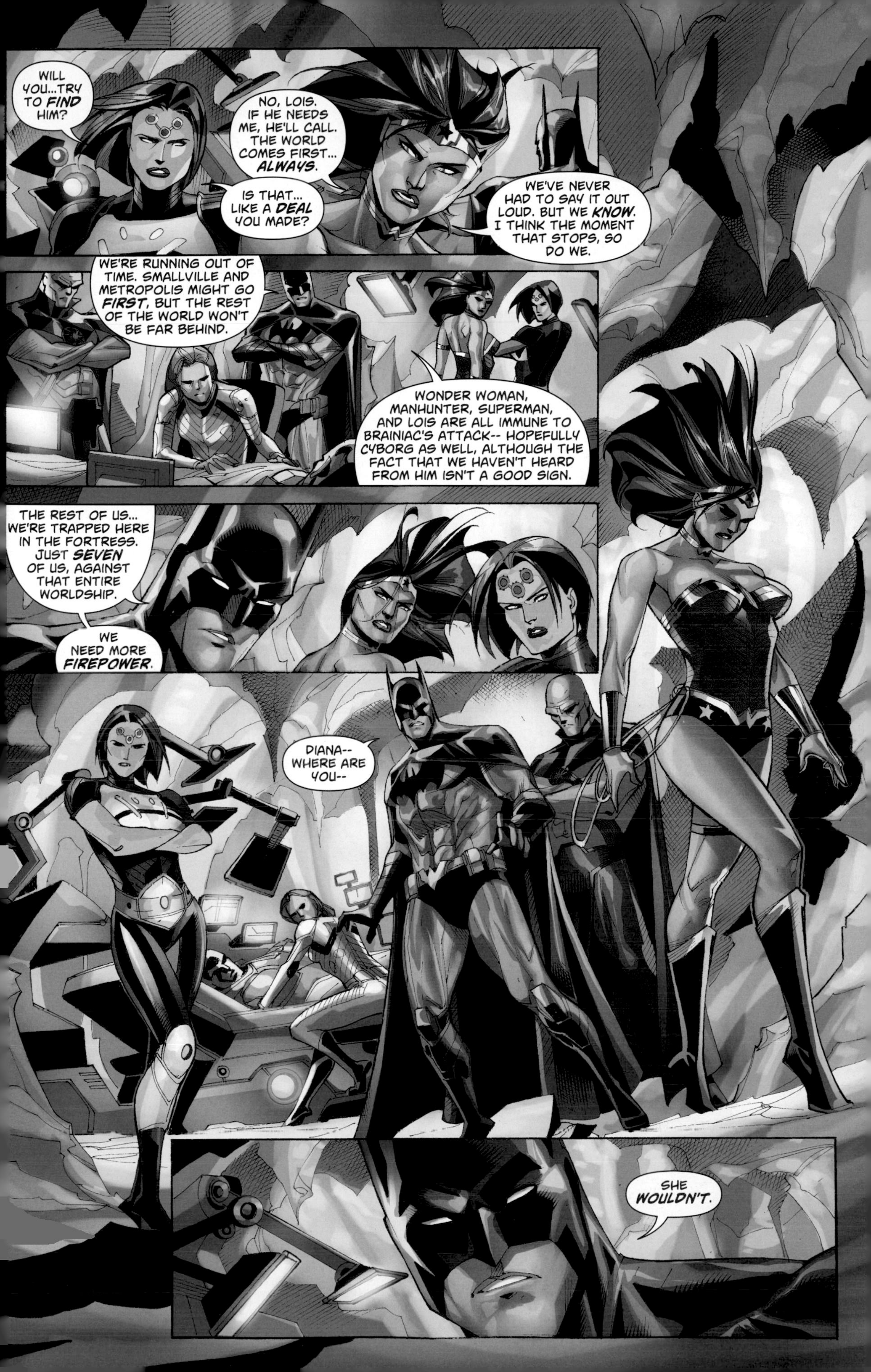
WILL YOU...TRY TO FIND HIM?
NO, LOIS. IF HE NEEDS ME, HE'LL CALL. THE WORLD COMES FIRST... ALWAYS.
IS THAT... LIKE A DEAL YOU MADE?
WE'VE NEVER HAD TO SAY IT OUT LOUD. BUT WE KNOW. I THINK THE MOMENT THAT STOPS, SO DO WE.
WE'RE RUNNING OUT OF TIME. SMALLVILLE AND METROPOLIS MIGHT GO FIRST, BUT THE REST OF THE WORLD WON'T BE FAR BEHIND.
WONDER WOMAN, MANHUNTER, SUPERMAN, AND LOIS ARE ALL IMMUNE TO BRAINIAC'S ATTACK-- HOPEFULLY CYBORG AS WELL, ALTHOUGH THE FACT THAT WE HAVEN'T HEARD FROM HIM ISN'T A GOOD SIGN.
THE REST OF US... WE'RE TRAPPED HERE IN THE FORTRESS. JUST SEVEN OF US, AGAINST THAT ENTIRE WORLDSHIP.
WE NEED MORE FIREPOWER.
DIANA-- WHERE ARE YOU--
SHE WOULDN'T.

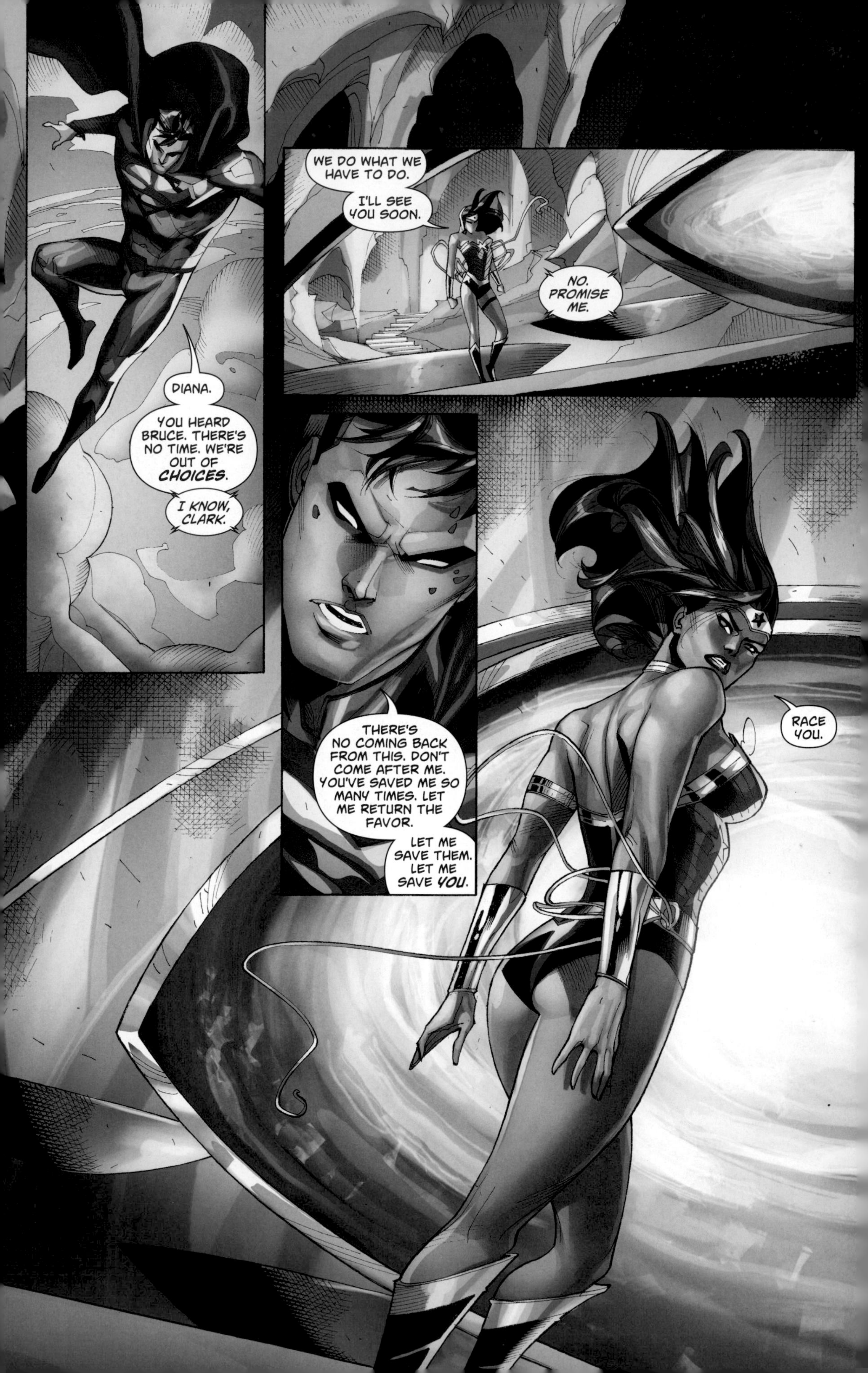
WE DO WHAT WE HAVE TO DO.
I'LL SEE YOU SOON.
NO. PROMISE ME.
DIANA.
YOU HEARD BRUCE. THERE'S NO TIME. WE'RE OUT OF CHOICES.
I KNOW, CLARK.
THERE'S NO COMING BACK FROM THIS. DON'T COME AFTER ME. YOU'VE SAVED ME SO MANY TIMES. LET ME RETURN THE FAVOR.
LET ME SAVE THEM. LET ME SAVE YOU.
RACE YOU.

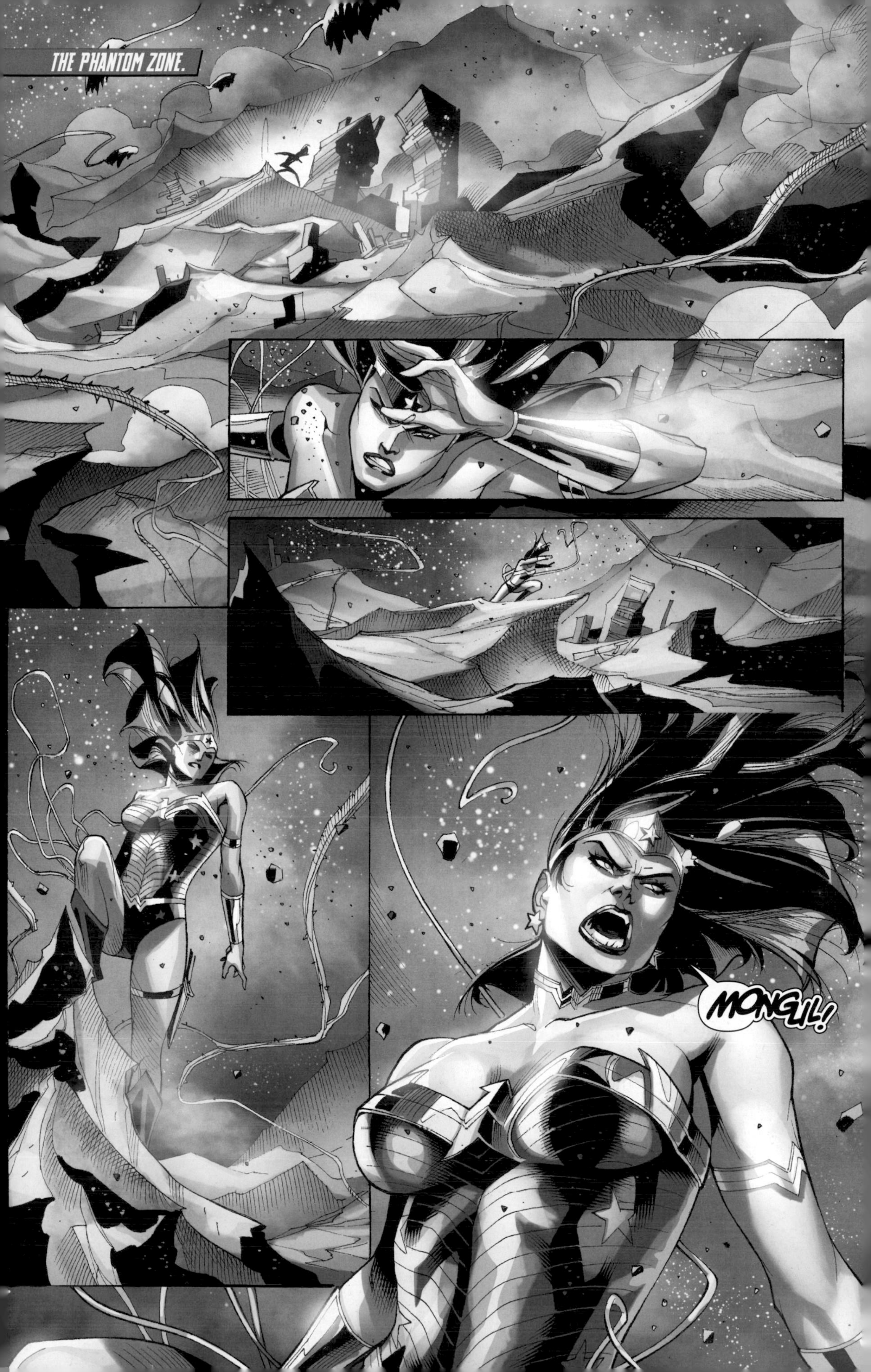
THE PHANTOM ZONE.
MONGUL!

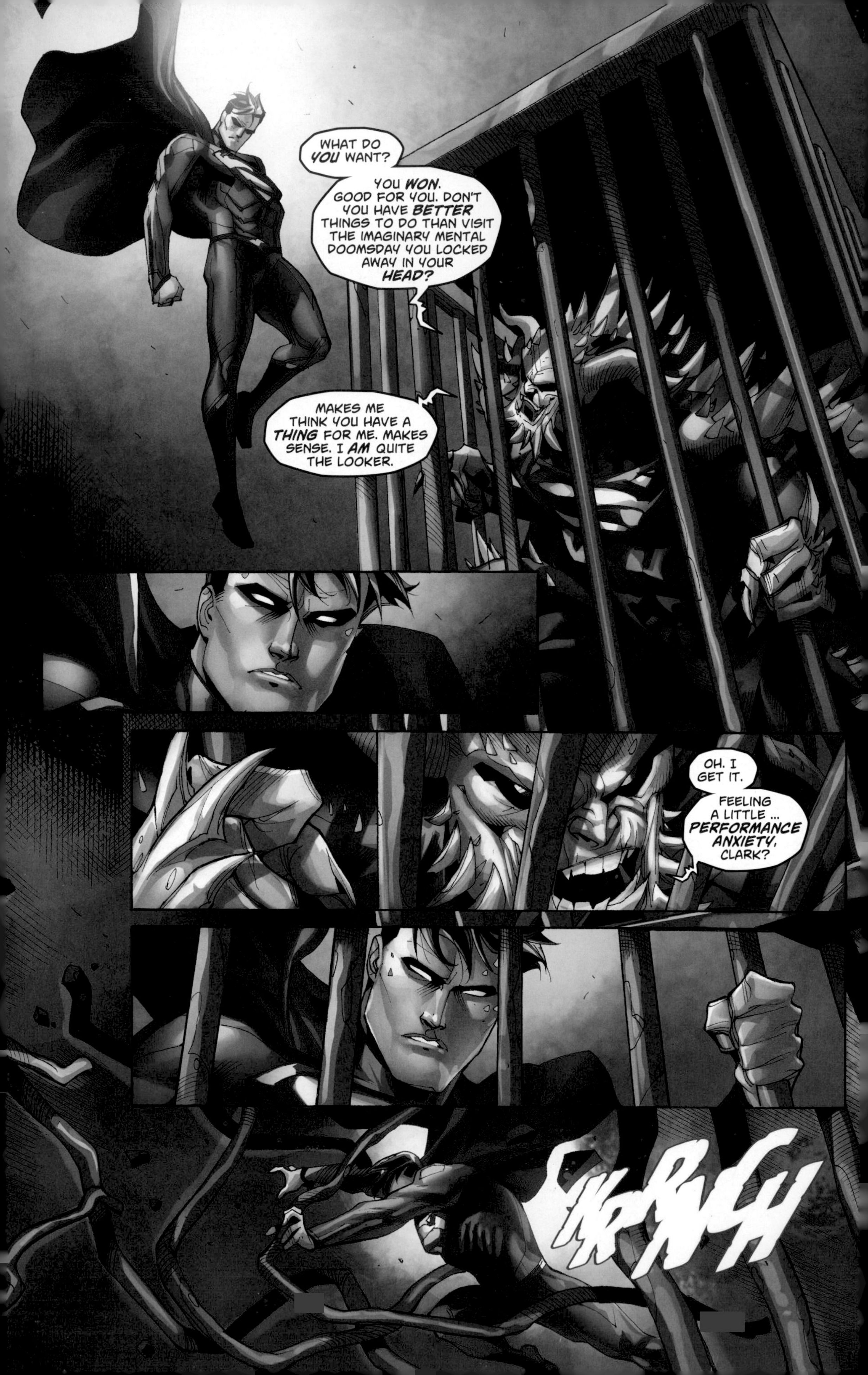
WHAT DO YOU WANT?
YOU WON. GOOD FOR YOU. DON'T YOU HAVE BETTER THINGS TO DO THAN VISIT THE IMAGINARY MENTAL DOOMSDAY YOU LOCKED AWAY IN YOUR HEAD?
MAKES ME THINK YOU HAVE A THING FOR ME. MAKES SENSE. I AM QUITE THE LOOKER.
OH. I GET IT.
FEELING A LITTLE ... PERFORMANCE ANXIETY, CLARK?

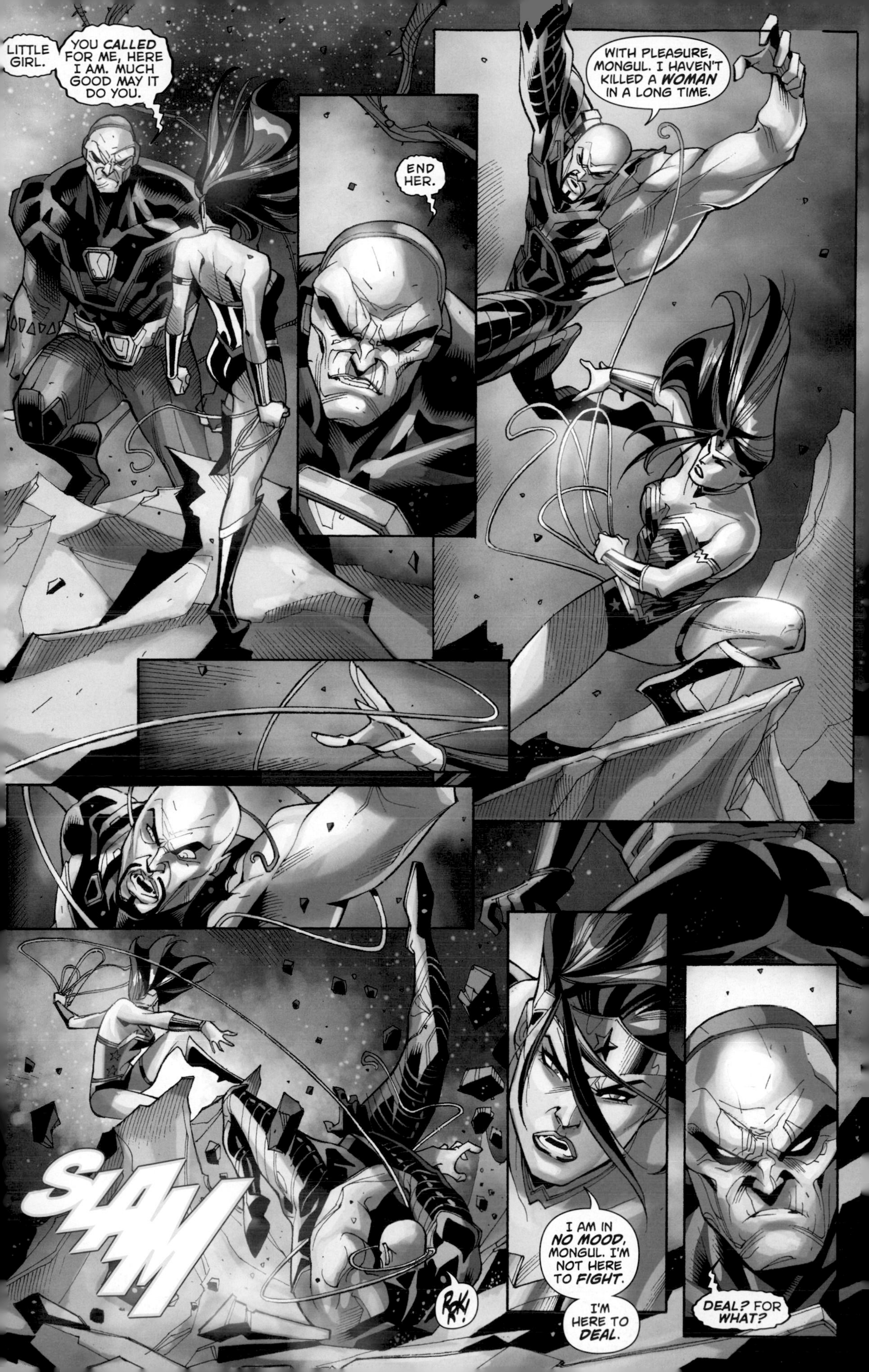
LITTLE GIRL.
YOU CALLED FOR ME, HERE I AM. MUCH GOOD MAY IT DO YOU.
END HER.
WITH PLEASURE, MONGUL. I HAVEN'T KILLED A WOMAN IN A LONG TIME.
SLAM
RAK!
I AM IN NO MOOD, MONGUL. I'M NOT HERE TO FIGHT.
I'M HERE TO DEAL.
DEAL? FOR WHAT?

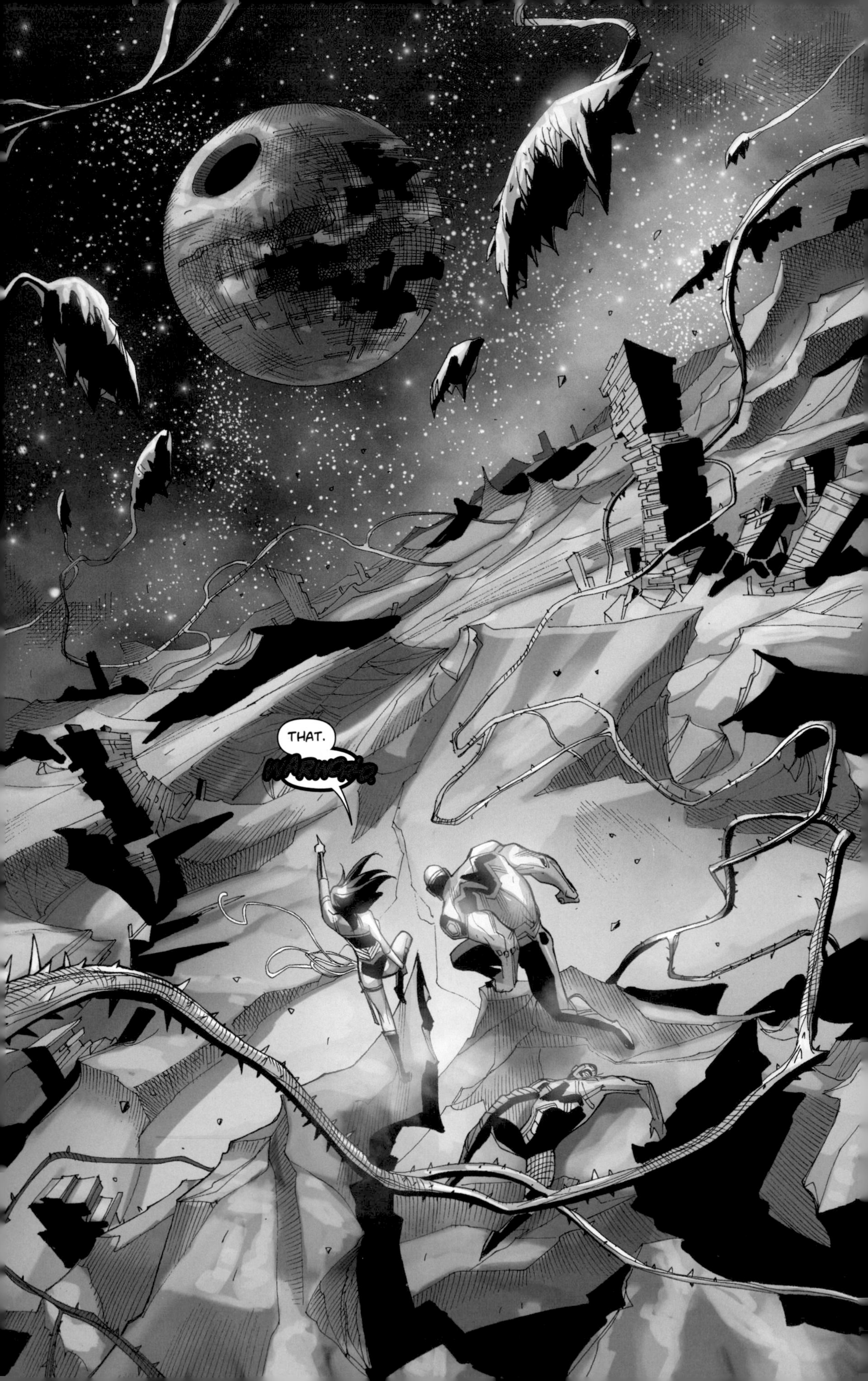
THAT.

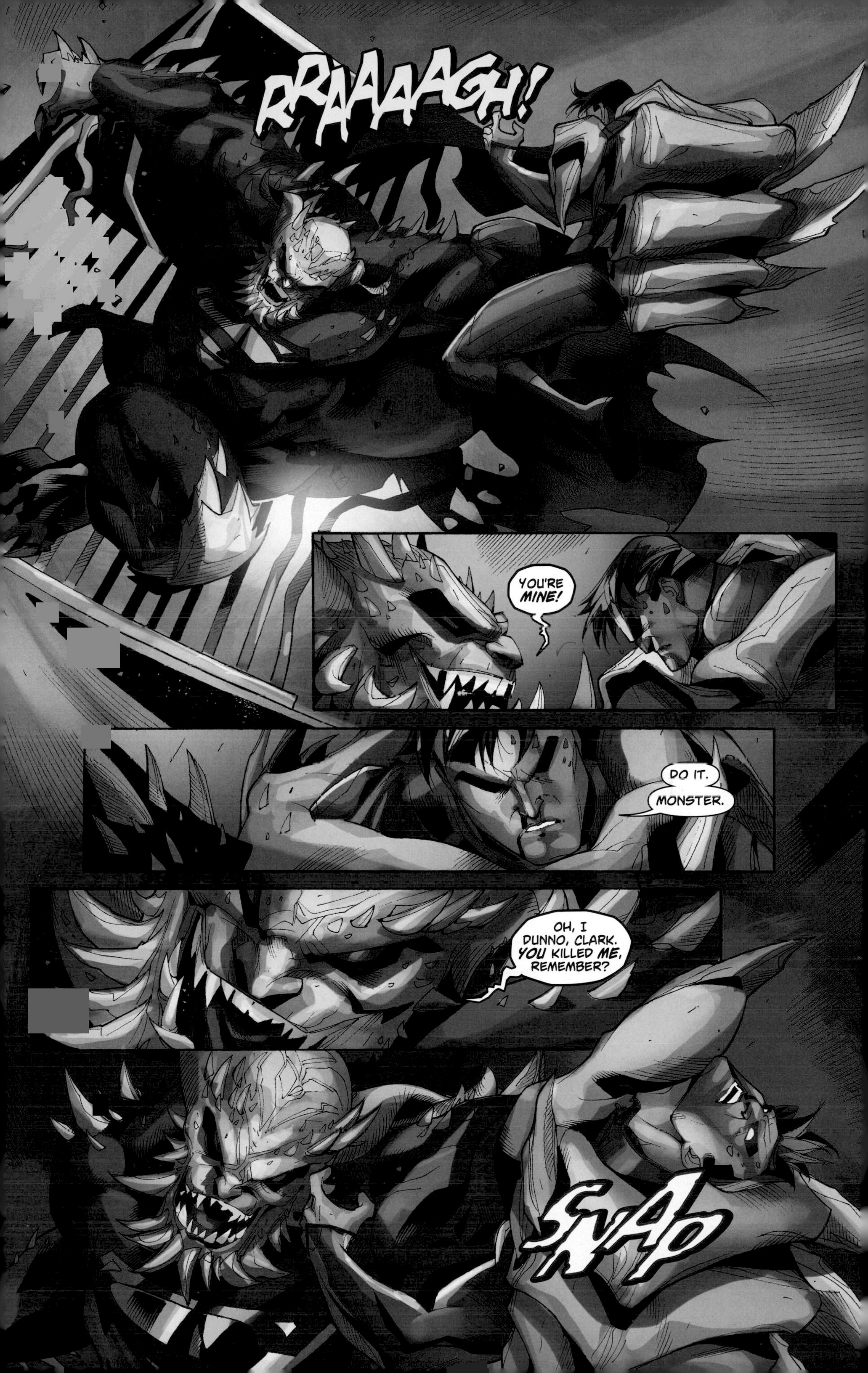
RRAAAAGH!
YOU'RE MINE!
DO IT.
MONSTER.
OH, I DUNNO, CLARK. YOU KILLED ME, REMEMBER?
SNAP

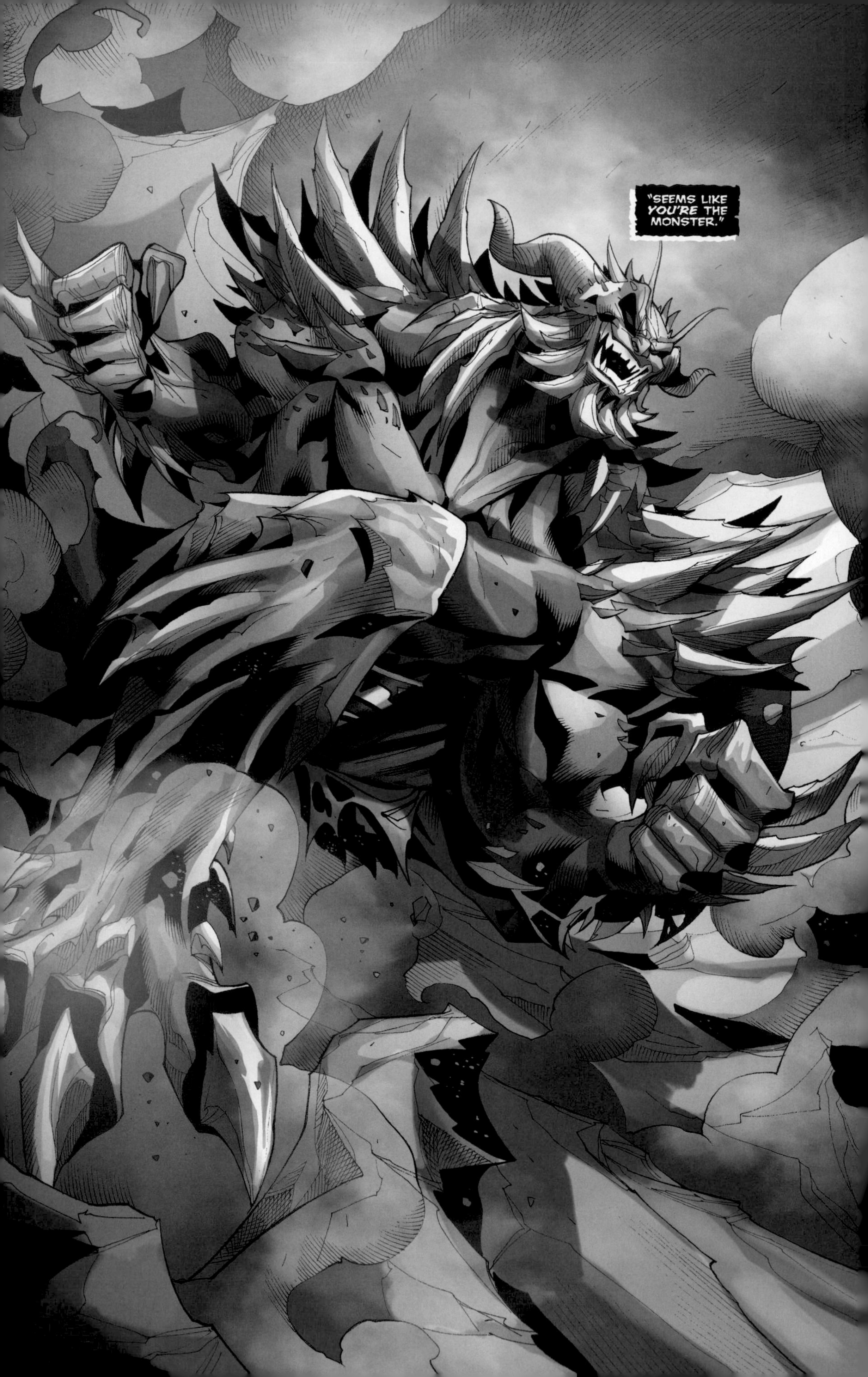
"SEEMS LIKE YOU'RE THE MONSTER."

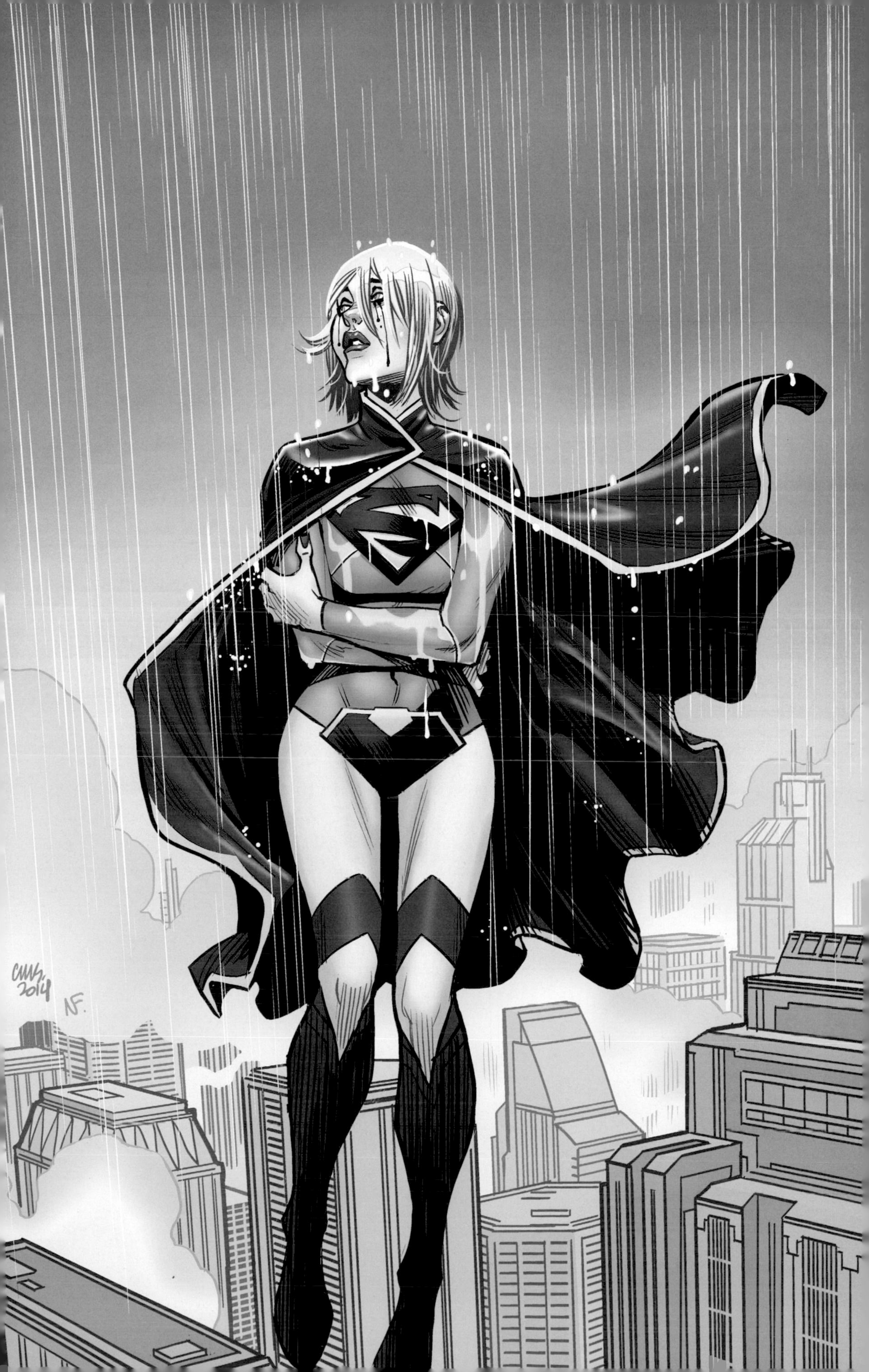

SUPERMAN

DOOMED

[LAST SUN] chapter **3**

"THE GIRL WHO FELL TO EARTH"

STORY
TONY BEDARD

PENCILS
KARL MOLINE

INKS
JOSÉ MARZÁN, JR.

COLORS
HI-FI

LETTERS
ROB LEIGH

COVER
CAMERON STEWART WITH **NATHAN FAIRBAIRN**

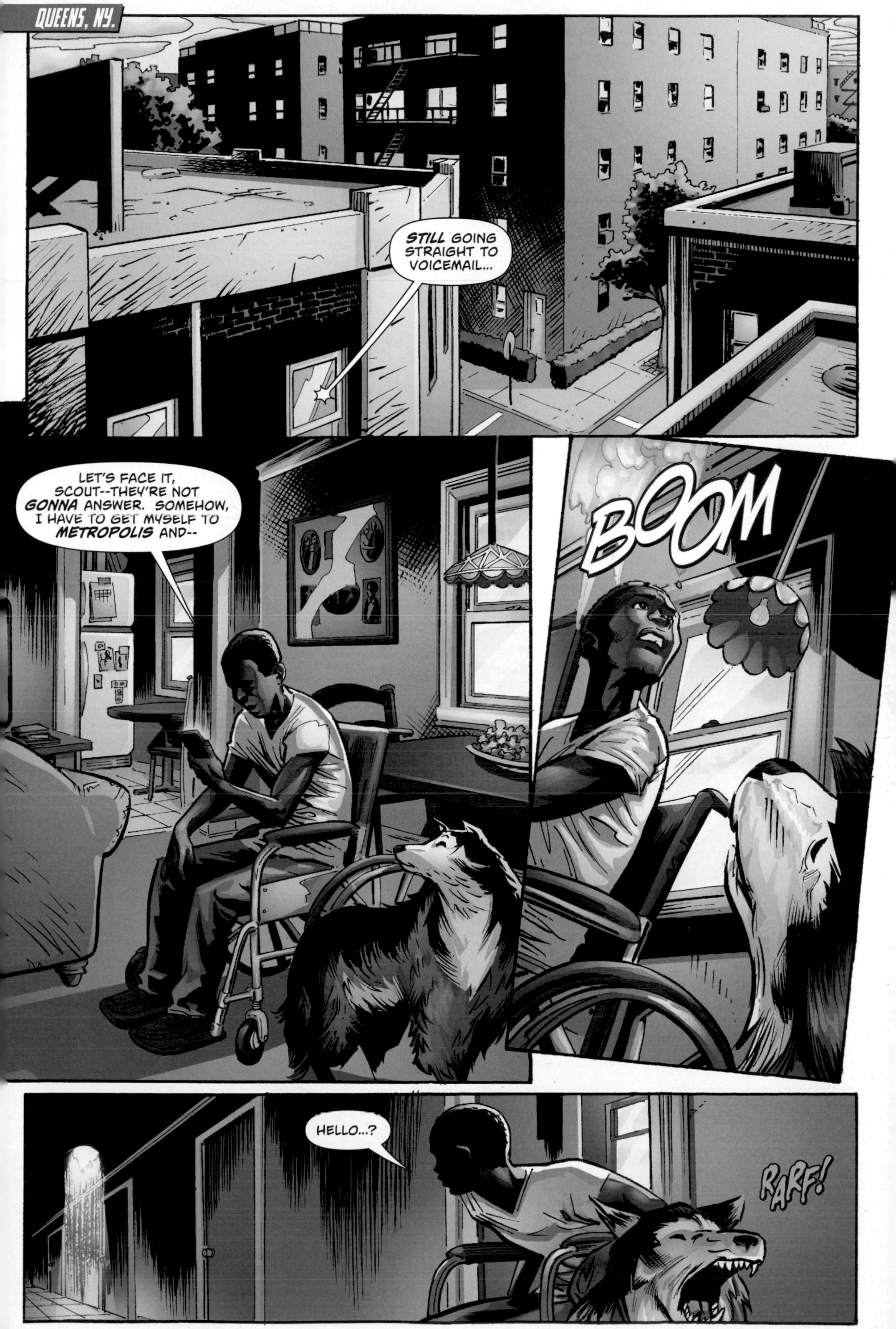
QUEENS, NY.
STILL GOING STRAIGHT TO VOICEMAIL...
LET'S FACE IT, SCOUT--THEY'RE NOT GONNA ANSWER. SOMEHOW, I HAVE TO GET MYSELF TO METROPOLIS AND--
BOOM
HELLO...?
RARF!

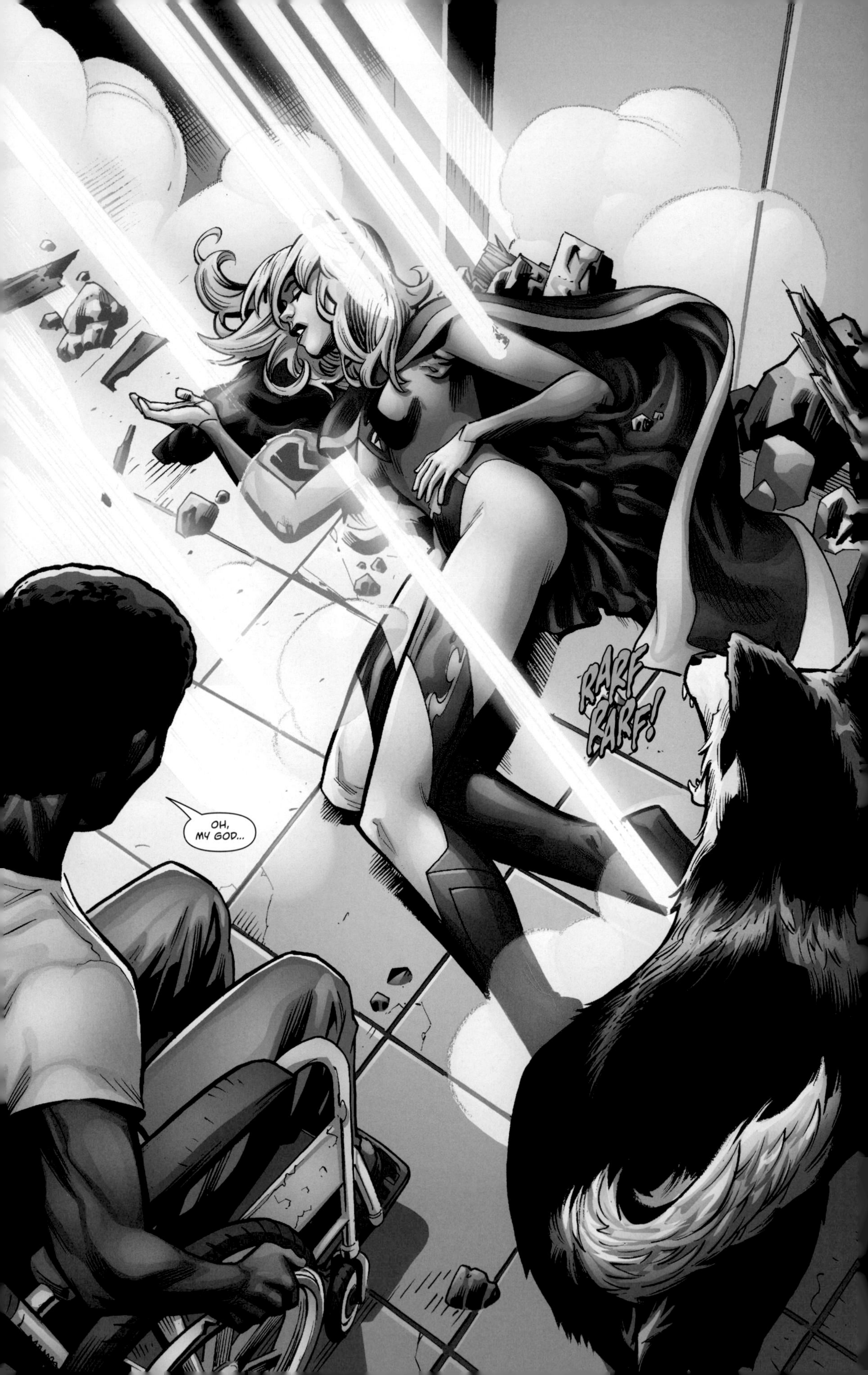
RARF RARF!
OH, MY GOD...

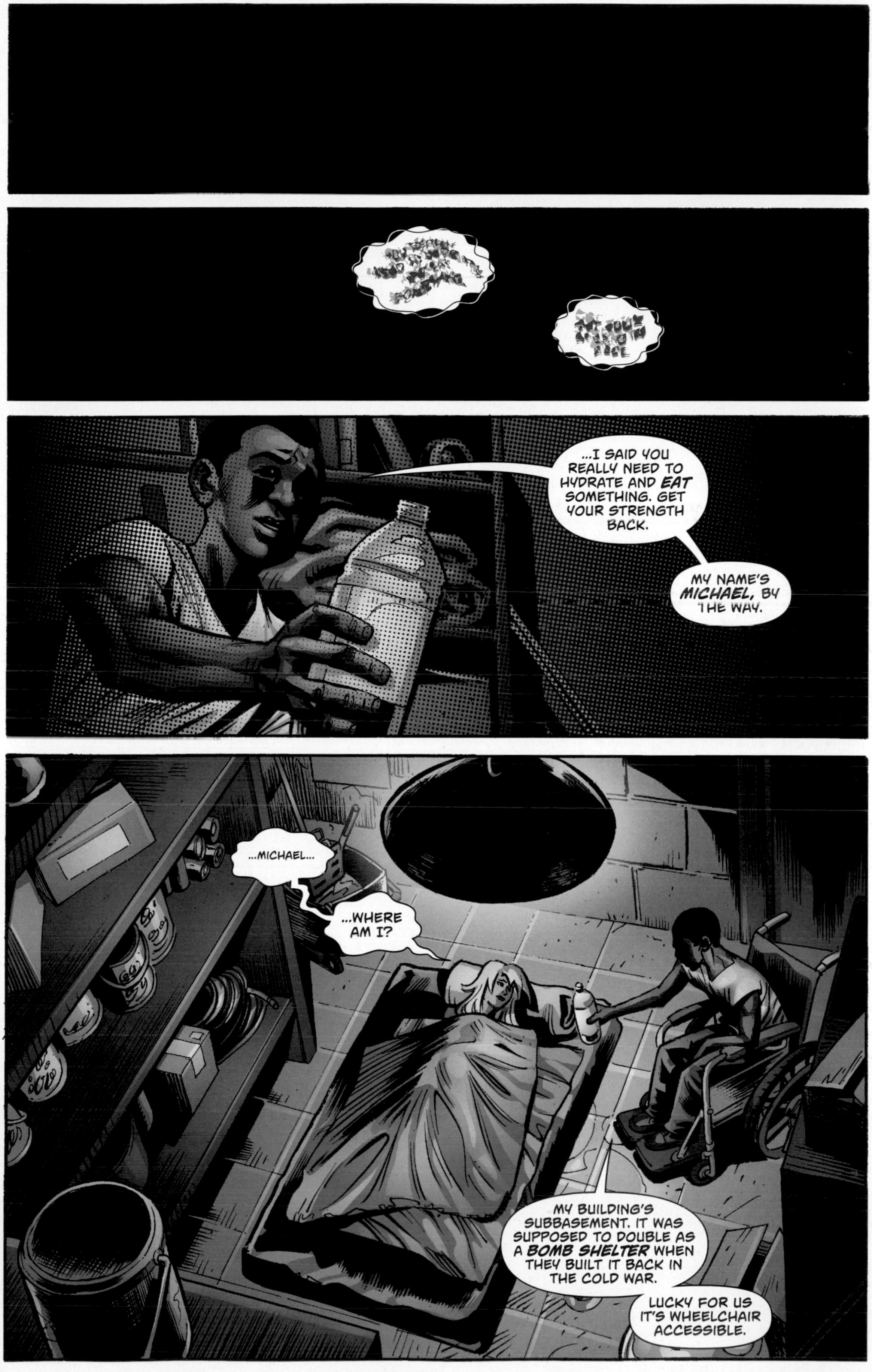
...I SAID YOU REALLY NEED TO HYDRATE AND EAT SOMETHING. GET YOUR STRENGTH BACK.
MY NAME'S MICHAEL, BY THE WAY.
...MICHAEL...
...WHERE AM I?
MY BUILDING'S SUBBASEMENT. IT WAS SUPPOSED TO DOUBLE AS A BOMB SHELTER WHEN THEY BUILT IT BACK IN THE COLD WAR.
LUCKY FOR US IT'S WHEELCHAIR ACCESSIBLE.

THEY SAID ON THE NEWS THAT ALL THE *KRYPTONITE* IN THE ATMOSPHERE GIVES OFF SOME KIND OF *RADIATION.*

YOU LOOKED LIKE YOU'D HAD ALL YOU COULD *TAKE.*

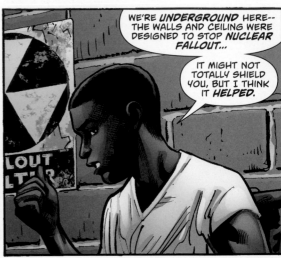

WE'RE *UNDERGROUND* HERE-- THE WALLS AND CEILING WERE DESIGNED TO STOP *NUCLEAR FALLOUT...*

IT MIGHT NOT TOTALLY SHIELD YOU, BUT I THINK IT *HELPED.*

Hnh....? CAN'T SEE THROUGH THESE...

WHAT ARE THESE BLANKETS MADE OF?

LINED WITH *LEAD.*

I HAVE A FRIEND WHO'S AN *X-RAY TECH* AT THE HOSPITAL. HE SORTA "LENT" THEM TO ME.

HOSPITAL? WHY DIDN'T YOU... JUST TAKE ME THERE?

I WASN'T SURE HOW THEY'D *REACT.*

YOU KNOW, CONSIDERING EVERYTHING THAT'S HAPPENED WITH *SUPERMAN...?*

SUPERMAN. YES. I WAS *THERE...*

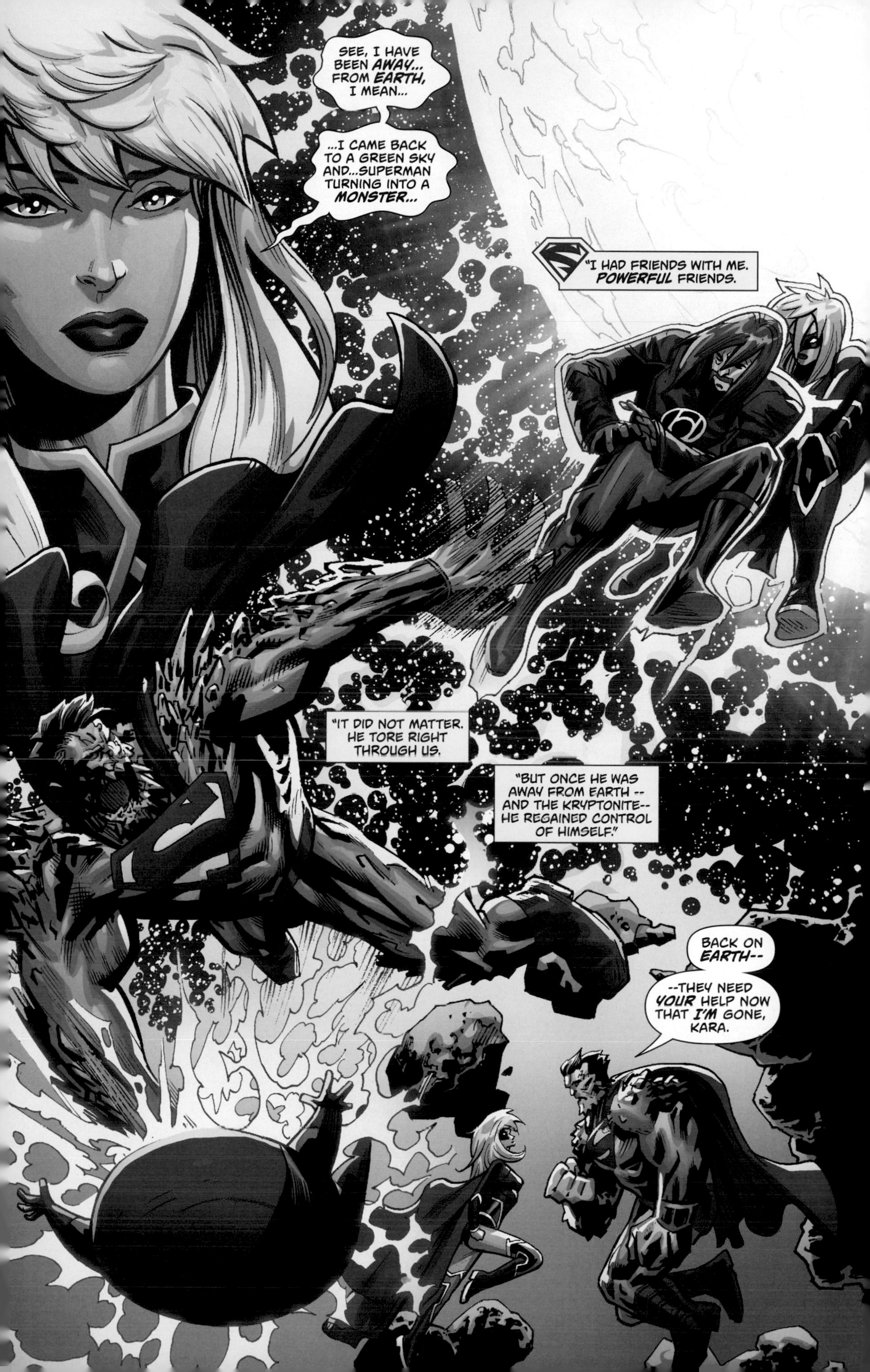
SEE, I HAVE BEEN AWAY... FROM EARTH, I MEAN...
...I CAME BACK TO A GREEN SKY AND...SUPERMAN TURNING INTO A MONSTER...
"I HAD FRIENDS WITH ME. POWERFUL FRIENDS.
"IT DID NOT MATTER. HE TORE RIGHT THROUGH US.
"BUT ONCE HE WAS AWAY FROM EARTH -- AND THE KRYPTONITE-- HE REGAINED CONTROL OF HIMSELF."
BACK ON EARTH--
--THEY NEED YOUR HELP NOW THAT I'M GONE, KARA.

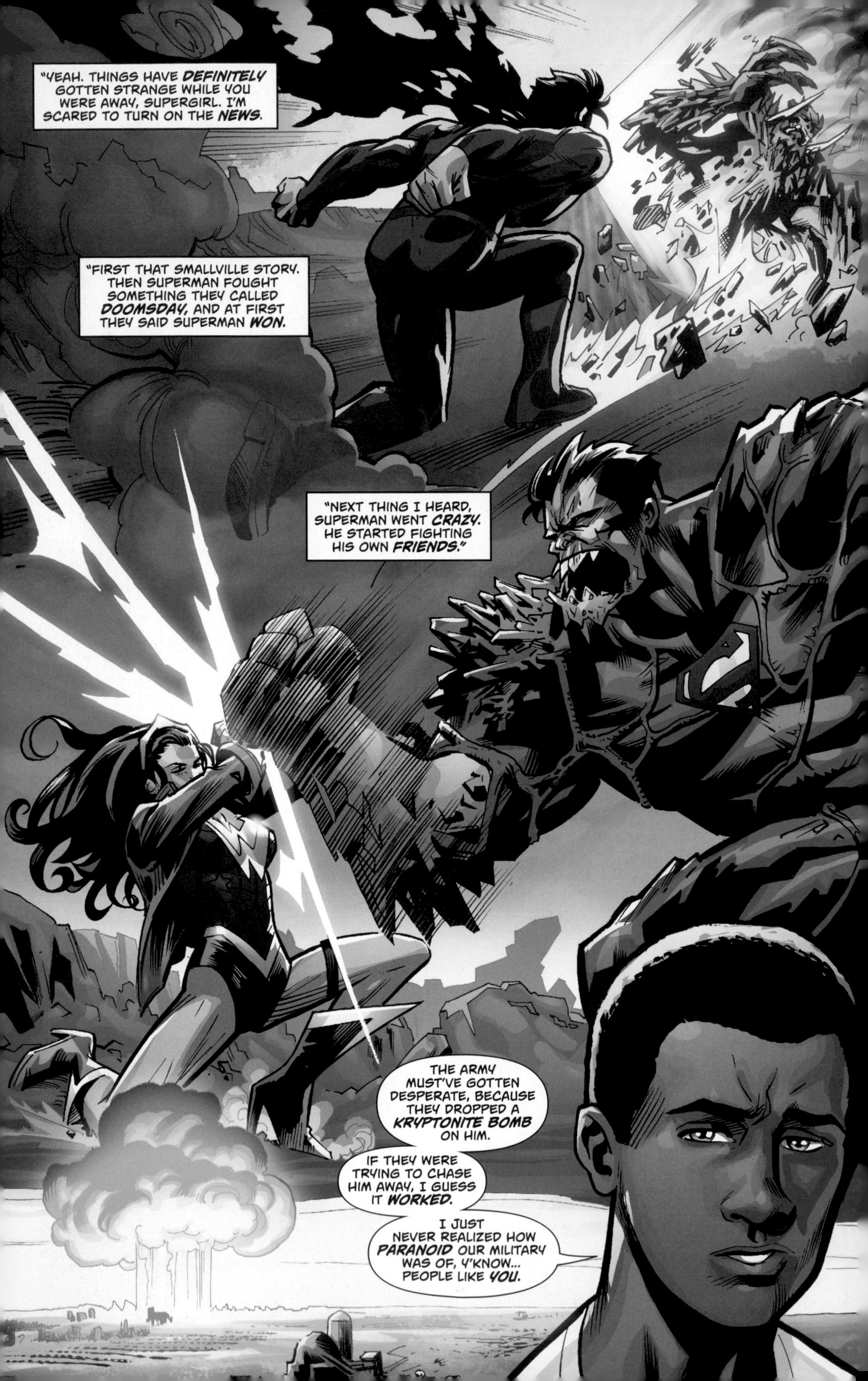
"YEAH. THINGS HAVE DEFINITELY GOTTEN STRANGE WHILE YOU WERE AWAY, SUPERGIRL. I'M SCARED TO TURN ON THE NEWS.
"FIRST THAT SMALLVILLE STORY. THEN SUPERMAN FOUGHT SOMETHING THEY CALLED DOOMSDAY, AND AT FIRST THEY SAID SUPERMAN WON.
"NEXT THING I HEARD, SUPERMAN WENT CRAZY. HE STARTED FIGHTING HIS OWN FRIENDS."
THE ARMY MUST'VE GOTTEN DESPERATE, BECAUSE THEY DROPPED A KRYPTONITE BOMB ON HIM.
IF THEY WERE TRYING TO CHASE HIM AWAY, I GUESS IT WORKED.
I JUST NEVER REALIZED HOW PARANOID OUR MILITARY WAS OF, Y'KNOW... PEOPLE LIKE YOU.

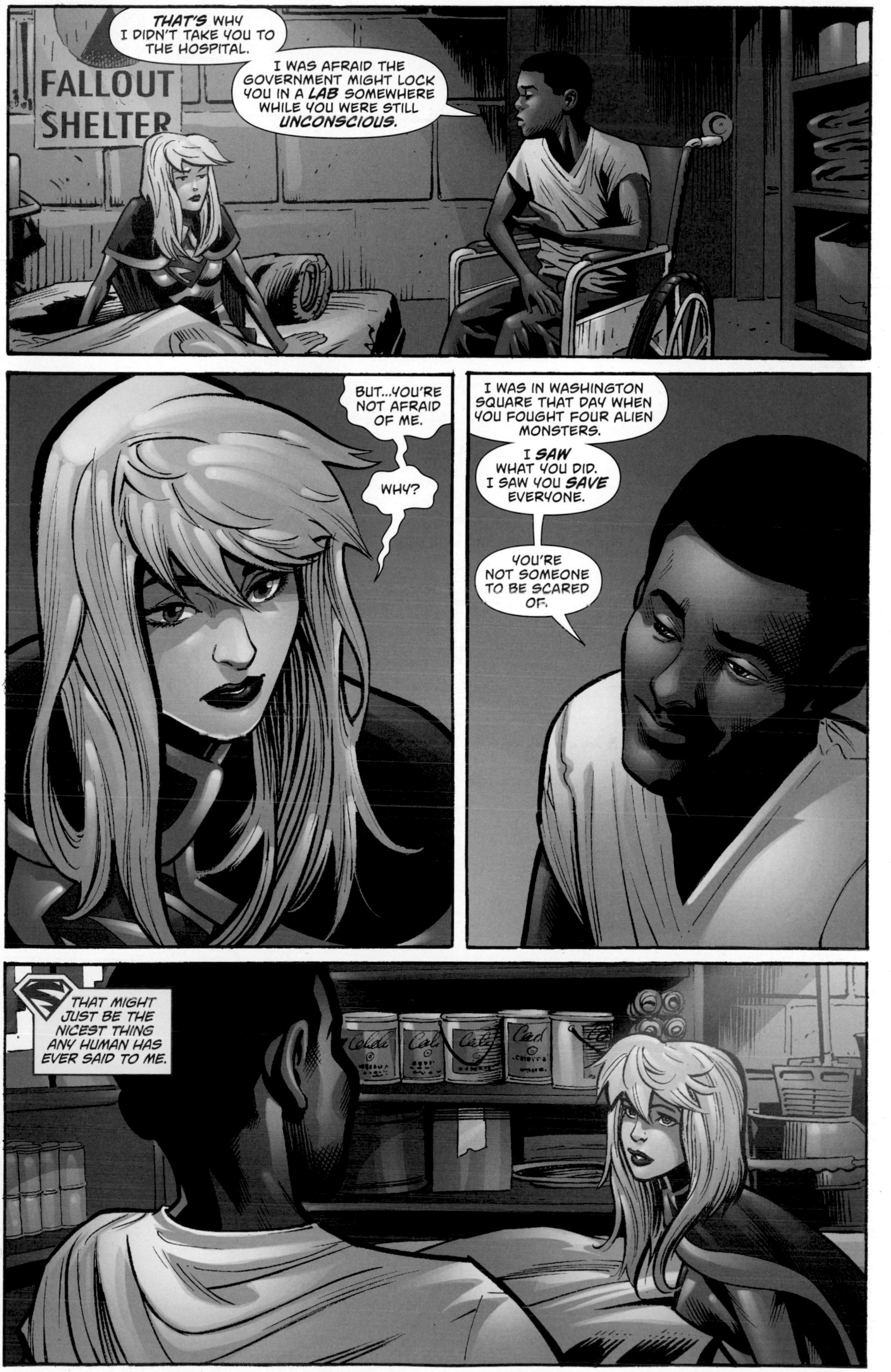
THAT'S WHY I DIDN'T TAKE YOU TO THE HOSPITAL.
I WAS AFRAID THE GOVERNMENT MIGHT LOCK YOU IN A LAB SOMEWHERE WHILE YOU WERE STILL UNCONSCIOUS.
FALLOUT SHELTER
BUT...YOU'RE NOT AFRAID OF ME.
WHY?
I WAS IN WASHINGTON SQUARE THAT DAY WHEN YOU FOUGHT FOUR ALIEN MONSTERS.
I SAW WHAT YOU DID. I SAW YOU SAVE EVERYONE.
YOU'RE NOT SOMEONE TO BE SCARED OF.
THAT MIGHT JUST BE THE NICEST THING ANY HUMAN HAS EVER SAID TO ME.

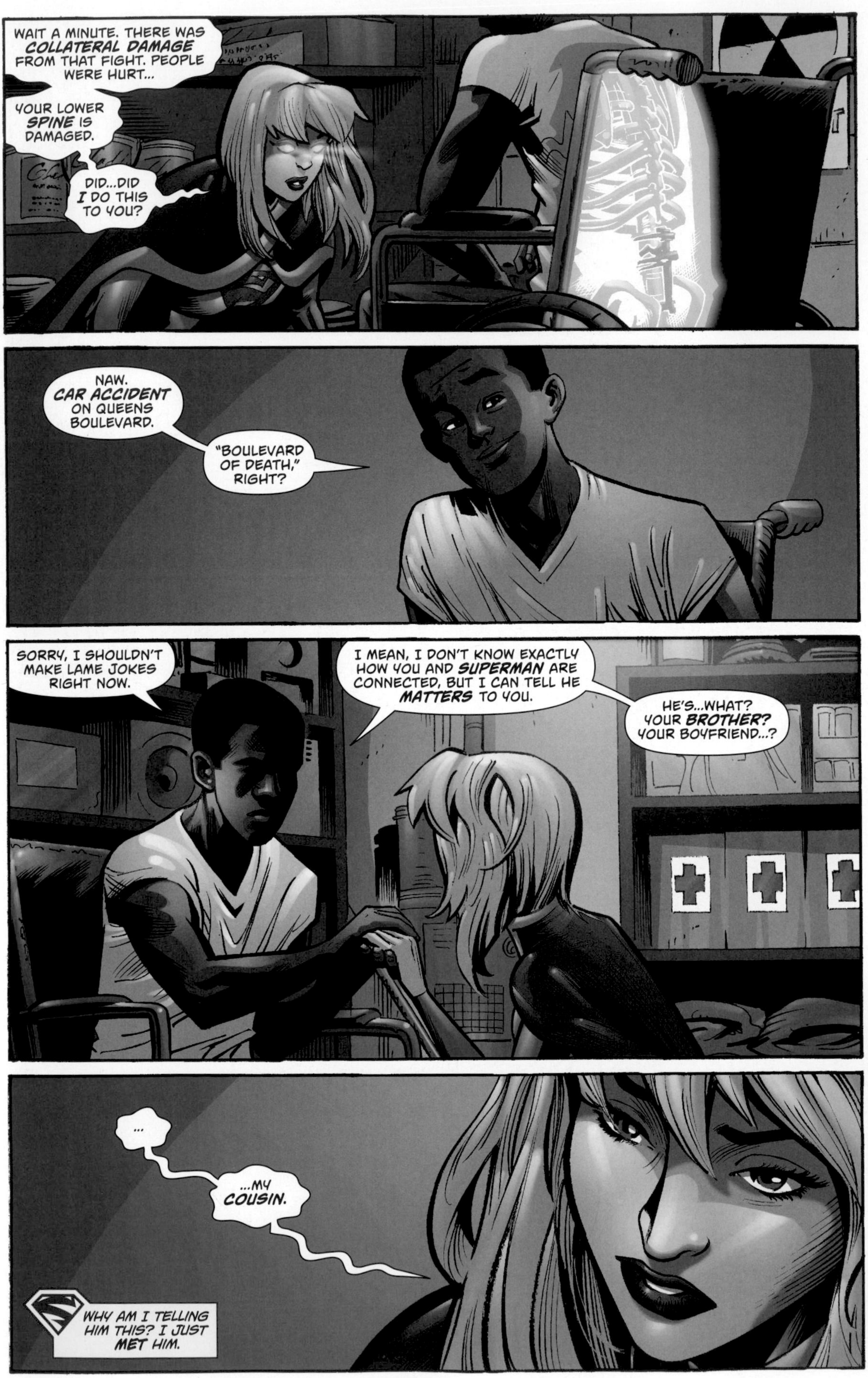
WAIT A MINUTE. THERE WAS COLLATERAL DAMAGE FROM THAT FIGHT. PEOPLE WERE HURT...
YOUR LOWER SPINE IS DAMAGED.
DID...DID I DO THIS TO YOU?
NAW. CAR ACCIDENT ON QUEENS BOULEVARD.
"BOULEVARD OF DEATH," RIGHT?
SORRY, I SHOULDN'T MAKE LAME JOKES RIGHT NOW.
I MEAN, I DON'T KNOW EXACTLY HOW YOU AND SUPERMAN ARE CONNECTED, BUT I CAN TELL HE MATTERS TO YOU.
HE'S...WHAT? YOUR BROTHER? YOUR BOYFRIEND...?
...
...MY COUSIN.
WHY AM I TELLING HIM THIS? I JUST MET HIM.

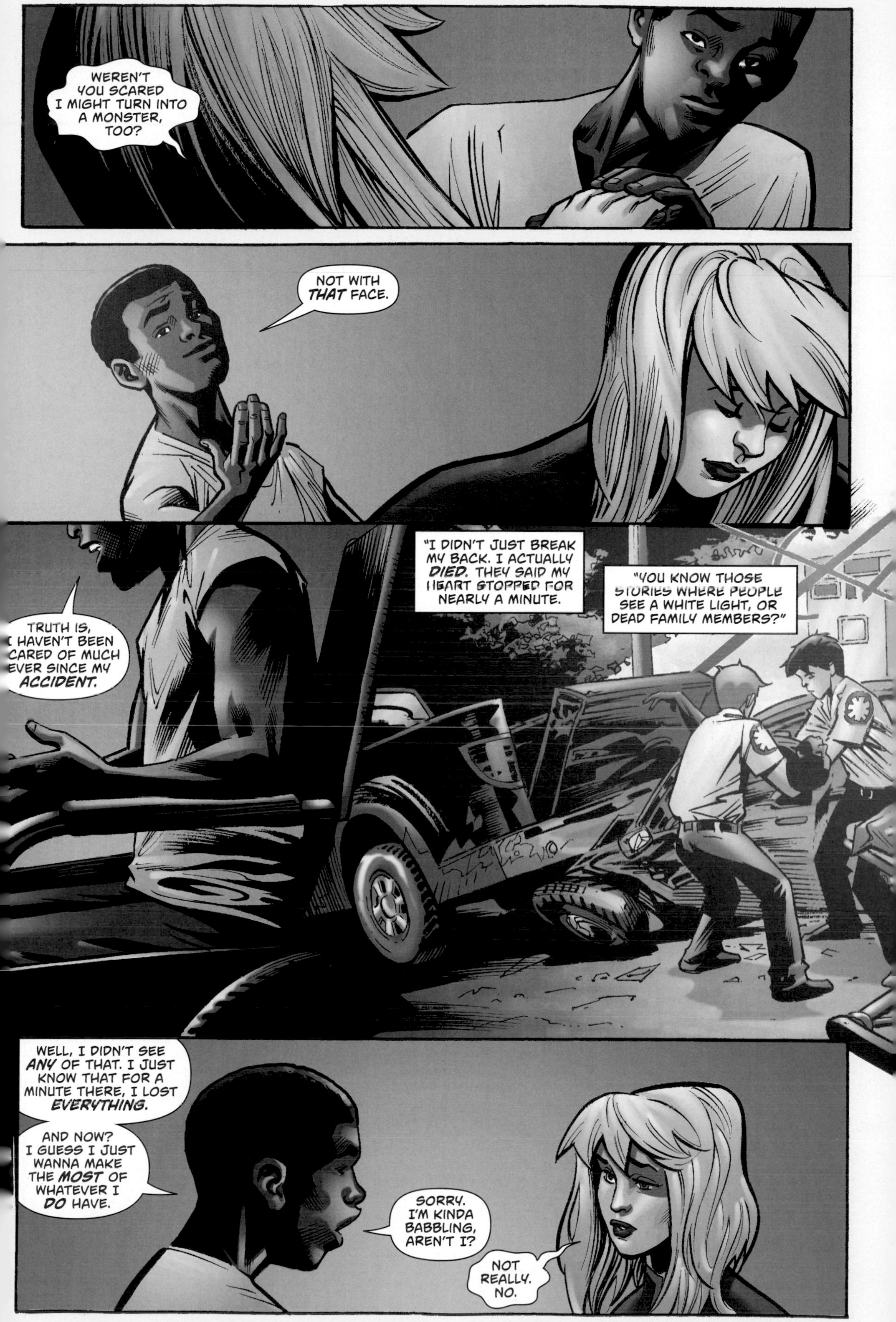
WEREN'T YOU SCARED I MIGHT TURN INTO A MONSTER, TOO?
NOT WITH *THAT* FACE.
TRUTH IS, I HAVEN'T BEEN SCARED OF MUCH EVER SINCE MY *ACCIDENT*.
"I DIDN'T JUST BREAK MY BACK. I ACTUALLY *DIED*. THEY SAID MY HEART STOPPED FOR NEARLY A MINUTE.
"YOU KNOW THOSE STORIES WHERE PEOPLE SEE A WHITE LIGHT, OR DEAD FAMILY MEMBERS?"
WELL, I DIDN'T SEE *ANY* OF THAT. I JUST KNOW THAT FOR A MINUTE THERE, I LOST *EVERYTHING*.
AND NOW? I GUESS I JUST WANNA MAKE THE *MOST* OF WHATEVER I *DO* HAVE.
SORRY. I'M KINDA BABBLING, AREN'T I?
NOT REALLY. NO.

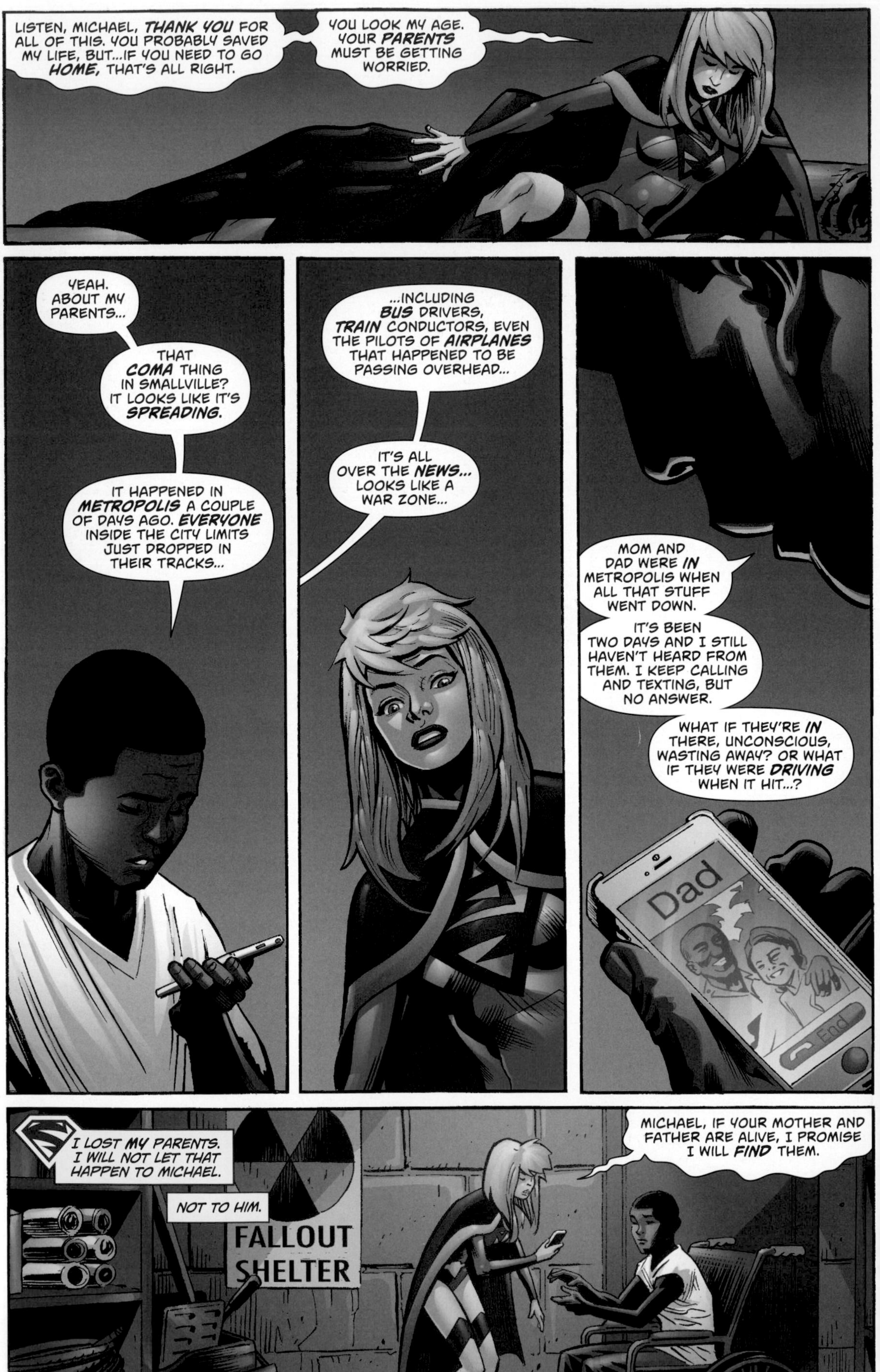
LISTEN, MICHAEL, THANK YOU FOR ALL OF THIS. YOU PROBABLY SAVED MY LIFE, BUT...IF YOU NEED TO GO HOME, THAT'S ALL RIGHT.
YOU LOOK MY AGE. YOUR PARENTS MUST BE GETTING WORRIED.
YEAH. ABOUT MY PARENTS...
THAT COMA THING IN SMALLVILLE? IT LOOKS LIKE IT'S SPREADING.
IT HAPPENED IN METROPOLIS A COUPLE OF DAYS AGO. EVERYONE INSIDE THE CITY LIMITS JUST DROPPED IN THEIR TRACKS...
...INCLUDING BUS DRIVERS, TRAIN CONDUCTORS, EVEN THE PILOTS OF AIRPLANES THAT HAPPENED TO BE PASSING OVERHEAD...
IT'S ALL OVER THE NEWS... LOOKS LIKE A WAR ZONE...
MOM AND DAD WERE IN METROPOLIS WHEN ALL THAT STUFF WENT DOWN.
IT'S BEEN TWO DAYS AND I STILL HAVEN'T HEARD FROM THEM. I KEEP CALLING AND TEXTING, BUT NO ANSWER.
WHAT IF THEY'RE IN THERE, UNCONSCIOUS, WASTING AWAY? OR WHAT IF THEY WERE DRIVING WHEN IT HIT...?
Dad
End
I LOST MY PARENTS. I WILL NOT LET THAT HAPPEN TO MICHAEL.
NOT TO HIM.
FALLOUT SHELTER
MICHAEL, IF YOUR MOTHER AND FATHER ARE ALIVE, I PROMISE I WILL FIND THEM.

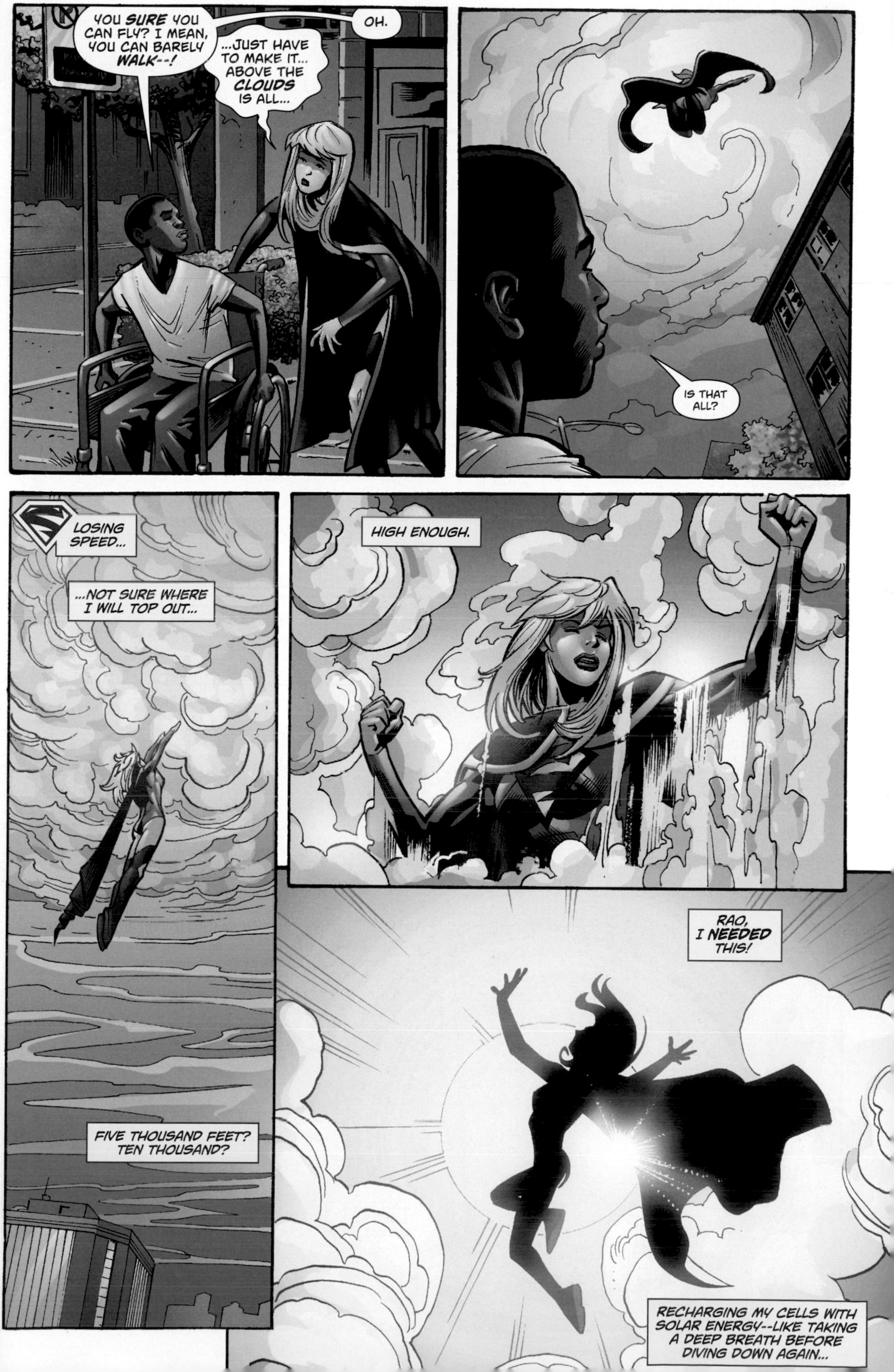
YOU SURE YOU CAN FLY? I MEAN, YOU CAN BARELY WALK--!
...JUST HAVE TO MAKE IT... ABOVE THE CLOUDS IS ALL...
OH.
IS THAT ALL?
LOSING SPEED...
...NOT SURE WHERE I WILL TOP OUT...
FIVE THOUSAND FEET? TEN THOUSAND?
HIGH ENOUGH.
RAO, I NEEDED THIS!
RECHARGING MY CELLS WITH SOLAR ENERGY--LIKE TAKING A DEEP BREATH BEFORE DIVING DOWN AGAIN...

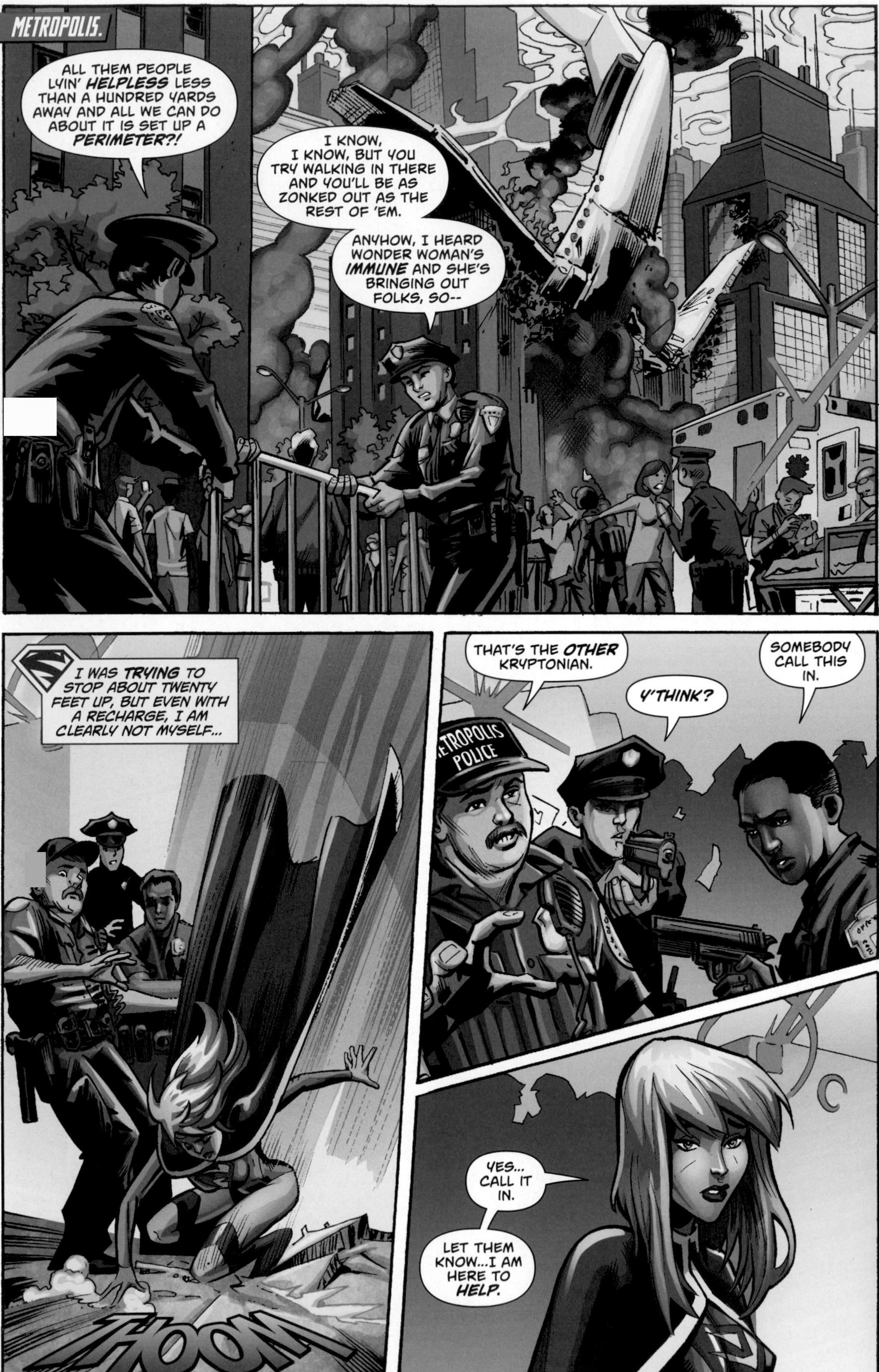
METROPOLIS.
ALL THEM PEOPLE LYIN' HELPLESS LESS THAN A HUNDRED YARDS AWAY AND ALL WE CAN DO ABOUT IT IS SET UP A PERIMETER?!
I KNOW, I KNOW, BUT YOU TRY WALKING IN THERE AND YOU'LL BE AS ZONKED OUT AS THE REST OF 'EM.
ANYHOW, I HEARD WONDER WOMAN'S IMMUNE AND SHE'S BRINGING OUT FOLKS, SO--
I WAS TRYING TO STOP ABOUT TWENTY FEET UP, BUT EVEN WITH A RECHARGE, I AM CLEARLY NOT MYSELF...
THOOM
THAT'S THE OTHER KRYPTONIAN.
Y'THINK?
SOMEBODY CALL THIS IN.
METROPOLIS POLICE
YES... CALL IT IN.
LET THEM KNOW...I AM HERE TO HELP.

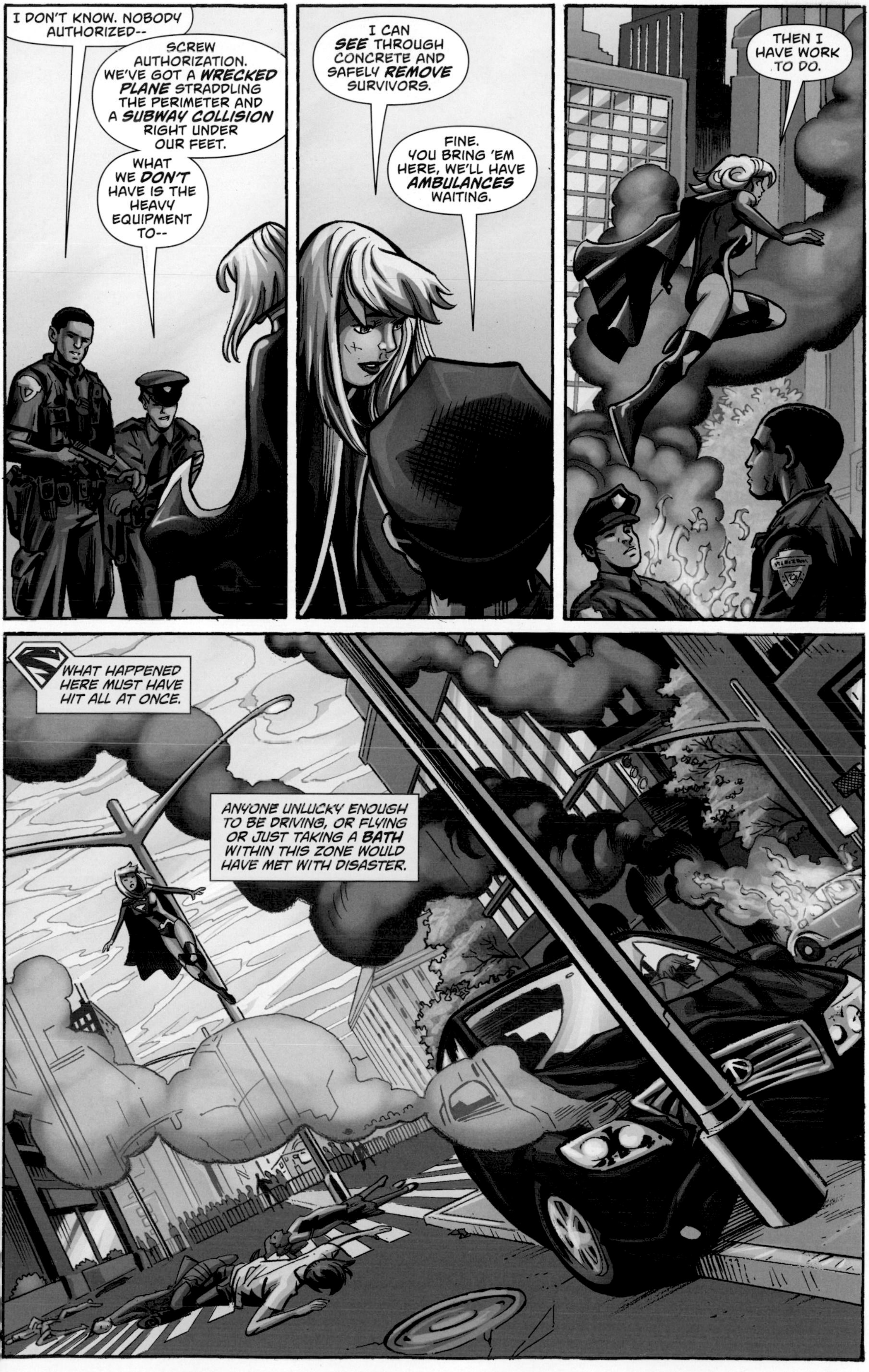
I DON'T KNOW. NOBODY AUTHORIZED--
SCREW AUTHORIZATION. WE'VE GOT A WRECKED PLANE STRADDLING THE PERIMETER AND A SUBWAY COLLISION RIGHT UNDER OUR FEET.
WHAT WE DON'T HAVE IS THE HEAVY EQUIPMENT TO--
I CAN SEE THROUGH CONCRETE AND SAFELY REMOVE SURVIVORS.
FINE. YOU BRING 'EM HERE, WE'LL HAVE AMBULANCES WAITING.
THEN I HAVE WORK TO DO.
WHAT HAPPENED HERE MUST HAVE HIT ALL AT ONCE.
ANYONE UNLUCKY ENOUGH TO BE DRIVING, OR FLYING OR JUST TAKING A BATH WITHIN THIS ZONE WOULD HAVE MET WITH DISASTER.

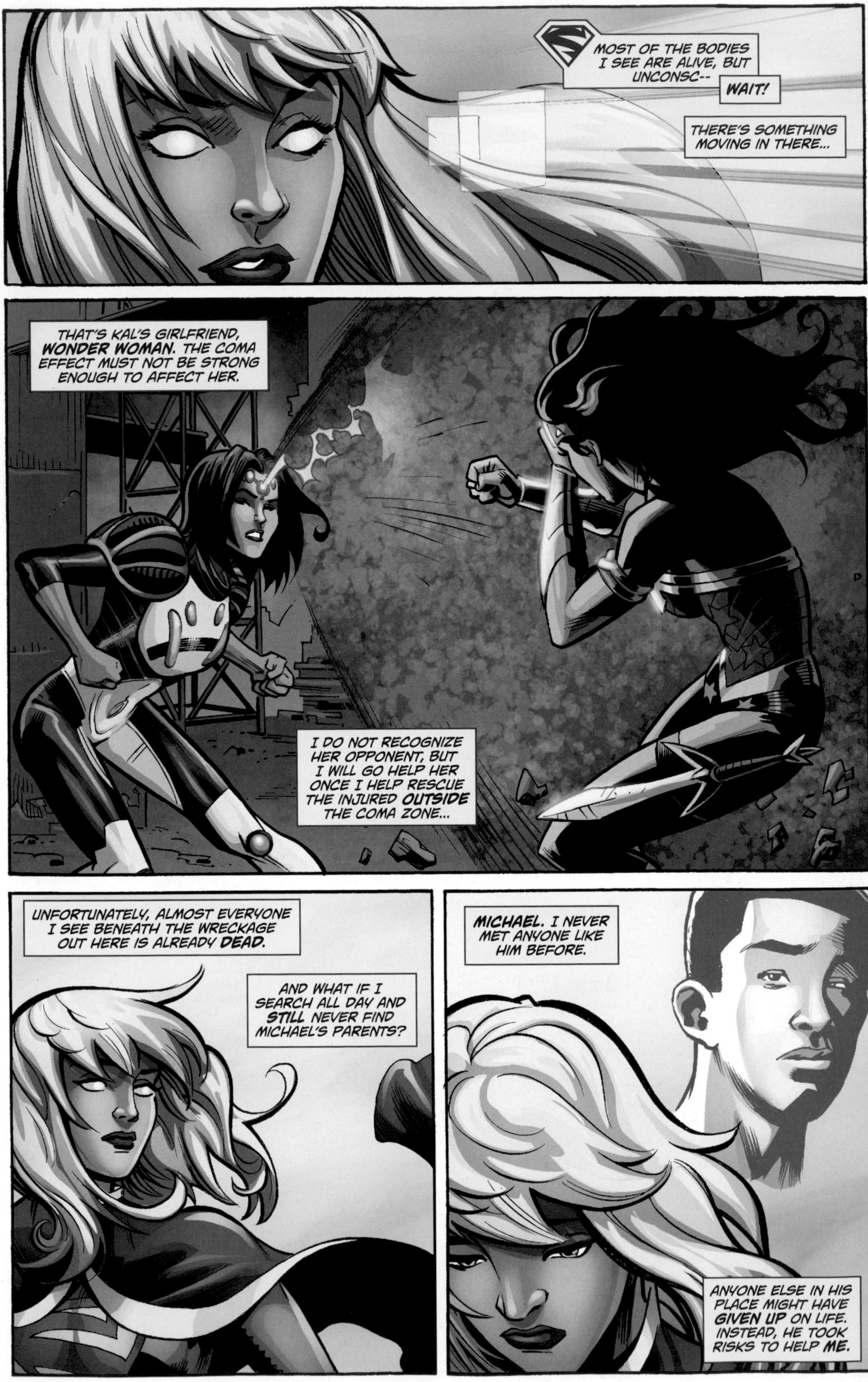
MOST OF THE BODIES I SEE ARE ALIVE, BUT UNCONSC--
WAIT!
THERE'S SOMETHING MOVING IN THERE...
THAT'S KAL'S GIRLFRIEND, WONDER WOMAN. THE COMA EFFECT MUST NOT BE STRONG ENOUGH TO AFFECT HER.
I DO NOT RECOGNIZE HER OPPONENT, BUT I WILL GO HELP HER ONCE I HELP RESCUE THE INJURED OUTSIDE THE COMA ZONE...
UNFORTUNATELY, ALMOST EVERYONE I SEE BENEATH THE WRECKAGE OUT HERE IS ALREADY DEAD.
AND WHAT IF I SEARCH ALL DAY AND STILL NEVER FIND MICHAEL'S PARENTS?
MICHAEL. I NEVER MET ANYONE LIKE HIM BEFORE.
ANYONE ELSE IN HIS PLACE MIGHT HAVE GIVEN UP ON LIFE. INSTEAD, HE TOOK RISKS TO HELP ME.

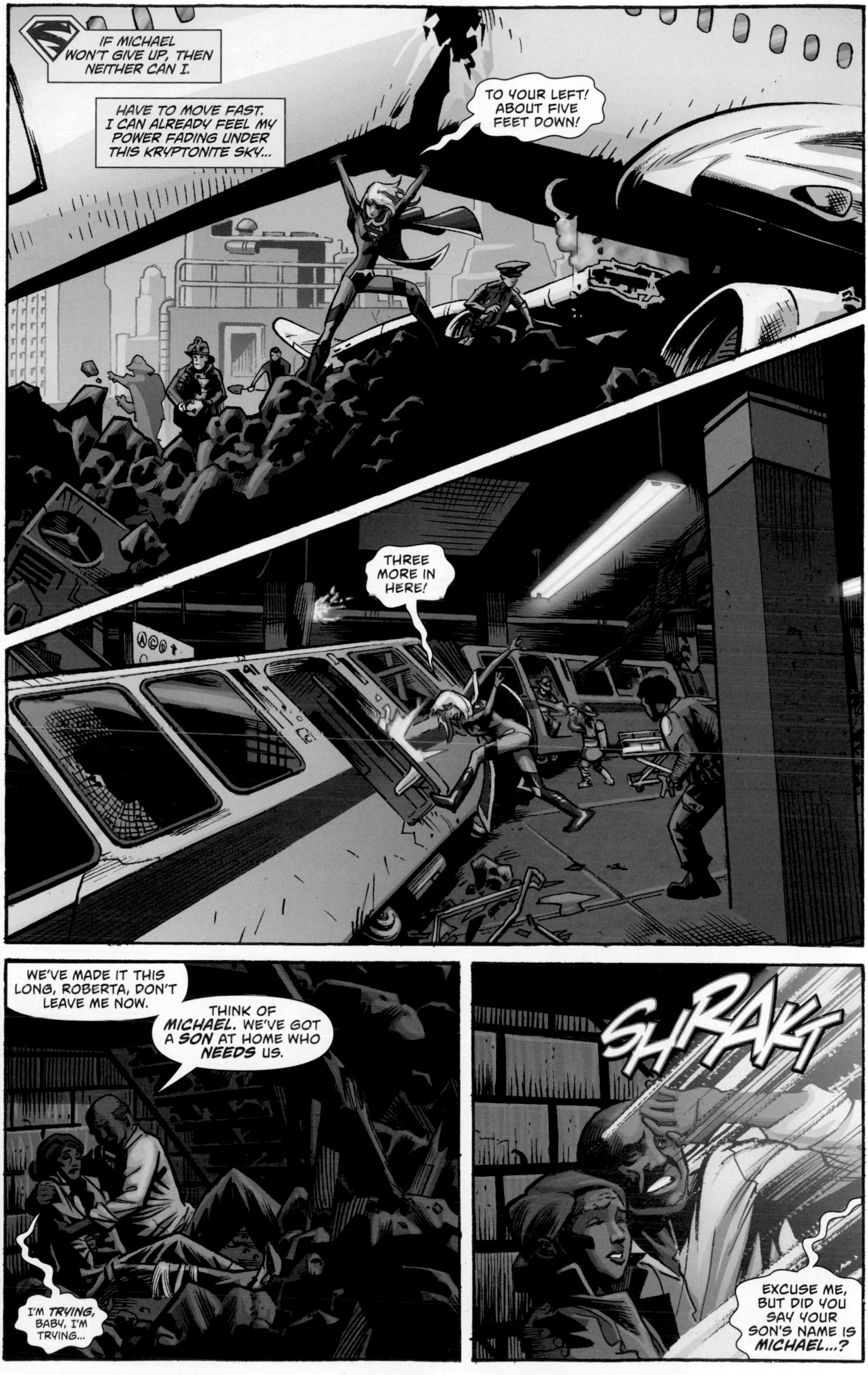

IF MICHAEL WON'T GIVE UP, THEN NEITHER CAN I.
HAVE TO MOVE FAST. I CAN ALREADY FEEL MY POWER FADING UNDER THIS KRYPTONITE SKY...
TO YOUR LEFT! ABOUT FIVE FEET DOWN!
THREE MORE IN HERE!
WE'VE MADE IT THIS LONG, ROBERTA, DON'T LEAVE ME NOW.
THINK OF MICHAEL. WE'VE GOT A SON AT HOME WHO NEEDS US.
I'M TRYING, BABY, I'M TRYING...
SHRAKT
EXCUSE ME, BUT DID YOU SAY YOUR SON'S NAME IS MICHAEL...?

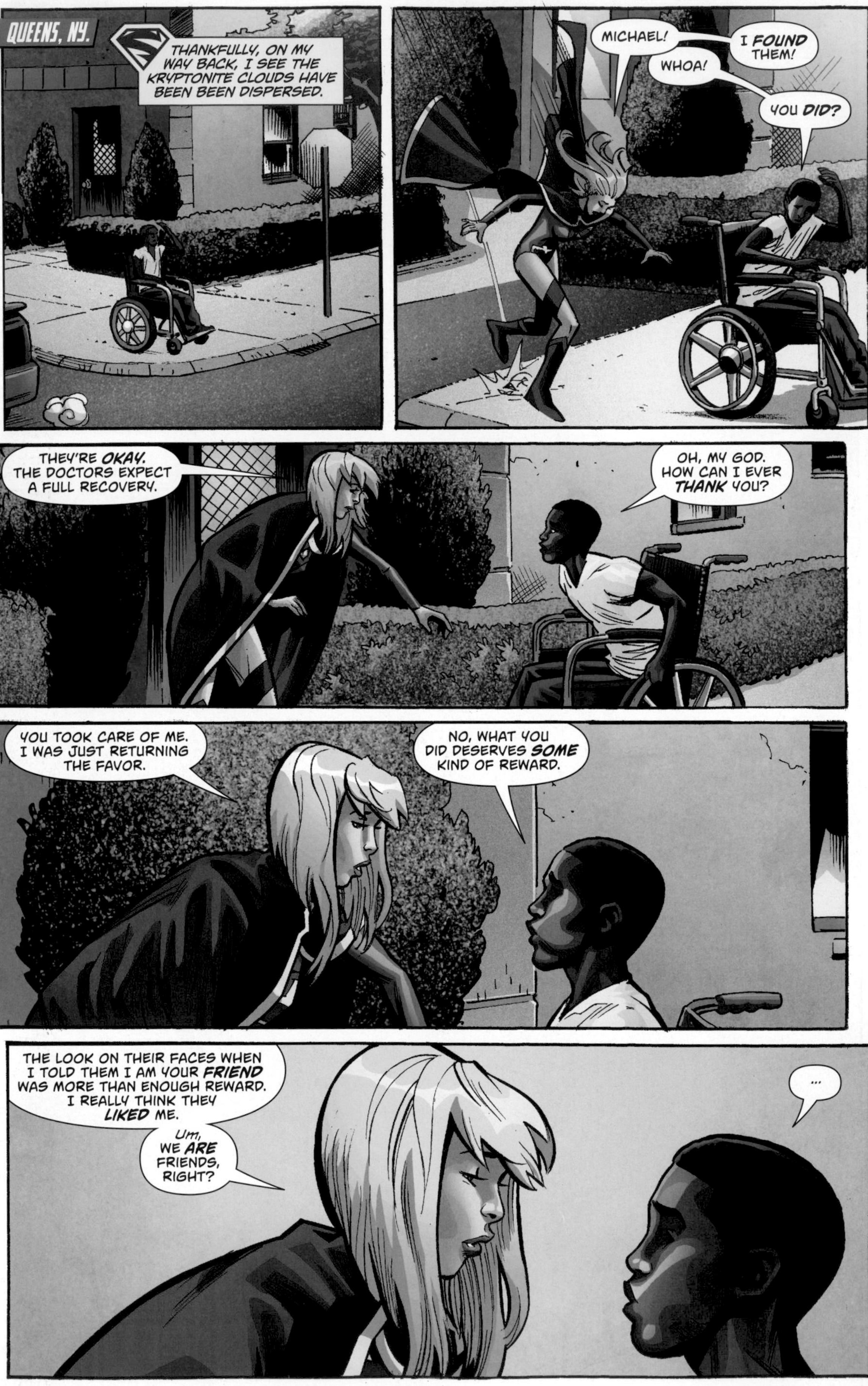
QUEENS, NY.
THANKFULLY, ON MY WAY BACK, I SEE THE KRYPTONITE CLOUDS HAVE BEEN BEEN DISPERSED.
MICHAEL!
I FOUND THEM!
WHOA!
YOU DID?
THEY'RE OKAY. THE DOCTORS EXPECT A FULL RECOVERY.
OH, MY GOD. HOW CAN I EVER THANK YOU?
YOU TOOK CARE OF ME. I WAS JUST RETURNING THE FAVOR.
NO, WHAT YOU DID DESERVES SOME KIND OF REWARD.
THE LOOK ON THEIR FACES WHEN I TOLD THEM I AM YOUR FRIEND WAS MORE THAN ENOUGH REWARD. I REALLY THINK THEY LIKED ME.
UM, WE ARE FRIENDS, RIGHT?
...

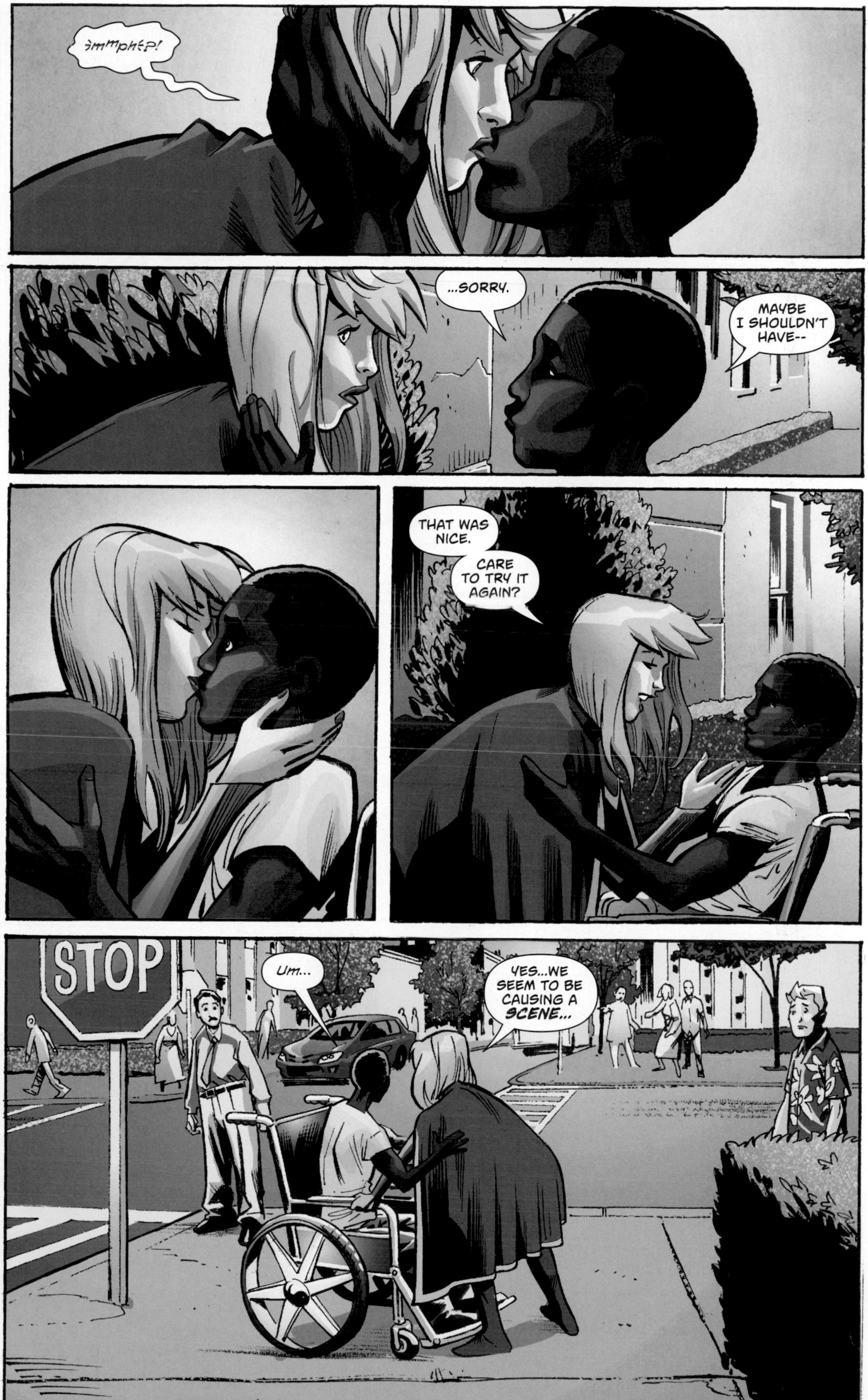

Mmmphff?!
...SORRY.
MAYBE I SHOULDN'T HAVE--
THAT WAS NICE.
CARE TO TRY IT AGAIN?
STOP
Um...
YES...WE SEEM TO BE CAUSING A SCENE...

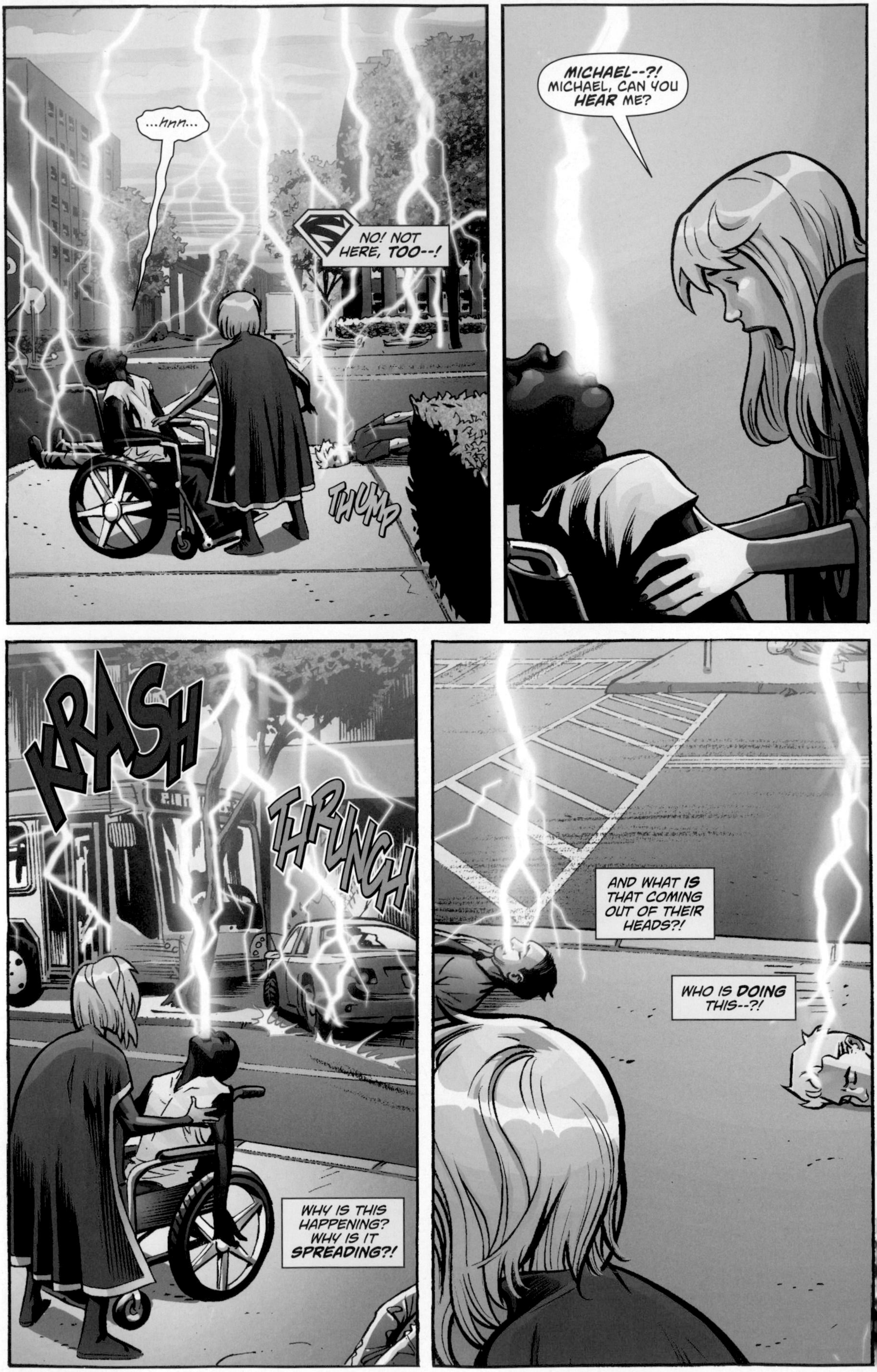
...hnn...
NO! NOT HERE, TOO--!
THUMP
MICHAEL--?! MICHAEL, CAN YOU HEAR ME?
KRASH
THRUNCH
WHY IS THIS HAPPENING? WHY IS IT SPREADING?!
AND WHAT IS THAT COMING OUT OF THEIR HEADS?!
WHO IS DOING THIS--?!

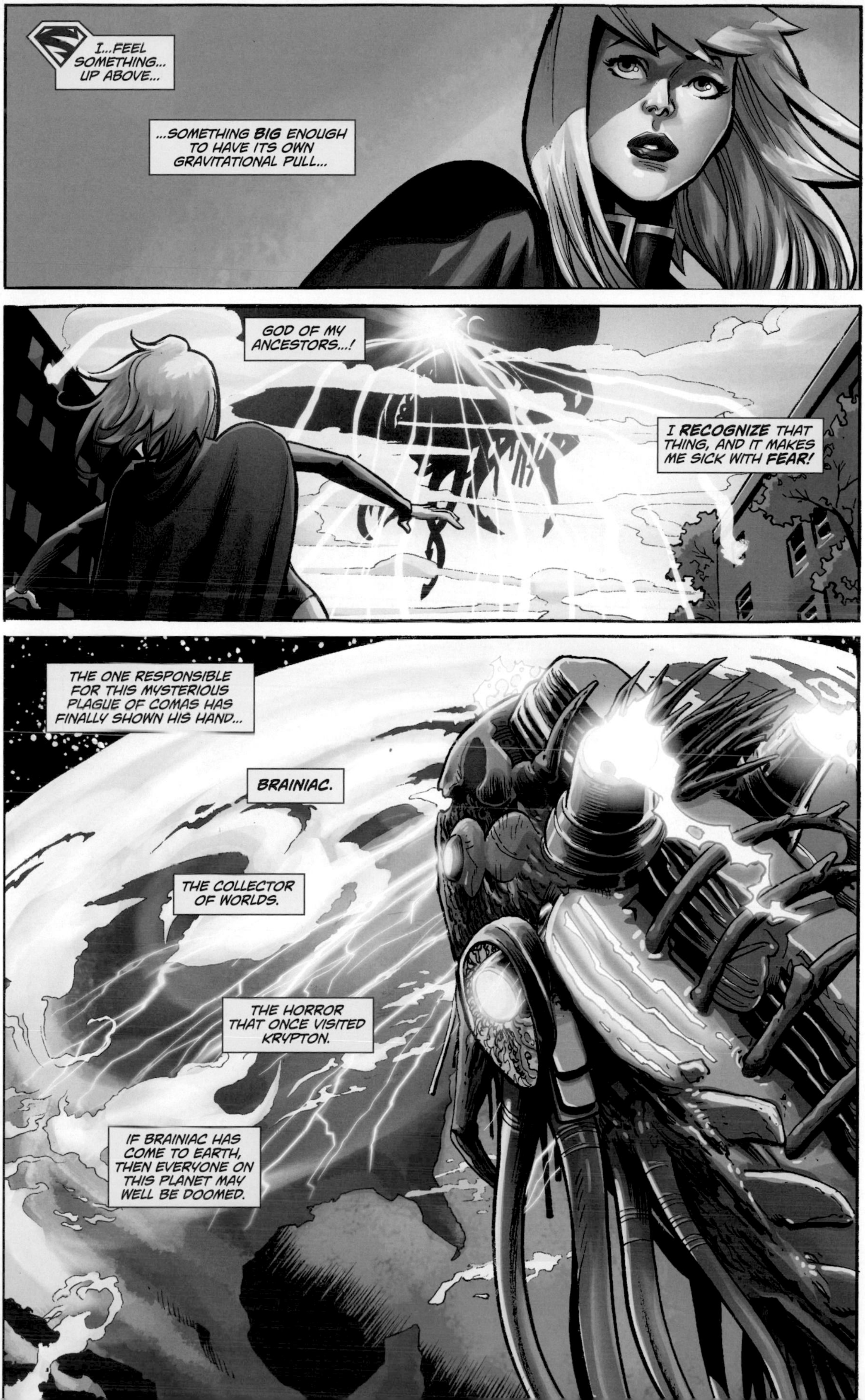
I...FEEL SOMETHING... UP ABOVE...
...SOMETHING BIG ENOUGH TO HAVE ITS OWN GRAVITATIONAL PULL...
GOD OF MY ANCESTORS...!
I RECOGNIZE THAT THING, AND IT MAKES ME SICK WITH FEAR!
THE ONE RESPONSIBLE FOR THIS MYSTERIOUS PLAGUE OF COMAS HAS FINALLY SHOWN HIS HAND...
BRAINIAC.
THE COLLECTOR OF WORLDS.
THE HORROR THAT ONCE VISITED KRYPTON.
IF BRAINIAC HAS COME TO EARTH, THEN EVERYONE ON THIS PLANET MAY WELL BE DOOMED.

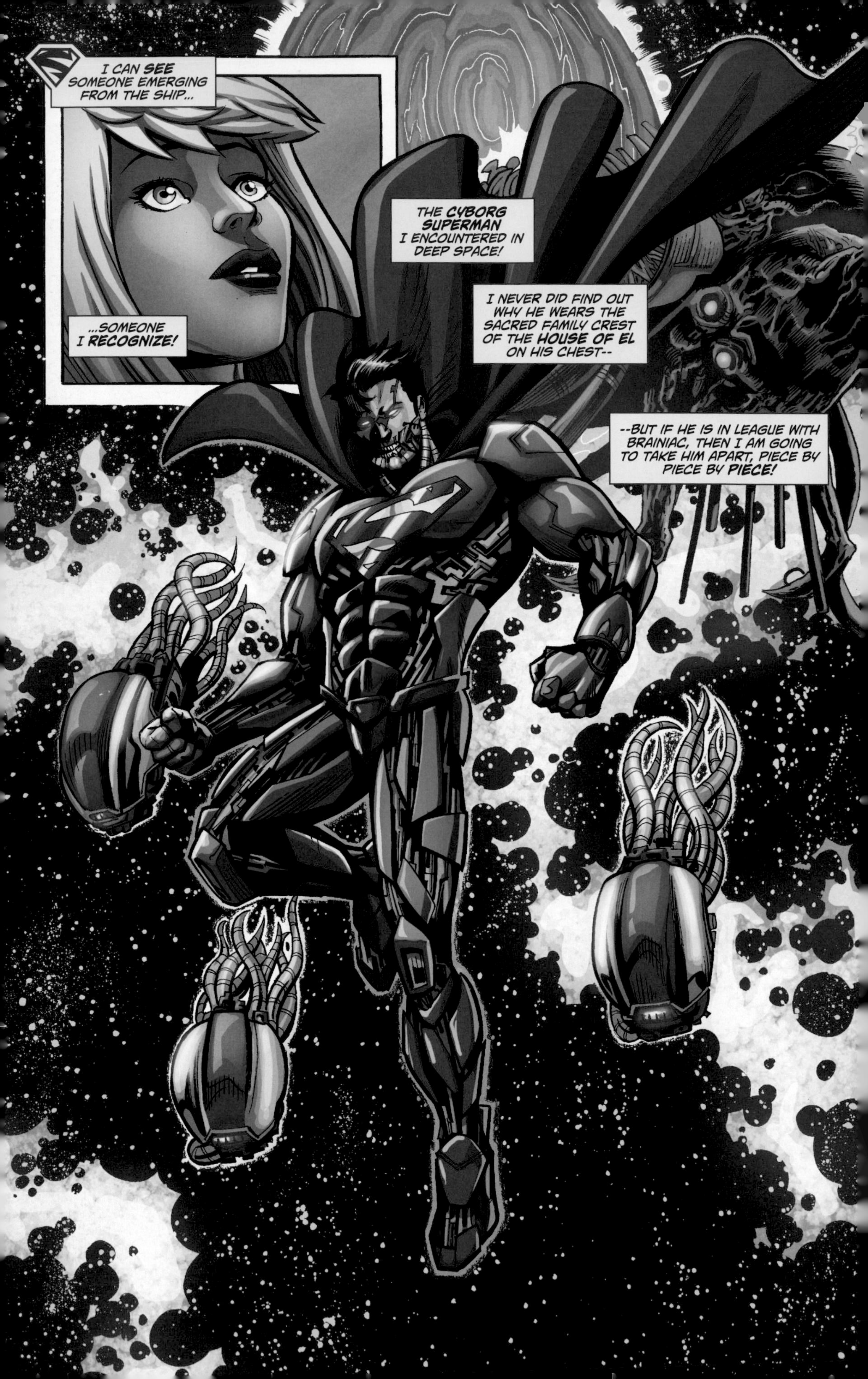
I CAN SEE SOMEONE EMERGING FROM THE SHIP...
...SOMEONE I RECOGNIZE!
THE CYBORG SUPERMAN I ENCOUNTERED IN DEEP SPACE!
I NEVER DID FIND OUT WHY HE WEARS THE SACRED FAMILY CREST OF THE HOUSE OF EL ON HIS CHEST--
--BUT IF HE IS IN LEAGUE WITH BRAINIAC, THEN I AM GOING TO TAKE HIM APART, PIECE BY PIECE BY PIECE!

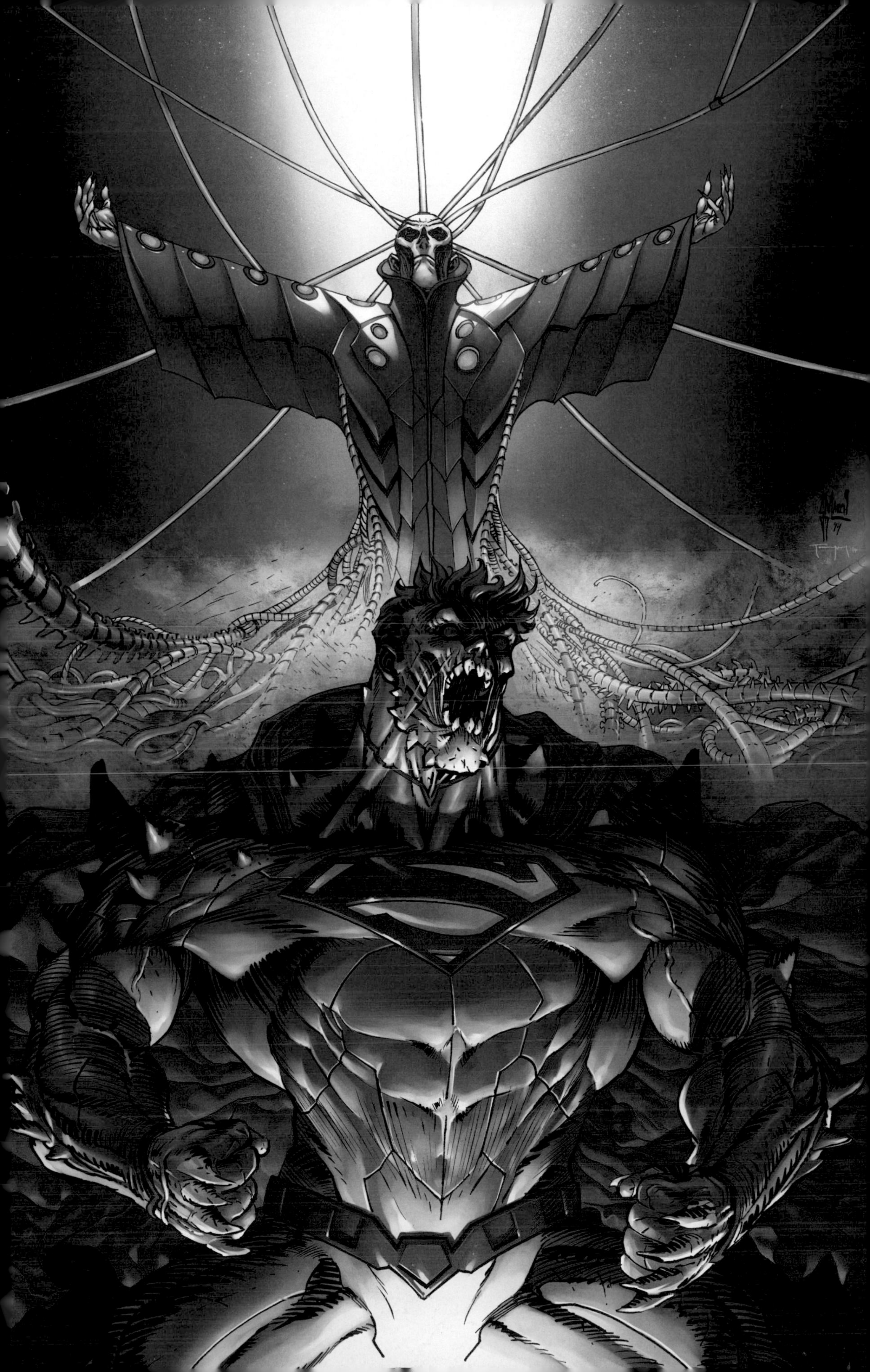

SUPERMAN DOOMED

[LAST SUN] chapter 4

"EVOLUTIONS"

STORY
GREG PAK & CHARLES SOULE

ART
**KEN LASHLEY, SZYMON KUDRANSKI, CORY SMITH,
DAVE BULLOCK, JACK HERBERT, IAN CHURCHILL,
AARON KUDER, VICENTE CIFUENTES & NORM RAPMUND**

COLORS
WIL QUINTANA

LETTERS
TAYLOR ESPOSITO

COVER
GUILLEM MARCH & TOMEU MOREY

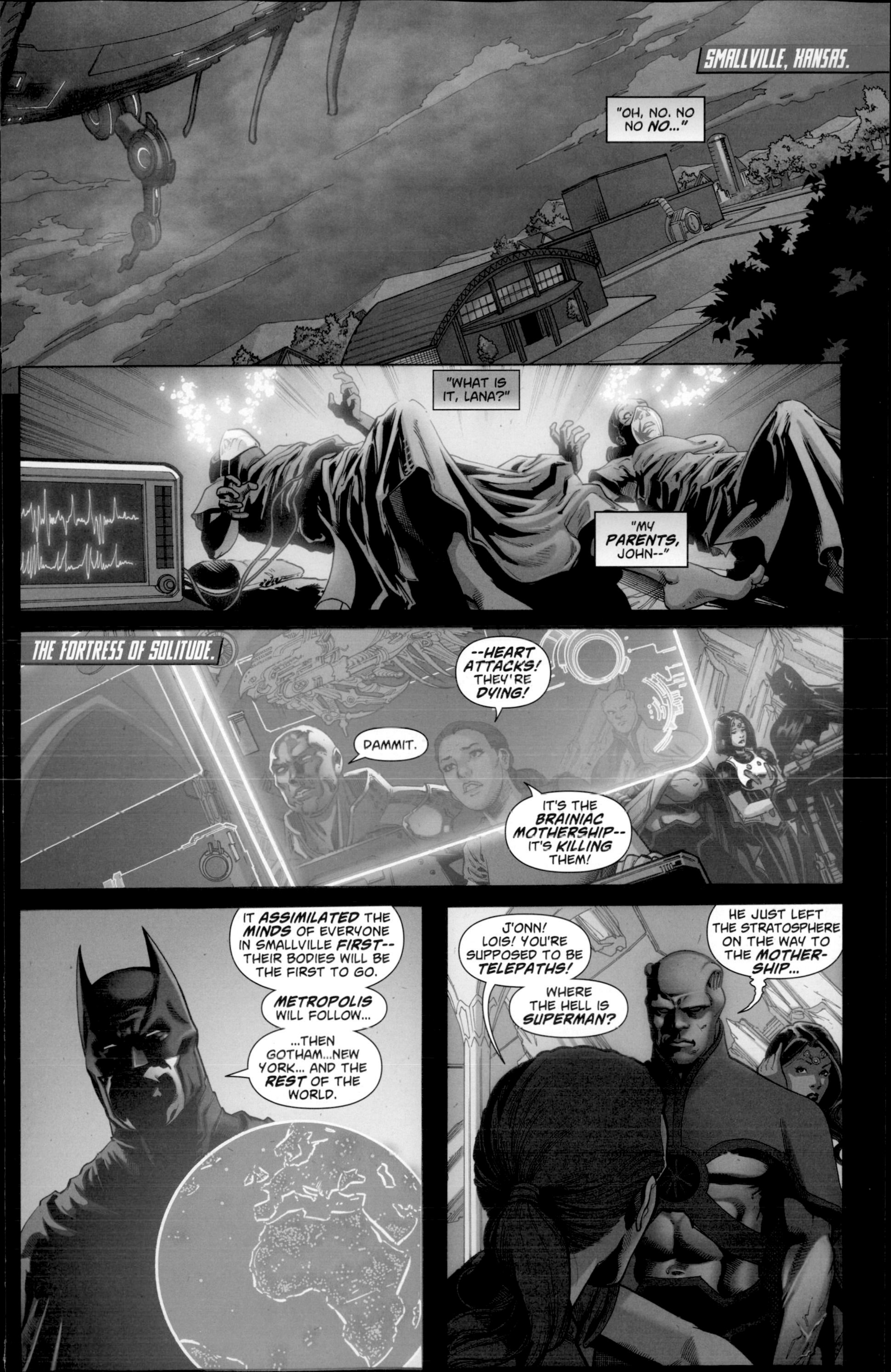
SMALLVILLE, KANSAS.
"OH, NO. NO NO NO..."
"WHAT IS IT, LANA?"
"MY PARENTS, JOHN--"
THE FORTRESS OF SOLITUDE.
--HEART ATTACKS! THEY'RE DYING!
DAMMIT.
IT'S THE BRAINIAC MOTHERSHIP-- IT'S KILLING THEM!
IT ASSIMILATED THE MINDS OF EVERYONE IN SMALLVILLE FIRST-- THEIR BODIES WILL BE THE FIRST TO GO.
METROPOLIS WILL FOLLOW...
...THEN GOTHAM...NEW YORK... AND THE REST OF THE WORLD.
J'ONN! LOIS! YOU'RE SUPPOSED TO BE TELEPATHS!
WHERE THE HELL IS SUPERMAN?
HE JUST LEFT THE STRATOSPHERE ON THE WAY TO THE MOTHER-SHIP...

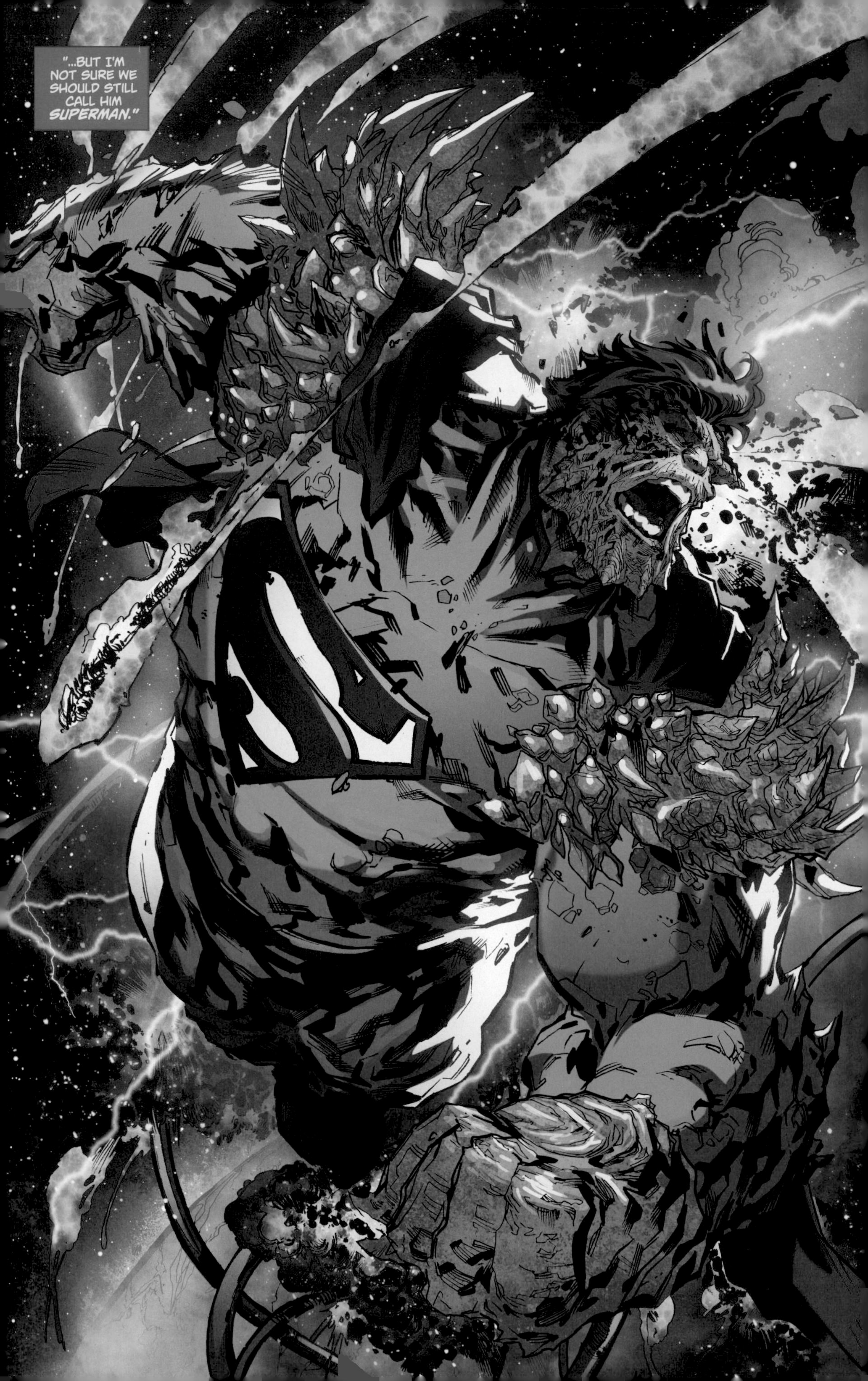
"...BUT I'M NOT SURE WE SHOULD STILL CALL HIM *SUPERMAN*."

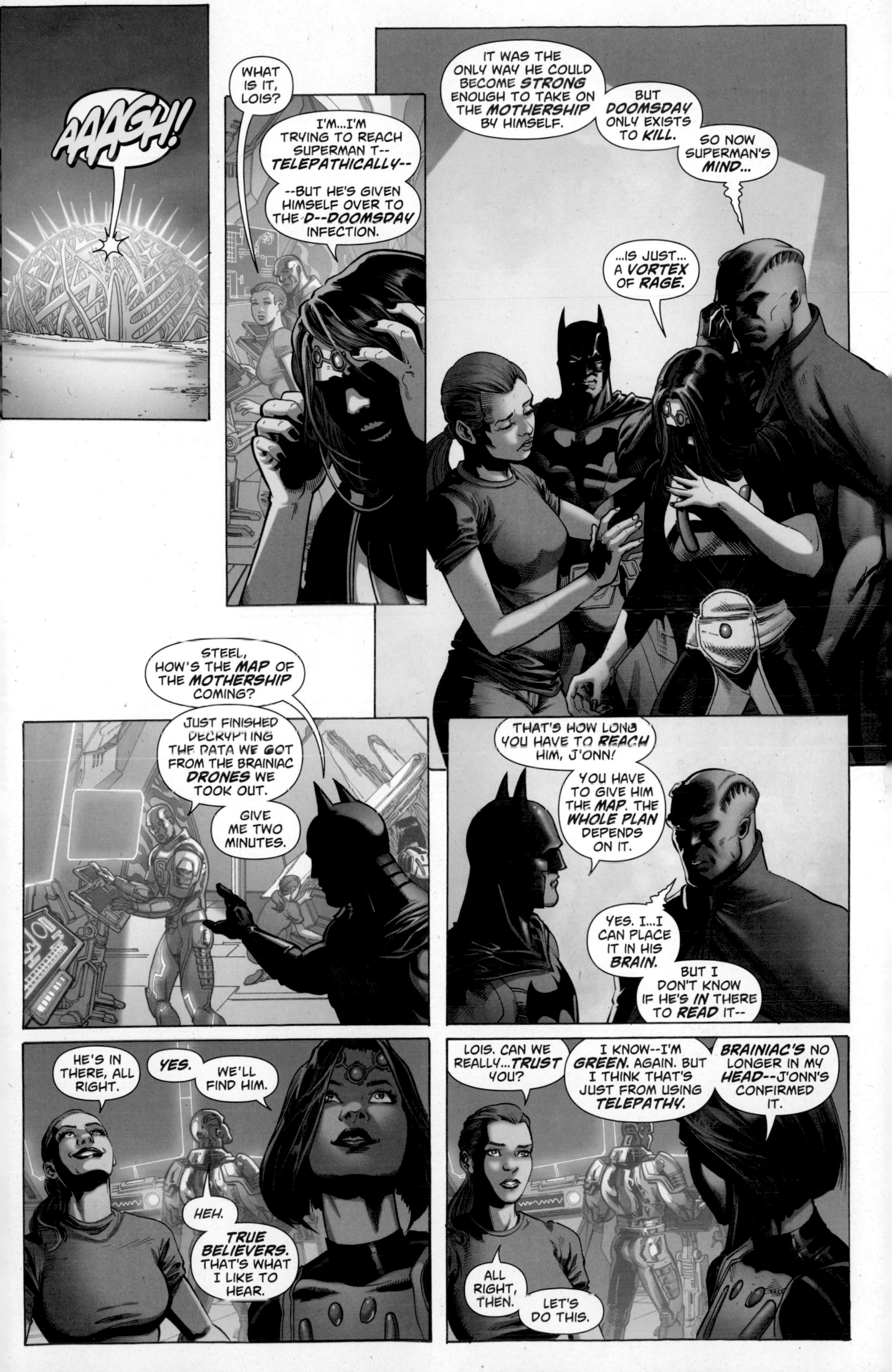
AAAGH!
WHAT IS IT, LOIS?
I'M...I'M TRYING TO REACH SUPERMAN T--TELEPATHICALLY--
--BUT HE'S GIVEN HIMSELF OVER TO THE D--DOOMSDAY INFECTION.
IT WAS THE ONLY WAY HE COULD BECOME STRONG ENOUGH TO TAKE ON THE MOTHERSHIP BY HIMSELF.
BUT DOOMSDAY ONLY EXISTS TO KILL.
SO NOW SUPERMAN'S MIND...
...IS JUST... A VORTEX OF RAGE.
STEEL, HOW'S THE MAP OF THE MOTHERSHIP COMING?
JUST FINISHED DECRYPTING THE DATA WE GOT FROM THE BRAINIAC DRONES WE TOOK OUT.
GIVE ME TWO MINUTES.
THAT'S HOW LONG YOU HAVE TO REACH HIM, J'ONN!
YOU HAVE TO GIVE HIM THE MAP. THE WHOLE PLAN DEPENDS ON IT.
YES. I...I CAN PLACE IT IN HIS BRAIN.
BUT I DON'T KNOW IF HE'S IN THERE TO READ IT--
HE'S IN THERE, ALL RIGHT.
YES.
WE'LL FIND HIM.
HEH.
TRUE BELIEVERS. THAT'S WHAT I LIKE TO HEAR.
LOIS. CAN WE REALLY...TRUST YOU?
I KNOW--I'M GREEN. AGAIN. BUT I THINK THAT'S JUST FROM USING TELEPATHY.
BRAINIAC'S NO LONGER IN MY HEAD--J'ONN'S CONFIRMED IT.
ALL RIGHT, THEN.
LET'S DO THIS.

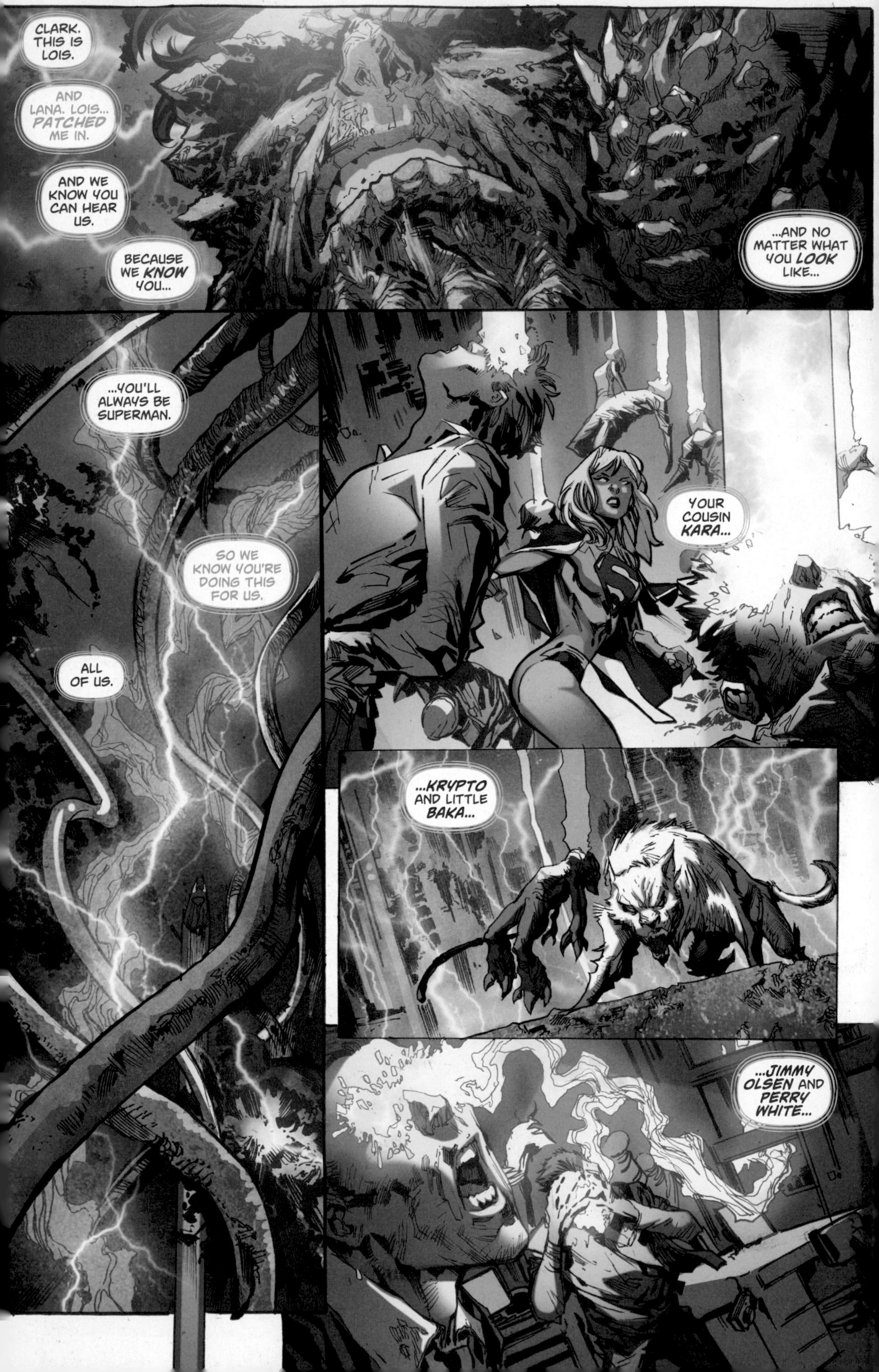
CLARK. THIS IS LOIS.
AND LANA. LOIS... PATCHED ME IN.
AND WE KNOW YOU CAN HEAR US.
BECAUSE WE KNOW YOU...
...AND NO MATTER WHAT YOU LOOK LIKE...
...YOU'LL ALWAYS BE SUPERMAN.
SO WE KNOW YOU'RE DOING THIS FOR US.
ALL OF US.
YOUR COUSIN KARA...
...KRYPTO AND LITTLE BAKA...
...JIMMY OLSEN AND PERRY WHITE...

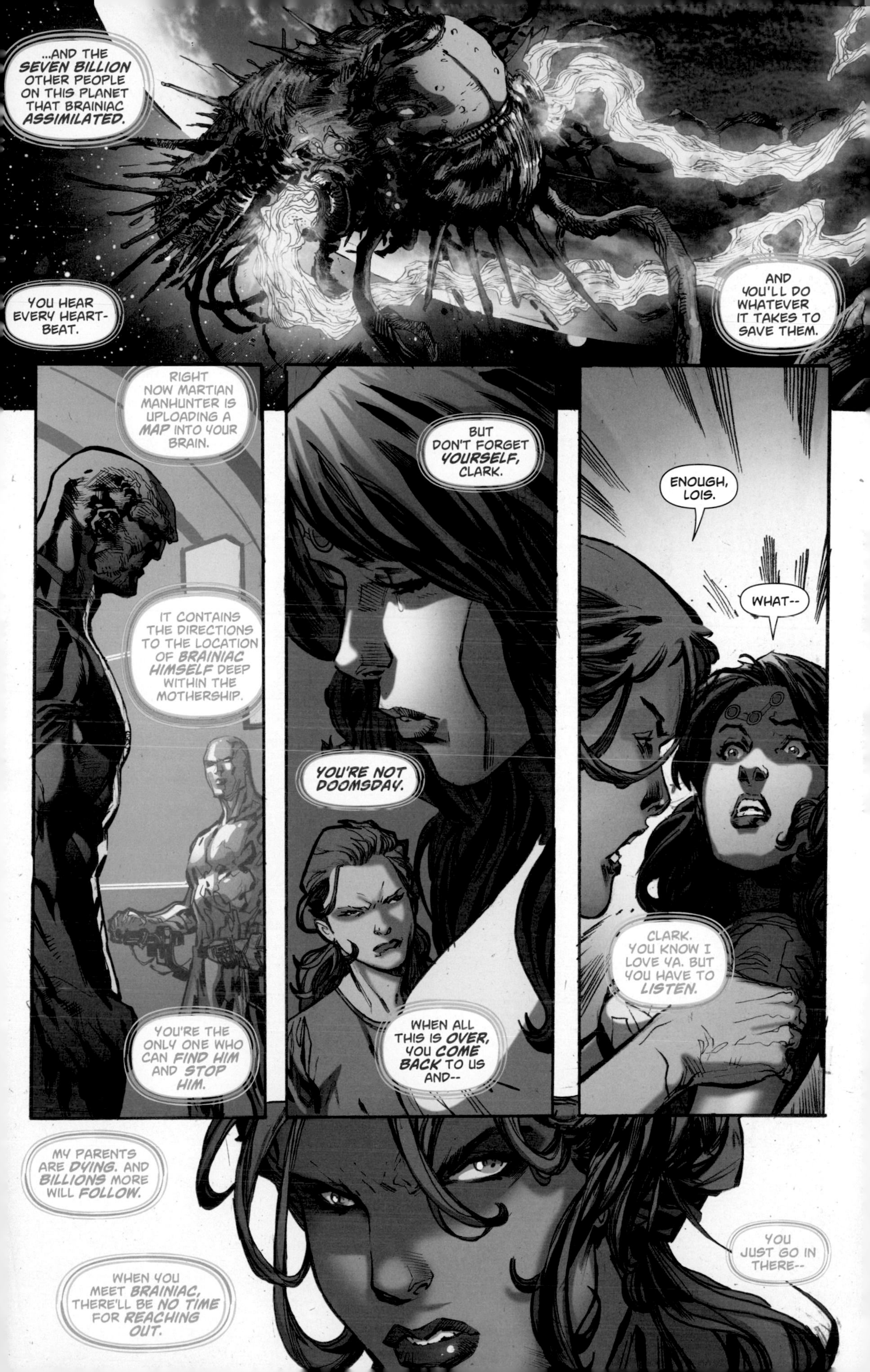
...AND THE SEVEN BILLION OTHER PEOPLE ON THIS PLANET THAT BRAINIAC ASSIMILATED.
YOU HEAR EVERY HEART-BEAT.
AND YOU'LL DO WHATEVER IT TAKES TO SAVE THEM.
RIGHT NOW MARTIAN MANHUNTER IS UPLOADING A MAP INTO YOUR BRAIN.
IT CONTAINS THE DIRECTIONS TO THE LOCATION OF BRAINIAC HIMSELF DEEP WITHIN THE MOTHERSHIP.
YOU'RE THE ONLY ONE WHO CAN FIND HIM AND STOP HIM.
BUT DON'T FORGET YOURSELF, CLARK.
YOU'RE NOT DOOMSDAY.
WHEN ALL THIS IS OVER, YOU COME BACK TO US AND--
ENOUGH, LOIS.
WHAT--
CLARK. YOU KNOW I LOVE YA. BUT YOU HAVE TO LISTEN.
MY PARENTS ARE DYING. AND BILLIONS MORE WILL FOLLOW.
WHEN YOU MEET BRAINIAC, THERE'LL BE NO TIME FOR REACHING OUT.
YOU JUST GO IN THERE--

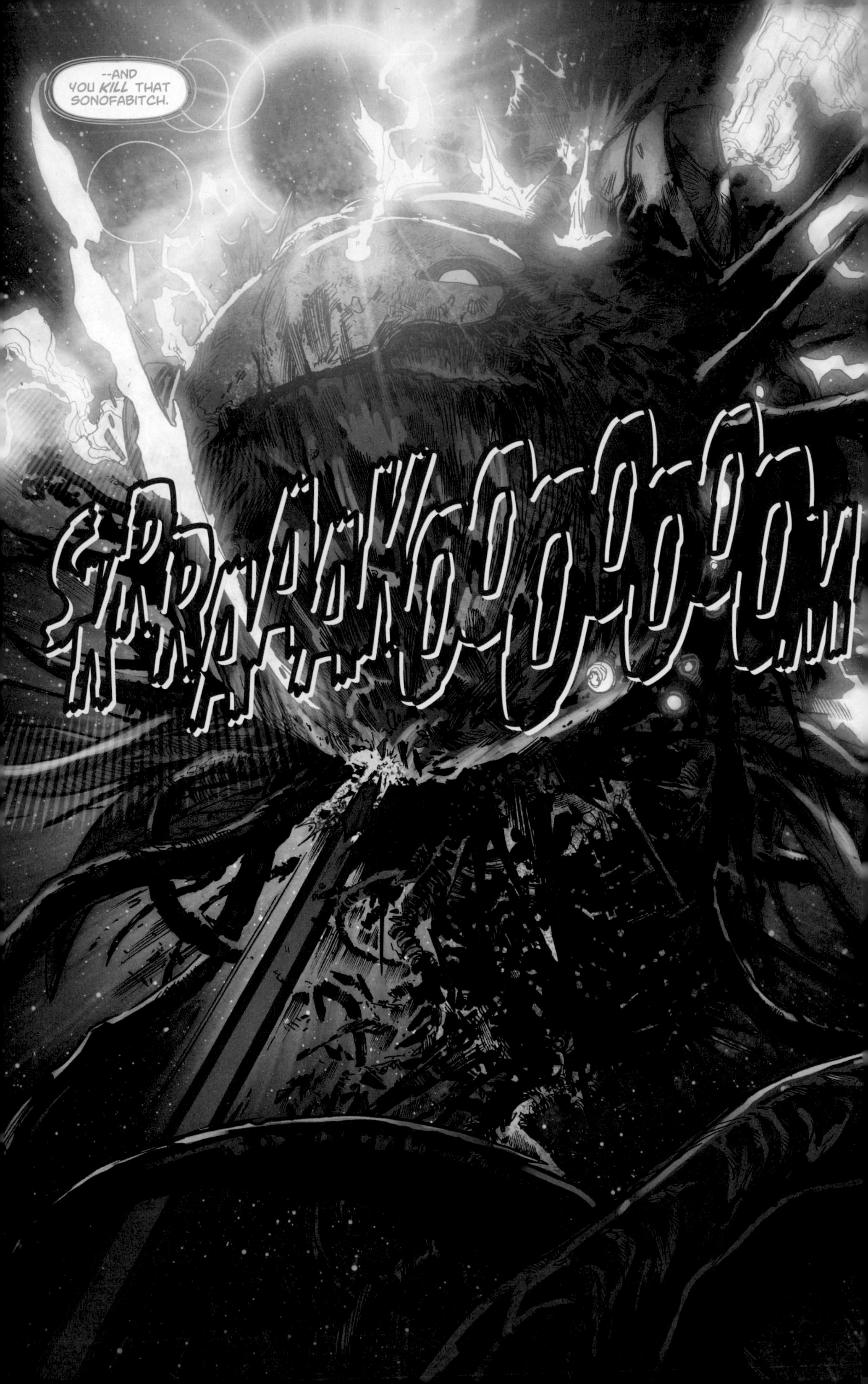
--AND YOU KILL THAT SONOFABITCH.

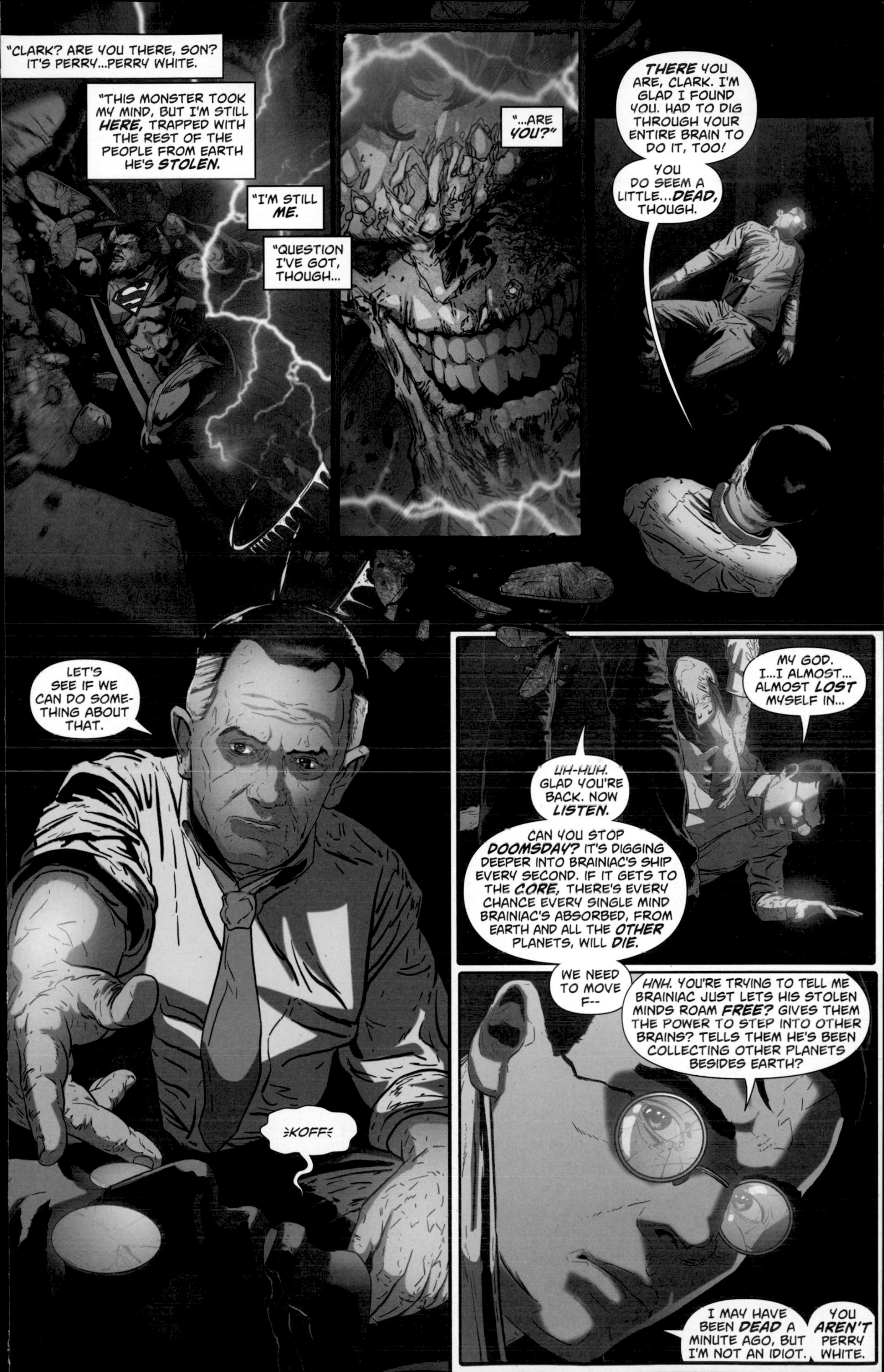
"CLARK? ARE YOU THERE, SON? IT'S PERRY...PERRY WHITE.
"THIS MONSTER TOOK MY MIND, BUT I'M STILL HERE, TRAPPED WITH THE REST OF THE PEOPLE FROM EARTH HE'S STOLEN.
"I'M STILL ME.
"QUESTION I'VE GOT, THOUGH...
"...ARE YOU?"
THERE YOU ARE, CLARK. I'M GLAD I FOUND YOU. HAD TO DIG THROUGH YOUR ENTIRE BRAIN TO DO IT, TOO!
YOU DO SEEM A LITTLE...DEAD, THOUGH.
LET'S SEE IF WE CAN DO SOMETHING ABOUT THAT.
KOFF
MY GOD. I...I ALMOST... ALMOST LOST MYSELF IN...
UH-HUH. GLAD YOU'RE BACK. NOW LISTEN.
CAN YOU STOP DOOMSDAY? IT'S DIGGING DEEPER INTO BRAINIAC'S SHIP EVERY SECOND. IF IT GETS TO THE CORE, THERE'S EVERY CHANCE EVERY SINGLE MIND BRAINIAC'S ABSORBED, FROM EARTH AND ALL THE OTHER PLANETS, WILL DIE.
WE NEED TO MOVE F--
HNH. YOU'RE TRYING TO TELL ME BRAINIAC JUST LETS HIS STOLEN MINDS ROAM FREE? GIVES THEM THE POWER TO STEP INTO OTHER BRAINS? TELLS THEM HE'S BEEN COLLECTING OTHER PLANETS BESIDES EARTH?
I MAY HAVE BEEN DEAD A MINUTE AGO, BUT I'M NOT AN IDIOT.
YOU AREN'T PERRY WHITE.

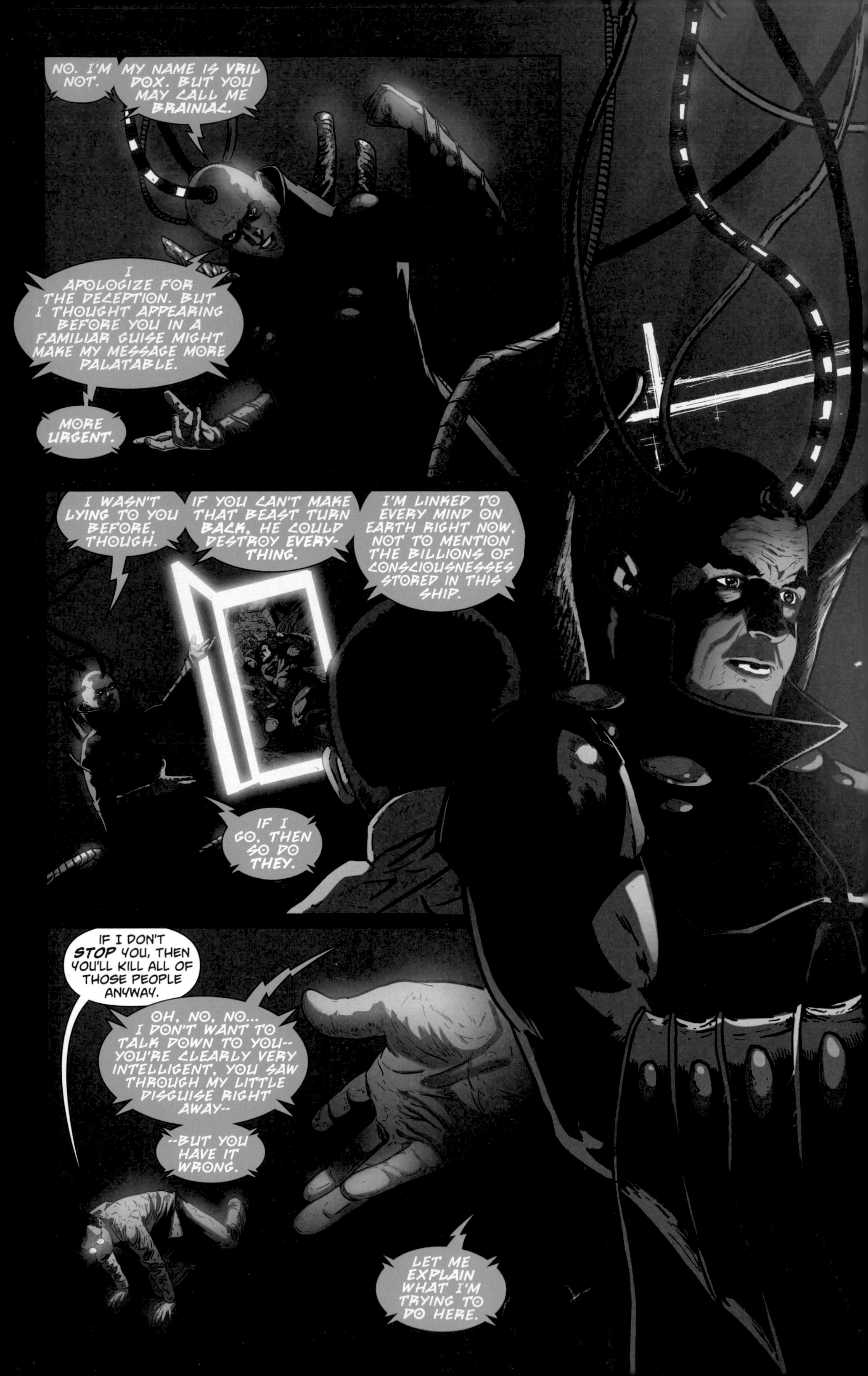
NO. I'M NOT.
MY NAME IS VRIL DOX. BUT YOU MAY CALL ME BRAINIAC.
I APOLOGIZE FOR THE DECEPTION. BUT I THOUGHT APPEARING BEFORE YOU IN A FAMILIAR GUISE MIGHT MAKE MY MESSAGE MORE PALATABLE.
MORE URGENT.
I WASN'T LYING TO YOU BEFORE, THOUGH.
IF YOU CAN'T MAKE THAT BEAST TURN BACK, HE COULD DESTROY EVERY-THING.
I'M LINKED TO EVERY MIND ON EARTH RIGHT NOW, NOT TO MENTION THE BILLIONS OF CONSCIOUSNESSES STORED IN THIS SHIP.
IF I GO, THEN SO DO THEY.
IF I DON'T STOP YOU, THEN YOU'LL KILL ALL OF THOSE PEOPLE ANYWAY.
OH, NO, NO... I DON'T WANT TO TALK DOWN TO YOU-- YOU'RE CLEARLY VERY INTELLIGENT. YOU SAW THROUGH MY LITTLE DISGUISE RIGHT AWAY--
--BUT YOU HAVE IT WRONG.
LET ME EXPLAIN WHAT I'M TRYING TO DO HERE.

THE UNIVERSE IS CREATED BY CONSCIOUS MINDS. WE OBSERVE PHENOMENA, AND SO THEY EXIST.
WITHOUT OUR PERCEPTION TO SHAPE THINGS, THINGS WOULD NOT BE.
IF YOU COULD COLLECT ENOUGH OF THOSE MINDS, UNIFY THEM, AND TELL THEM WHAT TO PERCEIVE, WHY...
...YOU COULD MAKE THE UNIVERSE...
...WHATEVER YOU WANT IT TO BE.

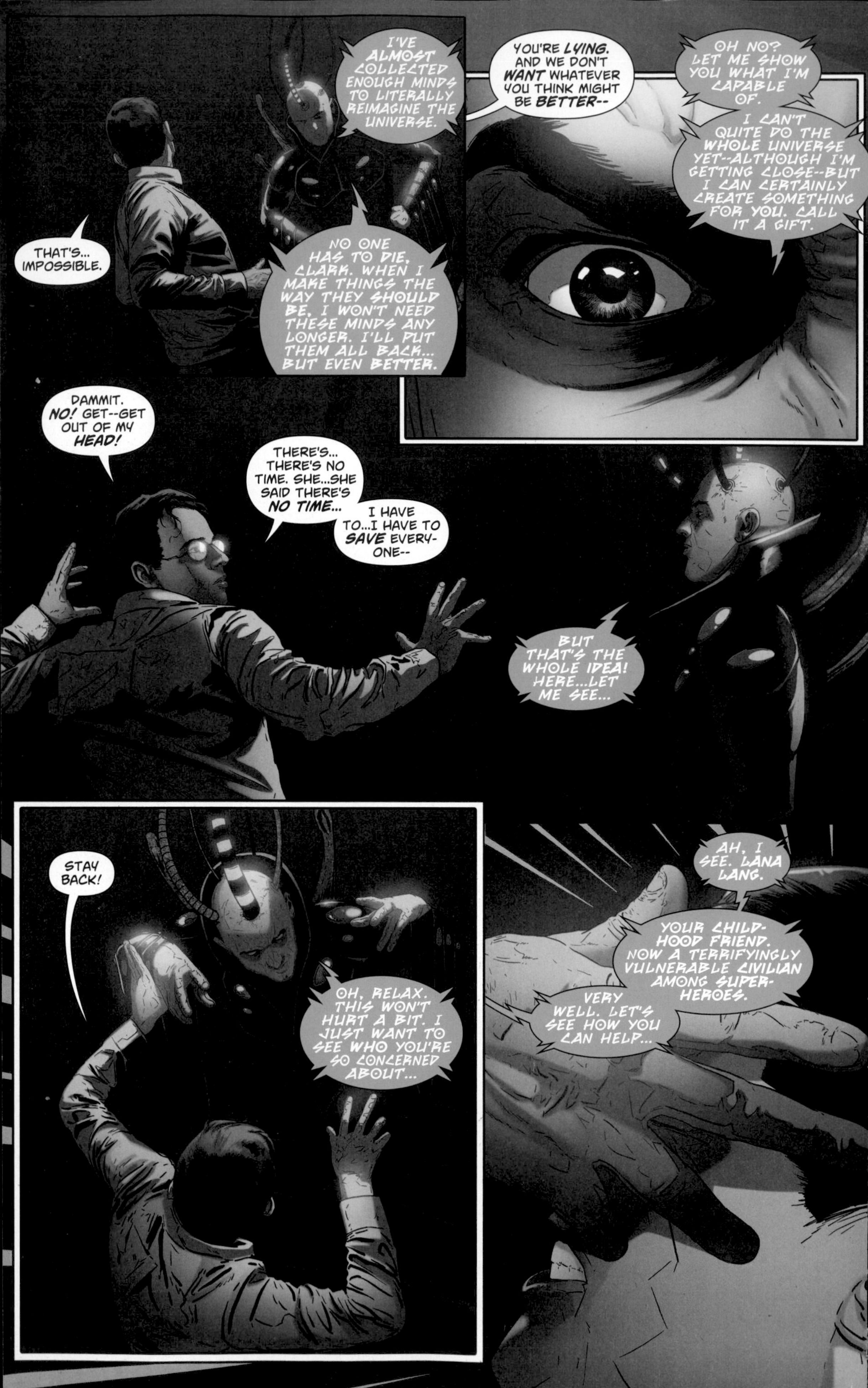
I'VE ALMOST COLLECTED ENOUGH MINDS TO LITERALLY REIMAGINE THE UNIVERSE.
THAT'S... IMPOSSIBLE.
NO ONE HAS TO DIE, CLARK. WHEN I MAKE THINGS THE WAY THEY SHOULD BE, I WON'T NEED THESE MINDS ANY LONGER. I'LL PUT THEM ALL BACK... BUT EVEN BETTER.
YOU'RE LYING. AND WE DON'T WANT WHATEVER YOU THINK MIGHT BE BETTER--
OH NO? LET ME SHOW YOU WHAT I'M CAPABLE OF.
I CAN'T QUITE DO THE WHOLE UNIVERSE YET--ALTHOUGH I'M GETTING CLOSE--BUT I CAN CERTAINLY CREATE SOMETHING FOR YOU. CALL IT A GIFT.
DAMMIT. NO! GET--GET OUT OF MY HEAD!
THERE'S... THERE'S NO TIME. SHE...SHE SAID THERE'S NO TIME...
I HAVE TO...I HAVE TO SAVE EVERY-ONE--
BUT THAT'S THE WHOLE IDEA! HERE...LET ME SEE...
STAY BACK!
OH, RELAX. THIS WON'T HURT A BIT. I JUST WANT TO SEE WHO YOU'RE SO CONCERNED ABOUT...
AH, I SEE. LANA LANG.
YOUR CHILD-HOOD FRIEND. NOW A TERRIFYINGLY VULNERABLE CIVILIAN AMONG SUPER-HEROES.
VERY WELL. LET'S SEE HOW YOU CAN HELP...

"...LANA...
"...AND WHY NOT TOSS IN HER SPECIAL NEW FRIEND, JOHN HENRY."
"WHA-- WHERE--?"
"METROPOLIS, CLARK.
"NOW PROTECTED BY IT'S MAN AND WOMAN OF STEEL.
"A WORLD WITH ALL THE TIME IN THE WORLD...
"...SO STRONG THAT YOU AREN'T NEEDED ANY LONGER."

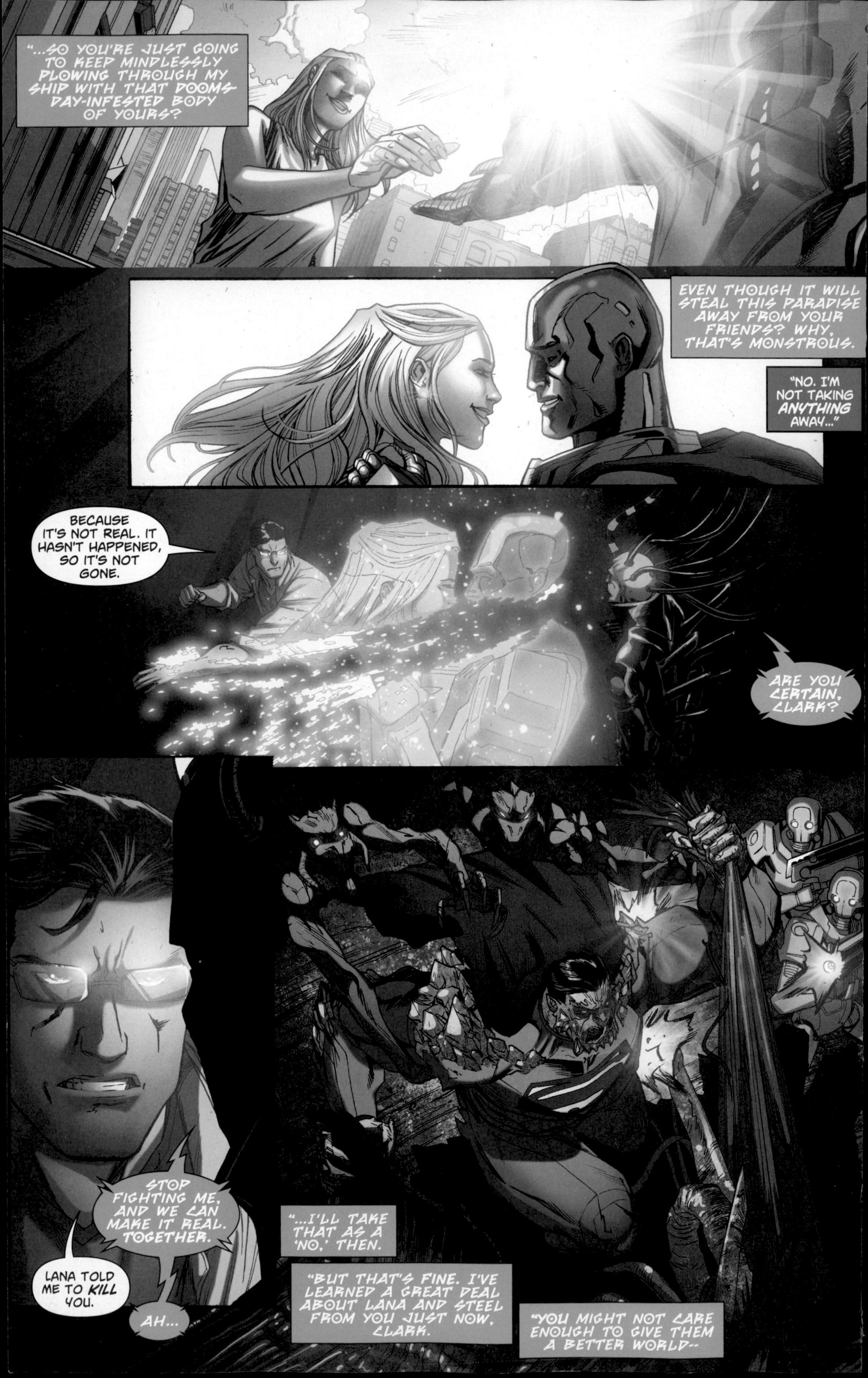
"...SO YOU'RE JUST GOING TO KEEP MINDLESSLY PLOWING THROUGH MY SHIP WITH THAT DOOMS-DAY-INFESTED BODY OF YOURS?
EVEN THOUGH IT WILL STEAL THIS PARADISE AWAY FROM YOUR FRIENDS? WHY, THAT'S MONSTROUS.
"NO. I'M NOT TAKING ANYTHING AWAY..."
BECAUSE IT'S NOT REAL. IT HASN'T HAPPENED, SO IT'S NOT GONE.
ARE YOU CERTAIN, CLARK?
STOP FIGHTING ME, AND WE CAN MAKE IT REAL. TOGETHER.
LANA TOLD ME TO KILL YOU.
AH...
"...I'LL TAKE THAT AS A 'NO,' THEN.
"BUT THAT'S FINE. I'VE LEARNED A GREAT DEAL ABOUT LANA AND STEEL FROM YOU JUST NOW, CLARK.
"YOU MIGHT NOT CARE ENOUGH TO GIVE THEM A BETTER WORLD--

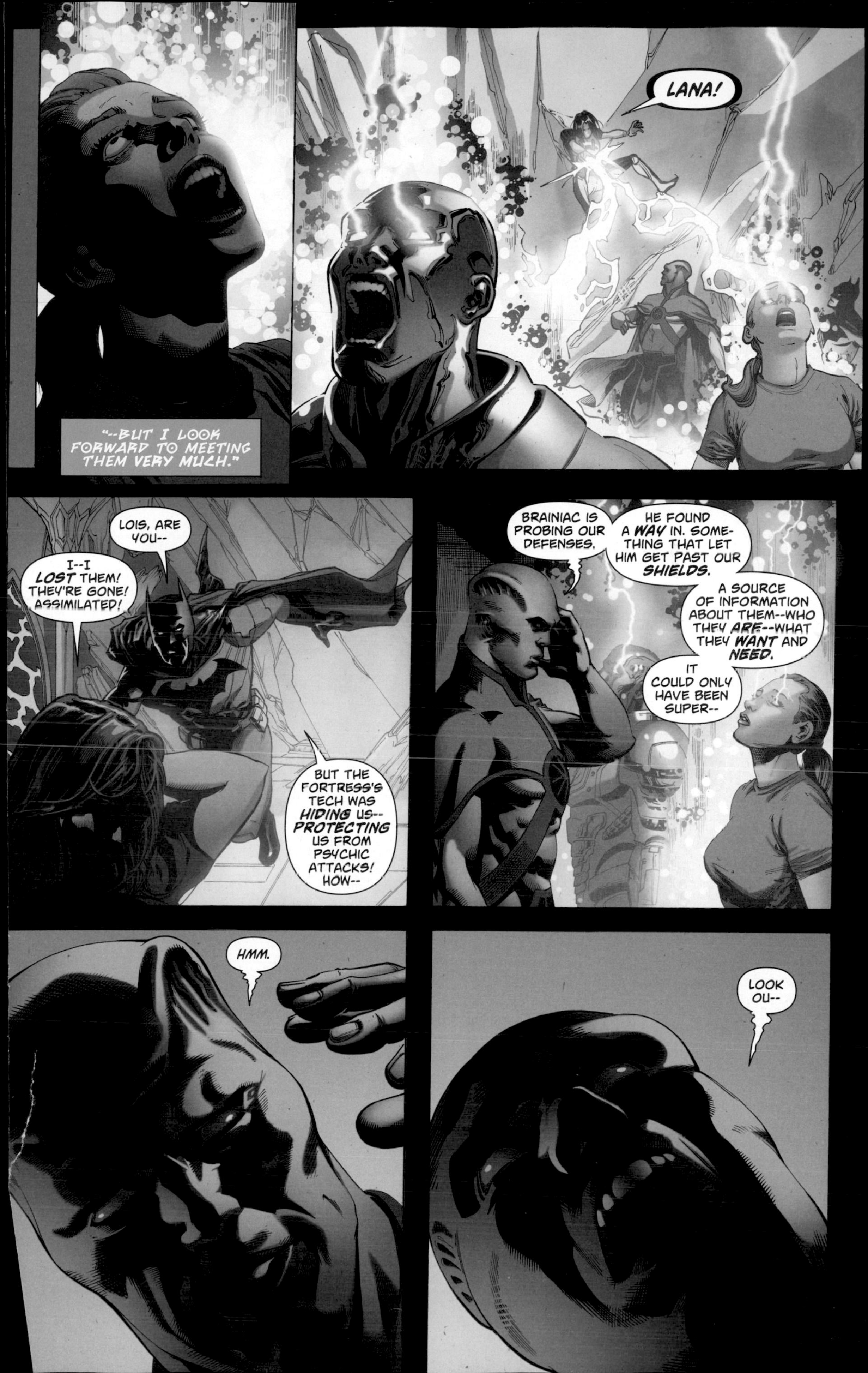
"--BUT I LOOK FORWARD TO MEETING THEM VERY MUCH."
LANA!
LOIS, ARE YOU--
I--I **LOST** THEM! THEY'RE GONE! ASSIMILATED!
BUT THE FORTRESS'S TECH WAS **HIDING** US-- **PROTECTING** US FROM PSYCHIC ATTACKS! HOW--
BRAINIAC IS PROBING OUR DEFENSES.
HE FOUND A **WAY** IN. SOMETHING THAT LET HIM GET PAST OUR **SHIELDS**.
A SOURCE OF INFORMATION ABOUT THEM--WHO THEY **ARE**--WHAT THEY **WANT** AND **NEED**.
IT COULD ONLY HAVE BEEN SUPER--
HMM.
LOOK OU--

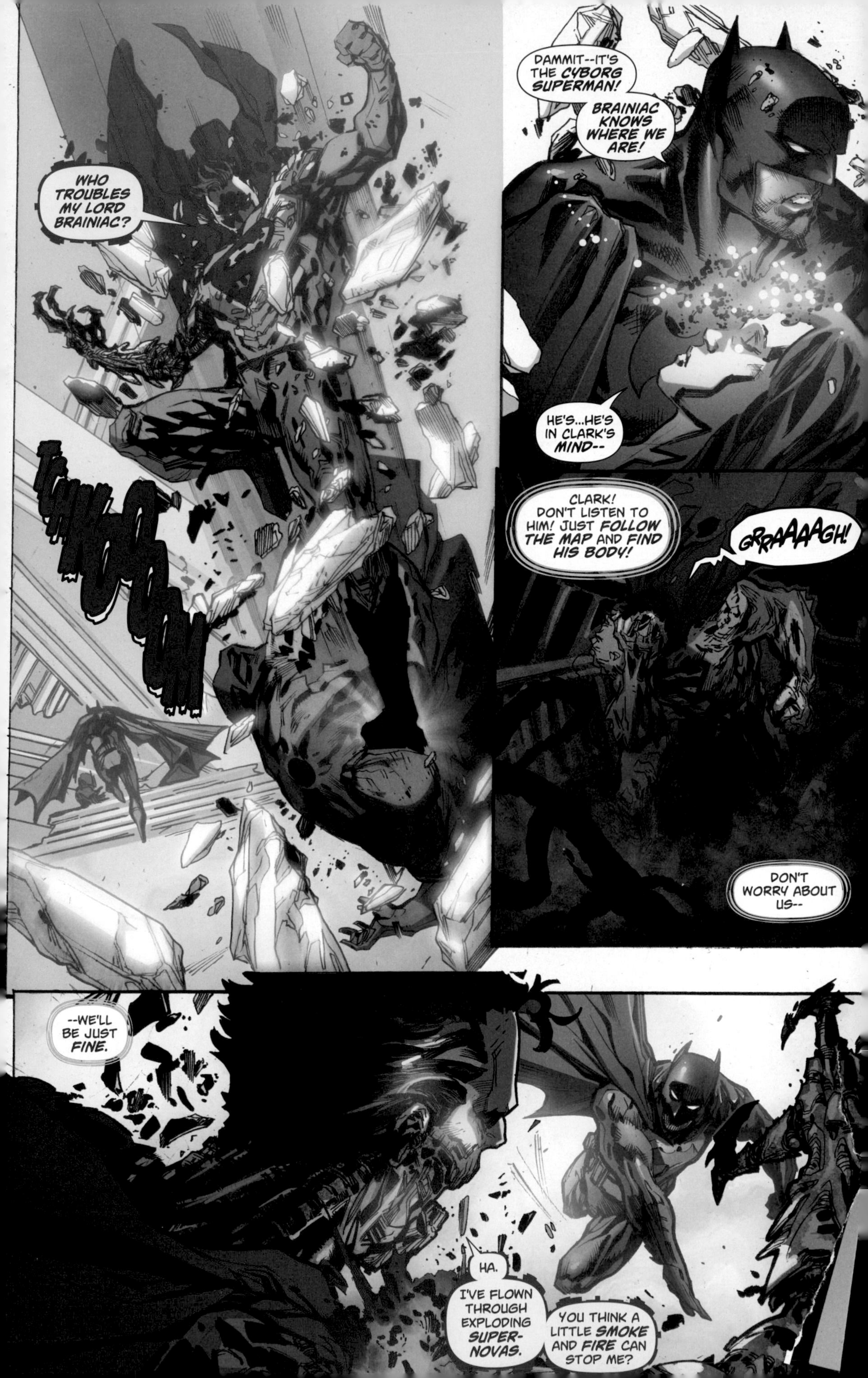
WHO TROUBLES MY LORD BRAINIAC?
TCHKOOOOOM
DAMMIT--IT'S THE CYBORG SUPERMAN!
BRAINIAC KNOWS WHERE WE ARE!
HE'S...HE'S IN CLARK'S MIND--
CLARK! DON'T LISTEN TO HIM! JUST FOLLOW THE MAP AND FIND HIS BODY!
GRRAAAAGH!
DON'T WORRY ABOUT US--
--WE'LL BE JUST FINE.
HA.
I'VE FLOWN THROUGH EXPLODING SUPER-NOVAS.
YOU THINK A LITTLE SMOKE AND FIRE CAN STOP ME?

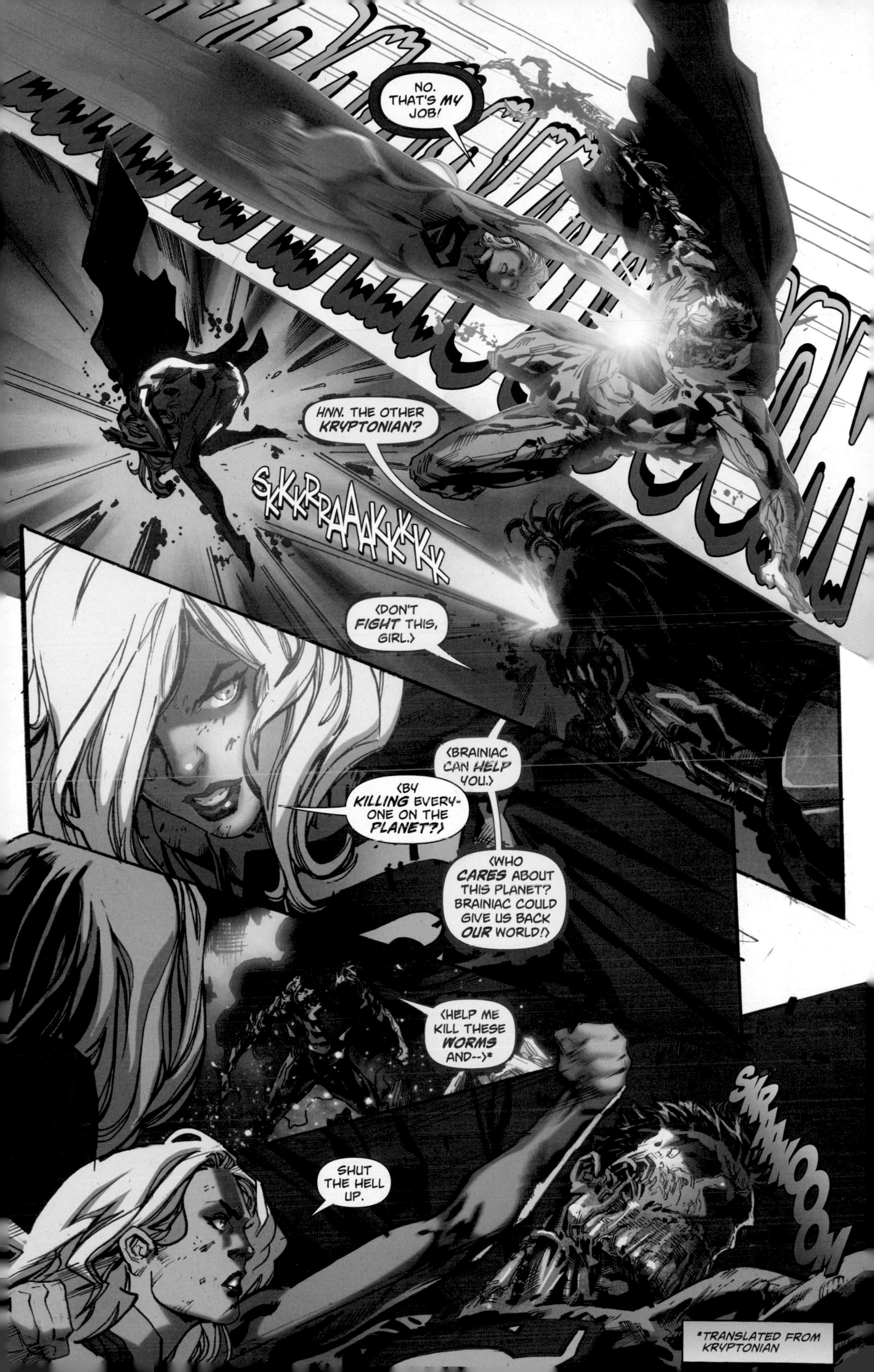
NO. THAT'S MY JOB!
HNN. THE OTHER KRYPTONIAN?
SKKKRRAAAKKKKK
‹DON'T FIGHT THIS, GIRL.›
‹BRAINIAC CAN HELP YOU.›
‹BY KILLING EVERY-ONE ON THE PLANET?›
‹WHO CARES ABOUT THIS PLANET? BRAINIAC COULD GIVE US BACK OUR WORLD!›
‹HELP ME KILL THESE WORMS AND--›*
SHUT THE HELL UP.
SKRAAKOOOM
*TRANSLATED FROM KRYPTONIAN

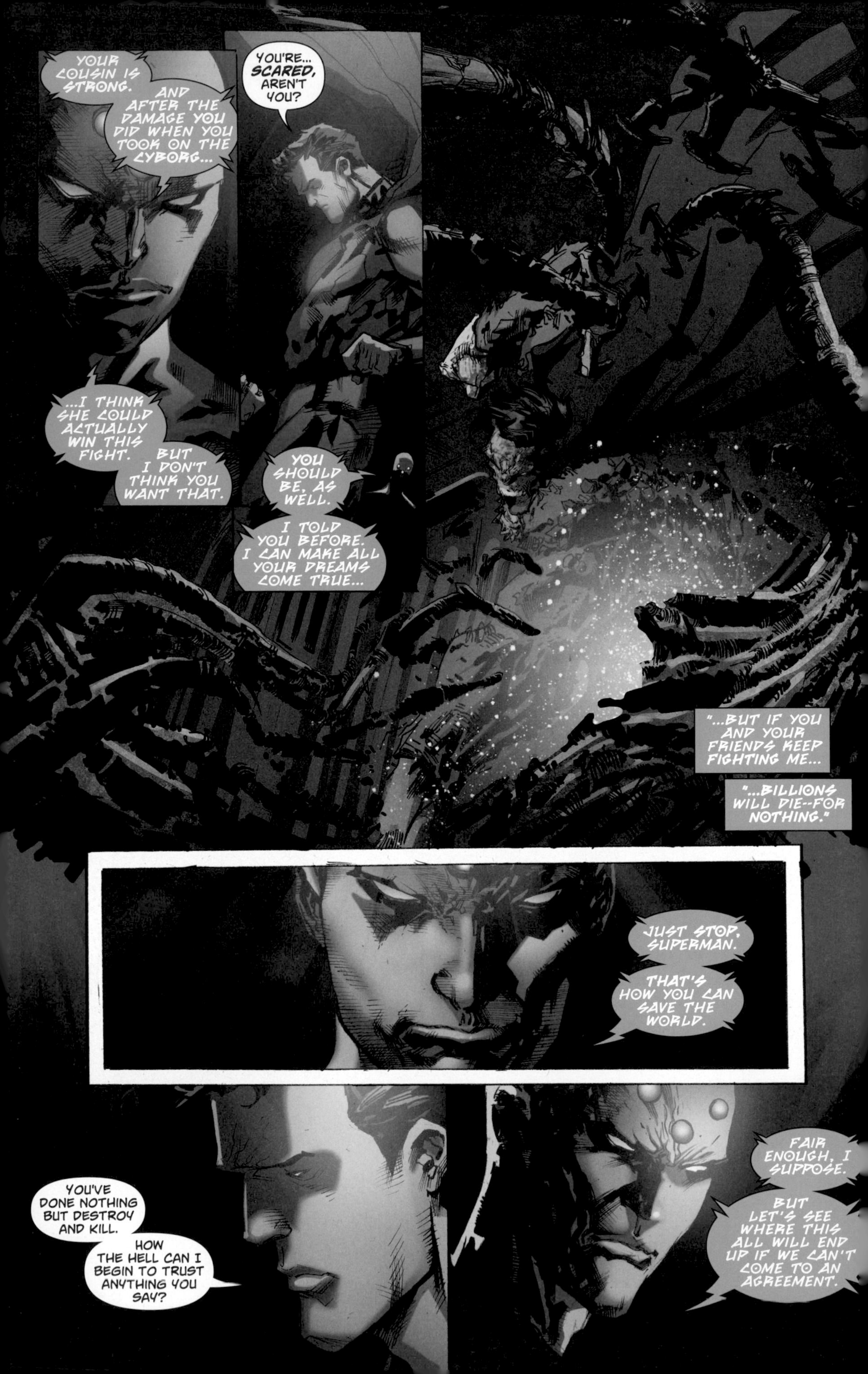
YOUR COUSIN IS STRONG.
AND AFTER THE DAMAGE YOU DID WHEN YOU TOOK ON THE CYBORG...
YOU'RE... SCARED, AREN'T YOU?
...I THINK SHE COULD ACTUALLY WIN THIS FIGHT.
BUT I DON'T THINK YOU WANT THAT.
YOU SHOULD BE, AS WELL.
I TOLD YOU BEFORE. I CAN MAKE ALL YOUR DREAMS COME TRUE...
"...BUT IF YOU AND YOUR FRIENDS KEEP FIGHTING ME...
"...BILLIONS WILL DIE--FOR NOTHING."
JUST STOP, SUPERMAN.
THAT'S HOW YOU CAN SAVE THE WORLD.
YOU'VE DONE NOTHING BUT DESTROY AND KILL.
HOW THE HELL CAN I BEGIN TO TRUST ANYTHING YOU SAY?
FAIR ENOUGH, I SUPPOSE.
BUT LET'S SEE WHERE THIS ALL WILL END UP IF WE CAN'T COME TO AN AGREEMENT.

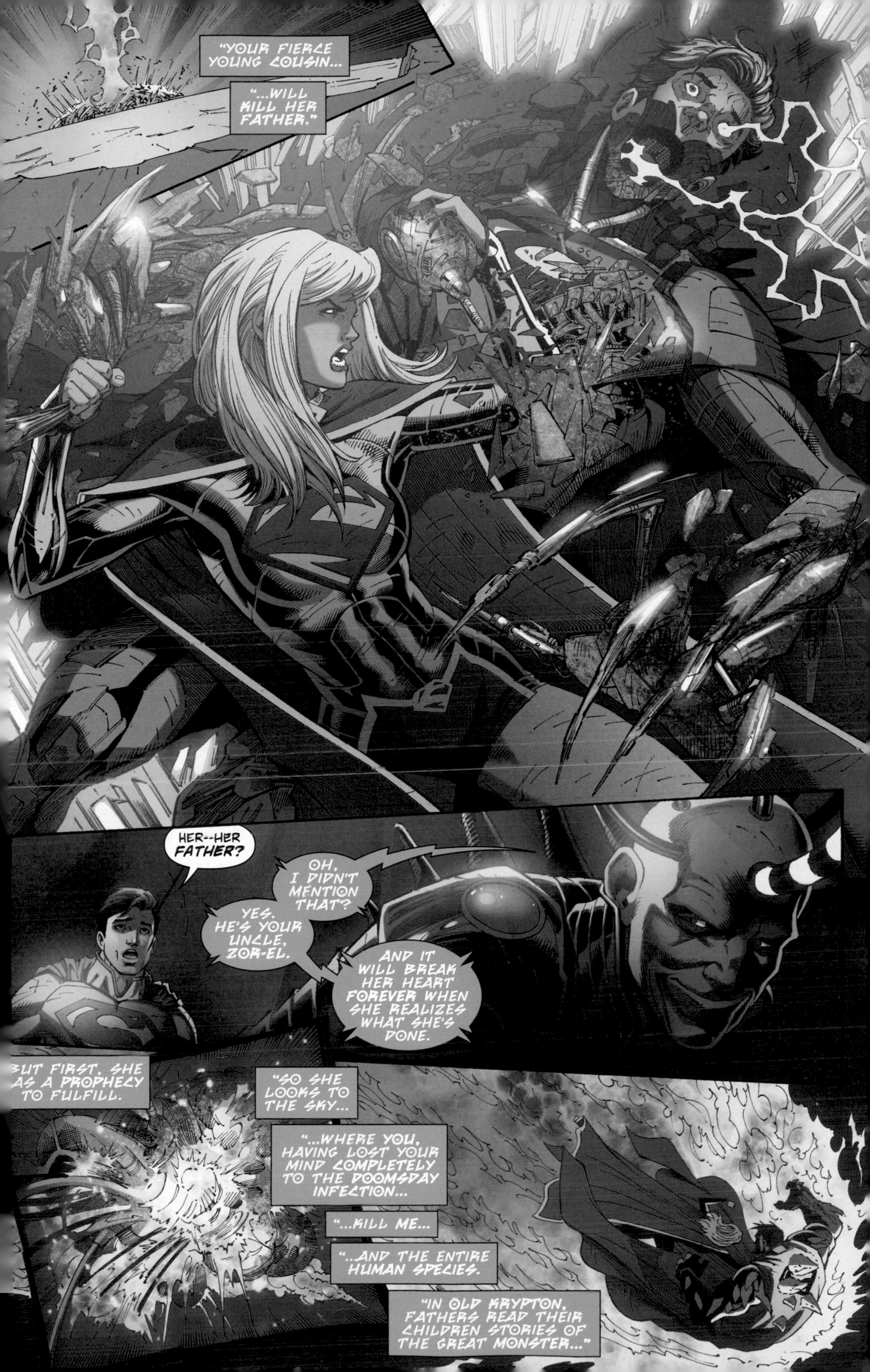
"YOUR FIERCE YOUNG COUSIN...
"...WILL KILL HER FATHER."
HER--HER FATHER?
OH, I DIDN'T MENTION THAT?
YES. HE'S YOUR UNCLE, ZOR-EL.
AND IT WILL BREAK HER HEART FOREVER WHEN SHE REALIZES WHAT SHE'S DONE.
UT FIRST, SHE AS A PROPHECY TO FULFILL.
"SO SHE LOOKS TO THE SKY...
"...WHERE YOU, HAVING LOST YOUR MIND COMPLETELY TO THE DOOMSDAY INFECTION...
"...KILL ME...
"...AND THE ENTIRE HUMAN SPECIES.
"IN OLD KRYPTON, FATHERS READ THEIR CHILDREN STORIES OF THE GREAT MONSTER..."

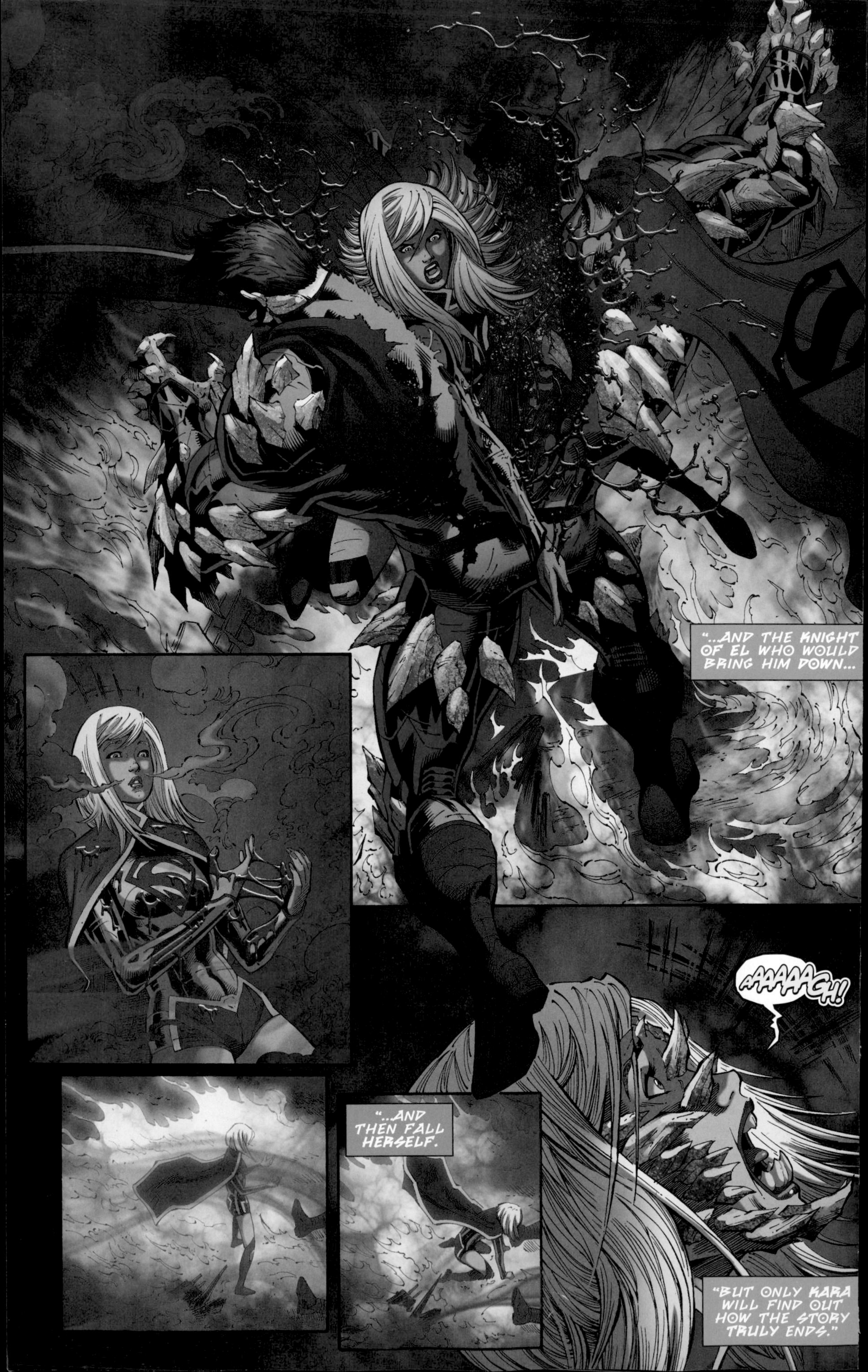
"...AND THE KNIGHT OF EL WHO WOULD BRING HIM DOWN...
AAAAAGH!
"...AND THEN FALL HERSELF.
"BUT ONLY KARA WILL FIND OUT HOW THE STORY TRULY ENDS."

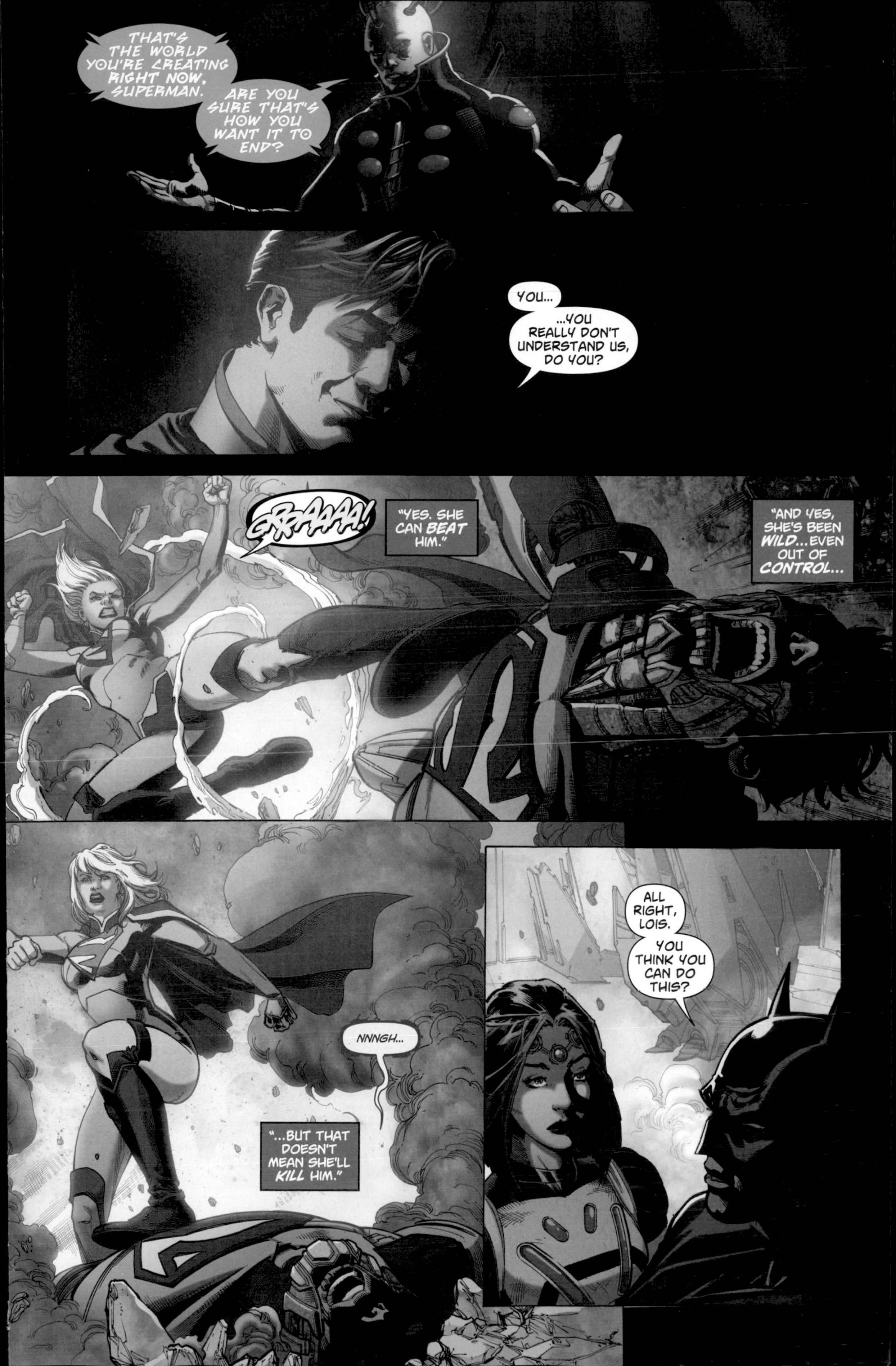
THAT'S THE WORLD YOU'RE CREATING RIGHT NOW, SUPERMAN.
ARE YOU SURE THAT'S HOW YOU WANT IT TO END?
YOU...
...YOU REALLY DON'T UNDERSTAND US, DO YOU?
GRRAAAA!
"YES. SHE CAN BEAT HIM."
"AND YES, SHE'S BEEN WILD...EVEN OUT OF CONTROL...
NNNGH...
"...BUT THAT DOESN'T MEAN SHE'LL KILL HIM."
ALL RIGHT, LOIS.
YOU THINK YOU CAN DO THIS?

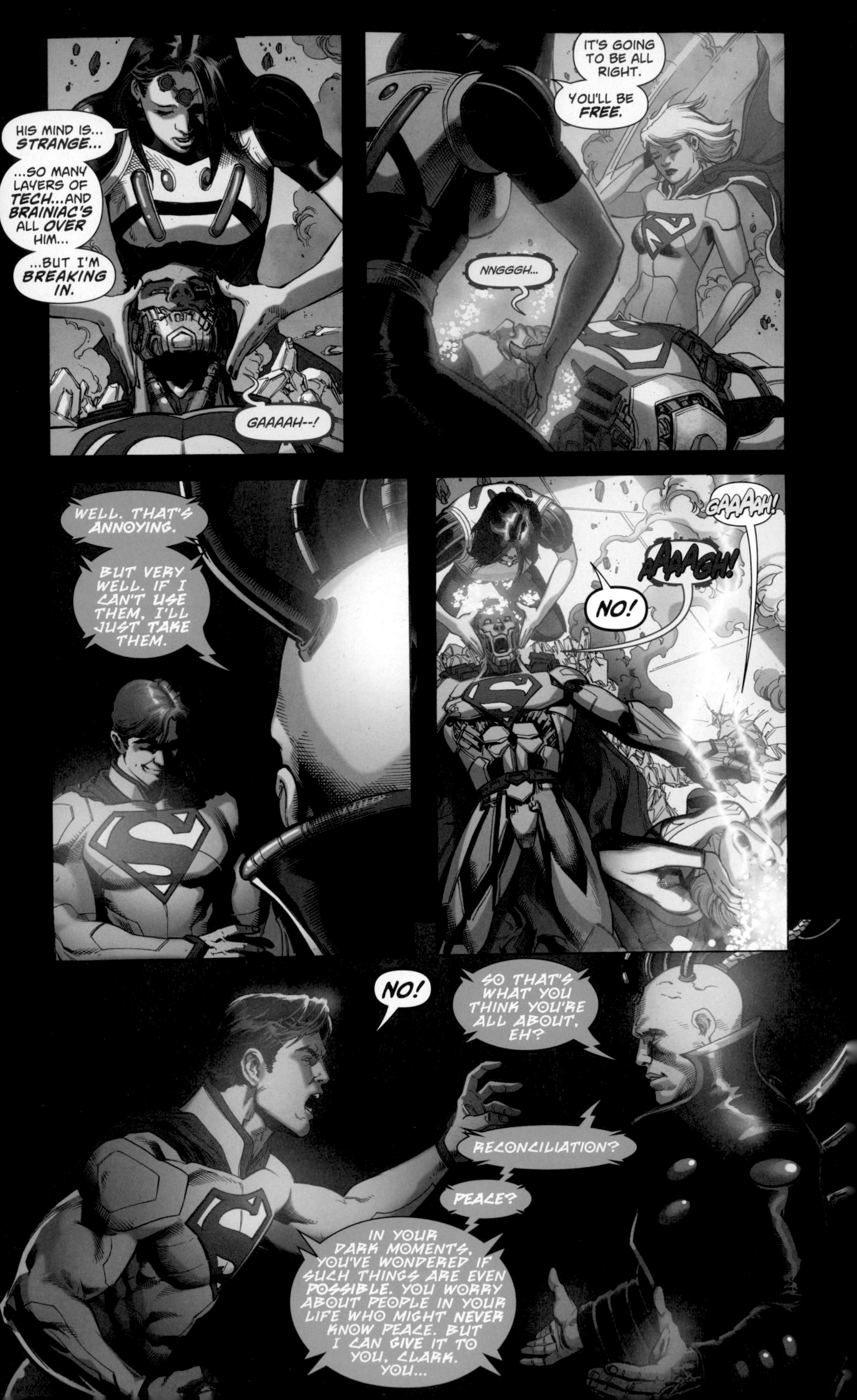
HIS MIND IS... STRANGE...
...SO MANY LAYERS OF TECH...AND BRAINIAC'S ALL OVER HIM...
...BUT I'M BREAKING IN.
GAAAAH--!
IT'S GOING TO BE ALL RIGHT.
YOU'LL BE FREE.
NNGGGH...
WELL. THAT'S ANNOYING.
BUT VERY WELL. IF I CAN'T USE THEM, I'LL JUST TAKE THEM.
GAAAAH!
AAAAGH!
NO!
NO!
SO THAT'S WHAT YOU THINK YOU'RE ALL ABOUT, EH?
RECONCILIATION?
PEACE?
IN YOUR DARK MOMENTS, YOU'VE WONDERED IF SUCH THINGS ARE EVEN POSSIBLE. YOU WORRY ABOUT PEOPLE IN YOUR LIFE WHO MIGHT NEVER KNOW PEACE. BUT I CAN GIVE IT TO YOU, CLARK. YOU...

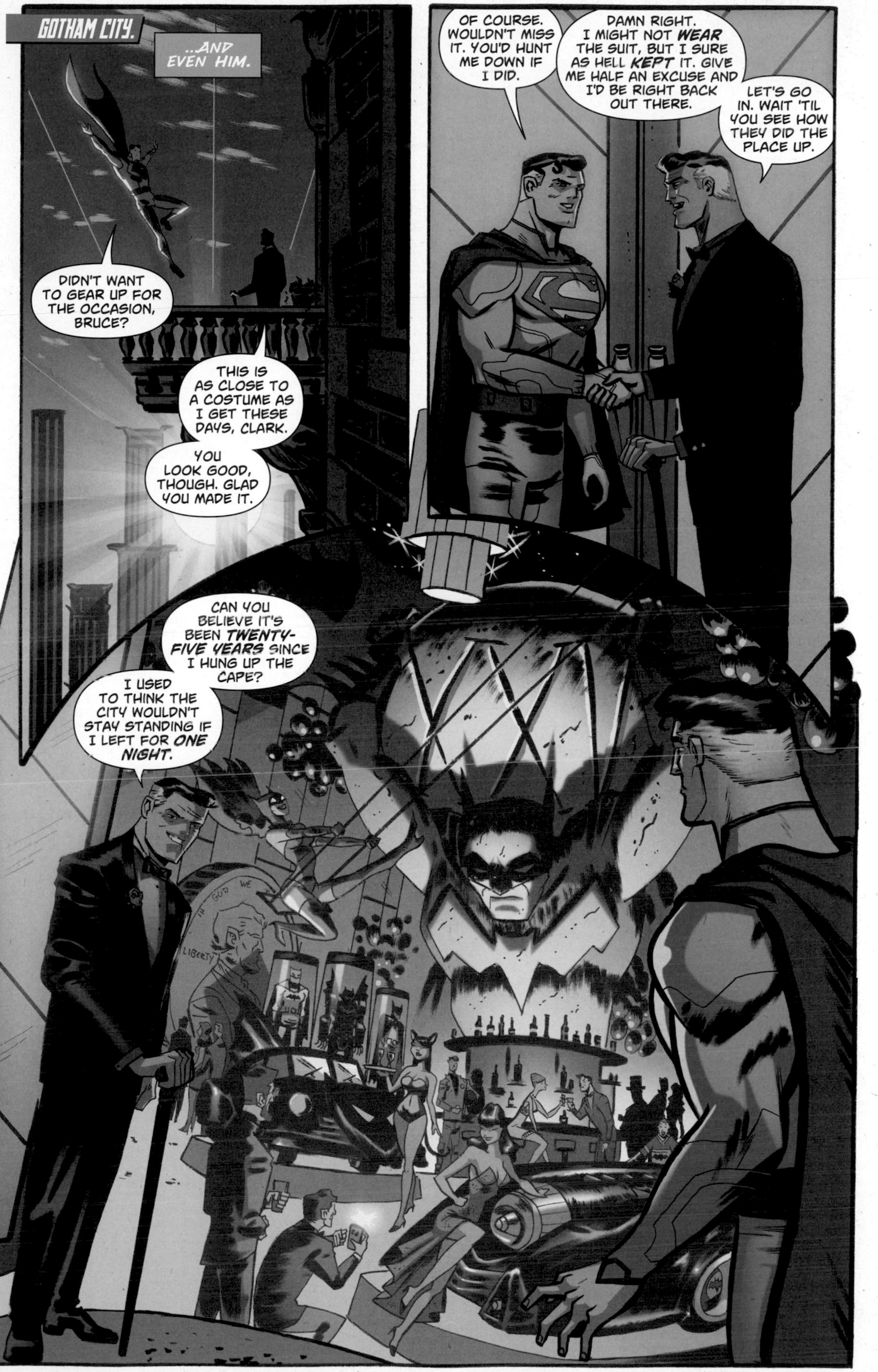
GOTHAM CITY.
...AND EVEN HIM.
DIDN'T WANT TO GEAR UP FOR THE OCCASION, BRUCE?
THIS IS AS CLOSE TO A COSTUME AS I GET THESE DAYS, CLARK.
YOU LOOK GOOD, THOUGH. GLAD YOU MADE IT.
OF COURSE. WOULDN'T MISS IT. YOU'D HUNT ME DOWN IF I DID.
DAMN RIGHT. I MIGHT NOT WEAR THE SUIT, BUT I SURE AS HELL KEPT IT. GIVE ME HALF AN EXCUSE AND I'D BE RIGHT BACK OUT THERE.
LET'S GO IN. WAIT 'TIL YOU SEE HOW THEY DID THE PLACE UP.
CAN YOU BELIEVE IT'S BEEN TWENTY-FIVE YEARS SINCE I HUNG UP THE CAPE?
I USED TO THINK THE CITY WOULDN'T STAY STANDING IF I LEFT FOR ONE NIGHT.

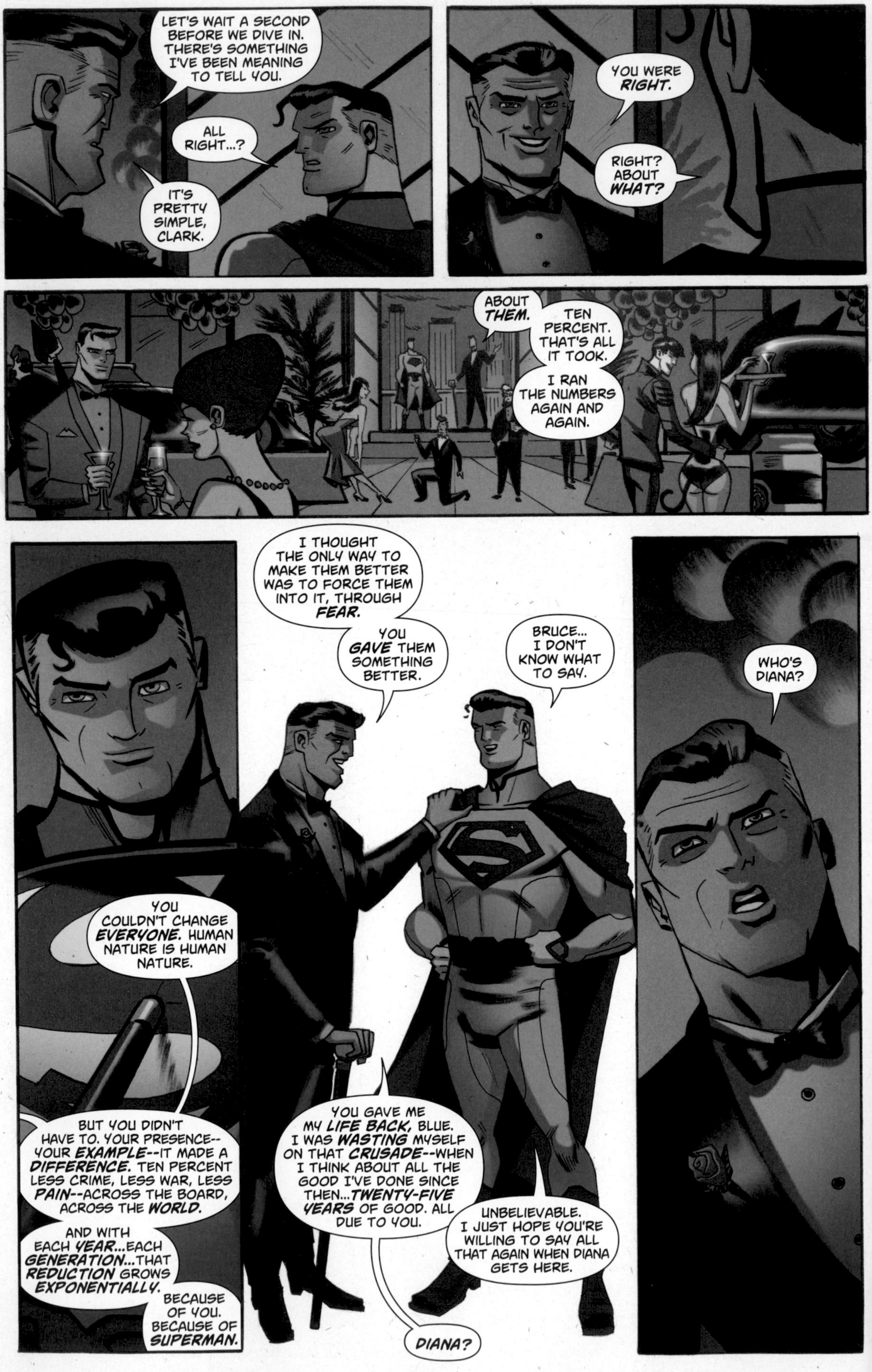
LET'S WAIT A SECOND BEFORE WE DIVE IN. THERE'S SOMETHING I'VE BEEN MEANING TO TELL YOU.
ALL RIGHT...?
IT'S PRETTY SIMPLE, CLARK.
YOU WERE RIGHT.
RIGHT? ABOUT WHAT?
ABOUT THEM.
TEN PERCENT. THAT'S ALL IT TOOK.
I RAN THE NUMBERS AGAIN AND AGAIN.
YOU COULDN'T CHANGE EVERYONE. HUMAN NATURE IS HUMAN NATURE.
BUT YOU DIDN'T HAVE TO. YOUR PRESENCE--YOUR EXAMPLE--IT MADE A DIFFERENCE. TEN PERCENT LESS CRIME, LESS WAR, LESS PAIN--ACROSS THE BOARD, ACROSS THE WORLD.
AND WITH EACH YEAR...EACH GENERATION...THAT REDUCTION GROWS EXPONENTIALLY.
BECAUSE OF YOU. BECAUSE OF SUPERMAN.
I THOUGHT THE ONLY WAY TO MAKE THEM BETTER WAS TO FORCE THEM INTO IT, THROUGH FEAR.
YOU GAVE THEM SOMETHING BETTER.
BRUCE... I DON'T KNOW WHAT TO SAY.
YOU GAVE ME MY LIFE BACK, BLUE. I WAS WASTING MYSELF ON THAT CRUSADE--WHEN I THINK ABOUT ALL THE GOOD I'VE DONE SINCE THEN...TWENTY-FIVE YEARS OF GOOD. ALL DUE TO YOU.
UNBELIEVABLE. I JUST HOPE YOU'RE WILLING TO SAY ALL THAT AGAIN WHEN DIANA GETS HERE.
DIANA?
WHO'S DIANA?

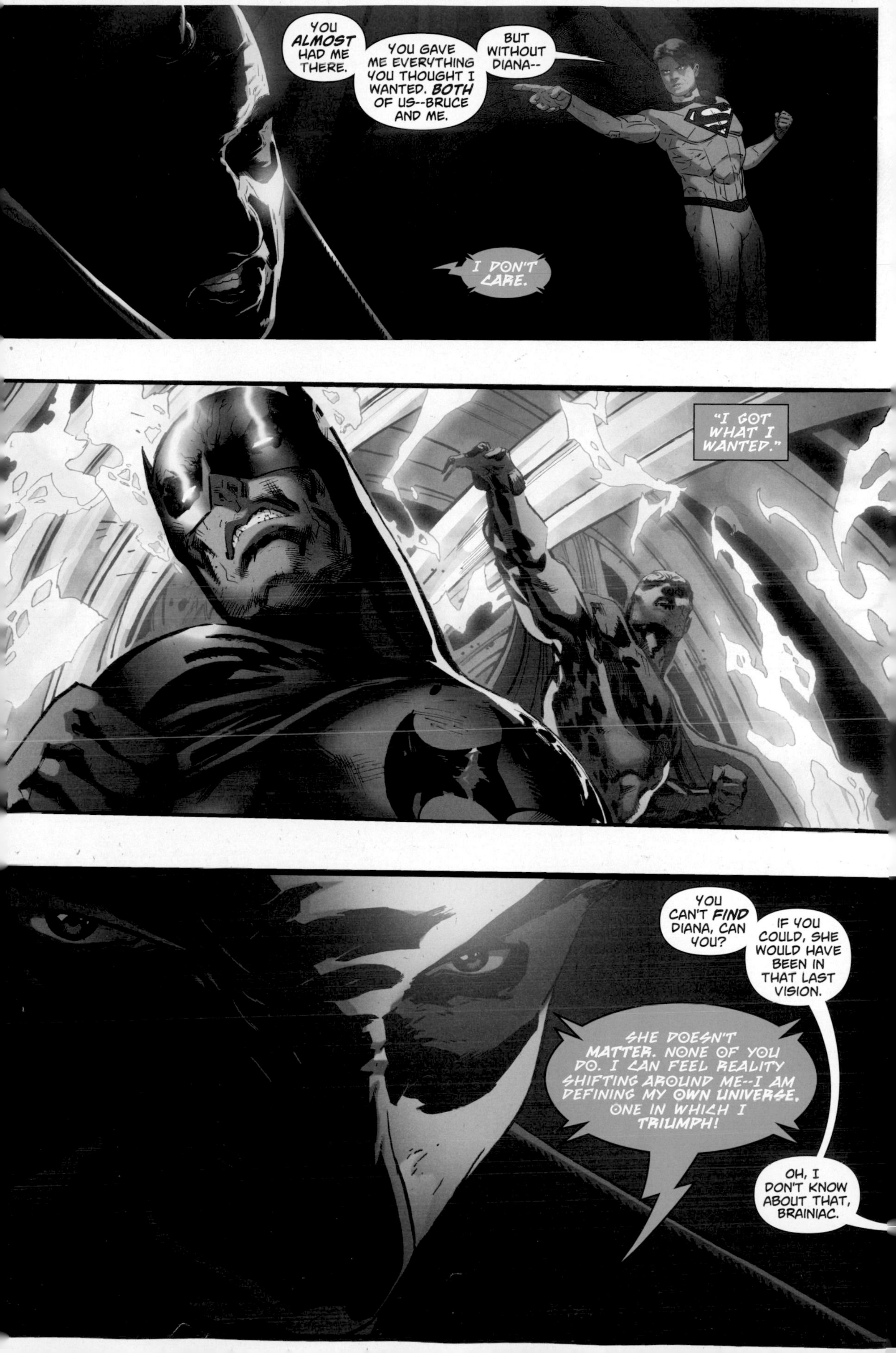
YOU ALMOST HAD ME THERE.
YOU GAVE ME EVERYTHING YOU THOUGHT I WANTED. BOTH OF US--BRUCE AND ME.
BUT WITHOUT DIANA--
I DON'T CARE.
"I GOT WHAT I WANTED."
YOU CAN'T FIND DIANA, CAN YOU?
IF YOU COULD, SHE WOULD HAVE BEEN IN THAT LAST VISION.
SHE DOESN'T MATTER. NONE OF YOU DO. I CAN FEEL REALITY SHIFTING AROUND ME--I AM DEFINING MY OWN UNIVERSE. ONE IN WHICH I TRIUMPH!
OH, I DON'T KNOW ABOUT THAT, BRAINIAC.

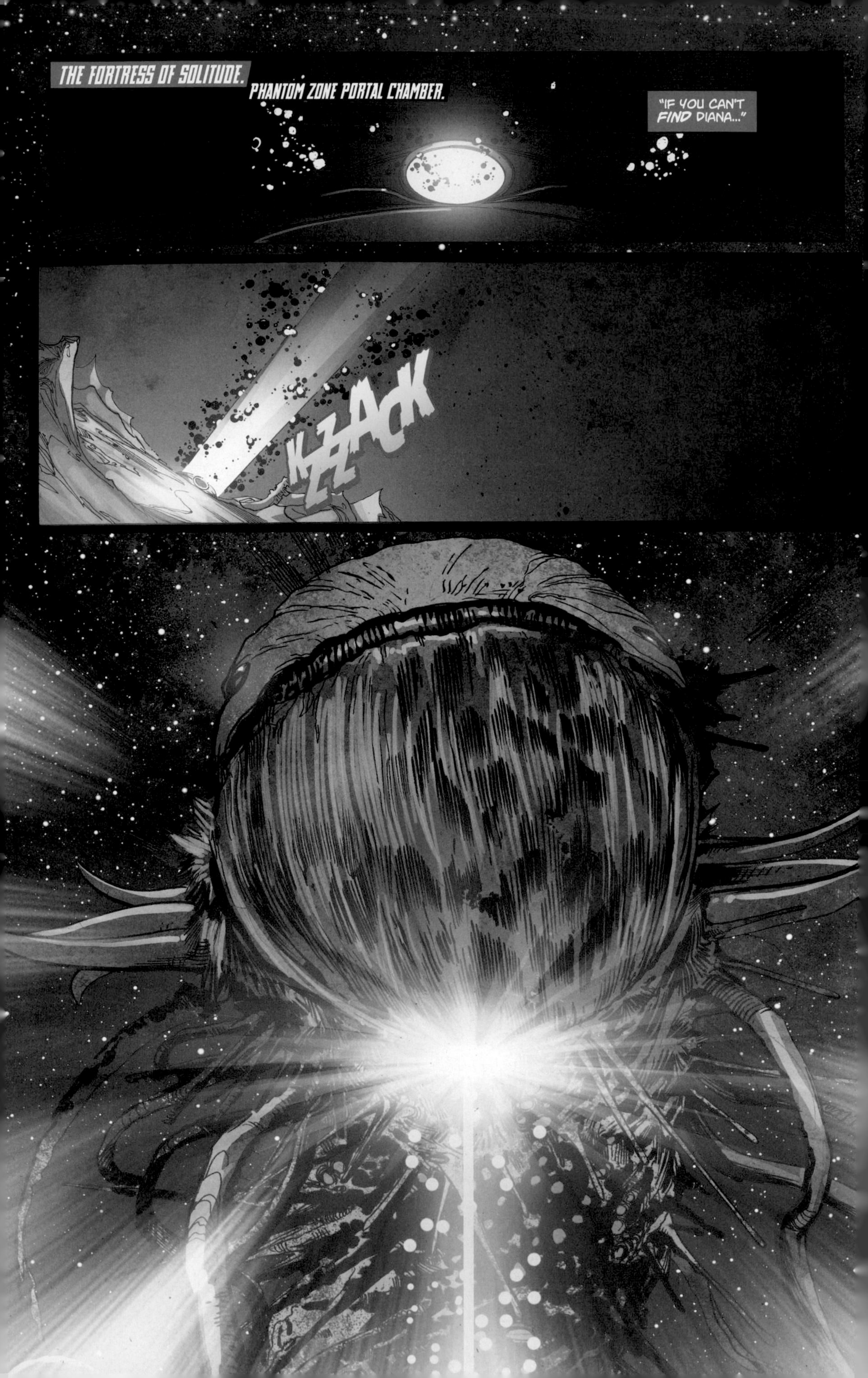
THE FORTRESS OF SOLITUDE.
PHANTOM ZONE PORTAL CHAMBER.
"IF YOU CAN'T FIND DIANA..."
KZZACK

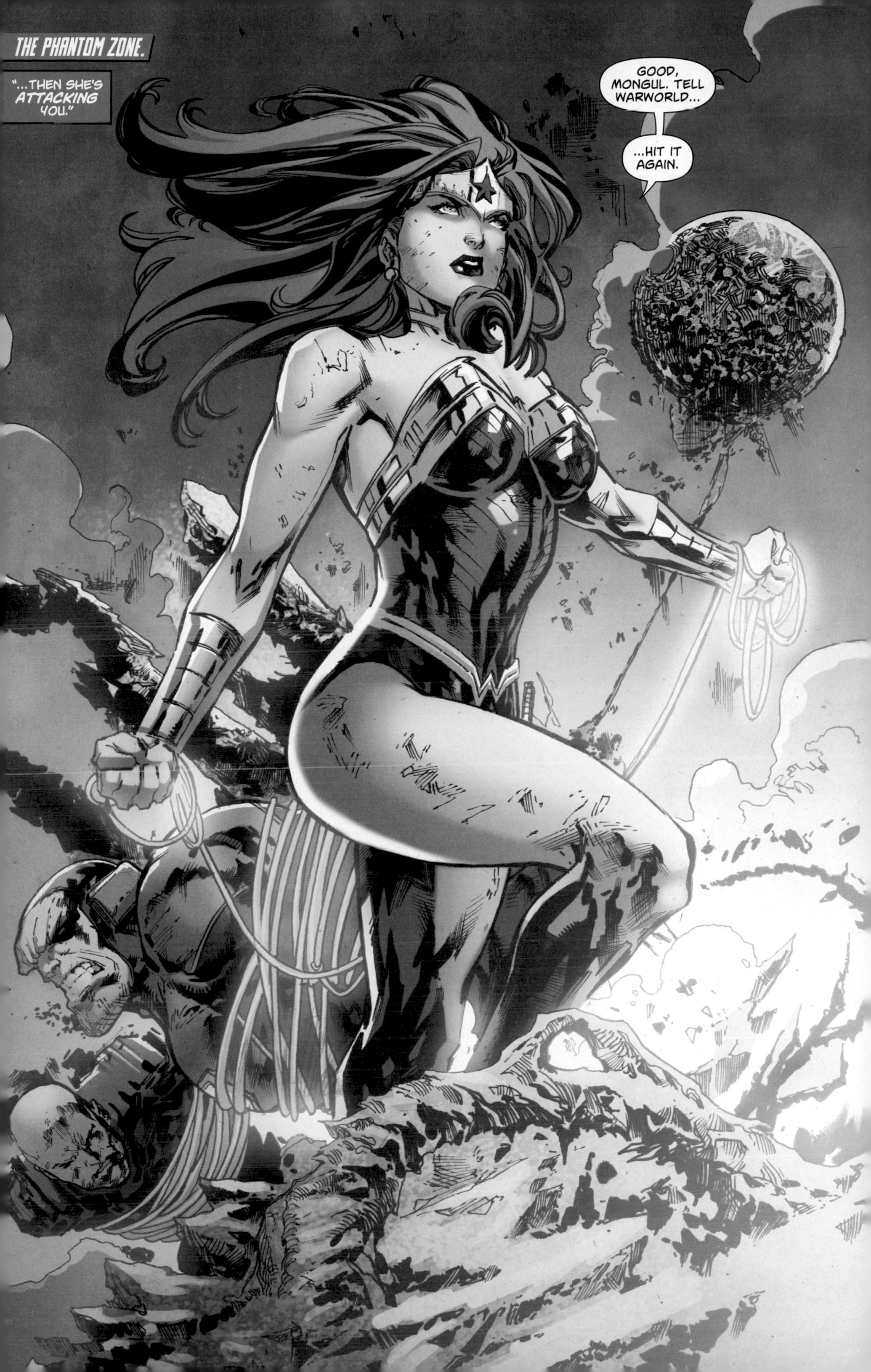
THE PHANTOM ZONE.
"...THEN SHE'S ATTACKING YOU."
GOOD, MONGUL. TELL WARWORLD...
...HIT IT AGAIN.

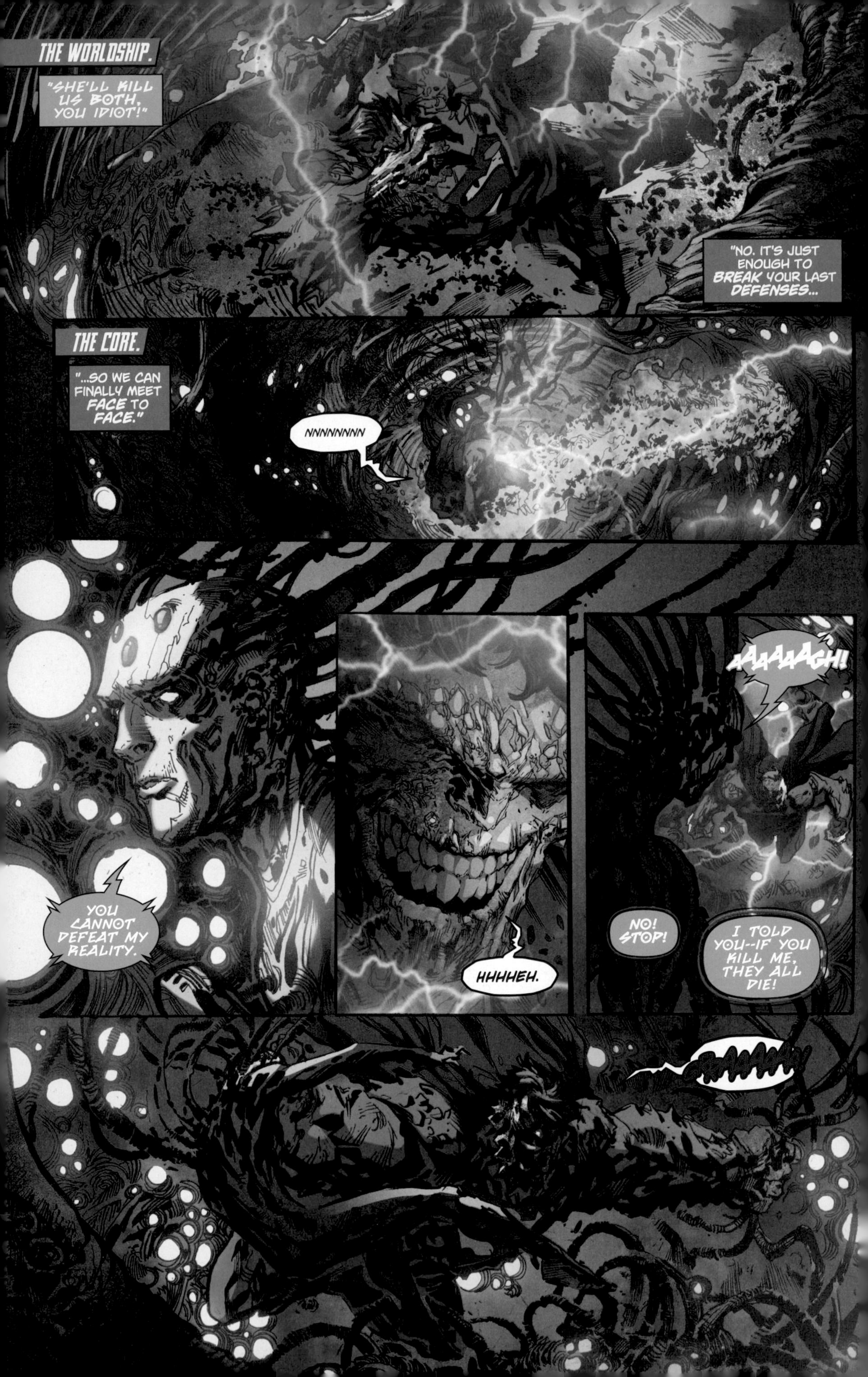
THE WORLDSHIP.
"SHE'LL KILL US BOTH, YOU IDIOT!"
"NO. IT'S JUST ENOUGH TO BREAK YOUR LAST DEFENSES...
THE CORE.
"...SO WE CAN FINALLY MEET FACE TO FACE."
NNNNNNNN
YOU CANNOT DEFEAT MY REALITY.
HHHHEH.
AAAAAAGH!
NO! STOP!
I TOLD YOU--IF YOU KILL ME, THEY ALL DIE!

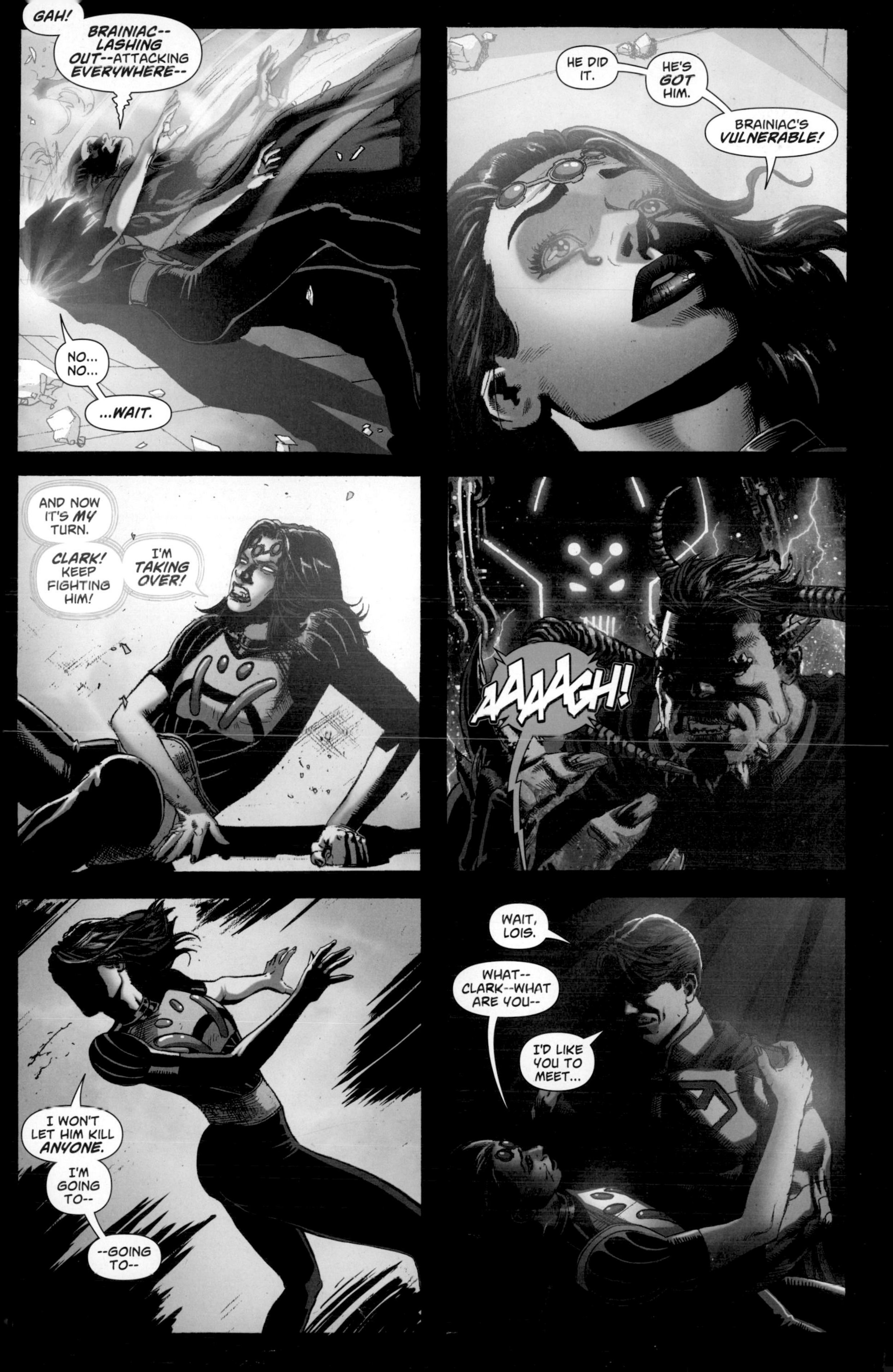
GAH!
BRAINIAC--LASHING OUT--ATTACKING EVERYWHERE--
NO... NO...
...WAIT.
HE DID IT.
HE'S GOT HIM.
BRAINIAC'S VULNERABLE!
AND NOW IT'S MY TURN.
CLARK! KEEP FIGHTING HIM!
I'M TAKING OVER!
AAAAGH!
I WON'T LET HIM KILL ANYONE.
I'M GOING TO--
--GOING TO--
WAIT, LOIS.
WHAT--CLARK--WHAT ARE YOU--
I'D LIKE YOU TO MEET...

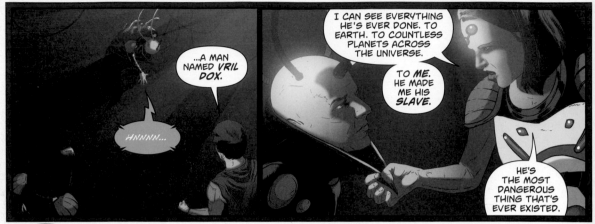

...A MAN NAMED *VRIL DOX.*

HNNNN...

I CAN SEE EVERYTHING HE'S EVER DONE. TO EARTH. TO COUNTLESS PLANETS ACROSS THE UNIVERSE.

TO *ME.* HE MADE ME HIS *SLAVE.*

HE'S THE MOST DANGEROUS THING THAT'S EVER EXISTED.

LANA WAS *RIGHT.* IT'S TIME TO *FINISH--*

THERE'S ANOTHER WAY.

ANOTHER WAY? DAMMIT, CLARK, DIDN'T YOU HEAR WHAT SHE SAID?

YOU'RE HOLDING HIS MIND IN YOUR HANDS, AND ALL HIS POWER ALONG WITH IT. ALMOST ANY-THING IS POSSIBLE FOR YOU NOW.

BUT FIRST...

CLARK...

...JUST TAKE A LOOK.

I...

"...I WAS A SCIENTIST."

"I HAD A WIFE."

"I HAD A SON.

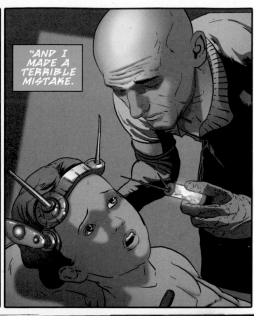

"AND I MADE A TERRIBLE MISTAKE."

"I TRIED TO EXPLAIN--I THOUGHT I WAS DOING THE RIGHT THING.

"THE PLANET WAS UNDER ATTACK. MY EXPERIMENTS WERE GOING TO SAVE THE WORLD.

"YOU UNDERSTAND, DON'T YOU?"

"BUT I FAILED...

"AND I LOST EVERYTHING.

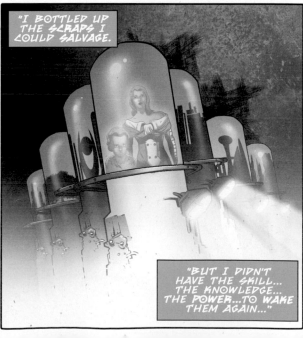

"I BOTTLED UP THE SCRAPS I COULD SALVAGE.

"BUT I DIDN'T HAVE THE SKILL... THE KNOWLEDGE... THE POWER...TO WAKE THEM AGAIN..."

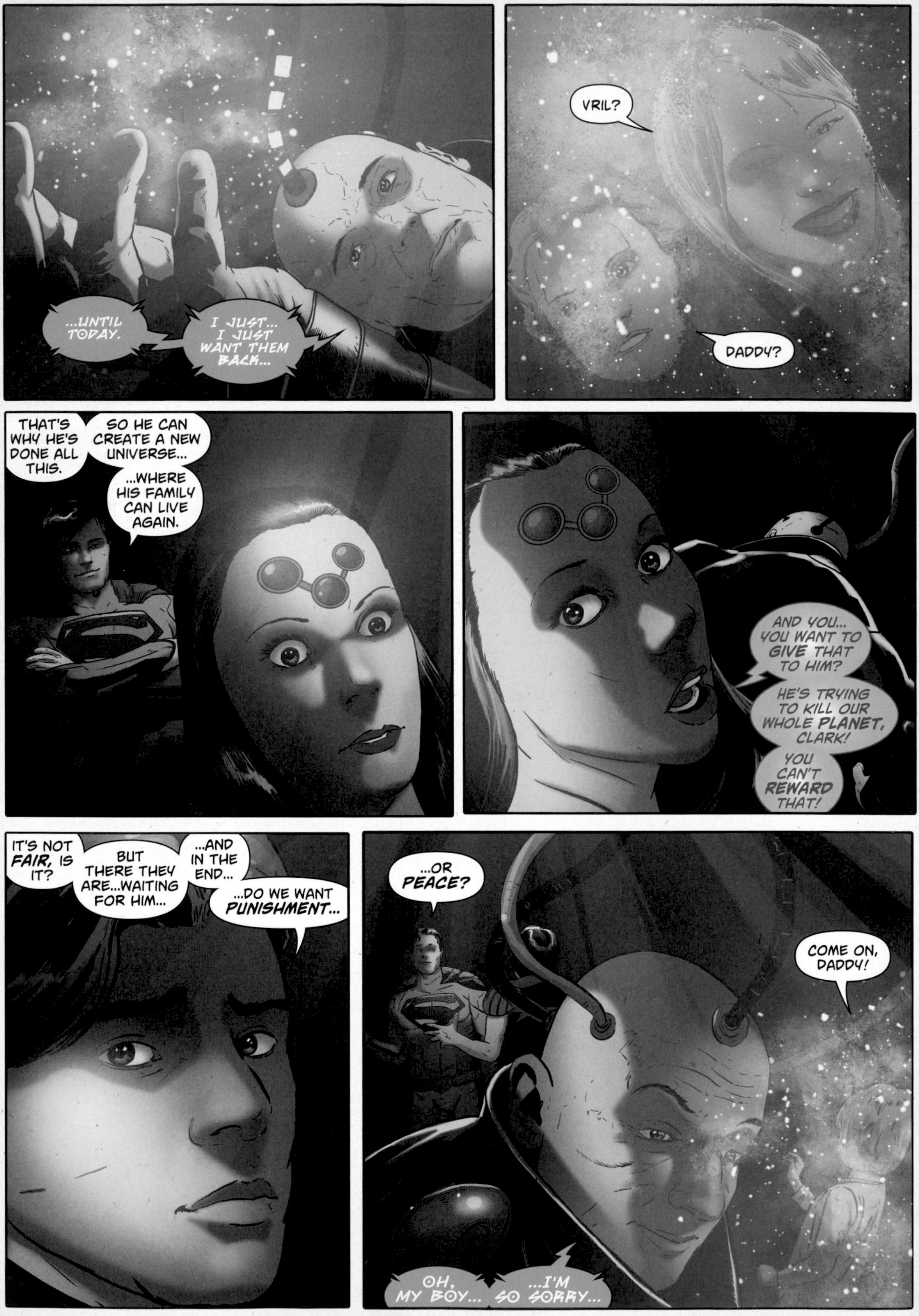
...UNTIL TODAY.
I JUST... I JUST WANT THEM BACK...
VRIL?
DADDY?
THAT'S WHY HE'S DONE ALL THIS.
SO HE CAN CREATE A NEW UNIVERSE...
...WHERE HIS FAMILY CAN LIVE AGAIN.
AND YOU... YOU WANT TO GIVE THAT TO HIM?
HE'S TRYING TO KILL OUR WHOLE PLANET, CLARK!
YOU CAN'T REWARD THAT!
IT'S NOT FAIR, IS IT?
BUT THERE THEY ARE...WAITING FOR HIM...
...AND IN THE END...
...DO WE WANT PUNISHMENT...
...OR PEACE?
COME ON, DADDY!
OH, MY BOY...
...I'M SO SORRY...

...BUT DADDY'S WORKING.

NO! BRAINIAC--

--YOU'RE KILLING THEM!

DAAAADDDY!

DOESN'T MATTER. I CAN RECREATE THEM, AGAIN AND AGAIN, UNTIL I GET IT RIGHT.

ONCE I TAKE BACK THE POWER YOU STOLE, I CAN DO ANYTHING.

NO! LOIS!

...HE'S--HE'S BREAKING IN.

MY BRAIN... JUST HUMAN... TOO VULNERABLE...

CLARK...

...THERE'S ANOTHER WAY...

...BUT... WILL...

...WILL YOU DO WHAT HAS TO BE DONE?

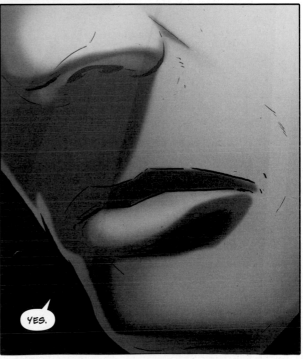

YES.

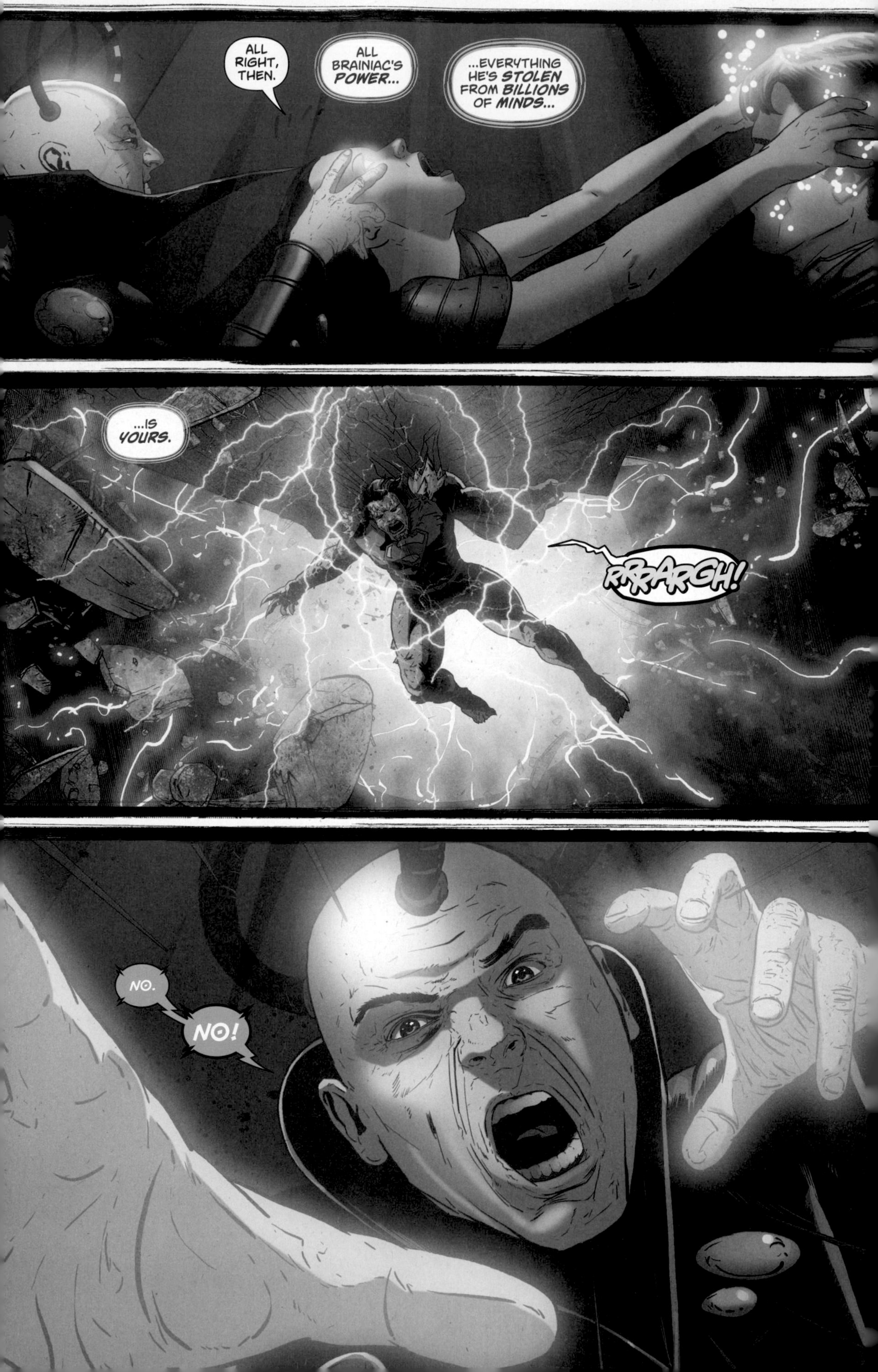
ALL RIGHT, THEN.
ALL BRAINIAC'S POWER...
...EVERYTHING HE'S STOLEN FROM BILLIONS OF MINDS...
...IS YOURS.
RRRARGH!
NO.
NO!

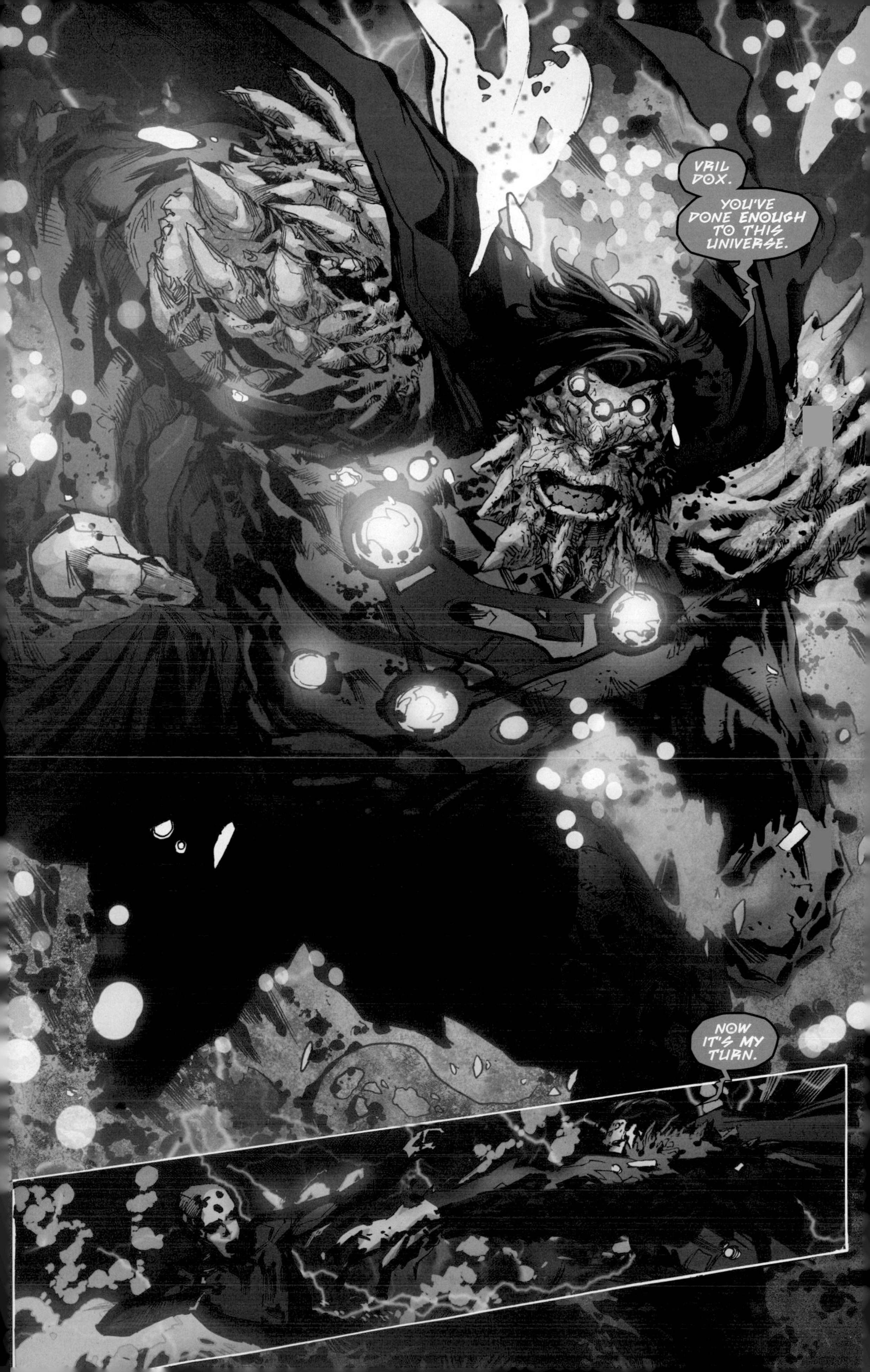
VRIL DOX.
YOU'VE DONE ENOUGH TO THIS UNIVERSE.
NOW IT'S MY TURN.

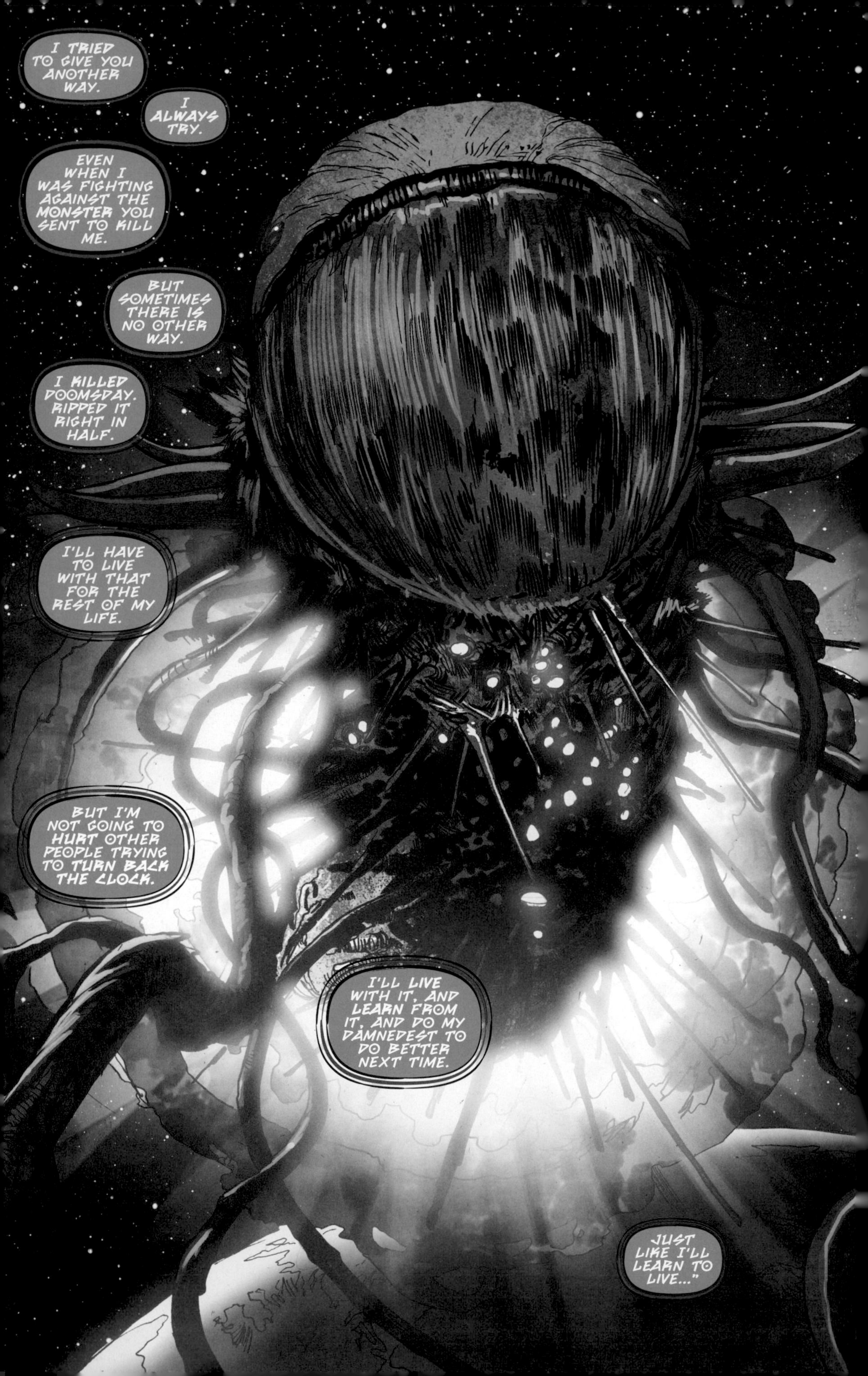
I TRIED TO GIVE YOU ANOTHER WAY.
I ALWAYS TRY.
EVEN WHEN I WAS FIGHTING AGAINST THE MONSTER YOU SENT TO KILL ME.
BUT SOMETIMES THERE IS NO OTHER WAY.
I KILLED DOOMSDAY. RIPPED IT RIGHT IN HALF.
I'LL HAVE TO LIVE WITH THAT FOR THE REST OF MY LIFE.
BUT I'M NOT GOING TO HURT OTHER PEOPLE TRYING TO TURN BACK THE CLOCK.
I'LL LIVE WITH IT, AND LEARN FROM IT, AND DO MY DAMNEDEST TO DO BETTER NEXT TIME.
JUST LIKE I'LL LEARN TO LIVE..."

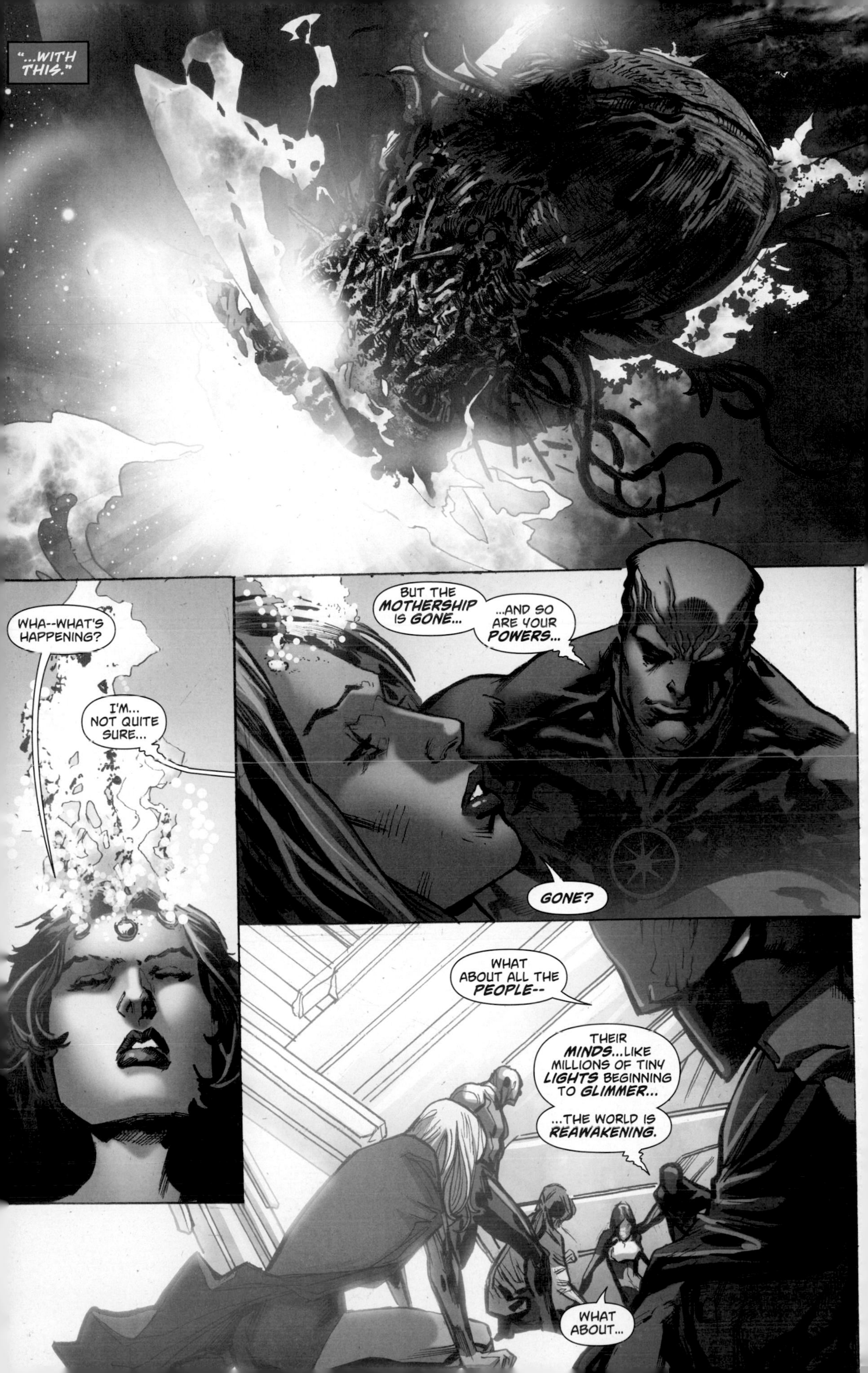
"...WITH THIS."
WHA--WHAT'S HAPPENING?
I'M... NOT QUITE SURE...
BUT THE MOTHERSHIP IS GONE...
...AND SO ARE YOUR POWERS...
GONE?
WHAT ABOUT ALL THE PEOPLE--
THEIR MINDS...LIKE MILLIONS OF TINY LIGHTS BEGINNING TO GLIMMER...
...THE WORLD IS REAWAKENING.
WHAT ABOUT...

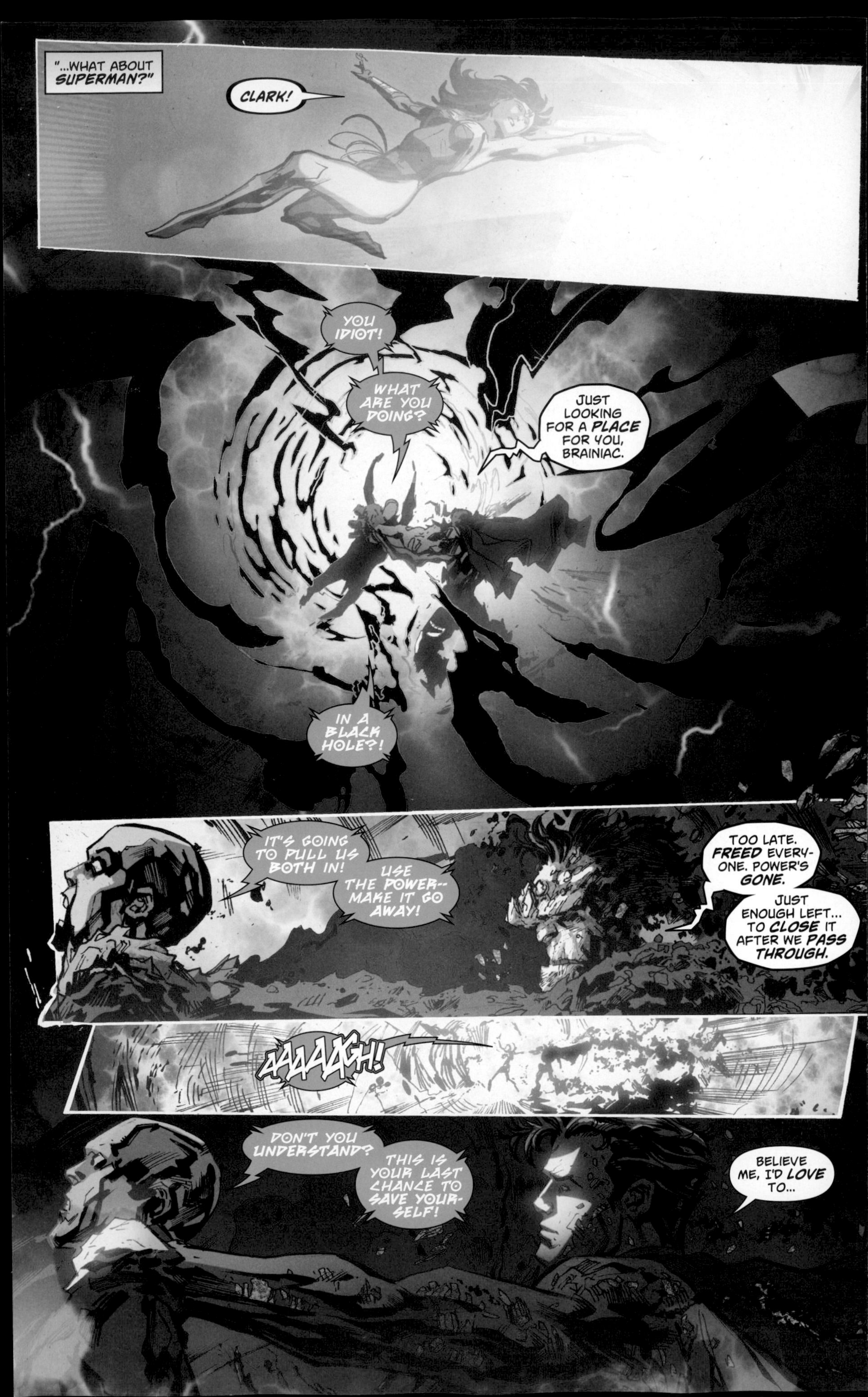
"...WHAT ABOUT SUPERMAN?"
CLARK!
YOU IDIOT!
WHAT ARE YOU DOING?
JUST LOOKING FOR A PLACE FOR YOU, BRAINIAC.
IN A BLACK HOLE?!
IT'S GOING TO PULL US BOTH IN!
USE THE POWER-- MAKE IT GO AWAY!
TOO LATE. FREED EVERY-ONE. POWER'S GONE.
JUST ENOUGH LEFT... TO CLOSE IT AFTER WE PASS THROUGH.
AAAAAGH!
DON'T YOU UNDERSTAND?
THIS IS YOUR LAST CHANCE TO SAVE YOUR-SELF!
BELIEVE ME, I'D LOVE TO...

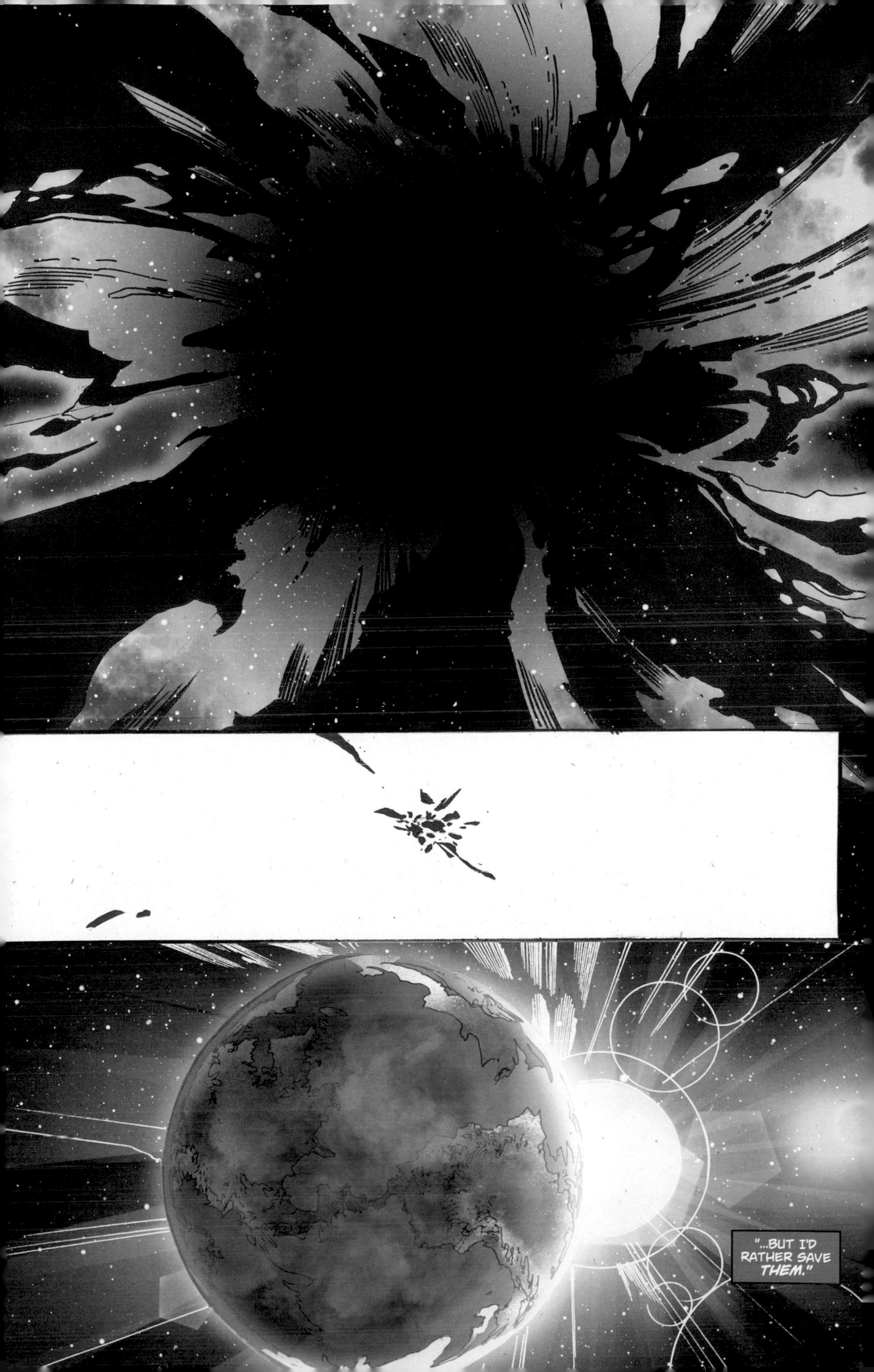
"...BUT I'D RATHER SAVE THEM."

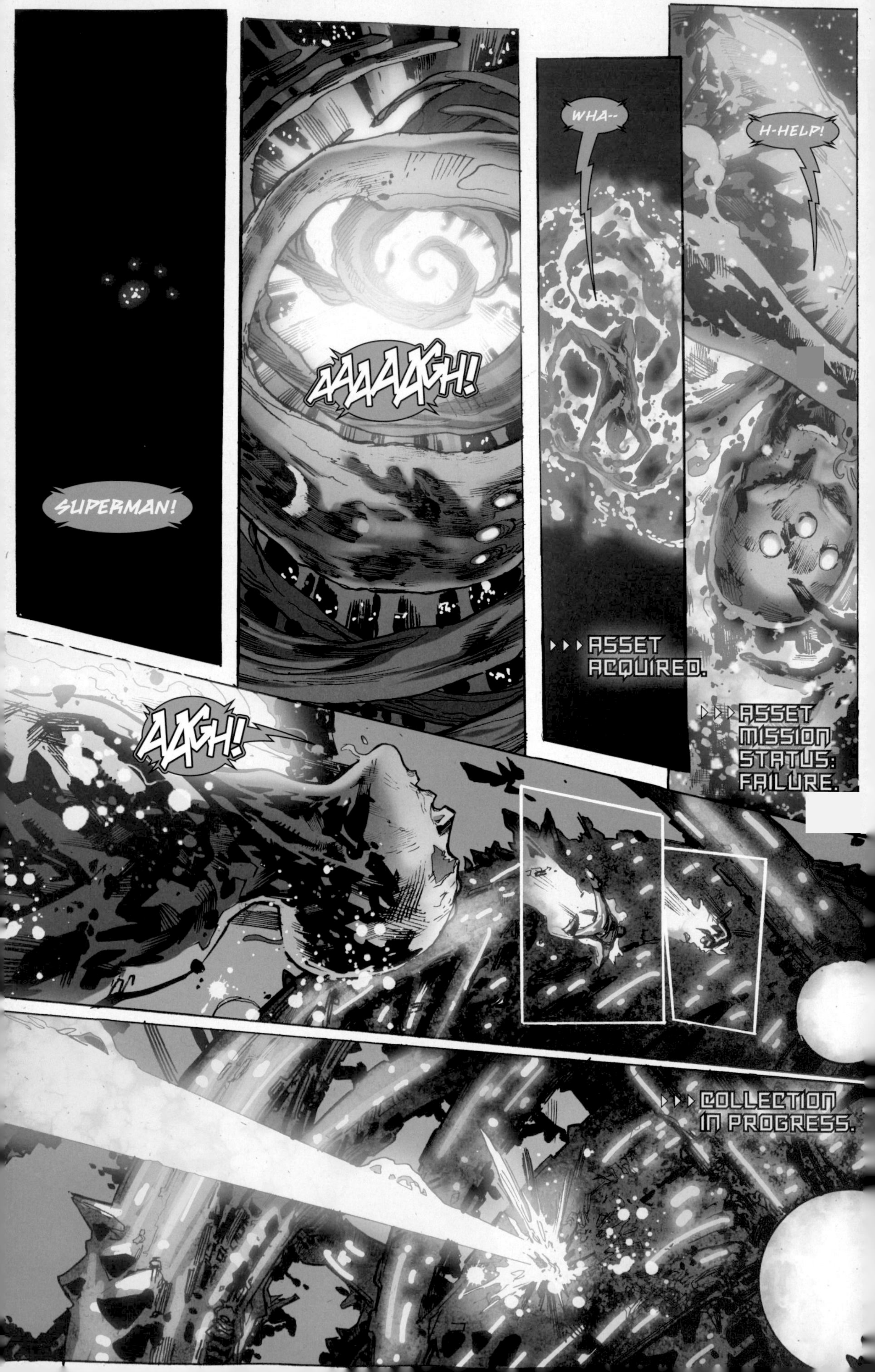
SUPERMAN!
AAAAAGH!
WHA--
H-HELP!
ASSET ACQUIRED.
ASSET MISSION STATUS: FAILURE.
AAGH!
COLLECTION IN PROGRESS.

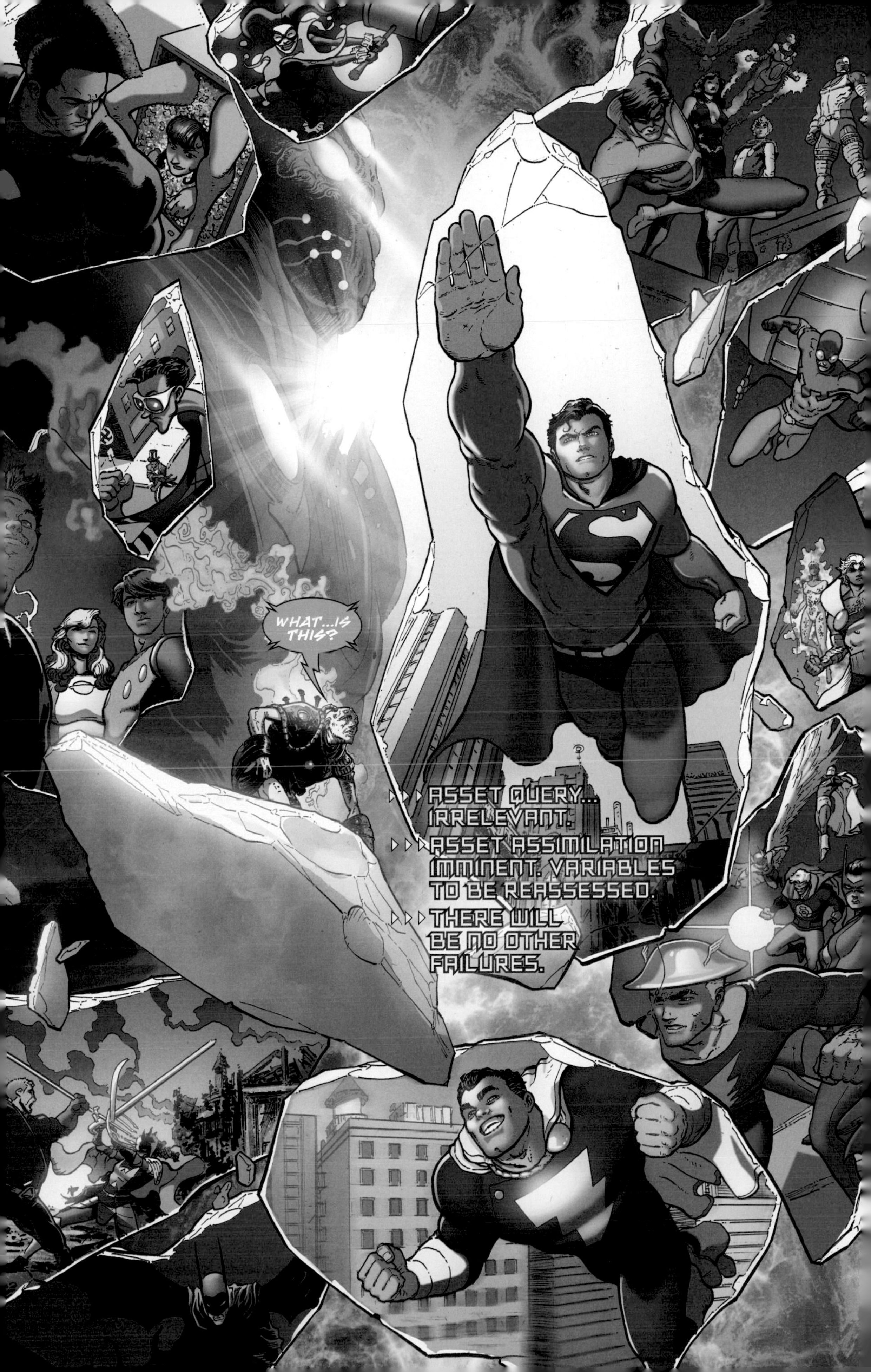
WHAT...IS THIS?
ASSET QUERY... IRRELEVANT.
ASSET ASSIMILATION IMMINENT. VARIABLES TO BE REASSESSED.
THERE WILL BE NO OTHER FAILURES.

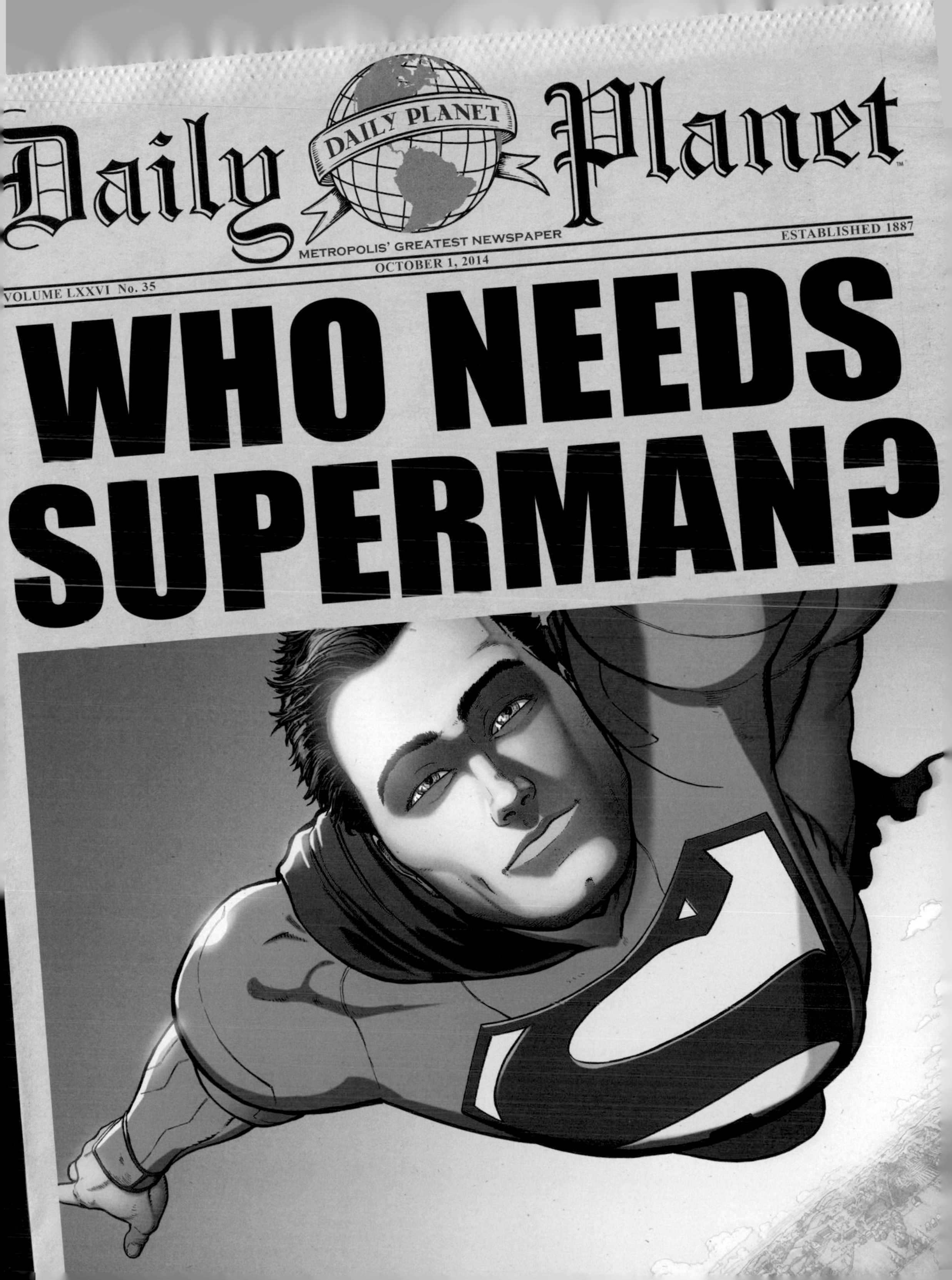
Daily Planet
DAILY PLANET
METROPOLIS' GREATEST NEWSPAPER
ESTABLISHED 1887
OCTOBER 1, 2014
VOLUME LXXVI No. 35
WHO NEEDS SUPERMAN?

SUPERMAN

DOOMED

[AFTERMATH] chapter 1

"AFTER DOOMED"

STORY
GREG PAK

ART
SCOTT KOLINS AND **VICENTE CIFUENTES**

COLORS
WIL QUINTANA

LETTERS
CARLOS M. MANGUAL

COVER
AARON KUDER AND **WIL QUINTANA**

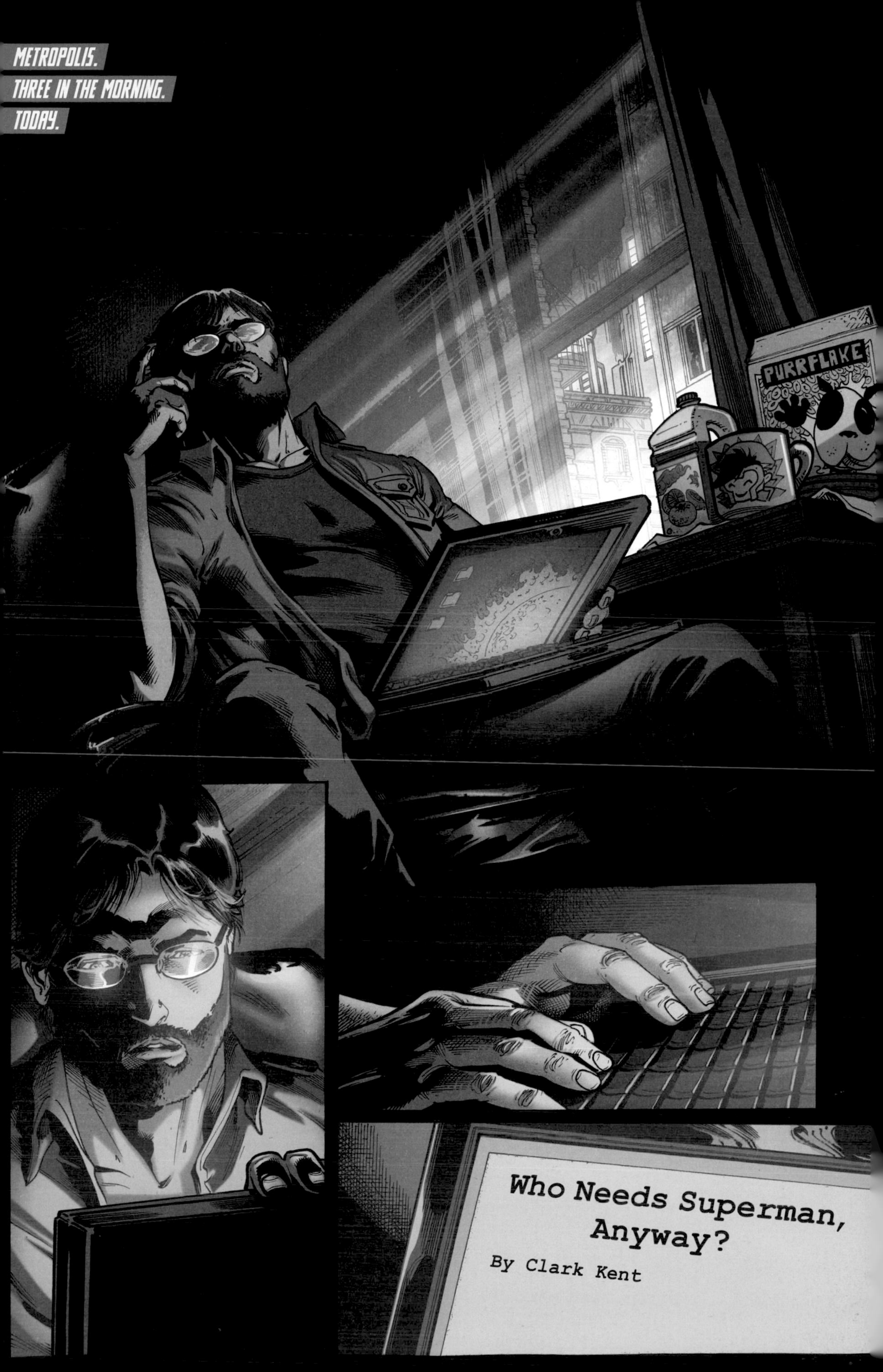
METROPOLIS.
THREE IN THE MORNING.
TODAY.
PURRFLAKE
Who Needs Superman, Anyway?
By Clark Kent

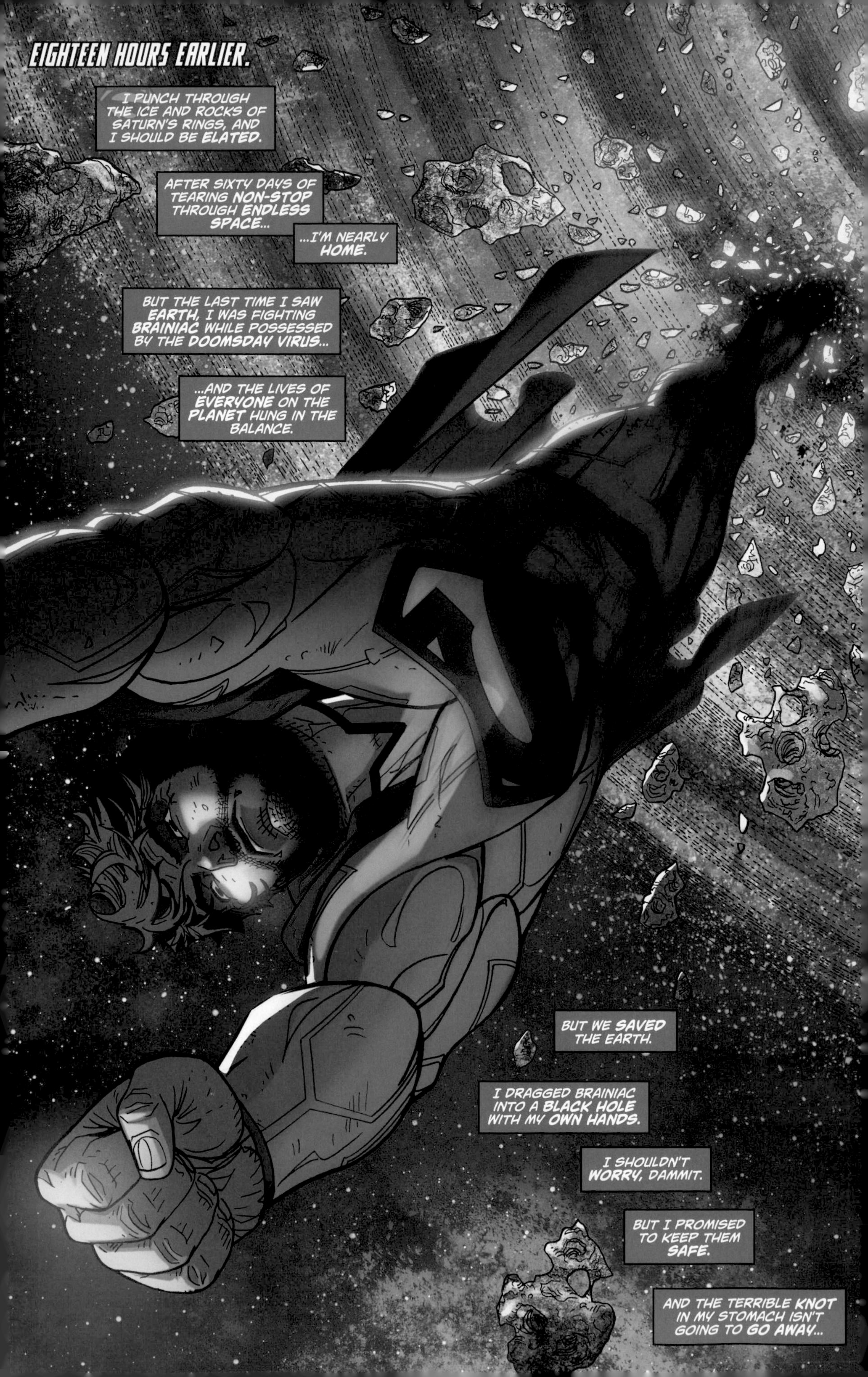
EIGHTEEN HOURS EARLIER.
I PUNCH THROUGH THE ICE AND ROCKS OF SATURN'S RINGS, AND I SHOULD BE ELATED.
AFTER SIXTY DAYS OF TEARING NON-STOP THROUGH ENDLESS SPACE...
...I'M NEARLY HOME.
BUT THE LAST TIME I SAW EARTH, I WAS FIGHTING BRAINIAC WHILE POSSESSED BY THE DOOMSDAY VIRUS...
...AND THE LIVES OF EVERYONE ON THE PLANET HUNG IN THE BALANCE.
BUT WE SAVED THE EARTH.
I DRAGGED BRAINIAC INTO A BLACK HOLE WITH MY OWN HANDS.
I SHOULDN'T WORRY, DAMMIT.
BUT I PROMISED TO KEEP THEM SAFE.
AND THE TERRIBLE KNOT IN MY STOMACH ISN'T GOING TO GO AWAY...

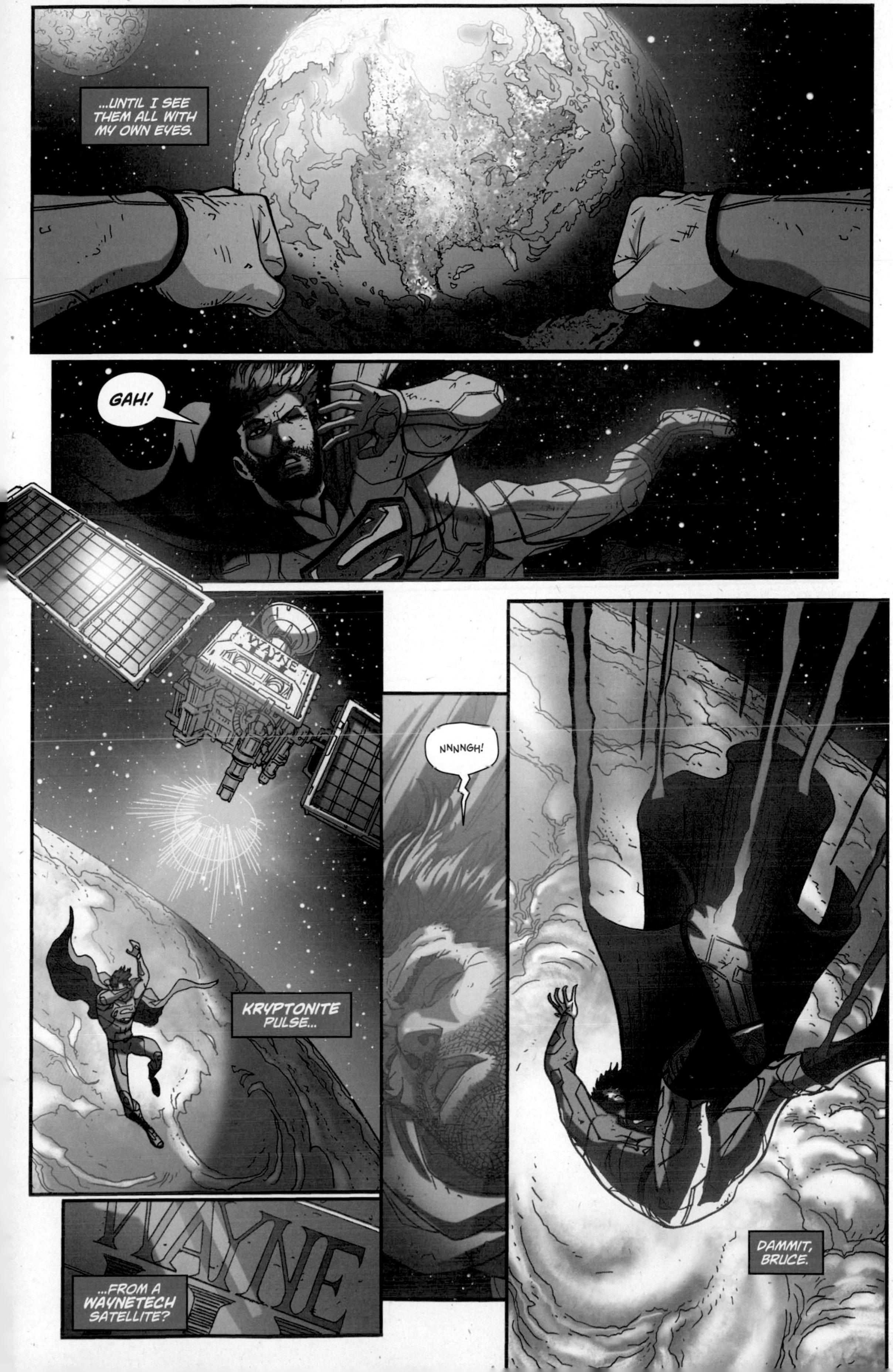
...UNTIL I SEE THEM ALL WITH MY OWN EYES.
GAH!
WAYNE
KRYPTONITE PULSE...
WAYNE
...FROM A WAYNETECH SATELLITE?
NNNNGH!
DAMMIT, BRUCE.

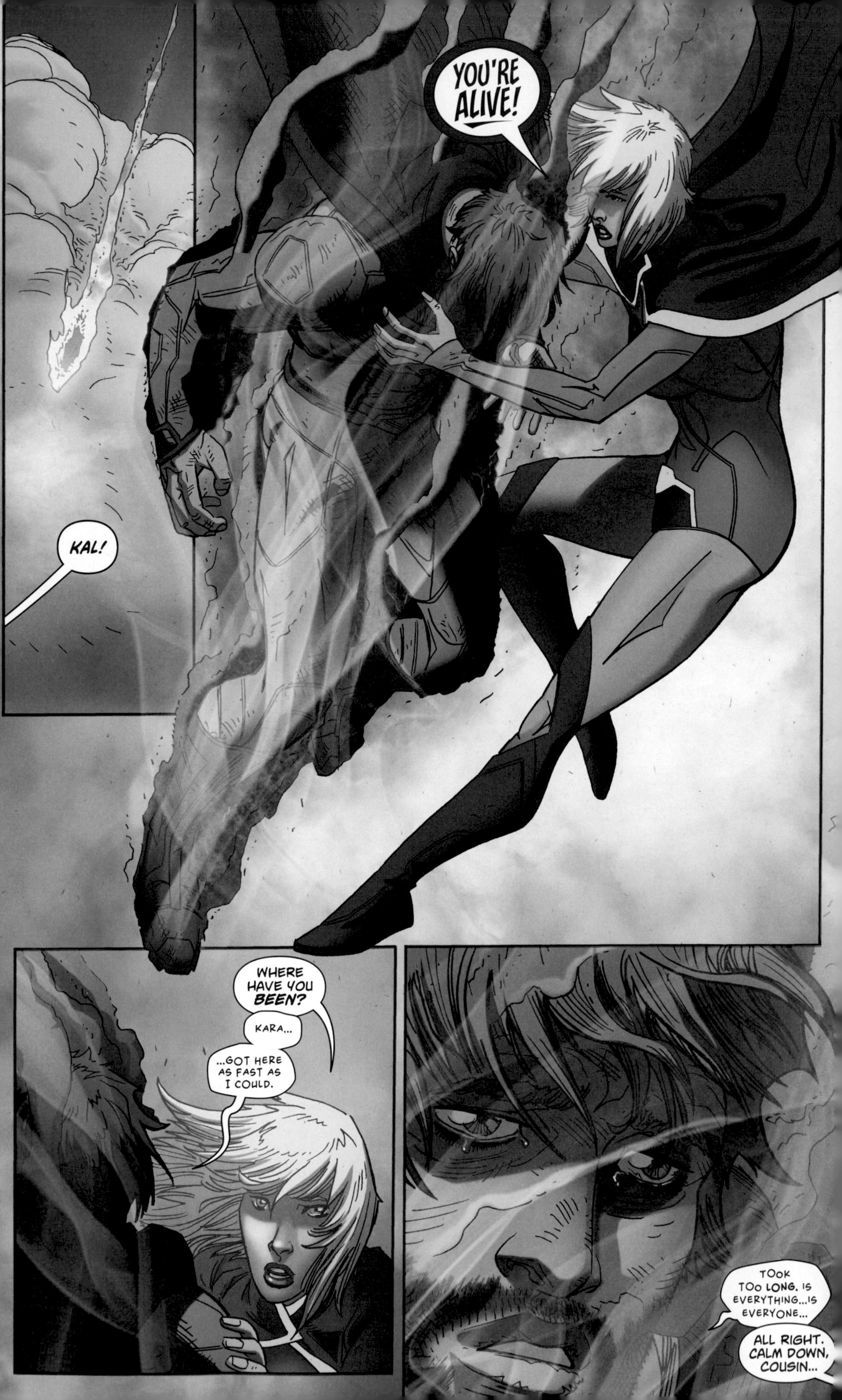
YOU'RE ALIVE!
KAL!
WHERE HAVE YOU BEEN?
KARA...
...GOT HERE AS FAST AS I COULD.
TOOK TOO LONG. IS EVERYTHING...IS EVERYONE...
ALL RIGHT. CALM DOWN, COUSIN...

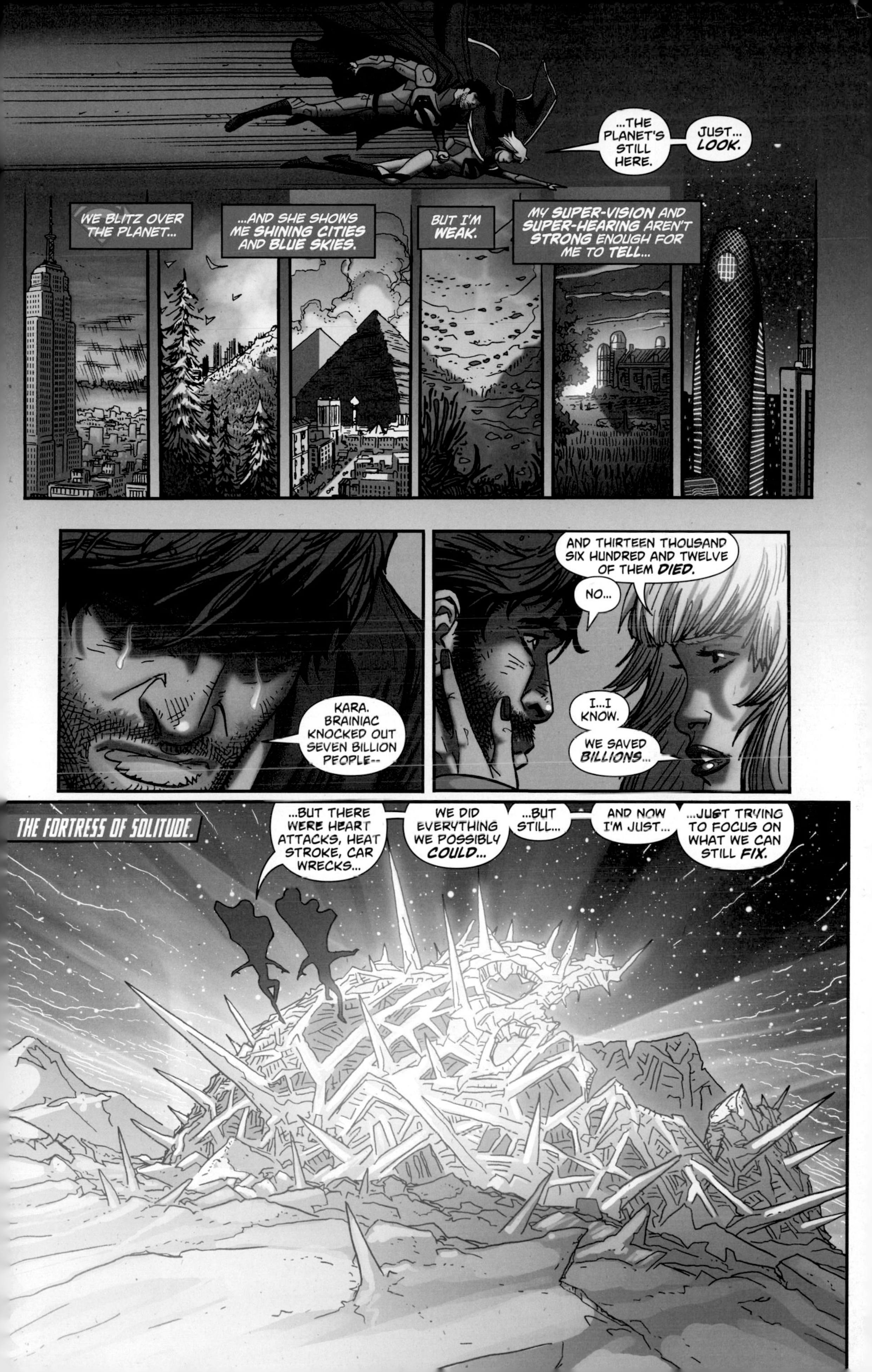
...THE PLANET'S STILL HERE.
JUST... LOOK.
WE BLITZ OVER THE PLANET...
...AND SHE SHOWS ME SHINING CITIES AND BLUE SKIES.
BUT I'M WEAK.
MY SUPER-VISION AND SUPER-HEARING AREN'T STRONG ENOUGH FOR ME TO TELL...
KARA. BRAINIAC KNOCKED OUT SEVEN BILLION PEOPLE--
AND THIRTEEN THOUSAND SIX HUNDRED AND TWELVE OF THEM DIED.
NO...
I...I KNOW.
WE SAVED BILLIONS...
THE FORTRESS OF SOLITUDE.
...BUT THERE WERE HEART ATTACKS, HEAT STROKE, CAR WRECKS...
WE DID EVERYTHING WE POSSIBLY COULD...
...BUT STILL...
AND NOW I'M JUST...
...JUST TRYING TO FOCUS ON WHAT WE CAN STILL FIX.

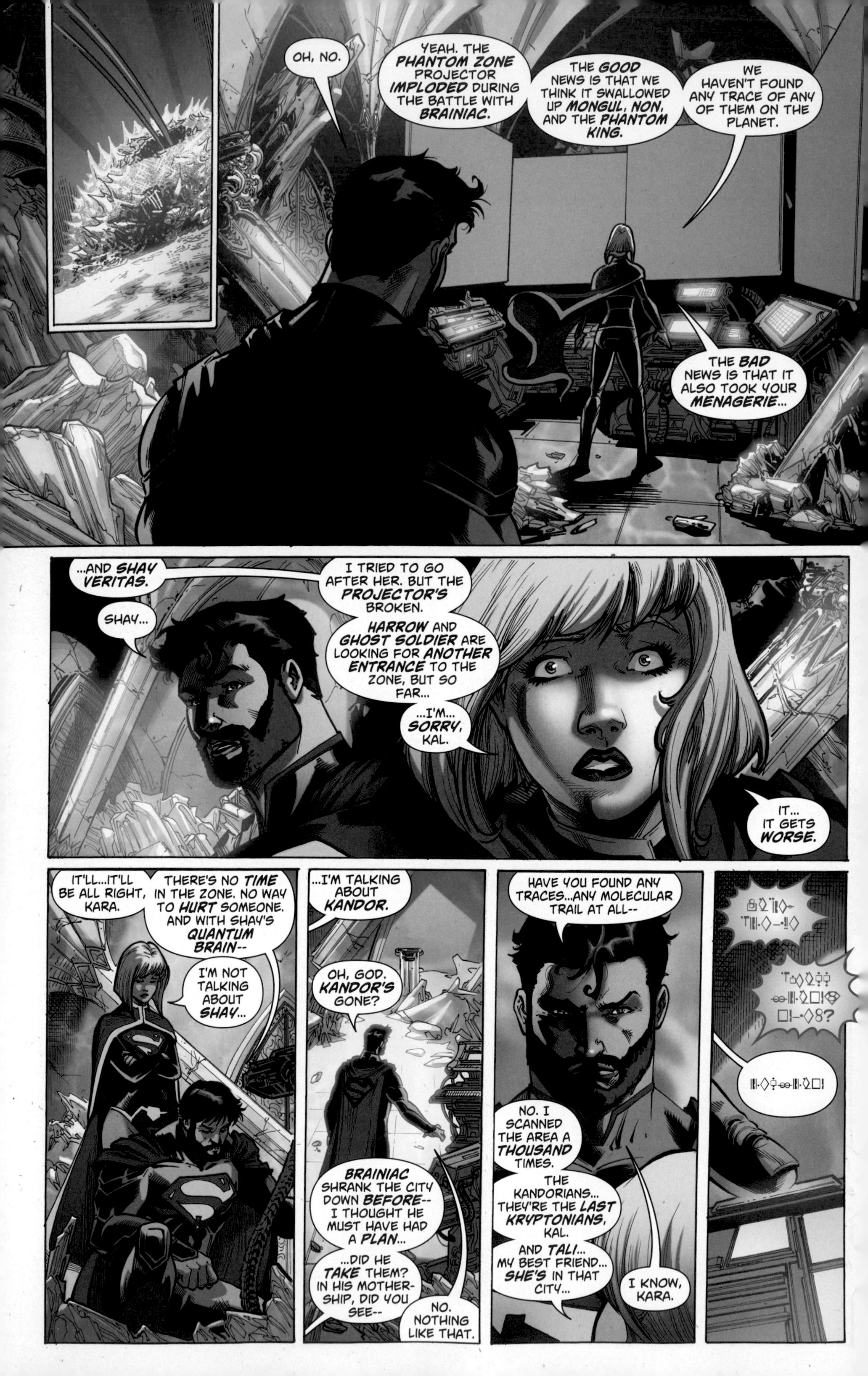
OH, NO.
YEAH. THE PHANTOM ZONE PROJECTOR IMPLODED DURING THE BATTLE WITH BRAINIAC.
THE GOOD NEWS IS THAT WE THINK IT SWALLOWED UP MONGUL, NON, AND THE PHANTOM KING.
WE HAVEN'T FOUND ANY TRACE OF ANY OF THEM ON THE PLANET.
THE BAD NEWS IS THAT IT ALSO TOOK YOUR MENAGERIE...
...AND SHAY VERITAS.
SHAY...
I TRIED TO GO AFTER HER. BUT THE PROJECTOR'S BROKEN.
HARROW AND GHOST SOLDIER ARE LOOKING FOR ANOTHER ENTRANCE TO THE ZONE, BUT SO FAR...
...I'M... SORRY, KAL.
IT... IT GETS WORSE.
IT'LL...IT'LL BE ALL RIGHT, KARA.
THERE'S NO TIME IN THE ZONE. NO WAY TO HURT SOMEONE. AND WITH SHAY'S QUANTUM BRAIN--
I'M NOT TALKING ABOUT SHAY...
...I'M TALKING ABOUT KANDOR.
OH, GOD. KANDOR'S GONE?
BRAINIAC SHRANK THE CITY DOWN BEFORE-- I THOUGHT HE MUST HAVE HAD A PLAN...
...DID HE TAKE THEM? IN HIS MOTHER-SHIP, DID YOU SEE--
NO. NOTHING LIKE THAT.
HAVE YOU FOUND ANY TRACES...ANY MOLECULAR TRAIL AT ALL--
NO. I SCANNED THE AREA A THOUSAND TIMES.
THE KANDORIANS... THEY'RE THE LAST KRYPTONIANS, KAL.
AND TALI... MY BEST FRIEND... SHE'S IN THAT CITY...
I KNOW, KARA.

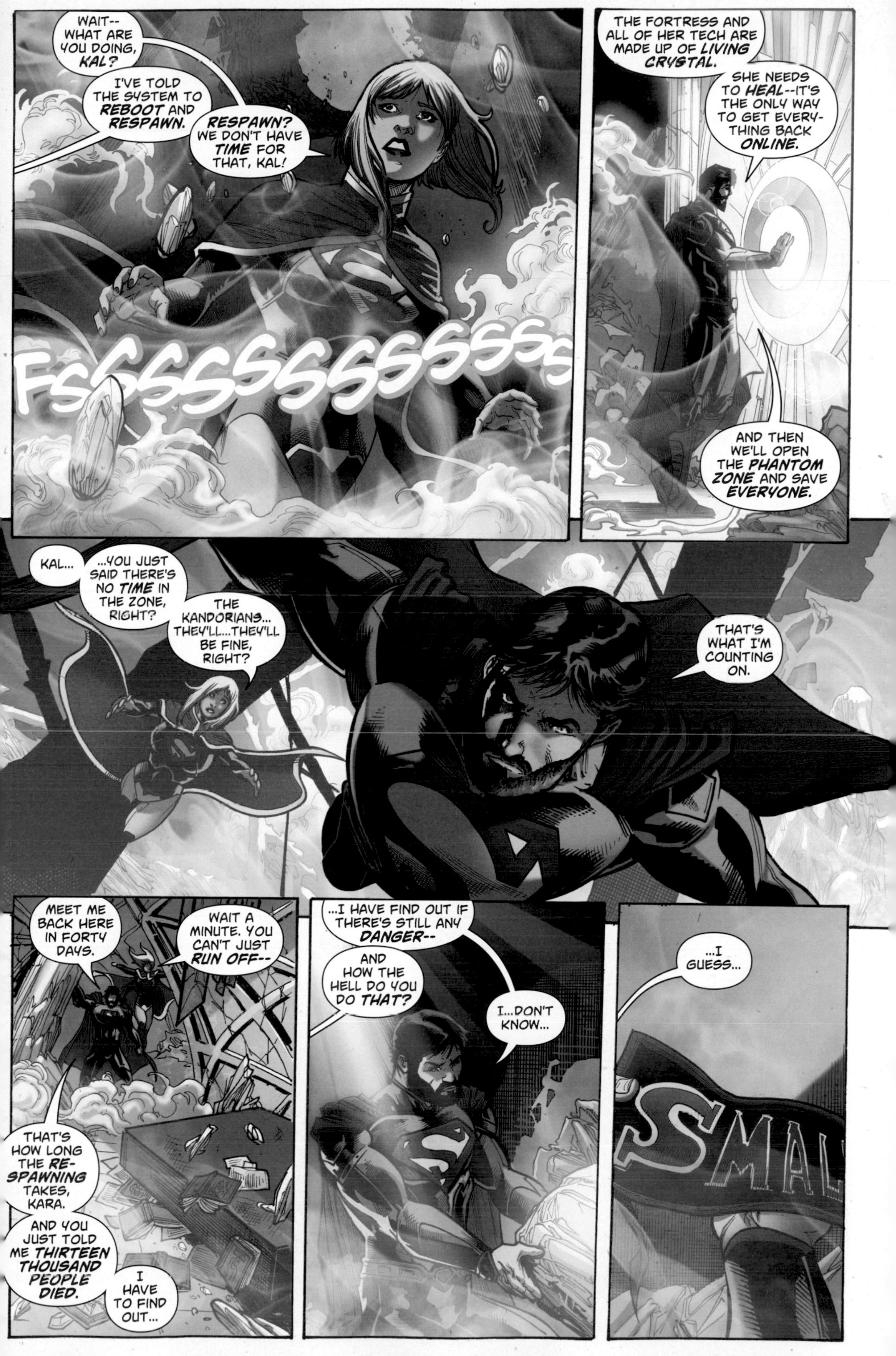
WAIT-- WHAT ARE YOU DOING, KAL?
I'VE TOLD THE SYSTEM TO REBOOT AND RESPAWN.
RESPAWN? WE DON'T HAVE TIME FOR THAT, KAL!
FSSSSSSSSSSSS
THE FORTRESS AND ALL OF HER TECH ARE MADE UP OF LIVING CRYSTAL.
SHE NEEDS TO HEAL--IT'S THE ONLY WAY TO GET EVERY-THING BACK ONLINE.
AND THEN WE'LL OPEN THE PHANTOM ZONE AND SAVE EVERYONE.
KAL...
...YOU JUST SAID THERE'S NO TIME IN THE ZONE, RIGHT?
THE KANDORIANS... THEY'LL...THEY'LL BE FINE, RIGHT?
THAT'S WHAT I'M COUNTING ON.
MEET ME BACK HERE IN FORTY DAYS.
WAIT A MINUTE. YOU CAN'T JUST RUN OFF--
THAT'S HOW LONG THE RE-SPAWNING TAKES, KARA.
AND YOU JUST TOLD ME THIRTEEN THOUSAND PEOPLE DIED.
I HAVE TO FIND OUT...
...I HAVE FIND OUT IF THERE'S STILL ANY DANGER--
AND HOW THE HELL DO YOU DO THAT?
I...DON'T KNOW...
...I GUESS...

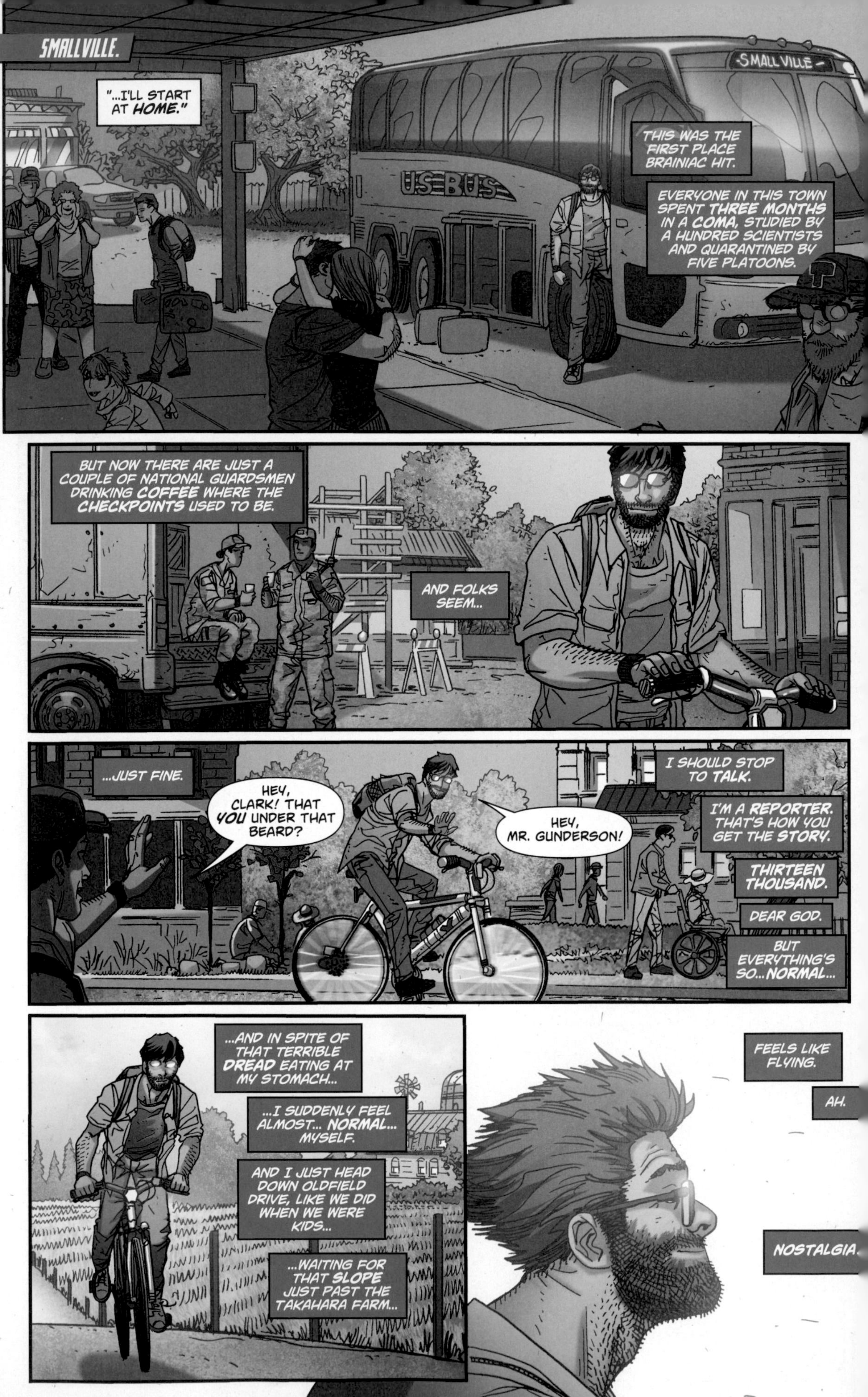
SMALLVILLE.
-SMALLVILLE-
"...I'LL START AT HOME."
US BUS
THIS WAS THE FIRST PLACE BRAINIAC HIT.
EVERYONE IN THIS TOWN SPENT THREE MONTHS IN A COMA, STUDIED BY A HUNDRED SCIENTISTS AND QUARANTINED BY FIVE PLATOONS.
BUT NOW THERE ARE JUST A COUPLE OF NATIONAL GUARDSMEN DRINKING COFFEE WHERE THE CHECKPOINTS USED TO BE.
AND FOLKS SEEM...
...JUST FINE.
HEY, CLARK! THAT YOU UNDER THAT BEARD?
HEY, MR. GUNDERSON!
I SHOULD STOP TO TALK.
I'M A REPORTER. THAT'S HOW YOU GET THE STORY.
THIRTEEN THOUSAND.
DEAR GOD.
BUT EVERYTHING'S SO...NORMAL...
...AND IN SPITE OF THAT TERRIBLE DREAD EATING AT MY STOMACH...
...I SUDDENLY FEEL ALMOST... NORMAL... MYSELF.
AND I JUST HEAD DOWN OLDFIELD DRIVE, LIKE WE DID WHEN WE WERE KIDS...
...WAITING FOR THAT SLOPE JUST PAST THE TAKAHARA FARM...
FEELS LIKE FLYING.
AH.
NOSTALGIA.

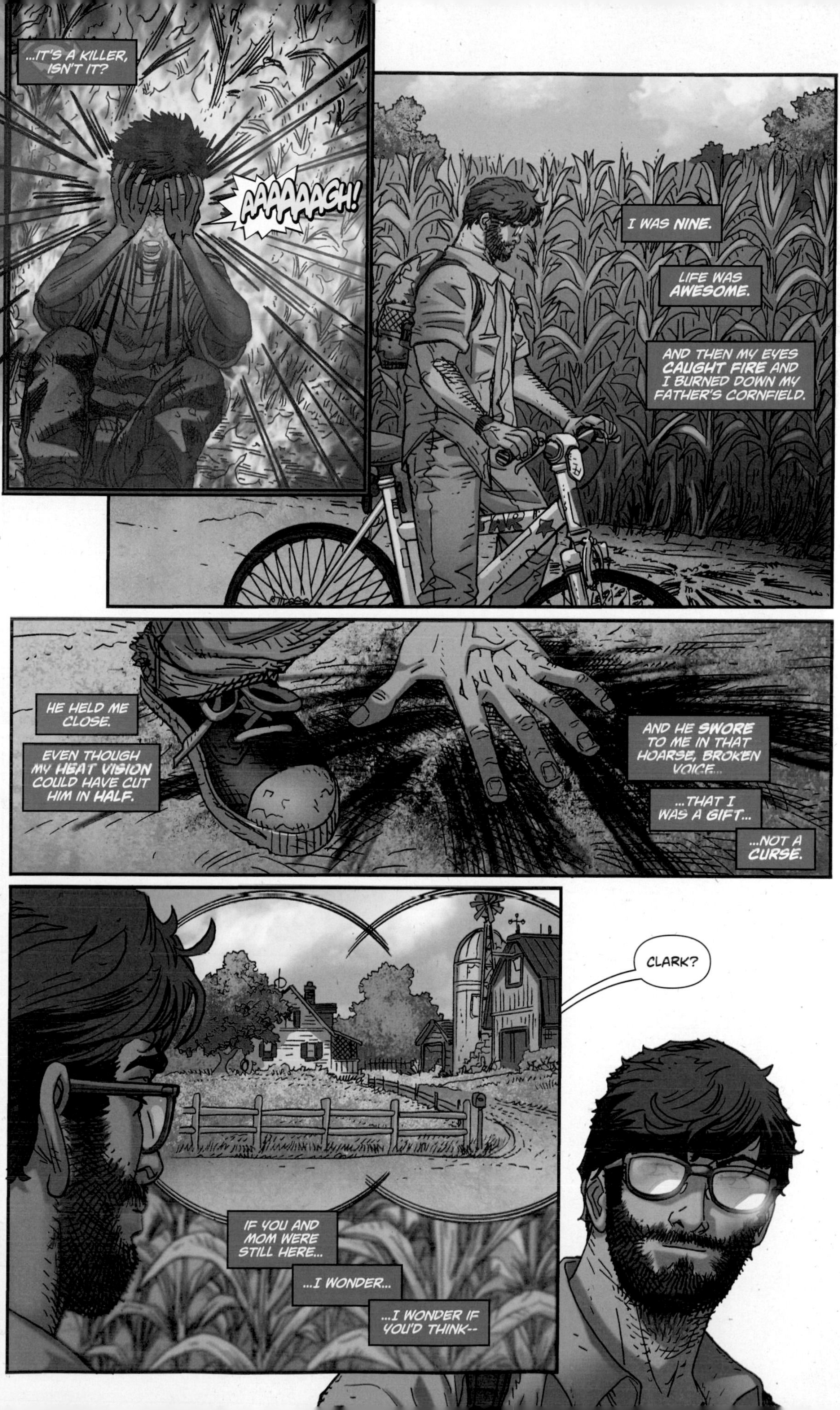

...IT'S A KILLER, ISN'T IT?
AAAAAAGH!
I WAS NINE.
LIFE WAS AWESOME.
AND THEN MY EYES CAUGHT FIRE AND I BURNED DOWN MY FATHER'S CORNFIELD.
HE HELD ME CLOSE.
EVEN THOUGH MY HEAT VISION COULD HAVE CUT HIM IN HALF.
AND HE SWORE TO ME IN THAT HOARSE, BROKEN VOICE...
...THAT I WAS A GIFT...
...NOT A CURSE.
CLARK?
IF YOU AND MOM WERE STILL HERE...
...I WONDER...
...I WONDER IF YOU'D THINK--

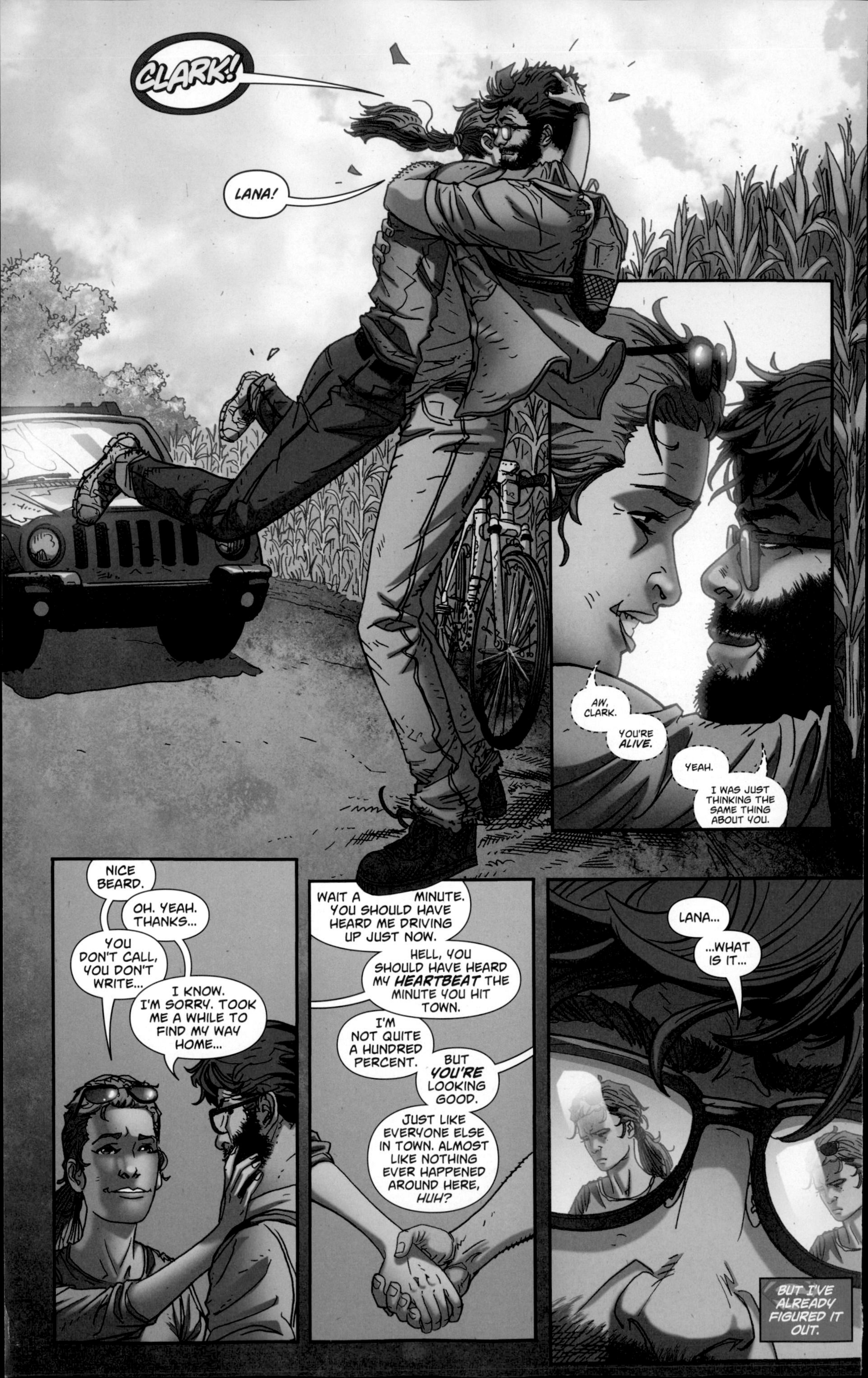

CLARK!
LANA!
AW, CLARK.
YOU'RE *ALIVE*.
YEAH.
I WAS JUST THINKING THE SAME THING ABOUT YOU.
NICE BEARD.
OH. YEAH. THANKS...
YOU DON'T CALL, YOU DON'T WRITE...
I KNOW. I'M SORRY. TOOK ME A WHILE TO FIND MY WAY HOME...
WAIT A MINUTE. YOU SHOULD HAVE HEARD ME DRIVING UP JUST NOW.
HELL, YOU SHOULD HAVE HEARD MY *HEARTBEAT* THE MINUTE YOU HIT TOWN.
I'M NOT QUITE A HUNDRED PERCENT.
BUT *YOU'RE* LOOKING GOOD.
JUST LIKE EVERYONE ELSE IN TOWN. ALMOST LIKE NOTHING EVER HAPPENED AROUND HERE, HUH?
LANA...
...WHAT IS IT...
BUT I'VE ALREADY FIGURED IT OUT.

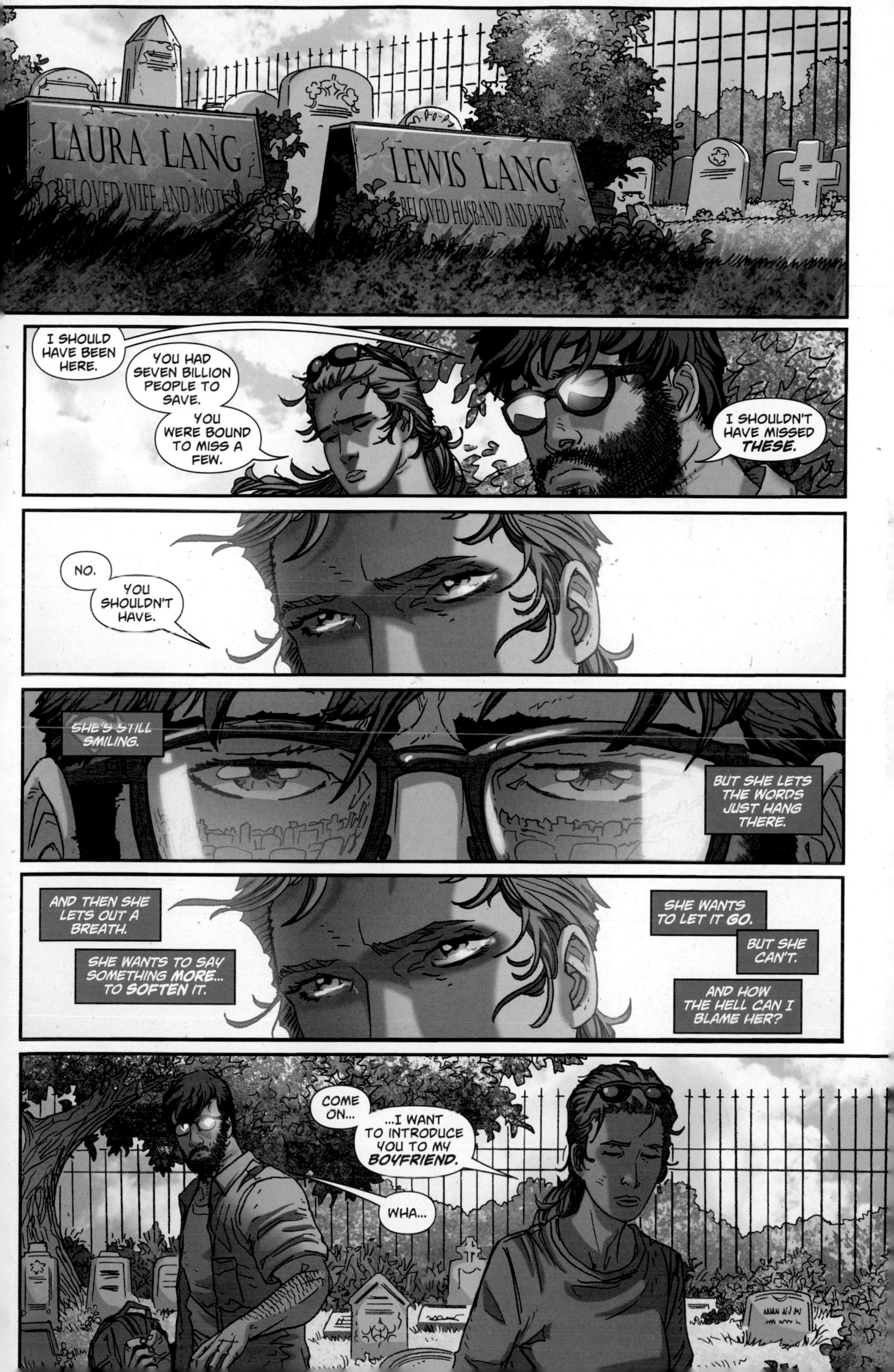
LAURA LANG
BELOVED WIFE AND MOTHER
LEWIS LANG
BELOVED HUSBAND AND FATHER
I SHOULD HAVE BEEN HERE.
YOU HAD SEVEN BILLION PEOPLE TO SAVE.
YOU WERE BOUND TO MISS A FEW.
I SHOULDN'T HAVE MISSED THESE.
NO.
YOU SHOULDN'T HAVE.
SHE'S STILL SMILING.
BUT SHE LETS THE WORDS JUST HANG THERE.
AND THEN SHE LETS OUT A BREATH.
SHE WANTS TO SAY SOMETHING MORE... TO SOFTEN IT.
SHE WANTS TO LET IT GO.
BUT SHE CAN'T.
AND HOW THE HELL CAN I BLAME HER?
COME ON...
...I WANT TO INTRODUCE YOU TO MY BOYFRIEND.
WHA...

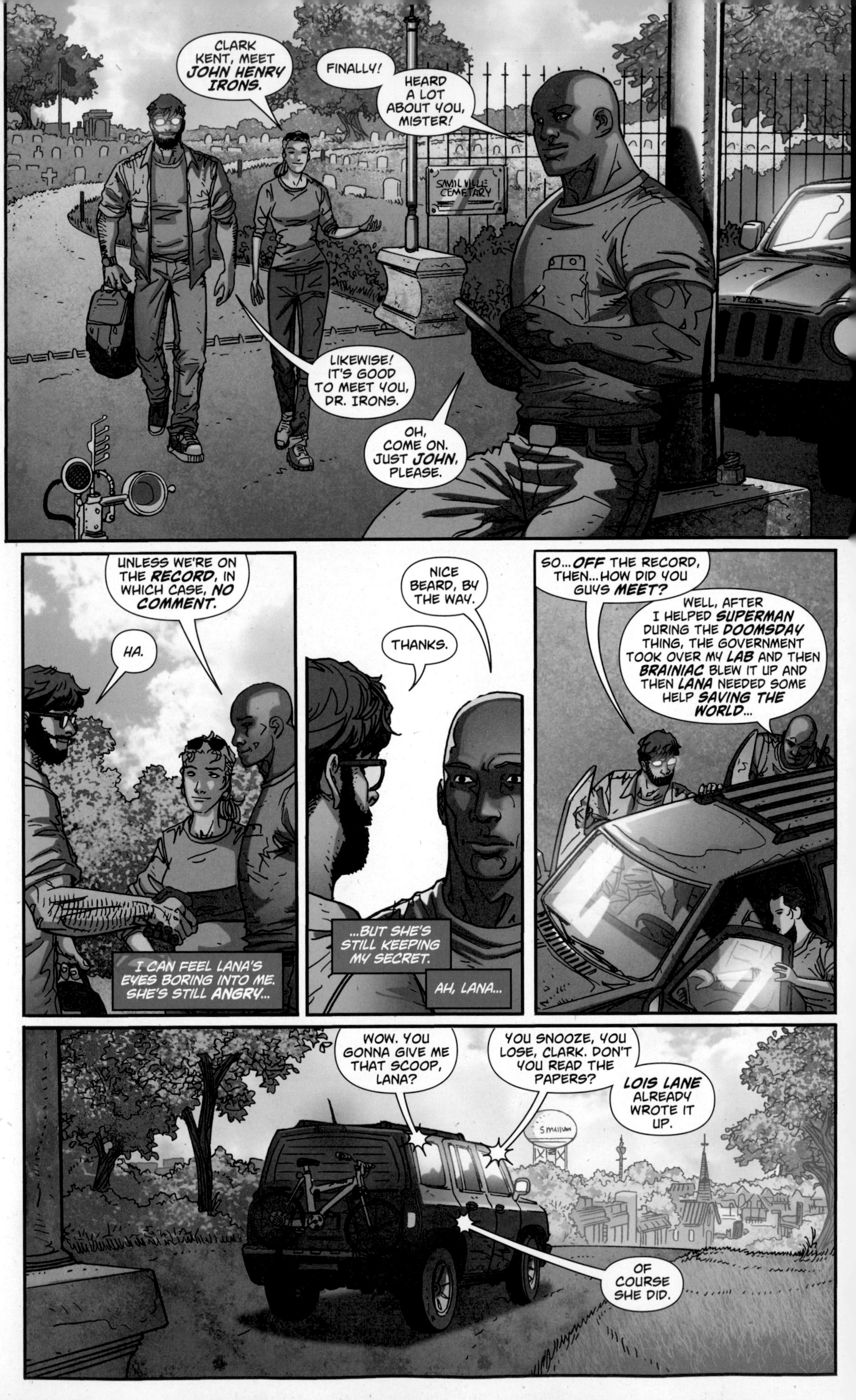
CLARK KENT, MEET JOHN HENRY IRONS.
FINALLY!
HEARD A LOT ABOUT YOU, MISTER!
SAVILVILLE CEMETARY
LIKEWISE! IT'S GOOD TO MEET YOU, DR. IRONS.
OH, COME ON. JUST JOHN, PLEASE.
UNLESS WE'RE ON THE RECORD, IN WHICH CASE, NO COMMENT.
HA.
I CAN FEEL LANA'S EYES BORING INTO ME. SHE'S STILL ANGRY...
NICE BEARD, BY THE WAY.
THANKS.
...BUT SHE'S STILL KEEPING MY SECRET.
AH, LANA...
SO...OFF THE RECORD, THEN...HOW DID YOU GUYS MEET?
WELL, AFTER I HELPED SUPERMAN DURING THE DOOMSDAY THING, THE GOVERNMENT TOOK OVER MY LAB AND THEN BRAINIAC BLEW IT UP AND THEN LANA NEEDED SOME HELP SAVING THE WORLD...
WOW. YOU GONNA GIVE ME THAT SCOOP, LANA?
YOU SNOOZE, YOU LOSE, CLARK. DON'T YOU READ THE PAPERS?
LOIS LANE ALREADY WROTE IT UP.
SMALLVILLE
OF COURSE SHE DID.

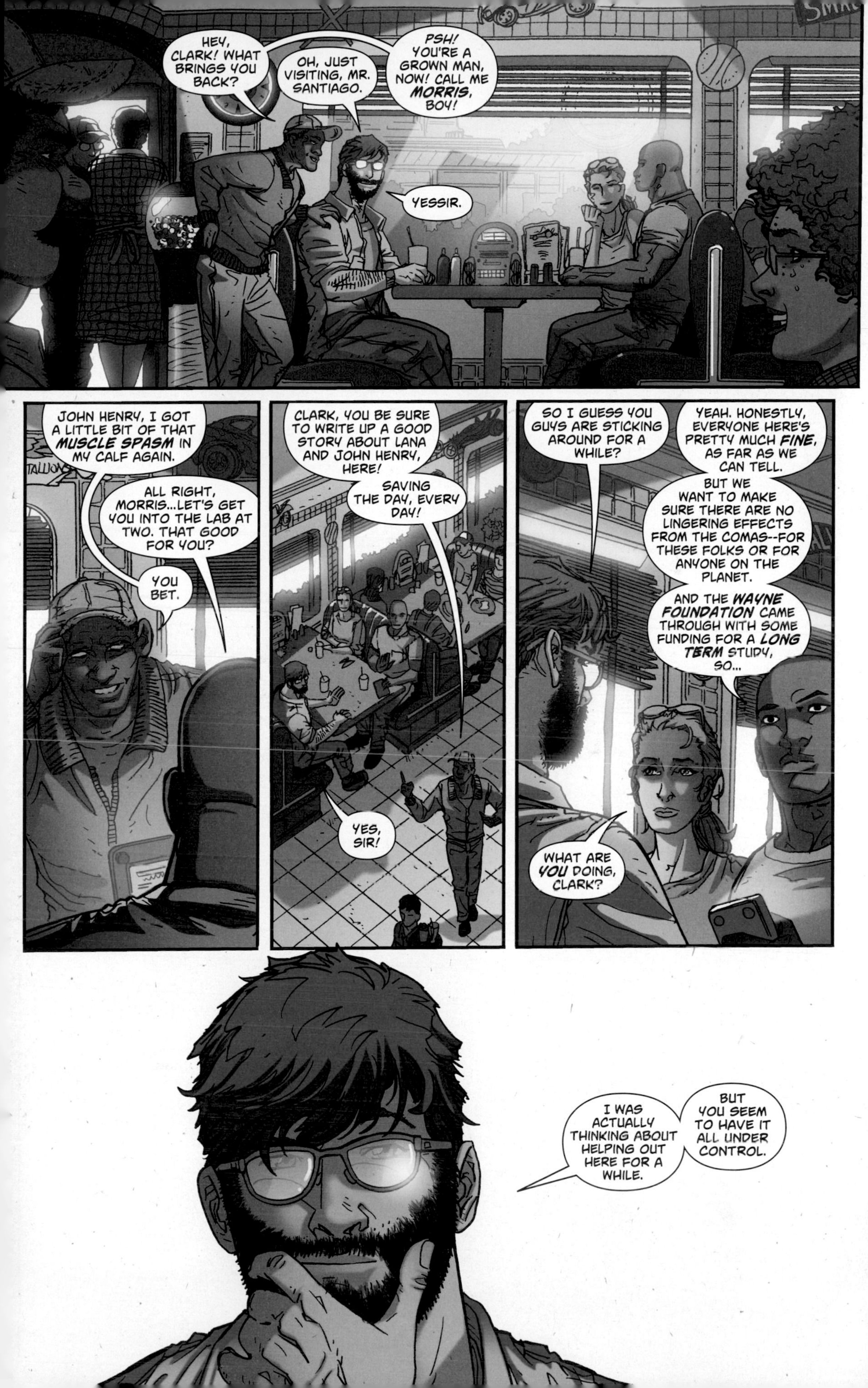
HEY, CLARK! WHAT BRINGS YOU BACK?
OH, JUST VISITING, MR. SANTIAGO.
PSH! YOU'RE A GROWN MAN, NOW! CALL ME MORRIS, BOY!
YESSIR.
JOHN HENRY, I GOT A LITTLE BIT OF THAT MUSCLE SPASM IN MY CALF AGAIN.
ALL RIGHT, MORRIS...LET'S GET YOU INTO THE LAB AT TWO. THAT GOOD FOR YOU?
YOU BET.
CLARK, YOU BE SURE TO WRITE UP A GOOD STORY ABOUT LANA AND JOHN HENRY, HERE!
SAVING THE DAY, EVERY DAY!
YES, SIR!
SO I GUESS YOU GUYS ARE STICKING AROUND FOR A WHILE?
YEAH. HONESTLY, EVERYONE HERE'S PRETTY MUCH FINE, AS FAR AS WE CAN TELL.
BUT WE WANT TO MAKE SURE THERE ARE NO LINGERING EFFECTS FROM THE COMAS--FOR THESE FOLKS OR FOR ANYONE ON THE PLANET.
AND THE WAYNE FOUNDATION CAME THROUGH WITH SOME FUNDING FOR A LONG TERM STUDY, SO...
WHAT ARE YOU DOING, CLARK?
I WAS ACTUALLY THINKING ABOUT HELPING OUT HERE FOR A WHILE.
BUT YOU SEEM TO HAVE IT ALL UNDER CONTROL.

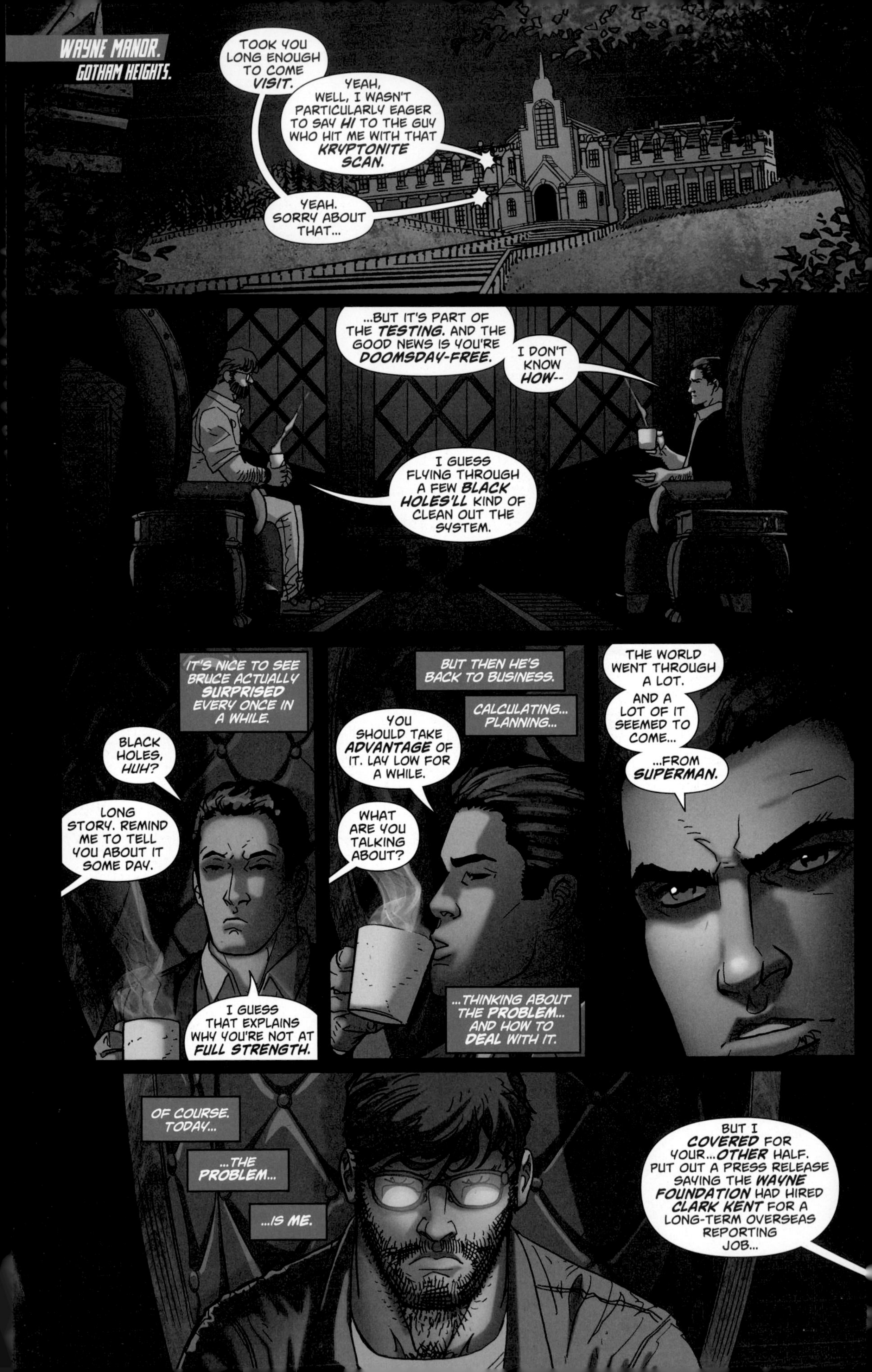
WAYNE MANOR.
GOTHAM HEIGHTS.
TOOK YOU LONG ENOUGH TO COME VISIT.
YEAH, WELL, I WASN'T PARTICULARLY EAGER TO SAY HI TO THE GUY WHO HIT ME WITH THAT KRYPTONITE SCAN.
YEAH. SORRY ABOUT THAT...
...BUT IT'S PART OF THE TESTING. AND THE GOOD NEWS IS YOU'RE DOOMSDAY-FREE.
I DON'T KNOW HOW--
I GUESS FLYING THROUGH A FEW BLACK HOLES'LL KIND OF CLEAN OUT THE SYSTEM.
IT'S NICE TO SEE BRUCE ACTUALLY SURPRISED EVERY ONCE IN A WHILE.
BLACK HOLES, HUH?
LONG STORY. REMIND ME TO TELL YOU ABOUT IT SOME DAY.
I GUESS THAT EXPLAINS WHY YOU'RE NOT AT FULL STRENGTH.
BUT THEN HE'S BACK TO BUSINESS.
CALCULATING... PLANNING...
YOU SHOULD TAKE ADVANTAGE OF IT. LAY LOW FOR A WHILE.
WHAT ARE YOU TALKING ABOUT?
...THINKING ABOUT THE PROBLEM... AND HOW TO DEAL WITH IT.
THE WORLD WENT THROUGH A LOT.
AND A LOT OF IT SEEMED TO COME...
...FROM SUPERMAN.
OF COURSE. TODAY...
...THE PROBLEM...
...IS ME.
BUT I COVERED FOR YOUR...OTHER HALF. PUT OUT A PRESS RELEASE SAYING THE WAYNE FOUNDATION HAD HIRED CLARK KENT FOR A LONG-TERM OVERSEAS REPORTING JOB...

"...SO GO HOME, CLARK.

"GO HOME...

"...AND GIVE IT SOME *TIME.*"

METROPOLIS.

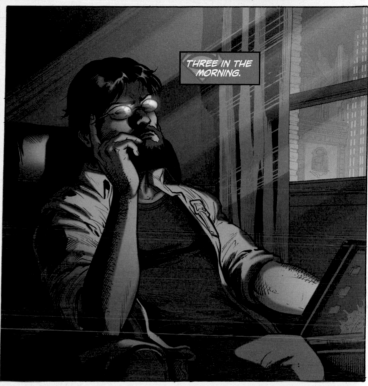

THREE IN THE MORNING.

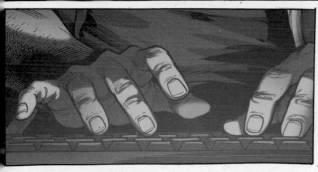

Who Needs Superman, Anyway?

By Clark Kent

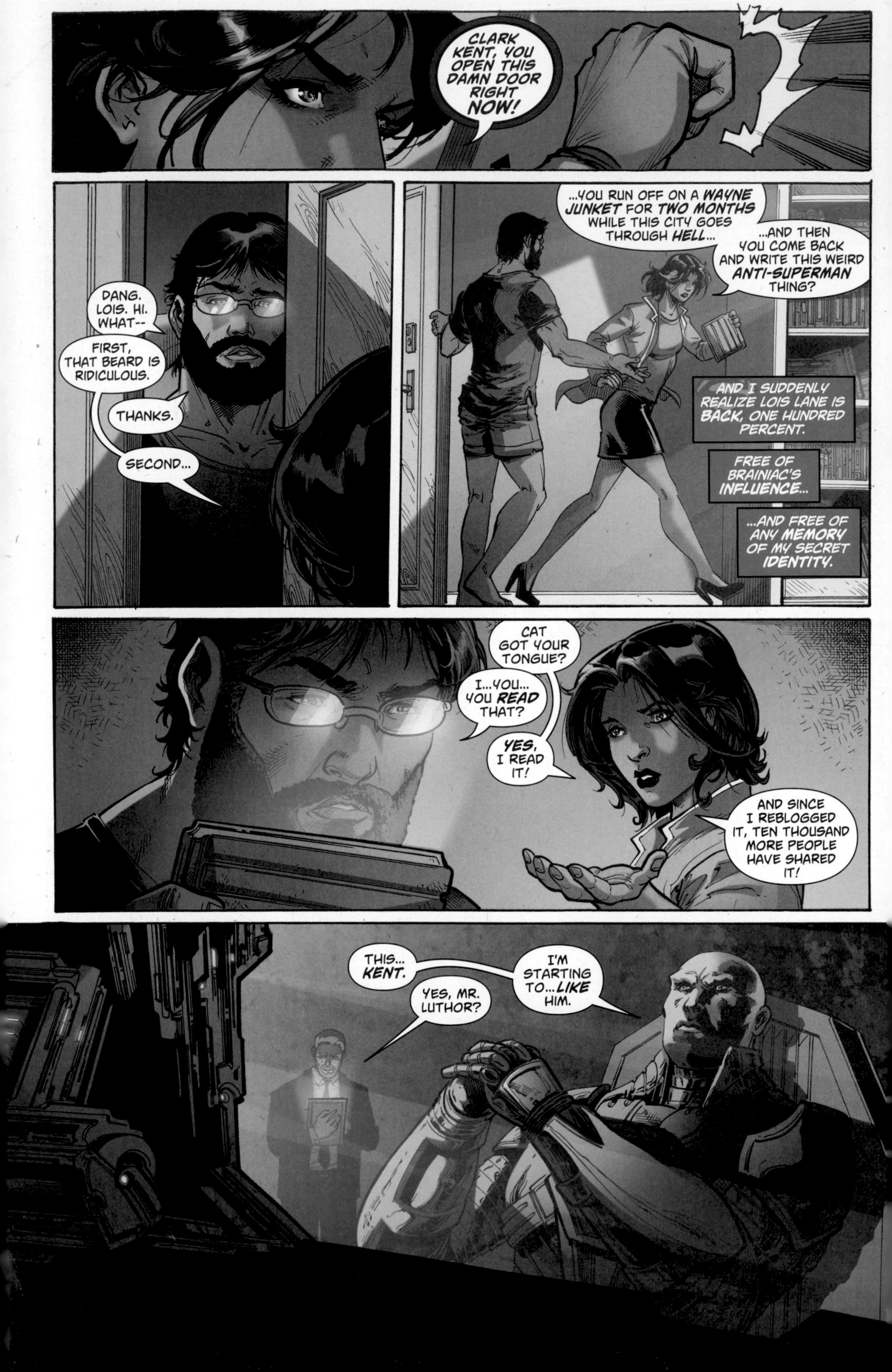
CLARK KENT, YOU OPEN THIS DAMN DOOR RIGHT NOW!
DANG. LOIS. HI. WHAT--
FIRST, THAT BEARD IS RIDICULOUS.
THANKS.
SECOND...
...YOU RUN OFF ON A WAYNE JUNKET FOR TWO MONTHS WHILE THIS CITY GOES THROUGH HELL...
...AND THEN YOU COME BACK AND WRITE THIS WEIRD ANTI-SUPERMAN THING?
AND I SUDDENLY REALIZE LOIS LANE IS BACK, ONE HUNDRED PERCENT.
FREE OF BRAINIAC'S INFLUENCE...
...AND FREE OF ANY MEMORY OF MY SECRET IDENTITY.
CAT GOT YOUR TONGUE?
I...YOU... YOU READ THAT?
YES, I READ IT!
AND SINCE I REBLOGGED IT, TEN THOUSAND MORE PEOPLE HAVE SHARED IT!
THIS... KENT.
YES, MR. LUTHOR?
I'M STARTING TO...LIKE HIM.

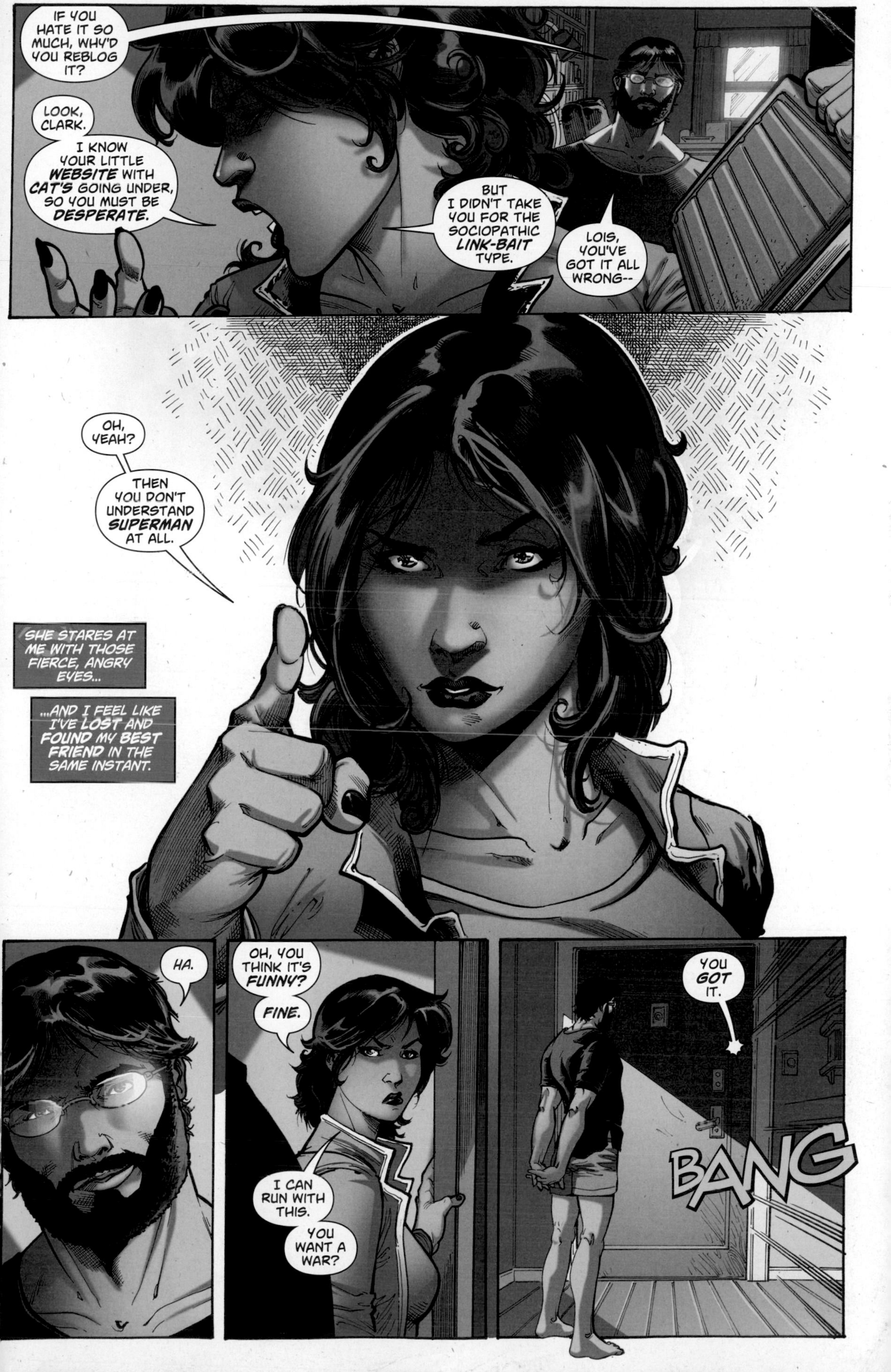
IF YOU HATE IT SO MUCH, WHY'D YOU REBLOG IT?
LOOK, CLARK.
I KNOW YOUR LITTLE WEBSITE WITH CAT'S GOING UNDER, SO YOU MUST BE DESPERATE.
BUT I DIDN'T TAKE YOU FOR THE SOCIOPATHIC LINK-BAIT TYPE.
LOIS, YOU'VE GOT IT ALL WRONG--
OH, YEAH?
THEN YOU DON'T UNDERSTAND SUPERMAN AT ALL.
SHE STARES AT ME WITH THOSE FIERCE, ANGRY EYES...
...AND I FEEL LIKE I'VE LOST AND FOUND MY BEST FRIEND IN THE SAME INSTANT.
HA.
OH, YOU THINK IT'S FUNNY?
FINE.
I CAN RUN WITH THIS.
YOU WANT A WAR?
YOU GOT IT.
BANG

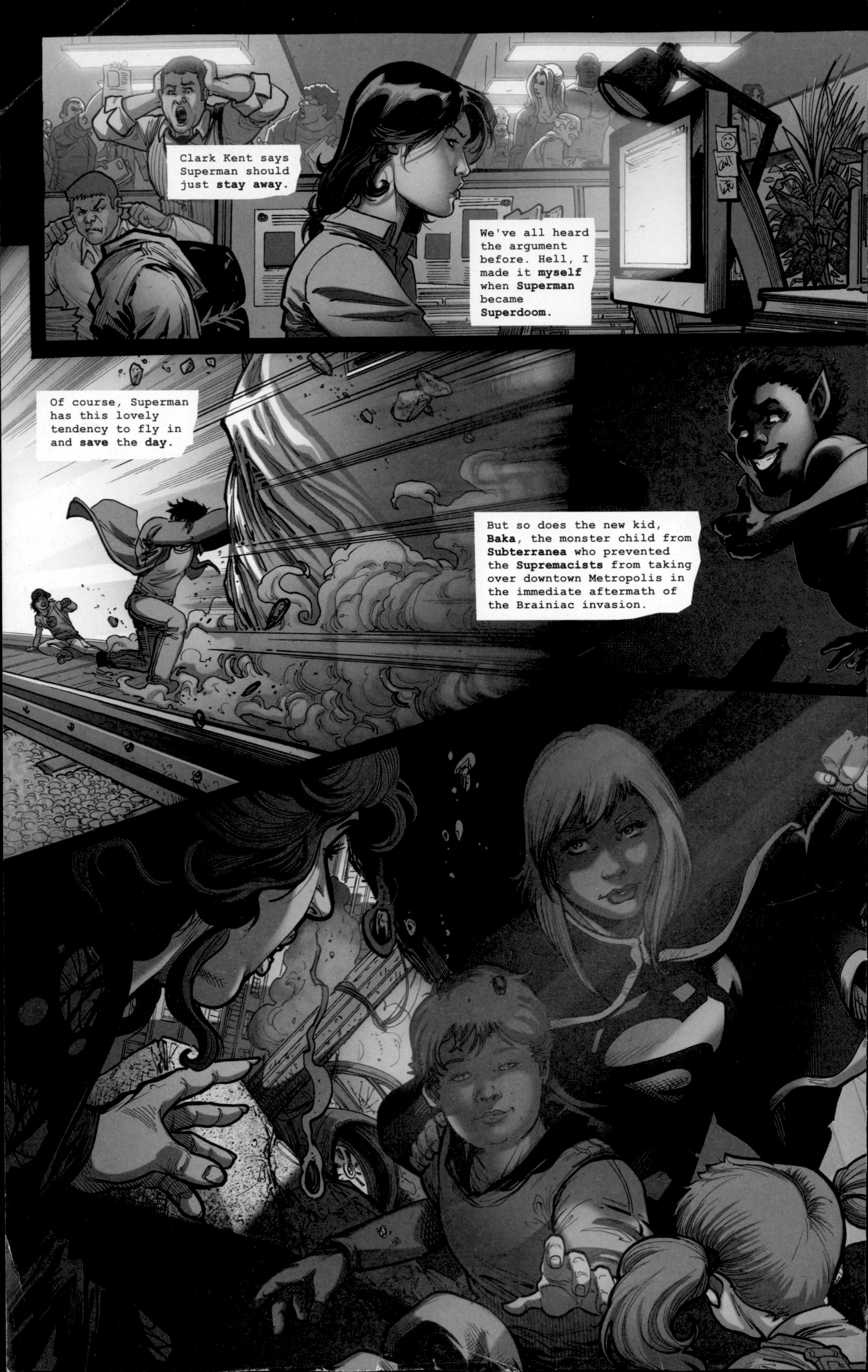

Clark Kent says Superman should just **stay away**.
We've all heard the argument before. Hell, I made it **myself** when **Superman** became **Superdoom**.
Of course, Superman has this lovely tendency to fly in and **save** the **day**.
But so does the new kid, **Baka**, the monster child from **Subterranea** who prevented the **Supremacists** from taking over downtown Metropolis in the immediate aftermath of the Brainiac invasion.

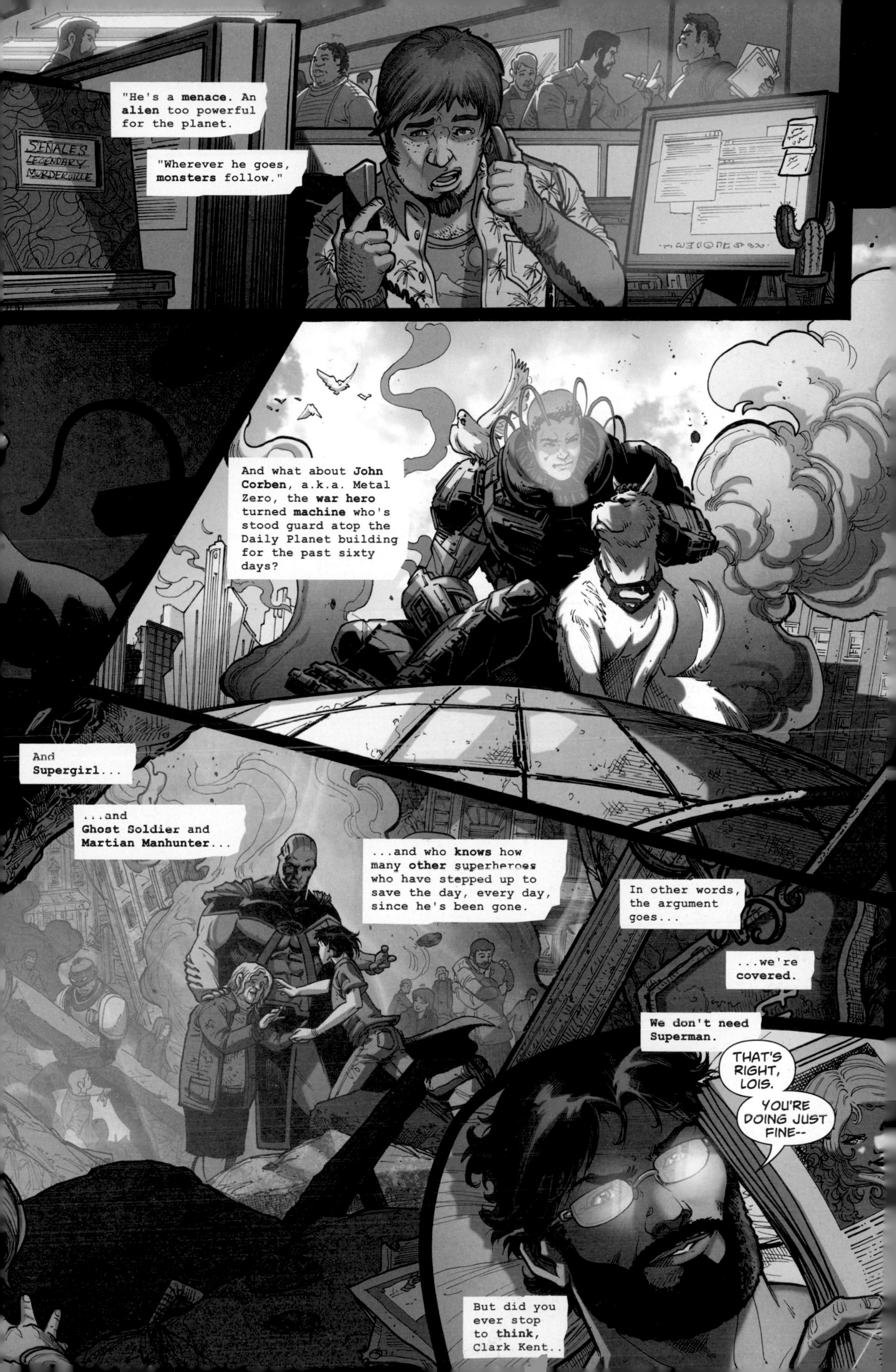
"He's a menace. An alien too powerful for the planet.
"Wherever he goes, monsters follow."
SEÑALES LEGENDARY MURDERVILLE
And what about John Corben, a.k.a. Metal Zero, the war hero turned machine who's stood guard atop the Daily Planet building for the past sixty days?
And Supergirl...
...and Ghost Soldier and Martian Manhunter...
...and who knows how many other superheroes who have stepped up to save the day, every day, since he's been gone.
In other words, the argument goes...
...we're covered.
We don't need Superman.
THAT'S RIGHT, LOIS.
YOU'RE DOING JUST FINE--
But did you ever stop to think, Clark Kent..

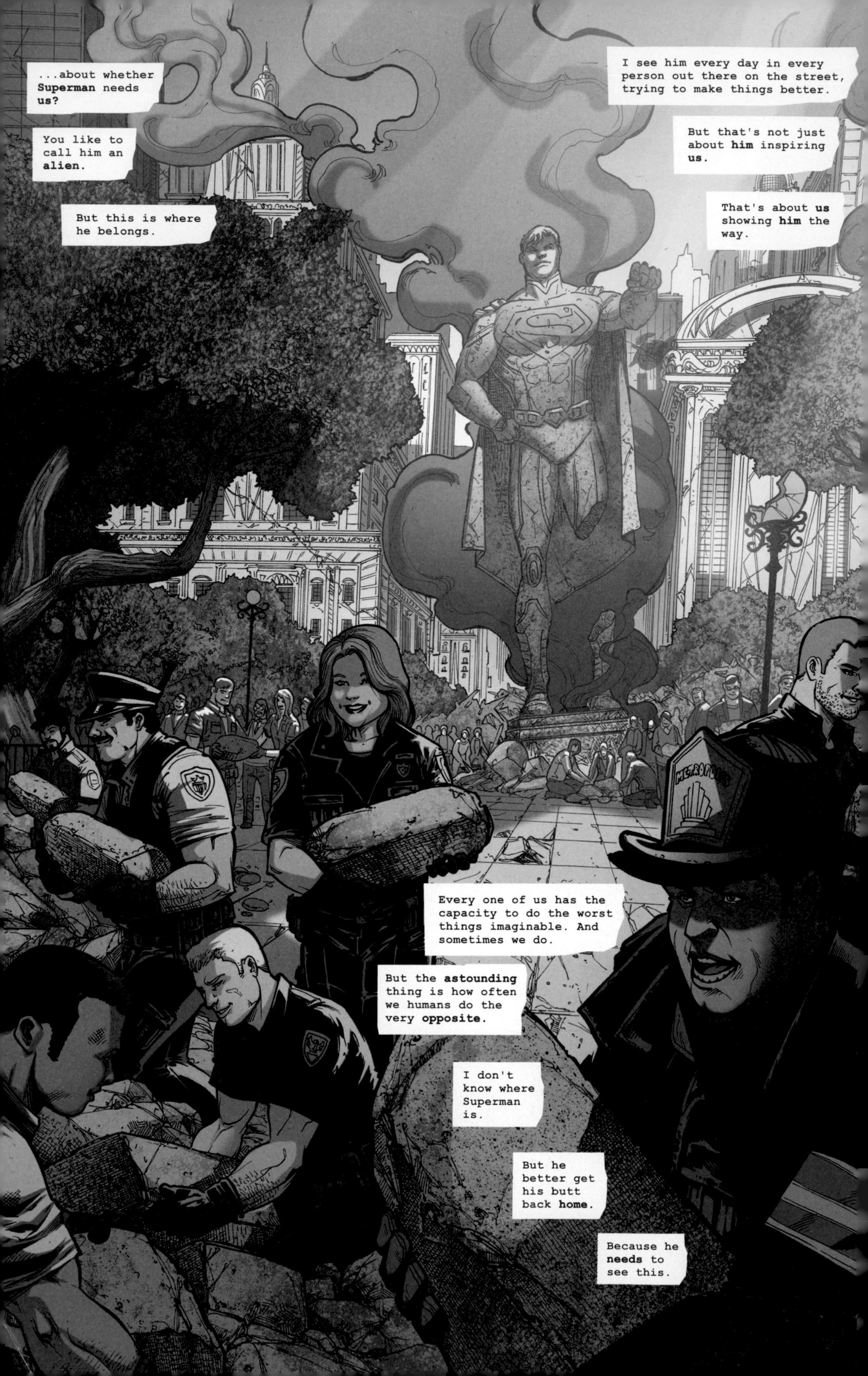
...about whether **Superman** needs **us?**
You like to call him an **alien.**
But this is where he belongs.
I see him every day in every person out there on the street, trying to make things better.
But that's not just about **him** inspiring **us.**
That's about **us** showing **him** the way.
METROPOLIS
Every one of us has the capacity to do the worst things imaginable. And sometimes we do.
But the **astounding** thing is how often we humans do the very **opposite.**
I don't know where Superman is.
But he better get his butt back **home.**
Because he **needs** to see this.

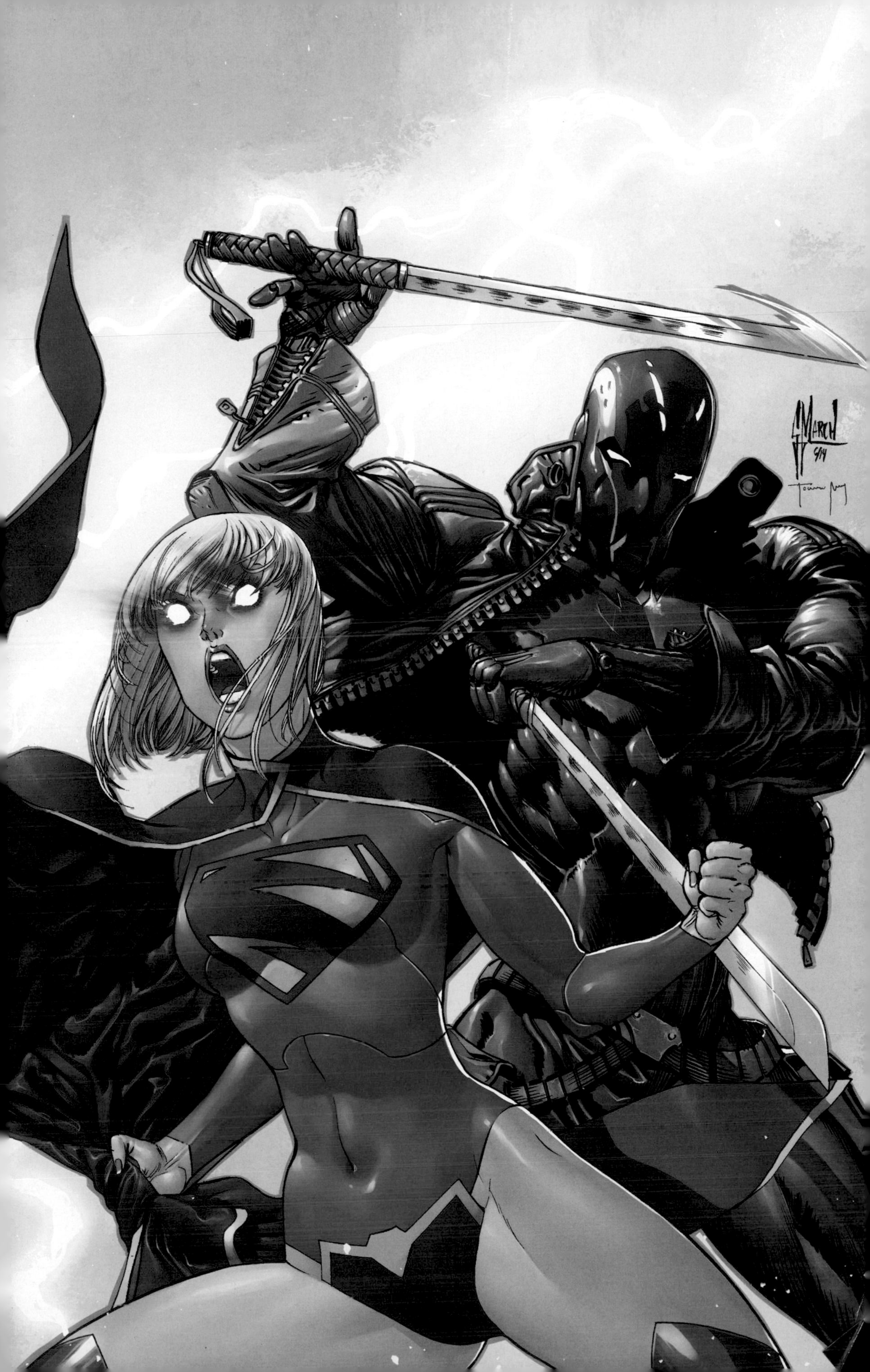

SUPERMAN DOOMED

[AFTERMATH] chapter 2

"NORMAL"

STORY
TONY BEDARD

ART
JONBOY MEYERS

COLORS
HI-FI

LETTERS
ROB LEIGH

COVER
GUILLEM MARCH AND **TOMEU MOREY**

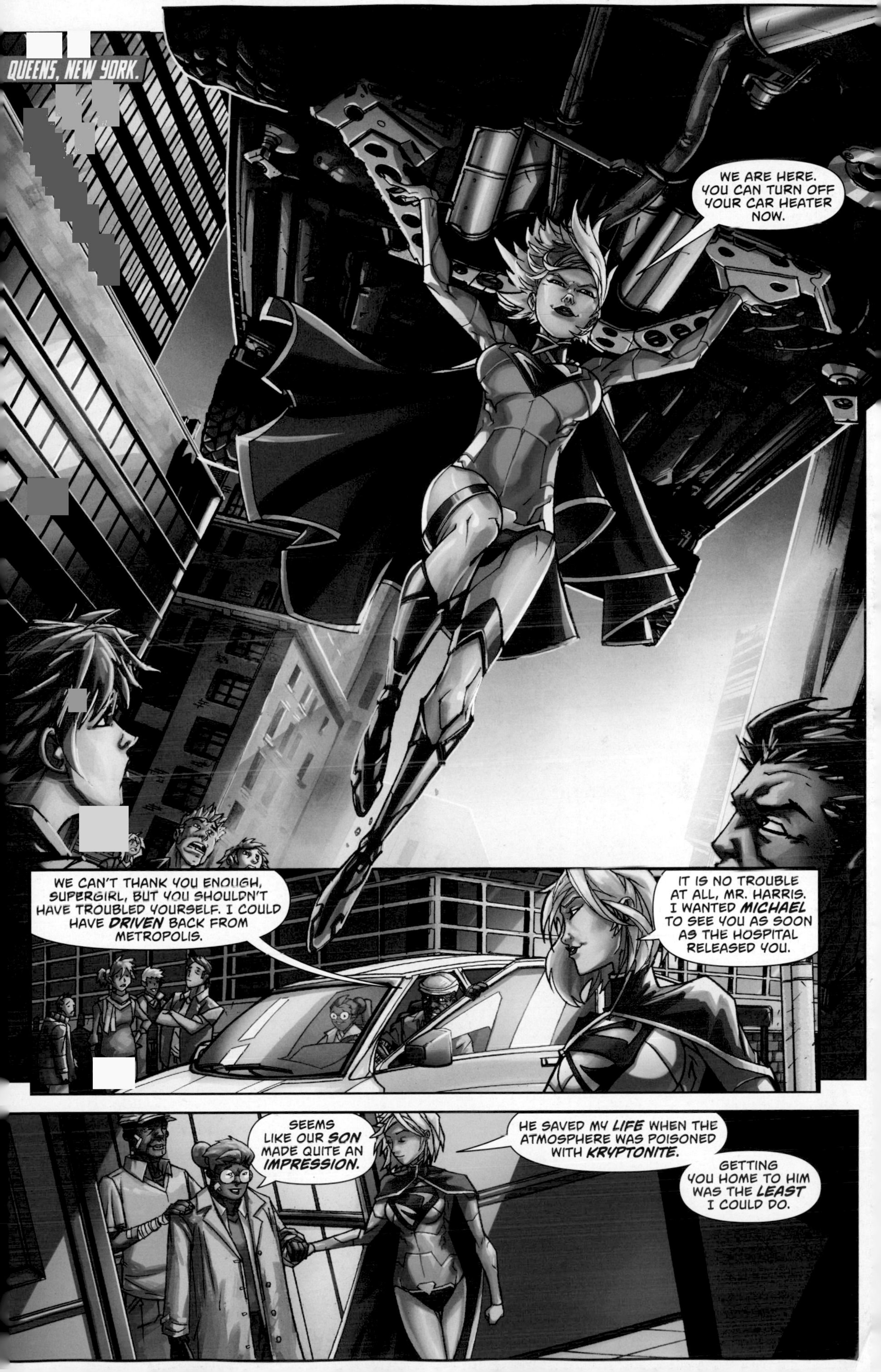
QUEENS, NEW YORK.
WE ARE HERE. YOU CAN TURN OFF YOUR CAR HEATER NOW.
WE CAN'T THANK YOU ENOUGH, SUPERGIRL, BUT YOU SHOULDN'T HAVE TROUBLED YOURSELF. I COULD HAVE DRIVEN BACK FROM METROPOLIS.
IT IS NO TROUBLE AT ALL, MR. HARRIS. I WANTED MICHAEL TO SEE YOU AS SOON AS THE HOSPITAL RELEASED YOU.
SEEMS LIKE OUR SON MADE QUITE AN IMPRESSION.
HE SAVED MY LIFE WHEN THE ATMOSPHERE WAS POISONED WITH KRYPTONITE.
GETTING YOU HOME TO HIM WAS THE LEAST I COULD DO.

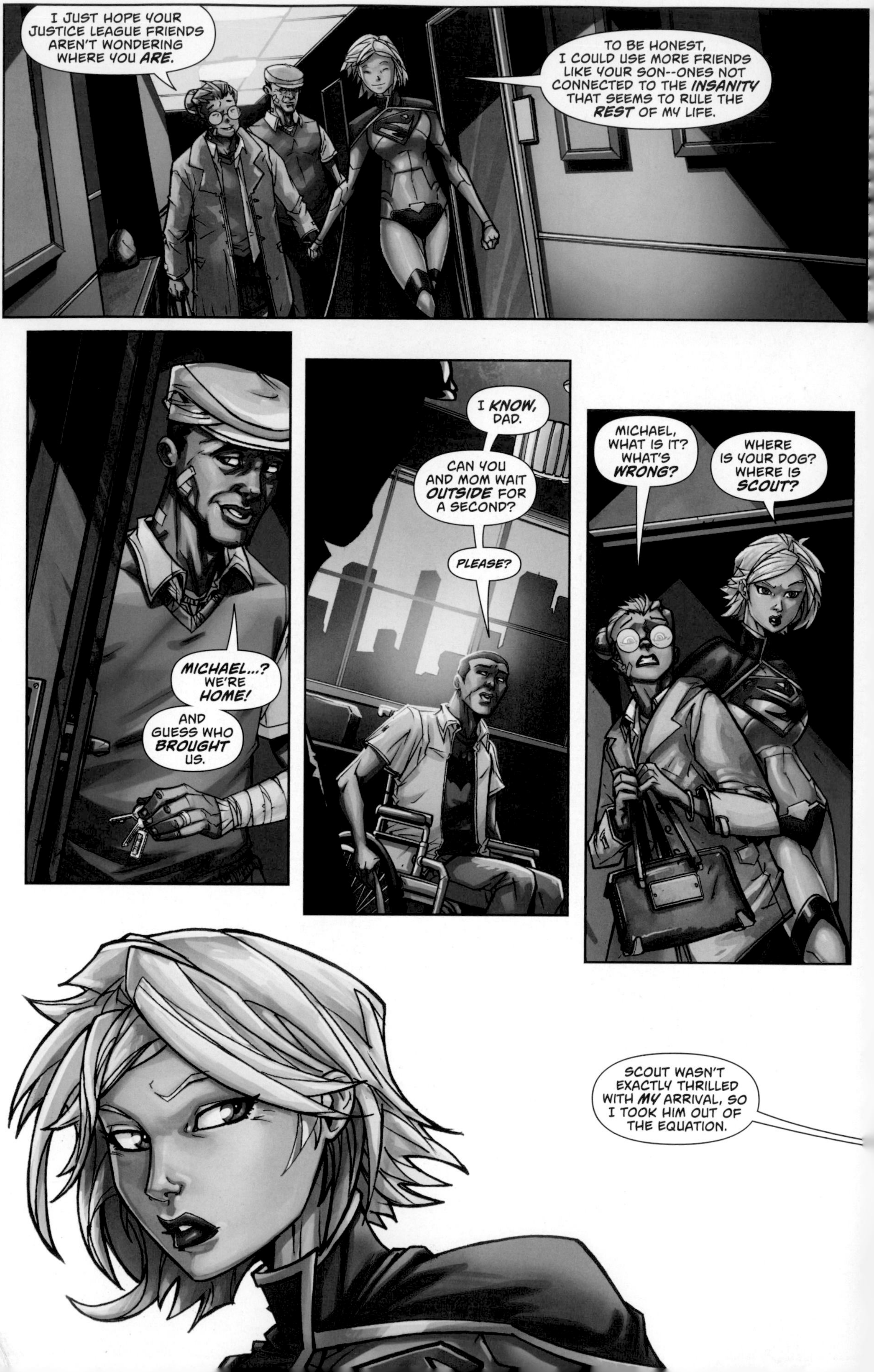
I JUST HOPE YOUR JUSTICE LEAGUE FRIENDS AREN'T WONDERING WHERE YOU ARE.
TO BE HONEST, I COULD USE MORE FRIENDS LIKE YOUR SON--ONES NOT CONNECTED TO THE INSANITY THAT SEEMS TO RULE THE REST OF MY LIFE.
MICHAEL...? WE'RE HOME!
AND GUESS WHO BROUGHT US.
I KNOW, DAD.
CAN YOU AND MOM WAIT OUTSIDE FOR A SECOND?
PLEASE?
MICHAEL, WHAT IS IT? WHAT'S WRONG?
WHERE IS YOUR DOG? WHERE IS SCOUT?
SCOUT WASN'T EXACTLY THRILLED WITH MY ARRIVAL, SO I TOOK HIM OUT OF THE EQUATION.

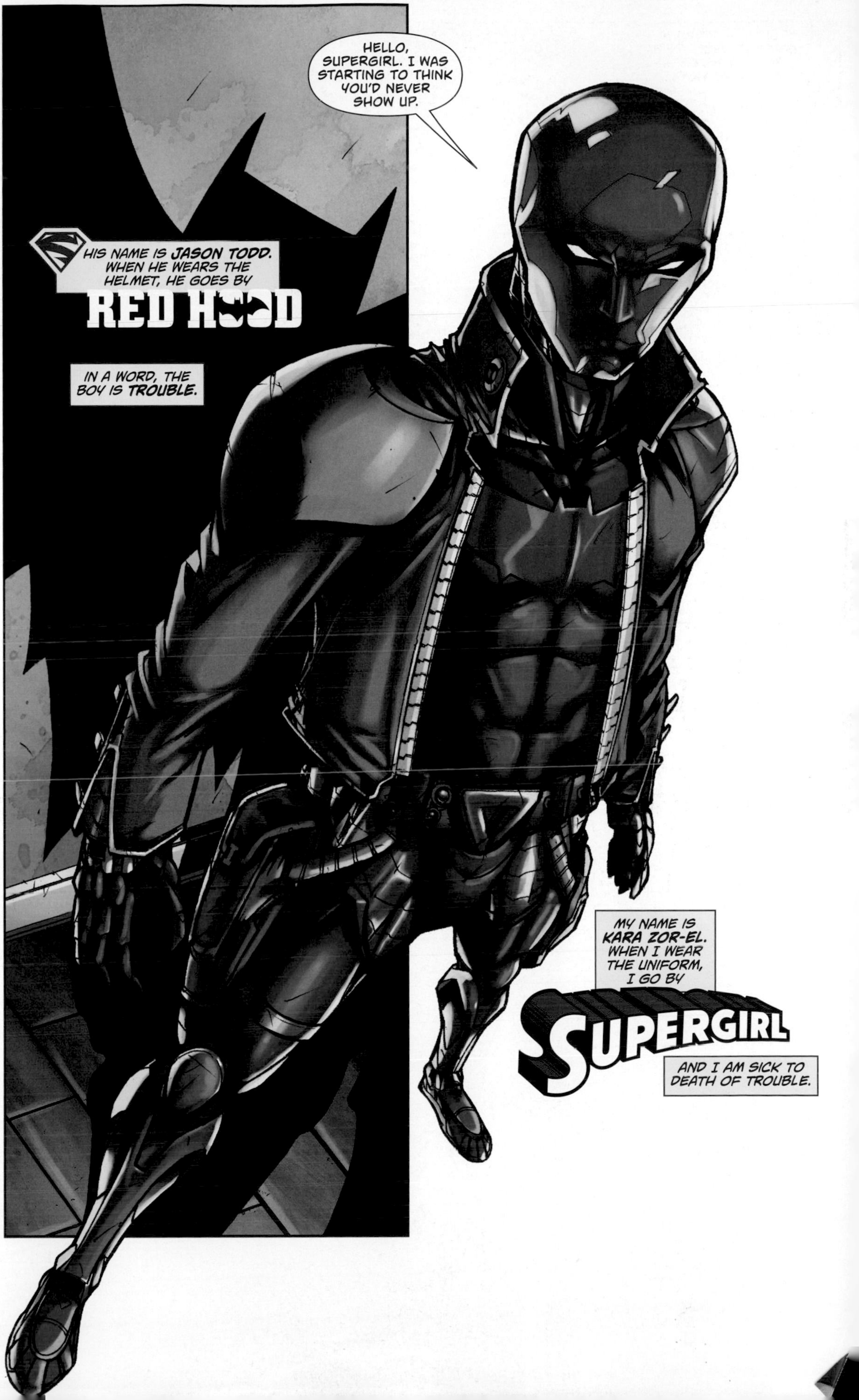
HELLO, SUPERGIRL. I WAS STARTING TO THINK YOU'D NEVER SHOW UP.
HIS NAME IS JASON TODD. WHEN HE WEARS THE HELMET, HE GOES BY
RED HOOD
IN A WORD, THE BOY IS TROUBLE.
MY NAME IS KARA ZOR-EL. WHEN I WEAR THE UNIFORM, I GO BY
SUPERGIRL
AND I AM SICK TO DEATH OF TROUBLE.

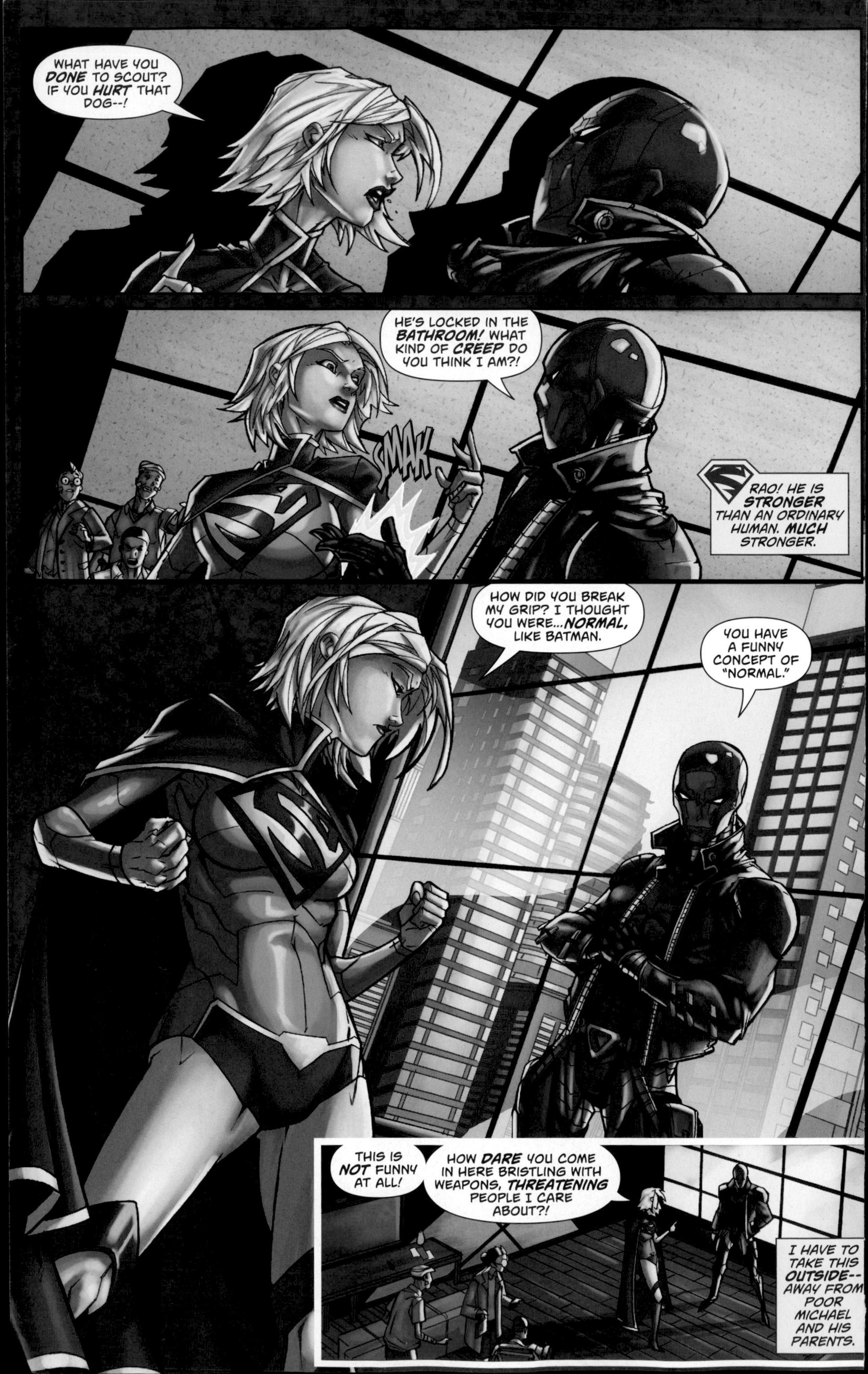
WHAT HAVE YOU DONE TO SCOUT? IF YOU HURT THAT DOG--!
HE'S LOCKED IN THE BATHROOM! WHAT KIND OF CREEP DO YOU THINK I AM?!
SMAK
RAO! HE IS STRONGER THAN AN ORDINARY HUMAN. MUCH STRONGER.
HOW DID YOU BREAK MY GRIP? I THOUGHT YOU WERE...NORMAL, LIKE BATMAN.
YOU HAVE A FUNNY CONCEPT OF "NORMAL."
THIS IS NOT FUNNY AT ALL!
HOW DARE YOU COME IN HERE BRISTLING WITH WEAPONS, THREATENING PEOPLE I CARE ABOUT?!
I HAVE TO TAKE THIS OUTSIDE-- AWAY FROM POOR MICHAEL AND HIS PARENTS.

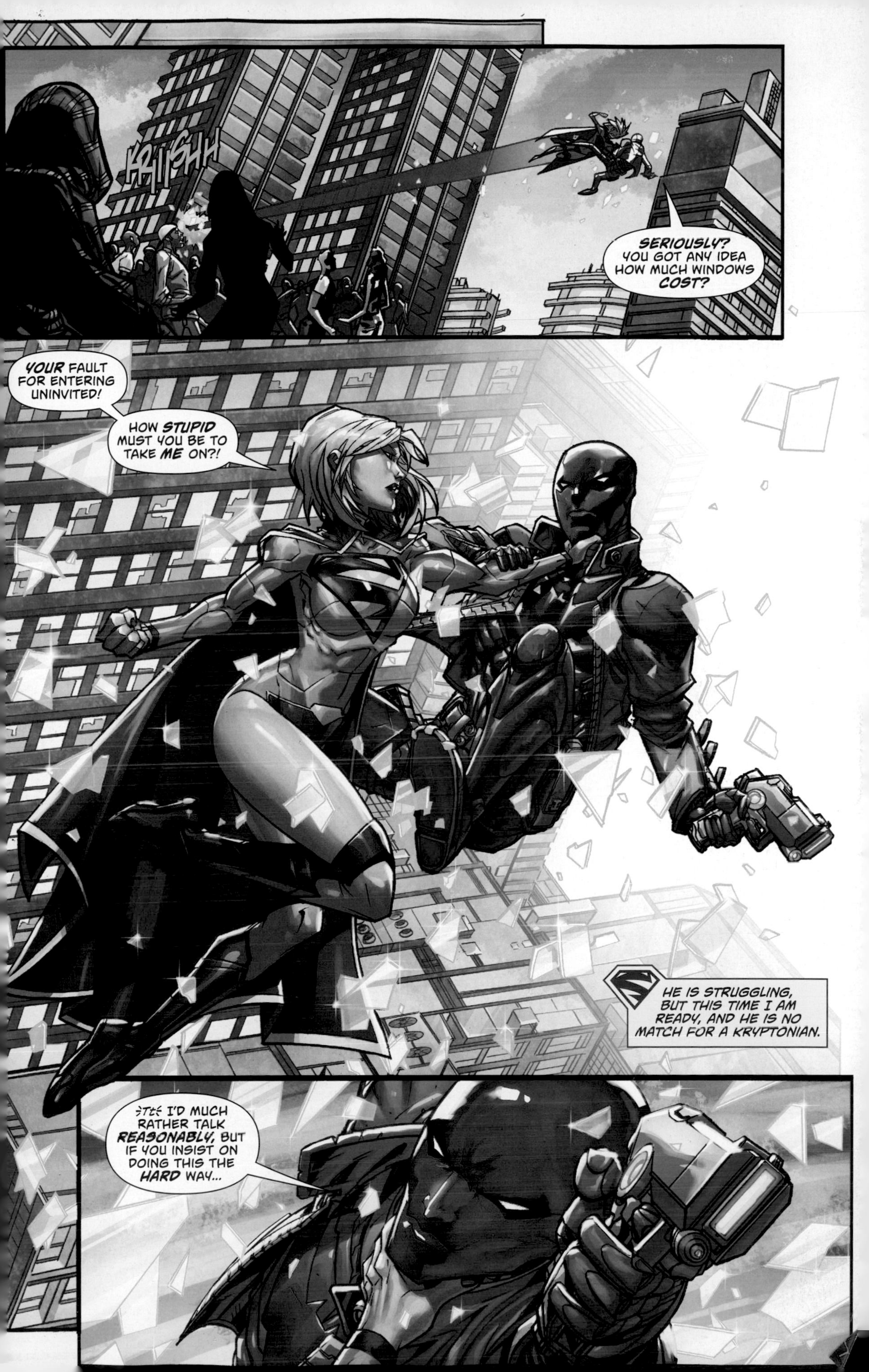
KRIISHH
SERIOUSLY? YOU GOT ANY IDEA HOW MUCH WINDOWS COST?
YOUR FAULT FOR ENTERING UNINVITED!
HOW STUPID MUST YOU BE TO TAKE ME ON?!
HE IS STRUGGLING, BUT THIS TIME I AM READY, AND HE IS NO MATCH FOR A KRYPTONIAN.
I'D MUCH RATHER TALK REASONABLY, BUT IF YOU INSIST ON DOING THIS THE HARD WAY...

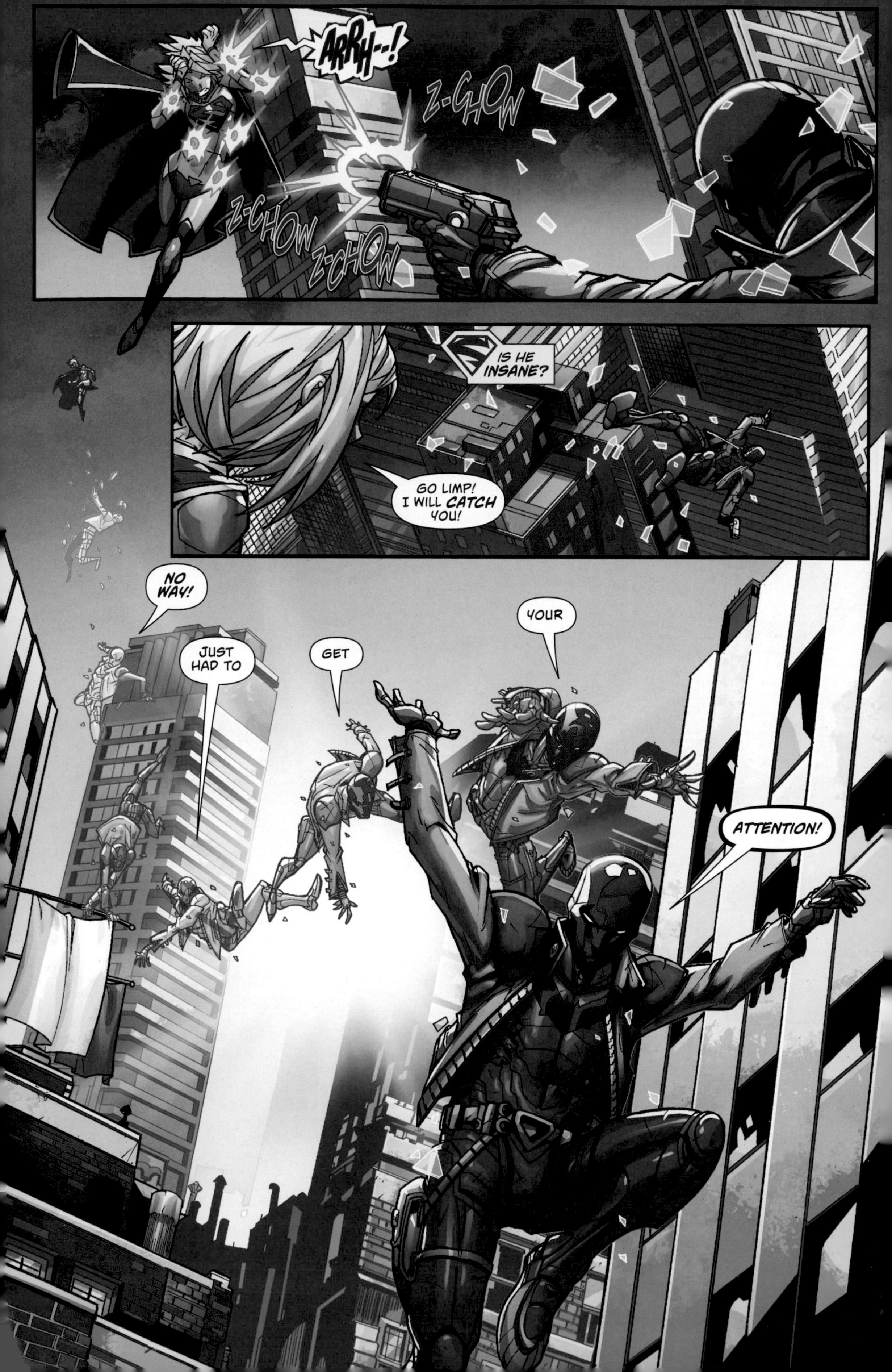

ARRH--!
Z-CHOW
Z-CHOW
Z-CHOW
IS HE INSANE?
GO LIMP! I WILL CATCH YOU!
NO WAY!
JUST HAD TO
GET
YOUR
ATTENTION!

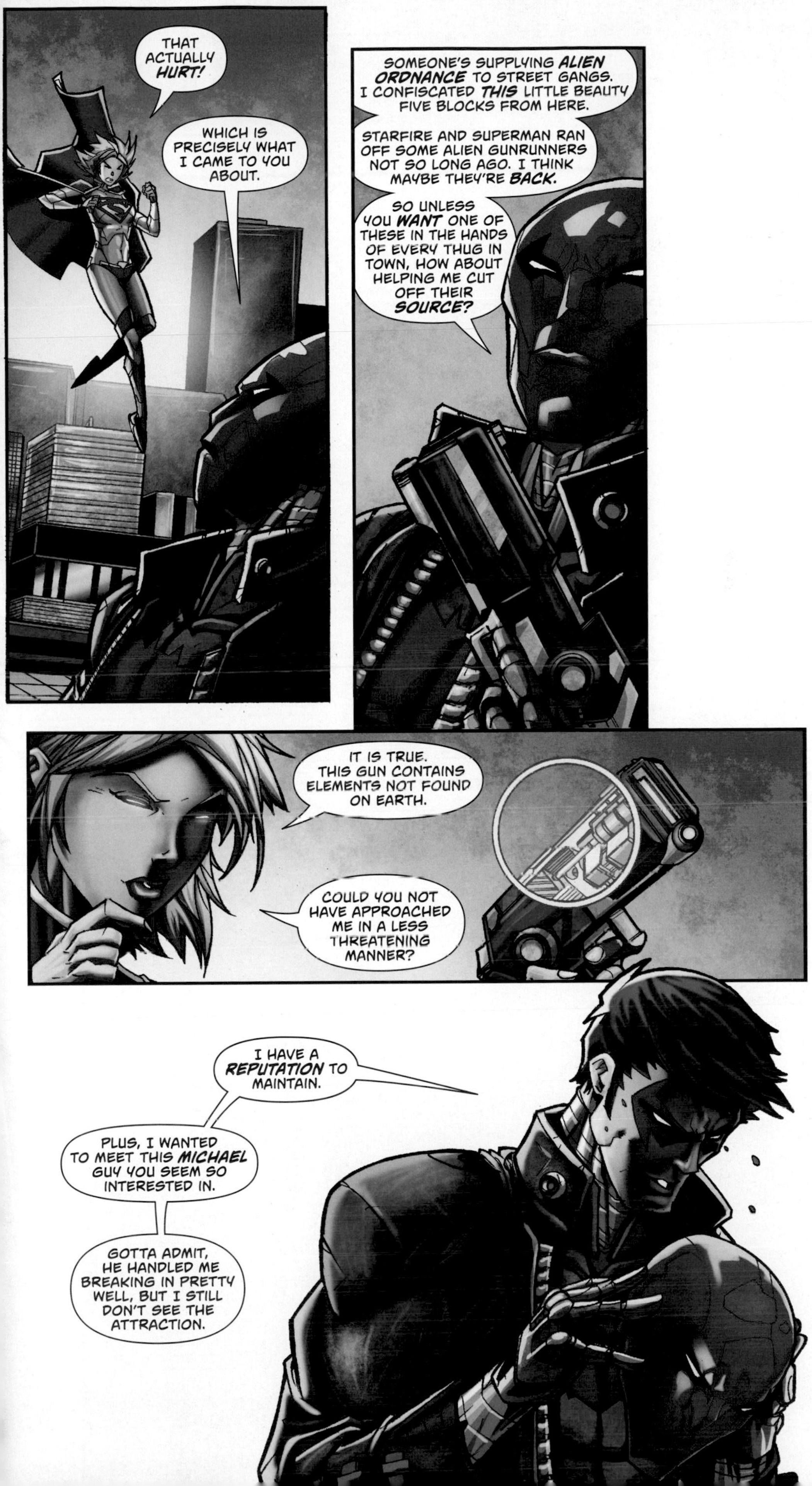
THAT ACTUALLY HURT!
WHICH IS PRECISELY WHAT I CAME TO YOU ABOUT.
SOMEONE'S SUPPLYING ALIEN ORDNANCE TO STREET GANGS. I CONFISCATED THIS LITTLE BEAUTY FIVE BLOCKS FROM HERE.
STARFIRE AND SUPERMAN RAN OFF SOME ALIEN GUNRUNNERS NOT SO LONG AGO. I THINK MAYBE THEY'RE BACK.
SO UNLESS YOU WANT ONE OF THESE IN THE HANDS OF EVERY THUG IN TOWN, HOW ABOUT HELPING ME CUT OFF THEIR SOURCE?
IT IS TRUE. THIS GUN CONTAINS ELEMENTS NOT FOUND ON EARTH.
COULD YOU NOT HAVE APPROACHED ME IN A LESS THREATENING MANNER?
I HAVE A REPUTATION TO MAINTAIN.
PLUS, I WANTED TO MEET THIS MICHAEL GUY YOU SEEM SO INTERESTED IN.
GOTTA ADMIT, HE HANDLED ME BREAKING IN PRETTY WELL, BUT I STILL DON'T SEE THE ATTRACTION.

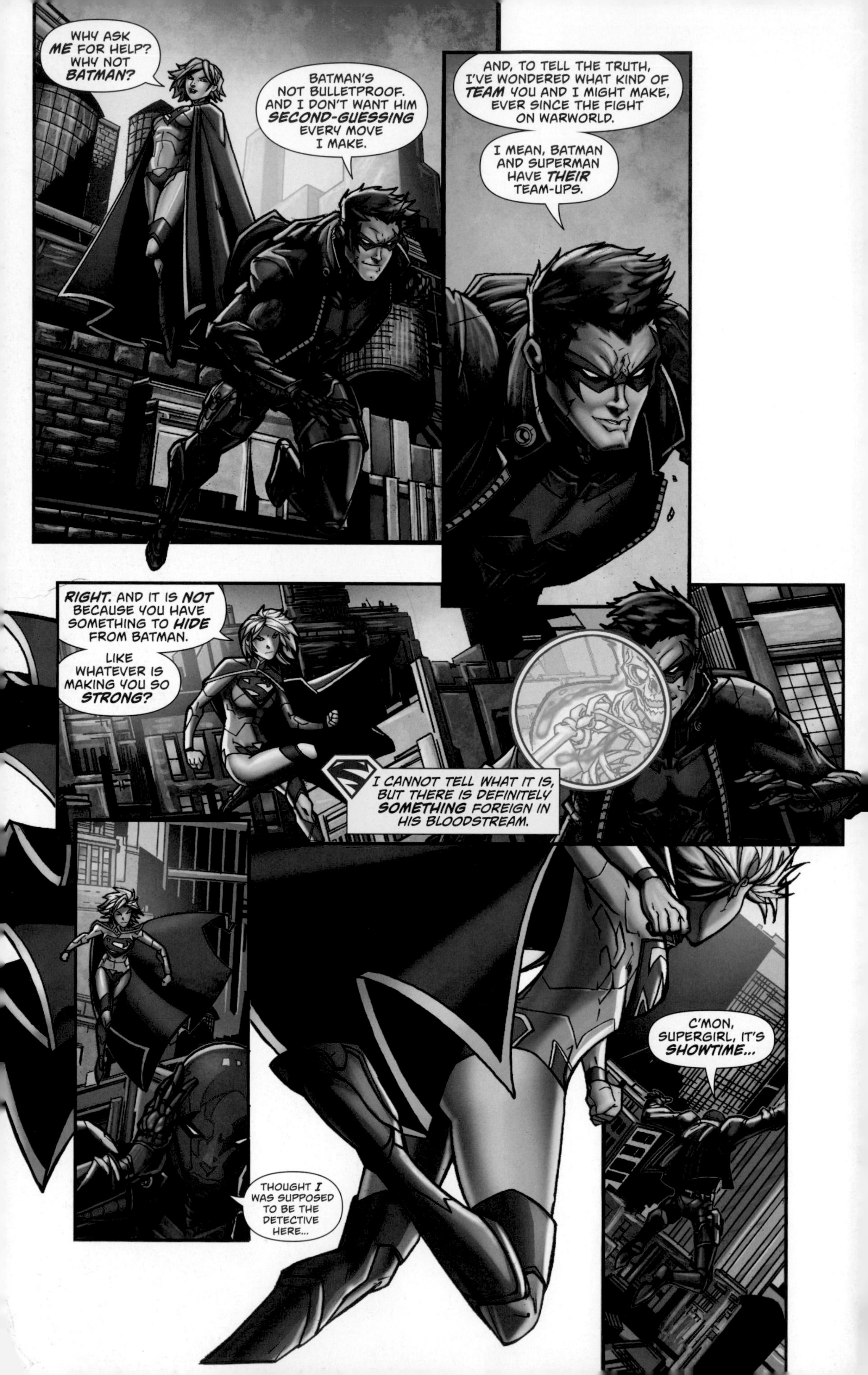

WHY ASK ME FOR HELP? WHY NOT BATMAN?
BATMAN'S NOT BULLETPROOF. AND I DON'T WANT HIM SECOND-GUESSING EVERY MOVE I MAKE.
AND, TO TELL THE TRUTH, I'VE WONDERED WHAT KIND OF TEAM YOU AND I MIGHT MAKE, EVER SINCE THE FIGHT ON WARWORLD.
I MEAN, BATMAN AND SUPERMAN HAVE THEIR TEAM-UPS.
RIGHT. AND IT IS NOT BECAUSE YOU HAVE SOMETHING TO HIDE FROM BATMAN.
LIKE WHATEVER IS MAKING YOU SO STRONG?
I CANNOT TELL WHAT IT IS, BUT THERE IS DEFINITELY SOMETHING FOREIGN IN HIS BLOODSTREAM.
THOUGHT I WAS SUPPOSED TO BE THE DETECTIVE HERE...
C'MON, SUPERGIRL, IT'S SHOWTIME...

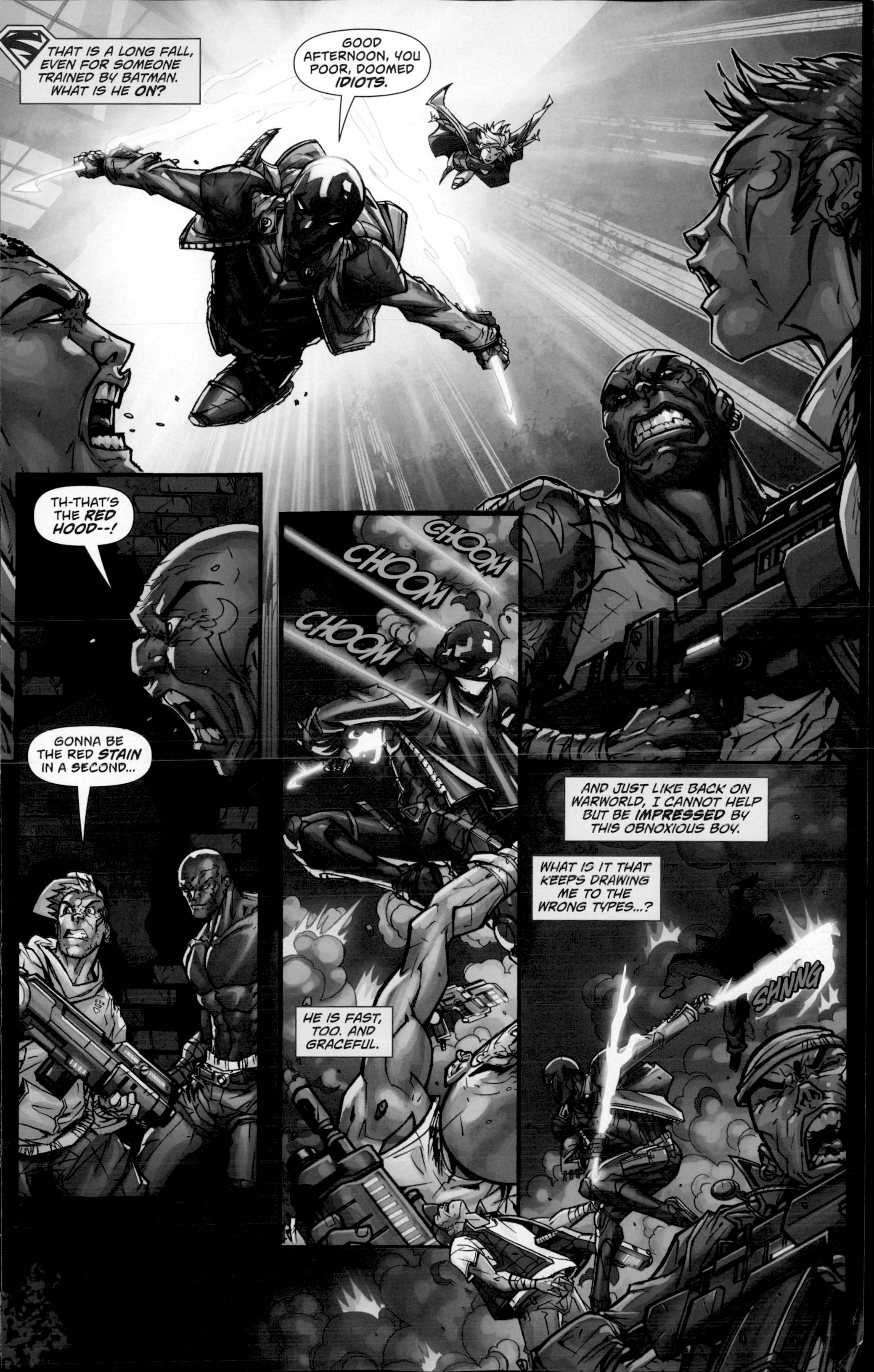

THAT IS A LONG FALL, EVEN FOR SOMEONE TRAINED BY BATMAN. WHAT IS HE ON?
GOOD AFTERNOON, YOU POOR, DOOMED IDIOTS.
TH-THAT'S THE RED HOOD--!
GONNA BE THE RED STAIN IN A SECOND...
CHOOM
CHOOM
CHOOM
HE IS FAST, TOO. AND GRACEFUL.
AND JUST LIKE BACK ON WARWORLD, I CANNOT HELP BUT BE IMPRESSED BY THIS OBNOXIOUS BOY.
WHAT IS IT THAT KEEPS DRAWING ME TO THE WRONG TYPES...?
SHNNG

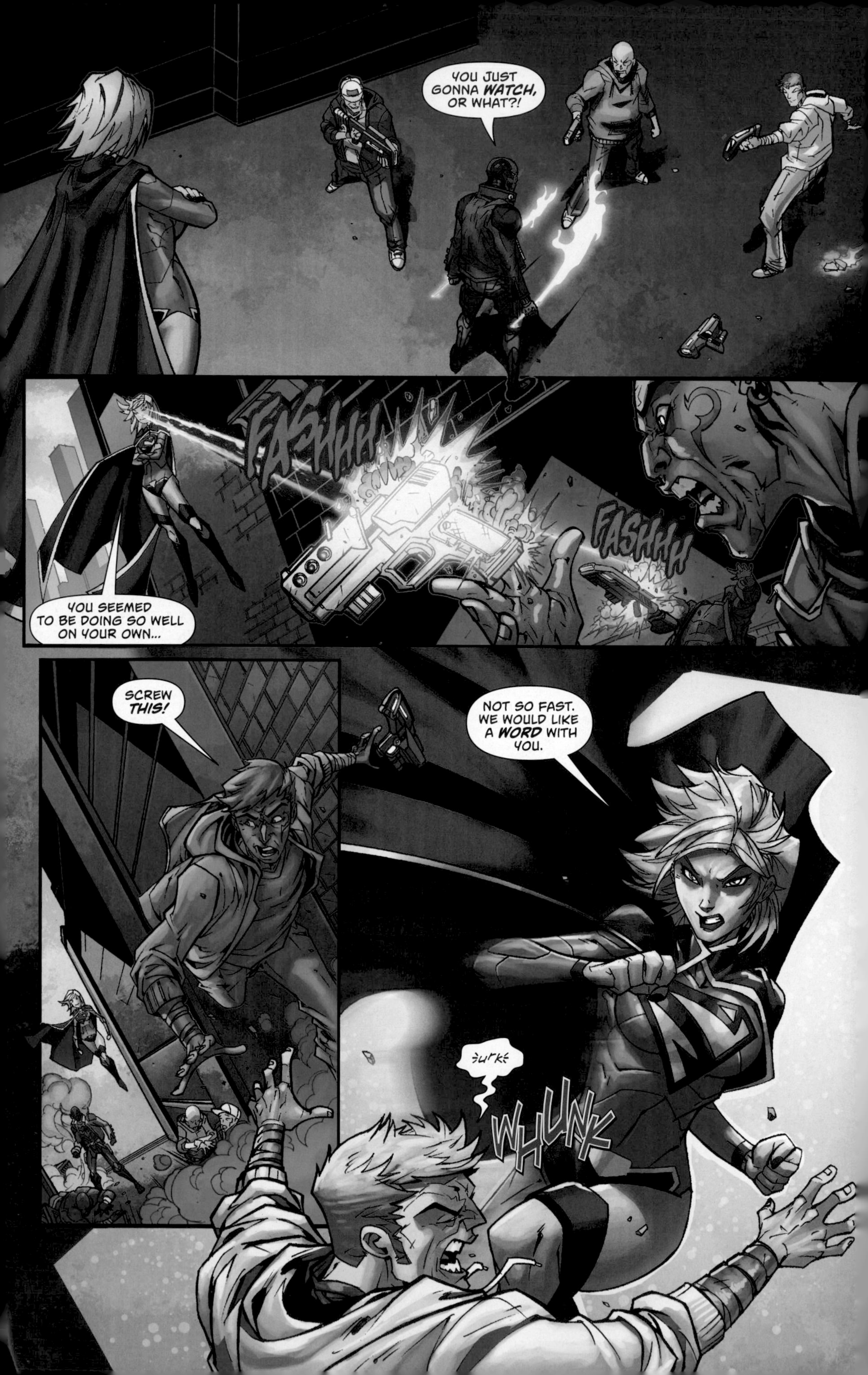
YOU JUST GONNA WATCH, OR WHAT?!
FASHHH
FASHHH
YOU SEEMED TO BE DOING SO WELL ON YOUR OWN...
SCREW THIS!
NOT SO FAST. WE WOULD LIKE A WORD WITH YOU.
urk
WHUNK

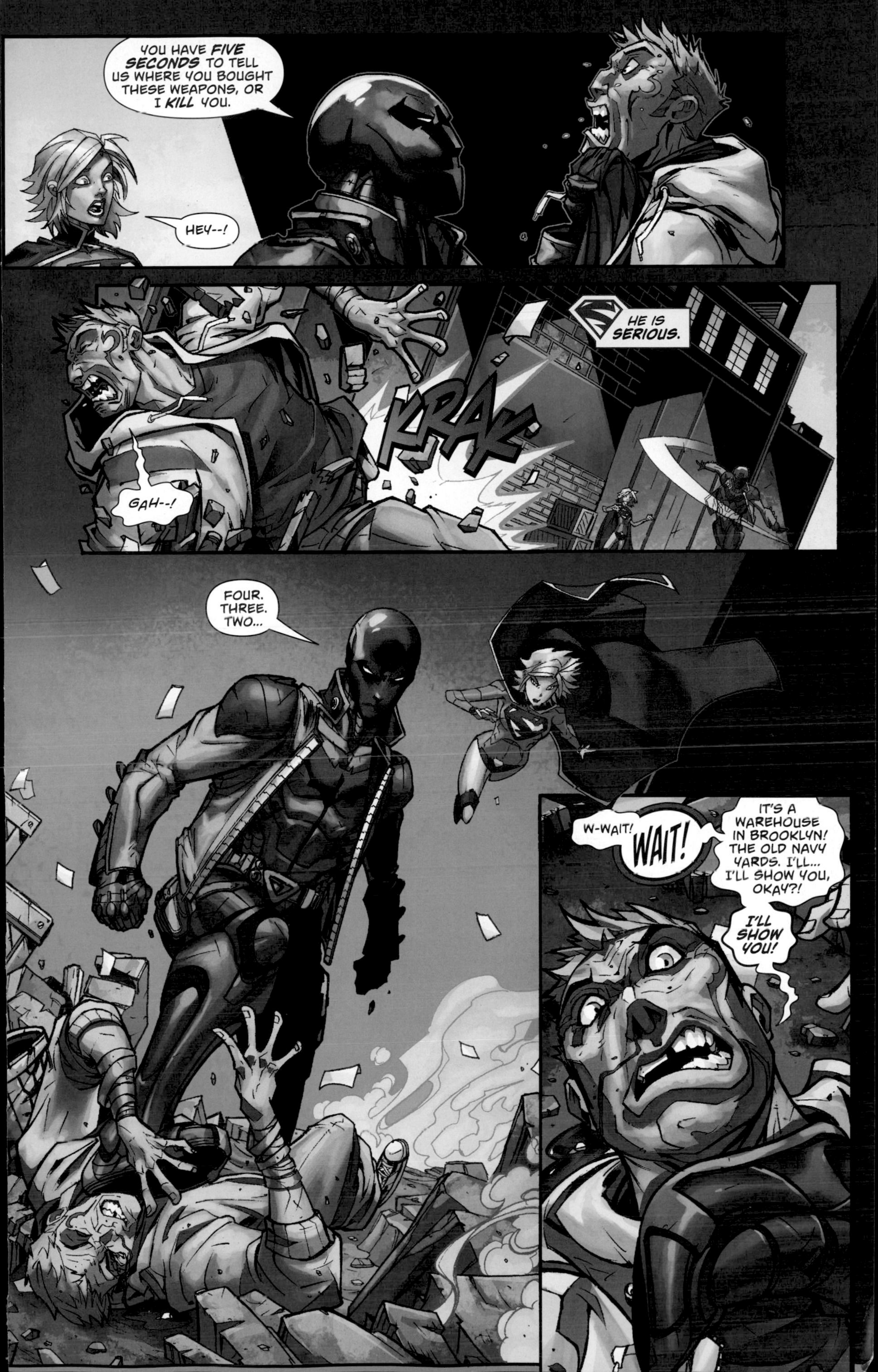
YOU HAVE FIVE SECONDS TO TELL US WHERE YOU BOUGHT THESE WEAPONS, OR I KILL YOU.
HEY--!
HE IS SERIOUS.
KRAK
GAH--!
FOUR. THREE. TWO...
W-WAIT!
WAIT!
IT'S A WAREHOUSE IN BROOKLYN! THE OLD NAVY YARDS. I'LL... I'LL SHOW YOU, OKAY?!
I'LL SHOW YOU!

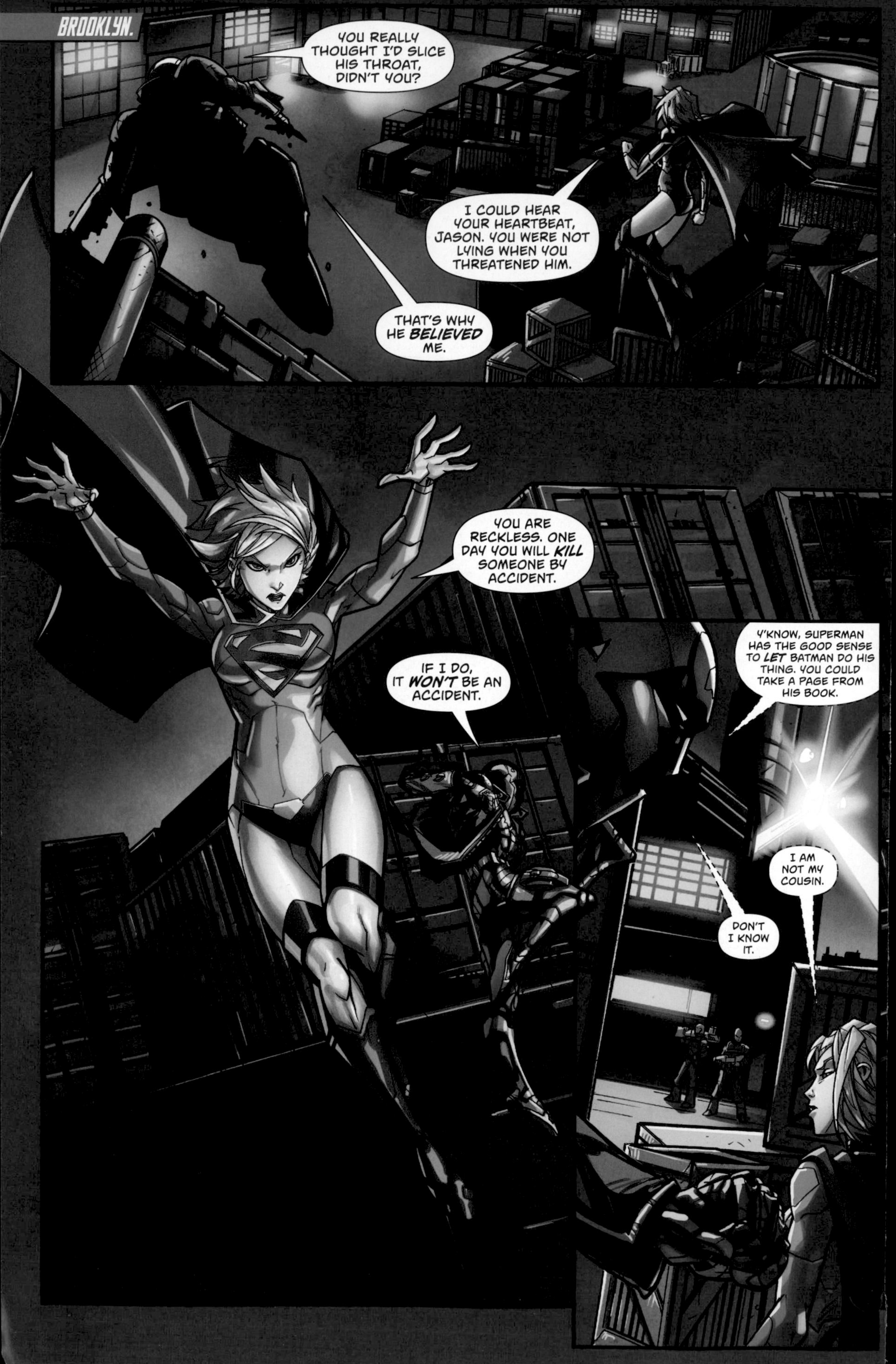
BROOKLYN.
YOU REALLY THOUGHT I'D SLICE HIS THROAT, DIDN'T YOU?
I COULD HEAR YOUR HEARTBEAT, JASON. YOU WERE NOT LYING WHEN YOU THREATENED HIM.
THAT'S WHY HE BELIEVED ME.
YOU ARE RECKLESS. ONE DAY YOU WILL KILL SOMEONE BY ACCIDENT.
IF I DO, IT WON'T BE AN ACCIDENT.
Y'KNOW, SUPERMAN HAS THE GOOD SENSE TO LET BATMAN DO HIS THING. YOU COULD TAKE A PAGE FROM HIS BOOK.
I AM NOT MY COUSIN.
DON'T I KNOW IT.

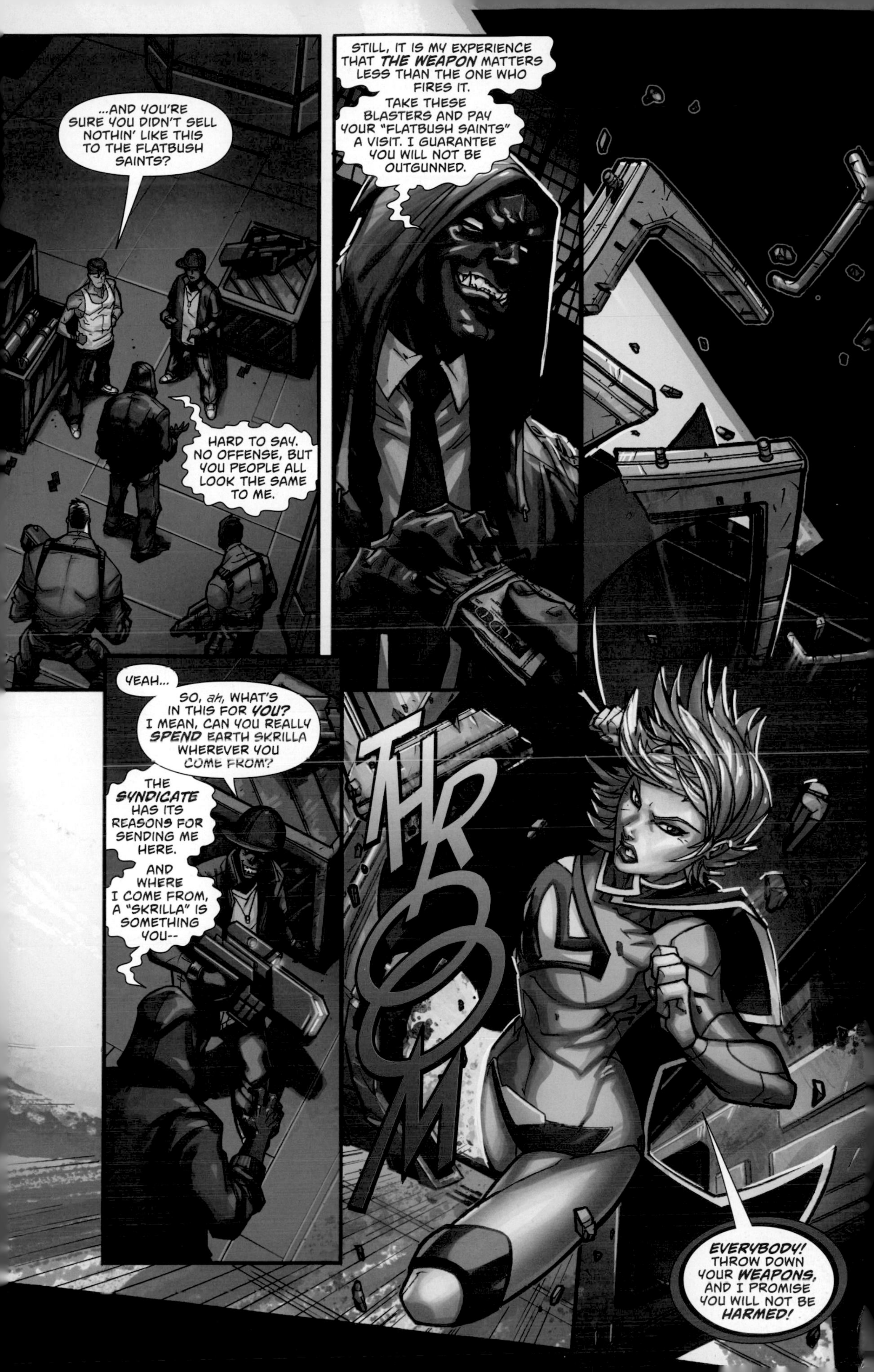
...AND YOU'RE SURE YOU DIDN'T SELL NOTHIN' LIKE THIS TO THE FLATBUSH SAINTS?
HARD TO SAY. NO OFFENSE, BUT YOU PEOPLE ALL LOOK THE SAME TO ME.
STILL, IT IS MY EXPERIENCE THAT THE WEAPON MATTERS LESS THAN THE ONE WHO FIRES IT.
TAKE THESE BLASTERS AND PAY YOUR "FLATBUSH SAINTS" A VISIT. I GUARANTEE YOU WILL NOT BE OUTGUNNED.
YEAH...
SO, ah, WHAT'S IN THIS FOR YOU? I MEAN, CAN YOU REALLY SPEND EARTH SKRILLA WHEREVER YOU COME FROM?
THE SYNDICATE HAS ITS REASONS FOR SENDING ME HERE.
AND WHERE I COME FROM, A "SKRILLA" IS SOMETHING YOU--
THROOM
EVERYBODY! THROW DOWN YOUR WEAPONS, AND I PROMISE YOU WILL NOT BE HARMED!

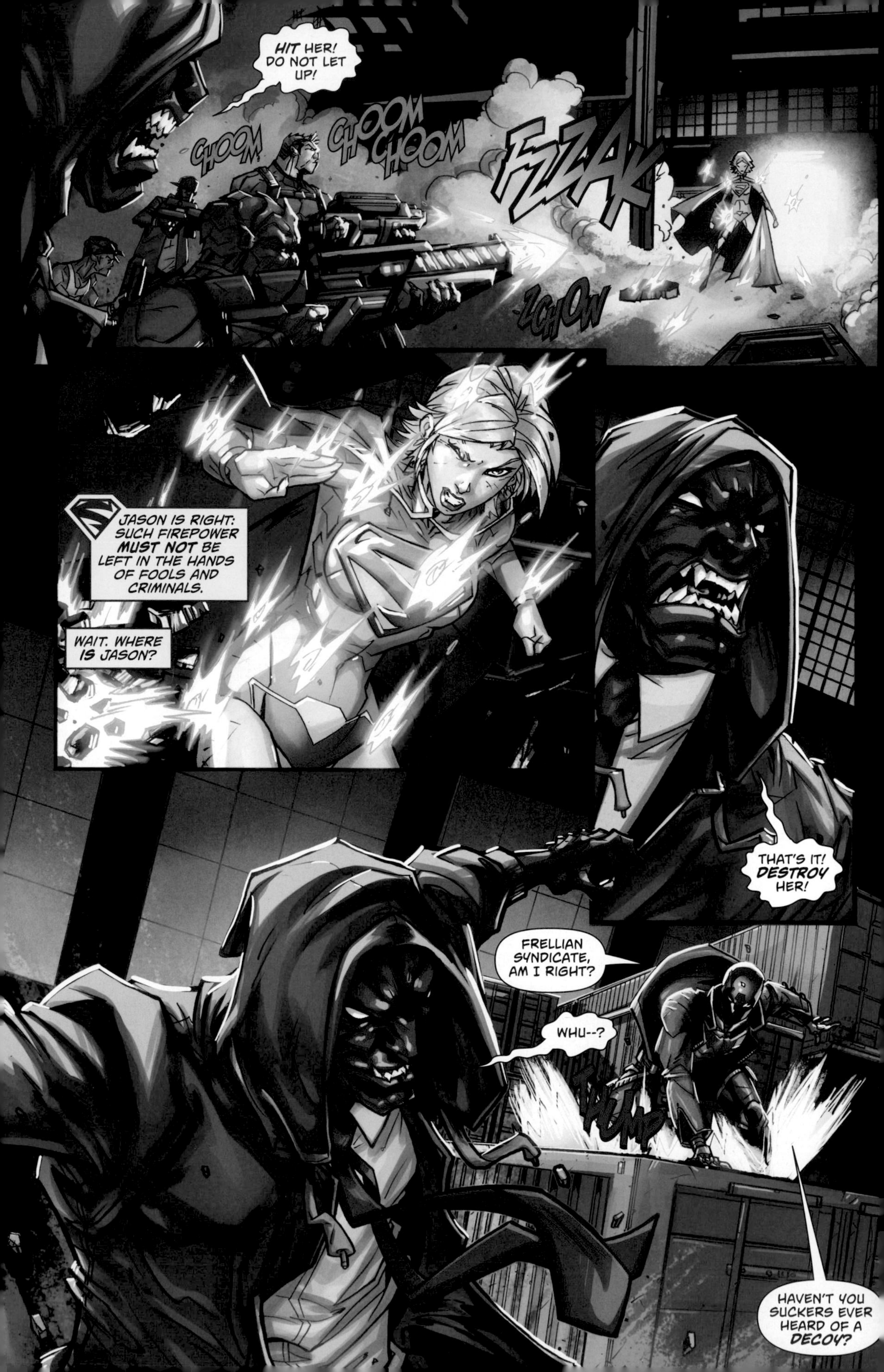
HIT HER! DO NOT LET UP!
CHOOM
CHOOM CHOOM CHOOM
FZZAK
ZCHOW
JASON IS RIGHT: SUCH FIREPOWER MUST NOT BE LEFT IN THE HANDS OF FOOLS AND CRIMINALS.
WAIT. WHERE IS JASON?
THAT'S IT! DESTROY HER!
FRELLIAN SYNDICATE, AM I RIGHT?
WHU--?
HAVEN'T YOU SUCKERS EVER HEARD OF A DECOY?

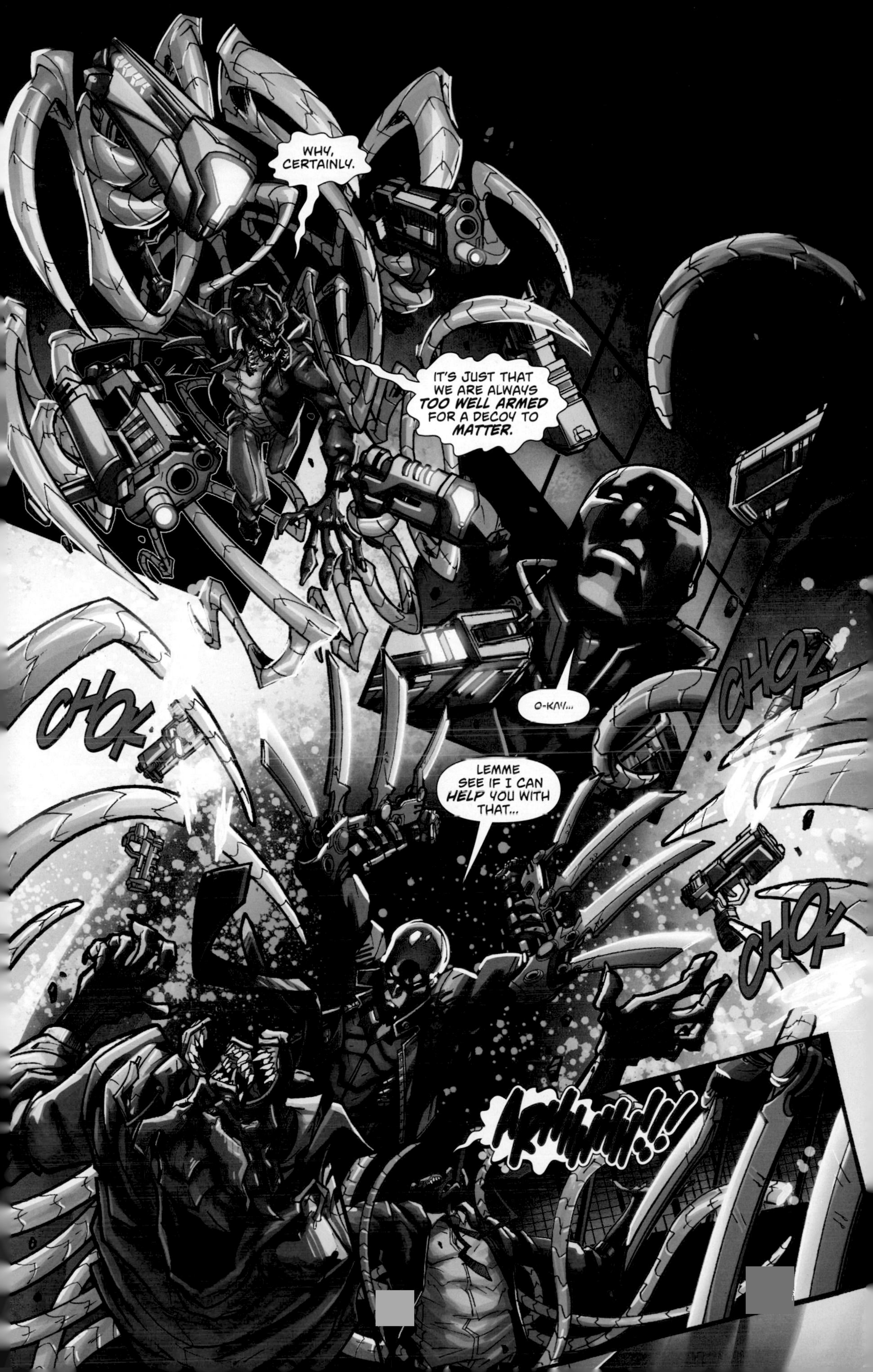
WHY, CERTAINLY.
IT'S JUST THAT WE ARE ALWAYS **TOO WELL ARMED** FOR A DECOY TO **MATTER.**
CHOK
O-KAY...
CHOK
LEMME SEE IF I CAN **HELP** YOU WITH THAT...
CHOK
ARHHHH!!!

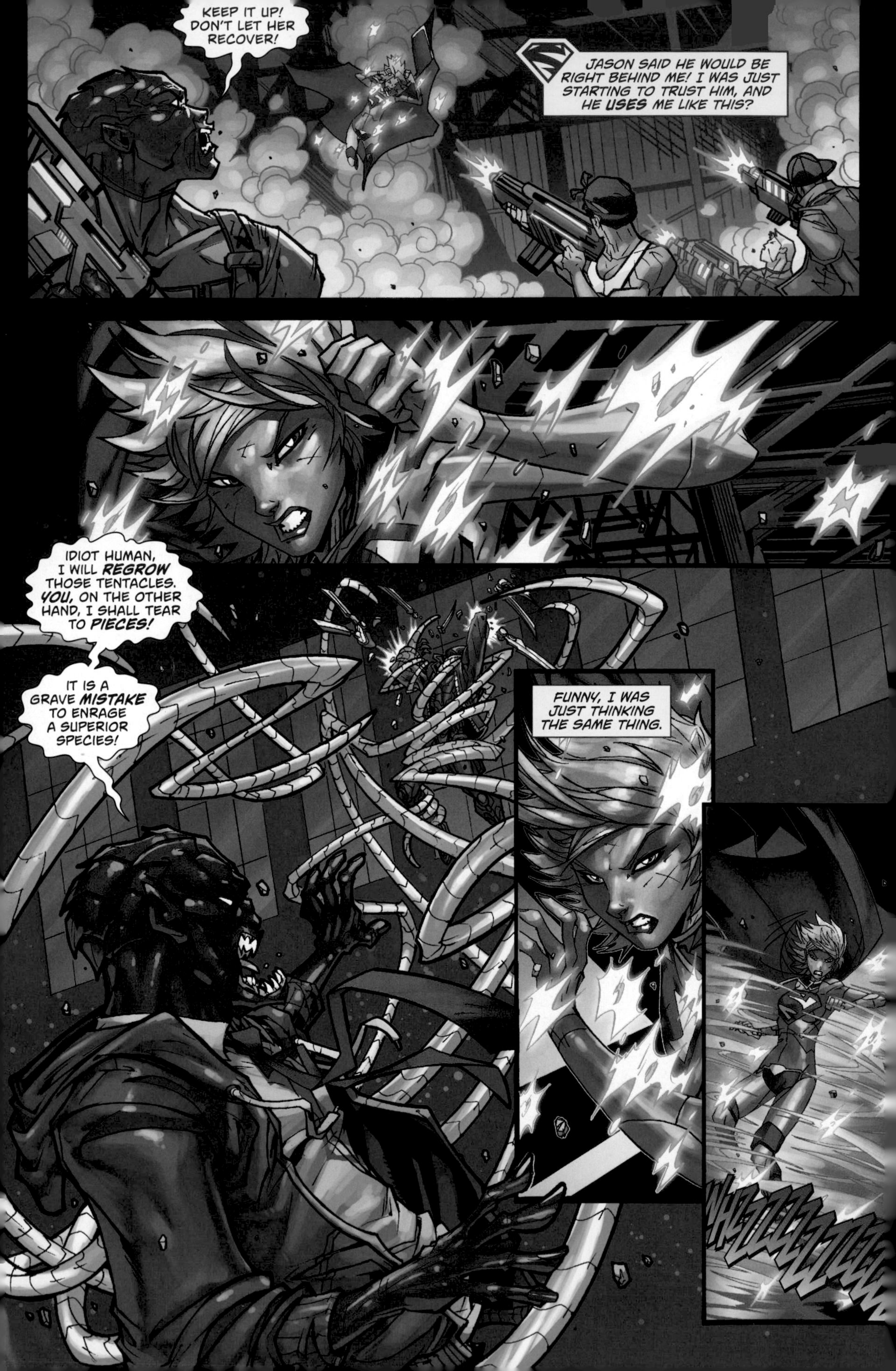
KEEP IT UP! DON'T LET HER RECOVER!
JASON SAID HE WOULD BE RIGHT BEHIND ME! I WAS JUST STARTING TO TRUST HIM, AND HE USES ME LIKE THIS?
IDIOT HUMAN, I WILL REGROW THOSE TENTACLES. YOU, ON THE OTHER HAND, I SHALL TEAR TO PIECES!
IT IS A GRAVE MISTAKE TO ENRAGE A SUPERIOR SPECIES!
FUNNY, I WAS JUST THINKING THE SAME THING.

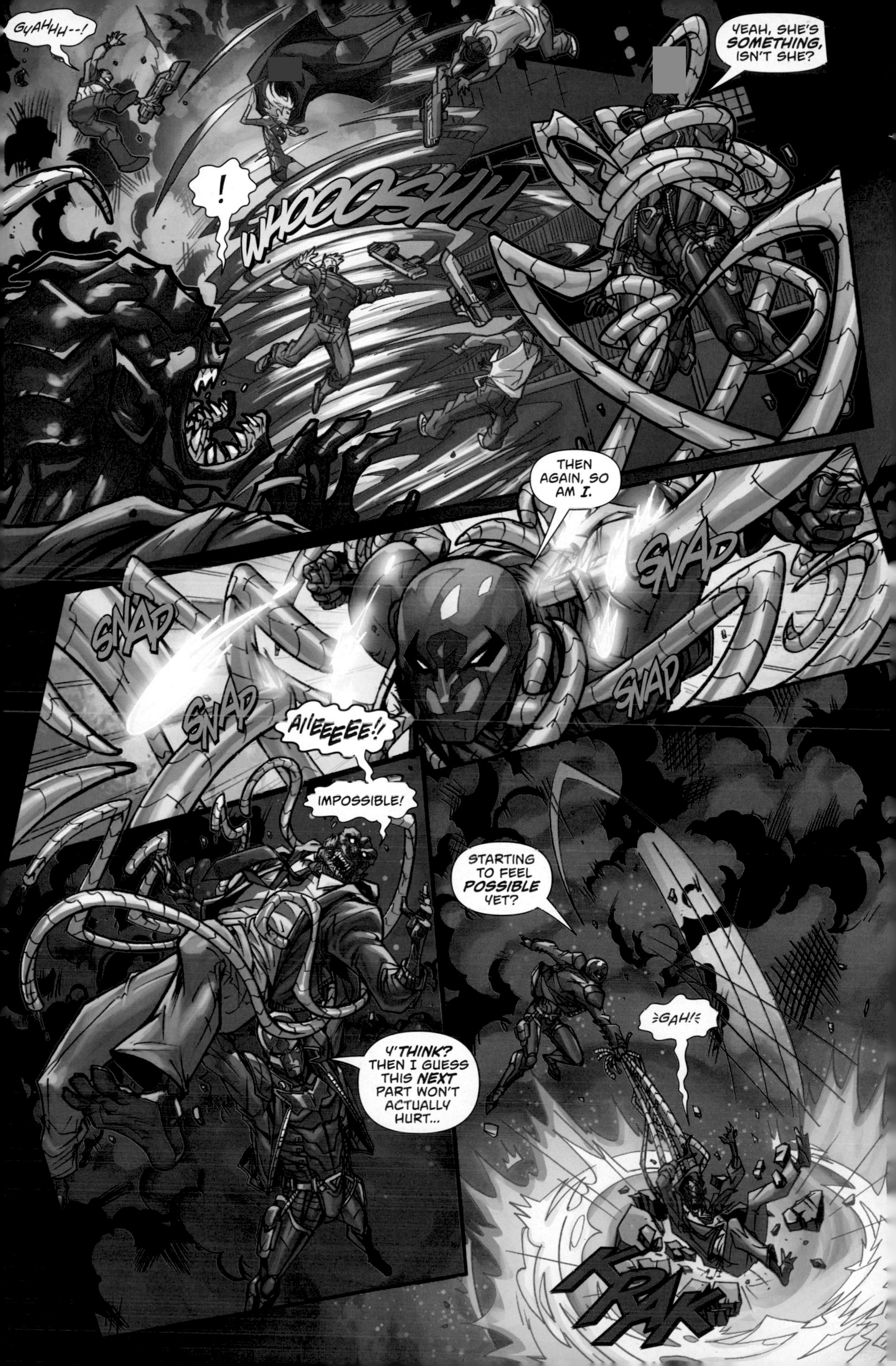
GYAHHH--!
YEAH, SHE'S SOMETHING, ISN'T SHE?
!
WHOOOOSHH
THEN AGAIN, SO AM I.
SNAP
SNAP
SNAP
SNAP
AIIEEEEE!!
IMPOSSIBLE!
STARTING TO FEEL POSSIBLE YET?
GAH!
Y'THINK? THEN I GUESS THIS NEXT PART WON'T ACTUALLY HURT...
KRAK

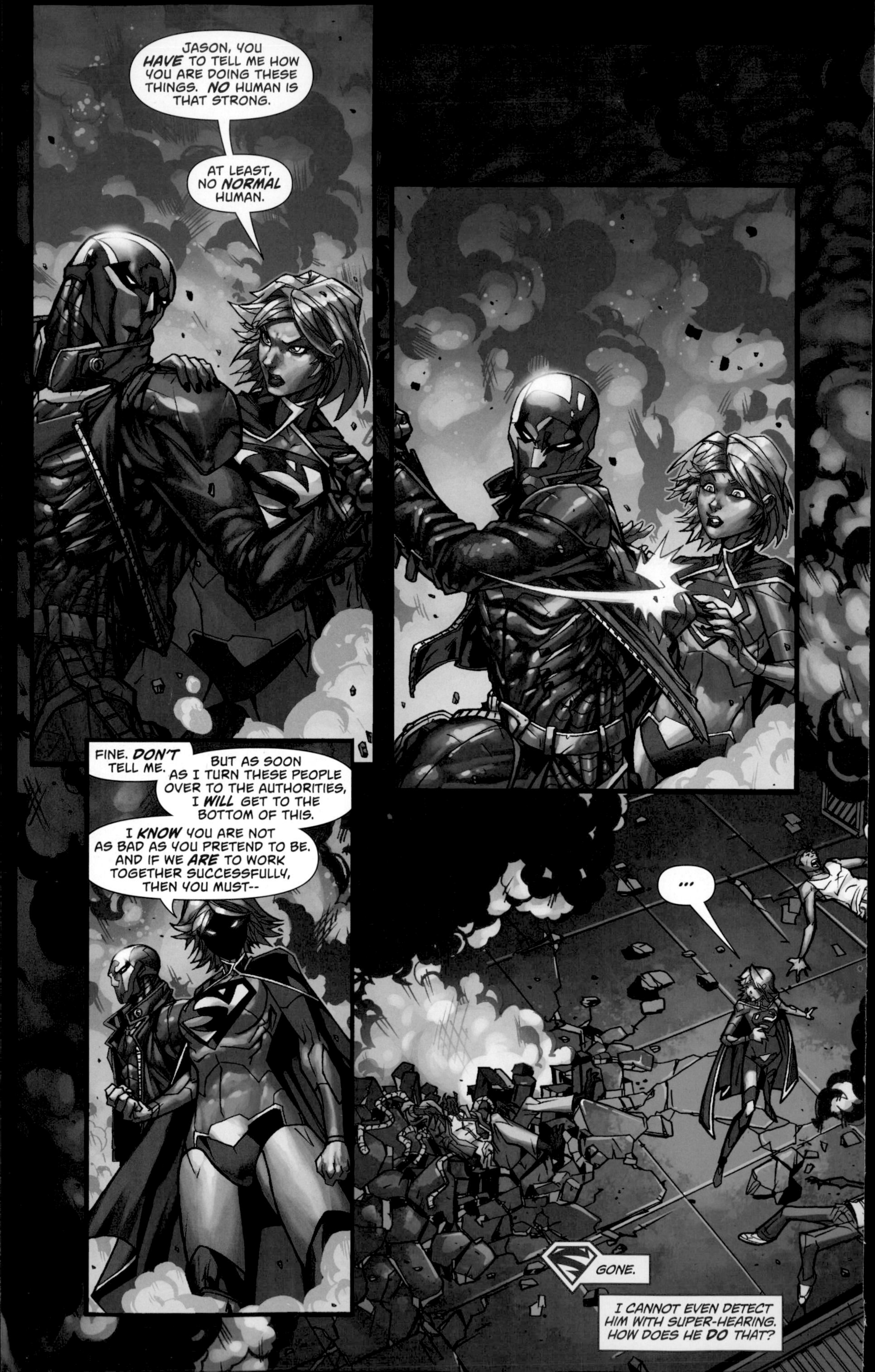
JASON, YOU HAVE TO TELL ME HOW YOU ARE DOING THESE THINGS. NO HUMAN IS THAT STRONG.
AT LEAST, NO NORMAL HUMAN.
FINE. DON'T TELL ME.
BUT AS SOON AS I TURN THESE PEOPLE OVER TO THE AUTHORITIES, I WILL GET TO THE BOTTOM OF THIS.
I KNOW YOU ARE NOT AS BAD AS YOU PRETEND TO BE. AND IF WE ARE TO WORK TOGETHER SUCCESSFULLY, THEN YOU MUST--
...
GONE.
I CANNOT EVEN DETECT HIM WITH SUPER-HEARING. HOW DOES HE DO THAT?

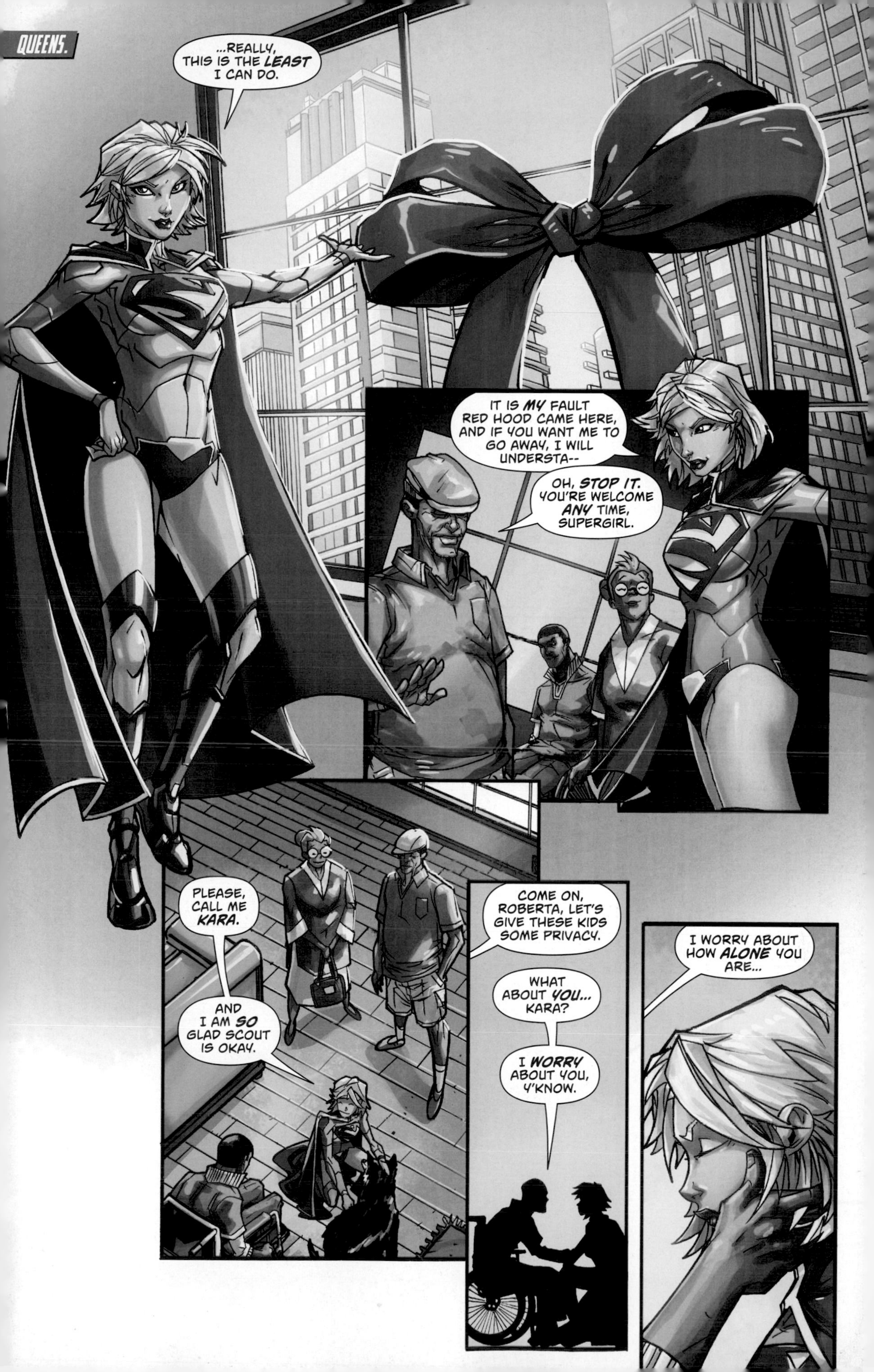
QUEENS.
...REALLY, THIS IS THE LEAST I CAN DO.
IT IS MY FAULT RED HOOD CAME HERE, AND IF YOU WANT ME TO GO AWAY, I WILL UNDERSTA--
OH, STOP IT. YOU'RE WELCOME ANY TIME, SUPERGIRL.
PLEASE, CALL ME KARA.
AND I AM SO GLAD SCOUT IS OKAY.
COME ON, ROBERTA, LET'S GIVE THESE KIDS SOME PRIVACY.
WHAT ABOUT YOU... KARA?
I WORRY ABOUT YOU, Y'KNOW.
I WORRY ABOUT HOW ALONE YOU ARE...

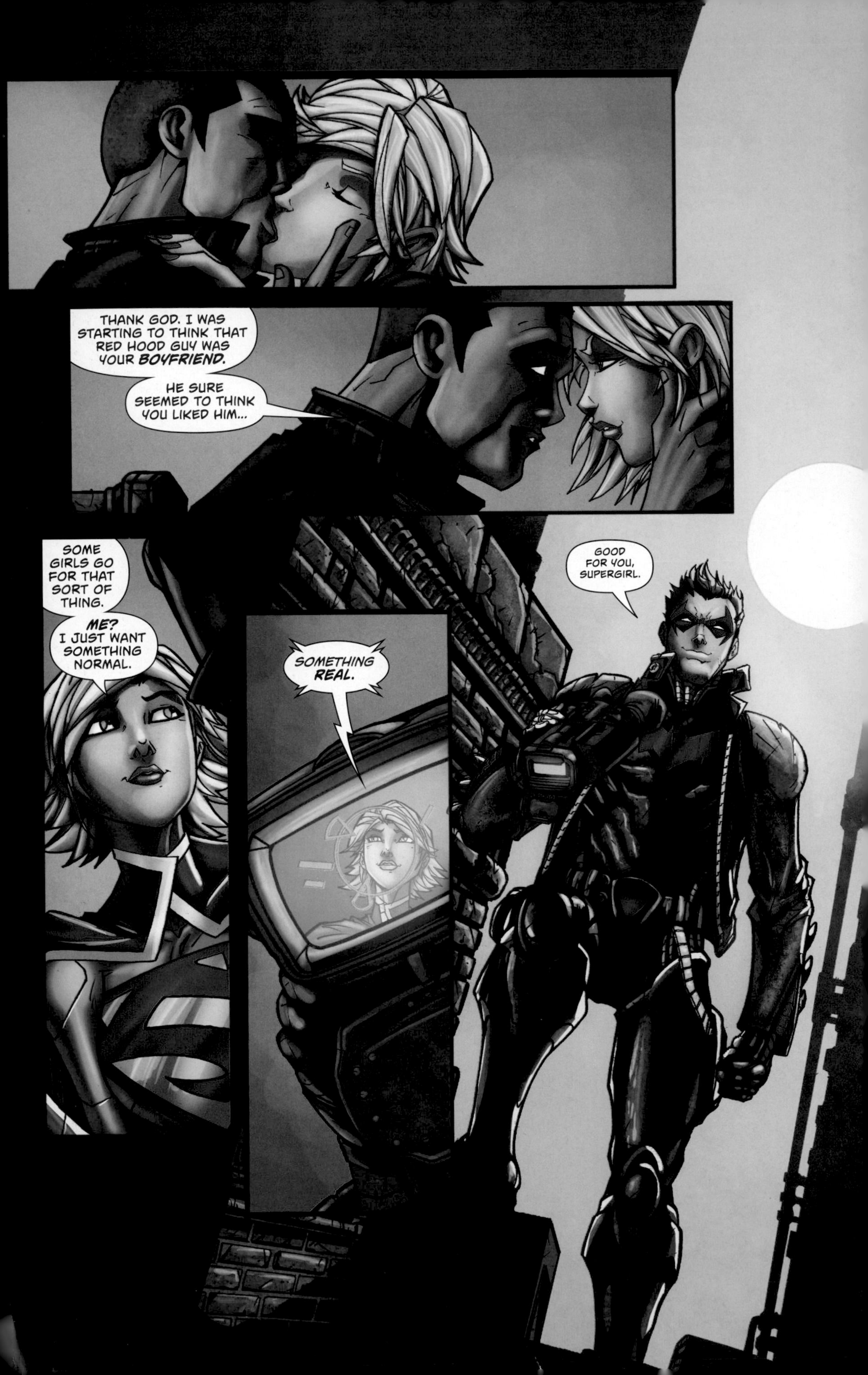
THANK GOD. I WAS STARTING TO THINK THAT RED HOOD GUY WAS YOUR **BOYFRIEND**.
HE SURE SEEMED TO THINK YOU LIKED HIM...
SOME GIRLS GO FOR THAT SORT OF THING.
ME? I JUST WANT SOMETHING NORMAL.
SOMETHING ***REAL***.
GOOD FOR YOU, SUPERGIRL.

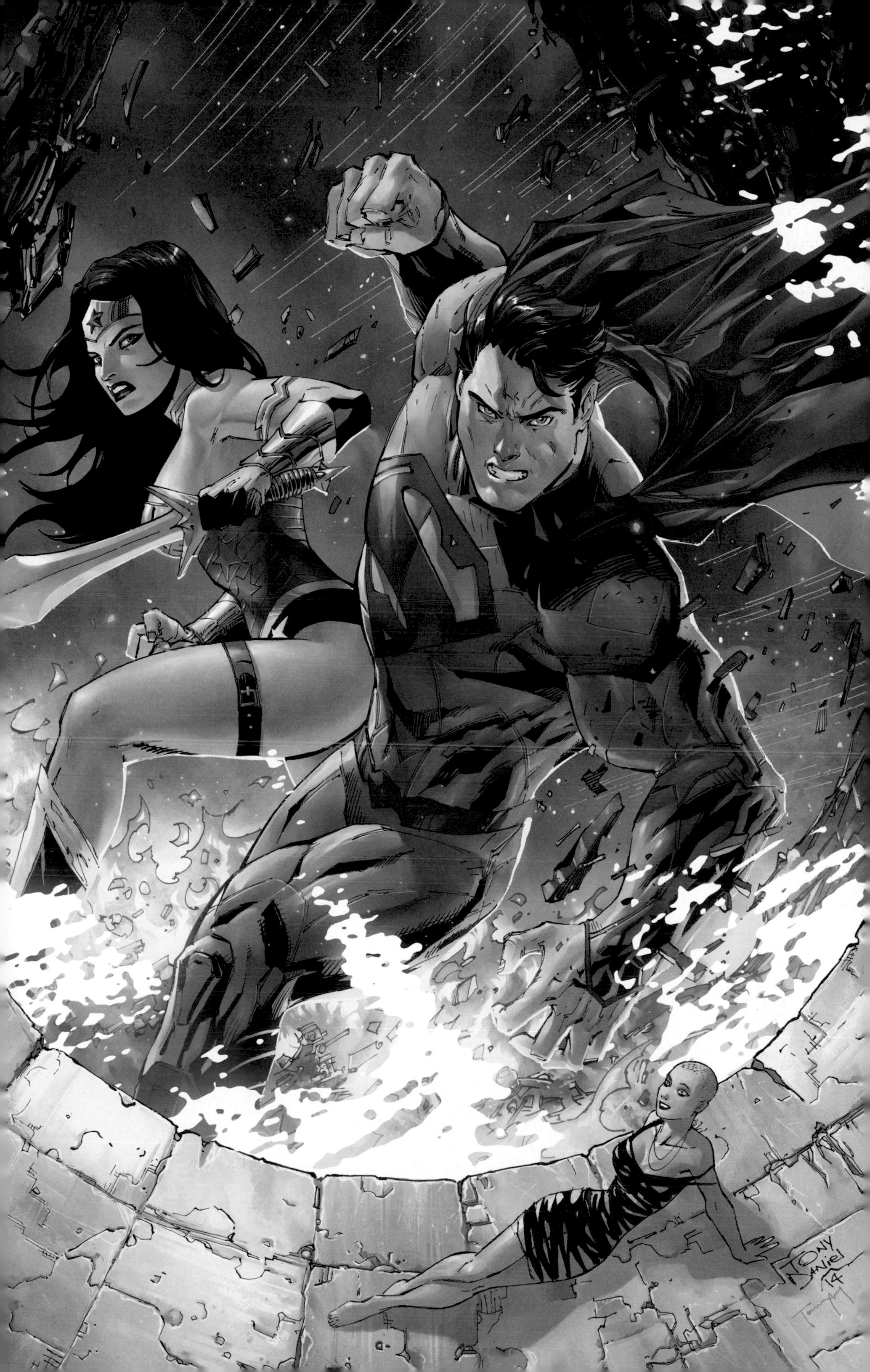
TONY DANIEL '14

SUPERMAN DOOMED

[AFTERMATH] chapter 3

"METAPHORMORPHOSIS"

STORY
CHARLES SOULE

ART
JACK HERBERT, WALDEN WONG
AND **CLIFF RICHARDS**

COLORS
TOMEU MOREY

LETTERS
CARLOS M. MANGUAL

COVER
TONY S. DANIEL AND **TOMEU MOREY**

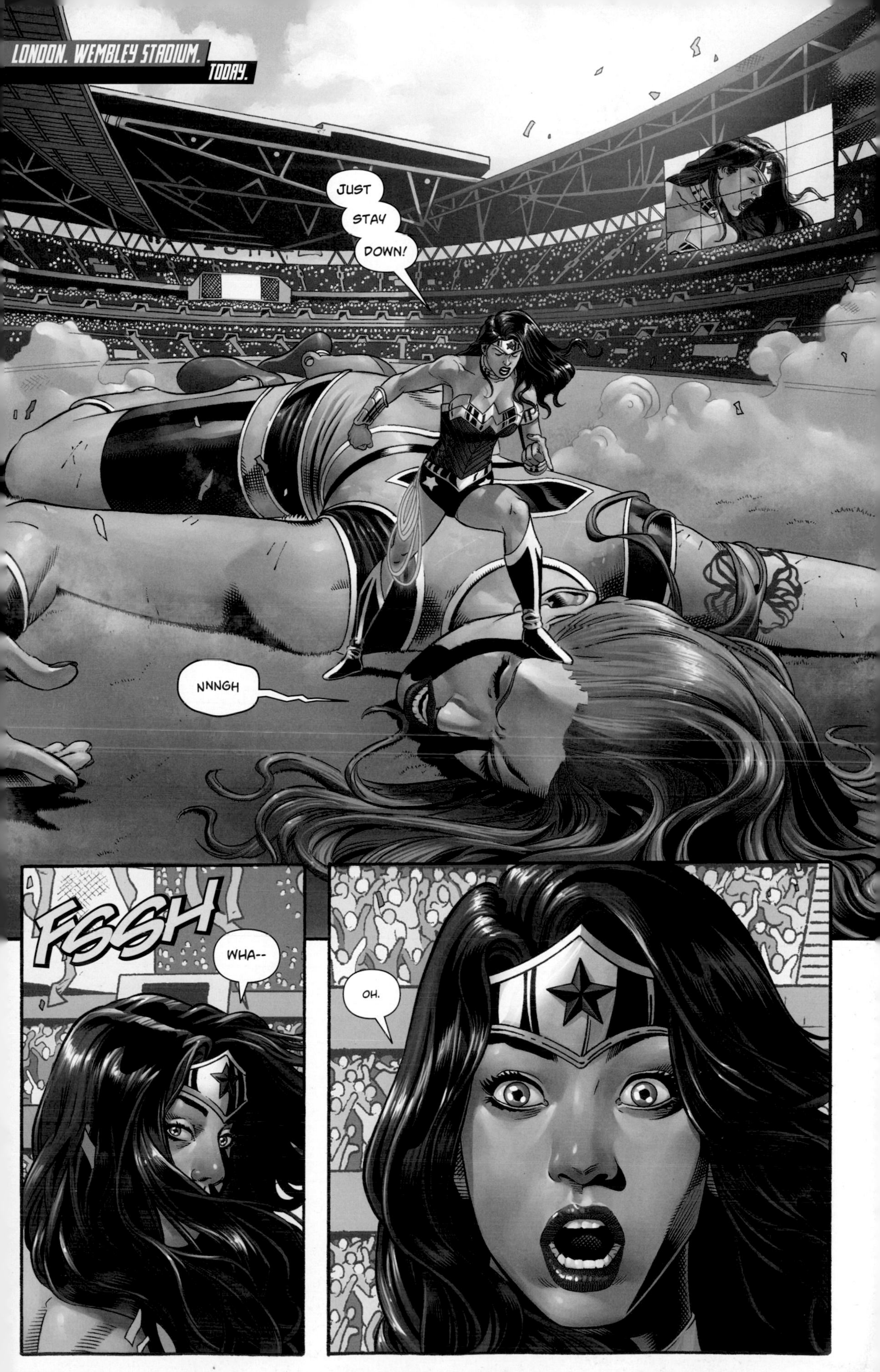
LONDON. WEMBLEY STADIUM.
TODAY.
JUST STAY DOWN!
NNNGH
FSSH
WHA--
OH.

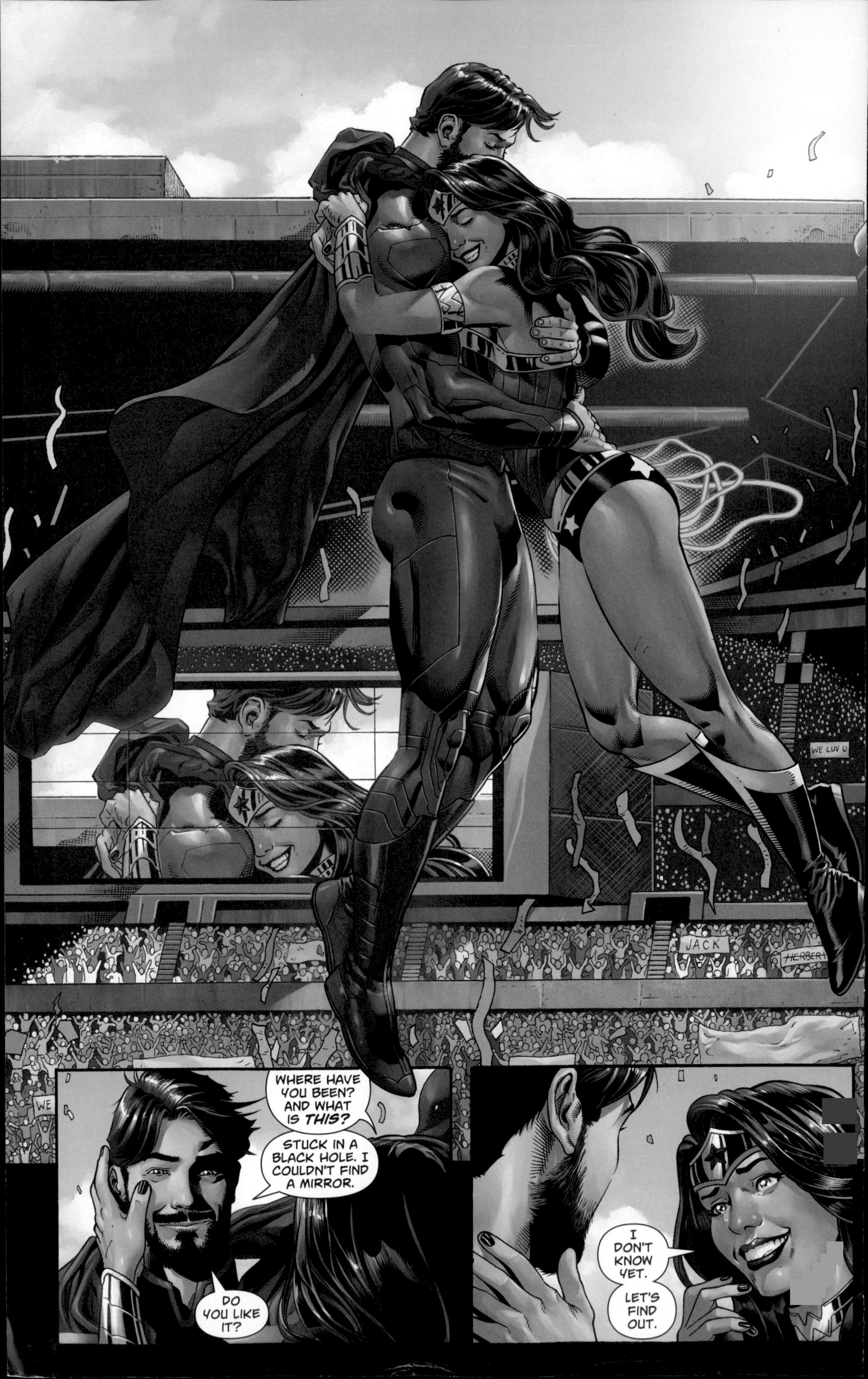
WE LUV U
JACK
HERBERT
WE
WHERE HAVE YOU BEEN? AND WHAT IS THIS?
STUCK IN A BLACK HOLE. I COULDN'T FIND A MIRROR.
DO YOU LIKE IT?
I DON'T KNOW YET.
LET'S FIND OUT.

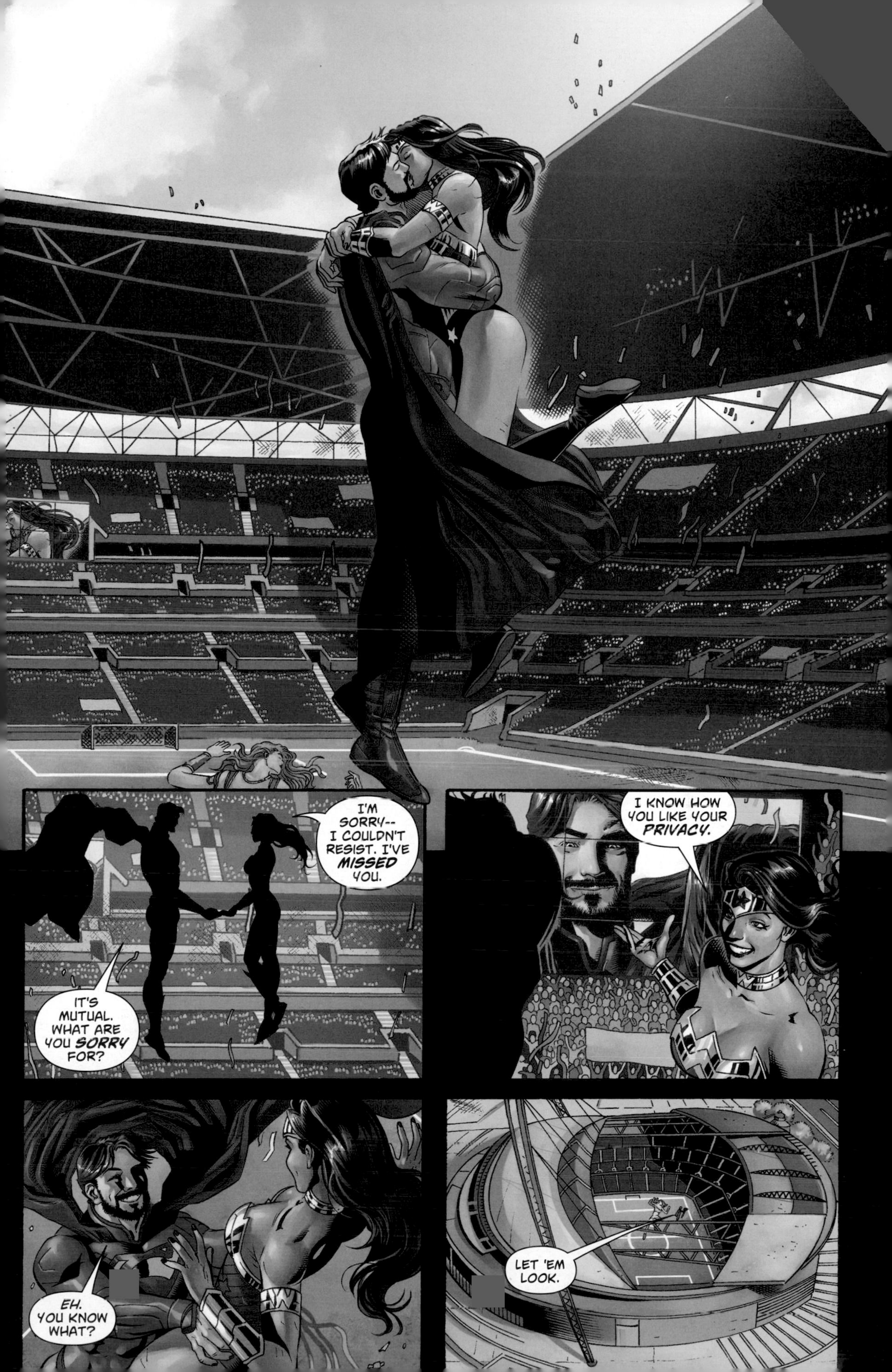
I'M SORRY-- I COULDN'T RESIST. I'VE MISSED YOU.
IT'S MUTUAL. WHAT ARE YOU SORRY FOR?
I KNOW HOW YOU LIKE YOUR PRIVACY.
EH. YOU KNOW WHAT?
LET 'EM LOOK.

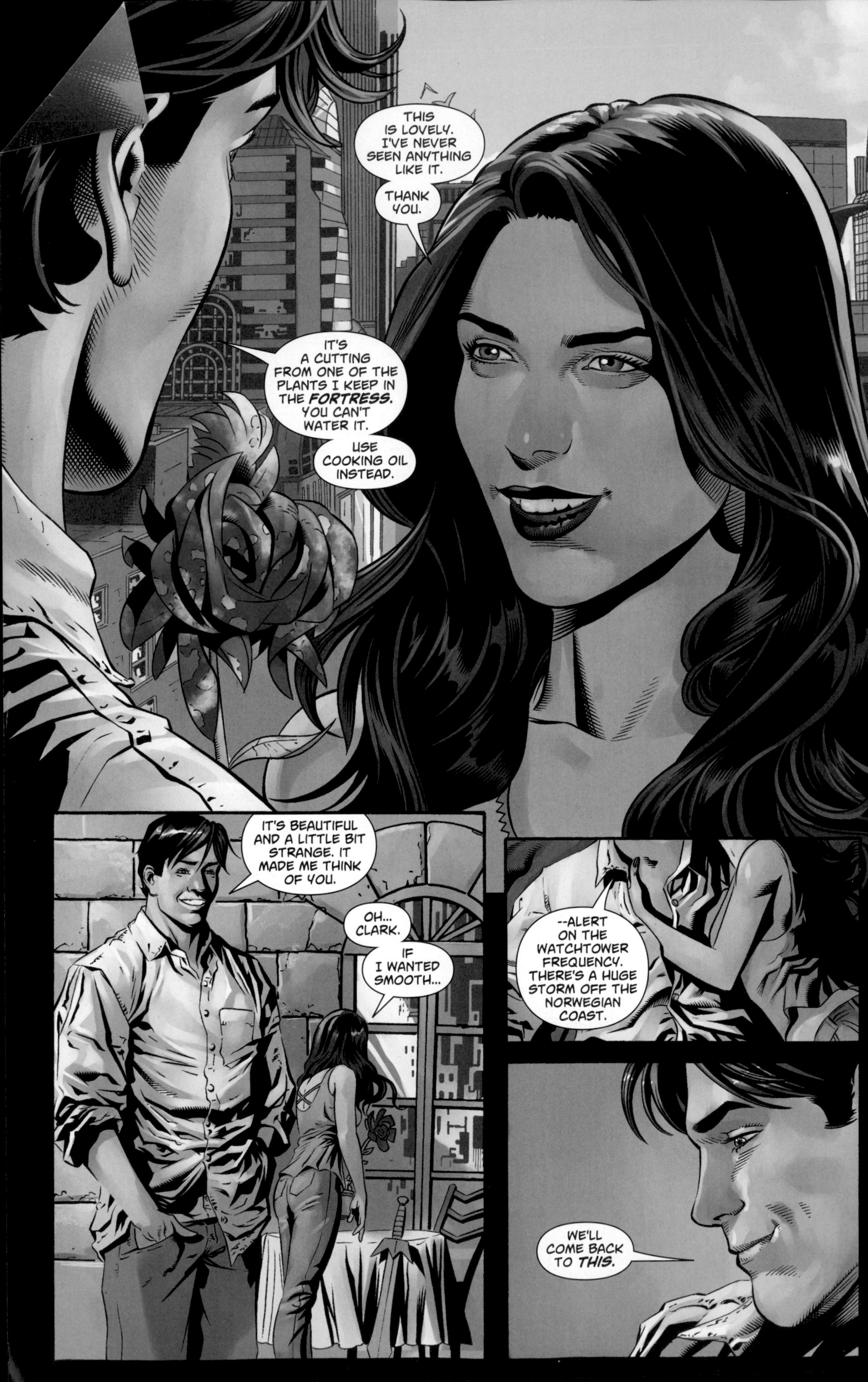
THIS IS LOVELY. I'VE NEVER SEEN ANYTHING LIKE IT.
THANK YOU.
IT'S A CUTTING FROM ONE OF THE PLANTS I KEEP IN THE FORTRESS. YOU CAN'T WATER IT.
USE COOKING OIL INSTEAD.
IT'S BEAUTIFUL AND A LITTLE BIT STRANGE. IT MADE ME THINK OF YOU.
OH... CLARK.
IF I WANTED SMOOTH...
--ALERT ON THE WATCHTOWER FREQUENCY. THERE'S A HUGE STORM OFF THE NORWEGIAN COAST.
WE'LL COME BACK TO THIS.

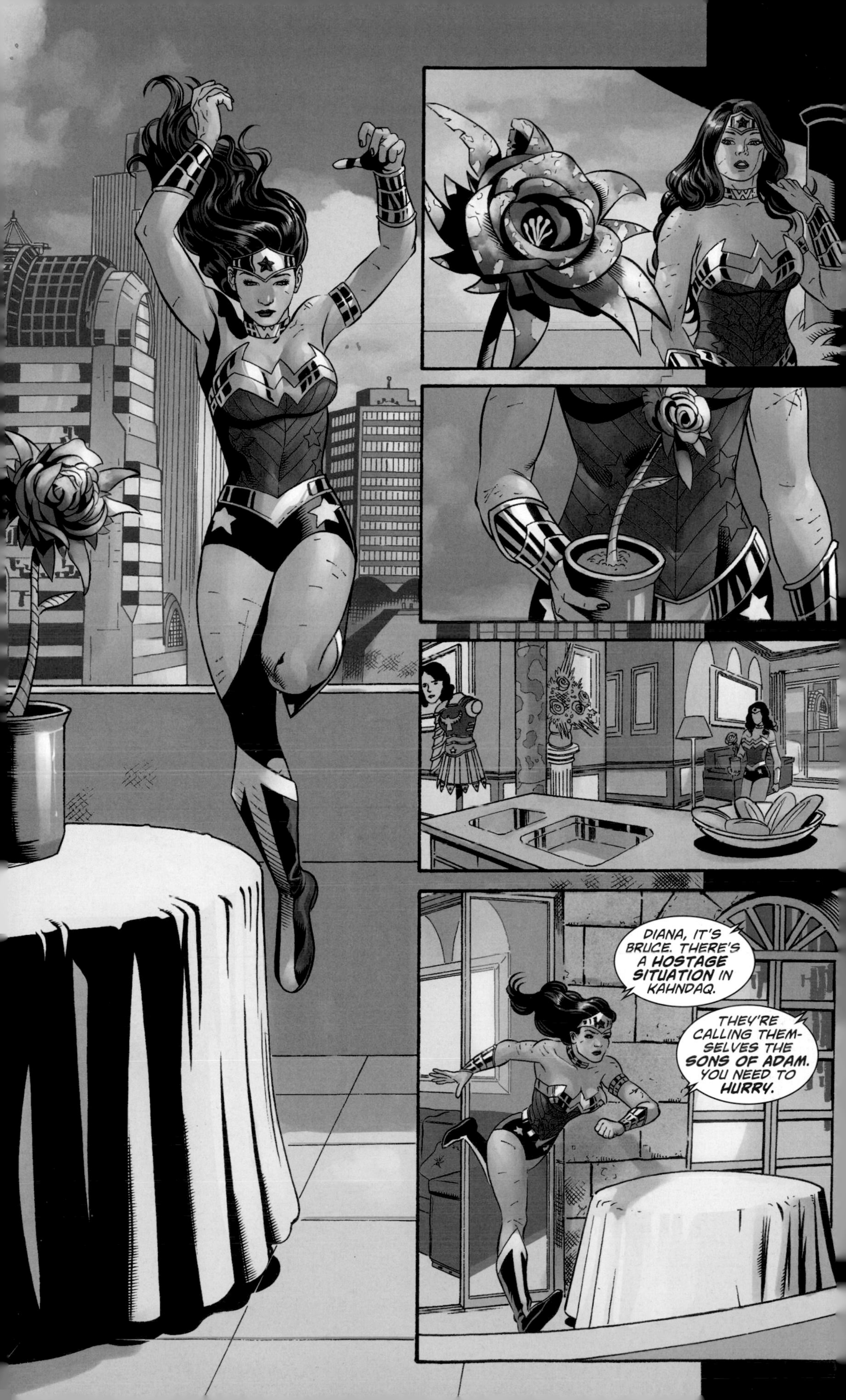
DIANA, IT'S BRUCE. THERE'S A HOSTAGE SITUATION IN KAHNDAQ.
THEY'RE CALLING THEMSELVES THE SONS OF ADAM. YOU NEED TO HURRY.

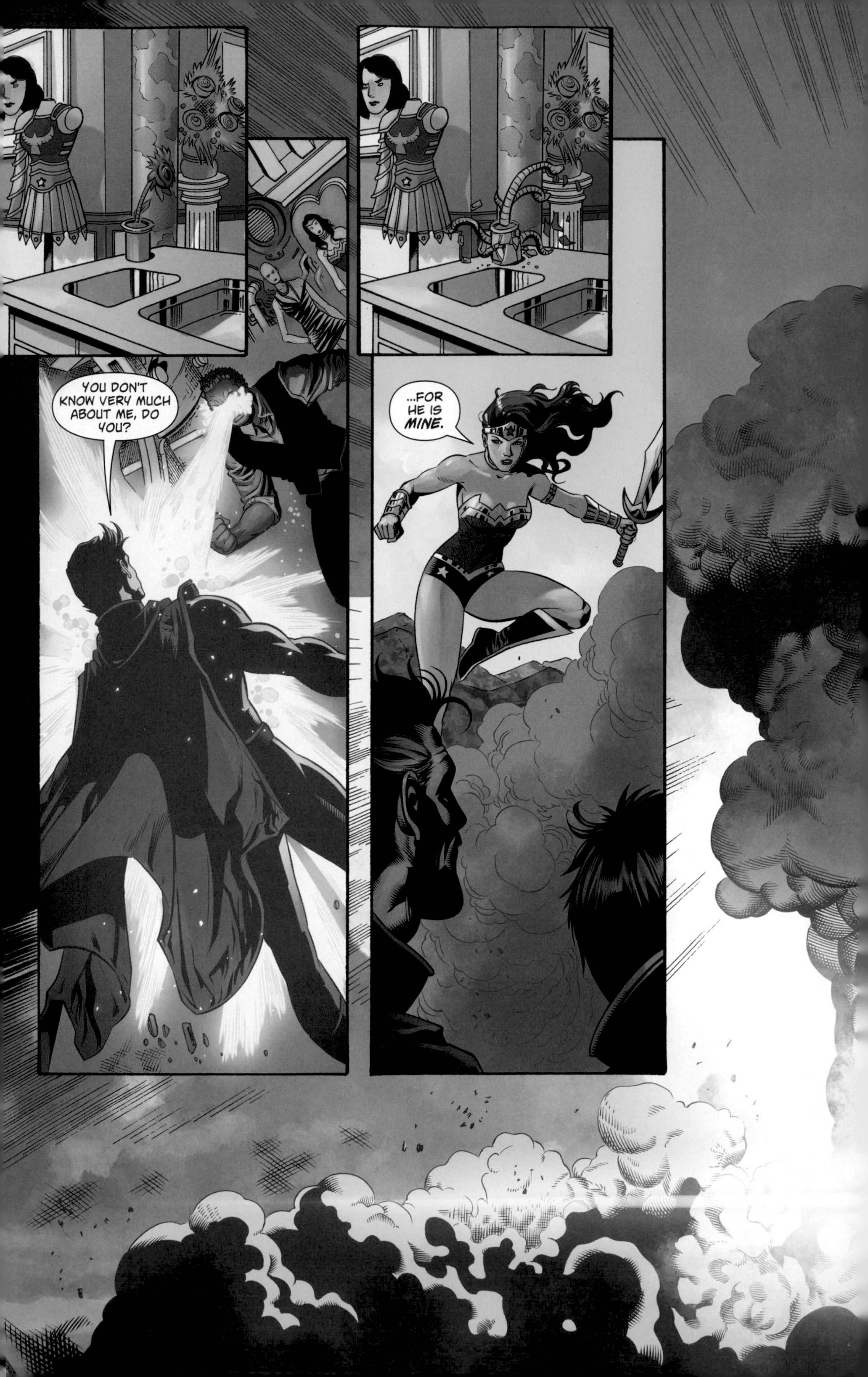
YOU DON'T KNOW VERY MUCH ABOUT ME, DO YOU?
...FOR HE IS *MINE*.

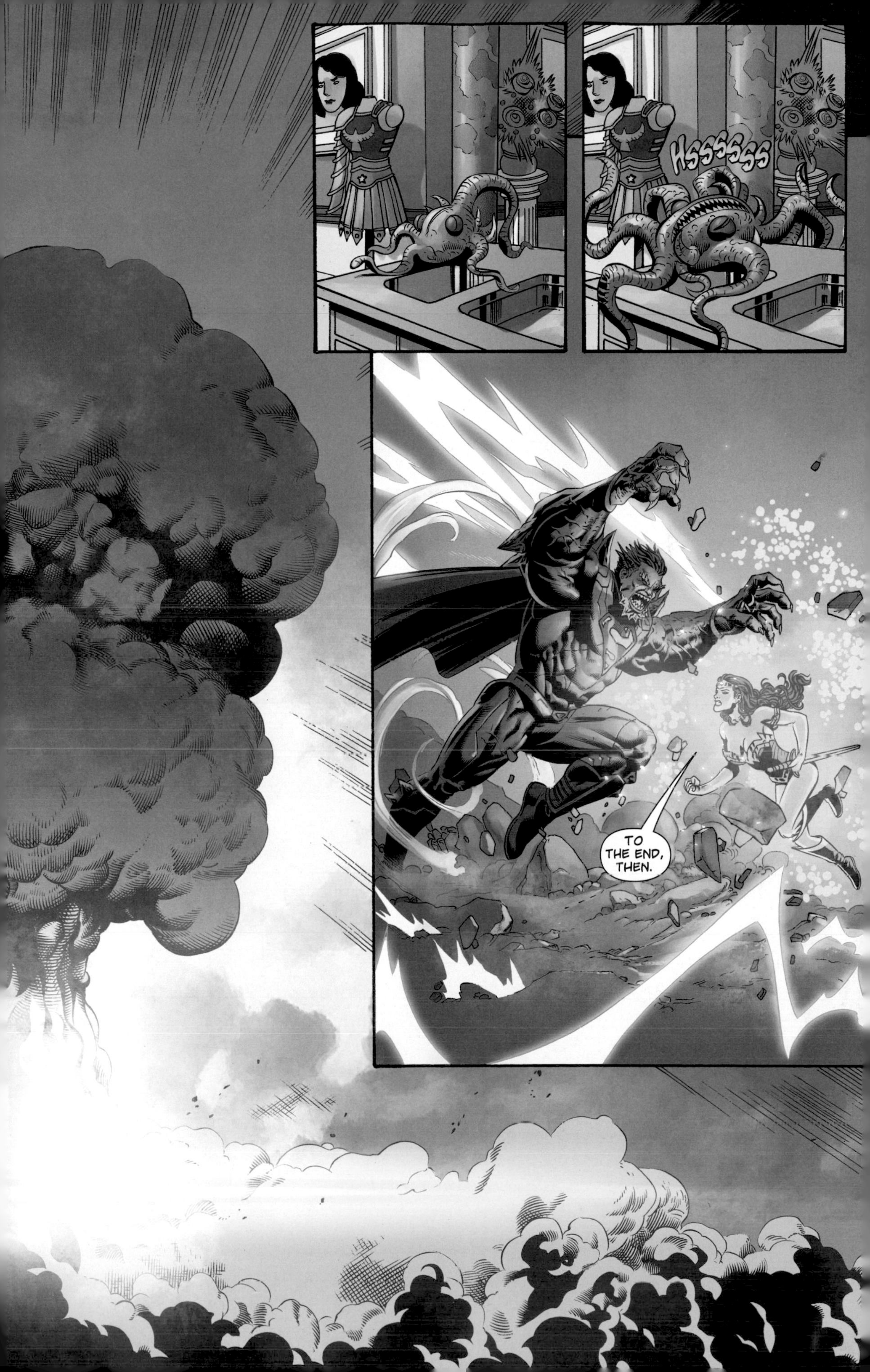
HSSSSSS
TO THE END, THEN.

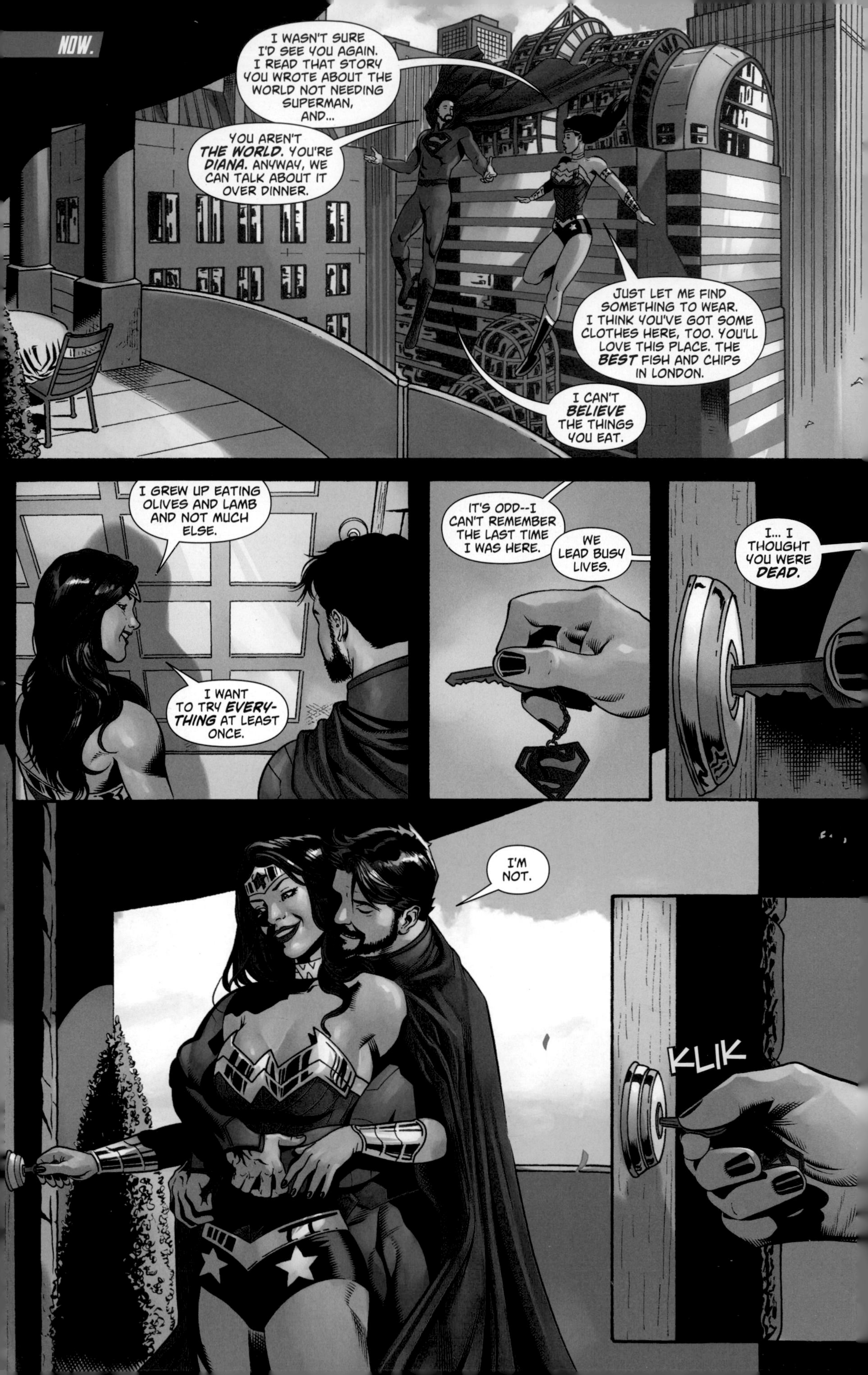
NOW.
I WASN'T SURE I'D SEE YOU AGAIN. I READ THAT STORY YOU WROTE ABOUT THE WORLD NOT NEEDING SUPERMAN, AND...
YOU AREN'T **THE WORLD.** YOU'RE **DIANA.** ANYWAY, WE CAN TALK ABOUT IT OVER DINNER.
JUST LET ME FIND SOMETHING TO WEAR. I THINK YOU'VE GOT SOME CLOTHES HERE, TOO. YOU'LL LOVE THIS PLACE. THE **BEST** FISH AND CHIPS IN LONDON.
I CAN'T **BELIEVE** THE THINGS YOU EAT.
I GREW UP EATING OLIVES AND LAMB AND NOT MUCH ELSE.
I WANT TO TRY **EVERYTHING** AT LEAST ONCE.
IT'S ODD--I CAN'T REMEMBER THE LAST TIME I WAS HERE.
WE LEAD BUSY LIVES.
I... I THOUGHT YOU WERE **DEAD.**
I'M NOT.
KLIK

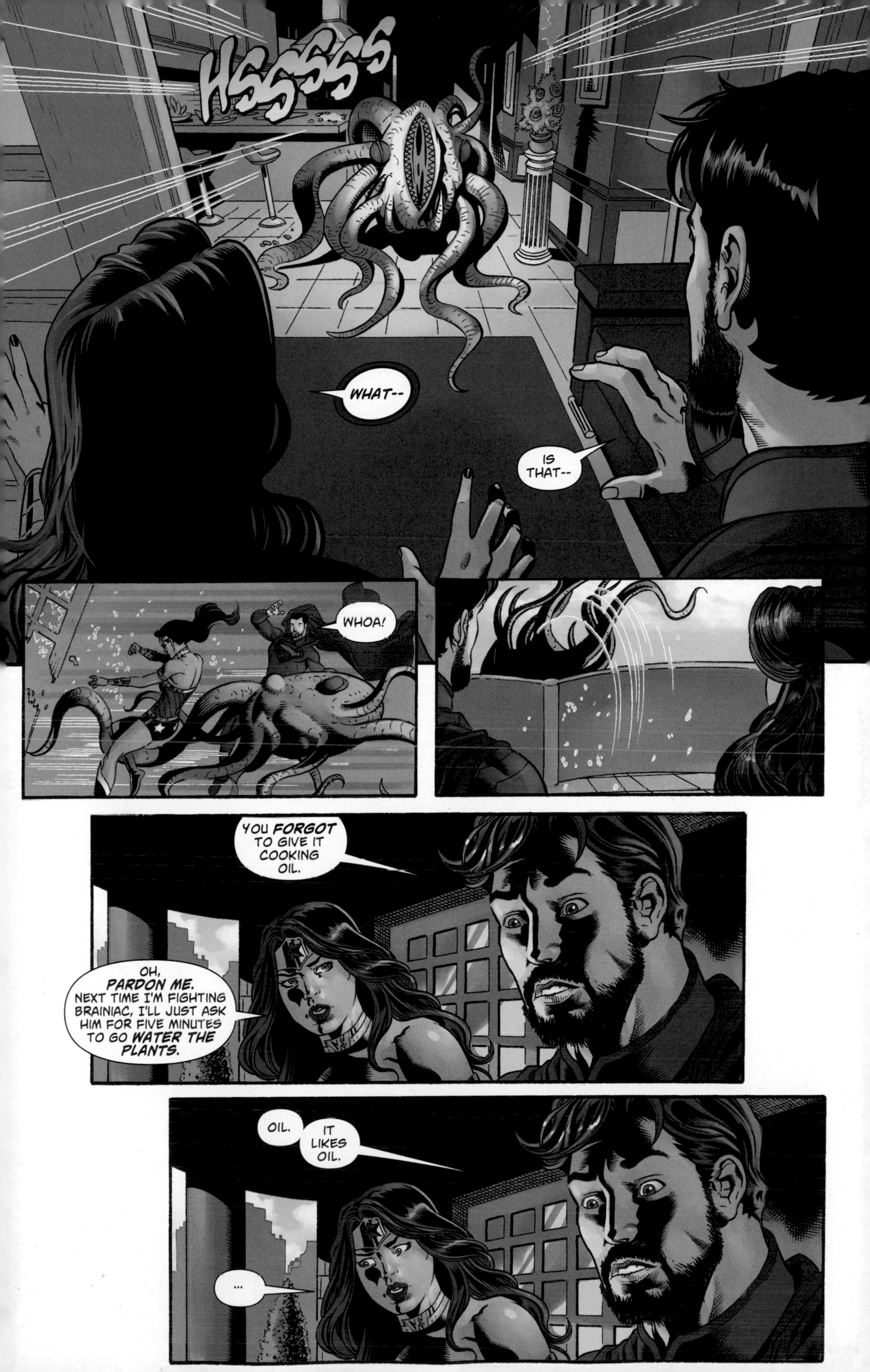
HSSSSS
WHAT--
IS THAT--
WHOA!
YOU FORGOT TO GIVE IT COOKING OIL.
OH, PARDON ME. NEXT TIME I'M FIGHTING BRAINIAC, I'LL JUST ASK HIM FOR FIVE MINUTES TO GO WATER THE PLANTS.
OIL.
IT LIKES OIL.
...

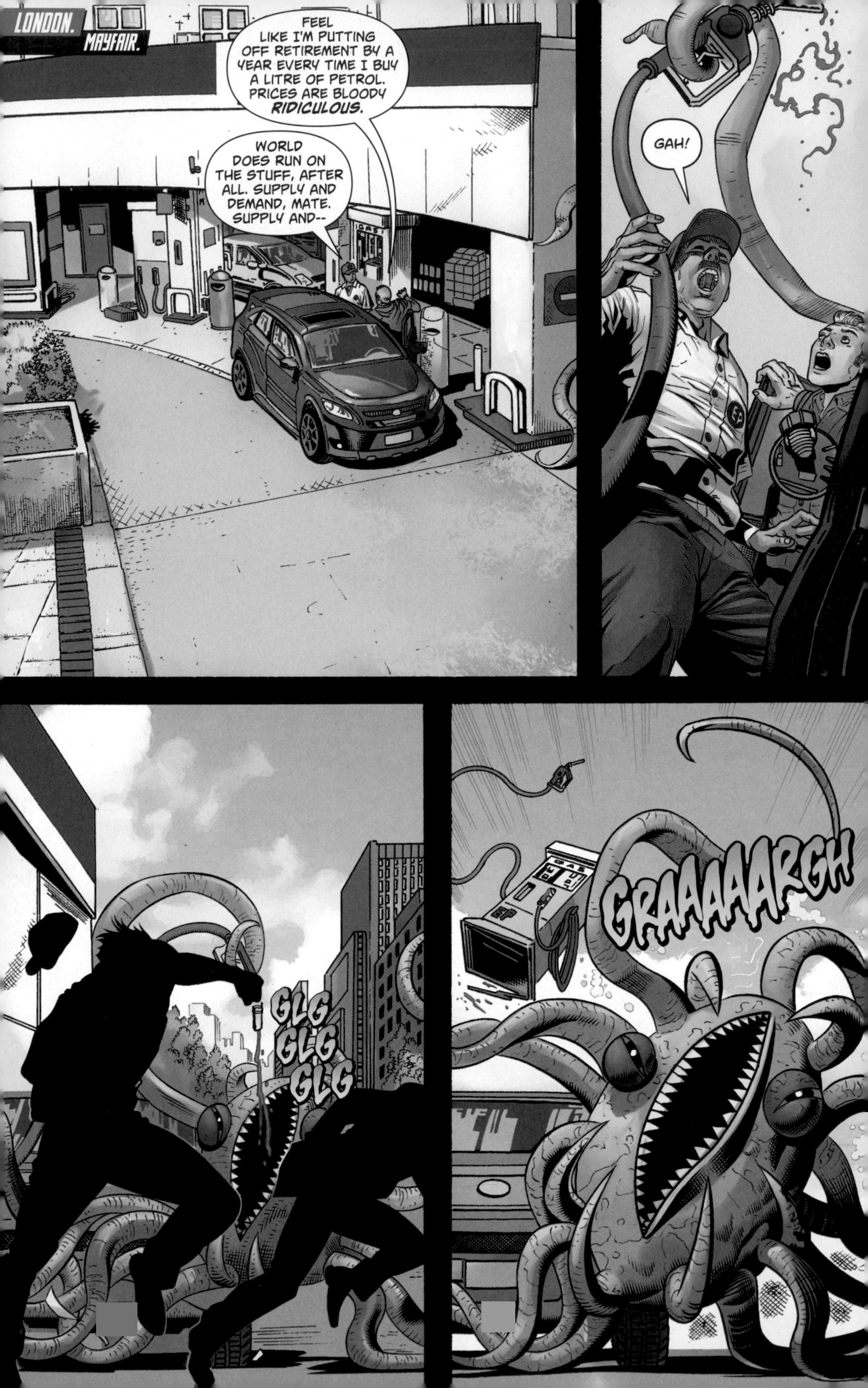
LONDON.
MAYFAIR.
FEEL LIKE I'M PUTTING OFF RETIREMENT BY A YEAR EVERY TIME I BUY A LITRE OF PETROL. PRICES ARE BLOODY RIDICULOUS.
WORLD DOES RUN ON THE STUFF, AFTER ALL. SUPPLY AND DEMAND, MATE. SUPPLY AND--
GAH!
GLG GLG GLG
GRAAAAARGH

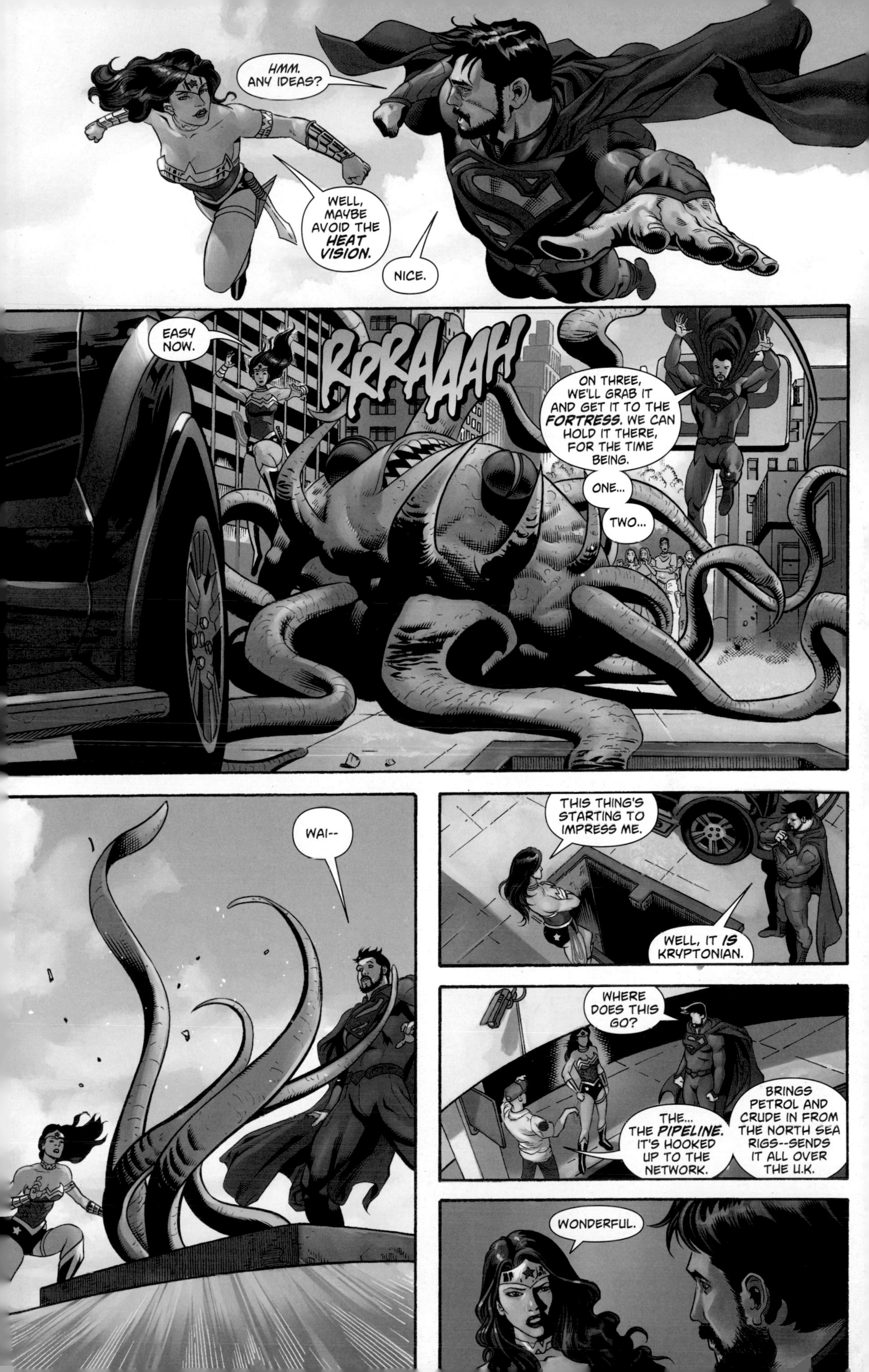

HMM. ANY IDEAS?
WELL, MAYBE AVOID THE **HEAT VISION.**
NICE.
EASY NOW.
RRRAAAAH
ON THREE, WE'LL GRAB IT AND GET IT TO THE **FORTRESS.** WE CAN HOLD IT THERE, FOR THE TIME BEING.
ONE...
TWO...
WAI--
THIS THING'S STARTING TO IMPRESS ME.
WELL, IT **IS** KRYPTONIAN.
WHERE DOES THIS GO?
THE... THE **PIPELINE.** IT'S HOOKED UP TO THE NETWORK.
BRINGS PETROL AND CRUDE IN FROM THE NORTH SEA RIGS--SENDS IT ALL OVER THE U.K.
WONDERFUL.

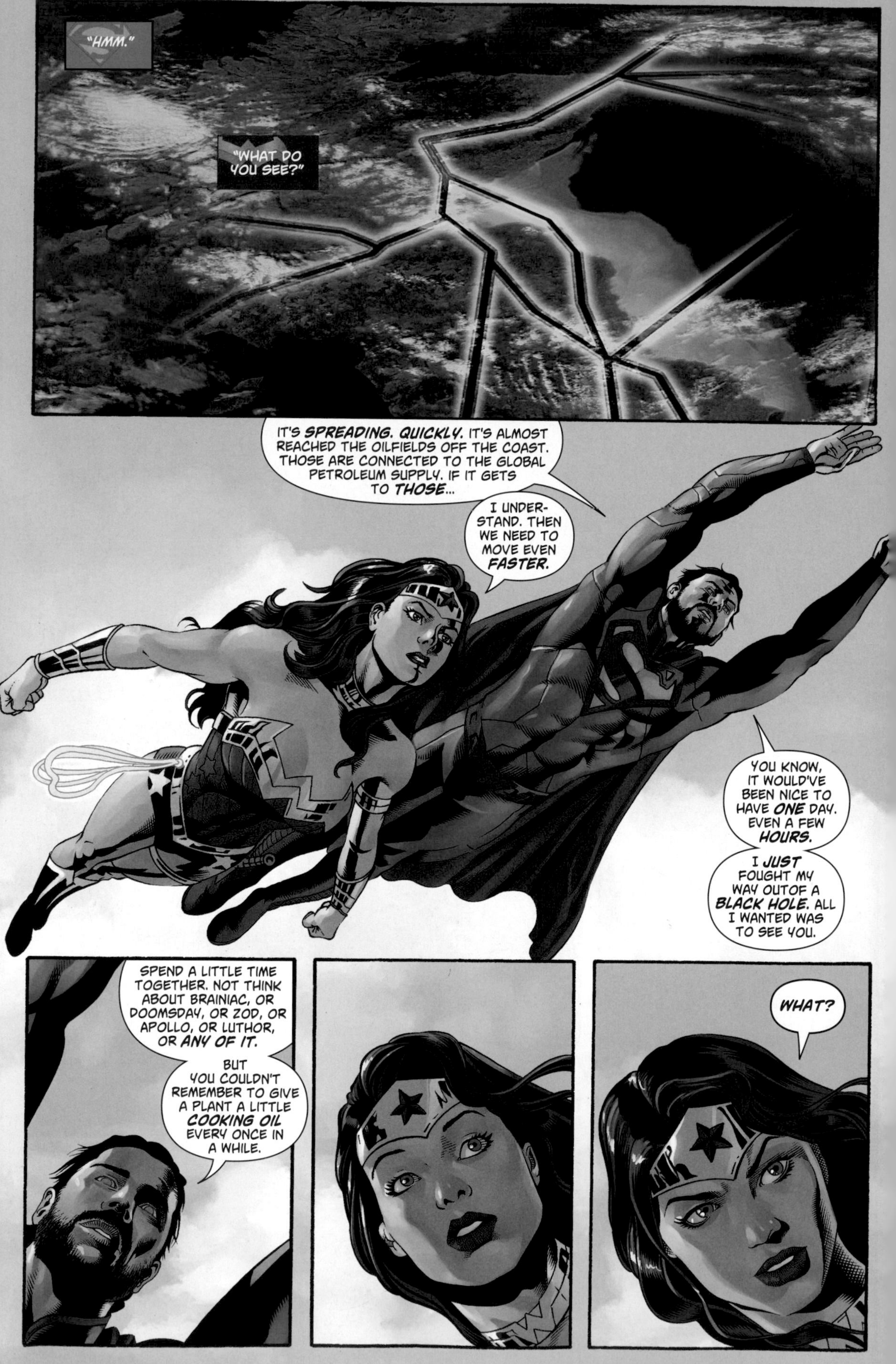
"HMM."
"WHAT DO YOU SEE?"
IT'S SPREADING. QUICKLY. IT'S ALMOST REACHED THE OILFIELDS OFF THE COAST. THOSE ARE CONNECTED TO THE GLOBAL PETROLEUM SUPPLY. IF IT GETS TO THOSE...
I UNDER-STAND. THEN WE NEED TO MOVE EVEN FASTER.
YOU KNOW, IT WOULD'VE BEEN NICE TO HAVE ONE DAY. EVEN A FEW HOURS.
I JUST FOUGHT MY WAY OUT OF A BLACK HOLE. ALL I WANTED WAS TO SEE YOU.
SPEND A LITTLE TIME TOGETHER. NOT THINK ABOUT BRAINIAC, OR DOOMSDAY, OR ZOD, OR APOLLO, OR LUTHOR, OR ANY OF IT.
BUT YOU COULDN'T REMEMBER TO GIVE A PLANT A LITTLE COOKING OIL EVERY ONCE IN A WHILE.
WHAT?

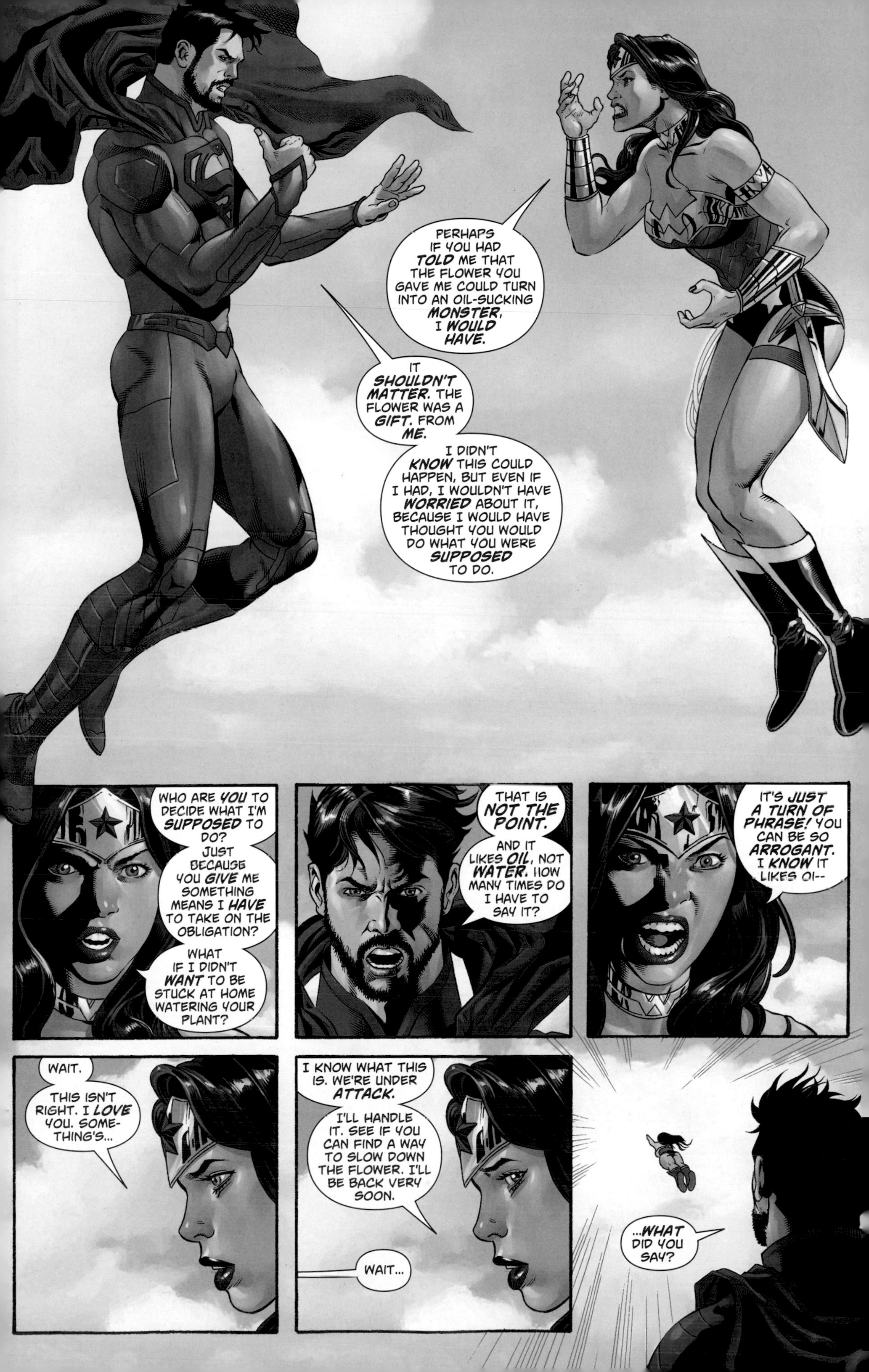
PERHAPS IF YOU HAD TOLD ME THAT THE FLOWER YOU GAVE ME COULD TURN INTO AN OIL-SUCKING MONSTER, I WOULD HAVE.
IT SHOULDN'T MATTER. THE FLOWER WAS A GIFT. FROM ME.
I DIDN'T KNOW THIS COULD HAPPEN, BUT EVEN IF I HAD, I WOULDN'T HAVE WORRIED ABOUT IT, BECAUSE I WOULD HAVE THOUGHT YOU WOULD DO WHAT YOU WERE SUPPOSED TO DO.
WHO ARE YOU TO DECIDE WHAT I'M SUPPOSED TO DO?
JUST BECAUSE YOU GIVE ME SOMETHING MEANS I HAVE TO TAKE ON THE OBLIGATION?
WHAT IF I DIDN'T WANT TO BE STUCK AT HOME WATERING YOUR PLANT?
THAT IS NOT THE POINT.
AND IT LIKES OIL, NOT WATER. HOW MANY TIMES DO I HAVE TO SAY IT?
IT'S JUST A TURN OF PHRASE! YOU CAN BE SO ARROGANT. I KNOW IT LIKES OI--
WAIT.
THIS ISN'T RIGHT. I LOVE YOU. SOME-THING'S...
I KNOW WHAT THIS IS. WE'RE UNDER ATTACK.
I'LL HANDLE IT. SEE IF YOU CAN FIND A WAY TO SLOW DOWN THE FLOWER. I'LL BE BACK VERY SOON.
WAIT...
...WHAT DID YOU SAY?

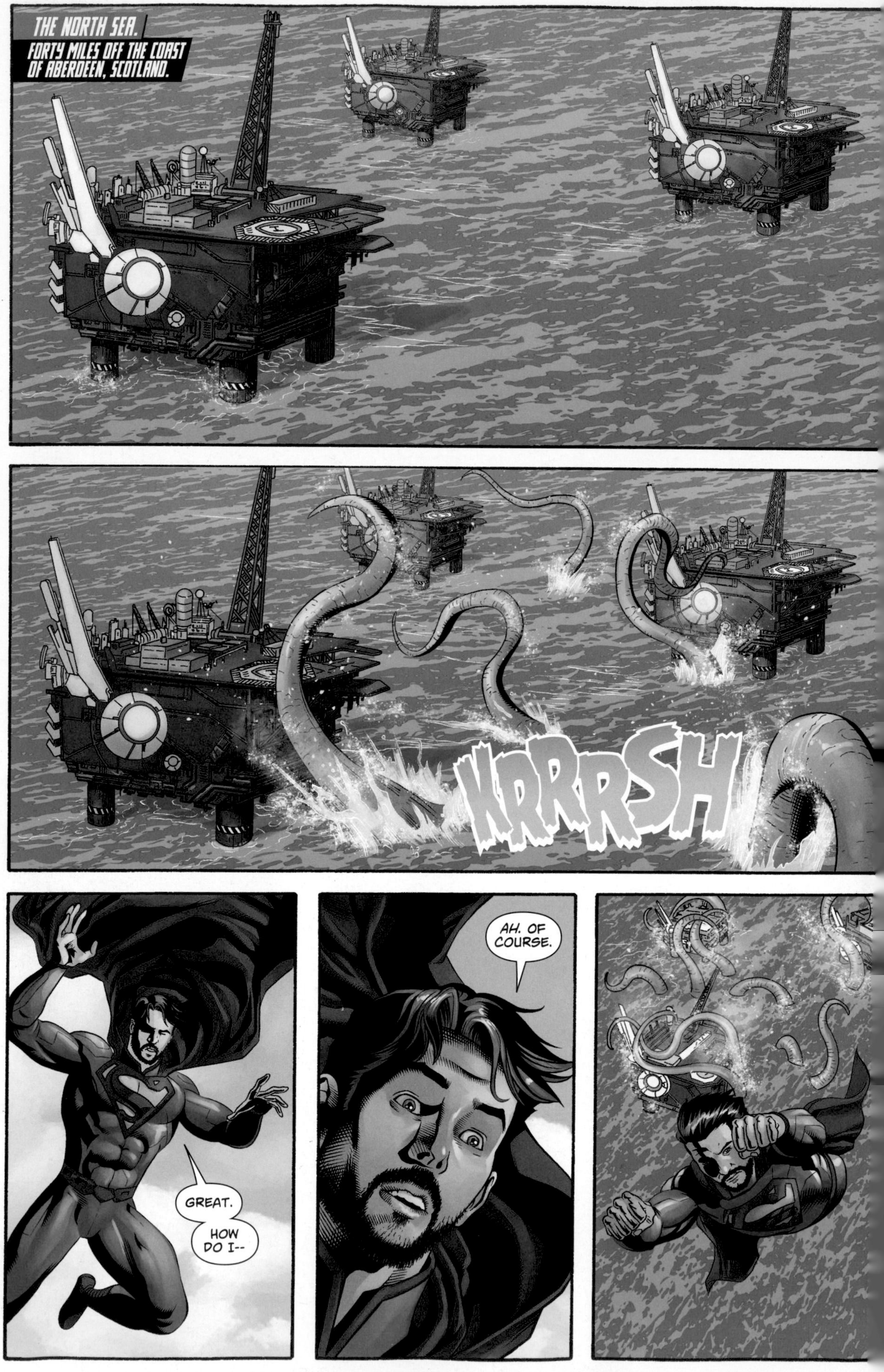
THE NORTH SEA.
FORTY MILES OFF THE COAST OF ABERDEEN, SCOTLAND.
KRRRSH
GREAT.
HOW DO I--
AH. OF COURSE.

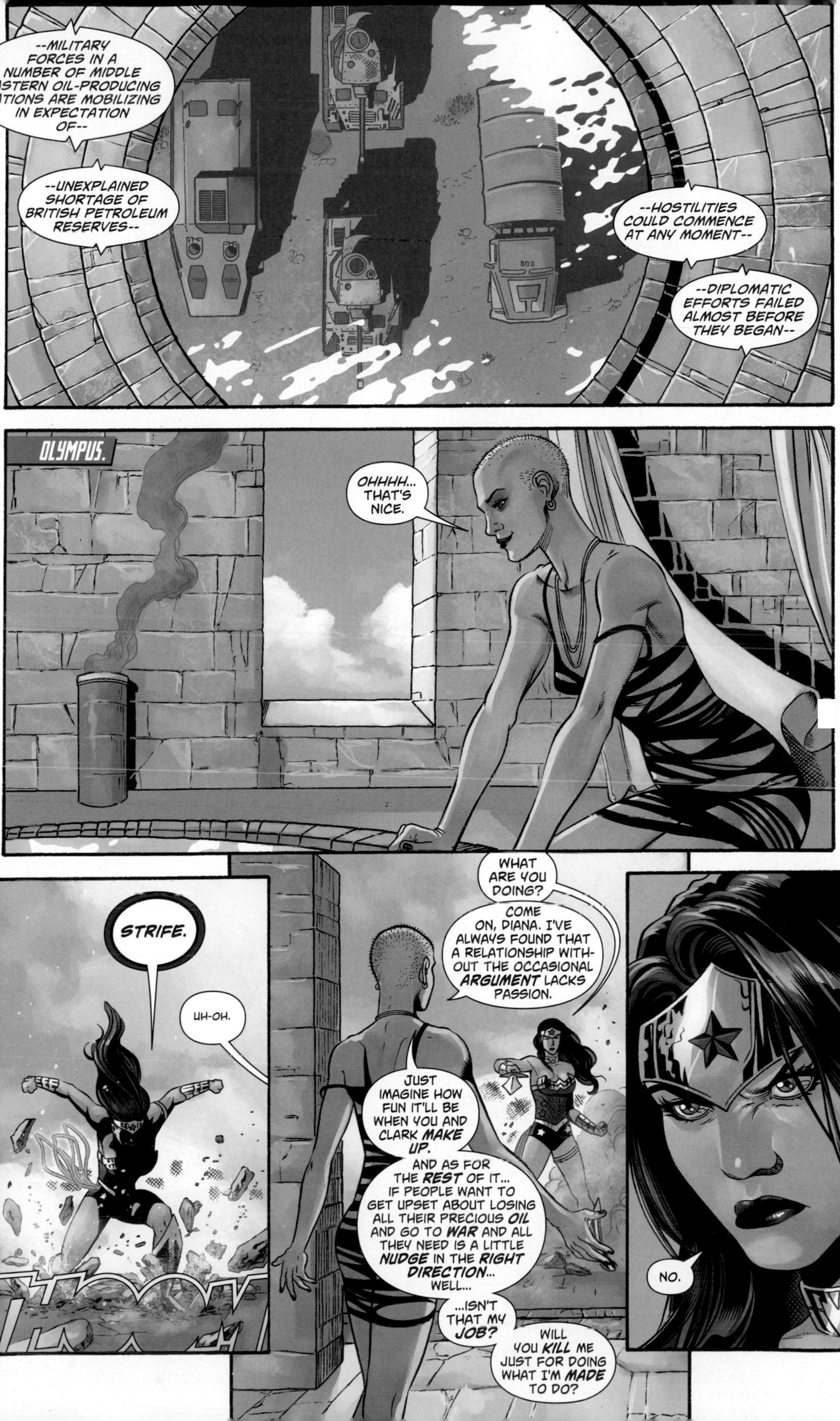
--MILITARY FORCES IN A NUMBER OF MIDDLE EASTERN OIL-PRODUCING NATIONS ARE MOBILIZING IN EXPECTATION OF--
--UNEXPLAINED SHORTAGE OF BRITISH PETROLEUM RESERVES--
--HOSTILITIES COULD COMMENCE AT ANY MOMENT--
--DIPLOMATIC EFFORTS FAILED ALMOST BEFORE THEY BEGAN--
OLYMPUS.
OHHHH... THAT'S NICE.
STRIFE.
UH-OH.
WHAT ARE YOU DOING?
COME ON, DIANA. I'VE ALWAYS FOUND THAT A RELATIONSHIP WITHOUT THE OCCASIONAL ARGUMENT LACKS PASSION.
JUST IMAGINE HOW FUN IT'LL BE WHEN YOU AND CLARK MAKE UP.
AND AS FOR THE REST OF IT... IF PEOPLE WANT TO GET UPSET ABOUT LOSING ALL THEIR PRECIOUS OIL AND GO TO WAR AND ALL THEY NEED IS A LITTLE NUDGE IN THE RIGHT DIRECTION... WELL...
...ISN'T THAT MY JOB?
WILL YOU KILL ME JUST FOR DOING WHAT I'M MADE TO DO?
NO.

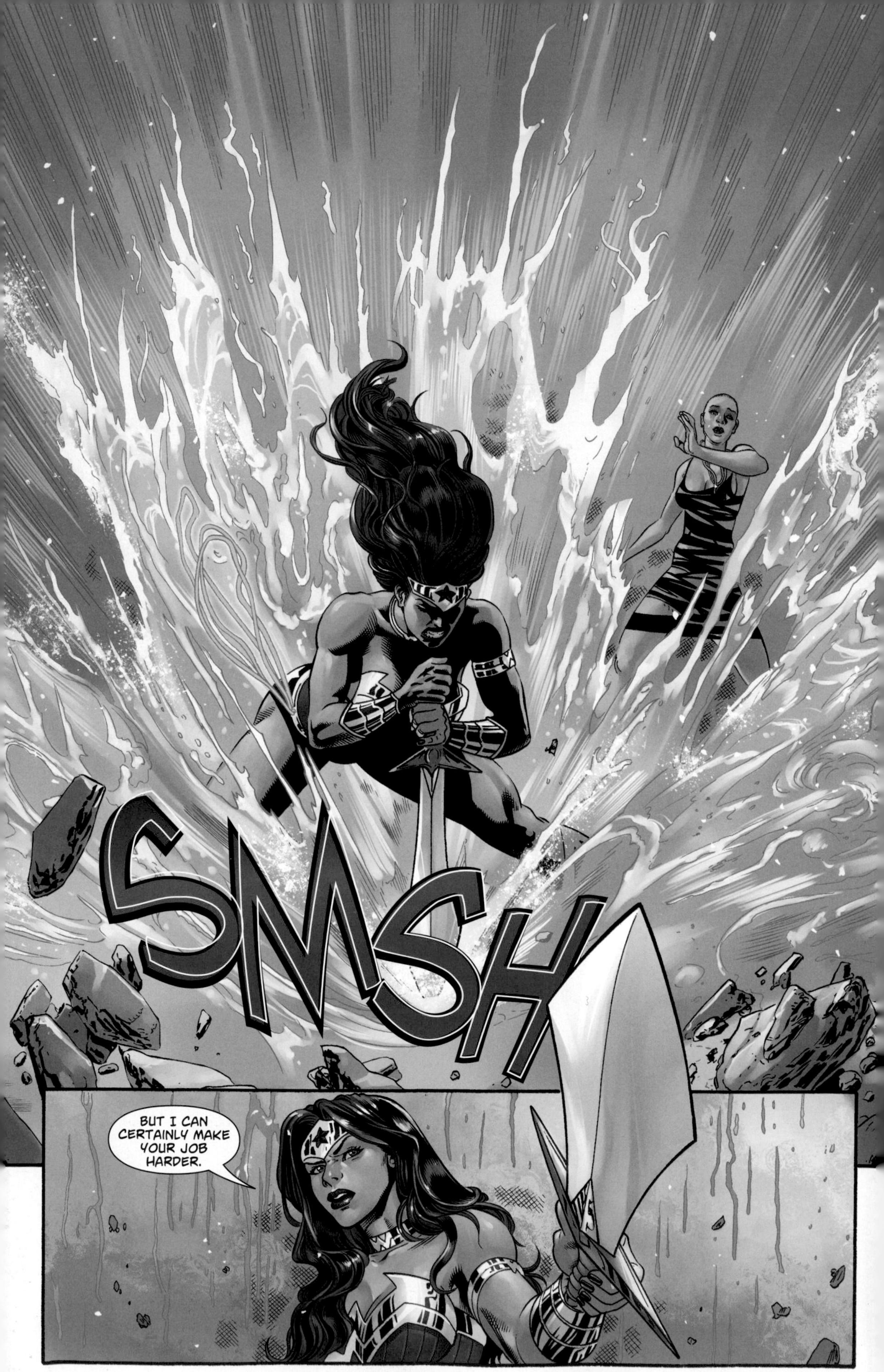
SMSH
BUT I CAN CERTAINLY MAKE YOUR JOB HARDER.

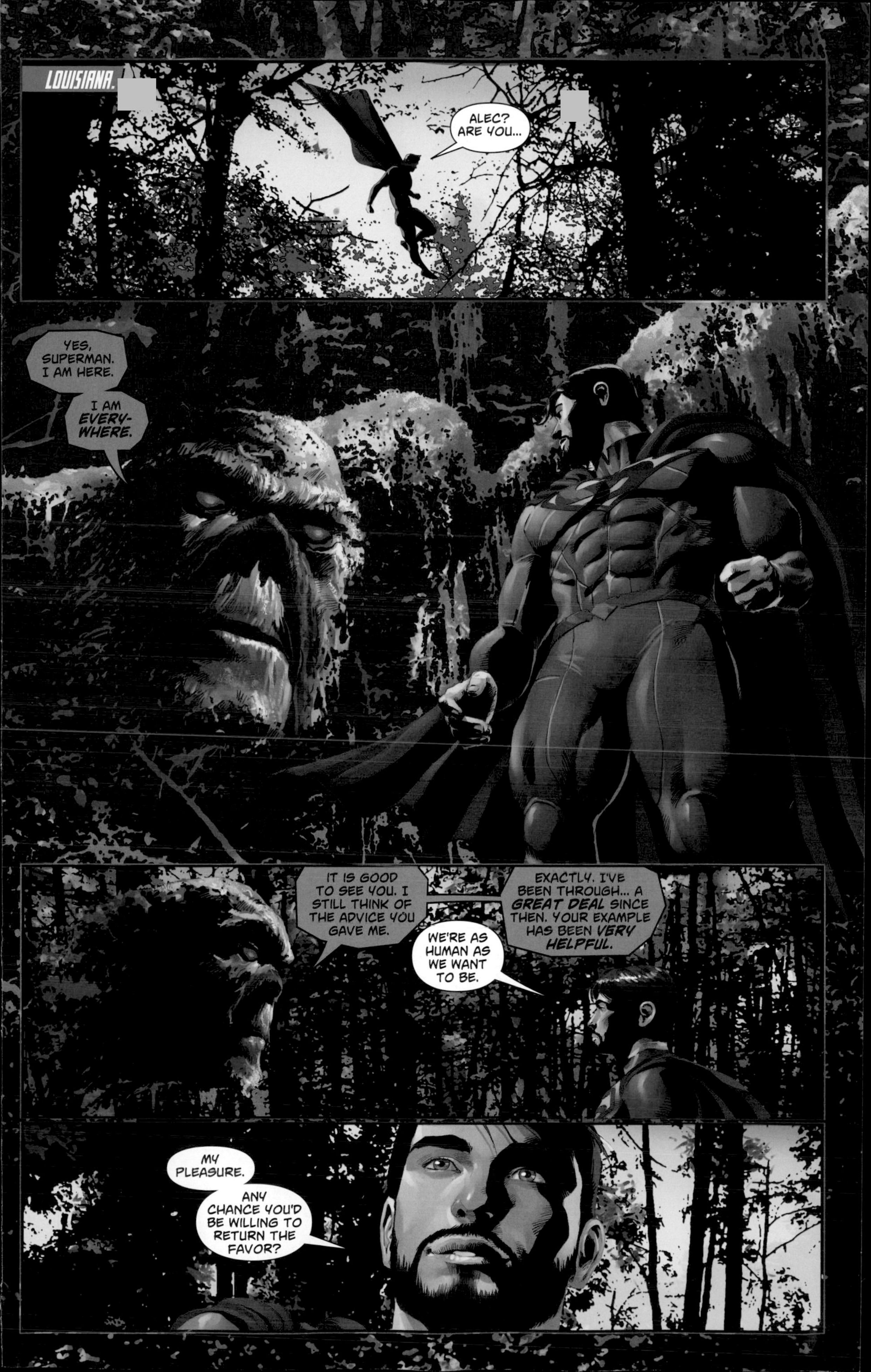
LOUISIANA.
ALEC? ARE YOU...
YES, SUPERMAN. I AM HERE.
I AM EVERY-WHERE.
IT IS GOOD TO SEE YOU. I STILL THINK OF THE ADVICE YOU GAVE ME.
WE'RE AS HUMAN AS WE WANT TO BE.
EXACTLY. I'VE BEEN THROUGH... A GREAT DEAL SINCE THEN. YOUR EXAMPLE HAS BEEN VERY HELPFUL.
MY PLEASURE.
ANY CHANCE YOU'D BE WILLING TO RETURN THE FAVOR?

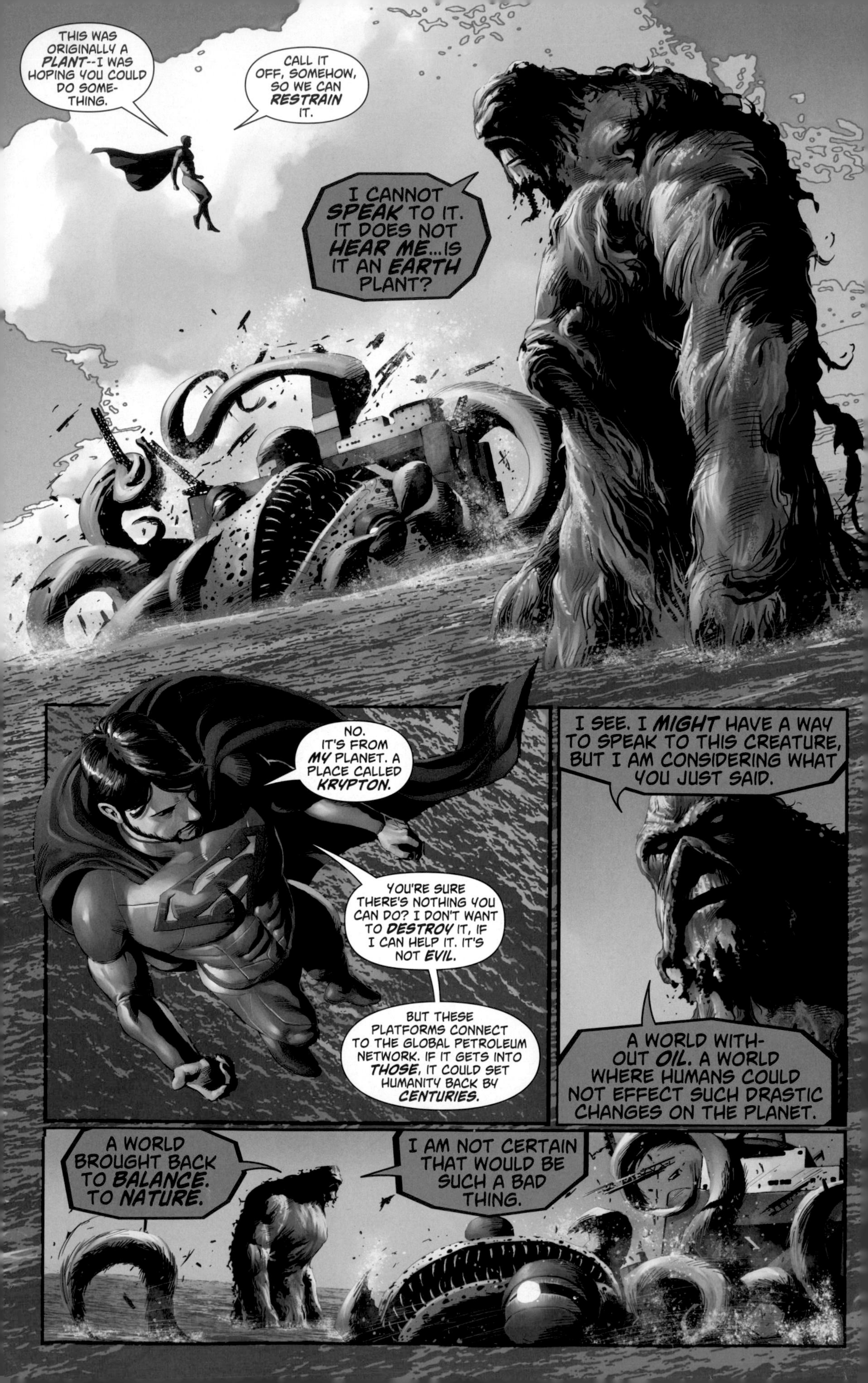
THIS WAS ORIGINALLY A PLANT--I WAS HOPING YOU COULD DO SOMETHING.
CALL IT OFF, SOMEHOW, SO WE CAN RESTRAIN IT.
I CANNOT SPEAK TO IT. IT DOES NOT HEAR ME...IS IT AN EARTH PLANT?
NO. IT'S FROM MY PLANET. A PLACE CALLED KRYPTON.
YOU'RE SURE THERE'S NOTHING YOU CAN DO? I DON'T WANT TO DESTROY IT, IF I CAN HELP IT. IT'S NOT EVIL.
BUT THESE PLATFORMS CONNECT TO THE GLOBAL PETROLEUM NETWORK. IF IT GETS INTO THOSE, IT COULD SET HUMANITY BACK BY CENTURIES.
I SEE. I MIGHT HAVE A WAY TO SPEAK TO THIS CREATURE, BUT I AM CONSIDERING WHAT YOU JUST SAID.
A WORLD WITHOUT OIL. A WORLD WHERE HUMANS COULD NOT EFFECT SUCH DRASTIC CHANGES ON THE PLANET.
A WORLD BROUGHT BACK TO BALANCE. TO NATURE.
I AM NOT CERTAIN THAT WOULD BE SUCH A BAD THING.

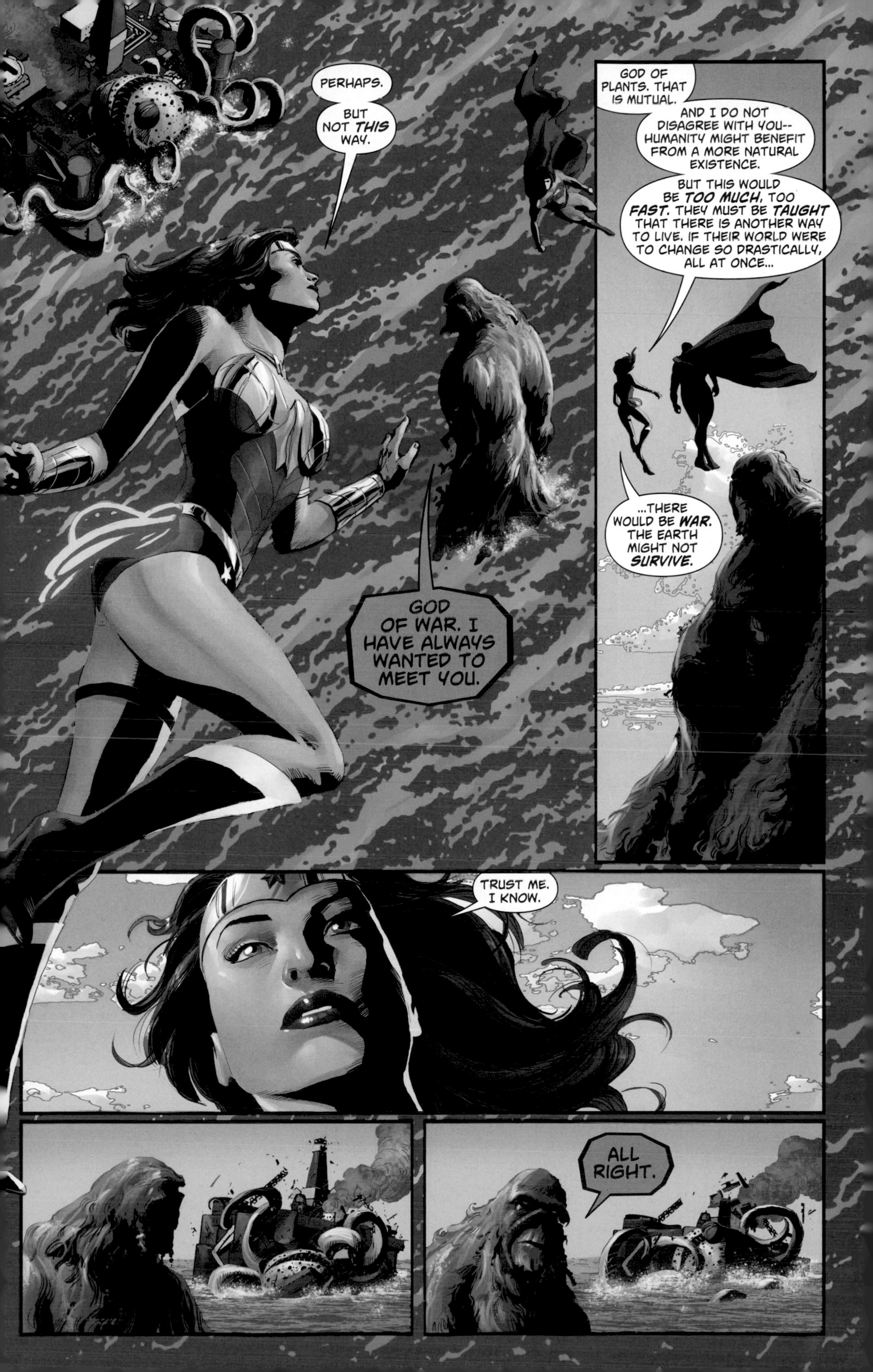
PERHAPS.
BUT NOT THIS WAY.
GOD OF WAR. I HAVE ALWAYS WANTED TO MEET YOU.
GOD OF PLANTS. THAT IS MUTUAL.
AND I DO NOT DISAGREE WITH YOU-- HUMANITY MIGHT BENEFIT FROM A MORE NATURAL EXISTENCE.
BUT THIS WOULD BE TOO MUCH, TOO FAST. THEY MUST BE TAUGHT THAT THERE IS ANOTHER WAY TO LIVE. IF THEIR WORLD WERE TO CHANGE SO DRASTICALLY, ALL AT ONCE...
...THERE WOULD BE WAR. THE EARTH MIGHT NOT SURVIVE.
TRUST ME. I KNOW.
ALL RIGHT.

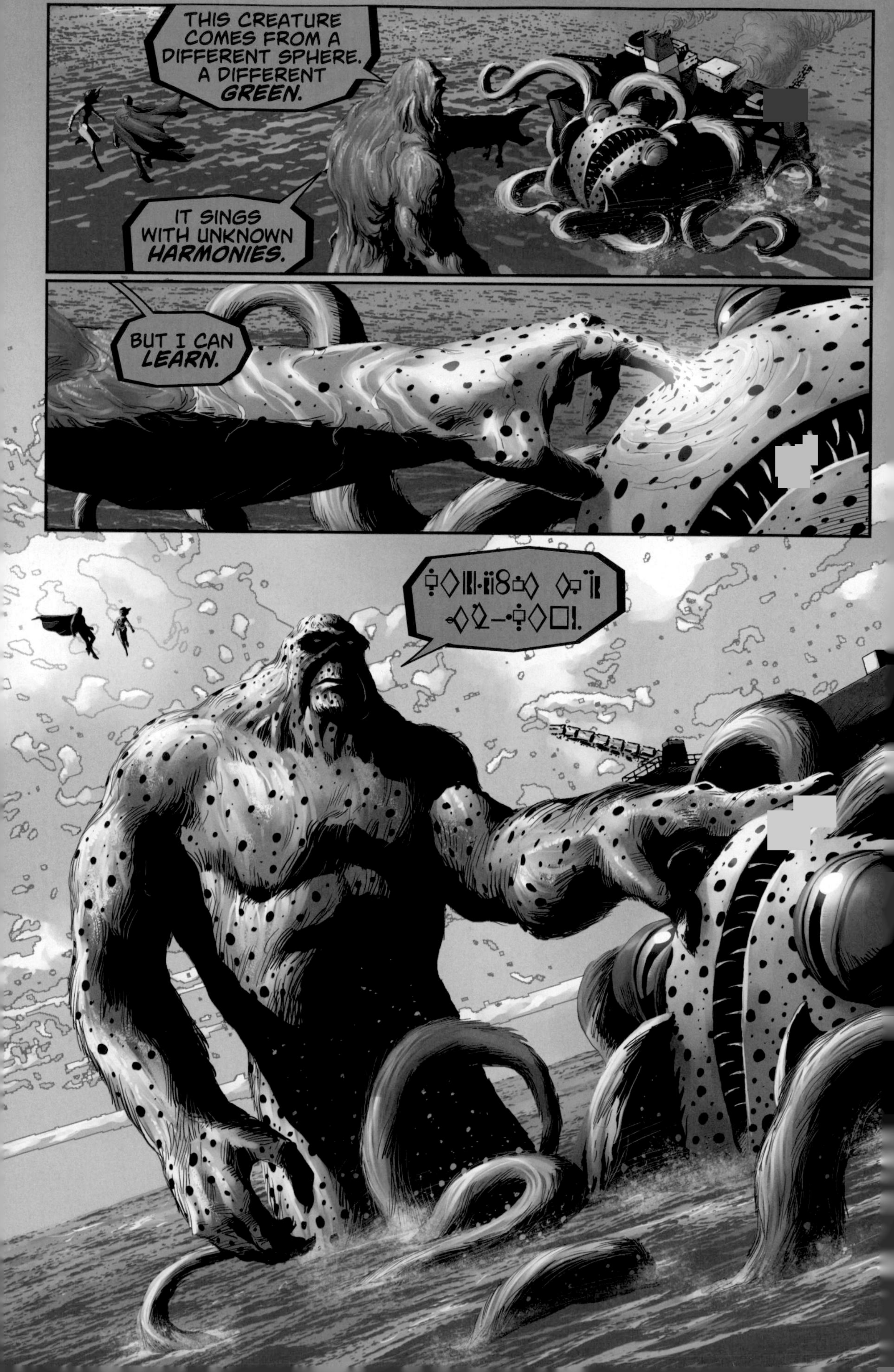
THIS CREATURE COMES FROM A DIFFERENT SPHERE. A DIFFERENT *GREEN.*
IT SINGS WITH UNKNOWN *HARMONIES.*
BUT I CAN *LEARN.*

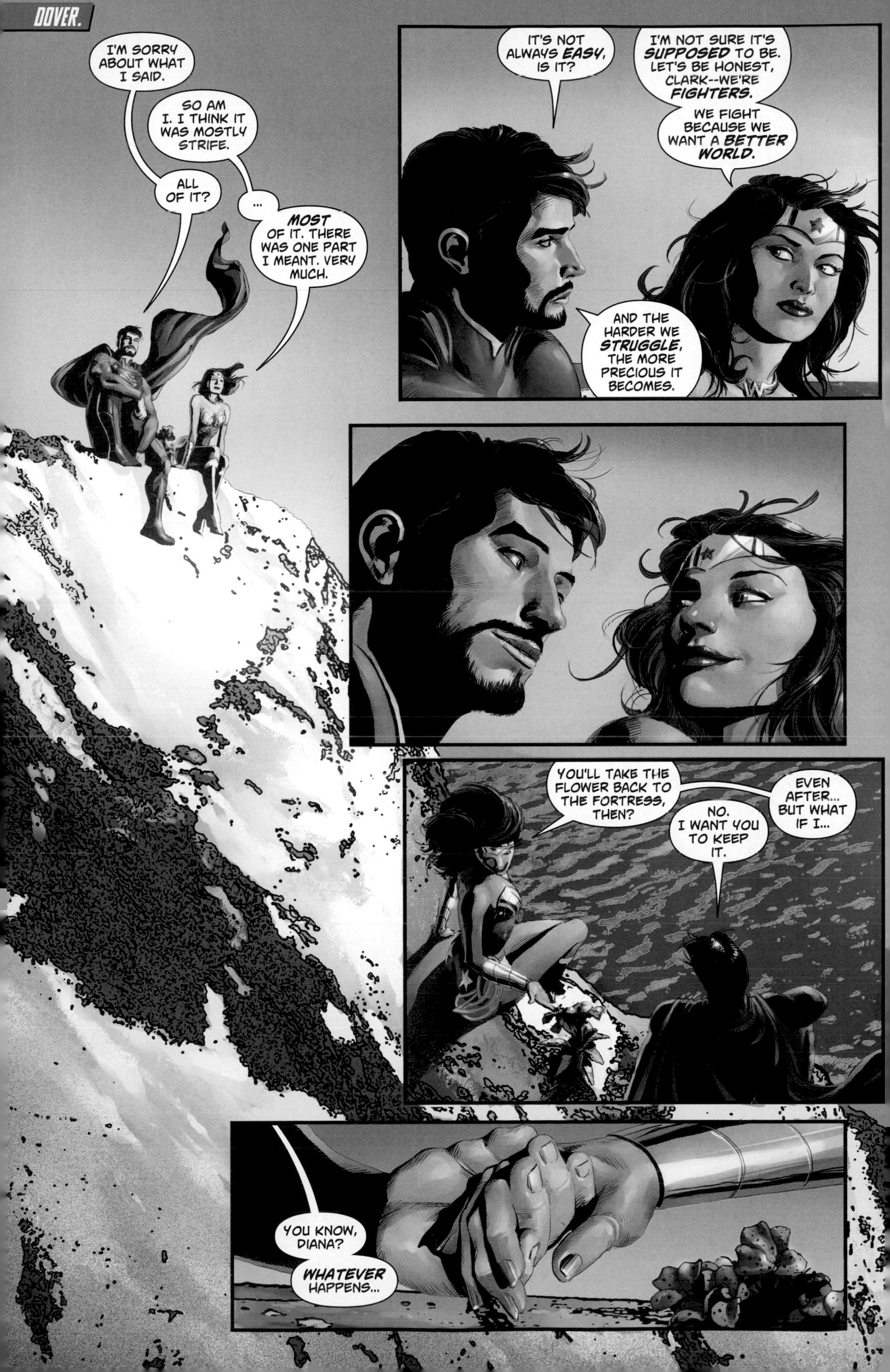
DOVER.
I'M SORRY ABOUT WHAT I SAID.
SO AM I. I THINK IT WAS MOSTLY STRIFE.
ALL OF IT?
...
MOST OF IT. THERE WAS ONE PART I MEANT. VERY MUCH.
IT'S NOT ALWAYS EASY, IS IT?
I'M NOT SURE IT'S SUPPOSED TO BE. LET'S BE HONEST, CLARK--WE'RE FIGHTERS.
WE FIGHT BECAUSE WE WANT A BETTER WORLD.
AND THE HARDER WE STRUGGLE, THE MORE PRECIOUS IT BECOMES.
YOU'LL TAKE THE FLOWER BACK TO THE FORTRESS, THEN?
NO. I WANT YOU TO KEEP IT.
EVEN AFTER... BUT WHAT IF I...
YOU KNOW, DIANA?
WHATEVER HAPPENS...

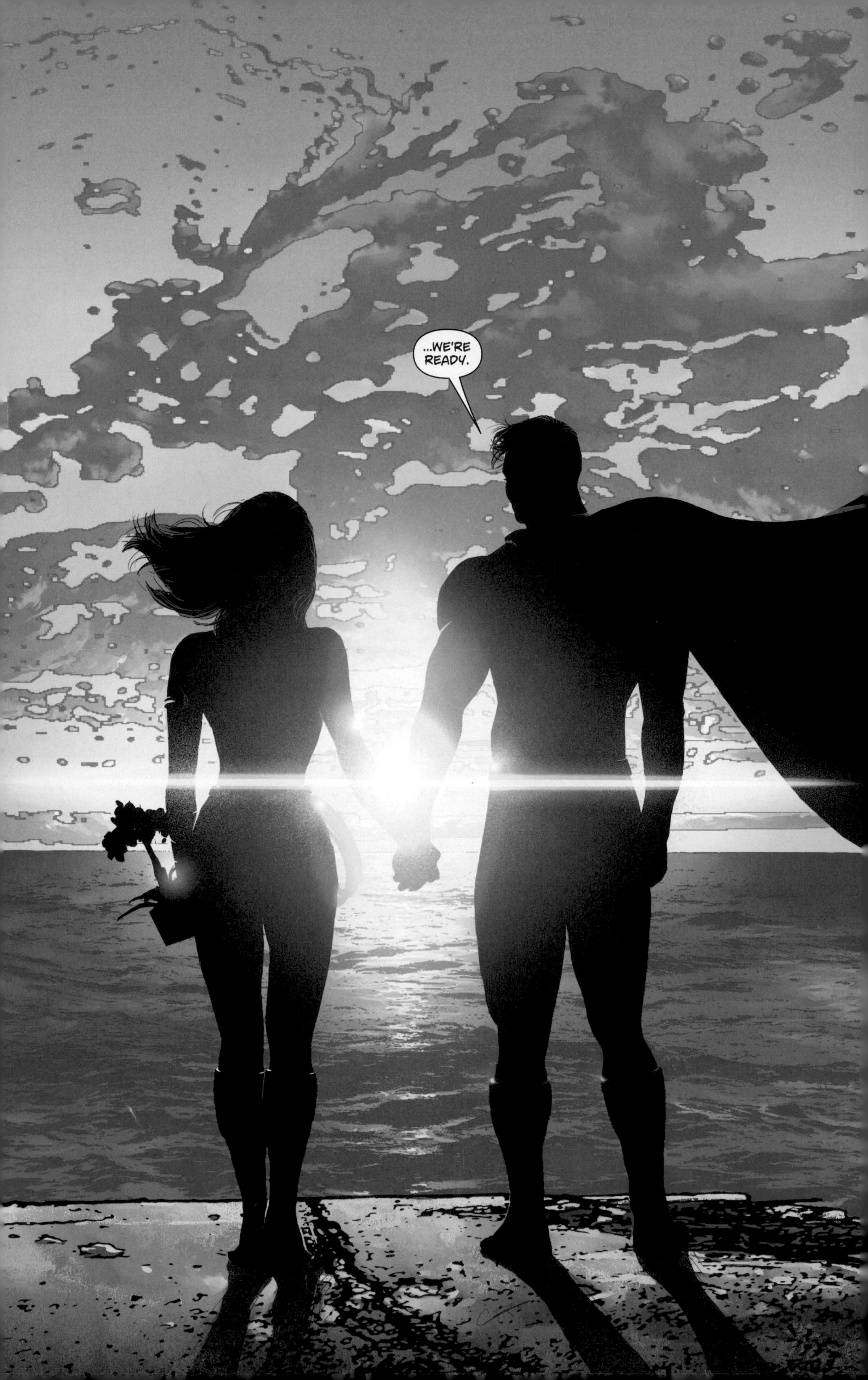
...WE'RE READY.

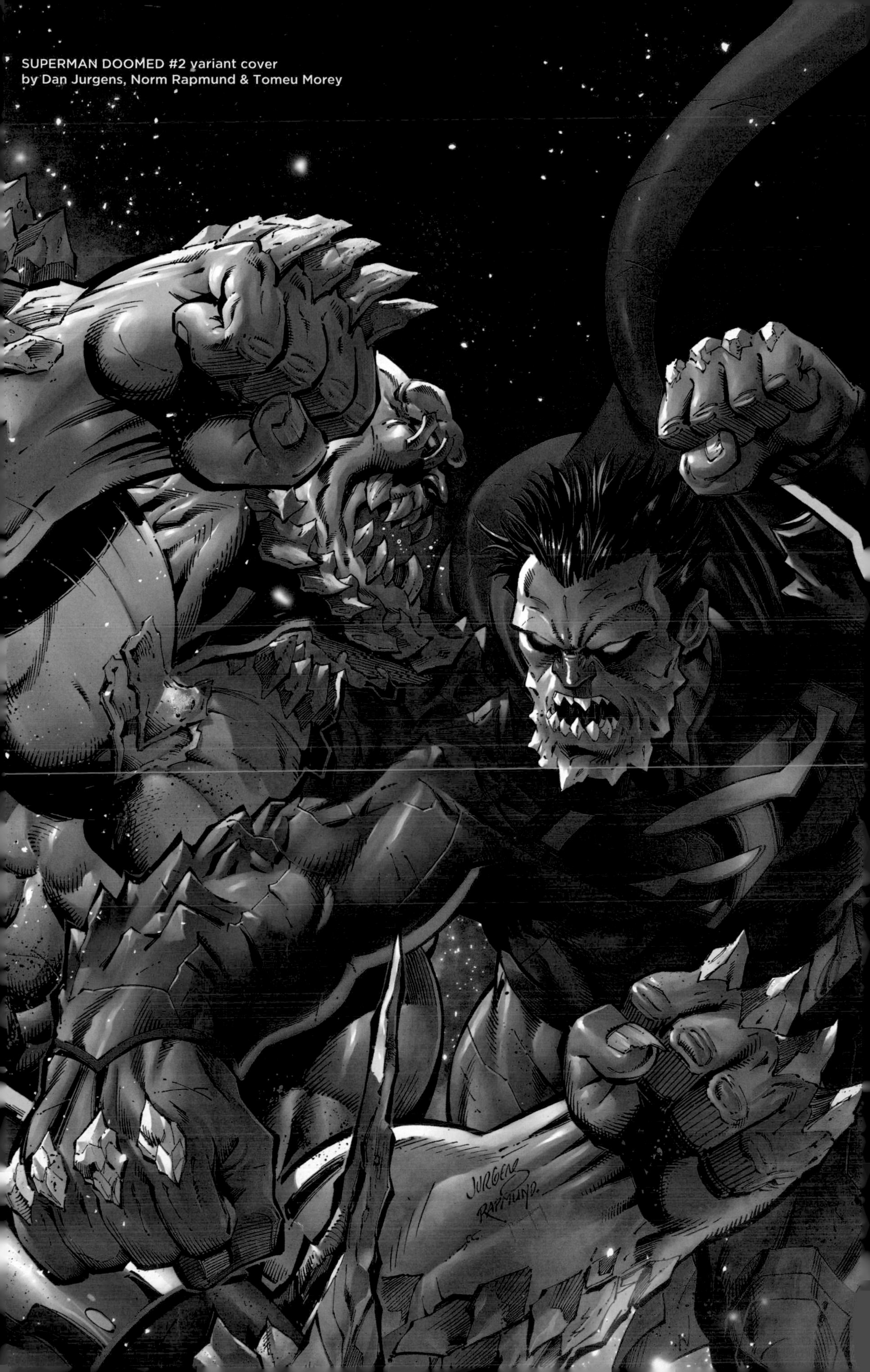
JURGENS
RAPMUND

SUPERMAN DOOMED #2 variant cover
by Dan Jurgens, Norm Rapmund & Tomeu Morey

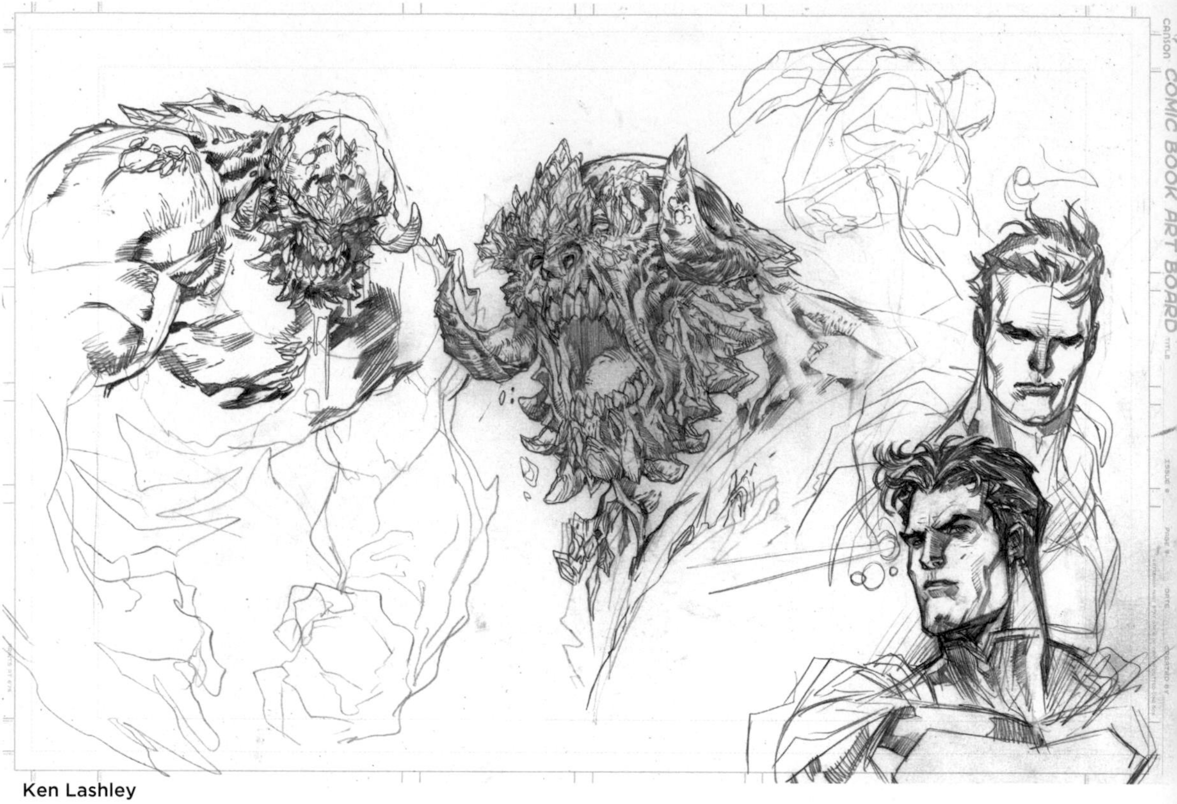
COMIC BOOK ART BOARD

Ken Lashley

Here and on the next page are the evolution of Superdoom.

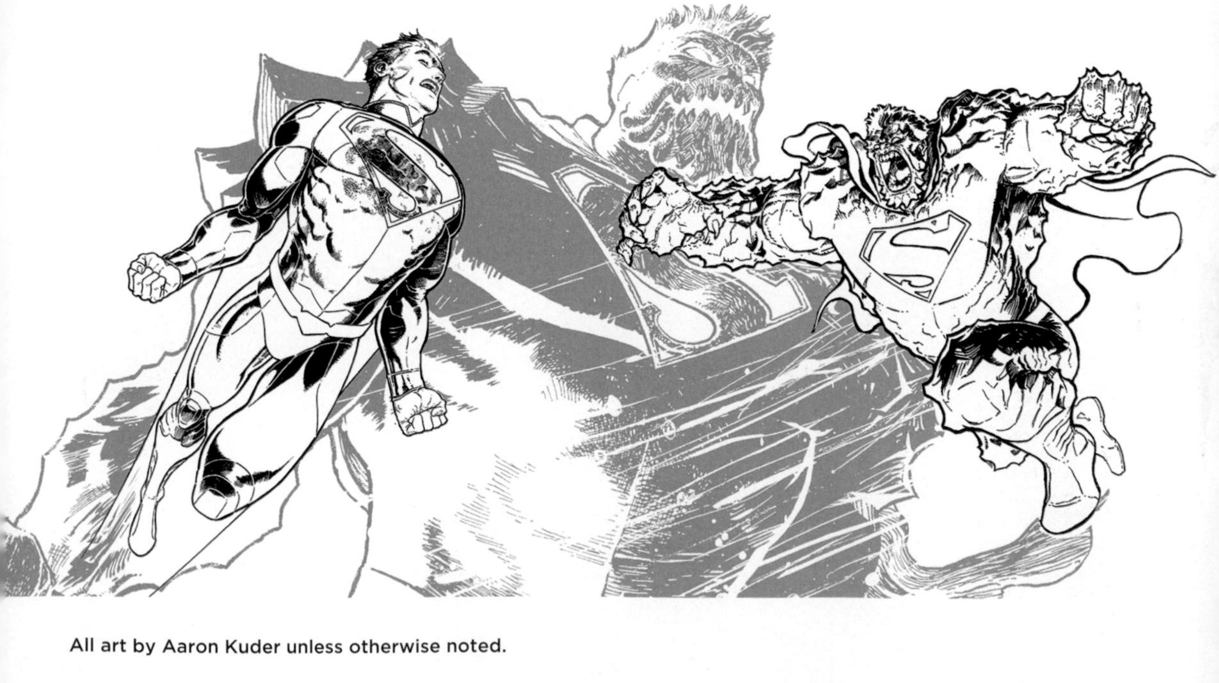

All art by Aaron Kuder unless otherwise noted.

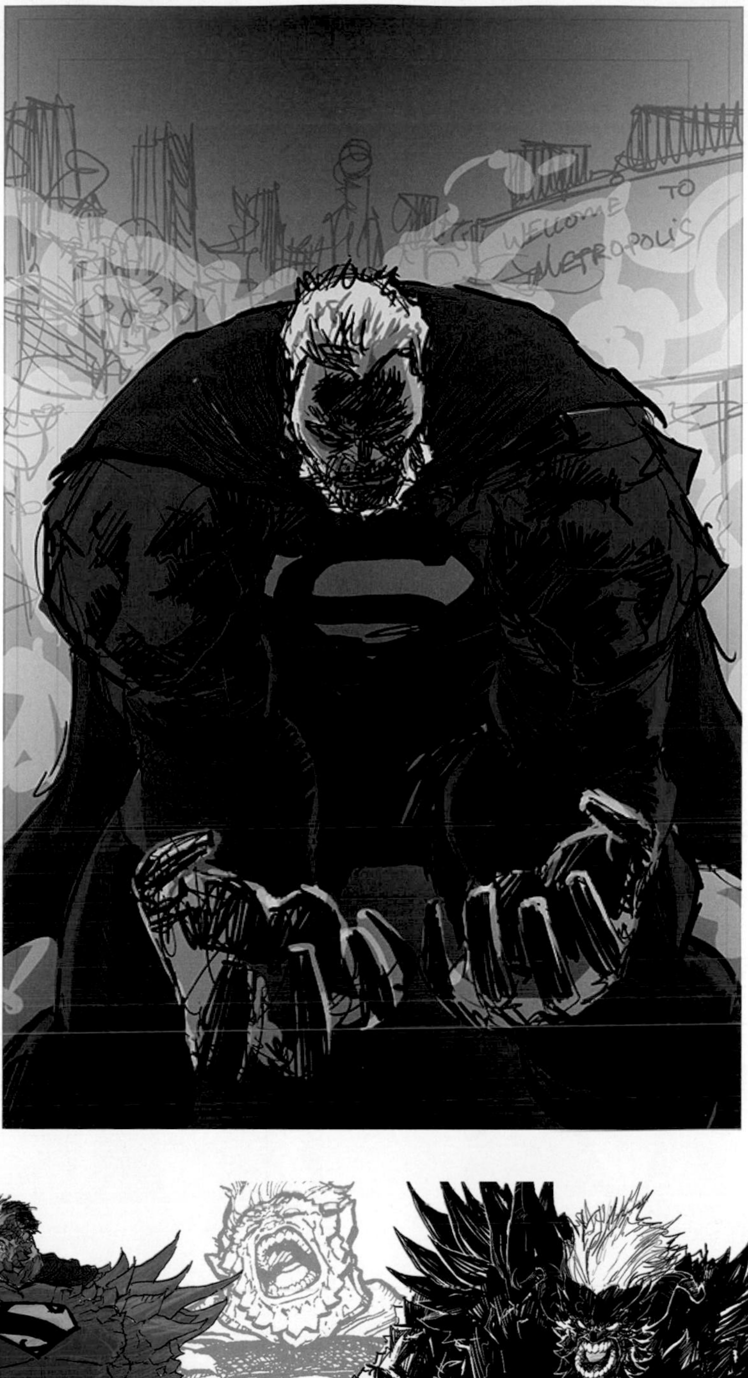
WELCOME TO
METROPOLIS

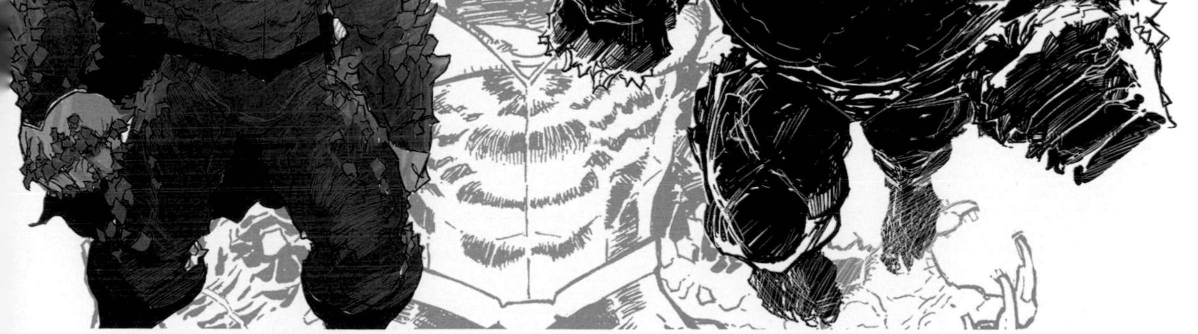

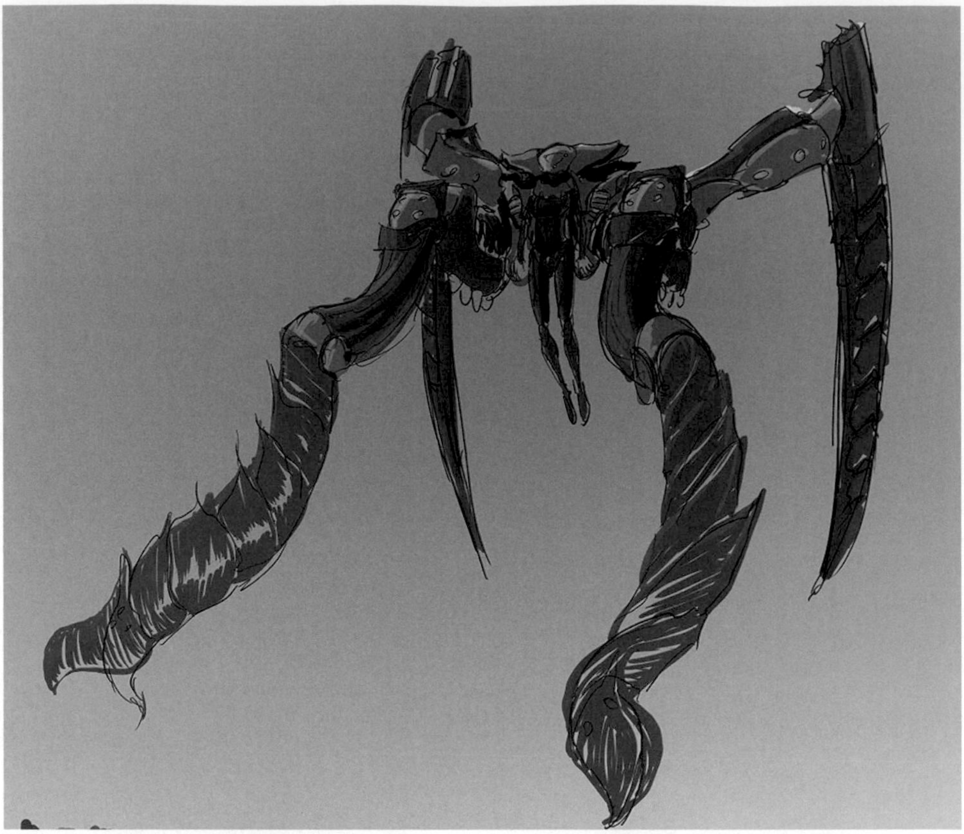

Above is Aaron Kuder's unused Braniac Lois.

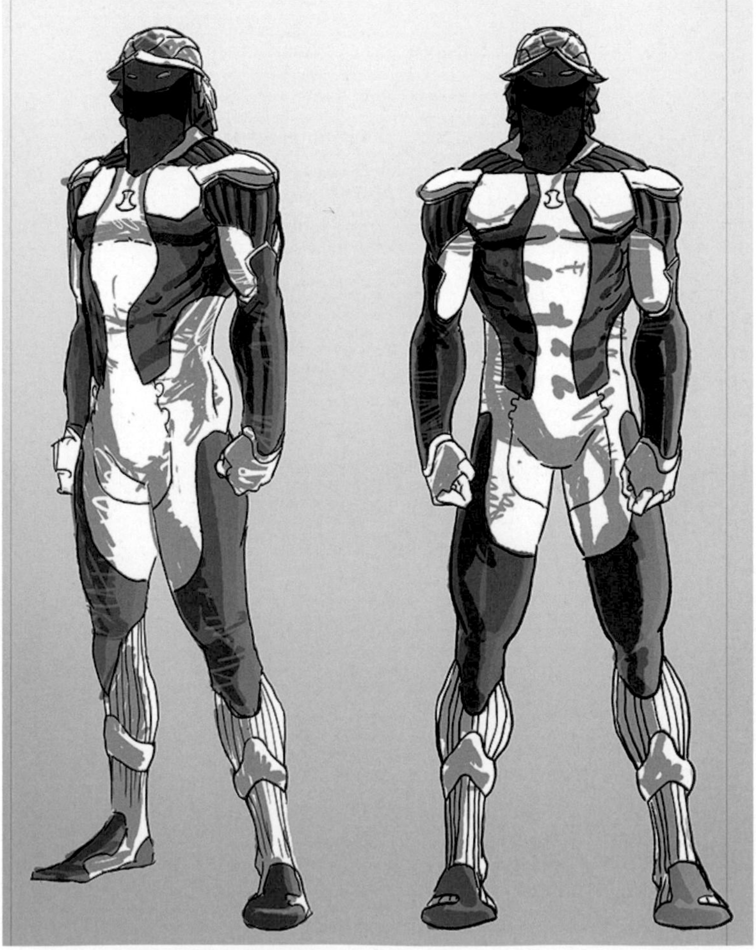

A variation of the alien defender Superdoom faced.

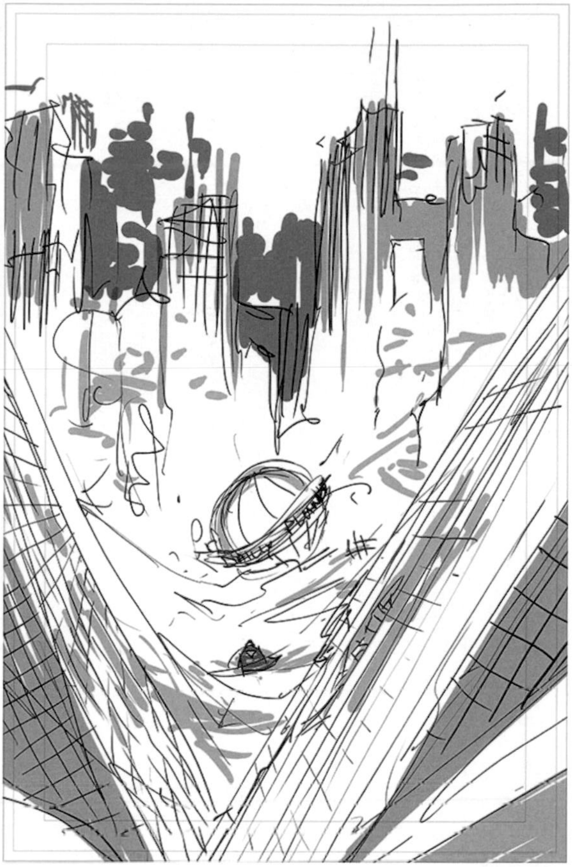
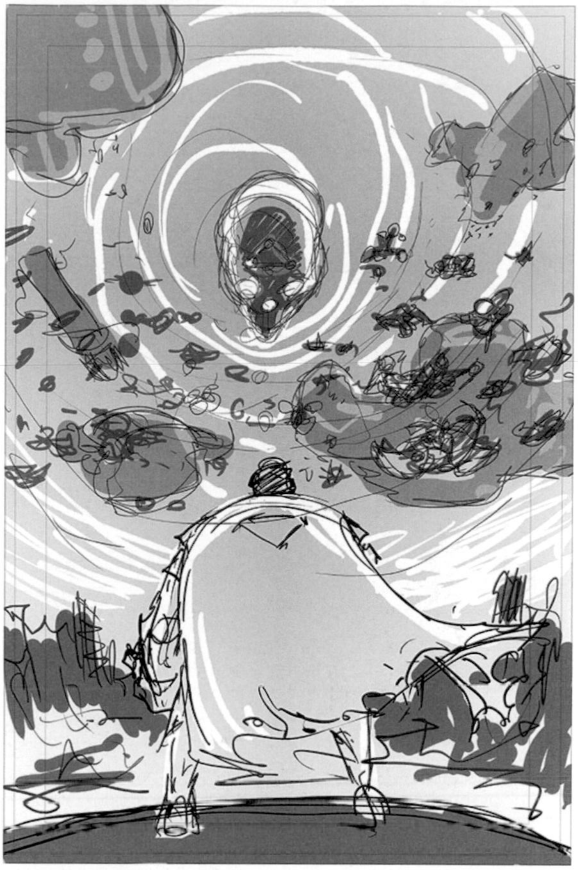

Cover sketches for Superdoom's last stand against Brainiac.

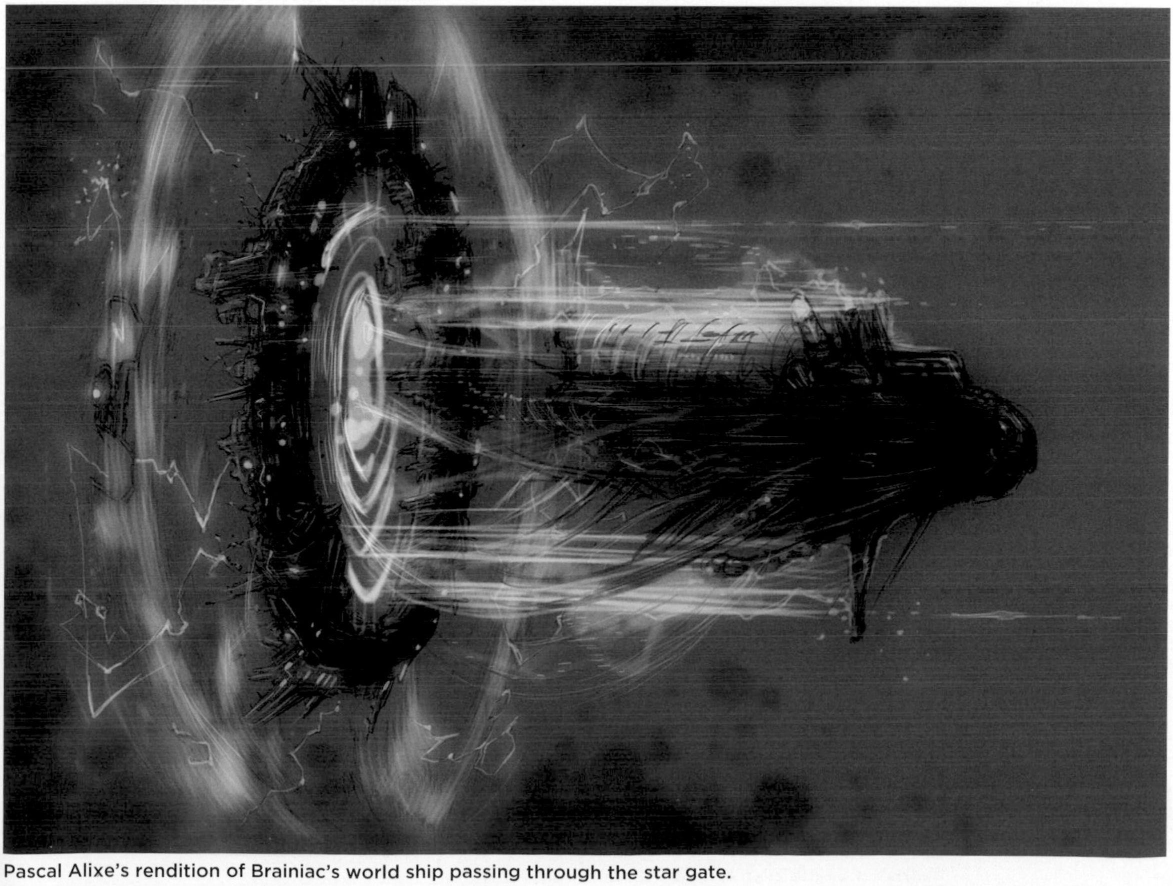

Pascal Alixe's rendition of Brainiac's world ship passing through the star gate.

Cover sketches for ACTION COMICS #32-33 by Aaron Kuder.
The task was to properly convey the dark side of the Man of Steel.

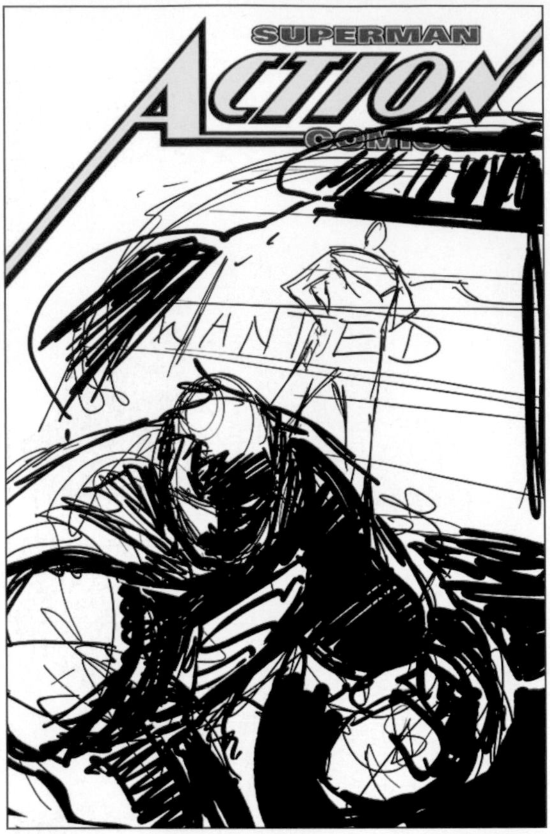
SUPERMAN
ACTION
COMICS
WANTED

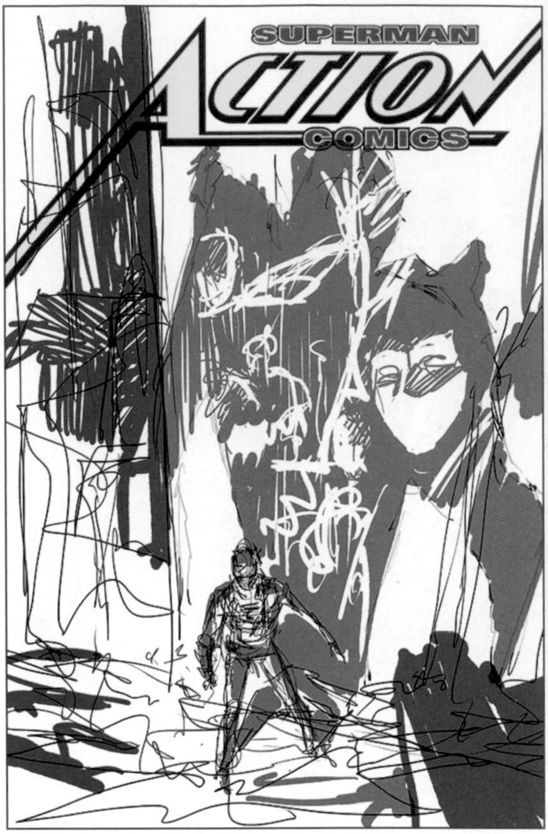
SUPERMAN
ACTION
COMICS

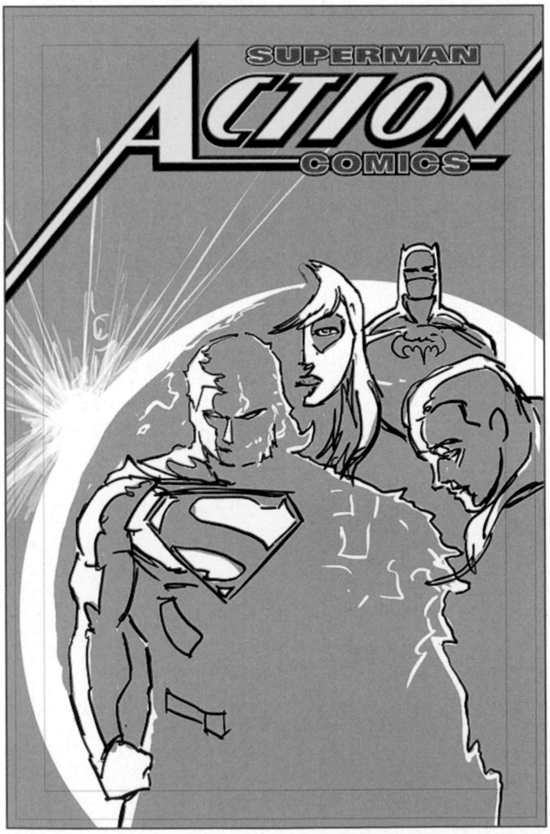
SUPERMAN
ACTION
COMICS

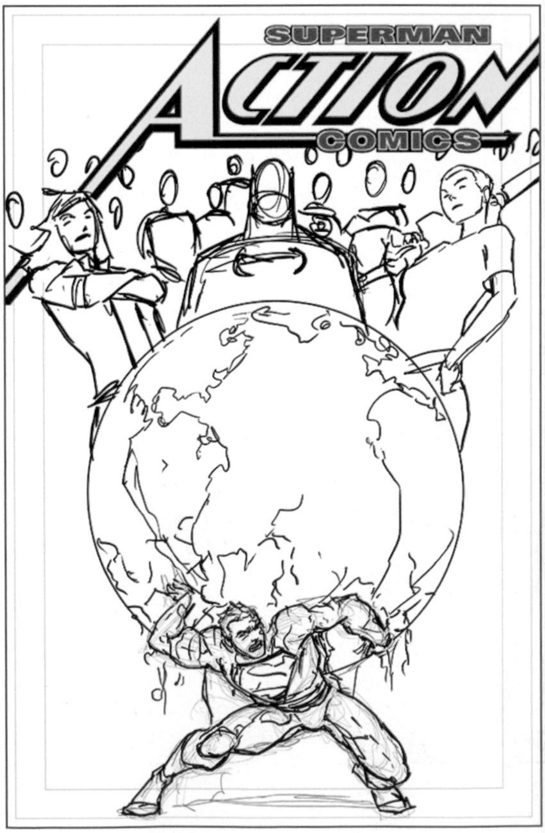
SUPERMAN
ACTION
COMICS

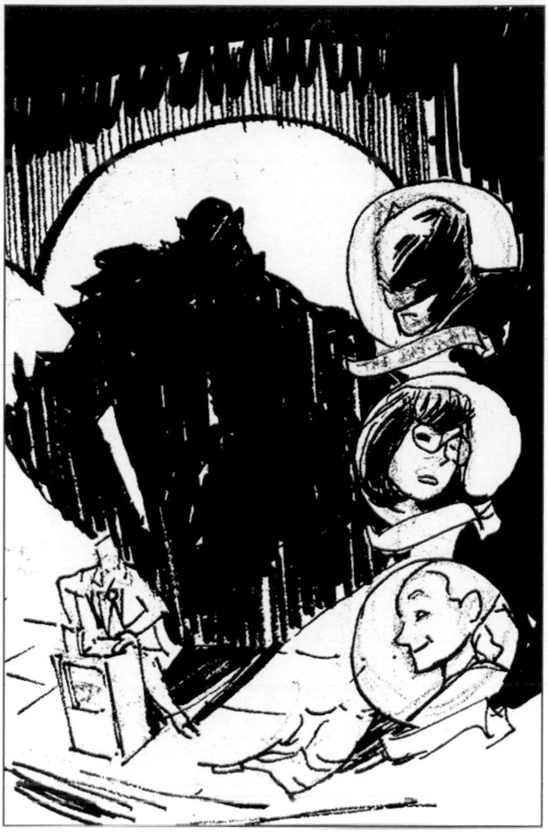
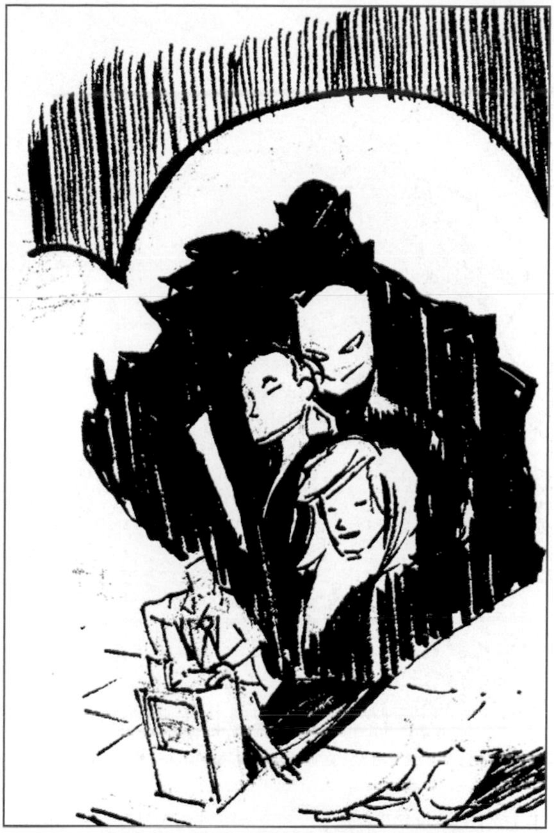
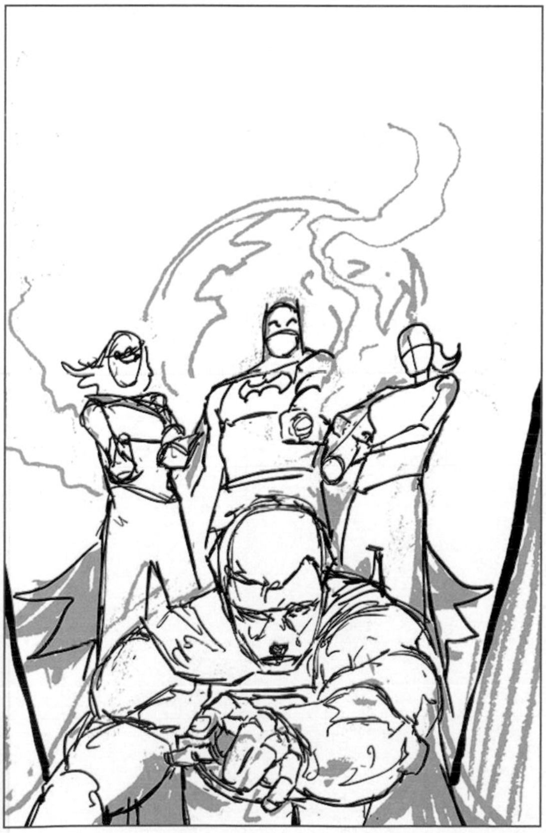
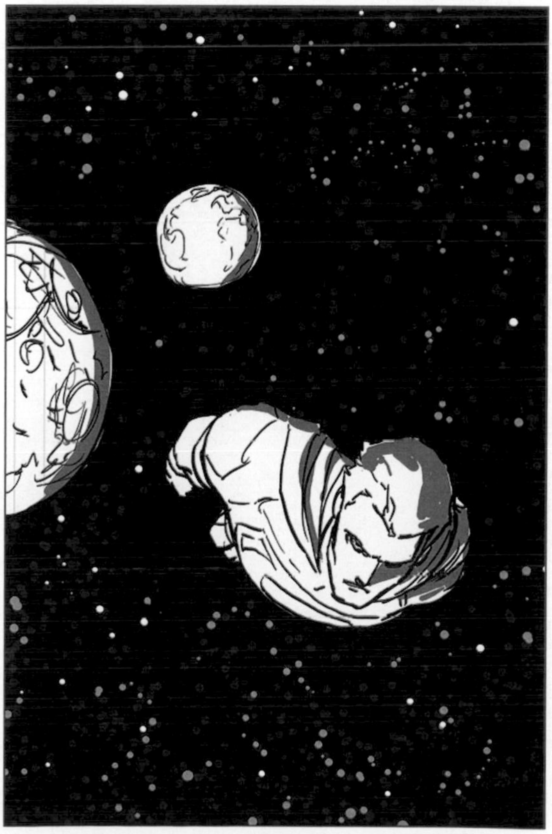

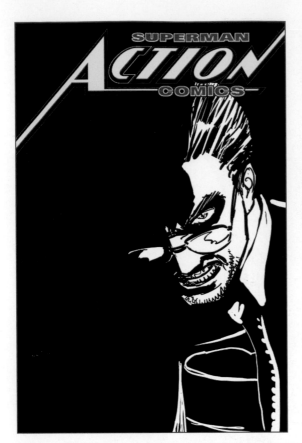
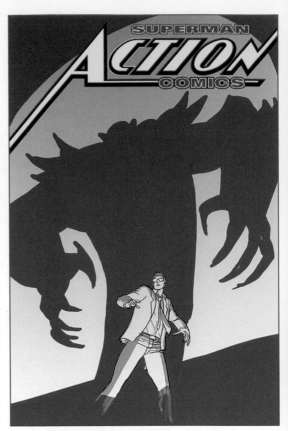
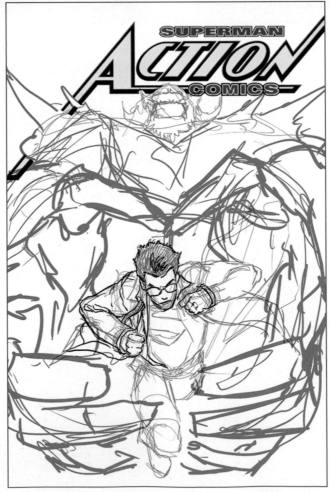

more energy

saps
- more Navy blue
  than Aqua
& more shade

more little highlights.

The purple here and
the purple space are a
bit too close, could we
change this one?